T5-DGS-614

POEMS OF AMERICAN HISTORY

AMERICA

My country, 't is of thee,
Sweet land of liberty,
    Of thee I sing ;
Land where my fathers died,
Land of the pilgrims' pride,
From every mountain-side
    Let freedom ring.

My native country. thee,
Land of the noble free,
    Thy name I love ;
I love thy rocks and rills,
Thy woods and templed hills ;
My heart with rapture thrills
    Like that above.

Let music swell the breeze,
And ring from all the trees
    Sweet freedom's song ;
Let mortal tongues awake,
Let all that breathe partake,
Let rocks their silence break, —
    The sound prolong.

Our fathers' God, to Thee,
Author of liberty,
    To Thee we sing ;
Long may our land be bright
With freedom's holy light ;
Protect us by Thy might,
    Great God, our King.

SAMUEL FRANCIS SMITH.

POEMS OF AMERICAN HISTORY

COLLECTED AND EDITED

BY

BURTON EGBERT STEVENSON

REVISED EDITION

Granger Index Reprint Series

 BOOKS FOR LIBRARIES PRESS
FREEPORT, NEW YORK

STANDARD BOOK NUMBER:
8369-6159-5

LIBRARY OF CONGRESS CATALOG CARD NUMBER:
72-116416

MANUFACTURED BY
HALLMARK LITHOGRAPHERS, INC.
IN THE U.S.A.

COPYRIGHT NOTICE

COPYRIGHT NOTICE FOR NEW EDITION

TO

E. B. S.

HELPMATE

ONE who underrates the significance of our literature, prose or verse, as both the expression and stimulant of national feeling, as of import in the past and to the future of America, and therefore of the world, is deficient in that critical insight which can judge even of its own day unwarped by personal taste or deference to public impression. He shuts his eyes to the fact that at times, notably throughout the years resulting in the Civil War, this literature has been a "force."—EDMUND CLARENCE STEDMAN.

INTRODUCTION

THE poetry relating to American history falls naturally into two classes:
that written, so to speak, from the inside, on the spot, and that written from
the outside, long afterwards. Of the first class, "The Star-Spangled Banner"
is the most famous example, as well as perhaps the best. Even at this distant
day, reading it with a knowledge of the circumstances which produced it, it
has a power of touching the heart and gripping the imagination which goes
far toward proving the genuineness of its art. Of the second class, "Paul
Revere's Ride" is probably the most widely known, though Mr. Longfel-
low's own "Ballad of the French Fleet" is a better poem.

It is evident that, in compiling an anthology such as this, different stand-
ards must be used in judging these two classes. The first, aside from any
quality as poetry which it may have, is of value because of its historical or
political interest, because it is an expression and an interpretation of the
hour which gave it birth. With it, poetic merit is not the first consideration,
which is, perhaps, as well. Yet, however slight their merit as poetry may be,
many of the early ballads possess an admirable energy, directness, and apt-
ness of phrase, and there is about them a childlike simplicity impossible of
reproduction in this sophisticated age — as where Stephen Tilden, in his
epitaph on Braddock, requests the great commanders who have preceded
that unfortunate soldier to the grave to

> "Edge close and give him room."

With the retrospective ballad, on the other hand, poetic merit is a sine
qua non. It has little value historically, however accurate its facts. It differs
from the contemporary ballad in the same way that the "New Canterbury
Tales" differ from Froissart; or as the "Idylls of the King" differ from
"Le Morte Arthur." It is less authentic, less convincing, less vital. It may
have atmosphere, but there is no infallible way of telling whether the at-
mosphere is right. Unless it is something more, then, than mere metrical
history, the modern ballad has little claim to consideration.

These are the two principles which the present compiler has had con-
stantly in mind. Yet the second principle has been violated more than once,
since, in a collection such as this, one must cut one's coat according to the
cloth; or, rather, one must make sure that one is decently covered, though
the covering may here and there be somewhat inferior in quality. So it has
been necessary, in order to keep the thread of history unbroken, to admit
some strands anything but silken; and if the choice has sometimes been of
ills, rather than of goods, the compiler can only hope that he chose wisely.

The most difficult and trying portion of his task has been, not to get his material together, but to compress it into reasonable limits. Especially in the colonial period was the temptation great to include more early American verse. Peter Folger's "A Looking-Glass for the Times," Benjamin Tompson's "New England's Crisis," Michael Wigglesworth's "God's Controversy with New England," the "Sot-Weed Factor," and many others, which it is recalling an old sorrow to name here, were excluded only after long and bitter debate. No doubt other exclusions will be noticed by nearly every reader of the volume — and it may interest him to know that the material gathered together would have made four such books as this.

The thread of narrative upon which the poems have been strung together has been made as slight as possible, just strong enough to carry the reader understandingly from one poem to the next. The notes, too, have been limited to the explanation of such allusions as are not likely to be found in the ordinary works of reference, with here and there an account of the circumstances which caused the lines to be written, or an indication of source, where the source is unusual. Every available source has been drawn upon — the works of all the better known and many of the minor American and English poets, anthologies, newspaper collections, magazines, collections of Americana and especially of broadsides — in a word, American and English poetry generally.

In this connection, the compiler wishes to make grateful acknowledgment of the assistance he has received on every hand, especially from Mr. Herbert Putnam and Miss Margaret McGuffey, of the Library of Congress; Mr. N. D. C. Hodges, librarian of the Cincinnati, Ohio, Public Library; Mr. C. B. Galbreath, librarian of the Ohio State Library; Mr. Charles F. Lummis, librarian of the Los Angeles, California, Public Library; Dr. Edward Everett Hale, Mr. William Henry Venable, Mr. Isaac R. Pennypacker, Mr. Arthur Guiterman, and Mr. Wallace Rice. He might add that it is a matter of deep personal gratification to him that in no instance has any author refused to permit the use of his work in this collection. On the contrary, many of them have been most helpful in suggestions.

A special effort has been made to secure accuracy of text, — no light task, especially with the early ballads. Where the text varied, as was often the case, that has been followed which seemed to have the greater authority, except that obvious misprints have been corrected. In this, the compiler has had the coöperation of The Riverside Press, and has had frequent occasion to admire the care and knowledge of the corrector and his assistants.

B. E. S.

CHILLICOTHE, OHIO, July 23, 1908.

TABLE OF CONTENTS

PART I

THE COLONIAL PERIOD

CHAPTER I

The Discovery of America

CHAPTER II

In the Wake of Columbus

CHAPTER III

The Settlement of Virginia

CHAPTER VII

King Philip's War and the Witchcraft Delusion

CHAPTER VIII

The Struggle for the Continent

PART II

THE REVOLUTION

CHAPTER I

The Coming of Discontent

CHAPTER II

The Bursting of the Storm

CHAPTER III

The Colonists take the Offensive

CHAPTER IV
Independence

CHAPTER V
The First Campaign

CHAPTER VI
"The Fate of Sir Jack Brag"

CHAPTER VII
The Second Stage

CHAPTER VIII

The War on the Water

CHAPTER IX

New York and the "Neutral Ground"

CHAPTER X

The War in the South

TABLE OF CONTENTS

CHAPTER XI

Peace

PART III

THE PERIOD OF GROWTH

CHAPTER I

The New Nation

CHAPTER II

The Second War with England

CHAPTER III

The West

CHAPTER IV

Through Five Administrations

CHAPTER V

The War with Mexico

CHAPTER VI

Fourteen Years of Peace

PART IV

THE CIVIL WAR

CHAPTER I

The Slavery Question

CHAPTER II

The Gauntlet

CHAPTER III

The North gets its Lesson

CHAPTER IV
The Grand Army of the Potomac

CHAPTER V
The War in the West

CHAPTER VI
The Coast and the River

CHAPTER VII

Emancipation

CHAPTER VIII

The "Grand Army's" Second Campaign

CHAPTER IX

With Grant on the Mississippi

CHAPTER X

The Final Struggle

CHAPTER XI

Winslow and Farragut

CHAPTER XII

The Martyr President

CHAPTER XIII

Peace

PART V

THE PERIOD OF EXPANSION

CHAPTER I

Reconstruction and After

CHAPTER II

The Year of a Hundred Years

CHAPTER III

The Conquest of the Plains

CHAPTER IV

The Second Assassination

CHAPTER V

The War with Spain

CHAPTER VI

The New Century

CHAPTER VII

The World War

PART I

THE COLONIAL PERIOD

AMERICA

Oh, who has not heard of the Northmen of yore,
How flew, like the sea-bird, their sails from the shore;
How westward they stayed not till, breasting the brine,
They hailed Narragansett, the land of the vine?

Then the war-songs of Rollo, his pennon and glaive,
Were heard as they danced by the moon-lighted wave,
And their golden-haired wives bore them sons of the soil,
While raged with the redskins their feud and turmoil.

And who has not seen, mid the summer's gay crowd,
That old pillared tower of their fortalice proud,
How it stands solid proof of the sea chieftains' reign
Ere came with Columbus those galleys of Spain?

'T was a claim for their kindred; an earnest of sway, —
By the stout-hearted Cabot made good in its day, —
Of the Cross of St. George on the Chesapeake's tide,
Where lovely Virginia arose like a bride.

Came the pilgrims with Winthrop; and, saint of the West,
Came Robert of Jamestown, the brave and the blest;
Came Smith, the bold rover, and Rolfe — with his ring,
To wed sweet Matoäka, child of a king.

Undaunted they came, every peril to dare,
Of tribes fiercer far than the wolf in his lair;
Of the wild irksome woods, where in ambush they lay;
Of their terror by night and their arrow by day.

And so where our capes cleave the ice of the poles,
Where groves of the orange scent sea-coast and shoals,
Where the froward Atlantic uplifts its last crest,
Where the sun, when he sets, seeks the East from the West;

The clime that from ocean to ocean expands,
The fields to the snow-drifts that stretch from the sands,
The wilds they have conquered of mountain and plain,
Those pilgrims have made them fair Freedom's domain.

And the bread of dependence if proudly they spurned,
'T was the soul of their fathers that kindled and burned,
'T was the blood of the Saxon within them that ran;
They held — to be free is the birthright of man.

So oft the old lion, majestic of mane,
Sees cubs of his cave breaking loose from his reign;
Unmeet to be his if they braved not his eye,
He gave them the spirit his own to defy.

Arthur Cleveland Coxe.

POEMS OF AMERICAN HISTORY

CHAPTER I

THE DISCOVERY OF AMERICA

Bjarni, son of Herjulf, speeding westward from Iceland in 986, to spend the Yuletide in Greenland with his father, encountered foggy weather and steered by guesswork for many days. At last he sighted land, but a land covered with dense woods, — not at all the land of fiords and glaciers he was seeking. So, without stopping, he turned his prow to the north, and ten days later was telling his story to the listening circle before the blazing logs in his father's house at Brattahlid. The tale came, in time, to the ears of Leif, the famous son of Red Eric, and in the year 1000 he set out from Greenland, with a crew of thirty-five, in search of the strange land to the south. He reached the barren coast of Labrador and named it Helluland, or "slate-land;" south of it was a coast so densely wooded that he named it Markland, or "woodland." At last he ran his ship ashore at a spot where "a river, issuing from a lake, fell into the sea." Wild grapes abounded, and he named the country Vinland.

THE STORY OF VINLAND[1]

From ".Psalm of the West"

FAR spread, below
The sea that fast hath locked in his loose flow
All secrets of Atlantis' drownèd woe
    Lay bound about with night on every hand,
    Save down the eastern brink a shining band
    Of day made out a little way from land.
Then from that shore the wind upbore a cry:
Thou Sea, thou Sea of Darkness ! why, oh why
Dost waste thy West in unthrift mystery ?
    But ever the idiot sea-mouths foam and fill,
    And never a wave doth good for man, or ill,
    And Blank is king, and Nothing hath his will;
And like as grim-beaked pelicans level file
Across the sunset toward their nightly isle
On solemn wings that wave but seldomwhile,
    So leanly sails the day behind the day
    To where the Past's lone Rock o'erglooms the spray,
    And down its mortal fissures sinks away.

[1] From Poems by Sidney Lanier; copyright, 1884, 1891, by Mary D. Lanier; published by Charles Scribner's Sons.

Master, Master, break this ban:
    The wave lacks Thee.
Oh, is it not to widen man
    Stretches the sea ?
Oh, must the sea-bird's idle van
    Alone be free ?

Into the Sea of the Dark doth creep
    Björne's pallid sail,
As the face of a walker in his sleep,
    Set rigid and most pale,
About the night doth peer and peep
    In a dream of an ancient tale.

Lo, here is made a hasty cry:
    Land, land, upon the west ! —
God save such land ! Go by, go by :
    Here may no mortal rest,
Where this waste hell of slate doth lie
    And grind the glacier's breast.

The sail goeth limp: hey, flap and strain
    Round eastward slanteth the mast;
As the sleep-walker waked with pain,
    White-clothed in the midnight blast,
Doth stare and quake, and stride again
    To houseward all aghast.

Yet as — A ghost ! his household cry:
    He hath followed a ghost in flight.
Let us see the ghost — his household fly
    With lamps to search the night —
So Norsemen's sails run out and try
    The Sea of the Dark with light.

Stout Are Marson, southward whirled
    From out the tempest's hand,
Doth skip the sloping of the world
    To Huitramannaland,
Where Georgia's oaks with moss-beards curled
    Wave by the shining strand,

And sway in sighs from Florida's Spring
    Or Carolina's Palm —

What time the mocking-bird doth bring
  The woods his artist's-balm,
Singing the Song of Everything
  Consummate-sweet and calm —

Land of large merciful-hearted skies,
  Big bounties, rich increase,
Green rests for Trade's blood-shotten eyes,
  For o'er-beat brains surcease,
For Love the dear woods' sympathies,
  For Grief the wise woods' peace.

For Need rich givings of hid powers
  In hills and vales quick-won,
For Greed large exemplary flowers
  That ne'er have toiled nor spun,
For Heat fair-tempered winds and showers,
  For Cold the neighbor sun.

.   .   .   .

Then Leif, bold son of Eric the Red,
  To the South of the West doth flee —
Past slaty Helluland is sped,
  Past Markland's woody lea,
Till round about fair Vinland's head,
  Where Taunton helps the sea,

The Norseman calls, the anchor falls,
  The mariners hurry a-strand:
They wassail with fore-drunken skals
  Where prophet wild grapes stand;
They lift the Leifsbooth's hasty walls,
  They stride about the land —

New England, thee! whose ne'er-spent wine
  As blood doth stretch each vein,
And urge thee, sinewed like thy vine,
  Through peril and all pain
To grasp Endeavor's towering Pine,
  And, once ahold, remain —

Land where the strenuous-handed Wind
  With sarcasm of a friend
Doth smite the man would lag behind
  To frontward of his end;
Yea, where the taunting fall and grind
  Of Nature's Ill doth send

Such mortal challenge of a clown
  Rude-thrust upon the soul,
That men but smile where mountains frown
  Or scowling waters roll,
And Nature's front of battle down
  Do hurl from pole to pole.

Now long the Sea of Darkness glimmers low
  With sails from Northland flickering to and
    fro —
Thorwald, Karlsefne, and those twin heirs
    of woe,
  Hellboge and Finnge, in treasonable bed
  Slain by the ill-born child of Eric Red,
  Freydisa false. Till, as much time is fled,
Once more the vacant airs with darkness fill,
Once more the wave doth never good nor ill,
And Blank is king, and Nothing works his
    will;
  And leanly sails the day behind the day
  To where the Past's lone Rock o'erglooms
    the spray,
And down its mortal fissures sinks away,
As when the grim-beaked pelicans level file
Across the sunset to their seaward isle
On solemn wings that wave but seldomwhile.
                                SIDNEY LANIER.

Leif and his crew spent the winter in Vinland,
and in the following spring took back to Green-
land news of the pleasant country they had dis-
covered. Other voyages followed, but the new-
comers became embroiled with the natives, who
attacked them in such numbers that all projects
of colonization were abandoned; and finally, in
1012, the Norsemen sailed away forever from this
land of promise.

THE NORSEMEN

[On a fragment of statue found at Bradford.]

GIFT from the cold and silent Past!
A relic to the present cast;
Left on the ever-changing strand
Of shifting and unstable sand,
Which wastes beneath the steady chime
And beating of the waves of Time!
Who from its bed of primal rock
First wrenched thy dark, unshapely block?
Whose hand, of curious skill untaught,
Thy rude and savage outline wrought?

The waters of my native stream
Are glancing in the sun's warm beam;
From sail-urged keel and flashing oar
The circles widen to its shore:
And cultured field and peopled town
Slope to its willowed margin down.
Yet, while this morning breeze is bringing
The home-life sound of school-bells ringing,
And rolling wheel, and rapid jar
Of the fire-winged and steedless car,

And voices from the wayside near
Come quick and blended on my ear, —
A spell is in this old gray stone,
My thoughts are with the Past alone!

A change! — The steepled town no more
Stretches along the sail-thronged shore;
Like palace-domes in sunset's cloud,
Fade sun-gilt spire and mansion proud:
Spectrally rising where they stood,
I see the old, primeval wood;
Dark, shadow-like, on either hand
I see its solemn waste expand;
It climbs the green and cultured hill,
It arches o'er the valley's rill,
And leans from cliff and crag to throw
Its wild arms o'er the stream below.
Unchanged, alone, the same bright river
Flows on, as it will flow forever!
I listen, and I hear the low
Soft ripple where its waters go;
I hear behind the panther's cry,
The wild-bird's scream goes thrilling by,
And shyly on the river's brink
The deer is stooping down to drink.

But hark! — from wood and rock flung
    back,
What sound comes up the Merrimac?
What sea-worn barks are those which throw
The light spray from each rushing prow?
Have they not in the North Sea's blast
Bowed to the waves the straining mast?
Their frozen sails the low, pale sun
Of Thulë's night has shone upon;
Flapped by the sea-wind's gusty sweep
Round icy drift, and headland steep.
Wild Jutland's wives and Lochlin's daugh-
    ters
Have watched them fading o'er the waters,
Lessening through driving mist and spray,
Like white-winged sea-birds on their way!

Onward they glide, — and now I view
Their iron-armed and stalwart crew;
Joy glistens in each wild blue eye,
Turned to green earth and summer sky.
Each broad, seamed breast has cast aside
Its cumbering vest of shaggy hide;
Bared to the sun and soft warm air,
Streams back the Northmen's yellow hair.
I see the gleam of axe and spear,
A sound of smitten shields I hear,
Keeping a harsh and fitting time
To Saga's chant, and Runic rhyme;

Such lays as Zetland's Scald has sung,
His gray and naked isles among;
Or muttered low at midnight hour
Round Odin's mossy stone of power.
The wolf beneath the Arctic moon
Has answered to that startling rune;
The Gael has heard its stormy swell,
The light Frank knows its summons well;
Iona's sable-stoled Culdee
Has heard it sounding o'er the sea,
And swept, with hoary beard and hair,
His altar's foot in trembling prayer!

'T is past, — the 'wildering vision dies
In darkness on my dreaming eyes!
The forest vanishes in air,
Hill-slope and vale lie starkly bare;
I hear the common tread of men,
And hum of work-day life again;
The mystic relic seems alone
A broken mass of common stone;
And if it be the chiselled limb
Of Berserker or idol grim,
A fragment of Valhalla's Thor,
The stormy Viking's god of War,
Or Praga of the Runic lay,
Or love-awakening Siona,
I know not, — for no graven line,
Nor Druid mark, nor Runic sign,
Is left me here, by which to trace
Its name, or origin, or place.
Yet, for this vision of the Past,
This glance upon its darkness cast,
My spirit bows in gratitude
Before the Giver of all good,
Who fashioned so the human mind,
That, from the waste of Time behind,
A simple stone, or mound of earth,
Can summon the departed forth;
Quicken the Past to life again,
The Present lose in what hath been,
And in their primal freshness show
The buried forms of long ago.
As if a portion of that Thought
By which the Eternal will is wrought,
Whose impulse fills anew with breath
The frozen solitude of Death,
To mortal mind were sometimes lent,
To mortal musings sometimes sent,
To whisper — even when it seems
But Memory's fantasy of dreams —
Through the mind's waste of woe and
    sin,
Of an immortal origin!
                JOHN GREENLEAF WHITTIER.

This, in mere outline, is the story of Vinland, as told in the Icelandic Chronicle. Of its substantial accuracy there can be little doubt. Many proofs of Norse occupation have been found on the shores of Massachusetts Bay. The "skeleton in armor," however, which was unearthed in 1835 near Fall River, Mass., was probably that of an Indian.

THE SKELETON IN ARMOR

"Speak! speak! thou fearful guest!
    Who, with thy hollow breast
    Still in rude armor drest,
        Comest to daunt me!
Wrapt not in Eastern balms,
But with thy fleshless palms
Stretched, as if asking alms,
        Why dost thou haunt me?"

Then, from those cavernous eyes
    Pale flashes seemed to rise,
    As when the Northern skies
        Gleam in December;
And, like the water's flow
Under December's snow,
Came a dull voice of woe
        From the heart's chamber.

"I was a Viking old!
    My deeds, though manifold,
    No Skald in song has told,
        No Saga taught thee!
Take heed, that in thy verse
Thou dost the tale rehearse,
Else dread a dead man's curse;
        For this I sought thee.

"Far in the Northern Land,
    By the wild Baltic's strand,
    I, with my childish hand,
        Tamed the gerfalcon;
And, with my skates fast-bound,
Skimmed the half-frozen Sound,
That the poor whimpering hound
        Trembled to walk on.

"Oft to his frozen lair
    Tracked I the grisly bear,
    While from my path the hare
        Fled like a shadow;
Oft through the forest dark
Followed the were-wolf's bark,
Until the soaring lark
        Sang from the meadow.

"But when I older grew,
    Joining a corsair's crew,
    O'er the dark sea I flew
        With the marauders.
Wild was the life we led;
Many the souls that sped,
Many the hearts that bled,
        By our stern orders.

"Many a wassail-bout
    Wore the long winter out;
    Often our midnight shout
        Set the cocks crowing,
As we the Berserk's tale
Measured in cups of ale,
Draining the oaken pail,
        Filled to o'erflowing.

"Once as I told in glee
    Tales of the stormy sea,
    Soft eyes did gaze on me,
        Burning yet tender;
And as the white stars shine
On the dark Norway pine,
On that dark heart of mine
        Fell their soft splendor.

"I wooed the blue-eyed maid,
    Yielding, yet half afraid,
    And in the forest's shade
        Our vows were plighted.
Under its loosened vest
Fluttered her little breast,
Like birds within their nest
        By the hawk frighted.

"Bright in her father's hall
    Shields gleamed upon the wall,
    Loud sang the minstrels all,
        Chanting his glory;
When of old Hildebrand
I asked his daughter's hand,
Mute did the minstrels stand
        To hear my story.

"While the brown ale he quaffed,
    Loud then the champion laughed
    And as the wind-gusts waft
        The sea-foam brightly,
So the loud laugh of scorn,
Out of those lips unshorn,
From the deep drinking-horn
        Blew the foam lightly.

"She was a Prince's child,
    I but a Viking wild,
And though she blushed and smiled,
        I was discarded!
Should not the dove so white
Follow the sea-mew's flight,
Why did they leave that night
        Her nest unguarded?

"Scarce had I put to sea,
Bearing the maid with me,
Fairest of all was she
        Among the Norsemen!
When on the white sea-strand,
Waving his armèd hand,
Saw we old Hildebrand,
        With twenty horsemen.

"Then launched they to the blast,
Bent like a reed each mast,
Yet we were gaining fast,
        When the wind failed us;
And with a sudden flaw
Came round the gusty Skaw,
So that our foe we saw
        Laugh as he hailed us.

"And as to catch the gale
    Round veered the flapping sail,
    'Death!' was the helmsman's hail,
        'Death without quarter!'
Mid-ships with iron keel
Struck we her ribs of steel!
Down her black hulk did reel
        Through the black water!

"As with his wings aslant,
    Sails the fierce cormorant,
    Seeking some rocky haunt,
        With his prey laden,—
So toward the open main,
Beating to sea again,
Through the wild hurricane,
        Bore I the maiden.

"Three weeks we westward bore,
And when the storm was o'er,
Cloud-like we saw the shore
        Stretching to leeward;
There for my lady's bower
Built I the lofty tower,
Which, to this very hour,
        Stands looking seaward.

"There lived we many years;
    Time dried the maiden's tears;
    She had forgot her fears,
        She was a mother;
Death closed her mild blue eyes,
Under that tower she lies;
Ne'er shall the sun arise
        On such another!

"Still grew my bosom then,
Still as a stagnant fen!
Hateful to me were men,
    The sunlight hateful!
In the vast forest here,
Clad in my warlike gear,
Fell I upon my spear,
    Oh, death was grateful!

"Thus, seamed with many scars,
Bursting these prison bars,
Up to its native stars
    My soul ascended!
There from the flowing bowl
Deep drinks the warrior's soul,
Skoal! to the Northland! *skoal!*"
        Thus the tale ended.
        HENRY WADSWORTH LONGFELLOW.

The centuries passed, and no more of the white-skinned race came to the New World. But a new era was at hand; the day drew near when a little fleet was to be put out from Spain and turn its prows westward on the grandest voyage the world has ever known.

PROPHECY

From "Il Morgante Maggiore"
1485

His bark
The daring mariner shall urge far o'er
The Western wave, a smooth and level plain,
Albeit the earth is fashioned like a wheel.
Man was in ancient days of grosser mould,
And Hercules might blush to learn how far
Beyond the limits he had vainly set
The dullest sea-boat soon shall wing her way.
Man shall descry another hemisphere,
Since to one common centre all things tend.
So earth, by curious mystery divine
Well balanced, hangs amid the starry spheres.
At our antipodes are cities, states,
And throngèd empires, ne'er divined of yore.

But see, the sun speeds on his western path
To glad the nations with expected light.
LUIGI PULCI.

About 1436 a son was born to Dominico Co-
lombo, wool-comber, of Genoa, and in due time
christened Cristoforo. Of his boyhood little is
known save that he early went to sea. About
1470 he followed his brother Bartholomew to
Lisbon, and in 1474 he was given a map by Tos-
canelli, the Florentine astronomer, showing Japan
and the Indies directly west of Portugal, together
with a long letter in which Toscanelli explained
his reasons for believing that by sailing west one
could reach the East. Columbus, studying the
problem month by month, became convinced of
the feasibility of such a route to the Indies, and
determined himself to traverse it.

THE INSPIRATION

From "The West Indies"

LONG lay the ocean-paths from man conceal'd;
Light came from heaven, — the magnet was
    reveal'd,
A surer star to guide the seaman's eye
Than the pale glory of the northern sky;
Alike ordain'd to shine by night and day,
Through calm and tempest, with unsetting
    ray;
Where'er the mountains rise, the billows
    roll,
Still with strong impulse turning to the pole,
True as the sun is to the morning true,
Though light as film, and trembling as the
    dew.

Then man no longer plied with timid oar,
And failing heart, along the windward shore;
Broad to the sky he turn'd his fearless sail,
Defied the adverse, woo'd the favoring gale,
Bared to the storm his adamantine breast,
Or soft on ocean's lap lay down to rest;
While free, as clouds the liquid ether sweep,
His white-wing'd vessels coursed the un-
    bounded deep;
From clime to clime the wanderer loved to
    roam,
The waves his heritage, the world his home.

Then first Columbus, with the mighty hand
Of grasping genius, weigh'd the sea and land;
The floods o'erbalanced: — where the tide of
    light,
Day after day, roll'd down the gulf of night,

There seem'd one waste of waters: — long
    in vain
His spirit brooded o'er the Atlantic main;
When sudden, as creation burst from nought,
Sprang a new world through his stupendous
    thought,
Light, order, beauty! — While his mind
    explored
The unveiling mystery, his heart adored;
Where er sublime imagination trod,
He heard the voice, he saw the face of God.

Far from the western cliffs he cast his eye,
O'er the wide ocean stretching to the sky:
In calm magnificence the sun declined,
And left a paradise of clouds behind:
Proud at his feet, with pomp of pearl and
    gold,
The billows in a sea of glory roll'd.

" — Ah! on this sea of glory might I sail,
Track the bright sun, and pierce the eternal
    veil
That hides those lands, beneath Hesperian
    skies,
Where daylight sojourns till our morrow
    rise!"

Thoughtful he wander'd on the beach alone;
Mild o'er the deep the vesper planet shone,
The eye of evening, brightening through the
    west
Till the sweet moment when it shut to rest:
"Whither, O golden Venus! art thou fled?
Not in the ocean-chambers lies thy bed;
Round the dim world thy glittering chariot
    drawn
Pursues the twilight, or precedes the dawn;
Thy beauty noon and midnight never see,
The morn and eve divide the year with
    thee."

Soft fell the shades, till Cynthia's slender bow
Crested the furthest wave, then sunk be-
    low:
"Tell me, resplendent guardian of the night,
Circling the sphere in thy perennial flight,
What secret path of heaven thy smiles adorn,
What nameless sea reflects thy gleaming
    horn?"

Now earth and ocean vanish'd, all serene
The starry firmament alone was seen;
Through the slow, silent hours, he watch'd
    the host

Of midnight suns in western darkness lost,
Till Night himself, on shadowy pinions borne,
Fled o'er the mighty waters, and the morn
Danced on the mountains: — "Lights of
    heaven!" he cried,
"Lead on; — I go to win a glorious bride;
Fearless o'er gulfs unknown I urge my way,
Where peril prowls, and shipwreck lurks for
    prey:
Hope swells my sail; — in spirit I behold
That maiden-world, twin-sister of the old,
By nature nursed beyond the jealous sea,
Denied to ages, but betroth'd to me."
                            JAMES MONTGOMERY.

In 1484 Columbus laid his plan before King
John II, of Portugal, but became so disgusted
with his treachery and double-dealing, that he
left Portugal and entered the service of Ferdinand
and Isabella. The Spanish monarchs listened to
him with attention, and ordered that the greatest
astronomers and cosmographers of the kingdom
should assemble at Salamanca and pass upon the
feasibility of the project.

COLUMBUS

[January, 1487]

St. Stephen's cloistered hall was proud
    In learning's pomp that day,
For there a robed and stately crowd
    Pressed on in long array.
A mariner with simple chart
    Confronts that conclave high,
While strong ambition stirs his heart,
And burning thoughts of wonder part
    From lip and sparkling eye.

What hath he said? With frowning face,
    In whispered tones they speak,
And lines upon their tablets trace,
    Which flush each ashen cheek;
The Inquisition's mystic doom
    Sits on their brows severe,
And bursting forth in visioned gloom,
Sad heresy from burning tomb
    Groans on the startled ear.

Courage, thou Genoese! Old Time
    Thy splendid dream shall crown:
Yon Western Hemisphere sublime,
    Where unshorn forests frown,
The awful Andes' cloud-wrapt brow,
    The Indian hunter's bow

Bold streams untamed by helm or prow,
And rocks of gold and diamonds, thou
    To thankless Spain shalt show.

Courage, World-finder! Thou hast need!
    In Fate's unfolding scroll,
Dark woes and ingrate wrongs I read,
    That rack the noble soul.
On! on! Creation's secrets probe,
    Then drink thy cup of scorn,
And wrapped in fallen Cæsar's robe,
Sleep like that master of the globe,
    All glorious, — yet forlorn.
                    LYDIA HUNTLEY SIGOURNEY.

The council convened at Salamanca and ex-
amined Columbus; but it presented to him an
almost impenetrable wall of bigotry and prejudice.
Long delays and adjournments followed; and for
three years the suppliant was put off with excuses
and evasions. At last, worn out with waiting and
anxiety, he appealed to Ferdinand to give him a
definite answer.

COLUMBUS TO FERDINAND

[January, 1491]

Illustrious monarch of Iberia's soil,
Too long I wait permission to depart;
Sick of delays, I beg thy list'ning ear —
Shine forth the patron and the prince of
    art.

While yet Columbus breathes the vital air,
Grant his request to pass the western main:
Reserve this glory for thy native soil,
And what must please thee more — for thy
    own reign.

Of this huge globe, how small a part we
    know —
Does heaven their worlds to western suns
    deny? —
How disproportion'd to the mighty deep
The lands that yet in human prospect lie!

Does Cynthia, when to western skies arriv'd,
Spend her sweet beam upon the barren main,
And ne'er illume with midnight splendor, she,
The natives dancing on the lightsome
    green? —

Should the vast circuit of the world contain
Such wastes of ocean, and such scanty land?

'T is reason's voice that bids me think not so,
I think more nobly of the Almighty hand.

Does yon fair lamp trace half the circle round
To light the waves and monsters of the
    seas ? —
No — be there must beyond the billowy waste
Islands, and men, and animals, and trees.

An unremitting flame my breast inspires
To seek new lands amidst the barren waves,
Where falling low, the source of day descends,
And the blue sea his evening visage laves.

Hear, in his tragic lay, Cordova's sage:
"*The time shall come, when numerous years
        are past,*
The ocean shall dissolve the bonds of things,
And an extended region rise at last;

"*And Typhis shall disclose the mighty land*
Far, far away, where none have rov'd before;
Nor shall the world's remotest region be
Gibraltar's rock, or Thule's savage shore."

Fir'd at the theme, I languish to depart,
Supply the barque, and bid Columbus sail;
He fears no storms upon the untravell'd deep;
Reason shall steer, and skill disarm the gale.

Nor does he dread to lose the intended course,
Though far from land the reeling galley stray,
And skies above and gulphy seas below
Be the sole objects seen for many a day.

Think not that Nature has unveil'd in vain
The mystic magnet to the mortal eye:
So late have we the guiding needle plann'd
Only to sail beneath our native sky?

Ere this was found, the ruling power of all
Found for our use an ocean in the land,
Its breadth so small we could not wander long,
Nor long be absent from the neighboring
        strand.

Short was the course, and guided by the stars,
But stars no more shall point our daring way;
The Bear shall sink, and every guard be
        drown'd,
And great Arcturus scarce escape the sea,

When southward we shall steer — O grant
    my wish,
Supply the barque, and bid Columbus sail,

He dreads no tempests on the untravell'd deep,
Reason shall steer, and skill disarm the gale.
                    PHILIP FRENEAU.

Early in 1491 the council of Salamanca re-
ported that the proposed enterprise was vain and
impossible of execution, and Ferdinand accepted
the decision. Indignant at thought of the years
he had wasted, Columbus started for Paris, to lay
his plan before the King of France. He was ac-
companied by his son, Diego, and stopped one
night at the convent of La Rabida, near Palos, to
ask for food and shelter. The prior, Juan Perez
de Marchena, became interested in his project,
detained him, and finally secured for him another
audience of Isabella.

COLUMBUS AT THE CONVENT

[July, 1491]

DREARY and brown the night comes down,
    Gloomy, without a star.
On Palos town the night comes down;
The day departs with a stormy frown;
    The sad sea moans afar.

A convent-gate is near; 't is late;
    Ting-ling! the bell they ring.
They ring the bell, they ask for bread —
"Just for my child," the father said.
    Kind hands the bread will bring.

White was his hair, his mien was fair,
    His look was calm and great.
The porter ran and called a friar;
The friar made haste and told the prior;
    The prior came to the gate.

He took them in, he gave them food;
    The traveller's dreams he heard;
And fast the midnight moments flew,
And fast the good man's wonder grew,
    And all his heart was stirred.

The child the while, with soft, sweet smile,
    Forgetful of all sorrow,
Lay soundly sleeping in his bed.
The good man kissed him then, and said:
    "You leave us not to-morrow!

"I pray you rest the convent's guest;
    The child shall be our own —
A precious care, while you prepare
Your business with the court, and bear
    Your message to the throne."

And so his guest he comforted.
  O wise, good prior! to you,
Who cheered the stranger's darkest days,
And helped him on his way, what praise
  And gratitude are due!
                JOHN T. TROWBRIDGE.

Isabella and Ferdinand were with their army before Granada, and received Columbus well; but his demands for emoluments and honors in the event of success were pronounced absurd; the negotiations were broken off, and again Columbus started for France. The few converts to his theories were in despair, and one of them, Luis de Santangel, receiver of the ecclesiastical revenues of Aragon, obtained an audience of the Queen, and enkindled her patriotic spirit. When Ferdinand still hesitated, she exclaimed, "I undertake the enterprise for my own crown of Castile. I will pledge my jewels to raise the money that is needed!" Santangel assured her that he himself was ready to provide the money, and advanced seventeen thousand florins from the coffers of Aragon, so that Ferdinand really paid for the expedition, after all.

THE FINAL STRUGGLE

From "The New World"

[January 6 — April 17, 1492]

YET had his sun not risen; from his lips
  Fell in swift fervid accents his desire,
    And Talavera's eyes of smouldering
      fire
Shone with a myriad doubts, a dark eclipse
Of faith hung round him, and the longed-
    for ships
  Ploughed but the ocean of his star-lit
    dreams;
Time had not tried his soul enough with
    whips
And scorns, for so the rigid Master deems
      He makes his servants fit
      For the hard toils which knit
The perfect garment, firm and without
    seams,
  The world shall wear at last; his hurt
    brain teems
With indignation and he turns away
Undaunted, and he girds him for the
    fray
Once more; but first he hears the words of
    his good friend,
Marchena, strong with trust in the far-shining
    end.

His wanderings reached at last the lonely
    door
  Of calm La Rabida; there the silence
    came
  Grateful upon his grief's consuming
    flame;
The simple cloisters gave him peace once
    more,
And the live ocean rolled up to the shore
  In ceaseless voice of promise; through
    the pines
The sun looked down benignant, and the
    roar
Of the far world of rivalries declines
      Into an inward murmur
      With each day growing firmer,
  Whose sense is conquest at the last; as
    shines
A lamp across a rocky path's confines,
  Making the outlet clear, Juan Perez' faith
Who heard him and conceived his words
    no wraith
Of fevered fancy but the very truth, was light
To bring the Queen to know his purposes
    aright.

O noble priest and friend! you reached
    the court
  And turned the Queen from conquest's
    mid career
  To hearken; other triumphs glittered
    clear
Before her, and again from Huelva's port
The seeker came; he saw Granada's fort
  Open its gates reluctant, and the King,
El Zogoibi, bewail his bitter sort
  And loss which made the rich *Te Deums*
    ring
      When on La Vela's tower
      The cross bloomed like a flower
Of heaven's own growing; but the sud-
    den spring,
  Loud with birds silent long that strove
    to sing,
After the winter's weary voiceless reign,
Was overcast with storms of cold disdain;
Haughtily forth he fared and reached Gra-
    nada's gates
When the clouds lifted and the persecuting
    fates

Relented from their fury; for the Queen
  Listened unto the urgings manifold
    Of Santangel, and counsel, wise and
    bold,

Of the far-seeing Marchioness, whose keen
Divinings pierced the misty ocean's screen
    And felt the deed must surely come to
        pass;
So they recalled him, and his life's changed
        scene
    Grew bright with blooms and smile of
        thickening grass;
            O royal woman then
            Your hand received again
    The keys of a great realm; in the clear
        glass
Of actions yet to be whose fires amass
Infinite stores of impulse toward the good,
Your image permanent lies; forth from the
        wood
Of beasts malicious and the unrelenting
        dread
You showed the way, but sought not from
        the gloom to tread.

    The wind was fair, the ships lay in the
        bay,
        And the blue sky looked down upon the
            earth;
        Prophetic time laughed toward the
            nearing birth
    Of the strong child with whom should come
        a day
    That dulled all earlier hours. Forth on the
        way
        With holy blessings said, and bellied
            sails,
    And mounting joy that knows not let nor
        stay!
        Lo! the undaunted purpose never fails!
            O patient master, seer,
            For whom the far is near,
        The vision true, and the mere present
            pales
        Its lustre, what mild seas and blossomed
            vales
Awaited you? haply a paradise
But not the one which drew your swerve-
        less eyes;
Could you have known what lands were there
        beyond the main,
You surelier would have turned to gladsome-
        ness from pain.
                    LOUIS JAMES BLOCK.

With the greatest difficulty, Columbus managed
to secure three little vessels, the Santa Maria, the
Pinta, and the Niña, and to enlist about a hundred
and twenty men for the enterprise. Early in the

morning of Friday, August 3, 1492, this tiny fleet
sailed out from Palos and turned their prows to
the west.

STEER, BOLD MARINER, ON!

[August 3, 1492]

STEER, bold mariner, on! albeit witlings
        deride thee,
And the steersman drop idly his hand at the
        helm.
Ever and ever to westward! there must the
        coast be discovered,
If it but lie distinct, luminous lie in thy mind.
Trust to the God that leads thee, and follow
        the sea that is silent;
Did it not yet exist, now would it rise from
        the flood.
Nature with Genius stands united in league
        everlasting;
What is promised by one, surely the other
        performs.
                    FRIEDRICH VON SCHILLER.

The fleet reached the Canaries without misad-
venture, but when the shores of Ferro sank from
sight, the sailors gave themselves up for lost.
Their terror increased day by day; the compass
behaved strangely, the boats became entangled
in vast meadows of floating seaweed; and finally
the trade-winds wafted them so steadily westward
that they became convinced they could never
return. By October 4 there were ominous signs
of mutiny, and finally, on the 11th, affairs reached
a crisis.

THE TRIUMPH[1]

From "Psalm of the West"

[Dawn, October 12, 1492]

SANTA MARIA, well thou tremblest down the
        wave,
    Thy Pinta far abow, thy Niña nigh astern:
Columbus stands in the night alone, and,
        passing grave,
    Yearns o'er the sea as tones o'er under-
        silence yearn.
Heartens his heart as friend befriends his
        friend less brave,
    Makes burn the faiths that cool, and cools
        the doubts that burn: —

[1] From Poems by Sidney Lanier; copyright,
1884, 1891, by Mary D. Lanier; published by
Charles Scribner's Sons.

*'Twixt this and dawn, three hours my soul
will smite
  With prickly seconds, or less tolerably
  With dull-blade minutes flatwise slapping
me.
Wait, Heart! Time moves. — Thou lithe
young Western Night,
Just-crownèd king, slow riding to thy right,
  Would God that I might straddle mutiny
Calm as thou sitt'st yon never-managed
sea,
Balk'st with his balking, fliest with his flight,
Giv'st supple to his rearings and his falls,
  Nor dropp'st one coronal star above thy
brow
  Whilst ever dayward thou art steadfast
drawn!
Yea, would I rode these mad contentious
brawls
  No damage taking from their If and How,
  Nor no result save galloping to my Dawn!

"My Dawn? my Dawn? How if it never
break?
  How if this West by other Wests is pieced,
  And these by vacant Wests on Wests in-
creased —
One Pain of Space, with hollow ache on ache
Throbbing and ceasing not for Christ's own
sake? —
  Big perilous theorem, hard for king and
priest:
  Pursue the West but long enough, 't is East!
Oh, if this watery world no turning take!
Oh, if for all my logic, all my dreams,
  Provings of that which is by that which
seems,
Fears, hopes, chills, heats, hastes, patiences,
droughts, tears,
Wife-grievings, slights on love, embezzled
years,
  Hates, treaties, scorns, upliftings, loss and
gain, —
  This earth, no sphere, be all one sickening
plane!

"Or, haply, how if this contrarious West,
  That me by turns hath starved, by turns
hath fed,
  Embraced, disgraced, beat back, solicited,
Have no fixed heart of Law within his breast,
Or with some different rhythm doth e'er
contest
  Nature in the East? Why, 't is but three
weeks fled

I saw my Judas needle shake his head
And flout the Pole that, East, he Lord con-
fessed!
  God! if this West should own some other
Pole,
  And with his tangled ways perplex my soul
Until the maze grow mortal, and I die
  Where distraught Nature clean hath gone
astray,
  On earth some other wit than Time's at
play,
Some other God than mine above the sky!

"Now speaks mine other heart with cheerier
seeming:
  Ho, Admiral! o'er-defalking to thy crew
  Against thyself, thyself far overfew
To front yon multitudes of rebel scheming?
Come, ye wild twenty years of heavenly
dreaming!
  Come, ye wild weeks since first this canvas
drew
  Out of vexed Palos ere the dawn was blue,
O'er milky waves about the bows full-cream-
ing!
Come set me round with many faithful spears
  Of confident remembrance— how I crushed
  Cat-lived rebellions, pitfalled treasons,
hushed
Scared husbands' heart-break cries on distant
wives,
Made cowards blush at whining for their lives,
Watered my parching souls, and dried their
tears.

"Ere we Gomera cleared, a coward cried,
  Turn, turn: here be three caravels ahead,
  From Portugal, to take us: we are dead! —
Hold Westward, pilot, calmly I replied.
So when the last land down the horizon died,
  Go back, go back! they prayed: *our hearts
are lead.* —
  Friends, we are bound into the West, I said.
Then passed the wreck of a mast upon our
side.
  See (so they wept) *God's Warning! Admiral,
turn!* —
  Steersman, I said, *hold straight into the
West.*
Then down the night we saw the meteor
burn.
  So do the very heavens in fire protest:
  *Good Admiral, put about! O Spain, dear
Spain!* —
Hold straight into the West, I said again.

"Next drive we o'er the slimy-weeded sea.
Lo! herebeneath (another coward cries)
The cursèd land of sunk Atlantis lies!
This slime will suck us down — turn while
    thou'rt free! —
But no! I said, Freedom bears West for me!
Yet when the long-time stagnant winds
    arise,
And day by day the keel to westward flies,
My Good my people's Ill doth come to be:
Ever the winds into the West do blow;
Never a ship, once turned, might homeward
    go;
Meanwhile we speed into the lonesome main.
For Christ's sake, parley, Admiral! Turn,
    before
We sail outside all bounds of help from pain!—
Our help is in the West, I said once more.

"So when there came a mighty cry of *Land!*
And we clomb up and saw, and shouted
    strong
Salve Regina! all the ropes along,
But knew at morn how that a counterfeit
    band
Of level clouds had aped a silver strand;
So when we heard the orchard-bird's small
    song,
And all the people cried, *A hellish throng*
To tempt us onward by the Devil planned,
Yea, all from hell — keen heron, fresh green
    weeds,
Pelican, tunny-fish, fair tapering reeds,
Lie-telling lands that ever shine and die
In clouds of nothing round the empty sky.
Tired Admiral, get thee from this hell, and
    rest! —
Steersman, I said, *hold straight into the West.*

"I marvel how mine eye, ranging the Night,
From its big circling ever absently
    Returns, thou large low Star, to fix on
    thee.
Maria! Star? No star: a Light, a Light!
Wouldst leap ashore, Heart? Yonder burns
    — a Light.
Pedro Gutierrez, wake! come up to me.
I prithee stand and gaze about the sea:
What seest? *Admiral, like as land — a Light!*
Well! Sanchez of Segovia, come and try:
What seest? *Admiral, naught but sea and*
    sky!
Well! but *I* saw It. Wait! the Pinta's gun!
Why, look, 't is dawn, the land is clear:
    't is done!

Two dawns do break at once from **Time's**
    full hand —
God's, East — mine, West: good friends,
    behold my Land!"
                              SIDNEY LANIER.

At daybreak of Friday, October 12 (N. S. Oc-
tober 22), the boats were lowered and Columbus,
with a large part of his company, went ashore,
wild with exultation. They found that they were
on a small island, and Columbus named it San
Salvador. It was one of the Bahamas, but which
one is not certainly known.

COLUMBUS

BEHIND him lay the gray Azores,
    Behind the Gates of Hercules;
Before him not the ghost of shores,
    Before him only shoreless seas.
The good mate said: "Now must we pray,
    For lo! the very stars are gone.
Brave Admiral, speak, what shall I say?"
    "Why, say 'Sail on! sail on! and on!'"

"My men grow mutinous day by day;
    My men grow ghastly wan, and weak."
The stout mate thought of home; a spray
    Of salt wave washed his swarthy cheek.
"What shall I say, brave Admiral, say,
    If we sight naught but seas at dawn?"
"Why, you shall say at break of day,
    'Sail on! sail on! sail on! and on!'"

They sailed and sailed, as winds might blow,
    Until at last the blanched mate said:
"Why, now not even God would know
    Should I and all my men fall dead.
These very winds forget their way,
    For God from these dread seas is gone.
Now speak, brave Admiral, speak and say" —
    He said: "Sail on! sail on! and on!"

They sailed. They sailed. Then spake the
    mate:
"This mad sea shows his teeth to-night.
He lifts his lip, he lies in wait,
    With lifted teeth, as if to bite!
Brave Admiral, say but one good word:
    What shall we do when hope is gone?"
The words leapt like a leaping sword:
    "Sail on! sail on! sail on! and on!"

Then, pale and worn, he kept his deck,
    And peered through darkness. Ah, that night

Of all dark nights! And then a speck —
A light! a light! a light! a light!
It grew, a starlit flag unfurled!
It grew to be Time's burst of dawn.
He gained a world; he gave that world
Its grandest lesson: "On! sail on!"

JOAQUIN MILLER.

Columbus reached Spain again on March 15,
1493, and at once sent word of his arrival to Ferdi-
nand and Isabella, who were at Barcelona. He
was summoned to appear before them and was
received with triumphal honors. The King and
Queen arose at his approach, directed him to seat
himself in their presence, and listened with in-
tense interest to his story of the voyage. When
he had finished, they sank to their knees, as did
all present, and thanked God for this mark of his
favor.

THE THANKSGIVING FOR AMERICA

[Barcelona, April, 1493]

I

'T WAS night upon the Darro.
The risen moon above the silvery tower
Of Comares shone, the silver sun of night,
And poured its lustrous splendors through
    the halls
Of the Alhambra.
    The air was breathless,
Yet filled with ceaseless songs of nightingales,
And odors sweet of falling orange blooms;
The misty lamps were burning odorous oil;
The uncurtained balconies were full of life,
And laugh and song, and airy castanets
And gay guitars.
    Afar Sierras rose,
Domes, towers, and pinnacles, over royal
    heights,
Whose crowns were gemmed with stars.
    The Generaliffe,
The summer palace of old Moorish kings
In vanished years, stood sentinel afar,
A pile of shade, as brighter grew the moon,
Impearling fountain sprays, and shimmer-
    ing
On seas of citron orchards cool and green,
And terraces embowered with vernal vines
And breathing flowers.
    In shadowy arcades
Were loitering priests, and here and there
A water-carrier passed with tinkling bells.
    There came a peal of horns
That woke Granada, city of delights,

From its long moonlight reverie. Again: —
The suave lute ceased to play, the casta-
    net;
The water-bearer stopped. and ceased his
    song
The wandering troubadour.
    Then rent the air
Another joyous peal, and oped the gates
And entered there a train of cavaliers,
Their helmets glittering in the low red moon.
    The streets and balconies
All danced with wondering life. The train
    moved on,
And filled the air again the horns melodious,
And loud the heralds shouted: —

"*Thy name, O Fernando, through all earth
    shall be sounded,
Columbus has triumphed, his foes are con-
    founded !*"

    A silence followed.
Could such tidings be? Men heard and
    whispered,
Eyes glanced to eyes, feet uncertain moved,
Never on mortal ears had fallen words
Like these. And was the earth a star?
    On marched the cavaliers,
And pealed again the horns, and again cried
The heralds: —

"*Thy name, Isabella, through all earth shall
    be sounded,
Columbus has triumphed, his foes are con-
    founded !*"

    All hearts were thrilled.
"Isabella!" That name breathed faith and
    hope
And lofty aim. Emotion swayed the crowds;
Tears flowed, and acclamations rose, and
    rushed
The wondering multitudes toward the plaza.
"Isabella! Isabella!" it filled
The air — that one word "Isabella!"
    And now
'T is noon of night. The moon hangs near
    the earth —
A golden moon in golden air; the peaks
Like silver tents of shadowy sentinels
Glint 'gainst the sky. The plaza gleams and
    surges
Like a sea. The joyful horns peal forth
    again,
And falls a hush, and cry the heralds: —

"*Thy name, Isabella, shall be praised by all
    the living;*
*Haste, haste to Barcelona, and join the Great
    Thanksgiving!*"

What nights had seen Granada!
Yet never one like this! The moon went down
And fell the wings of shadow, yet the streets
Still swarmed with people hurrying on and
    on.

II

        Morn came,
With bursts of nightingales and quivering
    fires.
The cavaliers rode forth toward Barcelona.
The city followed, throbbing with delight.
The happy troubadour, the muleteer,
The craftsmen all, the boy and girl, and e'en
The mother — 't was a soft spring morn;
The fairest skies of earth those April morns
In Andalusia. Long was the journey,
But the land was flowers and the nights were
    not,
And birds sang all the hours, and breezes cool
Fanned all the ways along the sea.
        The roads were filled
With hurrying multitudes. For well 't was
    known
That he, the conqueror, viceroy of the isles,
Was riding from Seville to meet the king.
And what were conquerors before to him
    whose eye
Had seen the world a star, and found the star
    a world?
        Once he had walked
The self-same ways, roofless and poor and
    sad,
A beggar at old convent doors, and heard
The very children jeer him in the streets,
And ate his crust and made his roofless bed
Upon the flowers beside his boy, and prayed,
And found in trust a pillow radiant
With dreams immortal. Now?

III

        That was a glorious day
That dawned on Barcelona. Banners filled
The thronging towers, the old bells rung, and
    blasts
Of lordly trumpets seemed to reach the sky
Cerulean. All Spain had gathered there,
And waited there his coming; Castilian
    knights,
Gay cavaliers, hidalgos young, and e'en the old

Puissant grandees of far Aragon,
With glittering mail, and waving plumes, and
    all
The peasant multitude with bannerets
And charms and flowers.
        Beneath pavilions
Of brocades of gold, the Court had met.
The dual crowns of Leon old and proud Cas-
    tile
There waited him, the peasant mariner.
        The trumpets waited
Near the open gates; the minstrels young and
    fair
Upon the tapestried and arrased walls,
And everywhere from all the happy provinces
The wandering troubadours.
        Afar was heard
A cry, a long acclaim. Afar was seen
A proud and stately steed with nodding
    plumes,
Bridled with gold, whose rider stately rode,
And still afar a long and sinuous train
Of silvery cavaliers. A shout arose,
And all the city, all the vales and hills,
With silver trumpets rung.
        He came, the Genoese,
With reverent look and calm and lofty mien,
And saw the wondering eyes and heard the
    cries
And trumpet peals, as one who followed still
Some Guide unseen.
        Before his steed
Crowned Indians marched with lowly faces,
And wondered at the new world that they
    saw;
Gay parrots shouted from their gold-bound
    arms,
And from their crests swept airy plumes.
        The sun
Shone full in splendor on the scene, and here
The old and new world met. But —

IV

        Hark! the heralds!
How they thrill all hearts and fill all eyes with
    tears!
The very air seems throbbing with delight;
Hark! hark! they cry, in chorus all they
    cry: —

"*Á Castilla y á Leon, á Castilla y á Leon,
Nuevo mundo dio Colon!*"

        Every heart now beats with his,
The stately rider on whose calm face shines

A heaven-born inspiration. Still the shout:
"*Nuevo mundo dio Colon!*" how it rings!
From wall to wall, from knights and cava-
    liers,
And from the multitudinous throngs,
A mighty chorus of the vales and hills!
"*Á Castilla y á Leon!*"
    And now the golden steed
Draws near the throne; the crowds move
    back, and rise
The reverent crowns of Leon and Castile;
And stands before the tear-filled eyes of all
The multitudes the form of Isabella.
Semiramis? Zenobia? What were they
To her, as met her eyes again the eyes of
    him
Into whose hands her love a year before
Emptied its jewels!
    He told his tale:
The untried deep, the green Sargasso Sea,
The varying compass, the affrighted crews,
The hymn they sung on every doubtful eve,
The sweet hymn to the Virgin. How there
    came
The land birds singing, and the drifting weeds,
How broke the morn on fair San Salvador,
How the *Te Deum* on that isle was sung,
And how the cross was lifted in the name
Of Leon and Castile. And then he turned
His face towards Heaven, "O Queen! O
    Queen!
There kingdoms wait the triumphs of the
    cross!"

Then Isabella rose,
With face illumined: then overcome with joy
She sank upon her knees, and king and court
And nobles rose and knelt beside her,
And followed them the sobbing multitude;
Then came a burst of joy, a chorus grand,
And mighty antiphon —

"*We praise thee, Lord, and, Lord, acknow-
    ledge thee,
And give thee glory! — Holy, Holy, Holy!*"

Loud and long it swelled and thrilled the air,
That first Thanksgiving for the new-found
    world!

VI

The twilight roses bloomed
In the far skies o'er Barcelona.
The gentle Indians came and stood before

The throne, and smiled the queen, and
    said:
"I see my gems again." The shadow fell,
And trilled all night beneath the moon and
    stars
The happy nightingales.
                    HEZEKIAH BUTTERWORTH.

Royal favor is capricious and Columbus had his
full share of enemies at court. These, in the end,
succeeded in gaining the King's ear; Columbus was
arrested in San Domingo and sent back to Spain
in chains. Isabella ordered them struck off, and
promised him that he should be reimbursed for
his losses and restored to all his dignities; but the
promise was never kept.

COLUMBUS IN CHAINS

[August, 1500]

ARE these the honors they reserve for me,
Chains for the man who gave new worlds to
    Spain!
Rest here, my swelling heart! — O kings, O
    queens,
Patrons of monsters, and their progeny,
Authors of wrong, and slaves to fortune
    merely!
Why was I seated by my prince's side,
Honor'd, caress'd like some first peer of
    Spain?
Was it that I might fall most suddenly
From honor's summit to the sink of scandal?
'T is done, 't is done! — what madness is
    ambition!
What is there in that little breath of men,
Which they call Fame, that should induce
    the brave
To forfeit ease and that domestic bliss
Which is the lot of happy ignorance,
Less glorious aims, and dull humility? —
Whoe'er thou art that shalt aspire to honor,
And on the strength and vigor of the mind
Vainly depending, court a monarch's favor,
Pointing the way to vast extended empire;
First count your pay to be ingratitude,
Then chains and prisons, and disgrace like
    mine!
Each wretched pilot now shall spread his
    sails,
And treading in my footsteps, hail new worlds,
Which, but for me, had still been empty
    visions.
                        PHILIP FRENEAU.

On November 7, 1504, Columbus landed in Spain after a fourth voyage to America, during which he had endured sufferings and privations almost beyond description. He was a broken man, and the last blow was the death of Isabella, nineteen days after he reached Seville. Her death left him without patron or protector, and the last eighteen months of his life were spent in sickness and poverty. He died at Valladolid, May 20, 1506.

COLUMBUS DYING

[May 20, 1506]

HARK! do I hear again the roar
Of the tides by the Indies sweeping down?
Or is it the surge from the viewless shore
That swells to bear me to my crown?
Life is hollow and cold and drear
With smiles that darken and hopes that flee;
And, far from its winds that faint and veer,
I am ready to sail the vaster sea!

Lord, Thou knowest I love Thee best;
And that scorning peril and toil and pain,
I held my way to the mystic West,
Glory for Thee and Thy Church to gain.
And Thou didst lead me, only Thou,
Cheering my heart in cloud and calm,
Till the dawn my glad, victorious prow
Greeted Thine isles of bloom and balm.

And then, O gracious, glorious Lord,
I saw Thy face, and all heaven came nigh
And my soul was lost in that rich reward,
And ravished with hope of the bliss on high,
So, I can meet the sovereign's frown —
My dear Queen gone — with a large disdain;
For the time will come when his chief renown
Will be that I sailed from his realm of Spain.

I have found new Lands — a World, maybe,
Whose splendor will yet the Old outshine;
And life and death are alike to me,
For earth will honor, and heaven is mine.
Is mine! — What songs of sweet accord!
What billows that nearer, gentler roll!
Is mine! — Into Thy hands, O Lord,
Into Thy hands I give my soul!
EDNA DEAN PROCTOR.

COLUMBUS

GIVE me white paper!
This which you use is black and rough with smears
Of sweat and grime and fraud and blood and tears,
Crossed with the story of men's sins and fears,
Of battle and of famine all these years,
When all God's children had forgot their birth,
And drudged and fought and died like beasts of earth.

"Give me white paper!"
One storm-trained seaman listened to the word;
What no man saw he saw; he heard what no man heard.
In answer he compelled the sea
To eager man to tell
The secret she had kept so well!
Left blood and guilt and tyranny behind, —
Sailing still West the hidden shore to find;
For all mankind that unstained scroll unfurled,
Where God might write anew the story of the World.
EDWARD EVERETT HALE.

COLUMBUS AND THE MAYFLOWER

O LITTLE fleet! that on thy quest divine
Sailedst from Palos one bright autumn morn,
Say, has old Ocean's bosom ever borne
A freight of faith and hope to match with thine?

Say, too, has Heaven's high favor given again
Such consummation of desire as shone
About Columbus when he rested on
The new-found world and married it to Spain?

Answer, — thou refuge of the freeman's need, —
Thou for whose destinies no kings looked out,
Nor sages to resolve some mighty doubt, —
Thou simple Mayflower of the salt-sea mead!

When thou wert wafted to that distant shore,
Gay flowers, bright birds, rich odors met thee not;
Stern Nature hailed thee to a sterner lot, —
God gave free earth and air, and gave no more.

Thus to men cast in that heroic mould
Came empire such as Spaniard never knew,
Such empire as beseems the just and true;
And at the last, almost unsought, came gold.

But He who rules both calm and stormy days,
Can guard that people's heart, that nation's health,
Safe on the perilous heights of power and wealth,
As in the straitness of the ancient ways
LORD HOUGHTON.

CHAPTER II

IN THE WAKE OF COLUMBUS

The news of Columbus's discoveries soon spread through western Europe, and in May, 1497, John Cabot sailed from Bristol, England, in the Matthew, and discovered what he supposed to be the Chinese coast on June 24. The thrifty Henry VII gave him the sum of £10 as a reward for this achievement. Cabot was the first European since the vikings to set foot on the North American continent.

THE FIRST VOYAGE OF JOHN CABOT

[1497]

"HE chases shadows," sneered the British tars.
"As well fling nets to catch the golden stars
As climb the surges of earth's utmost sea."
But for the Venice pilot, meagre, wan,
His swarthy sons beside him, life began
With that slipt cable, when his dream rode free.

And Henry, on his battle-wrested throne,
The Councils done, would speak in musing tone
Of Cabot, not the cargo he might bring.
"Man's heart, though morsel scant for hungry crow,
Is greater than a world can fill, and so
Fair fall the shadow-seekers!' quoth the king.

Colonies were planted by the Spaniards in Cuba and Hispaniola, but the New World continued to be for them a land of wonder and mystery. They were quite ready to believe any marvel, — among others, that somewhere to the north lay an island named Bimini, on which was a fountain whose waters gave perpetual youth to all who bathed therein.

THE LEGEND OF WAUKULLA

[1513]

THROUGH darkening pines the cavaliers marched on their sunset way,
While crimson in the trade-winds rolled far Appalachee Bay,
Above the water-levels rose palmetto crowns like ghosts
Of kings primeval; them, behind, the shadowy pines in hosts.
"O cacique, brav and trusty guide,
Are we not near the spring,
The fountai of eternal youth that health to age doth bring?"
The cacique sighed,
And Indian guide,
"The fount is fair,
Waukulla!

"But vainly to the blossomed flower will come the autumn rain,
And never youth's departed days come back to age again;
The future in the spirit lies, the earthly life is brief,
'T is you that say the fount hath life," so said the Indian chief.
"Nay, Indian king; nay, Indian king,
Thou knowest well the spring,
And thou shalt die if thou dost fail our feet to it to bring."
The cacique sighed,
And Indian guide,
"The spring is bright,
Waukulla!"

Then said the guide, "O men of Spain, a
    wondrous fountain flows
From deep abodes of gods below, and health
    on men bestows.
Blue are its deeps and green its walls, and
    from its waters gleam
The water-stars, and from it runs the pure
    Waukulla's stream.
    But men of Spain, but men of Spain,
    'T is *you* who say that spring
Eternal youth and happiness to men again
    will bring."
      The cacique sighed,
      And Indian guide,
      "The fount is clear,
        Waukulla!"

March on, the land enchanted is; march on,
    ye men of Spain;
Who would not taste the bliss of youth and
    all its hopes again.
Enchanted is the land; behold! enchanted
    is the air;
The very heaven is domed with gold; there's
    beauty everywhere!"
    So said De Leon. "Cavaliers,
    We're marching to the spring,
The fountain of eternal youth that health to
    age will bring!"
      The cacique sighed,
      And Indian guide,
      "The fount is pure,
        Waukulla!"

Beneath the pines, beneath the yews, the
    deep magnolia shades,
The clear Waukulla swift pursues its way
    through floral glades;
Beneath the pines, beneath the yews, beneath
    night's falling shade,
Beneath the low and dusky moon still marched
    the cavalcade.
    "The river widens," said the men;
    "Are we not near the spring,
The fountain of eternal youth that health
    to age doth bring?"
      The cacique sighed,
      And Indian guide,
      "The spring is near,
        Waukulla!

"The fount is fair and bright and clear, and
    pure its waters run;
Waukulla, lovely in the moon and beauteous
    in the sun.

But vainly to the blossomed flower will come
    the autumn rain,
And never youth's departed days come back
    to man again.
    O men of Spain! O men of Spain!
    'T is you that say the spring
Eternal youth and happiness to withered
    years will bring!"
      The cacique sighed,
      And Indian guide,
      "The fount is deep,
        Waukulla!"

The river to a grotto led, as to a god's
    abode;
There lay the fountain bright with stars;
    stars in its waters flowed;
The mighty live-oaks round it rose, in ancient
    mosses clad;
De Leon's heart beat high for joy; the cava-
    liers were glad,
    "O men of Spain! O men of Spain!
    This surely is the spring,
The fountain fair that health and joy to faces
    old doth bring!
      The cacique sighed,
      And Indian guide,
      "The spring is old,
        Waukulla!"

"Avalla, O my trusty friend that we this day
    should see!
Strip off thy doublet and descend the glowing
    fount with me!"
"The saints! I will," Avalla said. "Already
    young I feel,
And younger than my sons shall I return to
    old Castile."
    Then plunged De Leon in the spring
    And then Avalla old,
Then slowly rose each wrinkled face above
    the waters cold.
      The cacique sighed,
      And Indian guide,
      "The fount is false,
        Waukulla!"

O vainly to the blossomed flower will come
    the autumn rain,
And never youth's departed days come back
    to man again;
The crowns Castilian could not bring the
    withered stalk a leaf,
But came a sabre flash that morn, and fell
    the Indian chief.

Another sabre flash, and then
The guide beside him lay,
And red the clear Waukulla ran toward
Appalachee Bay.
Then from the dead
The Spaniards fled,
And cursed the spring,
Waukulla.

"Like comrades life was left behind, the
years shall o'er me roll,
For all the hopes that man can find lies hidden
in the soul.
Ye white sails lift, and drift again across the
southern main;
There wait for me, there wait us all, the hol-
low tombs of Spain!"
Beneath the liquid stars the sails
Arose and went their way,
And bore the gray-haired cavaliers from
Appalachee Bay.
The young chief slept,
The maiden wept,
Beside the bright
Waukulla.
HEZEKIAH BUTTERWORTH.

In 1512 Juan Ponce de Leon received a grant
to discover and settle this fabulous island. He
sailed from Porto Rico in search of it in March,
1513, and found an island but no fountain. Push-
ing on, he discovered the mainland March 27,
and, on April 2, landed and took possession of the
country for the King of Spain, calling it Florida.

THE FOUNTAIN OF YOUTH

A DREAM OF PONCE DE LEON

[1513]

I

A STORY of Ponce de Leon,
A voyager, withered and old,
Who came to the sunny Antilles,
In quest of a country of gold.
He was wafted past islands of spices,
As bright as the Emerald seas,
Where all the forests seem singing,
So thick were the birds on the trees;
The sea was as clear as the azure,
And so deep and so pure was the sky
That the jasper-walled city seemed shining
Just out of the reach of the eye.

By day his light canvas he shifted,
And rounded strange harbors and bars;
By night, on the full tides he drifted,
'Neath the low-hanging lamps of the stars.
Near the glimmering gates of the sunset,
In the twilight empurpled and dim,
The sailors uplifted their voices,
And sang to the Virgin a hymn.
"Thank the Lord!" said De Leon, the sailor,
At the close of the rounded refrain;
"Thank the Lord, the Almighty, who blesses
The ocean-swept banner of Spain!
The shadowy world is behind us,
The shining Cèpango, before;
Each morning the sun rises brighter
On ocean, and island, and shore.
And still shall our spirits grow lighter,
As prospects more glowing enfold;
Then on, merry men! to Cèpango,
To the west, and the regions of gold!"

II

There came to De Leon, the sailor,
Some Indian sages, who told
Of a region so bright that the waters
Were sprinkled with islands of gold.
And they added: "The leafy Bimini,
A fair land of grottos and bowers,
Is there; and a wonderful fountain
Upsprings from its gardens of flowers.
That fountain gives life to the dying,
And youth to the aged restores;
They flourish in beauty eternal,
Who set but their foot on its shores!"
Then answered De Leon, the sailor:
"I am withered, and wrinkled, and old;
I would rather discover that fountain
Than a country of diamonds and gold."

III

Away sailed De Leon, the sailor;
Away with a wonderful glee,
Till the birds were more rare in the azure,
The dolphins more rare in the sea.
Away from the shady Bahamas,
Over waters no sailor had seen,
Till again on his wondering vision,
Rose clustering islands of green.
Still onward he sped till the breezes
Were laden with odors, and lo!
A country embedded with flowers,
A country with rivers aglow!
More bright than the sunny Antilles,
More fair than the shady Azores.

"Thank the Lord!" said De Leon, the sailor
  As feasted his eye on the shores,
"We have come to a region, my brothers,
  More lovely than earth, of a truth;
And here is the life-giving fountain, —
  The beautiful Fountain of Youth."

IV

Then landed De Leon, the sailor,
  Unfurled his old banner, and sung;
But he felt very wrinkled and withered,
  All around was so fresh and so young.
The palms, ever-verdant, were blooming,
  Their blossoms e'en margined the seas;
O'er the streams of the forests bright flowers
  Hung deep from the branches of trees.
"Praise the Lord!" sung De Leon, the sailor;
  His heart was with rapture aflame;
And he said: "Be the name of this region
  By Florida given to fame.
'T is a fair, a delectable country,
  More lovely than earth, of a truth;
I soon shall partake of the fountain, —
  The beautiful Fountain of Youth!"

V

But wandered De Leon, the sailor,
  In search of that fountain in vain;
No waters were there to restore him
  To freshness and beauty again.
And his anchor he lifted, and murmured,
  As the tears gathered fast in his eye,
"I must leave this fair land of the flowers,
  Go back o'er the ocean, and die."
Then back by the dreary Tortugas,
  And back by the shady Azores,
He was borne on the storm-smitten waters
  To the calm of his own native shores.
And that he grew older and older,
  His footsteps enfeebled gave proof,
Still he thirsted in dreams for the fountain,
  The beautiful Fountain of Youth.

* * * * * * * *

VI

One day the old sailor lay dying
  On the shores of a tropical isle,
And his heart was enkindled with rapture,
  And his face lighted up with a smile.
He thought of the sunny Antilles,
  He thought of the shady Azores,
He thought of the dreamy Bahamas,
  He thought of fair Florida's shores.

And, when in his mind he passed over
  His wonderful travels of old,
He thought of the heavenly country,
  Of the city of jasper and gold.
"Thank the Lord!" said De Leon, the sailor,
  "Thank the Lord for the light of the truth,
I now am approaching the fountain,
  The beautiful Fountain of Youth."

VII

The cabin was silent: at twilight
  They heard the birds singing a psalm,
And the wind of the ocean low sighing
  Through groves of the orange and palm.
The sailor still lay on his pallet,
  'Neath the low-hanging vines of the roof;
His soul had gone forth to discover
  The beautiful Fountain of Youth.

HEZEKIAH BUTTERWORTH.

In March, 1521, De Leon led a large party to Florida and attempted to plant a colony there; but they were driven away by the Indians. De Leon himself was wounded in the thigh by an arrow. The wound was unskillfully treated, and the old adventurer died of it in Cuba shortly afterwards.

PONCE DE LEON

[1521]

You that crossed the ocean old,
Not from greed of Inca's gold,
But to search by vale and mount,
Wood and rock, the wizard fount
Where Time's harm is well undone, —
Here's to Ponce de Leon,
And your liegemen every one!
Surely, still beneath the sun,
In some region further west,
You live on and have your rest,
While the world goes spinning round,
And the sky hears the resound
Of a thousand shrill new fames,
Which your jovial silence shames!
Strength and joy your days endow,
Youth's eyes glow beneath your brow;
Wars and vigils are forgot,
And the Scytheman threats you not.
Tell us, of your knightly grace,
Tell us, left you not some trace
Leading to that wellspring true
Where old souls their age renew ?

EDITH M. THOMAS.

The Spaniards, meanwhile, had pushed on across the Caribbean Sea and founded Darien, whither, in 1510, came one Vasco Nuñez Balboa. He made numerous explorations, and, learning from the Indians that there was a great sea to the south, determined to search for it. He started from Darien September 1, 1513, and on the 25th reached the top of a mountain from which he first saw the Pacific. He gained the shore four days later, and, wading into the water, took possession of it for the King of Spain.

BALBOA

[September 25, 1513]

With restless step of discontent,
Day after day he fretting went
Along the old accustomed ways
That led to easeful length of days.

But far beyond the fragrant shade
Of orange groves his glances strayed
To where the white horizon line
Caught from the sea its silvery shine.

He knew the taste of that salt spray,
He knew the wind that blew that way;
Ah, once again to mount and ride
Upon that pulsing ocean tide, —

To find new lands of virgin gold,
To wrest them from the savage hold,
To conquer with the sword and brain
Fresh fields and fair for royal Spain!

This was the dream of wild desire
That set his gallant heart on fire,
And stirred with feverish discontent
That soul for nobler issues meant.

Sometimes his children's laughter brought
A thrill that checked his restless thought;
Sometimes a voice more tender yet
Would soothe the fever and the fret.

Thus day by day, until one day
Came news that in the harbor lay
A ship bound outward to explore
The treasures of that western shore,

Which bold adventurers as yet
Had failed to conquer or forget;
"Yet where they failed, and failing died,
My will shall conquer!" Balboa cried.

But when on Darien's shore he stept,
And fast and far his vision swept,
He saw before him, white and still,
The Andes mocking at his will.

Then like a flint he set his face;
Let others falter from their place,
His hand and foot, his sturdy soul
Should seek and gain that distant goal!

With speech like this he fired the land,
And gathered to his bold command
A troop of twenty score or more,
To follow where he led before.

They followed him day after day
O'er burning lands where ambushed lay
The waiting savage in his lair,
And fever poisoned all the air.

But like a sweeping wind of flame
A conqueror through all he came;
The savage fell beneath his hand,
Or led him on to seek the land

That richer yet for golden gain
Stretched out beyond the mountain chain.
Steep after steep of rough ascent
They followed, followed, worn and spent,

Until at length they came to where
The last peak lifted near and fair;
Then Balboa turned and waved aside
His panting troops. "Rest here," he cried,

"And wait for me." And with a tread
Of trembling haste, he quickly sped
Along the trackless height, alone
To seek, to reach, his mountain throne.

Step after step he mounted swift;
The wind blew down a cloudy drift;
From some strange source he seemed to hear
The music of another sphere.

Step after step; the cloud-winds blew
Their blinding mists, then through and through
Sun-cleft, they broke, and all alone
He stood upon his mountain throne.

Before him spread no paltry lands,
To wrest with spoils from savage hands;
But, fresh and fair, an unknown world
Of mighty sea and shore unfurled

Its wondrous scroll beneath the skies.
Ah, what to this the flimsy prize
Of gold and lands for which he came
With hot ambition's sordid aim!

Silent he stood with streaming eyes
In that first moment of surprise,
Then on the mountain-top he bent,
This conqueror of a continent,

In wordless ecstasy of prayer, —
Forgetting in that moment there,
With Nature's God brought face to face,
All vainer dreams of pomp and place.

Thus to the world a world was given.
Where lesser men had vainly striven,
And striving died, — this gallant soul,
Divinely guided, reached the goal.

NORA PERRY.

In 1518 a great expedition, under Hernando
Cortez, sailed from Cuba in search of a land of
marvellous wealth which was said to exist some-
where north of Darien. The result was the dis-
covery of Mexico, which the Spaniards subdued
with indescribable cruelties.

WITH CORTEZ IN MEXICO

[1519]

"MATER á Dios, preserve us
And give us the Mexican gold,
Viva España forever!"
Light-hearted, treacherous, bold,
With clashing of drums and of cymbals,
With clatter of hoofs and of arms,
Into the Tezcucan city,
Over the Tezcucan farms;
In through the hordes of Aztecs,
Past glitter of city and lake,
Brave for death or for conquest,
And the Mother of God's sweet sake.

Perchance from distant Granada,
Perchance from the Danube's far blue,
He had fought with Moor and Saracen,
Where the death hail of battle-fields flew.
Down through the smoke and the battle,
Trolling an old Moorish song,
Chanting an Ave or Pater,
To whiten the red of his wrong,
Dreaming of Seville, Toledo,
And dark, soft catholic eyes,

Light-hearted, reckless, and daring,
He rides under Mexican skies.

Child of valor and fortune,
Nurtured to ride and to strike,
Fearless in defeat or in conquest,
Of man and of devil alike;
Out through the clamor of battle,
Up through rivers of blood,
"Viva España forever!
God and the bold Brotherhood!
Strike for the memories left us,
Strike for the lives that we keep,
Strike for the present and future,
In the name of our comrades who sleep;
Strike! for Jesus' sweet Mother.
For the arms and the vows that we hold;
Strike for fortune and lover,
God, and the Mexican gold!"

.   .   .   .

At morning gay, careless in battle,
With love on his lips, in his eyes;
At even stretched pallid and silent,
Out under Mexican skies.
And far in some old Spanish city
Two dark eyes wait patient and long
For a lover who sailed to the westward,
Trolling an old Moorish song.

W. W. CAMPBELL.

Shortly afterwards, Pizarro completed the
conquest of Peru. Heavily-laden treasure-ships
were sent homeward across the Atlantic, and at
last the Spanish lust of gold seemed in a fair way
to be satisfied.

THE LUST OF GOLD

From "The West Indies"

RAPACIOUS Spain
Follow'd her hero's triumphs o'er the main,
Her hardy sons in fields of battle tried,
Where Moor and Christian desperately died.
A rabid race, fanatically bold,
And steel'd to cruelty by lust of gold,
Traversed the waves, the unknown world
explored,
The cross their standard, but their faith the
sword;
Their steps were graves; o'er prostrate realms
they trod;
They worshipp'd Mammon while they vow
to God.

Let nobler bards in loftier numbers tell
How Cortez conquer'd, Montezuma fell;
How fierce Pizarro's ruffian arm o'erthrew
The sun's resplendent empire in Peru;
How, like a prophet, old Las Casas stood,
And raised his voice against a sea of blood,
Whose chilling waves recoil'd while he fore-
    told
His country's ruin by avenging gold.
— That gold, for which unpitied Indians fell,
That gold, at once the snare and scourge of
    hell,
Thenceforth by righteous Heaven was doom'd
    to shed
Unmingled curses on the spoiler's head;
For gold the Spaniard cast his soul away, —
His gold and he were every nation's prey.

But themes like these would ask an angel-
    lyre,
Language of light and sentiment of fire;
Give me to sing, in melancholy strains,
Of Charib martyrdoms and Negro chains;
One race by tyrants rooted from the earth,
One doom'd to slavery by the taint of birth!

.   .   .   .

Dreadful as hurricanes, athwart the main
Rush'd the fell legions of invading Spain;
With fraud and force, with false and fatal
    breath
(Submission bondage, and resistance death),
They swept the isles. In vain the simple race
Kneel'd to the iron sceptre of their grace,
Or with weak arms their fiery vengeance
    braved;
They came, they saw, they conquer'd, they
    enslaved,
And they destroy'd; — the generous heart
    they broke,
They crush'd the timid neck beneath the
    yoke;
Where'er to battle march'd their fell array,
The sword of conquest plough'd resistless
    way;
Where'er from cruel toil they sought repose,
Around the fires of devastation rose.
The Indian, as he turn'd his head in flight,
Beheld his cottage flaming through the night,
And, midst the shrieks of murder on the wind,
Heard the mute bloodhound's death-step
    close behind.

The conflict o'er, the valiant in their graves,
The wretched remnant dwindled into slaves;
Condemn'd in pestilential cells to pine,

Delving for gold amidst the gloomy mine.
The sufferer, sick of life-protracting breath,
Inhaled with joy the fire-damp blast of death:
— Condemn'd to fell the mountain palm on
    high,
That cast its shadow from the evening sky,
Ere the tree trembled to his feeble stroke,
The woodman languish'd, and his heart-
    strings broke;
— Condemn'd in torrid noon, with palsied
    hand,
To urge the slow plough o'er the obdurate
    land,
The laborer, smitten by the sun's quick ray,
A corpse along the unfinish'd furrow lay.
O'erwhelm'd at length with ignominious toil,
Mingling their barren ashes with the soil,
Down to the dust the Charib people pass'd,
Like autumn foliage withering in the blast:
The whole race sunk beneath the oppressor's
    rod,
And left a blank among the works of God.

JAMES MONTGOMERY.

Although Pope Alexander VI had, in 1493
issued a bull dividing the New World between
Spain and Portugal, neither France nor England
paid any heed to it. One of France's most active
corsairs was Giovanni da Verazzano. In 1524
he crossed the Atlantic, and, sighting the coast at
Cape Fear, turned northward, discovered the
Hudson, landed at Rhode Island, and kept on,
perhaps, as far as Newfoundland.

VERAZZANO

AT RHODES AND RHODE ISLAND

[1524]

IN the tides of the warm south wind it lay,
    And its grapes turned wine in the fires of
        noon,
And its roses blossomed from May to May,
    And their fragrance lingered from June to
        June.

There dwelt old heroes at Ilium famed,
    There, bards reclusive, of olden odes;
And so fair were the fields of roses, they named
    The bright sea-garden the Isle of Rhodes.

Fair temples graced each blossoming field,
    And columned halls in gems arrayed;
Night shaded the sea with her jewelled shield
    And sweet the lyres of Orpheus played.

The Helios spanned the sea: its flame
  Drew hither the ships of Pelion's pines,
And twice a thousand statues of fame
  Stood mute in twice a thousand shrines.

And her mariners went, and her mariners
    came,
  And sang on the seas the olden odes,
And at night they remembered the Helios'
    flame,
  And at morn the sweet fields of the roses
    of Rhodes.

From the palm land's shade to the land of
    pines,
  A Florentine crossed the Western Sea;
He sought new lands and golden mines,
  And he sailed 'neath the flag of the Fleur-
    de-lis.

He saw at last in the sunset's gold,
  A wonderful island so fair to view
That it seemed like the Island of Roses old
  That his eyes in his wondering boyhood
    knew.

'T was summer time, and the glad birds sung
  In the hush of noon in the solitudes;
From the oak's broad arms the green vines
    hung;
  Sweet odors blew from the resinous woods.

He rounded the shores of the summer sea,
  And he said as his feet the white sands
    pressed,
And he planted the flag of the Fleur-de-lis:
  "I have come to the Island of Rhodes in
    the West.

"While the mariners go, and the mariners
    come,
  And sing on lone waters the olden odes
Of the Grecian seas and the ports of Rome,
  They will ever think of the roses of Rhodes."

To the isle of the West he gave the name
  Of the isle he had loved in the Grecian sea;
And the Florentine went away as he came,
  'Neath the silver flag of the Fleur-de-lis.

O fair Rhode Island, thy guest was true,
  He felt the spirit of beauteous things;
The sea-wet roses were faint and few,
  But memory made them the gardens of
    kings.

The Florentine corsair sailed once more,
  Out into the West o'er a rainy sea,
In search of another wonderful shore
  For the crown of France and the Fleur-de-lis.

But returned no more the Florentine brave
  To the courtly knights of fair Rochelle;
'Neath the lilies of France he found a grave,
  And not 'neath the roses he loved so well.

But the lessons of beauty his fond heart bore
  From the gardens of God were never lost;
And the fairest name of the Eastern shore
  Bears the fairest isle of the Western coast.
            HEZEKIAH BUTTERWORTH.

The Spaniards still dreamed of a great empire
somewhere in Florida, and in 1528 Pánfilo de
Narvaez set out with an expedition in search of
it. Only four members of the party got back to
Cuba alive, the others having been killed or cap-
tured by the Indians. Among those captured and
enslaved was Juan Ortiz. He was rescued by De
Soto nearly ten years later.

ORTIZ

[1528]

"Go bring the captive, he shall die,"
  He said, with faltering breath;
"Him stretch upon a scaffold high,
  And light the fire of death!"
The young Creeks danced the captive round,
  And sang the Song of Doom, —
"Fly, fly, ye hawks, in the open sky,
  Fly, wings of the warrior's plume!"

They brought the fagots for the flame,
  The braves and maids together,
When came the princess — sweet her name:
  The Red Flamingo Feather.
Then danced the Creeks the scaffold round,
  And sang the Song of Doom, —
"Fly, fly, ye hawks, in the open sky,
  Fly, wings of the warrior's plume!"

In shaded plumes of silver gray,
  The young Creeks danced together,
But she danced not with them that day,
  The Red Flamingo Feather.
Wild sped the feet the scaffold round,
  Wild rose the Song of Doom, —
"Fly, fly, ye hawks, in the open sky,
  Fly, wings of the warrior's plume!"

They stretched the stranger from the sea,
  Above the fagots lighted, —
Ortiz, — a courtly man was he,
  With deeds heroic knighted.
And sped the feet the scaffold round,
  And rose the Song of Doom, —
"Fly, fly, ye hawks, in the open sky,
  Fly, wings of the warrior's plume!"

The white smoke rose, the braves were
    gay,
  The war drums beat together,
But sad in heart and face that day
  Was Red Flamingo Feather.
They streaked with flames the dusky air,
  They shrieked the Song of Doom, —
"Fly, fly, ye hawks, in the open sky,
  Fly, wings of the warrior's plume!"

"Dance, dance, my girl, the torches gleam,
  Dance, dance, the gray plumes gather,
Dance, dance, my girl, the war-hawks
    scream,
  Dance, Red Flamingo Feather!"
More swiftly now the torches sped,
  Amid the Dance of Doom, —
"Fly, fly, ye hawks, in the open sky,
  Fly, wings of the warrior's plume!"

She knelt upon the green moss there,
  And clasped her father's knees:
"My heart is weak, O father, spare
  The wanderer from the seas!"
Like madness now swept on the dance,
  And rose the Song of Doom, —
"Fly, fly, ye hawks, in the open sky,
  Ye wings of the warrior's plume!'

"Grand were the men who sailed away,
  And he is young and brave ;
'T is small in heart the weak to slay,
  'T is great in heart to save."
He saw the torches sweep the air,
  He heard the Song of Doom, —
"Fly, fly, ye hawks, in the open sky,
  Fly, wings of the warrior's plume!'

"My girl, I know thy heart would spare
  The wanderer from the sea."
"The man is fair, and I am fair,
  And thou art great," said she.
The dance of fire went on and on,
  And on the Song of Doom, —
"Fly, fly, ye hawks, in the open sky,
  Fly, wings of the warrior's plume !"

The dark chief felt his pride abate:
  "I will the wanderer spare,
My Bird of Peace, since I am great,
  And he, like thee, is fair !"
They dropped the torches, stopped the dance,
  And died the Song of Doom, —
"Fly, fly, ye hawks, in the open sky,
  Away with the warrior's plume !"
                    HEZEKIAH BUTTERWORTH.

In 1538 Hernando de Soto was appointed governor of Cuba and Florida, with orders to explore and settle the latter country. He landed at Tampa Bay with nearly a thousand men and started into the interior. He was forced to fight his way across the country against the tribes of the Creek confederacy, and in October, 1540, had a desperate battle with them at a palisaded village called Maubila, at the mouth of the Alabama River.

THE FALL OF MAUBILA

[October 18, 1540]

HEARKEN the stirring story
  The soldier has to tell,
Of fierce and bloody battle,
  Contested long and well,
Ere walled Maubila, stoutly held,
  Before our forces fell.

Now many years have circled
  Since that October day,
When proudly to Maubila
  De Soto took his way,
With men-at-arms and cavaliers
  In terrible array.

Oh, never sight more goodly
  In any land was seen;
And never better soldiers
  Than those he led have been,
More prompt to handle arquebus,
  Or wield their sabres keen.

The sun was at meridian,
  His hottest rays fell down
Alike on soldier's corselet
  And on the friar's gown;
The breeze was hushed as on we rode
  Right proudly to the town.

First came the bold De Soto,
  In all his manly pride,
The gallant Don Diego,
  His nephew, by his side;

A yard behind Juan Ortiz rode,
  Interpreter and guide.

Baltasar de Gallegos,
  Impetuous, fierce and hot;
Francisco de Figarro,
  Since by an arrow shot;
And slender Juan de Guzman, who
  In battle faltered not.

Luis Bravo de Xeres,
  That gallant cavalier;
Alonzo de Carmono,
  Whose spirit knew no fear;
The marquis of Astorga, and
  Vasquez, the cannoneer.

Andres de Vasconcellos,
  Juan Cales, young and fair,
Roma de Cardenoso,
  Him of the yellow hair —
Rode gallant in their bravery,
  Straight to the public square.

And there, in sombre garments,
  Were monks of Cuba four,
Fray Juan de Gallegos,
  And other priests a score,
Who sacramental bread and wine
  And holy relics bore.

And next eight hundred soldiers
  In closest order come,
Some with Biscayan lances,
  With arquebuses some,
Timing their tread to martial notes
  Of trump and fife and drum.

Loud sang the gay Mobilians,
  Light danced their daughters brown;
Sweet sounded pleasant music
  Through all the swarming town;
But 'mid the joy one sullen brow
  Was lowering with a frown.

The haughty Tuscaloosa,
  The sovereign of the land,
With moody face, and thoughtful,
  Rode at our chief's right hand,
And cast from time to time a glance
  Of hatred at the band.

And when that gay procession
  Made halt to take a rest,

And eagerly the people
  To see the strangers prest,
The frowning King, in wrathful tones,
  De Soto thus addressed:

"To bonds and to dishonor
  By faithless friends trepanned,
For days beside you, Spaniard.
  The ruler of the land
Has ridden as a prisoner,
  Subject to your command.

" He was not born the fetters
  Of baser men to wear,
And tells you this, De Soto,
  Hard though it be to bear —
Let those beware the panther's rage
  Who follow to his lair.

"Back to your isle of Cuba!
  Slink to your den again,
And tell your robber sovereign,
  The mighty lord of Spain,
Whoso would strive this land to win
  Shall find his efforts vain.

"And, save it be your purpose
  Within my realm to die,
Let not your forces linger
  Our deadly anger nigh,
Lest food for vultures and for wolves
  Your mangled forms should lie."

Then, spurning courtly offers
  He left our chieftain's side,
And crossing the enclosure
  With quick and lengthened stride,
He passed within his palace gates,
  And there our wrath defied.

Now came up Charamilla,
  Who led our troop of spies,
And said unto our captain,
  With tones that showed surprise,
"A mighty force within the town,
  In wait to crush us, lies.

"The babes and elder women
  Were sent at break of day
Into the forest yonder,
  Five leagues or more away;
Within yon huts ten thousand men
  Wait eager for the fray."

"What say ye now, my comrades?"
 De Soto asked his men;
"Shall we, before these traitors,
 Go backward, baffled, then;
Or, sword in hand, attack the foe
 Who crouches in his den?"

Before their loud responses
 Had died upon the ear,
A savage stood before them,
 Who said, in accents clear,
"Ho! robbers base and coward thieves!
 Assassin Spaniards, hear!

"No longer shall our sovereign,
 Born noble, great, and free,
Be led beside your master,
 A shameful sight to see,
While weapons here to strike you down
 Or hands to grasp them be."

As spoke the brawny savage,
 Full wroth our comrades grew —
Baltasar de Gallegos
 His heavy weapon drew,
And dealt the boaster such a stroke
 As clove his body through.

Then rushed the swart Mobilians
 Like hornets from their nest;
Against our bristling lances
 Was bared each savage breast;
With arrow-head and club and stone,
 Upon our band they prest.

"Retreat in steady order!
 But slay them as ye go!"
Exclaimed the brave De Soto,
 And with each word a blow
That sent a savage soul to doom
 He dealt upon the foe.

"Strike well who would our honor
 From spot or tarnish save!
Strike down the haughty Pagan,
 The infidel and slave!
Saint Mary Mother sits above,
 And smiles upon the brave.

"Strike! all my gallant comrades!
 Strike! gentlemen of Spain!
Upon the traitor wretches
 Your deadly anger rain,
Or never to your native land
 Return in pride again!"

Then hosts of angry foemen
 We fiercely held at bay,
Through living walls of Pagans
 We cut our bloody way;
And though by thousands round they swarmed,
 We kept our firm array.

At length they feared to follow;
 We stood upon the plain,
And dressed our shattered column;
 When, slacking bridle rein,
De Soto, wounded as he was,
 Led to the charge again.

For now our gallant horsemen
 Their steeds again had found,
That had been fastly tethered
 Unto the trees around,
Though some of these, by arrows slain,
 Lay stretched upon the ground.

And as the riders mounted,
 The foe, in joyous tones,
Gave vent to shouts of triumph,
 And hurled a shower of stones;
But soon the shouts were changed to wails,
 The cries of joy to moans.

Down on the scared Mobilians
 The furious rush was led;
Down fell the howling victims
 Beneath the horses' tread;
The angered chargers trod alike
 On dying and on dead.

Back to the wooden ramparts,
 With cut and thrust and blow,
We drove the panting savage,
 The very walls below,
Till those above upon our heads
 Huge rocks began to throw.

Whenever we retreated
 The swarming foemen came —
Their wild and matchless courage
 Put even ours to shame —
Rushing upon our lances' points,
 And arquebuses' flame.

Three weary hours we fought them,
 And often each gave way;
Three weary hours, uncertain
 The fortune of the day;
And ever where they fiercest fought
 De Soto led the fray.

Baltasar de Gallegos
  Right well displayed his might:
His sword fell ever fatal,
  Death rode its flash of light;
And where his horse's head was turned
  The foe gave way in fright.

At length before our daring
  The Pagans had to yield,
And in their stout enclosure
  They sought to find a shield,
And left us, wearied with our toil,
  The masters of the field.

Now worn and spent and weary,
  Our force was scattered round,
Some seeking for their comrades,
  Some seated on the ground,
When sudden fell upon our ears
  A single trumpet's sound.

"Up! ready make for storming!"
  That speaks Moscoso near;
He comes with stainless sabre,
  He comes with spotless spear;
But stains of blood and spots of gore
  Await his weapons here.

Soon, formed in four divisions,
  Around the order goes —
"To front with battle-axes!
  No moment for repose.
At signal of an arquebus,
  Rain on the gates your blows."

Not long that fearful crashing,
  The gates in splinters fall;
And some, though sorely wounded,
  Climb o'er the crowded wall;
No rampart's height can keep them back,
  No danger can appall.

Then redly rained the carnage —
  None asked for quarter there;
Men fought with all the fury
  Born of a wild despair;
And shrieks and groans and yells of hate
  Were mingled in the air.

Four times they backward beat us,
  Four times our force returned;
We quenched in bloody torrents
  The fire that in us burned;
We slew who fought, and those who knelt
  With stroke of sword we spurned.

And what are these new forces,
  With long, black, streaming hair?
They are the singing maidens
  Who met us in the square;
And now they spring upon our ranks
  Like she-wolves from their lair.

Their sex no shield to save them,
  Their youth no weapon stayed;
De Soto with his falchion
  A lane amid them made,
And in the skulls of blooming girls
  Sank battle-axe and blade.

Forth came a wingèd arrow,
  And struck our leader's thigh;
The man who sent it shouted,
  And looked to see him die;
The wound but made the tide of rage
  Run twice as fierce and high.

Then came our stout camp-master,
  "The night is coming down;
Already twilight darkness
  Is casting shadows brown;
We would not lack for light on strife
  If once we burned the town."

With that we fired the houses;
  The ranks before us broke;
The fugitives we followed,
  And dealt them many a stroke,
While round us rose the crackling flame,
  And o'er us hung the smoke.

And what with flames around them,
  And what with smoke o'erhead,
And what with cuts of sabre,
  And what with horses' tread,
And what with lance and arquebus,
  The town was filled with dead.

Six thousand of the foemen
  Upon that day were slain,
Including those who fought us
  Outside upon the plain —
Six thousand of the foemen fell,
  And eighty-two of Spain.

Not one of us unwounded
  Came from the fearful fray;
And when the fight was over
  And scattered round we lay,
Some sixteen hundred wounds we bore
  As tokens of the day.

And through that weary darkness,
    And all that dreary night,
We lay in bitter anguish,
    But never mourned our plight,
Although we watched with eagerness
    To see the morning light.

And when the early dawning
    Had marked the sky with red,
We saw the Moloch incense
    Rise slowly overhead
From smoking ruins and the heaps
    Of charred and mangled dead.

I knew the slain were Pagans,
    While we in Christ were free,
And yet it seemed that moment
    A spirit said to me:
"Henceforth be doomed while life re-
        mains
    This sight of fear to see."

And ever since that dawning
    Which chased the night away,
I wake to see the corses
    That thus before me lay:
And this is why in cloistered cell
    I wait my latter day.
            THOMAS DUNN ENGLISH.

Early in 1540 a great expedition under Fran-
cisco de Coronado started northward from Mexico
in search of the Seven Cities of Cibola, of whose
glories and riches many stories had been told.
The cities were really the pueblos of the Zuñis,
and the ballad tells the story of the march.

QUIVÍRA

[1540-1541]

FRANCISCO CORONADO rode forth with all
        his train,
Eight hundred savage bowmen, three hun-
        dred spears of Spain,
To seek the rumored glory that pathless
        deserts hold —
The city of Quivíra whose walls are rich
        with gold.

Oh, gay they rode with plume on crest and
        gilded spur at heel,
With gonfalon of Aragon and banner of
        Castile!

While High Emprise and Joyous Youth, twin
        marshals of the throng,
Awoke Sonora's mountain peaks with trum-
        pet-note and song.

Beside that brilliant army, beloved of serf
        and lord,
There walked as brave a soldier as ever
        smote with sword,
Though nought of knightly harness his rus-
        set gown revealed —
The cross he bore as weapon, the missal
        was his shield.

But rugged oaths were changed to prayers,
        and angry hearts grew tame,
And fainting spirits waxed in faith where
        Fray Padilla came;
And brawny spearmen bowed their heads to
        kiss the helpful hand
Of him who spake the simple truth that brave
        men understand.

What pen may paint their daring — those
        doughty cavaliers!
The cities of the Zuñi were humbled by
        their spears.
Wild Arizona's barrens grew pallid in the
        glow
Of blades that won Granada and conquered
        Mexico.

They fared by lofty Acoma; their rally-call
        was blown
Where Colorado rushes down through God-
        hewn walls of stone;
Still, North and East, where deserts spread,
        and treeless prairies rolled,
A Fairy City lured them on with pinnacles
        of gold.

Through all their weary marches toward
        that flitting goal
They turned to Fray Padilla for aid of
        heart and soul.
He bound the wounds that lance-thrust
        and flinty arrow made;
He cheered the sick and failing; above the
        dead he prayed.

Two thousand miles of war and woe behind
        their banners lay:
And sadly fever, drought and toil had lessened
        their array,

When came a message fraught with hope to
    all the steadfast band:
"Good tidings from the northward, friends!
    Quivíra lies at hand!"

    How joyously they spurred them! How
        sadly drew the rein!
    There shone no golden palace, there blazed
        no jewelled fane.
    Rude tents of hide of bison, dog-guarded,
        met their view —
    A squalid Indian village; the lodges of the
        Sioux!

Then Coronado bowed his head. He spake
    unto his men:
"Our quest is vain, true hearts of Spain!
    Now ride we home again.
And would to God that I might give that
    phantom city's pride
In ransom for the gallant souls that here have
    sunk and died!"

    Back, back to Compostela the wayworn
        handful bore;
    But sturdy Fray Padilla took up the quest
        once more.
    His soul still longed for conquest, though
        not by lance and sword;
    He burned to show the Heathen the path-
        way to the Lord.

Again he trudged the flinty hills and dazzling
    desert sands,
And few were they that walked with him,
    and weaponless their hands —
But and the trusty man-at-arms, Docampo,
    rode him near
Like Great Heart, guarding Christian's way
    through wastes of Doubt and Fear.

    Where still in silken harvests the prairie-
        lilies toss,
    Among the dark Quivíras Padilla reared
        his cross.
    Within its sacred shadow the warriors of
        the Kaw
    In wonder heard the Gospel of Love and
        Peace and Law.

They gloried in their Brown-robed Priest;
    and oft in twilight's gold
The warriors grouped, a silent ring, to hear
    the tale he told,

While round the gentle man-at-arms their
    lithe-limbed children played
And shot their arrows at his shield and rode
    his guarded blade.

    When thrice the silver crescent had filled
        its curving shell,
    The Friar rose at dawning and spake his
        flock farewell:
    "— And if your Brothers northward be
        cruel, as ye say,
    My Master bids me seek them — and
        dare I answer 'Nay'?"

Again he strode the path of thorns; but ere
    the evening star
A savage cohort swept the plain in paint and
    plumes of war.
Then Fray Padilla spake to them whose
    hearts were most his own:
"My children, bear the tidings home — let
    me die here alone."

    He knelt upon the prairie, begirt by yelling
        Sioux. —
    "Forgive them, oh, my Father! they know
        not what they do!"
    The twanging bow-strings answered.
           Before his eyes, unrolled
    The City of Quivíra whose streets are
        paved with gold.
              ARTHUR GUITERMAN.

The Spaniards were not the only people who
searched in vain for fabulous cities. South of
Cape Breton lay a country which the early French
explorers named Norembega, and there was sup-
posed to exist, somewhere within its boundaries,
a magnificent city of the same name. Roberval
and Jacques Cartier spent a number of years
after 1541 seeking it, and in 1604 Champlain ex-
plored the Penobscot River, on whose banks it
was supposed to be situated, but found no trace
of it, nor any evidence of civilization except a
cross, very old and mossy, in the woods.

NOREMBEGA

[c. 1543]

THE winding way the serpent takes
    The mystic water took,
From where, to count its beaded lakes,
    The forest sped its brook.

A narrow space 'twixt shore and shor'
    For sun or stars to fall.

While evermore, behind, before,
  Closed in the forest wall.

The dim wood hiding underneath
  Wan flowers without a name;
Life tangled with decay and death,
  League after league the same.

Unbroken over swamp and hill
  The rounding shadow lay,
Save where the river cut at will
  A pathway to the day.

Beside that track of air and light,
  Weak as a child unweaned,
At shut of day a Christian knight
  Upon his henchman leaned.

The embers of the sunset's fires
  Along the clouds burned down;
"I see," he said, "the domes and spires
  Of Norembega town."

"Alack! the domes, O master mine,
  Are golden clouds on high;
Yon spire is but the branchless pine
  That cuts the evening sky."

"Oh, hush and hark! What sounds are these
  But chants and holy hymns?"
"Thou hear'st the breeze that stirs the trees
  Through all their leafy limbs."

"Is it a chapel bell that fills
  The air with its low tone?"
"Thou hear'st the tinkle of the rills,
  The insect's vesper drone."

"The Christ be praised! — He sets for me
  A blessed cross in sight!"
"Now, nay, 't is but yon blasted tree
  With two gaunt arms outright!"

"Be it wind so sad or tree so stark,
  It mattereth not, my knave;
Methinks to funeral hymns I hark,
  The cross is for my grave!

"My life is sped; I shall not see
  My home-set sails again;
The sweetest eyes of Normandie
  Shall watch for me in vain.

"Yet onward still to ear and eye
  The baffling marvel calls;

I fain would look before I die
  On Norembega's walls.

"So, haply, it shall be thy part
  At Christian feet to lay
The mystery of the desert's heart
  My dead hand plucked away.

"Leave me an hour of rest; go thou
  And look from yonder heights;
Perchance the valley even now
  Is starred with city lights."

The henchman climbed the nearest hill,
  He saw nor tower nor town,
But, through the drear woods, lone and still,
  The river rolling down.

He heard the stealthy feet of things
  Whose shapes he could not see,
A flutter as of evil wings,
  The fall of a dead tree.

The pines stood black against the moon
  A sword of fire beyond;
He heard the wolf howl, and the loon
  Laugh from his reedy pond.

He turned him back; "O master dear,
  We are but men misled;
And thou hast sought a city here
  To find a grave instead."

"As God shall will! what matters where
  A true man's cross may stand,
So Heaven be o'er it here as there
  In pleasant Norman land?

"These woods, perchance, no secret hide
  Of lordly tower and hall;
Yon river in its wanderings wide
  Has washed no city wall;

"Yet mirrored in the sullen stream
  The holy stars are given:
Is Norembega, then, a dream
  Whose waking is in Heaven?

"No builded wonder of these lands
  My weary eyes shall see;
A city never made with hands
  Alone awaiteth me —

"'*Urbs Syon mystica*;' I see
  Its mansions passing fair.

'*Condita cœlo;*' let me be,
Dear Lord, a dweller there!"

Above the dying exile hung
The vision of the bard,
As faltered on his failing tongue
The song of good Bernard.

The henchman dug at dawn a grave
Beneath the hemlocks brown,
And to the desert's keeping gave
The lord of fief and town.

Years after, when the Sieur Champlain
Sailed up the unknown stream,
And Norembega proved again
A shadow and a dream,

He found the Norman's nameless grave
Within the hemlock's shade,
And, stretching wide its arms to save,
The sign that God had made,

The cross-boughed tree that marked the spot
And made it holy ground:
He needs the earthly city not
Who hath the heavenly found.

JOHN GREENLEAF WHITTIER.

Until the middle of the sixteenth century, Spain
was the only nation which had succeeded in es-
tablishing colonies in the New World. In 1583
Sir Humphrey Gilbert secured permission from
Queen Elizabeth to set out on a voyage of dis-
covery and colonization, for the glory of England.
He landed at St. John's, Newfoundland, August 5,
and established there the first English colony in
North America. Then he sailed away to explore
further, and met the fate described in the poem.
The colony proved a failure.

SIR HUMPHREY GILBERT

[1583]

SOUTHWARD with fleet of ice
Sailed the corsair Death;
Wild and fast blew the blast,
And the east-wind was his breath.

His lordly ships of ice
Glisten in the sun;
On each side, like pennons wide,
Flashing crystal streamlets run.

His sails of white sea-mist
Dripped with silver rain;

But where he passed there were cast
Leaden shadows o'er the main.

Eastward from Campobello
Sir Humphrey Gilbert sailed;
Three days or more seaward he bore,
Then, alas! the land-wind failed.

Alas! the land-wind failed,
And ice-cold grew the night;
And nevermore, on sea or shore,
Should Sir Humphrey see the light.

He sat upon the deck,
The Book was in his hand;
"Do not fear! Heaven is as near,"
He said, "by water as by land!"

In the first watch of the night,
Without a signal's sound,
Out of the sea, mysteriously,
The fleet of Death rose all around.

The moon and the evening star
Were hanging in the shrouds;
Every mast, as it passed,
Seemed to rake the passing clouds.

They grappled with their prize,
At midnight black and cold!
As of a rock was the shock;
Heavily the ground-swell rolled.

Southward through day and dark,
They drift in close embrace,
With mist and rain, o'er the open main;
Yet there seems no change of place.

Southward, forever southward,
They drift through dark and day;
And like a dream, in the Gulf-Stream
Sinking, vanish all away.

HENRY WADSWORTH LONGFELLOW.

With the destruction of the Armada in 1588,
Spain's sea power was so shattered that the At-
lantic ceased to be a battleground, English sailors
could come and go with a fair degree of safety,
and before long the American coast was alive
with these daring and adventurous voyagers.

THE FIRST AMERICAN SAILORS

*Five fearless knights of the first renown
In Elizabeth's great array,*

From Plymouth in Devon sailed up and down—
  American sailors they;
    Who went to the West,
    For they all knew best
      Where the silver was gray
      As a moonlit night,
      And the gold as bright
      As a midsummer day —
    A-sailing away
Through the salt sea spray,
  The first American sailors.

Sir HUMPHREY GILBERT, he was ONE
  And Devon was heaven to him,
He loved the sea as he loved the sun
  And hated the Don as the Devil's limb —
    Hated him up to the brim :
In Holland the Spanish hide he tanned,
He roughed and routed their braggart band,
And God was with him on sea and land;
  Newfoundland knew him, and all that coast
  For he was one of America's host —
And now there is nothing but English speech
For leagues and leagues, and reach on reach,
  From near the Equator away to the Pole;
  While the billows beat and the oceans roll
    On the Three Americas.

Sir FRANCIS DRAKE, and he was TWO
  And Devon was heaven to him,
He loved in his heart the waters blue
  And hated the Don as the Devil's limb —
    Hated him up to the brim!
At Cadiz he singed the King's black beard,
The Armada met him and fled afeard,
Great Philip's golden fleece he sheared;
  Oregon knew him, and all that coast,
  For he was one of America's host —
And now there is nothing but English speech
For leagues and leagues, and reach on reach,
  From California away to the Pole;
  While the billows beat and the oceans roll
    On the Three Americas.

Sir WALTER RALEIGH, he was THREE
  And Devon was heaven to him,
There was nothing he loved so well as the sea —
  He hated the Don as the Devil's limb —
    Hated him up to the brim!
He settled full many a Spanish score,
Full many 's the banner his bullets tore
On English, American, Spanish shore;
  Guiana knew him, and all that coast,
  For he was one of America's host —

And now there is nothing but English speech
For leagues and leagues, and reach on reach,
  From Guiana northward to the Pole;
  While the billows beat and the oceans roll
    On the Three Americas.

Sir RICHARD GRENVILLE, he was FOUR
  And Devon was heaven to him,
He loved the waves and their windy roar
  And hated the Don as the Devil's limb —
    Hated him up to the brim !
He whipped him on land and mocked him at
    sea,
He laughed to scorn his sovereignty,
And with the Revenge beat his fifty-three;
  Virginia knew him, and all that coast,
  For he was one of America's host —
And now there is nothing but English speech
For leagues and leagues, and reach on reach,
  From the Old Dominion away to the Pole;
  While the billows beat and the oceans roll
    On the Three Americas.

And Sir JOHN HAWKINS, he was FIVE
  And Devon was heaven to him,
He worshipped the water while he was alive
  And hated the Don as the Devil's limb —
    Hated him up to the brim !
He chased him over the Spanish Main,
He scoffed and defied the navies of Spain —
His cities he ravished again and again;
  The Gulf it knew him, and all that coast,
  For he was one of America's host —
And now there is nothing but English speech
For leagues and leagues, and reach on reach,
  From the Rio Grandè away to the Pole;
  While the billows beat and the oceans roll
    On the Three Americas.

Five fearless knights have filled gallant graves
  This many and many a day,
Some under the willows, some under the
    waves —
  American sailors they;
    And still in the West
    Is their valor blest,
      Where a banner bright
      With the ocean's blue
      And the red wrack's hue
      And the spoondrift's white
        Is smiling to-day
  Through the salt sea spray
  Upon American sailors.
                              WALLACE RICE.

CHAPTER III

THE SETTLEMENT OF VIRGINIA

England laid claim to the continent of North America by virtue of the discoveries of John Cabot in 1497, but little effort was made toward colonization until 1584, when an expedition sent out by Sir Walter Raleigh explored Albemarle Sound and the adjacent coast, and brought back so glowing a description of the country that Elizabeth named the whole region Virginia, in honor of her maidenhood. An abortive attempt to settle Roanoke Island was made in 1585, and in 1587 another expedition under John White landed there. White returned to England in the fall to represent the needs of the settlement, leaving behind him his daughter and little granddaughter, — Virginia Dare, the first white child born in America. He promised to return within a year, but was intercepted by Spaniards, and it was not until August, 1590, that he again dropped anchor off the island. When he went ashore next day, not a trace of the colonists could be found, nor was their fate ever certainly discovered.

THE MYSTERY OF CRO-A-TÀN

I

[August 27, 1587]

THE home-bound ship stood out to sea,
    And on the island's marge,
Sir Richard waited restlessly
    To step into the barge.

"The Governor tarrieth long," he chode,
    "As he were loth to go:
With food before, and want behind,
    There should be haste, I trow."

Even as he spake, the Governor came: —
    "Nay, fret not, for the men
Have held me back with frantic let,
    To have them home again.

"The women weep; — 'Ay, ay, the ship
    Will come again' (he saith),
'Before the May; — Before the May
    We shall have starved to death!'

"I've sworn return by God's dear leave,
    I've vowed by court and crown,
Nor yet appeased them. Comrade, thou,
    Mayhap canst soothe them down."

Sir Richard loosed his helm, and stretched
    Impatient hands abroad: —
"Have ye no trust in man?" he cried,
    "Have ye no faith in God?

"Your Governor goes, as needs he must,
    To bear through royal grace,
Hither, such food-supply, that want
    May never blench a face.

"Of freest choice ye willed to leave
    What so ye had of ease;
For neither stress of liege nor law
    Hath forced you over seas.

"Your Governor leaves fair hostages
    As costliest pledge of care, —
His daughter yonder, and her child,
    The child Virginia Dare!

"Come hither, little sweetheart! Lo!
    Thou'lt be the first, I ween,
To bend the knee, and send through me
Thy birthland's virgin fealty
    Unto its Virgin Queen.

"And now, good folk, for my commands:
    If ye are fain to roam
Beyond this island's narrow bounds,
    To seek elsewhere a home, —

"Upon some pine-tree's smoothen trunk
    Score deep the Indian name
Of tribe or village where ye haunt,
    That we may read the same.

"And if ye leave your haven here
    Through dire distress or loss,
Cut deep within the wood above
    The symbol of the cross.

"And now on my good blade, I swear,
    And seal it with this sign,
That if the fleet that sails to-day
Return not hither by the May,
    The fault shall not be mine!"

II

[August 15, 1590]

The breath of spring was on the sea;
  Anon the Governor stepped
His good ship's deck right merrily, —
  His promise had been kept.

"See, see! the coast-line comes in view!"
  He heard the mariners shout, —
"We'll drop our anchors in the Sound
  Before a star is out!"

"Now God be praised!" he inly breathed,
  "Who saves from all that harms;
The morrow morn my pretty ones
  Will rest within my arms."

At dawn of day they moored their ship,
  And dared the breakers' roar:
What meant it? not a man was there
  To welcome them ashore!

They sprang to find the cabins rude;
  The quick green sedge had thrown
Its knotted web o'er every door,
  And climbed the chimney-stone.

The spring was choked with winter's leaves,
  And feebly gurgled on;
And from the pathway, strewn with wrack,
  All trace of feet was gone.

Their fingers thrid the matted grass,
  If there, perchance, a mound
Unseen might heave the broken turf;
  But not a grave was found.

They beat the tangled cypress swamp,
  If haply in despair
They might have strayed into its glade:
  But found no vestige there.

"The pine! the pine!" the Governor groaned;
  And there each staring man
Read in a maze, one single word,
  Deep carven, — CRO-A-TÀN!

But cut above, no cross, no sign,
  No symbol of distress;
Naught else beside that mystic line
  Within the wilderness!

And where and what was "CRO-A-TÀN"?
  But not an answer came;

And none of all who read it there
  Had ever heard the name.

The Governor drew his jerkin sleeve
  Across his misty eyes;
"Some land, maybe, of savagery
  Beyond the coast that lies;

"And skulking there the wily foe
  In ambush may have lain:
God's mercy! Could such sweetest heads
  Lie scalped among the slain?

"O daughter! daughter! with the thought
  My harrowed brain is wild!
Up with the anchors! I must find
  The mother and the child!"

They scoured the mainland near and far:
  The search no tidings brought;
Till mid a forest's dusky tribe
  They heard the name they sought.

The kindly natives came with gifts
  Of corn and slaughtered deer;
What room for savage treachery
  Or foul suspicion here?

Unhindered of a chief or brave,
  They searched the wigwam through;
But neither lance nor helm nor spear,
  Nor shred of child's nor woman's gear,
  Could furnish forth a clue.

How could a hundred souls be caught
  Straight out of life, nor find
Device through which to mark their fate,
  Or leave some hint behind?

Had winter's ocean inland rolled
  An eagre's deadly spray,
That overwhelmed the island's breadth
  And swept them all away?

In vain, in vain, their heart-sick search!
  No tidings reached them more;
No record save that silent word
  Upon that silent shore.

The mystery rests a mystery still,
  Unsolved of mortal man:
Sphinx-like untold, the ages hold
  The tale of CRO-A-TÀN!
          MARGARET JUNKIN PRESTON

In April, 1606, James I sanctioned the forma-
tion of two Virginia colonies, and the first colony
set sail on the following New Year's day — three
vessels, with one hundred and five men, under
command of Christopher Newport. Twelve weeks
later, they landed at a place they named "Point
Comfort," and proceeded up a great river which
they named the King's and afterwards the James.
On May 13, 1607, the colonists landed on a low
peninsula fifty miles up the river, and Captain
Newport selected this, against many protests,
as the site for the settlement. They christened
the place Jamestown. Captains Newport, Gos-
nold, Smith, and Sicklemore were named as the
resident council for the colony, but time soon
proved Smith the ablest man in the company,
and the leadership fell to him.

JOHN SMITH'S APPROACH TO JAMESTOWN

[May 13, 1607]

I PAUSE not now to speak of Raleigh's dreams,
Though they might give a loftier bard fit
　　　themes:
I pause not now to tell of Ocracock,
Where Saxon spray broke on the red-brown
　　　rock;
Nor of my native river which glides down
Through scenes where rose a happy Indian
　　　town;
But, leaving these and Chesapeake's broad bay,
Resume my story in the month of May,
Where England's cross — St. George's en-
　　　sign — flowed
Where ne'er before emblazoned banner
　　　glowed;
Where English breasts throbbed fast as Eng-
　　　lish eyes
Looked o'er the waters with a glad surprise, —
Looked gladly out upon the varied scene
Where stretched the woods in all their pomp
　　　of green;
Flinging great shadows, beautiful and vast
As e'er upon Arcadian lake were cast.
Turn where they would, in what direction rove,
They found some bay, or wild, romantic cove,
On which they coasted through those forests
　　　dim,
Wherein they heard the never-ceasing hymn
That swelled from all the tall, majestic
　　　pines, —
Fit choristers of Nature's sylvan shrines.

For though no priest their solitudes had trod,
The trees were vocal in their praise of God.

And then, when capes and jutting headlands
　　　past,
The sails were furled against each idle mast,
They saw the sunset in its pomp descend,
And sky and water gloriously contend
For gorgeousness of colors, red and gold,
And tints of amethyst together rolled,
Making a scene of splendor and of rest
As vanquished day lit camp-fires in the West.
And when the light grew faint on wave and
　　　strand,
New beauties woke in this enchanted land,
For through heaven's lattice-work of crimson
　　　bars
Like angels looked the bright eternal stars,
And then, when gathered tints of purplish
　　　brown,
A golden sickle, reaping darkness down,
The new moon shone above the lofty trees,
Which made low music in the evening
　　　breeze, —
The breeze which floating blandly from the
　　　shore
The perfumed breath of flowering jasmine
　　　bore;
For smiling Spring had kissed its clustering
　　　vines,
And breathed her fragrance on the lofty pines.

　　　　　　　　JAMES BARRON HOPE.

Captain Smith proved himself an energetic
and effective leader, and led numerous expedi-
tions into the country in search of food. On one
of these, in December, 1607, he was taken prisoner
and was conducted to the camp of Powhatan,
over-king of the tribes from the Atlantic coast
to the " falls of the river." According to the story
he sent to England a few months later, he was
well treated, and was sent back to Jamestown
with an escort. Eight years afterwards, when
writing an account of Powhatan's younger daugh-
ter, Pocahontas, who was then in England, for
the entertainment of Queen Anne, he embellished
this plain and probably truthful tale with the ro-
mantic incidents so long received as history.

POCAHONTAS

[January 5, 1608]

WEARIED arm and broken sword
　　Wage in vain the desperate fight;
Round him press a countless horde,
　　He is but a single knight.
Hark! a cry of triumph shrill
　　Through the wilderness resounds,
　　As, with twenty bleeding wounds,
Sinks the warrior, fighting still.

Now they heap the funeral pyre,
  And the torch of death they light;
Ah! 't is hard to die by fire!
  Who will shield the captive knight?
Round the stake with fiendish cry
Wheel and dance the savage crowd,
Cold the victim's mien and proud,
  And his breast is bared to die.

Who will shield the fearless heart?
  Who avert the murderous blade?
From the throng with sudden start
  See, there springs an Indian maid.
Quick she stands before the knight:
  "Loose the chain, unbind the ring!
I am daughter of the king,
  And I claim the Indian right!"

Dauntlessly aside she flings
  Lifted axe and thirsty knife,
Fondly to his heart she clings,
  And her bosom guards his life!
In the woods of Powhatan,
  Still 't is told by Indian fires
How a daughter of their sires
Saved a captive Englishman.
      WILLIAM MAKEPEACE THACKERAY.

The way in which the Pocahontas incident has
been handled by the poets is an interesting and
joyous study. These stanzas of Morris's are too
delicious to be omitted.

POCAHONTAS

UPON the barren sand
  A single captive stood;
Around him came, with bow and brand,
  The red men of the wood.
Like him of old, his doom he hears,
  Rock-bound on ocean's brim —
The chieftain's daughter knelt in tears,
  And breathed a prayer for him.

Above his head in air
  The savage war-club swung:
The frantic girl, in wild despair,
  Her arms about him flung.
Then shook the warriors of the shade,
  Like leaves on aspen limb,
Subdued by that heroic maid
  Who breathed a prayer for him!

"Unbind him!" gasped the chief:
  "It is your king's decree!"

He kiss'd away the tears of grief,
  And set the captive free!
'T is ever thus, when in life's storm
  Hope's star to man grows dim,
An angel kneels, in woman's form,
  And breathes a prayer for him.
      GEORGE POPE MORRIS.

The colony did not flourish as had been hoped,
and in May, 1609, the King granted a new charter
with larger powers and privileges, and a new
company was formed, of which Sir Thomas Gates,
Lord De La Warr, and Sir George Somers were
made the officers. A large expedition sailed from
England June 2, 1609, in charge of Gates, Somers,
and Captain Newport, who were on the Sea Ven-
ture. During a violent hurricane, their ship was
separated from the rest of the fleet and cast ashore
upon the Bermudas, whose beauties were so
eloquently sung by Andrew Marvell.

BERMUDAS

WHERE the remote Bermudas ride
In the ocean's bosom unespied,
From a small boat, that rowed along,
The listening winds received this song:

"What should we do but sing His praise,
That led us through the watery maze,
Unto an isle so long unknown,
And yet far kinder than our own?
Where He the huge sea-monsters wracks,
That lift the deep upon their backs,
He lands us on a grassy stage,
Safe from the storms, and prelates' rage.
He gave us this eternal Spring
Which here enamels every thing,
And sends the fowls to us in care,
On daily visits through the air;
He hangs in shades the orange bright,
Like golden lamps in a green night,
And does in the pomegranates close
Jewels more rich than Ormus shows;
He makes the figs our mouths to meet,
And throws the melons at our feet;
But apples plants of such a price,
No tree could ever bear them twice.
With cedars chosen by His hand
From Lebanon He stores the land,
And makes the hollow seas that roar
Proclaim the ambergris on shore;
He cast (of which we rather boast)
The Gospel's pearl upon our coast,
And in these rocks for us did frame
A temple where to sound His name.

Oh! let our voice His praise exalt,
Till it arrive at Heaven's vault,
Which thence (perhaps) rebounding may
Echo beyond the Mexique Bay."

Thus sung they, in the English boat,
A holy and a cheerful note:
And all the way, to guide their chime,
With falling oars they kept the time.
                    ANDREW MARVELL.

The passengers and crew of the Sea Venture
managed to get to land, and finally built two
pinnaces, in which they reached Virginia May 24,
1610. They found the colonists in a desolate and
miserable condition, and only the timely arrival
of Lord De La Warr in the following month (June
9, 1610), with fresh supplies and colonists, pre-
vented them from burning the town and sailing
back to England. Among the passengers on the
Sea Venture was one Richard Rich. He shared
in all the adventures and hardships of the voyage,
and finally got back to England in the fall of 1610.
On October 1 he published an account of the
voyage, called "Newes from Virginia," the first
poem written by a visitor to America.

NEWES FROM VIRGINIA

[September, 1610]

It is no idle fabulous tale, nor is it fayned
        newes:
For Truth herself is heere arriv'd, because
        you should not muse.
With her both Gates and Newport come, to
        tell Report doth lye,
Which did divulge unto the world, that they
        at sea did dye.

Tis true that eleaven months and more,
        these gallant worthy wights
War in the shippe Sea-venture nam'd de-
        priv'd Virginia's sight.
And bravely did they glyde the maine, till
        Neptune gan to frowne,
As if a courser proudly backt would throwe
        his ryder downe.

The seas did rage, the windes did blowe,
        distressèd were they then;
Their ship did leake, her tacklings breake,
        in daunger were her men.
But heaven was pylotte in this storme, and to
        an iland nere,
Bermoothawes call'd, conducted then, which
        did abate their feare.

But yet these worthies forcèd were, opprest
        with weather againe,
To runne their ship betweene two rockes,
        where she doth still remaine.
And then on shoare the iland came, inhabited
        by hogges,
Some foule and tortoyses there were, they
        only had one dogge.

To kill these swyne, to yeild them foode that
        little had to eate,
Their store was spent, and all things scant,
        alas! they wanted meate.
A thousand hogges that dogge did kill, their
        hunger to sustaine,
And with such foode did in that ile two and
        forty weekes remaine.

And there two gallant pynases did build of
        seader-tree;
The brave Deliverance one was call'd; of
        seaventy tonne was shee.
The other Patience had to name, her burthen
        thirty tonne;
Two only of their men which there pale death
        did overcome.

And for the losse of these two soules, which
        were accounted deere,
A son and daughter then was borne, and were
        baptizèd there.
The two and forty weekes being past, they
        hoyst sayle and away;
Their ships with hogges well freighted were,
        their harts with mickle joy.

And so unto Virginia came, where these brave
        soldiers finde
The English-men opprest with greife and
        discontent in minde.
They seem'd distracted and forlorne, for
        those two worthyes losse,
Yet at their home returne they joy'd, among'st
        them some were crosse.

And in the mid'st of discontent came noble
        Delaware;
He heard the greifes on either part, and sett
        them free from care.
He comforts them and cheeres their hearts,
        that they abound with joy;
He feedes them full and feedes their souls
        with Gods word every day.

A discreet counsell he creates of men of worthy fame,
That noble Gates leiftenant was the admirall had to name.
The worthy Sir George Somers knight, and others of commaund;
Maister Georg Pearcy, which is brother unto Northumberland.

Sir Fardinando Wayneman Knight, and others of good fame,
That noble lord his company, which to Virginia came,
And landed there; his number was one hundred seaventy; then
Ad to the rest, and they make full foure hundred able men.

Where they unto their labour fall, as men that meane to thrive;
Let's pray that heaven may blesse them all, and keep them long alive.
Those men that vagrants liv'd with us, have there deserved well;
Their governour writes in their praise, as divers letters tel.

And to th' adventurers thus he writes be not dismayed at all,
For scandall cannot doe us wrong, God will not let us fall.
Let England knowe our willingnesse, for that our worke is goode;
Wee hope to plant a nation, where none before hath stood.

To glorifie the lord tis done; and to no other end;
He that would crosse so good a work, to God can be no friend.
There is no feare of hunger here for corne much store here growes,
Much fish the gallant rivers yeild, tis truth without suppose.

Great store of fowle, of venison, of grapes and mulberries,
Of chestnuts, walnuts, and such like, of fruits and strawberries,
There is indeed no want at all, but some, condiciond ill,
That wish the worke should not goe on with words doe seeme to kill.

And for an instance of their store, the noble Delaware
Hath for the present hither sent, to testify his care
In mannaging so good a worke, to gallant ships, by name,
The Blessing and the Hercules, well fraught, and in the same

Two ships, as these commodities, furres, sturgeon, caviare,
Black walnut-tree, and some deale boards, with such they laden are;
Some pearle, some wainscot and clapboards, with some sassafras wood,
And iron promist, for tis true their mynes are very good.

Then maugre scandall, false report, or any opposition,
Th' adventurers doe thus devulge to men of good condition,
That he that wants shall have reliefe, be he of honest minde,
Apparel, coyne, or any thing, to such they will be kinde.

To such as to Virginia do purpose to repaire;
And when that they shall hither come, each man shall have his share.
Day wages for the laborer, and for his more content,
A house and garden plot shall have; besides, tis further ment

That every man shall have a part, and not thereof denaid,
Of generall profit, as if that he twelve pounds ten shillings paid;
And he that in Virginia shall copper coyne receive,
For hyer or commodities, and will the coun try leave

Upon delivery of such coyne unto the Gov ernour,
Shall by exchange at his returne be by their treasurer
Paid him in London at first sight, no man shall cause to grieve,
For tis their generall will and wish that every man should live

The number of adventurers, that are for this
    plantation,
Are full eight hundred worthy men, some
    noble, all of fashion.
Good, discreete, their worke is good, and as
    they have begun,
May Heaven assist them in their worke, and
    thus our newes is done.
                  RICHARD RICH.

Lord Delaware's stay in Virginia marked the
turning-point in the fortunes of the colony. New
settlements were made, tobacco culture was be-
gun, and Virginia seemed at last fairly started
on the road to prosperity.

TO THE VIRGINIAN VOYAGE

[1611]

You brave heroic minds,
Worthy your country's name,
    That honor still pursue,
    Go and subdue,
Whilst loitering hinds
Lurk here at home, with shame.

Britons, you stay too long:
Quickly aboard bestow you,
    And with a merry gale
    Swell your stretch'd sail,
With vows as strong
As the winds that blow you.

Your course securely steer,
West and by south forth keep!
    Rocks, lee-shores, nor shoals,
    When Eolus scowls,
You need not fear,
So absolute the deep.

And cheerfully at sea,
Success you still entice,
    To get the pearl and gold,
    And ours to hold
Virginia,
Earth's only paradise.

Where nature hath in store
Fowl, venison, and fish,
    And the fruitful'st soil,
    Without your toil,
Three harvests more,
All greater than your wish.

And the ambitious vine
Crowns with his purple mass
    The cedar reaching high
    To kiss the sky,
The cypress, pine,
And useful sassafras.

To whom the Golden Age
Still nature's laws doth give,
    No other cares attend,
    But them to defend
From winter's rage,
That long there doth not live.

When as the luscious smell
Of that delicious land,
    Above the seas that flows,
    The clear wind throws,
Your hearts to swell
Approaching the dear strand;

In kenning of the shore
(Thanks to God first given)
    O you the happiest men,
    Be frolic then!
Let cannons roar,
Frighting the wide heaven;

And in regions far
Such heroes bring ye forth
    As those from whom we came,
    And plant our name
Under that star
Not known unto our North;

And as there plenty grows
Of laurel everywhere, —
    Apollo's sacred tree, —
    You it may see,
A poet's brows
To crown, that may sing there.

Thy *Voyages* attend
Industrious Hackluit,
    Whose reading shall inflame
    Men to seek fame,
And much commend
To after-times thy wit.
                MICHAEL DRAYTON.

Among the planters at Jamestown was John
Rolfe, a zealous Christian, who became interested
in Pocahontas. Finally, either captivated by
her grace and beauty as the romancists believe,
or in spite of personal scruples and "for the good

of the colony," as Hamor wrote, he proposed marriage. The Princess was willing, her father consented, though he refused to be present at the ceremony (April 5, 1614), and the bride was given away by her uncle Opachisco. They had one son, Thomas Rolfe, whose descendants are still living in Virginia.

THE MARRIAGE OF POCAHONTAS

[April 5, 1614]

THAT balmy eve. within a trellised bower,
Rudely constructed on the sounding shore,
Her plighted troth the forest maiden gave
Ere sought the skiff that bore them o'er the
 wave
To the dark home-bound ship, whose restless
 sway
Rocked to the winds and waves, impatient
 of delay.

. . . .

Short was the word that pledged triumphant
 love;
That vow, that claims its registry above.
And low the cadence of that hymn of praise
Whose hallowed incense rose, as rose its lays;
And few the worshippers 'neath that pure
 cope
Which emblems to the soul eternal hope.

One native maiden waited the command
Of the young Princess of Virginia's strand;
And that dark youth, the Page of Cedar Isle,
Who wept her woes, and shared her sad exile,
With his loved bride, who owned the royal
 blood,
And near the forest Queen majestically stood.

Some others bent beside the rural shrine
In adoration to the Power divine;
When at the altar knelt, with minds serene,
The gallant Soldier and the dark-browed
 Queen.

These, for the love they bore her guileless
 youth,
Paid the high fealty of the warm heart's truth;
And with its homage satisfied, gone o'er
Each vision bright that graced their natal
 shore.

Those, with forebodings dread and brimful
 eyes,
Bade holy angels guard the destinies

Of one on whom had fallen the chrism of light
With unction pure; the youthful neophyte
Of that fair clime where millions yet unborn
Shall raise the choral hymn from eve till
 morn.

MRS. M. M. WEBSTER.

In 1616 Pocahontas was taken to England, where she was received with marked attention by the Queen and court. She renewed her acquaintance with Captain John Smith, who was busy weaving fairy tales about her, had her portrait painted and led a fashionable life generally. It did not agree with her, she developed consumption, and died at Gravesend, March 27, 1617.

THE LAST MEETING OF POCAHON-TAS AND THE GREAT CAPTAIN

[June, 1616]

IN a stately hall at Brentford, when the English June was green,
Sat the Indian Princess, summoned that her
 graces might be seen,
For the rumor of her beauty filled the ear
 of court and Queen.

There for audience as she waited, with half-scornful, silent air
All undazzled by the splendor gleaming
 round her everywhere,
Dight in broidered hose and doublet, came
 a courtier down the stair.

As with striding step he hasted, burdened
 with the Queen's command,
Loud he cried, in tones that tingled, "*Welcome, welcome, to my land!*"
But a tremor seized the Princess, and she
 drooped upon her hand.

"What! no word, my Sparkling-Water? must I come on bended knee?
I were slain within the forest, I were dead
 beyond the sea;
On the banks of wild Pamunkey, I had perished *but for thee*.

"Ah, I keep a heart right loyal, that can never
 more forget
I can hear the rush, the breathing; I can see
 the eyelids wet;
I can feel the sudden tightening of thine arms
 about me yet.

"Nay, look up. Thy father's daughter never
    feared the face of man,
Shrank not from the forest darkness when
    her doe-like footsteps ran
To my cabin, bringing tidings of the craft
    of Powhatan."

With extended arms, entreating, stood the
    stalwart Captain there,
While the courtiers press around her, and
    the passing pages stare;
But no sign gave Pocahontas underneath her
    veil of hair.

All her lithe and willowy figure quivered like
    an aspen-leaf,
And she crouched as if she shrivelled, frost-
    touched by some sudden grief,
Turning only on her husband, Rolfe, one
    glance, sharp, searching, brief.

At the Captain's haughty gesture, back the
    curious courtiers fell,
And with soothest word and accent he be-
    sought that she would tell
Why she turned away, nor greeted him whom
    she had served so well.

But for two long hours the Princess dumbly
    sate and bowed her head,
Moveless as the statue near her. When at
    last she spake, she said:
"White man's tongue is false. It told me —
    told me — *that my brave was dead.*

"And I lay upon my deer-skins all one moon
    of falling leaves
(Who hath care for song or corn-dance, when
    the voice within her grieves?),
Looking westward where the souls go, up the
    path the sunset weaves.

"Call me 'child' now. It is over. On my
    husband's arm I lean;
Never shadow, *Nenemoosa,* our twain hearts
    shall come between;
Take my hand, and let us follow the great
    Captain to his Queen."
                    MARGARET JUNKIN PRESTON.

In 1676 the colony was shaken by a struggle
which presaged that other one which was to occur
just a century later. An Indian war had broken
out along the frontier, but Governor Berkeley
disbanded the forces gathered to repress it. Where-
upon a young man named Nathaniel Bacon ga-
thered a force of his own, marched against the
Indians, and was proclaimed a rebel and traitor
by the royal governor, who had collected at James-
town a force of nearly a thousand men. Bacon,
after a campaign in which the hostile Indians
were practically wiped out of existence, marched
back to Jamestown and besieged the place. After
a sally in which he was repulsed, Berkeley sailed
away and left the town to its fate. Bacon entered
it next morning (September 19, 1676), and, de-
ciding that he could not hold it, set fire to it that
evening. It was totally destroyed.

THE BURNING OF JAMESTOWN

[September 19, 1676]

MAD Berkeley believed, with his gay cavaliers,
    And the ruffians he brought from the
        Accomac shore,
He could ruffle our spirit by rousing our fears,
    And lord it again as he lorded before:
        It was — "Traitors, be dumb!"
        And — "Surrender, ye scum!"
And that Bacon, our leader, was rebel, he
    swore.

A rebel? Not he! He was true to the throne;
    For the King, at a word, he would lay
        down his life;
But to listen unmoved to the piteous moan
    When the redskin was plying the hatchet
        and knife,
        And shrink from the fray,
        Was not the man's way —
It was Berkeley, not Bacon, who stirred up
    the strife.

On the outer plantations the savages burst,
    And scattered around desolation and woe;
And Berkeley, possessed by some spirit accurst,
    Forbade us to deal for our kinsfolk a blow;
        Though when, weapons in hand,
        We made our demand,
He sullenly suffered our forces to go.

Then while we were doing our work for the
    crown,
    And risking our lives in the perilous fight,
He sent lying messengers out, up and down,
    To denounce us as outlaws — mere malice
        and spite;
        Then from Accomac's shore
        Brought a thousand or more,
Who swaggered the country around, day
    and night.

Returning in triumph, instead of reward
  For the marches we made and the battles
    we won,
There were threats of the fetters or bullet or
    sword —
  Were these a fair guerdon for what we had
    done?
    When this madman abhorred
    Appealed to the sword,
And our leader said "fight!" did he think we
    would run?

Battle-scarred, and a handful of men as we
    were,
  We feared not to combat with lord or with
    lown,
So we took the old wretch at his word —
    that was fair;
  But he dared not come out from his hold
    in the town
    Where he lay with his men,
    Like a wolf in his den;
And in siege of the place we sat steadily down.

He made a fierce sally, — his force was so
    strong
  He thought the mere numbers would put
    us to flight, —
But we met in close column his ruffianly
    throng,
  And smote it so sore that we filled him
    with fright;
    Then while ready we lay
    For the storming next day,
He embarked in his ships, and escaped in
    the night.

The place was our own; could we hold it?
    why, no!
  Not if Berkeley should gather more force
    and return;
But one course was left us to baffle the foe —
  The birds would not come if the nest we
    should burn;
    So the red, crackling fire
    Climbed to roof-top and spire,
A lesson for black-hearted Berkeley to learn.

That our torches destroyed what our fathers
    had raised
  On that beautiful isle, is it matter of blame?
That the houses we dwelt in, the church
    where they praised
  The God of our Fathers, we gave to the
    flame?

    That we smiled when there lay
    Smoking ruins next day,
And nothing was left of the town but its
    name?

We won; but we lost when brave Nicholas
    died;
  The spirit that nerved us was gone from
    us then;
And Berkeley came back in his arrogant
    pride
  To give to the gallows the best of our men;
    But while the grass grows
    And the clear water flows,
The town shall not rise from its ashes again.

So, you come for your victim! I'm ready;
    but, pray,
  Ere I go, some good fellow a full goblet
    bring.
Thanks, comrade! Now hear the last words
    I shall say
  With the last drink I take. Here's a health
    to the King,
    Who reigns o'er a land
    Where, against his command,
The rogues rule and ruin, while honest men
    swing.

              Thomas Dunn English.

    Jamestown soon avenged itself. Before Bacon
left the place he was ill with fever, and on the
first day of October, at the house of a friend in
Gloucester County, he "surrendered up that fort
he was no longer able to keep, into the hands of
the grim and all-conquering Captain, Death." His
death was celebrated in a poem which is perhaps
the most brilliant example of sustained poetic art
produced in Colonial America. It was written "by
his man," of whom absolutely nothing is known.

BACON'S EPITAPH, MADE BY HIS MAN

[October 1, 1676]

Death, why so cruel? What! no other way
To manifest thy spleen, but thus to slay
Our hopes of safety, liberty, our all,
Which, through thy tyranny, with him must
    fall
To its late chaos? Had thy rigid force
Been dealt by retail, and not thus in gross,
Grief had been silent. Now we must com-
    plain,

Since thou, in him, hast more than thousands
    slain,
Whose lives and safeties did so much depend
On him their life, with him their lives must
    end.
If 't be a sin to think Death brib'd can be
We must be guilty; say 't was bribery
Guided the fatal shaft. Virginia's foes,
To whom for secret crimes just vengeance
    owes
Deservèd plagues, dreading their just desert,
Corrupted Death by Paracelsian art
Him to destroy; whose well-tried courage
    such,
Their heartless hearts, nor arms, nor strength
    could touch.
    Who now must heal those wounds   r stop
        that blood
The Heathen made, and drew into a flood?
Who is 't must plead our cause? nor trump,
    nor drum,
Nor Deputation; these, alas! are dumb
And cannot speak. Our arms (though ne'er
    so strong)
Will want the aid of his commanding tongue,
Which conquer'd more than Cæsar. He
    o'erthrew
Only the outward frame; this could subdue
The rugged works . nature. Souls replete
With dull chill cc d, he'd animate with heat
Drawn forth of reason's limbec. In a word,
Mars and Minerva both in him concurred
For arts, for arms, whose pen and sword alike
As Cato's did, may admiration strike
Into his foes; while they confess withal
It was their guilt styl'd him a criminal.
Only this difference does from truth pro-
    ceed:
They in the guilt, he in the name must bleed.
While none shall dare his obsequies to sing
In deserv'd measures; until time shall bring
Truth crown'd with freedom, and from dan-
    ger free
To sound his praises to posterity.
    Here let him rest; while we this truth
        report,
He's gone from hence unto a higher Court
To plead his cause, where he by this doth
    know
Whether to Cæsar he was friend or foe.

Jamestown never recovered from the blow
which Bacon dealt it. The location was so un-
healthy that it could not attract new settlers,
and though some of the houses which had been
burned were subsequently rebuilt, the town's
day of greatness was past. The seat of govern-
ment was removed to Williamsburg, and the old
settlement dropped gradually to decay.

ODE TO JAMESTOWN

OLD cradle of an infant world,
    In which a nestling empire lay,
Struggling awhile, ere she unfurled
    Her gallant wing and soared away;
All hail! thou birthplace of the glowing west,
Thou seem'st the towering eagle's ruined
    nest!

What solemn recollections throng,
    What touching visions rise,
As, wandering these old stones among,
    I backward turn mine eyes,
And see the shadows of the dead flit round,
Like spirits, when the last dread trump shall
    sound.

The wonders of an age combined
    In one short moment memory supplies;
They throng upon my wakened mind,
    As time's dark curtains rise.
The volume of a hundred buried years,
Condensed in one bright sheet, appears.

I hear the angry ocean rave,
    I see the lonely little bark
Scudding along the crested wave,
    Freighted like old Noah's ark,
As o'er the drownèd earth 't was hurled,
With the forefathers of another world.

I see the train of exiles stand,
    Amid the desert, desolate,
The fathers of my native land,
    The daring pioneers of fate,
Who braved the perils of the sea and earth,
And gave a boundless empire birth.

I see the sovereign Indian range
    His woodland empire, free as air;
I see the gloomy forest change,
    The shadowy earth laid bare;
And where the red man chased the bounding
    deer,
The smiling labors of the white appear.

I see the haughty warrior gaze
    In wonder or in scorn,

As the pale faces sweat to raise
  Their scanty fields of corn,
While he, the monarch of the boundless
    wood,
By sport, or hair-brained rapine, wins his
    food.

A moment, and the pageant's gone;
  The red men are no more;
The pale-faced strangers stand alone
  Upon the river's shore;
And the proud wood-king, who their arts
    disdained,
Finds but a bloody grave where once he
    reigned.

The forest reels beneath the stroke
  Of sturdy woodman's axe;
The earth receives the white man's yoke,
  And pays her willing tax
Of fruits, and flowers, and golden harvest
    fields,
And all that nature to blithe labor yields.

Then growing hamlets rear their heads,
  And gathering crowds expand,
Far as my fancy's vision spreads,
  O'er many a boundless land,
Till what was once a world of savage strife
Teems with the richest gifts of social life.

Empire to empire swift succeeds,
  Each happy, great, and free;
One empire still another breeds,
  A giant progeny,
Destined their daring race to run,
Each to the regions of yon setting sun.

Then, as I turn my thoughts to trace
  The fount whence these rich waters
    sprung,
I glance towards this lonely place,
  And find it these rude stones among.
Here rest the sires of millions, sleeping round,
The Argonauts, the golden fleece that found.

Their names have been forgotten long;
  The stone, but not a word, remains;
They cannot live in deathless song,
  Nor breathe in pious strains.
Yet this sublime obscurity to me
More touching is than poet's rhapsody.

They live in millions that now breathe;
  They live in millions yet unborn,

And pious gratitude shall wreathe
  As bright a crown as e'er was worn,
And hang it on the green-leaved bough,
That whispers to the nameless dead below.

No one that inspiration drinks,
  No one that loves his native land,
No one that reasons, feels, or thinks,
  Can mid these lonely ruins stand
Without a moistened eye, a grateful tear
Of reverent gratitude to those that moulder
    here.

The mighty shade now hovers round,
  Of him whose strange, yet bright career
Is written on this sacred ground
  In letters that no time shall sere;
Who in the Old World smote the turbaned
    crew,
And founded Christian empires in the New.

And she! the glorious Indian maid,
  The tutelary of this land,
The angel of the woodland shade,
  The miracle of God's own hand,
Who joined man's heart to woman's softest
    grace,
And thrice redeemed the scourges of her
    race.

Sister of charity and love,
  Whose life-blood was soft Pity's tide,
Dear goddess of the sylvan grove,
  Flower of the forest, nature's pride,
He is no man who does not bend the knee,
And she no woman who is not like thee!

Jamestown, and Plymouth's hallowed rock
  To me shall ever sacred be, —
I care not who my themes may mock,
  Or sneer at them and me.
I envy not the brute who here can stand
Without a thrill for his own native land.

And if the recreant crawl her earth,
  Or breathe Virginia's air,
Or in New England claim his birth,
  From the old pilgrims there,
He is a bastard if he dare to mock
Old Jamestown's shrine or Plymouth's
    famous rock.
                      JAMES KIRKE PAULDING.

In the early part of the eighteenth century,
pirates did a thriving trade along the American

coast. One of the most redoubtable of these was Captain Teach, better known as "Blackbeard." After a long career of variegated villainy, he was cornered in Pamlico Inlet, in 1718, and killed, together with most of his crew, by a force sent after him by Governor Spottiswood of Virginia. His death was celebrated in a ballad said to have been written by Benjamin Franklin.

THE DOWNFALL OF PIRACY

[November 22, 1718]

WILL you hear of a bloody Battle,
  Lately fought upon the Seas?
It will make your Ears to rattle,
  And your Admiration cease;
Have you heard of Teach the Rover,
  And his Knavery on the Main;
How of Gold he was a Lover,
  How he lov'd all ill-got Gain?

When the Act of Grace appeared,
  Captain Teach, with all his Men,
Unto Carolina steered,
  Where they kindly us'd him then;
There he marry'd to a Lady,
  And gave her five hundred Pound,
But to her he prov'd unsteady,
  For he soon march'd off the Ground.

And returned, as I tell you,
  To his Robbery as before,
Burning, sinking Ships of value,
  Filling them with Purple Gore;
When he was at Carolina,
  There the Governor did send
To the Governor of Virginia,
  That he might assistance lend.

Then the Man-of-War's Commander,
  Two small Sloops he fitted out,
Fifty Men he put on board, Sir,
  Who resolv'd to stand it out;
The Lieutenant he commanded
  Both the Sloops, and you shall hear
How, before he landed,
  He suppress'd them without fear.

Valiant Maynard as he sailed,
  Soon the Pirate did espy,
With his Trumpet he then hailed,
  And to him they did reply:
Captain Teach is our Commander,
  Maynard said, he is the Man

Whom I am resolv'd to hang, Sir,
  Let him do the best he can.

Teach replyed unto Maynard,
  You no Quarter here shall see,
But be hang'd on the Mainyard,
  You and all your Company;
Maynard said, I none desire
  Of such Knaves as thee and thine,
None I'll give, Teach then replyed,
  My Boys, give me a Glass of Wine.

He took the Glass, and drank Damnation
  Unto Maynard and his Crew;
To himself and Generation,
  Then the Glass away he threw;
Brave Maynard was resolv'd to have him,
  Tho' he'd Cannons nine or ten;
Teach a broadside quickly gave him,
  Killing sixteen valiant Men.

Maynard boarded him, and to it
  They fell with Sword and Pistol too;
They had Courage, and did show it,
  Killing of the Pirate's Crew.
Teach and Maynard on the Quarter,
  Fought it out most manfully,
Maynard's Sword did cut him shorter,
  Losing his head, he there did die.

Every Sailor fought while he, Sir,
  Power had to wield the Sword,
Not a Coward could you see, Sir,
  Fear was driven from aboard;
Wounded Men on both Sides fell, Sir,
  'T was a doleful Sight to see,
Nothing could their Courage quell, Sir,
  O, they fought courageously.

When the bloody Fight was over,
  We're informed by a Letter writ,
Teach's Head was made a Cover,
  To the Jack Staff of the Ship;
Thus they sailed to Virginia,
  And when they the Story told,
How they kill'd the Pirates many,
  They'd Applause from young and old.
                    BENJAMIN FRANKLIN. (?)

On the twenty-second day of February, 1732 (February 12, O. S.), there was born in Westmoreland County, Virginia, a son to Augustine and Mary (Ball) Washington. The baby was

christened George, and lived to become the most
famous personage in American history.

FROM POTOMAC TO MERRIMAC

[February 11, 1732]

I. POTOMAC SIDE

Do you know how the people of all the land
Knew at last that the time was at hand
When He should be sent to give command
To armies and people, to father and son!
How the glad tidings of joy should run
Which tell of the birth of Washington?

Three women keep watch of the midnight
    sky
  Where Potomac ripples below;
They watch till the light in the window hard
    by
  The birth of the child shall show.
    Is it peace? Is it strife?
    Is it death? Is it life?
  The light in the window shall show!
      Weal or woe!
      We shall know!

The women have builded a signal pile
For the birthday's welcome flame,
That the light may show for many a mile
  To tell when the baby came!
    And south and north
    The word go forth
    That the boy is born
    On that blessèd morn;
    The boy of deathless fame!

II. SIGNAL FIRES

The watchmen have waited on Capitol Hill
  And they light the signal flame;
And at Baltimore Bay they waited till
  The welcome tidings came;
And then across the starlit night,
At the head of Elk the joyful light

Told to the Quaker town the story
Of new-born life and coming glory!
To Trenton Ferry and Brooklyn Height
They sent the signal clear and bright,
    And far away,
    Before the day,
To Kaatskill and Greylock the joyful flame
And everywhere the message came,
    As the signal flew
    The people knew
That the man of men was born!

III. MERRIMAC SIDE, AND AGIOCHOOK

So it is, they say, that the men in the bay,
  In winter's ice and snow,
See the welcome light on Wachusett Height
  While the Merrimac rolls below.
    The cheery fire
    Rose higher and higher,
Monadnock and Carrigain catch the flame,
And on and on, and on it came,
    And as men look
      Far away in the north
      The word goes forth,
    To Agiochook.
    The welcome fire
    Flashed higher and higher
To our mountain ways,
And the dome, and Moat and Pequawket
    blaze!

So the farmers in the Intervale
See the light that shall never fail,
The beacon light which shines to tell
  To all the world to say
    That the boy has been born
    On that winter's morn
  By Potomac far away.
    Whose great command
    Shall bless that land
    Whom the land shall bless
    In joy and distress
  Forever and a day!
          EDWARD EVERETT HALE.

CHAPTER IV

THE DUTCH AT NEW AMSTERDAM

On the fourth day of April, 1609, there put out from the port of Amsterdam a little craft of about eighty tons, called the Half Moon. It had been chartered by the Dutch East India Company to search for the Northwest Passage. Its captain was Henry Hudson, and on September 3 he cast anchor inside Sandy Hook.

HENRY HUDSON'S QUEST

[1609]

Out from the harbor of Amsterdam
    The Half Moon turned her prow to sea;
The coast of Norway dropped behind,
    Yet Northward still kept she
Through the drifting fog and the driving
    snow,
Where never before man dared to go:
"O Pilot, shall we find the strait that leads
    to the Eastern Sea?"
"A waste of ice before us lies — we must
    turn back," said he.

Westward they steered their tiny bark,
    Westward through weary weeks they sped,
Till the cold gray strand of a stranger-land
    Loomed through the mist ahead.
League after league they hugged the coast,
    And their Captain never left his post:
"O Pilot, see you yet the strait that leads
    to the Eastern Sea?"
"I see but the rocks and the barren shore;
    no strait is there," quoth he.

They sailed to the North — they sailed to
    the South —
    And at last they rounded an arm of sand
Which held the sea from a harbor's
    mouth —
    The loveliest in the land;
They kept their course across the bay,
    And the shore before them fell away:
"O Pilot, see you not the strait that leads to
    the Eastern Sea?"
"Hold the rudder true! Praise Christ Jesu!
    the strait is here," said he.

Onward they glide with wind and tide,
    Past marshes gray and crags sun-kist;

They skirt the sills of green-clad hills,
    And meadows white with mist —
But alas! the hope and the brave, brave
    dream!
For rock and shallow bar the stream:
"O Pilot, can this be the strait that leads to
    the Eastern Sea?"
"Nay, Captain, nay; 't is not this way; turn
    back we must," said he.

Full sad was Hudson's heart as he turned
    The Half Moon's prow to the South
    once more;
He saw no beauty in crag or hill,
    No beauty in curving shore;
For they shut him away from that fabled
    main
He sought his whole life long, in vain:
"O Pilot, say, can there be a strait that leads
    to the Eastern Sea?"
"God's crypt is sealed! 'T will stand revealed
    in His own good time," quoth he.
          Burton Egbert Stevenson.

A few days were spent in exploring the bay, and on September 6 occurred the only fatality that marked the voyage. A seaman named John Colman, with four sailors, was sent out in a small boat to sound the Narrows, and encountered some Indians, who sent a flight of arrows toward the strangers. One of the arrows pierced Colman's throat, killing him.

THE DEATH OF COLMAN

[September 6, 1609]

'T was Juet spoke — the Half Moon's mate·
And they who Holland's ship of state
Compass'd with wisdom, listening sate:

Discovery's near-extinguished spark
    Flared up into a blaze,
When Man-na-hat-ta's virgin hills,
    Enriched by Autumn's days,
First fell on our impatient sight,
And soothed us with a strange delight

Bidden by fevered trade, our keel
    Had ploughed unbeaten deeps:

From many a perfume-laden isle
  To the dark land that sleeps
Forever in its winter robe,
Th' unsocial hermit of the globe.

But we, who sought for China's strand
  By ocean ways untried,
Forgot our mission when we cast
  Our anchor in a tide
That kissed a gem too wondrous fair
For any eastern sea to wear!

Entranced, we saw the golden woods
  Slope gently to the sands;
The grassy meads, the oaks that dwarfed
  Their kin of other lands;
And from the shore the balmy wind
Blew sweeter than the spice of Ind.

As he whose eyes, though opened wide,
  Are fixed upon a dream,
So Colman — one who long had held
  Our Hudson's warm esteem —
Gazed on the gorgeous scene, and said,
"Ere even's shades are overspread,

"Proudly our flag on yonder height
  Shall tell of Holland's gain;
Proclaiming her to all the earth
  The sovereign of the main."
And quickly from the Half Moon's bow
We turned the longboat's yielding prow.

The measured flashing of the oars
  Broke harshly on the ear;
And eye asked eye — for lips were mute —
  What Holland hearts should fear;
For true it is our hearts were soft,
Save his, who held the flag aloft.

And suddenly our unshaped dread
  Took direful form and sound.
For from a near nook's rocky shade,
  Swift as pursuing hound,
A savage shallop sped, to hold
From stranger feet that strand of gold.

And rageful cries disturbed the peace
  That on the waters slept;
And Echo whispered on the hills,
  As though an army crept,
With flinty axe and brutal blade,
Through the imperforate forest shade.

"What! are ye cravens?" Colman said;
  For each had shipped his oar.
He waved the flag: "For Netherland,
  Pull for yon jutting shore!"
Then prone he fell within the boat,
A flinthead arrow through his throat!

And now full many a stealthy skiff
  Shot out into the bay;
And swiftly, sadly, pulled we back
  To where the Half Moon lay;
But he was dead — our master wept —
He smiled, brave heart, as though he slept.

Then to the seaward breeze our sail
  With woful hearts we threw;
And anchored near a sandy strip
  That looks o'er ocean blue:
And there we kissed and buried him,
While surges sang his funeral hymn.

And many a pitying glance we gave,
  And many a prayer we said,
As from that grave we turned, and left
  The dark sea with her dead;
For — God of Waves! — none could repress
One choking thought — *the loneliness!*
                              THOMAS FROST.

Hudson ascended the river to a point a little above the present town of Albany, then turned back and returned to Holland. His report of the rich country he had discovered was received with enthusiasm there, and preparations were begun on an extensive scale to colonize the new country. Dutch voyagers explored all the adjacent coasts, among the most active being Adrian Block.

ADRIAN BLOCK'S SONG

[July, 1615]

HARD aport! Now close to shore sail!
  Starboard now, and drop your foresail!
See, boys, what yon bay discloses,
What yon open bay discloses!
Where the breeze so gently blows is
Heaven's own land of ruddy roses.

  Past the Cormorant we sail,
  Past the rippling Beaver Tail,
Green with summer, red with flowers,
Green with summer, fresh with showers,
Sweet with song and red with flowers,
Is this new-found land of ours!

Roses close above the sand,
Roses on the trees on land,
I shall take this land for my land,
Rosy beach and rosy highland,
And I name it Roses Island.
                EDWARD EVERETT HALE.

But troubles at home prevented any extensive effort at colonization until 1621, when the States-General chartered the Dutch West India Company, which in 1623 sent Captain Cornelius Jacobsen Mey, with thirty families, to start the colony.

THE PRAISE OF NEW NETHER-LAND

WITH sharpened pen and wit, one tunes his lays,
To sing the vanity of fame and praise;
His moping thoughts, bewildered in a maze,
            In darkness wander.
What brings disgrace, what constitutes a wrong,
These form the burden of the tuneful song:
And honor saved, his senses then among
            The dark holes ponder.
For me, it is a nobler thing I sing.
New Netherland springs forth my heroine;
Where Amstel's folk did erst their people bring,
            And still they flourish.
New Netherland, thou noblest spot of earth,
Where Bounteous Heaven ever poureth forth
The fulness of His gifts, of greatest worth,
            Mankind to nourish.
Whoe'er to you a judgment fair applies,
And knowing, comprehends your qualities,
Will justify the man who, to the skies,
            Extols your glories.
Who studies well your natural elements,
And with the plumb of science, gains a sense
Of all the four: fails not in their defence,
            Before free juries.
Your *Air*, so clear, so sharp to penetrate,
The western breezes softly moderate;
And, tempering the heat, they separate
            It from all moisture.
From damp, and mist, and fog, they set it free;
From smells of pools, they give it liberty:
The struggling stenches made to mount on high,
            And be at peace there.

No deadly pest its purity assails,
To spread infection o'er your hills and vales,
Save when a guilty race, great sins bewails
            In expiating.
Your Sun, th' original of *Fire* and heat,
The common nutriment of both to eat,
Is warm and pure; in plants most delicate,
            Much sap creating.
Nor turf, nor dried manure, — within your doors,
Nor coal, extracted from earth's secret stores,
Nor sods, uplifted from the barren moors,
            For fuel given;
Which, with foul stench the brain intoxicate,
And thus, by the foul gas which they create
The intellects of many, wise and great,
            Men are out-driven.
The forests do, with better means, supply
The hearth and house; the stately hickory,
Not planted, does the winter fell defy, —
            A valiant warden;
So closely grained, so rich with fragrant oil,
Before its blaze both wet and cold recoil;
And sweetest perfumes float around the while,
            Like 'n Eden's garden.
The *Water* clear and fresh, and pure and sweet,
Springs up continually beneath the feet,
And everywhere the gushing fountains meet,
            In brooks o'erflowing,
Which animals refresh, both tame and wild;
And plants conduce to grow on hill and field;
And these to man unnumbered comforts yield,
            And quickly growing.
The *Earth* in soils of different shades appears,
Black, blue and white, and red; its bosom bears
Abundant harvests; and, what pleases, spares
            Not to surrender.
No bounds exist to their variety.
They nourishment afford most plenteously
To creatures which, in turn, man's wants supply
            And health engender.
O fruitful land! heaped up with blessings kind,
Whoe'er your several virtues brings to mind, —
Its proper value to each gift assigned,
            Will soon discover,
If ever land perfection have attained,
That you in all things have that glory gained;
Ungrateful mortal, who, your worth disdained,
            Would pass you over.

In North America, behold your *Seat*,
Where all that heart can wish you satiate,
And where oppressed with wealth inordinate,
    You have the power
To bless the people with whate'er they need,
The melancholy, from their sorrows lead,
The light of heart, exulting pleasures cede,
    Who never cower.
The *Ocean* laves secure the outer shore,
Which, like a dyke, is raised your fields before;
And streams, like arteries, all veinèd o'er,
    The woods refreshing;
And rolling down from mountains and the
    hills,
Afford, upon their banks, fit sites for mills;
And furnish, what the heart with transport fills,
    The finest fishing.

.　.　.　.　.　.　.

JACOB STEENDAM.

Other expeditions followed, but though the
colony prospered, the mother country could pro-
vide little means of defence, and it was practically
at the mercy of the English — the "swine" of
Steendam's verses.

THE COMPLAINT OF NEW
AMSTERDAM

[1659]

I'M a grandchild of the gods
Who on th' Amstel have abodes;
Whence their orders forth are sent,
Swift for aid and punishment.
I, of Amsterdam, was born,
Early of her breasts forlorn;
From her care so quickly weaned
Oft have I my fate bemoaned.
    From my youth up left alone,
Naught save hardship have I known;
Dangers have beset my way
From the first I saw the day.
    Think you this a cause for marvel?
This will then the thread unravel,
And the circumstances trace,
Which upon my birth took place.
    Would you ask for my descent?
Long the time was it I spent
In the loins of warlike Mars.
'T seems my mother, seized with fears,
    Prematurely brought me forth.
But I now am very loth
To inform how this befel;
Though 't was thus, I know full well,
    Bacchus, too, — it is no dream, —

First beheld the daylight's beam
From the thigh of Jupiter.
But my reasons go too far.
    My own matter must I say,
And not loiter by the way,
E'en though Bacchus oft has proven
Friend to me in my misfortune.
    Now the midwife who received me,
Was Bellona; in suspense, she
Long did sit in trembling fear,
For the travail was severe.
    From the moment I was born,
Indian neighbors made me mourn.
They pursued me night and day,
While my mother kept away.
    But my sponsors did supply
Better my necessity;
They sustained my feeble life;
They procured a bounteous wife
    As my nurse, who did not spare
To my lips her paps to bear.
This was Ceres; freely she
Rendered what has nurtured me.
    Her most dearly I will prize;
She has made my horns to rise;
Trained my growth through tender years,
'Midst my burdens and my cares.
    True both simple 't was and scant,
What I had to feed my want.
Oft 't was naught except Sapawn
And the flesh of buck or fawn.
    When I thus began to grow,
No more care did they bestow,
Yet my breasts are full and neat,
And my hips are firmly set.
    Neptune shows me his good will;
Merc'ry, quick, exerts his skill
Me t' adorn with silk and gold;
Whence I'm sought by suitors bold.
    Stricken by my cheek's fresh bloom,
By my beauteous youthful form,
They attempt to seize the treasure
To enjoy their wanton pleasure.
    They, my orchards too, would plunder;
Truly 't is a special wonder,
That a maid with such a portion
Does not suffer more misfortune:
    For, I venture to proclaim,
No one can a maiden name
Who with richer land is blessed
Than th' estate by me possessed.
    See: two streams my garden bind,
From the East and North they wind, —
Rivers pouring in the sea,
Rich in fish, beyond degree.

Milk and butter; fruits to eat
No one can enumerate;
Ev'ry vegetable known;
Grain the best that e'er was grown.
All the blessings man e'er knew,
Here does Our Great Giver strew
(And a climate ne'er more pure),
But for me, — yet immature,
Fraught with danger, for the swine
Trample down these crops of mine;
Up-root, too, my choicest land;
Still and dumb, the while I stand,
In the hope, my mother's arm
Will protect me from the harm.
She can succor my distress.
Now my wish, my sole request, —
Is for men to till my land;
So I'll not in silence stand.
I have lab'rors almost none;
Let my household large become;
I'll my mother's kitchen furnish
With my knick-knacks, with my surplus;
With tobacco, furs and grain;
So that Prussia she'll disdain.

JACOB STEENDAM,
noch vaster.

In spite of this neglect, the new town thrived
apace. Friendly relations were established with
the settlers at Plymouth, and the colony seemed
to be moving steadily toward a golden future.
In May, 1647, there arrived from Holland the new
director, Peter Stuyvesant. He ruled supreme
until 1664, when New Amsterdam surrendered to
an English fleet.

PETER STUYVESANT'S NEW YEAR'S CALL

[I. Jan. A. C. 1661]

WHERE nowadays the Battery lies,
New York had just begun,
A new-born babe, to rub its eyes,
In Sixteen Sixty-One.
They christened it Nieuw Amsterdam,
Those burghers grave and stately,
And so, with schnapps and smoke and psalm,
Lived out their lives sedately.

Two windmills topped their wooden wall,
On Stadthuys gazing down,
On fort, and cabbage-plots, and all
The quaintly gabled town·

These flapped their wings and shifted backs,
As ancient scrolls determine,
To scare the savage Hackensacks,
Paumanks, and other vermin.

At night the loyal settlers lay
Betwixt their feather-beds;
In hose and breeches walked by day,
And smoked, and wagged their heads.
No changeful fashions came from France,
The freulen to bewilder,
And cost the burgher's purse, perchance
Its every other guilder.

In petticoats of linsey-red,
And jackets neatly kept,
The vrouws their knitting-needles sped
And deftly spun and swept.
Few modern-school flirtations there
Set wheels of scandal trundling,
But youths and maidens did their share
Of staid, old-fashioned bundling.

— The New Year opened clear and cold:
The snow, a Flemish ell
In depth, lay over Beeckman's Wold
And Wolfert's frozen well.
Each burgher shook his kitchen-doors,
Drew on his Holland leather,
Then stamped through drifts to do the chores,
Beshrewing all such weather.

But — after herring, ham, and kraut —
To all the gathered town
The Dominie preached the morning out,
In Calvinistic gown;
While tough old Peter Stuyvesant
Sat pewed in foremost station, —
The potent, sage, and valiant
Third Governor of the nation.

Prayer over, at his mansion hall,
With cake and courtly smile,
He met the people, one and all,
In gubernatorial style;
Yet missed, though now the day was old,
An ancient fellow-feaster, —
Heer Govert Loockermans, that bold
Brewer and burgomeester;

Who, in his farmhouse, close without
The picket's eastern end,
Sat growling at the twinge of gout
That kept him from his friend.

But Peter strapped his wooden peg,
  When tea and cake were ended
(Meanwhile the sound remaining leg
  Its high jack-boot defended),

A woolsey cloak about him threw,
  And swore, by wind and limb,
Since Govert kept from Peter's view,
  Peter would visit him;
Then sallied forth, through snow and blast,
  While many a humbler greeter
Stood wondering whereaway so fast
  Strode bluff Hardkoppig Pieter.

Past quay and cowpath, through a lane
  Of vats and mounded tans,
He puffed along, with might and main,
  To Govert Loockermans;
Once there, his right of entry took,
  And hailed his ancient crony:
"Myn Gód! in dese Manhattoes, Loock,
  Ve gets more snow as money!"

To which, and after whiffs profound,
  With doubtful wink and nod,
There came at last responsive sound:
  "Yah, Peter; yah, Myn Gód!"
Then goedevrouw Marie sat her guest
  Beneath the chimney-gable,
And courtesied, bustling at her best
  To spread the New Year's table.

She brought the pure and genial schnapps,
  That years before had come —
In the "Nieuw Nederlandts," perhaps —
  To cheer the settlers' home;
The long-stemmed pipes; the fragrant roll
  Of pressed and crispy Spanish;
Then placed the earthen mugs and bowl,
  Nor long delayed to vanish.

Thereat, with cheery nod and wink,
  And honors of the day,
The trader mixed the Governor's drink
  As evening sped away.
That ancient room! I see it now:
  The carven nutwood dresser;
The drawers, that many a burgher's vrouw
  Begrudged their rich possessor;

The brace of high-backed leathern chairs,
  Brass-nailed at every seam;
Six others, ranged in equal pairs;
  The bacon hung abeam;

The chimney-front, with porcelain shelft;
  The hearty wooden fire;
The picture, on the steaming delft,
  Of David and Goliah.

I see the two old Dutchmen sit
  Like Magog and his mate,
And hear them, when their pipes are lit,
  Discuss affairs of state:
The clique that would their sway demean;
  The pestilent importation
Of wooden nutmegs, from the lean
  And losel Yankee nation.

But when the subtle juniper
  Assumed its sure command,
They drank the buxom loves that were, —
  They drank the Motherland;
They drank the famous Swedish wars,
  Stout Peter's special glory,
While Govert proudly showed the scars
  Of Indian contests gory.

Erelong, the berry's power awoke
  Some music in their brains,
And, trumpet-like, through rolling smoke,
  Rang long-forgotten strains, —
Old Flemish snatches, full of blood,
  Of phantom ships and battle;
And Peter, with his leg of wood,
  Made floor and casement rattle.

Then round and round the dresser pranced,
  The chairs began to wheel,
And on the board the punch-bowl danced
  A Netherlandish reel;
Till midnight o'er the farmhouse spread
  Her New Year's skirts of sable,
And inch by inch, each puzzled head
  Dropt down upon the table.

But still to Peter, as he dreamed,
  The table spread and turned;
The chimney-log blazed high, and seemed
  To circle as it burned;
The town into the vision grew
  From ending to beginning;
Fort, wall, and windmill met his view,
  All widening and spinning.

The cowpaths, leading to the docks,
  Grew broader, whirling past.
And checkered into shining blocks, —
  A city fair and vast;

Stores, churches, mansions, overspread
  The metamorphosed island,
While not a beaver showed his head
  From Swamp to Kalchook highland.

Eftsoons the picture passed away;
  Hours after, Peter woke
To see a spectral streak of day
  Gleam in through fading smoke;
Still slept old Govert, snoring on
  In most melodious numbers;

No dreams of Eighteen Sixty-One
  Commingled with his slumbers.

But Peter, from the farmhouse door,
  Gazed doubtfully around,
Rejoiced to find himself once more
  On sure and solid ground.
The sky was somewhat dark ahead,
  Wind east, the morning lowery;
And on he pushed, a two-miles' tread,
  To breakfast at his Bouwery.
            EDMUND CLARENCE STEDMAN.

CHAPTER V

THE SETTLEMENT OF NEW ENGLAND

The Northern or Plymouth Branch of the Virginia Company, which had been chartered by James I in 1606, did, to some extent, for the north what the sister company did for the south. Sir Ferdinando Gorges was its Raleigh, and sent out a number of exploring ships, one of which made what is now reckoned the first permanent settlement in New England. Captain George Popham was in command, and in August, 1607, three months after the planting of Jamestown, built Fort Popham, or Fort St. George, at the mouth of the Kennebec. But it is not this settlement which has been celebrated in song and story. It is that made at New Plymouth in the winter of 1620 by a shipload of Separatists from the Church of England, who have come down through history as the "Pilgrim Fathers."

Driven from England by religious persecution, the Separatist congregation from the little town of Scrooby, about a hundred in number, had fled to Amsterdam, and finally, in 1609, to Leyden. But they were not in sympathy with the Dutch, and their thoughts turned to America. The Plymouth company was approached, but could not guarantee religious freedom. It gave the suppliants to understand, however, that there was little likelihood they would be interfered with, and after long debate and hesitation, they decided to take the risk.

THE WORD OF GOD TO LEYDEN CAME

[August 15 (N. S.), 1620]

THE word of God to Leyden came,
  Dutch town by Zuyder Zee:
Rise up, my children of no name,
  My kings and priests to be.
There is an empire in the West,
  Which I will soon unfold:

A thousand harvests in her breast,
  Rocks ribbed with iron and gold.

Rise up, my children, time is ripe!
  Old things are passed away.
Bishops and kings from earth I wipe;
  Too long they've had their day.
A little ship have I prepared
  To bear you o'er the seas;
And in your souls my will declared
  Shall grow by slow degrees.

Beneath my throne the martyrs cry;
  I hear their voice, How long?
It mingles with their praises high,
  And with their victor song.
The thing they longed and waited for,
  But died without the sight;
So, this shall be! I wrong abhor,
  The world I'll now set right.

Leave, then, the hammer and the loom,
  You've other work to do;
For Freedom's commonwealth there's room,
  And you shall build it too.
I'm tired of bishops and their pride,
  I'm tired of kings as well;
Henceforth I take the people's side,
  And with the people dwell.

Tear off the mitre from the priest,
  And from the king, his crown;
Let all my captives be released;
  Lift up, whom men cast down.
Their pastors let the people choose,
  And choose their rulers too;

Whom they select, I'll not refuse,
But bless the work they do.

The Pilgrims rose, at this, God's word,
And sailed the wintry seas:
With their own flesh nor blood conferred,
Nor thought of wealth or ease.
They left the towers of Leyden town,
They left the Zuyder Zee;
And where they cast their anchor down,
Rose Freedom's realm to be.
                    JEREMIAH EAMES RANKIN.

A vessel of one hundred and eighty tons, named
the Mayflower, was fitted out, and, on August 5
(N. S. 15), 1620, the emigrants sailed from South-
ampton, whither they had gone to join the ship.
There were ninety persons aboard the Mayflower
and thirty aboard a smaller vessel, the Speedwell.
But the Speedwell proved unseaworthy, and after
twice putting back for repairs, twelve of her pas-
sengers were crowded into the Mayflower, which
finally, on September 6 (N. S. 16), turned her prow
to the west, and began the most famous voyage
in American history, after that of Columbus.

SONG OF THE PILGRIMS

[September 16 (N. S.), 1620]

THE breeze has swelled the whitening sail,
The blue waves curl beneath the gale,
And, bounding with the wave and wind,
We leave Old England's shores behind —
    Leave behind our native shore,
    Homes, and all we loved before.

The deep may dash, the winds may blow,
The storm spread out its wings of woe,
Till sailors' eyes can see a shroud
Hung in the folds of every cloud;
    Still, as long as life shall last,
    From that shore we'll speed us fast.

For we would rather never be,
Than dwell where mind cannot be free,
But bows beneath a despot's rod
Even where it seeks to worship God.
    Blasts of heaven, onward sweep!
    Bear us o'er the troubled deep!

O see what wonders meet our eyes!
Another land, and other skies!
Columbian hills have met our view!
Adieu! Old England's shores, adieu!

Here, at length, our feet shall rest,
Hearts be free, and homes be blessed.

As long as yonder firs shall spread
Their green arms o'er the mountain's head, —
As long as yonder cliffs shall stand,
Where join the ocean and the land, —
    Shall those cliffs and mountains be
    Proud retreats for liberty.

Now to the King of kings we'll raise
The pæan loud of sacred praise;
More loud than sounds the swelling breeze,
More loud than speak the rolling seas!
    Happier lands have met our view!
    England's shores, adieu! adieu!
                    THOMAS COGSWELL UPHAM.

On November 19 (N. S.), nine weeks after
leaving Plymouth, land was sighted, and in the
evening of that day, the "band of exiles moored
their bark" in Cape Cod harbor.

LANDING OF THE PILGRIM FATHERS

[November 19 (N. S.), 1620]

THE breaking waves dashed high
    On the stern and rock-bound coast,
And the woods, against a stormy sky,
    Their giant branches tossed;

And the heavy night hung dark
    The hills and waters o'er,
When a band of exiles moored their bark
    On the wild New England shore.

Not as the conqueror comes,
    They, the true-hearted, came:
Not with the roll of the stirring drums,
    And the trumpet that sings of fame;

Not as the flying come,
    In silence and in fear, —
They shook the depths of the desert's gloom
    With their hymns of lofty cheer.

Amidst the storm they sang,
    And the stars heard, and the sea;
And the sounding aisles of the dim woods rang
    To the anthem of the free!

The ocean-eagle soared
    From his nest by the white wave's foam,

And the rocking pines of the forest roared:
　This was their welcome home!

There were men with hoary hair
　Amidst that pilgrim band;
Why have they come to wither there,
　Away from their childhood's land?

There was woman's fearless eye,
　Lit by her deep love's truth;
There was manhood's brow, serenely high,
　And the fiery heart of youth.

What sought they thus afar?
　Bright jewels of the mine?
The wealth of seas, the spoils of war? —
　They sought a faith's pure shrine!

Aye, call it holy ground,
　The soil where first they trod!
They have left unstained what there they
　　found —
　Freedom to worship God!
　　　　　　　　　FELICIA HEMANS.

Two days later, on Saturday, November 21,
the Mayflower dropped her anchor in what is now
the harbor of Provincetown, and a force of six-
teen, "every one his Musket, Sword and Corslet,
under the command of Captaine Myles Standish,"
went ashore to explore. The next day, being
Sunday, praise service was held on board, and
on the following Monday occurred the first wash-
ing-day.

THE FIRST PROCLAMATION OF
MILES STANDISH

[November 23 (N. S.), 1620]

"Ho, Rose!" quoth the stout Miles Stand-
　　ish,
　As he stood on the Mayflower's deck,
And gazed on the sandy coast-line
　That loomed as a misty speck

On the edge of the distant offing, —
　"See! yonder we have in view
Bartholomew Gosnold's ' headlands.'
　'T was in sixteen hundred and two

"That the Concord of Dartmouth anchored
　Just there where the beach is broad,
And the merry old captain named it
　(Half swamped by the fish) — Cape Cod.

"And so as his mighty 'headlands'
　Are scarcely a league away,
What say you to landing, sweetheart,
　And having a washing-day?

"For did not the mighty Leader
　Who guided the chosen band
Pause under the peaks of Sinai,
　And issue his strict command —

"(For even the least assoilment
　Of Egypt the spirit loathes) —
Or ever they entered Canaan,
　The people should wash their clothes?

"The land we have left is noisome, —
　And rank with the smirch of sin;
The land that we seek should find us
　Clean-vestured without and within."

"Dear heart" — and the sweet Rose Stand
　　ish
　Looked up with a tear in her eye;
She was back in the flag-stoned kitchen
　Where she watched, in the days gone by,

Her mother among her maidens
　(She should watch them no more, alas!),
And saw as they stretched the linen
　To bleach on the Suffolk grass.

In a moment her brow was cloudless,
　As she leaned on the vessel's rail,
And thought of the sea-stained garments,
　Of coif and of farthingale;

And the doublets of fine Welsh flannel,
　The tuckers and homespun gowns,
And the piles of the hosen knitted
　From the wool of the Devon downs.

So the matrons aboard the Mayflower
　Made ready with eager hand
To drop from the deck their baskets
　As soon as the prow touched land.

And there did the Pilgrim Mothers,
　"On a Monday," the record says,
Ordain for their new-found England
　The first of her washing-days.

And there did the Pilgrim Fathers,
　With matchlock and axe well slung,
Keep guard o'er the smoking kettles
　That propt on the crotches hung.

For the trail of the startled savage
  Was over the marshy grass,
And the glint of his eyes kept peering
  Through cedar and sassafras.

And the children were mad with pleasure
  As they gathered the twigs in sheaves,
And piled on the fire the fagots,
  And heaped up the autumn leaves.

"Do the thing that is next," saith the pro-
    verb,
  And a nobler shall yet succeed: —
'T is the motive exalts the action;
  'T is the doing, and not the deed;

For the earliest act of the heroes
  Whose fame has a world-wide sway
Was — to fashion a crane for a kettle,
  And order a washing-day!
                MARGARET JUNKIN PRESTON.

A shallop which the Pilgrims had brought with
them in the Mayflower was put together, and
in it a party explored the neighboring shores,
in search of a suitable place for the settlement.
They finally selected Plymouth Harbor, and on
Monday, December 21 (O. S. 11), they "marched
into the land and found divers corn-fields and
little running brooks, — a place (as they sup-
posed) fit for situation; at least it was the best
they could find."

THE MAYFLOWER

DOWN in the bleak December bay
The ghostly vessel stands away;
Her spars and halyards white with ice,
Under the dark December skies.
A hundred souls, in company,
Have left the vessel pensively, —
Have reached the frosty desert there,
And touched it with the knees of prayer.
  And now the day begins to dip,
The night begins to lower
  Over the bay, and over the ship
    Mayflower.

Neither the desert nor the sea
Imposes rites: their prayers are free;
Danger and toil the wild imposes,
And thorns must grow before the roses.
And who are these? — and what distress
The savage-acred wilderness
On mother, maid, and child may bring,

Beseems them for a fearful thing;
  For now the day begins to dip,
The night begins to lower
  Over the bay, and over the ship
    Mayflower.

But Carver leads (in heart and health
A hero of the commonwealth)
The axes that the camp requires,
To build the lodge and heap the fires,
And Standish from his warlike store
Arrays his men along the shore,
Distributes weapons resonant,
And dons his harness militant;
  For now the day begins to dip,
The night begins to lower
  Over the bay, and over the ship
    Mayflower;

And Rose, his wife, unlocks a chest —
She sees a Book, in vellum drest,
She drops a tear and kisses the tome,
Thinking of England and of home:
Might they — the Pilgrims, there and then
Ordained to do the work of men —
Have seen, in visions of the air,
While pillowed on the breast of prayer
  (When now the day began to dip,
The night began to lower
  Over the bay, and over the ship
    Mayflower),

The Canaan of their wilderness
A boundless empire of success;
And seen the years of future nights
Jewelled with myriad household lights;
And seen the honey fill the hive;
And seen a thousand ships arrive;
And heard the wheels of travel go;
It would have cheered a thought of woe.
  When now the day began to dip,
The night began to lower
  Over the bay, and over the ship
    Mayflower.
                ERASTUS WOLCOTT ELLSWORTH.

On March 16 an Indian came into the hamlet,
and in broken English bade the strangers "Wel-
come." He said his name was Samoset, that he
came from Monhegan, distant five days' journey
toward the southeast, where he had learned
something of the language from the crews of
fishing-boats, and that he was an envoy from
"the greatest commander in the country," a
sachem named Massasoit. Massasoit himself
appeared a few days later (March 21), and a

treaty offensive and defensive was entered into, which remained in force for fifty-four years.

THE PEACE MESSAGE

[March 16, 162[.]]

At the door of his hut sat Massasoit,
    And his face was lined with care,
For the Yellow Pest had stalked from the
        West
    And swept his wigwams bare;
Mother and child had it stricken down,
    And the warrior in his pride,
Till for one that lived when the plague was
        past,
    A full half-score had died.

Now from the Eastern Shore there came
    Word of a white-skinned race
Who had risen from out the mighty deep
    In search of a dwelling-place.
Houses they fashioned of tree and stone,
    Turkey and deer they slew
With a breath of flame like the lightning-
        flash
    Of the great God, Manitu.

Was it war or peace? The Chief looked
        round
    On the wreck of his mighty band.
His heart was sad as he rose from the
        ground
    And held on high his hand.
"We must treat with the stranger, my chil-
        dren," he said,
    And he called to him Samoset:
"You will go to the men on the Eastern
        Shore
    With wampum and calumet."

Warm was the welcome he received,
    For the Pilgrims' hearts did thrill
At the message he brought from Massa-
        soit,
    With its earnest of good-will.
They bade him eat and they bade him
        drink,
    Gave bracelet, knife, and ring,
And sent him again to Monhegan
    To lay them before his king.

So the treaty was made, and the treaty was
        kept
    For fifty years and four;

The white men wrought, and waked, and slept
    Secure on the Eastern Shore;
From the door of his hut, old Massasoit
    Noted their swift increase,
And blessed the day he had sent that way
    His messenger of peace.
                    BURTON EGBERT STEVENSON.

The colonists set about the work of planting their fields as soon as spring opened. The harvest proved a good one; "there was great store of wild turkeys, of which they took many, besides venison," the fowlers having been sent out by the governor, "that so they might, after a special manner, rejoice together after they had gathered the fruit of their labors." This festival was New England's "First Thanksgiving Day." For three days a great feast was spread not only for the colonists, but for Massasoit and some ninety of his people, who had contributed five deer to the larder.

THE FIRST THANKSGIVING DAY

[November, 1621]

"And now," said the Governor, gazing
        abroad on the piled-up store
Of the sheaves that dotted the clearings and
        covered the meadows o'er,
"'T is meet that we render praises because of
        this yield of grain;
'T is meet that the Lord of the harvest be
        thanked for His sun and rain.

"And therefore, I, William Bradford (by the
        grace of God to-day,
And the franchise of this good people), Gov-
        ernor of Plymouth, say,
Through virtue of vested power — ye shall
        gather with one accord,
And hold, in the month November, thanks-
        giving unto the Lord.

"He hath granted us peace and plenty, and
        the quiet we've sought so long;
He hath thwarted the wily savage, and kept
        him from wrack and wrong;
And unto our feast the Sachem shall be
        bidden, that he may know
We worship his own Great Spirit who maketh
        the harvests grow.

"So shoulder your matchlocks, masters:
        there is hunting of all degrees;
And fishermen, take your tackle, and scour
        for spoil the seas;

And maidens and dames of Plymouth, your
    delicate crafts employ
To honor our First Thanksgiving, and make
    it a feast of joy!

"We fail of the fruits and dainties — we
    fail of the old home cheer;
Ah, these are the lightest losses, mayhap,
    that befall us here;
But see, in our open clearings, how golden
    the melons lie;
Enrich them with sweets and spices, and
    give us the pumpkin-pie!"

So, bravely the preparations went on for
    the autumn feast;
The deer and the bear were slaughtered;
    wild game from the greatest to least
Was heaped in the colony cabins; brown
    home-brew served for wine,
And the plum and the grape of the forest, for
    orange and peach and pine.

At length came the day appointed: the snow
    had begun to fall,
But the clang from the meeting-house belfry
    rang merrily over all,
And summoned the folk of Plymouth, who
    hastened with glad accord
To listen to Elder Brewster as he fervently
    thanked the Lord.

In his seat sate Governor Bradford; men,
    matrons, and maidens fair;
Miles Standish and all his soldiers, with
    corselet and sword, were there;
And sobbing and tears and gladness had
    each in its turn the sway,
For the grave of the sweet Rose Standish
    o'ershadowed Thanksgiving Day.

And when Massasoit, the Sachem, sate down
    with his hundred braves,
And ate of the varied riches of gardens and
    woods and waves,
And looked on the granaried harvest, —
    with a blow on his brawny chest,
He muttered, "The good Great Spirit loves
    His white children best!"
                    MARGARET JUNKIN PRESTON.

The colonists, through the friendship of Mas-
sasoit, had had little trouble with the Indians,
but in April, 1622, a messenger from the Narra-
gansetts brought to Plymouth a sheaf of arrows
tied round with a rattlesnake skin. which the
Indians there interpreted as a declaration of
war. Governor Bradford, at the advice of the
doughty Standish, stuffed the skin with powder
and ball, and sent it back to the Narragansetts.
Their chief, Canonicus, was so alarmed at the
look of this missive that he refused to receive it.
and it finally found its way back to Plymouth.

THE WAR–TOKEN

From "The Courtship of Miles Standish"

[April 1, 1622]

MEANWHILE the choleric Captain strode
    wrathful away to the council,
Found it already assembled, impatiently
    waiting his coming;
Men in the middle of life, austere and grave
    in deportment,
Only one of them old, the hill that was nearest
    to heaven,
Covered with snow, but erect, the excellent
    Elder of Plymouth.
God had sifted three kingdoms to find the
    wheat for this planting,
Then had sifted the wheat, as the living seed
    of a nation;
So say the chronicles old, and such is the
    faith of the people!
Near them was standing an Indian, in atti-
    tude stern and defiant,
Naked down to the waist, and grim and
    ferocious in aspect;
While on the table before them was lying
    unopened a Bible,
Ponderous, bound in leather, brass-studded,
    printed in Holland,
And beside it outstretched the skin of a
    rattlesnake glittered,
Filled, like a quiver, with arrows; a signal
    and challenge of warfare,
Brought by the Indian, and speaking with
    arrowy tongues of defiance.
This Miles Standish beheld, as he entered,
    and heard them debating
What were an answer befitting the hostile
    message and menace,
Talking of this and of that, contriving, sug-
    gesting, objecting;
One voice only for peace, and that the voice
    of the Elder,
Judging it wise and well that some at least
    were converted,
Rather than any were slain, for this was but
    Christian behavior!

Then out spake Miles Standish, the stal-
    wart Captain of Plymouth,
Muttering deep in his throat, for his voice
    was husky with anger,
"What! do you mean to make war with milk
    and the water of roses?
Is it to shoot red squirrels you have your
    howitzer planted
There on the roof of the church, or is it to
    shoot red devils?
Truly the only tongue that is understood
    by a savage
Must be the tongue of fire that speaks from
    the mouth of the cannon!"
Thereupon answered and said the excellent
    Elder of Plymouth,
Somewhat amazed and alarmed at this irrev-
    erent language:
"Not so thought St. Paul, nor yet the other
    Apostles;
Not from the cannon's mouth were the
    tongues of fire they spake with!"
But unheeded fell this mild rebuke on the
    Captain,
Who had advanced to the table, and thus
    continued discoursing:
"Leave this matter to me, for to me by right
    it pertaineth.
War is a terrible trade; but in the cause that
    is righteous,
Sweet is the smell of powder; and thus I
    answer the challenge!"

Then from the rattlesnake's skin, with a
    sudden, contemptuous gesture,
Jerking the Indian arrows, he filled it with
    powder and bullets
Full to the very jaws, and handed it back
    to the savage,
Saying, in thundering tones: "Here, take
    it! this is your answer!"
Silently out of the room then glided the
    glistening savage,
Bearing the serpent's skin, and seeming him-
    self like a serpent,
Winding his sinuous way in the dark to the
    depths of the forest.
        HENRY WADSWORTH LONGFELLOW.

The period of prosperity, which had been
marked by the first Thanksgiving, was short-lived.
Through nearly the whole of the next two years,
the colony was pinched with famine. A crisis
was reached in the month of April, 1622, when,
so tradition says, the daily ration for each person
was reduced to five kernels of corn.

FIVE KERNELS OF CORN

[April, 1622]

I

'T WAS the year of the famine in Plymouth
    of old,
The ice and the snow from the thatched roofs
    had rolled;
Through the warm purple skies steered the
    geese o'er the seas,
And the woodpeckers tapped in the clocks
    of the trees;
And the boughs on the slopes to the south
    winds lay bare,
And dreaming of summer the buds swelled
    in the air.
The pale Pilgrims welcomed each reddening
    morn;
There were left but for rations Five Kernels
    of Corn.
        Five Kernels of Corn!
        Five Kernels of Corn!
But to Bradford a feast were Five Kernels
    of Corn!

II

"Five Kernels of Corn! Five Kernels of Corn!
Ye people, be glad for Five Kernels of Corn!"
So Bradford cried out on bleak Burial Hill,
And the thin women stood in their doors,
    white and still.
"Lo, the harbor of Plymouth rolls bright in
    the Spring,
The maples grow red, and the wood robins
    sing,
The west wind is blowing, and fading the snow,
And the pleasant pines sing, and the arbu-
    tuses blow.
        Five Kernels of Corn!
        Five Kernels of Corn!
To each one be given Five Kernels of Corn!"

III

O Bradford of Austerfield haste on thy way,
The west winds are blowing o'er Province-
    town Bay,
The white avens bloom, but the pine domes
    are chill,
And new graves have furrowed Precisioners'
    Hill!
"Give thanks, all ye people, the warm skies
    have come,
The hilltops are sunny, and green grows the
    holm,

And the trumpets of winds, and the white
    March is gone,
And ye still have left you Five Kernels of
    Corn.
        Five Kernels of Corn!
        Five Kernels of Corn!
Ye have for Thanksgiving Five Kernels of
    Corn!

IV

'The raven's gift eat and be humble and
    pray,
A new light is breaking, and Truth leads
    your way;
One taper a thousand shall kindle: rejoice
That to you has been given the wilderness
    voice!"
O Bradford of Austerfield, daring the wave,
And safe through the sounding blasts leading
    the brave,
Of deeds such as thine was the free nation
    born,
And the festal world sings the "Five Kernels
    of Corn."
        Five Kernels of Corn!
        Five Kernels of Corn!
The nation gives thanks for Five Kernels of
    Corn!
To the Thanksgiving Feast bring Five Ker-
    nels of Corn!
            HEZEKIAH BUTTERWORTH.

In June, 1622, a colony of adventurers from
England settled at Wessagusset, now Weymouth,
and when their supplies ran short, the following
winter, broke open and robbed some of the Indian
granaries. The Indians were naturally enraged,
and formed a plot for the extirpation of the
whites. Warned by Massasoit, the Plymouth
settlers determined to strike the first blow, and
on March 23, 1623, Standish and eight men were
dispatched to Wessagusset. The poem tells the
story of the events which followed.

THE EXPEDITION TO WESSA-
GUSSET

From "The Courtship of Miles Standish"

[March, 1623]

JUST in the gray of the dawn, as the mists
    uprose from the meadows,
There was a stir and a sound in the slum-
    bering village of Plymouth;
Clanging and clicking of arms, and the order
    imperative "Forward!"

Given in tone suppressed, a tramp of feet,
    and then silence.
Figures ten, in the mist, marched slowly out
    of the village.
Standish the stalwart it was, with eight of
    his valorous army,
Led by their Indian guide, by Hobomok
    friend of the white men,
Northward marching to quell the sudden
    revolt of the savage.
Giants they seemed in the mist, or the mighty
    men of King David;
Giants in heart they were, who believed in
    God and the Bible, —
Ay, who believed in the smiting of Midianites
    and Philistines.
Over them gleamed far off the crimson ban-
    ners of morning;
Under them loud on the sands, the serried
    billows, advancing,
Fired along the line, and in regular order
    retreated.
.   .   .   .   .   .

Meanwhile the stalwart Miles Standish was
    marching steadily northward,
Winding through forest and swamp, and
    along the trend of the sea-shore.
.   .   .   .   .   .

After a three days' march he came to an
    Indian encampment
Pitched on the edge of a meadow, between
    the sea and the forest;
Women at work by the tents, and warriors,
    horrid with war-paint,
Seated about a fire, and smoking and talk-
    ing together;
Who, when they saw from afar the sudden
    approach of the white men,
Saw the flash of the sun on breastplate and
    sabre and musket,
Straightway leaped to their feet, and two,
    from among them advancing,
Came to parley with Standish, and offer him
    furs as a present;
Friendship was in their looks, but in their
    hearts there was hatred.
Braves of the tribe were these, and brothers,
    gigantic in stature,
Huge as Goliath of Gath, or the terrible Og
    king of Bashan;
One was Pecksuot named, and the other
    was called Wattawamat.
Round their necks were suspended their
    knives in scabbards of wampum.

Two-edged, trenchant knives, with points as
　　sharp as a needle.
Other arms had they none, for they were
　　cunning and crafty.
"Welcome, English!" they said, — these
　　words they had learned from the
　　traders
Touching at times on the coast, to barter
　　and chaffer for peltries.
Then in their native tongue they began to
　　parley with Standish,
Through his guide and interpreter, Hobo-
　　mok, friend of the white man,
Begging for blankets and knives, but mostly
　　for muskets and powder,
Kept by the white man, they said, con-
　　cealed, with the plague, in his cel-
　　lars,
Ready to be let loose, and destroy his brother
　　the red man!
But when Standish refused, and said he
　　would give them the Bible,
Suddenly changing their tone, they began
　　to boast and to bluster.
Then Wattawamat advanced with a stride
　　in front of the other,
And, with a lofty demeanor, thus vauntingly
　　spake to the Captain:
"Now Wattawamat can see, by the fiery
　　eyes of the Captain,
Angry is he in his heart; but the heart of the
　　brave Wattawamat
Is not afraid of the sight. He was not born
　　of a woman,
But on a mountain at night, from an oak-
　　tree riven by lightning,
Forth he sprang at a bound, with all his
　　weapons about him,
Shouting, 'Who is there here to fight with
　　the brave Wattawamat?'"
Then he unsheathed his knife, and, whetting
　　the blade on his left hand,
Held it aloft and displayed a woman's face
　　on the handle;
Saying, with bitter expression and look of
　　sinister meaning:
"I have another at home, with the face of a
　　man on the handle;
By and by they shall marry; and there will
　　be plenty of children!"

Then stood Pecksuot forth, self-vaunting,
　　insulting Miles Standish:
While with his fingers he patted the knife
　　that hung at his bosom,

Drawing it half from its sheath, and plung-
　　ing it back, as he muttered,
"By and by it shall see; it shall eat; ah, ha!
　　but shall speak not!
This is the mighty Captain the white men
　　have sent to destroy us!
He is a little man; let him go and work with
　　the women!"

Meanwhile Standish had noted the faces
　　and figures of Indians
Peeping and creeping about from bush to
　　tree in the forest,
Feigning to look for game, with arrows set
　　on their bow-strings,
Drawing about him still closer and closer
　　the net of their ambush.
But undaunted he stood, and dissembled
　　and treated them smoothly;
So the old chronicles say, that were writ in
　　the days of the fathers.
But when he heard their defiance, the boast,
　　the taunt, and the insult,
All the hot blood of his race, of Sir Hugh
　　and of Thurston de Standish,
Boiled and beat in his heart, and swelled in
　　the veins of his temples.
Headlong he leaped on the boaster, and,
　　snatching his knife from its scab-
　　bard,
Plunged it into his heart, and, reeling back-
　　ward, the savage
Fell with his face to the sky, and a fiendlike
　　fierceness upon it.
Straight there arose from the forest the awful
　　sound of the war-whoop.
And, like a flurry of snow on the whistling
　　wind of December,
Swift and sudden and keen came a flight of
　　feathery arrows.
Then came a cloud of smoke, and out of the
　　cloud came the lightning,
Out of the lightning thunder; and death
　　unseen ran before it.
Frightened the savages fled for shelter in
　　swamp and in thicket,
Hotly pursued and beset; but their sachem
　　the brave Wattawamat,
Fled not; he was dead. Unswerving and
　　swift had a bullet
Passed through his brain, and he fell with
　　both hands clutching the green
　　sward,
Seeming in death to hold back from his foe
　　the land of his fathers.

There on the flowers of the meadow the
    warriors lay, and above them,
Silent, with folded arms, stood Hobomok,
    friend of the white man.
Smiling at length he exclaimed to the stal-
    wart Captain of Plymouth: —
"Pecksuot bragged very loud, of his cour-
    age, his strength, and his stature, —
Mocked the great Captain, and called him
    a little man; but I see now
Big enough have you been to lay him speech-
    less before you!"

Thus the first battle was fought and won
    by the stalwart Miles Standish.
When the tidings thereof were brought to
    the village of Plymouth,
And as a trophy of war the head of the brave
    Wattawamat
Scowled from the roof of the fort, which at
    once was a church and a fortress,
All who beheld it rejoiced, and praised the
    Lord, and took courage.
    HENRY WADSWORTH LONGFELLOW.

By the end of 1624 Plymouth was in a thriving
condition. Its inhabitants numbered nearly two
hundred, and it boasted thirty-two dwelling-
houses. Other colonies soon sprang up about the
Bay — Piscataqua (Portsmouth), Naumkeag
(Salem), Nantasket (Hull), and Winnisimmet
(Chelsea). The trials and pleasures of life in New
England at about this time are humorously de-
scribed in what are perhaps the first verses written
by an American colonist.

NEW ENGLAND'S ANNOYANCES

[1630]

NEW England's annoyances, you that would
    know them,
Pray ponder these verses which briefly doth
    shew them.

The Place where we live is a wilderness
    Wood,
Where Grass is much wanting that's fruitful
    and good:
Our Mountains and Hills and our Vallies
    below
Being commonly cover'd with Ice and with
    Snow;
And when the North-west Wind with vio-
    lence blows,
Then every Man pulls his Cap over his Nose:

But if any's so hardy and will it withstand,
He forfeits a Finger, a Foot, or a Hand.

But when the Spring opens, we then take
    the Hoe,
And make the Ground ready to plant and to
    sow;
Our Corn being planted and Seed being
    sown,
The Worms destroy much before it is grown;
And when it is growing, some spoil there is
    made
By Birds and by Squirrels that pluck up the
    Blade;
And when it is come to full Corn in the Ear,
It is often destroy'd by Raccoon and by
    Deer.

And now do our Garments begin to grow
    thin,
And Wool is much wanted to card and to
    spin;
If we can get a Garment to cover without,
Our other In-Garments are Clout upon
    Clout:
Our Clothes we brought with us are apt to
    be torn,
They need to be clouted soon after they 're
    worn;
But clouting our Garments they hinder us
    nothing:
Clouts double are warmer than single whole
    Clothing.

If fresh Meat be wanting, to fill up our Dish,
We have Carrots and Turnips as much as
    we wish;
And is there a mind for a delicate Dish,
We repair to the Clam-banks, and there we
    catch Fish.
For Pottage and Puddings, and Custards and
    Pies,
Our Pumpkins and Parsnips are common
    supplies;
We have Pumpkins at morning, and Pump-
    kins at noon;
If it was not for Pumpkins we should be
    undone.

If Barley be wanting to make into Malt,
We must be contented, and think it no fault;
For we can make Liquor to sweeten our Lips
Of Pumpkins and Parsnips and Walnut-
    Tree Chips.

.   .   .   .

Now while some are going let others be
     coming,
For while Liquor's boiling it must have a
     scumming;
But I will not blame them, for Birds of a
     Feather,
By seeking their Fellows, are flocking together.
But you whom the Lord intends hither to
     bring,
Forsake not the Honey for fear of the Sting;
But bring both a quiet and contented Mind,
And all needful Blessings you surely will
     find.

The Old Colony's palmy days were of short
duration, for it was soon overshadowed by a
more wealthy and vigorous neighbor, founded by
the powerful Puritan party.

THE PILGRIM FATHERS

I

WELL worthy to be magnified are they
Who, with sad hearts, of friends and country
     took
A last farewell, their loved abodes forsook,
And hallowed ground in which their fathers
     lay;
Then to the new-found World explored their
     way,
That so a Church, unforced, uncalled to
     brook
Ritual restraints, within some sheltering
     nook
Her Lord might worship and his word obey
In freedom. Men they were who could not
     bend;
Blest Pilgrims, surely, as they took for guide
A will by sovereign Conscience sanctified;
Blest while their Spirits from the woods
     ascend
Along a Galaxy that knows no end,
But in His glory who for Sinners died.

II

From Rite and Ordinance abused they fled
To Wilds where both were utterly unknown;
But not to them had Providence foreshown
What benefits are missed, what evils bred,
In worship neither raised nor limited
Save by Self-will. Lo! from that distant shore,
For Rite and Ordinance, Piety is led
Back to the Land those Pilgrims left of yore,

Led by her own free choice. So Truth and
     Love
By Conscience governed do their steps re-
     trace. —
Fathers! your Virtues, such the power of
     grace,
Their spirit, in your Children, thus approve.
Transcendent over time, unbound by place,
Concord and Charity in circles move.
                    WILLIAM WORDSWORTH.

When Charles I came to the throne, in 1625,
with the expressed determination to harry the
Puritans out of England, the latter decided
to seek an asylum in the New World. In 1628
John Endicott and a few others secured a patent
from the New England Council for a trading-com-
pany, the grant including a strip of land across
the continent from a line three miles north of
the Merrimac to another three miles south of the
Charles. It was into this colony, known as Massa-
chusetts, that the older colony of Plymouth was
finally absorbed.

THE PILGRIM FATHERS

THE Pilgrim Fathers, — where are they?
     The waves that brought them o'er
Still roll in the bay, and throw their spray
     As they break along the shore;
Still roll in the bay, as they rolled that day
     When the Mayflower moored below;
When the sea around was black with storms,
     And white the shore with snow.

The mists that wrapped the Pilgrim's sleep
     Still brood upon the tide;
And his rocks yet keep their watch by the
     deep
     To stay its waves of pride.
But the snow-white sail that he gave to the
     gale,
     When the heavens looked dark, is gone, —
As an angel's wing through an opening cloud
     Is seen, and then withdrawn.

The pilgrim exile, — sainted name!
     The hill whose icy brow
Rejoiced, when he came, in the morning's
     flame,
     In the morning's flame burns now.
And the moon's cold light, as it lay that
     night
     On the hillside and the sea,
Still lies where he laid his houseless head, —
     But the Pilgrim! where is he?

The Pilgrim Fathers are at rest:
  When summer's throned on high,
And the world's warm breast is in verdure
    drest,
  Go, stand on the hill where they lie.
The earliest ray of the golden day
  On that hallowed spot is cast;
And the evening sun, as he leaves the world,
  Looks kindly on that spot last.

The Pilgrim spirit has not fled:
  It walks in noon's broad light;
And it watches the bed of the glorious dead,
  With the holy stars by night.
It watches the bed of the brave who have bled,
  And still guard this ice-bound shore,
Till the waves of the bay, where the May-
    flower lay,
  Shall foam and freeze no more.
                              JOHN PIERPONT.

King Charles, little suspecting that he was
providing an asylum for the Puritans, confirmed
the patent by a royal charter to " The Governor
and Company of the Massachusetts Bay in New
England." No place for the meetings of the com-
pany had been named in the charter, and the
audacious plan was formed to remove it, patents,
charter, and all, to New England. Secret meetings
were held, the old officers were finally got rid of,
and John Winthrop was elected governor. Win-
throp sailed for America on April 7, 1630, and
arrived at Salem June 12. It was the beginning
of a great emigration, for, in the four months that
followed, seventeen ships arrived, with nearly a
thousand passengers.

THE THANKSGIVING IN BOSTON HARBOR

[June 12, 1630]

"PRAISE ye the Lord!" The psalm to-day
  Still rises on our ears,
Borne from the hills of Boston Bay
  Through five times fifty years,
When Winthrop's fleet from Yarmouth crept
  Out to the open main,
And through the widening waters swept,
  In April sun and rain.
    "Pray to the Lord with fervent lips,"
      The leader shouted, "pray;"
    And prayer arose from all the ships
      As faded Yarmouth Bay.

They passed the Scilly Isles that day,
  And May-days came, and June,

And thrice upon the ocean lay
  The full orb of the moon.
And as that day, on Yarmouth Bay,
  Ere England sunk from view,
While yet the rippling Solent lay
  In April skies of blue,
    "Pray to the Lord with fervent lips,"
      Each morn was shouted, "pray;"
    And prayer arose from all the ships,
      As first in Yarmouth Bay;

Blew warm the breeze o'er Western seas,
  Through Maytime morns, and June,
Till hailed these souls the Isles of Shoals,
  Low 'neath the summer moon;
And as Cape Ann arose to view,
  And Norman's Woe they passed,
The wood-doves came the white mists through,
  And circlèd round each mast.
    "Pray to the Lord with fervent lips,"
      Then called the leader, "pray;"
    And prayer arose from all the ships,
      As first in Yarmouth Bay.

Above the sea the hill-tops fair —
  God's towers — began to rise,
And odors rare breathe through the air,
  Like balms of Paradise.
Through burning skies the ospreys flew,
  And near the pine-cooled shores
Danced airy boat and thin canoe,
  To flash of sunlit oars.
    "Pray to the Lord with fervent lips,"
      The leader shouted, "pray!"
    Then prayer arose, and all the ships
      Sailed into Boston Bay.

The white wings folded, anchors down,
  The sea-worn fleet in line,
Fair rose the hills where Boston town
  Should rise from clouds of pine;
Fair was the harbor, summit-walled,
  And placid lay the sea.
"Praise ye the Lord," the leader called;
  "Praise ye the Lord," spake he.
    "Give thanks to God with fervent lips,
      Give thanks to God to-day,"
    The anthem rose from all the ships,
      Safe moored in Boston Bay.

"Praise ye the Lord!" Primeval woods
  First heard the ancient song,
And summer hills and solitudes
  The echoes rolled along.

The Red Cross flag of England blew
  Above the fleet that day,
While Shawmut's triple peaks in view
  In amber hazes lay.
    "Praise ye the Lord with fervent lips,
      Praise ye the Lord to-day,"
    The anthem rose from all the ships
      Safe moored in Boston Bay.

The Arabella leads the song —
  The Mayflower sings below,
That erst the Pilgrims bore along
  The Plymouth reefs of snow.
Oh! never be that psalm forgot
  That rose o'er Boston Bay,
When Winthrop sang, and Endicott,
  And Saltonstall, that day:
    "Praise ye the Lord with fervent lips,
      Praise ye the Lord to-day:"
    And praise arose from all the ships,
      Like prayers in Yarmouth Bay.

That psalm our fathers sang we sing,
  That psalm of peace and wars,
While o'er our heads unfolds its wing
  The flag of forty stars.
And while the nation finds a tongue
  For nobler gifts to pray,
'T will ever sing the song they sung
  That first Thanksgiving Day:
    "Praise ye the Lord with fervent lips,
      Praise ye the Lord to-day:"
    So rose the song from all the ships,
      Safe moored in Boston Bay.

Our fathers' prayers have changed to psalms,
  As David's treasures old
Turned, on the Temple's giant arms,
  To lily-work of gold.
Ho! vanished ships from Yarmouth's tide,
  Ho! ships of Boston Bay,
Your prayers have crossed the centuries wide
  To this Thanksgiving Day!
    We pray to God with fervent lips,
      We praise the Lord to-day,
    As prayers arose from Yarmouth ships,
      But psalms from Boston Bay.
        HEZEKIAH BUTTERWORTH.

But the condition of the colonists was for the most part pitiful, and food was so scarce that shell-fish served for meat and acorns for bread. Winthrop had foreseen this and had engaged Captain William Pierce, of the ship Lion, to go in all haste to the nearest port in Ireland for provisions. Food-stuffs were nearly as scarce there as in America, and Pierce was forced to go on to London, where he was again delayed. A fast was appointed throughout the settlements for February 22, 1631, to implore divine succor. On the 21st, as Winthrop " was distributing the last handful of meal in the barrel unto a poor man distressed by the wolf at the door, at that instant they spied a ship arrived at the harbour's mouth, laden with provisions for them all." The ship was the Lion, and the fast day was changed into a day of feasting and thanksgiving.

THE FIRST THANKSGIVING

[February 22, 1631]

IT was Captain Pierce of the Lion who strode
  the streets of London,
  Who stalked the streets in the blear of
    morn and growled in his grisly beard;
By Neptune ! quoth this grim sea-dog, *I fear*
  that my master 's undone !
'T is a bitter thing if all for naught through
  the drench of the deep I 've steered !

He had come from out of the ultimate West
  through the spinning drift and the
  smother,
  Come for a guerdon of golden grain for a
    hungry land afar;
And he thought of many a wasting maid, and
  of many a sad-eyed mother,
  And how their gaze would turn and turn
    for a sail at the harbor bar.

But famine lay on the English isle, and grain
  was a hoarded treasure,
  So ruddy the coin must gleam to loose the
    lock of the store-house door;
And under his breath the Captain groaned
  because of his meagre measure,
  And the grasping souls of those that held
    the keys to the precious store.

But he flung a laugh and a fleer at doubt, and
  braving the roaring city
  He faced them out — those moiling men
    whose greed had grown to a curse —
Till at last he found in the strenuous press a
  heart that was moved to pity,
  And he gave the Governor's bond and word
    for what he lacked in his purse.

So the Lion put her prow to the West in the
  wild and windy weather,
  Her sails all set, though her decks were wet
    with the driving scud and the foam;

Never an hour would the Captain hold his
  staunch little craft in tether,
For the haunting thought of hungry eyes
  was the lure that called him home.

Sooth, in the streets of Boston-town was the
  heavy sound of sorrow,
For an iron frost had bound the wold, and
  the sky hung bleak and dread;
Despair sat dark on the face of him who dared
  to think of the morrow,
When not a crust could the goodwife give if
  the children moaned for bread.

But hark, from the wintry waterside a loud
  and lusty cheering,
That sweeps the sullen streets of the town
  as a wave the level strand!
A sail! a sail! upswelled the cry, speeding the
  vessel steering
Out of the vast of the misty sea in to the
  waiting land.

Turn the dimming page of the past that the
  dust of the years is dry on,
And see the tears in the eyes of Joy as the
  ship draws in to the shore,
And see the genial glow on the face of Captain
  Pierce of the Lion,
  As the Governor grips his faithful hand and
  blesses him o'er and o'er!

Oh, the rapture of that release! Feasting
  instead of fasting!
Happiness in the heart of the home, and
  hope with its silver ray!
Oh, the songs of prayer and praise to the
  Lord God everlasting
That mounted morn and noon and eve on
  that first Thanksgiving Day!
              CLINTON SCOLLARD.

In the four years that followed, the worst hard-
ships of the new plantation were outlived, and
between three and four thousand Englishmen
were distributed among the twenty hamlets along
and near the seashore. The fight for a foothold
had been won.

NEW ENGLAND'S GROWTH

From a fragmentary poem on " New England "

FAMINE once we had,
But other things God gave us in full store,
As fish and ground-nuts to supply our strait,
That we might learn on Providence to wait;
And know, by bread man lives not in his need,
But by each word that doth from God proceed.
But a while after plenty did come in,
From His hand only who doth pardon sin,
And all did flourish like the pleasant green,
Which in the joyful spring is to be seen.

Almost ten years we lived here alone,
In other places there were few or none;
For Salem was the next of any fame,
That began to augment New England's name;
But after multitudes began to flow,
More than well knew themselves where to
  bestow;
Boston then began her roots to spread,
And quickly soon she grew to be the head,
Not only of the Massachusetts Bay,
But all trade and commerce fell in her way.
And truly it was admirable to know,
How greatly all things here began to grow.
New plantations were in each place begun,
And with inhabitants were filled soon.
All sorts of grain which our own land doth
  yield,
Was hither brought and sown in every field:
As wheat and rye, barley, oats, beans and
  pease,
Here all thrive, and they profit from them
  raise.
All sorts of roots and herbs in gardens grow,
Parsnips, carrots, turnips, or what you'll sow.
Onions, melons, cucumbers, radishes,
Skirets, beets, coleworts, and fair cabbages.
Here grow fine flowers many, and 'mongst
  those,
The fair white lily and sweet fragrant rose.
Many good wholesome berries here you'll find,
Fit for man's use, almost of every kind,
Pears, apples, cherries, plumbs, quinces, and
  peach,
Are now no dainties; you may have of each.
Nuts and grapes of several sorts are here,
If you will take the pains them to seek for.
             WILLIAM BRADFORD.

There remained but one danger, the Indians;
and most feared of all were the Pequots, who
dwelt just west of what is now Rhode Island,
and in 1637 began open hostilities. A force of
about a hundred men marched against the prin-
cipal Pequot stronghold, a palisaded village which
stood on a hilltop near the Mystic. The attack
was made on the night of May 25, 1637, the Indians
were taken by surprise, their thatched houses

were set on fire, and of the six or seven hundred persons in the village, scarcely one escaped.

THE ASSAULT ON THE FORTRESS

From " The Destruction of the Pequods "

[May 25, 1637]

THROUGH verdant banks where Thames's
    branches glide,
Long held the Pequods an extensive sway;
Bold, savage, fierce, of arms the glorious
    pride,
And bidding all the circling realms obey.
Jealous, they saw the tribes, beyond the sea,
Plant in their climes; and towns, and cities,
    rise;
Ascending castles foreign flags display;
Mysterious art new scenes of life devise;
And steeds insult the plains, and cannon rend
    the skies.

The rising clouds the savage chief descried,
And, round the forest, bade his heroes arm;
To arms the painted warriors proudly hied,
And through surrounding nations rung the
    alarm.
The nations heard; but smiled, to see the
    storm,
With ruin fraught, o'er Pequod mountains
    driven
And felt infernal joy the bosom warm,
To see their light hang o'er the skirts of even,
And other suns arise, to gild a kinder heaven.

Swift to the Pequod fortress Mason sped,
Far in the wildering wood's impervious
    gloom;
A lonely castle, brown with twilight dread;
Where oft the embowelled captive met his
    doom,
And frequent heaved, around the hollow tomb,
Scalps hung in rows, and whitening bones
    were strew'd;
Where, round the broiling babe, fresh from the
    womb,
With howls the Powow fill'd the dark abode,
And screams and midnight prayers invoked
    the evil god.

But now no awful rites, nor potent spell,
To silence charm'd the peals of coming war;
Or told the dread recesses of the dell,
Where glowing Mason led his bands from far:

No spirit, buoyant on his airy car,
Controll'd the whirlwind of invading fight:
Deep died in blood, dun evening's falling star
Sent sad o'er western hills its parting light,
And no returning morn dispersed the long,
    dark night.

On the drear walls a sudden splendor glow'd,
There Mason shone, and there his veterans
    pour'd.
Anew the hero claim'd the fiends of blood,
While answering storms of arrows round him
    shower'd,
And the war-scream the ear with anguish
    gored.
Alone, he burst the gate; the forest round
Reëchoed death; the peal of onset roar'd,
In rush'd the squadrons; earth in blood was
    drown'd;
And gloomy spirits fled, and corses hid the
    ground.

Not long in dubious fight the host had striven,
When, kindled by the musket's potent flame,
In clouds, and fire, the castle rose to heaven,
And gloom'd the world, with melancholy
    beam.
Then hoarser groans, with deeper anguish,
    came;
And fiercer fight the keen assault repell'd:
Nor e'en these ills the savage breast could
    tame;
Like hell's deep caves, the hideous region
    yell'd,
Till death, and sweeping fire, laid waste the
    hostile field.
                        TIMOTHY DWIGHT.

Sassacus, the Pequot chief, escaped and sought
refuge with the Mohawks, but was slain by them.

DEATH SONG

[1673]

GREAT Sassacus fled from the eastern shores,
Where the sun first shines, and the great sea
    roars,
For the white men came from the world afar.
And their fury burnt like the bison star.

His sannops were slain by their thunder's
    power,
And his children fell like the star-eyed flower;

His wigwams were burnt by the white man's
    flame,
And the home of his youth has a stranger
    name —

His ancestor once was our countryman's foe,
And the arrow was plac'd in the new-strung
    bow,
The wild deer ranged through the forest
    free,
While we fought with his tribe by the distant
    sea.

But the foe never came to the Mohawk's
    tent,
With his hair untied, and his bow unbent,
And found not the blood of the wild deer
    shed,
And the calumet lit and the bear-skin bed.

But sing ye the Death Song, and kindle the
    pine,
And bid its broad light like his valor to shine;
Then raise high his pile by our warriors'
    heaps,
And tell to his tribe that his murderer sleeps.
                    ALONZO LEWIS.

OUR COUNTRY

ON primal rocks she wrote her name;
    Her towers were reared on holy graves;
The golden seed that bore her came
    Swift-winged with prayer o'er ocean waves.

The Forest bowed his solemn crest,
    And open flung his sylvan doors;
Meek Rivers led the appointed guest
    To clasp the wide-embracing shores;

Till, fold by fold, the broidered land
    To swell her virgin vestments grew,
While sages, strong in heart and hand,
    Her virtue's fiery girdle drew.

O Exile of the wrath of kings!
    O Pilgrim Ark of Liberty!
The refuge of divinest things,
    Their record must abide in thee!

First in the glories of thy front
    Let the crown-jewel, Truth, be found;
Thy right hand fling, with generous wont,
    Love's happy chain to farthest bound!

Let Justice, with the faultless scales,
    Hold fast the worship of thy sons;
Thy Commerce spread her shining sails
    Where no dark tide of rapine runs!

So link thy ways to those of God,
    So follow firm the heavenly laws,
That stars may greet thee, warrior-browed,
    And storm-sped angels hail thy cause!

O Lord, the measure of our prayers,
    Hope of the world in grief and wrong,
Be thine the tribute of the years,
    The gift of Faith, the crown of Song!
                  JULIA WARD HOWE.

CHAPTER VI

RELIGIOUS PERSECUTIONS IN NEW ENGLAND

The Puritans, who had come to New England to escape a religious despotism, lost no time in establishing one of their own. At the first meeting of the General Council, in the autumn of 1630, it was agreed that no one should be admitted to membership in the company who was not a member of some church approved by it, and a religious oligarchy was thus established which kept itself in power for over thirty years.

PROLOGUE

From "John Endicott"

TO-NIGHT we strive to read, as we may best,
This city, like an ancient palimpsest;

And bring to light, upon the blotted page,
The mournful record of an earlier age,
That, pale and half effaced, lies hidden away
Beneath the fresher writing of to-day.

Rise, then, O buried city that hast been;
Rise up, rebuilded in the painted scene,
And let our curious eyes behold once more
The pointed gable and the pent-house door,
The meeting-house with leaden-latticed panes,
The narrow thoroughfares, the crooked lanes!

Rise, too, ye shapes and shadows of the Past,
Rise from your long-forgotten graves at last;

Let us behold your faces, let us hear
The words ye uttered in those days of fear!
Revisit your familiar haunts again, —
The scenes of triumph, and the scenes of pain,
And leave the footprints of your bleeding feet
Once more upon the pavement of the street!

Nor let the Historian blame the Poet here,
If he perchance misdate the day or year,
And group events together, by his art,
That in the Chronicles lie far apart;
For as the double stars, though sundered
      far,
Seem to the naked eye a single star,
So facts of history, at a distance seen,
Into one common point of light convene.

"Why touch upon such themes?" perhaps
      some friend
May ask, incredulous; "and to what good
      end?
Why drag again into the light of day
The errors of an age long passed away?"
I answer: "For the lesson that they teach:
The tolerance of opinion and of speech.
Hope, Faith, and Charity remain, — these
      three;
And greatest of them all is Charity."

Let us remember, if these words be true,
That unto all men Charity is due;
Give what we ask; and pity, while we blame,
Lest we become copartners in the shame,
Lest we condemn, and yet ourselves partake,
And persecute the dead for conscience' sake.
                HENRY WADSWORTH LONGFELLOW.

One of the earliest to feel the displeasure of
the ruling powers of the Colony was Roger Wil-
liams, who came to Boston in 1631. He made
himself obnoxious to the government by denying
the right of the magistrates to punish Sabbath
breaking; and continued to occasion so much
excitement that it was decided to send him back
to England. Williams got wind of this, and took
to the woods in January, 1636.

ROGER WILLIAMS

[January, 1636]

WHY do I sleep amid the snows,
   Why do the pine boughs cover me,
While dark the wind of winter blows
   Across the Narragansett's sea?

O sense of right! O sense of right.
   Whate'er my lot in life may be,
Thou art to me God's inner light,
   And these tired feet must follow thee.

Yes, still my feet must onward go,
   With nothing for my hope but prayer,
Amid the winds, amid the snow,
   And trust the ravens of the air.

But though alone, and grieved at heart,
   Bereft of human brotherhood,
I trust the whole and not the part,
   And know that Providence is good.

Self-sacrifice is never lost,
   But bears the seed of its reward;
They who for others leave the most,
   For others gain the most from God.

O sense of right! I must obey,
   And hope and trust, whate'er betide;
I cannot always know my way,
   But I can always know my Guide.

And so for me the winter blows
   Across the Narragansett's sea,
And so I sleep beneath the snows,
   And so the pine boughs cover me.
                HEZEKIAH BUTTERWORTH.

Williams had a hard time of it. Thirty years
later, he related how he was "sorely tossed for
fourteen weeks in a bitter winter season, not
knowing what bread or bed did mean."

GOD MAKES A PATH

GOD makes a path, provides a guide,
   And feeds in wilderness!
His glorious name while breath remains,
   O that I may confess.

Lost many a time, I have had no guide,
   No house, but hollow tree!
In stormy winter night no fire,
   No food, no company:

In him I found a house, a bed,
   A table, company:
No cup so bitter, but's made sweet,
   When God shall sweetning be.
                ROGER WILLIAMS.

Williams went to Narragansett Bay, where he bargained with Canonicus for the land he wanted, and laid the foundations of the present city of Providence.

CANONICUS AND ROGER WILLIAMS

[1636]

CONTENT within his wigwam warm,
Canonicus sate by the fire;
Without, the voices of the storm
Shrieked ever high and higher.

Eager and wild, the spiteful wind
Tore at the thatch with fingers strong;
The Sachem fed the fire within
And hummed a hunting-song.

Sudden upon the crusted snow
He caught a sound not of the storm —
A sound of footsteps dragging slow
Towards his shelter warm.

He drew aside the flap of skin;
A stranger at the threshold stood;
Canonicus bade him enter in,
And gave him drink and food.

His hand he gave in friendship true,
Land for a home gave he;
And he learned of the love of Christ Jesu,
Who died upon the tree.

To the stranger guest sweet life he gave;
For a State he saved its Sire;
Yea, and his own soul did he save
From burning in hell-fire.

Scarcely were the Massachusetts magistrates rid of Williams, when they found themselves engaged in a much more threatening controversy with Mrs. Anne Hutchinson and her adherents, who believed in various "dangerous errors," and carried their contempt for the constituted ministry to the point of rising and marching out of the Boston church when its respected pastor, John Wilson, arose to speak. The other ministers of the colony rallied to Wilson's support, the General Court summoned Mrs. Hutchinson before it in November, 1637, and pronounced sentence of banishment, which was put into effect March 28, 1638.

ANNE HUTCHINSON'S EXILE

[March 28, 1638]

"HOME, home — where's my baby's home?
Here we seek, there we seek, my baby's
home to find.

Come, come, come, my baby, come!
We found her home, we lost her home, and
home is far behind.
Come, my baby, come!
Find my baby's home!"

The baby clings; the mother sings; the pony
stumbles on;
The father leads the beast along the tangled,
muddy way;
The boys and girls trail on behind; the sun
will soon be gone,
And starlight bright will take again the
place of sunny day.
"Home, home — where's my baby's home?
Here we seek, there we seek, my baby's
home to find.
Come, come, come, my baby, come!
We found her home, we lost her home, and
home is far behind.
Come, my baby, come!
Find my baby's home!"

The sun goes down behind the lake; the night
fogs gather chill,
The children's clothes are torn; and the
children's feet are sore.
"Keep on, my boys, keep on, my girls, till
all have passed the hill;
Then ho, my girls, and ho, my boys, for
fire and sleep once more!"
And all the time she sings to the baby on her
breast,
"Home, my darling, sleep, my darling, find a
place for rest;
Who gives the fox his burrow will give my
bird a nest.
Come, my baby, come!
Find my baby's home!"

He lifts the mother from the beast; the hem-
lock boughs they spread,
And make the baby's cradle sweet with
fern-leaves and with bays.
The baby and her mother are resting on their
bed;
He strikes the flint, he blows the spark,
and sets the twigs ablaze.
"Sleep, my child; sleep, my child!
Baby, find her rest,
Here beneath the gracious skies, upon her
father's breast;
Who gives the fox his burrow will give my
bird her nest.

Come, come, with her mother, come!
Home, home, find my baby's home!"

The guardian stars above the trees their loving
vigil keep;
The cricket sings her lullaby, the whippoor-
will his cheer.
The father knows his Father's arms are round
them as they sleep;
The mother knows that in His arms her
darling need not fear.
"Home, home, my baby's home is here;
With God we seek, with God we find the
place for baby's rest.
Hist, my child, list, my child; angels guard
us here.
The God of heaven is here to make and
keep my birdie's nest.
Home, home, here's my baby's home !"
EDWARD EVERETT HALE.

Among the converts made by Mrs. Hutchinson
during her stay in Boston was John Underhill,
commander of the colony's troops. He became
involved in the controversy that followed, and
as a result was disarmed, disfranchised, and finally
banished. In September, 1638, he betook him-
self to Cocheco (Dover), on the Piscataqua, where
some of Mrs. Hutchinson's adherents had started
a settlement, and where he afterwards held various
offices.

JOHN UNDERHILL

[September, 1638]

A SCORE of years had come and gone
Since the Pilgrims landed on Plymouth stone,
When Captain Underhill, bearing scars
From Indian ambush and Flemish wars,
Left three-hilled Boston and wandered down,
East by north, to Cocheco town.

With Vane the younger, in council sweet,
He had sat at Anna Hutchinson's feet,
And, when the bolt of banishment fell
On the head of his saintly oracle,
He had shared her ill as her good report,
And braved the wrath of the General Court.

He shook from his feet as he rode away
The dust of the Massachusetts Bay.
The world might bless and the world might
ban,
What did it matter the perfect man,
To whom the freedom of earth was given,
Proof against sin, and sure of heaven?

He cheered his heart as he rode along
With screed of Scripture and holy song,
Or thought how he rode with his lances
free
By the Lower Rhine and the Zuyder-Zee,
Till his wood-path grew to a trodden road,
And Hilton Point in the distance showed.

He saw the church with the block-house nigh,
The two fair rivers, the flakes thereby,
And, tacking to windward, low and crank,
The little shallop from Strawberry Bank;
And he rose in his stirrups and looked abroad
Over land and water, and praised the Lord.

Goodly and stately and grave to see,
Into the clearing's space rode he,
With the sun on the hilt of his sword in sheath,
And his silver buckles and spurs beneath,
And the settlers welcomed him, one and all,
From swift Quampeagan to Gonic Fall.

And he said to the elders: "Lo, I come
As the way seemed open to seek a home.
Somewhat the Lord hath wrought by my
hands
In the Narragansett and Netherlands,
And if here ye have work for a Christian man,
I will tarry, and serve ye as best I can.

"I boast not of gifts, but fain would own
The wonderful favor God hath shown,
The special mercy vouchsafed one day
On the shore of Narragansett Bay,
As I sat, with my pipe, from the camp aside,
And mused like Isaac at eventide.

"A sudden sweetness of peace I found,
A garment of gladness wrapped me round;
I felt from the law of works released,
The strife of the flesh and spirit ceased,
My faith to a full assurance grew,
And all I had hoped for myself I knew.

"Now, as God appointeth, I keep my way,
I shall not stumble, I shall not stray;
He hath taken away my fig-leaf dress,
I wear the robe of His righteousness;
And the shafts of Satan no more avail
Than Pequot arrows on Christian mail."

"Tarry with us," the settlers cried,
"Thou man of God, as our ruler and guide."
And Captain Underhill bowed his head,
"The will of the Lord be done!" he said.

And the morrow beheld him sitting down
In the ruler's seat in Cocheco town.

And he judged therein as a just man should;
His words were wise and his rule was good;
He coveted not his neighbor's land,
From the holding of bribes he shook his hand;
And through the camps of the heathen ran
A wholesome fear of the valiant man.

But the heart is deceitful, the good Book saith,
And life hath ever a savor of death.
Through hymns of triumph the tempter calls,
And whoso thinketh he standeth falls.
Alas! ere their round the seasons ran,
There was grief in the soul of the saintly man.

The tempter's arrows that rarely fail
Had found the joints of his spiritual mail;
And men took note of his gloomy air,
The shame in his eye, the halt in his prayer,
The signs of a battle lost within,
The pain of a soul in the coils of sin.

Then a whisper of scandal linked his name
With broken vows and a life of blame;
And the people looked askance on him
As he walked among them sullen and grim,
Ill at ease, and bitter of word,
And prompt of quarrel with hand or sword.

None knew how, with prayer and fasting still,
He strove in the bonds of his evil will;
But he shook himself like Samson at length,
And girded anew his loins of strength,
And bade the crier go up and down
And call together the wondering town.

Jeer and murmur and shaking of head
Ceased as he rose in his place and said:
"Men, brethren, and fathers, well ye know
How I came among you a year ago,
Strong in the faith that my soul was freed
From sin of feeling, or thought, or deed.

"I have sinned, I own it with grief and shame,
But not with a lie on my lips I came.
In my blindness I verily thought my heart
Swept and garnished in every part.
He chargeth His angels with folly; He sees
The heavens unclean. Was I more than these?

"I urge no plea. At your feet I lay
The trust you gave me, and go my way.
Hate me or pity me, as you will,
The Lord will have mercy on sinners still;
And I, who am chiefest, say to all,
Watch and pray, lest ye also fall."

No voice made answer: a sob so low
That only his quickened ear could know
Smote his heart with a bitter pain,
As into the forest he rode again,
And the veil of its oaken leaves shut down
On his latest glimpse of Cocheco town.

Crystal-clear on the man of sin
The streams flashed up, and the sky shone in;
On his cheek of fever the cool wind blew,
The leaves dropped on him their tears of dew,
And angels of God, in the pure, sweet guise
Of flowers, looked on him with sad surprise.

Was his ear at fault that brook and breeze
Sang in their saddest of minor keys?
What was it the mournful wood-thrush said?
What whispered the pine-trees overhead?
Did he hear the Voice on his lonely way
That Adam heard in the cool of day?

Into the desert alone rode he,
Alone with the Infinite Purity;
And, bowing his soul to its tender rebuke,
As Peter did to the Master's look,
He measured his path with prayers of pain
For peace with God and nature again.

And in after years to Cocheco came
The bruit of a once familiar name;
How among the Dutch of New Netherlands,
From wild Danskamer to Haarlem sands,
A penitent soldier preached the Word,
And smote the heathen with Gideon's sword!

And the heart of Boston was glad to hear
How he harried the foe on the long frontier,
And heaped on the land against him barred
The coals of his generous watch and ward.
Frailest and bravest! the Bay State still
Counts with her worthies John Underhill.

JOHN GREENLEAF WHITTIER.

In 1656 a new danger threatened, for in July the first Quakers landed in New England. The preachers of this sect were generally believed to be either Franciscan monks in disguise, or publishers of irreligious fancies, and in an evil hour the authorities resolved to keep them out of Massachusetts. When the General Court met in October, it passed the law of which Mr. Longfellow gives an accurate résumé. This law was "forthwith published, in several places of Boston, by beat of drum," October 21, 1656.

THE PROCLAMATION

From " John Endicott "

[October 21, 1656]

COLE

HERE comes the Marshal.

MERRY (*within*)

Make room for the Marshal.

KEMPTHORN

How pompous and imposing he appears!
His great buff doublet bellying like a mainsail,
And all his streamers fluttering in the wind.
What holds he in his hand?

COLE

A proclamation.

Enter the MARSHAL, *with a proclamation ; and* MERRY, *with a halberd. They are preceded by a drummer, and followed by the hangman, with an armful of books, and a crowd of people, among whom are* UPSALL *and* JOHN ENDICOTT. *A pile is made of the books.*

MERRY

Silence, the drum! Good citizens, attend
To the new laws enacted by the Court.

MARSHAL (*reads*)

"Whereas a cursed sect of Heretics
Has lately risen, commonly called Quakers,
Who take upon themselves to be commissioned
Immediately of God, and furthermore
Infallibly assisted by the Spirit
To write and utter blasphemous opinions,
Despising Government and the order of God
In Church and Commonwealth, and speaking evil
Of Dignities, reproaching and reviling
The Magistrates and Ministers, and seeking
To turn the people from their faith, and thus
Gain proselytes to their pernicious ways; —
This Court, considering the premises,

And to prevent like mischief as is wrought
By their means in our land, doth hereby order,
That whatsoever master or commander
Of any ship, bark, pink, or catch shall bring
To any roadstead, harbor, creek, or cove
Within this Jurisdiction any Quakers,
Or other blasphemous Heretics, shall pay
Unto the Treasurer of the Commonwealth
One hundred pounds, and for default thereof
Be put in prison, and continue there
Till the said sum be satisfied and paid."

COLE

Now, Simon Kempthorn, what say you to that?

KEMPTHORN

I pray you, Cole, lend me a hundred pounds!

MARSHAL (*reads*)

"If any one within this Jurisdiction
Shall henceforth entertain, or shall conceal
Quakers, or other blasphemous Heretics,
Knowing them so to be, every such person
Shall forfeit to the country forty shillings
For each hour's entertainment or concealment,
And shall be sent to prison, as aforesaid,
Until the forfeiture be wholly paid."

Murmurs in the crowd.

KEMPTHORN

Now, Goodman Cole, I think your turn has come!

COLE

Knowing them so to be!

KEMPTHORN

At forty shillings
The hour, your fine will be some forty pounds!

COLE

Knowing them so to be! That is the law.

MARSHAL (*reads*)

" And it is further ordered and enacted,
If any Quaker or Quakers shall presume
To come henceforth into this Jurisdiction,
Every male Quaker for the first offence
Shall have one ear cut off; and shall be kept
At labor in the Workhouse, till such time
As he be sent away at his own charge.
And for the repetition of the offence

Shall have his other ear cut off, and then
Be branded in the palm of his right hand.
And every woman Quaker shall be whipt
Severely in three towns; and every Quaker,
Or he or she, that shall for a third time
Herein again offend, shall have their tongues
Bored through with a hot iron, and shall be
Sentenced to Banishment on pain of Death."

Loud murmurs. The voice of CHRISTISON *in
the crowd*

O patience of the Lord! How long, how long,
Ere thou avenge the blood of Thine Elect?

MERRY

Silence, there, silence! Do not break the peace!

MARSHAL (*reads*)

"Every inhabitant of this Jurisdiction
Who shall defend the horrible opinions
Of Quakers, by denying due respect
To equals and superiors, and withdrawing
From Church Assemblies, and thereby ap-
proving
The abusive and destructive practices
Of this accursed sect, in opposition
To all the orthodox received opinions
Of godly men, shall be forthwith committed
Unto close prison for one month; and then
Refusing to retract and to reform
The opinions as aforesaid, he shall be
Sentenced to Banishment on pain of Death.
By the Court. Edward Rawson, Secretary."
Now, hangman, do your duty. Burn those
books.

*Loud murmurs in the crowd. The pile of books
is lighted.*

UPSALL

I testify against these cruel laws!
Forerunners are they of some judgment on us;
And, in the love and tenderness I bear
Unto this town and people, I beseech you,
O Magistrates, take heed, lest ye be found
As fighters against God!

HENRY WADSWORTH LONGFELLOW.

The law was soon to be enforced, and among
the earliest to endure its penalties were Christopher
Holden and John Copeland, who were whipped
and imprisoned, while Lawrence and Cassandra
Southwick, of Salem, were also imprisoned for
having harbored them. The Southwicks were in
advanced years, and had three grown children —
Provided, Josiah, and Daniel. The whole family
had united with the Society of Friends, and the
parents were banished from the colony upon pain
of death. While they and one son, Josiah, were in
prison, Provided and Daniel were fined ten pounds
for not attending public worship at Salem. They
refused to pay, and were ordered to be sold into
slavery in Virginia or Barbadoes, but no master of
a vessel could be found to carry out the sentence.

CASSANDRA SOUTHWICK

[1658]

To the God of all sure mercies let my blessing
rise to-day,
From the scoffer and the cruel He hath
plucked the spoil away;
Yea, He who cooled the furnace around the
faithful three,
And tamed the Chaldean lions, hath set His
handmaid free!

Last night I saw the sunset melt through my
prison bars,
Last night across my damp earth-floor fell
the pale gleam of stars;
In the coldness and the darkness all through
the long night-time,
My grated casement whitened with autumn's
early rime.

Alone, in that dark sorrow, hour after hour
crept by;
Star after star looked palely in and sank
adown the sky;
No sound amid night's stillness, save that
which seemed to be
The dull and heavy beating of the pulses of
the sea;

All night I sat unsleeping, for I knew that on
the morrow
The ruler and the cruel priest would mock
me in my sorrow,
Dragged to their place of market, and bar-
gained for and sold,
Like a lamb before the shambles, like a
heifer from the fold!

Oh, the weakness of the flesh was there, —
the shrinking and the shame;
And the low voice of the Tempter like whis-
pers to me came:
"Why sit'st thou thus forlornly," the wicked
murmur said,
"Damp walls thy bower of beauty, cold earth
thy maiden bed?

"Where be the smiling faces, and voices soft
        and sweet,
Seen in thy father's dwelling, heard in the
        pleasant street?
Where be the youths whose glances, the sum-
        mer Sabba.h through,
Turned tenderly and timidly unto thy father's
        pew?

"Why sit'st thou here, Cassandra? — Be-
        think thee with what mirth
Thy happy schoolmates gather around the
        warm, bright hearth;
How the crimson shadows tremble on fore-
        heads white and fair,
On eyes of merry girlhood, half hid in golden
        hair.

"Not for thee the hearth-fire brightens, not
        for thee kind words are spoken,
Not for thee the nuts of Wenham woods by
        laughing boys are broken;
No first-fruits of the orchard within thy lap
        are laid,
For thee no flowers of autumn the youthful
        hunters braid.

"O weak, deluded maiden! — by crazy fan-
        cies led,
With wild and raving railers an evil path to
        tread;
To leave a wholesome worship, and teaching
        pure and sound,
And mate with maniac women, loose-haired
        and sackcloth bound, —

"Mad scoffers of the priesthood, who mock
        at things divine,
Who rail against the pulpit, and holy bread
        and wine;
Sore from their cart-tail scourgings, and from
        the pillory lame,
Rejoicing in their wretchedness, and glorying
        in their shame.

And what a fate awaits thee! — a sadly
        toiling slave,
Dragging the slowly lengthening chain of
        bondage to the grave!
Think of thy woman's nature, subdued in
        hopeless thrall,
The easy prey of any, the scoff and scorn
        of all!"

Oh, ever as the Tempter spoke, and feeble
        Nature's fears
Wrung drop by drop the scalding flow of
        unavailing tears,
I wrestled down the evil thoughts, and strove
        in silent prayer,
To feel, O Helper of the weak! that Thou
        indeed wert there!

I thought of Paul and Silas, within Philippi's
        cell,
And how from Peter's sleeping limbs the
        prison shackles fell,
Till I seemed to hear the trailing of an angel's
        robe of white,
And to feel a blessed presence invisible to
        sight.

Bless the Lord for all his mercies! — for the
        peace and love I felt,
Like dew of Hermon's holy hill, upon my
        spirit melt;
When "Get behind me, Satan!" was the
        language of my heart,
And I felt the Evil Tempter with all his
        doubts depart.

Slow broke the gray cold morning; again the
        sunshine fell,
Flecked with the shade of bar and grate
        within my lonely cell;
The hoar-frost melted on the wall, and up-
        ward from the street
Came careless laugh and idle word, and tread
        of passing feet.

At length the heavy bolts fell back, my door
        was open cast,
And slowly at the sheriff's side, up the long
        street I passed;
I heard the murmur round me, and felt, but
        dared not see,
How, from every door and window, the people
        gazed on me.

And doubt and fear fell on me, shame
        burned upon my cheek,
Swam earth and sky around me, my trem-
        bling limbs grew weak:
"O Lord! support thy handmaid; and from
        her soul cast out
The fear of man, which brings a snare, the
        weakness and the doubt."

Then the dreary shadows scattered, like a
cloud in morning's breeze,
And a low deep voice within me seemed
whispering words like these:
"Though thy earth be as the iron, and thy
heaven a brazen wall,
Trust still His loving-kindness whose power
is over all."

We paused at length, where at my feet the
sunlit waters broke
On glaring reach of shining beach, and
shingly wall of rock;
The merchant-ships lay idly there, in hard
clear lines on high,
Tracing with rope and slender spar their net-
work on the sky.

And there were ancient citizens, cloak-
wrapped and grave and cold,
And grim and stout sea-captains with faces
bronzed and old,
And on his horse, with Rawson, his cruel
clerk at hand,
Sat dark and haughty Endicott, the ruler
of the land.

And poisoning with his evil words the ruler's
ready ear,
The priest leaned o'er his saddle, with laugh
and scoff and jeer;
It stirred my soul, and from my lips the seal
of silence broke,
As if through woman's weakness a warning
spirit spoke.

I cried, "The Lord rebuke thee, thou smiter
of the meek,
Thou robber of the righteous, thou trampler
of the weak!
Go light the dark, cold hearth-stones, — go
turn the prison lock
Of the poor hearts thou hast hunted, thou
wolf amid the flock!"

Dark lowered the brows of Endicott, and
with a deeper red
O'er Rawson's wine-empurpled cheek the
flush of anger spread;
"Good people," quoth the white-lipped priest,
"heed not her words so wild,
Her Master speaks within her, — the Devil
owns his child!"

But gray heads shook, and young brows
knit, the while the sheriff read
That law the wicked rulers against the poor
have made,
Who to their house of Rimmon and idol priest-
hood bring
No bended knee of worship, nor gainful
offering.

Then to the stout sea-captains the sheriff,
turning, said, —
"Which of ye, worthy seamen, will take this
Quaker maid?
In the Isle of fair Barbadoes, or on Virginia's
shore,
You may hold her at a higher price than
Indian girl or Moor."

Grim and silent stood· the captains; and
when again he cried,
"Speak out, my worthy seamen!" — no
voice, no sign replied;
But I felt a hard hand press my own, and
kind words met my ear, —
"God bless thee, and preserve thee, my
gentle girl and dear!"

A weight seemed lifted from my heart, a
pitying friend was nigh, —
I felt it in his hard, rough hand, and saw it
in his eye;
And when again the sheriff spoke, that voice,
so kind to me,
Growled back its stormy answer like the
roaring of the sea, —

"Pile my ship with bars of silver, pack with
coins of Spanish gold,
From keel-piece up to deck-plank, the room-
age of her hold,
By the living God who made me! — I would
sooner in your bay
Sink ship and crew and cargo, than bear this
child away!"

"Well answered, worthy captain, shame on
their cruel laws!"
Ran through the crowd in murmurs loud
the people's just applause.
"Like the herdsman of Tekoa, in Israel of
old,
Shall we see the poor and righteous again
for silver sold?"

I looked on haughty Endicott; with weapon
  half-way drawn,
Swept round the throng his lion glare of bitter
  hate and scorn;
Fiercely he drew his bridle-rein, and turned in
  silence back,
And sneering priest and baffled clerk rode
  murmuring in his track.

Hard after them the sheriff looked, in bitter-
  ness of soul;
Thrice smote his staff upon the ground, and
  crushed his parchment roll.
"Good friends," he said, "since both have
  fled, the ruler and the priest,
Judge ye, if from their further work I be not
  well released."

Loud was the cheer which, full and clear,
  swept round the silent bay,
As, with kind words and kinder looks, he
  bade me go my way;
For He who turns the courses of the stream-
  let of the glen,
And the river of great waters, had turned the
  hearts of men.

Oh, at that hour the very earth seemed
  changed beneath my eye,
A holier wonder round me rose the blue walls
  of the sky,
A lovelier light on rock and hill and stream
  and woodland lay,
And softer lapsed on sunnier sands the waters
  of the bay.

Thanksgiving to the Lord of life! to Him all
  praises be,
Who from the hands of evil men hath set his
  handmaid free;
All praise to Him before whose power the
  mighty are afraid,
Who takes the crafty in the snare which for
  the poor is laid!

Sing, O my soul, rejoicingly, on evening's
  twilight calm
Uplift the loud thanksgiving, pour forth the
  grateful psalm;
Let all dear hearts with me rejoice, as did
  the saints of old,
When of the Lord's good angel the rescued
  Peter told.

And weep and howl, ye evil priests and
  mighty men of wrong,
The Lord shall smite the proud, and lay His
  hand upon the strong.
Woe to the wicked rulers in His avenging
  hour!
Woe to the wolves who seek the flocks to
  raven and devour!

But let the humble ones arise, the poor in
  heart be glad,
And let the mourning ones again with robes
  of praise be clad.
For He who cooled the furnace, and smoothed
  the stormy wave,
And tamed the Chaldean lions, is mighty
  still to save!
                    JOHN GREENLEAF WHITTIER.

In September, 1661, Edward Burrough, a
prominent Quaker of England, obtained an audi-
ence of King Charles II and laid the grievances
of the New England Quakers before him. That
careless King, who always found it more easy to
grant a request than to refuse it, so long as it cost
him nothing, directed that a letter be written to
Endicott and the governors of the other New
England colonies, commanding that "if there
were any of those people called Quakers amongst
them, now already condemned to suffer death, or
other corporal punishment, or that were im-
prisoned, and obnoxious to the like condemna-
tion, they were to forbear to proceed any further
therein," and to send such persons to England for
trial. This letter was given in charge to Samuel
Shattuck, a Quaker of Salem, then in England
under sentence of banishment, with the usual
condition of being hanged should he return. He
reached Boston in November, 1661, and presented
himself with all haste at the governor's door·
The ballad very accurately describes the inter
view which followed.

THE KING'S MISSIVE

[November, 1661]

UNDER the great hill sloping bare
  To cove and meadow and Common lot,
In his council chamber and oaken chair,
  Sat the worshipful Governor Endicott.
A grave, strong man, who knew no peer
In the pilgrim land, where he ruled in fear
Of God, not man, and for good or ill
Held his trust with an iron will.

He had shorn with his sword the cross from out
  The flag, and cloven the May-pole down.

Harried the heathen round about,
  And whipped the Quakers from town to
      town.
Earnest and honest, a man at need
To burn like a torch for his own harsh creed,
He kept with the flaming brand of his zeal
The gate of the holy common weal.

His brow was clouded, his eye was stern,
  With a look of mingled sorrow and wrath;
"Woe 's me!" he murmured: "at every turn
  The pestilent Quakers are in my path!
Some we have scourged, and banished some,
Some hanged, more doomed, and still they
      come,
Fast as the tide of yon bay sets in,
Sowing their heresy's seed of sin.

"Did we count on this? Did we leave behind
  The graves of our kin, the comfort and ease
Of our English hearths and homes, to find
  Troublers of Israel such as these?
Shall I spare? Shall I pity them? God for-
      bid!
I will do as the prophet to Agag did:
They come to poison the wells of the Word,
I will hew them in pieces before the Lord!"

The door swung open, and Rawson the clerk
  Entered, and whispered under breath,
"There waits below for the hangman's work
  A fellow banished on pain of death —
Shattuck, of Salem, unhealed of the whip,
Brought over in Master Goldsmith's ship
At anchor here in a Christian port,
With freight of the devil and all his sort!"

Twice and thrice on the chamber floor
  Striding fiercely from wall to wall,
"The Lord do so to me and more,"
  The Governor cried, "if I hang not all!
Bring hither the Quaker." Calm, sedate,
With the look of a man at ease with fate,
Into that presence grim and dread
Came Samuel Shattuck, with hat on head.

"Off with the knave's hat!" An angry hand
  Smote down the offence; but the wearer
      said,
With a quiet smile, "By the king's command
  I bear his message and stand in his stead."
In the Governor's hand a missive he laid
With the royal arms on its seal displayed,
And the proud man spake as he gazed thereat,
Uncovering, "Give Mr. Shattuck his hat."

He turned to the Quaker, bowing low, —
  "The king commandeth your friends'
      release;
Doubt not he shall be obeyed, although
  To his subjects' sorrow and sin's increase.
What he here enjoineth, John Endicott,
His loyal servant, questioneth not.
You are free! God grant the spirit you own
May take you from us to parts unknown."

So the door of the jail was open cast,
  And, like Daniel, out of the lion's den
Tender youth and girlhood passed,
  With age-bowed women and gray-locked
      men.
And the voice of one appointed to die
Was lifted in praise and thanks on high,
And the little maid from New Netherlands
Kissed, in her joy, the doomed man's hand.

And one, whose call was to minister
  To the souls in prison, beside him went,
An ancient woman, bearing with her
  The linen shroud for his burial meant.
For she, not counting her own life dear,
In the strength of a love that cast out fear,
Had watched and served where her brethren
      died,
Like those who waited the cross beside.

One moment they paused on their way to
      look
  On the martyr graves by the Common side,
And much scourged Wharton of Salem took
  His burden of prophecy up and cried:
"Rest, souls of the valiant! Not in vain
Have ye borne the Master's cross of pain;
Ye have fought the fight, ye are victors
      crowned,
With a fourfold chain ye have Satan bound!"

The autumn haze lay soft and still
  On wood and meadow and upland farms;
On the brow of Snow Hill the great windmill
  Slowly and lazily swung its arms;
Broad in the sunshine stretched away,
With its capes and islands, the turquoise
      bay;
And over water and dusk of pines
Blue hills lifted their faint outlines.

The topaz leaves of the walnut glowed,
  The sumach added its crimson fleck,
And double in air and water showed
  The tinted maples along the Neck;

Through frost flower clusters of pale star-
mist,
And gentian fringes of amethyst,
And royal plumes of golden-rod,
The grazing cattle on Centry trod.

But as they who see not, the Quakers saw
The world about them; they only thought
With deep thanksgiving and pious awe
On the great deliverance God had wrought.
Through lane and alley the gazing town
Noisily followed them up and down;
Some with scoffing and brutal jeer,
Some with pity and words of cheer.

One brave voice rose above the din.
Upsall, gray with his length of days,
Cried from the door of his Red Lion Inn:
"Men of Boston, give God the praise!
No more shall innocent blood call down
The bolts of wrath on your guilty town.
The freedom of worship, dear to you,
Is dear to all, and to all is due.

"I see the vision of days to come,
When your beautiful City of the Bay

Shall be Christian liberty's chosen home,
And none shall his neighbor's rights gainsay.
The varying notes of worship shall blend
And as one great prayer to God ascend,
And hands of mutual charity raise
Walls of salvation and gates of praise."

So passed the Quakers through Boston town,
Whose painful ministers sighed to see
The walls of their sheep-fold falling down,
And wolves of heresy prowling free.
But the years went on, and brought no wrong;
With milder counsels the State grew strong,
As outward Letter and inward Light
Kept the balance of truth aright.

The Puritan spirit perishing not,
To Concord's yeomen the signal sent,
And spake in the voice of the cannon-shot
That severed the chains of a continent.
With its gentler mission of peace and good-
will
The thought of the Quaker is living still,
And the freedom of soul he prophesied
Is gospel and law where the martyrs died.
JOHN GREENLEAF WHITTIER.

CHAPTER VII

KING PHILIP'S WAR AND THE WITCHCRAFT DELUSION

Metacomet, or Philip, had succeeded his father,
Massasoit, as chief of the Wampanoags, and en-
deavored to maintain friendly relations with the
English, but in June, 1675, some of his young
men attacked the village of Swansea, and started
the desperate struggle known as King Philip's
War. For months the Indians ravaged the fron-
tier, and on September 18 all but annihilated a
picked force of eighty men, the "Flower of Essex,"
under Captain Thomas Lathrop, which had been
sent to Deerfield to save a quantity of grain which
had been abandoned there. Only nine of the eighty
survived.

THE LAMENTABLE BALLAD OF
THE BLOODY BROOK

[September 18, 1675]

COME listen to the Story of brave Lathrop
and his Men, —
How they fought, how they died,
When they marched against the Red Skins
in the Autumn Days, and then

How they fell, in their pride,
By Pocumtuck Side.

"Who will go to Deerfield Meadows and
bring the ripened Grain?"
Said old Mosely to his men in Array.
"Take the Wagons and the Horses, and
bring it back again;
But be sure that no Man stray
All the Day, on the Way."

Then the Flower of Essex started, with
Lathrop at their head,
Wise and brave, bold and true.
He had fought the Pequots long ago, and
now to Mosely said,
"Be there Many, be there Few,
I will bring the Grain to you."

They gathered all the Harvest, and marched
back on their Way
Through the Woods which blazed like Fire.

No Soldier left the Line of march to wander
    or to stray,
  Till the Wagons were stalled in the
    Mire,
And the Beasts began to tire.

The Wagons have all forded the Brook as it
    flows,
  And then the Rear-Guard stays
To pick the Purple Grapes that are hanging
    from the Boughs,
  When, crack! — to their Amaze,
A hundred Fire-locks blaze!

Brave Lathrop, he lay dying; but as he fell he
    cried,
  "Each Man to his Tree," said he,
"Let no one yield an Inch;" and so the
    Soldier died;
  And not a Man of all can see
Where the Foe can be.

And Philip and his Devils pour in their Shot
    so fast,
  From behind and before,
That Man after Man is shot down and
    breathes his last.
  Every Man lies dead in his Gore
To fight no more, — no more!

Oh, weep, ye Maids of Essex, for the Lads
    who have died, —
  The Flower of Essex they!
The Bloody Brook still ripples by the black
    Mountain-side,
But never shall they come again to see the
    ocean-tide,
And never shall the Bridegroom return to his
    Bride,
  From that dark and cruel Day, — cruel
    Day!

            EDWARD EVERETT HALE.

At the approach of winter, the Indians with-
drew to the Narragansett country, and the col-
onists decided to strike a decisive blow. An army
of a thousand men was raised and on the morning
of Sunday, December 19, approached the Narra-
gansett stronghold, a well-fortified position on
an island in the midst of a swamp. A murderous
fire greeted the assailants, but they forced an
entrance into the fort, set fire to the wigwams,
and after a terrific struggle, in which they lost
nearly three hundred killed and wounded, drove
the Indians out and destroyed their store of
winter provisions.

THE GREAT SWAMP FIGHT

[December 19, 1675]

I

Oh, rouse you, rouse you, men at arms,
  And hear the tale I tell,
From Pettaquamscut town I come,
  Now hear what there befell.

The houses stand upon the hill,
  Not large, each house is full,
But largest of them all there stood
  The house of Justice Bull

'T was there the court sat every year,
  The governor came in state,
From there the couriers through the town
  Served summons soon and late.

And there, 't is but three years agone,
  George Fox preached, you remember;
That was in May when he preached peace,
  And now it is December.

Peace, peace, he cried, but righteous God,
  How can there be true peace,
When war and tumult stalk at night,
  And deeds of blood increase?

Revenge, revenge, good captains bold,
  Revenge, my people cry;
Where stood the house of Justice Bull
  But piled-up ashes lie.

How fared it then, who may dare tell?
  The shutters barred the light,
As one by one the windows closed,
  And all was black as night.

Strong was the house, and strong brave
    men
  All armed lay down to sleep,
And women fair, and children, too,
  They were to guard and keep.

And then a horror in the night,
  And shouts, and fire, and knives,
And demons yelling in delight,
  As men fought for their lives.

And where there stood that goodly house
  And lived those goodly men,
Full seven goodly souls are gone.
  Revenge, we cry again!

II

Up, up, ye men of English blood!
  The gallant governor cried,
And we shall dare to find their lair,
  Where'er it be they hide.

For never men of English blood
  Could brook so foul a deed,
For all these sins the fierce redskins
  Shall reap their lawful meed.

Up rose the little army then,
  All armed as best they could,
With pike and sword and axes broad,
  Flint-locks and staves of wood.

And motley was the company,
  Recruits from wood and field,
But strong young men were with them then,
  Who'd sooner die than yield.

Connecticut had sent her men
  With Major Robert Treat;
Each colony in its degree
  Sent in its quota meet.

And Massachusetts led the way,
  And Plymouth had next post,
Winslow commands the gathered bands,
  A thousand men they boast.

The winter sun hung in the sky
  And frost bound all things fast;
As they set forth, from out the north,
  There blew a bitter blast.

The meadow grass was stiff with rime,
  The frozen brook lay dead;
Like stone did sound the frozen ground
  Beneath the martial tread.

All day they marched in bitter cold,
  And when, as fell the night,
They reached the hill and gazed their fill
  Upon the piteous sight,

No need to urge the rapid chase,
  The cinders did that well,
And in the air a woman's hair
  Told more than words could tell.

In stern resolve they lay them down,
  For rest they needed sore,
But long ere dawn the swords were drawn
  And open stood the door.

Out to the gloom of morning passed
  Full silently those men,
And what 'twixt light and fall of night
  Should come, no soul might ken.

III

They turned their faces toward the west,
  The morning air was cold,
And softly stepped, while still men slept,
  With courage high and bold.

An Indian they met ere long,
  'T was Peter, whom they knew;
They asked their way, naught would he say,
  To his own comrades true.

In anger cried the governor:
  Then let the man be hung,
For he can tell, he knows full well,
  So let him find his tongue.

To save his life that wretched man
  Agreed to be their guide,
As they marched on, the Indian
  Marched onward by their side.

And soon they reached a dreadful swamp,
  With cedar trees o'ergrown,
And thick and dark with dead trees stark
  And great trunks lying prone.

'T was frozen hard, and Indians there!
  They fired as they ran,
And with a bound that spurned the ground
  The fierce assault began.

And then a wonder in the wood, —
  A little rising ground,
With palisade for shelter made
  Of timber planted round.

And but one place of entrance there
  Across a watery way,
A tall felled tree gave access free,
  From shore to shore it lay.

Full many a gallant man that day
  His life left at that tree,
The bravest men pressed forward then,
  And there fell captains three.

A dreadful day, and of our men
  Short work would have been made,
But that by grace they found a place
  Weak in the palisade.

Then they poured in, within the fort
  Soon filled with Indians dead,
And many a one great deeds had done
  Within that place of dread.

Then with a torch the whole was fired,
  The wigwams caught the blaze,
The fire roared and spread abroad
  And fed on tubs of maize.

The night came on, the governor called,
  The soldiers gathered round;
The fort was theirs, and dying prayers
  Were rising from the ground.

With care they gathered up their dead,
  The few who had been spared,
All through the cold, in pain untold.
  To Warwick they repaired.

So was the Indians' power gone,
  Avenged were Englishmen,
For from the night of that Swamp fight
  They never rose again.

In Narragansett there was peace,
  The soldiers went their way,
All that remains are some few grains
  Of corn parched on that day.

Gone is the wrong, the toil, the pain,
  The Indians, they are gone.
Please God we use, and not abuse
  The land so hardly won!
                            CAROLINE HAZARD.

This assault by the colonists drove the Narra-
gansetts, who had hitherto taken no active part
in the war, into alliance with Philip, and two
months later, on February 21, 1676, Medfield,
less than twenty miles from Boston, was attacked
and partially burned. Groton soon suffered a
similar fate, and the leaders of the savages boasted
that they would march on Cambridge, Concord,
Roxbury, and Boston itself. It was at this juncture
that the "Amazonian Dames" mentioned in the
poem became so frightened at the prospect that
they resolved to fortify Boston neck.

ON A FORTIFICATION AT BOSTON BEGUN BY WOMEN

DUX FOEMINA FACTI

[March, 1676]

A GRAND attempt some Amazonian Dames
Contrive whereby to glorify their names,

A ruff for Boston Neck of mud and turfe,
Reaching from side to side, from surf to surf,
Their nimble hands spin up like Christmas
      pyes,
Their pastry by degrees on high doth rise.
The wheel at home counts it an holiday,
Since while the mistress worketh it may play.
A tribe of female hands, but manly hearts,
Forsake at home their pasty crust and tarts,
To knead the dirt, the samplers down they
      hurl,
Their undulating silks they closely furl.
The pick-axe one as a commandress holds,
While t'other at her awk'ness gently scolds.
One puffs and sweats, the other mutters why
Cant you promove your work so fast as I?
Some dig, some delve, and others' hands do
      feel
The little waggon's weight with single wheel.
And least some fainting-fits the weak surprize,
They want no sack nor cakes, they are more
      wise.
These brave essays draw forth male, stronger
      hands,
More like to dawbers than to marshal bands;
These do the work, the sturdy bulwarks raise,
But the beginners well deserve the praise.
                            BENJAMIN TOMPSON.

On April 21 an attack was made on Sudbury;
a portion of the town was burned, and a relief
party of over fifty which hurried up was lured
into an ambush and all but annihilated. The
Indians in this battle were bolder than they had
ever been before, and their strategy was unusually
effective.

THE SUDBURY FIGHT

[April 21, 1676]

YE sons of Massachusetts, all who love that
      honored name,
Ye children of New England, holding dear
      your fathers' fame,
Hear tell of Sudbury's battle through a day
      of death and flame!

The painted Wampanoags, Philip's hateful
      warriors, creep
  Upon the town at springtide while the skies
      deny us rain;
We see their shadows lurking in the forest's
      whispering deep,
  And speed the sorry tidings past dry field
      and rustling lane:

*Come hastily or never when the wild beast
    lusts for gore,*
*And send your best and bravest if you wish to
    see us more!*

The Commonwealth is quiet now, and peace
    her measure fills,
Content in homes and farmsteads, busy marts
    and buzzing mills
From the Atlantic's roaring to the tranquil
    Berkshire hills.

But through that day our fathers, speaking
    low their breathless words,
    Their wives and babes in safety, toil to save
        their little all;
They fetch their slender food-stores, drive
    indoors their scanty herds,
    They clean the bell-mouthed musket, melt
        the lead and mould the ball;
Please God they'll keep their battle till their
    countrymen shall haste
With succor from the eastward, iron-hearted,
    flinty-faced.

A hundred dragging twelvemonths ere the
    welcome joy-bells ring
The dawn of Independence did King Philip's
    devils spring
Through April on the little spot, like wolves
    a-ravening.

The morning lifts in fury as they come with
    torch in hand,
    And howl about the houses in the shrunken
        frontier town;
Our garrisons hold steady while the flames
    by breezes fanned
    Disclose the painted demons, fierce and
        cunning, lithe and brown;
At every loophole firing, women close at hand
    to load,
The children bringing bullets, thus the Sud-
    bury men abode.

By night, through generations, have the eager
    children come
Beside their grandsire's settle, listening to the
    droning hum
Of this old tale, with backward glances, open-
    mouthed and dumb.

The burning hours stretch slowly — then a
    welcome sight appears!
    Along the tawny upland where stout Haynes
    keeps faithful guard!

From Watertown speeds Mason, young in
    everything but years;
    Our men rush down to meet him; then,
        together, swift and hard,
They force the Indians backward to the
    Musketaquid's side,
And slaying, ever slaying, drive them o'er the
    reddened tide.

There stand stout Haynes and Mason by the
    bridge upon the flood;
In vain the braves attack them, thick as sap-
    lings in the wood:
Praise God for men so valiant, who have such
    a foe withstood!

But Green Hill looks with anguish down upon
    the painted horde
    Their stealthy ambush keeping as the Con-
        cord men draw near,
To dart with hideous noises as they reach the
    lower ford,
    A thousand 'gainst a dozen; but their every
        life costs dear
As, sinking 'neath such numbers, one by one
    our neighbors fail:
One sole survivor in his blood brings on the
    dreadful tale.

Through sun and evening shadow, through
    the night till weary morn,
Speeds Wadsworth with his soldiers, forth
    from Boston, spent and worn,
And Brocklebank at Marlboro' joins that
    little hope forlorn.

They hear the muskets snap afar, they hear
    the savage whoop —
    All weariness forgotten, on they hasten in
        relief;
They see the braves before them — with a
    cheer the little group
    Bends down and charges forward; from
        above the cunning Chief,
His wild-cat eyes dilating, sees his bushes
    bloom with fire,
The tree-trunks at his bidding blaze with
    fiendish lust and ire.

A thousand warriors lurk there, and a thou-
    sand warriors shout,
Exulting, aiming, flaming, happy in our
    coming rout;
But Wadsworth never pauses, every musket
    ringing out.

He gains the lifting hillside, and his sixscore
  win their way
Defiant through the coppice till upon the
  summit placed;
With every bullet counting, there they load
  and aim and slay,
Against all comers warring, iron-hearted,
  flinty-faced;
Hold Philip as for scorning, drive him down
  the bloodstained slope,
And stand there, firm and dauntless, stead-
  fast in their faith and hope.

With Mason at the river, Wadsworth staunch
  upon the hill,
The certain reinforcements, and black night
  the foe to chill,
An hour or less and hideous Death might
  have been baffled still.

But in that droughty woodland Philip fires
  the leaves and grass:
The flames dance up the hillside, in their
  rear less savage foes.
No courage can avail us, down the slope the
  English pass —
A day in flame beginning lights with hell
  its awful close,
As swifter, louder, fiercer, o'er the crest the
  reek runs past
And headlong hurls bold Wadsworth, con-
  quered by the cruel blast.

Ye men of Massachusetts, weep the awful
  slaughter there!
The panther heart of Philip drives the Eng-
  lish to despair,
As scalping-knife and tomahawk gleam in
  th' affrighted glare.

There Wadsworth yields his spirit, Brockle-
  bank must meet his doom;
Within the stone mill's shelter fights the
  remnant of their force;
When swift upon the foemen, rushing through
  the gathering gloom,
Cheer Cowell's men from Brookfield,
  gallant Prentice with his horse!
And Mason from the river, and Haynes join
  in the fight,
Till Philip's host is routed, hurled on shriek-
  ing through the night.

Defeated, cursing, weeping, flees King Philip
  to his den,

Our speedy vengeance glutted on the flower
  of his men;
In pomp and pride the Wampanoags ne'er
  shall march again.

We mourn our stricken Captains, but not
  vainly did they fall:
The King of Pocanoket has received their
  stern command;
Their lives were laid down gladly at their
  country's trumpet-call,
And on their savage foemen have they set
  the heavier hand;
Against our day-long valor was the red man's
  fortune spent
And that one day at Sudbury has saved a
  continent.

In graves adown the hemisphere, in graves
  across the seas,
The sons of Massachusetts sleep, as here
  beneath her trees,
Nor Brocklebank nor Wadsworth is the first
  or last of these.

Oh, blue hills of New England, slanting to
  the morning beams
Where suns and clouds of April have their
  balmy power sped;
Oh, greening woods and meadows, pleasant
  ponds and babbling streams,
And clematis soft-blooming where War
  once his banners led;
How hungers many an exile for that home-
  land far away,
And all the happy dreaming of a bygone April
  day!

Wherever speaks New England, wheresoever
  spreads her shade,
We praise our fathers' valor, and our fathers'
  prayer is said,
That, fearing God's Wrath only, firm may
  stand the State they made.
                              WALLACE RICE.

The victory at Sudbury was the last considerable
success the Indians gained in the war. Jealousies
broke out among them, many deserted to the
whites, and the final blow was struck when, at
daybreak of August 12, 1676, Captain Church
surprised Philip's camp at Mt. Hope, and Philip
himself was shot by an Indian while trying to
escape. His head was cut off, sent to Plymouth,
and fixed upon a pole, where it remained for twenty
years. His wife and son, a boy of nine, were taken

prisoners and sold into slavery. With them, the race of Massasoit, that true and tried friend of the early settlers, vanishes from the pages of history.

KING PHILIP'S LAST STAND

[August 12, 1676]

'T was Captain Church, bescarred and brown,
  And armèd cap-a-pie,
Came ambling into Plymouth-town;
And from far riding up and down
  A weary man was he.

Now, where is my good wife? he quoth
  Before the goodmen all;
And they replied, *What of thine oath?*
And he looked on them lorn and loath,
  As he were like to fall.

What of thine oath? to him they cried,
  And wilt thou let him slip
Who harrieth fair New England-side
Till every path is slaughter-dyed, —
  The murderous King Philip!

His cheek went flush and swelled his girth;
  Upon him be God's ban!
His voice ran loud in grisly mirth:
Now, who with me will run to earth
  This bloody Indiàn?

Then *I!* and *I!* the lusty peal
  Made thrill the Plymouth air;
And forth with him for woe or weal,
Their hands agrip on musket-steel,
  Hied many a godly pair.

They sped them through the summer-land
  By ferry and by ford,
Until they saw before them stand
A redman of that cursèd band,
  His features ochre-scored.

Would the pale-faces find, he said,
  Where lurks their fiercest foe?
Now, by the spirit of the dead, —
My brother, whose heart's blood he shed, —
  Follow, and they shall know!

This Indian brave, they followed him;
  In caution crawled and crept;
Till in a marish deep and dim
They came to where the Sachem grim
  In leafy hiding slept.

(The quiet August morn's at bud,
  King Philip, woe's the day!
And woe that one of thine own blood,
Now that ill-fortune roars to flood,
  Should be the man to slay!)

Around him spread a girdling line;
  The fatal snare was laid;
And when down aisles of birch and pine
They saw the first slant sun-rays shine,
  They sprang their ambuscade.

And did he slink, or did he shrink
  From that relentless ring?
Nay, not a coward did he sink,
But leaped across Death's darkling brink
  A savage, yet a king!

Then unto him whose bolt of lead
  Had struck King Philip down,
They gave the Sachem's hand and head;
Then back they marched, with triumph tread,
  To joyful Plymouth-town.

On Philip's name a bloody blot
  The white man's writ has thrown, —
The ruthless raid, the inhuman plot;
And yet what one of us would not
  Do battle for his own!
                    CLINTON SCOLLARD.

The Indians conquered, the people of Massachusetts set themselves resolutely to fight the devil. They were firm believers in the actual presence of the powers of darkness, and almost from the beginning of the colony there had been prosecutions for witchcraft. But it was not until 1692 that the great outbreak of superstition, vindictiveness, and fear occurred, which forms the darkest blot on New England's history.

PROLOGUE

From "Giles Corey of the Salem Farms"

DELUSIONS of the days that once have been,
Witchcraft and wonders of the world un-
  seen,
Phantoms of air, and necromantic arts
That crushed the weak and awed the stoutest
  hearts, —
These are our theme to-night; and vaguely
  here,
Through the dim mists that crowd the atmos-
  phere,

We draw the outlines of weird figures cast
In shadow on the background of the Past.

Who would believe that in the quiet town
Of Salem, and amid the woods that crown
The neighboring hillsides, and the sunny
  farms
That fold it safe in their paternal arms, —
Who would believe that in those peaceful
  streets,
Where the great elms shut out the summer
  heats,
Where quiet reigns, and breathes through
  brain and breast
The benediction of unbroken rest, —
Who would believe such deeds could find a
  place
As these whose tragic history we retrace?

'T was but a village then: the goodman
  ploughed
His ample acres under sun or cloud;
The goodwife at her doorstep sat and spun,
And gossiped with her neighbors in the sun;
The only men of dignity and state
Were then the Minister and the Magistrate,
Who ruled their little realm with iron rod,
Less in the love than in the fear of God;
And who believed devoutly in the Powers
Of Darkness, working in this world of ours,
In spells of Witchcraft, incantations dread,
And shrouded apparitions of the dead.

Upon this simple folk "with fire and flame,"
Saith the old Chronicle, "the Devil came;
Scattering his firebrands and his poisonous
  darts,
To set on fire of Hell all tongues and hearts!
And 't is no wonder; for, with all his host,
There most he rages where he hateth most,
And is most hated; so on us he brings
All these stupendous and portentous things!"

Something of this our scene to-night will
  show;
And ye who listen to the Tale of Woe,
Be not too swift in casting the first stone,
Nor think New England bears the guilt
  alone.
This sudden burst of wickedness and crime
Was but the common madness of the time,
When in all lands, that lie within the sound
Of Sabbath bells, a Witch was burned or
  drowned.
HENRY WADSWORTH LONGFELLOW.

The outbreak occurred in that part of Salem then called Salem Village, now the separate town of Danvers, and was brought about by three or four children who pretended to be bewitched and who "cried out" against various persons. They were countenanced, not to say encouraged, by Samuel Parris, the minister of the place, and there is evidence to show that he used them to gratify his private enmities.

SALEM

[A. D. 1692]

SOE, Mistress Anne, faire neighbour myne,
  How rides a witch when night-winds blowe?
Folk say that you are none too goode
To joyne the crewe in Salem woode,
When one you wot of gives the signe:
  Righte well, methinks, the pathe you knowe.

In meetinge-time I watched you well,
  Whiles godly Master Parris prayed:
Your folded hands laye on your booke;
But Richard answered to a looke
That fain would tempt him unto hell,
  Where, Mistress Anne, your place is made.

You looke into my Richard's eyes
  With evill glances shamelesse growne;
I found about his wriste a hair,
And guesse what fingers tyed it there!
He shall not lightly be your prize —
  Your Master first shall take his owne.

'T is not in nature he should be
  (Who loved me soe when Springe was
    greene)
A childe, to hange upon your gowne!
He loved me well in Salem towne
Until this wanton witcherie
  His heart and myne crept dark betweene.

Last Sabbath nighte, the gossips saye,
  Your goodman missed you from his side.
He had no strength to move, until
Agen, as if in slumber still,
Beside him at the dawne you laye.
  Tell, nowe, what meanwhile did betide.

Dame Anne, mye hate goe with you fleete
  As drifts the Bay fogg overhead —
Or over yonder hill-topp, where
There is a tree ripe fruit shall bear
When, neighbour myne, your wicked feet
  The stones of Gallows Hill shall tread.
EDMUND CLARENCE STEDMAN.

A special jury, instituted to try the suspects, went to work without delay. On June 2, 1692, Bridget Bishop was tried and condemned and was hanged a week later. On June 30 the court sentenced five persons to death, and all of them were executed soon afterwards. Among those condemned was Rebecca Nourse, seventy-one years of age, universally beloved and of excellent character. The jury was with great difficulty persuaded to convict her; the governor granted a reprieve, but Parris, who had an ancient grudge against her, finally got it repealed, and on July 19, 1692, she was carted to the summit of Gallows Hill and hanged.

THE DEATH OF GOODY NURSE

[July 19, 1692]

THE chill New England sunshine
    Lay on the kitchen floor;
The wild New England north wind
    Came rattling at the door.

And by the wide old fire-place,
    Deep in her cushioned chair,
Lay back an ancient woman,
    With shining snow-white hair.

The peace of God was on her face,
    Her eyes were sweet and calm,
And when you heard her earnest voice
    It sounded like a psalm.

In all the land they loved her well;
    From country and from town
Came many a heart for counsel,
    And many a soul cast down.

Her hands had fed the hungry poor
    With blessing and with bread;
Her face was like a comforting
    From out the Gospel read.

So weak and silent as she lay,
    Her warm hands clasped in prayer,
A sudden knocking at the door
    Came on her unaware.

And as she turned her hoary head,
    Beside her chair there stood
Four grim and grisly Puritans —
    No visitants for good.

They came upon her like a host,
    And bade her speak and tell
Why she had sworn a wicked oath
    To serve the powers of hell;

To work the works of darkness
    On children of the light,
A witch they might not suffer here
    Who read the Word aright.

Like one who sees her fireside yawn,
    A pit of black despair,
Or one who wakes from quiet dreams
    Within a lion's lair,

She glared at them with starting eyes,
    Her voice essayed no sound;
She gasped like any hunted deer
    The eager dogs surround.

"Answer us!" hoarse and loud they cry;
    She looked from side to side —
No human help — "Oh, gracious God!"
    In agony she cried.

Then, calling back her feeble life,
    The white lips uttered slow,
"I am as pure as babe unborn
    From this foul thing, ye know.

"If God doth visit me for sin,
    Beneath His rod I bend,"
But pitiless and wroth were they,
    And bent upon their end.

They tortured her with taunt and jeer,
    They vexed her night and day —
No husband's arm nor sister's tears
    Availed their rage to stay.

Before the church they haled her then;
    The minister arose
And poured upon her patient head
    The worst of all its woes:

He bade her be accursed of God
    Forever here and there;
He cursed her with a heavy curse
    No mortal man may bear.

She stood among the cowering crowd
    As calm as saints in heaven,
Her eyes as sweet as summer skies,
    Her face like summer's even.

The devils wrought their wicked will
    On matron and on maid.
"Thou hast bewitched us!" cried they all,
    But not a word she said

They fastened chains about her feet,
  And carried her away;
For many days in Salem jail
  Alone and ill she lay

She heard the scythe along the field
  Ring through the fragrant air,
She smelt the wild-rose on the wind
  That bloweth everywhere.

Reviled and hated and bereft,
  The soul had plenteous rest,
Though sorrow like a frantic flood
  Beat sore upon her breast.

At last the prison door stood wide,
  They led the saint abroad;
By many an old familiar place
  Her trembling footsteps trod.

Till faint with weakness and distress,
  She climbed a hillside bleak,
And faced the gallows built thereon,
  Still undisturbed and meek.

They hanged this weary woman there,
  Like any felon stout;
Her white hairs on the cruel rope
  Were scattered all about.

The body swung upon the tree
  In every flitting wind,
Reviled and mocked by passengers
  And folk of evil mind.

A woman old and innocent,
  To die a death of shame,
With kindred, neighbors, friends thereby,
  And none to utter blame.

Oh, God, that such a thing should be
  On earth which Thou hast made!
A voice from heaven answered me,
  "Father forgive," He said.
          ROSE TERRY COOKE.

At the August session, six persons were tried and, of course, condemned, among them Elizabeth and John Proctor. The former had been arrested April 11, and when her husband came to her defence, he was also arrested. They were tried together August 5, and both were convicted and sentenced to be hanged. Proctor was executed August 19. His wife escaped by pleading pregnancy. Some months later she gave birth to a child, and her execution was again ordered early in 1693, but Governor Phips granted a reprieve, and she ultimately escaped.

A SALEM WITCH

[August 19, 1692]

THE wind blows east, — the wind blows
    west, —
  It blows upon the gallows tree:
Oh, little babe beneath my breast,
  He died for thee! — he died for me!

The judges came, — the children came
  (Some mother's heart o'er each had
    yearned),
They set their black lies on my name: —
  "A God-accursèd witch who learned

"Each night (they said) the Devil's art,
  Through Salem wood by devils drawn."—
I, whose heart beat against his heart
  From dark till dawn! — from dark till dawn!

He faced them in his fearless scorn
  (The sun was on him as he stood):
"No purer is her babe unborn;
  I prove her sinless with my blood."

They spared the babe beneath my breast, —
  They bound his hands, — they set me
    free, —
Hush, hush, my babe! hush, hush and rest;
  He died for thee! — he died for me!

They dragged him, bound, to Gallows Hill
  (I saw the flowers among the grass);
The women came, — I hear them still, —
  They held their babes to see him pass.

God curse them! — Nay, — Oh God forgive!
  He said it while their lips reviled;
He kissed my lips, — he whispered: "Live!
  The father loves thee in the child."

Then earth and sky grew black, — I fell —
  I lay as stone beside their stone.
They did their work. They earned their Hell.
  I woke on Gallows Hill, alone.

Oh Christ who suffered, Christ who blessed,
  Shield him upon the gallows tree!
O babe, his babe, beneath my breast,
  He died for thee! — he died for me!
          EDNAH PROCTOR CLARKE.

The case of Giles Corey is one of the most tragic in all this hideous drama. When arrested and brought before the court, he refused to plead — "stood mute," as the law termed it. The penalty for "standing mute," according to the English law of the time, was that the prisoner "be remanded to prison . . . and there be laid on his back on the bare floor . . . ; that there be placed upon his body as great a weight of iron as he can bear, and more," until death should ensue. This was the penalty Giles Corey suffered.

THE TRIAL

From "Giles Corey of the Salem Farms"

[September 7, 1692]

SCENE II. — *Interior of the Meeting-house.* MATHER *and the Magistrates seated in front of the pulpit. Before them a raised platform.* MARTHA *in chains.* COREY *near her.* MARY WALCOT *in a chair. A crowd of spectators, among them* GLOYD. *Confusion and murmurs during the scene.*

HATHORNE

CALL Martha Corey.

MARTHA

I am here.

HATHORNE

                         Come forward.
She ascends the platform.
The Jurors of our Sovereign Lord and Lady
The King and Queen, here present, do accuse you
Of having on the tenth of June last past,
And divers other times before and after,
Wickedly used and practised certain arts
Called Witchcrafts, Sorceries, and Incantations,
Against one Mary Walcot, single woman,
Of Salem Village: by which wicked arts
The aforesaid Mary Walcot was tormented,
Tortured, afflicted, pined, consumed, and wasted,
Against the peace of our Sovereign Lord and Lady
The King and Queen, as well as of the Statute
Made and provided in that case. What say you?

MARTHA

Before I answer, give me leave to pray.

HATHORNE

We have not sent for you, nor are we here,
To hear you pray, but to examine you
In whatsoever is alleged against you
Why do you hurt this person?

MARTHA

                         I do not.
I am not guilty of the charge against me.

MARY

Avoid, she-devil! You may torment me now!
Avoid, avoid, Witch!

MARTHA

                         I am innocent.
I never had to do with any Witchcraft
Since I was born. I am a gospel woman.

MARY

You are a gospel Witch!

MARTHA (*clasping her hands*)

                         Ah me! ah me!
Oh, give me leave to pray!

MARY (*stretching out her hands*)

                         She hurts me now.
See, she has pinched my hands!

HATHORNE

                         Who made these marks
Upon her hands?

MARTHA

                         I do not know. I stand
Apart from her. I did not touch her hands.

HATHORNE

Who hurt her then?

MARTHA

                         I know not.

HATHORNE

                         Do you think
She is bewitched?

MARTHA

                         Indeed I do not think so.
I am no Witch, and have no faith in Witches.

HATHORNE

Then answer me: When certain person came

To see you yesterday, how did you know
Beforehand why they came?

MARTHA

        I had had speech;
The children said I hurt them, and I thought
These people came to question me about it.

HATHORNE

How did you know the children had been
    told
To note the clothes you wore?

MARTHA

        My husband told me
What others said about it.

HATHORNE

        Goodman Corey,
Say, did you tell her?

COREY

        I must speak the truth;
I did not tell her. It was some one else.

HATHORNE

Did you not say your husband told you so?
How dare you tell a lie in this assembly?
Who told you of the clothes? Confess the
    truth.
   MARTHA *bites her lips, and is silent.*
You bite your lips, but do not answer me!

MARY

Ah, she is biting me! Avoid, avoid!

HATHORNE

You said your husband told you.

MARTHA

        Yes, he told me
The children said I troubled them.

HATHORNE

        Then tell me,
Why do you trouble them?

MARTHA

        I have denied it.

MARY

he threatened me; stabbed at me with her
    spindle;
nd, when my brother thrust her with his
    sword,

He tore her gown, and cut a piece away.
Here are they both, the spindle and the cloth.
        Shows them.

HATHORNE

And there are persons here who know the
    truth
Of what has now been said. What answer
    make you?

MARTHA

I make no answer. Give me leave to pray.

HATHORNE

Whom would you pray to?

MARTHA

        To my God and Father.

HATHORNE

Who is your God and Father?

MARTHA

        The Almighty!

HATHORNE

Doth he you pray to say that he is God?
It is the Prince of Darkness, and not God.

MARY

There is a dark shape whispering in her ear.

HATHORNE

What does it say to you?

MARTHA

        I see no shape.

HATHORNE

Did you not hear it whisper?

MARTHA

        I heard nothing

MARY

What torture! Ah, what agony I suffer!
        Falls into a swoon.

HATHORNE

You see this woman cannot stand before
    you.
If you would look for mercy, you must look
In God's way, by confession of your guilt.
Why does your spectre haunt and hurt this
    person?

MARTHA

I do not know. He who appeared of old
In Samuel's shape, a saint and glorified,
May come in whatsoever shape he chooses.
I cannot help it. I am sick at heart!

COREY

O Martha, Martha! let me hold your hand.

HATHORNE

No; stand aside, old man.

MARY (*starting up*)
                    Look there! Look there!
I see a little bird, a yellow bird,
Perched on her finger; and it pecks at me.
Ah, it will tear mine eyes out!

MARTHA

                    I see nothing.

HATHORNE

'T is the Familiar Spirit that attends her.

MARY

Now it has flown away. It sits up there
Upon the rafters. It is gone; is vanished.

MARTHA

Giles, wipe these tears of anger from mine eyes.
Wipe the sweat from my forehead. I am faint.
    She leans against the railing.

MARY

Oh, she is crushing me with all her weight!

HATHORNE

Did you not carry once the Devil's Book
To this young woman?

MARTHA

                    Never.

HATHORNE

                    Have you signed it,
Or touched it?

MARTHA

            No; I never saw it.

HATHORNE

Did you not scourge her with an iron rod?

MARTHA

No, I did not. If any Evil Spirit

Has taken my shape to do these evil deeds,
I cannot help it. I am innocent.

HATHORNE

Did you not say the Magistrates were blind?
That you would open their eyes?

MARTHA (*with a scornful laugh*)
                    Yes, I said that;
If you call me a sorceress, you are blind!
If you accuse the innocent, you are blind!
Can the innocent be guilty?

HATHORNE

                    Did you not
On one occasion hide your husband's saddle
To hinder him from coming to the Ses-
    sions?

MARTHA

I thought it was a folly in a farmer
To waste his time pursuing such illusions.

HATHORNE

What was the bird that this young woman
    saw
Just now upon your hand?

MARTHA

                    I know no bird.

HATHORNE

Have you not dealt with a Familiar Spirit?

MARTHA

No, never, never!

HATHORNE

                    What then was the Book
You showed to this young woman, and be-
    sought her
To write in it?

MARTHA

            Where should I have a book?
I showed her none, nor have none.

MARY

                    The next Sabbath
Is the Communion Day, but Martha Corey
Will not be there!

MARTHA

                    Ah, you are all against me!
What can I do or say?

HATHORNE

You can confess.

MARTHA

No, I cannot, for I am innocent.

HATHORNE

We have the proof of many witnesses
That you are guilty.

MARTHA

Give me leave to speak.
Will you condemn me on such evidence, —
You who have known me for so many years?
Will you condemn me in this house of God,
Where I so long have worshipped with you all?
Where I have eaten the bread and drunk the
wine
So many times at our Lord's Table with you?
Bear witness, you that hear me; you all know
That I have led a blameless life among you,
That never any whisper of suspicion
Was breathed against me till this accusation.
And shall this count for nothing? Will you
take
My life away from me, because this girl,
Who is distraught, and not in her right mind,
Accuses me of things I blush to name?

HATHORNE

What! is it not enough? Would you hear
more?
Giles Corey!

COREY

I am here.

HATHORNE

Come forward, then.
COREY *ascends the platform.*
Is it not true, that on a certain night
You were impeded strangely in your prayers?
That something hindered you? and that you
left
This woman here, your wife, kneeling alone
Upon the hearth?

COREY

Yes; I cannot deny it.

HATHORNE

Did you not say the Devil hindered you?

COREY

think I said some words to that effect.

HATHORNE

Is it not true, that fourteen head of cattle,
To you belonging, broke from their enclosure
And leaped into the river, and were drowned?

COREY

It is most true.

HATHORNE

And did you not then say
That they were overlooked?

COREY

So much I said.
I see; they 're drawing round me closer, closer,
A net I cannot break, cannot escape from!
(Aside.)

HATHORNE

Who did these things?

COREY

I do not know who did them.

HATHORNE

Then I will tell you. It is some one near
you;
You see her now; this woman, your own wife.

COREY

I call the heavens to witness, it is false!
She never harmed me, never hindered me
In anything but what I should not do.
And I bear witness in the sight of heaven,
And in God's house here, that I never knew
her
As otherwise than patient, brave, and true,
Faithful, forgiving, full of charity,
A virtuous and industrious and good wife!

HATHORNE

Tut, tut, man; do not rant so in your speech;
You are a witness, not an advocate!
Here, Sheriff, take this woman back to prison.

MARTHA

O Giles, this day you 've sworn away my life!

MARY

Go, go and join the Witches at the door.
Do you not hear the drum? Do you not see
them?
Go quick. They 're waiting for you. You are
late!
[*Exit* MARTHA; COREY *following.*

COREY

The dream! the dream! the dream!

HATHORNE

What does he say?
Giles Corey, go not hence. You are yourself
Accused of Witchcraft and of Sorcery
By many witnesses. Say, are you guilty?

COREY

I know my death is foreordained by you, —
Mine and my wife's. Therefore I will not
answer.

During the rest of the scene he remains silent.

HATHORNE

Do you refuse to plead? — 'T were better
for you
To make confession, or to plead Not Guilty. —
Do you not hear me? — Answer, are you
guilty?
Do you not know a heavier doom awaits you,
If you refuse to plead, than if found guilty?
Where is John Gloyd?

GLOYD (*coming forward*)

Here am I.

HATHORNE

Tell the Court;
Have you not seen the supernatural power
Of this old man? Have you not seen him do
Strange feats of strength?

GLOYD

I've seen him lead the field,
On a hot day, in mowing, and against
Us younger men; and I have wrestled with
him.
He threw me like a feather. I have seen him
Lift up a barrel with his single hands,
Which two strong men could hardly lift
together,
And, holding it above his head, drink from it.

HATHORNE

That is enough; we need not question further.
What answer do you make to this, Giles
Corey?

MARY

See there! See there!

HATHORNE

What is it? I see nothing.

MARY

Look! Look! It is the ghost of Robert
Goodell,
Whom fifteen years ago this man did murder
By stamping on his body! In his shroud
He comes here to bear witness to the crime!
The crowd shrinks back from COREY *in horror.*

HATHORNE

Ghosts of the dead and voices of the living
Bear witness to your guilt, and you must die!
It might have been an easier death. Your
doom
Will be on your own head, and not on ours.
Twice more will you be questioned of these
things;
Twice more have room to plead or to confess.
If you are contumacious to the Court,
And if, when questioned, you refuse to answer,
Then by the Statute you will be condemned
To the *peine forte et dure!* To have your body
Pressed by great weights until you shall be
dead!
And may the Lord have mercy on your soul!
HENRY WADSWORTH LONGFELLOW.

GILES COREY

[September 19, 1692]

Giles Corey was a Wizzard strong,
    A stubborn wretch was he;
And fitt was he to hang on high
    Upon the Locust-tree.

So when before the magistrates
    For triall he did come,
He would no true confession make,
    But was compleatlie dumbe.

"Giles Corey," said the Magistrate,
    "What hast thou heare to pleade
To these that now accuse thy soule
    Of crimes and horrid deed?"

Giles Corey, he said not a worde,
    No single worde spoke he.
"Giles Corey," saith the Magistrate,
    "We'll press it out of thee."

They got them then a heavy beam,
    They laid it on his breast;
They loaded it with heavy stones,
    And hard upon him prest.

"More weight!" now said this wretched man;
   "More weight!" again he cried;
And he did no confession make,
   But wickedly he dyed.

One of the most assiduous of the prosecutors had been John Hale, minister of the First Church at Beverly. In October the accusers "cried out" against his wife, who was widely known for generous and disinterested virtues. Hale knew the "innocence and piety of his wife, and stood between her and the storm he had helped to raise. The whole community became convinced that the accusers in crying out upon Mrs. Hale had perjured themselves, and from that moment their power was destroyed."

MISTRESS HALE OF BEVERLY

[October, 1692]

THE roadside forests here and there were
   touched with tawny gold;
The days were shortening, and at dusk the
   sea looked blue and cold;
Through his long fields the minister paced,
   restless, up and down;
Before, the land-locked harbor lay; behind,
   the little town.

No careless chant of harvester or fisherman
   awoke
The silent air; no clanging hoof, no curling
   weft of smoke,
Where late the blacksmith's anvil rang; all
   dumb as death, — and why?
Why? echoed back the minister's chilled
   heart, for sole reply.

His wife was watching from the door; she
   came to meet him now
A weary sadness in her voice, a care upon her
   brow.
A vague, oppressive mystery, a hint of un-
   known fear,
Hung hovering over every roof: it was the
   witchcraft year.

She laid her hand upon his arm, and looked
   into his face,
And as he turned away she turned, beside him
   keeping pace:
And, "Oh, my husband, let me speak!" said
   gentle Mistress Hale,
"For truth is fallen in the street, and false-
   hoods vile prevail.

"The very air we breathe is thick with whis-
   perings of hell;
The foolish trust the quaking bog, where wise
   men sink as well,
Who follow them: O husband mine, for love
   of me, beware
Of touching slime that from the pit is oozing
   everywhere!

"The rulers and the ministers, tell me, what
   have they done,
Through all the dreadful weeks since this
   dark inquest was begun,
Save to encourage thoughtless girls in their
   unhallowed ways,
And bring to an untimely end many a good
   woman's days?

"Think of our neighbor, Goodwife Hoar;
   because she would not say
She was in league with evil powers, she pines
   in jail to-day.
Think of our trusty field-hand, Job, — a
   swaggerer, it is true, —
Boasting he feared no Devil, they have con-
   demned him, too.

"And Bridget Bishop, when she lived yonder
   at Ryal-side,
What if she kept a shovel-board, and trimmed
   with laces wide
Her scarlet bodice: grant she was too frivo-
   lous and vain;
How dared they take away the life they could
   not give again?

"Nor soberness availeth aught; for who hath
   suffered worse,
Through persecutions undeserved, than good
   Rebecca Nurse?
Forsaken of her kith and kin, alone in her
   despair,
It almost seemed as if God's ear were closed
   against her prayer.

"They spare not even infancy: poor little
   Dorcas Good,
The vagrant's child — but four years old! —
   who says that baby could
To Satan sign her soul away condemns this
   business blind,
As but the senseless babbling of a weak and
   wicked mind.

"Is it not like the ancient tale they tell of
　Phaeton,
Whose ignorant hands were trusted with the
　horses of the sun?
Our teachers now by witless youths are led
　on and beguiled:
Woe to the land, the Scripture saith, whose
　ruler is a child!

"God grant this dismal day be short! Except
　help soon arrive,
To ruin these deluded ones will our fair
　country drive.
If I to-morrow were accused, what further
　could I plead
Than those who died, whom neither judge
　nor minister would heed?

"I pray thee, husband, enter not their councils
　any more!
My heart aches with forebodings! Do not
　leave me, I implore!
Yet if to turn this curse aside my life might
　but avail,
In Christ's name would I yield it up," said
　gentle Mistress Hale.

The minister of Beverly dreamed a strange
　dream that night:
He dreamed the tide came up, blood-red,
　through inlet, cove, and bight,
Till Salem village was submerged; until Bass
　River rose,
A threatening crimson gulf, that yawned the
　hamlet to inclose.

It rushed in at the cottage-doors whence
　women fled and wept;
Close to the little meeting-house with serpent
　curves it crept;
The grave-mounds in the burying-ground
　were sunk beneath its flood;
The doorstone of the parsonage was dashed
　with spray of blood.

And on the threshold, praying, knelt his dear
　and honored wife,
As one who would that deluge stay at cost of
　her own life. —
"Oh, save her! save us, Christ!" the cry un-
　locked him from his dream,
And at his casement in the east he saw the
　day-star gleam.

The minister that morning said, "Only this
　once I go,
Beloved wife; I cannot tell if witches be or
　no.
We on the judgment-throne have sat in place
　of God too long;
I fear me much lest we have done His flock
　a grievous wrong:

"And this before my brethren will I testify
　to-day."
Around him quiet wooded isles and placid
　waters lay,
As unto Salem-Side he crossed. He reached
　the court-room small,
Just as a shrill, unearthly shriek echoed from
　wall to wall.

"Woe! Mistress Hale tormenteth me! She
　came in like a bird,
Perched on her husband's shoulder!" Then
　silence fell; no word
Spake either judge or minister, while with
　profound amaze
Each fixed upon the other's face his horror-
　stricken gaze.

But, while the accuser writhed in wild con-
　tortions on the floor,
One rose and said, "Let all withdraw! the
　court is closed!" no more:
For well the land knew Mistress Hale's rare
　loveliness and worth;
Her virtues bloomed like flowers of heaven
　along the paths of earth.

The minister of Beverly went homeward rid-
　ing fast;
His wife shrank back from his strange look,
　affrighted and aghast.
"Dear wife thou ailest! Shut thyself into thy
　room!" said he;
"Whoever comes, the latch-string keep
　drawn in from all save me!"

Nor his life's treasure from close guard did he
　one moment lose,
Until across the ferry came a messenger with
　news
That the bewitched ones acted now vain
　mummeries of woe;
The judges looked and wondered still, but
　all the accused let go.

The dark cloud rolled from off the land; the
    golden leaves dropped down
Along the winding wood-paths of the little
    sea-side town:
In Salem Village there was peace; with witch-
    craft-trials passed
The nightmare-terror from the vexed New
    England air at last.

Again in natural tones men dared to laugh
    aloud and speak;
From Naugus Head the fisher's shout rang
    back to Jeffrey's Creek;
The phantom-soldiery withdrew, that haunted
    Gloucester shore;
The teamster's voice through Wenham Woods
    broke into psalms once more.

The minister of Beverly thereafter sorely
    grieved
That he had inquisition held with counsellors
    deceived;
Forsaking love's unerring light and duty's
    solid ground,
And groping in the shadowy void, where
    truth is never found.

Errors are almost trespasses; rarely indeed
    we know
How our mistakes hurt other hearts, until
    some random blow

Has well-nigh broken our own. Alas! regret
    could not restore
To lonely hearths the presences that glad-
    dened them before.

As with the grain our fathers sowed sprang
    up Old England's weeds,
So to their lofty piety clung superstition's seeds.
Though tares grow with it, wheat is wheat:
    by food from heaven we live:
Yet whoso asks for daily bread must add,
    "Our sins forgive!"

Truth made transparent in a life, tried gold of
    character,
Were Mistress Hale's, and this is all that his-
    tory says of her;
Their simple force, like sunlight, broke the
    hideous midnight spell,
And sight restored again to eyes obscured
    by films of hell.

The minister's long fields are still with dews
    of summer wet;
The roof that sheltered Mistress Hale tradi-
    tion points to yet.
Green be her memory ever kept all over
    Cape-Ann-Side,
Whose unobtrusive excellence awed back
    delusion's tide!

Lucy Larcom.

CHAPTER VIII

THE STRUGGLE FOR THE CONTINENT

While England was colonizing the Atlantic
seaboard, France was firmly establishing herself
to the north along the St. Lawrence. It was in-
evitable that war should follow; and as early as
1613 the English had destroyed the French settle-
ments in Nova Scotia. The country had scarcely
rallied from the blow, when it was torn asunder
by the contest between Charles la Tour and the
Chevalier D'Aulnay — a contest which, after
twelve years, resulted in victory for the latter.

ST. JOHN

[April, 1647]

"To the winds give our banner!
    Bear homeward again!"
Cried the Lord of Acadia,
    Cried Charles of Estienne!

From the prow of his shallop
    He gazed, as the sun
From its bed in the ocean,
    Streamed up the St. John.

O'er the blue western waters
    That shallop had passed,
Where the mists of Penobscot
    Clung damp on her mast.
St. Saviour had looked
    On the heretic sail,
As the songs of the Huguenot
    Rose on the gale.

The pale, ghostly fathers
    Remembered her well,
And had cursed her while passing,
    With taper and bell:

But the men of Monhegan,
　Of Papists abhorred,
Had welcomed and feasted
　The heretic Lord.

They had loaded his shallop
　With dun-fish and ball,
With stores for his larder,
　And steel for his wall.
Pemaquid, from her bastions
　And turrets of stone,
Had welcomed his coming
　With banner and gun.

And the prayers of the elders
　Had followed his way,
As homeward he glided,
　Down Pentecost Bay.
Oh, well sped La Tour!
　For, in peril and pain,
His lady kept watch,
　For his coming again.

O'er the Isle of the Pheasant
　The morning sun shone,
On the plane-trees which shaded
　The shores of St. John.
'Now, why from yon battlements
　Speaks not my love!
Why waves there no banner
　My fortress above?"

Dark and wild, from his deck
　St. Estienne gazed about,
On fire-wasted dwellings,
　And silent redoubt;
From the low, shattered walls
　Which the flame had o'errun,
There floated no banner,
　There thundered no gun!

But beneath the low arch
　Of its doorway there stood
A pale priest of Rome,
　In his cloak and his hood.
With the bound of a lion,
　La Tour sprang to land,
On the throat of the Papist
　He fastened his hand.

'Speak, son of the Woman
　Of scarlet and sin!
What wolf has been prowling
　My castle within?"

From the grasp of the soldier
　The Jesuit broke,
Half in scorn, half in sorrow,
　He smiled as he spoke:

"No wolf, Lord of Estienne,
　Has ravaged thy hall,
But thy red-handed rival,
　With fire, steel, and ball!
On an errand of mercy
　I hitherward came,
While the walls of thy castle
　Yet spouted with flame.

"Pentagoet's dark vessels
　Were moored in the bay,
Grim sea-lions, roaring
　Aloud for their prey."
"But what of my lady?"
　Cried Charles of Estienne.
"On the shot-crumbled turret
　Thy lady was seen:

"Half-veiled in the smoke-cloud,
　Her hand grasped thy pennon,
While her dark tresses swayed
　In the hot breath of cannon!
But woe to the heretic,
　Evermore woe!
When the son of the church
　And the cross is his foe!

"In the track of the shell,
　In the path of the ball,
Pentagoet swept over
　The breach of the wall!
Steel to steel, gun to gun,
　One moment, — and then
Alone stood the victor,
　Alone with his men!

"Of its sturdy defenders,
　Thy lady alone
Saw the cross-blazoned banner
　Float over St. John."
"Let the dastard look to it!"
　Cried fiery Estienne,
"Were D'Aulnay King Louis,
　I'd free her again!"

"Alas for thy lady!
　No service from thee
Is needed by her
　Whom the Lord hath set free:

Nine days, in stern silence,
  Her thraldom she bore,
But the tenth morning came,
  And Death opened her door!"

As if suddenly smitten
  La Tour staggered back;
His hand grasped his sword-hilt,
  His forehead grew black.
He sprang on the deck
  Of his shallop again.
"We cruise now for vengeance!
  Give away!" cried Estienne.

"Massachusetts shall hear
  Of the Huguenot's wrong,
And from island and creekside
  Her fishers shall throng!
Pentagoet shall rue
  What his Papists have done,
When his palisades echo
  The Puritan's gun!"

Oh, the loveliest of heavens
  Hung tenderly o'er him,
There were waves in the sunshine,
  And green isles before him;
But a pale hand was beckoning
  The Huguenot on;
And in blackness and ashes
  Behind was St. John!
            JOHN GREENLEAF WHITTIER.

The rivalry between the colonists for the fur
trade grew steadily more bitter, and in 1690 (King
William's War) Canada undertook the conquest
of New York and destroyed a number of frontier
towns. The English made some reprisals; Sir
William Phips capturing Acadia and Major Peter
Schuyler leading a raid into the country south of
Montreal, where he defeated a considerable body
of French and Indians under Valrennes, in a
spirited fight at La Prairie.

THE BATTLE OF LA PRAIRIE

[1691]

THAT was a brave old epoch,
  Our age of chivalry,
When the Briton met the Frenchman
  At the fight of La Prairie;
And the manhood of New England,
  And the Netherlanders true
And Mohawks sworn, gave battle
  To the Bourbon's lilied blue.

That was a brave old governor
  Who gathered his array,
And stood to meet, he knew not what,
  On that alarming day.
Eight hundred, amid rumors vast
  That filled the wild wood's gloom,
With all New England's flower of youth,
  Fierce for New France's doom.

And the brave old half five hundred!
  Theirs should in truth be fame;
Borne down the savage Richelieu,
  On what emprise they came!
Your hearts are great enough, O few:
  Only your numbers fail, —
New France asks more for conquerors,
  All glorious though your tale.

It was a brave old battle
  That surged around the fort,
When D'Hosta fell in charging,
  And 't was deadly strife and short;
When in the very quarters
  They contested face and hand,
And many a goodly fellow
  Crimsoned yon La Prairie sand.

And those were brave old orders
  The colonel gave to meet
That forest force with trees entrenched
  Opposing the retreat:
"De Callière's strength's behind us,
  And in front your Richelieu;
We must go straightforth at them;
  There is nothing else to do."

And then the brave old story comes,
  Of Schuyler and Valrennes,
When "Fight" the British colonel called,
  Encouraging his men,
" For the Protestant Religion
  And the honor of our King!" —
"Sir, I am here to answer you!"
  Valrennes cried, forthstepping.

Were not those brave old races?
  Well, here they still abide;
And yours is one or other,
  And the second's at your side;
So when you hear your brother say,
  "Some loyal deed I'll do,"
Like old Valrennes, be ready with
  "I'm here to answer you!"
WILLIAM DOUW SCHUYLER-LIGHTHALL.

Peace was declared in 1697, but hostilities began again five years later, and early in 1704 Vaudreuil, governor of Canada, dispatched a force of three hundred, under Hertel de Rouville, against Deerfield, on the northwestern frontier of Massachusetts. They reached their destination a little before daylight of February 29, and, finding the sentinels asleep and the snow drifted over the palisades, rushed the place, and carried it, with the exception of one block-house, which held out successfully.

THE SACK OF DEERFIELD

[February 29, 1704]

Of the onset, fear-inspiring, and the firing and the pillage
  Of our village, when De Rouville with his forces on us fell,
When, ere dawning of the morning, with no death-portending warning,
  With no token shown or spoken, came the foeman, hear me tell.

High against the palisadoes, on the meadows, banks, and hill-sides,
  At the rill-sides, over fences, lay the lingering winter snow;
And so high by tempest rifted, at our pickets it was drifted,
  That its frozen crust was chosen as a bridge to bear the foe.

We had set at night a sentry, lest an entry, while the sombre
  Heavy slumber was upon us, by the Frenchman should be made;
But the faithless knave we posted, though of wakefulness he boasted,
  'Stead of keeping watch was sleeping, and his solemn trust betrayed.

Than our slumber none profounder; never sounder fell on sleeper,
  Never deeper sleep its shadow cast on dull and listless frames;
But it fled before the crashing of the portals, and the flashing,
  And the soaring, and the roaring, and the crackling of the flames.

Fell the shining hatchets quickly 'mid the thickly crowded women,
  Growing dim in crimson currents from the pulses of the brain·

Rained the balls from firelocks deadly, till the melted snow ran redly
  With the glowing torrent flowing from the bodies of the slain.

I, from pleasant dreams awaking at the breaking of my casement,
  With amazement saw the foemen enter quickly where I lay;
Heard my wife and children's screaming, as the hatchets woke their dreaming,
  Heard their groaning and their moaning as their spirits passed away.

'T was in vain I struggled madly as the sadly sounding pleading
  Of my bleeding, dying darlings fell upon my tortured ears;
'T was in vain I wrestled, raging, fight against their numbers waging,
  Crowding round me there they bound me, while my manhood sank in tears.

At the spot to which they bore me, no one o'er me watched or warded;
  There unguarded, bound and shivering, on the snow I lay alone;
Watching by the firelight ruddy, as the butchers dark and bloody,
  Slew the nearest friends and dearest to my memory ever known.

And it seemed, as rose the roaring blaze up soaring, redly streaming
  O'er the gleaming snow around me through the shadows of the night,
That the figures flitting fastly were the fiend at revels ghastly,
  Madly urging on the surging, seething billows of the fight.

Suddenly my gloom was lightened, hope was heightened, though the shrieking,
  Malice-wreaking, ruthless wretches death were scattering to and fro;
For a knife lay there — I spied it, and a tomahawk beside it
  Glittering brightly, buried lightly, keen edge upward, in the snow.

Naught knew I how came they thither, nor from whither; naught to me then
  If the heathen dark, my captors, dropped those weapons there or no;

Quickly drawn o'er axe-edge lightly, cords
    were cut that held me tightly,
  Then, with engines of my vengeance in my
    hands, I sought the foe.

Oh, what anger dark, consuming, fearful,
    glooming, looming horrid,
  Lit my forehead, draped my figure, leapt
    with fury from my glance;
'Midst the foemen rushing frantic, to their
    sight I seemed gigantic,
  Like the motion of the ocean, like a tempest
    my advance.

Stoutest of them all, one savage left the ravage
    round and faced me;
  Fury braced me, for I knew him — he my
    pleading wife had slain.
Huge he was, and brave and brawny, but I
    met the slayer tawny,
  And with rigorous blow, and vigorous,
    clove his tufted skull in twain —
Madly dashing down the crashing bloody
    hatchet in his brain.

As I brained him rose their calling, "Lo!
    appalling from yon meadow
  The Monedo of the white man comes with
    vengeance in his train!"
As they fled, my blows Titanic falling fast
    increased their panic,
  Till their shattered forces scattered widely
    o'er the snowy plain.

Stern De Rouville then their error, born of
    terror, soon dispersing,
  Loudly cursing them for folly, roused their
    pride with words of scorn;
Peering cautiously they knew me, then by
    numbers overthrew me;
  Fettered surely, bound securely, there again
    I lay forlorn.

Well I knew their purpose horrid, on each
    forehead it was written —
  Pride was smitten that their bravest had
    retreated at my ire;
For the rest the captive's durance, but for me
    there was assurance
  Of the tortures known to martyrs — of the
    terrible death by fire.

Then I felt, though horror-stricken, pulses
    quicken as the swarthy
  Savage, or the savage Frenchman, fiercest
    of the cruel band,

Darted in and out the shadows, through the
    shivered palisadoes,
  Death-blows dealing with unfeeling heart
    and never-sparing hand.

Soon the sense of horror left me, and bereft
    me of all feeling;
  Soon, revealing all my early golden mo-
    ments, memory came;
Showing how, when young and sprightly, with
    a footstep falling lightly,
  I had pondered as I wandered on the maid
    I loved to name.

Her, so young, so pure, so dove-like, that the
    love-like angels whom a
  Sweet aroma circles ever wheresoe'er they
    move their wings,
Felt with her the air grow sweeter, felt with
    her their joy completer,
  Felt their gladness swell to madness, silent
    grow their silver strings.

Then I heard her voice's murmur breathing
    summer, while my spirit
  Leaned to hear it and to drink it like a
    draught of pleasant wine;
Felt her head upon my shoulder drooping as
    my love I told her;
  Felt the utterly pleased flutter of her heart
    respond to mine.

Then I saw our darlings clearly that more
    nearly linked our gladness;
  Saw our sadness as a lost one sank from
    pain to happy rest;
Mingled tears with hers and chid her, bade
    her by our love consider
  How our dearest now was nearest to the
    blessed Master's breast.

I had lost that wife so cherished, who had
    perished, passed from being,
  In my seeing — I, unable to protect her or
    defend;
At that thought dispersed those fancies, born
    of woe-begotten trances,
  While unto me came the gloomy present
    hour my heart to rend.

For I heard the firelocks ringing fiercely
    flinging forth the whirring,
  Blood-preferring leaden bullets from a gar-
    risoned abode;

There it stood so grim and lonely, speaking
  of its tenants only,
  When the furious leaden couriers from its
    loopholes fastly rode.

And the seven who kept it stoutly, though
  devoutly triumph praying,
  Ceased not slaying, trusting somewhat to
    their firelocks and their wives;
For while they the house were holding, balls
  the wives were quickly moulding —
  Neither fearful, wild, nor tearful, toiling
    earnest for their lives.

Onward rushed each dusky leaguer, hot and
  eager, but the seven
  Rained the levin from their firelocks as the
    Pagans forward pressed;
Melting at that murderous firing, back that
  baffled foe retiring,
  Left there lying, dead or dying, ten, their
    bravest and their best.

Rose the red sun, straightly throwing from
  his glowing disk his brightness
  On the whiteness of the snowdrifts and the
    ruins of the town —
On those houses well defended, where the foe
  in vain expended
  Ball and powder, standing prouder, smoke-
    begrimed and scarred and brown.

Not for us those rays shone fairly, tinting
  rarely dawning early
  With the pearly light and glistering of the
    March's snowy morn;
Some were wounded, some were weary, some
  were sullen, all were dreary,
  As the sorrow of that morrow shed its cloud
    of woe forlorn.

Then we heard De Rouville's orders, "To the
  borders!" and the dismal,
  Dark abysmal fate before us opened widely
    as he spoke;
But we heard a shout in distance — into
  fluttering existence,
  Brief but splendid, quickly ended, at the
    sound our hopes awoke.

'T was our kinsmen armed and ready, sweep-
  ing steady to the nor'ward,
  Pressing forward fleet and fearless, though
    in scanty force they came —

Cried De Rouville, grimly speaking, "Is't our
  captives you are seeking?
  Well, with iron we environ them, and wall
    them round with flame.

"With the toil of blood we won them, we've
  undone them with our bravery;
  Off to slavery, then, we carry them or leave
    them lifeless here.
Foul my shame so far to wander, and my
  soldiers' blood to squander
  'Mid the slaughter free as water, should our
    prey escape us clear.

"Off, ye scum of peasants Saxon, and your
  backs on Frenchmen turning,
  To our burning, dauntless courage proper
    tribute promptly pay;
Do you come to seize and beat us? Are you
  here to slay and eat us?
  If your meat be Gaul and Mohawk, we will
    starve you out to-day."

How my spirit raged to hear him, standing
  near him bound and helpless!
  Never whelpless tigress fiercer howled at
    slayer of her young,
When secure behind his engines, he has baf-
  fled her of vengeance,
  Than did I there, forced to lie there while
    his bitter taunts he flung.

For I heard each leaden missile whirr and
  whistle from the trusty
  Firelock rusty, brought there after long
    time absence from the strife,
And was forced to stand in quiet, with my
  warm blood running riot,
  When for power to give an hour to battle
    I had bartered life.

All in vain they thus had striven; backward
  driven, beat and broken,
  Leaving token of their coming in the dead
    around the dell,
They retreated — well it served us! their
  retreat from death preserved us,
  Though the order for our murder from the
    dark De Rouville fell.

As we left our homes in ashes, through the
  lashes of the sternest
  Welled the earnest tears of anguish for the
    dear ones passed away:

Sick at heart and heavily loaded, though with
 cruel blows they goaded,
Sorely cumbered, miles we numbered four
 alone that weary day.

They were tired themselves of tramping, for
 encamping they were ready,
 Ere the steady twilight newer pallor threw
  upon the snow;
So they built them huts of branches, in the
 snow they scooped out trenches,
 Heaped up firing, then, retiring, let us sleep
  our sleep of woe.

By the wrist — and by no light hand — to the
 right hand of a painted,
Murder-tainted, loathsome Pagan, with a
 jeer, I soon was tied;
And the one to whom they bound me, 'mid the
 scoffs of those around me,
 Bowing to me, mocking, drew me down
  to slumber at his side.

As for me, be sure I slept not: slumber crept
 not on my senses;
 Less intense is lover's musing than a cap-
  tive's bent on ways
To escape from fearful thralling, and a death
 by fire appalling;
 So, unsleeping, I was keeping on the
  Northern Star my gaze.

There I lay — no muscle stirring, mind un-
 erring, thought unswerving,
 Body nerving, till a death-like, breathless
  slumber fell around;
Then my right hand cautious stealing, o'er
 my bed-mate's person feeling,
 Till each finger stooped to linger on the belt
  his waist that bound.

'T was his knife — the handle clasping,
 firmly grasping, forth I drew it,
 Clinging to it firm, but softly, with a more
  than robber's art;
As I drove it to its utter length of blade, I
 heard the flutter
 Of a snow-bird — ah! 't was *no* bird!
  t was the flutter of my heart.

Then I cut the cord that bound me, peered
 around me, rose uprightly,
 Stepped as lightly as a lover on his blessed
  bridal day ·

Swiftly as my need inclined me, kept the
 bright North Star behind me,
And, ere dawning of the morning, I was
 twenty miles away.
     THOMAS DUNN ENGLISH.

Under French officers and priests, the war con-
tinued to be conducted with a cruelty as aimless
as it was brutal. Isolated hamlets were burned,
and their inhabitants tortured or taken prisoners,
only, for the most part, to be butchered on the
way to Canada. On August 29, 1708, a party of
French and Indians, under De Chaillons and the
infamous De Rouville, surprised the town of
Haverhill. Rushing upon it, as their custom was,
just before daylight, they fired several houses,
plundered others, and killed some thirty or forty
of the inhabitants. The townspeople rallied, and
after an hour's fighting drove away the assailants,
killing nearly thirty, among them De Rouville
himself.

PENTUCKET

[August 29, 1708]

How sweetly on the wood-girt town
The mellow light of sunset shone!
Each small, bright lake, whose waters still
Mirror the forest and the hill,
Reflected from its waveless breast
The beauty of a cloudless west,
Glorious as if a glimpse were given
Within the western gates of heaven,
Left, by the spirit of the star
Of sunset's holy hour, ajar!

Beside the river's tranquil flood
The dark and low-walled dwellings stood,
Where many a rood of open land
Stretched up and down on either hand,
With corn-leaves waving freshly green
The thick and blackened stumps between
Behind, unbroken, deep and dread,
The wild, untravelled forest spread,
Back to those mountains, white and cold,
Of which the Indian trapper told,
Upon whose summits never yet
Was mortal foot in safety set.

Quiet and calm without a fear
Of danger darkly lurking near,
The weary laborer left his plough,
The milkmaid carolled by her cow;
From cottage door and household hearth
Rose songs of praise, or tones of mirth.
At length the murmur died away,
And silence on that village lay.

— So slept Pompeii, tower and hall,
Ere the quick earthquake swallowed all,
Undreaming of the fiery fate
Which made its dwellings desolate!

Hours passed away. By moonlight sped
The Merrimac along his bed.
Bathed in the pallid lustre, stood
Dark cottage-wall and rock and wood,
Silent, beneath that tranquil beam,
As the hushed grouping of a dream.
Yet on the still air crept a sound,
No bark of fox, nor rabbit's bound,
No stir of wings, nor waters flowing,
Nor leaves in midnight breezes blowing.

Was that the tread of many feet,
Which downward from the hillside beat?
What forms were those which darkly stood
Just on the margin of the wood?
Charred tree-stumps in the moonlight dim,
Or paling rude, or leafless limb?
No, — through the trees fierce eyeballs glowed,
Dark human forms in moonshine showed,
Wild from their native wilderness,
With painted limbs and battle-dress!

A yell the dead might wake to hear
Swelled on the night air, far and clear;
Then smote the Indian tomahawk
On crashing door and shattering lock;
Then rang the rifle-shot, and then
The shrill death-scream of stricken men, —
Sank the red axe in woman's brain,
And childhood's cry arose in vain.
Bursting through roof and window came,
Red, fast, and fierce, the kindled flame,
And blended fire and moonlight glared
On still dead men and scalp-knives bared.

The morning sun looked brightly through
The river willows, wet with dew.
No sound of combat filled the air,
No shout was heard, nor gunshot there;
Yet still the thick and sullen smoke
From smouldering ruins slowly broke;
And on the greensward many a stain,
And, here and there, the mangled slain,
Told how that midnight bolt had sped,
Pentucket, on thy fated head!

Even now the villager can tell
Where Rolfe beside his hearthstone fell,
Still show the door of wasting oak,
Through which the fatal death-stroke broke,

And point the curious stranger where
De Rouville's corse lay grim and bare;
Whose hideous head, in death still feared,
Bore not a trace of hair or beard;
And still, within the churchyard ground,
Heaves darkly up the ancient mound,
Whose grass-grown surface overlies
The victims of that sacrifice.

                    JOHN GREENLEAF WHITTIER.

Though the Peace of Utrecht (1714) closed the war, desultory raids continued. In April, 1725, John Lovewell, of Dunstable, with forty-six men, marched against the Indian town of Pigwacket, or Pequawket (now Fryeburg). On the morning of May 8 they were suddenly attacked by a large force of Indians who had formed an ambuscade. Twelve men fell at the first fire, among them Lovewell himself. The survivors fought against heavy odds until sunset, when the Indians drew off without having been able to scalp the dead. It was this battle, in its day "as famous in New England as was Chevy Chase on the Scottish border," which inspired the earliest military ballad, still extant, composed in America. Its author is unknown, but it was for many years "the best beloved song in all New England."

LOVEWELL'S FIGHT

[May 8, 1725]

Of worthy Captain Lovewell I purpose now
        to sing,
How valiantly he served his country and his
        King;
He and his valiant soldiers did range the
        woods full wide,
And hardships they endured to quell the
        Indian's pride.

'Twas nigh unto Pigwacket, on the eighth
        day of May,
They spied a rebel Indian soon after break of
        day;
He on a bank was walking, upon a neck of
        land,
Which leads into a pond as we're made to
        understand.

Our men resolv'd to have him, and travell'd
        two miles round,
Until they met the Indian, who boldly stood
        his ground;
Then spake up Captain Lovewell, "Take
        you good heed," says he,
"This rogue is to decoy us, I very plainly see.

"The Indians lie in ambush, in some place
　　nigh at hand,
In order to surround us upon this neck of
　　land;
Therefore we'll march in order, and each man
　　leave his pack
That we may briskly fight them, when they
　　make their attack."

They came unto this Indian, who did them
　　thus defy,
As soon as they came nigh him, two guns he
　　did let fly,
Which wounded Captain Lovewell, and like-
　　wise one man more,
But when this rogue was running, they laid him
　　in his gore.

Then having scalp'd the Indian, they went
　　back to the spot
Where they had laid their packs down, but
　　there they found them not,
For the Indians having spy'd them, when they
　　them down did lay,
Did seize them for their plunder, and carry
　　them away.

These rebels lay in ambush, this very place
　　hard by,
So that an English soldier did one of them
　　espy,
And cried out, "Here's an Indian," with that
　　they started out,
As fiercely as old lions, and hideously did
　　shout.

With that our valiant English all gave a loud
　　huzza,
To show the rebel Indians they fear'd them
　　not a straw:
So now the fight began, and as fiercely as
　　could be,
The Indians ran up to them, but soon were
　　forced to flee.

Then spake up Captain Lovewell, when first
　　the fight began:
"Fight on, my valiant heroes! you see they
　　fall like rain."
For as we are inform'd, the Indians were so
　　thick
A man could scarcely fire a gun and not some
　　of them hit.

Then did the rebels try their best our soldiers
　　to surround,
But they could not accomplish it, because
　　there was a pond,
To which our men retreated, and covered all
　　the rear,
The rogues were forc'd to face them, altho
　　they skulked for fear.

Two logs there were behind them that close
　　together lay,
Without being discovered, they could not
　　get away;
Therefore our valiant English they travell'd
　　in a row,
And at a handsome distance, as they were
　　wont to go.

'T was ten o'clock in the morning when first
　　the fight begun,
And fiercely did continue until the setting
　　sun;
Excepting that the Indians some hours be-
　　fore 't was night
Drew off into the bushes and ceas'd awhile
　　to fight,

But soon again returned, in fierce and furious
　　mood,
Shouting as in the morning, but yet not half so
　　loud;
For as we are informed, so thick and fast they
　　fell,
Scarce twenty of their number at night did
　　get home well.

And that our valiant English till midnight
　　there did stay,
To see whether the rebels would have another
　　fray;
But they no more returning, they made off
　　towards their home,
And brought away their wounded as far as
　　they could come.

Of all our valiant English there were but
　　thirty-four,
And of the rebel Indians there were about
　　fourscore.
And sixteen of our English did safely home
　　return,
The rest were kill'd and wounded, for which
　　we all must mourn.

Our worthy Captain Lovewell among them
    there did die,
They killed Lieutenant Robbins, and wounded
    good young Frye,
Who was our English Chaplain; he many
    Indians slew,
And some of them he scalp'd when bullets
    round him flew.

Young Fullam, too, I'll mention, because he
    fought so well,
Endeavoring to save a man, a sacrifice he fell:
But yet our valiant Englishmen in fight were
    ne'er dismay'd,
But still they kept their motion, and Wymans
    Captain made,

Who shot the old chief Paugus, which did the
    foe defeat,
Then set his men in order, and brought off
    the retreat;
And braving many dangers and hardships in
    the way,
They safe arriv'd at Dunstable, the thirteenth
    day of May.

The story of Lovewell's fight is told in another
ballad printed in Farmer and Moore's Historical
Collections in 1824. It is an excellent example of
ballad literature, describing the struggle in great
detail and with unusual accuracy.

LOVEWELL'S FIGHT

[May 8, 1725]

WHAT time the noble Lovewell came,
    With fifty men from Dunstable,
The cruel Pequa'tt tribe to tame,
    With arms and bloodshed terrible,

Then did the crimson streams, that flowed,
    Seem like the waters of the brook,
That brightly shine, that loudly dash
    Far down the cliffs of Agiochook.

With Lovewell brave, John Harwood came;
    From wife and babes 't was hard to part,
Young Harwood took her by the hand,
    And bound the weeper to his heart.

Repress that tear, my Mary, dear,
    Said Harwood to his loving wife,
It tries me hard to leave thee here,
    And seek in distant woods the strife.

When gone, my Mary, think of me,
    And pray to God, that I may be,
Such as one ought that lives for thee,
    And come at last in victory.

Thus left young Harwood babe and wife,
    With accent wild she bade adieu;
It grieved those lovers much to part,
    So fond and fair, so kind and true.

Seth Wyman, who in Woburn lived
    (A marksman he of courage true),
Shot the first Indian whom they saw,
    Sheer through his heart the bullet flew.

The savage had been seeking game,
    Two guns and eke a knife he bore,
And two black ducks were in his hand,
    He shrieked, and fell, to rise no more.

Anon, there eighty Indians rose,
    Who'd hid themselves in ambush dread;
Their knives they shook, their guns they
    aimed,
    The famous Paugus at their head.

Good heavens! they dance the Powow dance,
    What horrid yells the forest fill?
The grim bear crouches in his den,
    The eagle seeks the distant hill.

What means this dance, this Powow dance?
    Stern Wyman said; with wonderous art,
He crept full near, his rifle aimed,
    And shot the leader through the heart.

John Lovewell, captain of the band,
    His sword he waved, that glittered bright,
For the last time he cheered his men,
    And led them onward to the fight.

Fight on, fight on, brave Lovewell said,
    Fight on, while heaven shall give you breath
An Indian ball then pierced him through,
    And Lovewell closed his eyes in death.

John Harwood died all bathed in blood,
    When he had fought, till set of day;
And many more we may not name,
    Fell in that bloody battle fray.

When news did come to Harwood's wife,
    That he with Lovewell fought and died
Far in the wilds had given his life,
    Nor more would in their home abide,

Such grief did seize upon her mind,
  Such sorrow filled her faithful breast;
On earth, she ne'er found peace again,
  But followed Harwood to his rest.

'T was Paugus led the Pequa'tt tribe; —
  As runs the Fox, would Paugus run;
As howls the wild wolf, would he howl,
  A large bear skin had Paugus on.

But Chamberlain, of Dunstable
  (One whom a savage ne'er shall slay),
Met Paugus by the water side,
  And shot him dead upon that day.

Good heavens! Is this a time for pray'r?
  Is this a time to worship God?
When Lovewell's men are dying fast,
  And Paugus' tribe hath felt the rod?

The Chaplain's name was Jonathan Frye;
  In Andover his father dwelt,
And oft with Lovewell's men he'd prayed,
  Before the mortal wound he felt.

A man was he of comely form,
  Polished and brave, well learnt and kind;
Old Harvard's learned halls he left,
  Far in the wilds a grave to find.

Ah! now his blood-red arm he lifts,
  His closing lids he tries to raise;
And speak once more before he dies,
  In supplication and in praise.

He prays kind heaven to grant success,
  Brave Lovewell's men to guide and bless,
And when they've shed their heart blood true,
  To raise them all to happiness.

Come hither, Farwell, said young Frye,
  You see that I'm about to die;
Now for the love I bear to you,
  When cold in death my bones shall lie;

Go thou and see my parents dear,
  And tell them you stood by me here;
Console them when they cry, Alas!
  And wipe away the falling tear.

Lieutenant Farwell took his hand,
  His arm around his neck he threw,
And said, brave Chaplain, I could wish,
  That heaven had made me die for you.

The Chaplain on kind Farwell's breast,
  Bloody and languishing he fell;
Nor after this said more, but this,
  "I love thee, soldier, fare thee well."

Ah! many a wife shall rend her hair,
  And many a child cry, "Wo is me!"
When messengers the news shall bear,
  Of Lovewell's dear bought victory.

With footsteps slow shall travellers go,
  Where Lovewell's pond shines clear and
    bright,
And mark the place, where those are laid,
  Who fell in Lovewell's bloody fight.

Old men shall shake their heads, and say,
  Sad was the hour and terrible,
When Lóvewell brave 'gainst Paugus went,
  With fifty men from Dunstable.

The fight near Lovewell's Pond was the
ground of still another case of literary priority.
Nearly a hundred years after its occurrence, on
November 17, 1820, the Portland *Gazette* printed
the first poetical venture of a lad of thirteen years.
It bore the title of "The Battle of Lovell's Pond."
Its author was Henry Wadsworth Longfellow.

THE BATTLE OF LOVELL'S POND

[May 8, 1725]

COLD, cold is the north wind and rude is the
    blast
That sweeps like a hurricane loudly and
    fast,
As it moans through the tall waving pines
    lone and drear,
Sighs a requiem sad o'er the warrior's bier.

The war-whoop is still, and the savage's yell
Has sunk into silence along the wild dell;
The din of the battle, the tumult, is o'er,
And the war-clarion's voice is now heard no
    more.

The warriors that fought for their country,
    and bled,
Have sunk to their rest; the damp earth is
    their bed;
No stone tells the place where their ashes
    repose,
Nor points out the spot from the graves of
    their foes.

They died in their glory, surrounded by
  fame,
And Victory's loud trump their death did
  proclaim;
They are dead; but they live in each Patriot's
  breast,
And their names are engraven on honor's
  bright crest.
        HENRY WADSWORTH LONGFELLOW.

The English gained a notable victory in the
summer of 1745 when they captured the formida-
ble fortress of Louisburg, which had been built
by the French on the eastern coast of Cape Breton
Island. News of the victory created the greatest
joy throughout the colonies.

LOUISBURG

[June 17, 1745]

NEPTUNE and Mars in Council sate
  To humble France's pride,
Whose vain unbridled insolence
  All other Powers defied.

The gods having sat in deep debate
  Upon the puzzling theme,
Broke up perplexed and both agreed
  Shirley should form the scheme.

Shirley, with Britain's glory fired,
  Heaven's favoring smile implored:
"Let Louisburg return," — he said,
  "Unto its ancient Lord."

At once the Camp and Fleet were filled
  With Britain's loyal sons,
Whose hearts are filled with generous strife
  T' avenge their Country's wrongs.

With Liberty their breasts are filled,
  Fair Liberty's their shield;
'T is Liberty their banner waves
  And hovers o'er their field.

Louis! — behold the unequal strife,
  Thy slaves in walls immured!
While George's sons laugh at those walls —
  Of victory assured.

One key to your oppressive pride
  Your Western Dunkirk's gone;
So Pepperell and Warren bade
  And what they bade was done!

Forbear, proud Prince, your gasconades,
  Te Deums cease to sing, —
When Britains fight the *Grand Monarque*
  Must yield to Britain's King.
      BOSTON, December, 1745.

Louis XV felt the loss of Louisburg keenly,
and in 1746, to avenge its fall, sent a strong fleet,
under Admiral D'Anville, against Boston. The
town was terror-stricken; but after many mis-
haps the fleet was finally dispersed by a great
storm off Cape Sable, on October 15, 1746, and
such of the ships as lived through it were forced
to make their way back to France.

A BALLAD OF THE FRENCH FLEET

[October 15, 1746]

MR. THOMAS PRINCE, *loquitur*

A FLEET with flags arrayed
  Sailed from the port of Brest,
And the Admiral's ship displayed
  The signal: "Steer southwest."
For this Admiral D'Anville
  Had sworn by cross and crown
To ravage with fire and steel
  Our helpless Boston Town.

There were rumors in the street,
  In the houses there was fear
Of the coming of the fleet,
  And the danger hovering near.
And while from mouth to mouth
  Spread the tidings of dismay,
I stood in the Old South,
  Saying humbly: "Let us pray!

'O Lord! we would not advise;
  But if in thy Providence
A tempest should arise
  To drive the French Fleet hence,
And scatter it far and wide,
  Or sink it in the sea,
We should be satisfied,
  And thine the glory be."

This was the prayer I made,
  For my soul was all on flame,
And even as I prayed
  The answering tempest came;
It came with a mighty power,
  Shaking the windows and walls,
And tolling the bell in the tower,
  As it tolls at funerals.

The lightning suddenly
    Unsheathed its flaming sword,
And I cried: "Stand still, and see
    The salvation of the Lord!"
The heavens were black with cloud,
    The sea was white with hail,
And ever more fierce and loud
    Blew the October gale.

The fleet it overtook,
    And the broad sails in the van
Like, the tents of Cushan shook,
    Or the curtains of Midian.
Down on the reeling decks
    Crashed the o'erwhelming seas;
Ah, never were there wrecks
    So pitiful as these!

Like a potter's vessel broke
    The great ships of the line;
They were carried away as a smoke,
    Or sank like lead in the brine.
O Lord! before thy path
    They vanished and ceased to be,
When thou didst walk in wrath
    With thine horses through the sea!
        HENRY WADSWORTH LONGFELLOW.

Peace was made at Aix-la-Chapelle in 1748,
but it was really only a truce. England and
France could not be permanently at peace until
one or the other was undisputed master of the
North American continent. The French claimed
all the country west of the Alleghanies and en-
forced their claims by building a string of forts,
among them Fort Duquesne at the head of the
Ohio. At last, in 1755, was "the British Lyon
roused."

THE BRITISH LYON ROUSED

[1755]

HAIL, great Apollo! guide my feeble pen,
To rouse the august lion from his den,
Exciting vengeance on the worst of men.

Rouse, *British Lion*, from thy soft repose,
And take revenge upon the worst of foes,
Who try to ring and hawl you by the nose.

They always did thy quiet breast annoy,
Raising rebellion with the Rival boy,
Seeking thy faith and interest to destroy.

Treaties and oaths they always did break
    thro',
They never did nor wou'd keep faith with
    you
By popes and priests indulged so to do.

All neighboring powers and neutral standers
    by
Look on our cause with an impartial eye,
And see their falseness and their perfidy.

Their grand encroachments on us ne'er did
    cease,
But by indulgence mightily increase,
Killing and scalping us in times of peace.

They buy our scalps exciting savage clans,
In children's blood for to imbue their hands,
Assisted by their cruel Gallic bands.

Britains, strike home, strike home decisive
    blows
Upon the heads of your perfidious foes,
Who always truth and justice did oppose.

Go brave the ocean with your war-like ships,
And speak your terror o'er the western deeps,
And crush the squadrons of the Gallic fleets.

Cleave liquid mountains of the foaming flood,
And tinge the billows with the Gallic blood,
A faithful drubbing to their future good.

Bury their squadrons ill in watery tombs;
And when the news unto Versailles it comes,
Let Lewis swear by Gar and gnaw his thumbs.

Oh! ride triumphant o'er the Gallic powers,
And conquer all these cursed foes of ours,
And sweep the ocean with your iron showers.

While all the tribes in Neptune's spacious
    hall,
Shall stand astonish'd at the cannon ball;
To see such hail-stones down among them fall.

Some of their tribes perhaps are killed dead,
And others in a vast amazement fled,
While Neptune stands aghast and scratch's
    his head.

My roving muse the surface reach again,
Search every part of the Atlantic plain,
And see if any Gallics yet remain;

And if they do, let British cannon roar;
And let thy thunders reach the western shore,
While I shall strive to rouse her sons once
more.
STEPHEN TILDEN.

Active hostilities began early in 1755. On February 20 General Edward Braddock landed at Hampton. Va., and proceeded at once to organize an expedition to march against Fort Duquesne. George Washington, who had already had some bitter experience with the French, was made one of his aides-de-camp. On May 29 the army, with an immense wagon train, began its long journey across the mountains.

THE SONG OF BRADDOCK'S MEN

[May 29, 1755]

To arms, to arms! my jolly grenadiers!
Hark, how the drums do roll it along!
To horse, to horse, with valiant good cheer;
We'll meet our proud foe before it is long.
Let not your courage fail you;
Be valiant, stout and bold;
And it will soon avail you,
My loyal hearts of gold.
Huzzah, my valiant countrymen! again I say
huzzah!
'T is nobly done, — the day's our own, —
huzzah, huzzah!

March on, march on, brave Braddock leads
the foremost;
The battle is begun as you may fairly see.
Stand firm, be bold, and it will soon be over;
We'll soon gain the field from our proud
enemy.
A squadron now appears, my boys;
If that they do but stand!
Boys, never fear, be sure you mind
The word of command!
Huzzah, my valiant countrymen! again I say
huzzah!
'T is nobly done, — the day's our own, —
huzzah, huzzah!

See how, see how, they break and fly before us!
See how they are scattered all over the
plain!
Now, now — now, now our country will
adore us!
In peace and in triumph, boys, when we
return again!
Then laurels shall our glory crown
For all our actions told:

The hills shall echo all around,
My loyal hearts of gold.
Huzzah, my valiant countrymen! again I say
huzzah!
'T is nobly done, — the day's our own, —
huzzah, huzzah!

Braddock, with a picked force of about twelve hundred men, reached the Monongahela July 8 in excellent order, and, on the following morning, with colors flying and drums beating, marched against the fort. The French garrison, under Contrecœur, was in a panic, and ready for flight, but a young captain of regulars named Beaujeu with difficulty obtained permission to take out a small party, mostly Indians, to harass the advancing column. They encountered the English about seven miles from the fort, marching in close order along a narrow road which the pioneers had made. The Indians opened fire, spreading along either flank, and protected by the underbrush. The English, crowded together in the open road, could not see their enemies, and were thrown into confusion. Braddock, wild with rage, refused to permit them to fight in Indian fashion, but beat them back into line with his sword. At last a bullet struck him down, and his troops fled in panic from the field.

BRADDOCK'S FATE, WITH AN INCITEMENT TO REVENGE

[July 9, 1755]

COME all ye sons of Brittany,
Assist my muse in tragedy,
And mourn brave Braddock's destiny,
And spend a mournful day,
Upon Monongahela fields,
The mighty're fallen o'er their shields;
And British blood bedews the hills
Of western Gilboa.

July the ninth, oh! Fatal Day,
They had a bold and bloody fray,
Our host was smote with a dismay;
Some basely did retire,
And left brave Braddock in the field,
Who had much rather die than yield,
A while his sword he bravely wield
In clouds of smoke and fire.

Some time he bravely stood his ground,
A thousand foes did him surround,
Till he received a mortal wound,
Which forc'd him to retreat.
He dy'd upon the thirteenth day,
As he was home-ward on his way;

Alas! alas! we all must say,
  A sore and sad defeat.

Now to his grave this hero's borne,
While savage foes triumph and scorn,
And drooping banners dress his urn,
  And guard him to his tomb.
Heralds and monarchs of the dead,
You that so many worms have fed,
He's coming to your chilly bed,
  Edge close and give him room.

HIS EPITAPH

Beneath this stone brave Braddock lies,
Who always hated cowardice,
But fell a savage sacrifice
  Amidst his Indian foes.
I charge you, heroes, of the ground,
To guard his dark pavilion round,
And keep off all obtruding sound,
  And cherish his repose.

Sleep, sleep, I say, brave valiant man,
Bold death, at last, has bid thee stand
And to resign thy great command,
  And cancel thy commission.
Altho' thou didst not much incline
Thy post and honors to resign;
Now iron slumber doth confine;
  None envy's thy condition.

A SURVEY OF THE FIELD OF BATTLE

Return my muse unto the field,
See what a prospect it doth yield;
Ingrateful to the eyes and smell
  A carnage bath'd in gore,
Lies scalp'd and mangled o'er the hills,
While sanguine rivers fill the dales,
And pale-fac'd horror spreads the fields,
  The like ne'er here before.

And must these sons of Brittany
Be clouded, set in western skies,
And fall a savage sacrifice?
  Oh! 't is a gloomy hour!
My blood boils high in every vein,
To climb the mountains of the slain,
And break the iron jaws in twain,
  Of savage Gallic power.

Our children with their mothers die,
While they aloud for mercy cry;
They kill, and scalp them instantly,

Then fly into the woods,
And make a mock of all their cries,
And bring their scalps a sacrifice
To their infernal deities,
  And praise their demon gods.

Revenge, revenge the harmless blood
Which their inhuman dogs have shed
In every frontier neighborhood,
  For near these hundred years.
Their murdering clan in ambush lies,
To kill and scalp them by surprize,
And free from tender parents' eyes
  Ten hundred thousand tears.

Their sculking, scalping, murdering tricks
Have so enraged old sixty-six,
With legs and arms like withered sticks,
  And youthful vigor gone;
That if he lives another year,
Complete in armor he'll appear,
And laugh at death and scoff at fear,
  To right his country's wrong.

Let young and old, both high and low,
Arm well against this savage foe,
Who all around inviron us so,
  The sons of black delusion.
New England's sons you know their way,
And how to cross them in their play,
And drive these murdering dogs away,
  Unto their last confusion.

One bold effort, oh, let us make,
And at one blow behead the snake,
And then these savage powers will break,
  Which long have us oppress'd.
And this, brave soldiers, will we do
If Heaven and George shall say so too;
And if we drive the matter thro',
  The land will be at rest.

Come every soldier charge your gun,
And let your task be killing one;
Take aim until the work is done;
  Don't throw away your fire,
For he that fires without an aim,
May kill his friend and be to blame,
And in the end come off with shame,
  When forced to retire.

O mother land, we think we're sure.
Sufficient is thy marine powers
To dissipate all eastern showers:
  And if our arms be blest,

Thy sons in *North America*
Will drive these hell-born dogs away
As far beyond the realms of day,
  As east is from the west.

Forbear my muse thy barbarous song,
Upon this theme thou'st dwelt too long,
It is too high and much too strong,
  The learned won't allow.
Much honor should accrue to him
Who ne'er was at their Academ
Come blot out every telesem;
  Get home unto thy plow.
                    STEPHEN TILDEN.

Composed August 20, 1755.

NED BRADDOCK

[July 9, 1755]

SAID the Sword to the Ax, 'twixt the whacks
    and the hacks,
"Who's your bold Berserker, cleaving of
    tracks?
Hewing a highway through greenwood and
    glen,
Foot-free for cattle and heart-free for men?"
— "Braddock of Fontenoy, stubborn and
    grim,
Carving a cross on the wilderness rim;
In his own doom building large for the Lord,
Steeple and State!" said the Ax to the Sword.

Said the Blade to the Ax, "And shall none say
    him Nay?
Never a broadsword to bar him the way?
Never a bush where a Huron may hide,
Or the shot of a Shawnee spit red on his side?"
— Down the long trail from the Fort to the
    ford,
Naked and streaked, plunge a moccasin'd
    horde:
Huron and Wyandot, hot for the bout;
Shawnee and Ottawa, barring him out!

Red'ning the ridge, 'twixt a gorge and a
    gorge,
Bold to the sky, loom the ranks of St. George;
Braddock of Fontenoy, belted and horsed,
For a foe to be struck and a pass to be forced.
— 'Twixt the pit and the crest, 'twixt the
    rocks and the grass,
Where the bush hides the foe, and the foe
    holds the pass,

Beaujeu and Pontiac, striving amain;
Huron and Wyandot, jeering the slain!

Beaujeu, bon camarade! Beaujeu the **Gay**
Beaujeu and Death cast their blades in the
    fray.
Never a rifle that spared when they spoke,
Never a scalp-knife that balked in its stroke.
Till the red hillocks marked where the
    standards had danced,
And the Grenadiers gasped where their sabres
    had glanced.
— But Braddock raged fierce in that storm by
    the ford,
And railed at his "curs" with the flat of his
    sword!

Said the Sword to the Ax, "Where's your
    Berserker now?
Lo! his bones mark a path for a countryman's
    cow.
And Beaujeu the Gay? Give him place, right
    or wrong,
In your tale of a camp, or your stave of a
    song."
— "But Braddock of Fontenoy, stubborn and
    grim,
Who but he carved a cross on the wilderness
    rim?
In his own doom building large for the Lord,
Steeple and State!" said the Ax to the Sword.
                    JOHN WILLIAMSON PALMER.

After Braddock's defeat, the Pennsylvania and
Virginia frontiers were left, for a time, to the
ravages of the Indians. The colonies were slow
to defend themselves, and could get no aid what-
ever from England, who had her hands full else-
where.

ODE TO THE INHABITANTS OF PENNSYLVANIA

[September 30, 1756]

STILL shall the tyrant scourge of Gaul
With wasteful rage resistless fall
  On Britain's slumbering race?
Still shall she wave her bloody hand
And threatening banners o'er this land,
  To Britain's fell disgrace?

And not one generous chieftain rise
(Who dares the frown of war despise,
  And treacherous fear disclaim)

His country's ruin to oppose,
To hurl destruction on her foes,
    And blast their rising fame?

In Britain's cause, with valor fired,
Braddock, unhappy chief! expired,
    And claim'd a nation's tear;
Nor could Oswego's bulwarks stand
The fury of a savage band,
    Though Schuyler's arm was there.

Still shall this motley, murderous crew
Their deep, destructive arts pursue,
    And general horror spread?
No — see Britannia's genius rise!
Swift o'er the Atlantic foam she flies
    And lifts her laurell'd head!

Lo! streaming through the dear blue sky,
Great Loudon's awful banners fly,
    In British pomp display'd!
Soon shall the gallant chief advance;
Before him shrink the sons of France,
    Confounded and dismay'd.

Then rise, illustrious Britons, rise!
Great Freedom calls, pursue her voice,
    And save your country's shame!
Let every hand for Britain arm'd,
And every breast with virtue warm'd,
    Aspire at deathless fame!

But chief, let Pennsylvania wake,
And on her foes let terrors shake,
    Their gloomy troops defy;
For, lo! her smoking farms and plains,
Her captured youths, and murder'd swains,
    For vengeance louder cry.

Why should we seek inglorious rest,
Or sink, with thoughtless ease oppress'd,
    While war insults so near?
While ruthless, fierce, athirst for blood,
Bellona's sons, a desperate brood!
    In furious bands appear!

Rouse, rouse at once, and boldly chase
From their deep haunts, the savage race,
    Till they confess you men.
Let other Armstrongs grace the field!
Let other slaves before them yield,
    And tremble round Duquesne.

And thou, our chief, and martial guide,
Of worth approved, of valor tried

In many a hard campaign,
O Denny, warmed with British fire,
Our inexperienced troops inspire,
    And conquest's laurels gain!
Pennsylvania Gazette, September 30, 1756.

Meanwhile things were in a troubled condition in Acadia, where the so-called " French neutrals" were discovered to be in arms against England. "Every resource of patience and persuasion" had been used to secure their loyalty to Great Britain, but in vain. At last it was decided to disperse them among the southern provinces, and the deportation began in October. At the end of two months, about six thousand of the Acadians had been sent away, and their homes destroyed.

THE EMBARKATION

From " Evangeline "

[October 8, 1755]

FOUR times the sun had risen and set; and
    now on the fifth day
Cheerily called the cock to the sleeping maids
    of the farm-house.
Soon o'er the yellow fields, in silent and
    mournful procession,
Came from the neighboring hamlets and
    farms the Acadian women,
Driving in ponderous wains their household
    goods to the sea-shore,
Pausing and looking back to gaze once more
    on their dwellings,
Ere they were shut from sight by the winding
    road and the woodland.
Close at their sides their children ran, and
    urged on the oxen,
While in their little hands they clasped some
    fragments of playthings.

Thus to the Gaspereau's mouth they hur-
    ried; and there on the sea-beach
Piled in confusion lay the household goods of
    the peasants.
All day long between the shore and the ships
    did the boats ply;
All day long the wains came laboring down
    from the village.
Late in the afternoon, when the sun was near
    to his setting,
Echoed far o'er the fields came the roll of
    drums from the churchyard.
Thither the women and children thronged.
    On a sudden the church-doors

Opened, and forth came the guard, and
    marching in gloomy procession
Followed the long-imprisoned, but patient,
    Acadian farmers.
Even as pilgrims, who journey afar from their
    homes and their country,
Sing as they go, and in singing forget they are
    weary and wayworn,
So with songs on their lips the Acadian
    peasants descended
Down from the church to the shore, amid
    their wives and their daughters.
Foremost the young men came; and, raising
    together their voices,
Sang with tremulous lips a chant of the Catho-
    lic Missions: —
"Sacred heart of the Saviour! O inexhausti-
    ble fountain!
Fill our hearts this day with strength and sub-
    mission and patience!"
Then the old men, as they marched, and the
    women that stood by the wayside
Joined in the sacred psalm, and the birds in
    the sunshine above them
Mingled their notes therewith, like voices of
    spirits departed.

.   .   .   .

Thus to the Gaspereau's mouth moved on
    that mournful procession.

There disorder prevailed, and the tumult
    and stir of embarking.
Busily plied the freighted boats; and in the
    confusion
Wives were torn from their husbands, and
    mothers, too late, saw their children
Left on the land, extending their arms, with
    wildest entreaties.
So unto separate ships were Basil and Gabriel
    carried,
While in despair on the shore Evangeline
    stood with her father.
Half the task was not done when the sun went
    down, and the twilight
Deepened and darkened around; and in haste
    the refluent ocean
Fled away from the shore, and left the line of
    the sand-beach
Covered with waifs of the tide, with kelp and
    the slippery sea-weed.
Farther back in the midst of the household
    goods and the wagons,
Like to a gypsy camp, or a leaguer after a
    battle,

All escape cut off by the sea, and the sentinels
    near them,
Lay encamped for the night the houseless
    Acadian farmers.
Back to its nethermost caves retreated the
    bellowing ocean,
Dragging adown the beach the rattling peb-
    bles, and leaving
Inland and far up the shore the stranded boats
    of the sailors.
Then, as the night descended, the herds re-
    turned from their pastures;
Sweet was the moist still air with the odor of
    milk from their udders;
Lowing they waited, and long, at the well-
    known bars of the farm-yard, —
Waited and looked in vain for the voice and
    the hand of the milk-maid.
Silence reigned in the streets; from the church
    no Angelus sounded,
Rose no smoke from the roofs, and gleamed
    no lights from the windows.

.   .   .   .

Suddenly rose from the south a light, as in
    autumn the blood-red
Moon climbs the crystal walls of heaven, and
    o'er the horizon
Titan-like stretches its hundred hands upon
    the mountain and meadow,
Seizing the rocks and the rivers and piling
    huge shadows together.
Broader and ever broader it gleamed on the
    roofs of the village,
Gleamed on the sky and sea, and the ships
    that lay in the roadstead.
Columns of shining smoke uprose, and flashes
    of flame were
Thrust through their folds and withdrawn,
    like the quivering hands of a martyr.
Then as the wind seized the gleeds and the
    burning thatch, and, uplifting,
Whirled them aloft through the air, at once
    from a hundred house-tops
Started the sheeted smoke with flashes of
    flame intermingled.

These things beheld in dismay the crowd
    on the shore and on shipboard.
Speechless at first they stood, then cried aloud
    in their anguish,
"We shall behold no more our homes in the
    village of Grand-Pré!"
Loud on a sudden the cocks began to crow in
    the farm-yards.

Thinking the day had dawned; and anon the
    lowing of cattle
Came on the evening breeze, by the barking
    of dogs interrupted.
Then rose a sound of dread, such as startles
    the sleeping encampments
Far in the western prairies or forests that skirt
    the Nebraska,
When the wild horses affrighted sweep by
    with the speed of the whirlwind,
Or the loud bellowing herds of buffaloes rush
    to the river.
Such was the sound that arose on the night,
    as the herds and the horses
Broke through their folds and fences, and
    madly rushed o'er the meadows.

.   .   .   .

Lo! with a mournful sound, like the voice of a
    vast congregation,
Solemnly answered the sea, and mingled its
    roar with the dirges.
'T was the returning tide, that afar from the
    waste of the ocean,
With the first dawn of the day, came heaving
    and hurrying landward.
Then recommenced once more the stir and
    noise of embarking:
And with the ebb of the tide the ships sailed
    out of the harbor,
Leaving behind them the dead on the shore,
    and the village in ruins.
HENRY WADSWORTH LONGFELLOW.

In July, 1758, an army of fifteen thousand,
under General James Abercromby and Brigadier
Lord Howe, attempted to take Ticonderoga,
where Montcalm was stationed at the head of
about three thousand men. Lord Howe, the very
life of the army, was killed in the first skirmish,
and Abercromby handled the army so badly that
it was repulsed with a loss of nearly two thousand,
and fled in a panic. The French loss was less than
four hundred, and the victory was hailed as one
of the greatest ever achieved by French arms in
America.

ON THE DEFEAT AT TICONDEROGA
OR CARILONG

[July 8, 1758]

NEGLECTED long had been my useless lyre,
And heartfelt grief represt the poet's fire;
But rous'd by dire alarms of wasting war,
Again, O muse, the solemn dirge prepare,

And join the widow's, orphan's, parent's tear.
Unwept, unsung shall Britain's chiefs remain;
Doomed in this stranger clime to bleed in
    vain:
Here a last refuge hapless Braddock found,
When the grim savage gave the deadly
    wound:
Ah! hide Monongahel thy hateful head
(Still as thy waves roll near the injur'd dead)
On whose gore-moistened banks the num'rous
    slain,
Now spring in vegetative life again,
Whilst their wan ghosts as night's dark gloom
    prevail
Murmur to whistling winds the mournful
    tale;
Cease, cease, ye grisly forms, nor wail the past.
Lo! a new scene of death exceeds the last;
Th' empurpled fields of Carilong survey
Rich with the spoils of one disastrous day!
Bold to the charge the ready vet'ran stood
And thrice repell'd, as oft the fight renewed,
Till (life's warm current drain'd) they sunk in
    blood,
Uncheck'd their ardor, unallay'd their fire,
See Beaver, Proby, Rutherford, expire;
Silent Britannia's tardy thunder lay
While clouds of Gallick smoke obscur'd the
    day.
Th' intrepid race nursed on the mountain's
    brow
O'er-leap the mound, and dare th' astonish'd
    foe:
Whilst Albion's sons (mow'd down in ranks)
    bemoan
Their much lov'd country's wrongs nor feel
    their own;
Cheerless they hear the drum discordant
    beat —
And with slow motion sullenly retreat.
    But where wert thou, oh! first in martial
    fame,
Whose early cares distinguish'd praises claim,
Who ev'ry welcome toil didst gladly share
And taught th' enervate warrior want to bear?
Illustrious Howe! whose ev'ry deed confest
The patriot wish that fill'd thy generous
    breast:
Alas! too swift t' explore the hostile land,
Thou dy'dst sad victim to an ambush band,
Nor e'er this hour of wild confusion view'd
Like Braddock, falling in the pathless wood;
Still near the spot where thy pale corse is
    laid,
May the fresh laurel spread its amplest shade'

Still may thy name be utter'd with a sigh,
And the big drops swell ev'ry grateful eye;
Oh! would each leader who deplores thy fate
Thy zeal and active virtues emulate,
Soon should proud Carilong be humbled low
Nor Montcalm's self, prevent th' avenging
    blow.

London Magazine, 1759.

But at last the tide turned. In 1757 William
Pitt forced his way to the leadership of the gov-
ernment in England, and at once formed a com-
prehensive plan for a combined attack on the
French forts in America. The first point of attack
was Louisburg, which had been ceded back to
France in 1748, and in the spring of 1758 a strong
expedition under Lord Amherst was dispatched
against it. The siege commenced June 8 — the
very day of the disaster at Ticonderoga — and
after a tremendous bombardment which destroyed
the town and badly breached the fortress, the
garrison, numbering nearly six thousand, sur-
rendered July 26, 1758.

ON THE LATE SUCCESSFUL EXPE-
DITION AGAINST LOUISBOURG

[July 26, 1758]

AT length 't is done, the glorious conflict's
    done,
And British valor hath the conquest won:
Success our arms, our heroes, honor crowns,
And Louisbourg an English monarch owns!
Swift, to the scene where late the valiant
    fought,
Waft me, ye muses, on the wings of thought —
That awful scene where the dread od of war
O'er field of death roll'd his triumphant car:
There yet, with fancy's eye, methinks I view
The pressing throng, the fierce assault renew:
With dauntless front advance, and boldly
    brave
The cannon's thunder and th' expecting
    grave.

On yonder cliff, high hanging o'er the deep,
Where trembling joy climbs the darksome
    steep;
Britannia lonely sitting, from afar
Waits the event, and overlooks the war;
Thence, rolls her eager wand'ring eyes about
In all the dread anxiety of doubt;
Sees her fierce sons, her foes with vengeance
    smite
Grasp deathless honors, and maintain the
    fight.

Whilst thus her breast alternate passions
    sway,
And hope and fear wear the slow hours away
See! from the realms of everlasting light,
A radiant form wings her aerial flight.
The palm she carries, and the crown she
    wears,
Plainly denote 't is *Victory* appears;
Her crimson vestment loosely flows behind,
The clouds her chariot, and the wings her
    wind:
Trumpets shrill sounding all around her
    play,
And laurell'd honors gild her azure way —
Now she alights — the trumpets cease to
    sound,
Her presence spreads expecting silence
    round: —
And thus she speaks; whilst from her heav'nly
    face
Effulgent glories brighten all the place —

"Britannia, hail! thine is at length the day,
And lasting triumphs shall thy cares repay;
Thy godlike sons, by *this*, their names shall
    raise,
And tongues remote shall joy to swell their
    praise.
I to the list'ning world shall soon proclaim
Of *Wolfe's* brave deeds, the never-dying
    fame,
And swell with glory Amherst's patriot name.
Such are the heroes that shall ever bring
Wealth to their country, honor to their
    king:
Opposing foes, in vain attempt to quell
The native fires that in such bosoms dwell.
To thee, with joy, this laurel I resign,
Smile, smile, *Britannia!* victory is thine.
Long may it flourish on thy sacred brow!
Long may thy foes a forc'd subjection know!
See, see their pow'r, their boasted pow'r
    decline!
Rejoice, *Britannia,* victory is thine."

Give your loose canvas to the breezes free,
Ye floating thund'rers, bulwarks of the sea:
Go, bear the joyful tidings to your king,
And, in the voice of war, declare 't is victory
    you bring;
Let the wild crowd that catch the breath of
    fame,
In mad huzzas their ruder joy proclaim.
Let their loud thanks to heav'n in flames
    ascend,

While mingling shouts the azure concave rend.
But let the few, whom reason makes more wise,
With glowing gratitude uplift their eyes:
Oh! let their breasts dilate with sober joy.
Let pious praise their hearts and tongues employ;
To bless our *God* with me let all unite,
He guides the conq'ring sword, *he* governs in the fight.

                    FRANCIS HOPKINSON.

The fall of Louisburg was followed a few months later by the capture of Fort Duquesne (November 25, 1758), by General John Forbes. Forbes, at the head of an excellent army, had proceeded slowly and carefully. As the English approached, the French realized that to remain was simply to be captured, so they deserted the hopeless post, and Forbes marched in unmolested. He named his conquest Fort Pitt, after the great minister.

FORT DUQUESNE

A HISTORICAL CENTENNIAL BALLAD

[November 25, 1758–1858]

I

COME, fill the beaker, while we chaunt a pean of old days:
By Mars! no men shall live again more worthy of our praise,
Than they who stormed at Louisburg and Frontenac amain,
And shook the English standard out o'er the ruins of Duquesne.

For glorious were the days they came, the soldiers strong and true,
And glorious were the days, they came for Pennsylvania, too;
When marched the troopers sternly on through forest's autumn brown,
And where St. George's cross was raised, the oriflame went down.

Virginia sent her chivalry and Maryland her brave,
And Pennsylvania to the cause her noblest yeomen gave:
Oh, and proud were they who wore the garb of Indian hunters then,
For every sturdy youth was worth a score of common men!

They came from Carolina's pines, from fruitful Delaware —
The staunchest and the stoutest of the chivalrous were there;
And calm and tall above them all, i' the red November sun,
Like Saul above his brethren, rode Colonel Washington.

O'er leagues of wild and waste they passed, they forded stream and fen,
Where danger lurked in every glade, and death in every glen;
They heard the Indian ranger's cry, the Frenchman's far-off hail,
From purple distance echoed back through the hollows of the vale.

And ever and anon they came, along their dangerous way,
Where, ghastly, 'mid the yellow leaves, their slaughtered comrades lay;
The tartans of Grant's Highlanders were sodden yet and red,
As routed in the rash assault, they perished as they fled.

— Ah! many a lass ayont the Tweed shall rue the fatal fray,
And high Virginian dames shall mourn the ruin of that day,
When gallant lad and cavalier i' the wilderness were slain,
'Twixt laurelled Loyalhanna and the outposts of Duquesne.

And there before them was the field of massacre and blood,
Of panic, rout and shameful flight, in that disastrous wood
Where Halket fell and Braddock died, with many a noble one
Whose white bones glistened through the leaves i' the pale November sun.

Then spoke the men of Braddock's Field, and hung their heads in shame,
For England's tarnished honor and for England's sullied fame;
"And, by St. George. the soldiers swore, "we'll wipe away the stain
Before to-morrow's sunset. at the trenches of Duquesne."

II

'T was night along the autumn hills, the
sun's November gleam
Had left its crimson on the leaves, its tinge
upon the stream;
And Hermit Silence kept his watch 'mid
ancient rocks and trees,
And placed his finger on the lip of babbling
brook and breeze.

The bivouac's set by Turtle Creek; and
while the soldiers sleep,
The swarthy chiefs around the fires an
anxious council keep;
Some spoke of murmurs in the camp, scarce
whispered to the air,
But tokens of discouragement, the presage
of despair.

Some a retreat advised; 't was late; the
winter drawing on;
The forage and provision, too, — so Ormsby
said, — were gone.
Men could not feed on air and fight; what-
ever Pitt might say;
In praise or censure, still, they thought, 't were
wiser to delay.

Then up spoke iron-headed Forbes, and
through his feeble frame
There ran the lightning of a will that put
them all to shame!
"I'll hear no more," he roundly swore;
"we'll storm the fort amain!
I'll sleep in hell to-morrow night, or sleep
in Fort Duquesne!"

So said: and each to sleep addressed his
wearied limbs and mind,
And all was hushed i' the forest, save the
sobbing of the wind,
And the tramp, tramp, tramp of the sentinel,
who started oft in fright
At the shadows wrought 'mid the giant trees
by the fitful camp-fire light.

Good Lord! what sudden glare is that that
reddens all the sky,
As though hell's legions rode the air and
tossed their torches high!
Up, men! the alarm drum beats to arms!
and the solid ground seems riven
By the shock of warring thunderbolts in the
lurid depth of heaven!

O there was clattering of steel, and muster-
ing in array,
And shouts and wild huzzas of men, impatient
of delay,
As came the scouts swift-footed in — "They
fly! the foe! they fly!
They've fired the powder magazine and
blown it to the sky!"

III

Now morning o'er the frosty hills in autumn
splendor came,
And touched the rolling mists with gold, and
flecked the clouds with flame;
And through the brown woods on the hills —
those altars of the world —
The blue smoke from the settler's hut and
Indian's wigwam curled.

Yet never, here, had morning dawned on
such a glorious din
Of twanging trump, and rattling drum, and
clanging culverin,
And glittering arms and sabre gleams and
serried ranks of men,
Who marched with banners high advanced
along the river glen.

Oh, and royally they bore themselves who
knew that o'er the seas
Would speed the glorious tidings from the
loyal colonies,
Of the fall of French dominion with the fall
of Fort Duquesne,
And the triumph of the English arms from
Erie to Champlain.

Before high noon they halted; and while
they stood at rest,
They saw, unfolded gloriously, the "Gate-
way of the West,"
There flashed the Allegheny, like a scimetar
of gold,
And king-like in its majesty, Monongahela
rolled.

Beyond, the River Beautiful swept down
the woody vales,
Where Commerce, ere a century passed,
should spread her thousand sails;
Between the hazy hills they saw Contrecœur's
armed batteaux,
And the flying, flashing, feathery oars of the
Ottawa's canoes.

Then, on from rank to rank of men, a shout
of triumph ran,
And while the cannon thundered, the leader
of the van,
The tall Virginian, mounted on the walls
that smouldered yet,
And shook the English standard out, and
named the place Fort Pitt.

Again with wild huzzas the hills and river
valleys ring,
And they swing their loyal caps in air, and
shout — "Long live the King!
Long life unto King George!" they cry,
"and glorious be the reign
That adds to English statesmen Pitt. to
English arms Duquesne!"

FLORUS B. PLIMPTON.

Pitt determined to strike a blow at the very
centre of French power, and on June 26, 1759, an
English fleet of twenty-two ships of the line, with
frigates, sloops-of-war, and transports carrying
nine thousand regulars, appeared before Quebec.
In command of this great expedition was Major-
General James Wolfe, who had played so dashing a
part in the capture of Louisburg the year before,
and was soon to win immortal glory.

HOT STUFF

[June, 1759]

COME, each death-doing dog who dares ven-
ture his neck,
Come, follow the hero that goes to Quebec;
Jump aboard of the transports, and loose
every sail,
Pay your debts at the tavern by giving leg-
bail;
And ye that love fighting shall soon have
enough:
Wolfe commands us, my boys; we shall give
them Hot Stuff.

Up the River St. Lawrence our troops shall
advance,
To the Grenadiers' March we will teach
them to dance.
Cape Breton we have taken, and next we will
try
At their capital to give them another black eye.
Vaudreuil, 't is in vain you pretend to look
gruff, —
Those are coming who know how to give
you Hot Stuff.

With powder in his periwig, and snuff in his
nose,
Monsieur will run down our descent to op-
pose;
And the Indians will come: but the light
infantry
Will soon oblige *them* to betake to a tree.
From such rascals as these may we fear a
rebuff?
Advance, grenadiers, and let fly your Hot Stuff!

When the forty-seventh regiment is dashing
ashore,
While bullets are whistling and cannon do
roar,
Says Montcalm: "Those are Shirley's — I
know the lappels."
"You lie," says Ned Botwood, "we belong
to Lascelles'!
Tho' our clothing is changed, yet we scorn
a powder-puff;
So at you, ye bitches, here's give you Hot
Stuff."

EDWARD BOTWOOD.

About the end of August a place was found
where the heights might be scaled, and an assault
was ordered for the night of Wednesday, Sep-
tember 12. The night arrived; every preparation
had been made and every order given; it only
remained to wait the turning of the tide. Wolfe
was on board the flagship Sutherland, and to
while away the hours of waiting he is said to have
written the little song, ":How Stands the Glass
Around?"

HOW STANDS THE GLASS AROUND?

[September 12, 1759]

How stands the glass around?
For shame ye take no care, my boys,
How stands the glass around?
Let mirth and wine abound,
The trumpets sound,
The colors they are flying, boys,
To fight, kill, or wound,
May we still be found
Content with our hard fate, my boys,
On the cold ground.

Why, soldiers, why,
Should we be melancholy, boys?
Why, soldiers, why?
Whose business 't is to die!
What, sighing? fie!

Don't fear, drink on, be jolly, boys!
  'T is he, you or I!
Cold, hot, wet or dry,
We're always bound to follow, boys,
  And scorn to fly!

  'T is but in vain, —
I mean not to upbraid you, boys, —
  'T is but in vain,
  For soldiers to complain:
Should next campaign
Send us to him who made us, boys,
  We're free from pain!
  But if we remain,
A bottle and a kind landlady
  Cure all again.

                              JAMES WOLFE.

Montcalm, riding out from Quebec early in the morning of Thursday, September 13, 1759, found the English drawn up in line of battle on the Plains of Abraham — they had scaled the cliffs in safety. He attacked about ten o'clock, but his troops were repulsed at the second volley and fled in confusion back to the fort. Wolfe was killed in the charge which followed, and Montcalm was fatally wounded and died that night. The French were demoralized; a council was called and the incredible resolution reached to abandon the fort without further resistance. The retreat commenced at once, and Quebec was left to its fate. It was never again to pass into the hands of France.

BRAVE WOLFE

[September 13, 1759]

CHEER up, my young men all,
  Let nothing fright you;
Though oft objections rise,
  Let it delight you.

Let not your fancy move
  Whene'er it comes to trial;
Nor let your courage fail
  At the first denial.

I sat down by my love,
  Thinking that I woo'd her;
I sat down by my love,
  But sure not to delude her.

But when I got to speak,
  My tongue it doth so quiver,
I dare not speak my mind,
  Whenever I am with her.

Love, here's a ring of gold,
  'T is long that I have kept it.
My dear, now for my sake,
  I pray you to accept it.

When you the posy read,
  Pray think upon the giver,
My dear, remember me,
  Or I'm undone forever.

Then Wolfe he took his leave,
  Of his most lovely jewel;
Although it seemed to be
  To him, an act most cruel.

Although it's for a space
  I'm forced to leave my love.
My dear, where'er I rove,
  I'll ne'er forget my dove.

So then this valiant youth
  Embarked on the ocean,
To free America
  From faction's dire commotion.

He landed at Quebec,
  Being all brave and hearty;
The city to attack,
  With his most gallant party.

Then Wolfe drew up his men,
  In rank and file so pretty
On Abraham's lofty heights,
  Before this noble city.

A distance from the town
  The noble French did meet them,
In double numbers there,
  Resolved for to beat them.

A Parley: WOLFE *and* MONTCALM *together*
Montcalm and this brave youth,
  Together they are walking;
So well they do agree,
  Like brothers they are talking.

Then each one to his post,
  As they do now retire;
Oh, then their numerous hosts
  Began their dreadful fire.

Then instant from his horse,
  Fell this most noble hero,
May we lament his loss
  In words of deepest sorrow.

The French are seen to break,
    Their columns all are flying;
Then Wolfe he seems to wake,
    Though in the act of dying.

And lifting up his head
    (The drums and trumpets rattle),
And to his army said,
    "I pray how goes the battle?"

His aide-de-camp replied,
    "Brave general, 't is in our favor,
Quebec and all her pride,
    'T is nothing now can save her.

"She falls into our hands,
    With all her wealth and treasure."
"O then," brave Wolfe replied,
    "I quit the world with pleasure."

Wolfe's death almost overshadowed the victory.
Major Knox, in his diary, writes, "our joy at this
success is inexpressibly damped by the loss we
sustained of one of the greatest heroes which this
or any other age can boast of."

THE DEATH OF WOLFE

[September 13, 1759]

THY merits, Wolfe, transcend all human
    praise,
The breathing marble or the muses' lays.
Art is but vain — the force of language weak,
To paint thy virtues, or thy actions speak.
Had I Duché's or Godfrey's magic skill,
Each line to raise, and animate at will —
To rouse each passion dormant in the soul,
Point out its object, or its rage control —
Then, Wolfe, some faint resemblance should
    we find
Of those great virtues that adorned thy mind.
Like Britain's genius shouldst thou then
    appear,
Hurling destruction on the Gallic rear —
While France, astonished, trembled at thy
    sight,
And placed her safety in ignoble flight.
Thy last great scene should melt each Briton's
    heart,
And rage and grief alternately impart.
    With foes surrounded, midst the shades of
        death,
These were the words that closed the war-
    rior's breath —

"My eyesight fails! — but does the foe retreat?
If they retire, I'm happy in my fate!"
A generous chief, to whom the hero spoke,
Cried, "Sir, they fly! — their ranks entirely
    broke:
Whilst thy bold troops o'er slaughtered heaps
    advance,
And deal due vengeance on the sons of
    France."
The pleasing truth recalls his parting soul,
And from his lips these dying accents stole: —
"I'm satisfied!" he said, then wing'd his way
Guarded by angels to celestial day.
    An awful band! — Britannia's mighty
        dead,
Receives to glory his immortal shade.
Marlborough and Talbot hail the warlike
    chief —
Halket and Howe, late objects of our grief,
With joyful song conduct their welcome guest
To the bright mansions of eternal rest —
For those prepared who merit just applause
By bravely dying in their country's cause.
    Pennsylvania Gazette, November 8, 1759.

The fall of Quebec settled the fate of Canada.
On September 8, 1760, Vaudreuil surrendered
Montreal to a great besieging force under Am-
herst. By the terms of the capitulation, Canada
and all its dependencies passed to the British crown.
The fight for the continent was ended. Indian
hostilities continued for some years, and it was
not until October, 1764, that peace was made
with them. One of its conditions was the return
of all captives taken by the Indians, and they
were assembled at Carlisle, Pa., December 31
1764. It was there the incident took place which
is related in the following verses.

THE CAPTIVE'S HYMN

(Carlisle, Pa., December 31, 1764)

THE Indian war was over,
    And Pennsylvania's towns
Welcomed the blessed calm that comes
    When peace a conflict crowns.
Bitter and long had been the strife,
    But gallant Colonel Bouquet
Had forced the foe to sue for grace,
    And named the joyful day
When Shawnees, Tuscarawas,
    Miamis, Delawares,
And every band that roved the land
    And called a captive theirs —
From the pathless depths of the forest,
    By stream and dark defile,

Should bring their prisoners, on their lives,
  In safety to Carlisle;
Carlisle in the Cumberland valley,
  Where Conodogwinnet flows,
And the guardian ranges, north and south,
  In mountain pride repose.

Like the wind the Colonel's order
  To hamlet and clearing flew;
And mourning mothers and wives and sons
From banks where Delaware seaward runs,
From Erie's wave, and Ohio's tide,
And the vales where the southern hills divide,
  Flocked to the town, perchance to view,
At last, 'mid the crowds by the startled square,
The faces lost, but in memory fair.

How strange the scene on the village green
  That morning cold and gray!
To right the Indian tents were set,
And in groups the dusky warriors met,
While their captives clung to the captors yet,
  As wild and bronzed as they —
In rags and skins, with moccasined feet,
Some loath to part, some fain to greet
  The friends of a vanished day;
And, eagerly watching the tents, to left
Stood mothers and sons and wives bereft,
While, beyond, were the throngs from hill
    and valley,
And, waiting the keen-eyed Colonel's rally,
  The troops in their brave array.

Now friends and captives mingle,
  And cries of joy or woe
Thrill the broad street as loved ones meet,
Or in vain the tale of the past repeat,
  And back in anguish go.
Among them lingered a widow —
  From the Suabian land was she —
And one fell morning she had lost
  Husband and children three,
All slain save the young Regina,
  A captive spared to be.
Nine weary years had followed,
  But the wilderness was dumb,
And never a word to her aching heart
  Through friend or foe had come,
And now, from Tulpehocken,
  Full seventy miles away,
She had walked to seek her daughter,
  The Lord her only stay.

She scanned the sun-browned maidens;
  But the tunic's rough disguise,

The savage tongue, the forest ways,
Baffled and mocked her yearning gaze,
  And with sobs and streaming eyes
She turned to the Colonel and told him
  How hopeless was her quest —
Moaning, "Alas, Regina!
  The grave for me is best!"
"Nay, Madam," gently he replied,
"Don't be disheartened yet, but bide,
  And try some other test.
What pleasant song or story
  Did the love from your lips to hear?"
"O Sir, I taught her 'Our Father;'
  And the 'Creed' we hold so dear,
And she said them over and over
  While I was spinning near;
And every eve, by her little bed,
  When the light was growing dim,
I sung her to sleep, my darling!
  With Schmolke's beautiful hymn."
"Then sing it *now*," said the Colonel,
  And close to the captive band
He brought the mother with her hymn
  From the far Suabian land;
And with faltering voice and quivering
    lips,
  While all was hushed, she sung
The strain of lofty faith and cheer
  In her rich German tongue:

"Allein, und doch nicht ganz allein "
  (How near the listeners press!),
Alone, yet not alone am I,
  Though all may deem my days go by
    In utter dreariness;
The Lord is still my company,
I am with Him, and He with me,
  The solitude to bless.

He speaks to me within His word
As if His very voice I heard,
  And when I pray, apart,
He meets me in the quiet there
With counsel for each cross and care,
  And comfort for my heart.

The world may say my life is lone,
With every joy and blessing flown
  Its vision can descry;
I shall not sorrow nor repine,
For glorious company is mine
  With God and angels nigh.

As she sung, a maid of the captives
  Threw back her tangled hair,

And forward leaned as if to list
  The lightest murmur there;
Her breath came fast, her brown cheek
    flushed,
  Her eyes grew bright and wide
As if some spell the song had cast,
  And, ere the low notes died,
With a bound like a deer in the forest
  She sprang to the singer's side,
And, "Liebe, kleine Mutter!"
  Enfolding her, she cried —
"My dear, dear, little Mother!" —
  Then swift before her knelt
As in the long, long buried days
  When by the wood they dwelt;
And, "Vater unser, der du bist
  Im Himmel," chanted she,
The sweet "Our Father" she had learned
  Beside that mother's knee;
And then the grand "Apostles' Creed"
  That in her heart had lain:
"Ich glaube an Gott den Vater,"
  Like a child she said again —
"I believe in God the Father" —
  Down to the blest "Amen."
Stooping and clasping the maiden
  Whose soul the song had freed,
"Now God be praised!" said the mother,
  "This is my child indeed! —
My own, my darling Regina,
  Come back in my sorest need,
For she knows the Hymn, and 'Our Father,'
  And the holy 'Apostles' Creed'!"

Then, while the throng was silent,
  And the Colonel bowed his head,
With tears and glad thanksgivings
  Her daughter forth she led;
And the sky was lit with sunshine,
  And the cold earth caught its smile
For the mother and ransomed maiden,
  That morning in Carlisle.

EDNA DEAN PROCTOR.

A PROPHECY

[1764]

ERE five score years have run their tedious
    rounds, —
If yet Oppression breaks o'er human bounds,
As it has done the last sad passing year,
Made the New World in anger shed the tear, —
Unmindful of their native, once-loved isle,
They'll bid Allegiance cease her peaceful
    smile,
While from their arms they tear Oppression's
    chain,
And make lost Liberty once more to reign.
But let them live, as they would choose to be,
Loyal to King, and as true Britons free,
They'll ne'er by fell revolt oppose that crown
Which first has raised them, though now pulls
    them down:
If but the rights of subjects they receive,
'T is all they ask — or all a crown can give.

ARTHUR LEE (?).

PART II

THE REVOLUTION

FLAWLESS HIS HEART

FLAWLESS his heart and tempered to the core
Who, beckoned by the forward-leaning wave,
First left behind him the firm-footed shore,
And, urged by every nerve of sail and oar,
Steered for the Unknown which gods to mortals gave,
Of thought and action the mysterious door,
Bugbear of fools, a summons to the brave:
Strength found he in the unsympathizing sun,
And strange stars from beneath the horizon won,
And the dumb ocean pitilessly grave:
High-hearted surely he;
But bolder they who first off-cast
Their moorings from the habitable Past
And ventured chartless on the sea
Of storm-engendering Liberty:
For all earth's width of waters is a span,
And their convulsed existence mere repose,
Matched with the unstable heart of man,
Shoreless in wants, mist-girt in all it knows,
Open to every wind of sect or clan,
And sudden-passionate in ebbs and flows.

JAMES RUSSELL LOWELL.

CHAPTER I

THE COMING OF DISCONTENT

The close of the struggle with the French for the possession of the continent may be fairly said to mark the beginning of that series of aggressions on the part of England which ended in the revolt of her colonies. True there had been before that arbitrary and tyrannical royal governors, and absurdly perverse enactments on the part of the Lords of Trade; but not until the French troubles had been disposed of did the British government bend its energies seriously to regulating the affairs of a people which it considered fractious and turbulent. In the *Virginia Gazette* for May 2, 1766, appeared one of the first of those songs, afterwards so numerous, which expressed the discontent of the colonies under this régime.

THE VIRGINIA SONG

[May 2, 1766]

SURE never was picture drawn more to the life,
Or affectionate husband more fond of his wife,
Than America copies and loves Britain's sons,
Who, conscious of Freedom, are bold as great guns,
 "Hearts of Oak are we still, for we're sons of those men
  Who always are ready, steady, boys, steady,
  To fight for their freedom again and again."

Tho' we feast and grow fat on America's soil,
Yet we own ourselves subjects of Britain's fair isle;
And who's so absurd to deny us the name,
Since true British blood flows in every vein?
 "Hearts of Oak," etc.

Then cheer up, my lads, to your country be firm,
Like kings of the ocean, we'll weather each storm;
Integrity calls out, fair liberty, see,
Waves her Flag o'er our heads and her words are *be free !*
 "Hearts of Oak," etc.

To King George, as true subjects, we loyal bow down,
But hope we may call Magna Charta our own.
Let the rest of the world slavish worship decree,
Great Britain has ordered her sons to be free.
 "Hearts of Oak," etc.

Poor Esau his birthright gave up for a bribe,
Americans scorn th' mean soul-selling tribe;
Beyond life our freedom we chuse to possess,
Which thro' life we'll defend, and abjure a broad S.
 "Hearts of Oak are we still, and we're sons of those men
  Who fear not the ocean, brave roarings of cannon,
  To stop all oppression, again and again."

On our brow while we laurel-crown'd Liberty wear,
What Englishmen ought we Americans dare;
Though tempests and terrors around us we see,
Bribes nor fears can prevail o'er the hearts that are free.
 "Hearts of Oak," etc.

With Loyalty, Liberty let us entwine,
Our blood shall for both flow as free as our wine;
Let us set an example, what all men should be,
And a Toast give the World, "Here's to those dare be free.
 "Hearts of Oak," etc.

In 1766 William Pitt, perhaps the most enlightened friend America had in England, became Prime Minister, and adopted toward the colonies a policy so conciliatory that it occasioned much disgust in England — as is evident from the following verses which appeared originally in the *Gentleman's Magazine.*

THE WORLD TURNED UPSIDE DOWN

OR, THE OLD WOMAN TAUGHT WISDOM

[1767]

GOODY BULL and her daughter together fell
 out,
Both squabbled, and wrangled, and made a
 —— rout,
But the cause of the quarrel remains to be told,
Then lend both your ears, and a tale I'll
 unfold.

The old lady, it seems, took a freak in her
 head,
That her daughter, grown woman, might earn
 her own bread:
Self-applauding her scheme, she was ready to
 dance;
But we're often too sanguine in what we
 advance.

For mark the event; thus by fortune we're
 crossed,
Nor should people reckon without their good
 host;
The daughter was sulky, and would n't come
 to,
And pray, what in this case could the old
 woman do?

In vain did the matron hold forth in the cause,
That the young one was able; her duty, the
 laws;
Ingratitude vile, disobedience far worse;
But she might e'en as well sung psalms to a
 horse.

Young, froward, and sullen, and vain of her
 beauty,
She tartly replied, that she knew well her duty,
That other folks' children were kept by their
 friends,
And that some folks loved people but for their
 own ends.

"Zounds, neighbor!" quoth Pitt, "what the
 devil's the matter?
A man cannot rest in his house for your clat-
 ter;"
"Alas!" cries the daughter, "here's dainty
 fine work,
The old woman grown harder than Jew or
 than Turk."

"She be——," says the farmer, and to her
 he goes,
First roars in her ears, then tweaks her old
 nose,
"Hallo, Goody, what ails you? Wake! wo-
 man, I say;
I am come to make peace, in this desperate
 fray.

"Adzooks, ope thine eyes, what a pother is
 here!
You 've no right to compel her, you have not, I
 swear;
Be ruled by your friends, kneel down and ask
 pardon,
You 'd be sorry, I'm sure, should she walk
 Covent Garden."

"Alas!" cries the old woman, "and must I
 comply?
But I'd rather submit than the huzzy should
 die;"
"Pooh, prithee be quiet, be friends and agree,
You must surely be right, *if you 're guided by
 me*."

Unwillingly awkward, the mother knelt down,
While the absolute farmer went on with a
 frown,
"Come, kiss the poor child, there come, kiss
 and be friends!
There, kiss your poor daughter, and make her
 amends."

"No thanks to you, mother," the daughter
 replied:
"But thanks to my friend here, I've hum-
 bled your pride."

But Pitt was soon incapacitated by illness from
taking any active part in the government, and
Charles Townshend, chancellor of the exchequer,
was able to pass his "port bills," and other op-
pressive measures. Many prominent Americans,
among them Samuel Adams, decided that the col-
onies must be independent.

A SONG

[January 26, 1769]

COME, cheer up, my lads, like a true British
 band,
In the cause of our country who join heart and
 hand:

Fair Freedom invites — she cries out, "Agree!
And be steadfast for those that are steadfast
    for me."
   Hearts of oak are we all, hearts of oak
   we'll remain:
        We always are ready —
        Steady, boys, steady —
   To give them our voices again and
   again.

With the brave sons of Freedom, of every
   degree,
Unite all the good — and united are we:
But still be the lot of the villains disgrace,
Whose foul, rotten hearts give the lie to their
   face.
   Hearts of oak, etc.

See! their unblushing chieftain! perverter of
   laws!
His teeth are the shark's, and a vulture's his
   claws —
As soon would I venture, howe'er he may
   talk,
My lambs with a wolf, or my fowls with a
   hawk.
   Hearts of oak, etc.

First — the worth of good Cruger let's crown
   with applause,
Who has join'd us again in fair Liberty's
   cause —
Sour Envy, herself, is afraid of his name,
And weeps that she finds not a blot in his
   fame.
   Hearts of oak, etc.

To Jauncey, my souls, let your praises re-
   sound!
With health and success may his goodness be
   crown'd:
May the cup of his joy never cease to run
   o'er —
For he gave to us all when he gave to the poor!
   Hearts of oak, etc.

What Briton, undaunted, that pants to be
   free,
But warms at the mention of brave De
   Launcey?
"Happy Freedom!" said Fame, "what a son
   have you here!
Whose head is approved, and whose heart is
   sincere."
   Hearts of oak, etc.

For worth and for truth, and good nature
   renown'd,
Let the name and applauses of Walton go
   round:
His prudence attracts — but his free, honest
   soul
Gives a grace to the rest, and enlivens the
   whole.
   Hearts of oak, etc.

Huzza! for the patriots whose virtue is tried —
Unbiass'd by faction, untainted by pride:
Who Liberty's welfare undaunted pursue,
With heads ever clear, and hearts ever true.
   Hearts of oak, etc.

New York Journal, January 26, 1769.

Associations known as Sons of Liberty were
organized in the larger cities, and in February,
1770, the first Liberty Pole in America was raised
at New York city, in what is now City Hall Park.
A struggle ensued with the British troops, during
which the pole was twice cut down, but it was
hooped with iron and set up a third time. A Tory
versifier celebrated the event in a burlesque
cantata, from which the following description of
the pole is taken.

THE LIBERTY POLE

[February, 1770]

Come listen, good neighbors of every degree,
Whose hearts, like your purses, are open and
   free,
Let this pole a monument ever remain,
Of the folly and arts of the time-serving train.
   Derry down, down, hey derry down.

Its bottom, so artfully fix'd under ground,
Resembles their scheming, so low and pro
   found;
The dark underminings, and base dirty ends.
On which the success of the faction depends.
   Derry down, etc.

The vane, mark'd with freedom, may put us
   in mind,
As it varies, and flutters, and turns, with the
   wind,
That no faith can be plac'd in the words of our
   foes,
Who change as the wind of their interest
   blows.
   Derry down, etc.

The iron clasp'd around it, so firm and so neat,
Resembles too closely their fraud and deceit,
If the outside's but guarded, they care not a pin
How rotten and hollow the heart is within.
    Derry down, etc.

Then away, ye pretenders to freedom, away,
Who strive to cajole us in hopes to betray;
Leave the pole for the stroke of the lightning
        to sever,
And, huzzah for King George and our coun-
        try forever!
    Derry down, etc.

Two regiments of British troops arrived at
Boston on March 5, 1768, and annoyed the people
in many ways. Brawls were frequent, and by the
beginning of 1770 the tension of feeling had
reached the snapping point. The "Massachusetts
Liberty Song" and "The British Grenadier" did
not go well together.

THE BRITISH GRENADIER

COME, come fill up your glasses,
    And drink a health to those
Who carry caps and pouches,
    And wear their looped clothes.
For be you Whig or Tory,
    Or any mortal thing,
Be sure that you give glory
    To George, our gracious King.
For if you prove rebellious,
    He'll thunder in your ears
Huzza! Huzza! Huzza! Huzza!
    For the British Grenadiers!

And when the wars are over,
    We'll march by beat of drum,
The ladies cry "So, Ho girls,
    The Grenadiers have come!
The Grenadiers who always
    With love our hearts do cheer.
Then Huzza! Huzza! Huzza! Huzza!
    For the British Grenadier!"

On the evening of March 5 a crowd collected
near the barracks and some blows were exchanged;
a sentinel in King Street knocked down a boy, and
was about to be mobbed, when Captain Preston
and seven privates came to his assistance. The
crowd pressed upon their levelled pieces, which
were suddenly discharged, killing four men and
wounding seven. Crispus Attucks, a mulatto
slave, was the first to fall.

CRISPUS ATTUCKS

[March 5, 1770]

WHERE shall we seek for a hero, and where
        shall we find a story?
Our laurels are wreathed for conquest, our
        songs for completed glory.
But we honor a shrine unfinished, a column
        uncapped with pride,
If we sing the deed that was sown like seed
        when Crispus Attucks died.

Shall we take for a sign this Negro slave with
        unfamiliar name —
With his poor companions, nameless too, till
        their lives leaped forth in flame?
Yea, surely, the verdict is not for us, to render
        or deny;
We can only interpret the symbol; God chose
        these men to die —
As teachers and types, that to humble lives
        may chief award be made;
That from lowly ones, and rejected stones,
        the temple's base is laid!

When the bullets leaped from the British guns,
        no chance decreed their aim;
Men see what the royal hirelings saw — a
        multitude and a flame;
But beyond the flame, a mystery; five dying
        men in the street,
While the streams of severed races in the well
        of a nation meet!

O blood of the people! changeless tide,
        through century, creed, and race!
Still one as the sweet salt air is one, though
        tempered by sun and place;
The same in the ocean currents, and the same
        in the sheltered seas;
Forever the fountain of common hopes and
        kindly sympathies;
Indian and Negro, Saxon and Celt, Teuton
        and Latin and Gaul —
Mere surface shadow and sunshine; while the
        sounding unifies all!
One love, one hope, one duty theirs! No
        matter the time or ken,
There never was separate heart-beat in all the
        races of men!

But alien is one — of class, not race — he has
        drawn the line for himself;
His roots drink life from inhuman soil, from
        garbage of pomp and pelf;

His heart beats not with the common beat,
  he has changed his life-stream's hue;
He deems his flesh to be finer flesh, he boasts
  that his blood is blue:
Patrician, aristocrat, Tory — whatever his
  age or name,
To the people's rights and liberties, a traitor
  ever the same.
The natural crowd is a mob to him, their
  prayer a vulgar rhyme;
The freeman's speech is sedition, and the
  patriot's deed a crime.
Wherever the race, the law, the land, — what-
  ever the time or throne,
The Tory is always a traitor to every class but
  his own.

Thank God for a land where pride is clipped,
  where arrogance stalks apart;
Where law and song and loathing of wrong
  are words of the common heart;
Where the masses honor straightforward
  strength, and know, when veins are
  bled,
That the bluest blood is putrid blood — that
  the people's blood is red!

And honor to Crispus Attucks, who was
  leader and voice that day;
The first to defy and the first to die, with
  Maverick, Carr, and Gray.
Call it riot or revolution, his hand first
  clenched at the crown;
His feet were the first in perilous place to pull
  the king's flag down;
His breast was the first one rent apart that
  liberty's stream might flow;
For our freedom now and forever, his head
  was the first laid low.

Call it riot or revolution, or mob or crowd, as
  you may,
Such deaths have been seed of nations, such
  lives shall be honored for aye.
They were lawless hinds to the lackeys — but
  martyrs to Paul Revere;
And Otis and Hancock and Warren read spirit
  and meaning clear.
Ye teachers, answer: what shall be done when
  just men stand in the dock;
When the caitiff is robed in ermine, and his
  sworders keep the lock;
When torture is robbed of clemency, and
  guilt is without remorse;

When tiger and panther are gentler than the
  Christian slaver's curse;
When law is a satrap's menace, and order the
  drill of a horde —
Shall the people kneel to be trampled, and
  bare their neck to the sword?

Not so! by this Stone of Resistance that
  Boston raises here!
By the old North Church's lantern, and the
  watching of Paul Revere!
Not so! by Paris of 'Ninety-Three, and Ulster
  of 'Ninety-Eight!
By Toussaint in St. Domingo! by the horror
  of Delhi's gate!
By Adams's word to Hutchinson! by the tea
  that is brewing still!
By the farmers that met the soldiers at Con-
  cord and Bunker Hill!

Not so! not so! Till the world is done, the
  shadow of wrong is dread;
The crowd that bends to a lord to-day, to-
  morrow shall strike him dead.
There is only one thing changeless: the earth
  steals from under our feet,
The times and manners are passing moods,
  and the laws are incomplete;
There is only one thing changes not, one
  word that still survives —
The slave is the wretch who wields the lash,
  and not the man in gyves!

There is only one test of contract: is it willing,
  is it good?
There is only one guard of equal right: the
  unity of blood;
There is never a mind unchained and true that
  class or race allows;
There is never a law to be obeyed that reason
  disavows;
There is never a legal sin but grows to the
  law's disaster,
The master shall drop the whip, and the slave
  shall enslave the master!

Oh, Planter of seed in thought and deed has
  the year of right revolved,
And brought the Negro patriot's cause with
  its problem to be solved?
His blood streamed first for the building, and
  through all the century's years,
Our growth of story and fame of glory are
  mixed with his blood and tears.

He lived with men like a soul condemned —
    derided, defamed, and mute;
Debased to the brutal level, and instructed to
    be a brute.
His virtue was shorn of benefit, his industry
    of reward;
His love! — O men, it were mercy to have cut
    affection's cord;
Through the night of his woe, no pity save
    that of his fellow-slave;
For the wage of his priceless labor, the scourg-
    ing block and the grave!

And now, is the tree to blossom? Is the bowl
    of agony filled?
Shall the price be paid and the honor said, and
    the word of outrage stilled?
And we who have toiled for freedom's law,
    have we sought for freedom's soul?
Have we learned at last that human right is
    not a part but the whole?
That nothing is told while the clinging sin
    remains part unconfessed?
That the health of the nation is perilled if one
    man be oppressed?

Has he learned — the slave from the rice-
    swamps, whose children were sold —
    has he,
With broken chains on his limbs, and the cry
    in his blood, "I am free!"
Has he learned through affliction's teaching
    what our Crispus Attucks knew —
When Right is stricken, the white and black
    are counted as one, not two?
Has he learned that his century of grief was
    worth a thousand years
In blending his life and blood with ours, and
    that all his toils and tears
Were heaped and poured on him suddenly,
    to give him a right to stand
From the gloom of African forests, in the blaze
    of the freest land?
That his hundred years have earned for him a
    place in the human van
Which others have fought for and thought for
    since the world of wrong began?

For this, shall his vengeance change to love,
    and his retribution burn,
Defending the right, the weak, and the poor,
    when each shall have his turn;
For this, shall he set his woeful past afloat on
    the stream of night;

For this, he forgets as we all forget when dark-
    ness turns to light;
For this, he forgives as we all forgive when
    wrong has changed to right.

And so, must we come to the learning of Bos-
    ton's lesson to-day;
The moral that Crispus Attucks taught in the
    old heroic way;
God made mankind to be one in blood, as one
    in spirit and thought;
And so great a boon, by a brave man's death,
    is never dearly bought!
                          JOHN BOYLE O'REILLY.

This insignificant street riot was the famous
"Boston Massacre." It created a great stir, and
the victims were buried with military honors on
March 8, the bodies being deposited in a single
vault. A few days later, Paul Revere engraved
and printed a large hand-bill giving a picture of
the scene, accompanied by the following lines:

UNHAPPY BOSTON

[March 8, 1770]

UNHAPPY Boston! see thy sons deplore
Thy hallowed walks besmear'd with guiltless
    gore.
While faithless Preston and his savage bands,
With murderous rancor stretch their bloody
    hands;
Like fierce barbarians grinning o'er their
    prey,
Approve the carnage and enjoy the day.
If scalding drops, from rage, from anguish
    wrung,
If speechless sorrows lab'ring for a tongue,
Or if a weeping world can aught appease
The plaintive ghosts of victims such as these;
The patriot's copious tears for each are shed,
A glorious tribute which embalms the dead.
But know, Fate summons to that awful goal,
Where justice strips the murderer of his soul:
Should venal C——ts, the scandal of the land,
Snatch the relentless villain from her hand,
Keen execrations on this plate inscrib'd
Shall reach a judge who never can be bribed.
                          PAUL REVERE.

A conflict of a much more serious nature took
place at Alamance, N. C., on May 7, 1771, be-
tween a body of colonists, goaded to rebellion
by repeated acts of extortion, and a force of
British regulars under Governor Tryon. The col-

onists were totally defeated and left two hundred dead and wounded on the field.

ALAMANCE

[May 7, 1771]

No stately column marks the hallowed place
  Where silent sleeps, un-urned, their sacred dust:
The first free martyrs of a glorious race,
  Their fame a people's wealth, a nation's trust.

The rustic ploughman at the early morn
  The yielding furrow turns with heedless tread,
Or tends with frugal care the springing corn,
  Where tyrants conquered and where heroes bled.

Above their rest the golden harvest waves,
  The glorious stars stand sentinels on high,
While in sad requiem, near their turfless graves,
  The winding river murmurs, mourning, by.

No stern ambition moved them to the deed:
  In Freedom's cause they nobly dared to die.
The first to conquer, or the first to bleed,
  "God and their country's right" their battle cry.

But holier watchers here their vigils keep
  Than storied urn or monumental stone;
For Law and Justice guard their dreamless sleep,
  And Plenty smiles above their bloody home.

Immortal youth shall crown their deathless fame;
  And as their country's glories shall advance,
Shall brighter blaze, o'er all the earth, thy name,
  Thou first-fought field of Freedom — Alamance.
                              SEYMOUR W. WHITING.

The first American "victory" occurred on the night of June 9, 1772, when the British eight-gun schooner Gaspee was captured and burned to the water's edge. For some months the crew of the Gaspee, commissioned to enforce the revenue acts in Narragansett Bay, had been stopping vessels, seizing goods, stealing sheep and hogs, and committing other depredations along the shore. On June 9, while pursuing the Providence Packet, the schooner ran aground, and that night was boarded by a party of Rhode Islanders, the crew overpowered, and the boat burned.

A NEW SONG CALLED THE GASPEE

[June 9–10, 1772]

'T WAS in the reign of George the Third
The public peace was much disturb'd
By ships of war, that came and laid
Within our ports to stop our trade.

In seventeen hundred seventy-two,
In Newport harbor lay a crew
That play'd the parts of pirates there,
The sons of Freedom could not bear.

Sometimes they'd weigh and give them chase —
Such actions, sure, were very base;
No honest coasters could pass by
But what they would let some shot fly.

Which did provoke to high degree
Those true-born sons of Liberty,
So that they could no longer bear
Those sons of Belial staying there.

But 't was not long 'fore it fell out,
That William Doddington so stout,
Commander of the Gaspee tender,
Which he had reason to remember —

Because, as people do assert,
He almost had his just desert
Here, on the tenth day of last June,
Between the hours of twelve and one —

Did chase the sloop call'd the Hannah,
Of whom one Linsey was commander;
They dogg'd her up to Providence Sound,
And there the rascal got aground.

The news of it flew, that very day,
That they on Nanquit Point did lay,
That night, about half after ten,
Some Narragansett Indian-men —

Being sixty-four, if I remember,
Soon made this stout coxcomb surrender:
And what was best of all their tricks,
They in his breech a ball did fix.

They set the men upon the land,
And burn'd her up, we understand;
Which thing provoked the king so high,
He said, "those men should surely die."

So, if he can but find them out,
The hangman he 'll employ, no doubt:
For he has declared, in his passion,
"He 'll have them tried in a new fashion."

Now for to find those people out,
King George has offered, very stout,
One thousand pounds to find out one
That wounded William Doddington.

One thousand more he says he 'll spare,
For those who say they sheriffs were:
One thousand more there doth remain
For to find out the leader's name.

Likewise, one hundred pounds per man,
For any one of all the clan.
But let him try his utmost skill,
I 'm apt to think he never will
Find out any of those hearts of gold,
Though he should offer fifty fold.

The duty on tea, imposed five years before
by Townshend, had been retained by the British
government as a matter of principle, and in the
autumn of 1773 the King determined to assert
the obnoxious principle which the tax involved.
Several ships loaded with tea were accordingly
started for America. On Sunday, November 28,
the first of these arrived at Boston, and two others
came in a few days later. The town went wild,
meeting after meeting was held, and on the night
of Tuesday, December 16, 1773, a band of about
twenty, disguised as Indians, boarded the ships,
cut open the tea-chests and flung the contents into
the water.

A BALLAD OF THE BOSTON TEA-PARTY

[December 16, 1773]

No! never such a draught was poured
  Since Hebe served with nectar
The bright Olympians and their Lord,
  Her over-kind protector, —
Since Father Noah squeezed the grape
  And took to such behaving
As would have shamed our grandsire ape
  Before the days of shaving, —
No! ne'er was mingled such a draught
  In palace, hall. or arbor,

As freemen brewed and tyrants quaffed
  That night in Boston Harbor!
It kept King George so long awake
  His brain at last got addled,
It made the nerves of Britain shake,
  With sevenscore millions saddled;
Before that bitter cup was drained
  Amid the roar of cannon,
The Western war-cloud's crimson stained
  The Thames, the Clyde, the Shannon;
Full many a six-foot grenadier
  The flattened grass had measured,
And many a mother many a year
  Her tearful memories treasured;
Fast spread the tempest's darkening pall,
  The mighty realms were troubled,
The storm broke loose, but first of all
  The Boston teapot bubbled!

An evening party, — only that,
  No formal invitation,
No gold-laced coat, no stiff cravat,
  No feast in contemplation,
No silk-robed dames, no fiddling band,
  No flowers, no songs, no dancing, —
A tribe of red men, axe in hand, —
  Behold the guests advancing!
How fast the stragglers join the throng,
  From stall and workshop gathered!
The lively barber skips along
  And leaves a chin half-lathered;
The smith has flung his hammer down, —
  The horseshoe still is glowing;
The truant tapster at the Crown
  Has left a beer-cask flowing;
The cooper's boys have dropped the adze,
  And trot behind their master;
Up run the tarry ship-yard lads, —
  The crowd is hurrying faster, —
Out from the Millpond's purlieus gush
  The streams of white-faced millers,
And down their slippery alleys rush
  The lusty young Fort-Hillers;
The ropewalk lends its 'prentice crew, —
  The tories seize the omen:
"Ay, boys, you 'll soon have work to do
  For England's rebel foemen,
'King Hancock,' Adams, and their gang,
  That fire the mob with treason, —
When these we shoot and those we hang
  The town will come to reason."

On — on to where the tea-ships ride!
  And now their ranks are forming, —

A rush, and up the Dartmouth's side
  The Mohawk band is swarming!
See the fierce natives! What a glimpse
  Of paint and fur and feather,
As all at once the full-grown imps
  Light on the deck together!
A scarf the pigtail's secret keeps,
  A blanket hides the breeches, —
And out the cursèd cargo leaps,
  And overboard it pitches!

O woman, at the evening board
  So gracious, sweet, and purring,
So happy while the tea is poured,
  So blest while spoons are stirring,
What martyr can compare with thee,
  The mother, wife, or daughter,
That night, instead of best Bohea,
  Condemned to milk and water!

Ah, little dreams the quiet dame
  Who plies with rock and spindle
The patient flax, how great a flame
  Yon little spark shall kindle!
The lurid morning shall reveal
  A fire no king can smother
Where British flint and Boston steel
  Have clashed against each other!
Old charters shrivel in its track,
  His Worship's bench has crumbled,
It climbs and clasps the union-jack,
  Its blazoned pomp is humbled,
The flags go down on land and sea
  Like corn before the reapers;
So burned the fire that brewed the tea
  That Boston served her keepers!

The waves that wrought a century's wreck
  Have rolled o'er whig and tory;
The Mohawks on the Dartmouth's deck
  Still live in song and story;
The waters in the rebel bay
  Have kept the tea-leaf savor;
Our old North-Enders in their spray
  Still taste a Hyson flavor;
And Freedom's teacup still o'erflows
  With ever fresh libations,
To cheat of slumber all her foes
  And cheer the wakening nations!
                OLIVER WENDELL HOLMES.

Next morning, Paul Revere, booted and spurred, started for Philadelphia with the news that Boston had at last thrown down the gauntlet. The following song appeared in the *Pennsylvania Packet* a few days after Revere reached Philadelphia.

A NEW SONG

[December 16, 1773]

As near beauteous Boston lying,
  On the gently swelling flood,
Without jack or pendant flying,
  Three ill-fated tea-ships rode.

Just as glorious Sol was setting,
  On the wharf, a numerous crew,
Sons of freedom, fear forgetting,
  Suddenly appeared in view.

Armed with hammers, axe, and chisels,
  Weapons new for warlike deed,
Towards the herbage-freighted vessels,
  They approached with dreadful speed.

O'er their heads aloft in mid-sky,
  Three bright angel forms were seen;
This was Hampden, that was Sidney,
  With fair Liberty between.

"Soon," they cried, "your foes you'll banish,
  Soon the triumph shall be won;
Scarce shall setting Phœbus vanish,
  Ere the deathless deed be done."

Quick as thought the ships were boarded,
  Hatches burst and chests displayed;
Axes, hammers help afforded;
  What a glorious crash they made.

Squash into the deep descended,
  Cursed weed of China's coast;
Thus at once our fears were ended;
  British rights shall ne'er be lost.

Captains! once more hoist your streamers,
  Spread your sails, and plough the wave;
Tell your masters they were dreamers,
  When they thought to cheat the brave.

News of the insurrection was received in England with the greatest indignation, and measures of reprisal were at once undertaken. No ships were to be allowed to enter the port of Boston until the rebellious town should have repaid the East India Company for the loss of its tea; the charter of Massachusetts was annulled and her free government destroyed; and General Gage was sent over with four regiments to take possession of the town.

HOW WE BECAME A NATION

[April 15, 1774]

WHEN George the King would punish folk
    Who dared resist his angry will —
Resist him with their hearts of oak
That neither King nor Council broke —
    He told Lord North to mend his quill,
    And sent his Parliament a Bill.

The Boston Port Bill was the thing
    He flourished in his royal hand;
A subtle lash with scorpion sting,
Across the seas he made it swing,
    And with its cruel thong he planned
    To quell the disobedient land.

His minions heard it sing, and bare
    The port of Boston felt his wrath;
They let no ship cast anchor there,
They summoned Hunger and Despair, —
    And curses in an aftermath
    Followed their desolating path.

No coal might enter there, nor wood,
    Nor Holland flax, nor silk from France;
No drugs for dying pangs, no food
    For any mother's little brood.
    "Now," said the King, "we have our chance,
    We'll lead the haughty knaves a dance."

No other flags lit up the bay,
    Like full-blown blossoms in the air,
Than where the British war-ships lay;
The wharves were idle; all the day
    The idle men, grown gaunt and spare,
    Saw trouble, pall-like, everywhere.

Then in across the meadow land,
    From lonely farm and hunter's tent,
From fertile field and fallow strand,
Pouring it out with lavish hand,
    The neighboring burghs their bounty sent,
    And laughed at King and Parliament.

To bring them succor, Marblehead
    Joyous her deep-sea fishing sought.
Her trees, with ringing stroke and tread,
Old many-rivered Newbury sped,
    And Groton in her granaries wrought,
    And generous flocks old Windham brought.

Rice from the Carolinas came,
    Iron from Pennsylvania's forge,
And, with a spirit all aflame,
Tobacco-leaf and corn and game
    The Midlands sent; and in his gorge
    The Colonies defied King George!

And Hartford hung, in black array,
    Her town-house, and at half-mast there
The flags flowed, and the bells all day
Tolled heavily; and far away
    In great Virginia's solemn air
    The House of Burgesses held prayer.

Down long glades of the forest floor
    The same thrill ran through every vein,
And down the long Atlantic's shore;
Its heat the tyrant's fetters tore
    And welded them through stress and strain
    Of long years to a mightier chain.

That mighty chain with links of steel
    Bound all the Old Thirteen at last,
Through one electric pulse to feel
The common woe, the common weal.
    And that great day the Port Bill passed
    Made us a nation hard and fast.
                    HARRIET PRESCOTT SPOFFORD.

Gage arrived at Boston in May, 1774, and at once issued a proclamation calling upon the inhabitants to be loyal, and warning them of his intention to maintain the authority of the King at any cost.

A PROCLAMATION

[May, 1774]

AMERICA! thou fractious nation,
Attend thy master's proclamation!
Tremble! for know, I, Thomas Gage,
Determin'd come the war to wage.

With the united powers sent forth,
Of Bute, of Mansfield, and of North;
To scourge your insolence, my choice,
While England mourns and Scots rejoice!

Bostonia first shall feel my power,
And gasping midst the dreadful shower
Of ministerial rage, shall cry,
Oh, save me, Bute! I yield! and die.

Then shall my thundering cannons rattle,
My hardy veterans march to battle,
Against Virginia's hostile land,
To humble that rebellious band.

At my approach her trembling swains
Shall quit well-cultivated plains,
To seek the inhospitable wood;
Or try, like swine of old, the flood.

Rejoice! ye happy Scots rejoice!
Your voice lift up, a mighty voice,
The voice of gladness on each tongue,
The mighty praise of Bute be sung.

The praise of Mansfield, and of North,
Let next your hymns of joy set forth,
Nor shall the rapturous strain assuage,
'Till sung's your own proclaiming Gage.

Whistle ye pipes! ye drones drone on.
Ye bellows blow! Virginia's won!
Your Gage has won Virginia's shore,
And Scotia's sons shall mourn no more.

Hail, Middlesex! oh happy county!
Thou too shalt share thy master's bounty,
Thy sons obedient, naught shall fear,
Thy wives and widows drop no tear.

Thrice happy people, ne'er shall feel
The force of unrelenting steel;
What brute would give the ox a stroke
Who bends his neck to meet the yoke?

To Murray bend the humble knee;
He shall protect you under me;
His generous pen shall not be mute,
But sound your praise thro' Fox to Bute.

By Scotchmen lov'd, by Scotchmen taught,
By all your country Scotchmen thought;
Fear Bute, fear Mansfield, North and me,
And be as blest as slaves can be.

The Virginia Gazette, 1774.

The colonies rallied nobly to Boston's support;
provisions of all sorts were sent over-land to the
devoted city; the 1st of June, the day on which
the Port Bill went into effect, was observed as a
day of fasting and prayer throughout the country,
and it became a point of honor with all good pa-
triots to refrain from indulgence in "the blasted
herb."

THE BLASTED HERB

[1774]

ROUSE every generous, thoughtful mind,
The rising danger flee,
If you would lasting freedom find,
Now then abandon tea.

Scorn to be bound with golden chains,
Though they allure the sight;
Bid them defiance, if they claim
Our freedom and birthright.

Shall we our freedom give away,
And all our comfort place,
In drinking of outlandish tea,
Only to please our taste?

Forbid it Heaven, let us be wise,
And seek our country's good;
Nor ever let a thought arise
That tea should be our food.

Since we so great a plenty have,
Of all that's for our health,
Shall we that blasted herb receive,
Impoverishing our wealth?

When we survey the breathless corpse,
With putrid matter filled,
For crawling worms a sweet resort,
By us reputed ill.

Noxious effluvia sending out
From its pernicious store,
Not only from the foaming mouth,
But every lifeless pore.

To view the same enrolled in tea,
Besmeared with such perfumes,
And then the herb sent o'er the sea,
To us it tainted comes —

Some of it tinctured with a filth
Of carcasses embalmed;
Taste of this herb, then, if thou wilt!
Sure me it cannot charm.

Adieu! away, oh tea! begone!
Salute our taste no more;
Though thou art coveted by some,
Who're destined to be poor.

MESECH WEARE.

Fowle's *Gazette*. July 22. 1774.

EPIGRAM

ON THE POOR OF BOSTON BEING EMPLOYED
IN PAVING THE STREETS, 1774

In spite of *Rice*, in spite of *Wheat*,
Sent for the Boston Poor — to eat:
In spite of *Brandy*, one would think,
Sent for the Boston Poor — to drink:
Poor are the Boston Poor, indeed,
And needy, tho' there is no Need:
They cry for Bread; the mighty Ones
Instead of *Bread*, give only *Stones*.

Rivington's *New York Gazetteer*, September 2,
1774.

It was plain that, in this crisis, the colonies
must stick together, and the proposal for a Con-
tinental Congress, first made by the Sons of Lib-
erty in New York, was approved by colony after
colony, and the Congress was finally called to
meet at Philadelphia, September 1.

THE DAUGHTER'S REBELLION

When fair Columbia was a child,
And mother Britain on her smil'd
With kind regard, and strok'd her head,
And gave her dolls and gingerbread,
And sugar plumbs, and many a toy,
Which prompted gratitude and joy —
Then a more duteous maid, I ween,
Ne'er frisked it o'er the playful green;
Whate'er the mother said, approv'd,
And with sincere affection lov'd —
With reverence listen'd to her dreams,
And bowed obsequious to her schemes —
Barter'd the products of her garden,
For trinkets, worth more than a farthing —
And whensoe'er the mother sigh'd,
She, sympathetic daughter, cri'd,
Fearing the heavy, long-drawn breath,
Betoken'd her approaching death.
But when at puberty arriv'd,
Forgot the power in whom she liv'd,
And 'gan to make preposterous splutter,
'Bout spreading her own bread and butter,
And stubbornly refus'd t' agree,
In form, to drink her bohea-tea,
And like a base, ungrateful daughter,
Hurl'd a whole tea box in the water —
'Bout writing paper made a pother,
And dared to argue with her mother —
Contended pertly, that the nurse,
Should not be keeper of the purse;

But that herself, now older grown,
Would have a pocket of her own,
In which the purse she would deposit,
As safely as in nurse's closet.

FRANCIS HOPKINSON.

The Whig papers generally at this time adopted
for a headpiece a snake broken into parts repre-
senting the several colonies, with the motto,
"Unite or Die."

ON THE SNAKE

DEPICTED AT THE HEAD OF SOME AMERICAN
NEWSPAPERS

Ye sons of Sedition, how comes it to pass
That America's typ'd by a Snake — in the
grass?
Don't you think 't is a scandalous, saucy
reflection,
That merits the soundest, severest correction?
New-England's the Head, too; — New-
England's abus'd,
For the Head of the Serpent we know should
be bruis'd.

From Rivington's *New York Gazetteer*, Au-
gust 25, 1774.

The feeling of the entire country was aptly
voiced in "Free America," which appeared at
that time, and which was ascribed to Dr. Joseph
Warren.

FREE AMERICA

[1774]

That seat of Science, Athens,
And earth's proud mistress, Rome;
Where now are all their glories?
We scarce can find a tomb.
Then guard your rights, Americans,
Nor stoop to lawless sway;
Oppose, oppose, oppose, oppose,
For North America.

We led fair Freedom hither,
And lo, the desert smiled!
A paradise of pleasure
Was opened in the wild!
Your harvest, bold Americans,
No power shall snatch away!
Huzza, huzza, huzza, huzza,
For free America.

Torn from a world of tyrants,
Beneath this western sky,

We formed a new dominion,
A land of liberty:
The world shall own we're masters here;
Then hasten on the day:
Huzza, huzza, huzza, huzza,
    For free America.

Proud Albion bowed to Cæsar,
And numerous lords before;
To Picts, to Danes, to Normans,
And many masters more:
But we can boast, Americans,
We've never fallen a prey;
Huzza, huzza, huzza, huzza,
    For free America.

God bless this maiden climate,
And through its vast domain
May hosts of heroes cluster,
Who scorn to wear a chain:
And blast the venal sycophant
That dares our rights betray;
Huzza, huzza, huzza, huzza,
    For free America.

Lift up your hands, ye heroes,
And swear with proud disdain,
The wretch that would ensnare you,
Shall lay his snares in vain:
Should Europe empty all her force,
We'll meet her in array,
And fight and shout, and shout and fight
    For North America.

Some future day shall crown us,
The masters of the main,
Our fleets shall speak in thunder
To England, France, and Spain;
And the nations over the ocean spread
Shall tremble and obey
The sons, the sons, the sons, the sons
    Of brave America.
                    JOSEPH WARREN.

The Continental Congress assembled at Phila-
delphia, September 5, 1774, and, after four weeks'
deliberation, agreed upon a declaration of rights,
claiming for the American people the right of
free legislation and calling for the repeal of eleven
acts of Parliament.

LIBERTY TREE

In a chariot of light from the regions of day,
    The Goddess of Liberty came;

Ten thousand celestials directed the way
    And hither conducted the dame.
A fair budding branch from the gardens
        above,
    Where millions with millions agree,
She brought in her hand as a pledge of her
        love,
    And the plant she named *Liberty Tree*.

The celestial exotic struck deep in the ground,
    Like a native it flourished and bore;
The fame of its fruit drew the nations around,
    To seek out this peaceable shore.
Unmindful of names or distinction they came,
    For freemen like brothers agree;
With one spirit endued, they one friendship
        pursued,
    And their temple was *Liberty Tree*.

Beneath this fair tree, like the patriarchs of
        old,
    Their bread in contentment they ate,
Unvexed with the troubles of silver and
        gold,
    The cares of the grand and the great.
With timber and tar they Old England sup-
        plied,
    And supported her power on the sea;
Her battles they fought, without getting a
        groat,
    For the honor of *Liberty Tree*.

But hear, O ye swains, 't is a tale most pro-
        fane,
    How all the tyrannical powers,
Kings, Commons, and Lords, are uniting
        amain,
    To cut down this guardian of ours;
From the east to the west blow the trumpet to
        arms
    Through the land let the sound of it
        flee,
Let the far and the near, all unite with a
        cheer,
    In defence of our *Liberty Tree*.
                    THOMAS PAINE.
Pennsylvania Magazine, 1775.

The duty of presenting to the British govern-
ment the Declaration of Rights prepared by the
Congress devolved upon Benjamin Franklin, who
was in England at the time. Lord Dartmouth
received the document, but permission was re-
fused Franklin to present the case for the Con-
tinental Congress, and to defend it, before the
House of Commons.

THE MOTHER COUNTRY

[1775]

WE have an old mother that peevish is
    grown;
She snubs us like children that scarce walk
    alone;
She forgets we're grown up and have sense
    of our own;
        Which nobody can deny, deny,
        Which nobody can deny.

If we don't obey orders, whatever the case,
She frowns, and she chides, and she loses all
    pati-
Ence, and sometimes she hits us a slap in the
    face;
        Which nobody, etc.

Her orders so odd are, we often suspect
That age has impaired her sound intellect;
But still an old mother should have due re-
    spect;
        Which nobody, etc.

Let's bear with her humors as well as we can;
But why should we bear the abuse of her
    man?
When servants make mischief, they earn the
    rattan;
        Which nobody, etc.

Know, too, ye bad neighbors, who aim to
    divide
The sons from the mother, that still she's
    our pride;
And if ye attack her, we're all of her side;
        Which nobody, etc.

We'll join in her lawsuits, to baffle all those
Who, to get what she has, will be often her
    foes;
For we know it must all be our own, when
    she goes;
        Which nobody can deny, deny,
        Which nobody can deny.
                    BENJAMIN FRANKLIN.

Very few Englishmen believed that the Ameri-
cans would fight. Lord Sandwich said that they
were a lot of undisciplined cowards, who would
take to their heels at the first sound of a cannon,
and that it would be easy to frighten them into
submission. The "Pennsylvania Song" was evi-
dently written to answer this assertion.

PENNSYLVANIA SONG

WE are the troop that ne'er will stoop
    To wretched slavery,
Nor shall our seed, by our base deed,
    Despisèd vassals be;
Freedom we will bequeath to them,
    Or we will bravely die;
Our greatest foe, ere long shall know,
    How much did Sandwich lie.
        And all the world shall know,
        Americans are free;
        Nor slaves nor cowards we will prove,
        Great Britain soon shall see.

We'll not give up our birthright,
    Our foes shall find us men;
As good as they, in any shape,
    The British troops shall ken.
Huzza! brave boys, we'll beat them
    On any hostile plain;
For Freedom, wives, and children dear,
    The battle we'll maintain.
        And all the world, etc.

What! can those British tyrants think,
    Our fathers cross'd the main,
And savage foes, and dangers met,
    To be enslav'd by them?
If so, they are mistaken,
    For we will rather die;
And since they have become our foes,
    Their forces we defy.
        And all the world, etc.

Dunlap's *Packet*, 1775.

About the middle of December, 1774, deputies
appointed by the freemen of Maryland met at
Annapolis, and unanimously resolved to resist
the attempts of Parliament to tax the colonies
and to support the acts of the Continental Con-
gress. They also recommended that every man
should provide himself with "a good firelock,
with bayonet attached, powder and ball," to be
in readiness to act in any emergency.

MARYLAND RESOLVES

[December, 1774]

ON Calvert's plains new faction reigns,
    Great Britain we defy, sir,
True Liberty lies gagg'd in chains,
    Though freedom is the cry, sir.

The Congress, and their factious tools,
  Most wantonly oppress us,
Hypocrisy triumphant rules,
  And sorely does distress us.

The British bands with glory crown'd,
  No longer shall withstand us;
Our martial deeds loud fame shall sound
  Since mad Lee now commands us.

Triumphant soon a blow he'll strike,
  That all the world shall awe, sir,
And General Gage, Sir Perseus like,
  Behind his wheels he'll draw, sir.

When Gallic hosts, ungrateful men,
  Our race meant to extermine,
Pray did committees save us then,
  Or Hancock, or such vermin?

Then faction spurn! think for yourselves!
  Your parent state, believe me,
From real griefs, from factious elves,
  Will speedily relieve ye.

  Rivington's *Gazetteer.*

Such effusions as the "Massachusetts Liberty Song" became immensely popular, and bands of liberty-loving souls met nightly to sing them.

MASSACHUSETTS SONG OF LIBERTY

COME swallow your bumpers, ye *Tories,* and
    roar
That the Sons of fair Freedom are hamper'd
    once more;
But know that no *Cut-throats* our spirits can
    tame,
Nor a host of *Oppressors* shall smother the
    flame.
  In Freedom we're born, and, like Sons
  of the brave,
    Will never surrender,
    But swear to defend her,
  And scorn to survive, if unable to save.

Our grandsires, bless'd heroes, we'll give
    them a tear,
Nor sully their honors by stooping to fear;
Through deaths and through dangers their
    Trophies they won,
We dare be their *Rivals,* nor will be outdone.
  In Freedom we're born, etc.

Let tyrants and minions presume to despise,
Encroach on our RIGHTS, and make FREEDOM
    their prize;
The fruits of their rapine they never shall
    keep,
Though Vengeance may nod, yet how short
    is her sleep.
  In Freedom we're born, etc.

The tree which proud *Haman* for *Mordecai*
    rear'd
Stands recorded, that virtue endanger'd is
    spared;
That *rogues,* whom no bounds and no laws
    can restrain,
Must be stripp'd of their honors and humbled
    again.
  In Freedom we're born, etc.

Our wives and our babes, still protected, shall
    know
Those who dare to be free shall forever be
    so;
On these arms and these hearts they may
    safely rely
For in freedom we'll live, or like *Heroes* we'll
    die.
  In Freedom we're born, etc.

Ye insolent *Tyrants!* who wish to enthrall;
Ye *Minions,* ye *Placemen, Pimps, Pensioners,*
    all;
How short is your triumph, how feeble your
    trust,
Your honor must wither and nod to the dust.
  In Freedom we're born, etc.

When oppress'd and approach'd, our KING
    we implore,
Still firmly persuaded our RIGHTS he'll re-
    store;
When our hearts beat to arms to defend a
    just right,
Our monarch rules there, and forbids us to
    fight.
  In Freedom we're born, etc.

Not the glitter of arms nor the dread of a
    fray
Could make us submit to their chains for a
    day;
Withheld by affection, on *Britons* we call,
Prevent the fierce conflict which threatens
    your fall.
  In Freedom we're born, etc.

All ages should speak with amaze and applause
Of the prudence we show in support of our cause:
Assured of our safety, a BRUNSWICK still reigns,
Whose free loyal subjects are strangers to chains.
In Freedom we're born, etc.

Then join hand in hand, brave Americans all,
To be free is to live, to be slaves is to fall;
Has the land such a dastard as scorns not a LORD,
Who dreads not a fetter much more than a sword?
In Freedom we're born, etc.
Attributed to MRS. MERCY WARREN.

EPIGRAM

RUDELY forced to drink tea, Massachusetts, in anger,
Spills the tea on John Bull. John falls on to bang her.
Massachusetts, enraged, calls her neighbors to aid
And give Master John a severe bastinade.
Now, good men of the law, who is at fault,
The one who begins or resists the assault?
Anderson's *Constitutional Gazette*, 1775.

TO THE BOSTON WOMEN

O BOSTON wives and maids, draw near and see
Our delicate Souchong and Hyson tea,
Buy it, my charming girls, fair, black, or brown,
If not, we'll cut your throats, and burn your town.
St. James Chronicle.

It was evident that, in the excited state of the country, a single incident might turn the balance between peace and war and produce a general explosion. That incident was not long in coming.

"PROPHECY"

[1774]

HAIL, happy Britain, Freedom's blest retreat,
Great is thy power, thy wealth, thy glory great,
But wealth and power have no immortal day,
For all things ripen only to decay.
And when that time arrives, the lot of all,
When Britain's glory, power and wealth shall fall;
Then shall thy sons by Fate's unchanged decree
In other worlds another Britain see,
And what thou art, America shall be.
GULIAN VERPLANCK.

CHAPTER II

THE BURSTING OF THE STORM

All through the winter of 1774-75, the people of Massachusetts had offered a passive but effective resistance to General Gage. Not a councillor, judge, sheriff, or juryman could be found to serve under the royal commission; and for nine months the ordinary functions of government were suspended. At eventide, on every village-green, a company of yeomen drilled, and a supply of powder and ball was gradually collected at Concord; but every man in the province was given to understand that England must fire the first shot. At the beginning of spring, Gage received peremptory orders to arrest Samuel Adams and John Hancock, and send them to England to be tried for treason. He learned that they would be at a friend's house at Lexington, during the middle of April, and on the night of April 18 dispatched a force of eight hundred men to seize them, and then to proceed to Concord and destroy the military stores collected there. Although the movement was conducted with the greatest secrecy, Joseph Warren divined its purpose, and sent out Paul Revere by way of Charlestown to give the alarm.

PAUL REVERE'S RIDE

[April 18-19, 1775]

LISTEN, my children, and you shall hear
Of the midnight ride of Paul Revere,
On the eighteenth of April, in Seventy-five;
Hardly a man is now alive
Who remembers that famous day and year.

He said to his friend, "If the British march
By land or sea from the town to-night,

Hang a lantern aloft in the belfry arch
Of the North Church tower as a signal light,—
One, if by land, and two, if by sea;
And I on the opposite shore will be,
Ready to ride and spread the alarm
Through every Middlesex village and farm,
For the country folk to be up and to arm.''

Then he said, "Good night!" and with
    muffled oar
Silently rowed to the Charlestown shore,
Just as the moon rose over the bay,
Where swinging wide at her moorings lay
The Somerset, British man-of-war;
A phantom ship, with each mast and spar
Across the moon like a prison bar,
And a huge black hulk, that was magnified
By its own reflection in the tide.

Meanwhile, his friend, through alley and
    street,
Wanders and watches with eager ears,
Till in the silence around him he hears
The muster of men at the barrack door,
The sound of arms, and the tramp of feet,
And the measured tread of the grenadiers,
Marching down to their boats on the shore.

Then he climbed the tower of the Old North
    Church,
By the wooden stairs, with stealthy tread,
To the belfry-chamber overhead,
And startled the pigeons from their perch
On the sombre rafters, that round him made
Masses and moving shapes of shade, —
By the trembling ladder, steep and tall,
To the highest window in the wall,
Where he paused to listen and look down
A moment on the roofs of the town,
And the moonlight flowing over all.

Beneath, in the churchyard, lay the dead,
In their night-encampment on the hill,
Wrapped in silence so deep and still
That he could hear, like a sentinel's tread,
The watchful night-wind, as it went
Creeping along from tent to tent,
And seeming to whisper, "All is well!"
A moment only he feels the spell
Of the place and the hour, and the secret
    dread
Of the lonely belfry and the dead;
For suddenly all his thoughts are bent
On a shadowy something far away,
Where the river widens to meet the bay, —

A line of black that bends and floats
On the rising tide, like a bridge of boats.

Meanwhile, impatient to mount and ride,
Booted and spurred, with a heavy stride
On the opposite shore walked Paul Revere.
Now he patted his horse's side,
Now gazed at the landscape far and near,
Then, impetuous, stamped the earth,
And turned and tightened his saddle-girth;
But mostly he watched with eager search
The belfry-tower of the Old North Church,
As it rose above the graves on the hill,
Lonely and spectral and sombre and still.
And lo! as he looks, on the belfry's height
A glimmer, and then a gleam of light!
He springs to the saddle, the bridle he turns,
But lingers and gazes, till full on his sight
A second lamp in the belfry burns!

A hurry of hoofs in a village street,
A shape in the moonlight, a bulk in the dark,
And beneath, from the pebbles, in passing, a
    spark
Struck out by a steed flying fearless and fleet:
That was all! And yet, through the gloom
    and the light,
The fate of a nation was riding that night;
And the spark struck out by that steed, in his
    flight,
Kindled the land into flame with its heat.

He has left the village and mounted the steep,
And beneath him, tranquil and broad and
    deep,
Is the Mystic, meeting the ocean tides;
And under the alders that skirt its edge,
Now soft on the sand, now loud on the ledge,
Is heard the tramp of his steed as he rides.

It was twelve by the village clock,
When he crossed the bridge into Medford
    town.
He heard the crowing of the cock,
And the barking of the farmer's dog,
And felt the damp of the river fog,
That rises after the sun goes down.

It was one by the village clock,
When he galloped into Lexington.
He saw the gilded weathercock
Swim in the moonlight as he passed,
And the meeting-house windows, blank and
    bare,
Gaze at him with a spectral glare,

As if they already stood aghast
At the bloody work they would look upon.

It was two by the village clock,
When he came to the bridge in Concord town.
He heard the bleating of the flock,
And the twitter of birds among the trees,
And felt the breath of the morning breeze
Blowing over the meadows brown.
And one was safe and asleep in his bed
Who at the bridge would be first to fall,
Who that day would be lying dead,
Pierced by a British musket-ball.

You know the rest. In the books you have
read,
How the British Regulars fired and fled, —
How the farmers gave them ball for ball,
From behind each fence and farm-yard wall,
Chasing the red-coats down the lane,
Then crossing the fields to emerge again
Under the trees at the turn of the road,
And only pausing to fire and load.

So through the night rode Paul Revere;
And so through the night went his cry of
alarm
To every Middlesex village and farm, —
A cry of defiance and not of fear,
A voice in the darkness, a knock at the door,
And a word that shall echo forevermore!
For, borne on the night-wind of the Past,
Through all our history, to the last,
In the hour of darkness and peril and need,
The people will waken and listen to hear
The hurrying hoof-beats of that steed,
And the midnight message of Paul Revere.

HENRY WADSWORTH LONGFELLOW.

At the same time Warren dispatched William
Dawes by way of Roxbury; but though Dawes
played an important part in the events of the
night, his exploits have been completely over-
shadowed in the popular imagination by those
of the other courier.

WHAT'S IN A NAME?

I AM a wandering, bitter shade;
Never of me was a hero made;
Poets have never sung my praise,
Nobody crowned my brow with bays;
And if you ask me the fatal cause,
I answer only, "My name was Dawes."

'T is all very well for the children to hear
Of the midnight ride of Paul Revere;
But why should my name be quite forgot,
Who rode as boldly and well, God wot?
Why should I ask? The reason is clear —
My name was Dawes and his Revere.

When the lights from the old North Church
flashed out,
Paul Revere was waiting about,
But I was already on my way.
The shadows of night fell cold and gray
As I rode, with never a break or pause;
But what was the use, when my name was
Dawes?

History rings with his silvery name;
Closed to me are the portals of fame.
Had he been Dawes and I Revere,
No one had heard of him, I fear.
No one has heard of me because
He was Revere and I was Dawes.

HELEN F. MORE.

Revere galloped at top speed to Lexington, and
warned Hancock and Adams, who left the town
shortly before daybreak. Meanwhile the minute-
men of the village had gathered, and the vanguard
of the English column was confronted by about
fifty colonials under command of Captain John
Parker. The British commander, Major Pitcairn,
ordered them to disperse, and as they stood motion-
less, he gave the order to fire. His men hesitated,
but he discharged his own pistol and repeated the
order, whereupon a deadly volley killed eight of the
minute-men and wounded ten. A moment later,
the main body of the British came up, and Parker,
seeing the folly of resistance, ordered his men to
retire.

LEXINGTON [1]

[April 19, 1775]

From "Psalm of the West"

O'ER Cambridge set the yeoman's mark:
Climb, patriot, through the April dark.
O lanthorn! kindle fast thy light,
Thou budding star in the April night,
For never a star more news hath told,
Or later flame in heaven shall hold.
Ay, lanthorn on the North Church tower,
When that thy church hath had her hour,
Still from the top of Reverence high
Shalt thou illume Fame's ampler sky;

[1] From Poems by Sidney Lanier, copyright,
1884, 1891, by Mary D. Lanier; published by
Charles Scribner's Sons.

For, statured large o'er town and tree,
Time's tallest Figure stands by thee,
And, dim as now thy wick may shine,
The Future lights his lamp at thine.

Now haste thee while the way is cléar,
        Paul Revere!
Haste, Dawes! but haste thou not, O Sun!
        To Lexington.

Then Devens looked and saw the light:
He got him forth into the night,
And watched alone on the river-shore,
And marked the British ferrying o'er.

John Parker! rub thine eyes and yawn,
But one o'clock and yet 't is Dawn!
Quick, rub thine eyes and draw thy hose:
The Morning comes ere darkness goes.
Have forth and call the yeomen out,
For somewhere, somewhere close about
Full soon a Thing must come to be
Thine honest eyes shall stare to see —
Full soon before thy patriot eyes
Freedom from out of a Wound shall rise.

Then haste ye, Prescott and Revere!
Bring all the men of Lincoln here;
Let Chelmsford, Littleton, Carlisle,
Let Acton, Bedford, hither file —
Oh hither file, and plainly see
Out of a wound leap Liberty.
Say, Woodman April! all in green,
Say, Robin April! hast thou seen
In all thy travel round the earth
Ever a morn of calmer birth?
But Morning's eye alone serene
Can gaze across yon village-green
To where the trooping British run
        Through Lexington.

Good men in fustian, stand ye still;
The men in red come o'er the hill.
Lay down your arms, damned Rebels! cry
The men in red full haughtily.
But never a grounding gun is heard;
The men in fustian stand unstirred;
Dead calm, save maybe a wise bluebird
Puts in his little heavenly word.
O men in red! if ye but knew
The half as much as bluebirds do,
Now in this little tender calm
Each hand would out, and every palm
With patriot palm strike brotherhood's stroke
Or ere these lines of battle broke.

O men in red! if ye but knew
The least of the all that bluebirds do,
Now in this little godly calm
Yon voice might sing the Future's Psalm —
The Psalm of Love with the brotherly eyes
Who pardons and is very wise —
Yon voice that shouts, high-hoarse with ire,
        Fire!
The red-coats fire, the homespuns fall:
The homespuns' anxious voices call,
Brother, art hurt? and *Where hit, John?*
And, *Wipe this blood,* and, *Men, come on,*
And, *Neighbor, do but lift my head,*
And, *Who is wounded? Who is dead?*
Seven are killed. My God! my God!
Seven lie dead on the village sod.
Two Harringtons, Parker, Hadley, Brown,
Monroe and Porter, — these are down.
Nay, look! Stout Harrington not yet dead!
He crooks his eibow, lifts his head.
He lies at the step of his own house-door;
He crawls and makes a path of gore.
The wife from the window hath seen, and
        rushed;
He hath reached the step, but the blood hath
        gushed;
He hath crawled to the step of his own house-
        door,
But his head hath dropped: he will crawl no
        more.
Clasp, Wife, and kiss, and lift the head:
Harrington lies at his doorstep dead.

But, O ye Six that round him lay
And bloodied up that April day!
As Harrington fell, ye likewise fell —
At the door of the House wherein ye dwell;
As Harrington came, ye likewise came
And died at the door of your House of Fame.
                        SIDNEY LANIER.

LEXINGTON

[April 19, 1775]

SLOWLY the mist o'er the meadow was creep-
        ing,
    Bright on the dewy buds glistened the
        sun,
When from his couch, while his children were
        sleeping,
    Rose the bold rebel and shouldered his gun.
        Waving her golden veil
        Over the silent dale,

Blithe looked the morning on cottage and
    spire;
    Hushed was his parting sigh,
    While from his noble eye
Flashed the last sparkle of liberty's fire.

On the smooth green where the fresh leaf is
    springing
    Calmly the first-born of glory have met;
Hark! the death-volley around them is ring-
    ing!
    Look! with their life-blood the young grass
    is wet!
    Faint is the feeble breath,
    Murmuring low in death,
"Tell to our sons how their fathers have
    died;"
    Nerveless the iron hand,
    Raised for its native land,
Lies by the weapon that gleams at its side.

Over the hillsides the wild knell is tolling,
    From their far hamlets the yeomanry come;
As through the storm-clouds the thunder-burst
    rolling,
    Circles the beat of the mustering drum.
    Fast on the soldier's path
    Darken the waves of wrath, —
Long have they gathered and loud shall they
    fall;
    Red glares the musket's flash,
    Sharp rings the rifle's crash,
Blazing and clanging from thicket and wall.

Gayly the plume of the horseman was dancing,
    Never to shadow his cold brow again;
Proudly at morning the war-steed was pranc-
    ing,
    Reeking and panting he droops on the rein;
    Pale is the lip of scorn,
    Voiceless the trumpet horn,
Torn is the silken-fringed red cross on high;
    Many a belted breast
    Low on the turf shall rest
Ere the dark hunters the herd have passed by.

Snow-girdled crags where the hoarse wind is
    raving,
    Rocks where the weary floods murmur and
    wail,
Wilds where the fern by the furrow is waving,
    Reeled with the echoes that rode on the
    gale;
    Far as the tempest thrills
    Over the darkened hills,

Far as the sunshine streams over the plain,
    Roused by the tyrant band,
    Woke all the mighty land,
Girdled for battle, from mountain to main.

Green be the graves where her martyrs are
    lying!
    Shroudless and tombless they sunk to their
    rest,
While o'er their ashes the starry fold flying
    Wraps the proud eagle they roused from
    his nest.
    Borne on her Northern pine,
    Long o'er the foaming brine
Spread her broad banner to storm and to
    sun;
    Heaven keep her ever free,
    Wide as o'er land and sea
Floats the fair emblem her heroes have won!
                OLIVER WENDELL HOLMES.

    The British pressed on to Concord, but the
greater part of the stores had been hidden, and
minute-men were gathering from all directions.
Colonel Smith, commanding the British, began to
realize the dangers of his position and about noon
started to retreat to Boston. And none too soon,
for the whole country was aroused. Minute-men
swarmed in from all directions, and taking advan-
tage of every tree and hillock by the roadside,
poured into the British a fire so deadly that the
retreat soon became a disorderly flight. The
timely arrival of strong reinforcements was all
that saved the British from annihilation.

NEW ENGLAND'S CHEVY CHASE

[April 19, 1775]

'T was the dead of the night. By the pine-
    knot's red light
    Brooks lay, half-asleep, when he heard the
    alarm, —
Only this, and no more, from a voice at the
    door:
    "The Red-Coats are out, and have passed
    Phips's farm."

Brooks was booted and spurred; he said never
    a word;
    Took his horn from its peg, and his gun
    from its rack;
To the cold midnight air he led out his white
    mare,
    Strapped the girths and the bridle, and
    sprang to her back.

Up the North Country road at her full pace
she strode,
    Till Brooks reined her up at John Tarbell's
to say,
"We have got the alarm, — they have left
Phips's farm;
    You rouse the East Precinct, and I 'll go this
way."

John called his hired man, and they harnessed
the span;
    They roused Abram Garfield, and Abram
called me:
"Turn out right away; let no minute-man
stay;
    The Red-Coats have landed at Phips's,"
says he.

By the Powder-House Green seven others fell
in;
    At Nahum's, the men from the Saw-Mill
came down;
So that when Jabez Bland gave the word of
command,
    And said, "Forward, march!" there
marched forward THE TOWN.

Parson Wilderspin stood by the side of the
road,
    And he took off his hat, and he said, "Let
us pray!
O Lord, God of might, let thine angels of
light
    Lead thy children to-night to the glories of
day!
And let thy stars fight all the foes of the
Right
    As the stars fought of old against Sisera."

And from heaven's high arch those stars
blessed our march,
    Till the last of them faded in twilight away;
And with morning's bright beam, by the bank
of the stream,
    Half the county marched in, and we heard
Davis say:

"On the King's own highway I may travel
all day,
    And no man hath warrant to stop me,"
says he;
"I've no man that's afraid, and I 'll march
at their head."
    Then he turned to the boys, — "Forward,
march! Follow me."

And we marched as he said, and the Fifer he
played
    The old "White Cockade," and he played
it right well.
We saw Davis fall dead, but no man was
afraid;
    That bridge we'd have had, though a
thousand men fell.

This opened the play, and it lasted all day.
    We made Concord too hot for the Red-
Coats to stay;
Down the Lexington way we stormed, black,
white, and gray;
    We were first in the feast, and were last in
the fray.

They would turn in dismay, as red wolves
turn at bay.
    They levelled, they fired, they charged up
the road.
Cephas Willard fell dead; he was shot in the
head
    As he knelt by Aunt Prudence's well-
sweep to load.

John Danforth was hit just in Lexington
Street,
    John Bridge at that lane where you cross
Beaver Falls,
And Winch and the Snows just above John
Munroe's, —
    Swept away by one swoop of the big can-
non-balls.

I took Bridge on my knee, but he said, "Don't
mind me;
    Fill your horn from mine, — let me lie where
I be.
Our fathers," says he, "that their sons might
be free,
    Left their king on his throne, and came over
the sea;
And that man is a knave or a fool who, to
save
    His life for a minute, would live like a slave."

Well, all would not do! There were men
good as new, —
    From Rumford, from Saugus, from towns
far away, —
Who filled up quick and well for each soldier
that fell;
    And we drove them, and drove them, and
drove them, all day.

We knew, every one, it was war that begun,
When that morning's marching was only half
 done.

In the hazy twilight, at the coming of night,
I crowded three buckshot and one bullet
 down.
'T was my last charge of lead; and I aimed
 her and said,
 "Good luck to you, lobsters, in old Boston
 Town."

In a barn at Milk Row, Ephraim Bates and
 Munroe
And Baker and Abram and I made a bed.
We had mighty sore feet, and we'd nothing
 to eat;
 But we'd driven the Red-Coats, and Amos,
 he said:
"It's the first time," says he, "that it's
 happened to me
 To march to the sea by this road where
 we've come;
But confound this whole day, but we'd all
 of us say
 We'd rather have spent it this way than
 to home."

 ———

The hunt had begun with the dawn of the sun,
 And night saw the wolf driven back to his
 den.
And never since then, in the memory of men,
 Has the Old Bay State seen such a hunting
 again.
 EDWARD EVERETT HALE.
 April 19, 1882.

THE KING'S OWN REGULARS

AND THEIR TRIUMPH OVER THE IRREGULARS

SINCE you all will have singing, and won't
 be said nay,
I cannot refuse, when you so beg and pray;
So I'll sing you a song, — as a body may say,
'T is of the King's Regulars, who ne'er ran
 away.
 *Oh! the old soldiers of the King, and the
 King's own Regulars.*

At Prestonpans we met with some rebels one
 day,
We marshalled ourselves all in comely array;

Our hearts were all stout, and bid our legs
 stay,
But our feet were wrong-headed and took us
 away.

At Falkirk we resolved to be braver,
And recover some credit by better behavior:
We would n't acknowledge feet had done us
 a favor,
So feet swore they would stand, but — legs
 ran however.

No troops perform better than we at reviews,
We march and we wheel, and whatever you
 choose,
George would see how we fight, and we never
 refuse,
There we all fight with courage — you may
 see't in the news.

To Monongahela, with fifes and with drums,
We marched in fine order, with cannon and
 bombs;
That great expedition cost infinite sums,
But a few irregulars cut us all into crumbs.

It was not fair to shoot at us from behind
 trees,
If they had stood open, as they ought, before
 our great guns, we should have beat
 them with ease,
They may fight with one another that way if
 they please,
But it is not *regular* to stand, and fight with
 such rascals as these.

At Fort George and Oswego, to our great
 reputation,
We show'd our vast skill in fortification;
The French fired three guns; — of the fourth
 they had no occasion;
For we gave up those forts, not through fear,
 but mere persuasion.

To Ticonderoga we went in a passion,
Swearing to be revenged on the whole French
 nation;
But we soon turned tail, without hesitation,
Because they fought behind trees, which is
 not the *regular* fashion.

Lord Loudon, he was a regular general, they
 say;
With a great regular army he went on his
 way,

Against Louisburg, to make it his prey,
But returned — without seeing it, — for he
did n't *feel bold* that day.

Grown proud at reviews, great George had
no rest,
Each grandsire, he had heard, a rebellion
suppressed,
He wish'd a rebellion, looked round and saw
none,
So resolved a rebellion to make — of his
own.

The Yankees he bravely pitched on, because
he thought they would n't fight,
And so he sent us over to take away their
right;
But lest they should spoil our review clothes,
he cried braver and louder,
For God's sake, brother kings, don't sell the
cowards any powder.

Our general with his council of war did ad-
vise
How at Lexington we might the Yankees
surprise;
We march'd — and re-marched — all sur-
prised — at being beat;
And so our wise general's plan of *surprise* —
was complete.

For fifteen miles, they follow'd and pelted
us, we scarce had time to pull a trig-
ger;
But did you ever know a retreat performed
with more vigor?
For we did it in two hours, which saved us
from perdition;
'T was not in *going out*, but in *returning*,
consisted our EXPEDITION.

Says our general, "We were forced to take
to our *arms* in our defence
(For *arms* read *legs*, and it will be both truth
and sense),
Lord Percy (says he), I must say something
of him in civility,
And that is — 'I can never enough praise
him for his great — agility.'"

Of their firing from behind fences he makes
a great pother;
Every fence has two sides, they made use of
one, and we only forgot to use the
other;

Then we turned our backs and ran away so
fast; don't let that disgrace us,
'T was only to make good what Sandwich
said, that the Yankees — could not face
us.

As they could not get before us, how could
they look us in the face?
We took care they should n't, by scampering
away apace.
That they had not much to brag of, is a very
plain case;
For if they beat us in the fight, we beat them
in the race.

Pennsylvania Evening Post, March 30, 1776.

How the alarm of the fight spread through the
countryside, how men left the plough, the loom,
the anvil, and hastened, musket in hand, to the
land's defence that day, has been told and retold
in song and story. Here is the story of Morgan
Stanwood, one among hundreds such.

MORGAN STANWOOD

CAPE ANN, 1775

MORGAN STANWOOD, patriot!
Little more is known;
Nothing of his home is left
But the door-step stone.

Morgan Stanwood, to our thought
You return once more;
Once again the meadows lift
Daisies to your door.

Once again the morn is sweet,
Half the hay is down, —
Hark! what means that sudden clang
From the distant town?

Larum bell and rolling drum
Answer sea-borne guns;
Larum bell and rolling drum
Summon Freedom's sons!

And the mower thinks to him
Cry both bell and drum,
"Morgan Stanwood, where art thou?
Here th' invaders come!"

"Morgan Stanwood" need no more
Bell and drum-beat call;
He is one who, hearing once,
Answers once for all.

Ne'er the mower murmured then,
　"Half my grass is mown,
Homespun is n't soldier-wear,
　Each may save his own."

Fallen scythe and aftermath
　Lie forgotten now;
Winter need may come and find
　But a barren mow.

Down the musket comes. "Good wife, —
　Wife, a quicker flint!"
And the face that questions face
　Hath no color in 't.

"Wife, if I am late to-night,
　Milk the heifer first; —
Ruth, if I'm not home at all, —
　Worse has come to worst."

Morgan Stanwood sped along,
　Not the common road;
Over wall and hill-top straight,
　Straight to death, he strode;

Leaving her to hear at night
　Tread of burdened men,
By the gate and through the gate,
　At the door, and then —

Ever after that to hear,
　When the grass is sweet,
Through the gate and through the night,
　Slowly coming feet.

Morgan Stanwood's roof is gone;
　Here the door-step lies;
One may stand thereon and think, —
　For the thought will rise, —

Were we where the meadow was,
　Mowing grass alone,
Would we go the way he went,
　From this very stone?

Were we on the door-step here,
　Parting for a day,
Would we utter words as though
　Parting were for aye?

Would we? Heart, the hearth is dear,
　Meadow-math is sweet;
Parting be as parting may,
　After all, we meet.
　　　　　　　　　　HIRAM RICH.

Tidings of the fight reached Northboro' early in the afternoon, while a company of minute-men were listening to a patriotic address. They shouldered their muskets and started at once for the firing line.

THE MINUTE-MEN OF NORTH-BORO'

[April 19, 1775]

'T IS noonday by the buttonwood, with
　　slender-shadowed bud;
'T is April by the Assabet, whose banks
　　scarce hold his flood;
　When down the road from Marlboro' we
　　　hear a sound of speed —
　A cracking whip and clanking hoofs — a
　　　case of crying need!
And there a dusty rider hastes to tell of flow-
　　ing blood,
　Of troops a-field, of war abroad, and many
　　　a desperate deed.

The Minute-Men of Northboro' were gather-
　　ing that day
　To hear the Parson talk of God, of Free-
　　　dom and the State;
They throng about the horseman, drinking
　　in all he should say,
　Beside the perfumed lilacs blooming by
　　　the Parson's gate:

"The British march from Boston through
　　the night to Lexington;
Revere alarms the countryside to meet them
　　ere the sun;
　Upon the common, in the dawn, the red-
　　　coat butchers slay;
　On Concord march, and there again pur-
　　　sue their murderous way;
We drive them back; we follow on; they
　　have begun to run:
　All Middlesex and Worcester's up: Pray
　　　God, ours is the day!"

The Minute-Men of Northboro' let rust the
　　standing plough,
　The seed may wait, the fertile ground up-
　　　smiling to the spring.
They seize their guns and powder-horns,
　　there is no halting now,
　At thought of homes made fatherless by
　　　order of the King.

The pewter-ware is melted into bullets —
    long past due,
The flints are picked, the powder's dry, the
    rifles shine like new.
  Within their Captain's yard enranked they
    hear the Parson's prayer
  Unto the God of armies for the battles they
    must share;
He asks that to their Fathers and their Altars
    they be true,
  For Country and for Liberty unswervingly
    to dare.

The Minute-Men of Northboro' set out with
    drum and fife;
  With shining eyes they've blest their babes
    and bid their wives good-by.
The hands that here release the plough have
    taken up a strife
  That shall not end until all earth has heard
    the battle-cry.

At every town new streams of men join in the
    mighty flow;
At every crossroad comes the message of a
    fleeing foe:
  The British force, though trebled, fails
    against the advancing tide.
  Our rifles speak from fence and tree — in
    front, on every side.
The British fall: the Minute-Men have
    mixed with bitterest woe
  Their late vainglorious vaunting and their
    military pride.

The Minute-Men of Northboro' they boast
    no martial air;
  No uniforms gleam in the sun where on
    and on they plod;
But generations yet unborn their valor shall
    declare;
  They strike for Massachusetts Bay; they
    serve New England's God.

The hirelings who would make us slaves them-
    selves are backward hurled,
On Worcester and on Middlesex their flag's
    forever furled.
  Theirs was the glinting pomp of war; ours
    is the victor's prize:
  That day of bourgeoning has seen a race
    of freemen rise.
A Nation born in fearlessness stands forth
    before the world
  With God her shield, the Right her sword,
    and Freedom in her eyes.

The Minute-Men of Northboro' sit down
    by Boston-town;
  They fight and bleed at Bunker Hill; they
    cheer for Washington.
In thankfulness they speed their bolt against
    the British Crown;
  And take the plough again in peace, their
    warrior's duty done.
              WALLACE RICE.

LEXINGTON

[1775]

No Berserk thirst of blood had they,
  No battle-joy was theirs, who set
    Against the alien bayonet
Their homespun breasts in that old day.

Their feet had trodden peaceful ways;
  They loved not strife, they dreaded pain;
    They saw not, what to us is plain,
That God would make man's wrath His
    praise.

No seers were they, but simple men;
  Its vast results the future hid:
    The meaning of the work they did
Was strange and dark and doubtful then.

Swift as their summons came they left
  The plough mid-furrow standing still,
    The half-ground corn grist in the mill,
The spade in earth, the axe in cleft.

They went where duty seemed to call,
  They scarcely asked the reason why;
    They only knew they could but die,
And death was not the worst of all!

Of man for man the sacrifice,
  All that was theirs to give, they gave.
    The flowers that blossomed from their
    grave
Have sown themselves beneath all skies.

Their death-shot shook the feudal tower,
  And shattered slavery's chain as well;
    On the sky's dome, as on a bell,
Its echo struck the world's great hour.

That fateful echo is not dumb:
  The nations listening to its sound
    Wait, from a century's vantage-ground
The holier triumphs yet to come, —

The bridal time of Law and Love,
  The gladness of the world's release,
  When, war-sick, at the feet of Peace
The hawk shall nestle with the dove! —

The golden age of brotherhood
  Unknown to other rivalries
  Than of the mild humanities,
And gracious interchange of good,

When closer strand shall lean to strand,
  Till meet, beneath saluting flags,
  The eagle of our mountain-crags,
The lion of our Motherland!
            JOHN GREENLEAF WHITTIER.

The news of the fight at Lexington spread with
remarkable rapidity throughout the whole coun-
try, and nearly every colony at once took steps
for the enlistment and training of a colonial militia.
No stronger proof of the electric condition of the
country could be offered than the way in which
men everywhere rushed to arms.

THE RISING

From "The Wagoner of the Alleghanies"

OUT of the North the wild news came,
Far flashing on its wings of flame,
Swift as the boreal light which flies
At midnight through the startled skies.

And there was tumult in the air,
  The fife's shrill note, the drum's loud beat,
And through the wild land everywhere
  The answering tread of hurrying feet,
While the first oath of Freedom's gun
Came on the blast from Lexington;
And Concord, roused, no longer tame,
Forgot her old baptismal name,
Made bare her patriot arm of power,
And swell'd the discord of the hour.

  .   .   .   .

Within its shade of elm and oak
  The church of Berkeley Manor stood;
There Sunday found the rural folk,
  And some esteem'd of gentle blood.
  In vain their feet with loitering tread
Pass'd mid the graves where rank is naught;
All could not read the lesson taught
  In that republic of the dead.

  .   .   .   .

The pastor rose; the prayer was strong;
The psalm was warrior David's song;
The text, a few short words of might, —
"The Lord of hosts shall arm the right!"
He spoke of wrongs too long endured,
Of sacred rights to be secured;
Then from his patriot tongue of flame
The startling words for Freedom came.
The stirring sentences he spake
Compell'd the heart to glow or quake,
And, rising on his theme's broad wing,
  And grasping in his nervous hand
  The imaginary battle-brand,
In face of death he dared to fling
Defiance to a tyrant King.

Even as he spoke, his frame, renewed
In eloquence of attitude,
Rose, as it seem'd, a shoulder higher;
Then swept his kindling glance of fire
From startled pew to breathless choir;
When suddenly his mantle wide
His hands impatient flung aside,
And, lo! he met their wondering eyes
Complete in all a warrior's guise.

A moment there was awful pause, —
When Berkeley cried, "Cease, traitor!
    cease!
God's temple is the house of peace!"
  The other shouted, "Nay, not so,
When God is with our righteous cause;
His holiest places then are ours,
His temples are our forts and towers
  That frown upon the tyrant foe;
In this, the dawn of Freedom's day,
There is a time to fight and pray!"

And now before the open door —
  The warrior priest had order'd so —
The enlisting trumpet's sudden soar
Rang through the chapel, o'er and o'er,
  Its long reverberating blow,
So loud and clear, it seem'd the ear
Of dusty death must wake and hear.
And there the startling drum and fife
Fired the living with fiercer life;
While overhead, with wild increase,
Forgetting its ancient toll of peace,
  The great bell swung as ne'er before.
It seemed as it would never cease;
And every word its ardor flung
From off its jubilant iron tongue
  Was, "War! war! war!"

"Who dares" — this was the patriot's cry,
  As striding from the desk he came —
  "Come out with me, in Freedom's name,
For her to live, for her to die?"
A hundred hands flung up reply,
A hundred voices answer'd, "I!"

Thomas Buchanan Read.

Early in May, news of the fight at Lexington reached Machias, Maine, and on the 11th a party of young men boarded the British armed schooner, Margaretta, which was in the harbor there, and forced her to surrender, after a loss of about twenty on each side.

THE PRIZE OF THE MARGARETTA [1]

[May 11, 1775]

I

Four young men, of a Monday morn,
Heard that the flag of peace was torn;

Heard that "rebels" with sword and gun,
Had fought the British at Lexington,

While they were far from that bloody plain,
Safe on the green-clad shores of Maine.

With eyes that glittered, and hearts that burned,
They talked of the glory their friends had earned,

And asked each other, "What can we do,
So our hands may prove that our hearts are true?"

II

Silent the Margaretta lay,
Out on the bosom of the bay;

On her masts rich bunting gleamed:
Bravely the flag of England streamed.

The young men gazed at the tempting prize —
They wistfully glanced in each other's eyes;

Said one, "We can lower that cloth of dread
And hoist the pine-tree flag instead.

"We are only boys to the old and sage;
We have not yet come to manhood's age;

[1] From *Poems for Young Americans*, published by Harper & Bros.

"But we can show them that, when there's need,
Men may follow and boys may lead."

Tightly each other's hand they pressed,
Loudly they cried, "We will do our best;

"The pine-tree flag, ere day is passed,
Shall float from the Margaretta's mast."

III

They ran to a sloop that lay near by;
They roused their neighbors, with hue and cry;

They doffed their hats, gave three loud cheers,
And called for a crew of volunteers.

Their bold, brave spirit spread far and wide,
And men came running from every side.

Curious armed were the dauntless ones,
With axes, pitchforks, scythes, and guns;

They shouted, "Ere yet this day be passed,
The pine-tree grows from the schooner's mast!"

IV

With sails all set, trim as could be,
The Margaretta stood out to sea.

With every man and boy in place,
The gallant Yankee sloop gave chase.

Rippled and foamed the sunlit seas;
Freshened and sung the soft May breeze;

And came from the sloop's low deck, "Hurray!
We're gaining on her! We'll win the day!"

A sound of thunder, echoing wide,
Came from the Margaretta's side;

A deadly crash, and a loud death-yell,
And one of the brave pursuers fell.

They aimed a gun at the schooner then,
And sent the compliment back again;

He who at the helm of the schooner stood,
Covered the deck with his rich life-blood.

V

Each burning to pay a bloody debt,
The crews of the hostile vessels met;

The Western nation now to be,
Made her first fight upon the sea.

And not till forty men were slain,
Did the pine-tree flag a victory gain;

But at last the hearts of the Britons quailed,
And grandly the patriot arm prevailed.

One of the youths, the deed to crown,
Grasped the colors and pulled them down;

And raised, 'mid cries of wild delight,
The pine-tree flag of blue and white.

And the truth was shown, for the world to
    read,
That men may follow and boys may lead.
                        WILL CARLETON.

In North Carolina, the men of Mecklenburg
County met, May 31, and adopted their famous
"Resolves," declaring that each provincial con-
gress was invested with all legislative and execu-
tive powers for the government of the colonies,
and should exercise them independently of Great
Britain, until Parliament should resign its arbi-
trary pretensions. It was from these "Resolves"
that the legend of the Mecklenburg "Declaration
of Independence, said to have been signed May
20," originated.

THE MECKLENBURG DECLARA-
TION

[May 20, 1775]

OPPRESSED and few, but freemen yet,
The men of Mecklenburg had met
    Determined to be free,
    And crook no coward knee,
Though Might in front and Treason at the
    back
Brought death and ruin in their joint attack.

The tyrant's heel was on the land
When Polk convoked his gallant band,
    And told in words full strong
    The bitter tale of wrong,
Then came a whisper, like the storm's first
    waves:
"We must be independent, or be slaves!"

But, hark! What hurried rider, this,
With jaded horse and garb amiss,
    Whose look some woe proclaims,
    Ere he his mission names?
He rides amain from far-off Lexington,
And tells the blood-red news of war begun!

Then Brevard, Balch, and Kennon spoke
The wise bold words that aye invoke
    Men to defend the right
    And scorn the despot's might;
Until from all there rose the answering cry:
"We will be independent, or we die."

When Alexander called the vote,
No dastard "nay's" discordant note
    Broke on that holy air —
    For dastard none was there!
But in prompt answer to their country's
    call,
They pledged life, fortune, sacred honor —
    all!

In solemn hush the people heard;
With shout and cheer they caught the word:
    Independence! In that sign
    We grasp our right divine;
For the tyrant's might and the traitor's
    hate
Must yield to men who fight for God and
    State!

The hero shout flew on the breeze;
Rushed from the mountains to the seas;
    Till all the land uprose,
    Their faces to their foes,
Shook off the thraldom they so long had
    borne,
And swore the oath that Mecklenburg had
    sworn!

And well those men maintained the right;
They kept the faith, and fought the fight;
    Till Might and Treason both
    Fled fast before the oath
Which brought the God of Freedom's battles
    down
To place on patriot brows the victor's crown!
                        WILLIAM C. ELAM.

Up and down the land, in every city, town, and
hamlet, men were drilling — with brooms and
corn-stalks, when no muskets were available. The
storm, which had been gathering for years, had
burst at last.

A SONG

HARK! 't is Freedom that calls. come, patri-
      ots, awake!
To arms, my brave boys, and away:
'T is Honor, 't is Virtue, 't is Liberty calls,
  And upbraids the too tedious delay.
What pleasure we find in pursuing our foes,
  Thro' blood and thro' carnage we'll fly;
Then follow, we'll soon overtake them, huzza!
  The tyrants are seized on, they die!

Triumphant returning with Freedom secur'd,
  Like men, we'll be joyful and gay —
With our wives and our friends, we'll sport,
      love, and drink,
  And lose the fatigues of the day.
'T is freedom alone gives a relish to mirth,
  But oppression all happiness sours;
It will smooth life's dull passage, 't will slope
      the descent,
  And strew the way over with flowers.
                Pennsylvania Journal, May 31, 1775.

CHAPTER III

THE COLONISTS TAKE THE OFFENSIVE

A rustic army of nearly twenty thousand men quickly gathered about Boston to besiege Gage there; but its warlike spirit ran too high to be contented with passive and defensive measures. Benedict Arnold suggested that expeditions be sent against the fortresses at Ticonderoga and Crown Point, which commanded the northern approach to the Hudson and were of great strategic importance. The suggestion was at once adopted. Arnold was created colonel and set out to raise a regiment among the Berkshire Hills. When he arrived there, he found that Ethan Allen had already raised a force of Vermonters and started for Ticonderoga.

THE GREEN MOUNTAIN BOYS

[May 9, 1775]

I

HERE halt we our march, and pitch our tent
  On the rugged forest-ground,
And light our fire with the branches rent
  By winds from the beeches round.
Wild storms have torn this ancient wood,
  But a wilder is at hand,
With hail of iron and rain of blood,
  To sweep and waste the land.

II

How the dark wood rings with our voices
      shrill,
  That startle the sleeping bird!
To-morrow eve must the voice be still,
  And the step must fall unheard.
The Briton lies by the blue Champlain,
  In Ticonderoga's towers,
And ere the sun rise twice again,
  Must they and the lake be ours.

III

Fill up the bowl from the brook that glides
  Where the fire-flies light the brake;
A ruddier juice the Briton hides
  In his fortress by the lake.
Build high the fire, till the panther leap
  From his lofty perch in flight,
And we'll strengthen our weary arms with
      sleep
  For the deeds of to-morrow night.
                    WILLIAM CULLEN BRYANT.

Arnold overtook Allen and his "Green Mountain Boys" on May 9, and accompanied the expedition as a volunteer. At daybreak of the 10th, Allen and Arnold, with eighty-three men, crossed Lake Champlain and entered Ticonderoga side by side. The garrison was completely surprised and surrendered the stronghold without a blow.

THE SURPRISE AT TICONDEROGA

[May 10, 1775]

'T WAS May upon the mountains, and on the
      airy wing
Of every floating zephyr came pleasant sounds
      of spring, —
Of robins in the orchards, brooks running
      clear and warm,
Or chanticleer's shrill challenge from busy
      farm to farm.

But, ranged in serried order, attent on sterner
      noise,
Stood stalwart Ethan Allen and his "Green
      Mountain Boys," —

Two hundred patriots listening, as with the ears of one,
To the echo of the muskets that blazed at Lexington!

"My comrades," — thus the leader spake to his gallant band, —
"The key of all the Canadas is in King George's hand,
Yet, while his careless warders our slender armies mock,
Good Yankee swords — God willing — may pick his rusty lock!"

At every pass a sentinel was set to guard the way,
Lest the secret of their purpose some idle lip betray,
As on the rocky highway they marched with steady feet
To the rhythm of the brave hearts that in their bosoms beat.

The curtain of the darkness closed 'round them like a tent,
When, travel-worn and weary, yet not with courage spent,
They halted on the border of slumbering Champlain,
And saw the watch lights glimmer across the glassy plain.

O proud Ticonderoga, enthroned amid the hills!
O bastions of old Carillon, the "Fort of Chiming Rills!"
Well might your quiet garrison have trembled where they lay,
And, dreaming, grasped their sabres against the dawn of day!

In silence and in shadow the boats were pushed from shore,
Strong hands laid down the musket to ply the muffled oar;
The startled ripples whitened and whispered in their wake,
Then sank again, reposing, upon the peaceful lake.

Fourscore and three they landed, just as the morning gray
Gave warning on the hilltops to rest not or delay;

Behind, their comrades waited, the fortress frowned before,
And the voice of Ethan Allen was in their ears once more:

"Soldiers, so long united — dread scourge of lawless power!
Our country, torn and bleeding, calls to this desperate hour.
One choice alone is left us, who hear that high behest —
To quit our claims to valor, or put them to the test!

"I lead the storming column up yonder fateful hill,
Yet not a man shall follow save at his ready will!
There leads no pathway backward — 't is death or victory!
Poise each his trusty firelock, ye that will come with me!"

From man to man a tremor ran at their captain's word
(Like the "going" in the mulberry-trees that once King David heard), —
While his eagle glances sweeping adown the triple line,
Saw, in the glowing twilight, each even barrel shine!

"Right face, my men, and forward!" Low-spoken, swift-obeyed!
They mount the slope unfaltering — they gain the esplanade!
A single drowsy sentry beside the wicket-gate,
Snapping his aimless fusil, shouts the alarm — too late!

They swarm before the barracks — the quaking guards take flight,
And such a shout resultant resounds along the height,
As rang from shore and headland scarce twenty years ago,
When brave Montcalm's defenders charged on a British foe!

Leaps from his bed in terror the ill-starred Delaplace,
To meet across his threshold a wall he may not pass!

The bayonets' lightning flashes athwart his
    dazzled eyes,
And, in tones of sudden thunder, "Surren-
    der!" Allen cries.

"Then in whose name the summons?" the
    ashen lips reply.
The mountaineer's stern visage turns proudly
    to the sky, —
"In the name of great Jehovah!" he speaks
    with lifted sword,
"And the Continental Congress, who wait
    upon his word!"

Light clouds, like crimson banners, trailed
    bright across the east,
As the great sun rose in splendor above a
    conflict ceased,
Gilding the bloodless triumph for equal rights
    and laws,
As with the smile of heaven upon a holy
    cause.

Still, wave on wave of verdure, the emerald
    hills arise,
Where once were heroes mustered from men
    of common guise,
And still, on Freedom's roster, through all
    her glorious years,
Shine the names of Ethan Allen and his bold
    volunteers!
            MARY A. P. STANSBURY.

The Continental army at Cambridge, meanwhile,
was busy day and night, drilling and getting into
shape. It was at this time that "a gentleman of
Connecticut," whose name, it is said, was Edward
Bangs, described his visit to the camp in verses
destined to become famous. They were printed
originally as a broadside.

THE YANKEE'S RETURN FROM
CAMP

[June, 1775]

FATHER and I went down to camp,
    Along with Captain Gooding,
And there we see the men and boys,
    As thick as hasty pudding.
Chorus — Yankee Doodle, keep it up,
        Yankee Doodle, dandy,
        Mind the music and the step,
        And with the girls be handy.

And there we see a thousand men,
    As rich as 'Squire David;
And what they wasted every day
    I wish it could be savèd.

The 'lasses they eat every day
    Would keep an house a winter;
They have as much that, I'll be bound
    They eat it when they're a mind to.

And there we see a swamping gun,
    Large as a log of maple,
Upon a deucèd little cart,
    A load for father's cattle.

And every time they shoot it off,
    It takes a horn of powder,
And makes a noise like father's gun,
    Only a nation louder.

I went as nigh to one myself
    As Siah's underpinning;
And father went as nigh again,
    I thought the deuce was in him.

Cousin Simon grew so bold,
    I thought he would have cocked it;
It scared me so, I shrinked it off,
    And hung by father's pocket.

And Captain Davis had a gun,
    He kind of clapt his hand on 't,
And stuck a crooked stabbing iron
    Upon the little end on 't.

And there I see a pumpkin shell
    As big as mother's bason;
And every time they touched it off,
    They scampered like the nation.

I see a little barrel, too,
    The heads were made of leather,
They knocked upon 't with little clubs
    And called the folks together.

And there was Captain Washington,
    And gentlefolks about him,
They say he's grown so tarnal proud
    He will not ride without 'em.

He got him on his meeting clothes,
    Upon a strapping stallion,
He set the world along in rows,
    In hundreds and in millions.

The flaming ribbons in his hat,
They looked so tearing fine ah,
I wanted pockily to get,
To give to my Jemimah.

I see another snarl of men
A digging graves, they told me,
So tarnal long, so tarnal deep,
They 'tended they should hold me.

It scared me so, I hooked it off,
Nor stopped, as I remember,
Nor turned about, till I got home,
Locked up in mother's chamber.
EDWARD BANGS.

Howe, Clinton, and Burgoyne arrived, May 25, with reinforcements which raised the British force in Boston to ten thousand men, and plans were at once made to extend the lines to cover Charlestown and Dorchester, the occupation of which by the Americans would render Boston untenable. Confident of victory, Gage, on June 12, issued a proclamation offering pardon to all rebels who should lay down their arms and return to their allegiance, save only John Hancock and Samuel Adams. At the same time, all who remained in arms were threatened with the gallows.

TOM GAGE'S PROCLAMATION;

OR BLUSTERING DENUNCIATION
(REPLETE WITH DEFAMATION)
THREATENING DEVASTATION,
AND SPEEDY JUGULATION,
OF THE NEW ENGLISH NATION. —
WHO SHALL HIS PIOUS WAYS SHUN?

[June 12, 1775]

WHEREAS the rebels hereabout
Are stubborn still, and still hold out;
Refusing yet to drink their tea,
In spite of Parliament and me;
And to maintain their hubble, Right,
Prognosticate a real fight;
Preparing flints, and guns, and ball,
My army and the fleet to maul;
Mounting their guilt to such a pitch,
As to let fly at soldiers' breech;
Pretending they design'd a trick,
Tho' ordered not to hurt a chick;
But peaceably, without alarm,
The men of Concord to disarm;
Or, if resisting, to annoy,
And every magazine destroy: —
All which, tho' long obliged to bear,
Thro' want of men, and not of fear;

I'm able now by augmentation,
To give a proper castigation;
For since th' addition to the troops,
Now reinforc'd as thick as hops;
I can, like Jeremey at the Boyne,
Look safely on — fight you, Burgoyne;
And now, like grass, the rebel Yankees,
I fancy not these doodle dances: —
Yet, e'er I draw the vengeful sword,
I have thought fit to send abroad,
This present gracious proclamation,
Of purpose mild the demonstration,
That whosoe'er keeps gun or pistol,
I'll spoil the motion of his systole;
Or, whip his ——, or cut his weason,
As haps the measure of his treason: —
But every one that will lay down
His hanger bright, and musket brown,
Shall not be beat, nor bruis'd, nor bang'd,
Much less for past offences hang'd;
But on surrendering his toledo,
Go to and fro unhurt as we do: —
But then I must, out of this plan, lock
Both Samuel Adams and John Hancock;
For those vile traitors (like debentures)
Must be tucked up at all adventures;
As any proffer of a pardon,
Would only tend those rogues to harden: -
But every other mother's son,
The instant he destroys his gun
(For thus doth run the King's command),
May, if he will, come kiss my hand. —
And to prevent such wicked game, as
Pleading the plea of ignoramus,
Be this my proclamation spread
To every reader that can read: —
And as nor law nor right was known
Since my arrival in this town,
To remedy this fatal flaw,
I hereby publish martial law.
Meanwhile, let all, and every one
Who loves his life, forsake his gun;
And all the council, by mandamus,
Who have been reckoned so infamous,
Return unto their habitation,
Without or let or molestation. —
Thus graciously the war I wage,
As witnesseth my hand, — TOM GAGE.
By command of MOTHER CARY,
Thomas Flucker, Secretary.

Pennsylvania Journal, June 28, 1775.

The Committee of Safety received intelligence of Gage's plans and ordered out a force of twelve hundred men to take possession of Bunker Hill

Charlestown. At sunset of June 16 this brigade started from Cambridge, under command of Colonel William Prescott, a veteran of the French War. On reaching Bunker Hill, a consultation was held, and it was decided to push on to Breed's Hill, and erect a fortification there. Breed's Hill was reached about midnight, and the work of throwing up intrenchments began at once.

THE EVE OF BUNKER HILL

[June 16, 1775]

'T WAS June on the face of the earth, June
    with the rose's breath,
When life is a gladsome thing, and a distant
    dream is death;
There was gossip of birds in the air, and a
    lowing of herds by the wood,
And a sunset gleam in the sky that the heart
    of a man holds good;
Then the nun-like Twilight came, violet-
    vestured and still,
And the night's first star outshone afar on the
    eve of Bunker Hill.

There rang a cry through the camp, with its
    word upon rousing word;
There was never a faltering foot in the ranks
    of those that heard; —
Lads from the Hampshire hills, and the rich
    Connecticut vales,
Sons of the old Bay Colony, from its shores
    and its inland dales;
Swiftly they fell in line; no fear could their
    valor chill;
Ah, brave the show as they ranged a-row on
    the eve of Bunker Hill!

Then a deep voice lifted a prayer to the God
    of the brave and the true,
And the heads of the men were bare in the
    gathering dusk and dew;
The heads of a thousand men were bowed as
    the pleading rose, —
*Smite Thou, Lord, as of old Thou smotest
    Thy people's foes!*
*Oh, nerve Thy servants' arms to work with a
    mighty will!*
hush, and then a loud *Amen!* on the eve of
    Bunker Hill!

Now they are gone through the night with
    never a thought of fame,
Gone to the field of a fight that shall win them
    a deathless name;

Some shall never again behold the set of the
    sun,
But lie like the Concord slain, and the slain of
    Lexington,
Martyrs to Freedom's cause. Ah, how at their
    deeds we thrill,
The men whose might made strong the height
    on the eve of Bunker Hill!

CLINTON SCOLLARD.

June 17 dawned fair and bright, and the intrenchments were at once discovered by the British. A lively cannonade was opened upon them by the ships in the harbor, but without effect. At noon, three thousand veterans were ordered forward to rout out the "peasants," and by three o'clock in the afternoon had crossed the river and were ready to storm the intrenchments. Commanded by General Howe and General Pigot, they advanced steadily up the hill, only to be met by so terrific a fire that they gave way and retreated in disorder.

WARREN'S ADDRESS TO THE AMERICAN SOLDIERS

[June 17, 1775]

STAND! the ground's your own, my
    braves!
Will ye give it up to slaves?
Will ye look for greener graves?
    Hope ye mercy still?
What's the mercy despots feel?
Hear it in that battle-peal!
Read it on yon bristling steel!
    Ask it, — ye who will.

Fear ye foes who kill for hire?
Will ye to your homes retire?
Look behind you! they're a-fire!
    And, before you, see
Who have done it! — From the vale
On they come! — And will ye quail? —
Leaden rain and iron hail
    Let their welcome be!

In the God of battles trust!
Die we may, — and die we must;
But, oh, where can dust to dust
    Be consigned so well,
As where Heaven its dews shall shed
On the martyred patriot's bed,
And the rocks shall raise their head,
    Of his deeds to tell!

JOHN PIERPONT.

A pause followed, during which Charlestown was set on fire by shells from the fleet and was soon in a roaring blaze. Then a second time the British advanced to the assault; again the Americans held their fire, and again, at thirty yards, poured into the Redcoats so deadly a volley that they were forced to retreat.

THE BALLAD OF BUNKER HILL

WE lay in the Trenches we'd dug in the
    Ground
    While *Phœbus* blazed down from his glory-
      lined Car,
And then from the lips of our Leader re-
    nown'd,
    These lessons we learn'd in the *Science of
    War*.
      "Let the Foeman draw nigh,
      Till the white of his Eye
Is in range with your Rifles, and then, Lads, let
    fly!
And shew to *Columbia*, to *Britain*, and *Fame*,
    How *Justice* smiles aweful. when *Freemen*
    take *aim!*"

The Regulars from Town to the Foot of the Hill
    Came in Barges and Rowboats, some great
    and some small,
But they potter'd and dawdl'd, and twaddled,
    until
    We fear'd there would be no *Attack* after all!
      Two men in red Coats
      Talk'd to one in long Boots,
And all of them *pinted* and *gestur'd* like *Coots*,
And we said, — as the Boys do upon *Training-
    Day* —
"If they waste all their *Time* so, the *Sham-
fight* won't pay."

But when they got Ready, and All came along,
    The way they march'd up the *Hill-side*
    was n't slow,
But we were not a-fear'd, and we welcomed
    'em strong,
    Held our *Fire* till the Word, and then laid
    the Lads low!
      . . . But who shall declare
      The *End* of the Affair?
At Sundown there was n't a Man of us there!
But we did n't depart till we'd given them
    Some!
When we burned up our Powder, we had to go
    Home!

        EDWARD EVERETT HALE.

So long a time elapsed after the second assault that it seemed for a time that the Americans would be left in possession of the field. In the confusion of the moment, no reinforcements were sent them, and Prescott, to his dismay, discovered that his supply of powder and ball was nearly exhausted.

BUNKER HILL

"NOT yet, not yet; steady, steady!"
On came the foe, in even line:
Nearer and nearer to thrice paces nine.
    We looked into their eyes. "Ready!"
    A sheet of flame! A roll of death!
    They fell by scores; we held our breath!
      Then nearer still they came;
      Another sheet of flame!
And brave men fled who never fled before.
      Immortal fight!
      Foreshadowing flight
Back to the astounded shore.

    Quickly they rallied, reinforced.
Mid louder roar of ship's artillery,
And bursting bombs and whistling musketry
    And shouts and groans, anear, afar,
    All the new din of dreadful war,
    Through their broad bosoms calmly
    coursed
    The blood of those stout farmers, aiming
    For freedom, manhood's birthrights
    claiming.
    Onward once more they came;
    Another sheet of deathful flame!
    Another and another still:
      They broke, they fled:
      Again they sped
Down the green, bloody hill.

    Howe, Burgoyne, Clinton, Gage,
    Stormed with commander's rage.
    Into each emptied barge
They crowd fresh men for a new charge
    Up that great hill.
Again their gallant blood we spill:
    That volley was the last:
      Our powder failed.
      On three sides fast
    The foe pressed in; nor quailed
A man. Their barrels empty, with musket
    stocks
    They fought, and gave death-dealing
    knocks,
    Till Prescott ordered the retreat.
Then Warren fell; and through a leaden sleet
    From Bunker Hill and Breed,

Stark, Putnam, Pomeroy, Knowlton, Read,
Led off the remnant of those heroes true,
The foe too shattered to pursue.
    The ground they gained; but we
      The victory.

The tidings of that chosen band
    Flowed in a wave of power
Over the shaken, anxious land,
    To men, to man, a sudden dower.
From that stanch, beaming hour
History took a fresh higher start;
And when the speeding messenger, that bare
    The news that strengthened every heart,
      Met near the Delaware
      Riding to take command,
The leader, who had just been named,
    Who was to be so famed,
The steadfast, earnest Washington
    With hand uplifted cries,
His great soul flashing to his eyes,
"Our liberties are safe; tne cause is won."
    A thankful look he cast to heaven, and
      then
His steed he spurred, in haste to lead such
    noble men.
              GEORGE H. CALVERT.

There was, in fact, a difference of opinion among
the British generals as to continuing the assault.
But Howe insisted that a third attempt be made,
and at five o'clock it was ordered. For a moment,
the advancing column was again shaken by the
American fire, but the last cartridges were soon
spent, and, at the bayonet point, the Americans
were driven from their works and forced to re-
treat across Charlestown neck.

GRANDMOTHER'S STORY OF BUNKER-HILL BATTLE

AS SHE SAW IT FROM THE BELFRY

'T is like stirring living embers when, at
    eighty, one remembers
All the achings and the quakings of "the
    times that tried men's souls;"
When I talk of *Whig* and *Tory*, when I tell
    the *Rebel* story,
To you the words are ashes, but to me they're
    burning coals.

I had heard the muskets' rattle of the April
    running battle;
Lord Percy's hunted soldiers, I can see their
    red coats still;

But a deadly chill comes o'er me, as the day
    looms up before me,
When a thousand men lay bleeding on the
    slopes of Bunker's Hill.

'T was a peaceful summer's morning, when
    the first thing gave us warning
Was the booming of the cannon from the
    river and the shore:
"Child," says grandma, "what's the matter,
    what is all this noise and clatter?
Have those scalping Indian devils come to
    murder us once more?"

Poor old soul! my sides were shaking in the
    midst of all my quaking,
To hear her talk of Indians when the guns
    began to roar:
She had seen the burning village, and the
    slaughter and the pillage,
When the Mohawks killed her father with
    their bullets through his door.

Then I said, "Now, dear old granny, don't
    you fret and worry any,
For I'll soon come back and tell you whether
    this is work or play;
There can't be mischief in it, so I won't be
    gone a minute" —
For a minute then I started. I was gone the
    livelong day.

No time for bodice-lacing or for looking-glass
    grimacing;
Down my hair went as I hurried, tumbling
    half-way to my heels;
God forbid your ever knowing, when there's
    blood around her flowing,
How the lonely, helpless daughter of a quiet
    household feels!

In the street I heard a thumping; and I knew
    it was the stumping
Of the Corporal, our old neighbor, on that
    wooden leg he wore,
With a knot of women round him, — it was
    lucky I had found him,
So I followed with the others, and the Cor-
    poral marched before.

They were making for the steeple, — the
    old soldier and his people;
The pigeons circled round us as we climbed
    the creaking stair.

Just across the narrow river — oh, so close
    it made me shiver! —
Stood a fortress on the hill-top that but yes-
    terday was bare.

Not slow our eyes to find it; well we knew
    who stood behind it,
Though the earthwork hid them from us,
    and the stubborn walls were dumb:
Here were sister, wife, and mother, looking
    wild upon each other,
And their lips were white with terror as they
    said, THE HOUR HAS COME!

The morning slowly wasted, not a morsel
    had we tasted
And our heads were almost splitting with
    the cannons' deafening thrill,
When a figure tall and stately round the
    rampart strode sedately;
It was PRESCOTT, one since told me; he com-
    manded on the hill.

Every woman's heart grew bigger when we
    saw his manly figure,
With the banyan buckled round it, standing
    up so straight and tall;
Like a gentleman of leisure who is strolling
    out for pleasure,
Through the storm of shells and cannon-
    shot he walked around the wall.

At eleven the streets were swarming, for the
    redcoats' ranks were forming;
At noon in marching order they were moving
    to the piers;
How the bayonets gleamed and glistened,
    as we looked far down, and listened
To the trampling and the drum-beat of the
    belted grenadiers!

At length the men have started, with a cheer
    (it seemed faint-hearted),
In their scarlet regimentals, with their knap-
    sacks on their backs,
And the reddening, rippling water, as after
    a sea-fight's slaughter,
Round the barges gliding onward blushed
    like blood along their tracks.

So they crossed to the other border, and
    again they formed in order;
And the boats came back for soldiers, came
    for soldiers, soldiers still:

The time seemed everlasting to us women
    faint and fasting, —
At last they're moving, marching, marching
    proudly up the hill.

We can see the bright steel glancing all along
    the lines advancing, —
Now the front rank fires a volley, — they
    have thrown away their shot;
For behind their earthwork lying, all the
    balls above them flying,
Our people need not hurry; so they wait and
    answer not.

Then the Corporal, our old cripple (he would
    swear sometimes and tipple), —
He had heard the bullets whistle (in the old
    French war) before, —
Calls out in words of jeering, just as if they
    all were hearing, —
And his wooden leg thumps fiercely on the
    dusty belfry floor: —

"Oh! fire away, ye villains, and earn King
    George's shillin's,
But ye'll waste a ton of powder afore a 'rebel'
    falls;
You may bang the dirt and welcome, they're
    as safe as Dan'l Malcolm
Ten foot beneath the gravestone that you've
    splintered with your balls!"

In the hush of expectation, in the awe and
    trepidation
Of the dread approaching moment, we are
    well-nigh breathless all;
Though the rotten bars are failing on the
    rickety belfry railing,
We are crowding up against them like the
    waves against a wall.

Just a glimpse (the air is clearer), they are
    nearer, — nearer, — nearer,
When a flash — a curling smoke-wreath —
    then a crash — the steeple shakes —
The deadly truce is ended; the tempest'
    shroud is rended;
Like a morning mist it gathered, like a thun-
    dercloud it breaks!

Oh the sight our eyes discover as the blue-
    black smoke blows over!
The redcoats stretched in windrows as
    mower rakes his hay;

Here a scarlet heap is lying, there a head-
long crowd is flying
Like a billow that has broken and is shivered
into spray.

Then we cried, "The troops are routed! they
are beat — it can't be doubted!
God be thanked, the fight is over!" — Ah!
the grim old soldier's smile!
"Tell us, tell us why you look so?" (we could
hardly speak, we shook so), —
"Are they beaten? *Are* they beaten? ARE
they beaten?" — "Wait a while."

Oh the trembling and the terror! for too soon
we saw our error:
They are baffled, not defeated; we have
driven them back in vain;
And the columns that were scattered, round
the colors that were tattered,
Toward the sullen, silent fortress turn their
belted breasts again.

All at once, as we are gazing, lo the roofs of
Charlestown blazing!
They have fired the harmless village; in an
hour it will be down!
The Lord in heaven confound them, rain
his fire and brimstone round them, —
The robbing, murdering redcoats, that would
burn a peaceful town!

They are marching, stern and solemn; we
can see each massive column
As they near the naked earth-mound with
the slanting walls so steep.
Have our soldiers got faint-hearted, and in
noiseless haste departed?
Are they panic-struck and helpless? Are
they palsied or asleep?

Now! the walls they're almost under! scarce
a rod the foes asunder!
Not a firelock flashed against them! up the
earthwork they will swarm!
But the words have scarce been spoken, when
the ominous calm is broken,
And a bellowing crash has emptied all the
vengeance of the storm!

So again, with murderous slaughter, pelted
backwards to the water,
fly Pigot's running heroes and the frightened
braves of Howe:

And we shout, "At last they're done for, it's
their barges they have run for:
They are beaten, beaten, beaten; and the
battle's over now!"

And we looked, poor timid creatures, on the
rough old soldier's features,
Our lips afraid to question, but he knew what
we would ask:
"Not sure," he said; "keep quiet, — once
more, I guess, they'll try it —
Here's damnation to the cut-throats!" —
then he handed me his flask,

Saying, "Gal, you're looking shaky; have
a drop of old Jamaiky;
I'm afeard there'll be more trouble afore
the job is done;"
So I took one scorching swallow; dreadful
faint I felt and hollow,
Standing there from early morning when the
firing was begun.

All through those hours of trial I had watched
a calm clock dial,
As the hands kept creeping, creeping, — they
were creeping round to four,
When the old man said, "They're forming
with their bagonets fixed for storming:
It's the death-grip that's a-coming, — they
will try the works once more."

With brazen trumpets blaring, the flames
behind them glaring,
The deadly wall before them, in close array
they come;
Still onward, upward toiling, like a dragon's
fold uncoiling, —
Like the rattlesnake's shrill warning the re-
verberating drum!

Over heaps all torn and gory — shall I tell
the fearful story,
How they surged above the breastwork, as
a sea breaks over a deck;
How, driven, yet scarce defeated, our worn-
out men retreated,
With their powder-horns all emptied, like
the swimmers from a wreck?

It has all been told and painted; as for me,
they say I fainted,
And the wooden-legged old Corporal stumped
with me down the stair:

When I woke from dreams affrighted the
    evening lamps were lighted, —
On the floor a youth was lying; his bleeding
    breast was bare.

And I heard through all the flurry, "Send
    for WARREN! hurry! hurry!
Tell him here's a soldier bleeding, and he'll
    come and dress his wound!"
Ah, we knew not till the morrow told its tale
    of death and sorrow,
How the starlight found him stiffened on the
    dark and bloody ground.

Who the youth was, what his name was,
    where the place from which he came
    was,
Who had brought him from the battle, and
    had left him at our door,
He could not speak to tell us; but 't was one
    of our brave fellows,
As the homespun plainly showed us which
    the dying soldier wore.

For they all thought he was dying, as they
    gathered round him crying, —
And they said, "Oh, how they'll miss him!"
    and, "What *will* his mother do?"
Then, his eyelids just unclosing like a child's
    that has been dozing,
He faintly murmured, "Mother!" — and —
    I saw his eyes were blue.

"Why, grandma, how you're winking!" Ah,
    my child, it sets me thinking
Of a story not like this one. Well, he some-
    how lived along;
So we came to know each other, and I nursed
    him like a — mother,
Till at last he stood before me, tall, and rosy-
    cheeked, and strong.

And we sometimes walked together in the
    pleasant summer weather, —
"Please to tell us what his name was?"
    Just your own, my little dear, —
There's his picture Copley painted: we be-
    came so well acquainted,
That — in short, that's why I'm grandma,
    and you children all are here!
        OLIVER WENDELL HOLMES.

In this last charge, the Americans met with an
irreparable loss in the death of General Joseph
Warren, who was shot through the head as he
lingered on the field, loath to join in the retreat.
He had hastened to the battlefield in the early
morning, replying to the remonstrance of a friend,
"Dulce et decorum est pro patria mori." He had
just been appointed major-general, but refused
the command tendered him by Prescott, saying
that he was only too glad to serve as a volunteer
aid.

THE DEATH OF WARREN

[June 17, 1775]

WHEN the war-cry of Liberty rang through
    the land,
To arms sprang our fathers the foe to with-
    stand;
On old Bunker Hill their entrenchments they
    rear,
When the army is joined by a young volunteer.
"Tempt not death!" cried his friends; but
    he bade them good-by,
Saying, "Oh! it is sweet for our country to die!"

The tempest of battle now rages and swells,
'Mid the thunder of cannon, the pealing of
    bells;
And a light, not of battle, illumes yonder
    spire —
Scene of woe and destruction; — 't is Charles-
    town on fire!
The young volunteer heedeth not the sad cry
But murmurs, "'T is sweet for our country
    to die!"

With trumpets and banners the foe draweth
    near:
A volley of musketry checks their career!
With the dead and the dying the hill-side is
    strown,
And the shout through our lines is, "The day
    is our own!"
"Not yet," cries the young volunteer, "do
    they fly!
Stand firm! — it is sweet for our country to
    die!"

Now our powder is spent, and they rally
    again; —
"Retreat," says our chief, "since unarmed
    we remain!"
But the young volunteer lingers yet on the
    field,
Reluctant to fly, and disdaining to yield.
A shot! Ah! he falls! but his life's latest sigh
Is, "'T is sweet, oh, 't is sweet for our country
    to die!"

And thus Warren fell! Happy death! noble
    fall!
To perish for country at Liberty's call!
Should the flag of invasion profane evermore
The blue of our seas or the green of our shore,
May the hearts of our people re-echo that
    cry, —
"'T is sweet, oh, 't is sweet for our country
    to die!"

EPES SARGENT.

The British loss in killed and wounded was
1054, while the American loss, incurred mainly
in the last hand-to-hand struggle, was 449. The
British had gained the victory, but the moral
advantage was wholly with the Americans.

THE BATTLE OF BUNKER HILL

COMPOSED BY A BRITISH OFFICER, THE DAY
AFTER THE BATTLE

IT was on the seventeenth, by break of day,
    The Yankees did surprise us,
With their strong works they had thrown up
To burn the town and drive us.

But soon we had an order come,
    An order to defeat them;
Like rebels stout, they stood it out,
    And thought we ne'er could beat them.

About the hour of twelve that day,
    An order came for marching,
With three good flints and sixty rounds,
    Each man hoped to discharge them.

We marchèd down to the Long Wharf,
    Where boats were ready waiting;
With expedition we embark'd,
    Our ships kept cannonading.

And when our boats all fillèd were
    With officers and soldiers,
With as good troops as England had,
    To oppose who dare controul us?

And when our boats all fillèd were,
    We row'd in line of battle,
Where showers of ball like hail did fly,
    Our cannon loud did rattle.

There was Copps' Hill battery, near Charles-
    town,
    Our twenty-fours they played:

And the three frigates in the stream,
    That very well behaved.

The Glasgow frigate clear'd the shore,
    All at the time of landing,
With her grape-shot and cannon-balls,
    No Yankee e'er could stand them.

And when we landed on the shore,
    We draw'd up all together;
The Yankees they all mann'd their works,
    And thought we'd ne'er come thither.

But soon they did perceive brave Howe,
    Brave Howe, our bold commander;
With grenadiers, and infantry,
    We made them to surrender.

Brave William Howe, on our right wing,
    Cried, "Boys, fight on like thunder;
You soon will see the rebels flee,
    With great amaze and wonder."

Now some lay bleeding on the ground,
    And some fell fast a-running
O'er hills and dales, and mountains high,
    Crying, "Zounds! brave Howe's a-coming."

They 'gan to play on our left wing,
    Where Pigot, he commanded;
But we returned it back again,
    With courage most undaunted.

To our grape-shot and musket-balls,
    To which they were but strangers,
They thought to come with sword in hand,
    But soon they found their danger.

And when their works we got into,
    And put them to the flight, sirs,
Some of them did hide themselves,
    And others died of fright, sirs.

And when their works we got into,
    Without great fear or danger,
The works they'd made were firm and strong,
    The Yankees are great strangers.

But as for our artillery,
    They all behavèd dinty;
For while our ammunition held,
    We gave it to them plenty.

But our conductor, he got broke
    For his misconduct sure, sir;

The shot he sent for twelve-pound guns,
　Were made for twenty-fours, sir.

There's some in Boston pleased to say,
　As we the field were taking,
We went to kill their countrymen,
　While they their hay were making.

For such stout whigs I never saw,
　To hang them all I'd rather;
For making hay with musket-balls,
　And buckshot mixt together.

Brave Howe is so considerate,
　As to guard against all dangers:
He allows us half a pint a day —
　To rum we are no strangers.

Long may he live by land and sea,
　For he's belov'd by many;
The name of Howe the Yankees dread,
　We see it very plainly.

And now my song is at an end:
　And to conclude my ditty,
It is the poor and ignorant,
　And only them, I pity.

But as for their king, John Hancock,
　And Adams, if they're taken,
Their heads for signs shall hang up high,
　Upon that hill call'd Beacon.

On July 2, 1775, George Washington, who had,
a fortnight before, been appointed commander-
in-chief of the Continental army by the Congress
then assembled in Philadelphia, arrived at Cam-
bridge, and on the following day, under the shade
of the great elm which is still standing near Cam-
bridge Common, he took command of the sixteen
thousand men composing the American forces.

THE NEW-COME CHIEF

From "Under the Old Elm"

[July 3, 1775]

BENEATH our consecrated elm
A century ago he stood,
Famed vaguely for that old fight in the wood
Whose red surge sought, but could not over-
　whelm
The life foredoomed to wield our rough-
　hewn helm: —

From colleges, where now the gown
To arms had yielded, from the town,
Our rude self-summoned levies flocked to see
The new-come chief and wonder which was
　he.
No need to question long; close-lipped and
　tall,
Long trained in murder-brooding forests lone
To bridle others' clamors and his own,
Firmly erect, he towered above them all,
The incarnate discipline that was to free
With iron curb that armed democracy.

A motley rout was that which came to stare,
In raiment tanned by years of sun and storm,
Of every shape that was not uniform,
Dotted with regimentals here and there;
An army all of captains, used to pray
And stiff in fight, but serious drill's despair,
Skilled to debate their orders, not obey;
Deacons were there, selectmen, men of note
In half-tamed hamlets ambushed round with
　woods,
Ready to settle Freewill by a vote,
But largely liberal to its private moods;
Prompt to assert by manners, voice, or pen,
Or ruder arms, their rights as Englishmen,
Nor much fastidious as to how and when:
Yet seasoned stuff and fittest to create
A thought-staid army or a lasting state:
Haughty they said he was, at first; severe;
But owned, as all men own, the steady hand
Upon the bridle, patient to command,
Prized, as all prize, the justice pure from
　fear,
And learned to honor first, then love him, then
　revere.
Such power there is in clear-eyed self-re-
　straint
And purpose clean as light from every selfish
　taint.

．　．　．　．　．　．　．　．

Never to see a nation born
Hath been given to mortal man,
Unless to those who, on that summer morn
Gazed silent when the great Virginian
Unsheathed the sword whose fatal flash
Shot union through the incoherent clash
Of our loose atoms, crystallizing them
Around a single will's unpliant stem,
And making purpose of emotion rash.
Out of that scabbard sprang, as from its
　womb,
Nebulous at first but hardening to a star.

Through mutual share of sunburst and of
    gloom,
The common faith that made us what we are.

That lifted blade transformed our jangling
    clans,
Till then provincial, to Americans,
And made a unity of wildering plans;
Here was the doom fixed; here is marked the
    date
When this New World awoke to man's estate,
Burnt its last ship and ceased to look behind:
Nor thoughtless was the choice; no love or
    hate
Could from its poise move that deliberate
    mind,
Weighing between too early and too late
Those pitfalls of the man refused by Fate:
His was the impartial vision of the great
Who see not as they wish, but as they find.
He saw the dangers of defeat, nor less
The incomputable perils of success;
The sacred past thrown by, an empty rind;
The future, cloud-land, snare of prophets
    blind;
The waste of war, the ignominy of peace;
On either hand a sullen rear of woes,
Whose garnered lightnings none could guess,
Piling its thunder-heads and muttering
    "Cease!"
Yet drew not back his hand, but gravely chose
The seeming-desperate task whence our new
    nation rose.
          JAMES RUSSELL LOWELL.

Tory balladists found rich material for their
rhymes in the undisciplined and motley army of
which Washington was the head, but, strangely
enough, the commander himself was the object
of very few attacks of this kind. The following
is almost the only one which has survived.

THE TRIP TO CAMBRIDGE

[July 3, 1775]

WHEN Congress sent great Washington
    All clothed in power and breeches,
To meet old Britain's warlike sons
    And make some rebel speeches;

'T was then he took his gloomy way
    Astride his dapple donkeys,
And travelled well, both night and day,
    Until he reach'd the Yankees.

Away from camp, 'bout three miles off,
    From Lily he dismounted,
His sergeant brush'd his sun-burnt wig
    While he the specie counted.

All prinkèd up in *full* bag-wig;
    The shaking notwithstanding,
In leathers tight, oh! glorious sight!
    He reach'd the Yankee landing.

The women ran, the darkeys too;
    And all the bells, they tollèd;
For Britain's sons, by Doodle doo,
    We're sure to be — consolèd.

Old mother Hancock with a pan
    All crowded full of butter,
Unto the lovely Georgius ran,
    And added to the splutter.

Says she, "Our brindle has just calved,
    And John is wondrous happy.
He sent this present to you, dear,
    As you're the 'country's papa.'" —

"You'll butter bread and bread butter,
    But do not butt your speeches.
You'll butter bread and bread butter,
    But do not grease your breeches."

Full many a child went into camp,
    All dressed in homespun kersey,
To see the greatest rebel scamp
    That ever cross'd o'er Jersey.

The rebel clowns, oh! what a sight!
    Too awkward was their figure.
'T was yonder stood a pious wight,
    And here and there a nigger.

Upon a stump he placed (himself),
    Great Washington did he,
And through the nose of lawyer Close,
    Proclaimed great Liberty.

The patriot brave, the patriot fair,
    From fervor had grown thinner,
So off they march'd, with patriot zeal,
    And took a patriot dinner.

The Colonials, on the other hand, among whom
he seems to have inspired almost instant respect
and affection, made him the subject of many
songs, the most popular of which was Sewall's
"War and Washington," which was sung by sol-
diers and civilians during the whole Revolution.

WAR AND WASHINGTON

VAIN Britons, boast no longer with proud
  indignity,
By land your conquering legions, your match-
  less strength at sea,
Since we, your braver sons incensed, our
  swords have girded on,
Huzza, huzza, huzza, huzza, for war and
  Washington.

Urged on by North and vengeance those val-
  iant champions came,
Loud bellowing Tea and Treason, and George
  was all on flame,
Yet sacrilegious as it seems, we rebels still live
  on,
And laugh at all their empty puffs, huzza for
  Washington!

Still deaf to mild entreaties, still blind to Eng-
  land's good,
You have for thirty pieces betrayed your coun-
  try's blood.
Like Esop's greedy cur you'll gain a shadow
  for your bone,
Yet find us fearful shades indeed inspired by
  Washington.

Mysterious! unexampled! incomprehensible!
The blundering schemes of Britain their folly,
  pride, and zeal,
Like lions how ye growl and threat! mere asses
  have you shown,
And ye shall share an ass's fate, and drudge
  for Washington!

Your dark unfathomed councils our weakest
  heads defeat,
Our children rout your armies, our boats de-
  stroy your fleet,
And to complete the dire disgrace, cooped up
  within a town,
You live the scorn of all our host, the slaves of
  Washington!

Great Heaven! is this the nation whose thun-
  dering arms were hurled,
Through Europe, Afric, India? whose navy
  ruled a world?
The lustre of your former deeds, whole ages
  of renown,
Lost in a moment, or transferred to us and
  Washington!

Yet think not thirst of glory unsheaths our
  vengeful swords
To rend your bands asunder, or cast away
  your cords,
'T is heaven-born freedom fires us all, and
  strengthens each brave son,
From him who humbly guides the plough, to
  god-like Washington.

For this, oh could our wishes your ancient rage
  inspire,
Your armies should be doubled, in numbers,
  force, and fire,
Then might the glorious conflict prove which
  best deserved the boon,
America or Albion, a George or Washing-
  ton!

Fired with the great idea, our Fathers' shades
  would rise,
To view the stern contention, the gods desert
  their skies;
And Wolfe, 'midst hosts of heroes, superior
  bending down,
Cry out with eager transport, God save great
  Washington!

Should George, too choice of Britons, to for-
  eign realms apply,
And madly arm half Europe, yet still we would
  defy
Turk, Hessian, Jew, and Infidel, or all those
  powers in one,
While Adams guards our senate, our camp
  great Washington!

Should warlike weapons fail us, disdaining
  slavish fears,
To swords we'll beat our ploughshares, our
  pruning-hooks to spears,
And rush, all desperate, on our foe, nor
  breathe till battle won,
Then shout, and shout America! and conquer-
  ing Washington!

Proud France should view with terror, and
  haughty Spain revere,
While every warlike nation would court alli-
  ance here;
And George, his minions trembling round,
  dismounting from his throne
Pay homage to America and glorious Wash-
  ington!

JONATHAN MITCHELL SEWALL.

While the army at Cambridge was getting into shape to assume the offensive, the British were by no means idle. They recovered St. John's, which Arnold had captured in May, and a fleet under Admiral Wallace ravaged the shores of Narragansett Bay. On October 7, 1775, he bombarded the town of Bristol, which had refused to furnish him with supplies, — an incident which is described in one of the most ingenuous and amusing of Revolutionary ballads.

THE BOMBARDMENT OF BRISTOL

[October 7, 1775]

In seventeen hundred and seventy-five,
Our Bristol town was much surprised
By a pack of thievish villains,
That will not work to earn their livings.

October 't was the seventh day,
As I have heard the people say,
Wallace, his name be ever curst,
Came on our harbor just at dusk.

And there his ship did safely moor,
And quickly sent his barge on shore,
With orders that should not be broke,
Or they might expect a smoke.

Demanding that the magistrates
Should quickly come on board his ship,
And let him have some sheep and cattle,
Or they might expect a battle.

At eight o'clock, by signal given,
Our peaceful atmosphere was riven
By British balls, both grape and round,
As plenty afterwards were found.

But oh! to hear the doleful cries
Of people running for their lives!
Women, with children in their arms,
Running away to the farms!

With all their firing and their skill
They did not any person kill;
Neither was any person hurt
But the Reverend Parson Burt.

And he was not killed by a ball,
As judged by jurors one and all;
But being in a sickly state,
He, frightened, fell, which proved his fate.

Another truth to you I'll tell,
That you may see they levelled well;

For aiming for to kill the people,
They fired their shot into a steeple.

They fired low, they fired high,
The women scream, the children cry;
And all their firing and their racket
Shot off the topmast of a packet.

From the moment, almost, of the fight at Lexington, the conquest of Canada had been dreamed of, and in September, 1775, a force of two thousand men, under General Richard Montgomery, started for Quebec. He was joined by another force under Benedict Arnold, and an attempt was made to carry the citadel by storm. But Montgomery fell as he led the way over the walls, Arnold was wounded, and the Americans were beaten back.

MONTGOMERY AT QUEBEC

[December 31, 1775]

Round Quebec's embattled walls
    Moodily the patriots lay;
Dread disease within its thralls
    Drew them closer day by day;
Till from suffering man to man,
Mutinous, a murmur ran.

Footsore, they had wandered far,
    They had fasted, they had bled;
They had slept beneath the star
    With no pillow for the head;
Was it but to freeze to stone
In this cruel icy zone?

Yet their leader held his heart,
    Naught discouraged, naught dismayed;
Quelled with unobtrusive art
    Those that muttered; unafraid
Waited, watchful, for the hour
When his golden chance should flower.

'T was the death-tide of the year;
    Night had passed its murky noon;
Through the bitter atmosphere
    Pierced nor ray of star nor moon;
But upon the bleak earth beat
Blinding arrows of the sleet.

While the trumpets of the storm
    Pealed the bastioned heights around,
Did the dauntless heroes form,
    Did the low, sharp order sound.
"Be the watchword *Liberty!*"
Cried the brave Montgomery.

Here, where he had won applause,
    When Wolfe faced the Gallic foe,
For a nobler, grander cause
    Would he strike the fearless blow, —
Smite at Wrong upon the throne,
At Injustice giant grown.

"Men, you will not fear to tread
    Where your general dares to lead!
On, my valiant boys!" he said,
    And his foot was first to speed;
Swiftly up the beetling steep,
Lion-hearted, did he leap.

Flashed a sudden blinding glare;
    Roared a fearsome battle-peal;
Rang the gloomy vasts of air;
    Seemed the earth to rock and reel;
While adown that fiery breath
Rode the hurtling bolts of death.

Woe for him, the valorous one,
    Now a silent clod of clay!
Nevermore for him the sun
    Would make glad the paths of day;
Yet 't were better thus to die
Than to cringe to tyranny! —

Better thus the life to yield,
    Striking for the right and God,
Upon Freedom's gory field,
    Than to kiss Oppression's rod!
Honor, then, for all time be
To the brave Montgomery!
                    CLINTON SCOLLARD.

Though the Americans had lost Canada, they
were soon to gain Boston. During the winter of
1775–76, a great number of captured cannon had
been dragged on sledges from Ticonderoga, the
drilling of the army had gone steadily on, and at
last Washington felt that he was able to assume
the offensive, and on the night of March 4, 1776,
he seized and fortified Dorchester Heights.

A SONG

[1776]

SMILE, Massachusetts, smile,
    Thy virtue still outbraves
The frowns of Britain's isle,
    The rage of home-born slaves.
Thy free-born sons disdain their ease,
When purchased by their liberties.

Thy genius, once the pride
    Of Britain's ancient isle,
Brought o'er the raging tide
    By our forefathers' toil;
In spite of North's despotic power,
Shines glorious on this western shore.

In Hancock's generous mind
    Awakes the noble strife,
Which so conspicuous shined
    In gallant Sydney's life;
While in its cause the hero bled,
Immortal honors crown'd his head.

Let zeal your breasts inspire;
    Let wisdom guide your plans;
'T is not your cause entire,
    On doubtful conflict hangs;
The fate of this vast continent,
And unborn millions share th' event.

To close the gloomy scenes
    Of this alarming day,
A happy union reigns
    Through wide America.
While awful Wisdom hourly waits
To adorn the councils of her states.

Brave Washington arrives,
    Arrayed in warlike fame,
While in his soul revives
    Great Marlboro's martial flame,
To lead your conquering armies on
To lasting glory and renown.

To aid the glorious cause,
    Experienc'd Lee has come,
Renown'd in foreign wars,
    A patriot at home.
While valiant Putnam's warlike deeds
Amongst the foe a terror spreads.

Let Britons proudly boast,
    "That their two thousand braves
Can drive our numerous host,
    And make us all their slaves,"
While twice six thousand quake with fear,
Nor dare without their lines appear.

Kind Heaven has deign'd to own
    Our bold resistance just,
Since murderous Gage began
    The bloody carnage first.
Near ten to one has been their cost,
For each American we've lost.

Stand firm in your defence,
Like Sons of Freedom fight,
Your haughty foes convince
That you 'll maintain your right.
Defiance bid to tyrants' frown,
And glory will your valor crown.
        The Connecticut Gazette, 1776.

Howe realized that Boston was untenable un-
less the Americans could be dislodged; but with
the memory of Bunker Hill before him, he had no
heart for the enterprise. While he hesitated, the
American works were made well-nigh impregnable,
and Howe decided to abandon the town. On
March 17, 1776, the British troops, eight thousand
in number, sailed away for Halifax. Washington
at once took possession of the city.

A POEM CONTAINING SOME RE-MARKS ON THE PRESENT WAR

[March 17, 1776]

BRITONS grown big with pride
And wanton ease,
And tyranny beside,
They sought to please
Their craving appetite,
They strove with all their might,
They vow'd to rise and fight,
To make us bow.

The plan they laid was deep
Even like hell;
With sympathy I weep,
While here I tell
Of that base murderous brood,
Void of the fear of God,
Who came to spill our blood
In our own land.

They bid their armies sail
Though billows roar,
And take the first fair gale
For Boston's shore;
They cross'd the Atlantic sea
A long and watery way,
Poor Boston fell a prey
To tyranny.

.   .   .   .   .   .

Gage was both base and mean,
He dare not fight,
The men he sent were seen
Like owls in night:
It was in Lexington
Where patriots' blood did run

Before the rising sun
In crimson gore.

Here sons of freedom fell
Rather than flee,
Unto those brutes of hell
They fell a prey;
But they shall live again,
Their names shall rise and reign
Among the noble slain
In all our land.

But oh! this cruel foe
Went on in haste,
To Concord they did go,
And there did waste
Some stores in their rage,
To gratify old Gage,
His name in every page
Shall be defam'd.

Their practice thus so base,
And murder too,
Rouz'd up the patriot race,
Who did pursue,
And put this foe to flight,
They could not bear the light,
Some rued the very night
They left their den.

And now this cruelty
Was spread abroad,
The sons of liberty
This act abhorr'd,
Their noble blood did boil,
Forgetting all the toil,
In troubles they could smile,
And went in haste.

Our army willingly
Did then engage,
To stop the cruelty
Of tyrants' rage!
They did not fear our foe,
But ready were to go,
And let the tyrants know
Whose sons they were.

But when old Gage did see
All us withstand,
And strive for liberty
Through all our land,
He strove with all his might,
For rage was his delight,
With fire he did fight,
A monster he.

On Charlestown he display'd
His fire abroad;
He it in ashes laid,
An act abhorr'd
By sons of liberty,
Who saw the flames on high
Piercing their native sky,
And now lies waste.

To Bunker-Hill they came
Most rapidly,
And many there were slain,
And there did die.
They call'd it bloody hill,
Altho' they gain'd their will
In triumph they were still,
'Cause of their slain.

Here sons of freedom fought
Right manfully,
A wonder here was wrought
Though some did die.
Here WARREN bow'd to death,
His last expiring breath,
In language mild he saith,
Fight on, brave boys.

Oh! this did stain the pride
Of British troops,
They saw they were deny'd
Of their vain hopes
Of marching thro' our land,
When twice a feeble band,
Did fight and boldly stand
In our defence.

Brave WASHINGTON did come
To our relief;
He left his native home,
Filled with grief,
He did not covet gain,
The cause he would maintain
And die among the slain
Rather than flee.

His bosom glow'd with love
For liberty,
His passions much did move
To orphans' cry,
He let proud tyrants know,
How far their bounds should go
And then his bombs did throw
Into their den.

This frighted them full sore
When bombs were sent.

When cannon loud did roar
They left each tent:
Oh! thus did the tyrants fly,
Went precipitately,
Their shipping being nigh,
They sailed off.

And now Boston is free
From tyrants base,
The sons of liberty
Possess the place;
They now in safety dwell.
Free from those brutes of hell,
Their raptur'd tongues do tell
Their joys great.

A portion of the British fleet remained in Boston harbor, and apprehensions began to be felt that an effort would be made to recapture the town. It was at this juncture that Captain James Mugford, of the schooner Franklin, captured the British ship Hope, bound for Boston with supplies and fifteen hundred barrels of powder. Two days later, on May 19, the Franklin ran aground at Point Shirley, at the mouth of the harbor, and was at once attacked by boats from the British vessels. A sharp engagement ensued, in which Mugford was killed. His last words are said to have been those used by Lawrence nearly forty years later: "Don't give up the ship! You will beat them off!" And they did.

MUGFORD'S VICTORY

[May 17-19, 1776]

OUR mother, the pride of us all,
  She sits on her crags by the shore,
And her feet they are wet with the waves
Whose foam is as flowers from the graves
    Of her sons whom she welcomes no
      more,
And who answer no more to her call.

Amid weeds and sea-tangle and shells
  They are buried far down in the deep, —
The deep which they loved to career.
  Oh, might we awake them from sleep!
Oh, might they our voices but hear,
And the sound of our holiday bells!

Can it be she is thinking of them,
  Her face is so proud and so still,
And her lashes are moistened with tears?
Ho, little ones! pluck at her hem,
  Her lap with your jollity fill,
And ask of her thoughts and her fears.

"Fears!" — we have roused her at last;
  See! her lips part with a smile,
And laughter breaks forth from her eyes, —
"Fears! whence should they ever arise
  In our hearts, O my children, the while
We can remember the past?

"Can remember that morning of May,
  When Mugford went forth with his men,
Twenty, and all of them ours.
'T is a hundred years to a day,
  And the sea and the shore are as then,
And as bright are the grass and the flowers;
  But our twenty — they come not again!

"He had heard of the terrible need
  Of the patriot army there
In Boston town. Now for a deed
  To save it from despair!
To thrill with joy the great commander's
    heart,
And hope new-born to all the land impart!

"Hope! ay; that was the very name
Of the good ship that came
  From England far away,
Laden with enginery of death,
Food for the cannon's fiery breath;
Hope-laden for great Washington,
Who, but for her, was quite undone
  A hundred years ago to-day.

" 'Oh, but to meet her there,
And grapple with her fair,
  Out in the open bay!'
Mugford to Glover said.
  How could he answer nay?
  And Mugford sailed away,
Brave heart and newly wed.

"But what are woman's tears,
  And rosy cheeks made pale,
To one who far off hears
  The generations hail
A deed like this we celebrate to-day,
A hundred years since Mugford sailed away!

"I love to picture him,
Clear-eyed and strong of limb,
Gazing his last upon the rocky shore
His feet should press no more;
Seeing the tall church-steeples fade away
In distance soft and gray;
So dropping down below the horizon's rim
Where fame awaited him.

"Slow sailing from the east his victim came.
They met; brief parley struggle brief and
    tame,
  And she was ours;
In Boston harbor safe ere set of sun,
Great joy for Washington!
  But heavy grew the hours
On Mugford's hands, longing to bring to me
His mother proud, news of his victory;
But that was not to be!

"Abreast Nantasket's narrow strip of gray
The British cruisers lay:
They saw the daring skipper dropping down
From the much-hated rebel-haunted town,
  And in the twilight dim
Their boats awaited him,
While wind and tide conspired
  To grant what they desired.

"Thickly they swarmed about his tiny craft;
  But Mugford gayly laughed
And gave them blow for blow;
  And many a hapless foe
Went hurtling down below.
    Upon the schooner's rail
    Fell, like a thresher's flail,
The strokes that beat the soul and sense apart,
And pistol-crack through many an eager heart
    Sent deadly hail.
But when the fight was o'er,
Brave Mugford was no more.
    Crying, with death-white lip,
    'Boys, don't give up the ship!'
His soul struck out for heaven's peaceful shore.

    "We gave him burial meet;
    Through every sobbing street
A thousand men marched with their arms
    reversed;
    And Parson Story told,
    In sentences of gold,
The tale since then a thousand times re-
    hearsed."

Such is the story she tells,
  Our mother, the pride of us all.
Ring out your music, O bells,
  That ever such things could befall!
Ring not for Mugford alone,
Ring for the twenty unknown,
Who fought hand-to-hand at his side,
Who saw his last look when he died,
And who brought him, though dead, to his own!
                JOHN WHITE CHADWICK.

A month later, on June 14, 1775, the Continentals occupied various islands and points in the bay, and opened so hot a fire upon the British ships that they were finally forced to weigh anchor and sail away. The news of the capture of Boston and departure of the British was received with the greatest rejoicing throughout the country. Among the many songs composed to celebrate the event, one, "Off from Boston," gained wide popularity.

OFF FROM BOSTON

Sons of valor, taste the glories
  Of celestial liberty,
Sing a triumph o'er the Tories,
  Let the pulse of joy beat high.

Heaven hath this day foil'd the many
  Fallacies of George the King;
Let the echo reach Britan'y,
  Bid her mountain summits ring.

See yon navy swell the bosom
  Of the late enragèd sea;
Where'er they go, we shall oppose them,
  Sons of valor must be free.

Should they touch at fair Rhode Island,
  There to combat with the brave,
Driven from each dale and highland,
  They shall plough the purple wave.

Should they thence to fair Virginia,
  Bend a squadron to Dunmore,
Still with fear and ignominy,
  They shall quit the hostile shore.

To Carolina or to Georg'y,
  Should they next advance their fame,
This land of heroes shall disgorge the
  Sons of tyranny and shame.

Let them rove to climes far distant,
  Situate under Arctic skies,
Call on Hessian troops assistant,
  And the savages to rise.

Boast of wild brigades from Russia,
  To fix down the galling chain,
Canada and Nova Scotia,
  Shall disgorge these hordes again.

In New York state, rejoin'd by Clinton,
  Should their standards mock the air,
Many a surgeon shall put lint on
  Wounds of death receivèd there.

War, fierce war, shall break their forces,
  Nerves of Tory men shall fail,
Seeing Howe, with alter'd courses,
  Bending to the western gale.

Thus from every bay of ocean,
  Flying back with sails unfurl'd,
Tossed with ever-troubled motion,
  They shall quit this smiling world.

Like Satan banishèd from heaven,
  Never see the smiling shore;
From this land, so happy, driven,
  Never stain its bosom more.

CHAPTER IV

INDEPENDENCE

At the outbreak of the Revolution very few, even of the more radical colonial leaders, thought of or desired complete independence from Great Britain. Samuel Adams was perhaps the first to proclaim this as the only solution of the problem which confronted the colonies. But the sentiment for independence grew steadily.

EMANCIPATION FROM BRITISH DEPENDENCE

[1775]

Libera nos, Domine — Deliver us, O Lord,
Not only from British dependence, but also,

From a junto that labor for absolute power,
Whose schemes disappointed have made them look sour;
From the lords of the council, who fight against freedom
Who still follow on where delusion shall lead 'em.

From groups at St. James's who slight our Petitions,
And fools that are waiting for further submissions;

From a nation whose manners are rough and abrupt,
From scoundrels and rascals whom gold can corrupt.

From pirates sent out by command of the king
To murder and plunder, but never to swing;
From Wallace, and Graves, and *Vipers*, and *Roses*,
Whom, if Heaven pleases, we'll give bloody noses.

From the valiant Dunmore, with his crew of banditti
Who plunder Virginians at Williamsburg city,
From hot-headed Montague, mighty to swear,
The little fat man with his pretty white hair.

From bishops in Britain, who butchers are grown,
From slaves that would die for a smile from the throne,
From assemblies that vote against Congress' proceedings
(Who now see the fruit of their stupid mis-leadings).

From Tryon, the mighty, who flies from our city,
And swelled with importance, disdains the committee
(But since he is pleased to proclaim us his foes,
What the devil care we where the devil he goes).

From the caitiff, Lord North, who would bind us in chains,
From our noble King Log, with his toothful of brains,
Who dreams, and is certain (when taking a nap),
He has conquered our lands as they lay on his map.

From a kingdom that bullies, and hectors, and swears,
I send up to Heaven my wishes and prayers
That we, disunited, may freemen be still,
And Britain go on — to be damn'd if she will.
                              PHILIP FRENEAU.

On June 8 Richard Henry Lee submitted to the Continental Congress a motion "That these United Colonies are, and of right ought to be, free and independent States; that they are absolved from all allegiance to the British Crown; and that all political connection between them and the state of Great Britain is, and ought to be, totally dissolved." The debate on the motion began July 1.

RODNEY'S RIDE

[July 3, 1776]

IN that soft mid-land where the breezes bear
The North and South on the genial air,
Through the county of Kent, on affairs of state,
Rode Cæsar Rodney, the delegate.

Burly and big, and bold and bluff,
In his three-cornered hat and coat of snuff,
A foe to King George and the English State,
Was Cæsar Rodney, the delegate.

Into Dover village he rode apace,
And his kinsfolk knew, from his anxious face,
It was matter grave that brought him there,
To the counties three on the Delaware.

"Money and men we must have," he said,
"Or the Congress fails and our cause is dead;
Give us both and the King shall not work his will.
We are men, since the blood of Bunker Hill!"

Comes a rider swift on a panting bay:
"Ho, Rodney, ho! you must save the day,
For the Congress halts at a deed so great,
And your vote alone may decide its fate."

Answered Rodney then: "I will ride with speed;
It is Liberty's stress; it is Freedom's need.
When stands it?" "To-night. Not a moment to spare,
But ride like the wind from the Delaware."

"Ho, saddle the black! I've but half a day,
And the Congress sits eighty miles away —
But I'll be in time, if God grants me grace,
To shake my fist in King George's face."

He is up; he is off! and the black horse flies
On the northward road ere the "God-speed" dies;
It is gallop and spur, as the leagues they clear,
And the clustering mile-stones move a-rear.

It is two of the clock; and the fleet hoofs fling
The Fieldboro's dust with a clang and a cling;
It is three; and he gallops with slack rein
where
The road winds down to the Delaware.

Four; and he spurs into New Castle town,
From his panting steed he gets him down —
"A fresh one, quick! not a moment's wait!"
And off speeds Rodney, the delegate.

It is five; and the beams of the western sun
Tinge the spires of Wilmington gold and dun;
Six; and the dust of Chester Street
Flies back in a cloud from the courser's feet.

It is seven; the horse-boat broad of beam,
At the Schuylkill ferry crawls over the
stream —
And at seven-fifteen by the Rittenhouse
clock,
He flings his reins to the tavern jock.

The Congress is met; the debate's begun,
And Liberty lags for the vote of one —
When into the hall, not a moment late,
Walks Cæsar Rodney, the delegate.

Not a moment late! and that half day's ride
Forwards the world with a mighty stride;
For the act was passed; ere the midnight
stroke
O'er the Quaker City its echoes woke.

At Tyranny's feet was the gauntlet flung;
"We are free!" all the bells through the
colonies rung,
And the sons of the free may recall with pride
The day of Delegate Rodney's ride.

The motion was put to a vote the following
day, July 2, 1776, and was adopted by the unani-
mous vote of twelve colonies, the delegates from
New York being excused from voting, as they had
no sufficient instructions. This having been de-
cided, the Congress at once went into committee
of the whole, to consider the form of declaration
which should be adopted.

AMERICAN INDEPENDENCE

MAKE room, all ye kingdoms, in history
renown'd,
Whose arms have in battle with victory been
crown'd,

Make room for America, another great na-
tion;
She rises to claim in your councils a station.

Her sons fought for freedom, and by their
own bravery
Have rescued themselves from the shackles of
slavery;
America is free; and Britain's abhorr'd;
And America's fame is forever restored.

Fair Freedom in Britain her throne had
erected;
Her sons they grew venal, and she disre-
spected.
The goddess, offended, forsook that base
nation,
And fix'd on our mountains: a more honor'd
station.

With glory immortal she here sits en-
throned,
Nor fears the vain vengeance of Britain dis-
own'd,
Great Washington guards her, with heroes
surrounded;
Her foes he, with shameful defeat, has con-
founded.

To arms! we to arms flew! 't was Freedom
invited us,
The trumpet, shrill sounding, to battle excited
us;
The banners of virtue, unfurl'd, did wave o'er
us,
Our hero led on, and the foe flew before us.

In Heaven and Washington we placed reli-
ance,
We met the proud Britons, and bid them
defiance;
The cause we supported was just, and was
glorious;
When men fight for freedom, they must be
victorious.

FRANCIS HOPKINSON.

A committee had already been appointed to
draw up a paper which should be worthy this sol-
emn occasion. Thomas Jefferson was its chairman,
and was chosen to be the author of the Declara-
tion. On the evening of July 4, 1776, the Decla-
ration of Independence was unanimously adopted
by twelve colonies, the New York delegates being
still unable to act.

THE FOURTH OF JULY

DAY of glory! Welcome day!
Freedom's banners greet thy ray;
See! how cheerfully they play
    With thy morning breeze,
On the rocks where pilgrims kneeled,
On the heights where squadrons wheeled,
When a tyrant's thunder pealed
    O'er the trembling seas.

God of armies! did thy stars
On their courses smite his cars;
Blast his arm, and wrest his bars
    From the heaving tide?
On our standard, lo! they burn,
And, when days like this return,
Sparkle o'er the soldier's urn
    Who for freedom died.

God of peace! whose spirit fills
All the echoes of our hills,
All the murmur of our rills,
    Now the storm is o'er,
O let freemen be our sons,
And let future Washingtons
Rise, to lead their valiant ones
    Till there's war no more!

                    JOHN PIERPONT.

News of its adoption was received throughout
the country with the greatest rejoicing. On the
9th of July it was ratified by New York, and the
soldiers there celebrated the occasion by throw-
ing down the leaden statue of George III on the
Bowling Green, and casting it into bullets.
Everywhere there were bonfires, torchlight pro-
cessions, and ratification meetings.

INDEPENDENCE DAY

SQUEAK the fife, and beat the drum,
Independence day is come!
Let the roasting pig be bled,
Quick twist off the cockerel's head,
Quickly rub the pewter platter,
Heap the nutcakes, fried in butter.
Set the cups and beaker glass,
The pumpkin and the apple sauce;
Send the keg to shop for brandy;
Maple sugar we have handy.
Independent, staggering Dick.
A noggin mix of swingeing thick;
Sal, put on your russet skirt,
Jotham, get your *boughten* shirt.

To-day we dance to tiddle diddle.
— Here comes Sambo with his fiddle;
Sambo, take a dram of whiskey,
And play up Yankee Doodle frisky.
Moll, come leave your witched tricks,
And let us have a reel of six.
Father and mother shall make two;
Sal, Moll, and I stand all a-row;
Sambo, play and dance with quality;
This is the day of blest equality.
Father and mother are but *men*,
And Sambo — is a citizen.
Come foot it, Sal — Moll, figure in,
And mother, you dance up to him;
Now saw as fast as e'er you can do,
And father, you cross o'er to Sambo.
— Thus we dance, and thus we play,
On glorious independence day. —
Rub more rosin on your bow,
And let us have another go.
Zounds! as sure as eggs and bacon,
Here's ensign Sneak, and Uncle Deacon,
Aunt Thiah, and their Bets behind her,
On blundering mare, than beetle blinder.
And there's the 'Squire too, with his lady —
Sal, hold the beast, I'll take the baby,
Moll, bring the 'Squire our great armchair;
Good folks, we're glad to see you here.
Jotham, get the great case bottle,
Your teeth can pull its corn-cob stopple.
Ensign, — Deacon, never mind;
'Squire, drink until you're blind.
Come, here's the French, the Guillotine,
And here is good 'Squire Gallatin,
And here's each noisy Jacobin.
Here's friend Madison so hearty,
And here's confusion to the treaty.
Come, one more swig to Southern Demos
Who represent our brother negroes.
Thus we drink and dance away,
This glorious INDEPENDENCE DAY!

                    ROYALL TYLER.

ON INDEPENDENCE

[August 17, 1776]

COME all you brave soldiers, both valiant and
    free,
It's for Independence we all now agree;
Let us gird on our swords and prepare to
    defend
Our liberty, property, ourselves and our
    friends.

In a cause that's so righteous, come let us
    agree,
And from hostile invaders set America free,
The cause is so glorious we need not to fear
But from merciless tyrants we'll set ourselves
    clear.

Heaven's blessing attending us, no tyrant shall
    say
That Americans e'er to such monsters gave
    way,
But fighting we'll die in America's cause
Before we'll submit to tyrannical laws.

George the Third, of Great Britain, no more
    shall he reign,
With unlimited sway o'er these free States
    again;
Lord North, nor old Bute, nor none of their
    clan,
Shall ever be honor'd by an American.

May Heaven's blessing descend on our United
    States,
And grant that the union may never abate;
May love, peace, and harmony ever be found,
For to go hand in hand America round.

Upon our grand Congress may Heaven bestow
Both wisdom and skill our good to pursue;
On Heaven alone dependent we'll be,
But from all earthly tyrants we mean to be
    free.

Unto our brave Generals may Heaven give
    skill
Our armies to guide, and the sword for to
    wield,
May their hands taught to war, and their
    fingers to fight,
Be able to put British armies to flight.

And now, brave Americans, since it is so,
That we are independent, we'll have them to
    know
That united we are, and united we'll be,
And from all British tyrants we'll try to keep
    free.

May Heaven smile on us in all our endeavors,
Safe guard our seaports, our towns, and our
    rivers,
Keep us from invaders by land and by sea,
And from all who'd deprive us of our liberty.
                JONATHAN MITCHELL SEWALL.

THE AMERICAN PATRIOT'S PRAYER

[1776]

Parent of all, omnipotent
    In heav'n, and earth below,
Thro' all creation's bounds unspent,
    Whose streams of goodness flow.

Teach me to know from whence I rose,
    And unto what design'd;
No private aims let me propose,
    Since link'd with human kind.

But chief to hear my country's voice,
    May all my thoughts incline,
'T is reason's law, 't is virtue's choice,
    'T is nature's call and thine.

Me from fair freedom's sacred cause
    Let nothing e'er divide;
Grandeur, nor gold, nor vain applause,
    Nor friendship false misguide.

Let me not faction's partial hate
    Pursue to *this land's* woe;
Nor grasp the thunder of the state
    To wound a private foe.

If, for the right, to wish the wrong
    My country shall combine,
Single to serve th' erron'ous throng,
    Spite of themselves, be mine.

COLUMBIA

Columbia, Columbia, to glory arise,
The queen of the world, and the child of the
    skies;
Thy genius commands thee; with rapture
    behold,
While ages on ages thy splendor unfold,
Thy reign is the last, and the noblest of time,
Most fruitful thy soil, most inviting thy clime;
Let the crimes of the east ne'er encrimson thy
    name,
Be freedom, and science, and virtue thy fame.

To conquest and slaughter let Europe aspire;
Whelm nations in blood, and wrap cities in fire;
Thy heroes the rights of mankind shall defend,
And triumph pursue them, and glory attend.
A world is thy realm: for a world be thy laws,

Enlarged as thine empire, and just as thy
    cause;
On Freedom's broad basis, that empire shall
    rise,
Extend with the main, and dissolve with the
    skies.

Fair science her gates to thy sons shall unbar,
And the east see the morn hide the beams of
    her star.
New bards, and new sages, unrivalled shall
    soar
To fame unextinguished, when time is no
    more;
To thee, the last refuge of virtue designed,
Shall fly from all nations the best of man-
    kind;
Here, grateful to heaven, with transport shall
    bring
Their incense, more fragrant than odors of
    spring,

Nor less shall thy fair ones to glory ascend,
And genius and beauty in harmony blend;
The graces of form shall awake pure desire,
And the charms of the soul ever cherish the fire;
Their sweetness unmingled, their manners
    refined,
And virtue's bright image, instamped on the
    mind,

With peace and soft rapture shall teach life to
    glow,
And light up a smile in the aspect of woe.

Thy fleets to all regions thy power shall display,
The nations admire and the ocean obey;
Each shore to thy glory its tribute unfold,
And the east and the south yield their spices
    and gold.
As the day-spring unbounded, thy splendor
    shall flow,
And earth's little kingdoms before thee shall
    bow;
While the ensigns of union, in triumph unfurled,
Hush the tumult of war and give peace to the
    world.

Thus, as down a lone valley, with cedars o'er-
    spread,
From war's dread confusion I pensively
    strayed,
The gloom from the face of fair heaven retired;
The winds ceased to murmur; the thunders
    expired;
Perfumes as of Eden flowed sweetly along,
And a voice as of angels, enchantingly sung:
"Columbia, Columbia, to glory arise,
The queen of the world, and the child of the
    skies."

TIMOTHY DWIGHT.

CHAPTER V

THE FIRST CAMPAIGN

News of the Declaration of Independence was
accompanied over the country by that of a bril-
liant success at the South. Early in June, the Brit-
ish, under Sir Peter Parker, Sir Henry Clinton, and
Lord Cornwallis, prepared to capture Charleston,
S. C. To oppose them there was practically nothing
but a fort of palmetto logs built on Sullivan's Island
in Charleston harbor by Colonel William Moultrie.
On June 28, 1776, the British advanced to the at-
tack, but were beaten off with heavy loss.

THE BOASTING OF SIR PETER PARKER

[June 28, 1776]

'T was the proud Sir Peter Parker came sail-
    ing in from the sea,
With his serried ships-of-line a-port, and his
    ships-of-line a-lee;
A little lead for a cure, he said, *for these rebel
    sires and sons!*

And the folk on the Charleston roof-tops
    heard the roar of the shotted guns;
They heard the roar of the guns off shore, but
    they marked, with a hopeful smile,
The answering ire of a storm of fire from
    Sullivan's sandy isle.

'T was the proud Sir Peter Parker who saw
    with the climbing noon
Ruin and wreck on each blood-stained deck
    that day in the wane of June, —
The shivered spar and the shattered beam and
    the torn and toppling mast
And the grimy gunners wounded sore, and the
    seamen falling fast;
But from the stubborn fort ashore no sight of
    a single sign
That the rebel sires and sons had quailed
    before his ships-of-the-line.

'T was the proud Sir Peter Parker who saw
　　the fall of the flag
From the fortress wall; then rang his call: —
　　They have lost their rebel rag!
And the fifty guns of the Bristol flamed, and
　　the volumed thunder rolled;
'*T is now*, the haughty Admiral cried, *we'll*
　　drive them out of their hold!
But little he knew, and his British crew, how
　　small was their vaunted power,
For lo, to the rampart's crest there leaped the
　　dauntless man of the hour!

'T was the proud Sir Peter Parker who saw
　　with a wild amaze
This hero spring from the fortress height
　　'mid the hail and the fiery haze;
Under the wall he strode, each step with the
　　deadliest danger fraught,
And up from the sand with a triumph hand
　　the splintered staff he caught.
Then, still unscathed by the iron rain, he
　　clambered the parapet,
And 'mid the burst of his comrades' cheers
　　the flag on the bastion set.

'T was the proud Sir Peter Parker who slunk
　　through the night to sea,
With his shattered ships-of-line a-port and his
　　ships-of-line a-lee;
Above there was wreck, and below was wreck,
　　and the sense of loss and woe,
For the sneered-at rebel sires and sons had
　　proved them a direful foe;
But War's dark blight on the land lay light,
　　and they hailed with a joyful smile
The stars of victory burning bright over Sul-
　　livan's sandy isle.

CLINTON SCOLLARD.

The British fleet remained in the neighborhood
for three weeks to refit and then sailed away to
New York to coöperate with Howe. Charleston
was saved and for two years the Southern States
were free from the invader.

A NEW WAR SONG BY SIR PETER
PARKER

MY lords, with your leave,
An account I will give,
Which deserves to be written in metre;
How the rebels and I
Have been pretty nigh,
Faith, 't was almost too nigh for Sir Peter!

De'il take 'em! their shot
Came so swift and so hot,
And the cowardly dogs stood so stiff, sirs,
That I put ship about
And was glad to get out,
Or they would not have left me a skiff, sirs.

With much labor and toil
Unto Sullivan's Isle,
I came, swift as Falstaff, or Pistol;
But the Yankees, od rat 'em —
I could not get at 'em,
They so terribly maul'd my poor Bristol

Behold, Clinton, by land,
Did quietly stand,
While I made a thundering clatter;
But the channel was deep,
So he only could peep,
And not venture over the water.

Now, bold as a Turk,
I proceeded to York,
Where, with Clinton and Howe, you may find
　　me:
I've the wind in my tail,
And am hoisting my sail,
To leave Sullivan's Island behind me.

But, my lords, do not fear,
For, before the next year,
Although a small island should fret us,
The continent, whole,
We will take, by my soul,
If the cowardly Yankees will let us.

The victory at Charleston was the last success
which American arms were to achieve for many
months. The British had decided to capture and
hold the line of the Hudson in order to cut the
colonies in two. Howe, with a trained army of
twenty-five thousand men, prepared to attack
New York, while, to oppose him, Washington
had only eighteen thousand undisciplined levies.
Half this force was concentrated at Brooklyn
Heights, which was strongly fortified, and here,
on August 27, 1776, Howe delivered his attack.
Overwhelming superiority of numbers enabled
the British to press back their opponents to their
works on the heights. Not daring to storm, the
British prepared to lay siege to this position.
Washington had no way to withstand a siege,
which must have resulted in the loss of his whole
army, and after nightfall of August 29, he suc-
ceeded in ferrying the entire force, with their
cannon, arms, ammunition, horses, and larder,
over to the New York side.

THE MARYLAND BATTALION

[August 27, 1776]

SPRUCE Macaronis, and pretty to see,
Tidy and dapper and gallant were we;
Blooded fine gentlemen, proper and tall,
Bold in a fox-hunt and gay at a ball;
Prancing soldados, so martial and bluff,
Billets for bullets, in scarlet and buff —
But our cockades were clasped with a
    mother's low prayer.
And the sweethearts that braided the sword-
    knots were fair.

There was grummer of drums humming
    hoarse in the hills,
And the bugles sang fanfaron down by the
    mills,
By Flatbush the bagpipes were droning
    amain,
And keen cracked the rifles in Martense's
    lane;
For the Hessians were flecking the hedges
    with red,
And the Grenadiers' tramp marked the roll
    of the dead.

Three to one, flank and rear, flashed the files
    of St. George,
The fierce gleam of their steel as the glow of a
    forge.
The brutal boom-boom of their swart can-
    noneers
Was sweet music compared with the taunt of
    their cheers —
For the brunt of their onset, our crippled
    array,
And the light of God's leading gone out in the
    fray!

Oh, the rout on the left and the tug on the
    right!
The mad plunge of the charge and the wreck
    of the flight!
When the cohorts of Grant held stout Stirling
    at strain,
And the mongrels of Hesse went tearing the
    slain;
When at Freeke's Mill the flumes and the
    sluices ran red,
And the dead choked the dyke and the marsh
    choked the dead!

"Oh, Stirling, good Stirling! How long must
    we wait?
Shall the shout of your trumpet unleash us too
    late?
Have you never a dash for brave Mordecai
    Gist
With his heart in his throat, and his blade in
    his fist?
Are we good for no more than to prance in a
    ball,
When the drums beat the charge and the
    clarions call?"

Tralára! Tralára! Now praise we the Lord,
For the clang of His call and the flash of His
    sword!
Tralára! Tralára! Now forward to die;
For the banner, hurrah! and for sweethearts,
    good-by!
"Four hundred wild lads!" Maybe so. I'll be
    bound
'T will be easy to count us, face up, on the
    ground.
If we hold the road open, though Death take
    the toll,
We'll be missed on parade when the States
    call the roll —
When the flags meet in peace and the guns are
    at rest,
And fair Freedom is singing Sweet Home in
    the West.

JOHN WILLIAMSON PALMER.

On September 15, 1776, the British took pos-
session of New York, and the American lines were
withdrawn to the line of the Harlem River. On
September 16 the British attempted to break
through their centre at Harlem Heights. The
attack was repulsed, and for nearly a month the
lines remained where they had been formed.

HAARLEM HEIGHTS

Captain Stephen Brown of Knowlton's Con-
necticut Rangers tells of the affair of September
16, 1776.

THEY'VE turned at last! Good-by, King
    George,
    Despite your hireling band!
The farmer boys have borne a brunt,
    The 'prentice lads will stand!

Though Peace may lag and Fortune flag,
    Our fight as good as won;

We've made them yield in open field!
  We've made the Redcoats run!

Our Rangers sallied forth at dawn
  With Knowlton at their head
To rout the British pickets out
  And spend a little lead.

We gave them eight brisk rounds a-piece,
  And hurried, fighting, back;
For, eighteen score, the Light Armed Corps
  Were keen upon our track.

Along the vale of Bloomingdale
  They pressed our scant array;
They swarmed the crag and jeered our flag
  Across the Hollow Way.

Their skirmishers bawled "Hark, away!"
  Their buglers, from the wall,
In braggart vaunt and bitter taunt
  Brayed out the hunting call!

Oh, sound of shame! It woke a flame
  In every sunburned face,
And every soul was hot as coal
  To cleanse the foul disgrace.

And some that blenched on Brooklyn Heights
  And fled at Turtle Bay
Fair wept for wrath, and thronged my path
  And clamored for the fray.

Our General came spurring! —
  There rolled a signal drum. —
His eye was bright; he rose his height;
  He knew the time had come.

He gave the word to Knowlton
  To lead us on once more —
The pick of old Connecticut, —
  And Leitch with Weedon's corps

Of proud Virginia Riflemen,
  Tall hunters of the deer, —
To round the boastful Briton's flank
  And take him in the rear.

We left the dell, we scaled the fell,
  And up the crest we sprang,
When swift and sharp along the scarp
  A deadly volley rang;

And down went Leitch of Weedon's corps!
  Deep hurt, but gallant still;

And down went Knowlton! — he that bore
  The sword of Bunker Hill.

I raised his head. But this he said,
  Death-wounded as he lay:
"Lead on the fight! I hold it light
  If we but get the day!"

In open rank we struck their flank,
  And oh! the fight was hot!
Up came the Hessian Yagers!
  Up came the kilted Scot!

Up came the men of Linsingen,
  Von Donop's Grenadiers!
But soon we sped the vengeful lead
  A-whistling 'bout their ears!

They buckled front to Varnum's brunt;
  We crumpled up their right,
And hurling back the crimson wrack
  We swept along the height.

The helmets of the Hessians
  Are tumbled in the wheat;
The tartan of the Highlander
  Shall be his winding-sheet!

A mingled rout, we drove them out
  From orchard, field, and glen;
In goodly case it seemed to chase
  Our hunters home again!

We flaunted in their faces
  The flag they thought to scorn,
And left them with a loud "Hurrah!"
  To choke their bugle-horn!

Upon a ledge embattled
  Above the Hudson's shore
We dug the grave for Knowlton
  And Leitch of Weedon's corps.

And though in plight of War's despite
  We yield this island throne,
Upon that ledge we left a pledge
  That we shall claim our own!
                          ARTHUR GUITERMAN.

  At this time occurred the first of the two most
dramatic and moving tragedies of the Revolution.
It was important that Washington should obtain
detailed and accurate information as to the posi-
tion and intentions of the British, and Nathan
Hale, a captain in Knowlton's regiment, volun-
teered for the service, and passed into the British

lines in disguise. He was captured and taken before Sir William Howe, to whom he frankly acknowledged his errand. Howe ordered him hanged next day.

NATHAN HALE

[September 22, 1776]

THE breezes went steadily thro' the tall pines,
  A-saying "Oh! hu-ush!" a-saying "Oh! hu-ush!"
As stilly stole by a bold legion of horse,
  For Hale in the bush; for Hale in the bush.

"Keep still!" said the thrush as she nestled her young,
  In a nest by the road; in a nest by the road.
"For the tyrants are near, and with them appear
  What bodes us no good; what bodes us no good."

The brave captain heard it, and thought of his home,
  In a cot by the brook; in a cot by the brook.
With mother and sister and memories dear,
  He so gayly forsook; he so gayly forsook.

Cooling shades of the night were coming apace,
  The tattoo had beat; the tattoo had beat.
The noble one sprang from his dark lurking-place,
  To make his retreat; to make his retreat.

He warily trod on the dry rustling leaves,
  As he pass'd thro' the wood; as he pass'd thro' the wood;
And silently gain'd his rude launch on the shore,
  As she play'd with the flood; as she play'd with the flood.

The guards of the camp, on that dark, dreary night,
  Had a murderous will; had a murderous will.
They took him and bore him afar from the shore,
  To a hut on the hill; to a hut on the hill.

No mother was there, nor a friend who could cheer,
  In that little stone cell; in that little stone cell.

But he trusted in love, from his Father above.
  In his heart, all was well; in his heart, all was well.

An ominous owl with his solemn bass voice,
  Sat moaning hard by; sat moaning hard by.
"The tyrant's proud minions most gladly rejoice,
  For he must soon die; for he must soon die."

The brave fellow told them, no thing he restrain'd,
  The cruel gen'ral; the cruel gen'ral.
His errand from camp, of the ends to be gain'd,
  And said that was all; and said that was all.

They took him and bound him and bore him away,
  Down the hill's grassy side; down the hill's grassy side.
'T was there the base hirelings, in royal array,
  His cause did deride; his cause did deride.

Five minutes were given, short moments, no more,
  For him to repent; for him to repent.
He pray'd for his mother, he ask'd not another,
  To Heaven he went; to Heaven he went.

The faith of a martyr, the tragedy show'd,
  As he trod the last stage; as he trod the last stage.
And Britons will shudder at gallant Hale's blood,
  As his words do presage; as his words do presage.

"Thou pale king of terrors, thou life's gloomy foe,
  Go frighten the slave; go frighten the slave;
Tell tyrants, to you their allegiance they owe.
  No fears for the brave; no fears for the brave."

The execution took place shortly after sunrise, the scaffold being erected in an orchard near the present junction of Market Street and East Broadway. Hale's last words were the famous, "I only regret that I have but one life to lose for my country."

NATHAN HALE

[September 22, 1776]

To drum-beat and heart-beat,
 A soldier marches by;
There is color in his cheek,
 There is courage in his eye,
Yet to drum-beat and heart-beat
 In a moment he must die.

By the starlight and moonlight,
 He seeks the Briton's camp;
He hears the rustling flag
 And the armèd sentry's tramp;
And the starlight and moonlight
 His silent wanderings lamp.

With slow tread and still tread,
 He scans the tented line;
And he counts the battery guns,
 By the gaunt and shadowy pine;
And his slow tread and still tread
 Gives no warning sign.

The dark wave, the plumed wave,
 It meets his eager glance;
And it sparkles 'neath the stars,
 Like the glimmer of a lance —
A dark wave, a plumed wave,
 On an emerald expanse.

A sharp clang, a still clang,
 And terror in the sound!
For the sentry, falcon-eyed,
 In the camp a spy hath found;
With a sharp clang, a steel clang,
 The patriot is bound.

With calm brow, and steady brow,
 He listens to his doom;
In his look there is no fear,
 Nor a shadow-trace of gloom;
But with calm brow and steady brow,
 He robes him for the tomb.

In the long night, the still night,
 He kneels upon the sod;
And the brutal guards withhold
 E'en the solemn word of God!
In the long night, the still night,
 He walks where Christ hath trod.

'Neath the blue morn, the sunny morn,
 He dies upon the tree;

And he mourns that he can lose
 But one life for Liberty;
And in the blue morn, the sunny morn,
 His spirit wings are free.

But his last words, his message-words,
 They burn, lest friendly eye
Should read how proud and calm
 A patriot could die,
With his last words, his dying words,
 A soldier's battle-cry.

From Fame-leaf and Angel-leaf,
 From monument and urn,
The sad of earth, the glad of heaven,
 His tragic fate shall learn;
But on Fame-leaf and Angel-leaf
 The name of HALE shall burn!
    FRANCIS MILES FINCH.

Washington soon found himself unable to cope with Howe's superior force, retreated across New Jersey, and on December 8 reached the west bank of the Delaware River. The British came up the next day and took a position on the east bank, with their centre at Trenton. Never did America's future look darker than on that Christmas night of 1776.

THE BALLAD OF SWEET P

[December 25, 1776]

MISTRESS PENELOPE PENWICK, she,
Called by her father, "My Sweet P,"
Painted by Peale, she won renown
In a clinging, short-waisted satin gown;
A red rose touched by her finger-tips
And a smile held back from her roguish lips.

Thus, William Penwick, the jolly wight,
In clouds of smoke, night after night,
Would tell a tale in delighted pride,
To cronies, who came from far and wide;
Always ending (with candle, he)
"And this is the picture of my Sweet P!"

The tale? 'T was how Sweet P did chance
To give to the British a Christmas dance.
Penwick's house past the outpost stood,
Flanked by the ferry and banked by the wood.
Hessian and British quartered there
Swarmed through chamber and hall and
 stair.

Fires ablaze and candles alight,
Soldier and officer feasted that night.
The enemy? Safe, with a river between,
Black and deadly and fierce and keen;
A river of ice and a blinding storm! —
So they made them merry and kept them
    warm.

But while they mirth and roistering made,
Up in her dormer window stayed
Mistress Penelope Penwick apart,
With fearful thought and sorrowful heart.
Night by night had her candle's gleam
Sent through the dark its hopeful beam.

But the nights they came and they passed
    again,
With never a sign from her countrymen;
For where beat the heart so brave, so bold,
Which could baffle that river's bulwark
    cold?
Penelope's eyes and her candle's light
Were mocked by the storm that Christmas
    night.

But lo, full sudden a missile stung
And shattered her casement pane and rung
At her feet! 'T was a word from the storm
    outside.
She opened her dormer window wide.
A wind-swept figure halted below —
The ferryman, old and bent and slow.
Then a murmur rose upward — only one,
Thrilling and powerful — "*Washington!*"

With jest and laughter and candles bright,
'T was two by the stairway clock that night,
When Penelope Penwick tripped her down,
Dressed in a short-waisted satin gown,
With a red rose (cut from her potted bush).
There fell on the rollicking crowd a hush.

She stood in the soldiers' midst, I ween,
The daintiest thing they e'er had seen!
And swept their gaze with her eyes most
    sweet,
And patted her little slippered feet.
"'T is Christmas night, sirs," quoth Sweet P,
"I should like to dance! Will you dance with
    me?"

Oh, but they cheered; ran to and fro,
And each for the honor bowed him low.
With smiling charm and witching grace
She chose him pranked with officer's lace

And shining buttons and dangling sword;
No doubt he strutted him proud as a lord!

Doffed with enmity, donned with glee, —
Oh, she was charming, that Sweet P!
And when it was over, and blood aflame,
Came an eager cry for "A game!" "A
    game!"
"We'll play at forfeits," Penelope cried.
"If one holdeth aught in his love and pride,

"Let each lay it down at my feet in turn,
And a fine from me shall he straightway learn!"
What held they all in their love and pride?
Straight flew a hand unto every side;
Each man had a sword and nothing more,
And the swords they clanged in a heap on the
    floor.

Standing there, in her satin gown,
With candlelight on her yellow crown,
And at her feet a bank of steel
(I'll wager that look was caught by Peale!)
Penelope held her rose on high —
"I fine each one for a leaf to try!"

She plucked the petals and blew them out,
A rain of red they fluttered about.
Over the floor and through the air
Rushed the officers here and there;
When lo! a cry! The door burst in!
"*The enemy!*" Tumult, terror, and din!

Flew a hand unto every side, —
Swords? — Penelope, arms thrown wide
Leapt that heap of steel before;
Swords behind her upon the floor;
Facing her countrymen staunch and bold,
Who dared the river of death and cold,
Who swept them down on a rollicking horde
And found they never a man with sword!

And so it happened (but not by chance),
In '76 there was given a dance
By a witch with a rose and a satin gown
(Painted in Philadelphia town),
Mistress Penelope Penwick, she,
Called by her father, "My Sweet P."
      VIRGINIA WOODWARD CLOUD.

The British soldiers, thinking the war virtually
ended, had grown careless, and Howe and Corn-
wallis had returned to New York to celebrate
Christmas. It was at this juncture that Washing-
ton decided to attack. More than ten hours were

consumed in getting across the river, which was blocked with ice. At daybreak on the 26th, Washington entered Trenton, and surprised the enemy.

ACROSS THE DELAWARE

THE winter night is cold and drear,
 Along the river's sullen flow;
The cruel frost is camping here —
 The air has living blades of snow.
Look! pushing from the icy strand,
 With ensigns freezing in the air,
There sails a small but mighty band,
 Across the dang'rous Delaware.

Oh, wherefore, soldiers, would you fight
 The bayonets of a winter storm?
In truth it were a better night
 For blazing fire and blankets warm!
We seek to trap a foreign foe,
 Who fill themselves with stolen fare;
We carry freedom as we go
 Across the storm-swept Delaware!

The night is full of lusty cheer
 Within the Hessians' merry camp;
And faint and fainter on the ear
 Doth fall the heedless sentry's tramp.
O hirelings, this new nation's rage
 Is something 't is not well to dare;
You are not fitted to engage
 These men from o'er the Delaware!

A rush — a shout — a clarion call,
 Salute the early morning's gray:
Now, roused invaders, yield or fall:
 The refuge-land has won the day!
Soon shall the glorious news be hurled
 Wherever men have wrongs to bear;
For freedom's torch illumes the world,
 And God has crossed the Delaware!
                    WILL CARLETON.

The surprise was complete. Eighteen of the enemy were killed and over a thousand made prisoners, while the American loss was only four. The remainder of the enemy retreated in disorder to Princeton, leaving their sick and wounded, and all their heavy arms and baggage behind them.

THE BATTLE OF TRENTON

ON Christmas-day in seventy-six,
Our ragged troops, with bayonets fixed,
 For Trenton marched away.

The Delaware see! the boats below!
The light obscured by hail and snow!
 But no signs of dismay.

Our object was the Hessian band,
That dared invade fair freedom's land,
 And quarter in that place.
Great Washington he led us on,
Whose streaming flag, in storm or sun,
 Had never known disgrace.

In silent march we passed the night,
Each soldier panting for the fight,
 Though quite benumbed with frost.
Greene on the left at six began,
The right was led by Sullivan
 Who ne'er a moment lost.

Their pickets stormed, the alarm was spread,
That rebels risen from the dead
 Were marching into town.
Some scampered here, some scampered there,
And some for action did prepare;
 But soon their arms laid down.

Twelve hundred servile miscreants,
With all their colors, guns, and tents,
 Were trophies of the day.
The frolic o'er, the bright canteen,
In centre, front, and rear was seen
 Driving fatigue away.

Now, brothers of the patriot bands,
Let's sing deliverance from the hands
 Of arbitrary sway.
And as our life is but a span,
Let's touch the tankard while we can,
 In memory of that day.

At Princeton Cornwallis joined them, and on January 2, 1777, advanced against Trenton at the head of eight thousand men. By the time he reached there, Washington had withdrawn his whole force beyond a little stream called the Assunpink, where he repelled two British assaults. That night, he marched toward Princeton, routed a British detachment of two thousand, and took up a strong position on the heights at Morristown.

TRENTON AND PRINCETON

[December 26, 1776–January 3, 1777]

ON December, the sixth
 And the twentieth day,
Our troops attacked the Hessians,
 And show'd them gallant play.

Our roaring cannon taught them
  Our valor for to know;
We fought like brave Americans
  Against a haughty foe.

The chiefs were kill'd or taken,
  The rest were put to flight,
And some arrived at Princeton,
  Half-fainting with affright.

The third of January,
  The morning being clear,
Our troops attack'd the regulars,
  At Princeton, we do hear.

About a mile from Princeton,
  The battle is begun,
And many a haughty Briton fell
  Before the fight was done.

And what our gallant troops have done
  We'll let the British know;
We fought like brave Americans
  Against a haughty foe.

The British, struck with terror,
  And frighted, ran away:
They ran across the country
  Like men in deep dismay,

Crying to every one they met,
  "Oh! hide us! hide us! do!
The rebels will devour us,
  So hotly they pursue."

Oh, base, ungenerous Britons!
  To call us by that name;
We're fighting for our liberty,
  Our just and lawful claim.

We trust in Heaven's protection,
  Nor fear to win the day;
When time shall come we'll crown our deeds
  With many a loud huzza!

Our foes are fled to Brunswick,
  Where they are close confined;
Our men they are unanimous,
  In Freedom's cause combined.

Success to General Washington,
  And Gates and Putnam, too,
Both officers and privates,
  Who liberty pursue.

ASSUNPINK AND PRINCETON

[January 3, 1777]

GLORIOUS the day when in arms at Assun-
      pink,
  And after at Princeton the Briton we met;
Few in both armies — they'd skirmishes call
      them,
  Now hundreds of thousands in battle are
      set.
But for the numbers engaged, let me tell you,
  Smart brushes they were, and two battles
      that told;
There't was I first drew a bead on a foeman —
  I, a mere stripling, not twenty years old.

Tell it? Well, friends, that is just my inten-
      tion;
  There's nothing a veteran hates and abhors
More than a chance lost to tell his adventures,
  Or give you his story of battles and wars.
Nor is it wonder old men are loquacious,
  And talk, if you listen, from sun unto sun;
Youth has the power to be up and be doing,
  While age can but tell of the deeds it has
      done.

Ranged for a mile on the banks of Assun-
      pink,
  There, southward of Trenton, one morning
      we lay,
When, with his red-coats all marshalled to
      meet us,
  Cornwallis came fiercely at close of the
      day —
Driving some scouts who had gone out with
      Longstreet,
  From where they were crossing at Shabba-
      conk Run —
Trumpets loud blaring, drums beating, flags
      flying —
  Three hours, by the clock, before setting
      of sun.

Two ways were left them by which to assail
      us,
  And neither was perfectly to their desire —
One was the bridge we controlled by our
      cannon,
  The other the ford that was under our fire.
"Death upon one side, and Dismal on
      t' other,"
  Said Sambo, our cook, as he gazed on our
      foes:

Cheering and dauntless they marched to the
    battle,
    And, doubtful of choice, both the dangers
        they chose.

Down at the ford, it was said, that the water
    Was reddened with blood from the soldiers
        who fell:
As for the bridge, when they tried it, their
    forces
    Were beaten with terrible slaughter, as well.
Grape-shot swept causeway, and pattered
        on water,
    And riddled their columns, that broke and
        gave way;
Thrice they charged boldly, and thrice they
    retreated;
    Then darkness came down, and so ended
        the fray.

How did I get there? I came from our corn-
    mill
    At noon of the day when the battle begun,
Bringing in flour to the troops under Proctor;
    'Twas not very long ere that errand was
        done.
Up to that time I had never enlisted,
    Though Jacob, my brother, had entered
        with Wayne;
But the fight stirred me; I sent back the
    horses,
    And made up my mind with the rest to re-
        main.

We camped on *our* side — the south — of
    Assunpink,
    While *they* bivouacked for the night upon
        theirs;
Both posting sentries and building up watch-
    fires,
    With those on both sides talking over
        affairs.
"Washington 's caught in a trap!" said
    Cornwallis,
    And smiled with a smile that was joyous
        and grim;
"Fox! but I have him!" — the earl had mis-
    taken;
    The fox, by the coming of daylight, had
        him.

Early that night, when the leaders held
    council,
    Both St. Clair and Reed said our action
        was clear;

Useless to strike at the van of our foemen —
    His force was too strong; we must fall on
        his rear.
Washington thought so, and bade us re-
    plenish
    Our watchfires till nearly the dawn of the
        day;
Setting some more to make feint of intrench-
    ing,
    While swiftly in darkness the rest moved
        away.

Marching by Sandtown, and Quaker Bridge
        crossing,
    We passed Stony Creek a full hour before
        dawn,
Leaving there Mercer with one scant bat-
    talion
    Our foes to amuse, should they find we
        were gone;
Then the main force pushed its way into
    Princeton,
    All ready to strike those who dreamed of
        no blow;
Only a chance that we lost not our labor,
    And slipped through our fingers, unknow-
        ing, the foe.

Mawhood's brigade, never feeling its danger,
    Had started for Trenton at dawn of the
        day,
Crossed Stony Creek, after we had gone
        over,
    When Mercer's weak force they beheld on
        its way;
Turning contemptuously back to attack it,
    They drove it with ease in disorder ahead —
Firelocks alone were no match for their can-
    non —
    A fight, and then flight, and brave Mercer
        lay dead.

Murdered, some said, while imploring for
        quarter —
    A dastardly deed, if the thing had been
        true —
Cruel our foes, but in that thing we wronged
    them,
    And let us in all give the demon his due.
Gallant Hugh Mercer fell sturdily fighting,
    So long as his right arm his sabre could
        wield,
Stretching his enemies bleeding around him,
    And then, overpowered, fell prone on the
        field.

Hearing the firing, we turned and we met
      them,
   Our cannon replying to theirs with a will;
Fiercely with grape and with canister swept
      them,
   And chased them in wrath from the brow
      of the hill.

Racing and chasing it was into Princeton,
   Where, seeking the lore to be taught in that
      hall,
Redcoats by scores entered college, but stayed
      not —
   We rudely expelled them with powder and
      ball.

Only a skirmish, you see, though a sharp
      one —
   It did not last over the fourth of an hour;
But 't was a battle that did us this service —
   No more, from that day, had we fear of
      their power.
Trenton revived us, Assunpink encouraged,
   But Princeton gave hope that we held to
      the last;
Flood-tide had come on the black, sullen
      water
   And ebb-tide for ever and ever had passed.

Yes! 't was the turn of the tide in our favor —
   A turn of the tide to a haven that bore.
Had Lord Cornwallis crossed over Assunpink
   That day we repelled him, our fighting
      were o'er.
Had he o'ertaken us ere we smote Mawhood,
   All torn as we were, it seems certain to
      me,
I would not chatter to you about battles,
   And you and your children would not have
      been free.
                    THOMAS DUNN ENGLISH.

"Thus in a brief campaign of three weeks,
Washington had rallied the fragments of a de-
feated and broken army, fought two successful
battles, taken nearly two thousand prisoners, and
recovered the state of New Jersey."

SEVENTY-SIX

WHAT heroes from the woodland sprung,
   When, through the fresh-awakened land,
The thrilling cry of freedom rung
And to the work of warfare strung
   The yeoman's iron hand!

Hills flung the cry to hills around,
   And ocean-mart replied to mart,
And streams, whose springs were yet un-
      found,
Pealed far away the startling sound
   Into the forest's heart.

Then marched the brave from rocky steep,
   From mountain-river swift and cold;
The borders of the stormy deep,
The vales where gathered waters sleep,
   Sent up the strong and bold, —

As if the very earth again
   Grew quick with God's creating breath,
And, from the sods of grove and glen,
Rose ranks of lion-hearted men
   To battle to the death.

The wife, whose babe first smiled that day
   The fair fond bride of yestereve,
And aged sire and matron gray,
Saw the loved warriors haste away,
   And deemed it sin to grieve.

Already had the strife begun;
   Already blood, on Concord's plain,
Along the springing grass had run,
And blood had flowed at Lexington,
   Like brooks of April rain.

That death-stain on the vernal sward
   Hallowed to freedom all the shore;
In fragments fell the yoke abhorred —
The footstep of a foreign lord
   Profaned the soil no more.
                    WILLIAM CULLEN BRYANT.

The question of a national flag, which had been
under consideration for a long time, was now
finally settled. There is a tradition that in June,
1776, General Washington and a committee of
Congress had called upon Mrs. John Ross, of
Philadelphia, and requested her to make a flag
after a design which Washington furnished, which
she did, producing the first "stars and stripes."

BETSY'S BATTLE FLAG

FROM dusk till dawn the livelong night
She kept the tallow dips alight,
And fast her nimble fingers flew
To sew the stars upon the blue.
With weary eyes and aching head
She stitched the stripes of white and red,

And when the day came up the stair
Complete across a carven chair
    Hung Betsy's battle flag.

Like shadows in the evening gray
The Continentals filed away,
With broken boots and ragged coats,
But hoarse defiance in their throats;
They bore the marks of want and cold,
And some were lame and some were old,
And some with wounds untended bled,
But floating bravely overhead
    Was Betsy's battle flag.

When fell the battle's leaden rain,
The soldier hushed his moans of pain
And raised his dying head to see
King George's troopers turn and flee.
Their charging column reeled and broke,
And vanished in the rolling smoke,
Before the glory of the stars,
The snowy stripes, and scarlet bars
    Of Betsy's battle flag.

The simple stone of Betsy Ross
Is covered now with mold and moss,
But still her deathless banner flies,
And keeps the color of the skies.
A nation thrills, a nation bleeds,
A nation follows where it leads,
And every man is proud to yield
His life upon a crimson field
    For Betsy's battle flag!
              MINNA IRVING.

It was not, however, until Saturday, June 14, 1777, that a flag was formally adopted by Congress. On that day, Congress "Resolved, That the flag of the thirteen United States be thirteen stripes alternate red and white; that the union be thirteen stars, white in a blue field, representing a new constellation." Save for the addition of a star for each new state admitted to the Union, this is the flag of the United States to-day.

THE AMERICAN FLAG

I

WHEN Freedom from her mountain height
    Unfurled her standard to the air,
She tore the azure robe of night,
    And set the stars of glory there;
She mingled with its gorgeous dyes
The milky baldric of the skies,
And striped its pure, celestial white
With streakings of the morning light;

Then from his mansion in the sun
She called her eagle bearer down,
And gave into his mighty hand
The symbol of her chosen land.

II

Majestic monarch of the cloud!
    Who rear'st aloft thy regal form,
To hear the tempest-trumpings loud,
    And see the lightning lances driven,
    When strive the warriors of the storm,
And rolls the thunder-drum of heaven —
Child of the sun! to thee 't is given
    To guard the banner of the free,
To hover in the sulphur smoke,
To ward away the battle-stroke,
And bid its blendings shine afar,
Like rainbows on the cloud of war,
    The harbingers of victory!

III

Flag of the brave! thy folds shall fly,
    The sign of hope and triumph high,
When speaks the signal trumpet tone,
    And the long line comes gleaming on;
Ere yet the life-blood, warm and wet,
    Has dimmed the glistening bayonet,
Each soldier eye shall brightly turn
    To where thy sky-born glories burn,
And, as his springing steps advance,
Catch war and vengeance from the glance
And when the cannon-mouthings loud
    Heave in wild wreaths the battle-shroud
And gory sabres rise and fall,
Like shoots of flame on midnight's pall;
    Then shall thy meteor-glances glow,
And cowering foes shall sink beneath
    Each gallant arm that strikes below
That lovely messenger of death.

IV

Flag of the seas! on ocean wave
    Thy stars shall glitter o'er the brave;
When death, careering on the gale,
    Sweeps darkly round the bellied sail,
And frighted waves rush wildly back
    Before the broadside's reeling rack,
Each dying wanderer of the sea
    Shall look at once to heaven and thee,
And smile to see thy splendors fly
In triumph o'er his closing eye.

V

Flag of the free heart's hope and home,
    By angel hands to valor given;

The stars have lit the welkin dome,
  And all thy hues were born in heaven.
Forever float that standard sheet!
  Where breathes the foe but falls before us,

With Freedom's soil beneath our feet,
  And Freedom's banner streaming o'er
    us?

JOSEPH RODMAN DRAKE.

CHAPTER VI

"THE FATE OF SIR JACK BRAG"

Defeated in Jersey, the English turned with increased vigor to the task of securing the line of the Hudson. An army under General Burgoyne, starting from Canada, was to march down the Hudson to Albany; a second, under Colonel Saint Leger, was to descend the Mohawk valley and unite with Burgoyne; while a third, under Sir William Howe, was to ascend the river to Albany, thus completing the conquest of New York. Burgoyne began his advance early in June with an army of eight thousand men; but soon ran short of supplies, and finally, on August 13, detached an expedition to the little village of Bennington, where the Americans had collected horses and stores. Word of its approach was sent forward and Colonel John Stark prepared to give it a warm reception.

THE RIFLEMAN'S SONG AT BENNINGTON

WHY come ye hither, stranger?
  Your mind what madness fills?
In our valleys there is danger,
  And danger on our hills!
Hear ye not the singing
  Of the bugle, wild and free?
Full soon ye'll know the ringing
  Of the rifle from the tree!
    The rifle, the sharp rifle!
    In our hands it is no trifle!

Ye ride a goodly steed;
  He may know another master:
Ye forward come with speed,
  But ye'll learn to back much faster,
When ye meet our mountain boys
  And their leader, Johnny Stark!
Lads who make but little noise,
  But who always hit the mark
    With the rifle, the true rifle!
    In their hands will prove no trifle!

Had ye no graves at home
  Across the briny water,
That hither ye must come,
  Like bullocks to the slaughter?

If we the work must do,
  Why, the sooner 't is begun,
If flint and trigger hold but true,
  The quicker 't will be done
    By the rifle, the good rifle!
    In our hands it is no trifle!

Within a day, eight hundred yeomen were marching under Stark's orders. He was joined by a regiment under Colonel Seth Warner, and on August 15, 1777, in the midst of a drenching rain, set out to meet the enemy.

THE MARCHING SONG OF STARK'S MEN

[August 15, 1777]

MARCH! March! March! from sunrise till
    it's dark,
  And let no man straggle on the way!
March! March! March! as we follow old
    John Stark,
  For the old man needs us all to-day.

Load! Load! Load! Three buckshot and a
    ball,
  With a hymn-tune for a wad to make them
    stay!
But let no man dare to fire till he gives the
    word to all,
  Let no man let the buckshot go astray.

Fire! Fire! Fire! Fire all along the line,
  When we meet those bloody Hessians in
    array!
They shall have every grain from this pow-
    der-horn of mine,
  Unless the cowards turn and run away.

Home! Home! Home! When the fight is
    fought and won,
  To the home where the women watch and
    pray!

To tell them how John Stark finished what
   he had begun,
And to hear them thank our God for the
   day.
              EDWARD EVERETT HALE.

Stark found Baum and his Hessians about six
miles distant, and the latter hastily took up a
strong position on some rising ground, and began
to throw up intrenchments. Stark laid his plans
to storm this position on the morrow. During the
night, a company of Berkshire militia arrived, and
with them the warlike parson of Pittsfield, Thomas
Allen.

PARSON ALLEN'S RIDE

[August 15, 1777]

THE "Catamount Tavern" is lively to-night,
   The boys of Vermont and New Hampshire
     are here,
Assembled and grouped in the lingering light,
   To greet Parson Allen with shout and with
     cheer.

Over mountain and valley, from Pittsfield
     green,
   Through the driving rain of that August
     day,
The "Flock" marched on with martial mien,
   And the Parson rode in his "one-hoss
     shay."

"Three cheers for old Berkshire!" the Gen-
     eral said,
   As the boys of New England drew up
     face to face,
"Baum bids us a breakfast to-morrow to
     spread,
   And the Parson is here to say us the
     'grace.'"

"The lads who are with me have come here
     to fight,
   And we know of no grace," was the
     Parson's reply,
"Save the name of Jehovah, our country and
     right,
   Which your own Ethan Allen pronounced
     at Fort Ti."

"To-morrow," said Stark, "there'll be fight-
     ing to do,
   If you think you can wait for the morning
     light,

And, Parson, I'll conquer the British with
     you,
   Or Molly Stark sleeps a widow at night."

What the Parson dreamed in that Bennington
     camp,
   Neither Yankee nor Prophet would dare
     to guess;
A vision, perhaps, of the King David stamp,
   With a mixture of Cromwell and good
     Queen Bess.

But we know the result of that glorious day,
   And the victory won ere the night came
     down;
How Warner charged in the bitter fray,
   With Rossiter, Hobart, and old John
     Brown:

And how in the lull of the three hours' fight,
   The Parson harangued the Tory line,
As he stood on a stump, with his musket
     bright,
   And sprinkled his texts with the powder
     fine: —

The sword of the Lord is our battle-cry,
   A refuge sure in the hour of need,
And freedom and faith can never die,
   Is article first of the Puritan creed.

"Perhaps the 'occasion' was rather rash,"
   He remarked to his comrades after the rout,
"For behind a bush I saw a flash,
   But I fired that way and put it out."

And many the sayings, eccentric and queer,
   Repeated and sung through the whole
     country side,
And quoted in Berkshire for many a year,
   Of the Pittsfield march and the Parson's
     ride.

All honor to Stark and his resolute men,
   To the Green Mountain Boys all honor
     and praise,
While with shout and with cheer we welcome
     again,
   The Parson who came in his one-horse
     chaise.
              WALLACE BRUCE.

The next day, August 16, 1777, dawned clear
and bright, and the morning was consumed in
preparations for the attack. Stark managed to

throw half his force on Baum's rear and flanks, and, early in the afternoon, assaulted the enemy on all sides. The Germans stood their ground and fought desperately, but they were soon thrown into disorder, and at the end of two hours were all either killed or captured.

THE BATTLE OF BENNINGTON

[August 16, 1777]

Up through a cloudy sky, the sun
  Was buffeting his way,
On such a morn as ushers in
  A sultry August day.
Hot was the air — and hotter yet
  Men's thoughts within them grew:
They Britons, Hessians, Tories saw —
  They saw their homesteads too.

They thought of all their country's wrongs,
  They thought of noble lives
Pour'd out in battle with her foes,
  They thought upon their wives,
Their children, and their aged sires,
  Their firesides, churches, God —
And these deep thoughts made hallow'd
    ground
  Each foot of soil they trod.

Their leader was a brave old man,
  A man of earnest will;
His very presence was a host —
  He'd fought at Bunker Hill.
A living monument he stood
  Of stirring deeds of fame,
Of deeds that shed a fadeless light
  On his own deathless name.

Of Charlestown's flames, of Warren's blood,
  His presence told the tale,
It made each hero's heart beat high
  Though lip and cheek grew pale;
It spoke of Princeton, Morristown,
  Told Trenton's thrilling story —
It lit futurity with hope,
  And on the past shed glory.

Who were those men — their leader who?
  Where stood they on that morn?
The men were Berkshire yeomanry,
  Brave men as e'er were born, —
Who in the reaper's merry row
  Or warrior rank could stand
Right worthy such a noble troop,
  John Stark led on the band.

Wollamsac wanders by the spot
  Where they that morning stood;
Then roll'd the war-cloud o'er the stream,
  The waves were tinged with blood;
And the near hills that dark cloud girt,
  And fires like lightning flash'd,
And shrieks and groans, like howling blasts,
  Rose as the bayonets clash'd.

The night before, the Yankee host
  Came gathering from afar,
And in each belted bosom glow'd
  The spirit of the war.
As full of fight, through rainy storm,
  Night, cloudy, starless, dark,
They came, and gathered as they came,
  Around the valiant Stark.

There was a Berkshire parson — he
  And all his flock were there,
And like true churchmen militant
  The arm of flesh made bare.
Out spake the Dominie and said,
  "For battle have we come
These many times, and after this
  We mean to stay at home."

"If now we come in vain," said Stark,
  "What! will you go to-night
To battle it with yonder troops,
  God send us morning light,
And we will give you work enough:
  Let but the morning come,
And if ye hear no voice of war
  Go back and stay at home."

The morning came — there stood the
    foe,
  Stark eyed them as they stood —
Few words he spake — 't was not a time
  For moralizing mood.
"See there the enemy, my boys!
  Now strong in valor's might,
Beat them, or Molly Stark will sleep
  In widowhood to-night."

Each soldier there had left at home
  A sweetheart, wife, or mother,
A blooming sister, or, perchance,
  A fair-hair'd, blue-eyed brother.
Each from a fireside came, and thoughts
  Those simple words awoke
That nerved up every warrior's arm
  And guided every stroke.

Fireside and woman — mighty words!
    How wondrous is the spell
They work upon the manly heart,
    Who knoweth not full well?
And then the women of this land,
    That never land hath known
A truer, prouder hearted race,
    Each Yankee boy must own.

Brief eloquence was Stark's — nor vain —
    Scarce utter'd he the words,
When burst the musket's rattling peal
    Out-leap'd the flashing swords;
And when brave Stark in after time
    Told the proud tale of wonder,
He said the battle din was one
    "Continual clap of thunder."

Two hours they strove — then victory crown'd
    The gallant Yankee boys.
Nought but the memory of the dead
    Bedimm'd their glorious joys;
Ay — there's the rub — the hour of strife,
    Though follow years of fame,
Is still in mournful memory link'd
    With some death-hallow'd name.

The cypress with the laurel twines —
    The pæan sounds a knell,
The trophied column marks the spot
    Where friends and brothers fell.
Fame's mantle a funereal pall
    Seems to the grief-dimm'd eye,
For ever where the bravest fall
    The best beloved die.
                    THOMAS P. RODMAN.

Just at this moment, when the Americans, thinking the battle over, began to scatter to the plunder of the German camp, a relieving force of five hundred men, sent by Burgoyne, came upon the scene. Luckily, Seth Warner also arrived with fresh men at this juncture, charged furiously upon the British, and by nightfall had killed or captured the entire column, with the exception of six men, who succeeded in reaching the British camp.

BENNINGTON

[August 16, 1777]

A CYCLE was closed and rounded,
    A continent lost and won,
When Stark and his men went over
    The earthworks at Bennington.

Slowly down from the northward,
    Billowing fold on fold,
Whelming the land and crushing,
    The glimmering glacier rolled.

Down from the broad St. Lawrence,
    Bright with its thousand isles,
Through the Canadian woodlands,
    Sweet with the summer smiles,

On over field and fastness,
    Village and vantage coigne,
Rolled the resistless legions
    Led by the bold Burgoyne.

Roared the craggy ledges
    Looming o'er Lake Champlain;
Red with the blaze of navies
    Quivered the land-locked main;

Soared the Vancour eagle,
    Screaming, across the sun;
Deep dived the loon in terror
    Under Lake Horicon.

Panther and hart together
    Fled to the wilds afar,
From the flash and the crash of the can-
        non
    And the rush of the southward war.

But at last by the lordly river
    The trampling giant swayed,
And his massive arm swung eastward
    Like a blindly-plunging blade.

New England felt her bosom
    Menaced with deadly blow,
And her minute-men sprang up again
    And flew to bar the foe.

But Stark in his Hampshire valley
    Watched like a glowering bear,
That hears the cry go sweeping by
    Yet stirs not from his lair;

For on his daring spirit
    A wrath lay like a spell, —
The wrath of one rewarded ill
    For a great work wrought right well.

Neighbor and friend and brother
    Flocked to his side in vain, —
"What, can it be that they long for me
    To ruin their cause again?

"Surely the northern lights are bright.
  Surely the South lies still.
Would they have more? — Lo, I left my
    sword
  On the crest of Bunker Hill."

But at last from his own New Hampshire
  An urgent summons came,
That stirred his heart like the voice of
    God
  From Sinai's walls of flame.

He bowed his head, and he rose aloft;
  Again he grasped the brand, —
"For the cause of man and my native State,
  Not for an ingrate land!"

Through the mist-veil faintly struggling,
  The rays of the setting sun
Reddened the leafy village
  Of white-walled Bennington.

Then out of the dismal weather
  Came many a sound of war, —
The straggling shots and the volleys
  And the cries, now near now far.

For forms half seen were chasing
  The phantom forms that fled;
And ghostly figures grappled
  And spectres fought and bled;

Till the mist on a sudden settled
  And they saw before them fair,
Over a hill to the westward,
  An island in the air.

There were tree-trunks and waving branches,
  And greensward and flowers below;
It rose in a dome of verdure
  From the mist-waves' watery flow.

A flag from its summit floated
  And a circling earthwork grew,
As the arms of the swarming soldiers
  At their toil unwonted flew.

"Aha!" cried the Yankee leader,
  "So the panther has turned at bay
With his claws of steel and his breath of
    fire
  Behind that wall of clay!

"*Our* steel is in muscle and sinew.
  But I know," — and his voice rang free, —

"Right well I know we shall strike a blow
  That the world will leap to see."

I stood by a blazing city
  Till the fires had died away,
Save a flickering gleam in the ruins
  And a fitful gleam on the bay.

But a swarthy cove by the water
  Blue-bristled from point to base,
With the breath of demons, bursting
  Through the crust of their prison-place;

And another beside it flaunted
  A thousand rags of red,
Like the Plague King's dancing banners
  On a mound of the swollen dead.

Twin brothers of flame and evil,
  In their quivering living light,
They ruled with a frightful beauty
  The desolate waste of night.

Thus did the battle mountain
  Blazon with flashes dire;
The leaguered crest responded
  In a coronal of fire.

The tough old fowling-pieces
  In huddling tumult rang.
Louder the muskets' roaring!
  Shriller the rifles' clang!

Hour after hour the turmoil
  Gathered and swelled apace,
Till the hill seemed a volcano
  Bursting in every place.

Then the lights grew faint and meagre,
  Though the hideous noise rolled on;
And out of a bath of glory
  Uprose the noble sun.

It brightened the tossing banner;
  It yellowed the leafy crest;
It smote on the serried weapons,
  On helmet and scarlet breast.

It drove on the mist below them
  Where Stark and his foremost stood,
Flashing volley for volley
  Into the stubborn wood.

A thousand stalwart figures
  Sprang from the gulf profound,

A thousand guns uplifted
  Went whirling round and round.

Like some barbarian onslaught
  On a lofty Roman hold;
Like the upward rush of Titans
  On Olympian gods of old;

With a swirl of the wrangling torrents
  As they dash on a castle wall;
With the flame-seas skyward surging
  At the mountain demon's call,

Heedless of friend and brother
  Stricken to earth below,
The sons of New England bounded
  On the breastwork of the foe.

Each stalwart form on the ramparts
  Swaying his battered gun
Seemed a vengeful giant, looming
  Against the rising sun.

The pond'rous clubs swept crashing
  Through the bayonets round their feet
As a woodman's axe-edge crashes
  Through branches mailed in sleet,

Shattering head and shoulder,
  Splintering arm and thigh,
Hurling the redcoats earthward
  Like bolts from an angry sky.

Faster each minute and faster
  The yeomen swarm over the wall,
And narrower grows the circle
  And thicker the Britons fall;

Till Baum with his Hessian swordsmen
  Swift to the rescue flies,
The frown of the Northland on their brows
  And the war-light in their eyes.

Back reeled the men of Berkshire,
  The mountaineers gave back,
But Stark and his Hampshire yeomen
  Flung full across their track.

The stern Teutonic mother
  Well might she grandly eye
The prowess dread of her war-swarms red
  As they racked the earth and sky.

Like rival wrestling athletes
  Grappled the East and West.

With straining thews and staring eyes
They swayed and strove for the royal prize,
  A continent's virgin breast.

Till at last as a strong man's wrenching
  Shatters a brittle vase,
The lustier arms of the Westland
  Shattered the elder race.

Baum and his bravest cohorts
  Lay on the trampled sod,
And Stark's strong cry rose clear and high,
  "Yield in the name of God!"

Then the sullen Hessians yielded,
  Girt by an iron ring,
And down from the summit fluttered
  The flag of the British king.

Vainly the tardy Breyman
  May strive that height to gain;
More work for the Hampshire war-clubs!
  More room for the Hessian slain!

The giant's arm is severed,
  The giant's blood flows free,
And he staggers in the pathway
  That leads to the distant sea.

The Berkshire and Hampshire yeomen
  With the men of the Hudson join,
And the gathering flood rolls over
  The host of the bold Burgoyne.

For a cycle was closed and rounded,
  A continent lost and won,
When Stark and his men went over
  The earthworks at Bennington.
                    W. H. BABCOCK.

Saint Leger, meanwhile, had landed at Oswego
and advanced against Fort Stanwix. General
Nicholas Herkimer, commander of the militia of
Tryon County, at the head of eight hundred men,
started to the rescue. He met the enemy, on
August 5, at Oriskany, and there followed the
most obstinate and murderous battle of the Revo-
lution. Both sides claimed the victory.

THE BATTLE OF ORISKANY

[August 6, 1777]

As men who fight for home and child and wife,
As men oblivious of life
  In holy martyrdom,

The yeomen of the valley fought that day,
Throughout thy fierce and deadly fray, —
  Blood-red Oriskany.

From rock and tree and clump of twisted
  brush
The hissing gusts of battle rush, —
  Hot-breathed and horrible!
The roar, the smoke, like mist on stormy
  seas,
Sweep through thy splintered trees, —
  Hard-fought Oriskany.

Heroes are born in such a chosen hour;
From common men they rise, and tower,
  Like thee, brave Herkimer!
Who wounded, steedless, still beside the
  beech
Cheered on thy men, with sword and speech,
  In grim Oriskany.

But ere the sun went toward the tardy night,
The valley then beheld the light
  Of freedom's victory;
And wooded Tryon snatched from British
  arms
The empire of a million farms —
  On bright Oriskany.

The guns of Stanwix thunder to the skies;
The rescued wilderness replies;
  Forth dash the garrison!
And routed Tories, with their savage aids,
Sink reddening through the sullied shades —
  From lost Oriskany.
          CHARLES D. HELMER.

Saint Leger rallied his shaken columns and set-
tled down to besiege the fort, which laughed at
his summons to surrender. Soon afterwards, news
of Oriskany and of the siege arrived at General
Schuyler's headquarters at Stillwater, and Bene-
dict Arnold set out at once for Fort Stanwix at the
head of twelve hundred men. Such exaggerated
reports of the size of his force were conveyed to
Saint Leger that, on August 22, he raised the siege
and retreated to Canada.

SAINT LEGER

[August, 1777]

FROM out of the North-land his leaguer he led,
  Saint Leger, Saint Leger;
And the war-lust was strong in his heart as
  he sped;

Their courage, he cried, *it shall die i' the
  throat
When they mark the proud standards that over
  us float —
See rover and ranger, redskin and redcoat!*
  Saint Leger, Saint Leger.

He hurried by water, he scurried by land,
  Saint Leger, Saint Leger,
Till closely he cordoned the patriot band:
Surrender, he bade, *or I tighten the net!
Surrender?* they mocked him, *we laugh at
  your threat!
By Heaven!* he thundered, *you'll live to regret*
  Saint Leger, Saint Leger!

He mounted his mortars, he smote with his
  shell,
    Saint Leger, Saint Leger;
Then fumed in a fury that futile they fell;
But he counselled with rum till he chuckled,
  elate,
As he sat in his tent-door, *Egad, we can wait,
For famine is famous to open a gate!*
  Saint Leger, Saint Leger.

But lo! as he waited, was borne to his ear —
  Saint Leger, Saint Leger —
A whisper of dread and a murmur of fear!
*They come, and as leaves are their numbers
  enrolled!
They come, and their onset may not be con-
  trolled,
For 't is Arnold who heads them, 't is Arnold
  the bold —*
  Saint Leger, Saint Leger!

Retreat! Was the word e'er more bitterly
  said,
    Saint Leger, Saint Leger,
Than when to the North-land your leaguer
  you led?
Alas, for Burgoyne in his peril and pain —
Who lists in the night for the tramp of that
  train!
And, alas, for the boasting, the vaunting, the
  vain
    Saint Leger!
          CLINTON SCOLLARD.

Saint Leger's retreat, joined to the disaster a
Bennington, left Burgoyne in an exceedingly
critical condition. The Americans hemmed him
in, front and rear, and increased rapidly in num-
bers; he had received no news from Howe, who

was supposed to be on his way up the Hudson to join him; and he found it more and more difficult to get provisions.

THE PROGRESS OF SIR JACK BRAG

SAID Burgoyne to his men, as they passed in review,
    Tullalo, tullalo, tullalo, boys!
These rebels their course very quickly will rue,
And fly as the leaves 'fore the autumn tempest flew,
When him who is your leader they know, boys!
    They with men have now to deal,
    And we soon will make them feel —
    Tullalo, tullalo, tullalo, boys!
That a loyal Briton's arm, and a loyal Briton's steel,
Can put to flight a rebel, as quick as other foe, boys!
    Tullalo, tullalo, tullalo,
    Tullalo, tullalo, tullalo-o-o-o, boys!

As to Sa-ra-tog' he came, thinking how to jo the game,
    Tullalo, tullalo, tullalo, boys!
He began to see the grubs, in the branches of his fame,
He began to have the trembles, lest a flash should be the flame
For which he had agreed his perfume to forego, boys!
    No lack of skill, but fates,
    Shall make us yield to Gates,
    Tullalo, tullalo, tullalo, boys!
The devils may have leagued, as you know, with the States.
But we never will be beat by any mortal foe, boys!
    Tullalo, tullalo, tullalo,
    Tullalo, tullalo, tullalo-o-o-o, boys!

The American army was stationed along the western bank of the Hudson; while Burgoyne's troops were encamped along the eastern bank. For nearly a month the armies remained in this position; then Burgoyne determined to advance to Albany, and on September 13, 1777, the British army crossed on a pontoon bridge to the west bank of the Hudson. Two desperate attempts were made to break through the American lines, but the British were routed by Benedict Arnold's superb and daring generalship, and forced to retreat to Saratoga.

ARNOLD AT STILLWATER

[October 7, 1777]

AH, you mistake me, comrades, to think that my heart is steel!
Cased in a cold endurance, nor pleasure nor pain to feel;
Cold as I am in my manner, yet over these cheeks so seared
Teardrops have fallen in torrents, thrice since my chin grew beard.

Thrice since my chin was bearded I suffered the tears to fall;
Benedict Arnold, the traitor, he was the cause of them all!
Once, when he carried Stillwater, proud of his valor, I cried;
Then, with my rage at his treason — with pity when André died.

Benedict Arnold, the traitor, sank deep in the pit of shame,
Bartered for vengeance his honor, blackened for profit his fame;
Yet never a gallanter soldier, whatever his after crime,
Fought on the red field of honor than he in his early time.

Ah, I remember Stillwater, as it were yesterday!
Then first I shouldered a firelock, and set out the foemen to slay.
The country was up all around us, racing and chasing Burgoyne,
And I had gone out with my neighbors, Gates and his forces to join.

Marched we with Poor and with Learned, ready and eager to fight;
There stood the foemen before us, cannon and men on the height;
Onward we trod with no shouting, forbidden to fire till the word;
As silent their long line of scarlet — not one of them whispered or stirred.

Suddenly, then, from among them smoke rose and spread on the breeze;
Grapeshot flew over us sharply, cutting the limbs from the trees:

But onward we pressed till the order of Cilley
    fell full on the ear;
Then we levelled our pieces and fired them,
    and rushed up the slope with a cheer.

Fiercely we charged on their centre, and beat
    back the stout grenadiers,
And wounded the brave Major Ackland, and
    grappled the swart cannoneers;
Five times we captured their cannons, and
    five times they took them again;
But the sixth time we had them we kept them,
    and with them a share of their men.

Our colonel who led us dismounted, high on
    a cannon he sprang;
Over the noise of our shouting clearly his
    joyous words rang:
"These are our own brazen beauties! Here
    to America's cause
I dedicate each, and to freedom! — foes to
    King George and his laws!"

Worn as we were with the struggle, wounded
    and bleeding and sore,
Some stood all pale and exhausted; some
    lay there stiff in their gore;
And round through the mass went a murmur,
    that grew to a whispering clear,
And then to reproaches outspoken —"If
    General Arnold were here!"

For Gates, in his folly and envy, had given
    the chief no command,
And far in the rear some had seen him horse-
    less and moodily stand,
Knitting his forehead in anger, gnawing his
    red lip in pain,
Fretting himself like a bloodhound held back
    from his prey by a chain.

Hark, at our right there is cheering! there
    is the ruffle of drums!
Here is the well-known brown charger! Spur-
    ring it madly he comes!
Learned's brigade have espied him, rending
    the air with a cheer;
Woe to the terrified foeman, now that our
    leader is here!

Piercing the tumult behind him, Armstrong
    is out on his track;
Gates has dispatched his lieutenant to sum-
    mon the fugitive back.

Armstrong might summon the tempest, order
    the whirlwind to stay,
Issue commands to the earthquake — would
    they the mandate obey?

Wounds, they were healed in a moment!
    weariness instantly gone!
Forward he pointed his sabre — led us, not
    ordered us on.
Down on the Hessians we thundered, he, like
    a madman ahead;
Vainly they strove to withstand us; raging,
    they shivered and fled.

On to their earthworks we drove them, shaking
    with ire and dismay;
There they made stand with a purpose to beat
    back the tide of the day.
Onward we followed, then faltered; deadly
    their balls whistled free.
Where was our death-daring leader? Arnold,
    our hope, where was he?

He? He was everywhere riding! hither and
    thither his form,
On the brown charger careering, showed us
    the path of the storm;
Over the roar of the cannon, over the mus-
    ketry's crash,
Sounded his voice, while his sabre lit up the
    way with its flash.

Throwing quick glances around him, reining
    a moment his steed —
"Brooks, that redoubt!" was his order; "let
    the rest follow my lead!
Mark where the smoke-cloud is parting!
    see where the gun-barrels glance!
Livingston, forward! On, Wesson, charge
    them! Let Morgan advance!"

"Forward!" he shouted, and, spurring on
    through the sally-port then,
Fell sword in hand on the Hessians, closely
    behind him our men.
Back shrank the foemen in terror; off went
    their forces pellmell,
Firing one Parthian volley; struck by it,
    Arnold, he fell.

Ours was the day. Up we raised him; spurted
    the blood from his knee —
"Take my cravat, boys, and bind it; I am
    not dead yet," said he.

"What! did you follow me, Armstrong?
  Pray, do you think it quite right,
Leaving your duties out yonder, to risk your
  dear self in the fight?"

"General Gates sent his orders" — faltering
  the aide-de-camp spoke —
"You're to return, lest some rashness —"
  Fiercely the speech Arnold broke:
"Rashness! Why, yes, tell the general the
  rashness he dreaded is done!
Tell him his kinsfolk are beaten! tell him
  the battle is won!"

Oh, that a soldier so glorious, ever victorious
  in fight,
Passed from a daylight of honor into the
  terrible night! —
Fell as the mighty archangel, ere the earth
  glowed in space, fell —
Fell from the patriot's heaven down to the
  loyalist's hell!
                    THOMAS DUNN ENGLISH.

Burgoyne was hotly pursued, and when he
reached the place where he had crossed the Hud-
son, found it occupied in force by the Americans.
The British army, in short, was surrounded, and,
after a week's indecision, Burgoyne sent a flag of
truce to Gates, inquiring what terms of surrender
would be accepted. Three days were spent in a
discussion of terms, and on October 17, 1777,
Burgoyne surrendered to the American forces.

THE FATE OF JOHN BURGOYNE

[October 17, 1777]

WHEN Jack the King's commander
Was going to his duty,
Through all the crowd he smiled and bowed
To every blooming beauty.

The city rung with feats he'd done
In Portugal and Flanders,
And all the town thought he'd be crowned
The first of Alexanders.

To Hampton Court he first repairs
To kiss great George's hand, sirs;
Then to harangue on state affairs
Before he left the land, sirs.

The "Lower House" sat mute as mouse
To hear his grand oration;
And "all the peers," with loudest cheers,
Proclaimed him to the nation.

Then off he went to Canada,
Next to Ticonderoga,
And quitting those away he goes
Straightway to Saratoga.

With great parade his march he made
To gain his wished-for station,
While far and wide his minions hied
To spread his "Proclamation."

To such as stayed he offers made
Of "pardon on submission;
But savage bands should waste the lands
Of all in opposition."

But ah, the cruel fates of war!
This boasted son of Britain,
When mounting his triumphal car,
With sudden fear was smitten.

The sons of Freedom gathered round,
His hostile bands confounded,
And when they'd fain have turned their back
They found themselves surrounded!

In vain they fought, in vain they fled;
Their chief, humane and tender,
To save the rest soon thought it best
His forces to surrender.

Brave St. Clair, when he first retired,
Knew what the fates portended;
And Arnold and heroic Gates
His conduct have defended.

Thus may America's brave sons
With honor be rewarded,
And be the fate of all her foes
The same as here recorded.

SARATOGA SONG

[October 17, 1777]

COME unto me, ye heroes
  Whose hearts are true and bold,
Who value more your honor
  Than others do their gold;
Give ear unto my story,
  And I the truth will tell,
Concerning many a soldier
  Who for his country fell.

Burgoyne, the King's commander,
  From Canada set sail;

With full eight thousand regulars,
  He thought he could not fail;
With Indians and Canadians,
  And his cursèd Tory crew,
On board his fleet of shipping
  He up the Champlain flew.

Before Ticonderoga,
  The first day of July,
Appeared his ships and army,
  And we did them espy.
Their motions we observed,
  Full well both night and day,
And our brave boys prepared
  To have a bloody fray.

Our garrison, they viewed them,
  And straight their troops did land;
And when St. Clair, our chieftain,
  The fact did understand,
That they the Mount Defiance
  Were bent to fortify,
He found we must surrender,
  Or else prepare to die.

The fifth day of July, then,
  He ordered a retreat;
And when next morn we started,
  Burgoyne thought we were beat.
And closely he pursued us,
  Till when near Hubbardton,
Our rear guards were defeated,
  He thought the country won.

And when 't was told in Congress
  That we our forts had left,
To Albany retreated,
  Of all the North bereft,
Brave General Gates they sent us,
  Our fortunes to retrieve,
And him, with shouts of gladness,
  The army did receive.

Where first the Mohawk's waters
  Do in the sunshine play,
For Herkimer's brave soldiers
  Sellinger ambushed lay;
And them he there defeated,
  But soon he had his due,
And scared by Brooks and Arnold,
  He to the north withdrew.

To take the stores and cattle
  That we had gathered then,
Burgoyne sent a detachment
  Of fifteen hundred men;

By Baum they were commanded,
  To Bennington they went;
To plunder and to murder
  Was fully their intent.

But little did they know then
  With whom they had to deal;
It was not quite so easy
  Our stores and stocks to steal,
Bold Stark would give them only
  A portion of his lead;
With half his crew, ere sunset,
  Baum lay among the dead.

The nineteenth of September,
  The morning cool and clear,
Brave Gates rode through our army,
  Each soldier's heart to cheer;
"Burgoyne," he cried, "advances,
  But we will never fly;
No — rather than surrender,
  We'll fight him till we die!"

The news was quickly brought us,
  The enemy was near,
And all along our lines then,
  There was no sign of fear;
It was above Stillwater
  We met at noon that day,
And every one expected
  To see a bloody fray.

Six hours the battle lasted,
  Each heart as true as gold,
The British fought like lions,
  And we like Yankees bold;
The leaves with blood were crimson,
  And then did brave Gates cry,
"'T is diamond now cut diamond!
  We'll beat them, boys, or die."

The darkness soon approaching,
  It forced us to retreat
Into our lines till morning,
  Which made them think us beat;
But ere the sun was risen,
  They saw before their eyes
Us ready to engage them,
  Which did them much surprise.

Of fighting they seem weary,
  Therefore to work they go
Their thousand dead to bury,
  And breastworks up to throw;
With grape and bombs intending
  Our army to destroy.

Or from our works our forces
     By stratagem decoy.

The seventh day of October
     The British tried again,
Shells from their cannon throwing,
     Which fell on us like rain;
To drive us from our stations,
     That they might thus retreat;
For now Burgoyne saw plainly
     He never could us beat.

But vain was his endeavor
     Our men to terrify;
Though death was all around us,
     Not one of us would fly.
But when an hour we'd fought them,
     And they began to yield,
Along our lines the cry ran,
     "The next blow wins the field!"

Great God who guides their battles
     Whose cause is just and true,
Inspired our bold commander
     The course he should pursue!
He ordered Arnold forward,
     And Brocks to follow on;
The enemy was routed!
     Our liberty was won!

Then, burning all their luggage,
     They fled with haste and fear,

Burgoyne with all his forces,
     To Saratoga did steer;
And Gates, our brave commander,
     Soon after him did hie,
Resolving he would take them,
     Or in the effort die.

As we came nigh the village,
     We overtook the foe;
They'd burned each house to ashes,
     Like all where'er they go.
The seventeenth of October,
     They did capitulate,
Burgoyne and his proud army
     Did we our prisoners make.

Now here's a health to Arnold,
     And our commander Gates,
To Lincoln and to Washington,
     Whom every Tory hates;
Likewise unto our Congress,
     God grant it long to reign;
Our Country, Right, and Justice
     Forever to maintain.

Now finished is my story,
     My song is at an end;
The freedom we're enjoying
     We're ready to defend;
For while our cause is righteous,
     Heaven nerves the soldier's arm,
And vain is their endeavor
     Who strive to do us harm.

CHAPTER VII

THE SECOND STAGE

News of the reverse at Saratoga was received in England with amazement and consternation, and its effect on the government was soon discernible. On February 17, 1778, Lord North astonished the House of Commons by rising in his place and moving that Parliament repeal the tea tax and other measures obnoxious to the Americans, that it renounce forever the right of raising a revenue in America, and that commissioners be sent to Congress, with full powers for negotiating a peace. So complete a political somersault has seldom been turned by an English minister.

LORD NORTH'S RECANTATION

[February 17, 1778]

WHEN North first began
     With his taxation plan,
The Colonies all to supplant,

To Britain's true cause,
     And her liberty, laws,
Oh, how did he scorn to recant.

Oh! how did he boast
     Of his pow'r and his host,
Alternately swagger and cant;
     Of freedom so dear,
     Not a word would he hear,
Nor believe he'd be forc'd to recant.

That freedom he swore
     They ne'er should have more,
Their money to give and to grant;
     Whene'er they addressed,
     What disdain he express'd,
Not thinking they'd make him recant.

He armies sent o'er
To America's shore,
New government there to transplant;
But every campaign
Prov'd his force to be vain,
Yet still he refus'd to recant.

But with all their bombast,
They were so beat at last,
As to silence his impious rant;
Who for want of success,
Could at last do no less
Than draw in his horns, and recant.

With his brother Burgoyne,
He's forc'd now to join,
And a treaty of peace for to want;
Says he ne'er will fight,
But will give up his right
To taxation, and freely recant.

With the great General Howe,
He'd be very glad now,
He ne'er had engag'd in the jaunt;
And ev'ry proud Scot
In the devilish plot,
With his Lordship, are forc'd to recant.

Old England, alas!
They have brought to such pass,
Too late are proposals extant;
America's lost,
Our glory at most
Is only that — tyrants recant.

But these proposals came too late. America
had just concluded with France a treaty by which
she agreed, in consideration of armed support to
be furnished by that power, never to entertain
proposals of peace from Great Britain until her
independence should be acknowledged. On March
13 this action on the part of France was commu-
nicated to the British government, and war against
France was instantly declared.

A NEW BALLAD

[1778]

ROUSE, Britons! at length,
And put forth your strength
Perfidious France to resist;
Ten Frenchmen will fly,
To shun a black eye,
If an Englishman doubles his fist.
Derry down, down, hey derry down.

But if they feel stout,
Why let them turn out,
With their maws stuff'd with frogs, soups,
and jellies,
Brave Hardy's sea thunder
Shall strike them with wonder,
And make the frogs leap in their bellies!

For their Dons and their ships
We care not three skips
Of a flea — and their threats turn into jest, O!
We'll bang their bare ribs
For the infamous fibs
Cramm'd into their fine manifesto.

Our brethren so frantic
Across the Atlantic,
Who quit their old friends in a huff,
In spite of their airs,
Are at their last prayers,
And of fighting have had quantum suff.

Then if powers at a distance
Should offer assistance,
Say boldly, "we want none, we thank ye,"
Old England's a match
And more for old scratch,
A Frenchman, a Spaniard, a Yankee!
Derry down, down, hey derry down.

In spite of this change in the complexion of
affairs abroad, the situation in America was still
critical. Howe had abandoned Burgoyne to his
fate, but he had not been inactive. He had set his
heart upon the capture of Philadelphia, and in
June, 1777, assembled his army at New Bruns-
wick, but finding Washington strongly posted on
the Heights of Middlebrook and not daring to
attack him, was forced to retire to New York.

GENERAL HOWE'S LETTER

The substance of Sir W.'s last letter from New
York, versified.

[June, 1777]

As to kidnap the Congress has long been my
aim,
I lately resolv'd to accomplish the same;
And, that none, in the glory, might want his
due share,
All the troops were to Brunswick desir'd to
repair.
Derry down, down, hey derry down.

There I met them in person, and took the
    command,
When I instantly told them the job upon
    hand;
I did not detain them with long-winded stuff,
But made a short speech, and each soldier
    look'd bluff.

With this omen elated, towards Quibbletown
I led them, concluding the day was our
    own;
For, till we went thither, the coast was quite
    clear, —
But Putnam and Washington, d—n them,
    were there!

I own I was stagger'd, to see with what skill
The rogues were intrenched, on the brow of
    the hill;
With a view to dismay them, I show'd my
    whole force,
But they kept their position, and car'd not a
    curse.

There were then but two ways, — to retreat
    or attack,
And to me it seem'd wisest, by far, to go back;
For I thought, if I rashly got into a fray,
There might both be the Devil and Piper to
    pay.

Then, to lose no more time, by parading in
    vain,
I determin'd elsewhere to transfer the cam-
    paign;
So just as we went, we return'd to this place,
With no other diff'rence, — than mending
    our pace.

Where next we proceed, is not yet very clear,
But, when we get there, be assur'd you shall
    hear;
I'll settle that point, when I meet with my
    brother, —
Meanwhile, we're embarking for some place
    or other.

Having briefly, my lord, told you, — how the
    land lies,
I hope there's enough — for a word to the
    wise;
'T is a good horse, they say, that never will
    stumble, —
But, fighting or flying, — I'm your very
    humble.

Howe, finding the approach to the "rebel capi-
tal" by land cut off, determined to reach it by
water, and about the middle of July put to sea
with a fleet of two hundred and twenty-eight sail,
carrying an army of eighteen thousand men. Not
until the 25th of August did he succeed in land-
ing this force at the head of Chesapeake Bay.
Washington, though he had only eleven thousand
men, decided to offer battle, rather than let Phila-
delphia be taken without a blow, and on Septem-
ber 11, 1777, the armies met at Brandywine Creek.
The Americans were forced to retire, with a loss
of about a thousand men, and the British entered
Philadelphia two weeks later.

CARMEN BELLICOSUM

In their ragged regimentals
Stood the old Continentals,
        Yielding not,
When the grenadiers were lunging,
And like hail fell the plunging
        Cannon-shot;
        When the files
        Of the isles,
From the smoky night-encampment, bore the
    banner of the rampant
        Unicorn,
And grummer, grummer, grummer, rolled
    the roll of the drummer,
        Through the morn!

Then with eyes to the front all,
And with guns horizontal,
        Stood our sires;
And the balls whistled deadly,
And in streams flashing redly
        Blazed the fires:
        As the roar
        Of the shore,
Swept the strong battle-breakers o'er the
    green-sodded acres
        Of the plain;
And louder, louder. louder, cracked the black
    gunpowder,
        Cracking amain!

Now like smiths at their forges
Worked the red St. George's
        Cannoneers;
And the "villainous saltpetre"
Rung a fierce, discordant metre
        Round their ears;
        As the swift
        Storm-drift.

With hot sweeping anger, came the horse-
 guards' clangor
  On our flanks:
Then higher, higher, higher, burned the old-
 fashioned fire
  Through the ranks!

  Then the bareheaded Colonel
  Galloped through the white infernal
   Powder-cloud;
 And his broadsword was swinging
 And his brazen throat was ringing
   Trumpet-loud.
  Then the blue
  Bullets flew,
And the trooper-jackets redden at the touch
 of the leaden
  Rifle-breath;
And rounder, rounder, rounder, roared the
 iron six-pounder,
  Hurling Death.
   GUY HUMPHREYS McMASTER.

Washington retired to winter quarters at Val-
ley Forge, where, through the neglect and mis-
management of Congress, the patriot army was
so ill-provided with food, clothing, and shelter,
and endured sufferings so intense that, from dis-
ease and desertion, it dwindled at times to less
than two thousand effective men.

VALLEY FORGE

From "The Wagoner of the Alleghanies "

[1777–78]

O'ER town and cottage, vale and height,
Down came the Winter, fierce and white,
And shuddering wildly, as distraught
At horrors his own hand had wrought.

His child, the young Year, newly born,
 Cheerless, cowering, and affrighted,
Wailed with a shivering voice forlorn,
 As on a frozen heath benighted.
In vain the hearths were set aglow,
 In vain the evening lamps were lighted,
To cheer the dreary realm of snow:
Old Winter's brow would not be smoothed,
Nor the young Year's wailing soothed.

How sad the wretch at morn or eve
Compelled his starving home to leave,
Who, plunged breast-deep from drift to drift,
Toils slowly on from rift to rift,

Still hearing in his aching ear
The cry his fancy whispers near,
Of little ones who weep for bread
Within an ill-provided shed!

But wilder, fiercer, sadder still,
 Freezing the tear it caused to start,
Was the inevitable chill
 Which pierced a nation's agued heart, —
A nation with its naked breast
Against the frozen barriers prest,
Heaving its tedious way and slow
Through shifting gulfs and drifts of woe,
Where every blast that whistled by
Was bitter with its children's cry.

Such was the winter's awful sight
For many a dreary day and night,
What time our country's hope forlorn,
Of every needed comfort shorn,
Lay housed within a hurried tent,
Where every keen blast found a rent,
And oft the snow was seen to sift
Along the floor its piling drift,
Or, mocking the scant blankets' fold,
Across the night-couch frequent rolled;
Where every path by a soldier beat,
 Or every track where a sentinel stood,
Still held the print of naked feet,
 And oft the crimson stains of blood;
Where Famine held her spectral court,
 And joined by all her fierce allies:
She ever loved a camp or fort
 Beleaguered by the wintry skies, —
But chiefly when Disease is by,
To sink the frame and dim the eye,
Until, with seeking forehead bent,
 In martial garments cold and damp,
Pale Death patrols from tent to tent,
 To count the charnels of the camp.

Such was the winter that prevailed
 Within the crowded, frozen gorge;
Such were the horrors that assailed
 The patriot band at Valley Forge.

It was a midnight storm of woes
 To clear the sky for Freedom's morn;
And such must ever be the throes
 The hour when Liberty is born.
   THOMAS BUCHANAN READ.

Howe's army, meanwhile, spent the winter in
Philadelphia; very pleasantly, for the most part,
and yet not without various alarms, one of which

was celebrated by Francis Hopkinson in some fa-
mous verses to the tune of " Yankee Doodle," pub-
lished in the *Pennsylvania Packet*, March 4, 1778.

BRITISH VALOR DISPLAYED;

OR, THE BATTLE OF THE KEGS

[January 5, 1778]

GALLANTS attend, and hear a friend
    Trill forth harmonious ditty;
Strange things I'll tell which late befel
    In Philadelphia city.

'T was early day, as Poets say,
    Just when the sun was rising,
A soldier stood on a log of wood,
    And saw a sight surprising.

As in a maze he stood to gaze
    (The truth can't be deny'd, Sir),
He spy'd a score of kegs, or more,
    Come floating down the tide, Sir.

A sailor, too, in jerkin blue,
    This strange appearance viewing,
First damn'd his eyes, in great surprise,
    Then said " Some mischief's brewing:

" These kegs now hold, the rebels bold,
    Packed up like pickl'd herring;
And they're come down t' attack the town
    In this new way of ferry'ng."

The soldier flew, the sailor too,
    And, scar'd almost to death, Sir,
Wore out their shoes to spread the news,
    And ran 'til out of breath, Sir.

Now up and down, throughout the town
    Most frantic scenes were acted;
And some ran here, and others there,
    Like men almost distracted.

Some fire cry'd, which some deny'd,
    But said the earth had quaked;
And girls and boys, with hideous noise,
    Ran thro' the streets half naked.

Sir William he, snug as a flea,
    Lay all this time a snoring;
Nor dream'd of harm as he lay warm
    In bed with Mrs. Loring.

Now in a fright, he starts upright,
    Awaked by such a clatter;

He rubs both eyes, and boldly cries,
    " For God's sake, what's the matter?"

At his bedside he then espy'd,
    Sir Erskine at command, Sir;
Upon one foot he had one boot,
    And t' other in his hand, Sir.

" Arise, arise," *Sir Erskine* cries,
    " The rebels — more's the pity —
Without a boat, are all afloat,
    And rang'd before the city.

" The motley crew, in vessels new,
    With Satan for their guide, Sir,
Pack'd up in bags, and wooden kegs,
    Come driving down the tide, Sir.

"Therefore prepare for bloody war;
    These kegs must all be routed;
Or surely we dispis'd shall be,
    And British valor doubted."

The royal band now ready stand,
    All ranged in dread array, Sir,
On every slip, on every ship,
    For to begin the fray, Sir.

The cannons roar from shore to shore;
    The small-arms loud did rattle;
Since wars began I'm sure no man
    E'er saw so strange a battle.

The *rebel* dales, the *rebel* vales,
    With *rebel* trees surrounded,
The distant woods, the hills and floods,
    With *rebel* echoes sounded.

The fish below swam to and fro,
    Attack'd from every quarter;
Why, sure (thought they), the De'il's to pay
    'Mong folks above the water.

The kegs, 't is said, though strongly made
    Of *rebel* staves and hoops, Sir,
Could not oppose their pow'rful foes,
    The conq'ering British troops, Sir.

From morn to night these men of might
    Display'd amazing courage;
And when the sun was fairly down,
    Retired to sup their porridge.

A hundred men, with each a pen,
    Or more, upon my word, Sir,

It is most true, would be too few,
  Their valor to record, Sir.

Such feats did they perform that day
  Against these wicked kegs, Sir,
That years to come, *if they get home,*
  They'll make their boasts and brags, Sir.
                            FRANCIS HOPKINSON.

Another pleasant story of the same period,
which also has its foundation in fact, is told by
Mr. Carleton in "The Little Black-Eyed Rebel."
The heroine's name was Mary Redmond, and she
succeeded more than once in helping to smuggle
through letters from soldiers in the Continental
army to their wives in Philadelphia.

THE LITTLE BLACK–EYED REBEL [1]

A BOY drove into the city, his wagon loaded
    down
With food to feed the people of the British-
    governed town;
And the little black-eyed rebel, so innocent
    and sly,
Was watching for his coming from the corner
    of her eye.

His face looked broad and honest, his hands
    were brown and tough,
The clothes he wore upon him were homespun,
    coarse, and rough;
But one there was who watched him, who
    long time lingered nigh,
And cast at him sweet glances from the corner
    of her eye.

He drove up to the market, he waited in the
    line;
His apples and potatoes were fresh and fair
    and fine;
But long and long he waited, and no one came
    to buy,
Save the black-eyed rebel, watching from the
    corner of her eye.

"Now who will buy my apples?" he shouted
    long and loud;
And "Who wants my potatoes?" he repeated
    to the crowd;

¹ From *Poems for Young Americans,* published
by Harper & Bros.

But from all the people round him came no
    word of a reply,
Save the black-eyed rebel, answering from
    the corner of her eye.

For she knew that 'neath the lining of the
    coat he wore that day,
Were long letters from the husbands and the
    fathers far away,
Who were fighting for the freedom that they
    meant to gain or die;
And a tear like silver glistened in the corner
    of her eye.

But the treasures — how to get them? crept
    the question through her mind,
Since keen enemies were watching for what
    prizes they might find:
And she paused awhile and pondered, with
    a pretty little sigh;
Then resolve crept through her features, and a
    shrewdness fired her eye.

So she resolutely walked up to the wagon
    old and red;
"May I have a dozen apples for a kiss?" she
    sweetly said:
And the brown face flushed to scarlet; for
    the boy was somewhat shy,
And he saw her laughing at him from the
    corner of her eye.

"You may have them all for nothing, and
    more, if you want," quoth he.
"I will have them, my good fellow, but can
    pay for them," said she;
And she clambered on the wagon, minding not
    who all were by,
With a laugh of reckless romping in the corner
    of her eye.

Clinging round his brawny neck, she clasped
    her fingers white and small,
And then whispered, "Quick! the letters!
    thrust them underneath my shawl!
Carry back again *this* package, and be sure
    that you are spry!"
And she sweetly smiled upon him from the
    corner of her eye.

Loud the motley crowd were laughing at the
    strange, ungirlish freak,
And the boy was scared and panting, and so
    dashed he could not speak;

And, "Miss, *I* have good apples," a bolder
    lad did cry;
But she answered, "No, I thank you," from
    the corner of her eye.

With the news of loved ones absent to the
    dear friends they would greet,
Searching them who hungered for them,
    swift she glided through the street,
"There is nothing worth the doing that it does
    not pay to try,"
Thought the little black-eyed rebel, with a
    twinkle in her eye.

                            WILL CARLETON.

Early in May, Sir Henry Clinton succeeded
Howe in command of the British forces, and on
June 18, 1778, evacuated Philadelphia, and
started, with his whole army, for New York.
Washington started in pursuit, and on Sunday,
June 28, ordered General Charles Lee, in com-
mand of the advance guard, to fall upon the Brit-
ish left wing near Monmouth Court-House. In-
stead of pressing forward, Lee ordered his men to
retire, and they began to fall into disorder. At
that moment, Washington, summoned by Lafay-
ette, galloped up, white with rage, ordered Lee to
the rear, re-formed the troops, and drove the Brit-
ish back. Night put an end to the conflict, and
Clinton managed to get away under cover of the
darkness, leaving his wounded behind.

THE BATTLE OF MONMOUTH

[June 28, 1778]

WHILST in peaceful quarters lying
    We indulge the glass till late,
Far remote the thought of dying,
    Hear, my friends, the soldier's fate:
From the summer's sun hot beaming,
    Where yon dust e'en clouds the skies,
To the plains where heroes bleeding,
    Shouts and dying groans arise.
        Halt! halt! halt! form every rank here;
            Mark yon dust that climbs the sky,
        To the front close up the long rear,
            See! the enemy is nigh;
        Platoons march at proper distance,
            Cover close each rank and file,
        They will make a bold resistance,
            Here, my lads, is gallant toil.

Now all you from downy slumber
    Roused to the soft joys of love,
Waked to pleasures without number,
    Peace and ease your bosoms prove:

Round us roars Bellona's thunder,
    Ah! how close the iron storm,
O'er the field wild stalks pale wonder,
    Pass the word there, form, lads, form.
        To the left display that column,
            Front, halt, dress, be bold and brave;
        Mark in air yon fiery volume,
            Who'd refuse a glorious grave;
        Ope your boxes, quick, be ready,
            See! our light-bobs gain the hill;
        Courage, boys, be firm and steady,
            Hence each care, each fear lie still.

Now the dismal cannon roaring
    Speaks loud terror to the soul,
Grape shot wing'd with death fast pour-
        ing,
    Ether rings from pole to pole;
See, the smoke, how black and dreary,
    Clouds sulphureous hide the sky,
Wounded, bloody, fainting, weary,
    How their groans ascend on high!
        Firm, my lads; who breaks the line thus?
            Oh! can brave men ever yield,
        Glorious danger now combines us,
            None but cowards quit the field.
        To the rear each gun dismounted;
            Close the breach, and brisk advance
        All your former acts recounted
            This day's merit shall enhance.

Now half-choked with dust and powder,
    Fiercely throbs each bursting vein:
Hark! the din of arms grows louder,
    Ah! what heaps of heroes slain!
See, from flank to flank wide flashing,
    How each volley rends the gloom;
Hear the trumpet; ah! what clashing,
    Man and horse now meet their doom;
        Bravely done! each gallant soldier
            Well sustained this heavy fire;
        Alexander ne'er was bolder;
            Now by regiments retire.
        See, our second line moves on us,
            Ope your columns, give them way,
        Heaven perhaps may smile upon us,
            These may yet regain the day.

Now our second line engaging,
    Charging close, spreads carnage round.
Fierce revenge and fury raging,
    Angry heroes bite the ground.
The souls of brave men here expiring
    Call for vengeance e'en in death,

Frowning still, the dead, the dying,
  Threaten with their latest breath.
    To the left obliquely flying,
      Oh! be ready, level well,
    Who could think of e'er retiring,
      See, my lads, those volleys tell.
  Ah! by heavens, our dragoons flying,
    How the squadrons fill the plain!
  Check them, boys, ye fear not dying,
    Sell your lives, nor fall in vain.

Now our left flank they are turning;
  Carnage is but just begun;
Desperate now, 't is useless mourning,
  Farewell, friends, adieu the sun!
Fix'd to die, we scorn retreating,
  To the shock our breasts oppose,
Hark! the shout, the signal beating,
  See, with bayonets they close:
    Front rank charge! the rear make ready!
      Forward, march — reserve your fire!
    Now present, fire brisk, be steady,
      March, march, see their lines retire!
  On the left, our light troops dashing,
    Now our dragoons charge the rear,
  Shout! huzza! what glorious slashing,
    They run, they run, hence banish fear!

Now the toil and danger 's over,
  Dress alike the wounded brave,
Hope again inspires the lover,
  Old and young forget the grave;
Seize the canteen, poise it higher,
  Rest to each brave soul that fell!
Death for this is ne'er the nigher,
  Welcome mirth, and fear farewell.
                              R. H.

THE BATTLE OF MONMOUTH

[June 28, 1778]

FOUR-AND-EIGHTY years are o'er me; great-
    grandchildren sit before me;
  These my locks are white and scanty, and
    my limbs are weak and worn;
Yet I've been where cannon roaring, firelocks
    rattling, blood outpouring,
  Stirred the souls of patriot soldiers, on the
    tide of battle borne;
Where they told me I was bolder far than
    many a comrade older,
    Though a stripling at that fight for the
      right

All that sultry day in summer beat his sullen
    march the drummer,
  Where the Briton strode the dusty road
    until the sun went down;
Then on Monmouth plain encamping, tired
    and footsore with the tramping,
  Lay all wearily and drearily the forces of
    the crown,
With their resting horses neighing and their
    evening bugles playing,
    And their sentries pacing slow to and fro.

Ere the day to night had shifted, camp was
    broken, knapsacks lifted,
  And in motion was the vanguard of our
    swift-retreating foes;
Grim Knyphausen rode before his brutal
    Hessians, bloody Tories —
  They were fit companions, truly, hirelings
    these and traitors those —
While the careless jest and laughter of the
    teamsters coming after
    Rang around each creaking wain of the
      train.

'T was a quiet Sabbath morning; nature gave
    no sign of warning
  Of the struggle that would follow when we
    met the Briton's might;
Of the horsemen fiercely spurring, of the bul-
    lets shrilly whirring,
  Of the bayonets brightly gleaming through
    the smoke that wrapped the fight;
Of the cannon thunder-pealing, and the
    wounded wretches reeling,
    And the corses gory red of the dead.

Quiet nature had no prescience; but the
    Tories and the Hessians
  Heard the baying of the bugles that were
    hanging on their track;
Heard the cries of eager ravens soaring high
    above the cravens;
  And they hurried, worn and worried, casting
    startled glances back,
Leaving Clinton there to meet us, with his
    bull-dogs fierce to greet us,
    With the veterans of the crown, scarred
      and brown.

For the fight our souls were eager, and each
    Continental leaguer,
  As he gripped his firelock firmly, scarce
    could wait the word to fire;

For his country rose such fervor, in his heart
     of hearts, to serve her,
   That it gladdened him and maddened him
     and kindled raging ire.
Never panther from his fastness, through the
     forest's gloomy vastness,
   Coursed more grimly night and day for
     his prey.

I was in the main force posted; Lee, of whom
     his minions boasted,
   Was commander of the vanguard, and with
     him were Scott and Wayne.
What they did I know not, cared not; in their
     march of shame I shared not;
   But it startled me to see them panic-stricken
     back again,
At the black morass's border, all in headlong,
     fierce disorder.
   With the Briton plying steel at their
     heel.

Outward cool when combat waging, howso-
     ever inward raging,
   Ne'er had Washington shown feeling when
     his forces fled the foe;
But to-day his forehead lowered, and we
     shrank his wrath untoward,
   As on Lee his bitter speech was hurled in
     hissing tones and low:
"Sir, what means this wild confusion? Is it
     cowardice or collusion?
   Is it treachery or fear brings you here?"

Lee grew crimson in his anger — rang his
     curses o'er the clangor,
   O'er the roaring din of battle, as he wrath-
     fully replied;
But his raging was unheeded; fastly on our
     chieftain speeded,
   Rallied quick the fleeing forces, stayed the
     dark, retreating tide;
Then, on foaming steed returning, said to Lee,
     with wrath still burning,
   "Will you now strike a blow at the
     foe?"

At the words Lee drew up proudly, curled his
     lip and answered loudly;
   "Ay!" his voice rang out, "and will not be
     the first to leave the field;"
And his word redeeming fairly, with a skill
     surpassed but rarely,
   Struck the Briton with such ardor that the
     scarlet column reeled;

Then, again, but in good order, past the black
     morass's border,
   Brought his forces rent and torn, spent
     and worn.

As we turned on flanks and centre, in the
     path of death to enter,
   One of Knox's brass six-pounders lost its
     Irish cannoneer;
And his wife who, 'mid the slaughter, had
     been bearing pails of water
   For the gun and for the gunner, o'er his
     body shed no tear.
"Move the piece!" — but there they found
     her loading, firing that six-pounder,
   And she gayly, till we won, worked the gun.

Loud we cheered as Captain Molly waved
     the rammer; then a volley
   Pouring in upon the grenadiers, we sternly
     drove them back;
Though like tigers fierce they fought us, to
     such zeal had Molly brought us
   That, though struck with heat, and thirst-
     ing, yet of drink we felt no lack:
There she stood amid the clamor, busily
     handling sponge and rammer,
   While we swept with wrath condign on
     their line.

From our centre backward driven, with his
     forces rent and riven,
   Soon the foe re-formed in order, dressed
     again his shattered ranks;
In a column firm advancing, from his bayo-
     nets hot rays glancing
   Showed in waving lines of brilliance as he
     fell upon our flanks,
Charging bravely for his master: thus he met
     renewed disaster
   From the stronghold that we held back
     repelled.

Monckton, gallant, cool, and fearless, 'mid
     his bravest comrades peerless,
   Brought his grenadiers to action but to fall
     amid the slain;
Everywhere their ruin found them; red de-
     struction rained around them
   From the mouth of Oswald's cannon, from
     the musketry of Wayne;
While our sturdy Continentals, in their dusty
     regimentals,
   Drove their plumed and scarlet force,
     man and horse.

Beamed the sunlight fierce and torrid o'er
    the raging battle horrid,
Till, in faint exhaustion sinking, death
    was looked on as a boon;
Heat, and not a drop of water — heat, that
    won the race of slaughter,
Fewer far with bullets dying than beneath
    the sun of June;
Only ceased 'he terrible firing, with the Briton
    slow retiring,
    As the sunbeams in the west sank to rest.

On our arms so heavily sleeping, careless
    watch our sentries keeping,
Ready to renew the contest when the dawn-
    ing day should show;
Worn with toil and heat, in slumber soon
    were wrapt our greatest number,
Seeking strength to rise again and fall upon
    the wearied foe;
For we felt his power was broken! but what
    rage was ours outspoken
    When, on waking at the dawn, he had
    gone.

In the midnight still and sombre, while our
    force was wrapt in slumber,
Clinton set his train in motion, sweeping
    fast to Sandy Hook;
Safely from our blows he bore his mingled
    Britons, Hessians, Tories —
Bore away his wounded soldiers, but his
    useless dead forsook;
Fleeing from a worse undoing, and too far
    for our pursuing:
    So we found the field our own, and alone.

How that stirring day comes o'er me! How
    those scenes arise before me!
How I feel a youthful vigor for a moment
    fill my frame!
Those who fought beside me seeing, from the
    dim past brought to being,
By their hands I fain would clasp them —
    ah! each lives but in a name;
But the freedom that they fought for, and
    the country grand they wrought for,
    Is their monument to-day, and for aye.
            THOMAS DUNN ENGLISH.

The most famous incident of the fight, next to
Washington's encounter with Lee, is the exploit
of a camp follower named Molly Pitcher or Molly
McGuire. She was a sturdy, red-haired, freckle-
faced Irishwoman, and during the battle was en-

gaged in carrying water to her husband, who was a
cannoneer. A bullet killed him at his post and
Molly, seizing his rammer as it fell, sprang to take
his place. She served the gun with skill and cour-
age, and on the following morning, covered with
dirt and blood, she was presented by General
Greene to Washington, who conferred upon her a
sergeant's commission.

MOLLY PITCHER

[June 28, 1778]

'T WAS hurry and scurry at Monmouth town,
  For Lee was beating a wild retreat;
The British were riding the Yankees down,
  And panic was pressing on flying feet.

Galloping down like a hurricane
  Washington rode with his sword swung
    high,
Mighty as he of the Trojan plain
  Fired by a courage from the sky.

"Halt, and stand to your guns!" he cried.
  And a bombardier made swift reply.
Wheeling his cannon into the tide,
  He fell 'neath the shot of a foeman nigh.

Molly Pitcher sprang to his side,
  Fired as she saw her husband do.
Telling the king in his stubborn pride
  Women like men to their homes are true.

Washington rode from the bloody fray
  Up to the gun that a woman manned.
"Molly Pitcher, you saved the day,"
  He said, as he gave her a hero's hand.

He named her sergeant with manly praise,
  While her war-brown face was wet with
    tears —
A woman has ever a woman's ways,
  And the army was wild with cheers.
        KATE BROWNLEE SHERWOOD.

MOLLY PITCHER

ALL day the great guns barked and roared;
All day the big balls screeched and soared;
All day, 'mid the sweating gunners grim,
Who toiled in their smoke-shroud dense and
    dim,
Sweet Molly labored with courage high,
With steady hand and watchful eye,

Till the day was ours, and the sinking sun
Looked down on the field of Monmouth won,
And Molly standing beside her gun.

Now, Molly, rest your weary arm!
Safe, Molly, all is safe from harm.
Now, woman, bow your aching head,
And weep in sorrow o'er your dead!

Next day on that field so hardly won,
Stately and calm stands Washington,
And looks where our gallant Greene doth
    lead
A figure clad in motley weed —
A soldier's cap and a soldier's coat
Masking a woman's petticoat.
He greets our Molly in kindly wise;
He bids her raise her tearful eyes;
And now he hails her before them all
Comrade and soldier, whate'er befall,
"And since she has played a man's full part,
A man's reward for her loyal heart!
And Sergeant Molly Pitcher's name
Be writ henceforth on the shield of fame!"

Oh, Molly, with your eyes so blue!
Oh, Molly, Molly, here's to you!
Sweet honor's roll will aye be richer
To hold the name of Molly Pitcher.
                    LAURA E. RICHARDS.

About the middle of July, a strong French fleet,
commanded by Count d'Estaing, arrived off Sandy
Hook, bringing with it M. Gérard, the first minister
from France to the United States. It was found
that the ships could not pass the bar at the mouth
of New York harbor, and it was decided to at-
tempt the capture of the British force which held
Newport, R. I., but the expedition proved a failure,
and the French sailed away to Boston to refit.

YANKEE DOODLE'S EXPEDITION
TO RHODE ISLAND

[August, 1778]

FROM Lewis, Monsieur Gérard came,
    To Congress in this town, sir,
They bow'd to him, and he to them,
    And then they all sat down, sir.

Begar, said Monsieur, one grand coup
    You shall bientot behold, sir;
This was believ'd as gospel true,
    And Jonathan felt bold, sir.

So Yankee Doodle did forget
    The sound of British drum, sir,
How oft it made him quake and sweat,
    In spite of Yankee rum, sir.

He took his wallet on his back,
    His rifle on his shoulder,
And veow'd Rhode Island to attack
    Before he was much older.

In dread array their tatter'd crew
    Advanc'd with colors spread, sir,
Their fifes played Yankee doodle, doo,
    King Hancock at their head, sir.

What numbers bravely cross'd the seas,
    I cannot well determine,
A swarm of rebels and of fleas,
    And every other vermin.

Their mighty hearts might shrink they
    tho't,
For all flesh only grass is,
A plenteous store they therefore bought
    Of whiskey and molasses.

They swore they'd make bold Pigot squeak,
    So did their good ally, sir,
And take him pris'ner in a week,
    But that was all my eye, sir.

As Jonathan so much desir'd
    To shine in martial story,
D'Estaing with politesse retir'd,
    To leave him all the glory.

He left him what was better yet,
    At least it was more use, sir,
He left him for a quick retreat
    A very good excuse, sir.

To stay, unless he rul'd the sea,
    He thought would not be right, sir,
And Continental troops, said he,
    On islands should not fight, sir.

Another cause with these combin'd
    To throw him in the dumps, sir,
For Clinton's name alarmed his mind,
    And made him stir his stumps, sir.

Lord Howe came up, soon afterwards, with the
British fleet, and made a pretence of blockading
the French in Boston harbor, but prudently with-
drew when he saw the French were ready to put

to sea again. The latter abandoned all attempt to coöperate with the Americans and sailed away for the West Indies.

RUNNING THE BLOCKADE

[September, 1778]

WHEN the French fleet lay
In Massachusetts bay
　　In that day

When the British squadron made
Its impudent parade
　　Of blockade;

All along and up and down
The harbor of the town, —
　　The brave, proud town

That had fought with all its might
Its bold, brave fight
　　For the right,

To win its way alone
And hold and rule its own,
　　Such a groan

From the stanch hearts and stout
Of the Yankees there went out:
　　But to rout

The British lion then
Were maddest folly, when
　　One to ten

Their gallant allies lay,
Scant of powder, day by day
　　In the bay.

Chafing thus, impatient, sore,
One day along the shore
　　Slowly bore

A clipper schooner, worn
And rough and forlorn,
　　With its torn

Sails fluttering in the air:
The British sailors stare
　　At her there,

So cool and unafraid.
"What! she's running the blockade,
　　The jade!"

They all at once roar out,
Then — "Damn the Yankee lout!"
　　They shout.

Athwart her bows red hot
They send a challenge shot;
　　But not

An inch to right or left she veers,
Straight on and on she steers,
　　Nor hears

Challenge or shout, until
Rings forth with British will
　　A shrill

"Heave to!" Then sharp and short
Question and quick retort
　　Make British sport.

"What is it that you say, —
Where do I hail from pray,
　　What is my cargo, eh?

"My cargo? I'll allow
You can hear 'em crowin' now,
　　At the bow.

"And I've long-faced gentry too,
For passengers and crew,
　　Just a few,

"To fatten up, you know,
For home use, and a show
　　Of garden sass and so.

"And from Taunton town I hail;
Good Lord, it was a gale
　　When I set sail!"

The British captain laught
As he leaned there abaft:
　　" 'T is a harmless craft,

"And a harmless fellow too,
With his long-faced gentry crew;
　　Let him through,"

He cried; and a gay "Heave ahead!"
Sounded forth, and there sped
　　Down the red

Sunset track, unafraid,
Straight through the blockade,
　　This jade

Of a harmless craft,
Packed full to her draught,
Fore and aft,

With powder and shot.
One day when, red hot
The British got

Their full share and more
Of this cargo, they swore,
With a roar,

At the trick she had played,
This "damned Yankee jade"
Who had run the blockade!
                    NORA PERRY.

The abortive expedition against Rhode Island
practically ended the war at the north, and for a
time the scene of activity was transferred to the
frontier. The Indians had naturally allied them-
selves with the British at the beginning of the war,
and early in September, 1777, attacked Fort Henry,
near Wheeling, but were beaten off after a desper-
ate fight, during which the garrison was saved by
the famous exploit of Elizabeth Zane.

BETTY ZANE

[September, 1777]

WOMEN are timid, cower and shrink
At show of danger, some folk think;
But men there are who for their lives
Dare not so far asperse their wives.
We let that pass — so much is clear,
Though little perils they may fear,
When greater perils men environ,
Then women show a front of iron;
And, gentle in their manner, they
Do bold things in a quiet way,
And so our wondering praise obtain,
As on a time did Betty Zane.

A century since, out in the West,
A block-house was by Girty pressed —
Girty, the renegade, the dread
Of all that border, fiercely led
Five hundred Wyandots, to gain
Plunder and scalp-locks from the slain;
And in this hold — Fort Henry then,
But Wheeling now — twelve boys and men
Guarded with watchful ward and care
Women and prattling children there,
Against their rude and savage foes,
And Betty Zane was one of those.

There had been forty-two at first
When Girty on the border burst;
But most of those who meant to stay
And keep the Wyandots at bay,
Outside by savage wiles were lured,
And ball and tomahawk endured,
Till few were left the place to hold,
And some were boys and some were old;
But all could use the rifle well,
And vainly from the Indians fell,
On puncheon roof and timber wall,
The fitful shower of leaden ball.

Now Betty's brothers and her sire
Were with her in this ring of fire,
And she was ready, in her way,
To aid their labor day by day,
In all a quiet maiden might.
To mould the bullets for the fight,
And, quick to note and so report,
Watch every act outside the fort;
Or, peering through the loopholes, see
Each phase of savage strategy —
These were her tasks, and thus the maid
The toil-worn garrison could aid.

Still, drearily the fight went on
Until a week had nearly gone,
When it was told — a whisper first,
And then in loud alarm it burst —
Their powder scarce was growing; they
Knew where a keg unopened lay
Outside the fort at Zane's — what now?
Their leader stood with anxious brow.
It must be had at any cost,
Or toil and fort and lives were lost.
Some one must do that work of fear;
What man of men would volunteer?

Two offered, and so earnest they,
Neither his purpose would give way;
And Shepherd, who commanded, dare
Not pick or choose between the pair.
But ere they settled on the one
By whom the errand should be done,
Young Betty interposed, and said,
"Let me essay the task instead.
Small matter 't were if Betty Zane,
A useless woman, should be slain;
But death, if dealt on one of those,
Gives too much vantage to our foes."

Her father smiled with pleasure grim —
Her pluck gave painful pride to him:

And while her brothers clamored "No!"
He uttered, "Boys, let Betty go!
She'll do it at less risk than you;
But keep her steady in your view,
And be your rifles shields for her.
If yonder foe make step or stir,
Pick off each wretch who draws a bead,
And so you'll serve her in her need.
Now I recover from surprise,
I think our Betty's purpose wise."

The gate was opened, on she sped;
The foe, astonished, gazed, 't is said,
And wondered at her purpose, till
She gained that log-hut by the hill.
But when, in apron wrapped, the cask
She backward bore, to close her task,
The foemen saw her aim at last,
And poured their fire upon her fast.
Bullet on bullet near her fell,
While rang the Indians' angry yell;
But safely through that whirring rain,
Powder in arms, came Betty Zane.

They filled their horns, both boys and men,
And so began the fight again.
Girty, who there so long had stayed,
By this new feat of feet dismayed,
Fired houses round and cattle slew,
And moved away — the fray was through.
But when the story round was told
How they maintained the leaguered hold,
It was agreed, though fame was due
To all who in that fight were true,
The highest meed of praise, 't was plain,
Fell to the share of Betty Zane.

A hundred years have passed since then;
The savage never came again.
Girty is dust; alike are dead
Those who assailed and those bestead.
Upon those half-cleared, rolling lands,
A crowded city proudly stands;
But of the many who reside
By green Ohio's rushing tide,
Not one has lineage prouder than
Be he or poor or rich) the man
Who boasts that in his spotless strain
Mingles the blood of Betty Zane.

THOMAS DUNN ENGLISH.

Early in July, 1778, the Indians struck a blow at
which the whole country stood aghast. The valley
of Wyoming, in northeastern Pennsylvania, had,
by its fertility, attracted many settlers. The

position of the settlement was peculiarly exposed,
and yet it had sent the best part of its militia to
serve with Washington. This circumstance did
not escape the eyes of the enemy, and on July 3,
1778, a force of twelve hundred Indians and Tories
fell upon the settlement, routed the garrison, tor-
tured the prisoners to death, and plundered and
burned the houses. The settlers fled to the woods,
where nearly a hundred women and children
perished of fatigue and starvation.

THE WYOMING MASSACRE

[July 3, 1778]

KIND Heaven, assist the trembling muse,
    While she attempts to tell
Of poor Wyoming's overthrow
    By savage sons of hell.

One hundred whites, in painted hue,
    Whom Butler there did lead,
Supported by a barb'rous crew
    Of the fierce savage breed.

The last of June the siege began,
    And several days it held,
While many a brave and valiant man
    Lay slaughtered on the field.

Our troops marched out from Forty Fort
    The third day of July,
Three hundred strong, they marched along
    The fate of war to try.

But oh! alas! three hundred men
    Is much too small a band
To meet eight hundred men complete,
    And make a glorious stand.

Four miles they marchèd from the Fort
    Their enemy to meet,
Too far indeed did Butler lead,
    To keep a safe retreat.

And now the fatal hour is come —
    They bravely charge the foe,
And they, with ire, returned the fire,
    Which prov'd our overthrow.

Some minutes they sustained the fire,
    But ere they were aware,
They were encompassed all around,
    Which prov'd a fatal snare.

And then they did attempt to fly,
    But all was now in vain,

Their little host — by far the most —
  Was by those Indians slain.

And as they fly, for quarters cry;
  Oh hear! indulgent Heav'n!
Hard to relate — their dreadful fate,
  No quarters must be given.

With bitter cries and mournful sighs,
  They seek some safe retreat,
Run here and there, they know not where,
  Till awful death they meet.

Their piercing cries salute the skies —
  Mercy is all their cry:
"Our souls prepare God's grace to share,
  We instantly must die."

Some men yet found are flying round
  Sagacious to get clear;
In vain to fly, their foes too nigh!
  They front the flank and rear.

And now the foe hath won the day,
  Methinks their words are these:
"Ye cursed, rebel, Yankee race,
  Will this your Congress please?

"Your pardons crave, you them shall have,
  Behold them in our hands;
We'll all agree to set you free,
  By dashing out your brains.

"And as for you, enlisted crew,
  We'll raise your honors higher:
Pray turn your eye, where you must lie,
  In yonder burning fire."

Then naked in those flames they're cast,
  Too dreadful 't is to tell,
Where they must fry, and burn and die,
  While cursed Indians yell.

Nor son, nor sire, these tigers spare, —
  The youth, and hoary head,
Were by those monsters murdered there,
  And numbered with the dead.

Methinks I hear some sprightly youth
  His mournful state condole:
"Oh, that my tender parents knew
  The anguish of my soul!

"But oh! there's none to save my life,
  Or heed my dreadful fear;

I see the tomahawk and knife,
  And the more glittering spear.

"When years ago, I dandled was
  Upon my parents' knees,
I little thought I should be brought
  To feel such pangs as these.

"I hoped for many a joyful day,
  I hoped for riches' store —
These golden dreams are fled away;
  I straight shall be no more.

"Farewell, fond mother; late I was
  Locked up in your embrace;
Your heart would ache, and even break,
  If you could know my case.

"Farewell, indulgent parents dear,
  I must resign my breath;
I now must die, and here must lie
  In the cold arms of death.

"For oh! the fatal hour is come,
  I see the bloody knife, —
The Lord have mercy on my soul!'"
  And quick resigned his life.

A doleful theme; yet, pensive muse,
  Pursue the doleful theme;
It is no fancy to delude,
  Nor transitory dream.

The Forty Fort was the resort
  For mother and for child,
To save them from the cruel rage
  Of the fierce savage wild.

Now, when the news of this defeat
  Had sounded in our ears,
You well may know our dreadful woe,
  And our foreboding fears.

A doleful sound is whispered round,
  The sun now hides his head;
The nightly gloom forebodes our doom,
  We all shall soon be dead.

How can we bear the dreadful spear,
  The tomahawk and knife?
And if we run, the awful gun
  Will rob us of our life.

But Heaven! kind Heaven, propitious power
  His hand we must adore.

He did assuage the savage rage,
  That they should kill no more.

The gloomy night now gone and past,
  The sun returns again,
The little birds from every bush
  Seem to lament the slain.

With aching hearts and trembling hands,
  We walkèd here and there,
Till through the northern pines we saw
  A flag approaching near.

Some men were chose to meet this flag,
  Our colonel was the chief,
Who soon returned and in his mouth
  He brought an olive leaf.

This olive leaf was granted life,
  But then we must no more
Pretend to fight with Britain's king,
  Until the wars are o'er.

And now poor Westmoreland is lost,
  Our forts are all resigned,
Our buildings they are all on fire, —
  What shelter can we find?

They did agree in black and white,
  If we'd lay down our arms,
That all who pleased might quietly
  Remain upon their farms.

But oh! they've robbed us of our all,
  They've taken all but life,
And we'll rejoice and bless the Lord,
  If this may end the strife.

And now I've told my mournful tale,
  I hope you'll all agree
To help our cause and break the jaws
  Of cruel tyranny.

URIAH TERRY

CHAPTER VIII

THE WAR ON THE WATER

At the outbreak of the Revolution, the colonies had no navy, but a number of cruisers and privateers were soon fitted out, and by the end of 1776 nearly three hundred British vessels had fallen into the hands of the Americans. This activity was kept up during the succeeding year, the cruise of the Fair American, as described in the old ballad of that name, being one of the most noteworthy.

THE CRUISE OF THE FAIR AMERICAN

[1777]

THE twenty-second of August,
  Before the close of day,
All hands on board of our privateer,
  We got her under weigh;
We kept the Eastern shore along,
  For forty leagues or more,
Then our departure took for sea,
  From the isle of Mauhegan shore.

Bold Hawthorne was commander,
  A man of real worth,
Old England's cruel tyranny
  Induced him to go forth;

She, with relentless fury,
  Was plundering all our coast,
And thought, because her strength was great,
  Our glorious cause was lost.

Yet boast not, haughty Britons,
  Of power and dignity,
By land thy conquering armies,
  Thy matchless strength at sea;
Since taught by numerous instances
  Americans can fight,
With valor can equip their stand,
  Your armies put to flight.

Now farewell to fair America,
  Farewell our friends and wives;
We trust in Heaven's peculiar care
  For to protect their lives;
To prosper our intended cruise
  Upon the raging main,
And to preserve our dearest friends
  Till we return again.

The wind it being leading,
  It bore us on our way,

As far unto the southward
  As the Gulf of Florida;
Where we fell in with a British ship,
  Bound homeward from the main;
We gave her two bow-chasers,
  And she returned the same.

We haulèd up our courses,
  And so prepared for fight;
The contest held four glasses,
  Until the dusk of night;
Then having sprung our main-mast,
  And had so large a sea,
We dropped astern and left our chase
  Till the returning day.

Next morn we fished our main-mast,
  The ship still being nigh,
All hands made for engaging,
  Our chance once more to try;
But wind and sea being boisterous,
  Our cannon would not bear,
We thought it quite imprudent
  And so we left her there.

We cruisèd to the eastward,
  Near the coast of Portugal,
In longitude of twenty-seven
  We saw a lofty sail;
We gave her chase, and soon perceived
  She was a British snow
Standing for fair America,
  With troops for General Howe.

Our captain did inspect her
  With glasses, and he said,
"My boys, she means to fight us,
  But be you not afraid;
All hands repair to quarters,
  See everything is clear,
We'll give her a broadside, my boys,
  As soon as she comes near."

She was prepared with nettings,
  And her men were well secured,
And bore directly for us,
  And put us close on board;
When the cannon roared like thunder,
  And the muskets fired amain,
But soon we were alongside
  And grappled to her chain.

And now the scene it altered,
  The cannon ceased to roar,
We fought with swords and boarding-pikes
  One glass or something more,

Till British pride and glory
  No longer dared to stay,
But cut the Yankee grapplings,
  And quickly bore away.

Our case was not so desperate
  As plainly might appear;
Yet sudden death did enter
  On board our privateer.
Mahoney, Crew, and Clemmons,
  The valiant and the brave,
Fell glorious in the contest,
  And met a watery grave.

Ten other men were wounded
  Among our warlike crew,
With them our noble captain,
  To whom all praise is due;
To him and all our officers
  Let's give a hearty cheer;
Success to fair America
  And our good privateer.

The Americans were not without their losses,
and one of the most serious occurred early in 1778.
On the morning of March 7, the 32-gun frigate
Randolph, Captain Nicholas Biddle, while cruis-
ing off Barbadoes, fell in with the English 64-gun
ship of the line Yarmouth, and attacked imme-
diately. The fight had lasted about an hour when
the Randolph's magazine was in some way fired,
and the ship blew up. Of the crew of three hundred
and fifteen, only four were saved.

ON THE DEATH OF CAPTAIN
NICHOLAS BIDDLE

[March 7, 1778]

WHAT distant thunders rend the skies,
What clouds of smoke in volumes rise,
  What means this dreadful roar!
Is from his base Vesuvius thrown,
Is sky-topt Atlas tumbled down,
  Or Etna's self no more!

Shock after shock torments my ear;
And lo! two hostile ships appear,
  Red lightnings round them glow:
The Yarmouth boasts of sixty-four,
The Randolph thirty-two — no more —
  And will she fight this foe!

The Randolph soon on Stygian streams
Shall coast along the land of dreams,
  The islands of the dead!

But fate, that parts them on the deep,
Shall save the Briton, still to weep
 His ancient honors fled.

Say, who commands that dismal blaze,
Where yonder starry streamer plays;
 Does Mars with Jove engage!
'T is Biddle wings those angry fires,
Biddle, whose bosom Jove inspires
 With more than mortal rage.

Tremendous flash! and hark, the ball
Drives through old Yarmouth, flames and all;
 Her bravest sons expire;
Did Mars himself approach so nigh,
Even Mars, without disgrace, might fly
 The Randolph's fiercer fire.

The Briton views his mangled crew,
"And shall we strike to *thirty-two*"
 (Said Hector, stained with gore);
"Shall Britain's flag to these descend —
Rise, and the glorious conflict end,
 Britons, I ask no more!"

He spoke — they charged their cannon round,
Again the vaulted heavens resound,
 The Randolph bore it all,
Then fixed her pointed cannons true —
Away the unwieldy vengeance flew;
 Britain, the warriors fall.

The Yarmouth saw, with dire dismay,
Her wounded hull, shrouds shot away,
 Her boldest heroes dead —
She saw amidst her floating slain
The conquering Randolph stem the main —
 She saw, she turned, and fled!

That hour, blest chief, had she been thine,
Dear Biddle, had the powers divine
 Been kind as thou wert brave;
But fate, who doomed thee to expire,
Prepared an arrow tipped with fire,
 And marked a watery grave,

And in that hour when conquest came
Winged at his ship a pointed flame
 That not even *he* could shun —
The conquest ceased, the Yarmouth fled,
The bursting Randolph ruin spread,
 And lost what honor won.
     PHILIP FRENEAU.

Among the most successful of the Yankee privateers was the Providence, and her most famous exploit was performed in July, 1779, when she attacked a fleet of merchantmen, under convoy of a ship of the line and some cruisers, and captured ten prizes, nine of which, valued at over a million dollars, were got safely to Boston. The Providence was commanded by Abraham Whipple, the hero of the Gaspee exploit and of a hundred others.

THE YANKEE PRIVATEER

[July, 1779]

COME listen and I'll tell you
 How first I went to sea,
To fight against the British
 And earn our liberty.
We shipped with Cap'n Whipple
 Who never knew a fear,
The Captain of the Providence,
 The Yankee Privateer.

We sailed and we sailed
 And made good cheer,
There were many pretty men
 On the Yankee Privateer.

The British Lord High Admiral
 He wished old Whipple harm,
He wrote that he would hang him
 At the end of his yard arm.
"My Lord," wrote Cap'n Whipple back,
 "It seems to me it's clear
That if you want to hang him,
 You must catch your Privateer."

We sailed and we sailed
 And made good cheer,
For not a British frigate
 Could come near the Privateer.

We sailed to the south'ard,
 And nothing did we meet,
Till we found three British frigates
 And their West Indian fleet.
Old Whipple shut our ports
 As we crawled up near,
And he sent us all below
 On the Yankee Privateer.

So slowly he sailed
 We dropped to the rear,
And not a soul suspected
 The Yankee Privateer.

At night we put the lights out
  And forward we ran
And silently we boarded
  The biggest merchantman.
We knocked down the watch, —
  And the lubbers shook for fear,
She's a prize without a shot
  To the Yankee Privateer.

We sent the prize north
  While we lay near
And all day we slept
  On the bold Privateer.

For ten nights we followed,
  And ere the moon rose,
Each night a prize we'd taken
  Beneath the Lion's nose.
When the British looked to see
  Why their ships should disappear,
They found they had in convoy
  A Yankee Privateer.

But we sailed and sailed
  And made good cheer!
Not a coward was on board
  Of the Yankee Privateer.

The biggest British frigate
  Bore round to give us chase,
But though he was the fleeter
  Old Whipple would n't race,
Till he'd raked her fore and aft,
  For the lubbers could n't steer,
Then he showed them the heels
  Of the Yankee Privateer.

Then we sailed and we sailed
  And we made good cheer,
For not a British frigate
  Could come near the Privateer.

Then northward we sailed
  To the town we all know,
And there lay our prizes
  All anchored in a row;
And welcome were we
  To our friends so dear,
And we shared a million dollars
  On the bold Privateer.

We'd sailed and we'd sailed
  And we made good cheer,
We had all full pockets
  On the bold Privateer.

Then we each manned a ship
  And our sails we unfurled,
And we bore the Stars and Stripes
  O'er the oceans of the world.
From the proud flag of Britain
  We swept the seas clear,
And we earned our independence
  On the Yankee Privateer.

Then landsmen and sailors,
  One more cheer!
Here is three times three
  For the Yankee Privateer!

ARTHUR HALE.

The achievements of other American naval captains were soon eclipsed by those of John Paul Jones, a Scotch sailor, settled in Virginia, who, at the outbreak of the war, offered his services to Congress. In 1776, on board the Alfred, in the Delaware River, he raised the first flag of the Revolution, — a pine tree, with a rattlesnake coiled at the foot, and the motto, "Don't tread on me."

PAUL JONES

A SONG unto Liberty's brave Buccaneer,
  Ever bright be the fame of the patriot
    Rover,
For our rights he first fought in his "black
    privateer,"
  And faced the proud foe ere our sea they
    cross'd over,
      In their channel and coast,
      He scattered their host,
And proud Britain robbed of her sea-ruling
    boast,
And her rich merchants' barks shunned the
    ocean in fear
Of Paul Jones, fair Liberty's brave Buccaneer.

In the first fleet that sailed in defence of our
    land,
  Paul Jones forward stood to defend freedom's arbor,
He led the bold Alfred at Hopkins' command,
  And drove the fierce foeman from Providence harbor,
      'T was his hand that raised
      The first flag that blazed,
And his deeds 'neath the "Pine tree" all
    ocean amaz'd,
For hundreds of foes met a watery bier
From Paul Jones, fair Liberty's brave Buccaneer.

His arm crushed the Tory and mutinous crew
   That strove to have freemen inhumanly
      butchered;
Remember his valor at proud Flamborough,
   When he made the bold Serapis strike to
      the Richard;
      Oh! he robbed of their store
      The vessels sent o'er
To feed all the Tories and foes on our
      shore,
He gave freemen the spoils and long may they
      revere
The name of fair Liberty's bold Buccaneer.

In 1778 he was sent with the 18-gun ship Ranger to prowl about the British coasts. He entered the Irish Channel, seized the Lord Chatham, set fire to the shipping at Whitehaven, and captured the British 20-gun sloop Drake, after a fierce fight. With the Drake and several merchant prizes, he made his way to Brest, and prepared for a more important expedition which was fitting out for the following year.

THE YANKEE MAN–OF–WAR

[1778]

'T is of a gallant Yankee ship that flew the
   stripes and stars,
And the whistling wind from the west-nor'-
   west blew through the pitch-pine
   spars, —
With her starboard tacks aboard, my boys,
   she hung upon the gale,
On an autumn night we raised the light on
   the old head of Kinsale.

t was a clear and cloudless night, and the
   wind blew steady and strong,
As gayly over the sparkling deep our good ship
   bowled along;
With the foaming seas beneath her bow the
   fiery waves she spread,
And bending low her bosom of snow, she
   buried her lee cat-head.

There was no talk of short'ning sail by him
   who walked the poop,
And under the press of her pond'ring jib, the
   boom bent like a hoop!
And the groaning water-ways told the strain
   that held her stout main-tack,
But he only laughed as he glanced aloft at a
   white and silv'ry track.

The mid-tide meets in the channel waves that
   flow from shore to shore,
And the mist hung heavy upon the land from
   Featherstone to Dunmore,
And that sterling light in Tusker Rock where
   the old bell tolls each hour,
And the beacon light that shone so bright was
   quench'd on Waterford Tower.

The nightly robes our good ship wore were
   her own top-sails three,
Her spanker and her standing jib — the
   courses being free;
"Now, lay aloft! my heroes bold, let not a
   moment pass!"
And royals and top-gallant sails were quickly
   on each mast.

What looms upon our starboard bow? What
   hangs upon the breeze?
'T is time our good ship hauled her wind
   abreast the old Saltee's,
For by her ponderous press of sail and by her
   consorts four
We saw our morning visitor was a British
   man-of-war.

Up spake our noble Captain then, as a shot
   ahead of us past —
"Haul snug your flowing courses! lay your
   top-sail to the mast!"
Those Englishmen gave three loud hur-
   rahs from the deck of their covered
   ark,
And we answered back by a solid broadside
   from the decks of our patriot bark.

"Out booms! out booms." our skipper cried,
   "out booms and give her sheet,"
And the swiftest keel that was ever launched
   shot ahead of the British fleet,
And amidst a thundering shower of shot with
   stun'-sails hoisting away,
Down the North Channel Paul Jones did steer
   just at the break of day.

The new squadron sailed for the English coast in the summer of 1779. It consisted of the flagship — a clumsy old Indiaman called the Duras, whose name Jones changed to Bon Homme Richard — and four consorts. The summer was spent in cruising about the British coast and so much damage was done that Paul Jones became a sort of bogey to all England.

PAUL JONES — A NEW SONG

Of heroes and statesmen I'll just mention
        four,
That cannot be match'd, if we trace the world
        o'er,
For none of such fame ever stept o'er the
        stones,
As Green, Jemmy Twitcher, Lord North, and
        Paul Jones.

Thro' a mad-hearted war, which old England
        will rue,
At London, at Dublin, and Edinburgh, too,
The tradesmen stand still, and the merchant
        bemoans
The losses he meets with from such as Paul
        Jones.

How happy for England, would Fortune but
        sweep
At once all her treacherous foes to the
        deep;
For the land under burthens most bitterly
        groans,
To get rid of some that are worse than Paul
        Jones.

To each honest heart that is Britain's true
        friend,
In bumpers I'll freely this toast recom-
        mend,
May Paul be converted, the Ministry purg'd,
Old England be free, and her enemies
        scourg'd!

If success to our fleets be not quickly re-
        stor'd,
The Leaders in office to shove from the
        board;
May they all fare alike, and the De'il pick
        the bones
Of Green, Jemmy Twitcher, Lord North, and
        Paul Jones!

On September 23, 1779, the little squadron
sighted a British fleet of forty sail off Flambor-
ough Head. They were merchantmen bound for
the Baltic under convoy of the Serapis, forty-
four, and the Countess of Scarborough, twenty.
Captain Jones instantly gave chase, ordering his
consorts to form in line of battle, but the Alliance,
whose command had been given to a Frenchman,
ran off to some distance, leaving the Richard to
attack the Serapis single-handed, while the Pallas
took care of the Scarborough.

PAUL JONES

[September 23, 1779]

An American frigate from Baltimore came,
Her guns mounted forty, the Richard by
        name;
Went to cruise in the channel of old Eng-
        land,
With a noble commander, Paul Jones was
        the man.

We had not sail'd long before we did espy
A large forty-four, and a twenty close by:
These two warlike ships, full laden with
        store,
Our captain pursued to the bold Yorkshire
        shore.

At the hour of twelve, Pierce came along-
        side.
With a loud speaking-trumpet, "Whence
        came you?" he cried;
"Quick give me an answer, I hail'd you
        before,
Or this very instant a broadside I'll pour."

Paul Jones he exclaimed, "My brave boys,
        we'll not run:
Let every brave seaman stand close to his
        gun;"
When a broadside was fired by these brave
        Englishmen,
We bold buckskin heroes return'd it again.

We fought them five glasses, five glasses most
        hot,
Till fifty brave seamen lay dead on the spot
And full seventy more lay bleeding in their
        gore,
Whilst Pierce's loud cannon on the Richard
        did roar.

Our gunner, affrighted, unto Paul Jones he
        came,
"Our ship is a-sinking, likewise in a flame;
Paul Jones he replied, in the height of his
        pride,
"If we can do no better, we'll sink along-
        side."

At length our shot flew so quick, they could
        not stand:
The flag of proud Britain was forced to come
        down,

The Alliance bore down and the Richard did rake,
Which caused the heart of Richard to ache.

Come now, my brave buckskin, we've taken a prize,
A large forty-four, and a twenty likewise;
They are both noble vessels, well laden with store!
We will toss off the can to our country once more.

God help the poor widows, who shortly must weep
For the loss of their husbands, now sunk in the deep!
We'll drink to brave Paul Jones, who, with sword in hand,
Shone foremost in action, and gave us command.

The Serapis was greatly superior to the Richard in armament and fighting qualities, but Jones succeeded in running his vessel into her and lashing fast. So close did they lie that their yardarms interlocked and both ships were soon covered with dead and wounded. At the end of two hours, the Serapis was on fire; but the Richard was ready sinking. Half an hour later the Serapis surrendered. The Richard was kept afloat with great difficulty until morning, when she sank.

THE BONHOMME RICHARD AND SERAPIS

[September 23, 1779]

OER the rough main, with flowing sheet,
The guardian of a numerous fleet,
Serapis from the Baltic came:
A ship of less tremendous force
Sail'd by her side the self-same course,
The Countess of Scarb'ro' was her name.

And now their native coasts appear,
Britannia's hills their summits rear
Above the German main;
And to suppose their dangers o'er,
They southward coast along the shore,
Thy waters, gentle Thames, to gain.

Full forty guns Serapis bore,
And Scarb'ro's Countess twenty-four,
Mann'd with Old England's boldest tars—
What flag that rides the Gallic seas
Will dare attack such piles as these,
Design'd for tumults and for wars!

Now from the top-mast's giddy height
A seaman cry'd — "Four sail in sight
Approach with favoring gales."
Pearson, resolv'd to save the fleet,
Stood off to sea, these ships to meet,
And closely brac'd his shivering sails.

With him advanc'd the Countess bold,
Like a black tar in wars grown old:
And now these floating piles drew nigh.
But, muse, unfold what chief of fame
In the other warlike squadron came,
Whose standards at his mast-head fly.

'T was Jones, brave Jones, to battle led
As bold a crew as ever bled
Upon the sky-surrounded main;
The standards of the western world
Were to the willing winds unfurl'd,
Denying Britain's tyrant reign.

The Good-Man-Richard led the line;
The Alliance next: with these combine
The Gallic ship they Pallas call,
The Vengeance arm'd with sword and flame;
These to attack the Britons came —
But two accomplish'd all.

Now Phœbus sought his pearly bed:
But who can tell the scenes of dread,
The horrors of that fatal night!
Close up these floating castles came:
The Good-Man-Richard bursts in flame;
Serapis trembled at the sight.

She felt the fury of her ball:
Down, prostrate, down the Britons fall;
The decks were strew'd with slain:
Jones to the foe his vessel lash'd;
And, while the black artillery flash'd,
Loud thunders shook the main.

Alas! that mortals should employ
Such murdering engines to destroy
That frame by heaven so nicely join'd;
Alas! that e'er the god decreed
That brother should by brother bleed,
And pour'd such madness in the mind.

But thou, brave Jones, no blame shalt bear,
The rights of man demand your care:
For these you dare the greedy waves.
No tyrant, on destruction bent,
Has plann'd thy conquest — thou art sent
To humble tyrants and their slaves.

See! — dread Serapis flames again —
And art thou, Jones, among the slain,
    And sunk to Neptune's caves below? —
He lives — though crowds around him
        fall,
Still he, unhurt, survives them all;
    Almost alone he fights the foe.

And can your ship these strokes sustain?
Behold your brave companions slain,
    All clasp'd in ocean's cold embrace;
STRIKE, OR BE SUNK — the Briton cries —
SINK IF YOU CAN — the chief replies,
    Fierce lightnings blazing in his face.

Then to the side three guns he drew
(Almost deserted by his crew),
    And charg'd them deep with woe;
By Pearson's flash he aim'd hot balls;
His main-mast totters — down it falls —
    O'erwhelming half below.

Pearson had yet disdain'd to yield,
But scarce his secret fears conceal'd,
    And thus was heard to cry —
"With hell, not mortals, I contend;
What art thou — human, or a fiend,
    That dost my force defy?

"Return, my lads, the fight renew!" —
So call'd bold Pearson to his crew;
    But call'd, alas! in vain;
Some on the decks lay maim'd and dead;
Some to their deep recesses fled,
    And hosts were shrouded in the main.

Distress'd, forsaken, and alone,
He haul'd his tatter'd standard down,
    And yielded to his gallant foe;
Bold Pallas soon the Countess took, —
Thus both their haughty colors struck,
    Confessing what the brave can do.

But, Jones, too dearly didst thou buy
These ships possest so gloriously,
    Too many deaths disgrac'd the fray:
Thy barque that bore the conquering
        flame,
That the proud Briton overcame,
    Even she forsook thee on thy way;

For when the morn began to shine,
Fatal to her, the ocean brine
    Pour'd through each spacious wound;

Quick in the deep she disappear'd —
But Jones to friendly Belgia steer'd,
    With conquest and with glory crown'd.

Go on, great man, to scourge the foe,
And bid these haughty Britons know
    They to our *Thirteen Stars* shall bend;
Those *Stars* that, veil'd in dark attire,
Long glimmer'd with a feeble fire,
    But radiant now ascend.

Bend to the Stars that flaming rise
In western, not in eastern, skies,
    Fair Freedom's reign restored —
So when the Magi, come from far,
Beheld the God-attending Star,
    They trembled and ador'd.

                        PHILIP FRENEAU.

Another remarkable action was that between
the Hyder Ali and the General Monk. The latter,
a cruiser mounting twenty nine-pounders, had
been harassing the American shipping in Delaware
Bay, and the merchants of Philadelphia finally
equipped the Hyder Ali, an old merchantman
with sixteen six-pounders, put Joshua Barney in
command and started him after the British ship.

BARNEY'S INVITATION

[April, 1782]

COME all ye lads who know no fear,
To wealth and honor with me steer
In the Hyder Ali privateer,
    Commanded by brave Barney.

She's new and true, and tight and sound,
Well rigged aloft, and all well found —
Come away and be with laurel crowned,
    Away — and leave your lasses.

Accept our terms without delay,
And make your fortunes while you may,
Such offers are not every day
    In the power of the jolly sailor.

Success and fame attend the brave,
But death the coward and the slave,
Who fears to plough the Atlantic wave,
    To seek the bold invaders.

Come, then, and take a cruising bout,
Our ship sails well, there is no doubt,
She has been tried both in and out,
    And answers expectation.

Let no proud foes whom Europe bore,
Distress our trade, insult our shore —
Teach them to know their reign is o'er,
    Bold Philadelphia sailors!

We'll teach them how to sail so near,
Or to venture on the Delaware,
When we in warlike trim appear
    And cruise without Henlopen.

Who cannot wounds and battle dare
Shall never clasp the blooming fair;
The brave alone their charms should share,
    The brave are their protectors.

With hand and heart united all,
Prepared to conquer or to fall,
Attend, my lads, to honor's call,
    Embark in our Hyder Ali.

From an Eastern prince she takes her
    name,
Who, smit with Freedom's sacred flame,
Usurping Britons brought to shame,
    His country's wrongs avenging;

See, on her stern the waving stars —
Inured to blood, inured to wars,
Come, enter quick, my jolly tars,
    To scourge these warlike Britons.

Here's grog enough — then drink a bout,
I know your hearts are firm and stout;
American blood will never give out,
    And often we have proved it.

Though stormy oceans round us roll,
We'll keep a firm undaunted soul,
Befriended by the cheering bowl,
    Sworn foes to melancholy·

When timorous landsmen lurk on shore,
'Tis ours to go where cannons roar —
On a coasting cruise we'll go once more,
    Despisers of all danger;

And Fortune still, who crowns the brave,
Shall guard us over the gloomy wave;
A fearful heart betrays the knave —
    Success to the Hyder Ali.
             PHILIP FRENEAU.

The Hyder Ali sailed down the bay April 8,
'82, and met the Englishman near the capes.
By skilful manœuvring, Barney was able to
rake his antagonist; then, lashing fast, poured
several broadsides in rapid succession into the
enemy, who struck their colors at the end of thirty
minutes.

SONG

ON CAPTAIN BARNEY'S VICTORY OVER THE SHIP GENERAL MONK

[April 8, 1782]

O'ER the waste of waters cruising,
    Long the General Monk had reigned;
All subduing, all reducing,
    None her lawless rage restrained:
Many a brave and hearty fellow
    Yielding to this warlike foe,
When her guns began to bellow
    Struck his humbled colors low.

But grown bold with long successes,
    Leaving the wide watery way,
She, a stranger to distresses,
    Came to cruise within Cape May:
"Now we soon (said Captain Rogers)
    Shall their men of commerce meet;
In our hold we'll have them lodgers,
    We shall capture half their fleet.

"Lo! I see their van appearing —
    Back our topsails to the mast —
They toward us full are steering
    With a gentle western blast:
I've a list of all their cargoes,
    All their guns, and all their men:
I am sure these modern Argos
    Can't escape us one in ten:

"Yonder comes the Charming Sally
    Sailing with the General Greene —
First we'll fight the Hyder Ali,
    Taking her is taking them:
She intends to give us battle,
    Bearing down with all her sail —
Now, boys, let our cannon rattle!
    To take her we cannot fail.

"Our eighteen guns, each a nine-pounder,
    Soon shall terrify this foe;
We shall maul her, we shall wound her,
    Bringing rebel colors low." —
While he thus anticipated
    Conquests that he could not gain,
He in the Cape May channel waited
    For the ship that caused his pain.

Captain Barney then preparing,
  Thus addressed his gallant crew —
"Now, brave lads, be bold and daring,
  Let your hearts be firm and true;
This is a proud English cruiser,
  Roving up and down the main,
We must fight her — must reduce her,
  Though our decks be strewed with slain.

"Let who will be the survivor,
  We must conquer or must die,
We must take her up the river,
  Whate'er comes of you or I:
Though she shows most formidable
  With her eighteen pointed nines,
And her quarters clad in sable,
  Let us balk her proud designs.

"With four nine-pounders, and twelve sixes
  We will face that daring band;
Let no dangers damp your courage,
  Nothing can the brave withstand.
Fighting for your country's honor,
  Now to gallant deeds aspire;
Helmsman, bear us down upon her,
  Gunner, give the word to fire!"

Then yardarm and yardarm meeting,
  Strait began the dismal fray,
Cannon mouths, each other greeting,
  Belched their smoky flames away:
Soon the langrage, grape and chain shot,
  That from Barney's cannons flew,
Swept the Monk, and cleared each round
      top,
  Killed and wounded half her crew.

Captain Rogers strove to rally
  But they from their quarters fled,
While the roaring Hyder Ali
  Covered o'er his decks with dead.
When from their tops their dead men
      tumbled,
  And the streams of blood did flow,
Then their proudest hopes were humbled
  By their brave inferior foe.

All aghast, and all confounded,
  They beheld their champions fall,
And their captain, sorely wounded,
  Bade them quick for quarters call.
Then the Monk's proud flag descended,
  And her cannon ceased to roar;
By her crew no more defended,
  She confessed the contest o'er.

Come, brave boys, and fill your glasses,
  You have humbled one proud foe,
No brave action this surpasses,
  Fame shall tell the nation so —
Thus be Britain's woes completed,
  Thus abridged her cruel reign,
Till she ever, thus defeated,
  Yields the sceptre of the main.
                    PHILIP FRENEAU.

The last naval action of the war occurred December 19, 1782, when the American ship, South Carolina, forty guns, was chased and captured off the Delaware, by the British ships Quebec, Diomede, and Astrea, carrying ninety-eight guns. A few days later a ballad describing the affair appeared in the loyalist papers as a letter "from a dejected Jonathan, a prisoner taken in the South Carolina, to his brother Ned at Philadelphia."

THE SOUTH CAROLINA

[December 19, 1782]

My dear brother Ned,
  We are knock'd on the head,
No more let America boast;
  We may all go to bed,
  And that's enough said,
For the South Carolina we've lost.

The pride of our eyes,
  I swear is a prize,
You never will see her again,
  Unless thro' surprise,
  You are brought where she lies,
A prisoner from the false main.

Oh Lord! what a sight! —
  I was struck with affright,
When the Diomede's shot round us fell
  I feared that in spite,
  They'd have slain us outright,
And sent us directly to h—l.

The Quebec did fire,
  Or I'm a curs'd liar,
And the Astrea came up apace;
  We could not retire
  From the confounded fire,
They all were so eager in chase.

The Diomede's shot
  Was damnation hot,
She was several times in a blaze;

It was not my lot
To go then to pot,
But I veow, I was struck with amaze.

And Ned, may I die,
Or be pok'd in a sty,
If ever I venture again
Where bullets do fly,
And the wounded do cry,
Tormented with anguish and pain.

The Hope, I can tell,
And the brig Constance fell,
I swear, and I veow, in our sight;
The first I can say,
Was taken by day,
But the latter was taken at night.

I die to relate
What has been our fate,
How sadly our navies are shrunk;
The pride of our State
Begins to abate,
For the branches are lopp'd from the
trunk.

The Congress must bend,
We shall fall in the end,
For the curs'd British sarpents are tough;
But, I think as you find,
I have enough penn'd
Of such cursèd, such vexatious stuff.

Yet how vexing to find
We are left all behind,
That by sad disappointment we're cross d;
Ah, fortune unkind!
Thou afflicted'st my mind,
When the South Carolina we lost.

Our enemy vile,
Cunning Digby does smile,
Is pleasèd at our mischance;
He useth each wile
Our fleets to beguile,
And to check our commerce with France.

No more as a friend,
Our ships to defend,
Of South Carolina we boast;
As a foe in the end,
She will us attend,
For the South Carolina we've lost.

CHAPTER IX

NEW YORK AND THE "NEUTRAL GROUND"

For more than a year following the battle of onmouth, Sir Henry Clinton remained cooped in New York, while Washington, established in mp at White Plains, kept a sharp eye upon him. he thirty miles between their lines, embracing arly all of Westchester County, was known as e "Neutral Ground." New York was naturally owded with Royalist refugees, whom Clinton t to work on the fortifications.

IR HENRY CLINTON'S INVITATION TO THE REFUGEES

[1779]

ME, gentlemen Tories, firm, loyal, and true,
re are axes and shovels, and something
to do!
For the sake of our King,
Come labor and sing.
u left all you had for his honor and glory,
d he will remember the suffering Tory.

We have, it is true,
Some small work to do;
But here's for your pay, twelve coppers a day,
And never regard what the rebels may say,
But throw off your jerkins and labor away.

To raise up the rampart, and pile up the
wall,
To pull down old houses and dig the canal,
To build and destroy,
Be this your employ,
In the daytime to work at our fortifications,
And steal in the night from the rebels your
rations.
The King wants your aid,
Not empty parade;
Advance to your places, ye men of long faces,
Nor ponder too much on your former dis-
graces;
This year, I presume, will quite alter your
cases.

Attend at the call of the fifer and drummer,
The French and the rebels are coming next
 summer,
  And the forts we must build
  Though the Tories are killed.
Take courage, my jockies, and work for your
 King,
For if you are taken, no doubt you will swing.
  If York we can hold,
  I'll have you enroll'd;
And after you're dead, your names shall be
 read,
As who for their monarch both labor'd and
 bled,
And ventur'd their necks for their beef and
 their bread.

'T is an hour to serve the bravest of nations,
And be left to be hanged in their capitulations.
  Then scour up your mortars,
  And stand to your quarters,
'T is nonsense for Tories in battle to run,
They never need fear sword, halberd, or gun;
  Their hearts should not fail 'em,
  No balls will assail 'em,
Forget your disgraces, and shorten your faces,
For 't is true as the gospel, believe it or not,
Who are born to be hang'd, will never be shot.
     PHILIP FRENEAU.

On the last day of May, Clinton had succeeded
in capturing the fortress at Stony Point, on the
Hudson, had thrown a garrison of six hundred
men into it, and added two lines of fortifications,
rendering it almost impregnable. Washington,
nevertheless, determined to recapture it, and in-
trusted the task to General Anthony Wayne, giv-
ing him twelve hundred men for the purpose.
At midnight of July 15, the Americans crossed
the swamp which divided the fort from the main-
land, reached the outworks before they were dis-
covered, and carried the fort by storm.

THE STORMING OF STONY POINT

[July 16, 1779]

HIGHLANDS of Hudson! ye saw them pass,
 Night on the stars of their battle-flag,
Threading the maze of the dark morass
 Under the frown of the Thunder Crag;

Flower and pride of the Light Armed Corps,
 Trim in their trappings of buff and blue,
Silent, they skirted the rugged shore,
 Grim in the promise of work to do.

"Cross ye the ford to the moated rock!
 Let not a whisper your march betray!
Out with the flint from the musket lock!
 Now! let the bayonet find the way!"

"Halt!" rang the sentinel's challenge clear.
 Swift came the shot of the waking foe.
Bright flashed the axe of the Pioneer
 Smashing the abatis, blow on blow.

Little they tarried for British might!
 Lightly they recked of the Tory jeers!
Laughing, they swarmed to the craggy height,
 Steel to the steel of the Grenadiers!

Storm King and Dunderberg! wake once
 more
 Sentinel giants of Freedom's throne,
Massive and proud! to the Eastern shore
 Bellow the watchword: "The fort's our
  own!"

Echo our cheers for the Men of old!
 Shout for the Hero who led his band
Braving the death that his heart foretold
 Over the parapet, "spear in hand!"
     ARTHUR GUITERMAN.

WAYNE AT STONY POINT

[July 16, 1779]

'T WAS the heart of the murky night, and th
 lowest ebb of the tide,
Silence lay on the land, and sleep on the water
 wide,
Save for the sentry's tramp, or the note of
 lone night bird,
Or the sough of the haunted pines as th
 south wind softly stirred.
Gloom above and around, and the broodin
 spirit of rest;
Only a single star over Dunderberg's loft
 crest.

Through the drench of ooze and slime at th
 marge of the river fen
File upon file slips by. See! are they ghos
 or men?
Fast do they forward press, on by a tra
 unbarred;
Now is the causeway won, now have th
 throttled the guard;

Now have they parted line to storm with a rush on the height,
Some by a path to the left, some by a path to the right.

Hark, — the peal of a gun! and the drummer's rude alarms!
Ringing down from the height there soundeth the cry, *To arms!*
Thundering down from the height there cometh the cannon's blare;
Flash upon blinding flash lightens the livid air:
Look! do the stormers quail? Nay, for their feet are set
Now at the bastion's base, now on the parapet'

Urging the vanguard on prone doth the leader fall,
Smitten sudden and sore by a foeman's musket-ball;
Waver the charging lines; swiftly they spring to his side,
Madcap Anthony Wayne, the patriot army's pride!
Forward, my braves! he cries, and the heroes hearten again;
Bear me into the fort, I'll die at the head of my men!

Die! — did he die that night, felled in his lusty prime?
Answer many a field in the stormy aftertime!
Still did his prowess shine, still did his courage soar,
From the Hudson's rocky steep to the James's level shore;
But never on Fame's fair scroll did he blazon a deed more bright
Than his charge on Stony Point in the heart of the murky night.

CLINTON SCOLLARD.

The raids over the "Neutral Ground" continued, and among the boldest of the leaders on the American side was Colonel Aaron Burr. But not all of his nights were occupied in warlike expeditions. Fifteen miles away, across the Hudson, dwelt the charming Widow Prevost, whom he afterwards married, and on at least two occasions, Burr, with boldness to touch the heart of any woman, succeeded in getting across to spend a few hours with her.

AARON BURR'S WOOING

FROM the commandant's quarters on Westchester height
The blue hills of Ramapo lie in full sight;
On their slope gleam the gables that shield his heart's queen,
But the redcoats are wary — the Hudson's between.
Through the camp runs a jest: "There's no moon — 't will be dark;
'T is odds little Aaron will go on a spark!"
And the toast of the troopers is: "Pickets, lie low,
And good luck to the colonel and Widow Prevost!"

Eight miles to the river he gallops his steed,
Lays him bound in the barge, bids his escort make speed,
Loose their swords, sit athwart, through the fleet reach yon shore.
Not a word — not a plash of the thick-muffled oar!
Once across, once again in the seat and away —
Five leagues are soon over when love has the say;
And "Old Put" and his rider a bridle-path know
To the Hermitage manor of Madame Prevost.

Lightly done! but he halts in the grove's deepest glade,
Ties his horse to a birch, trims his cue, slings his blade,
Wipes the dust and the dew from his smooth, handsome face,
With the 'kerchief she broidered and bordered in lace;
Then slips through the box-rows and taps at the hall,
Sees the glint of a waxlight, a hand white and small,
And the door is unbarred by herself all aglow —
Half in smiles, half in tears — Theodosia Prevost.

Alack for the soldier that's buried and gone!
What's a volley above him, a wreath on his stone,
Compared with sweet life and a wife for one's view

Like this dame, ripe and warm in her India
　　fichu?
She chides her bold lover, yet holds him more
　　dear,
For the daring that brings him a night-rider
　　here;
British gallants by day through her doors
　　come and go,
But a Yankee's the winner of Theo. Prevost.

Where's the widow or maid with a mouth to
　　be kist,
When Burr comes a-wooing, that long would
　　resist?
Lights and wine on the beaufet, the shutters
　　all fast,
And "Old Put" stamps in vain till an hour
　　has flown past —
But an hour, for eight leagues must be covered
　　ere day;
Laughs Aaron, " Let Washington frown as
　　he may,
When he hears of me next, in a raid on the
　　foe,
He'll forgive this night's tryst with the Widow
　　Prevost!"
　　　　　　EDMUND CLARENCE STEDMAN.

In June, 1780, Clinton made a desperate at-
tempt to capture the American stores at Morris-
town, N. J. At dawn of the 23d, he advanced
in great force upon Springfield, where General
Greene was stationed. Overwhelming numbers
compelled the Americans to fall back to a strong
position, which the enemy dared not attack, and
after setting fire to the village, Clinton retreated
toward Elizabethtown.

THE MODERN JONAS

[June 23, 1780]

You know there goes a tale,
How Jonas went on board a whale,
　　Once, for a frolic;
　　　And how the whale
　　　Set sail
　　And got the cholic;
And, after a great splutter,
　　Spew'd him up upon the coast,
　　Just like woodcock on a toast,
With trail and butter.

There also goes a joke,
How Clinton went on board the Duke

Count Rochambeau to fight;
　　As he did n't fail
　　To set sail
　　The first fair gale,
　　For once we thought him right;
But, after a great clutter,
　　He turn'd back along the coast,
　　And left the French to make their boast,
And Englishmen to mutter.

Just so, not long before,
　　Old Knyp,
　　And old Clip
Went to the Jersey shore,
The rebel rogues to beat;
　　　But, at Yankee farms,
　　　They took alarms,
　　　At little harms,
And quickly did retreat.

Then after two days' wonder,
March'd boldly up to Springfield town,
And swore they'd knock the rebels down.
　　　But as their foes
　　　Gave them some blows,
　　　They, like the wind,
　　　Soon changed their mind.
　　　And, in a crack,
　　　Returned back,
From not one third their number.

On June 6, while on their way to Springfield
the British passed through a village called Con-
necticut Farms. They set it on fire, destroying
almost every house, and one of them shot and
killed the wife of Rev. James Caldwell, as she was
kneeling at prayer in her bedroom. Her hus-
band took the revenge described in Mr. Harte's
poem.

CALDWELL OF SPRINGFIELD

[June 23, 1780]

HERE's the spot. Look around you. Above
　　on the height
Lay the Hessians encamped. By that church
　　on the right
Stood the gaunt Jersey farmers. And he
　　ran a wall, —
You may dig anywhere and you'll turn up a
　　ball.
Nothing more. Grasses spring, waters run,
　　flowers blow,
Pretty much as they did ninety-three years
　　ago.

Nothing more, did I say? Stay one moment;
  you've heard
Of Caldwell, the parson, who once preached
  the Word
Down at Springfield? What, No? Come —
  that's bad; why he had
All the Jerseys aflame. And they gave him
  the name
Of the "rebel high-priest." He stuck in their
  gorge,
For he loved the Lord God, — and he hated
  King George!

He had cause, you might say! When the
  Hessians that day
Marched up with Knyphausen they stopped
  on their way
At the "Farms," where his wife, with a child
  in her arms,
Sat alone in the house. How it happened
  none knew
But God — and that one of the hireling crew
Who fired the shot! Enough! — there she lay,
And Caldwell, the chaplain, her husband,
  away!

Did he preach — did he pray? Think of
  him as you stand
By the old church to-day; — think of him
  and his band
Of militant ploughboys! See the smoke and
  the heat
Of that reckless advance, — of that straggling
  retreat!
Keep the ghost of that wife, foully slain, in
  your view, —
And what could you, what should you, what
  would you do?

Why, just what he did! They were left in the
  lurch
For the want of more wadding. He ran to the
  church,
Broke the door, stripped the pews, and dashed
  out in the road
With his arms full of hymn-books and threw
  down his load
At their feet! Then above all the shouting
  and shots,
Rang his voice, — "Put Watts into 'em, —
  Boys, give 'em Watts!"

And they did. That is all. Grasses spring,
  flowers blow
Pretty much as they did ninety-three years ago.

You may dig anywhere and you'll turn up a
  ball, —
But not always a hero like this,—and that's all.
            BRET HARTE.

Among the posts occupied by the British on the
Hudson was a blockhouse just above Bergen
Neck. Pastured on the neck was a large number
of cattle and horses, and on July 21, 1780, General
Wayne was sent, with some Pennsylvania and
Maryland troops, to storm this blockhouse and
drive the stock within the American lines. The
attack on the blockhouse was repulsed by the
British, the Americans losing heavily. It was this
affair which was celebrated by Major John André
in the verses called "The Cow-Chace."

THE COW-CHACE

[July 21, 1780]

CANTO I

To drive the kine one summer's morn,
  The Tanner took his way;
The calf shall rue that is unborn
  The jumbling of that day.

And Wayne descending steers shall know,
  And tauntingly deride;
And call to mind in every low,
  The tanning of *his* hide.

Yet Bergen cows still ruminate,
  Unconscious in the stall,
What mighty means were used to get,
  And loose them after all.

For many heroes bold and brave,
  From Newbridge and Tappan,
And those that drink Passaic's wave,
  And those who eat supawn;

And sons of distant Delaware,
  And still remoter Shannon,
And Major Lee with horses rare,
  And Proctor with his cannon.

All wond'rous proud in arms they came,
  What hero could refuse
To tread the rugged path to fame,
  Who had a pair of shoes!

At six, the host with sweating buff,
  Arrived at Freedom's pole:
When Wayne, who thought he'd time enough,
  Thus speechified the whole:

"O ye, whom glory doth unite,
　Who Freedom's cause espouse;
Whether the wing that's doom'd to fight,
　Or that to drive the cows,

"Ere yet you tempt your further way,
　Or into action come,
Hear, soldiers, what I have to say,
　And take a pint of rum.

"Intemp'rate valor then will string
　Each nervous arm the better;
So all the land shall I O sing,
　And read the Gen'ral's letter.

"Know that some paltry refugees,
　Whom I've a mind to fright,
Are playing h—l amongst the trees
　That grow on yonder height.

"Their fort and blockhouses we'll level,
　And deal a horrid slaughter;
We'll drive the scoundrels to the devil,
　And ravish wife and daughter.

"I, under cover of th' attack,
　Whilst you are all at blows,
From English neighb'rhood and Nyack,
　Will drive away the cows;

"For well you know the latter is
　The serious operation,
And fighting with the refugees
　Is only demonstration."

His daring words, from all the crowd,
　Such great applause did gain,
That every man declar'd aloud
　For serious work with Wayne.

Then from the cask of rum once more,
　They took a heady gill;
When one and all, they loudly swore,
　They'd fight upon the hill.

But here — the Muse hath not a strain
　Befitting such great deeds;
Huzza! they cried, huzza! for Wayne,
　And shouting, — did their needs.

CANTO II

Near his meridian pomp, the sun
　Had journey'd from th' horizon;
When fierce the dusky tribe mov'd on,
　Of heroes drunk as pison.

The sounds confus'd of boasting oaths,
　Reëchoed through the wood;
Some vow'd to sleep in dead men's clothes,
　And some to swim in blood.

At Irving's nod 't was fine to see
　The left prepare to fight;
The while, the drovers, Wayne and Lee,
　Drew off upon the right.

Which Irving 't was, fame don't relate,
　Nor can the Muse assist her;
Whether 't was he that cocks a hat,
　Or he that gives a clyster.

For greatly one was signaliz'd,
　That fought on Chestnut Hill;
And Canada immortaliz'd
　The vender of the pill.

Yet their attendance upon Proctor,
　They both might have to boast of;
For there was business for the doctor,
　And hats to be disposed of.

Let none uncandidly infer,
　That Stirling wanted spunk;
The self-made peer had sure been there,
　But that the peer was drunk.

But turn we to the Hudson's banks,
　Where stood the modest train,
With purpose firm, tho' slender ranks,
　Nor car'd a pin for Wayne.

For them the unrelenting hand
　Of rebel fury drove,
And tore from ev'ry genial band
　Of friendship and of love.

And some within the dungeon's gloom,
　By mock tribunals laid,
Had waited long a cruel doom
　Impending o'er each head.

Here one bewails a brother's fate,
　There one a sire demands,
Cut off, alas! before their date,
　By ignominious hands.

And silver'd grandsires here appear'd
　In deep distress serene,
Of reverent manners that declar'd
　The better days they'd seen.

Oh, curs'd rebellion, these are thine,
  Thine all these tales of woe;
Shall at thy dire insatiate shrine
  Blood never cease to flow?

And now the foe began to lead
  His forces to th' attack;
Balls whistling unto balls succeed,
  And make the blockhouse crack.

No shot could pass, if you will take
  The Gen'ral's word for true;
But 't is a d——ble mistake,
  For ev'ry shot went thro'.

The firmer as the rebels press'd,
  The loyal heroes stand;
Virtue had nerv'd each honest breast,
  And industry each hand.

In valor's frenzy, Hamilton
  Rode like a soldier big,
And Secretary Harrison,
  With pen stuck in his wig.

But lest their chieftain, Washington,
  Should mourn them in the mumps,
The fate of Withrington to shun,
  They fought behind the stumps.

But ah, Thaddeus Posset, why
  Should thy poor soul elope?
And why should Titus Hooper die,
  Ay, die — without a rope?

Apostate Murphy, thou to whom
  Fair Shela ne'er was cruel,
In death shalt hear her mourn thy doom,
  "Och! would ye die, my jewel?"

Thee, Nathan Pumpkin, I lament,
  Of melancholy fate;
The gray goose stolen as he went,
  In his heart's blood was wet.

Now, as the fight was further fought,
  And balls began to thicken,
The fray assum'd, the gen'rals thought,
  The color of a lickin'.

Yet undismay'd the chiefs command,
  And to redeem the day,
Cry, SOLDIERS, CHARGE! they hear, they
    stand,
  They turn and run away.

CANTO III

Not all delights the bloody spear,
  Or horrid din of battle;
There are, I 'm sure, who 'd like to hear
  A word about the cattle.

The chief whom we beheld of late,
  Near Schralenberg haranging,
At Yan Van Poop's unconscious sat
  Of Irving's hearty banging.

Whilst valiant Lee, with courage wild,
  Most bravely did oppose
The tears of woman and of child,
  Who begg'd he 'd leave the cows.

But Wayne, of sympathizing heart,
  Required a relief,
Not all the blessings could impart
  Of battle or of beef.

For now a prey to female charms,
  His soul took more delight in
A lovely hamadryad's arms,
  Than cow-driving or fighting.

A nymph the refugees had drove
  Far from her native tree,
Just happen'd to be on the move,
  When up came Wayne and Lee.

She, in Mad Anthony's fierce eye,
  The hero saw portray'd,
And all in tears she took him by —
  The bridle of his jade.

"Hear," said the nymph, "oh, great com-
    mander!
  No human lamentations;
The trees you see them cutting yonder,
  Are all my near relations.

"And I, forlorn! implore thine aid,
  To free the sacred grove;
So shall thy prowess be repaid
  With an immortal's love."

Now some, to prove she was a goddess,
  Said this enchanting fair
Had late retirèd from the Bodies
  In all the pomp of war.

The drums and merry fifes had play'd
  To honor her retreat,

And Cunningham himself convey'd
  The lady through the street.

Great Wayne, by soft compassion sway'd,
  To no inquiry stoops,
But takes the fair afflicted maid
  Right into Yan Van Poop's.

So Roman Anthony, they say,
  Disgraced th' imperial banner,
And for a gypsy lost a day,
  Like Anthony the tanner.

The hamadryad had but half
  Receiv'd redress from Wayne,
When drums and colors, cow and calf,
  Came down the road amain.

And in a cloud of dust was seen
  The sheep, the horse, the goat,
The gentle heifer, ass obscene,
  The yearling and the shoat.

And pack-horses with fowls came by,
  Be-feather'd on each side,
Like Pegasus, the horse that I
  And other poets ride.

Sublime upon his stirrups rose
  The mighty Lee behind,
And drove the terror-smitten cows
  Like chaff before the wind.

But sudden see the woods above
  Pour down another corps,
All helter-skelter in a drove,
  Like that I sung before.

Irving and terror in the van,
  Came flying all abroad;
And cannon, colors, horse, and man,
  Ran tumbling to the road.

Still as he fled, 't was Irving's cry,
  And his example too,
"Run on, my merry men — for why?
  The shot will not go thro'."

As when two kennels in the street,
  Swell'd with a recent rain,
In gushing streams together meet
  And seek the neighboring drain;

So met these dung-born tribes in one,
  As swift in their career,

And so to Newbridge they ran on —
  But all the cows got clear.

Poor Parson Caldwell, all in wonder,
  Saw the returning train,
And mourn'd to Wayne the lack of plunder
  For them to steal again.

For 't was his right to steal the spoil, and
  To share with each commander,
As he had done at Staten Island
  With frost-bit Alexander.

In his dismay, the frantic priest
  Began to grow prophetic;
You'd swore, to see his laboring breast,
  He'd taken an emetic.

"I view a future day," said he,
  "Brighter than this dark day is;
And you shall see what you shall see,
  Ha! ha! one pretty Marquis!

"And he shall come to Paulus Hook,
  And great achievements think on;
And make a bow and take a look,
  Like Satan over Lincoln.

"And every one around shall glory
  To see the Frenchman caper;
And pretty Susan tell the story
  In the next Chatham paper."

This solemn prophecy, of course,
  Gave all much consolation,
Except to Wayne, who lost his horse
  Upon that great occasion.

His horse that carried all his prog,
  His military speeches,
His corn-stalk whiskey for his grog,
  Blue stockings and brown breeches.

And now I've clos'd my epic strain,
  I tremble as I show it,
Lest this same warrior-drover, Wayne,
  Should ever catch the poet.

                              JOHN ANDRÉ.

The last stanza was singularly prophetic. The
Americans relied for the defence of the Hudson
upon the impregnable position at West Point, to
the command of which Benedict Arnold had been
appointed in July, 1780. Arnold, one of the most
brilliant officers in the army, had been treated
with great injustice by Congress, and to revenge

himself determined to betray West Point into the hands of the British. He therefore opened communication with Clinton, and on September 21 Major André was sent to confer with the traitor. While returning to the British lines the following night, he was captured by an American outpost, who searched him, discovered the papers giving the details of the plot, and took him back to the American lines, refusing his offers of reward for his release.

BRAVE PAULDING AND THE SPY

[September 23, 1780]

COME all you brave Americans,
    And unto me give ear,
And I'll sing you a ditty
    That will your spirits cheer,
Concerning a young gentleman
    Whose age was twenty-two;
He fought for North America,
    His heart was just and true.

They took him from his dwelling,
    And they did him confine,
They cast him into prison,
    And kept him there a time.
But he with resolution
    Resolv'd not long to stay;
He set himself at liberty,
    And soon he ran away.

He with a scouting-party
    Went down to Tarrytown,
Where he met a British officer,
    A man of high renown,
Who says unto these gentlemen,
    "You're of the British cheer,
I trust that you can tell me
    If there's any danger near?"

Then up stept this young hero,
    John Paulding was his name,
"Sir, tell us where you're going,
    And, also, whence you came?"
"I bear the British flag, sir;
    I've a pass to go this way,
I'm on an expedition,
    And have no time to stay."

Then round him came this company,
    And bid him to dismount;
"Come, tell us where you're going,
    Give us a strict account;
For we are now resolvèd
    That you shall ne'er pass by."

Upon examination
    They found he was a spy.

He beggèd for his liberty,
    He plead for his discharge,
And oftentimes he told them,
    If they'd set him at large,
"Here's all the gold and silver
    I have laid up in store,
But when I reach the city,
    I'll give you ten times more."

"I scorn the gold and silver
    You have laid up in store,
And when you get to New York,
    You need not send us more;
But you may take your sword in hand
    To gain your liberty,
And if that you do conquer me,
    Oh, then you shall be free."

"The time it is improper
    Our valor for to try,
For if we take our swords in hand,
    Then one of us must die;
I am a man of honor,
    With courage true and bold,
And I fear not the man of clay,
    Although he's cloth'd in gold."

He saw that his conspiracy
    Would soon be brought to light;
He begg'd for pen and paper,
    And askèd leave to write
A line to General Arnold,
    To let him know his fate,
And beg for his assistance;
    But now it was too late.

When the news it came to Arnold,
    It put him in a fret;
He walk'd the room in trouble,
    Till tears his cheek did wet;
The story soon went through the camp
    And also through the fort;
And he callèd for the Vulture
    And sailèd for New York.

Now Arnold to New York has gone,
    A-fighting for his king,
And left poor Major André
    On the gallows for to swing;
When he was executed,
    He look'd both meek and mild;

He look'd upon the people,
  And pleasantly he smil'd.

It mov'd each eye with pity,
  Caus'd every heart to bleed,
And every one wished him releas'd
  And Arnold in his stead.
He was a man of honor,
  In Britain he was born;
To die upon the gallows
  Most highly he did scorn.

A bumper to John Paulding!
  Now let your voices sound,
Fill up your flowing glasses,
  And drink his health around;
Also to those young gentlemen
  Who bore him company;
Success to North America,
  Ye sons of liberty!

Arnold learned of André's capture just in time
to escape to a British ship in the river, and Wash-
ington, arriving soon after, prevented his treach-
erous disposition of the American forces from
being taken advantage of by the enemy.

ARNOLD

THE VILE TRAITOR

[September 25, 1780]

ARNOLD! the name, as heretofore,
Shall now be Benedict no more:
Since, instigated by the devil,
Thy ways are turned from good to evil.

'T is fit we brand thee with a name
To suit thy infamy and shame;
And, since of treason thou 'rt convicted,
Thy name shall be maledicted.
Unless, by way of contradiction,
We style thee Britain's Benediction.
Such blessings she, with lavish hand,
Confers on this devoted land.

For instance, only let us mention
Some proof of her benign intention;
The slaves she sends us o'er the deep,
And bribes to cut our throats in sleep.
To take our lives and scalps away,
The savage Indians keeps in pay,
And Tories worse, by half, than they.

Then, in this class of Britain's heroes, —
The Tories, savage Indians, negroes, —
Recorded Arnold's name shall stand,
While Freedom's blessings crown our land,
And odious for the blackest crimes,
Arnold shall stink to latest times.

EPIGRAM

Quoth Satan to Arnold: "My worthy good
    fellow,
I love you much better than ever I did;
You live like a prince, with Hal may get mel-
    low, —
But mind that you both do just what I bid."

Quoth Arnold to Satan: "My friend, do not
    doubt me!
I will strictly adhere to all your great views;
To you I'm devoted, with all things about
    me —
You'll permit me, I hope, to die in my
    shoes."
        New Jersey Gazette, November 1, 1780.

André was tried by court-martial September 29,
and condemned to be hanged as a spy. Clinton,
with whom André was a warm personal favorite,
made a desperate effort to save him, but in vain;
and a petition from André himself that he might
be shot instead of hanged was also rejected.

ANDRÉ'S REQUEST TO WASH-
INGTON

[October 1, 1780]

IT is not the fear of death
  That damps my brow,
It is not for another breath
  I ask thee now;
I can die with a lip unstirr'd
  And a quiet heart —
Let but this prayer be heard
  Ere I depart.

I can give up my mother's look —
  My sister's kiss;
I can think of love — yet brook
  A death like this!
I can give up the young fame
  I burn'd to win —
All — but the spotless name
  I glory in.

Thine is the power to give,
  Thine to deny,
Joy for the hour I live —
  Calmness to die.
By all the brave should cherish,
  By my dying breath,
I ask that I may perish
  By a soldier's death!
            NATHANIEL PARKER WILLIS.

Accordingly, on Monday, October 2, 1780, the adjutant-general of the British army was led to the gallows, and shared the fate which had befallen Nathan Hale four years before.

ANDRÉ

THIS is the place where André met that death
Whose infamy was keenest of its throes,
And in this place of bravely yielded breath
His ashes found a fifty years' repose;

And then, at last, a transatlantic grave,
With those who have been kings in blood or
      fame,
As Honor here some compensation gave
For that once forfeit to a hero's name.

But whether in the Abbey's glory laid,
Or on so fair but fatal Tappan's shore,
Still at his grave have noble hearts betrayed
The loving pity and regret they bore.

In view of all he lost, — his youth, his love,
And possibilities that wait the brave,
Inward and outward bound, dim visions
      move
Like passing sails upon the Hudson's wave.

The country's Father! how do we revere
His justice, — Brutus-like in its decree, —
With André-sparing mercy, still more dear
Had been his name, — if that, indeed, could
      be!
            CHARLOTTE FISKE BATES.

But Arnold, the chief offender, had escaped, and a plan was set on foot to abduct him from the midst of the British and bring him back to the American lines. The execution of this plot was intrusted to John Champe, a sergeant-major in Lee's cavalry. On the night of October 20, Champe mounted his horse and seemingly deserted to the British, escaping a hot pursuit. He gained Arnold's confidence, and made every arrangement to abduct him, but was foiled at the last moment by Arnold's embarkation on an expedition to the south.

SERGEANT CHAMPE

[October 20, 1780]

COME sheathe your swords! my gallant boys,
  And listen to the story,
How Sergeant Champe, one gloomy night,
  Set off to catch the Tory.

You see the general had got mad
  To think his plans were thwarted,
And swore by all, both good and bad,
  That Arnold should be carted.

So unto Lee he sent a line,
  And told him all his sorrow,
And said that he must start the hunt
  Before the coming morrow.

Lee found a sergeant in his camp,
  Made up of bone and muscle,
Who ne'er knew fear, and many a year
  With Tories had a tussle.

Bold Champe, when mounted on old Rip,
  All button'd up from weather,
Sang out, "good-by!" crack'd off his whip,
  And soon was in the heather.

He gallop'd on towards Paulus Hook,
  Improving every instant —
Until a patrol, wide awake,
  Descried him in the distance.

On coming up, the guard call'd out
  And asked him where he's going —
To which he answer'd with his spur,
  And left him in the mowing.

The bushes pass'd him like the wind,
  And pebbles flew asunder,
The guard was left far, far behind,
  All mix'd with mud and wonder.

Lee's troops paraded, all alive,
  Although 't was one the morning,
And counting o'er a dozen or more,
  One sergeant is found wanting.

A little hero, full of spunk,
  But not so full of judgment,
Press'd Major Lee to let him go,
  With the bravest of his reg'men?

Lee summon'd cornet Middleton,
  Expressèd what was urgent,
And gave him orders how to go
  To catch the rambling sergeant.

Then forty troopers, more or less,
  Set off across the meader;
'Bout thirty-nine went jogging on
  A-following their leader.

At early morn, adown a hill,
  They saw the sergeant sliding;
So fast he went, it was not ken't
  Whether he's rode, or riding.

None lookèd back, but on they spurr'd,
  A-gaining every minute.
To see them go, 't would done you good,
  You'd thought old Satan in it.

The sergeant miss'd 'em, by good luck,
  And took another tracing,
He turn'd his horse from Paulus Hook,
  Elizabethtown facing.

It was the custom of Sir Hal
  To send his galleys cruising,
And so it happenèd just then
  That two were at Van Deusen's.

Strait unto these the sergeant went,
  And left old Rip, all standing,
A-waiting for the blown cornet,
  At Squire Van Deusen's landing.

The troopers did n't gallop home,
  But rested from their labors;
And some 't is said took gingerbread
  And cider from the neighbors.

'T was just at eve the troopers reach'd
  The camp they left that morning.
Champe's empty saddle, unto Lee,
  Gave an unwelcome warning.

"If Champe has suffered, 't is my fault;"
  So thought the generous major;
" I would not have his garment touch'd
  For millions on a wager!"

The cornet told him all he knew,
  Excepting of the cider.
The troopers, all, spurred very well,
  But Champe was the best rider!

And so it happen'd that brave Champe
  Unto Sir Hal deserted,
Deceiving him, and you, and me,
  And into York was flirted.

He saw base Arnold in his camp,
  Surrounded by the legion,
And told him of the recent prank
  That threw him in that region.

Then Arnold grinn'd, and rubb'd his hands.
  And e'enmost choked with pleasure,
Not thinking Champe was all the while
  A "taking of his measure."

"Come now," says he, "my bold soldier,
  As you 're within our borders,
Let's drink our fill, old care to kill,
  To-morrow you'll have orders."

Full soon the British fleet set sail!
  Say! was n't that a pity?
For thus it was brave Sergeant Champe
  Was taken from the city.

To southern climes the shipping flew,
  And anchored in Virginia,
When Champe escaped and join'd his friends
  Among the picininni.

Base Arnold's head, by luck, was sav'd,
  Poor André was gibbeted;
Arnold's to blame for André's fame,
  And André's to be pitied.

After the flurry consequent upon André's capture and execution, affairs at New York settled back into the old routine. A sort of lethargy seemed to possess the British leaders, and the Americans grew bolder and bolder, sometimes pushing their foraging expeditions within the British lines, and on one occasion seizing a quantity of hay and setting fire to some houses within sight of Clinton's quarters. The next day, the Loyalist disgust was voiced in some verses written by Joseph Stansbury and stuck up about the town.

A NEW SONG

[1780]

  "Has the Marquis La Fayette
  Taken off all our hay yet?"
Says Clinton to the wise heads around
  him:

"Yes, faith, Sir Harry,
Each stack he did carry,
And likewise the cattle — confound him!

"Besides, he now goes,
Just under your nose,
To burn all the houses to cinder."
"If that be his project,
It is not an object
Worth a great man's attempting to hinder.

"For forage and house
I care not a louse;
For revenge, let the Loyalists bellow:
I swear I'll not do more
To keep them in humor,
Than play on my violoncello.

"Since Charleston is taken,
'T will sure save my bacon, —
I can live a whole year on that same, sir;
Ride about all the day,
At night, concert or play;
So a fig for the men that dare blame, sir.

"If growlers complain,
I inactive remain —
Will do nothing, nor let any others!
'T is sure no new thing
To serve thus our king —
Witness Burgoyne, and two famous Bro-
thers!"

JOSEPH STANSBURY.

Another of Stansbury's lyrics, and perhaps the
best he ever wrote, is "The Lords of the Main,"
intended for the use of the British sailors then
engaged in fighting their ancient foes, France and
Spain.

THE LORDS OF THE MAIN

[1780]

WHEN Faction, in league with the treacher-
ous Gaul,
Began to look big, and paraded in state,
A meeting was held at Credulity Hall,
And Echo proclaimed their ally good and
great.
By sea and by land
Such wonders are planned —
No less than the bold British lion to chain!
"Well hove!" says Jack Lanyard,
"French, Congo, and Spaniard,

Have at you! — remember, we're Lords of
the Main.
Lords of the Main, aye, Lords of the Main;
The Tars of old England are Lords of the
Main!"

Though party-contention awhile may perplex,
And lenity hold us in doubtful suspense,
If perfidy rouse, or ingratitude vex,
In defiance of hell we'll chastise the of-
fence.
When danger alarms,
'T is then that in arms
United we rush on the foe with disdain;
And when the storm rages,
It only presages
Fresh triumphs to Britons as Lords of the
Main!
Lords of the Main, aye, Lords of the Main —
Let thunder proclaim it, we're Lords of the
Main!

Then, Britons, strike home — make sure of
your blow:
The chase is in view — never mind a lea
shore.
With vengeance o'ertake the confederate foe:
'T is now we may rival our heroes of yore!
Brave Anson, and Drake,
Hawke, Russell, and Blake,
With ardor like yours, we defy France and
Spain!
Combining with treason,
They're deaf to all reason;
Once more let them feel we are Lords of the
Main.
Lords of the Main, aye, Lords of the Main —
The first-born of Neptune are Lords of the
Main!

JOSEPH STANSBURY.

Among the desperate and foolish expedients to
which the British resorted in the hope of winning
America back to her allegiance was that of send-
ing Prince William Henry, afterwards William IV,
to New York in 1781. The Tory authorities of the
city overwhelmed him with adulation, but in the
country at large, his visit excited only derision.

THE ROYAL ADVENTURER

[1781]

PRINCE WILLIAM, of the Brunswick race,
To witness George's sad disgrace
The royal lad came over,

Rebels to kill, by right divine —
Derived from that illustrious line,
   The beggars of Hanover.

So many chiefs got broken pates
In vanquishing the rebel states,
   So many nobles fell,
That George the Third in passion cried:
"Our royal blood must now be tried;
   'T is that must break the spell;

"To you [the fat pot-valiant swain
To Digby said], dear friend of mine,
   To you I trust my boy;
The rebel tribes shall quake with fears,
Rebellion die when he appears,
   My Tories leap with joy."

So said, so done — the lad was sent,
But never reached the continent,
   An island held him fast —
Yet there his friends danced rigadoons,
The Hessians sung in high Dutch tunes,
   "Prince William 's come at last!"

"Prince William 's come!" — the Briton
   cried —
"Our labors now will be repaid —
   Dominion be restored —
Our monarch is in William seen,
He is the image of our queen,
   Let William be adored!"

The Tories came with long address,
With poems groaned the royal press,
   And all in William's praise —
The youth, astonished, looked about
To find their vast dominions out,
   Then answered in amaze:

"Where all your vast domain can be,
Friends, for my soul I cannot see;
   'T is but an empty name;
Three wasted islands and a town
In rubbish buried — half burnt down,
   Is all that we can claim;

"I am of royal birth, 't is true.
But what, my sons, can princes do,
   No armies to command?
Cornwallis conquered and distrest —
Sir Henry Clinton grown a jest —
   I curse — and quit the land."
            PHILIP FRENEAU.

The war in the North thereafter was confined,
on the part of the British, to predatory raids along
the coasts, of which "The Descent on Middlesex"
is a fair example. On the afternoon of July 22,
1781, a party of Royalist refugees surrounded the
church, where the people of Middlesex were at
prayer, and took fifty of them captive, among
them Schoolmaster St. John, of Norwalk, the
author of the following ingenuous ballad describ-
ing their experiences.

THE DESCENT ON MIDDLESEX

[July 22, 1781]

JULY the twenty-second day,
The precise hour I will not say,
In seventeen hundred and eighty-one,
A horrid action was begun.

While to the Lord they sing and pray,
The Tories who in ambush lay,
Beset the house with brazen face,
At Middlesex, it was the place.

A guard was plac'd the house before,
Likewise behind and at each door;
Then void of shame, those men of sin
The sacred temple enter'd in.

The reverend Mather closed his book.
How did the congregation look!
Those demons plunder'd all they could,
Either in silver or in gold.

The silver buckles which we use,
Both at the knees and on the shoes,
These caitiffs took them in their rage,
Had no respect for sex or age.

As they were searching all around,
They several silver watches found;
While they who 're plac'd as guards without,
Like raging devils rang'd about.

Run forty horses to the shore,
Not many either less or more;
With bridles, saddles, pillions on;
In a few minutes all was done.

The men from hence they took away,
Upon that awful sacred day,
Was forty-eight, besides two more
They chanc'd to find upon the shore.

On board the shipping they were sent,
Their money gone, and spirits spent,

And greatly fearing their sad end,
This wicked seizure did portend.

They hoisted sail, the Sound they cross'd,
And near Lloyd's Neck they anchor'd first;
'T was here the Tories felt 't was wrong
To bring so many men along.

Then every man must tell his name,
A list they took, and kept the same;
When twenty-four of fifty men
Were order'd to go home again.

The twenty-six who stay'd behind,
Most cruelly they were confin'd;
On board the brig were order'd quick,
And then confin'd beneath the deck.

A dismal hole with filth besmear'd,
But 't was no more than what we fear'd;
Sad the confinement, dark the night,
But then the devil thought 't was right.

But to return whence I left off.
They at our misery made a scoff;
Like raving madmen tore about,
Swearing they 'd take our vitals out.

They said no quarter they would give
Nor let a cursèd rebel live;
But would their joints in pieces cut,
Then round the deck like turkeys strut.

July, the fourth and twentieth day,
We all marched off to Oyster Bay;
To increase our pains and make it worse,
They iron'd just six pair of us.

But as they wanted just one pair,
An iron stirrup lying there
Was taken and on anvil laid,
On which they with a hammer paid.

And as they beat it inch by inch,
They bruis'd their wrists, at which they flinch;
Those wretched caitiffs standing by,
Would laugh to hear the sufferers cry.

Although to call them not by name,
From Fairfield county many came;
And were delighted with the rout,
To see the rebels kick'd about.

At night we travell'd in the rain,
All begg'd for shelter, but in vain,

Though almost naked to the skin;
A dismal pickle we were in.

Then to the half-way house we came,
The "Half-way House" 't is called by name,
And there we found a soul's relief;
We almost miss'd our dreadful grief.

The people gen'rously behav'd,
Made a good fire, some brandy gave,
Of which we greatly stood in need,
As we were wet and cold indeed.

But ere the house we did attain,
We trembled so with cold and rain,
Our irons jingled — well they might —
We shiver'd so that stormy night.

In half an hour or thereabout,
The orders were, "Come, all turn out!
Ye rebel prisoners, shabby crew,
To loiter thus will never do."

'T was now about the break of day,
When all were forc'd to march away;
With what they order'd we complied,
Though cold, nor yet one quarter dried.

We made a halt one half mile short
Of what is term'd Brucklyn's fort;
Where all were hurried through the street:
Some overtook us, some we met.

We now traversing the parade,
The awful figure which we made,
Caus'd laughter, mirth, and merriment,
And some would curse us as we went.

Their grandest fort was now hard by us;
They show'd us that to terrify us;
They show'd us all their bulwarks there,
To let be known how strong they were.

Just then the Tory drums did sound,
And pipes rang out a warlike round;
Supposing we must thence conclude
That Britain ne'er could be subdued.

Up to the guard-house we were led,
Where each receiv'd a crumb of bread;
Not quite one mouthful, I believe,
For every man we did receive.

In boats, the ferry soon we pass'd,
And at New York arriv'd at last;

As through the streets we pass'd along,
Ten thousand curses round us rang.

But some would laugh, and some would sneer,
And some would grin, and others leer;
A mixèd mob, a medley crew,
I guess as e'er the devil knew.

To the Provost we then were haul'd,
Though we of war were prisoners call'd;
Our irons now were order'd off,
And we were left to sneeze and cough.

But oh! what company we found.
With great surprise we look'd around:
I must conclude that in that place,
We found the worst of Adam's race.

Thieves, murd'rers, and pickpockets too,
And everything that's bad they'd do;
One of our men found to his cost,
Three pounds, York money, he had lost.

They pick'd his pocket quite before
We had been there one single hour;
And while he lookèd o'er and o'er,
The vagrants from him stole some more.

We soon found out, but thought it strange
We never were to be exchang'd
By a cartel, but for some men
Whom they desir'd to have again.

A pack with whom they well agree,
Who're call'd the loyal company,
Or "Loyalists Associated,"
As by themselves incorporated.

Our food was call'd two-thirds in weight
Of what a soldier has to eat;
We had no blankets in our need,
Till a kind friend did intercede.

Said he, "The prisoners suffer so,
'T is quite unkind and cruel, too;
I'm sure it makes my heart to bleed,
So great their hardship and their need.'

And well to us was the event,
Fine blankets soon to us were sent;
Small the allowance, very small,
But better far than none at all.

An oaken plank, it was our bed,
An oaken pillow for the head,
And room as scanty as our meals,
For we lay crowded head and heels.

In seven days or thereabout,
One Jonas Weed was taken out,
And to his friends he was resign'd,
But many still were kept behind.

Soon after this some were parol'd,
Too tedious wholly to be told;
And some from bondage were unstrung,
Whose awful sufferings can't be sung.

The dread smallpox to some they gave,
Nor tried at all their lives to save,
But rather sought their desolation,
As they denied 'em 'noculation.

To the smallpox there did succeed
A putrid fever, bad indeed;
As they before were weak and spent,
Soon from the stage of life they went.

For wood we greatly stood in need,
For which we earnestly did plead;
But one tenth part of what we wanted
Of wood, to us was never granted.

The boiling kettles which we had,
Were wanting covers, good or bad;
The worst of rum that could be bought,
For a great price, to us was brought.

For bread and milk, and sugar, too,
We had to pay four times their due;
While cash and clothing which were sent,
Those wretched creatures did prevent.

Some time it was in dark November
But just the day I can't remember,
Full forty of us were confin'd
In a small room both damp and blind,

Because there had been two or three,
Who were not of our company,
Who did attempt the other day,
The Tories said, to get away.

In eighteen days we were exchang'd,
And through the town allowed to range;
Of twenty-five that were ta'en,
But just nineteen reach'd home again.

Four days before December's gone,
In seventeen hundred eighty-one,
I hail'd the place where months before,
The Tories took me from the shore.

PETER ST. JOHN.

CHAPTER X

THE WAR IN THE SOUTH

After the surrender of Burgoyne, the military attitude of the British in the Northern States was, as has been seen, purely defensive, but the Southern States were the scene of vigorous fighting. The King had set his heart on the reduction of Georgia and the Carolinas, and it looked for a time as though he would be gratified. In General Augustine Prevost there was at last found a man after the King's own heart, and his barbarities and vandalism were among the most monstrous of the war. General Benjamin Lincoln was sent south to oppose him, and was soon joined by Count Pulaski and his legion.

HYMN OF THE MORAVIAN NUNS OF BETHLEHEM

AT THE CONSECRATION OF PULASKI'S BANNER

WHEN the dying flame of day
Through the chancel shot its ray,
Far the glimmering tapers shed
Faint light on the cowlèd head;
And the censer burning swung,
Where, before the altar, hung
The crimson banner, that with prayer
Had been consecrated there.
And the nuns' sweet hymn was heard the
      while,
Sung low, in the dim, mysterious aisle.

"Take thy banner! May it wave
Proudly o'er the good and brave;
When the battle's distant wail
Breaks the sabbath of our vale,
When the clarion's music thrills
To the hearts of these lone hills,
When the spear in conflict shakes,
And the strong lance shivering breaks.

"Take thy banner! and, beneath
The battle-cloud's encircling wreath,
Guard it, till our homes are free!
Guard it! God will prosper thee!
In the dark and trying hour,
In the breaking forth of power,
In the rush of steeds and men,
His right hand will shield thee then.

"Take thy banner! But when night
Closes round the ghastly fight,

If the vanquished warrior bow,
Spare him! By our holy vow,
By our prayers and many tears,
By the mercy that endears,
Spare him! he our love hath shared!
Spare him! as thou wouldst be spared!

"Take thy banner! and if e'er
Thou shouldst press the soldier's bier,
And the muffled drum should beat
To the tread of mournful feet,
Then this crimson flag shall be
Martial cloak and shroud for thee."

The warrior took that banner proud,
And it was his martial cloak and shroud!
      HENRY WADSWORTH LONGFELLOW.

In August, 1779, the French fleet under D'Estaing appeared off the coast of Georgia, and plans were made for the capture of Savannah. The place was closely invested by the French and Americans, and for nearly a month the siege was vigorously carried on. But D'Estaing grew impatient, and on October 9 an attempt was made to carry the place by storm. The assailants were totally defeated, losing more than a thousand men, while the British loss was only fifty-five. Count Pulaski was among the slain.

ABOUT SAVANNAH

[October 9, 1779]

COME let us rejoice,
With heart and with voice,
Her triumphs let loyalty show, sir,
      While bumpers go round,
      Reëcho the sound,
Huzza for the King and Prevost, sir.

With warlike parade,
And his Irish brigade,
His ships and his spruce Gallic host, sir,
      As proud as an elf,
      D'Estaing came himself,
And landed on Georgia's coast, sir.

There joining a band
Under Lincoln's command,
Of rebels and traitors and Whigs, sir,

'Gainst the town of Savannah
He planted his banner,
And then he felt wondrous big, sir.

With thund'ring of guns,
And bursting of bombs,
He thought to have frighten'd our boys, sir:
But amidst all their din,
Brave Maitland push'd in,
And Moncrieffe cried, "A fig for your noise,"
    sir.

Chagrined at delay,
As he meant not to stay,
The Count form'd his troops in the morn, sir.
Van, centre, and rear
March'd up without fear,
Cock sure of success, by a storm, sir.

Though rude was the shock,
Unmov'd as a rock,
Stood our firm British bands to their works,
    sir,
While the brave German corps,
And Americans bore
Their parts as intrepid as Turks, sir.

Then muskets did rattle,
Fierce ragèd the battle,
Grape shot it flew thicker than hail, sir.
The ditch fill'd with slain,
Blood dyed all the plain,
When rebels and French turnèd tail, sir.

See! see! how they run!
Lord! what glorious fun!
How they tumble, by cannon mowed down,
    sir!
Brains fly all around,
Dying screeches resound,
And mangled limbs cover the ground, sir.

There Pulaski fell,
That imp of old Bell,
Who attempted to murder his king, sir.
But now he is gone
Whence he'll never return;
But will make hell with treason to ring, sir.

To Charleston with fear
The rebels repair,
D'Estaing scampers back to his boats, sir,
Each blaming the other,
Each cursing his brother,
And — may they cut each other's throats, sir.

Scarce three thousand men
The town did maintain,
'Gainst three times their number of foes, sir,
Who left on the plain,
Of wounded and slain,
Three thousand to fatten the crows, sir.

Three thousand! no less!
For the rebels confess
Some loss, as you very well know, sir.
Then let bumpers go round,
And reëcho the sound,
Huzza for the King and Prevost, sir.

As soon as Clinton learned of this victory, he
determined to capture Charleston, where General
Lincoln was stationed with three thousand men.
Lincoln decided to withstand a siege, hoping for
reinforcements; but none came, and on May 12,
1780, to avoid a wanton waste of life, he surren-
dered his army and the city to the British.

A SONG ABOUT CHARLESTON

[May 12, 1780]

KING HANCOCK sat in regal state,
And big with pride and vainly great,
    Address'd his rebel crew:
"These haughty Britons soon shall yield
The boasted honors of the field,
    While our brave sons pursue.

"Six thousand fighting men or more,
Protect the Carolina shore,
    And Freedom will defend;
And stubborn Britons soon shall feel,
'Gainst Charleston, and hearts of steel,
    How vainly they contend."

But ere he spake, in dread array,
To rebel foes, ill-fated day,
    The British boys appear;
Their mien with martial ardor fir'd,
And by their country's wrongs inspir'd,
    Shook Lincoln's heart with fear.

See Clinton brave, serene, and great,
For mighty deeds rever'd by fate,
    Direct the thund'ring fight,
While Mars, propitious god of war,
Looks down from his triumphal car
    With wonder and delight.

"Clinton," he cries, "the palm is thine,
'Midst heroes thou wert born to shine
    A great immortal name,

And Cornwallis' mighty deeds appear
Conspicuous each revolving year,
  The pledge of future fame."

Our tars, their share of glories won,
For they among the bravest shone,
  Undaunted, firm, and bold;
Whene'er engag'd, their ardor show'd
Hearts which with native valor glow'd,
  Hearts of true British mould.

The whole of South Carolina was soon overrun
by the British; estates were confiscated, houses
were burned, and alleged traitors hanged without
trial. Organized resistance was impossible, but
there soon sprang up in the state a number of
partisan leaders, foremost among whom was
Francis Marion, perhaps the most picturesque
figure of the Revolution. No act of cruelty ever
sullied the brightness of his fame, but no partisan
leader excelled him in ability to distress the enemy
in legitimate warfare.

THE SWAMP FOX

WE follow where the Swamp Fox guides,
  His friends and merry men are we;
And when the troop of Tarleton rides,
  We burrow in the cypress-tree.
The turfy hammock is our bed,
  Our home is in the red deer's den,
Our roof, the tree-top overhead,
  For we are wild and hunted men.

We fly by day and shun its light,
  But, prompt to strike the sudden blow,
We mount and start with early night,
  And through the forest track our foe.
And soon he hears our chargers leap,
  The flashing sabre blinds his eyes,
And ere he drives away his sleep,
  And rushes from his camp, he dies.

Free bridle-bit, good gallant steed,
  That will not ask a kind caress
To swim the Santee at our need,
  When on his heels the foemen press, —
The true heart and the ready hand,
  The spirit stubborn to be free,
The twisted bore, the smiting brand, —
  And we are Marion's men, you see.

Now light the fire and cook the meal,
  The last perhaps that we shall taste;
I hear the Swamp Fox round us steal,
  And that's a sign we move in haste.

He whistles to the scouts, and hark!
  You hear his order calm and low.
Come, wave your torch across the dark,
  And let us see the boys that go.

We may not see their forms again,
  God help 'em, should they find the strife!
For they are strong and fearless men,
  And make no coward terms for life;
They'll fight as long as Marion bids,
  And when he speaks the word to shy,
Then, not till then, they turn their steeds,
  Through thickening shade and swamp to
    fly.

Now stir the fire and lie at ease, —
  The scouts are gone, and on the brush
I see the Colonel bend his knee,
  To take his slumbers too. But hush!
He's praying, comrades; 't is not strange;
  The man that's fighting day by day
May well, when night comes, take a change,
  And down upon his knees to pray.

Break up that hoe-cake, boys, and hand
  The sly and silent jug that's there;
I love not it should idly stand
  When Marion's men have need of cheer.
'T is seldom that our luck affords
  A stuff like this we just have quaffed,
And dry potatoes on our boards
  May always call for such a draught.

Now pile the brush and roll the log;
  Hard pillow, but a soldier's head
That's half the time in brake and bog
  Must never think of softer bed.
The owl is hooting to the night,
  The cooter crawling o'er the bank,
And in that pond the flashing light
  Tells where the alligator sank.

What! 't is the signal! start so soon,
  And through the Santee swamp so deep,
Without the aid of friendly moon,
  And we, Heaven help us! half asleep!
But courage, comrades! Marion leads,
  The Swamp Fox takes us out to-night;
So clear your swords and spur your steeds,
  There's goodly chance, I think, of fight.

We follow where the Swamp Fox guides,
  We leave the swamp and cypress-tree,
Our spurs are in our coursers' sides,
  And ready for the strife are we.

The Tory camp is now in sight,
  And there he cowers within his den;
He hears our shouts, he dreads the fight,
  He fears, and flies from Marion's men.
                WILLIAM GILMORE SIMMS.

SONG OF MARION'S MEN

OUR band is few, but true and tried,
  Our leader frank and bold;
The British soldier trembles
  When Marion's name is told.
Our fortress is the good greenwood,
  Our tent the cypress-tree;
We know the forest round us
  As seamen know the sea.
We know its walls of thorny vines,
  Its glades of reedy grass,
Its safe and silent islands
  Within the dark morass.

Woe to the English soldiery
  That little dread us near!
On them shall light at midnight
  A strange and sudden fear;
When, waking to their tents on fire,
  They grasp their arms in vain,
And they who stand to face us
  Are beat to earth again;
And they who fly in terror deem
  A mighty host behind,
And hear the tramp of thousands
  Upon the hollow wind.

Then sweet the hour that brings release
  From danger and from toil;
We talk the battle over,
  We share the battle's spoil.
The woodland rings with laugh and shout,
  As if a hunt were up,
And woodland flowers are gathered
  To crown the soldier's cup.
With merry songs we mock the wind
  That in the pine-top grieves,
And slumber long and sweetly
  On beds of oaken leaves.

Well knows the fair and friendly moon
  The band that Marion leads —
The glitter of their rifles,
  The scampering of their steeds.
'T is life to guide the fiery barb
  Across the moonlight plain;

'T is life to feel the night-wind
  That lifts his tossing mane.
A moment in the British camp —
  A moment — and away,
Back to the pathless forest
  Before the peep of day.

Grave men there are by broad Santee,
  Grave men with hoary hairs;
Their hearts are all with Marion,
  For Marion are their prayers.
And lovely ladies greet our band
  With kindliest welcoming,
With smiles like those of summer,
  And tears like those of spring.
For them we wear these trusty arms,
  And lay them down no more
Till we have driven the Briton
  Forever from our shore.
                WILLIAM CULLEN BRYANT.

Among the members of Marion's band was a
gigantic Scotsman named Macdonald, the hero
of many daring escapades, of which his raid
through Georgetown, S. C., with only four troop-
ers, was the most remarkable. Georgetown was
a fortified place, defended by a garrison of three
hundred men.

MACDONALD'S RAID

[1780]

I REMEMBER it well; 't was a morn dull and
      gray,
And the legion lay idle and listless that day,
A thin drizzle of rain piercing chill to the
      soul,
And with not a spare bumper to brighten the
      bowl,
When Macdonald arose, and unsheathing
      his blade,
Cried, "Who'll back me, brave comrades?
      I'm hot for a raid.
Let the carbines be loaded, the war harness
      ring,
Then swift death to the Redcoats, and down
      with the King!"

We leaped up at his summons, all eager and
      bright,
To our finger-tips thrilling to join him in fight;
Yet he chose from our numbers *four* men and
      no more.
"Stalwart brothers," quoth he, "you'll be
      strong as fourscore,

If you follow me fast wheresoever I lead,
With keen sword and true pistol, stanch
    heart and bold steed.
Let the weapons be loaded, the bridle-bits ring,
Then swift death to the Redcoats, and down
    with the King!"

In a trice we were mounted; Macdonald's
    tall form
Seated firm in the saddle, his face like a storm
When the clouds on Ben Lomond hang
    heavy and stark,
And the red veins of lightning pulse hot
    through the dark;
His left hand on his sword-belt, his right
    lifted free,
With a prick from the spurred heel, a touch
    from the knee,
His lithe Arab was off like an eagle on wing —
Ha! death, death to the Redcoats, and down
    with the King!

'T was three leagues to the town, where, in
    insolent pride,
Of their disciplined numbers, their works
    strong and wide,
The big Britons, oblivious of warfare and
    arms,
A soft *dolce* were wrapped in, not dreaming
    of harms,
When fierce yells, as if borne on some fiend-
    ridden rout,
With strange cheer after cheer, are heard
    echoing without,
Over which, like the blast of ten trumpeters,
    ring,
"Death, death to the Redcoats, and down
    with the King!"

Such a tumult we raised with steel, hoof-
    stroke, and shout,
That the foemen made straight for their in-
    most redoubt,
And therein, with pale lips and cowed spirits,
    quoth they,
"Lord, the whole rebel army assaults us to-
    day.
Are the works, think you, strong? God of
    heaven, what a din!
'T is the front wall besieged — have the
    rebels rushed in?
It must be; for, hark! hark to that jubilant
    ring
Of 'death to the Redcoats, and down with
    the King!'"

Meanwhile, through the town like a whirl-
    wind we sped,
And ere long be assured that our broad-
    swords were red;
And the ground here and there by an ominous
    stain
Showed how the stark soldier beside it was
    slain:
A fat sergeant-major, who yawed like a
    goose,
With his waddling bow-legs, and his trappings
    all loose,
By one back-handed blow the Macdonald
    cuts down,
To the shoulder-blade cleaving him sheer
    through the crown,
And the last words that greet his dim con-
    sciousness ring
With "Death, death to the Redcoats, and
    down with the King!"

Having cleared all the streets, not an enemy
    left
Whose heart was unpierced, or whose head-
    piece uncleft,
What should we do next, but — as careless
    and calm
As if we were scenting a summer morn's
    balm
'Mid a land of pure peace — just serenely
    drop down
On the few constant friends who still stopped
    in the town.
What a welcome they gave us! One dear
    little thing,
As I kissed her sweet lips, did I dream of the
    King? —

Of the King or his minions? No; war and its
    scars
Seemed as distant just then as the fierce front
    of Mars
From a love-girdled earth; but, alack! on our
    bliss,
On the close clasp of arms and kiss showering
    on kiss,
Broke the rude bruit of battle, the rush thick
    and fast
Of the Britons made 'ware of our rash *ruse*
    at last;
So we haste to our coursers, yet flying, we
    fling
The old watch-words abroad, "Down with
    Redcoats and King!"

As we scampered pell-mell o'er the hard-
    beaten track
We had traversed that morn, we glanced
    momently back,
And beheld their long earth-works all com-
    passed in flame:
With a vile plunge and hiss the huge musket-
    balls came,
And the soil was ploughed up, and the space
    'twixt the trees
Seemed to hum with the war-song of Brob-
    dingnag bees;
Yet above them, beyond them, victoriously
    ring
The shouts, "Death to the Redcoats, and
    down with the King!"

Ah! *that* was a feat, lads, to boast of! What
    men
Like you weaklings to-day had durst cope
    with *us* then?
Though I say it who should not, I am ready
    to vow
I'd o'ermatch a half score of your fops even
    now —
The poor puny prigs, mincing up, mincing
    down,
Through the whole wasted day the thronged
    streets of the town:
Why, their dainty white necks 't were but
    pastime to wring —
Ay! *my* muscles are firm still; *I* fought 'gainst
    the King!

Dare you doubt it? well, give me the weight-
    iest of all
The sheathed sabres that hang there, un-
    looped on the wall;
Hurl the scabbard aside; yield the blade to
    my clasp;
Do you see, with one hand how I poise it and
    grasp
The rough iron-bound hilt? With this long
    hissing sweep
I have smitten full many a foeman with
    sleep —
That forlorn, final sleep! God! what memo-
    ries cling
To those gallant old times when we fought
    'gainst the King.
            PAUL HAMILTON HAYNE.

Second alone to Marion in this wild warfare was
Thomas Sumter, a Virginian, destined to serve
his country in other ways. During the summer of
1780, he kept up so brisk a guerrilla warfare that
Cornwallis called him " the greatest plague in the
country."

SUMTER'S BAND

WHEN Carolina's hope grew pale
    Before the British lion's tread,
And Freedom's sigh in every gale
    Was heard above her martyr'd dead;

When from her mountain heights subdued,
    In pride of place forbid to soar,
Her Eagle banner, quench'd in blood,
    Lay sullen on the indignant shore,

Breathing revenge, invoking doom,
    Tyrant! upon thy purple host,
When all stood wrapt in steadfast gloom,
    And silence brooded o'er her coast,

Stealthy, as when from thicket dun,
    The Indian springs upon his bow,
Up rose, South Mount, thy warrior son,
    And headlong darted on the foe.

Not in the pride of war he came,
    With bugle note and banner high,
And nodding plume, and steel of flame,
    Red battle's gorgeous panoply!

With followers few, but undismay'd,
    Each change and chance of fate withstood,
Beneath her sunshine and her shade,
    The same heroic brotherhood!

From secret nook, in other land,
    Emerging fleet along the pine,
Prone down he flew before his band,
    Like eagle on the British line!

Catacoba's waters smiled again,
    To see her Sumter's soul in arms;
And issuing from each glade and glen,
    Rekindled by war's fierce alarms,

Throng'd hundreds through the solitude
    Of the wild forest, to the call
Of him whose spirit, unsubdued,
    Fresh impulse gave to each, to all.

By day the burning sands they ply,
    Night sees them in the fell ravine;
Familiar to each follower's eye,
    The tangled brake, the hall of green.

Roused by their tread from covert deep,
  Springs the gaunt wolf, and thus while
     near
Is heard, forbidding thought of sleep,
  The rattling serpent's sound of fear!

Before or break of early morn,
  Or fox looks out from copse to close,
Before the hunter winds his horn,
  Sumter's already on his foes!

He beat them back! beneath the flame
  Of valor quailing, or the shock!
And carved, at last, a hero's name
  Upon the glorious Hanging Rock!

And time, that shades or sears the wreath,
  Where glory binds the soldier's brow,
Kept bright her Sumter's fame in death,
  His hour of proudest triumph, now.

And ne'er shall tyrant tread the shore
  Where Sumter bled, nor bled in vain;
A thousand hearts shall break, before
  They wear the oppressor's chains again.

O never can thy sons forget
  The mighty lessons taught by thee;
Since — treasured by the eternal debt —
  Their watchword is thy memory!
               J. W. SIMMONS.

South Carolina was too important to be left
dependent upon the skill of partisan commanders,
and General Gates was hurried to the scene, only
to be ignominiously defeated by Cornwallis at
Camden, and routed with a loss of two thousand
men. Cornwallis, elated by this victory, started
for North Carolina; but the country was thor-
oughly aroused, and on October 7 a detachment
of twelve hundred men was brought to bay on
King's Mountain, and either killed or captured.

THE BATTLE OF KING'S MOUNTAIN

[October 7, 1780]

'T WAS on a pleasant mountain
  The Tory heathens lay,
With a doughty major at their head,
  One Ferguson, they say.

Cornwallis had detach'd him
  A-thieving for to go,
And catch the Carolina men,
  Or bring the rebels low.

The scamp had rang'd the country
  In search of royal aid,
And with his owls, perchèd on high,
  He taught them all his trade.

But ah! that fatal morning,
  When Shelby brave drew near!
'T is certainly a warning
  That ministers should hear.

And Campbell, and Cleveland,
  And Colonel Sevier,
Each with a band of gallant men,
  To Ferguson appear.

Just as the sun was setting
  Behind the western hills,
Just then our trusty rifles sent
  A dose of leaden pills.

Up, up the steep together
  Brave Williams led his troop,
And join'd by Winston, bold and true,
  Disturb'd the Tory coop.

The royal slaves, the royal owls,
  Flew high on every hand;
But soon they settled — gave a howl,
  And quarter'd to Cleveland.

I would not tell the number
  Of Tories slain that day,
But surely it is certain
  That none did run away.

For all that were a-living,
  Were happy to give up;
So let us make thanksgiving,
  And pass the bright tin-cup.

To all the brave regiments,
  Let's toast 'em for their health,
And may our good country
  Have quietude and wealth.

This brilliant victory restored hope to the
patriots of the South, and Cornwallis soon found
himself in a dangerous position. He was finally
forced to detach Tarleton, with eleven hundred
men, to attack Daniel Morgan's little army of nine
hundred men, which was threatening his line of
communications. On Tarleton's approach, Morgan
retreated to a grazing ground known as the Cow-
pens near King's Mountain, and here, on January
17, 1781, Tarleton attacked him, only to be com-
pletely routed.

THE BATTLE OF THE COWPENS

[January 17, 1781]

To the Cowpens riding proudly, boasting
        loudly, rebels scorning,
    Tarleton hurried, hot and eager for the fight;
From the Cowpens, sore confounded, on that
        January morning,
    Tarleton hurried somewhat faster, fain to
        save himself by flight.

In the morn he scorned us rarely, but he
        fairly found his error,
    When his force was made our ready blows
        to feel;
When his horsemen and his footmen fled in
        wild and pallid terror
    At the leaping of our bullets and the sweep-
        ing of our steel.

All the day before we fled them, and we led
        them to pursue us,
    Then at night on Thickety Mountain
        made our camp;
There we lay upon our rifles, slumber quickly
        coming to us,
    Spite the crackling of our camp-fires and
        our sentries' heavy tramp.

Morning on the mountain border ranged in
        order found our forces,
    Ere our scouts announced the coming of
        the foe;
While the hoar-frost lying near us, and the
        distant water-courses,
    Gleamed like silver in the sunlight, seemed
        like silver in their glow.

Morgan ranged us there to meet them, and
        to greet them with such favor
    That they scarce would care to follow us
        again;
In the rear, the Continentals — none were
        readier, nor braver;
    In the van, with ready rifles, steady, stern,
        our mountain men.

Washington, our trooper peerless, gay and
        fearless, with his forces
    Waiting panther-like upon the foe to fall,
Formed upon the slope behind us, where, on
        raw-boned country horses,
    Sat the sudden-summoned levies brought
        from Georgia by M'Call.

Soon we heard a distant drumming, nearer
        coming, slow advancing —
    It was then upon the very nick of nine.
Soon upon the road from Spartanburg we
        saw their bayonets glancing,
    And the morning sunlight playing on their
        swaying scarlet line.

In the distance seen so dimly, they looked
        grimly; coming nearer,
    There was naught about them fearful,
        after all,
Until some one near me spoke in voice than
        falling water clearer,
    "Tarleton's quarter is the sword-blade,
        Tarleton's mercy is the ball."

Then the memory came unto me, heavy,
        gloomy, of my brother
    Who was slain while asking quarter at
        their hand;
Of that morning when was driven forth my
        sister and my mother
    From our cabin in the valley by the spoilers
        of the land.

I remembered of my brother slain, my mother
        spurned and beaten,
    Of my sister in her beauty brought to
        shame;
Of the wretches' jeers and laughter, as from
        mud-sill up to rafter
    Of the stripped and plundered cabin leapt
        the fierce, consuming flame.

But that memory had no power there in that
        hour there to depress me —
    No! it stirred within my spirit fiercer ire;
And I gripped my sword-hilt firmer, and my
        arm and heart grew stronger;
    And I longed to meet the wronger on the
        sea of steel and fire.

On they came, our might disdaining, where
        the raining bullets leaden
    Pattered fast from scattered rifles on each
        wing;
Here and there went down a foeman, and the
        ground began to redden;
    And they drew them back a moment, like
        the tiger ere his spring.

Then said Morgan, "Ball and powder kill
        much prouder men than George's;
    On your rifles and a careful aim rely.

They were trained in many battles — we in
  workshops, fields, and forges;
But we have our homes to fight for, and
  we do not fear to die."

Though our leader's words we cheered not,
  yet we feared not; we awaited,
Strong of heart, the threatened onset, and
  it came:
Up the sloping hill-side swiftly rushed the foe
  so fiercely hated;
On they came with gleaming bayonet 'mid
  the cannon's smoke and flame.

At their head rode Tarleton proudly; ringing
  loudly o'er the yelling
Of his men we heard his voice's brazen tone;
With his dark eyes flashing fiercely, and his
  sombre features telling
In their look the pride that filled him as the
  champion of the throne.

On they pressed, when sudden flashing,
  ringing, crashing, came the firing
Of our forward line upon their close-set
  ranks;
Then at coming of their steel, which moved
  with steadiness untiring,
Fled our mountaineers, re-forming in good
  order on our flanks.

Then the combat's raging anger, din, and
  clangor, round and o'er us
Filled the forest, stirred the air, and shook
  the ground;
Charged with thunder-tramp the horsemen,
  while their sabres shone before us,
Gleaming lightly, streaming brightly,
  through the smoky cloud around.

Through the pines and oaks resounding,
  madly bounding from the mountain,
Leapt the rattle of the battle and the roar;
Fierce the hand-to-hand engaging, and the
  human freshet raging
Of the surging current urging past a dark
  and bloody shore.

Soon the course of fight was altered; soon
  they faltered at the leaden
Storm that smote them, and we saw their
  centre swerve.
Tarleton's eye flashed fierce in anger; Tarle-
  ton's face began to redden;
Tarleton gave the closing order — "Bring
  to action the reserve!"

Up the slope his legion thundered, full three
  hundred; fiercely spurring,
Cheering lustily, they fell upon our flanks;
And their worn and wearied comrades, at the
  sound so spirit-stirring,
Felt a thrill of hope and courage pass along
  their shattered ranks.

By the wind the smoke-cloud lifted lightly
  drifted to the nor'ward,
And displayed in all their pride the scarlet
  foe;
We beheld them, with a steady tramp and
  fearless, moving forward,
With their banners proudly waving, and
  their bayonets levelled low.

Morgan gave his order clearly — "Fall back
  nearly to the border
Of the hill and let the enemy come nigher!"
Oh! they thought we had retreated, and they
  charged in fierce disorder,
When out rang the voice of Howard —
  "To the right about, face! — Fire!"

Then upon our very wheeling came the peal
  ing of our volley,
And our balls made red a pathway down
  the hill;
Broke the foe and shrank and cowered; rang
  again the voice of Howard —
"Give the hireling dogs the bayonet!" —
  and we did it with a will.

In the meanwhile one red-coated troop, un-
  noted, riding faster
Than their comrades on our rear in fury
  bore;
But the light-horse led by Washington soon
  brought it to disaster,
For they shattered it and scattered it, and
  smote it fast and sore.

Like a herd of startled cattle from the battle-
  field we drove them;
In disorder down the Mill-gap road they
  fled;
Tarleton led them in the racing, fast he fled
  before our chasing,
And he stopped not for the dying, and he
  stayed not for the dead.

Down the Mill-gap road they scurried and
  they hurried with such fleetness —
We had never seen such running in our
  lives!

Ran they swifter than if seeking homes to
    taste domestic sweetness,
  Having many years been parted from their
    children and their wives.

Ah! for some no wife to meet them, child to
    greet them, friend to shield them!
  To their home o'er ocean never sailing
    back;
After them the red avengers, bitter hate for
    death had sealed them,
  Yelped the dark and red-eyed sleuth-
    hound unrelenting on their track.

In their midst I saw one trooper, and around
    his waist I noted
  Tied a simple silken scarf of blue and
    white;
When my vision grasped it clearly to my
    hatred I devoted
  Him, from all the hireling wretches who
    were mingled there in flight.

For that token in the summer had been from
    our cabin taken
  By the robber-hands of wrongers of my
    kin;
'T was my sister's — for the moment things
    around me were forsaken;
  I was blind to fleeing foemen, I was deaf
    to battle's din.

Olden comrades round me lying dead or dy-
    ing were unheeded;
  Vain to me they looked for succor in their
    need.
O'er the corses of the soldiers, through the
    gory pools I speeded,
  Driving rowel-deep my spurs within my
    madly-bounding steed.

As I came he turned, and staring at my glar-
    ing eyes he shivered;
  Pallid fear went quickly o'er his features
    grim;
As he grasped his sword in terror, every nerve
    within him quivered,
  For his guilty spirit told him why I solely
    sought for him.

Though the stroke I dealt he parried, on-
    ward carried, down I bore him —
  Horse and rider — down together went
    the twain:

"Quarter!" — He! that scarf had doomed
    him! stood a son and brother o'er him;
  Down through plume and brass and leather
    went my sabre to the brain —
Ha! no music like that crushing through
    the skull-bone to the brain.
                        THOMAS DUNN ENGLISH.

Tarleton's defeat deprived Cornwallis of nearly
a third of his forces, and his situation became more
desperate than ever. He kept on across North
Carolina and engaged Greene in an indecisive
action at Guilford Court-House on March 15, and
then retreated to Wilmington. Greene, with
splendid strategy, started at once for South Caro-
lina, captured nearly all the forts there in British
hands, and on September 8 fell upon the British
at Eutaw Springs, compelling them to retreat to
Charleston.

THE BATTLE OF EUTAW

[September 8, 1781]

HARK! 't is the voice of the mountain,
  And it speaks to our heart in its pride,
As it tells of the bearing of heroes
  Who compassed its summits and died!
How they gathered to strife as the eagles,
  When the foeman had clambered the
    height!
How, with scent keen and eager as beagles,
  They hunted him down for the fight.

Hark! through the gorge of the valley,
  'T is the bugle that tells of the foe;
Our own quickly sounds for the rally,
  And we snatch down the rifle and go.
As the hunter who hears of the panther,
  Each arms him and leaps to his steed,
Rides forth through the desolate antre,
  With his knife and his rifle at need.

From a thousand deep gorges they gather,
  From the cot lowly perched by the rill,
The cabin half hid in the heather,
  'Neath the crag which the eagle keeps
    still;
Each lonely at first in his roaming,
  Till the vale to the sight opens fair,
And he sees the low cot through the gloam-
    ing,
  When his bugle gives tongue to the air.

Thus a thousand brave hunters assemble
  For the hunt of the insolent foe,

And soon shall his myrmidons tremble
   'Neath the shock of the thunderbolt's
     blow.
Down the lone heights now wind they to-
   gether,
   As the mountain-brooks flow to the vale,
And now, as they group on the heather,
   The keen scout delivers his tale:

"The British — the Tories are on us,
   And now is the moment to prove
To the women whose virtues have won us,
   That our virtues are worthy their love!
They have swept the vast valleys below us
   With fire, to the hills from the sea;
And here would they seek to o'erthrow us
   In a realm which our eagle makes free!"

No war-council suffered to trifle
   With the hours devote to the deed;
Swift followed the grasp of the rifle,
   Swift followed the bound to the steed;
And soon, to the eyes of our yeomen,
   All panting with rage at the sight,
Gleamed the long wavy tents of the foeman,
   As he lay in his camp on the height.

Grim dashed they away as they bounded,
   The hunters to hem in the prey,
And, with Deckard's long rifles surrounded,
   Then the British rose fast to the fray;
And never with arms of more vigor
   Did their bayonets press through the strife,
Where, with every swift pull of the trigger,
   The sharpshooters dashed out a life!

'T was the meeting of eagles and lions;
   'T was the rushing of tempests and waves;
Insolent triumph 'gainst patriot defiance,
   Born freemen 'gainst sycophant slaves;
Scotch Ferguson sounding his whistle,
   As from danger to danger he flies,
Feels the moral that lies in Scotch thistle,
   With its "touch me who dare!" and he
     dies!

An hour, and the battle is over;
   The eagles are rending the prey;
The serpents seek flight into cover,
   But the terror still stands in the way:
More dreadful the doom that on treason
   Avenges the wrongs of the state;
And the oak-tree for many a season
   Bears fruit for the vultures of fate!
         WILLIAM GILMORE SIMMS.

EUTAW SPRINGS

TO THE MEMORY OF THE BRAVE AMERICANS,
UNDER GENERAL GREENE, IN SOUTH CARO-
LINA, WHO FELL IN THE ACTION OF SEP-
TEMBER 8, 1781, AT EUTAW SPRINGS

AT Eutaw Springs the valiant died:
   Their limbs with dust are covered o'er —
Weep on, ye springs, your tearful tide;
   How many heroes are no more!

If in this wreck of ruin they
   Can yet be thought to claim a tear,
O smite thy gentle breast, and say
   The friends of freedom slumber here!

Thou who shalt trace this bloody plain,
   If goodness rules thy generous breast,
Sigh for the wasted, rural reign;
   Sigh for the shepherds, sunk to rest!

Stranger, their humble graves adorn;
   You too may fall and ask a tear;
'T is not the beauty of the morn
   That proves the evening shall be clear —

They saw their injured country's woe;
   The flaming town, the wasted field;
Then rushed to meet the insulting foe;
   They took the spear, — but left the
     shield.

Led by thy conquering genius, Greene,
   The Britons they compelled to fly;
None distant viewed the fatal plain,
   None grieved, in such a cause, to die —

But, like the Parthians famed of old,
   Who, flying, still their arrows threw,
These routed Britons, full as bold,
   Retreated, and retreating slew.

Now rest in peace, our patriot band;
   Though far from Nature's limits thrown,
We trust they find a happier land,
   A brighter sunshine of their own.
         PHILIP FRENEAU.

Cornwallis, meanwhile, had marched off toward
Virginia, reaching Petersburg May 20, 1781, join-
ing the British forces there and raising his army
to five thousand men. He marched down the
peninsula and established himself at Yorktown,
adding the garrison of Portsmouth to his army,
so that it numbered over seven thousand men.

THE DANCE

CORNWALLIS led a country dance,
  The like was never seen, sir,
Much retrograde and much advance,
  And all with General Greene, sir.

They rambled up and rambled down,
  Joined hands, then off they run, sir,
Our General Greene to Charlestown,
  The earl to Wilmington, sir.

Greene in the South then danced a set,
  And got a mighty name, sir,
Cornwallis jigged with young Fayette,
  But suffered in his fame, sir.

Then down he figured to the shore,
  Most like a lordly dancer,
And on his courtly honor swore
  He would no more advance, sir.

Quoth he, my guards are weary grown
  With footing country dances,
They never at St. James's shone,
  At capers, kicks, or prances.

Though men so gallant ne'er were seen,
  While sauntering on parade, sir,
Or wriggling o'er the park's smooth green,
  Or at a masquerade, sir.

Yet are red heels and long-laced skirts,
  For stumps and briars meet, sir?
Or stand they chance with hunting-shirts,
  Or hardy veteran feet, sir?

Now housed in York, he challenged all,
  At minuet or all 'amande,
And lessons for a courtly ball
  His guards by day and night conned.

This challenge known, full soon there came
  A set who had the bon ton,
De Grasse and Rochambeau, whose fame
  Fut brillant pour un long tems.

And Washington, Columbia's son,
  Whom easy nature taught, sir,
That grace which can't by pains be won,
  Or Plutus's gold be bought, sir.

Now hand in hand they circle round
  This ever-dancing peer, sir;

Their gentle movements soon confound
  The earl as they draw near, sir.

His music soon forgets to play —
  His feet can move no more, sir,
And all his bands now curse the day
  They jiggèd to our shore, sir.

Now Tories all, what can ye say?
  Come — is not this a griper,
That while your hopes are danced away,
  'T is you must pay the piper?

Here an unexpected factor entered upon the scene. A magnificent French fleet under Count de Grasse had sailed for the Chesapeake, and Washington, with a daring worthy of Cæsar or Napoleon, decided to transfer his army from the Hudson to Virginia and overwhelm Cornwallis. On August 19 Washington's army crossed the Hudson at King's Ferry and started on its four hundred mile march. On September 18 it appeared before Yorktown. The French squadron was already on the scene, and Cornwallis was in the trap. There was no escape. On October 17 he hoisted the white flag, and two days later the British army, over seven thousand in number, laid down its arms.

CORNWALLIS'S SURRENDER

[October 19, 1781]

WHEN British troops first landed here,
  With Howe commander o'er them,
They thought they'd make us quake for fear,
  And carry all before them;
With thirty thousand men or more,
  And she without assistance,
America must needs give o'er,
  And make no more resistance.

But Washington, her glorious son,
  Of British hosts the terror,
Soon, by repeated overthrows,
  Convinc'd them of their error;
Let Princeton, and let Trenton tell,
  What gallant deeds he's done, sir,
And Monmouth's plains where hundreds fell,
  And thousands more have run, sir.

Cornwallis, too, when he approach'd
  Virginia's old dominion,
Thought he would soon her conqu'ror be;
  And so was North's opinion.
From State to State with rapid stride,
  His troops had march'd before, sir,

Till quite elate with martial pride,
He thought all dangers o'er, sir.

But our allies, to his surprise,
The Chesapeake had enter'd;
And now too late, he curs'd his fate,
And wish'd he ne'er had ventur'd,
For Washington no sooner knew
The visit he had paid her,
Than to his parent State he flew,
To crush the bold invader.

When he sat down before the town,
His Lordship soon surrender'd;
His martial pride he laid aside,
And cas'd the British standard;
Gods! how this stroke will North provoke,
And all his thoughts confuse, sir!
And how the Peers will hang their ears,
When first they hear the news, sir.

Be peace, the glorious end of war,
By this event effected;
And be the name of Washington
To latest times respected;
Then let us toast America,
And France in union with her;
And may Great Britain rue the day
Her hostile bands came hither.

THE SURRENDER OF CORNWALLIS

COME, all ye bold Americans, to you the truth
I tell,
'T is of a sad disaster, which late on Britain
fell;
'T was near the height of Old Yorktown,
where the cannons loud did roar,
A summons to Cornwallis, to fight or else give
o'er.

A summons to surrender was sent unto the
lord,
Which made him feel like poor Burgoyne
and quickly draw his sword,
Saying, "Must I give o'er those glittering
troops, those ships and armies too.
And yield to General Washington, and his
brave noble crew?"

A council to surrender this lord did then com-
mand;
"What say you, my brave heroes, to yield
you must depend;

Don't you hear the bomb-shells flying, boys,
and the thundering cannon's roar?
De Grasse is in the harbor, and Washing-
ton's on shore."

'T was on the nineteenth of October, in the
year of '81,
Cornwallis did surrender to General Wash-
ington;
Six thousand chosen British troops march'd
out and grounded arms;
Huzza, ye bold Americans, for now sweet
music charms.

Six thousand chosen British troops to Wash-
ington resign'd,
Besides some thousand Hessians that could
not stay behind;
Both refugees and Tories all, when the devil
gets his due,
O now we have got thousands, boys, but then
we should have few.

Unto New York this lord has gone, surren-
dering you see,
And for to write these doleful lines unto his
majesty;
For to contradict those lines, which he before
had sent,
That he and his brave British crew were con-
querors where they went.

Here's a health to General Washington, and
his brave noble crew,
Likewise unto De Grasse, and all that liberty
pursue;
May they scourge these bloody tyrants, all
from our Yankee shore.
And with the arms of Freedom cause the
wars they are all o'er.

"Early on a dark morning of the fourth week
in October, an honest old German, slowly pacing
the streets of Philadelphia on his night watch,
began shouting, 'Basht dree o'glock, und Gorn-
vallis ish dakendt!' and light sleepers sprang out
of bed and threw up their windows." The whole
country burst into jubilation at the news, and
every village green was ablaze with bonfires.

NEWS FROM YORKTOWN

OCTOBER, 1781

"PAST two o'clock and Cornwallis is taken.'
How the voice rolled down the street

Till the silence rang and echoed
    With the stir of hurrying feet!
In the hush of the Quaker city,
    As the night drew on to morn,
How it startled the troubled sleepers,
    Like the cry for a man-child born!

"Past two o'clock and Cornwallis is taken."
    How they gathered, man and maid,
Here the child with a heart for the flint-lock,
    There the trembling grandsire staid!
From the stateliest homes of the city,
    From hovels that love might scorn,
How they followed that ringing summons.
    Like the cry for a king's heir born!

"Past two o'clock and Cornwallis is taken."
    I can see the quick lights flare,
See the glad, wild face at the window,
    Half dumb in a breathless stare.
In the pause of an hour portentous,
    In the gloom of a hope forlorn,
How it throbbed to the star-deep heavens,
    Like the cry for a nation born!

"Past two o'clock and Cornwallis is taken."
    How the message is sped and gone
To the farm and the town and the forest
    Till the world was one vast dawn!
To distant and slave-sunk races,
    Bowed down in their chains that morn,
How it swept on the winds of heaven,
    Like a cry for God's justice born!
                LEWIS WORTHINGTON SMITH.

AN ANCIENT PROPHECY

(Written soon after the surrender of Cornwallis)

WHEN a certain great King, whose initial is G.,
Forces stamps upon paper and folks to drink
        tea;

When these folks burn his tea and stampt-
        paper, like stubble,
You may guess that this King is then coming
        to trouble.

But when a Petition he treads under feet,
And sends over the ocean an army and
        fleet,
When that army, half famished, and frantic
        with rage,
Is cooped up with a leader whose name
        rhymes to *cage* ;
When that leader goes home, dejected and
        sad;
You may then be assur'd the King's pros-
        pects are bad.

But when B. and C. with their armies are
        taken
This King will do well if he saves his own
        bacon:
In the year Seventeen hundred and eighty
        and two
A stroke he shall get, that will make him look
        blue;
And soon, very soon, shall the season ar-
        rive,
When Nebuchadnezzar to pasture shall drive.

In the year eighty-three, the affair will be
        over
And he shall eat turnips that grow in Han-
        over;
The face of the Lion will then become pale,
He shall yield fifteen teeth and be sheared of
        his tail —
O King, my dear King, you shall be very
        sore,
From the *Stars* and the *Stripes* you will
        mercy implore,
And your Lion shall growl, but hardly bite
        more. —
                PHILIP FRENEAU.

CHAPTER XI

PEACE

The news of Cornwallis's surrender was received with consternation in Great Britain. The King declared that he would abdicate rather than acknowledge the independence of the United States, Lord North resigned, Lord Germaine was dismissed, and Sir Henry Clinton was superseded in command of the army by Sir Guy Carleton.

ON SIR HENRY CLINTON'S RECALL

[May, 1782]

The dog that is beat has a right to com-
    plain —
Sir Harry returns, a disconsolate swain,
To the face of his master, the devil's anointed,
To the country provided for thieves disap-
    pointed.

Our freedom, he thought, to a tyrant must
    fall:
He concluded the weakest must go to the
    wall.
The more he was flatter'd, the bolder he grew:
He quitted the old world to conquer the new.

But in spite of the deeds he has done in his
    garrison
(And they have been curious beyond all com-
    parison),
He now must go home, at the call of his king,
To answer the charges that Arnold may bring.

But what are the acts which this chief has
    achieved?
If good, it is hard he should now be aggrieved:
And the more, as he fought for his national
    glory,
Nor valued, a farthing, the *right* of the story.

This famous great man, and two birds of his
    feather,
In the Cerberus frigate came over together:
But of all the bold chiefs that remeasure the
    trip,
Not two have been known to return in one
    ship.

Like children that wrestle and scuffle in sport,
They are very well pleased as long as unhurt;
But a thump on the nose, or a blow in the eye,
Ends the fray; and they go to their daddy
    and cry.

Sir Clinton, thy deeds have been mighty and
    many!
You said all our paper was not worth a penny:
('T is nothing but rags, quoth honest Will
    Tryon:
Are rags to discourage the sons of the lion?)

But Clinton thought thus: "It is folly to fight,
When things may by easier methods come
    right:
There is such an art as counterfeit-ation,
And I 'll do my utmost to honor our nation:

"I 'll show this damn'd country that I can
    enslave her,
And that by the help of a skilful engraver;
And then let the rebels take care of their
    bacon;
We 'll play 'em a trick, or I 'm vastly mis-
    taken."

But the project succeeded not quite to your
    liking;
So you paid off your artist, and gave up bill-
    striking:
But 't is an affair I am glad you are quit on:
You had surely been hang'd had you tried it
    in Britain.

At the taking of Charlestown you cut a great
    figure,
The terms you propounded were terms full
    of rigor,
Yet could not foresee poor Charley's disgrace,
Nor how soon your own colors would go to
    the case.

When the town had surrender'd, the more
    to disgrace ye
(Like another true Briton that did it at
    'Statia),
You broke all the terms yourself had ex-
    tended,
Because you supposed the rebellion was
    ended.

Whoever the Tories mark'd out as a Whig,
If gentle, or simple, or little, or big,
No matter to you — to kill 'em and spite 'em,
You soon had 'em up where the dogs could n't
    bite 'em.

Then, thinking these rebels were snug and
    secure,
You left them to Rawdon and Nesbit Bal-
    four
(The face of the latter no mask need be
    draw'd on,
And to fish for the devil, my bait should be
    Rawdon).

Returning to York with your ships and your
    plunder,
And boasting that rebels must shortly knock
    under,
The first thing that struck you as soon as you
    landed
Was the fortress at West Point where Arnold
    commanded.

Thought you, "If friend Arnold this fort will
    deliver,
We then shall be masters of all Hudson's
    river;
The east and the south losing communication,
The Yankees will die by the act of starva-
    tion."

So off you sent André (not guided by Pallas),
Who soon purchased Arnold, and with him
    the gallows;
Your loss, I conceive, than your gain was far
    greater,
You lost a good fellow and got a damn'd
    traitor.

Now Carleton comes over to give you relief;
A knight, like yourself, and commander-in-
    chief;
But the *chief* he will get, you may tell the dear
    honey,
Will be a black eye, hard knocks, and no
    money.

Now, with "Britons, strike home!" your
    sorrows dispel;
Away to your master, and honestly tell,
That his arms and his artists can nothing
    avail;
His men are too few, and his tricks are too
    stale.

Advise him, at length to be just and sincere,
Of which not a symptom as yet doth appear;
As we plainly perceive from his sending Sir
    Guy,
Commission'd to steal, and commission'd to
    lie.

Freeman's Journal, May 22, 1782.

George III also declared that he would retain
the cities of New York and Charleston at all
hazards, but it was soon out of his power to retain
Charleston, at least. General Leslie, in command
there, found himself in dire straits for supplies,
and on December 14, 1782, evacuated the city
and sailed away for Halifax.

ON THE DEPARTURE OF THE BRITISH FROM CHARLESTON

[December 14, 1782]

HIS triumphs of a moment done;
His race of desolation run,
The Briton, yielding to his fears,
To other shores with sorrow steers:

To other shores — and coarser climes
He goes, reflecting on his crimes,
His broken oaths, a murder'd *Hayne*,
And blood of thousands, spilt in vain.

To *Cooper's* stream, advancing slow,
Ashley no longer tells his woe,
No longer mourns his limpid flood
Discolor'd deep with human blood.

Lo! where those social streams combine
Again the friends of Freedom join;
And, while they stray where once they bled,
Rejoice to find their tyrants fled,

Since memory paints that dismal day
When British squadrons held the sway,
And circling close on every side,
By sea and land retreat deny'd —

Shall she recall that mournful scene,
And not the virtues of a GREENE,
Who great in war — in danger try'd,
Has won the day, and crush'd their pride.

Through barren wastes and ravag'd lands
He led his bold undaunted bands,
Through sickly climes his standard bore
Where never army marched before:

By fortitude, with patience join'd
(The virtues of a noble mind),
He spread, where'er our wars are known,
His country's honor and his own.

Like Hercules, his generous plan
Was to redress the wrongs of men;
Like him, accustom'd to subdue,
He freed a world from *monsters* too.

Through every want and every ill
We saw him persevering still,
Through Autumn's damps and Summer's
    heat,
Till his great purpose was complete.

Like the bold eagle, from the skies
That stoops, to seize his trembling prize,
He darted on the slaves of kings
At Camden heights and Eutaw Springs.

Ah! had our friends that led the fray
Surviv'd the ruins of that day,
We should not damp our joy with pain,
Nor, sympathizing, now complain.

Strange! that of those who nobly dare
Death always claims so large a share,
That those of virtue most refin'd
Are soonest to the grave consign'd! —

But fame is theirs — and future days
On pillar'd brass shall tell their praise;
Shall tell — when cold neglect is dead —
"These for their country fought and bled."
                    PHILIP FRENEAU.

However the King might froth and bluster, it
was evident that he was beaten. He was forced
to bow to the inevitable, and on December 5,
1782, in his speech at the opening of Parliament,
he recommended that peace be made with the
colonies in America, and that they be declared
free and independent.

ON THE BRITISH KING'S SPEECH

RECOMMENDING PEACE WITH THE AMERI-
CAN STATES

[December 5, 1782]

GROWN sick of war, and war's alarms,
    Good George has changed his note at last —
Conquest and death have lost their charms;
    He and his nation stand aghast,

To think what fearful lengths they've
    gone,
And what a brink they stand upon.

Old Bute and North, twin sons of hell,
    If you advised him to retreat
Before our vanquished thousands fell,
    Prostrate, submissive at his feet:
        Awake once more his latent flame,
        And bid us yield you all you claim.

The Macedonian wept and sighed
    Because no other world was found
Where he might glut his rage and pride,
    And by its ruin be renowned;
        The world that Sawney wished to view
        George fairly had — and lost it too!

Let jarring powers make war or peace,
    Monster! — no peace can greet your breast!
Our murdered friends can never cease
    To hover round and break your rest!
        The Furies will your bosom tear,
        Remorse, distraction, and despair
        And hell, with all its fiends, be there!

Cursed be the ship that e'er sets sail
    Hence, freighted for your odious shore;
May tempests o'er her strength prevail,
    Destruction round her roar!
May Nature all her aids deny,
    The sun refuse his light,
The needle from its object fly,
    No star appear by night:
        Till the base pilot, conscious of his
            crime,
        Directs the prow to some more Christian
            clime.

Genius! that first our race designed,
    To other kings impart
The finer feelings of the mind,
    The virtues of the heart;
Whene'er the honors of a throne
    Fall to the bloody and the base,
Like Britain's tyrant, pull them down,
    Like his, be their disgrace!

Hibernia, seize each native right!
    Neptune, exclude him from the main;
Like her that sunk with all her freight,
The Royal George, take all his fleet,
    And never let them rise again;
Confine him to his gloomy isle,
    Let Scotland rule her half,

Spare him to curse his fate awhile,
   And Whitehead, thou to write his epitaph.
                              PHILIP FRENEAU.

ENGLAND AND AMERICA IN 1782

O THOU, that sendest out the man
   To rule by land and sea,
Strong mother of a Lion-line,
Be proud of those strong sons of thine
   Who wrench'd their rights from thee!

What wonder if in noble heat
   Those men thine arms withstood,
Retaught the lesson thou had'st taught,
And in thy spirit with thee fought, —
   Who sprang from English blood!

But thou rejoice with liberal joy,
   Lift up thy rocky face,
And shatter, when the storms are black,
In many a streaming torrent back,
   The seas that shock thy base!

Whatever harmonies of law
   The growing world assume,
Thy work is thine — the single note
From that deep chord which Hampden
      smote
   Will vibrate to the doom.
                              ALFRED TENNYSON.

A preliminary treaty of peace was finally agreed
upon. Carleton received orders to evacuate New
York, and on October 18, 1783, Congress issued a
general order disbanding the American army.

ON DISBANDING THE ARMY

[October 18, 1783]

YE brave Columbian bands! a long farewell!
Well have ye fought for freedom — nobly
      done
Your martial task — the meed immortal
      won —
And Time's last records shall your triumphs
      tell.

Once friendship made their cup of suff'rings
      sweet —
The dregs how bitter, now those bands must
      part!
Ah! never, never more on earth to meet;

Distill'd from gall that inundates the heart,
What tears from heroes' eyes are seen to
      start!

Ye, too, farewell, who fell in fields of gore,
And chang'd tempestuous toil for rest serene;
Soon shall we join you on the peaceful shore
(Though gulfs irremeable roll between),
Thither by death-tides borne, as ye full soon
      have been.
                              DAVID HUMPHREYS.

November 25 was fixed upon as the date for
the evacuation of New York. Early on that day,
Carleton got his troops on shipboard, and by the
middle of the afternoon the city was in the hands
of the Americans. The song which is given below
was composed for and sung upon this occasion.

EVACUATION OF NEW YORK BY
THE BRITISH

[November 25, 1783]

THEY come! — they come! — the heroes
      come
With sounding fife, with thundering drum;
Their ranks advance in bright array, —
The heroes of America!

He comes! — 't is mighty Washington
(Words fail to tell all he has done),
Our hero, guardian, father, friend!
His fame can never, never end.

He comes! — he comes! — our Clinton comes!
Justice her ancient seat resumes:
From shore to shore let shouts resound,
For Justice comes, with Freedom crown'd.

She comes! — the angelic virgin — Peace,
And bids stern War his horrors cease;
Oh! blooming virgin, with us stay,
And bless, oh! bless America.

Since Freedom has our efforts crown'd,
Let flowing bumpers pass around:
The toast is, "Freedom's favorite son,
Health, peace, and joy to Washington!"

On Thursday, December 4, the principal officers
of the army assembled at Fraunce's Tavern to
take a final leave of their beloved chief. A few
days later, at Annapolis, Washington resigned his
commission, and betook himself to the quiet of
his estate at Mount Vernon.

OCCASIONED BY GENERAL WASH-
INGTON'S ARRIVAL IN PHILA-
DELPHIA, ON HIS WAY TO HIS
RESIDENCE IN VIRGINIA

[December, 1783]

THE great unequal conflict past,
  The Briton banished from our shore,
Peace, heaven-descended, comes at last,
  And hostile nations rage no more;
    From fields of death the weary swain
    Returning, seeks his native plain.

In every vale she smiles serene,
  Freedom's bright stars more radiant rise,
New charms she adds to every scene,
  Her brighter sun illumes our skies.
    Remotest realms admiring stand,
    And hail the *Hero* of our land:

He comes! — the Genius of these lands —
  Fame's thousand tongues his worth con-
    fess,
Who conquer'd with his suffering bands,
  And grew immortal by distress:
    Thus calms succeed the stormy blast,
    And valor is repaid at last.

O WASHINGTON! — thrice glorious name,
  What due rewards can man decree —
Empires are far below thy aim,
  And sceptres have no charms for thee;
    Virtue alone has your regard,
    And she must be your great reward.

Encircled by extorted power,
  Monarchs must envy your *Retreat*
Who cast, in some ill-fated hour,
  Their country's freedom at their feet;
    'T was yours to act a nobler part,
    For injur'd Freedom had your heart.

For ravag'd realms and conquer'd seas
  Rome gave the great imperial prize,
And, swell'd with pride, for feats like these,
  Transferr'd her heroes to the skies: —
    A brighter scene your deeds display,
    You gain those heights a different way.

When *Faction* rear'd her bristly head,
  And join'd with tyrants to destroy,
Where'er you march'd the monster fled,
  Timorous her arrows to employ:
    Hosts catch'd from you a bolder flame,
    And despots trembled at your name.

Ere war's dread horrors ceas'd to reign,
  What leader could your place supply? —
Chiefs crowded to the embattled plain,
  Prepar'd to conquer or to die —
    Heroes arose — but none, like you,
    Could save our lives and freedom too.

In swelling verse let kings be read,
  And princes shine in polish'd prose;
Without such aid your triumphs spread
  Where'er the convex ocean flows,
    To Indian worlds by seas embrac'd,
    And Tartar, tyrant of the waste.

Throughout the east you gain applause,
  And soon the *Old World*, taught by you,
Shall blush to own her barbarous laws,
  Shall learn instruction from the *New*.
    Monarchs shall hear the humble plea,
    Nor urge too far the proud decree.

Despising pomp and vain parade,
  At home you stay, while France and Spain
The secret, ardent wish convey'd,
  And hail'd you to their shores in vain:
    In *Vernon's* groves you shun the throne,
    Admir'd by kings, but seen by none.

Your fame, thus spread to distant lands,
  May envy's fiercest blasts endure,
Like Egypt's pyramids it stands,
  Built on a basis more secure;
    Time's latest age shall own in you
    The patriot and the statesman too.

Now hurrying from the busy scene,
  Where thy *Potowmack's* waters flow,
May'st thou enjoy thy rural reign,
  And every earthly blessing know;
    Thus he, who Rome's proud legions
      sway'd,
    Return'd, and sought his sylvan shade.

Not less in wisdom than in war
  Freedom shall still employ your mind,
Slavery must vanish, wide and far,
  Till not a trace is left behind;
    Your counsels not bestow'd in vain,
    Shall still protect this infant reign.

So, when the bright, all-cheering sun
  From our contracted view retires,
Though folly deems his race is run,
  On other worlds he lights his fires:
    Cold climes beneath his influence glow,
    And frozen rivers learn to flow.

O say, thou great, exalted name!
　What Muse can boast of equal lays,
Thy worth disdains all vulgar fame,
　　Transcends the noblest poet's praise.
　　Art soars, unequal to the flight,
　　And genius sickens at the height.

For States redeem'd — our western reign
　Restor'd by thee to milder sway,
Thy conscious glory shall remain
　　When this great globe is swept away
　　And *all* is lost that pride admires,
　　And all the pageant scene expires.
　　　　　　　　　PHILIP FRENEAU.

Early in January, word reached America that
the definite treaty of peace had been signed at
Paris on November 30, 1783. The independence
of the United States was acknowledged; the
Mississippi was set as the western boundary of
the country, the St. Croix and the Great Lakes
as the northern, and the Gulf of Mexico as the
southern. On January 14, 1784, this treaty was
ratified by Congress.

THE AMERICAN SOLDIER'S HYMN

'T is God that girds our armor on,
And all our just designs fulfils;
Through Him our feet can swiftly run,
And nimbly climb the steepest hills.

Lessons of war from Him we take,
And manly weapons learn to wield;
Strong bows of steel with ease we break,
Forced by our stronger arms to yield.

'T is God that still supports our right,
His just revenge our foes pursues;
'T is He that with resistless might,
Fierce nations to His power subdues.

Our universal safeguard He!
From Whom our lasting honors flow;
He made us great, and set us free
From our remorseless bloody foe.

Therefore to celebrate His fame,
Our grateful voice to Heaven we'll raise;
And nations, strangers to His name,
Shall thus be taught to sing His praise.

A day of solemn thanksgiving was set apart
and universally observed throughout the country,
which set its face toward the future, with a heart
full of hope and high resolve.

THANKSGIVING HYMN

THE Lord above, in tender love,
　Hath sav'd us from our foes;
Through Washington the thing is done,
　The war is at a close.

America has won the day,
　Through Washington, our chief;
Come let's rejoice with heart and voice,
　And bid adieu to grief.

Now we have peace, and may increase
　In number, wealth, and arts,
If every one, like Washington,
　Will strive to do their parts.

Then let's agree, since we are free,
　All needless things to shun;
And lay aside all pomp and pride,
　Like our great Washington.

Use industry, and frugal be,
　Like Washington the brave;
So shall we see, 't will easy be,
　Our country for to save,

From present wars and future foes,
　And all that we may fear;
While Washington, the great brave one,
　Shall as our chief appear.

Industry and frugality
　Will all our taxes pay;
In virtuous ways, we'll spend our days,
　And for our rulers pray.

The Thirteen States, united sets,
　In Congress simply grand;
The Lord himself preserve their health,
　That they may rule the land.

Whilst every State, without its mate,
　Doth rule itself by laws,
Will sovereign be, and always free;
　To grieve there is no cause.

But all should try, both low and high,
　Our freedom to maintain;
Pray God to bless our grand Congress,
　And cease from every sin.

Then sure am I, true liberty
　Of every sort will thrive;
With one accord we'll praise the Lord,
　All glory to Him give.

To whom all praise is due always,
For He is all in all;
George Washington, that noble one,
On His great name doth call.

Our Congress too, before they do,
Acknowledge Him supreme;
Come let us all before Him fall,
And glorify His name.

LAND OF THE WILFUL GOSPEL [1]

From "Psalm of the West"

LAND of the Wilful Gospel, thou worst and
thou best;
Tall Adam of lands, new-made of the dust
of the West;
Thou wroughtest alone in the Garden of God,
unblest
Till He fashioned lithe Freedom to lie for
thine Eve on thy breast —
Till out of thy heart's dear neighborhood,
out of thy side,
He fashioned an intimate Sweet one and
brought thee a Bride.
Cry hail! nor bewail that the wound of her
coming was wide.

[1] From Poems by Sidney Lanier; copyright,
1884, 1891, by Mary D. Lanier; published by
Charles Scribner's Sons.

Lo, Freedom reached forth where the world
as an apple hung red;
Let us taste the whole radiant round of it,
gayly she said:
*If we die, at the worst we shall lie as the first
of the dead.*
Knowledge of Good and of Ill, O Land!
she hath given thee;
Perilous godhoods of choosing have rent
thee and riven thee;
Will's high adoring to Ill's low exploring
hath driven thee —
Freedom, thy Wife, hath uplifted thy life
and clean shriven thee!
Her shalt thou clasp for a balm to the scars of
thy breast,
Her shalt thou kiss for a calm to thy wars of
unrest,
Her shalt thou extol in the psalm of the soul of the
West.
For Weakness, in freedom, grows stronger
than Strength with a chain;
And Error, in freedom, will come to lament-
ing his stain,
Till freely repenting he whiten his spirit
again;
And Friendship, in freedom, will blot out the
bounding of race;
And straight Law, in freedom, will curve to
the rounding of grace;
And Fashion, in freedom, will die of the lie
in her face.
SIDNEY LANIER.

PART III

THE PERIOD OF GROWTH

"OH MOTHER OF A MIGHTY RACE"

Oh mother of a mighty race,
Yet lovely in thy youthful grace!
The elder dames, thy haughty peers,
Admire and hate thy blooming years.
    With words of shame
And taunts of scorn they join thy name.

For on thy cheeks the glow is spread
That tints thy morning hills with red;
Thy step — the wild deer's rustling feet
Within thy woods are not more fleet;
    Thy hopeful eye
Is bright as thine own sunny sky.

Ay, let them rail — those haughty ones,
While safe thou dwellest with thy sons.
They do not know how loved thou art.
How many a fond and fearless heart
    Would rise to throw
Its life between thee and the foe.

They know not, in their hate and pride,
What virtues with thy children bide;
How true, how good, thy graceful maids
Make bright, like flowers, the valley-shades
    What generous men
Spring, like thine oaks, by hill and glen; —

What cordial welcomes greet the guest
By thy lone rivers of the West;
How faith is kept, and truth revered,
And man is loved, and God is feared
    In woodland homes,
And where the ocean border foams.

There's freedom at thy gates and rest
For earth's down-trodden and opprest,
A shelter for the hunted head,
For the starved laborer toil and bread.
    Power, at thy bounds,
Stops and calls back his baffled hounds.

Oh, fair young mother! on thy brow
Shall sit a nobler grace than now.
Deep in the brightness of the skies
The thronging years in glory rise,
    And, as they fleet,
Drop strength and riches at thy feet.
            WILLIAM CULLEN BRYANT.

CHAPTER I

THE NEW NATION

The war was ended, but the five years following 1783 were perhaps the most critical in the history of the American people. The country was at the verge of bankruptcy, there was discontent everywhere. In Massachusetts, the malcontents found a leader in Daniel Shays, rose in rebellion, looted the country, and were not dispersed for nearly a year.

A RADICAL SONG OF 1786

Huzza, my Jo Bunkers! no taxes we'll pay;
Here's a pardon for Wheeler, Shays, Parsons,
    and Day;
Put green boughs in your hats, and renew the
    old cause;
Stop the courts in each county, and bully the
    laws:
Constitutions and oaths, sir, we mind not a
    rush;
Such trifles must yield to us lads of the bush.
New laws and new charters our books shall
    display,
Composed by conventions and Counsellor
    Grey.

Since Boston and Salem so haughty have
    grown,
We'll make them to know we can let them
    alone.
Of Glasgow or Pelham we'll make a seaport,
And there we'll assemble our General Court:
Our governor, now, boys, shall turn out to
    work,
And live, like ourselves, on molasses and pork;
In Adams or Greenwich he'll live like a peer
On three hundred pounds, paper money, a
    year.

Grand jurors, and sheriffs, and lawyers we'll
    spurn,
As judges, we'll all take the bench in our turn,
And sit the whole term, without pension or fee,
Nor Cushing nor Sewal look graver than we.
Our wigs, though they're rusty, are decent
    enough;
Our aprons, though black, are of durable
    stuff;
Array'd in such gear, the laws we'll explain,
That poor people no more shall have cause
    to complain.

To Congress and impost we'll plead a release;
The French we can beat half-a-dozen apiece;
We want not their guineas, their arms, or
    alliance;
And as for the Dutchmen, we bid them defiance.
Then huzza, my Jo Bunkers! no taxes we'll
    pay;
Here's a pardon for Wheeler, Shays, Parsons
    and Day;
Put green boughs in your hats, and renew the
    old cause;
Stop the courts in each county, and bully the
    laws.

ST. JOHN HONEYWOOD.

A federal convention was proposed, and in May, 1787, there assembled at Philadelphia fifty-five men appointed by the various states to devise an adequate constitution for a federal government.

THE FEDERAL CONVENTION

[May, 1787]

Concentred here th' united wisdom shines,
Of learn'd judges, and of sound divines:
Patriots, whose virtues searching time has
    tried,
Heroes, who fought, where brother heroes
    died;
Lawyers, who speak, as Tully spoke before,
Sages, deep read in philosophic lore;
Merchants, whose plans are to no realms confin'd,
Farmers — the noblest title 'mongst mankind:
Yeomen and tradesmen, pillars of the state;
On whose decision hangs Columbia's fate.
    September, 1787.

George Washington was chosen president of the convention; the doors were locked, and the Herculean task of making a constitution begun. Washington himself, in a burst of noble eloquence, braced the delegates for the task before them. The problem was to devise a government which should bind all the states without impairing their sovereignty.

TO THE FEDERAL CONVENTION

[1787]

BE then your counsels, as your subject, great,
A world their sphere, and time's long reign
    their date.
Each party-view, each private good, disclaim,
Each petty maxim, each colonial aim;
Let all Columbia's weal your views expand,
A mighty system rule a mighty land;
Yourselves her genuine sons let Europe own,
Not the small agents of a paltry town.
    Learn, cautious, what to alter, where to
    mend;
See to what close projected measures tend.
From pressing wants the mind averting still,
Thinks good remotest from the present ill:
From feuds anarchial to oppression's throne,
Misguided nations hence for safety run;
And through the miseries of a thousand years,
Their fatal folly mourn in bloody tears.
    Ten thousand follies thro' Columbia spread;
Ten thousand wars her darling realms in-
    vade.
The private interest of each jealous state;
Of rule th' impatience and of law the hate.
But ah! from narrow springs these evils
    flow,
A few base wretches mingle general woe;
Still the same mind her manly race pervades;
Still the same virtues haunt the hallow'd
    shades.
But when the peals of war her centre shook,
All private aims the anxious mind forsook.
In danger's iron-bond her race was one,
Each separate good, each little view unknown.
Now rule, unsystem'd, drives the mind astray;
Now private interest points the downward
    way:
Hence civil discord pours her muddy stream,
And fools and villains float upon the brim;
O'er all, the sad spectator casts his eye,
And wonders where the gems and minerals
    lie.
    But ne'er of freedom, glory, bliss, despond:
Uplift your eyes those little clouds beyond;
See there returning suns, with gladdening
    ray,
Roll on fair spring to chase this wint'ry day.
'T is yours to bid those days of Eden shine:
First, then, and last, the federal bands en-
    twine:
To this your every aim and effort bend:
Let all your efforts here commence and end.

O'er state concerns, let every state preside;
Its private tax controul; its justice guide;
Religion aid; the morals to secure;
And bid each private right thro' time endure.
Columbia's interests public sway demand,
Her commerce, impost, unlocated land;
Her war, her peace, her military power;
Treaties to seal with every distant shore;
    To bid contending states their discord cease;
To send thro' all the calumet of peace;
Science to wing thro' every noble flight;
And lift desponding genius into light.
    Be then your task to alter, aid, amend;
The weak to strengthen, and the rigid bend;
The prurient lop; what's wanted to supply;
And grant new scions from each friendly sky.
                TIMOTHY DWIGHT.

There was a natural antagonism between large
and small states, and more than once the conven-
tion was on the verge of dissolution; but a com-
promise was finally reached, the constitution as
we know it was evolved and signed by all the
delegates, and on September 17, 1787, the con-
vention adjourned. The constitution was famil-
iarly styled the "new roof."

THE NEW ROOF

A SONG FOR FEDERAL MECHANICS

[1787]

I

COME muster, my lads, your mechanical tools,
Your saws and your axes, your hammers and
    rules;
Bring your mallets and planes, your level and
    line,
And plenty of pins of American pine:
*For our roof we will raise, and our song still
    shall be,
Our government firm, and our citizens free.*

II

Come, up with *the plates*, lay them firm on
    the wall,
Like the people at large, they're the ground-
    work of all;
Examine them well, and see that they're
    sound,
Let no rotten part in our building be found:
*For our roof we will raise, and our song still
    shall be
A government firm, and our citizens free.*

III

Now hand up the *girders*, lay each in his place,
Between them the *joists*, must divide all the space;
Like assemblymen *these* should lie level along,
Like *girders*, our senate prove loyal and strong:
For our roof we will raise, and our song still shall be
A government firm over citizens free.

IV

The *rafters* now frame; your *king-posts* and *braces*,
And drive your pins home, to keep all in their places;
Let wisdom and strength in the fabric combine,
And your pins be all made of American pine:
For our roof we will raise, and our song still shall be,
A government firm over citizens free.

V

Our *king-posts* are *judges*; how upright they stand,
Supporting the *braces*; the laws of the land:
The laws of the land, which divide right from wrong,
And strengthen the weak, by weak'ning the strong:
For our roof we will raise, and our song still shall be,
Laws equal and just, for a people that's free.

VI

Up! up! with the *rafters*; each frame is a state:
How nobly they rise! their span, too, how great!
From the north to the south, o'er the whole they extend,
And rest on the walls, whilst the walls they defend:
For our roof we will raise, and our song still shall be
Combined in strength, yet as citizens free.

VII

Now enter the *purlins*, and drive your pins through;
And see that your joints are drawn home and all true.
The *purlins* will bind all the rafters together:
The strength of the whole shall defy wind and weather:

For our roof we will raise, and our song still shall be,
United as states, but as citizens free.

VIII

Come, raise up the *turret*; our glory and pride;
In the centre it stands, o'er the whole to preside:
The sons of Columbia shall view with delight
Its pillars, and arches, and towering height:
Our roof is now rais'd, and our song still shall be,
A federal head o'er a people that's free.

IX

Huzza! my brave boys, our work is complete;
The world shall admire Columbia's fair seat;
Its strength against tempest and time shall be proof,
And thousands shall come to dwell under our roof:
Whilst we drain the deep bowl, our toast still shall be,
Our government firm, and our citizens free.
                                    FRANCIS HOPKINSON.

The new constitution had still to be submitted to the several states for ratification. One after another they fell into line, but Massachusetts held back. On January 9, 1788, the convention met, and week after week dragged by in fierce debate; but finally, on February 6, 1788, the Constitution was ratified by a majority of nineteen votes.

CONVENTION SONG

[February 6, 1788]

THE 'Vention did in Boston meet
    But State House could not hold 'em,
So they went to Federal Street,
    And there the truth was told 'em.
        Yankee doodle, keep it up!
        Yankee doodle, dandy,
        Mind the music and the step,
        And with the girls be handy.

They every morning went to prayer;
    And then began disputing;
Till opposition silenced were,
    By arguments refuting.

Then 'Squire Hancock, like a man
    Who dearly loves the nation,
By a Concil'atory plan,
    Prevented much vexation.

He made a *woundy* Fed'ral speech,
  With sense and elocution;
And then the Yankees did beseech
  T' adopt the Constitution.

The question being outright put
  (Each voter independent),
The Fed'ralists agreed to adopt,
  And then propose amendments.

The other party seeing then
  The People were against them,
Agreed, like honest, faithful men,
  To mix in peace amongst 'em.

The Boston folks are deuced lads,
  And always full of notions;
The boys, the girls, their mams and dads,
  Were fill'd with joy's commotions.

So straightway they procession made,
  Lord, how *nation* fine, sir!
For every man of every trade
  Went with his tools — to dine, sir.

John Foster Williams in a ship
  Join'd with the social band, sir.
And made the lasses dance and skip,
  To see him sail on land, sir!

O then a whopping feast began,
  And all hands went to eating,
They drank their toasts, shook hands and
    sung —
  Huzza for 'Vention meeting!

Now, politicians, of all kinds,
  Who are not yet derided,
May see how Yankees speak their minds,
  And yet we 're not decided.

Then from this sample, let 'em cease
  Inflammatory writing;
For freedom, happiness, and peace,
  Are better far than fighting.

So here I end my Federal song,
  Composed of thirteen verses;
May agriculture flourish long,
  And commerce fill our purses.

Hot battles were still to be fought in some of
the other states, — hottest of all in New York, —
but by midsummer of 1788 all the states had
ratified the Constitution, and it stood an accomplished fact.

THE FEDERAL CONSTITUTION

POETS may sing of their Helicon streams;
Their gods and their heroes are fabulous
    dreams!
  They ne'er sang a line
  Half so grand, so divine
  As the glorious toast
  We Columbians boast —
The Federal Constitution, boys, and Liberty
  forever.

The man of our choice presides at the helm;
No tempest can harm us, no storm overwhelm;
  Our sheet anchor 's sure,
  And our bark rides secure;
  So here 's to the toast
  We Columbians boast —
The Federal Constitution and the President
  forever.

A free navigation, commerce, and trade,
We 'll seek for no foe, of no foe be afraid;
  Our frigates shall ride,
  Our defence and our pride;
  Our tars guard our coast,
  And huzza for our toast —
The Federal Constitution, trade and commerce forever.

Montgomery and Warren still live in our
  songs;
Like them our young heroes shall spurn at
  our wrongs:
  The world shall admire
  The zeal and the fire,
  Which blaze in the toast
  We Columbians boast —
The Federal Constitution and its advocates
  forever.

When an enemy threats, all party shall cease;
We bribe no intruders to buy a mean peace;
  Columbia will scorn
  Friends and foes to suborn;
  We 'll ne'er stain the toast
  Which as freemen we boast —
The Federal Constitution, and integrity
  forever.

Fame's trumpet shall swell in Washington's
  praise,
And time grant a furlough to lengthen his
  days;

May health weave the thread
Of delight round his head.
No nation can boast
Such a name, such a toast,
The Federal Constitution, boys, and Wash-
ington forever.

WILLIAM MILNS.

The Continental Congress, in putting an end
to its troubled existence, decreed that the first
presidential election should be held on the first
Wednesday of January, 1789, and that the Senate
and House of Representatives should assemble
on the first Wednesday in March.

THE FIRST AMERICAN CONGRESS

[April 6, 1789]

COLUMBUS looked; and still around them
spread,
From south to north, th' immeasurable shade;
At last, the central shadows burst away,
And rising regions open'd on the day.
He saw, once more, bright Del'ware's silver
stream,
And Penn's throng'd city cast a cheerful
gleam,
The dome of state, that met his eager eye,
Now heav'd its arches in a loftier sky.
The bursting gates unfold: and lo, within,
A solemn train in conscious glory shine.
The well-known forms his eye had trac'd
before,
In diff'rent realms along th' extended shore;
Here, grac'd with nobler fame, and rob'd in
state,
They look'd and mov'd magnificently great.
High on the foremost seat, in living light,
Majestic Randolph caught the hero's sight:
Fair on his head, the civic crown was plac'd,
And the first dignity his sceptre grac'd.
He opes the cause, and points in prospect
far,
Thro' all the toils that wait th' impending
war —
But, hapless sage, thy reign must soon be o'er,
To lend thy lustre, and to shine no more.
So the bright morning star, from shades of
ev'n,
Leads up the dawn, and lights the front of
heav'n,
Points to the waking world the sun's broad
way,
Then veils his own, and shines above the day.

And see great Washington behind thee rise,
Thy following sun, to gild our morning skies;
O'er shadowy climes to pour the enliv'ning
flame,
The charms of freedom and the fire of fame.
Th' ascending chief adorn'd his splendid seat,
Like Randolph, ensign'd with a crown of
state;
Where the green patriot bay beheld, with
pride,
The hero's laurel springing by its side;
His sword, hung useless, on his graceful thigh,
On Britain still he cast a filial eye;
But sov'reign fortitude his visage bore,
To meet their legions on th' invaded shore.
Sage Franklin next arose, in awful mien,
And smil'd, unruffled, o'er th' approaching
scene;
High, on his locks of age, a wreath was brac'd,
Palm of all arts, that e'er a mortal grac'd;
Beneath him lies the sceptre kings have borne,
And crowns and laurels from their temples
torn.
Nash, Rutledge, Jefferson, in council great,
And Jay and Laurens op'd the rolls of fate.
The Livingstons, fair Freedom's gen'rous
band,
The Lees, the Houstons, fathers of the land,
O'er climes and kingdoms turn'd their ardent
eyes,
Bade all th' oppressed to speedy vengeance
rise;
All pow'rs of state, in their extended plan,
Rise from consent to shield the rights of man.
Bold Wolcott urg'd the all-important cause;
With steady hand the solemn scene he draws;
Undaunted firmness with his wisdom join'd,
Nor kings nor worlds could warp his stedfast
mind.
Now, graceful rising from his purple throne,
In radiant robes, immortal Hosmer shone;
Myrtles and bays his learned temples bound,
The statesman's wreath, the poet's garland
crown'd:
Morals and laws expand his liberal soul,
Beam from his eyes, and in his accents roll.
But lo! an unseen hand the curtain drew,
And snatch'd the patriot from the hero's view;
Wrapp'd in the shroud of death, he sees de-
scend
The guide of nations and the muses' friend.
Columbus dropp'd a tear. The angel's eye
Trac'd the freed spirit mounting thro' the
sky.
Adams, enrag'd, a broken charter bore,

And lawless acts of ministerial pow'r;
Some injur'd right in each loose leaf appears,
A king in terrors and a land in tears;
From all the guileful plots the veil he drew,
With eye retortive look'd creation through;
Op'd the wide range of nature's boundless
          plan,
Trac'd all the steps of liberty and man;
Crowds rose to vengeance while his accents
          rung,
And Independence thunder'd from his tongue.
                    JOEL BARLOW.

The first business was the counting of the electoral votes. There were sixty-nine of them, and every one was for George Washington, of Virginia.

WASHINGTON

GOD wills no man a slave. The man most
          meek,
Who saw Him face to face on Horeb's peak,
Had slain a tyrant for a bondman's wrong,
And met his Lord with sinless soul and strong.
But when, years after, overfraught with care,
His feet once trod doubt's pathway to despair,
For that one treason lapse, the guiding hand
That led so far now barred the promised
          land.
God makes no man a slave, no doubter free;
Abiding faith alone wins liberty.

No angel led our Chieftain's steps aright;
No pilot cloud by day, no flame by night;
No plague nor portent spake to foe or friend;
No doubt assailed him, faithful to the end.

Weaklings there were, as in the tribes of old,
Who craved for fleshpots, worshipped calves
          of gold,
Murmured that right would harder be than
          wrong,
And freedom's narrow road so steep and long;
But he who ne'er on Sinai's summit trod,
Still walked the highest heights and spake
          with God;
Saw with anointed eyes no promised land
By petty bounds or pettier cycles spanned,
Its people curbed and broken to the ring,
Packed with a caste and saddled with a
          King, —
But freedom's heritage and training school,
Where men unruled should learn to wisely
          rule,

Till sun and moon should see at Ajalon
King's heads in dust and freemen's feet
          thereon.

His work well done, the leader stepped aside,
Spurning a crown with more than kingly pride,
Content to wear the higher crown of worth,
While time endures, First Citizen of earth.
                    JAMES JEFFREY ROCHE.

Washington left Mount Vernon on April 16, and started for New York, where, on April 30, 1789, he took the oath of office as President of the United States.

THE VOW OF WASHINGTON

[April 30, 1789]

THE sword was sheathed: in April's sun
Lay green the fields by Freedom won;
And severed sections, weary of debates,
Joined hands at last and were United States.

O City sitting by the Sea!
How proud the day that dawned on thee,
When the new era, long desired, began,
And, in its need, the hour had found the man!

One thought the cannon salvos spoke,
The resonant bell-tower's vibrant stroke,
The voiceful streets, the plaudit-echoing halls,
And prayer and hymn borne heavenward from
          St. Paul's!

How felt the land in every part
The strong throb of a nation's heart,
As its great leader gave, with reverent awe,
His pledge to Union, Liberty, and Law!

That pledge the heavens above him heard,
That vow the sleep of centuries stirred;
In world-wide wonder listening peoples bent
Their gaze on Freedom's great experiment.

Could it succeed? Of honor sold
And hopes deceived all history told.
Above the wrecks that strewed the mournful
          past,
Was the long dream of ages true at last?

Thank God! the people's choice was just,
The one man equal to his trust,
Wise beyond lore, and without weakness good,
Calm in the strength of flawless rectitude!

His rule of justice, order, peace,
Made possible the world's release;
Taught prince and serf that power is but a trust,
And rule alone, which serves the ruled, is just;

That Freedom generous is, but strong
In hate of fraud and selfish wrong,
Pretence that turns her holy truth to lies,
And lawless license masking in her guise.

Land of his love! with one glad voice
Let thy great sisterhood rejoice;
A century's suns o'er thee have risen and set,
And, God be praised, we are one nation yet.

And still we trust the years to be
Shall prove his hope was destiny,
Leaving our flag, with all its added stars,
Unrent by faction and unstained by wars.

Lo! where with patient toil he nursed
And trained the new-set plant at first,
The widening branches of a stately tree
Stretch from the sunrise to the sunset sea.

And in its broad and sheltering shade,
Sitting with none to make afraid,
Were we now silent, through each mighty limb,
The winds of heaven would sing the praise of him.

Our first and best! — his ashes lie
Beneath his own Virginian sky.
Forgive, forget, O true and just and brave,
The storm that swept above thy sacred grave!

For, ever in the awful strife
And dark hours of the nation's life,
Through the fierce tumult pierced his warning word,
Their father's voice his erring children heard!

The change for which he prayed and sought
In that sharp agony was wrought;
No partial interest draws its alien line
'Twixt North and South, the cypress and the pine!

One people now, all doubt beyond,
His name shall be our Union-bond;
We lift our hands to Heaven, and here and now
Take on our lips the old Centennial vow.

For rule and trust must needs be ours;
Chooser and chosen both are powers
Equal in service as in rights; the claim
Of Duty rests on each and all the same.

Then let the sovereign millions, where
Our banner floats in sun and air,
From the warm palm-lands to Alaska's cold,
Repeat with us the pledge a century old!

JOHN GREENLEAF WHITTIER.

Benjamin Franklin had been in ill-health for many months, and the end came at Philadelphia, April 17, 1790. He was born at Boston, January 17, 1706.

ON THE DEATH OF BENJAMIN FRANKLIN

[April 17, 1790]

THUS, some tall tree that long hath stood
The glory of its native wood,
By storms destroyed, or length of years,
Demands the tribute of our tears.

The pile, that took long time to raise,
To dust returns by slow decays;
But, when its destined years are o'er,
We must regret the loss the more.

So long accustomed to your aid,
The world laments your exit made;
So long befriended by your art,
Philosopher, 't is hard to part! —

When monarchs tumble to the ground
Successors easily are found;
But, matchless Franklin! what a few
Can hope to rival such as you,
Who seized from kings their sceptred pride,
And turned the lightning's darts aside!

PHILIP FRENEAU.

On November 6, 1792, George Washington was again unanimously chosen President of the United States, and was inaugurated on March 4, 1793.

GEORGE WASHINGTON

THIS was the man God gave us when the hour
Proclaimed the dawn of Liberty begun;
Who dared a deed and died when it was done
Patient in triumph, temperate in power, —
Not striving like the Corsican to tower

To heaven, nor like great Philip's greater son
To win the world and weep for worlds unwon,
Or lose the star to revel in the flower.
The lives that serve the eternal verities
Alone do mould mankind. Pleasure and pride
Sparkle awhile and perish, as the spray
Smoking across the crests of cavernous seas
Is impotent to hasten or delay
The everlasting surges of the tide.

JOHN HALL INGHAM.

On September 19, 1796, Washington issued his "farewell address," declining a third term as President.

WASHINGTON

WHERE may the wearied eye repose
  When gazing on the Great;
Where neither guilty glory glows,
  Nor despicable state?
Yes — one — the first — the last — the
    best —
The Cincinnatus of the West,
  Whom envy dared not hate,
Bequeath the name of Washington,
To make men blush there was but one!

LORD BYRON.

The election was held on November 8, 1796, and the electoral votes were counted February 8, 1797. John Adams received seventy-one, Thomas Jefferson sixty-eight, Thomas Pinckney fifty-nine, and Aaron Burr thirty. Adams assumed office March 4, 1797. Relations with both France and England had become more than ever strained, and a war, especially with the former, seemed certain. These circumstances gave birth to one of the most popular political songs ever written in America.

ADAMS AND LIBERTY

[1798]

YE sons of Columbia, who bravely have
    fought
  For those rights which unstained from
    your sires have descended,
May you long taste the blessings your valor
    has bought,
  And your sons reap the soil which their
    fathers defended.
    'Mid the reign of mild peace,
    May your nation increase,
With the glory of Rome and the wisdom of
    Greece;

And ne'er shall the sons of Columbia be
    slaves,
  While the earth bears a plant, or the sea
    rolls its waves.

In a clime, whose rich vales feed the marts of
    the world,
  Whose shores are unshaken by Europe's
    commotion.
The trident of commerce should never be
    hurl'd,
  To incense the legitimate powers of the
    ocean.
    But should pirates invade,
    Though in thunder array'd,
Let your cannon declare the free charter of
    trade.
  For ne'er shall the sons of Columbia be
    slaves,
  While the earth bears a plant, or the sea
    rolls its waves.

The fame of our arms, of our laws the mild
    sway,
  Had justly ennobled our nation in story,
Till the dark clouds of faction obscured our
    young day,
  And enveloped the sun of American glory.
    But let traitors be told,
    Who their country have sold,
And barter'd their God for his image in
    gold,
  That ne'er will the sons of Columbia be
    slaves,
  While the earth bears a plant, or the sea
    rolls its waves.

While France her huge limbs bathes recum-
    bent in blood,
  And society's base threats with wide dis-
    solution;
May peace, like the dove who return'd from
    the flood,
  Find an ark of abode in our mild consti-
    tution.
    But, though peace is our aim,
    Yet the boon we disclaim,
If bought by our sovereignty, justice, or
    fame;
  For ne'er shall the sons of Columbia be
    slaves,
  While the earth bears a plant, or the sea
    rolls its waves.

'T is the fire of the flint, each American warms:
Let Rome's haughty victors beware of collision,
Let them bring all the vassals of Europe in arms,
We're a world by ourselves, and disdain a division.
While, with patriot pride,
To our laws we're allied,
No foe can subdue us, no faction divide,
For ne'er shall the sons of Columbia be slaves,
While the earth bears a plant, or the sea rolls its waves.

Our mountains are crown'd with imperial oak;
Whose roots, like our liberties, ages have nourish'd;
But long ere our nation submits to the yoke,
Not a tree shall be left on the field where it flourish'd.
Should invasion impend,
Every grove would descend,
From the hill-tops, they shaded, our shores to defend.
For ne'er shall the sons of Columbia be slaves,
While the earth bears a plant, or the sea rolls its waves.

Let our patriots destroy Anarch's pestilent worm;
Lest our liberty's growth should be check'd by corrosion;
Then let clouds thicken round us; we heed not the storm;
Our realm fears no shock, but the earth's own explosion.
Foes assail us in vain,
Though their fleets bridge the main,
For our altars and laws with our lives we'll maintain.
For ne'er shall the sons of Columbia be slaves,
While the earth bears a plant, or the sea rolls its waves.

Should the tempest of war overshadow our land,
Its bolts could ne'er rend Freedom's temple asunder;

For, unmov'd, at its portal, would Washington stand,
And repulse, with his breast, the assaults of the thunder!
His sword from the sleep
Of its scabbard would leap,
And conduct, with its point, every flash to the deep!
For ne'er shall the sons of Columbia be slaves,
While the earth bears a plant, or the sea rolls its waves.

Let fame to the world sound America's voice;
No intrigues can her sons from their government sever;
Her pride is her Adams; her laws are his choice,
And shall flourish, till Liberty slumbers forever.
Then unite heart and hand,
Like Leonidas' band,
And swear to the God of the ocean and land,
That ne'er shall the sons of Columbia be slaves,
While the earth bears a plant, or the sea rolls its waves.

ROBERT TREAT PAINE.

On May 28, 1798, Congress authorized a provisional army of ten thousand men and empowered the President to instruct the commanders of American ships of war to seize French armed vessels attacking American merchantmen, or hovering about the coast for that purpose. Public excitement ran high, and when Hopkinson's "Hail Columbia" was sung one night at a Philadelphia theatre, it met with instantaneous success.

HAIL COLUMBIA

[First sung at the Chestnut Street Theatre, Philadelphia, May, 1798]

Hail! Columbia, happy land!
Hail! ye heroes, heav'n-born band,
Who fought and bled in freedom's cause,
Who fought and bled in freedom's cause,
And when the storm of war was gone,
Enjoyed the peace your valor won;
Let independence be your boast,
Ever mindful what it cost,
Ever grateful for the prize,
Let its altar reach the skies.

Chorus — Firm, united let us be,
        Rallying round our liberty,
        As a band of brothers joined,
        Peace and safety we shall find.

Immortal patriots, rise once more!
Defend your rights, defend your shore;
Let no rude foe with impious hand,
Let no rude foe with impious hand
Invade the shrine where sacred lies
Of toil and blood the well-earned prize;
While offering peace, sincere and just,
In heav'n we place a manly trust,
That truth and justice may prevail,
And ev'ry scheme of bondage fail.

Sound, sound the trump of fame!
Let Washington's great name
Ring thro' the world with loud applause!
Ring thro' the world with loud applause!
Let ev'ry clime to freedom dear
Listen with a joyful ear;
With equal skill, with steady pow'r,
He governs in the fearful hour
Of horrid war, or guides with ease
The happier time of honest peace.

Behold the chief, who now commands,
Once more to serve his country stands,
The rock on which the storm will beat!
The rock on which the storm will beat!
But armed in virtue, firm and true,
His hopes are fixed on heav'n and you.
When hope was sinking in dismay,
When gloom obscured Columbia's day,
His steady mind, from changes free,
Resolved on death or liberty.

                    JOSEPH HOPKINSON.

Word crossed the ocean that Napoleon was gathering a great fleet at Toulon and it was generally believed that he intended to invade America. The fleet, of course, was intended for his expedition to Egypt, and the idea that he hoped to conquer America seems ludicrous enough, but some verses written by Thomas Green Fessenden in July, 1798, show how seriously it was entertained.

YE SONS OF COLUMBIA

AN ODE

[July, 1798]

YE sons of Columbia, unite in the cause
Of liberty, justice, religion, and laws;

Should foes then invade us, to battle we'll
        hie,
For the GOD OF OUR FATHERS will be our
        ally!
        Let Frenchmen advance,
        And all Europe join France,
    Designing our conquest and plunder;
        United and free
        Forever we'll be,
    And our cannon shall tell them in thunder,
That foes to our freedom we'll' ever defy,
Till the continent sinks, and the ocean is dry!

When Britain assail'd us, undaunted we
        stood,
Defended the land we had purchas'd with
        blood,
Our liberty won, and it shall be our boast,
If the old world united should menace our
        coast: —
        Should millions invade,
        In terrour array'd,
    Our liberties bid us surrender,
        Our country they'd find
        With bayonets lin d,
    And Washington here to defend her,
For foes to our freedom we'll ever defy
Till the continent sinks, and the ocean is dry!

Should Buonapart' come with his sans culotte
        band,
And a new sort of freedom we don't under-
        stand,
And make us an offer to give us as much
As France has bestow'd on the Swiss and the
        Dutch,
        His fraud and his force
        Will be futile of course;
    We wish for no *Frenchified* Freedom:
        If folks beyond sea
        Are to bid us be free,
    We'll send for them when we shall need
        'em.
But sans culotte Frenchmen we'll ever defy,
Till the continent sinks, and the ocean is dry!

We're anxious that Peace may continue her
        reign,
We cherish the virtues which sport in her
        train;
Our hearts ever melt, when the fatherless
        sigh,
And we shiver at Horrour's funereal cry!
        But still, though we prize
        That child of the skies,

We'll never like slaves be accosted.
In a war of defence
Our means are immense,
And we'll fight till our *all* is exhausted:
For foes to our freedom we'll ever defy,
Till the continent sinks, and the ocean is dry!

The EAGLE of FREEDOM with rapture behold,
Overshadow our land with his plumage of
gold!
The flood-gates of glory are open on high,
And Warren and Mercer descend from the sky!
They come from above
With a message of love,
To bid us be firm and decided;
"At Liberty's call,
Unite one and all,
For you conquer, unless you're divided.
Unite, and the foes to your freedom defy,
Till the continent sinks and the ocean is dry!

"Americans, seek no occasion for war;
The rude deeds of rapine still ever abhor:
But if in 'efence of your rights you should
arm,
Let toils ne'er discourage, nor dangers alarm.
For foes to your peace
Will ever increase,
If freedom and fame you should barter,
Let those rights be yours,
While nature :ndures,
For OMNIPOTENCE gave you the charter!"
Then foes to our freedom we'' ever defy,
Till the continent sinks, and the ocean is dry!
THOMAS GREEN FESSENDEN.

Though there was to be no invasion to repel,
the new navy was s on to win its spurs. On February 9, 1799, the Constellation, Captain Truxton,
sighted the 36-g n frig te, Insurgente, off St. Kitts,
in the West I es, and promptly gave chase. The
Frenchman was overhauled about the middle of
the afternoon, and aft r a fierce engagement was
forced to surrender. Two months later, Napoleon
agreed to receive the American envoy "with the
respect due a powerful nation," and all danger of
war was soon over.

TRUXTON'S VICTORY

[February 9, 1799]

WHEN Freedom, fair Freedom, her banner
display'd,
Defying each foe whom her rights would
invade.

Columbia's brave sons swore those rights to
maintain,
And o'er ocean and earth to establish her
reign;
United they cry,
While that standard shall fly,
Resolved, firm, and steady,
We always are ready
To fight, and to conquer, to conquer or die.

Tho' Gallia through Europe has rushed like
a flood,
And deluged the earth with an ocean of
blood:
While by faction she's led, while she's governed by knaves,
We court not her smiles, and will ne'er be her
slaves:
Her threats we defy,
While our standard shall fly,
Resolved, firm, and steady,
We always are ready
To fight, and to conquer, to conquer or die.

Tho' France with caprice dares our Statesmen upbraid,
A tribute demands, or sets bounds to our
trade;
From our young rising Navy our thunders
shall roar,
And our Commerce extend to the earth's utmost shore.
Our cannon we'll ply,
While our standard shall fly;
Resolved, firm, and steady,
We always are ready
To fight, and to conquer, to conquer or die.

To know we're resolved, let them think on
the hour,
When Truxton, brave Truxton off Nevis's
shore,
His ship mann'd for battle, the standard
unfurl'd,
And at the Insurgent defiance he hurled;
And his valiant tars cry,
While our standard shall fly,
Resolved, firm, and steady,
We always are ready
To fight, and to conquer, to conquer or die.

Each heart beat exulting, inspir'd by the
cause;
They fought for their country, their freedom
and laws;

From their cannon loud volleys of vengeance
    they pour'd,
And the standard of France to Columbia was
    lower'd.
        Huzza! they now cry,
        Let the Eagle wave high;
        Resolved, firm, and steady,
        We always are ready
To fight, and to conquer, to conquer or die.

Then raise high the strain, pay the tribute
    that's due
To the fair Constellation, and all her brave
    Crew;
Be Truxton revered, and his name be enrolled,
'Mongst the chiefs of the ocean, the heroes of
    old.
        Each invader defy,
        While such heroes are nigh,
        Who always are ready,
        Resolved, firm, and steady
To fight, and to conquer, to conquer or die.

THE CONSTELLATION AND THE INSURGENTE

[February 9, 1799]

Come all ye Yankee sailors, with swords and
    pikes advance,
'T is time to try your courage and humble
    haughty France,
        The sons of France our seas invade,
        Destroy our commerce and our trade,
        'T is time the reck'ning should be paid!
            To brave Yankee boys.

On board the Constellation, from Baltimore
    we came,
We had a bold commander and Truxton was
    his name!
        Our ship she mounted forty guns,
        And on the main so swiftly runs,
        To prove to France Columbia's sons
            Are brave Yankee boys.

We sailed to the West Indies in order to
    annoy
The invaders of our commerce, to burn, sink,
    and destroy;
        Our Constellation shone so bright,
        The Frenchmen could not bear the sight,
        And away they scamper'd in affright,
            From the brave Yankee boys.

'T was on the 9th of February, at Montserrat
    we lay,
And there we spy'd the Insurgente just at the
    break of day,
        We raised the orange and the blue,
        To see if they our signals knew,
        The Constellation and her crew
            Of brave Yankee boys.

Then all hands were called to quarters, while
    we pursued in chase,
With well-prim'd guns, our tompions out,
    well spliced the main brace.
        Soon to the French we did draw nigh,
        Compelled to fight, they were, or fly,
        The word was passed, "Conquer or
            die,"
            My brave Yankee boys.

Lord! our Cannons thunder'd with peals
    tremendous roar,
And death upon our bullets' wings that
    drenched their decks with gore,
        The blood did from their scuppers run,
        Their chief exclaimed, "We are un-
            done!"
        Their flag they struck, the battle won,
            By the brave Yankee boys.

Then to St. Kitts we steered, we bro't her safe
    in port,
The grand salute was fired and answered from
    the fort,
        John Adams in full bumpers toast,
        George Washington, Columbia's boast,
        And now "the girl we love the most!"
            My brave Yankee boys.
1813.

On December 14, 1799, George Washington died
at Mount Vernon after an illness lasting only a few
days. The funeral took place four days later, with
only such ceremonials as the immediate neighbor-
hood provided.

WASHINGTON'S MONUMENT

For him who sought his country's good
In plains of war, mid scenes of blood;
Who, in the dubious battle's fray,
Spent the warm noon of life's bright day,
That to a world he might secure
Rights that forever shall endure,
        Rear the monument of fame!
        Deathless is the hero's name

For him, who, when the war was done,
And victory sure, and freedom won,
Left glory's theatre, the field,
The olive branch of peace to wield;
And proved, when at the helm of state,
Though great in war, in peace as great;
 Rear the monument of fame!
 Deathless is the hero's name!

For him, whose worth, though unexpress'd,
Lives cherish'd in each freeman's breast,
Whose name, to patriot souls so dear,
Time's latest children shall revere,
Whose brave achievements praised shall be,
While beats one breast for liberty;
 Rear the monument of fame!
 Deathless is the hero's name!

But why for him vain marbles raise?
Can the cold sculpture speak his praise?
Illustrious shade! we can proclaim
Our gratitude, but not thy fame.
Long as Columbia shall be free,
She lives a monument of thee;
 And may she ever rise in fame,
 To honor thy immortal name!

Since 1785 it had been necessary to protect American commerce from the Barbary corsairs by paying tribute, but their demands grew so exorbitant that war was at last declared against Tripoli, and a squadron dispatched to the Mediterranean. One of this squadron was the Philadelphia, which ran aground and was captured by the pirates on October 31, 1803. The ship was towed into the harbor of Tripoli and anchored under the guns of the fortress. On the night of February 15, 1804, a party of seventy-five headed by Lieutenants Decatur and Lawrence and Midshipman Bainbridge, entered the harbor, boarded the Philadelphia, drove the Turkish crew overboard, set fire to the ship, and escaped without losing a man, having performed what Lord Nelson called "the most daring act of the age."

HOW WE BURNED THE PHILA-
DELPHIA

[February 15, 1804]

By the beard of the Prophet the Bashaw swore
 He would scourge us from the seas;
Yankees should trouble his soul no more —
By the Prophet's beard the Bashaw swore,
 Then lighted his hookah, and took his
  ease,
And troubled his soul no more.

The moon was dim in the western sky,
 And a mist fell soft on the sea,
As we slipped away from the Siren brig
 And headed for Tripoli.

Behind us the hulk of the Siren lay,
 Before us the empty night;
And when again we looked behind
 The Siren was gone from our sight.

Nothing behind us, and nothing before,
 Only the silence and rain,
As the jaws of the sea took hold of our bows
 And cast us up again.

Through the rain and the silence we stole
  along,
 Cautious and stealthy and slow,
For we knew the waters were full of those
 Who might challenge the Mastico.

But nothing we saw till we saw the ghost
 Of the ship we had come to see,
Her ghostly lights and her ghostly frame
 Rolling uneasily.

And as we looked, the mist drew up
 And the moon threw off her veil,
And we saw the ship in the pale moonlight,
 Ghostly and drear and pale.

Then spoke Decatur low and said:
 "To the bulwarks shadow all!
But the six who wear the Tripoli dress
 Shall answer the sentinel's call."

"What ship is that?" cried the sentinel.
 "No ship," was the answer free;
"But only a Malta ketch in distress
 Wanting to moor in your lee.

"We have lost our anchor, and wait for day
 To sail into Tripoli town,
And the sea rolls fierce and high to-night,
 So cast a cable down."

Then close to the frigate's side we came,
 Made fast to her unforbid —
Six of us bold in the heathen dress,
 The rest of us lying hid.

But one who saw us hiding there
 "Americano!" cried.
Then straight we rose and made a rush
 Pellmell up the frigate's side.

Less than a hundred men were we,
  And the heathen were twenty score;
But a Yankee sailor in those old days
  Liked odds of one to four.

And first we cleaned the quarter-deck,
  And then from stern to stem
We charged into our enemies
  And quickly slaughtered them.

All around was the dreadful sound
  Of corpses striking the sea,
And the awful shrieks of dying men
  In their last agony.

The heathen fought like devils all,
  But one by one they fell,
Swept from the deck by our cutlasses
  To the water, and so to hell.

Some we found in the black of the hold,
  Some to the fo'c's'le fled,
But all in vain; we sought them out
  And left them lying dead;

Till at last no soul but Christian souls
  Upon that ship was found;
The twenty score were dead, and we,
  The hundred, safe and sound.

And, stumbling over the tangled dead,
  The deck a crimson tide,
We fired the ship from keel to shrouds
  And tumbled over the side.

Then out to sea we sailed once more
  With the world as light as day,
And the flames revealed a hundred sail
  Of the heathen there in the bay.

All suddenly the red light paled,
  And the rain rang out on the sea;
Then — a dazzling flash, a deafening roar,
  Between us and Tripoli!

Then, nothing behind us, and nothing be-
    fore,
  Only the silence and rain;
And the jaws of the sea took hold of our
    bows
  And cast us up again.

By the beard of the Prophet the Bashaw swore
  He would scourge us from the seas ;
Yankees should trouble his soul no more —

By the Prophet's beard the Bashaw swore,
  Then lighted his hookah and took his ease,
And troubled his soul no more.
                              BARRETT EASTMAN.

Arrangements were made to bombard the port
and a concerted attack was made August 3, 1804.
Two gunboats were captured and three sunk, and
the shore batteries badly damaged. Attack after
attack followed, and the war was finally ended by
Tripoli renouncing all claim to tribute and releas-
ing all American prisoners. It was during the first
assault that Reuben James saved Decatur's life.

REUBEN JAMES

[August 3, 1804]

THREE ships of war had Preble when he left
    the Naples shore,
And the knightly king of Naples lent him
    seven galleys more,
And never since the Argo floated in the middle
    sea
Such noble men and valiant have sailed in
    company
As the men who went with Preble to the siege
    of Tripoli.
Stewart, Bainbridge, Hull, Decatur — how
    their names ring out like gold! —
Lawrence, Porter, Trippe, Macdonough, and
    a score as true and bold;
Every star that lights their banner tells the
    glory that they won;
But one common sailor's glory is the splendor
    of the sun.

Reuben James was first to follow when De-
    catur laid aboard
Of the lofty Turkish galley and in battle broke
    his sword.
Then the pirate captain smote him, till his
    blood was running fast,
And they grappled and they struggled, and
    they fell beside the mast.
Close behind him Reuben battled with a
    dozen, undismayed,
Till a bullet broke his sword-arm, and he
    dropped the useless blade.
Then a swinging Turkish sabre clove his left
    and brought him low,
Like a gallant bark, dismasted, at the mercy
    of the foe.
Little mercy knows the corsair: high his blade
    was raised to slay,
When a richer prize allured him where Deca-
    tur struggling lay.

"Help!" the Turkish leader shouted, and his
    trusty comrade sprung,
And his scimetar like lightning o'er the Yan-
    kee captain swung.

Reuben James, disabled, armless, saw the
    sabre flashed on high,
Saw Decatur shrink before it, heard the pi-
    rate's taunting cry,
Saw, in half the time I tell it, how a sailor
    brave and true
Still might show a bloody pirate what a dying
    man can do.
Quick he struggled, stumbling, sliding in the
    blood around his feet,
As the Turk a moment waited to make ven-
    geance doubly sweet.
Swift the sabre fell, but swifter bent the sail-
    or's head below,
And upon his 'fenceless forehead Reuben
    James received the blow!

So was saved our brave Decatur; so the com-
    mon sailor died;
So the love that moves the lowly lifts the great
    to fame and pride.
Yet we grudge him not his honors, for whom
    love like this had birth —
For God never ranks His sailors by the Regis-
    ter of earth!
              JAMES JEFFREY ROCHE.

In the spring of 1808 the schooner Betsy, of
Marblehead, commanded by "Skipper Ireson,"
sighted a wreck while passing Cape Cod on her
way home from the West Indies. It was dark at
the time, and the sea was running high, so that
she was unable to render any assistance. An-
other vessel soon afterwards rescued the people
on the wreck, and they reached shore in season
for news of the occurrence to reach Marblehead
before the Betsy's arrival. A crowd met the vessel
at the wharf, and the sailors, when called to ac-
count, protested that Ireson would not let them
go to the relief of the wrecked vessel. The mob
thereupon seized the unfortunate skipper, and
putting him into an old dory, started to drag him
to Beverly, where they said he belonged, in order
to show him to his own people.

SKIPPER IRESON'S RIDE

[1808]

Of all the rides since the birth of time,
Told in story or sung in rhyme, —
On Apuleius's Golden Ass,
Or one-eyed Calender's horse of brass,

Witch astride of a human back,
Islam's prophet on Al-Borák, —
The strangest ride that ever was sped
Was Ireson's out from Marblehead!
    Old Floyd Ireson, for his hard heart,
    Tarred and feathered and carried in a
      cart
    By the women of Marblehead!

Body of turkey, head of fowl,
Wings a-droop like a rained-on fowl,
Feathered and ruffled in every part,
Skipper Ireson stood in the cart.
Scores of women, old and young,
Strong of muscle, and glib of tongue,
Pushed and pulled up the rocky lane,
Shouting and singing the shrill refrain:
    "Here's Flud Oirson, fur his horrd horrt,
    Torr'd an' futherr'd an' corr'd in a corrt
    By the women o' Morble'ead!"

Wrinkled scolds with hands on hips,
Girls in bloom of cheek and lips,
Wild-eyed, free-limbed, such as chase
Bacchus round some antique vase,
Brief of skirt, with ankles bare,
Loose of kerchief and loose of hair,
With conch-shells blowing and fish-horns'
    twang,
Over and over the Mænads sang:
    "Here's Flud Oirson, fur his horrd horrt,
    Torr'd an' futherr'd an' corr'd in a corrt
    By the women o' Morble'ead!"

Small pity for him! — He sailed away
From a leaking ship in Chaleur Bay, —
Sailed away from a sinking wreck,
With his own town's-people on her deck!
"Lay by! lay by!" they called to him.
Back he answered, "Sink or swim!
Brag of your catch of fish again!"
And off he sailed through the fog and rain!
    Old Floyd Ireson, for his hard heart,
    Tarred and feathered and carried in a
      cart
    By the women of Marblehead!

Fathoms deep in dark Chaleur
That wreck shall lie forevermore.
Mother and sister, wife and maid,
Looked from the rocks of Marblehead
Over the moaning and rainy sea, —
Looked for the coming that might not be!
What did the winds and the sea-birds say
Of the cruel captain who sailed away? —

Old Floyd Ireson, for his hard heart,
Tarred and feathered and carried in a cart
  By the women of Marblehead!

Through the street, on either side,
Up flew windows, doors swung wide;
Sharp-tongued spinsters, old wives gray,
Treble lent the fish-horn's bray,
Sea-worn grandsires, cripple-bound,
Hulks of old sailors run aground,
Shook head, and fist, and hat, and cane,
And cracked with curses the hoarse refrain:
  "Here's Flud Oirson, fur his horrd horrt,
  Torr'd an' futherr'd an' corr'd in a corrt
    By the women o' Morble'ead!"

Sweetly along the Salem road
Bloom of orchard and lilac showed.
Little the wicked skipper knew
Of the fields so green and the sky so blue.
Riding there in his sorry trim,
Like an Indian idol glum and grim,
Scarcely he seemed the sound to hear
Of voices shouting, far and near:
  "Here's Flud Oirson, fur his horrd horrt,
  Torr'd an' futherr'd an' corr'd in a corrt
    By the women o' Morble'ead!"

"Hear me, neighbors!" at last he cried, —
"What to me is this noisy ride?
What is the shame that clothes the skin
To the nameless horror that lives within?
Waking or sleeping, I see a wreck,
And hear a cry from a reeling deck!
Hate me and curse me, — I only dread
The hand of God and the face of the dead!"
  Said old Floyd Ireson, for his hard heart,
  Tarred and feathered and carried in a cart
    By the women of Marblehead!

Then the wife of the skipper lost at sea
Said," God has touched him! why should we!"
Said an old wife mourning her only son,
"Cut the rogue's tether and let him run!"
So with soft relentings and rude excuse,
Half scorn, half pity, they cut him loose,
And gave him a cloak to hide him in,
And left him alone with his shame and sin.
  Poor Floyd Ireson, for his hard heart,
  Tarred and feathered and carried in a cart
    By the women of Marblehead!
        JOHN GREENLEAF WHITTIER.

Later investigation proved that Ireson was in
no way responsible for the abandonment of the
disabled ship, and that his crew had lied in order
to save themselves.

A PLEA FOR FLOOD IRESON

[1808]

OLD Flood Ireson! all too long
Have jeer and gibe and ribald song
Done thy memory cruel wrong.

Old Flood Ireson, bending low
Under the weight of years and woe,
Crept to his refuge long ago.

Old Flood Ireson sleeps in his grave;
Howls of a mad mob, worse than the wave,
Now no more in his ear shall rave!

.   .   .   .

Gone is the pack and gone the prey,
Yet old Flood Ireson's ghost to-day
Is hunted still down Time's highway.

Old wife Fame, with a fish-horn's blare
Hooting and tooting the same old air,
Drags him along the old thoroughfare.

Mocked evermore with the old refrain,
Skilfully wrought to a tuneful strain,
Jingling and jolting he comes again

Over that road of old renown,
Fair broad avenue, leading down
Through South Fields to Salem town,

Scourged and stung by the Muses' thong,
Mounted high on the car of song,
Sight that cries, O Lord! how long

Shall heaven look on and not take part
With the poor old man and his fluttering
      heart,
Tarred and feathered and carried in a cart?

Old Flood Ireson, now when Fame
Wipes away with tears of shame
Stains from many an injured name,

Shall not, in the tuneful line,
Beams of truth and mercy shine
Through the clouds that darken thine?

Take henceforth, perturbèd sprite,
From the fever and the fright,
Take the rest, — thy well-earned right.

Along the track of that hard ride
The form of Penitence oft shall glide,
With tender Pity by her side;

And their tears, that mingling fall
On the dark record they recall,
Shall cleanse the stain and expiate all.

CHARLES TIMOTHY BROOKS.

CHAPTER II

THE SECOND WAR WITH ENGLAND

The treaty of peace with England which closed the Revolution provided for the payment of English creditors and the restoration of confiscated estates, but the individual states refused to carry out this agreement, and England, in consequence, retained possession of some of the Western posts. To this were soon added other causes of annoyance, principal among which was the right claimed by England to impress into her service seamen of British birth, wherever found, and to stop and search the ships of the United States for this purpose.

THE TIMES

YE brave sons of Freedom, come join in the chorus,
　At the dangers of war do not let us repine,
But sing and rejoice at the prospect before us,
　And drink it success in a bumper of wine.
　　At the call of the nation,
　　Let each to his station,
　　And resist depredation,
　　Which our country degrades;
　　Ere the conflict is over,
　　Our rights we'll recover,
　　Or punish whoever
　　Our honor invades.

We're abused and insulted, our country's degraded,
　Our rights are infringed both by land and by sea;
Let us rouse up, indignant, when those rights are invaded,
　And announce to the world, "We're united and free!"
　　By our navy's protection
　　We'll make our election,
　　And in every direction
　　Our trade shall be free;
　　No British oppression,
　　No Gallic aggression
　　Shall disturb the possession
　　We claim to the sea.

Then Columbia's ships shall sail on the ocean,
　And the nations of Europe respect us at last:
Our stars and our stripes shall command their devotion,
　And Liberty perch on the top of the mast.
　　Though *Bona* and *John Bull*
　　Continue their long pull,
　　Till ambition's cup-full
　　Be drain'd to the lees;
　　By wisdom directed,
　　By tyrants respected,
　　By cannon protected,
　　We'll traverse the seas.

Though vile combinations to sever the Union
　Be projected with caution and managed with care,
Though traitors and Britons, in sweetest communion,
　Their patriot virtue unite and compare,
　　American thunder
　　Shall rend it asunder,
　　And ages shall wonder
　　At the deeds we have done:
　　And every Tory
　　When he hears of the story,
　　Shall repine at the glory
　　Our heroes have won.

Let local attachments be condemn'd and discarded,
　Distrust and suspicion be banish'd the mind,
Let union, our safety, be ever regarded,
　When improved by example, by virtue refined.
　　Our ancestors brought it,
　　Our sages have taught it,
　　Our Washington bought it,
　　'T is our glory and boast!
　　No factions shall ever
　　Our government sever,
　　But "Union forever,"
　　Shall be our last toast.

Measures so outrageous made war seemingly inevitable; but Washington, through the Jay Treaty, managed to patch up a peace. In 1805 England, hard-pressed by Napoleon, again asserted the "right of search," and her war-vessels stopped merchantmen and cruisers alike and took off all persons whom the British commanders chose to regard as British subjects. Congress retaliated by prohibiting commerce with England. The embargo went into effect in January, 1808, and aroused sectional feeling to such an extent that New England threatened secession from the Union.

REPARATION OR WAR

WRITTEN DURING THE EMBARGO

REJOICE, rejoice, brave patriots, rejoice!
Our martial sons take a bold and manly stand!
Rejoice, rejoice, exulting raise your voice,
Let union pervade our happy land.
The altar of Liberty shall never be polluted,
But freedom expand and flourish, firm and deeply rooted.
   Our eagle, towering high,
   Triumphantly shall fly,
While men like JEFFERSON preside to serve their country!
   Huzza! huzza! boys, etc., etc.
With firmness we'll resent our wrongs sustain'd at sea;
   Huzza! huzza! etc., etc.
For none but slaves will bend to tyranny.

To arms, to arms, with ardor rush to arms,
Our injured rights have long for vengeance cried.
To arms, to arms, prepare for war's alarms,
If honest reparation be denied.
Though feeble counteracting plans, or foreign combinations,
May interdict awhile our trade, against the law of nations,
   The embargo on supplies
   Shall open Europe's eyes;
Proclaiming unto all the world, "Columbia will be free."
   Huzza! huzza! etc., etc.
With honor we'll maintain a just neutrality.
   Huzza! huzza! etc., etc.
For none but slaves will bend to tyranny.

Defend, defend, ye heroes and ye sages,
The gift divine — your independency!
Transmit with joy, down to future ages,
How Washington achieved your liberty.
When freemen are insulted, they send forth vengeful thunder,
Determined to maintain their rights, strike the foe with wonder.
   They cheerfully will toil,
   To cultivate the soil,
And rather live on humble fare than feast ignobly.
   Huzza! huzza! etc., etc.
United, firm we stand, invincible and free,
   Huzza! huzza! etc., etc.
Then none but slaves shall bend to tyranny.

The opponents of the embargo termed the conflict a "terrapin war," — the nation, by extinguishing commerce, drawing within its own shell like a terrapin; and at gatherings of the Federalists, a song by that title was very popular.

TERRAPIN WAR

HUZZA for our liberty, boys,
   These are the days of our glory —
The days of true national joys,
   When terrapins gallop before ye!
There's Porter and Grundy and Rhea,
   In Congress who manfully vapor,
Who draw their six dollars a day,
   And fight bloody battles *on paper !*
   Ah! this is true Terrapin war.

Poor Madison the tremors has got,
   'Bout this same arming the nation;
Too far to retract, he cannot
   Go on — and he loses his station.
Then bring up your "regulars," lads,
   In "attitude" nothing ye lack, sirs,
Ye'll frighten to death the Danads,
   With fire-coals blazing aback, sirs!
   Oh, this is true Terrapin war!

As to powder and bullets and swords,
   For, as they were never intended,
They're a parcel of high-sounding words,
   But never to *action* extended.
Ye must *frighten* the rascals away,
   In "*rapid descent*" on their quarters;
Then the plunder divide as ye may,
   And drive them headlong in the waters.
   Oh, this is *great* Terrapin war!

But the hostility to Great Britain grew steadily more bitter, and the war party was led by such able men as Henry Clay and John C. Calhoun. Various incidents tended to fan the flames, and on June 18, 1812, war was declared.

FAREWELL, PEACE

[June 18, 1812]

FAREWELL, Peace! another crisis
  Calls us to "the last appeal,"
Made when monarchs and their vices
  Leave no argument but *steel*.
When injustice and oppression
  Dare avow the tyrant's plea.
Who would recommend submission?
  Virtue bids us to be free.

History spreads her page before us,
  Time unrolls his ample scroll;
Truth unfolds them, to assure us,
  States, united, ne'er can fall.
See, in annals Greek and Roman,
  What immortal deeds we find;
When those gallant sons of woman
  In their country's cause combined.

Sons of Freedom! brave descendants
  From a race of heroes tried,
To preserve our independence
  Let all Europe be defied.
Let not all the world, united,
  Rob us of one sacred right:
Every patriot heart's delighted
  In his country's cause to fight.

Come then, War! with hearts elated
  To thy standard we will fly;
Every bosom animated
  Either to live free or die.
May the wretch that shrinks from duty,
  Or deserts the glorious strife,
Never know the smile of beauty,
  Nor the blessing of a wife.

The Federalists claimed that war had been declared, not to avenge the country's wrongs upon the ocean, but to conquer Canada. Canada was, indeed, the first objective, and troops were enlisted and hurried forward to the various northern posts.

COME, YE LADS, WHO WISH TO SHINE

COME, ye lads, who wish to shine
  Bright in future story,

Haste to arms, and form the line
  That leads to martial glory.
    Beat the drum, the trumpet sound,
      Manly and united,
    Danger face, maintain your ground,
      And see your country righted.

Columbia, when her eagle's roused,
  And her flag is rearing
Will always find her sons disposed
  To drub the foe that's daring.
    Beat the drum, etc

Hearts of oak, protect the coast,
  Pour your naval thunder,
While on shore a mighty host
  Shall strike the world with wonder.
    Beat the drum, etc.

Haste to Quebec's towering walls,
  Through the British regions;
Hark! Montgomery's spirit calls,
  Drive the hostile legions.
    Beat the drum, etc.

Honor for the brave to share
  Is the noblest booty;
Guard your rights, protect the fair,
  For that's a soldier's duty.
    Beat the drum, etc.

Charge the musket, point the lance,
  Brave the worst of dangers;
Tell to Britain and to France,
  That we to fear are strangers.
    Beat the drum, etc.

The Canadian campaign was soon to end ignominiously enough. In July, General Hull, governor of Michigan territory, crossed from Detroit into Canada, then crossed back again, and on August 16, without striking a blow, surrendered Detroit and his entire army to the British under General Brock. Hull was afterwards tried by court-martial, convicted of cowardice, and sentenced to be shot, but the sentence was commuted.

HULL'S SURRENDER

OR, VILLANY SOMEWHERE

[August 16, 1812]

YE Columbians so bold, attend while I sing;
Sure treason and treachery's not quite the
    thing,

At a time like the present, we ought, one and
all,
In defence of our rights, to stand nobly or fall.

Chorus

Then let traitors be banish'd Columbia's
fair shore,
And treason be known in her borders no
more.

With a brave, gallant army HULL went to
Detroit,
And swore he'd accomplish a noble exploit;
That the British and Indians he'd conquer
outright,
And give cause to his country of joy and
delight.

Chorus

But if traitors still dwell on Columbia's
fair shore,
O let it be known in her borders no more.

Ah! quickly alas! defeat and disgrace
Star'd our brave noble soldiers quite full in
the face,
When they thought that the victory was sure
to be won,
Their general gave up, *without firing a gun.*

Chorus

Then do traitors still dwell on Columbia's
fair shore,
IF THEY DO, let them dwell in her borders
no more!

Those heroes, who bravely on the Wabash
had fought,
Who for glory successfully nobly had sought,
Where the *favor* denied of asserting their
wrongs,
And deprived of that *right* which to freemen
belongs.

Chorus

Then if treason still dwell on Columbia's
fair shore,
O let it be known in her borders no more!

Is it true that our soldiers were wrongfully
us'd?
Is it true that they've been by their GENERAL
abus'd?
Is it true that an army so gallant were *sold?*
Is it true that COLUMBIANS were barter'd for
gold?

Chorus

If it is, then does treason still dwell on our
shore,
But let it be known in our country no more!

Ye heroes who fought by the side of brave
Floyd,
Ye heroes, conducted to glory by *Boyd,*
Think not that your brethren will quietly
bear,
From your brows that a traitor your laurels
should tear.

Chorus

No — if treason still dwell on Columbia's
fair shore,
It shall soon be expell'd to reside here no
more.

Then rouse ye brave freemen, and heed no
alarms,
Your dear native country now calls you to
arms,
Away to the battle, and count not the cost
Till the glory you gain, which so basely was
lost.

Chorus

For if treason still dwell on Columbia's
fair shore,
By our fathers we swear it shall dwell here
no more.

The fury which the news of this disaster aroused
was tempered by rejoicing for a remarkable vic-
tory on the ocean. Anxious to meet some of the
famous British frigates, Captain Isaac Hull put out
from Boston with the Constitution on August 2
He sailed without orders, and had the cruise re-
sulted disastrously, he would probably have been
court-martialed and shot. On the afternoon o
August 19, a sail was sighted off Halifax an
proved to be the British frigate Guerrière. Hu
at once attacked, and soon reduced the enem
to a "perfect wreck." The Constitution sustaine
little injury and got safely back to port.

THE CONSTITUTION AND THE GUERRIÈRE

[August 19, 1812]

I OFTEN have been told
That the British seamen bold
Could beat the tars of France neat a
handy O;

But they never found their match,
Till the Yankees did them catch,
For the Yankee tars for fighting are the
dandy O.

O, the Guerrière so bold
On the foaming ocean rolled,
Commanded by Dacres the grandee O;
For the choice of British crew
That a rammer ever drew
Could beat the Frenchmen two to one quite
handy O.

When the frigate hove in view,
"O," said Dacres to his crew,
"Prepare ye for action and be handy O;
On the weather-gauge we'll get her."
And to make his men fight better,
He gave to them gunpowder and good
brandy O.

Now this boasting Briton cries,
"Make that Yankee ship your prize,
You can in thirty minutes do it handy O,
Or twenty-five, I'm sure
You'll do it in a score,
I will give you a double share of good brandy
O.

"When prisoners we've made them,
With switchell we will treat them,
We will treat them with 'Yankee Doodle
Dandy' O;"
The British balls flew hot,
But the Yankees answered not,
Until they got a distance that was handy O.

"O," cried Hull unto his crew,
"We'll try what we can do;
If we beat those boasting Britons we're the
dandy O."
The first broadside we poured
Brought the mizzen by the board,
Which doused the royal ensign quite
handy O.

O Dacres he did sigh,
And to his officers did cry,
I did not think these Yankees were so
handy O."
The second told so well
That the fore and main-mast fell,
Which made this lofty frigate look quite
handy O.

"O," says Dacres, "we're undone,"
So he fires a lee gun.
Our drummer struck up "Yankee Doodle
Dandy" O;
When Dacres came on board
To deliver up his sword,
He was loth to part with it, it looked so
handy O.

"You may keep it," says brave Hull.
"What makes you look so dull?
Cheer up and take a glass of good brandy O;"
O Britons now be still,
Since we've hooked you in the gill,
Don't boast upon Dacres the grandee O.

HALIFAX STATION

[August 19, 1812]

From Halifax station a bully there came,
To take or be taken, call'd Dacres by name:
But 't was who but a Yankee he met on his
way —
Says the Yankee to him, "Will you stop and
take tea?"

Then Dacres steps up, thus addressing his
crew: —
"Don't you see that d—d flag that is red,
white, and blue;
Let us drum all to quarters, prepare for to
fight,
For in taking that ship boys, it will make me
a knight."

Then up to each mast-head he straight sent a
flag,
Which shows, on the ocean, a proud British
brag;
But Hull, being pleasant, he sent up but one,
And told every seaman to stand true to his gun.

Then Hull, like a hero, before them appears,
And with a short speech his sailors he cheers,
Saying, "We'll batter their sides, and we'll
do the neat thing:
We'll conquer their bully, and laugh at their
king."

Then we off with our hats and gave him a
cheer,
Swore we'd stick by brave Hull, while a sea-
man could steer:

And at it we went with mutual delight,
For to fight and to conquer's a sailor's free
    right.

Then we crowded all sail, and we ran along-
    side,
And we wellfed our bull-dogs with true Yan-
    kee pride.
'T was broadside for broadside we on them
    did pour,
While cannon's loud mouths at each other did
    roar.

Says Dacres, "Fight on, and we'll have her
    in tow,
We will drink to Great Britain, and the cans
    they shall flow;
So strike, you d—d Yankee, I'll make you
    with ease:"
But the man they call Hull, says, "O no, if
    you please."

Then Dacres wore ship, expecting to rake;
But quite in a hurry, found out his mistake;
For we luff'd round his bow, boys, and caught
    his jib-boom,
And, in raking them aft, we soon gave him his
    doom.

Then Dacres look'd wild, and then sheath'd
    his sword,
When he found that his masts were all gone
    by the board,
And dropping astern cries out to the stew-
    ard,
"Come up and be d—d, fire a gun to the lee-
    ward."

Then we off with our hats, and we gave them
    three cheers,
Which bitterly stung all those Englishmen's
    ears;
Saying, "We'll fight for our country, do all
    things that's right,
And let the world know, that green Yankees
    can fight."

ON THE CAPTURE OF THE GUER-
RIÈRE

[August 19, 1812]

Long the tyrant of our coast
    Reigned the famous Guerrière;

Our little navy she defied,
    Public ship and privateer:
On her sails in letters red,
To our captains were displayed
Words of warning, words of dread,
    "All who meet me, have a care!
    I am England's Guerrière."

On the wide, Atlantic deep
    (Not her equal for the fight)
The Constitution, on her way,
    Chanced to meet these men of might;
On her sails was nothing said,
But her waist the teeth displayed
That a deal of blood could shed,
    Which, if she would venture near,
    Would stain the decks of the Guerrière

Now our gallant ship they met —
    And, to struggle with John Bull —
Who had come, they little thought,
    Strangers, yet, to Isaac Hull:
Better soon to be acquainted:
Isaac hailed the Lord's anointed —
While the crew the cannon pointed,
    And the balls were so directed
    With a blaze so unexpected;

Isaac so did maul and rake her
That the decks of Captain Dacre
Were in such a woful pickle
As if death with scythe and sickle,
    With his sling, or with his shaft
    Had cut his harvest fore and aft.
Thus, in thirty minutes ended,
Mischiefs that could not be mended;
Masts, and yards, and ship descended
    All to David Jones's locker —
    Such a ship in such a pucker!

Drink a bout to the Constitution.
She performed some execution,
Did some share of retribution
    For the insults of the year
    When she took the Guerrière.
May success again await her,
    Let who will again command her,
Bainbridge, Rodgers, or Decatur —
    Nothing like her can withstand her
With a crew like that on board her
Who so boldly called "to order"
    One bold crew of English sailors,
    Long, too long our seamen's jailors,
        Dacre and the Guerrière!
                PHILIP FRENEAU

FIRSTFRUITS IN 1812

[August 19, 1812]

WHAT is that a-billowing there
Like a thunderhead in air?
Why *should such a sight be whitening the*
seas?
That's a Yankee man-o'-war,
And three things she's seeking for —
For a prize, and for a battle, and a breeze.

When the war blew o'er the sea
Out went Hull and out went we
In the Constitution, looking for the foe;
But five British ships came down —
And we got to Boston-town
By a mighty narrow margin, you must know!

Captain Hull can't fight their fleet,
But he fairly aches to meet
Quite the prettiest British ship of all there
were;
So he stands again to sea
In the hope that on his lee
He'll catch Dacres and his pretty Guerrière.

'T is an August afternoon
Not a day too late or soon,
When we raise a ship whose lettered mainsail
reads:
All who meet me have a care,
I am England's Guerrière;
So Hull gayly clears for action as he speeds.

Cheery bells had chanted five
On the happiest day alive
When we Yankees dance to quarters at his
call;
While the British bang away
With their broadsides' screech and bray;
But the Constitution never fires a ball.

We send up three times to ask
If we sha'n't begin our task?
Captain Hull sends back each time the answer
No;
Till to half a pistol-shot
The two frigates he had brought,
Then he whispers, *Lay along!* — and we let go.

Twice our broadside lights and lifts,
And the Briton, crippled, drifts
With her mizzen dangling hopeless at her
poop:

Laughs a Yankee, *She's a brig!*
Says our Captain, *That's too big;*
Try another, so we'll have her for a sloop!

We hurrah, and fire again,
Lay aboard of her like men,
And, like men, they beat us off, and try in
turn;
But we drive bold Dacres back
With our muskets' snap and crack —
All the while our crashing broadsides boom
and burn.

'T is but half an hour, bare,
When that pretty Guerrière
Not a stick calls hers aloft or hers alow,
Save the mizzen's shattered mast,
Where her "meteor flag" 's nailed fast
Till, a fallen star, we quench its ruddy
glow.

Dacres, injured, o'er our side
Slowly bears his sword of pride,
Holds it out, as Hull stands there in his re-
nown:
No, no! says th' American,
Never, from so brave a man —
But I see you're wounded, let me help you
down.

All that night we work in vain
Keeping her upon the main,
But we've hulled her far too often, and at
last
In a blaze of fire there
Dies the pretty Guerrière;
While away we cheerly sail upon the blast.

Oh, the breeze that blows so free!
Oh, the prize beneath the sea!
Oh, the battle! — was there ever better won?
Still the happy Yankee cheers
Are a-ringing in our ears
From old Boston, glorying in what we've
done.

What is that a-billowing there
Like a thunderhead in air?
Why should such a sight be whitening the
seas?
That's Old Ir'nsides, trim and taut,
And she's found the things she sought —
Found a prize, a bully battle, and a breeze!
                                   WALLACE RICE.

This victory, needless to say, greatly encouraged the Americans, and General Stephen van Rensselaer, in command of the northern army, determined to try another stroke at Canada. On October 13, 1812, he started to cross the Niagara River with six hundred men; but the crossing was mismanaged, the militia refused to obey orders, and after a gallant fight lasting all day, the Americans were forced to surrender to an overwhelming force of British and Indians.

THE BATTLE OF QUEENSTOWN

[October 13, 1812]

WHEN brave Van Rensselaer cross'd the stream,
　Just at the break of day,
Distressing thoughts, a restless dream,
　Disturb'd me where I lay.

But all the terrors of the night
　Did quickly flee away:
My opening eyes beheld the light,
　And hail'd the new-born day.

Soon did the murdering cannon's roar
　Put blood in all my veins;
Columbia's sons have trod the shore
　Where the proud Britain reigns.

To expose their breast to cannon's ball,
　Their country's rights to save,
O what a grief to see them fall!
　True heroes, bold and brave!

The musket's flash, the cannon's glow,
　Thunder'd and lighten'd round,
Struck dread on all the tawny foe,
　And swept them to the ground.

I thought what numbers must be slain,
　What weeping widows left!
And aged parents full of pain,
　Of every joy bereft.

The naked savage yelling round
　Our heroes where they stood,
And every weapon to be found
　Was bathed in human blood.

But bold Van Rensselaer, full of wounds,
　Was quickly carried back;
Brave Colonel Bloom did next command
　The bloody fierce attack.

Where Brock, the proud insulter, rides
　In pomp and splendor great;
Our valiant heroes he derides,
　And dared the power of fate.

" Here is a mark for Yankee boys,
　So shoot me if you can:"
A Yankee ball soon closed his eyes,
　Death found him but a man.

They slaughter'd down the tawny foe,
　And Britons that were near;
They dealt out death at every blow,
　The battle was severe.

Five battles fought all in one day,
　Through four victorious stood,
But ah! the fifth swept all away,
　And spilt our heroes' blood.

The tomahawk and scalping-knife
　On them did try their skill;
Some wounded, struggling for their life,
　Did black barbarians kill.

Brave Wadsworth boldly kept the field
　Till their last bullets flew;
Then all were prisoners forced to yield,
　What could the general do?

Militia men! O fie for shame!
　Thus you your country flee.
'T is you at last will bear the blame
　For loss of victory.

When mild Van Rensselaer did command,
　You would not him obey;
But stood spectators on the strand,
　To see the bloody fray.

The number kill'd was seventy-four,
　Prisoners, seven hundred sixty-nine,
Wounded, two hundred or more,
　Who languish'd in great pain.

Some have already lost their lives,
　And others like to go;
But few, I fear, will tell their wives
　The doleful tale of wo.

WILLIAM BANKER, JR.

But disasters on land seemed fated to be followed by victories on the water. About noon October 18, 1812, the American 18-gun sloop of war, Wasp, encountered the 20-gun British br

Frolic, off Albemarle Sound, and, after a severe action, boarded and compelled her to surrender. Shortly afterwards, a sail hove in sight, which proved to be the British 74, Poictiers, and, running down on the sloops, she seized both the Wasp and her prize and carried them to Bermuda.

THE WASP'S FROLIC

[October 18, 1812]

'T WAS on board the sloop of war Wasp, boys,
　We set sail from Delaware Bay,
To cruise on Columbia's fair coast, sirs,
　Our rights to maintain on the sea.

Three days were not passed on our sta-
　tion,
　When the Frolic came up to our view;
Says Jones, "Show the flag of our nation;"
　Three cheers were then gave by our crew.

We boldly bore up to this Briton,
　Whose cannon began for to roar;
The Wasp soon her stings from her side
　ran,
　When we on them a broadside did pour.

Each sailor stood firm at his quarters,
　'T was minutes past forth and three,
When fifty bold Britons were slaughtered,
　Whilst our guns swept their masts in the
　sea.

Their breasts then with valor still glowing,
　Acknowledged the battle we'd won,
On us then bright laurels bestowing,
　When to leeward they fired a gun.

On their decks we the twenty guns counted,
　With a crew for to answer the same;
Eighteen was the number we mounted,
　Being served by the lads of true game.

With the Frolic in tow, we were standing,
　All in for Columbia's fair shore;
But fate on our laurels was frowning,
　We were taken by a seventy-four.

A more signal victory was soon to be recorded. On the morning of October 25, 1812, near the Canary Islands, the British 38-gun frigate, Mace-donian, was overhauled by the American 44, United States, and an hour after the action began, was reduced to a wreck by the terrible fire of the American. A prize crew was put aboard, repaired her, and got her safely to New York.

THE UNITED STATES AND MACE-DONIAN

[October 25, 1812]

How glows each patriot bosom that boasts a
　Yankee heart,
To emulate such glorious deeds and nobly
　take a part;
　When sailors with their thund'ring guns,
　Prove to the English, French, and Danes
　That Neptune's chosen fav'rite sons
　Are brave Yankee boys.

The twenty-fifth of October, that glorious
　happy day,
When we beyond all precedent, from Britons
　bore the sway, —
　'T was in the ship United States,
　Four and forty guns the rates,
　That she should rule, decreed the Fates.
　And brave Yankee boys.

Decatur and his hardy tars were cruising on
　the deep,
When off the Western Islands they to and fro
　did sweep,
　The Macedonian they espied,
　"Huzza! bravo!" Decatur cried,
　"We'll humble Britain's boasted pride,
　My brave Yankee boys."

The decks were cleared, the hammocks
　stowed, the boatswain pipes all hands,
The tompions out, the guns well sponged, the
　Captain now commands;
　The boys who for their country fight,
　Their words, "Free Trade and Sailor's
　Rights!"
　Three times they cheered with all their
　might,
　　Those brave Yankee boys.

Now chain-shot, grape, and langrage pierce
　through her oaken sides,
And many a gallant sailor's blood runs
　purpling in the tides;
　While death flew nimbly o'er their decks,
　Some lost their legs, and some their necks
　And Glory's wreath our ship be-decks,
　For brave Yankee boys.

My boys, the proud St. George's Cross, the
　stripes above it wave,
And busy are our gen'rous tars, the conquered
　foe to save.

Our Captain cries " Give me your hand,"
Then of the ship who took command
But brave Yankee boys?

Our enemy lost her mizzen, her main and
fore-topmast,
For ev'ry shot with death was winged, which
slew her men so fast,
That they lost five to one in killed,
And ten to one their blood was spilled,
So Fate decreed and Heaven had willed,
For brave Yankee boys.

Then homeward steered the captive ship, now
safe in port she lies,
The old and young with rapture viewed our
sailors' noble prize;
Through seas of wine their health we'll
drink,
And wish them sweet-hearts, friends, and
chink,
Who 'fore they'd strike, will nobly sink
Our brave Yankee boys.

THE UNITED STATES AND MACEDONIAN

[October 25, 1812]

THE banner of Freedom high floated unfurled,
While the silver-tipt surges in low homage
curled,
Flashing bright round the bow of Decatur's
brave bark,
In contest, an "eagle" — in chasing, a "lark."
The bold United States,
Which four-and-forty rates,
Will ne'er be known to yield — be known to
yield or fly,
Her motto is " Glory! we conquer or we die."

All canvas expanded to woo the coy gale,
The ship cleared for action, in chase of a sail;
The foemen in view, every bosom beats high,
All eager for conquest, or ready to die.

Now havoc stands ready, with optics of flame,
And battle-hounds "strain on the start" for
the game;
The blood demons rise on the surge for their
prey,
While Pity, rejected, awaits the dread fray.

The gay floating streamers of Britain appear,
Waving light on the breeze as the stranger we
near;

And now could the quick-sighted Yankee
discern
" Macedonian," emblazoned at large on her
stern.

She waited our approach, and the contest be-
gan,
But to waste ammunition is no Yankee plan;
In awful suspense every match was withheld,
While the bull-dogs of Britain incessantly
yelled.

Unawed by her thunders, alongside we came,
While the foe seemed enwrapped in a mantle
of flame;
When, prompt to the word, such a flood we
return,
That Neptune, aghast, thought his trident
would burn.

Now the lightning of battle gleams horridly
red,
With a tempest of iron and hail-storm of lead;
And our fire on the foe we so copiously poured,
His mizzen and topmasts soon went by the
board.

So fierce and so bright did our flashes aspire,
They thought that their cannon had set us on
fire,
" The Yankee's in flames! " — every British
tar hears,
And hails the false omen with three hearty
cheers.

In seventeen minutes they found their mis-
take,
And were glad to surrender and fall in our
wake;
Her decks were with carnage and blood
deluged o'er,
Where welt'ring in blood lay an hundred and
four.

But though she was made so completely a
wreck,
With blood they had scarcely encrimsoned
our deck;
Only five valiant Yankees in the contest were
slain,
And our ship in five minutes was fitted again.

Let Britain no longer lay claim to the seas,
For the trident of Neptune is ours, if we
please,

While Hull and Decatur and Jones are our
  boast,
We dare their whole navy to come on our coast.

Rise, tars of Columbia! — and share in the
  fame,
Which gilds Hull's, Decatur's, and Jones's
  bright name;
Fill a bumper, and drink, "Here's success to
  the cause,
But Decatur supremely deserves our ap-
  plause."
    The bold United States,
    Which four-and-forty rates,
Shall ne'er be known to yield — be known to
  yield or fly,
Her motto is "Glory! we conquer or we die."

The United States was commanded by Captain
Stephen Decatur, and just before she engaged the
Macedonian an incident occurred which showed
his crew's unbounded confidence in him.

JACK CREAMER

[October 25, 1812]

THE boarding nettings are triced for fight;
Pike and cutlass are shining bright;
The boatswain's whistle pipes loud and shrill;
Gunner and topman work with a will;
Rough old sailor and reefer trim
Jest as they stand by the cannon grim;
There's a fighting glint in Decatur's eye,
And brave Old Glory floats out on high.

But many a heart beats fast below
The laughing lips as they near the foe;
For the pluckiest knows, though no man
  quails,
That the breath of death is filling the sails.
Only one little face is wan;
Only one childish mouth is drawn;
One little heart is sad and sore
To the watchful eye of the Commodore.
Little Jack Creamer, ten years old,
In no purser's book or watch enrolled,
Must mope or skulk while his shipmates
  fight, —
No wonder his little face is white!

"Why, Jack, old man, so blue and sad?
Afraid of the music?" The face of the lad
With mingled shame and anger burns.
Quick to the Commodore he turns:

"I'm not a coward, but I think if you —
Excuse me, Capt'n, I mean if you knew
(I s'pose it's because I'm young and small)
I'm not on the books! I'm no one at all!
And as soon as this fighting work is done,
And we get our prize-money, every one
Has his share of the plunder — I get none."

"And you're sure we shall take her?" "Sure?
  Why, sir,
She's only a blessed Britisher!
We'll take her easy enough, I bet;
But glory's all that I'm going to get!"
"Glory! I doubt if I get more,
If I get so much," said the Commodore;
"But faith goes far in the race for fame,
And down on the books shall go your name."

Bravely the little seaman stood
To his post while the scuppers ran with blood,
While grizzled veterans looked and smiled
And gathered new courage from the child;
Till the enemy, crippled in pride and might,
Struck his crimson flag and gave up the fight.
Then little Jack Creamer stood once more
Face to face with the Commodore.

"You have got your glory," he said, "my lad,
And money to make your sweetheart glad.
Now, who may she be?" "My mother, sir;
I want you to send the half to her."
"And the rest?" Jack blushed and hung his
  head;
"I'll buy some schoolin' with that," he said.

Decatur laughed; then in graver mood:
"The first is the better, but both are good.
Your mother shall never know want while I
Have a ship to sail, or a flag to fly;
And schooling you'll have till all is blue,
But little the lubbers can teach to you."

Midshipman Creamer's story is told —
They did such things in the days of old,
When faith and courage won sure reward,
And the quarter-deck was not triply barred,
To the forecastle hero; for men were men,
And the Nation was close to its Maker then.
                    JAMES JEFFREY ROCHE.

Encouraged by these successes, Congress, on
January 2, 1813, appropriated $2,500,000 to build
four 74-gun ships and six 44-gun ships. England
also took them to heart, and toward the end of
the month the entire British fleet was sent to
blockade the Atlantic coast.

YANKEE THUNDERS

[1813]

BRITANNIA S gallant streamers
  Float proudly o'er the tide,
And fairly wave Columbia's stripes,
  In battle side by side.
And ne'er did bolder seamen meet,
  Where ocean's surges pour;
O'er the tide now they ride,
  While the bell'wing thunders roar,
While the cannon's fire is flashing fast,
  And the bell'wing thunders roar.

When Yankee meets the Briton,
  Whose blood congenial flows,
By Heav'n created to be friends,
  By fortune rendered foes;
Hard then must be the battle fray,
  Ere well the fight is o'er;
Now they ride, side by side,
  While the bell'wing thunders roar,
While her cannon's fire is flashing fast,
  And the bell'wing thunders roar.

Still, still, for noble England
  Bold D'Acres' streamers fly;
And for Columbia, gallant Hull's
  As proudly and as high;
Now louder rings the battle din,
  And thick the volumes pour;
Still they ride, side by side,
  While the bell'wing thunders roar,
While the cannon's fire is flashing fast,
  And the bell'wing thunders roar.

Why lulls Britannia's thunder,
  That waked the wat'ry war?
Why stays the gallant Guerrière,
  Whose streamers waved so fair?
That streamer drinks the ocean wave,
  That warrior's fight is o'er!
Still they ride, side by side,
  While the bell'wing thunders roar,
While the cannon's fire is flashing fast,
  And the bell'wing thunders roar.

Hark! 't is the Briton's lee gun!
  Ne'er bolder warrior kneeled!
And ne'er to gallant mariners
  Did braver seamen yield.
Proud be the sires, whose hardy boys
  Then fell to fight no more:

With the brave, mid the wave;
  When the cannon's thunders roar,
Their spirits then shall trim the blast,
  And swell the thunder's roar.

Vain were the cheers of Britons,
  Their hearts did vainly swell,
Where virtue, skill, and bravery
  With gallant Morris fell.
That heart so well in battle tried,
  Along the Moorish shore,
And again o'er the main,
  When Columbia's thunders roar,
Shall prove its Yankee spirit true,
  When Columbia's thunders roar.

Hence be our floating bulwark
  Those oaks our mountains yield;
'T is mighty Heaven's plain decree —
  Then take the wat'ry field!
To ocean's farthest barrier then
  Your whit'ning sail shall pour;
Safe they 'll ride o'er the tide,
  While Columbia's thunders roar,
While her cannon's fire is flashing fast,
  And her Yankee thunders roar.

On March 11, 1813, the little privateer schooner, General Armstrong, Captain Guy R. Champlin, was cruising off Surinam River, when she sighted a sail, and on investigation found it to be a large vessel, apparently a British privateer. Champlin bore down and endeavored to board. The stranger kept off, and, suddenly raising her port covers, disclosed herself as a British 44-gun frigate. For forty-five minutes the Americans stood to their guns and endeavored to dismast the enemy, then gradually drew away and escaped.

THE GENERAL ARMSTRONG

[March 11, 1813]

COME, all you sons of Liberty, that to the sea
    belong,
It's worth your attention to listen to my
    song;
The history of a privateer I will detail in
    full,
That fought a "six-and-thirty" belonging to
    John Bull.

The General Armstrong she is called, and
    sailèd from New York,
With all our hearts undaunted, once more to
    try our luck;

THE GENERAL ARMSTRONG

She was a noble vessel, a privateer of fame:
She had a brave commander, George Champlin was his name.

We stood unto the eastward, all with a favoring gale,
In longitude of fifty we spied a lofty sail:
Our mainsail being lower'd and foresail to repair,
Our squaresail being set, my boys, the wind it provèd fair.

We very soon perceivèd the lofty sail to be
Bearing down upon us while we lay under her lee;
All hands we call'd, and sail did make, then splicèd the main-brace,
Night coming on, we sail'd so fast, she soon gave up the chase.

Then to Barbadoes we were bound, our course so well did steer;
We cruisèd there for several days, and nothing did appear.
'T was on the 11th of March, to windward of Surinam,
We spied a lofty ship, my boys, at anchor near the land;
All hands we call'd to quarters, and down upon her bore,
Thinking 't was some merchant-ship then lying near the shore.

She quickly weighèd anchor and from us did steer,
And setting her top-gallant sail as if she did us fear,
But soon we were alongside of her, and gave her a gun,
Determinèd to fight, my boys, and not from her to run.

We hoisted up the bloody flag and down upon her bore,
If she did not strike, my boys, no quarters we would show her;
Each man a brace of pistols, a boarding-pike and sword,
We'll give her a broadside, my boys, before we do her board.

All hands at their quarters lay, until we came alongside,
And gave them three hearty cheers, their British courage tried.

The lower ports she had shut in, the Armstrong to decoy,
And quickly she her ports did show, to daunt each Yankee boy.

The first broadside we gave them true, their colors shot away,
Their topsail, haulyards, mizen rigging, main and mizen stay,
Two ports we did knock into one, his starboard quarter tore,
They overboard their wounded flung, while cannons loud did roar.

She wore directly round, my boys, and piped all hands on deck,
For fear that we would board and serve a Yankee trick;
To board a six-and-thirty it was in vain to try,
While the grape, round, and langrage, like hailstones they did fly.

Brave Champlin on the quarter-deck so nobly gave command:
"Fight on, my brave Americans, dismast her if you can."
The round, grape, and star-shot so well did play,
A musket-ball from the maintop brave Champlin low did lay.

His wound was quickly dress'd, while he in his cabin lay;
The doctor, while attending, these words he heard him say:
"Our Yankee flag shall flourish," our noble captain cried,
"Before that we do strike, my boys, we'll sink alongside."

She was a six-and-thirty, and mounted forty-two,
We fought her four glasses, what more then could we do;
Till six brave seamen we had kill'd, which grievèd us full sore,
And thirteen more wounded lay bleeding in their gore.

Our foremast being wounded, and bowsprit likewise;
Our lower rigging fore and aft, and headstay beside;

Our haulyards, braces, bowling, and foretop sheet also,
We found we could not fight her, boys, so from her we did go.

Our foremast proving dangerous, we could not carry sail,
Although we had it fish'd and welded with a chain;
It grieved us to the heart to put up with such abuse,
For this damn'd English frigate had surely spoil'd our cruise.

Here's success attend brave Champlin, his officers and men,
That fought with courage keen, my boys, our lives to defend;
We fought with much superior force, what could we do more?
Then haul'd our wind and stood again for Freedom's happy shore.

On the land, the year opened badly with the disastrous defeat of an American column, under General Winchester, at Raisin River, Michigan; but on April 27 General Pike, at the head of fifteen hundred men, stormed and captured the British fort at York, now Toronto.

CAPTURE OF LITTLE YORK

[April 27, 1813]

WHEN Britain, with envy and malice inflamed,
    Dared dispute the dear rights of Columbia's bless'd union,
We thought of the time when our freedom we claim'd,
    And fought 'gainst oppression with fullest communion.
        Our foes on the ocean have been forced to yield,
        And fresh laurels we now gather up in the field.

Freedom's flag on the wilds of the west is unfurl'd,
    And our foes seem to find their resistance delusion;
For our eagle her arrows amongst them has hurl'd
    And their ranks of bold veterans fill'd with confusion.
        Our foes on the ocean, etc.

On the lakes of the west, full of national pride,
    See our brave little fleet most triumphantly riding!
And behold the brave tars on the fresh-water tide,
    In a noble commander, brave Chauncey, confiding.
        Our foes on the ocean, etc.

Their deeds of proud valor shall long stand enroll'd
    On the bright shining page of our national glory:
And oft, in the deep winter's night, shall be told
    The exploits of the tars of American story.
        Our foes on the ocean, etc.

Nor less shall the soldiers come in for their praise,
    Who engaged to accomplish the great expedition;
And a monument Fame shall for them cheerily raise,
    And their deeds shall in history find repetition.
        Our foes on the ocean, etc.

Let Britons still boast of their prowess and pluck;
    We care not a straw for their muskets and cannon.
In the field we will beat them, unless they've the luck
    To run from their foes like Tenedos and Shannon.
        Our foes on the ocean, etc.

Our sweet little bull-dogs, they thunder'd away,
    And our sailors and soldiers the foe still kept mauling,
Till they grew very sick of such tight Yankee play,
    And poor Sheaffe and his troops then ran away bawling.
        Our foes on the ocean, etc.

But the rascals on malice quite fully were bent:
    And as from the fort they were cowardly going,
In pursuance to what was at first their intent,
    The magazine they had resolved on up-blowing.
        Our foes on the ocean, etc.

Two hundred brave soldiers there met with
    their death;
  And while for their country they nobly were
    dying,
Full fifty bold Britons at once lost their
    breath,
  And with them in the air were their car-
    casses flying.
    Our foes on the ocean, etc.

The brave General Pike there met with his
    end;
  But his virtues his country forever will
    cherish:
And while o'er his grave fair Freedom shall
    bend,
  She will swear that his memory never shall
    perish.
    Our foes on the ocean, etc.

Let the minions of Britain swarm over our
    coast;
  Columbians, all cowardly conduct dis-
    daining,
We'll teach the invaders how vain is their
    boast,
  And contend, whilst a drop of their blood
    is remaining.
    Our foes on the ocean, etc.

Then, freemen, arise, and gird on your
    swords,
  And declare, while you still have the means
    of resistance,
That you ne'er will give up for the threatening
    of words,
  Nor of arms, those dear rights which you
    prize as existence.
    Our foes on the ocean, etc.

Forty of the enemy and more than two hundred
Americans were killed or wounded by the explo-
sion of a magazine, just as the place surrendered.
General Pike was mortally wounded, and died
with his head on the British flag which had been
brought to him.

THE DEATH OF GENERAL PIKE

[April 27, 1813]

'T was on the glorious day
  When our valiant triple band
Drove the British troops away
  From their strong and chosen stand;

When the city York was taken,
  And the Bloody Cross hauled down
  From the walls of the town
Its defenders had forsaken.

The gallant Pike had moved
  A hurt foe to a spot
A little more removed
  From the death-shower of the shot;
And he himself was seated
  On the fragment of an oak,
  And to a captive spoke,
Of the troops he had defeated.

He was seated in a place,
  Not to shun the leaden rain
He had been the first to face,
  And now burned to brave again,
But had chosen that position
  Till the officer's return
  The truth who'd gone to learn
Of the garrison's condition.

When suddenly the ground
  With a dread convulsion shook,
And arose a frightful sound,
  And the sun was hid in smoke;
And huge stones and rafters, driven
  Athwart the heavy rack,
  Fell, fatal on their track
As the thunderbolt of Heaven.

Then two hundred men and more,
  Of our bravest and our best,
Lay all ghastly in their gore,
  And the hero with the rest.
On their folded arms they laid him:
  But he raised his dying breath:
  "On, men, avenge the death
Of your general!" They obeyed him.

They obeyed. Three cheers they gave,
  Closed their scattered ranks, and on.
Though their leader found a grave,
  Yet the hostile town was won.
To a vessel straight they bore him
  Of the gallant Chauncey's fleet,
  And, the conquest complete,
Spread the British flag before him.

O'er his eyes the long, last night
  Was already falling fast;
But came back again the light
  For a moment; 't was the last.

With a victor's joy they fired,
　'Neath his head by signs he bade
The trophy should be laid;
And, thus pillowed, Pike expired.
　　　　　LAUGHTON OSBORN.

General William Henry Harrison, meanwhile,
at the head of the western army, was besieged in
Fort Meigs, at the mouth of the Maumee, by a
large force of Indians and British. On May 1 the
British made a determined assault, but were
beaten off; a few days later, after a desperate
battle with a relief column, the British raised the
siege and retreated to Canada.

OLD FORT MEIGS

[April 28–May 9, 1813]

OH! lonely is our old green fort,
　Where oft, in days of old,
Our gallant soldiers bravely fought
　'Gainst savage allies bold;
But with the change of years have pass'd
　That unrelenting foe,
Since we fought here with Harrison,
　A long time ago.

It seems but yesterday I heard,
　From yonder thicket nigh,
The unerring rifle's sharp report,
　The Indian's startling cry.
Yon brooklet flowing at our feet,
　With crimson gore did flow,
When we fought here with Harrison,
　A long time ago.

The river rolls between its banks,
　As when of old we came,
Each grassy path, each shady nook,
　Seems to me still the same;
But we are scatter'd now, whose faith
　Pledged here, through weal or woe,
With Harrison our soil to guard,
　A long time ago.

But many a soldier's lip is mute,
　And clouded many a brow,
And hearts that beat for honor then,
　Have ceased their throbbing now.
We ne'er shall meet again in life
　As then we met, I trow,
When we fought here with Harrison,
　A long time ago.

The remarkable list of victories on the ocean
was soon to be broken, for on June 1, 1813, the
36-gun frigate, Chesapeake, was defeated and cap-
tured by the British 38-gun frigate, Shannon.

THE SHANNON AND THE CHESA-
PEAKE

[June 1, 1813]

THE captain of the Shannon came sailing
　up the bay,
A reeling wind flung out behind his pennons
　bright and gay;
His cannon crashed a challenge; the smoke
　that hid the sea
Was driven hard to windward and drifted
　back to lee.

The captain of the Shannon sent word into
　the town:
Was Lawrence there, and would he dare to
　sail his frigate down
And meet him at the harbor's mouth and
　fight him, gun to gun,
For honor's sake, with pride at stake, until
　the fight was won?

Now, long the gallant Lawrence had scoured
　the bitter main;
With many a scar and wound of war his ship
　was home again;
His crew, relieved from service, were scattered
　far and wide,
And scarcely one, his duty done, had lingered
　by his side.

But to refuse the challenge? Could he outlive
　the shame?
Brave men and true, but deadly few, he
　gathered to his fame.
Once more the great ship Chesapeake pre-
　pared her for the fight, —
"I'll bring the foe to town in tow," he said,
　" before to-night!"

High on the hills of Hingham that overlooked
　the shore,
To watch the fray and hope and pray, for
　they could do no more,
The children of the country watched the
　children of the sea
When the smoke drove hard to windward and
　drifted back to lee.

"How can he fight," they whispered, "with
    only half a crew,
Though they be rare to do and dare, yet what
    can brave men do?"
But when the Chesapeake came down, the
    Stars and Stripes on high,
Stilled was each fear, and cheer on cheer re-
    sounded to the sky.

The Captain of the Shannon, he swore both
    long and loud:
"This victory, where'er it be, shall make two
    nations proud!
Now onward to this victory or downward to
    defeat!
A sailor's life is sweet with strife, a sailor's
    death as sweet."

And as when lightnings rend the sky and
    gloomy thunders roar,
And crashing surge plays devil's dirge upon
    the stricken shore,
With thunder and with sheets of flame the
    two ships rang with shot,
And every gun burst forth a sun of iron crim-
    son-hot.

And twice they lashed together and twice they
    tore apart,
And iron balls burst wooden walls and pierced
    each oaken heart.
Still from the hills of Hingham men watched
    with hopes and fears,
While all the bay was torn that day with shot
    that rained like tears.

The tall masts of the Chesapeake went groan-
    ing by the board;
The Shannon's spars were weak with scars
    when Broke cast down his sword;
"Now woe," he cried, "to England, and
    shame and woe to me!"
The smoke drove hard to windward and
    drifted back to lee.

"Give them one breaking broadside more,"
    he cried, "before we strike!"
But one grim ball that ruined all for hope and
    home alike
Laid Lawrence low in glory, yet from his
    pallid lip
Rang to the land his last command: "Boys,
    don't give up the ship!"
.   .   .   .

The wounded wept like women when they
    hauled her ensign down.
Men's cheeks were pale as with the tale from
    Hingham to the town
They hurried in swift silence, while toward
    the eastern night
The victor bore away from shore and vanished
    out of sight.

Hail to the great ship Chesapeake! Hail to
    the hero brave
Who fought her fast, and loved her last, and
    shared her sudden grave!
And glory be to those that died for all eter-
    nity;
They lie apart at the mother-heart of God's
    eternal sea.

                THOMAS TRACY BOUVÉ.

A British versifier celebrated the victory by
composing a ballad in imitation of the famous one
about the Constitution and Guerrière.

CHESAPEAKE AND SHANNON

[June 1, 1813]

THE Chesapeake so bold
Out of Boston, I've been told,
Came to take a British Frigate
    Neat and handy O!
While the people of the port
Flocked out to see the sport,
With their music playing
    Yankee Doodle Dandy O!

Now the British Frigate's name
Which for the purpose came
Of cooling Yankee courage
    Neat and handy O!
Was the Shannon, Captain Broke,
Whose crew were heart of oak,
And for the fighting were confessed
    To be the dandy O!

The engagement scarce begun
Ere they flinched from their guns,
Which at first they thought of working
    Neat and handy O!
The bold Broke he waved his sword,
Crying, "Now, my lads, on board,
And we'll stop their playing
    Yankee Doodle Dandy O!"

They no sooner heard the word
Than they quickly rushed aboard
And hauled down the Yankee ensign
  Neat and handy O!
Notwithstanding all their brag,
Now the glorious British flag
At the Yankee's mizzen-peak
  Was quite the dandy O!

Successful Broke to you,
And your officers and crew,
Who on board the Shannon frigate
  Fought so handy O!
And may it ever prove
That in fighting as in love
  The true British tar is the dandy O!

James Lawrence, commander of the Chesapeake, had been fatally wounded early in the action. Until the last, he kept crying from the cockpit, "Keep the guns going! Fight her till she strikes or sinks!" His last words were the famous, "Don't give up the ship!"

DEFEAT AND VICTORY

[June 1, 1813]

THROUGH the clangor of the cannon,
  Through the combat's wreck and reek,
Answer to th' o'ermastering Shannon
  Thunders from the Chesapeake:
Gallant Lawrence, wounded, dying,
  Speaks with still unconquered lip
Ere the bitter draught he drinks:
Keep the Flag flying!
  Fight her till she strikes or sinks!
    Don't give up the ship!

Still that voice is sounding o'er us,
  So bold Perry heard it call;
Farragut has joined its chorus;
  Porter, Dewey, Wainwright — all
Heard the voice of duty crying;
  Deathless word from dauntless lip
That our past and future links:
Keep the Flag flying!
  Fight her till she strikes or sinks!
    Don't give up the ship!
                    WALLACE RICE.

Another action which resulted very differently was that between the American 16-gun schooner, Enterprise, and the British 14-gun brig, Boxer.

The ships came together off Monhegan on September 5, 1813, and after a fierce fight lasting an hour, the Englishman surrendered.

ENTERPRISE AND BOXER

[September 5, 1813]

AGAIN Columbia's stripes, unfurl'd,
Have testified before the world,
  How brave are those who wear 'em;
The foe has now been taught again
His streamers cannot shade the main
  While Yankees live to share 'em.
    Huzza! once more for Yankee skill!
    The brave are very generous still
      But teach the foes submission:
    Now twice three times his flag we've
        gain'd,
    And more, much more can be obtain'd
      Upon the same condition.

The gallant Enterprise her name,
A vessel erst of little fame,
  Had sail'd and caught the foe, sirs;
'T was hers the glory and the gain,
To meet the Boxer on the main,
  And bring her home in tow, sirs.
    Huzza! once more for Yankee skill, etc.

Fierce lightnings gleam and thunders roar,
While round and grape in torrents pour,
  And echo through the skies, sirs;
When minutes forty-five had flown,
Behold the Briton's colors down! —
  She's yielded up a prize, sirs.
    Huzza! once more for Yankee skill, etc.

The victory gain'd, we count the cost,
We mourn, indeed, a hero lost!
  Who nobly fell, we know, sirs;
But Burrows, we with Lawrence find,
Has left a living name behind,
  Much honor'd by the foe, sirs.
    Huzza! once more for Yankee skill, etc.

And while we notice deeds of fame,
In which the gallant honors claim;
  As heroes of our story,
The name of Blyth a meed demands,
Whose tomb is deck'd by freemen's hands,
  Who well deserve the glory.
    Huzza! once more for Yankee skill, etc

Then, while we fill the sparkling glass,
And cause it cheerly round to pass,
  In social hours assembled;
Be Hull, Decatur, Bainbridge, Jones,
Lawrence and Burrows — Victory's sons,
  With gratitude remember'd.
        Huzza! once more for Yankee skill, etc.

This little victory was soon overshadowed by
a far more brilliant and important one on Lake
Erie, where, on September 10, 1813, Oliver Haz-
ard Perry, in command of a hastily constructed
fleet of nine ships, defeated and captured a British
squadron of superior strength.

PERRY'S VICTORY

[September 10, 1813]

WE sailed to and fro in Erie's broad lake,
To find British bullies or get into their wake,
When we hoisted our canvas with true Yan-
    kee speed,
And the brave Captain Perry our squadron
    did lead.

We sailed through the lake, boys, in search
    of the foe,
In the cause of Columbia our brav'ry to show,
To be equal in combat was all our delight,
As we wished the proud Britons to know we
    could fight.

And whether like Yeo, boys, they'd taken
    affright,
We could see not, nor find them by day or by
    night;
So cruising we went in a glorious cause,
In defence of our rights, our freedom, and
    laws.

At length to our liking, six sails hove in view,
Huzzah! says brave Perry, huzzah! says his
    crew,
And then for the chase, boys, with our brave
    little crew,
We fell in with the bullies and gave them
    " burgoo."

Though the force was unequal, determined to
    fight,
We brought them to action before it was night;
We let loose our thunder, our bullets did fly,
"Now give them your shot, boys," our com-
    mander did cry.

We gave them a broadside, our cannon to
    try,
"Well done," says brave Perry, "for quarter
    they'll cry,
Shot well home, my brave boys, they shortly
    shall see,
That quite brave as they are, still braver are
    we."

Then we drew up our squadron, each man
    full of fight,
And put the proud Britons in a terrible
    plight,
The brave Perry's movements will prove
    fully as bold,
As the fam'd Admiral Nelson's prowess of
    old.

The conflict was sharp, boys, each man to his
    gun,
For our country, her glory, the vict'ry was
    won,
So six sail (the whole fleet) was our fortune
    to take,
Here's a health to brave Perry, who governs
    the Lake.

THE BATTLE OF ERIE

[September 10, 1813]

AVAST, honest Jack! now, before you get
    mellow,
Come tip us that stave just, my hearty old
    fellow,
'Bout the young commodore, and his fresh-
    water crew,
Who keelhaul'd the Britons, and captured a
    few.

"'T was just at sunrise, and a glorious day,
Our squadron at anchor snug in Put-in-
    Bay,
When we saw the bold Britons, and cleared
    for a bout,
Instead of put in, by the Lord we put out.

"Up went union-jack, never up there before,
'Don't give up the ship' was the motto it
    bore;
And as soon as that motto our gallant lads
    saw,
They thought of their Lawrence, and shouted
    huzza!

"Oh! then it would have raised your hat three
    inches higher,
To see how we dash'd in among them like
    fire!
The Lawrence went first, and the rest as they
    could,
And a long time the brunt of the action she
    stood.

"'T was peppering work, — fire, fury, and
    smoke,
And groans that from wounded lads, spite of
    'em, broke.
The water grew red round our ship as she
    lay,
Though 't was never before so till that bloody
    day.

"They fell all around me like spars in a gale;
The shot made a sieve of each rag of a sail;
And out of our crew scarce a dozen remain'd;
But these gallant tars still the battle main-
    tain'd.

"'T was then our commander — God bless
    his young heart —
Thought it best from his well-peppered ship
    to depart,
And bring up the rest who were tugging be-
    hind —
For why — they were sadly in want of a wind.

"So to Yarnall he gave the command of his
    ship,
And set out, like a lark, on this desperate
    trip,
In a small open yawl, right through their
    whole fleet,
Who with many a broadside our cockboat
    did greet.

"I steer'd her and damme if every inch
Of these timbers of mine at each crack did n't
    flinch:
But our tight little commodore, cool and
    serene,
To stir ne'er a muscle by any was seen.

"Whole volleys of muskets were levell'd at
    him,
But the devil a one ever grazed e'en a limb,
Though he stood up aloft in the stern of the
    boat,
Till the crew pull'd him down by the skirt of
    his coat.

"At last, through Heaven's mercy. we reached
    t'other ship,
And the wind springing up, we gave her the
    whip,
And run down their line, boys, through thick
    and through thin,
And bother'd their crews with a horrible din.

"Then starboard and larboard, and this way
    and that,
We bang'd them and raked them, and laid
    their masts flat,
Till, one after t'other, they haul'd down their
    flag,
And an end, for that time, put to Johnny
    Bull's brag.

"The Detroit, and Queen Charlotte, and
    Lady Prevost,
Not able to fight or run, gave up the ghost:
And not one of them all from our grapplings
    got free,
Though we'd fifty-four guns, and they just
    sixty-three.

"Smite my limbs! but they all got their bellies
    full then,
And found what it was, boys, to buckle with
    men,
Who fight, or, what's just the same, think
    that they fight
For their country's free trade and their own
    native right.

"Now give us a bumper to Elliott and those
Who came up, in good time, to belabor our foes:
To our fresh-water sailors we'll toss off one
    more,
And a dozen, at least, to our young com-
    modore.

"And though Britons may brag of their ruling
    the ocean,
And that sort of thing, by the Lord, I've a
    notion,
I'll bet all I'm worth — who takes it — who
    takes?
Though they're lords of the sea, we'll be
    lords of the lakes."

Immediately on receiving the surrender, Perry
wrote with a pencil on the back of an old letter,
using his cap for a desk, his famous message, "We
have met the enemy and they are ours — two
ships, two brigs, one schooner, and one sloop," and
dispatched it to General Harrison.

PERRY'S VICTORY — A SONG

[September 10, 1813]

COLUMBIA, appear! — To thy mountains
ascend,
And pour thy bold hymn to the winds and
the woods;
Columbia, appear! — O'er thy tempest-harp
bend,
And far to the nations its trumpet-song send,—
Let thy cliff-echoes wake, with their sun-
nourish'd broods,
And chant to the desert — the skies — and
the floods,
And bid them remember,
The Tenth of September,
When our Eagle came down from her home
in the sky —
And the souls of our heroes were marshall'd
on high.

Columbia, ascend! — Let thy warriors be-
hold
Their flag like a firmament bend o'er thy
head.
The wide rainbow-flag with its star-clustered
fold!
Let the knell of dark Battle beneath it be
tolled,
While the anthem of Peace shall be pealed
for the dead,
And the rude waters heave, on whose bosom
they bled:
Oh, they will remember,
The Tenth of September,
When their souls were let loose in a tempest
of flame,
And wide Erie shook at the trumpet of
Fame.

Columbia, appear! — Let thy cloud minstrels
wake,
As they march on the storm, all the gran-
deur of song,
Till the far mountain reel — and the billow-
less lake
Shall be mantled in froth, and its Monarch
shall quake
On his green oozy throne, as their harping
comes strong,
With the chime of the winds as they're
bursting along.
For he will remember
The Tenth of September,

When he saw his dominions all covered with
foam,
And heard the loud war in its echoless
home.

Columbia, appear! — Be thine olive dis-
played,
O cheer with thy smile, all the land and the
tide!
Be the anthem we hear not the song that was
made,
When the victims of slaughter stood forth,
all arrayed
In blood-dripping garments — and shouted
— and died.
Let the hymning of peace o'er the blue
heavens ride;
O let us remember
The Tenth of September,
When the dark waves of Erie were bright-
ened to-day,
And the flames of the Battle were quenched
in the spray.

Harrison, at the head of his army, started in
hot pursuit of the British and Indians, who had
been compelled to evacuate Detroit, and on Octo-
ber 5 overtook them on the bank of the Thames,
and routed them with great loss, the Indian chief
Tecumseh being among the slain.

THE FALL OF TECUMSEH

[October 5, 1813]

WHAT heavy-hoofed coursers the wilderness
roam,
To the war-blast indignantly tramping?
Their mouths are all white, as if frosted with
foam,
The steel bit impatiently champing.

'T is the hand of the mighty that grasps the
rein,
Conducting the free and the fearless.
Ah! see them rush forward, with wild dis-
dain,
Through paths unfrequented and cheerless.

From the mountains had echoed the charge
of death,
Announcing that chivalrous sally;
The savage was heard, with untrembling
breath,
To pour his response from the valley.

One moment, and nought but the bugle was
heard,
And nought but the war-whoop given;
The next, and the sky seemed convulsively
stirred,
As if by the lightning riven.

The din of the steed, and the sabred stroke,
The blood-stifled gasp of the dying,
Were screened by the curling sulphur-smoke,
That upward went wildly flying.

In the mist that hung over the field of blood,
The chief of the horsemen contended;
His rowels were bathed in purple flood,
That fast from his charger descended.

That steed reeled, and fell, in the van of the
fight,
But the rider repressed not his daring,
Till met by a savage, whose rank and might
Were shown by the plume he was wearing.

The moment was fearful; a mightier foe
Had ne'er swung the battle-axe o'er him;
But hope nerved his arm for a desperate blow,
And Tecumseh fell prostrate before him.

O ne'er may the nations again be cursed
With conflict so dark and appalling! —
Foe grappled with foe, till the life-blood burst
From their agonized bosoms in falling.

Gloom, silence, and solitude rest on the spot
Where the hopes of the red man perished;
But the fame of the hero who fell shall not,
By the virtuous, cease to be cherished.

He fought, in defence of his kindred and king,
With a spirit most loving and loyal.
And long shall the Indian warrior sing
The deeds of Tecumseh the royal.

The lightning of intellect flashed from his eye,
In his arm slept the force of the thunder,
But the bolt passed the suppliant harmlessly
by,
And left the freed captive to wonder.

Above, near the path of the pilgrim, he sleeps,
With a rudely built tumulus o'er him;
And the bright-bosomed Thames, in his
majesty, sweeps,
By the mound where his followers bore
him.

The British took care to maintain as strictly
as possible the blockade of the American coast,
and the coast towns were kept in a constant state
of terror lest they be bombarded and burned.

THE LEGEND OF WALBACH TOWER

Scene. — *Fort Constitution on the Island of
Newcastle, off Portsmouth, N. H., Colonel
Walbach, commanding. Period, the fall of
1813.*

More ill at ease was never man than Wal-
bach, that Lord's day,
When, spent with speed, a trawler cried, "A
war-ship heads this way!"

His pipe, half filled, to shatters flew; he
climbed the ridge of knolls;
And, turning spy-glass toward the east, swept
the long reach of Shoals.

An hour he watched: behind his back the
Portsmouth spires waxed red;
Its harbor like a field of war, a brazen shield
o'erhead.

Another hour: the sundown gun the Sabbath
stillness brake;
When loud a second voice hallooed, "Two
war-ships hither make!"

Again the colonel scanned the east, where soon
white gleams arose:
Behind Star Isle they first appeared, then
flashed o'er Smuttynose.

Fleet-wing'd they left Duck Isle astern;
when, rounding full in view,
Lo! in the face of Appledore three Britishers
hove to.

"To arms, O townsfolk!" Walbach cried.
"Behold these black hawk three!
Whether they pluck old Portsmouth town
rests now with you and me.

"The guns of Kittery, and mine, may keep
the channel clear,
If but one pintle-stone be raised to ward me in
the rear.

"But scarce a score my muster-roll; the
earthworks lie unmanned
(Whereof some mouthing spy, no doubt, has
made them understand);

"And if, ere dawn, their long-boat keels once
  kiss the nether sands,
My every port-hole's mouth is stopped, and
  we be in their hands!"

Then straightway from his place upspake the
  parson of the town:
"Let us beseech Heaven's blessing first!" —
  and all the folk knelt down.

"O God, our hands are few and faint; our
  hope rests all with thee:
Lend us thy hand in this sore strait, — and
  thine the glory be!"

"Amen! Amen!" the chorus rose; "Amen!"
  the pines replied;
And through the churchyard's rustling grass
  an "Amen" softly sighed.

Astir the village was awhile, with hoof and
  iron clang;
Then all grew still, save where, aloft, a hun-
  dred trowels rang.

None supped, they say, that Lord's-day eve;
  none slept, they say, that night;
But all night long, with tireless arms, each
  toiled as best he might.

Four flax-haired boys of Amazeen the flicker-
  ing torches stay,
Peopling with titan shadow-groups the canopy
  of gray;

Grandsires, with frost above their brows, the
  steaming mortar mix;
Dame Tarlton's apron, crisp at dawn, helps
  hod the yellow bricks;

While pilot, cooper, mackerelman, parson
  and squire as well,
Make haste to plant the pintle-gun, and raise
  its citadel.

And one who wrought still tells the tale, that
  as his task he plied,
An unseen fellow-form he felt that labored at
  his side;

And still to wondering ears relates, that as
  each brick was squared,
Lo! unseen trowels clinked response, and a
  new course prepared.

O night of nights! The blinking dawn beheld
  the marvel done,
And from the new martello boomed the echo-
  ing morning gun.

One stormy cloud its lip upblew; and as its
  thunder rolled,
Old England saw, above the smoke, New
  England's flag unfold.

Then, slowly tacking to and fro, more near
  the cruisers made,
To see what force unheralded had flown to
  Walbach's aid.

"God be our stay," the parson cried, "who
  hearkened Israel's wail!"
And as he spake, — all in a line, seaward the
  ships set sail.

GEORGE HOUGHTON.

In order to draw British ships from this block-
ade, the government adopted the policy of send-
ing light squadrons into distant seas, and in
October, 1812, the 32-gun frigate Essex, Captain
David Porter, sailed to join the Constitution and
Hornet for a cruise in the Indian Ocean. Porter
failed to find the other ships and decided to double
Cape Horn and cruise in the Pacific. He captured
a number of prizes, and completely destroyed
British commerce in the south Pacific. A strong
force of British cruisers was sent out to intercept
him, and finally, on March 28, 1814, he was caught
in a disabled condition at Valparaiso by two
British ships, and attacked, notwithstanding the
neutrality of the port. After a desperate fight, he
was forced to surrender.

THE BATTLE OF VALPARAISO

Proeliis audax, neque te silebo. — Hor.

[March 28, 1814]

FROM the laurel's fairest bough,
  Let the muse her garland twine,
To adorn our Porter's brow,
  Who, beyond the burning line,
Led his caravan of tars o'er the tide.
  To the pilgrims fill the bowl,
  Who, around the southern pole,
Saw new constellations roll,
    For their guide.

"Heave the topmast from the board,
  And our ship for action clear,

By the cannon and the sword,
　　We will die or conquer here.
The foe, of twice our force, nears us fast:
　　To your posts, my faithful tars!
　　Mind your rigging, guns, and spars,
And defend your stripes and stars
　　　　To the last."

At the captain's bold command,
　　Flew each sailor to his gun,
And resolved he there would stand,
　　Though the odds was two to one,
To defend his flag and ship with his life:
　　High on every mast display'd,
　　"God, Our Country, and Free Trade,"
E'en the bravest braver made
　　　　For the strife.

Fierce the storm of battle pours:
　　But unmoved as ocean's rock,
When the tempest round it roars,
　　Every seaman breasts the shock,
Boldly stepping where his brave messmates
　　　　fall.
　　O'er his head, full oft and loud,
　　Like the vulture in a cloud,
As it cuts the twanging shroud,
　　　　Screams the ball.

Before the siroc blast
　　From its iron caverns driven,
Drops the sear'd and shiver'd mast,
　　By the bolt of battle riven,
And higher heaps the ruin of the deck —
　　As the sailor, bleeding, dies,
　　To his comrades lifts his eyes,
"Let our flag still wave," he cries,
　　　　O'er the wreck.

In echo to the sponge,
　　Hark! along the silent lee,
Oft is heard the solemn plunge,
　　In the bosom of the sea.
'T is not the sullen plunge of the dead,
　　But the self-devoted tar,
　　Who, to grace the victor's car,
Scorns from home and friends afar
　　　　To be led.

Long live the gallant crew
　　Who survived that day of blood:
And may fortune soon renew
　　Equal battle on the flood.
Long live the glorious names of the brave

O'er these martyrs of the deep,
　　Oft the roving tar shall weep,
Crying, "Sweetly may they sleep
　　　　'Neath the wave."

With the opening of the spring of 1814, the campaign along the Canadian border was begun with unusual activity. The army there was under Major-General Jacob Brown, and on July 25 met the British in the fiercely contested battle of Lundy's Lane, or Bridgewater.

THE BATTLE OF BRIDGEWATER

[July 25, 1814]

O'ER Huron's wave the sun was low,
The weary soldier watch'd the bow
Fast fading from the cloud below
　　The dashing of Niagara.
And while the phantom chain'd his sight,
Ah! little thought he of the fight —
The horrors of the dreamless night,
　　That posted on so rapidly.

Soon, soon is fled each softer charm;
The drum and trumpet sound alarm,
And bid each warrior nerve his arm
　　For boldest deeds of chivalry;
The burning red-cross, waving high,
Like meteor in the evening sky,
Proclaims the haughty foemen nigh
　　To try the strife of rivalry.

Columbia's banner floats as proud,
Her gallant band around it crowd,
And swear to guard or make their shroud
　　The starred flag of liberty.
"Haste, haste thee, Scott, to meet the foe,
And let the scornful Briton know,
Well strung the arm and firm the blow
　　Of him who strikes for liberty."

Loud, loud, the din of battle rings,
Shrill through the ranks the bullet sings,
And onward fierce each foeman springs
　　To meet his peer in gallantry.
Behind the hills descends the sun,
The work of death is but begun,
And red through twilight's shadows dun
　　Blazes the vollied musketry.

"Charge, Miller, charge the foe once more,'
And louder than Niagara's roar
Along the line is heard, encore,
　　"On, on to death or victory."

From line to line, with lurid glow,
High arching shoots the rocket's bow,
And lights the mingled scene below
    Of carnage, death, and misery.

The middle watch has now begun,
The horrid battle-fray is done,
No longer beats the furious drum,
    To death, to death or victory.
All, all is still — with silent tread
The watchman steals among the dead,
To guard his comrade's lowly bed,
    Till morning give him sepulture.

Low in the west, of splendor shorn,
The midnight moon with bloody horn
Sheds her last beam on him, forlorn,
    Who fell in fight so gloriously;
Oh! long her crescent wax and wane
Ere she behold such fray again,
Such dismal night, such heaps of slain,
    Foe mix'd with foe promiscuously.

Colonel Winfield Scott commanded a battalion
at this battle, and by a series of desperate charges
drove the British from the field. But so shaken
was the American army that it was compelled to
retreat to camp, after spending the night upon the
conquered ground.

THE HERO OF BRIDGEWATER

[July 25, 1814]

SEIZE, O seize the sounding lyre,
    With its quivering string!
Strike the chords, in ecstasy,
    Whilst loud the valleys ring!
Sing the chief, who, gloriously,
    From England's veteran band,
Pluck'd the wreaths of victory,
    To grace his native land!

Where Bridgewater's war-famed stream
    Saw the foemen reel,
Thrice repulsed, with burnish'd gleam
    Of bayonet, knife, and steel;
And its crimson'd waters run
    Red with gurgling flow,
As Albion's gathering hosts his arm,
    His mighty arm, laid low.

Strike the sounding string of fame,
    O lyre! Beat loud, ye drums!
Ye clarion blasts, exalt his name!
    Behold the hero comes!

I see Columbia, joyously,
    Her palmy circlet throw
Around his high victorious brow
    Who laid her foemen low!

Take him, Fame! for thine he is!
    On silvery columns, rear
The name of Scott, whence envious Time
    Shall ne'er its honors tear!
And thou, O Albion, quake with dread!
    Ye veterans shrink, the while,
Whene'er his glorious name shall sound
    To shake your sea-girt isle!
            CHARLES L. S. JONES.

The British, meanwhile, had extended their
blockade to the whole coast of the United States,
and were ordered to "destroy and lay waste all
towns and districts of the United States found
accessive to the attack of the British armaments."
In pursuance of these orders, town after town
along the coast was bombarded and burned. On
August 9, 1814, a squadron descended on the little
village of Stonington, but met a warm reception.

THE BATTLE OF STONINGTON ON THE SEABOARD OF CONNECTICUT

[August 9–12, 1814]

FOUR gallant ships from England came
Freighted deep with fire and flame,
And other things we need not name,
    To have a dash at Stonington.

Now safely moor'd, their work begun;
They thought to make the Yankees run,
And have a mighty deal of fun
    In stealing sheep at Stonington.

A deacon then popp'd up his head,
And parson Jones's sermon read,
In which the reverend doctor said
    That they must fight for Stonington.

A townsman bade them, next, attend
To sundry resolutions penn'd,
By which they promised to defend
    With sword and gun old Stonington

The ships advancing different ways,
The Britons soon began to blaze,
And put th' old women in amaze,
    Who fear'd the loss of Stonington

The Yankees to their fort repair'd,
And made as though they little cared
For all that came — though very hard
  The cannon play'd on Stonington.

The Ramillies began the attack,
Despatch came forward — bold and black —
And none can tell what kept them back
  From setting fire to Stonington.

The bombardiers with bomb and ball,
Soon made a farmer's barrack fall,
And did a cow-house sadly maul
  That stood a mile from Stonington.

They kill'd a goose, they kill'd a hen,
Three hogs they wounded in a pen —
They dash'd away, and pray what then?
  This was not taking Stonington.

The shells were thrown, the rockets flew,
But not a shell, of all they threw,
Though every house was full in view,
  Could burn a house at Stonington.

To have their turn they thought but fair; —
The Yankees brought two guns to bear,
And, sir, it would have made you stare,
  This smoke of smokes at Stonington.

They bored Pactolus through and through,
And kill'd and wounded of her crew
So many, that she bade adieu
  T' the gallant boys of Stonington.

The brig Despatch was hull'd and torn —
So crippled, riddled, so forlorn,
No more she cast an eye of scorn
  On the little fort at Stonington.

The Ramillies gave up th' affray,
And, with her comrades, sneak'd away,
Such was the valor, on that day,
  Of British tars near Stonington.

But some assert, on certain grounds
(Besides the damage and the wounds),
It cost the king ten thousand pounds
  To have a dash at Stonington.
                    PHILIP FRENEAU.

Occasionally, an American ship would manage
to deal a telling blow. The Wasp, cruising in the
English Channel, did especially effective work,
among her most famous actions being that with

the Avon on the night of September 1, 1814, in
which, after a spirited fight, the Avon was sunk.

THE OCEAN-FIGHT

[September 1, 1814]

THE sun had sunk beneath the west,
When two proud barks to battle press'd,
With swelling sail and streamers dress'd,
      So gallantly.

Proud Britain's pennon flouts the skies:
Columbia's flag more proudly flies,
Her emblem stars of victories
      Beam gloriously.

Sol's lingering rays, through vapors shed,
Have streak'd the sky of bloody red,
And now the ensanguined lustre spread
      Heaven's canopy.

Dread prelude to that awful night
When Britain's and Columbia's might
Join'd in the fierce and bloody fight,
      Hard rivalry.

Now, lowering o'er the stormy deep,
Dank, sable clouds more threatening sweep:
Yet still the barks their courses keep
      Unerringly.

The northern gales more fiercely blow,
The white foam dashing o'er the prow;
The starry crescent round each bow
      Beams vividly.

Near and more near the war-ships ride,
Till, ranged for battle, side by side,
Each warrior's heart beats high with pride
      Of chivalry.

'T was awful, ere the fight begun,
To see brave warriors round each gun,
While thoughts on home and carnage run,
      Stand silently.

As death-like stillness reigns around,
Nature seems wrapp'd in peace profound,
Ere fires, volcanic, mountain bound,
      Burst furiously.

So, bursting from Columbia's prow,
Her thunder on the red-cross foe,
The lurid cloud's sulphuric glow
      Glares awfully.

Reëchoing peals more fiercely roar,
Britannia's shatter'd sides run gore,
The foaming waves that raged before,
    Sink, tremulous.

Columbia's last sulphuric blaze,
That lights her stripes and starry rays,
The vanquish'd red-cross flag betrays,
    Struck fearfully.

And, hark! their piercing shrieks of wo!
Haste, haste and save the sinking foe:
Haste, e'er their wreck to bottom go,
    Brave conquerors.

Now, honor to the warriors brave,
Whose field of fame, the mountain wave,
Their corses bear to ocean's cave,
    Their sepulchre.

Their country's pæans swell their praise;
And whilst the warm tear, gushing, strays,
Full many a bard shall chant his lays,
    Their requiem.

The Wasp herself never returned to port. On September 21 she captured the Atalanta and put a crew on board to take the prize to America. They parted company, and the Wasp was never seen again.

THE LOST WAR–SLOOP

(THE WASP, 1814)

O THE pride of Portsmouth water,
Toast of every brimming beaker, —
Eighteen hundred and fourteen on land and
    sea, —
Was the Wasp, the gallant war-sloop,
Built of oaks Kearsarge had guarded,
Pines of Maine to lift her colors high and free!
Every timber scorning cowards;
Every port alert for foemen
From the masthead seen on weather-side or
    lee; —
With eleven guns to starboard,
And eleven guns to larboard,
All for glory on a morn of May sailed she.

British ships were in the offing;
Swift and light she sped between them, —
Well her daring crew knew shoal and wind
    and tide;
They had come from Portsmouth river,
Sea-girt Marblehead and Salem,

Bays and islands where the fisher-folk abide;
Come for love of home and country,
Come with wrongs that cried for vengeance,—
Every man among them brave and true and
    tried.
"Hearts of oak" are British seamen?
Hearts of fire were these, their kindred,
Flaming till the haughty foe should be de-
    scried!

From the mountains, from the prairies,
Blew the west winds glad to waft her; —
Ah, what goodly ships before her guns went
    down!
Ships with wealth of London laden,
Ships with treasures of the Indies,
Till her name brought fear to British wharf
    and town;
Till the war-sloops Reindeer, Avon,
To her valor struck their colors,
Making coast and ocean ring with her renown;
While her captain cried, exultant,
"Britain, to the bold Republic,
Of the empire of the seas shall yield the crown!"

Oh, the woful, woful ending
Of the pride of Portsmouth water!
Never more to harbor nor to shore came she!
Springs returned but brought no tidings;
Mothers, maidens, broken-hearted,
Wept the gallant lads that sailed away in glee.
Did the bolts of heaven blast her?
Did the hurricanes o'erwhelm her
With her starry banner and her tall masts
    three?
Was a pirate-fleet her captor?
Did she drift to polar oceans?
Who shall tell the awful secret of the sea!

Who shall tell? yet many a sailor
In his watch at dawn or midnight,
When the wind is wildest and the black waves
    moan,
Sees a stanch three-master looming;
Hears the hurried call to quarters,
The drum's quick beat and the bugle fiercely
    blown; —
Then the cannon's direful thunder
Echoes far along the billows;
Then the victor's shout for the foe over-
    thrown; —
And the watcher knows the phantom
Is the Wasp, the gallant war-sloop,
Still a rover of the seas and glory's own!
    EDNA DEAN PROCTOR.

The abdication of Napoleon enabled England to turn her undivided attention to the war with America, and a large body of troops was detailed for service here. Having lost control of Lake Erie and Lake Ontario, England determined to secure Lake Champlain and to invade New York by this route. A force of twelve thousand regulars, under General George Prevost, started from Montreal early in August, while the British naval force on the lake was augmented to nineteen vessels.

ON THE BRITISH INVASION

[1814]

From France, desponding and betray'd,
From liberty in ruins laid,
Exulting Britain has display'd
    Her flag, again to invade us.

Her myrmidons, with murdering eye,
Across the broad Atlantic fly,
Prepared again their strength to try,
    And strike our country's standard.

Lord Wellington's ten thousand slaves,
And thrice ten thousand, on the waves,
And thousands more of brags and braves
    Are under sail, and coming,

To burn our towns, to seize our soil,
To change our laws, our country spoil,
And Madison to Elba's isle
    To send without redemption.

In Boston state they hope to find
A Yankee host of kindred mind,
To aid their arms, to rise and bind
    Their countrymen in shackles.

But no such thing — it will not do —
At least, not while a Jersey Blue
Is to the cause of freedom true,
    Or the bold Pennsylvanian.

A curse on England's frantic schemes!
Both mad and blind, her monarch dreams
Of crowns and kingdoms in these climes,
    Where kings have had their sentence.

Though Washington has left our coast,
Yet other Washingtons we boast,
Who rise, instructed by his ghost,
    To punish all invaders.

Go where they will, where'er they land,
This pilfering, plundering, pirate band,
They liberty will find at hand
    To hurl them to perdition!

If in Virginia they appear,
Their fate is fix'd, their doom is near,
Death in their front, and hell their rear;
    So says the gallant buckskin.

All Carolina is prepared,
And Charleston doubly on her guard;
Where, once, Sir Peter badly fared,
    So blasted by Fort Moultrie.

If farther south they turn their views,
With veteran troops, or veteran crews,
The curse of Heaven their march pursues,
    To send them all a-packing.

The tallest mast that sails the wave,
The longest keel its waters lave,
Will bring them to an early grave
    On the shores of Pensacola.
                            Philip Freneau

The American commander on the lake was Thomas Macdonough, and by almost herculean efforts he managed to build and launch a ship, a schooner, and a number of gunboats, so that his total force was raised to fourteen sail. With this fleet, he proceeded to Plattsburg and anchored in Plattsburg Bay. On September 11 the British fleet, certain of victory, sailed in and attacked him, but was ignominiously defeated.

THE BATTLE OF LAKE CHAMPLAIN

[September 11, 1814]

Parading near Saint Peter's flood
Full fourteen thousand soldiers stood;
Allied with natives of the wood,
With frigates, sloops, and galleys near;
    Which southward, now, began to steer;
    Their object was, Ticonderogue.

Assembled at Missisqui bay
A feast they held, to hail the day,
When all should bend to British sway
    From Plattsburgh to Ticonderogue.

And who could tell, if reaching there
They might not other laurels share
And England's flag in triumph bear
    To the capitol, at Albany!

Sir George advanced, with fire and sword,
The frigates were with vengeance stored,
The strength of Mars was felt on board, —
When Downie gave the dreadful word,
   Huzza! for death or victory!

Sir George beheld the prize at stake,
And, with his veterans, made the attack,
Macomb's brave legions drove him back;
And England's fleet approached, to meet
   A desperate combat, on the lake.

From Isle La Motte to Saranac
With sulphurous clouds the heavens were
   black;
We saw advance the Confiance,
Shall blood and carnage mark her track,
   To gain dominion on the lake.

Then on our ships she poured her flame,
And many a tar did kill or maim,
Who suffered for their country's fame,
   Her soil to save, her rights to guard.

Macdonough, now, began his play,
And soon his seamen heard him say,
"No Saratoga yields, this day,
   To all the force that Britain sends.

"Disperse, my lads, and man the waist,
Be firm, and to your stations haste,
And England from Champlain is chased,
   If you behave as you see me."

The fire began with awful roar;
At our first flash the artillery tore,
From his proud stand, their commodore,
   A presage of the victory.

The skies were hid in flame and smoke,
Such thunders from the cannon spoke,
The contest such an aspect took
   As if all nature went to wreck!

Amidst his decks, with slaughter strewed,
Unmoved, the brave Macdonough stood,
Or waded through a scene of blood,
   At every step that round him streamed:

He stood amidst Columbia's sons,
He stood amidst dismounted guns,
He fought amidst heart-rending groans,
   The tattered sail, the tottering mast.

Then, round about, his ship he wore,
And charged his guns with vengeance sore,
And more than Etna shook the shore —
   The foe confessed the contest vain.

In vain they fought, in vain they sailed,
That day; for Britain's fortune failed,
And their best efforts naught availed
   To hold dominion on Champlain.

So, down their colors to the deck
The vanquished struck — their ships a
   wreck —
What dismal tidings for Quebec,
   What news for England and her prince!

For, in this fleet, from England won,
A favorite project is undone;
Her sorrows only are begun —
And she may want, and very soon,
   Her armies for her own defence.
               PHILIP FRENEAU.

THE BATTLE OF PLATTSBURG BAY

[September 11, 1814]

Plattsburg Bay! Plattsburg Bay!
Blue and gold in the dawning ray,
Crimson under the high noonday
With the reek of the fray!

It was Thomas Macdonough, as gallant a
   sailor
   As ever went scurrying over the main;
And he cried from his deck, *If they think I'm*
   a quailer,
     And deem they can capture this Lake of
     Champlain,
     We'll show them they're not fighting France,
     sir, nor Spain!

So from Cumberland Head to the little Crab
   Island
   He scattered his squadron in trim battle-
   line;
And when he saw Downie come rounding the
   highland,
   He knelt him, beseeching for guidance
   divine,
   Imploring that Heaven would crown his
   design.

Then thundered the Eagle her lusty de-
   fiance;
The stout Saratoga aroused with a roar;
Soon gunboat and galley in hearty alliance
   Their resonant volley of compliments pour;
   And ever Macdonough's the man to the
      fore!

And lo, when the fight toward its fiercest was
   swirling,
A game-cock, released by a splintering ball,
Flew high in the ratlines, the smoke round him
   curling,
   And over the din gave his trumpeting call,
   An omen of ultimate triumph to all!

Then a valianter light touched the powder-
   grimed faces;
   Then faster the shot seemed to plunge
     from the gun;
And we shattered their yards and we sundered
   their braces,
   And the fume of our cannon — it shrouded
     the sun;
   Cried Macdonough — *Once more, and the*
     battle is won!

Now, the flag of the haughty Confiance is
   trailing;
   The Linnet in woe staggers in toward the
     shore;
The Finch is a wreck from her keel to her
   railing;
   The galleys flee fast to the strain of the
     oar;
   Macdonough! 't is he is the man to the fore!

Oh, our main decks were grim and our gun
   decks were gory,
   And many a brave brow was pallid with
     pain;
And while some won to death, yet we all won
   to glory
   Who fought with Macdonough that day on
     Champlain,
   And humbled her pride who is queen of the
     main!

              CLINTON SCOLLARD.

While the naval battle was in progress, Prevost
made an assault on the American lines, but was
repulsed with loss, and learning of the fleet's de-
feat, ordered a retreat. This was so precipitate
that it was almost a flight, and great quantities
of artillery, stores, and provisions fell into the
hands of the Americans.

THE BATTLE OF PLATTSBURG

[September 11, 1814]

SIR GEORGE PREVOST, with all his host,
   March'd forth from Montreal, sir,
Both he and they as blithe and gay
   As going to a ball, sir.
The troops he chose were all of those
   That conquer'd Marshall Soult, sir;
Who at Garonne (the fact is known)
   Scarce brought they to a halt, sir.

With troops like these, he thought with ease
   To crush the Yankee faction:
His only thought was how he ought
   To bring them into action.
"Your very names," Sir George exclaims,
   "Without a gun or bayonet,
Will pierce like darts through Yankee hearts,
   And all their spirits stagnate.

"Oh! how I dread lest they have fled
   And left their puny fort, sir,
For sure Macomb won't stay at home,
   T' afford us any sport, sir.
Good-by!" he said to those that stay'd:
   "Keep close as mice or rats snug:
We'll just run out upon a scout,
   To burn the town of Plattsburg."

Then up Champlain with might and main
   He marched in dress array, sir;
With fife and drum to scare Macomb,
   And drive him quite away, sir.
And, side by side, their nation's pride
   Along the current beat, sir:
Sworn not to sup till they ate up
   M‘Donough and his fleet, sir.

Still onward came these men of fame,
   Resolved to give "no quarter;"
But to their cost they found at last
   That they had caught a Tartar.
At distant shot awhile they fought,
   By water and by land, sir:
His knightship ran from man to man,
   And gave his dread command, sir.

"Britons, strike home! this dog Macomb —
   So well the fellow knows us —
Will just as soon jump o'er the moon
   As venture to oppose us.
With quick despatch light every match,
   Man every gun and swivel,

Cross in a crack the Saranac,
  And drive 'em to the devil!"

The Vermont ranks that lined the banks,
  Then poised the unerring rifle,
And to oppose their haughty foes
  They found a perfect trifle.
Meanwhile the fort kept up such sport,
  They thought the devil was in it;
Their mighty train play'd off in vain —
  'T was silenced in a minute.

Sir George, amazed, so wildly gazed,
  Such frantic gambols acted,
Of all his men, not one in ten
  But thought him quite distracted.
He cursed and swore, his hair he tore,
  Then jump'd upon his pony,
And gallop'd off towards the bluff,
  To look for Captain Downie.

But when he spied M·Donough ride,
  In all the pomp of glory,
He hasten'd back to Saranac,
  To tell the dismal story:
"My gallant crews — Oh! shocking news —
  Are all or killed or taken!
Except a few that just withdrew
  In time to save their bacon.

"Old England's pride must now subside.
  Oh! how the news will shock her,
To have her fleet not only beat,
  But sent to Davy's locker.
From this sad day, let no one say
  Britannia rules the ocean:
We've dearly bought the humbling thought,
  That this is all a notion.

"With one to ten I'd fight 'gainst men,
  But these are Satan's legions,
With malice fraught, some piping hot
  From Pluto's darkest regions!
Hélas! mon Dieu! what shall I do?
  I smell the burning sulphur —
Set Britain's isle all rank and file,
  Such men would soon engulf her.

"That's full as bad — Oh! I'll run mad!
  Those western hounds are summon'd;
Gaines, Scott, and Brown are coming down,
  To serve me just like Drummond.
Thick, too, as bees, the Vermontese
  Are swarming to the lake, sir;

And Izard's men, come back again,
  Lie hid in every brake, sir.

"Good Brisbane, beat a quick retreat,
  Before their forces join, sir:
For, sure as fate, they've laid a bait
  To catch us like Burgoyne, sir.
All round about, keep good look out:
  We'll surely be surrounded;
Since I could crawl, my gallant soul
  Was never so astounded."

The rout begun, Sir George led on,
  His men ran helter skelter,
Each tried his best t' outrun the rest
  To gain a place of shelter;
To hide their fear, they gave a cheer,
  And thought it mighty cunning —
He'll fight, they say, another day,
  Who saves himself by running!

Although the blow at New York had been turned aside, another, aimed at the Nation's Capital, fell with deadly effect. On August 24, 1814, a strong force landed in Chesapeake Bay, routed a force of militia at Bladensburg, entered Washington, and burned the Capitol, White House, and many other public buildings. A few days later, Baltimore was attacked.

THE BATTLE OF BALTIMORE

[September 12, 1814]

OLD Ross, Cockburn, and Cochrane too,
  And many a bloody villain more,
Swore with their bloody savage crew,
  That they would plunder Baltimore.
But General Winder being afraid
  That his militia would not stand,
He sent away to crave the aid
  Of a few true Virginians.
    Then up we rose with hearts elate,
    To help our suffering sister state.

When first our orders we received,
  For to prepare without delay,
Our wives and sweethearts for to leave,
  And to the army march away,
Although it grieved our hearts full sore,
  To leave our sweet Virginia shore,
We kiss'd our sweethearts o'er and o'er,
  And march'd like true Virginians.
    Adieu awhile, sweet girls, adieu,
    With honor we'll return to you.

With rapid marches on we went,
  To leave our sweet Virginia shore,
No halt was made, no time was spent,
  Till we arrived at Baltimore.
The Baltimoreans did us greet,
  The ladies clapt their lily-white hands,
Exclaiming as we passed the street,
  "Welcome, ye brave Virginians.
    May Heaven all your foes confound,
    And send you home with laurels crown'd."

We had not been in quarters long,
  Before we heard the dread alarms,
The cannon roar'd, the bells did ring,
  The drum did beat to arms, to arms.
Then up we rose to face our foes,
  Determined to meet them on the strand,
And drive them back from fair Freedom's
    shore,
  Or die like brave Virginians.
    In Heaven above we placed our trust,
    Well knowing that our cause is just.

Then Ross he landed at North Point,
  With seven thousand men or more,
And swore by that time next night,
  That he would be in Baltimore.
But Striker met him on the strand,
  Attended by a chosen band,
Where he received a fatal shot
  From a brave Pennsylvanian —
    Whom Heaven directed to the field,
    To make this haughty Briton yield.

Then Cockburn he drew up his fleet,
  To bombard Fort McHenry,
A thinking that our men, of course,
  Would take affright and run away.
The fort was commanded by a patriotic
    band,
  As ever graced fair Freedom's land,
And he who did the fort command
  Was a true blue Virginian.
    Long may we have brave Armstead's
      name
    Recorded on the book of fame.

A day and a night they tried their might,
  But found their bombs did not prevail,
And seeing their army put to flight,
  They weigh'd their anchor and made sail,
Resolving to return again,
  To execute their former plan;
But if they do, they'll find us still
  That we are brave Virginians.

And they shall know before they've done,
  That they are not in Washington.

But now their shipping 's out of sight,
  And each man takes a parting glass,
Drinks to his true love and heart's delight,
  His only joy and bosom friend,
For I might as well drink a health,
  For I hate to see good liquor stand,
That America may always boast
  That we are brave Virginians.

The next day, Admiral Cochrane moved his
fleet into position to attack Fort McHenry, two
miles above the city, and began a terrific bom-
bardment, which lasted all the night. The fort
answered with such guns as would reach the ships,
and when morning dawned, the Stars and Stripes
were still floating over it. The British feared to
attack an intrenchment so gallantly defended, and
the next day retreated to their shipping.

FORT McHENRY

[September 13, 1814]

THY blue waves, Patapsco, flow'd soft and
    serene,
  Thy hills and thy valleys were cheerful and
    gay,
While the day-star of Peace shed its beams on
    the scene,
  And youth, love, and beauty reflected its ray.

Where white-bosom'd commerce late reign'd
    o'er thy tide,
  And zephyrs of gladness expanded each
    sail,
I saw hostile squadrons in dread array ride,
  While their thunders reëchoed o'er hill and
    o'er vale.

But our heroes, thy sons, proud in panoply
    rose,
  For their homes, — for their altars, — to
    conquer or die;
With the lightning of freedom encounter'd
    their foes;
  Taught the veteran to tremble, — the
    valiant to fly.

Now, how tranquil thy scenes when the
    clangors of war
  Late broke the soft dreams of the fair and
    the young!

To the tombs of thy heroes shall beauty re-
    pair,
  And their deeds by our bards shall forever
    be sung.

On the iron-crown'd fortress "that frowns
    o'er thy flood,"
  And tells the sad fate of the gay and the
    brave,
In mournful reflection Eliza late stood,
  And paid a soft tribute — a tear on their
    grave.

To the manes of the fallen, oh! how grateful
    that tear!
  Far sweeter to me than the Spring's richest
    bloom:
Such rewards light the fire of Chivalry here,
  And when the brave fall — ever hallow
    their tomb.

Just before the bombardment began, Francis
Scott Key had put out to the admiral's frigate to
arrange for an exchange of prisoners, and was
directed to remain till the action was over. All
that night he watched the flaming shells, and
when, by the first rays of the morning, he saw his
country's flag still waving above the fort, he
hastily wrote the stirring verses which have since
become America's national song.

THE STAR-SPANGLED BANNER

[September 13, 1814]

O SAY, can you see, by the dawn's early light,
  What so proudly we hailed at the twilight's
    last gleaming?
Whose broad stripes and bright stars, through
    the perilous fight,
  O'er the ramparts we watched were so gal-
    lantly streaming!
And the rocket's red glare, the bombs burst-
    ing in air,
Gave proof through the night that our flag
    was still there:
  O say, does that star-spangled banner yet
    wave
O'er the land of the free and the home of the
    brave?

On the shore, dimly seen through the mists of
    the deep,
  Where the foe's haughty host in dread
    silence reposes,

What is that which the breeze, o'er the tower-
    ing steep,
  As it fitfully blows, now conceals, now dis-
    closes?
Now it catches the gleam of the morning's
    first beam,
In full glory reflected now shines on the
    stream:
  'T is the star-spangled banner! O long
    may it wave
O'er the land of the free and the home of the
    brave!

And where is that band who so vauntingly
    swore
  That the havoc of war and the battle's con-
    fusion
A home and a country should leave us no
    more?
  Their blood has washed out their foul foot-
    steps' pollution.
No refuge could save the hireling and
    slave
From the terror of flight, or the gloom of the
    grave:
  And the star-spangled banner in triumph
    doth wave
O'er the land of the free and the home of the
    brave!

Oh! thus be it ever, when freemen shall
    stand
  Between their loved homes and the war's
    desolation!
Blest with victory and peace, may the heaven-
    rescued land
  Praise the Power that hath made and pre-
    served us a nation.
Then conquer we must, for our cause it is
    just,
And this be our motto: "In God is our
    trust."
  And the star-spangled banner in triumph
    shall wave
O'er the land of the free and the home of the
    brave.

                    FRANCIS SCOTT KEY.

The destruction of Washington, besides being
perhaps the most outrageous act of vandalism
ever committed by a Christian army, was a grave
tactical error. One feeling of wrath and cry for
vengeance swept the land; party differences were
forgotten, and the whole country pressed forward
to prosecute the war with an enthusiasm and
vigor which had before been sadly wanting.

YE PARLIAMENT OF ENGLAND

YE parliament of England,
  You lords and commons, too,
Consider well what you're about,
  And what you're going to do;
You're now to fight with Yankees,
  I'm sure you'll rue the day
You roused the sons of liberty,
  In North America.

You first confined our commerce,
  And said our ships shan't trade,
You next impressed our seamen,
  And used them as your slaves;
You then insulted Rogers,
  While ploughing o'er the main,
And had not we declarèd war,
  You'd have done it o'er again.

You thought our frigates were but few
  And Yankees could not fight,
Until brave Hull your Guerrière took
  And banished her from your sight.
The Wasp then took your Frolic,
  We'll nothing say to that,
The Poictiers being of the line,
  Of course she took her back.

The next, your Macedonian,
  No finer ship could swim,
Decatur took her gilt-work off,
  And then he sent her in.
The Java, by a Yankee ship
  Was sunk, you all must know;
The Peacock fine, in all her plume,
  By Lawrence down did go.

Then next you sent your Boxer,
  To box us all about,
But we had an Enterprising brig
  That beat your Boxer out;
We boxed her up to Portland,
  And moored her off the town,
To show the sons of liberty
  The Boxer of renown.

The next upon Lake Erie,
  Where Perry had some fun,
You own he beat your naval force,
  And caused them for to run;
This was to you a sore defeat,
  The like ne'er known before —
Your British squadron beat complete —
  Some took, some run ashore.

There's Rogers in the President,
  Will burn, sink, and destroy;
The Congress, on the Brazil coast,
  Your commerce will annoy;
The Essex, in the South Seas,
  Will put out all your lights,
The flag she waves at her mast-head —
  "Free Trade and Sailor's Rights."

Lament, ye sons of Britain,
  Far distant is the day,
When you'll regain by British force
  What you've lost in America;
Go tell your king and parliament,
  By all the world 't is known,
That British force, by sea and land,
  By Yankees is o'erthrown.

Use every endeavor,
  And strive to make a peace,
For Yankee ships are building fast,
  Their navy to increase;
They will enforce their commerce,
  The laws by heaven are made,
That Yankee ships in time of peace
  To any port may trade.

Nor was the outrage universally applauded;
even in England. An anti-war party had arisen
there, and was constantly growing in strength.

THE BOWER OF PEACE

From " Ode Written during the War with
America, 1814 "

WHEN shall the Island Queen of Ocean lay
    The thunderbolt aside,
And, twining olives with her laurel crown,
    Rest in the Bower of Peace?

Not long may this unnatural strife endure
    Beyond the Atlantic deep;
Not long may men, with vain ambition drunk,
    And insolent in wrong,
Afflict with their misrule the indignant land
    Where Washington hath left
      His awful memory
      A light for after-times!
  Vile instruments of fallen Tyranny
In their own annals, by their countrymen,
For lasting shame shall they be written down.
Soon may the better Genius there prevail!
Then will the Island Queen of Ocean lay
    The thunderbolt aside,

And, twining olives with her laurel crown,
   Rest in the Bower of Peace.
                 ROBERT SOUTHEY.

One of the most remarkable naval battles of
the war occurred on September 26, 1814, in Fayal
Roads. The General Armstrong, the famous pri-
vateer schooner, Captain Samuel Chester Reid, had
anchored there, trusting to the neutrality of the
harbor, and was attacked after nightfall by the
boats of a strong British squadron. A fearful
struggle followed, the British being finally beaten
off.

REID AT FAYAL

[September 26, 1814]

A CLIFF-LOCKED port and a bluff sea wall,
   And a craggy rampart, brown and bold;
Proud Pico's bastions towering tall,
   And a castle dumb and cold.

The scream of a gull where a porpoise rolls;
   And the flash of a home-bound fisher's
      blade,
Where the ghostly boom of the drumfish
      tolls
   For wrecks that the surf has made.

A grim dun ridge, and a thin gray beach,
   And the swish and the swash of the sleep-
      less tide;
And the moonlight masking the reef's long
      reach,
   Where the lurking breakers bide.

And under the castle's senseless walls
   (Santa Cruz, old and cold and dumb),
Where only the prying sea-mew calls,
   And the harbor beetles hum,

A Yankee craft at her cable swings:
"All's well!" the cheery lookout sings.
But the skipper counts his sleeping crew,
His guns, and his drowsy ensign, too.
   — Says he, "They'll do!"

For the skipper marks, tho' he makes no
      sign,
Frigate and corvette and ship of the line,
Rounding the headland into the light:
"Three Union Jacks and a moonlight night!"
   — Says he, "We'll fight!"

Twelve launches cutting the silver bay;
Twenty score boarders called away.

And it's "Lively, hearties, and let her go!"
With a rouse and a cheer and a "Yeo, ho, ho!"
   — Says Reid, "Lie low!"

'T is a song of havoc the rowlocks sing,
And Death marks time in the rower's swing;
'T is a baleful glow on the spouting spray,
As the keels in their cruel lust make way.
   "Now, up and slay!"

Now up and play in the mad old game —
Axe and cutlass, fury and flame
White breasts red-wat in the viler muck,
Proud hearts hurled back in the sprawling
      ruck.
   — Says Reid, "Well struck."

Pike and pistol and dripping blade
(So are the ghosts and the glory made);
A curse for a groan, and a cheer for a yell;
Pale glut of Hate and red rapture of Hell!
   — Says Reid, "All's well!"

All's well for the banner that dances free,
Where the mountains are shouting the news
   to the sea.
All's well for the bold, and all's ill for the
   strong,
In the fight and the flight that shall hold us
   long,
     In tale and song.
             JOHN WILLIAMSON PALMER.

THE FIGHT OF THE ARMSTRONG PRIVATEER

TELL the story to your sons
   Of the gallant days of yore,
When the brig of seven guns
   Fought the fleet of seven score,
From the set of sun till morn, through the
   long September night —
Ninety men against two thousand, and the
   ninety won the fight
   In the harbor of Fayal the Azore.

Three lofty British ships came a-sailing to
   Fayal:
One was a line-of-battle ship, and two were
   frigates tall;
Nelson's valiant men of war, brave as Britons
   ever are,
Manned the guns they served so well at Abou-
   kir and Trafalgar.

Lord Dundonald and his fleet at Jamaica far
    away
Waited eager for their coming, fretted sore at
    their delay.
There was loot for British valor on the Mis-
    sissippi coast
In the beauty and the booty that the Creole
    cities boast;
There were rebel knaves to swing, there were
    prisoners to bring
Home in fetters to old England for the glory
    of the King!

At the setting of the sun and the ebbing of
    the tide
Came the great ships one by one, with their
    portals opened wide,
And their cannon frowning down on the
    castle and the town
And the privateer that lay close inside;
Came the eighteen-gun Carnation, and the
    Rota, forty-four,
And the triple-decked Plantagenet an Ad-
    miral's pennon bore;
And the privateer grew smaller as their top-
    masts towered taller,
And she bent her springs and anchored by the
    castle on the shore.

Spoke the noble Portuguese to the stranger:
    "Have no fear;
They are neutral waters these, and your ship
    is sacred here
As if fifty stout armadas to shelter you from
    harm,
For the honor of the Briton will defend you
    from his arm."
But the privateersman said, "Well we know
    the Englishmen,
And their faith is written red in the Dartmoor
    slaughter-pen.
Come what fortune God may send, we will
    fight them to the end,
And the mercy of the sharks may spare us
    then."

"Seize the pirate where she lies!" cried the
    English Admiral:
"If the Portuguese protect her, all the worse
    for Portugal!"
And four launches at his bidding leaped im-
    patient for the fray,
Speeding shoreward where the Armstrong,
    grim and dark and ready, lay.

Twice she hailed and gave them warning;
    but the feeble menace scorning,
On they came in splendid silence, till a cable's
    length away.
Then the Yankee pivot spoke; Pico's thou-
    sand echoes woke;
And four baffled, beaten launches drifted
    helpless on the bay.

Then the wrath of Lloyd arose till the lion
    roared again,
And he called out all his launches and he
    called five hundred men;
And he gave the word "No quarter!" and he
    sent them forth to smite.
Heaven help the foe before him when the
    Briton comes in might!
Heaven helped the little Armstrong in her
    hour of bitter need;
God Almighty nerved the heart and guided
    well the arm of Reid.

Launches to port and starboard, launches
    forward and aft,
Fourteen launches together striking the little
    craft.
They hacked at the boarding-nettings, they
    swarmed above the rail;
But the Long Tom roared from his pivot and
    the grape-shot fell like hail;
Pike and pistol and cutlass, and hearts that
    knew not fear,
Bulwarks of brawn and mettle, guarded the
    privateer.
And ever where fight was fiercest the form of
    Reid was seen:
Ever where foes drew nearest, his quick sword
    fell between.
    Once in the deadly strife
    The boarder's leader pressed
    Forward of all the rest
    Challenging life for life;
    But ere their blades had crossed
    A dying sailor tossed
    His pistol to Reid, and cried,
    "Now riddle the lubber's hide!"
But the privateersman laughed, and flung the
    weapon aside,
And he drove his blade to the hilt, and the
    foeman gasped and died.
Then the boarders took to their launches,
    laden with hurt and dead,
But little with glory burdened, and out of the
    battle fled.

Now the tide was at flood again, and the
    night was almost done,
When the sloop-of-war came up with her
    odds of two to one,
And she opened fire; but the Armstrong
    answered her, gun for gun,
And the gay Carnation wilted in half an hour
    of sun.

Then the Armstrong, looking seaward, saw the
    mighty seventy-four,
With her triple tier of cannon, drawing slowly
    to the shore.
And the dauntless captain said: "Take our
    wounded and our dead,
Bear them tenderly to land, for the Arm-
    strong's days are o'er;
But no foe shall tread her deck, and no flag
    above it wave —
To the ship that saved our honor we will give
    a shipman's grave."
So they did as he commanded, and they
    bore their mates to land
With the figurehead of Armstrong and the
    good sword in his hand.
Then they turned the Long Tom downward,
    and they pierced her oaken side,
And they cheered her, and they blessed her,
    and they sunk her in the tide.

    Tell the story to your sons,
      When the haughty stranger boasts
    Of his mighty ships and guns
      And the muster of his hosts,
How the word of God was witnessed in the
    gallant days of yore
When the twenty fled from one ere the rising
    of the sun,
    In the harbor of Fayal the Azore!
        JAMES JEFFREY ROCHE.

Three boats, loaded with dead and dying, were
captured by the Americans, the survivors having
escaped by jumping overboard and swimming
ashore. At daybreak the whole British fleet moved
in to attack, and Captain Reid was forced to
scuttle his ship and abandon her.

THE ARMSTRONG AT FAYAL

[September 26, 1814]

OH, the sun sets red, the moon shines white,
    And blue is Fayal's clear sky;
The sun and moon and sky are bright,
    And the sea, and stars on high;

But the name of Reid and the fame of Reid
    And the flag of his ship and crew
Are brighter far than sea or star
    Or the heavens' red, white, and blue:
So lift your voices once again
    For the land we love so dear,
For the fighting Captain and the men
    Of the Yankee Privateer !

The moonbeams, like fine silver, shine
    Upon the blue Azores,
As twilight pours her purple wine
    Upon those storied shores;
The General Armstrong's flag of stars
    In the harbor of Fayal
Flies forth, remote from thought of wars
    Until the sunset call.

No glistening guns in serried line
    The slender schooner boasts,
A pivot and eight hearty nines
    Shall meet her foeman's hosts;
Her sides are oak, her masts are tall,
    Her captain's one to trust,
Her ninety men are free men all,
    Her quarrel wholly just.

On far Fayal the moon is fair
    To-night as it was when,
Glad in the gay September air,
    Reid laughed beside his men;
On far Fayal the sun to-day
    Was lord of all the sky
As when the General Armstrong lay,
    Our banner flung on high;
But now there rests a holier light
    Than theirs on land or sea:
The splendor of our sailors' might,
    And glorious bravery.

A moment, and the flag will sink
    As sinks the sun to rest
Beyond the billows' western brink
    Where towers the Eagle's nest,
When round the azure harbor-head
    Where sparkling ocean brims,
Her British ensign streaming red,
    The brig Carnation swims.

Ere with the sun her sails are set
    The Rota frigate glides
And the great ship Plantagenet
    To stations at her sides:
They carry six score guns and ten,
    They serve the British crown.

They muster o'er a thousand men —
　To win were small renown.

'T was by Fayal, where Portugal
　Still flaunts her Blue-and-White;
What cares their Floyd for Portugal
　Or what cares he for right?
He starts his signals down the line —
　Our flag is flying free —
His weapons in the moonbeams shine,
　His boats drop on the sea.
Straight to the Armstrong swift they come.
　Speak, or I fire! shouts Reid —
Their rattling rowlocks louder hum
　To mark their heightened speed.

Fierce o'er their moonlit path there stream
　Bright glares of crimson flame;
Our muskets but an instant gleam,
　Yet leave them wounded, lame.
They try a feeble, brief reply
　Ere back their course is sped.
Before our marksmanship they fly,
　Their living with their dead.

Floyd swears upon his faith and all
　The Armstrong shall be his;
He scorns rebuke from Portugal,
　But not such enemies;
So guns are charged with canister
　And picked men go to fight:
Brave hearts and doomed full many were
　In the Azores that night.

From nine until the nick of twelve
　Their boats are seen to throng
Where rocky islets slant and shelve
　Safe from our bullets' song;
Then out they dash, their small arms flash,
　While blare their carronades,
Their boarding-pikes and axes clash,
　Their guns and cutlass blades.
Our Long Tom speaks, our shrapnel shrieks;
　But ere we load again,
On every side the battle reeks
　Of thrice a hundred men.

Our rail is low, and there the foe
　Cling as they shoot and hack.
We stab them as they climb a-row,
　Slaying, nor turning back.
They dash up now upon our bow,
　And there our hearties haste;
Now at our stern their muskets burn,
　And now along our waist.

Our fo'c'sle weeps when Williams dies,
　When Worth falls in his blood,
But bleeding through the battle-cries
　Our gallant Johnson stood;
The British muskets snapt and spat
　Till Reid came in his wrath,
His brow so pale with purpose that
　It glistened down his path.

Forth from the quarter-deck he springs,
　He and his men with cheers;
On British skulls his cutlass rings,
　His pistols in their ears;
His men beside him hold him good
　Till spent the foeman's breath;
Where at our sides a Briton stood,
　A Briton sank in death;
Though weak our men with blood and sweat,
　Our sides a riddled wreck,
Yet ne'er a British foot is set
　Upon the Armstrong's deck.

Three hundred men their Admiral sent
　Our schooner's ways to mend:
A hundred British sailors went
　Down to a warrior's end.
Two of our lads in death are red,
　But safe the flag above:
God grant that never worse be sped
　The fray for all we love!

The General Armstrong lies beneath
　The waves in far Fayal,
But still his countrymen shall wreathe
　Reid's name with laurels tall;
The sun and moon are fair to see
　Above the blue Azores,
But fairer far Reid's victory
　Beside their storied shores.

Oh, the sun sets red, the moon shines white,
　And blue is Fayal's clear sky;
The sun and moon and sky are bright,
　And the sea, and stars on high;
But the name of Reid and the fame of
　Reid
　And the flag of his ship and crew
Are brighter far than sea or star
　O'er the heavens' red, white, and blue:
So lift your voices once again
　For the land we love so dear,
For the fighting Captain and the men
　Of the Yankee Privateer.
　　　　　　　　　WALLACE RICE.

Major-General Andrew Jackson had been intrusted with the task of defending the South, and especially New Orleans, from the expected British invasion. On September 15, 1814, a British fleet and land force invested Fort Bowyer, which commanded the entrance to Mobile, but were beaten off and forced to retire, after a desperate struggle, in which one of the British ships was blown up.

FORT BOWYER

[September 15, 1814]

WHERE the wild wave, from ocean proudly
    swelling,
Mexico's shores, wide stretching, with its
    billowy
Surge, in its sweep laves, and, with lashing
    foam, breaks,
    Rough in its whiteness;

See where the flag of Freedom, with its light
    wreaths,
Floats on the wind, in buoyancy expanded
High o'er the walls of Bowyer's dauntless
    breastwork,
    Proudly and fearless.

Loud roll thy thunders, Albion; and thy mis-
    sile
Boasts throng the air with lightning flash
    tremendous,
Whilst the dark wave, illuminated bright,
    shines
    Sparkling with death-lights.

Shrink then that band of freemen, at the on-
    slaught?
Palsy those arms that wield the unerring
    rifles?
Strikes chill the breast dread fear? or coward
    paleness
    Whiten the blanch'd cheek?

No! round that flag, undaunted, midst the
    loud din,
Like their own shores, which mountain surges
    move not
Breasted and firm, and heedless of the war-
    shock,
    Rallying they stand fast.

" Look," Lawrence cries, " brave comrades;
    how the foe proud
Quails at our charge, with recreant spirit
    flying:"

Like Rome's bold chief, he came and saw,
    but neither
    Awed us, nor conquer'd.
                          CHARLES L. S. JONES.

Jackson hastened to New Orleans, and reached there just as a great British fleet appeared in the offing. He determined to attack the enemy as soon as they started to land, and on the night of December 23 he drove in their advance guard. Then he intrenched his little army, and on January 8, 1815, was attacked by the full British force, seven thousand strong. Their advance was checked by the steady fire of Jackson's riflemen, and the enemy was finally routed with a loss of over two thousand. The American loss was eight killed and thirteen wounded.

THE BATTLE OF NEW ORLEANS

[January 8, 1815]

HERE, in my rude log cabin,
    Few poorer men there be
Among the mountain ranges
    Of Eastern Tennessee.
My limbs are weak and shrunken,
    White hairs upon my brow,
My dog — lie still old fellow! —
    My sole companion now.
Yet I, when young and lusty,
    Have gone through stirring scenes,
For I went down with Carroll
    To fight at New Orleans.

You say you'd like to hear me
    The stirring story tell,
Of those who stood the battle
    And those who fighting fell.
Short work to count our losses —
    We stood and dropped the foe
As easily as by firelight
    Men shoot the buck or doe.
And while they fell by hundreds
    Upon the bloody plain,
Of us, fourteen were wounded
    And only eight were slain.

The eighth of January,
    Before the break of day,
Our raw and hasty levies
    Were brought into array.
No cotton-bales before us —
    Some fool that falsehood told;
Before us was an earthwork
    Built from the swampy mould.
And there we stood in silence,
    And waited with a frown.

To greet with bloody welcome
  The bull-dogs of the Crown.

The heavy fog of morning
  Still hid the plain from sight,
When came a thread of scarlet
  Marked faintly in the white.
We fired a single cannon,
  And as its thunders rolled,
The mist before us lifted
  In many a heavy fold —
The mist before us lifted
  And in their bravery fine
Came rushing to their ruin
  The fearless British line.

Then from our waiting cannon
  Leaped forth the deadly flame,
To meet the advancing columns
  That swift and steady came.
The thirty-twos of Crowley
  And Bluchi's twenty-four
To Spotts's eighteen-pounders
  Responded with their roar,
Sending the grape-shot deadly
  That marked its pathway plain,
And paved the road it travelled
  With corpses of the slain.

Our rifles firmly grasping,
  And heedless of the din,
We stood in silence waiting
  For orders to begin.
Our fingers on the triggers,
  Our hearts, with anger stirred,
Grew still more fierce and eager
  As Jackson's voice was heard:
"Stand steady! Waste no powder!
  Wait till your shots will tell!
To-day the work you finish —
  See that you do it well!"

Their columns drawing nearer,
  We felt our patience tire,
When came the voice of Carroll,
  Distinct and measured, "Fire!"
Oh! then you should have marked us
  Our volleys on them pour —
Have heard our joyous rifles
  Ring sharply through the roar,
And seen their foremost columns
  Melt hastily away
As snow in mountain gorges
  Before the floods of May.

They soon re-formed their columns,
  And, mid the fatal rain
We never ceased to hurtle,
  Came to their work again.
The Forty-fourth is with them,
  That first its laurels won
With stout old Abercrombie
  Beneath an eastern sun.
It rushes to the battle,
  And, though within the rear
Its leader is a laggard,
  It shows no signs of fear.

It did not need its colonel,
  For soon there came instead
An eagle-eyed commander,
  And on its march he led.
'T was Pakenham in person,
  The leader of the field;
I knew it by the cheering
  That loudly round him pealed;
And by his quick, sharp movement
  We felt his heart was stirred,
As when at Salamanca
  He led the fighting Third.

I raised my rifle quickly,
  I sighted at his breast,
God save the gallant leader
  And take him to his rest!
I did not draw the trigger,
  I could not for my life.
So calm he sat his charger
  Amid the deadly strife,
That in my fiercest moment
  A prayer arose from me —
God save that gallant leader,
  Our foeman though he be!

Sir Edward's charger staggers;
  He leaps at once to ground.
And ere the beast falls bleeding
  Another horse is found.
His right arm falls — 't is wounded;
  He waves on high his left;
In vain he leads the movement,
  The ranks in twain are cleft.
The men in scarlet waver
  Before the men in brown,
And fly in utter panic —
  The soldiers of the Crown!

I thought the work was over,
  But nearer shouts were heard,

And came, with Gibbs to head it,
  The gallant Ninety-third.
Then Pakenham, exulting,
  With proud and joyous glance,
Cried, "Children of the tartan —
  Bold Highlanders — advance!
Advance to scale the breastworks,
  And drive them from their hold,
And show the stainless courage
  That marked your sires of old!"

His voice as yet was ringing,
  When, quick as light, there came
The roaring of a cannon,
  And earth seemed all aflame.
Who causes thus the thunder
  The doom of men to speak?
It is the Baratarian,
  The fearless Dominique.
Down through the marshalled Scotsmen
  The step of death is heard,
And by the fierce tornado
  Falls half the Ninety-third.

The smoke passed slowly upward
  And, as it soared on high,
I saw the brave commander
  In dying anguish lie.
They bear him from the battle
  Who never fled the foe;
Unmoved by death around them
  His bearers softly go.
In vain their care, so gentle,
  Fades earth and all its scenes;
The man of Salamanca
  Lies dead at New Orleans.

But where were his lieutenants?
  Had they in terror fled?
No! Keane was sorely wounded
  And Gibbs as good as dead.
Brave Wilkinson commanding,
  A major of brigade,
The shattered force to rally
  A final effort made.
He led it up our ramparts,
  Small glory did he gain —
Our captives some; some slaughtered,
  And he himself was slain.

The stormers had retreated,
  The bloody work was o'er;
The feet of the invaders
  Were soon to leave our shore.

We rested on our rifles
  And talked about the fight,
When came a sudden murmur
  Like fire from left to right;
We turned and saw our chieftain,
  And then, good friend of mine,
You should have heard the cheering
  That rang along the line.

For well our men remembered
  How little, when they came,
Had they but native courage,
  And trust in Jackson's name;
How through the day he labored,
  How kept the vigils still,
Till discipline controlled us —
  A stronger power than will;
And how he hurled us at them
  Within the evening hour,
That red night in December
  And made us feel our power.

In answer to our shouting
  Fire lit his eye of gray;
Erect, but thin and pallid,
  He passed upon his bay.
Weak from the baffled fever,
  And shrunken in each limb,
The swamps of Alabama
  Had done their work on him;
But spite of that and fasting,
  And hours of sleepless care,
The soul of Andrew Jackson
  Shone forth in glory there.
                THOMAS DUNN ENGLISH.

JACKSON AT NEW ORLEANS

HEAR through the morning drums and trum-
      pets sounding,
Rumbling of cannon, tramp of mighty armies;
Then the mist sunders, all the plain disclosing
      Scarlet for England.

Batteries roll on, halt, and flashing lightnings
Search out our earthworks, silent and por-
      tentous.
Fierce on our right with crimson banners toss-
      ing
      Their lines spring forward.

Lanyards in hand, Americans and seamen,
Gunners from warships, Lafitte's privateers-
      men,

Roar out our thunders till the grape and
shrapnel
    Shriek through their columns.

Shattered in fragments, thus their right is
riven;
But on our left a deadlier bolt is speeding:
Wellesley's Peninsulars, never yet defeated,
    Charge in their valor.

Closing their files, our cannon fire disdaining,
Dauntless they come with vict'ry on their
standards;
Then slowly rise the rifles of our marksmen,
    Tennessee hunters.

Cradles of flame and scythes of whistling
bullets
Lay them in windrows, war's infernal harvest.
High through the onslaught Tennessee is
shouting,
    Joying in battle.

Pakenham falls there, Keane and his High-
landers
Close from the centre, hopeless in their cour-
age;
Backward they stagger, dying and disabled,
    Gloriously routed.

Stilled are our rifles as our cheers grow
louder:
War clouds sweep back in January breezes,
Showing the dreadful proof of the great tri-
umph
    God hath vouchsafed us.

That gallant war-host, England's best and
bravest,
Met by raw levies, scores against its hun-
dreds,
Lies at our feet, a thing for woman's weeping,
    Reddening the meadows.

Freed are our States from European tyrants;
Lift then your voices for the little army
Led by our battle-loving Andrew Jackson,
    Blest of Jehovah.
                WALLACE RICE.

The British were permitted to retire unmolested
to their ships, and the sails of that mighty fleet
were soon fading away along the horizon. Neither
victor nor vanquished knew that a treaty of peace
had been signed at Ghent two weeks before, and
that the battle need never have been fought.

TO THE DEFENDERS OF NEW ORLEANS

HAIL sons of generous valor,
  Who now embattled stand,
To wield the brand of strife and blood,
  For Freedom and the land.
And hail to him your laurelled chief,
  Around whose trophied name
A nation's gratitude has twined
  The wreath of deathless fame.

Now round that gallant leader
  Your iron phalanx form,
And throw, like Ocean's barrier rocks,
  Your bosoms to the storm.
Though wild as Ocean's wave it rolls,
  Its fury shall be low,
For justice guides the warrior's steel,
  And vengeance strikes the blow.

High o'er the gleaming columns,
  The bannered star appears,
And proud amid its martial band,
  His crest the eagle rears.
And long as patriot valor's arm
  Shall win the battle's prize,
That star shall beam triumphantly,
  That eagle seek the skies.

Then on, ye daring spirits,
  To danger's tumults now,
The bowl is filled and wreathed the crown,
  To grace the victor's brow;
And they who for their country die,
  Shall fill an honored grave.
For glory lights the soldier's tomb,
  And beauty weeps the brave.
          JOSEPH RODMAN DRAKE.

Prominent among the forces under Jackson was
a brigade of eight hundred Kentucky riflemen,
commanded by General John Coffee. They had
marched eight hundred miles through a wilderness,
having covered the last hundred miles in less than
two days — a march almost unequalled in history.
Jackson spoke of this brigade as the right arm of
his army.

THE HUNTERS OF KENTUCKY

YE gentlemen and ladies fair,
  Who grace this famous city,
Just listen, if you've time to spare,
  While I rehearse a ditty;

And for the opportunity
  Conceive yourselves quite lucky,
For 't is but seldom that you see
  A hunter from Kentucky.
      Oh! Kentucky,
    The hunters of Kentucky.

We are a hardy free-born race,
  Each man to fear a stranger;
Whate'er the game, we join in chase,
  Despising toil and danger
And if a daring foe annoys,
  Whate'er his strength or force is,
We'll show him that Kentucky boys
  Are Alligator-horses.

I s'pose you've read it in the prints,
  How Pakenham attempted
To make old Hickory Jackson wince,
  But soon his schemes repented;
For we, with rifles ready cock'd,
  Thought such occasion lucky,
And soon around the general flock'd
  The hunters of Kentucky.

I s'pose you've heard how New Orleans
  Is famed for wealth and beauty;
They've gals of every hue, it seems,
  From snowy white to sooty:
So Pakenham he made his brags
  If he in fight was lucky,
He'd have their gals and cotton bags,
  In spite of Old Kentucky.

But Jackson he was wide awake,
  And was n't scared at trifles,
For well he knew what aim we take
  With our Kentucky rifles;
So he led us down to Cypress Swamp,
  The ground was low and mucky;
There stood John Bull in martial pomp —
  But here was Old Kentucky.

We raised a bank to hide our breasts,
  Not that we thought of dying,
But then we always like to rest,
  Unless the game is flying:
Behind it stood our little force —
  None wish'd it to be greater,
For every man was half a horse
  And half an alligator.

They did n't let our patience tire
  Before they show'd their faces:

We did n't choose to waste our fire,
  But snugly kept our places;
And when so near we saw them wink,
  We thought it time to stop 'em,
It would have done you good, I think,
  To see Kentuckians drop 'em.

They found, at length, 't was vain to fight,
  When lead was all their booty,
And so they wisely took to flight,
  And left us all the beauty.
And now, if danger e'er annoys,
  Remember what our trade is;
Just send for us Kentucky boys,
  And we'll protect you, ladies:
      Oh! Kentucky,
    The hunters of Kentucky.

Another useless action, but a most remarkable
one, was fought by the famous old Constitution,
near Madeira, on February 20, 1815. On the after-
noon of that day she sighted and overhauled the
British 32-gun frigate Cyane and the 20-gun sloop
Levant. She attacked them simultaneously, and
after a fierce fight compelled them both to sur-
render.

THE CONSTITUTION'S LAST FIGHT

[February 20, 1815]

A YANKEE ship and a Yankee crew —
  Constitution, where ye bound for?
Wherever, my lad, there's fight to be had
  Acrost the Western ocean.

Our captain was married in Boston town
  And sailed next day to sea;
For all must go when the State says so;
  Blow high, blow low, sailed we.

"Now, what shall I bring for a bridal gift
  When my home-bound pennant flies?
The rarest that be on land or sea
  It shall be my lady's prize."

"There's never a prize on sea or land
  Could bring such joy to me
As my true love sound and homeward bound
  With a king's ship under his lee."

The Western ocean is wide and deep,
  And wild its tempests blow,
But bravely rides "Old Ironsides,"
  A-cruising to and fro.

We cruised to the east and we cruised to north,
  And southing far went we,
And at last off Cape de Verd we raised
  Two frigates sailing free.

Oh, God made man, and man made ships,
  But God makes very few
Like him who sailed our ship that day,
  And fought her, one to two.

He gained the weather-gage of both,
  He held them both a-lee;
And gun for gun, till set of sun,
  He spoke them fair and free;

Till the night-fog fell on spar and sail,
  And ship, and sea, and shore,
And our only aim was the bursting flame
  And the hidden cannon's roar.

Then a long rift in the mist showed up
  The stout Cyane, close-hauled
To swing in our wake and our quarter rake,
  And a boasting Briton bawled:

"Starboard and larboard, we've got him fast
  Where his heels won't take him through;
Let him luff or wear, he'll find us there, —
  Ho, Yankee, which will you do?"

We did not luff and we did not wear,
  But braced our topsails back,
Till the sternway drew us fair and true
  Broadsides athwart her track.

Athwart her track and across her bows
  We raked her fore and aft,
And out of the fight and into the night
  Drifted the beaten craft.

The slow Levant came up too late;
  No need had we to stir;
Her decks we swept with fire, and kept
  The flies from troubling her.

We raked her again, and her flag came
    down, —
  The haughtiest flag that floats, —
And the lime-juice dogs lay there like logs,
  With never a bark in their throats.

With never a bark and never a bite,
  But only an oath to break,
As we squared away for Praya Bay
  With our prizes in our wake.

Parole they gave and parole they broke,
  What matters the cowardly cheat,
If the captain's bride was satisfied
  With the one prize laid at her feet?

A Yankee ship and a Yankee crew —
  Constitution, where ye bound for?
Wherever the British prizes be,
Though it's one to two, or one to three, —
"Old Ironsides" means victory,
  Acrost the Western ocean.
                    JAMES JEFFREY ROCHE.

News of the peace did not reach America until
February 11, 1815. It was hailed with rejoicing
everywhere.

SEA AND LAND VICTORIES

WITH half the Western world at stake,
See Perry on the midland lake,
  The unequal combat dare;
Unawed by vastly stronger pow'rs,
He met the foe and made him ours,
  And closed the savage war.

Macdonough, too, on Lake Champlain,
In ships outnumbered, guns, and men,
  Saw dangers thick increase;
His trust in God and virtue's cause
He conquer'd in the lion's jaws,
  And led the way to peace.

To sing each valiant hero's name
Whose deeds have swelled the files of fame,
  Requires immortal powers;
Columbia's warriors never yield
To equal force by sea or field,
  Her eagle never cowers.

Long as Niagara's cataract roars
Or Erie laves our Northern shores,
  Great Brown, thy fame shall rise;
Outnumber'd by a veteran host
Of conquering heroes, Britain's boast —
  Conquest was there thy prize.

At Plattsburg, see the Spartan band,
Where gallant Macomb held command,
  The unequal host oppose;
Provost confounded, vanquished flies,
Convinced that numbers won't suffice
  Where Freemen are the foes.

Our songs to noblest strains we'll raise
While we attempt thy matchless praise,
    Carolina's godlike son;
While Mississippi rolls his flood,
Or Freemen's hearts move patriots' blood,
    The palm shall be thine own.

At Orleans — lo! a savage band,
In countless numbers gain the strand,
    "Beauty and spoil" the word —
There Jackson with his fearless few,
The invincibles by thousands slew,
    And dire destruction poured.

O Britain! when the tale is told
Of Jackson's deeds by fame enrolled,
    Should grief and madness rise,
Remember God, the avenger, reigns,
Who witnessed Havre's smoking plains,
    And Hampton's female cries.

ODE TO PEACE

Oh! breathe upon this hapless world,
    And bid our pains and sorrows cease;
Broad be thy snowy flag unfurl'd,
    And may we hail thy coming, peace!

For long enough has ruin stalk'd,
    With force and terror o'er our earth;
Around them hideous spectres walk'd,
    And evil nurs'd his monstrous birth.

Ah! banish'd from these happy skies,
    By thee, be soon these boding stars,
Which erring made mankind arise,
    To deeds of sin, to blood and wars.

Philadelphia, 1816.

CHAPTER III

THE WEST

At the close of the Revolution, the country west of the Alleghanies was still virtually an unbroken wilderness. Boone had pushed forward into Kentucky, drawing a few settlers after him; the trading-posts in the Illinois country, which had been captured by George Rogers Clark, still dragged on a miserable existence; but these were mere pin-points in the great stretches of virgin forest, amid which the first settlers hewed out a home.

THE SETTLER

His echoing axe the settler swung
    Amid the sea-like solitude,
And, rushing, thundering, down were flung
    The Titans of the wood;
Loud shrieked the eagle, as he dashed
From out his mossy nest, which crashed
    With its supporting bough,
And the first sunlight, leaping, flashed
    On the wolf's haunt below.

Rude was the garb and strong the frame
    Of him who plied his ceaseless toil:
To form that garb the wildwood game
    Contributed their spoil;
The soul that warmed that frame disdained
The tinsel, gaud, and glare that reigned
    Where men their crowds collect;
The simple fur, untrimmed, unstained,
    This forest-tamer decked.

The paths which wound mid gorgeous trees,
    The stream whose bright lips kissed their flowers,
The winds that swelled their harmonies
    Through those sun-hiding bowers,
The temple vast, the green arcade,
The nestling vale, the grassy glade,
    Dark cave, and swampy lair;
These scenes and sounds majestic made
    His world, his pleasures, there.

His roof adorned a pleasant spot;
    Mid the black logs green glowed the grain,
And herbs and plants the woods knew not
    Throve in the sun and rain.

The smoke-wreath curling o'er the dell,
The low, the bleat, the tinkling bell,
  All made a landscape strange,
Which was the living chronicle
  Of deeds that wrought the change.

The violet sprung at spring's first tinge,
  The rose of summer spread its glow,
The maize hung out its autumn fringe,
  Rude winter brought his snow;
And still the lone one labored there,
His shout and whistle broke the air,
  As cheerily he plied
His garden-spade, or drove his share
  Along the hillock's side.

He marked the fire-storm's blazing flood
Roaring and crackling on its path,
And scorching earth, and melting wood,
  Beneath its greedy wrath;
He marked the rapid whirlwind shoot,
Trampling the pine-tree with its foot,
  And darkening thick the day
With streaming bough and severed root,
  Hurled whizzing on its way.

His gaunt hound yelled, his rifle flashed,
  The grim bear hushed his savage growl;
In blood and foam the panther gnashed
  His fangs, with dying howl;
The fleet deer ceased its flying bound,
Its snarling wolf-foe bit the ground,
  And, with its moaning cry,
The beaver sunk beneath the wound
  Its pond-built Venice by.

Humble the lot, yet his the race,
  When Liberty sent forth her cry,
Who thronged in conflict's deadliest place,
  To fight, — to bleed, — to die!
Who cumbered Bunker's height of red,
By hope through weary years were led,
  And witnessed Yorktown's sun
Blaze on a nation's banner spread,
  A nation's freedom won.
                        ALFRED B. STREET.

Danger was ever present — and in its most
hideous form. Northwest of the Ohio dwelt the
powerful Delawares and Shawanese, ever ready
to march against the border settlements and to
surprise isolated dwellings. In the incessant war-
fare against the Indians, the frontier women
played no little part.

THE MOTHERS OF THE WEST

THE Mothers of our Forest-Land!
  Stout-hearted dames were they;
With nerve to wield the battle-brand,
  And join the border-fray.
Our rough land had no braver,
  In its days of blood and strife —
Aye ready for severest toil,
  Aye free to peril life.

The Mothers of our Forest-Land!
  On old Kan-tuc-kee's soil,
How shared they, with each dauntless band,
  War's tempest and Life's toil!
They shrank not from the foeman, —
  They quailed not in the fight, —
But cheered their husbands through the
      day,
  And soothed them through the night.

The Mothers of our Forest-Land!
  Their bosoms pillowed men !
And proud were they by such to stand,
  In hammock, fort, or glen.
To load the sure old rifle, —
  To run the leaden ball, —
To watch a battling husband's place,
  And fill it should he fall.

The Mothers of our Forest-Land!
  Such were their daily deeds.
Their monument! — where does it stand?
  Their epitaph! — who reads?
No braver dames had Sparta,
  No nobler matrons Rome, —
Yet who or lauds or honors them,
  E'en in their own green home!

The Mothers of our Forest-Land!
  They sleep in unknown graves;
And had they borne and nursed a band
  Of ingrates, or of slaves,
They had not been more neglected!
  But their graves shall yet be found,
And their monuments dot here and there
  "The Dark and Bloody Ground."
                    WILLIAM D. GALLAGHER.

In 1784 Virginia ceded to the national govern-
ment her claim to the lands west of the moun-
tains. New York, Massachusetts, and Connecticut
soon followed suit, and the tide of emigration to
the West set in with steady and ever-increasing
volume.

ON THE EMIGRATION TO AMERICA AND PEOPLING THE WESTERN COUNTRY

[1784]

To western woods and lonely plains,
Palemon from the crowd departs,
Where Nature's wildest genius reigns,
To tame the soil, and plant the arts —
What wonders there shall freedom show,
What mighty states successive grow!

From Europe's proud, despotic shores
Hither the stranger takes his way,
And in our new-found world explores
A happier soil, a milder sway,
Where no proud despot holds him down,
No slaves insult him with a crown.

What charming scenes attract the eye,
On wild Ohio's savage stream!
There Nature reigns, whose works outvie
The boldest pattern art can frame;
There ages past have rolled away,
And forests bloomed but to decay.

From these fair plains, these rural seats,
So long concealed, so lately known,
The unsocial Indian far retreats,
To make some other clime his own,
Where other streams, less pleasing, flow,
And darker forests round him grow.

Great Sire of floods! whose varied wave
Through climes and countries takes its
way,
To whom creating Nature gave
Ten thousand streams to swell thy sway!
No longer shall they useless prove,
Nor idly through the forests rove;

Nor longer shall your princely flood
From distant lakes be swelled in vain,
Nor longer through a darksome wood
Advance unnoticed to the main;
Far other ends the heavens decree —
And commerce plans new freights for thee.

While virtue warms the generous breast,
There heaven-born freedom shall reside,
Nor shall the voice of war molest,
Nor Europe's all-aspiring pride —
There Reason shall new laws devise,
And order from confusion rise.

Forsaking kings and regal state,
With all their pomp and fancied bliss,
The traveller owns, convinced though late,
No realm so free, so blest as this —
The east is half to slaves consigned,
Where kings and priests enchain the mind.

O come the time, and haste the day,
When man shall man no longer crush,
When Reason shall enforce her sway,
Nor these fair regions raise our blush,
Where still the African complains,
And mourns his yet unbroken chains.

Far brighter scenes a future age,
The muse predicts, these States will hail,
Whose genius may the world engage,
Whose deeds may over death prevail,
And happier systems bring to view
Than all the eastern sages knew.

PHILIP FRENEAU.

In 1788 Marietta was founded at the mouth of the Muskingum by the Ohio Company, which had bought a great tract of land extending to the Scioto. Later in the same year, Matthias Denman, Robert Patterson, and John Filson laid out the town of Losantiville, now Cincinnati. Filson had been a schoolmaster and was responsible for the strange name, which he thought indicated that the town was opposite the mouth of the Licking. He was soon afterwards killed by the Indians while on an exploring expedition.

JOHN FILSON

[1788]

JOHN FILSON was a pedagogue —
A pioneer was he;
I know not what his nation was,
Nor what his pedigree.

Tradition's scanty records tell
But little of the man,
Save that he to the frontier came
In immigration's van.

Perhaps with phantoms of reform
His busy fancy teemed,
Perhaps of new Utopias
Hesperian he dreamed.

John Filson and companions bold
A frontier village planned,
In forest wild, on sloping hills,
By fair Ohio's strand.

John Filson from three languages
  With pedant skill did frame
The novel word Losantiville
  To be the new town's name.

Said Filson: "Comrades, hear my words:
  Ere threescore years have flown
Our town will be a city vast."
  Loud laughed Bob Patterson.

Still John exclaimed, with prophet-tongue,
  "A city fair and proud,
The Queen of Cities in the West!"
  Mat Denman laughed aloud.

Deep in the wild and solemn woods
  Unknown to white man's track,
John Filson went, one autumn day,
  But nevermore came back.

He struggled through the solitude
  The inland to explore,
And with romantic pleasure traced
  Miami's winding shore.

Across his path the startled deer
  Bounds to its shelter green;
He enters every lonely vale
  And cavernous ravine.

Too soon the murky twilight comes,
  The boding night-winds moan;
Bewildered wanders Filson, lost,
  Exhausted, and alone.

By lurking foes his steps are dogged,
  A yell his ear appalls!
A ghastly corpse, upon the ground,
  A murdered man, he falls.

The Indian, with instinctive hate,
  In him a herald saw
Of coming hosts of pioneers,
  The friends of light and law;

In him beheld the champion
  Of industries and arts,
The founder of encroaching roads
  And great commercial marts;

The spoiler of the hunting-ground,
  The plougher of the sod,
The builder of the Christian school
  And of the house of God.

And so the vengeful tomahawk
  John Filson's blood did spill, —
The spirit of the pedagogue
  No tomahawk could kill.

John Filson had no sepulchre,
  Except the wildwood dim;
The mournful voices of the air
  Made requiem for him.

The druid trees their waving arms
  Uplifted o'er his head;
The moon a pallid veil of light
  Upon his visage spread.

The rain and sun of many years
  Have worn his bones away,
And what he vaguely prophesied
  We realize to-day.

Losantiville, the prophet's word,
  The poet's hope fulfils, —
She sits a stately Queen to-day
  Amid her royal hills!

Then come, ye pedagogues, and join
  To sing a grateful lay
For him, the martyr pioneer,
  Who led for you the way.

And may my simple ballad be
  A monument to save
His name from blank oblivion,
  Who never had a grave.
                WILLIAM HENRY VENABLE.

These pioneers found the land northwest of the Ohio remarkably fertile; but it was the hunting-ground of the warlike Delawares and Shawanese, and the man who attempted to settle there took his life in his hands. In the fall of 1791, a large force was collected at Cincinnati, under General Arthur St. Clair, and marched against the Indians. On the morning of November 4, the Americans were surprised near the Miami villages, and routed, with great loss. A ballad describing the defeat was written soon afterwards, and achieved a wide popularity.

SAINCLAIRE'S DEFEAT

[November 4, 1791]

'T was November the fourth, in the year of
    ninety-one,
We had a sore engagement near to Fort
    Jefferson;

Sainclaire was our commander, which may
   remembered be,
For there we left nine hundred men in t'
   West'n Ter'tory.

At Bunker's Hill and Quebeck, there many a
   hero fell,
Likewise at Long Island (it is I the truth can
   tell),
But such a dreadful carnage may I never see
   again
As hap'ned near St. Mary's, upon the river
   plain.

Our army was attacked just as the day did
   dawn,
And soon was overpowered and driven from
   the lawn.
They killed Major Ouldham, Levin and
   Briggs likewise,
And horrid yells of savages resounded through
   the skies.

Major Butler was wounded the very second
   fire;
His manly bosom swell'd with rage when
   forc'd to retire;
And as he lay in anguish, nor scarcely could
   he see,
Exclaim'd, "Ye hounds of hell! Oh, revenged
   I will be!"

We had not been long broken when General
   Butler found
Himself so badly wounded, was forced to quit
   the ground;
"My God!" says he, "what shall we do?
   we're wounded every man;
Go charge them, valiant heroes, and beat
   them if you can."

He leaned his back against a tree, and there
   resigned his breath,
And like a valiant soldier sunk in the arms of
   death;
When blessed angels did await his spirit to
   convey,
And unto the celestial fields he quickly bent
   his way.

We charg'd again with courage firm, but soon
   again gave ground;
The war-whoop then redoubled, as did the
   foes around.

They killed Major Ferguson, which caused
   his men to cry,
"Our only safety is in flight, or fighting here
   to die."

"Stand to your guns," says valiant Ford;
   "let's die upon them here,
Before we let the sav'ges know we ever har-
   bored fear!"
Our cannon-balls exhausted, and artill'ry-
   men all slain,
Obliged were our musketmen the enemy to
   sustain.

Yet three hours more we fought them, and
   then were forc'd to yield,
When three hundred warriors lay stretched
   upon the field.
Says Colonel Gibson to his men, "My boys,
   be not dismayed;
I'm sure that true Virginians were never yet
   afraid.

"Ten thousand deaths I'd rather die than
   they should gain the field!"
With that he got a fatal shot, which causèd
   him to yield.
Says Major Clarke, "My heroes, I can here
   no longer stand;
We'll strive to form in order, and retreat the
   best we can."

The word "Retreat!" being passed around,
   there was a dismal cry,
Then helter-skelter through the woods like
   wolves and sheep they fly.
This well-appointed army, who but a day
   before
Defied and braved all danger, had like a
   cloud passed o'er.

Alas, the dying and wounded, how dreadful
   was the thought!
To the tomahawk and scalping-knife in
   misery are brought.
Some had a thigh and some an arm broke
   on the field that day,
Who writhed in torments at the stake to close
   the dire affray.

To mention our brave officers, is what I wish
   to do;
No sons of Mars e'er fought more brave, or
   with more courage true.

To Captain Bradford I belonged, in his artil-
lery,
He fell that day amongst the slain, a valiant
man was he.

After this victory, the Indians grew bolder than
ever, and attacks on the border settlements were
increasingly frequent. , More than one family was
saved from surprise and death by a queer char-
acter known as Johnny Appleseed, who travelled
through the wilderness planting apple-seeds which
in time grew into valuable orchards. The Indians
thought him mad and would not harm him.

JOHNNY APPLESEED

A BALLAD OF THE OLD NORTHWEST

A MIDNIGHT cry appalls the gloom,
The puncheon door is shaken:
"Awake! arouse! and flee the doom!
Man, woman, child, awaken!

"Your sky shall glow with fiery beams
Before the morn breaks ruddy!
The scalpknife in the moonlight gleams,
Athirst for vengeance bloody!"

Alarumed by the dreadful word
Some warning tongue thus utters,
The settler's wife, like mother bird,
About her young ones flutters.

Her first-born, rustling from a soft
Leaf-couch, the roof close under,
Glides down the ladder from the loft,
With eyes of dreamy wonder.

The pioneer flings open wide
The cabin door, naught fearing;
The grim woods drowse on every side,
Around the lonely clearing.

"Come in! come in! nor like an owl
Thus hoot your doleful humors;
What fiend possesses you to howl
Such crazy, coward rumors?"

The herald strode into the room;
That moment, through the ashes,
The back-log struggled into bloom
Of gold and crimson flashes.

The glimmer lighted up a face,
And o'er a figure dartled,

So eerie, of so solemn grace,
The bluff backwoodsman startled.

The brow was gathered to a frown,
The eyes were strangely glowing,
And, like a snow-fall drifting down,
The stormy beard went flowing.

The tattered cloak that round him clung
Had warred with foulest weather;
Across his shoulders broad were flung
Brown saddlebags of leather.

One pouch with hoarded seed was packed,
From Penn-land cider-presses;
The other garnered book and tract
Within its creased recesses.

A glance disdainful and austere,
Contemptuous of danger,
Cast he upon the pioneer,
Then spake the uncouth stranger:

"Heed what the Lord's anointed saith;
Hear one who would deliver
Your bodies and your souls from death;
List ye to John the Giver.

"Thou trustful boy, in spirit wise
Beyond thy father's measure,
Because of thy believing eyes
I share with thee my treasure.

"Of precious seed this handful take;
Take next this Bible Holy:
In good soil sow both gifts, for sake
Of Him, the meek and lowly.

"Farewell! I go! — the forest calls
My life to ceaseless labors;
Wherever danger's shadow falls
I fly to save my neighbors.

"I save; I neither curse nor slay;
I am a voice that crieth
In night and wilderness. Away!
Whoever doubteth, dieth!"

The prophet vanished in the night,
Like some fleet ghost belated:
Then, awe-struck, fled with panic fright
The household, evil-fated.

They hurried on with stumbling feet,
Foreboding ambuscado;

Bewildered hope told of retreat
In frontier palisado.

But ere a mile of tangled maze
Their bleeding hands had broken,
Their home-roof set the dark ablaze,
Fulfilling doom forespoken.

The savage death-whoop rent the air!
A howl of rage infernal!
The fugitives were in Thy care,
Almighty Power eternal!

Unscathed by tomahawk or knife,
In bosky dingle nested,
The hunted pioneer, with wife
And babes, hid unmolested.

The lad, when age his locks of gold
Had changed to silver glory,
Told grandchildren, as I have told,
This western wildwood story.

Told how the fertile seeds had grown
To famous trees, and thriven;
And oft the Sacred Book was shown,
By that weird Pilgrim given.

Remember Johnny Appleseed,
All ye who love the apple;
He served his kind by Word and Deed,
In God's grand greenwood chapel.
WILLIAM HENRY VENABLE.

On August 20, 1794, General Anthony Wayne defeated the Indians on the Maumee and compelled them to sue for peace. At Greenville, in the following year, they ceded 25,000 square miles to the Americans, and settlers flocked into the fertile country thrown open to them.

THE FOUNDERS OF OHIO

THE footsteps of a hundred years
Have echoed, since o'er Braddock's Road
Bold Putnam and the Pioneers
Led History the way they strode.

On wild Monongahela stream
They launched the Mayflower of the West,
A perfect State their civic dream,
A new New World their pilgrim quest.

When April robed the Buckeye trees
Muskingum's bosky shore they trod;
They pitched their tents, and to the breeze
Flung freedom's star-flag, thanking God.

As glides the Oyo's solemn flood,
So fleeted their eventful years;
Resurgent in their children's blood,
They still live on — the Pioneers.

Their fame shrinks not to names and dates
On votive stone, the prey of time; —
Behold where monumental States
Immortalize their lives sublime!
WILLIAM HENRY VENABLE.

Ohio was admitted to the Union in 1803. The serenity of the new state was rudely shaken, in 1806, by the remarkable bugbear known as the "Burr Conspiracy." Burr had incurred the enmity of Jefferson and most of the other leading politicians of the time, and they were led to believe that he was preparing an expedition against the southwest, to set up a separate empire there. Burr had interested in his plan — which was really directed against Mexico — one Harmon Blennerhassett, who owned the island of that name in the Ohio, and who undertook to finance the expedition.

BLENNERHASSETT'S ISLAND

From "The New Pastoral"

ONCE came an exile, longing to be free,
Born in the greenest island of the sea;
He sought out this, the fairest blooming isle
That ever gemmed a river; and its smile,
Of summer green and freedom, on his heart
Fell, like the light of Paradise. Apart
It lay, remote and wild; and in his breast
He fancied this an island of the blest;
And here he deemed the world might never mar
The tranquil air with its molesting jar.
Long had his soul, among the strife of men,
Gone out and fought, and fighting, failed;
and then
Withdrew into itself: as when some fount
Finds space within, and will no longer mount,
Content to hear its own secluded waves
Make lonely music in the new-found caves.
And here he brought his household; here his wife,
As happy as her children, round his life
Sang as she were an echo, or a part
Of the deep pleasure springing in his heart —
A silken string which with the heavier cord
Made music, such as well-strung harps afford.
She was the embodied spirit of the man,
His second self, but on a fairer plan.

And here they came, and here they built their
    home,
And set the rose and taught the vines to
    roam,
Until the place became an isle of bowers,
Where odors, mist-like, swam above the
    flowers.
It was a place where one might lie and dream,
And see the naiads, from the river-stream,
Stealing among the umbrous, drooping limbs;
Where Zephyr, 'mid the willows, tuned her
    hymns
Round rippling shores. Here would the first
    birds throng,
In early spring-time, and their latest song
Was given in autumn; when all else had fled,
They half forgot to go; such beauty here was
    spread.
It was, in sooth, a fair enchanted isle,
Round which the unbroken forest, many a
    mile,
Reached the horizon like a boundless sea; —
A sea whose waves, at last, were forced to flee
On either hand, before the westward host,
To meet no more upon its ancient coast.
But all things fair, save truth, are frail and
    doomed;
And brightest beauty is the first consumed
By envious Time; as if he crowned the brow
With loveliest flowers, before he gave the
    blow
Which laid the victim on the hungry shrine: —
Such was the dreamer's fate, and such, bright
    isle, was thine.
There came the stranger, heralded by fame,
Whose eloquent soul was like a tongue of
    flame,
Which brightened and despoiled whate'er it
    touched.
A violet, by an iron gauntlet clutched,
Were not more doomed than whosoe'er he
    won
To list his plans, with glowing words o'er-
    run:
And Blennerhassett hearkened as he planned.
  Far in the South there was a glorious land
Crowned with perpetual flowers, and where
    repute
Pictured the gold more plenteous than the
    fruit —
The Persia of the West. There would he steer
His conquering course; and o'er the bright
    land rear
His far-usurping banner, till his home
Should rest beneath a wide, imperial dome,

Where License, round his thronèd feet, should
    whirl
Her dizzy mazes like an Orient girl.
His followers should be lords; their ladies each
Wear wreaths of gems beyond the old world's
    reach;
And emperors, gazing to that land of bloom,
With impotent fire of envy should consume.
Such was the gorgeous vision which he drew.
The listeners aw; and, dazzled by the view, —
As one in some enchanter's misty room,
His senses poisoned by the strange perfume,
Beholds with fierce desire the picture fair,
And grasps at nothing in the painted air, —
Gave acquiescence, in a fatal hour,
And wealth, and hope, and peace were in the
    tempter's power.
The isle became a rendezvous; and then
Came in the noisy rule of lawless men.
Domestic calm, affrighted, fled afar,
And Riot revelled 'neath the midnight star;
Continuous music rustled through the trees,
Where banners danced responsive on the
    breeze;
Or in festoons, above the astonished bowers,
With flaming colors shamed the modest
    flowers.
There clanged the mimic combat of the sword,
Like daily glasses round the festive board;
Here lounged the chiefs, there marched the
    plumèd file,
And martial splendor over-ran the isle.
Already, the shrewd leader of the sport
The shadowy sceptre grasped, and swayed his
    court.
In dreams, or waking, revelling or alone,
Before him swam the visionary throne;
Until a voice, as if the insulted woods
Had risen to claim their ancient solitudes,
Broke on his spirit, like a trumpet rude,
Shattering his dream to nothing where he
    stood!
The revellers vanished, and the banners fell
Like the red leaves beneath November's spell.
Full of great hopes, sustained by mighty will,
Urged by ambition, confident of skill,
As fearless to perform as to devise,
A-flush, but now he saw the glittering prize
Flame like a cloud in day's descending track;
But, lo, the sun went down and left it black!
Alone, despised, defiance in his eye,
He heard the shout, and "treason!" was the
    cry;
And that harsh word, with its unpitying blight,
Swept o'er the island like an arctic night.

Cold grew the hearthstone, withered fell the
        flowers,
And desolation walked among the bowers.
   This was the mansion. Through the ruined
        hall
The loud winds sweep, with gusty rise and
        fall,
Or glide, like phantoms, through the open
        doors;
And winter drifts his snow along the floors,
Blown through the yawning rafters, where the
        stars
And moon look in as through dull prison bars.
On yonder gable, through the nightly dark,
   The owl replies unto the dreary bark
Of lonely fox, beside the grass-grown sill;
And here, on summer eves, the whip-poor-will
Exalts her voice, and to the traveller's ear
Proclaims how Ruin rules with full content-
        ment here.
                THOMAS BUCHANAN READ.

Soon word got abroad that a great expedition
was being fitted out at Blennerhassett; the gov-
ernor of Ohio called out the sheriffs and militia,
who gathered in force, seized ten boats laden with
corn-meal, but permitted the boats containing
Blennerhassett and his followers to get away. A
mob destroyed Blennerhassett's beautiful home
and desolated the "fairy isle."

THE BATTLE OF MUSKINGUM

OR, THE DEFEAT OF THE BURRITES

[November 30, 1806]

YE jovial throng, come join the song
   I sing of glorious feats, sirs;
Of bloodless wounds, of laurels, crowns,
   Of charges, and retreats, sirs;

Of thundering guns, and honors won,
   By men of daring courage;
Of such as dine on beef and wine,
   And such as sup their porridge.

When Blanny's fleet, so snug and neat,
   Came floating down the tide, sirs,
Ahead was seen one-eyed Clark Green,
   To work them, or to guide, sirs.

Our General brave the order gave,
   "To arms! To arms, in season!
Old Blanny's boats most careless float,
   Brim-full of death and treason!"

A few young boys, their mothers' joys,
   And five men there were found, sirs,
Floating at ease — each little sees
   Or dreams of death and wound, sirs.

"Fly to the bank! on either flank!
   We'll fire from every corner;
We'll stain with blood Muskingum's flood,
   And gain immortal honor.

"The cannon there shall rend the air,
   Loaded with broken spikes, boys;
While our cold lead, hurled by each head,
   Shall give the knaves the gripes, boys.

"Let not maids sigh, or children cry,
   Or mothers drop a tear, boys;
I have the Baron in my head,
   Therefore you've nought to fear, boys.

"Now to your posts, this numerous host,
   Be manly, firm, and steady.
But do not fire till I retire
   And say when I am ready."

The Deputy courageously
   Rode forth in power and pride, sirs;
Twitching his reins, the man of brains
   Was posted by his side, sirs.

The men in ranks stood on the banks,
   While, distant from its border,
The active aid scours the parade
   And gives the general order:

"First, at command, bid them to stand;
   Then, if one rascal gains out
Or lifts his poll, why, damn his soul
   And blow the traitor's brains out."

The night was dark, silent came Clark
   With twelve or fifteen more, sirs;
While Paddy Hill, with voice most shrill,
   Whooped! as was said before, sirs.

The trembling ranks along the banks
   Fly into Shipman's manger;
While old Clark Green, with voice serene,
   Cried, "Soldiers, there's no danger.

"Our guns, good souls, are setting-poles,
   Dead hogs I'm sure can't bite you;
Along each keel is Indian meal;
   There's nothing here need fright you."

Out of the barn, still in alarm,
  Came fifty men or more, sirs,
And seized each boat and other float
  And tied them to the shore, sirs.

This plunder rare, they sport and share,
  And each a portion grapples.
'T was half a kneel of Indian meal,
  And ten of Putnam's apples.

The boats they drop to Allen's shop,
  Commanded by O'Flannon,
Where, lashed ashore, without an oar,
  They lay beneath the cannon.

This band so bold, the night being cold,
  And blacksmith's shop being handy,
Around the forge they drink and gorge
  On whiskey and peach-brandy.

Two honest tars, who had some scars,
  Beheld their trepidation.
Cries Tom, "Come, Jack, let's fire a crack;
  'T will fright them like damnation.

"Tyler, they say, lies at Belpré,
  Snug in old Blanny's quarters;
Yet this pale host tremble like ghosts
  For fear he'll walk on waters."

No more was said, but off they sped
  To fix what they'd begun on;
At one o'clock, firm as a rock,
  They fired the spun-yarn cannon.

Trembling and wan stood every man;
  Then bounced and shouted murder,
While Sergeant Morse squealed like a horse
  To get the folks to order.

Ten men went out and looked about —
  A hardy set of fellows;
Some hid in holes behind the coals,
  And some behind the bellows.

The Cor'ner swore the western shore
  He saw with muskets bristle;
Some stamp'd the ground; —'t was cannon sound,
  They heard the grape-shot whistle.

The Deputy mounted "Old Bay,"
  When first he heard the rattle,
Then changed his course — "Great men are scarce,
  I'd better keep from battle."

The General flew to meet the crew,
  His jacket flying loose, sirs;
Instead of sword, he seized his board; —
  Instead of hat, his goose, sirs.

"Tyler 's," he cried, "on t'other side,
  Your spikes will never do it;
The cannon's bore will hold some more,"
  Then thrust his goose into it.

Sol raised his head, cold spectres fled;
  Each man resumed his courage;
Captain O'Flan dismissed each man
  To breakfast on cold porridge.
                    WILLIAM HARRISON SAFFORD.

The whole party, including Burr, were arrested February 19, 1807 near Fort Stoddart, Ala., and taken to Richmond, Va., where Burr was put on trial for treason. The trial lasted six months, and resulted in acquittal.

TO AARON BURR, UNDER TRIAL FOR HIGH TREASON

THOU wonder of the Atlantic shore,
  Whose deeds a million hearts appall;
Thy fate shall pity's eye deplore,
  Or vengeance for thy ruin call.

Thou man of soul! whose feeble form
  Seems as a leaf the gales defy,
Though scattered in sedition's storm,
  Yet borne by glorious hope on high.

Such did the youthful Ammon seem,
  And such does Europe's scourge appear,
As, of the sun, a vertic beam,
  The brightest in the golden year.

Nature, who many a gift bestowed,
  The strong herculean limbs denied,
But gave — a mind, where genius glowed,
  A soul, to valor's self allied.

Ambition as her curse was seen,
  Thy every blessing to annoy;
To blight thy laurels' tender green;
  The banner of thy fame destroy.

Ambition, by the bard defined
  The fault of godlike hearts alone,
Like fortune in her frenzy, blind,
  Here gives a prison, *there* a throne.
                    SARAH WENTWORTH MORTON.

Scarcely had this "peril" been escaped, when another far more serious threatened the state on its western border. Tecumseh, chief of the Shawanese, was working to unite the western and southern Indians in war against the United States. William Henry Harrison had been made governor of the Indiana territory, and, collecting a force of about six hundred and fifty men, he marched into the Indian country, and, on November 7, 1811, at Tippecanoe, on the Wabash, routed the Indians and destroyed their villages.

THE BATTLE OF TIPPECANOE

[November 7, 1811]

AWAKE! awake! my gallant friends;
　To arms! to arms! the foe is nigh;
The sentinel his warning sends;
　And hark! the treacherous savage cry.
　　Awake! to arms! the word goes round;
　　The drum's deep roll, the fife's shrill sound,
　　The trumpet's blast, proclaim through night,
　　An Indian band, a bloody fight.

O haste thee, Baen! alas! too late;
　A red chief's arm now aims the blow
(An early, but a glorious fate);
　The tomahawk has laid thee low.
　　Dread darkness reigns. On, Daviess, on.
　　Where's Boyd? And valiant Harrison,
　　Commander of the Christian force?
　　And Owen? He's a bleeding corse!

"Stand, comrades brave, stand to your post:
　Here Wells, and Floyd, and Barton; all
Must now be won, or must be lost;
　Ply briskly, bayonet, sword, and ball."
　　Thus spake the general; when a yell
　　Was heard, as though a hero fell.
　　And, hark! the Indian whoop again —
　　It is for daring Daviess slain!

Oh! fearful is the battle's rage;
　No lady's hand is in the fray;
But brawny limbs the contest wage,
　And struggle for the victor's bay.
　　Lo! Spencer sinks, and Warwick's slain,
　　And breathless bodies strew the plain:
　　And yells, and groans, and clang, and roar,
　　Echo along the Wabash shore.

But mark! where breaks upon the eye
　Aurora's beam. The coming day

Shall foil a frantic prophecy,
　And Christian valor well display.
　　Ne'er did Constantine's soldiers see
　　With more of joy for victory,
　　A cross the arch of heaven adorn,
　　Than these the blushing of the morn.

Bold Boyd led on his steady band,
　With bristling bayonets burnish'd bright:
Who could their dauntless charge withstand?
　What stay the warriors' matchless might?
　　Rushing amain, they clear'd the field,
　　The savage foe constrain'd to yield
　　To Harrison, who, near and far,
　　Gave form and spirit to the war.

Sound, sound the charge! spur, spur the steed,
　And swift the fugitives pursue —
'T is vain: rein in — your utmost speed
　Could not o'ertake the recreant crew.
　　In lowland marsh, in dell, or cave,
　　Each Indian sought his life to save;
　　Whence, peering forth, with fear and ire,
　　He saw his prophet's town on fire.

Now the great Eagle of the West
　Triumphant wing was seen to wave!
And now each soldier's manly breast
　Sigh'd o'er his fallen comrade's grave.
　　Some dropp'd a tear, and mused the while,
　　Then join'd in measured march their file;
　　And here and there cast wistful eye,
　　That might surviving friend descry.

But let a foe again appear,
　Or east, or west, or south, or north;
The soldier then shall dry his tear,
　And fearless, gayly sally forth.
　　With lightning eye, and warlike front,
　　He 'll meet the battle's deadly brunt:
　　Come Gaul or Briton; if array'd
　　For fight — he 'll feel a freeman's blade.

THE TOMB OF THE BRAVE

IN COMMEMORATION OF THE BATTLE ON THE WABASH

[November 7, 1811]

WHEN darkness prevail'd and aloud on the air
　No war-whoop was heard through the deep silence yelling,

Till, fiercely, like lions just wild from their lair,
  Our chiefs found the foe on their slumbers
    propelling.
        While the mantle of night
        Hid the savage from sight,
Undismay'd were our warriors slain in the
    fight:
  But the laurel shall ever continue to wave,
  And glory thus bloom o'er the tomb of the
    brave.

Brave Daviess, legitimate offspring of fame,
  Though new to the war, rush'd to battle
    undaunted;
And ere, bearing death, the dread rifle-ball
    came,
  In the breast of the foe oft his weapon he
    planted.
        Gallant Daviess, adieu!
        Tears thy destiny drew;
But yet o'er thy body shall tremble no yew,
  For the laurel, etc.

Great Owen, too bold from the fight to re-
    main,
  Rush'd on to the foe, every soldier's heart
    firing;
But he sinks, in the blood of his foes, on the
    plain,
  The pale lamp of life in its socket expiring;
        Closed in death are his eyes,
        And lamented he lies;
Yet o'er the sad spot shall no cypress arise!
  But the laurel, etc.

Long Warwick, M'Mahan, and Spencer, and
    Baen,
  And Berry, 'mid darkness their banners
    defended,
But when day drew the curtain of night, they
    were seen
  Cover'd o'er with the blood of the savage,
    extended.
        Though Freedom may weep
        Where they mouldering sleep,
Yet shall valor their death as a jubilee keep!
  For the laurel, etc.

Ye chiefs of the Wabash, who gallantly
    fought,
  And fearlessly heard the dread storm of
    war rattle,
Who lived to see conquest so terribly bought,
  While your brothers were lost in the uproar
    of battle,

Still fearless remain,
And, though stretch'd on the plain,
You shall rise on the records of freedom again:
  For the laurel, etc.

Ye sons of Columbia, when danger is nigh,
  And liberty calls, round her standard to
    rally,
For your country, your wives, and your chil-
    dren to die,
  Resolve undismay'd on oppression to sally.
        Every hero secure
        That his fame shall endure
Till eternity time in oblivion immure;
  For the laurel shall ever continue to wave,
  And glory thus bloom o'er the tomb of the
    brave.
                        JOSEPH HUTTON.

While this struggle was waging for the country
between the Alleghanies and the Mississippi, two
daring explorers traversed the country to the
west of the great river. On May 14, 1804, Captain
Meriwether Lewis and Lieutenant William Clark,
of the First Infantry, who had been appointed to
seek water communication with the Pacific Coast,
entered the Missouri River and started westward.

SA–CÁ–GA–WE–A

THE INDIAN GIRL WHO GUIDED LEWIS AND
CLARK IN THEIR EXPEDITION TO THE
PACIFIC

SHO-SHÓ-NE SA-CÁ-GA-WE-A — captive and
  wife was she
On the grassy plains of Dakota in the land
  of the Minnetaree;
But she heard the west wind calling, and
  longed to follow the sun
Back to the shining mountains and the glens
  where her life begun.
So, when the valiant Captains, fain for the
  Asian sea,
Stayed their marvellous journey in the land
  of the Minnetaree
(The Red Men wondering, wary — Omaha,
  Mandan, Sioux —
Friendly now, now hostile, as they toiled the
  wilderness through),
Glad she turned from the grassy plains and
  led their way to the West,
Her course as true as the swan's that flew
  north to its reedy nest;
Her eye as keen as the eagle's when the young
  lambs feed below;

Her ear alert as the stag's at morn guarding
    the fawn and doe.
Straight was she as a hillside fir, lithe as the
    willow-tree,
And her foot as fleet as the antelope's when
    the hunter rides the lea;
In broidered tunic and moccasins, with
    braided raven hair,
And closely belted buffalo robe with her baby
    nestling there —
Girl of but sixteen summers, the homing bird
    of the quest,
Free of the tongues of the mountains, deep on
    her heart imprest, —
Sho-shó-ne Sa-cá-ga-we-a led the way to the
    West! —
To Missouri's broad savannas dark with bison
    and deer,
While the grizzly roamed the savage shore
    and cougar and wolf prowled near;
To the cataract's leap, and the meadows with
    lily and rose abloom;
The sunless trails of the forest, and the can-
    yon's hush and gloom;
By the veins of gold and silver, and the moun-
    tains vast and grim —
Their snowy summits lost in clouds on the
    wide horizon's brim;
Through sombre pass, by soaring peak, till
    the Asian wind blew free,
And lo! the roar of the Oregon and the
    splendor of the Sea!

Some day, in the lordly upland where the
    snow-fed streams divide —
Afoam for the far Atlantic, afoam for Pacific's
    tide —
There, by the valiant Captains whose glory
    will never dim
While the sun goes down to the Asian sea
    and the stars in ether swim,
She will stand in bronze as richly brown as
    the hue of her girlish cheek,
With broidered robe and braided hair and
    lips just curved to speak;
And the mountain winds will murmur as
    they linger along the crest,
"Sho-shó-ne Sa-cá-ga-we-a, who led the way
    to the West!"
                EDNA DEAN PROCTOR.

They ascended the Missouri, crossed the moun-
tains, and descended the Columbia, reaching its
mouth November 15, 1805. They started on the
return journey in March, 1806, and reached St.
Louis in September. On January 14, 1807, a
dinner was given at Washington to the explorers,
in the course of which the following stanzas were
recited.

ON THE DISCOVERIES OF CAPTAIN LEWIS

[January 14, 1807]

LET the Nile cloak his head in the clouds, and
    defy
    The researches of science and time;
Let the Niger escape the keen traveller's
    eye,
    By plunging or changing his clime.

Columbus! not so shall thy boundless do-
    main
    Defraud thy brave sons of their right;
Streams, midlands, and shorelands elude us
    in vain.
    We shall drag their dark regions to light.

Look down, sainted sage, from thy synod of
    Gods;
    See, inspired by thy venturous soul,
Mackenzie roll northward his earth-draining
    floods,
    And surge the broad waves to the pole.

With the same soaring genius thy Lewis
    ascends,
    And, seizing the car of the sun,
O'er the sky-propping hills and high waters
    he bends,
    And gives the proud earth a new zone.

Potowmak, Ohio, Missouri had felt
    Half her globe in their cincture com-
    prest;
His long curving course has completed the
    belt,
    And tamed the last tide of the west.

Then hear the loud voice of the nation pro-
    claim,
    And all ages resound the decree:
Let our occident stream bear the young hero's
    name,
    Who taught him his path to the sea.

These four brother floods, like a garland of
    flowers,
    Shall entwine all our states in a band

Conform and confederate their wide-spreading
        powers,
And their wealth and their wisdom expand.

From Darien to Davis one garden shall bloom,
    Where war's weary banners are furl'd,
And the far scenting breezes that waft its
        perfume,
    Shall settle the storms of the world.

Then hear the loud voice of the nation pro-
        claim
    And all ages resound the decree:
Let our occident stream bear the young hero's
        name,
    Who taught him his path to the sea.
                        JOEL BARLOW.

For many years, the East showed little interest
in this far western land — it was too indistinct, too
distant. The British Hudson Bay Company had
its eye on the country, and in October, 1842, pre-
pared to bring in a large body of immigrants to
occupy it. Dr. Marcus Whitman, of the American
Board of Missions, learned of this design, and
started to ride across the country to Washington,
D. C., in order to lay the plot before the United
States government. After enduring almost in-
credible fatigue and hardship, he reached Wash-
ington March 3, 1843. The tidings he brought
spurred the government to retain this great terri-
tory.

WHITMAN'S RIDE FOR OREGON

[October, 1842–March 3, 1843]

I

"AN empire to be lost or won!"
    And who four thousand miles will ride
    And climb to heaven the Great Divide,
And find the way to Washington,
    Through mountain cañons, winter snows,
    O'er streams where free the north wind
        blows?
Who, who will ride from Walla-Walla,
    Four thousand miles for Oregon?

II

"An empire to be lost or won?
    In youth to man I gave my all,
    And nought is yonder mountain wall;
If but the will of Heaven be done,
    It is not mine to live or die,
    Or count the mountains low or high,
Or count the miles from Walla-Walla.
    I, I will ride for Oregon.

III

"An empire to be lost or won?
    Bring me my Cayuse pony then,
    And I will thread old ways again,
Beneath the gray skies' crystal sun.
    'T was on these altars of the air
    I raised the flag, and saw below
The measureless Columbia flow;
The Bible oped, and bowed in prayer,
    And gave myself to God anew,
    And felt my spirit newly born;
And to my mission I'll be true,
And from the vale of Walla-Walla,
    I'll ride again for Oregon.

IV

"I'm not my own, myself I've given,
    To bear to savage hordes the word;
If on the altars of the heaven
    I'm called to die, it is the Lord.
The herald may not wait or choose,
    'T is his the summons to obey;
To do his best, or gain or lose,
    To seek the Guide and not the way.
He must not miss the cross, and I
    Have ceased to think of life or death;
My ark I've builded — Heaven is nigh,
    And earth is but a morning's breath;
Go, then, my Cayuse pony bring,
    The hopes that seek myself are gone,
And from the vale of Walla-Walla,
    I'll ride again for Oregon."

V

He disappeared, as not his own,
    He heard the warning ice winds sigh;
The smoky sun flames o'er him shone,
    On whitened altars of the sky,
As up the mountain sides he rose;
    The wandering eagle round him wheeled,
The partridge fled, the gentle roes,
    And oft his Cayuse pony reeled
Upon some dizzy crag, and gazed
    Down cloudy chasms, falling storms,
While higher yet the peaks upraised
    Against the winds their giant forms.
On, on and on, past Idaho,
    On past the mighty Saline sea,
His covering at night the snow,
    His only sentinel a tree.
On, past Portneuf's basaltic heights,
    On where the San Juan mountains lay,
Through sunless days and starless nights,
    Towards Toas and far Sante Fé.

O'er table-lands of sleet and hail,
   Through pine-roofed gorges, cañons cold,
Now fording streams incased in mail
   Of ice, like Alpine knights of old:
Still on, and on, forgetful on,
   Till far behind lay Walla-Walla,
And far the fields of Oregon.

VI

The winter deepened, sharper grew
   The hail and sleet, the frost and snow,
Not e'en the eagle o'er him flew,
   And scarce the partridge's wing below.
The land became a long white sea,
   And then a deep with scarce a coast,
The stars refused their light, till he
   Was in the wildering mazes lost.
He dropped the rein, his stiffened hand
   Was like a statue's hand of clay;
"My trusty beast, 't is the command,
   Go on, I leave to thee the way.
I must go on, I must go on,
   Whatever lot may fall to me,
On, 't is for others' sake I ride, —
   For others I may never see, —
And dare thy clouds, O Great Divide;
   Not for myself, O Walla-Walla,
Not for myself, O Washington,
   But for thy future, Oregon."

VII

And on and on the dumb beast pressed,
   Uncertain, and without a guide,
And found the mountain's curves of rest
   And sheltered ways of the Divide.
His feet grew firm, he found the way
   With storm-beat limbs and frozen breath,
As keen his instincts to obey
   As was his master's eye of faith.
Still on and on, still on and on,
   And far and far grew Walla-Walla,
And far the fields of Oregon.

VIII

That spring, a man with frozen feet
   Came to the marble halls of State,
And told his mission but to meet
   The chill of scorn, the scoff of hate.
'Is Oregon worth saving?" asked
   The treaty-makers from the coast;
And him the church with questions tasked,
   And said, "Why did you leave your post?"
Was it for this that he had braved
   The warring storms of mount and sky?

Yes! — yet that empire he had saved,
   And to his post went back to die, —
Went back to die for others' sake,
   Went back to die from Washington,
Went back to die for Walla-Walla,
   For Idaho and Oregon.

IX

At fair Walla-Walla one may see
   The city of the Western North,
And near it graves unmarked there be
   That cover souls of royal worth.
The flag waves o'er them in the sky
   Beneath whose stars are cities born,
And round them mountain-castled lie
   The hundred states of Oregon.
              HEZEKIAH BUTTERWORTH.

Far to the south of the point reached by Lewis and Clark lay the country known as California. It had been explored by the Spaniards as early as 1540, and in 1769 an expedition under Portala discovered San Francisco Bay.

DISCOVERY OF SAN FRANCISCO BAY

[October 31, 1769]

GOOD Junipero, the Padre,
   Slowly read the King's commands,
In relation to the missions
   To be built in heathen lands.
And he said: "The good Saint Francis
   Surely has some little claim,
Yet I find that here no mission
   Is assigned unto his name."

Then the Visitador answered:
   "If the holy Francis care
For a mission to his honor,
   Surely he will lead you there;
And it may be by the harbor
   That the Indian legends say
Lies by greenest hills surrounded
   To the north of Monterey."

Spoke Junipero the Padre:
   "It is not for me to tell
Of the truth of Indian legends,
   Yet of this I know full well —
If there be such hidden harbor,
   And our hope and trust we place
In the care of good Saint Francis,
   He will guide us to the place."

Soon, the Governor Portala
  Started northward, on his way
Overland, to rediscover
  The lost port of Monterey.
Since the time within its waters
  Viscaino anchor cast,
It remained unknown to Spaniards,
  Though a century had passed.

On his journey went Portala
  With his band of pioneers,
Padres, Indian guides, and soldiers,
  And a train of muleteers;
And said Serra, as he blessed them,
  As he wished them all Godspeed:
"Trust Saint Francis — he will guide you
  In your direst hour of need."

On his journey went Portala
  Till he reached the crescent bay;
But he dreamed not he was gazing
  On the wished-for Monterey.
So a cross on shore he planted,
  And the ground about he blessed,
And then he and his companions
  Northward went upon their quest.

On his journey went Portala,
  And his army northward on,
And methinks I see them marching,
  Or in camp when day was done;
Or at night when stars were twinkling,
  As that travel-weary band
By the log-fire's light would gather,
  Telling of their far-off land.

And they told weird Indian legends,
  Tales of Cortes, too, they told,
And of peaceful reign of Incas,
  And of Montezuma's gold;
And they sang, as weary exiles
  Sing of home and vanished years,
Sweet, heart-treasured songs that always
  Bring the dumb applause of tears.

When the day was sunk in ocean,
  And the land around was dim,
On the tranquil air of midnight
  Rose the sweet Franciscan hymn;
And when bugle told the dawning,
  And the matin prayers were done,
On his journey went Portala,
  And his army northward on.

Far away they saw sierras,
  Clothed with an eternal spring,
While at times the mighty ocean
  In their path her spray would fling;
On amid such scenes they journeyed,
  Through the dreary wastes of sand,
Through ravines dark, deep, and narrow,
  And through cañons wild and grand.

And with what a thrill of pleasure,
  All their toils and dangers through,
Gazed they on this scene of beauty
  When it burst upon their view,
As Portala and his army,
  Standing where I stand to-day,
Saw before them spread in beauty
  Green-clad hills and noble bay.

Then the Governor Portala
  Broke the spell of silence thus:
"To this place, through Padre Serra,
  Hath Saint Francis guided us;
So the bay and all around it
  For the Spanish King I claim,
And forever, in the future,
  Let it bear Saint Francis' name."

Thus he spoke, and I am standing
  On the self-same spot to-day,
And my eyes rest on the landscape,
  And the green hills, and the bay,
And upon Saint Francis' city,
  As, with youth and hope elate,
She is gazing toward the ocean,
  Sitting by the Golden Gate.

Needless were such gifts as heaven
  Gave to holy seers of yore,
To foretell the meed of glory,
  Fairest town, for thee in store!
To foretell the seat of empire
  Here will be, nor for a day,
Where Balboa's sea doth mingle
  With the waters of thy bay!
                    RICHARD EDWARD WHITE.

In 1822 California became a province of
Mexico, and in 1844 Colonel John Charles Fré-
mont reached Sutter's Fort with an exploring ex-
pedition. Two years later, during the war with
Mexico, he assumed command of the American
forces in the country, and established the author-
ity of the United States there.

JOHN CHARLES FRÉMONT

PATHFINDER — and Path-clincher!
  Who blazed the way, indeed,
But more — who made the eternal Fact
  Whereto a path had need;
Who, while our Websters set at naught
  The thing that Was to Be,
Whipped-out our halting, half-way map
  Full to the Other Sea!

'T was well that there were some could
      read
    The logic of the West!
A Kansas-edged geography,
    Of provinces confessed,
Became potential Union
    And took a Nation's span
When God sent Opportunity
    And Benton found the Man!
            CHARLES F. LUMMIS.

In 1848 California was ceded to the United
States by Mexico. In the same year gold was
discovered near Coloma, and within a few months
the famous rush for the new El Dorado began.

"THE DAYS OF 'FORTY–NINE"

YOU are looking now on old Tom Moore,
  A relic of bygone days;
A Bummer, too, they call me now,
  But what care I for praise?
For my heart is filled with the days of yore,
  And oft I do repine
For the Days of Old, and the Days of Gold,
  And the Days of 'Forty-nine.
    Refrain — Oh, my heart is filled, etc.

I had comrades then who loved me well,
  A jovial, saucy crew:
There were some hard cases, I must confess,
  But they all were brave and true;
Who would never flinch, whate'er the pinch,
  Who never would fret nor whine,
But like good old Bricks they stood the
      kicks
    In the Days of 'Forty-Nine.
    Refrain — And my heart is filled, etc.

There was Monte Pete — I 'll ne'er forget
  The luck he always had.
He would deal for you both day and night,
  So long as you had a scad.

He would play you Draw, he would Ante
      sling,
  He would go you a hatfull Blind —
But in a game with Death Pete lost his breath
  In the Days of 'Forty-Nine.
    Refrain — Oh, my heart is filled, etc.

There was New York Jake, a butcher boy,
  That was always a-getting tight;
Whenever Jake got on a spree,
  He was spoiling for a fight.
One day he ran against a knife
  In the hands of old Bob Cline —
So over Jake we held a wake,
  In the Days of 'Forty-Nine.
    Refrain —Oh, my heart is filled, etc.

There was Rackensack Jim, who could out-
      roar
    A Buffalo Bull, you bet!
He would roar all night, he would roar all day,
  And I b'lieve he 's a-roaring yet!
One night he fell in a prospect-hole —
  'T was a roaring bad design —
For in that hole he roared out his soul
  In the Days of 'Forty-Nine.
    Refrain — Oh, my heart is filled, etc.

There was Poor Lame Ches, a hard old case
  Who never did repent.
Ches never missed a single meal,
  Nor he never paid a cent.
But Poor Lame Ches, like all the rest,
  Did to death at last resign,
For all in his bloom he went up the Flume
  In the Days of 'Forty-Nine.
    Refrain — Oh, my heart is filled, etc.

And now my comrades all are gone,
  Not one remains to toast;
They have left me here in my misery,
  Like some poor wandering ghost.
And as I go from place to place,
  Folks call me a "Travelling Sign,"
Saying "There goes Tom Moore, a Bummer,
      sure,
    From the Days of 'Forty-Nine."
    Refrain — But my heart is filled, etc.

Most of the emigrants crossed the plains, en-
countering dangers and hardships innumerable.
The trails were soon marked by the skeletons of
horses and oxen, and by the graves of those who
had perished from hardship or been butchered by
the Indians.

THE OLD SANTA FÉ TRAIL

It wound through strange scarred hills, down
    cañons lone
Where wild things screamed, with winds for
    company;
Its mile-stones were the bones of pioneers.
Bronzed, haggard men, often with thirst
    a-moan,
Lashed on their beasts of burden toward the
    sea:
An epic quest it was of elder years,
For fabled gardens or for good, red gold,
The trail men strove in iron days of old.

To-day the steam-god thunders through the
    vast,
While dominant Saxons from the hurtling trains
Smile at the aliens, Mexic, Indian,
Who offer wares, keen-colored, like their past;
Dread dramas of immitigable plains
Rebuke the softness of the modern man;
No menace, now, the desert's mood of sand;
Still westward lies a green and golden land.

For, at the magic touch of water, blooms
The wilderness, and where of yore the yoke
Tortured the toilers into dateless tombs,
Lo! brightsome fruits to feed a mighty folk.
                              RICHARD BURTON.

The importance of the new country grew so
rapidly that on September 9, 1850, California was
admitted to the Union, the thirty-first state.

CALIFORNIA

[September 9, 1850]

Land of gold! — thy sisters greet thee
    O'er the mountain and the main;
See, — they stretch the hand to meet thee,
    Youngest of our household train.

Many a form their love hath fostered
    Lingers 'neath thy sunny sky,
And their spirit-tokens brighten
    Every link of sympathy.

We 'mid storms of war were cradled,
    'Mid the shock of angry foes;
Thou, with sudden, dreamlike splendor,
    Pallas-born, — in vigor rose.

Children of one common country,
    Strong in friendship let us stand,
With united ardor earning
    Glory for our Mother Land.

They of gold and they of iron,
    They who reap the bearded wheat,
They who rear the snowy cotton,
    Pour their treasures at her feet·

While with smiling exultation,
    She, who marks the host of Pharaob;
Like the mother of the Gracchi,
    Folds her jewels to her heart.
                      LYDIA HUNTLEY SIGOURNEY.

CHAPTER IV

THROUGH FIVE ADMINISTRATIONS

Although Aaron Burr had been acquitted of the
charge of treason, the persecution of him still
continued. He was practically run out of the
country, and when he returned at last in 1812,
it was in disguise, under the name of Arnat.
Fate soon afterwards dealt him a cruel blow, for
in January, 1813, his daughter, Theodosia, the
idol of his heart, perished at sea while on a voyage
from Charleston to New York.

THEODOSIA BURR:

THE WRECKER'S STORY

[January, 1813]

In revel and carousing
We gave the New Year housing;

With wreckage for our firing,
And rum to heart's desiring,
Antigua and Jamaica,
Flagon and stoup and breaker.
Full cans and a ranting chorus;
Hard hearts for the bout before us —
To brave grim Death's grimaces
On dazed and staring faces.

With dirks and hangers bristling,
We for a gale went whistling,
Tornado or pampero,
To swamp the host of Pharaob;
To goad the mad Atlantic,
And drive the skippers frantic·

To jar the deep with thunder,
And make the waste a wonder,
And plunge the coasters under,
And pile the banks with plunder.

Then the wild rack came skirling,
Ragged and crazed, and whirling
Sea-stuff and sand in breakers,
Frothing the shelvy acres:
Over the banks high bounding,
Inlet and sound confounding.
Hatteras roared and rumbled,
Currituck heaved and tumbled;
And the sea-gulls screamed like witches,
And sprawled in the briny ditches.

Shelter and rest we flouted,
Jorum and pipe we scouted,
Fiddler and wench we routed.
"Fetch out the nag!" we shouted;
For a craft in the offing struggled.
"Now for a skipper juggled;
Now for a coaster stranded,
And loot in the lockers landed!"
With lantern cheerly rocking
On the nag's head, we went mocking —
Lilting of tipsy blisses,
And Bonnibel's squandered kisses.

Straight for that hell-spark steering,
Drove the doomed craft careering;
Men on her fore-deck huddled,
Sea in her wake all cruddled,
Kitty Hawk sheer before her,
And the breakers booming o'er her
Till the rocks in their lurking stove her,
And her riven spars went over,
And she lay on her side and shivered,
And groaned to be delivered.

Boats through the black rift storming,
Foes on her quarter swarming;
Dirks in the torchlight flashing,
And the wicked hangers slashing;
Lips that were praying mangled,
Throats that were screaming, strangled;
Souls in the surges tumbling,
Vainly for foothold fumbling;
Horror of staring faces,
Gruesome in Death's grimaces —
And God's wrath overpast us,
With never a bolt to blast us!

By the brunt of our doings daunted,
We crouched where the fore-deck slanted.

Scanning each other's faces,
Graved with that horror's traces.
One, peering aft, wild-staring,
Points through the torches flaring:
"Spook of the storm, or human?
Angel, or wraith, or woman?"
Havoc and wreck surveying,
Imploring not, nor praying,
Nor death nor life refusing;
Stony and still — accusing!

Black as our hearts the creature's
Vesture, her matchless features
White as the dead. Oh! wonder
Of women high heaven under!
So she moved down upon us
(Though Death and the Fiend might
        shun us),
And we made passage, cowering.
Rigid and mute and towering,
Never a frown she deigned us,
Never with curse arraigned us.
One, trembling, dropped his hanger,
And swooned at the awful clangor;
But she passed on, unharking,
Her steps our doom-strokes marking,
Straight to the plank, and mounted.
"One, two, three, four!" we counted;
Till she paused, o'er the flood suspended,
Poised, her lithe arms extended. —
And the storm stood still and waited
For the stroke of the Lord, belated!
                JOHN WILLIAMSON PALMER.

Oliver Hazard Perry, the victor of Lake Erie, while in command of a squadron in the West Indies, in the summer of 1819, was attacked by yellow fever, and died after a brief illness. His body was brought to the United States in 1826 and buried at Newport.

ON THE DEATH OF COMMODORE OLIVER H. PERRY

By strangers honor'd, and by strangers mourn'd.

[August 23, 1819]

How sad the note of that funereal drum,
    That's muffled by indifference to the dead!
And how reluctantly the echoes come,
    On air that sighs not o'er that stranger's
        bed,
    Who sleeps with death alone. O'er his
        young head

His native breezes never more shall sigh;
  On his lone grave the careless step shall
    tread,
And pestilential vapors soon shall dry
Each shrub that buds around — each flow'r
    that blushes nigh.

Let Genius, poising on her full-fledg'd wing,
  Fill the charm'd air with thy deservèd
    praise!
Of war, and blood, and carnage let her sing,
  Of victory and glory! — let her gaze
    On the dark smoke that shrouds the can-
      non's blaze,
On the red foam that crests the bloody bil-
    low;
  Then mourn the sad close of thy shorten'd
    days —
Place on thy country's brow the weeping wil-
    low,
And plant the laurels thick around thy last
    cold pillow.

No sparks of Grecian fire to me belong:
  Alike uncouth the poet and the lay;
Unskill'd to turn the mighty tide of song,
  He floats along the current as he may,
  The humble tribute of a tear to pay.
Another hand may choose another theme,
  May sing of Nelson's last and brightest
    day,
Of Wolfe's unequall'd and unrivall'd fame,
The wave of Trafalgar — the fields of Abra-
    ham:

But if the wild winds of thy western lake
  Might teach a harp that fain would mourn
    the brave,
And sweep those strings the minstrel may not
    wake,
  Or give an echo from some secret cave
  That opens on romantic Erie's wave,
The feeble cord would not be swept in vain;
  And though the sound might never reach
    thy grave,
Yet there are spirits here that to the strain
Would send a still small voice responsive back
    again.

JOHN G. C. BRAINARD.

The death of Joseph Rodman Drake, on Sep-
tember 21, 1820, deserves mention here, not so
much because of Drake's prominence as a poet
as because of the admirable lyric which it called
forth — one of the most perfect in American lit-
erature.

ON THE DEATH OF JOSEPH ROD-
MAN DRAKE

[September 21, 1820]

GREEN be the turf above thee,
  Friend of my better days!
None knew thee but to love thee,
  Nor named thee but to praise.

Tears fell, when thou wert dying,
  From eyes unused to weep,
And long where thou art lying,
  Will tears the cold turf steep.

When hearts, whose truth was proven,
  Like thine, are laid in earth,
There should a wreath be woven
  To tell the world their worth;

And I, who woke each morrow
  To clasp thy hand in mine,
Who shared thy joy and sorrow,
  Whose weal and woe were thine:

It should be mine to braid it
  Around thy faded brow,
But I've in vain essayed it,
  And feel I cannot now.

While memory bids me weep thee,
  Nor thoughts nor words are free,
The grief is fixed too deeply
  That mourns a man like thee.

FITZ-GREENE HALLECK.

In 1824, at the invitation of Congress and Presi-
dent Monroe, the Marquis de Lafayette, who had
played so important a part in the revolution,
visited the United States. He arrived in New
York August 15, and for the next fourteen months
travelled through the country, visiting every
state, and being everywhere received with rev-
erence and affection. On June 17, 1825, he laid
the corner-stone of the Bunker Hill Monument.

ON LAYING THE CORNER-STONE
OF THE BUNKER HILL MONU-
MENT

[June 17, 1825]

OH, is not this a holy spot?
  'T is the high place of Freedom's birth!
God of our fathers! is it not
  The holiest spot of all the earth?

Quenched is thy flame on Horeb's side;
   The robber roams o'er Sinai now;
And those old men, thy seers, abide
   No more on Zion's mournful brow.

But 'on *this* hill thou, Lord, hast dwelt,
   Since round its head the war-cloud curled,
And wrapped our fathers, where they knelt
   In prayer and battle for a world.

Here sleeps their dust: 't is holy ground:
   And we, the children of the brave,
From the four winds are gathering round,
   To lay our offering on their grave.

Free as the winds around us blow,
   Free as the waves below us spread,
We rear a pile, that long shall throw
   Its shadow on their sacred bed.

But on their deeds no shade shall fall,
   While o'er their couch thy sun shall flame.
Thine ear was bowed to hear their call,
   And thy right hand shall guard their fame.
            JOHN PIERPONT.

Lafayette's sixty-eighth birthday was celebrated at the White House September 6, 1825, and he sailed next day for France, where he died May 20, 1834. The verses by Dolly Madison which follow were only recently discovered.

LA FAYETTE

BORN, nurtured, wedded, prized, within the pale
   Of peers and princes, high in camp — at court —
He hears, in joyous youth, a wild report,
Swelling the murmurs of the Western gale,
Of a young people struggling to be free!
   Straight quitting all, across the wave he flies,
   Aids with his sword, wealth, blood, the high emprize!
And shares the glories of its victory.
   Then comes for fifty years a high romance
   Of toils, reverses, sufferings, in the cause
   Of man and justice, liberty and France,
Crowned, at the last, with hope and wide applause.

Champion of Freedom! Well thy race was run!
All time shall hail thee, *Europe's noblest Son!*
            DOLLY MADISON.
Washington, April 25, 1848.

John Adams, second President of the United States, died at his home in Braintree, Mass., July 4, 1826. His last words were, "Thomas Jefferson still lives." But by a curious coincidence, Jefferson had died at his home, Monticello, in Albemarle County, Va., a few hours before.

THE DEATH OF JEFFERSON

[July 4, 1826]

I

'T WAS midsummer; cooling breezes all the
   languid forests fanned,
And the angel of the evening drew her curtain
   o'er the land.
Like an isle rose Monticello through the
   cooled and rippling trees,
Like an isle in rippling starlight in the silence
   of the seas.
Ceased the mocking-bird his singing; said
   the slaves with faltering breath,
"'T is the Third, and on the morrow Heaven
   will send the Angel Death."

II

In his room at Monticello, lost in dreams the
   statesman slept,
Seeing not the still forms round him, seeing
   not the eyes that wept,
Hearing not the old clock ticking in life's
   final silence loud,
Knowing not when night came o'er him like
   the shadow of a cloud.
In the past his soul is living as in fifty years
   ago,
Hastes again to Philadelphia, hears again the
   Schuylkill flow —

III

Meets again the elder Adams — knowing not
   that far away
He is waiting for Death's morrow, on old
   Massachusetts Bay;
Meets with Hancock, young and courtly,
   meets with Hopkins, bent and old,
Meets again calm Roger Sherman, fiery Lee,
   and Carroll bold,
Meets the sturdy form of Franklin, meets the
   half a hundred men
Who have made themselves immortal, —
   breathes the ancient morn again.

IV

Once again the Declaration in his nerveless
hands he holds,
And before the waiting statesmen its pro-
phetic hope unfolds, —
Reads again the words puissant, "All men
are created free,"
Claims again for man his birthright, claims
the world's equality;
Hears the coming and the going of an hundred
firm-set feet,
Hears the summer breezes blowing 'mid the
oak trees cool and sweet.

V

Sees again tall Patrick Henry by the side of
Henry Lee,
Hears him cry, "And will ye sign it ? — it will
make all nations free!
Fear ye not the axe or gibbet; it shall topple
every throne.
Sign it for the world's redemption! — all man-
kind its truth shall own!
Stars may fall, but truth eternal shall not
falter, shall not fail.
Sign it, and the Declaration shall the voice of
ages hail.

VI

"Sign, and set yon dumb bell ringing, that the
people all may know
Man has found emancipation; sign, the Al-
mighty wills it so."
Sees one sign it, then another, till like magic
moves the pen,
Till all have signed it, and it lies there,
charter of the rights of men.
Hears the small bells, hears the great bell,
hanging idly in the sun,
Break the silence, and the people whisper,
awe-struck, "It is done."

VII

Then the dream began to vanish — bur-
gesses, the war's red flames,
Charging Tarleton, proud Cornwallis, navies
moving on the James,
Years of peace, and years of glory, all began
to melt away,
And the statesman woke from slumber in the
night, and tranquil lay,
And his lips moved; friends there gathered
with love's silken footstep near,
And he whispered, softly whispered in love's
low and tender ear, —

VIII

"It is the Fourth ? " "No, not yet," they an-
swered, " but 't will soon be early morn;
We will wake you, if you slumber, when the
day begins to dawn."
Then the statesman left the present, lived
again amid the past,
Saw, perhaps, the peopled future ope its
portals grand and vast,
Till the flashes of the morning lit the far
horizon low,
And the sun's rays o'er the forests in the east
began to glow.

IX

Rose the sun, and from the woodlands fell the
midnight dews like rain,
In magnolias cool and shady sang the mock-
ing-bird again;
And the statesman woke from slumber, saw
the risen sun, and heard
Rippling breezes 'mid the oak trees, and the
lattice singing bird,
And, his eye serene uplifted, as rejoicing in the
sun,
"It is the Fourth ? " his only question, — to
the world his final one.

X

Silence fell on Monticello — for the last dread
hour was near,
And the old clock's measured ticking only
broke upon the ear.
All the summer rooms were silent, where the
great of earth had trod,
All the summer blooms seemed silent as the
messengers of God;
Silent were the hall and chamber where old
councils oft had met,
Save the far boom of the cannon that recalled
the old day yet.

XI

Silent still is Monticello — he is breathing
slowly now,
In the splendors of the noon-tide, with the
death-dew on his brow —
Silent save the clock still ticking where his
soul had given birth
To the mighty thoughts of freedom, that
should free the fettered earth;
Silent save the boom of cannon on the sun
filled wave afar,
Bringing 'mid the peace eternal still the
memory of war.

XII

Evening in majestic shadows fell upon the
    fortress' walls;
Sweetly were the last bells ringing on the
    James and on the Charles.
'Mid the choruses of freedom two departed
    victors lay,
One beside the blue Rivanna, one by Massa-
    chusetts Bay.
He was gone, and night her sable curtain
    drew across the sky;
Gone his soul into all nations, gone to live and
    not to die.
HEZEKIAH BUTTERWORTH.

On September 14, 1830, the Boston *Adver-
tiser* contained a paragraph asserting that the
Secretary of the Navy had recommended to the
Board of Navy Commissioners that the old frigate
Constitution, popularly known as "Old Ironsides,"
be disposed of. Two days later appeared the
famous poem by Oliver Wendell Holmes, which
instantly became a sort of national battle-cry.
Instead of being sold, the Constitution was rebuilt.

OLD IRONSIDES

[September 14, 1830]

Ay, tear her tattered ensign down!
    Long has it waved on high,
And many an eye has danced to see
    That banner in the sky;
Beneath it rung the battle shout,
    And burst the cannon's roar; —
The meteor of the ocean air
    Shall sweep the clouds no more.

Her deck, once red with heroes' blood,
    Where knelt the vanquished foe,
When winds were hurrying o'er the flood,
    And waves were white below,
No more shall feel the victor's tread,
    Or know the conquered knee; —
The harpies of the shore shall pluck
    The eagle of the sea!

Oh better that her shattered hulk
    Should sink beneath the wave;
Her thunders shook the mighty deep,
    And there should be her grave;
Nail to the mast her holy flag,
    Set every threadbare sail,
And give her to the god of storms,
    The lightning and the gale!
OLIVER WENDELL HOLMES.

CONCORD HYMN

SUNG AT THE COMPLETION OF THE BATTLE
MONUMENT, APRIL 19, 1836

By the rude bridge that arched the flood,
    Their flag to April's breeze unfurled,
Here once the embattled farmers stood,
    And fired the shot heard round the world.

The foe long since in silence slept;
    Alike the conqueror silent sleeps;
And Time the ruined bridge has swept
    Down the dark stream which seaward
    creeps.

On this green bank, by this soft stream,
    We set to-day a votive stone;
That memory may their deed redeem,
    When, like our sires, our sons are gone.

Spirit that made those heroes dare
    To die, and leave their children free,
Bid Time and Nature gently spare
    The shaft we raise to them and thee.
RALPH WALDO EMERSON.

On December 17, 1839, Longfellow wrote in
his journal: "News of shipwrecks horrible on
the coast. Twenty bodies washed ashore near
Gloucester, one lashed to a piece of the wreck.
There is a reef called Norman's Woe where many
of these took place; among others the schooner
Hesperus. Also the Sea-Flower on Black Rock. I
must write a ballad on this." It was written
twelve days later.

THE WRECK OF THE HESPERUS

[December 17, 1839]

It was the schooner Hesperus,
    That sailed the wintry sea;
And the skipper had taken his little daughter,
    To bear him company.

Blue were her eyes as the fairy-flax,
    Her cheeks like the dawn of day,
And her bosom white as the hawthorn buds
    That ope in the month of May.

The skipper he stood beside the helm,
    His pipe was in his mouth,
And he watched how the veering flaw did
    blow
The smoke now West, now South.

Then up and spake an old Sailòr,
  Had sailed to the Spanish Main,
"I pray thee, put into yonder port,
  For I fear a hurricane.

"Last night, the moon had a golden ring,
  And to-night no moon we see!"
The skipper, he blew a whiff from his pipe,
  And a scornful laugh laughed he.

Colder and louder blew the wind,
  A gale from the Northeast,
The snow fell hissing in the brine,
  And the billows frothed like yeast.

Down came the storm, and smote amain
  The vessel in its strength;
She shuddered and paused, like a frighted
    steed,
  Then leaped her cable's length.

"Come hither, come hither, my little daugh-
    tèr,
  And do not tremble so;
For I can weather the roughest gale
  That ever wind did blow."

He wrapped her warm in his seaman's coat
  Against the stinging blast;
He cut a rope from a broken spar,
  And bound her to the mast.

"O father! I hear the church-bells ring,
  O say, what may it be?"
"'T is a fog-bell on a rock-bound coast!" —
  And he steered for the open sea.

"O father! I hear the sound of guns,
  Oh say, what may it be?"
"Some ship in distress, that cannot live
  In such an angry sea!"

"O father! I see a gleaming light,
  Oh say, what may it be?"
But the father answered never a word,
  A frozen corpse was he.

Lashed to the helm, all stiff and stark,
  With his face turned to the skies,
The lantern gleamed through the gleaming
    snow
  On his fixed and glassy eyes.

Then the maiden clasped her hands and prayed
  That savèd she might be;
And she thought of Christ, who stilled the
    wave,
  On the Lake of Galilee.

And fast through the midnight dark and drear,
  Through the whistling sleet and snow,
Like a sheeted ghost, the vessel swept
  Tow'rds the reef of Norman's Woe.

And ever the fitful gusts between
  A sound came from the land;
It was the sound of the trampling surf
  On the rocks and the hard sea-sand.

The breakers were right beneath her bows,
  She drifted a dreary wreck,
And a whooping billow swept the crew
  Like icicles from her deck.

She struck where the white and fleecy waves
  Looked soft as carded wool,
But the cruel rocks, they gored her side
  Like the horns of an angry bull.

Her rattling shrouds, all sheathed in ice,
  With the masts, went by the board;
Like a vessel of glass, she stove and sank,
  Ho! ho! the breakers roared!

At daybreak, on the bleak sea-beach,
  A fisherman stood aghast,
To see the form of a maiden fair,
  Lashed close to a drifting mast.

The salt sea was frozen on her breast,
  The salt tears in her eyes;
And he saw her hair, like the brown sea-weed
  On the billows fall and rise.

Such was the wreck of the Hesperus,
  In the midnight and the snow!
Christ save us all from a death like this,
  On the reef of Norman's Woe!
          HENRY WADSWORTH LONGFELLOW.

  The presidential campaign of 1840 was the
most exciting that had ever taken place in the
United States. William Henry Harrison was the
candidate of the Whigs and Martin Van Buren
of the Democrats. Harrison was elected by an
overwhelming majority.

OLD TIPPECANOE

[October, November, 1840]

COME, rouse up, ye bold-hearted Whigs of
    Kentucky,
  And show the nation what deeds you can
    do;
The high-road to victory lies open before ye
  While led to the charge by Old Tippecanoe.

When Indians were scalping our friends and
    our brothers,
  To Ohio's frontier he gallantly flew;
And thousands of innocent infants, and
    mothers,
  Were saved by the valor of Tippecanoe.

When savage Tecumseh was rallying his
    forces,
  In innocent blood his hands to imbrue;
Our hero despis'd all his bloody associates,
  And won the proud name of Old Tippe-
    canoe.

And when this Tecumseh and his brother
    Proctor,
  To capture Fort Meigs their utmost did
    do;
Our gallant old hero again play'd the Doctor,
  And gave them a dose like at Tippecanoe.

And then on the Thames, on the fifth of
    October,
  Where musket balls whizz'd as they flew;
He blasted their prospects, and rent them
    asunder,
  Just like he had done on the Tippecanoe.

Let Greece praise the deeds of her great
    Alexander
  And Rome boast of Cæsar and Scipio too;
Just like Cincinnatus, that noble commander,
  Is our old Hero of Tippecanoe.

Or when the foes of his country no longer
    could harm her,
  To the shades of retirement he quickly
    withdrew;
And now at North Bend see the HONEST OLD
    FARMER,
  Who won the green laurel at Tippecanoe.

And when to the National Council elected,
  The good of his country still see him pursue,

And every poor man by him thus protected,
  Should ever remember "Old Tippecanoe."

And now from retirement the People doth
    call him,
  Because he is Honest and Qualified too;
And for One Term they soon will install him
  As President — "Hero of Tippecanoe."

Let *knaves* call him "coward," and *fools* call
    him "*granny*"
  To answer their *purpose* — this never will
    do;
When rallied around him we'll rout *little*
    Vanny,
  And give him a Thames — or a full *Water-*
    loo.

The Republican banner of Freedom is flying,
  The Eagle of Liberty soars in your view;
Then rally my hearties — all slanders defy-
    ing,
  And thunder huzza! for "Old Tippecanoe."

Among the supporters of brave General Jack
    son,
  There are many Republicans, honest and
    true,
To such we say "come out from among
    them,"
  And "go it for" Tyler and "Tippecanoe."

Harrison was inaugurated March 4, 1841. He
was at that time sixty-eight years of age, but he
took up the work of his office with a vigor almost
youthful. On March 27, however, he contracted
a chill, pneumonia developed, and he died April 4.
The vice-president, John Tyler, at once took the
oath of office as president.

THE DEATH OF HARRISON

[April 4, 1841]

WHAT! soar'd the old eagle to die at the sun!
Lies he stiff with spread wings at the goal
    he had won!
Are there spirits more blest than the "Planet
    of Even,"
Who mount to their zenith, then melt into
    Heaven —
No waning of fire, no quenching of ray,
But rising, still rising, when passing away?
Farewell, gallant eagle! thou 'rt buried in light!
God-speed into Heaven, lost star of our night!

Death! Death in the White House! Ah, never
    before,
Trod his skeleton foot on the President's
    floor!
He is look'd for in hovel, and dreaded in
    hall —
The king in his closet keeps hatchment and
    pall —
The youth in his birthplace, the old man at
    home,
Make clean from the door-stone the path to
    the tomb; —
But the lord of this mansion was cradled not
    here —
In a churchyard far-off stands his beckoning
    bier!
He is here as the wave-crest heaves flashing
    on high —
As the arrow is stopp'd by its prize in the
    sky —
The arrow to earth, and the foam to the
    shore —
Death finds them when swiftness and sparkle
    are o'er —
But Harrison's death fills the climax of story —
He went with his old stride — from glory to
    glory!

Lay his sword on his breast! There's no
    spot on its blade
In whose cankering breath his bright laurels
    will fade!
'T was the first to lead on at humanity's call —
It was stay'd with sweet mercy when "glory"
    was all'
As calm in the council as gallant in war,
He fought for its country and not its "hur-
    rah!"

In the path of the hero with pity he trod —
Let him pass — with his sword — to the
    presence of God!

What more? Shall we on with his ashes? Yet,
    stay!
He hath ruled the wide realm of a king in his
    day!
At his word, like a monarch's, went treasure
    and land —
The bright gold of thousands has pass'd
    through his hand.
Is there nothing to show of his glittering hoard?
No jewel to deck the rude hilt of his sword —
No trappings — no horses? — what had he
    but now?
On! — on with his ashes! — HE LEFT BUT
    HIS PLOUGH!

Follow now, as ye list! The first mourner to-day
Is the nation — whose father is taken away
Wife, children, and neighbor, may moan o'
    his knell —
He was "lover and friend" to his country
    as well!
For the stars on our banner, grown sudden
    dim,
Let us weep, in our darkness — but weep no
    for him!
Not for him — who, departing, leaves million
    in tears!
Not for him — who has died full of honor an
    years!
Not for him — who ascended Fame's ladde
    so high
From the round at the top he has stepp'd
    the sky!
                    NATHANIEL PARKER WILLIS.

CHAPTER V

THE WAR WITH MEXICO

In 1821 Mexico acquired her independence of
Spain, but the country became the prey of mili-
tary adventurers, who were made presidents by
proclamation, and retained office as long as they
had an army to support them. In 1834 Santa
Anna, who was in power at the time, abolished
the constitution and established a military despot-
ism. The citizens of the province of Texas, which
had been largely settled from the United States,
revolted and declared their independence. General
Cos, the military governor, and fifteen hundred
men. were besieged at Bejar. and forced to sur-

render, after a desperate assault led by Benjam
R. Milam.

THE VALOR OF BEN MILAM

[December 5-11, 1835]

*OH, who will follow old Ben Milam into S
    Antonio?*
Such was the thrilling word we heard in
    chill December glow;

Such was the thrilling word we heard, and a
　　ringing, answering cry
Went up from the dun adobe walls to the
　　cloudless Texas sky.

He had won from the reek of a Mexique jail
　　back without map or chart,
With his mother-wit and his hero-grit and his
　　stanch Kentucky heart;
He had trudged by vale and by mountain trail,
　　and by thorny and thirsty plain,
And now, with joy on his grizzled brow, he had
　　come to his own again.

They're the spawn of Hell! we heard him tell;
　　they will knife and lie and cheat;
At the board of none of the swarthy horde would
　　I deign to sit at meat;
They hold it naught that I bled and fought
　　when Spain was their ruthless foe;
Oh, who will follow old Ben Milam into San
　　Antonio?

It was four to one, not gun for gun, but never
　　a curse cared we,
Three hundred faithful and fearless men who
　　had sworn to make Texas free.
It was mighty odds, by all the gods, this brute
　　of the Mexique dam,
But it was not much for heroes such as fol-
　　lowed old Ben Milam!

With rifle-crack and sabre-hack we drove
　　them back in the street;
From house to house in the red carouse we
　　hastened their flying feet;
And ever that shout kept pealing out with a
　　swift and sure death-blow:
Oh, who will follow old Ben Milam into San
　　Antonio?

Behind the walls from the hurtling balls Cos
　　cowered and swore in his beard,
While we slashed and slew from dawn till dew,
　　and, Bexar, how we cheered!
But ere failed each ruse, and the white
　　of truce on the failing day was
　　thrown,
Our fearless soul had gone to the goal, the
　　Land of the Great Unknown.

Death brought the darksome boon too soon to
　　this truest one of the true,
O men of the fated Alamo, Milam had died
　　with you!

So when their names that now are Fame's —
　　the scorner of braggart sham; —
In song be praised, let a rouse be raised for
　　the name of Ben Milam!
CLINTON SCOLLARD.

BEN MILAM

Oft shall the soldier think of thee,
　　Thou dauntless leader of the brave,
Who on the heights of Tyranny
　　Won Freedom and a glorious grave.

And o'er thy tomb shall pilgrims weep,
　　And pray to heaven in murmurs low
That peaceful be the hero's sleep
　　Who conquered San Antonio.

Enshrined on Honor's deathless scroll,
　　A nation's thanks will tell thy fame;
Long as her beauteous rivers roll
　　Shall Freedom's votaries hymn thy name.

For bravest of the Texan clime,
　　Who fought to make her children free,
Was Milam, and his death sublime
　　Linked with undying Liberty!
WILLIAM H. WHARTON.

On February 23, 1836, Santa Anna appeared at
the head of two thousand men before San Antonio.
The town was guarded by a fort called the Alamo,
held by Colonel William Travis and one hundred
and fifty Texans. Travis sent to Gonzales for
reinforcements and shut himself up in the fort.
A few days later, thirty-two men got through the
Mexican lines, swelling his force to one hundred
and eighty-three. After a terrific struggle, the
Mexicans carried the fort on March 6. Not one of
the garrison survived.

THE MEN OF THE ALAMO

[February 23–March 6, 1836]

To Houston at Gonzales town, ride, Ranger,
　　for your life,
Nor stop to say good-bye to-day to home, or
　　child, or wife;
But pass the word from ranch to ranch, to
　　every Texan sword,
That fifty hundred Mexicans have crossed the
　　Nueces ford,
With Castrillon and perjured Cos, Sesmá and
　　Almontè,
And Santa Anna ravenous for vengeance and
　　for prey!

They smite the land with fire and sword; the
grass shall never grow
Where northward sweeps that locust herd on
San Antonio!

Now who will bar the foeman's path, to gain
a breathing space,
Till Houston and his scattered men shall meet
him face to face?
Who holds his life as less than naught when
home and honor call,
And counts the guerdon full and fair for
liberty to fall?
Oh, who but Barrett Travis, the bravest of
them all!
With seven score of riflemen to play the
rancher's game,
And feed a counter-fire to halt the sweeping
prairie flame;
For Bowie of the broken blade is there to
cheer them on,
With Evans of Concepcion, who conquered
Castrillon,
And o'er their heads the Lone Star flag defiant
floats on high,
And no man thinks of yielding, and no man
fears to die.

But ere the siege is held a week a cry is
heard without,
A clash of arms, a rifle peal, the Ranger's
ringing shout,
And two-and-thirty beardless boys have
bravely hewed their way
To die with Travis if they must, to conquer if
they may.
Was ever valor held so cheap in Glory's mart
before
In all the days of chivalry, in all the deeds of
war?
But once again the foemen gaze in wonder-
ment and fear
To see a stranger break their lines and hear
the Texans cheer.
God! how they cheered to welcome him,
those spent and starving men!
For Davy Crockett by their side was worth an
army then.
The wounded ones forgot their wounds; the
dying drew a breath
To hail the king of border men, then turned
to laugh at death.
For all knew Davy Crockett, blithe and gen-
erous as bold,

And strong and rugged as the quartz that hides
its heart of gold.
His simple creed for word or deed true as the
bullet sped,
And rung the target straight: "Be sure you're
right, then go ahead!"

And were they right who fought the fight for
Texas by his side?
They questioned not; they faltered not; they
only fought and died.
Who hath an enemy like these, God's mercy
slay him straight! —
A thousand Mexicans lay dead outside the
convent gate,
And half a thousand more must die before the
fortress falls,
And still the tide of war beats high around the
leaguered walls.
At last the bloody breach is won; the weak-
ened lines give way;
The wolves are swarming in the court; th
lions stand at bay.
The leader meets them at the breach, and win
the soldier's prize;
A foeman's bosom sheathes his sword whe
gallant Travis dies.
Now let the victor feast at will until his cre
be red —
We may not know what raptures fill the vu
ture with the dead.
Let Santa Anna's valiant sword right brave
hew and hack
The senseless corse; its hands are cold; the
will not strike him back.
Let Bowie die, but 'ware the hand that wiel
his deadly knife;
Four went to slay, and one comes back,
dear he sells his life.
And last of all let Crockett fall, too proud
sue for grace,
So grand in death the butcher dared not lo
upon his face.

But far on San Jacinto's field the Texan to
are set,
And Alamo's dread memory the Texan st
shall whet.
And Fame shall tell their deeds who fell
all the years be run.
"Thermopylæ left one alive — the Ala
left none."

JAMES JEFFREY ROCHE

THE DEFENCE OF THE ALAMO

[March 6, 1835]

SANTA ANA came storming, as a storm might
    come;
    There was rumble of cannon; there was
        rattle of blade;
There was cavalry, infantry, bugle and drum —
    Full seven thousand in pomp and parade.
The chivalry, flower of Mexico;
And a gaunt two hundred in the Alamo!

And thirty lay sick, and some were shot
    through;
    For the siege had been bitter, and bloody,
        and long.
"Surrender, or die!" — "Men, what will *you*
    do?"
    And Travis, great Travis, drew sword, quick
        and strong;
Drew a line at his feet. . . . . "Will you come?
    Will you go?
    die with my wounded, in the Alamo."

The Bowie gasped, "Lead me over that line!"
    Then Crockett, one hand to the sick, one
        hand to his gun,
Crossed with him; then never a word or a
    sign
    Till all, sick or well, all, all save but one,
One man. Then a woman stepped, praying,
    and slow
    cross; to die at her post in the Alamo.

hen that one coward fled, in the night, in
    that night
    When all men silently prayed and thought
        of home; of to-morrow; of God and the
        right,
Till dawn; and with dawn came Travis's
    cannon-shot,
    answer to insolent Mexico,
om the old bell-tower of the Alamo.

hen came Santa Ana; a crescent of flame!
    Then the red escalade; then the fight hand
        to hand;
ch an unequal fight as never had name
    Since the Persian hordes butchered that
        doomed Spartan band.
day — all day and all night; and the
    morning? so slow,
    rough the battle smoke mantling the
        Alamo.

Now silence! Such silence! Two thousand
    lay dead
    In a crescent outside! And within? Not a
        breath
Save the gasp of a woman, with gory gashed
    head,
    All alone, all alone there, waiting for death;
And she but a nurse. Yet when shall we know
Another like this of the Alamo?

Shout "Victory, victory, victory ho!"
    I say 't is not always to the hosts that win!
I say that the victory, high or low,
    Is given the hero who grapples with sin,
Or legion or single; just asking to know
When duty fronts death in his Alamo.
                            JOAQUIN MILLER.

A few days later, at Goliad, Colonel Fannin and
four hundred soldiers surrendered to the Mexi-
cans under solemn assurances that their lives
would be spared. On March 27 the prisoners were
marched out under guard and shot down like
cattle in the shambles. This massacre aroused
the wildest indignation, and recruits flocked to
the army under Houston, and on April 21 sur-
prised Santa Anna at San Jacinto, routed the
Mexicans, and inflicted a terrible vengeance.

THE FIGHT AT SAN JACINTO

[April 21, 1836]

"Now for a brisk and cheerful fight!"
    Said Harman, big and droll,
As he coaxed his flint and steel for a light,
    And puffed at his cold clay bowl;
"For we are a skulking lot," says he,
    "Of land-thieves hereabout,
And the bold señores, two to one,
    Have come to smoke us out."

Santa Anna and Castrillon,
    Almonte brave and gay,
Portilla red from Goliad,
    And Cos with his smart array.
Dulces and cigaritos,
    And the light guitar, ting-tum!
Sant' Anna courts siesta —
    And Sam Houston taps his drum.

The buck stands still in the timber —
    "Is 't the patter of nuts that fall?"
The foal of the wild mare whinnies —
    "Did he hear the Comanche call?"

In the brake by the crawling bayou
  The slinking she-wolves howl,
And the mustang's snort in the river sedge
  Has startled the paddling fowl.

A soft low tap, and a muffled tap,
  And a roll not loud nor long —
We would not break Sant' Anna's nap,
  Nor spoil Almonte's song.
Saddles and knives and rifles!
  Lord! but the men were glad
When Deaf Smith muttered "Alamo!"
  And Karnes hissed "Goliad!"

The drummer tucked his sticks in his belt,
  And the fifer gripped his gun.
Oh, for one free, wild Texan yell,
  And we took the slope in a run!
But never a shout nor a shot we spent,
  Nor an oath nor a prayer that day,
Till we faced the bravos, eye to eye,
  And then we blazed away.

Then we knew the rapture of Ben Milam,
  And the glory that Travis made,
With Bowie's lunge and Crockett's shot,
  And Fannin's dancing blade;
And the heart of the fighter, bounding free
  In his joy so hot and mad —
When Millard charged for Alamo,
  Lamar for Goliad.

Deaf Smith rode straight, with reeking spur,
  Into the shock and rout:
"I've hacked and burned the bayou bridge,
  There's no sneak's back-way out!"
Muzzle or butt for Goliad,
  Pistol and blade and fist!
Oh, for the knife that never glanced,
  And the gun that never missed!

Dulces and cigaritos,
  Song and the mandolin!
That gory swamp was a gruesome grove
  To dance fandangos in.
We bridged the bog with the sprawling herd
  That fell in that frantic rout;
We slew and slew till the sun set red,
  And the Texan star flashed out.
    JOHN WILLIAMSON PALMER.

The victory at San Jacinto ended the war.
Santa Anna at once signed a treaty recognizing
the independence of Texas, and it was formally
ratified May 14, 1836. The Republic of Texas was
established, and commissioners were dispatched
to Washington to secure recognition and proffer
annexation.

SONG OF TEXAS

MAKE room on our banner bright
  That flaps in the lifting gale,
For the orb that lit the fight
  In Jacinto's storied vale.
Through clouds, all dark of hue,
  It arose with radiant face;
Oh, grant to a sister true,
  Ye stars, in your train a place!

The blood of the Saxon flows
  In the veins of the men who cry, —
"Give ear, give ear unto those
  Who pine for their native sky!
We call on our Motherland
  For a home in Freedom's hall, —
While stretching forth the hand,
  Oh, build no dividing wall!

"The Mexican vaunteth no more;
  In strife we have tamed his pride;
The coward raps not at your door,
  Speak out! shall it open wide?
Oh, the wish of our hearts is strong,
  That the star of Jacinto's fight
Have place in the flashing throng
  That spangle your banner bright."
    WILLIAM HENRY CUYLER HOSMER.

The question of the admission of Texas w
destined to occasion the bitterest controversy th
ever shook the Union. The struggle between t.
advocates of freedom and of slavery was at ⁵
height; the former feared that to annex Texas, wi
its two hundred thousand square miles, would
to seat the slave interests more firmly than ev
in power. It would also involve war with Mexi
The controversy raged with unexampled veno
but on December 29, 1845, Texas was admitt
to the Union.

TEXAS

VOICE OF NEW ENGLAND

UP the hillside, down the glen,
Rouse the sleeping citizen;
Summon out the might of men!

Like a lion growling low,
Like a night-storm rising slow,
Like the tread of unseen foe;

It is coming, it is nigh!
Stand your homes and altars by;
On your own free thresholds die.

Clang the bells in all your spires;
On the gray hills of your sires
Fling to heaven your signal-fires.

From Wachuset, lone and bleak,
Unto Berkshire's tallest peak,
Let the flame-tongued heralds speak.

Oh, for God and duty stand,
Heart to heart and hand to hand,
Round the old graves of the land.

Whoso shrinks or falters now,
Whoso to the yoke would bow,
Brand the craven on his brow!

Freedom's soil hath only place
For a free and fearless race,
None for traitors false and base.

Perish party, perish clan;
Strike together while ye can,
Like the arm of one strong man.

Like that angel's voice sublime,
Heard above a world of crime,
Crying of the end of time;

With one heart and with one mouth,
Let the North unto the South
Speak the word befitting both:

"What though Issachar be strong!
Ye may load his back with wrong
Overmuch and over long:

"Patience with her cup o'errun,
With her weary thread outspun,
Murmurs that her work is done.

"Make our Union-bond a chain,
Weak as tow in Freedom's strain
Link by link shall snap in twain.

"Vainly shall your sand-wrought rope
Bind the starry cluster up,
Shattered over heaven's blue cope!

'Give us bright though broken rays,
Rather than eternal haze,
Clouding o'er the full-orbed blaze.

"Take your land of sun and bloom;
Only leave to Freedom room
For her plough, and forge, and loom;

"Take your slavery-blackened vales;
Leave us but our own free gales,
Blowing on our thousand sails.

"Boldly, or with treacherous art,
Strike the blood-wrought chain apart;
Break the Union's mighty heart;

"Work the ruin, if ye will;
Pluck upon your heads an ill
Which shall grow and deepen still.

"With your bondman's right arm bare,
With his heart of black despair,
Stand alone, if stand ye dare!

"Onward with your fell design;
Dig the gulf and draw the line:
Fire beneath your feet the mine:

"Deeply, when the wide abyss
Yawns between your land and this,
Shall ye feel your helplessness.

"By the hearth and in the bed,
Shaken by a look or tread,
Ye shall own a guilty dread.

"And the curse of unpaid toil,
Downward through your generous soil
Like a fire shall burn and spoil.

"Our bleak hills shall bud and blow,
Vines our rocks shall overgrow,
Plenty in our valleys flow; —

"And when vengeance clouds your skies,
Hither shall ye turn your eyes,
As the lost on Paradise!

"We but ask our rocky strand,
Freedom's true and brother band,
Freedom's strong and honest hand;

"Valleys by the slave untrod,
And the Pilgrim's mountain sod,
Blessèd of our fathers' God!"
                    JOHN GREENLEAF WHITTIER.

The Mexican minister had already demanded
his passports, and the annexation of Texas to the

Union was regarded by Mexico as an act of war. A Mexican army was collected on the Rio Grande, while an American army of occupation under General Zachary Taylor was thrown into Texas. The war awakened the most violent hostility in the North, and especially in New England, where it was held to be merely a pretext for extending slave territory.

MR. HOSEA BIGLOW SPEAKS

Thrash away, you'll *hev* to rattle
  On them kittle-drums o' yourn, —
'Taint a knowin' kind o' cattle
  Thet is ketched with mouldy corn;
Put in stiff, you fifer feller,
  Let folks see how spry you be, —
Guess you'll toot till you are yeller
  'Fore you git ahold o' me!

Thet air flag's a leetle rotten,
  Hope it aint your Sunday's best; —
Fact! it takes a sight o' cotton
  To stuff out a soger's chest:
Sence we farmers hev to pay fer 't,
  Ef you must wear humps like these,
S'posin' you should try salt hay fer 't,
  It would du ez slick ez grease.

'T would n't suit them Southun fellers,
  They're a dreffle graspin' set,
We must ollers blow the bellers
  Wen they want their irons het;
May be it's all right ez preachin',
  But *my* narves it kind o' grates,
Wen I see the overreachin'
  O' them nigger-drivin' States.

Them thet rule us, them slave-traders,
  Haint they cut a thunderin' swarth
(Helped by Yankee renegaders),
  Thru the vartu o' the North!
We begin to think it's nater
  To take sarse an' not be riled; —
Who'd expect to see a tater
  All on eend at bein' biled?

Ez fer war, I call it murder, —
  There you hev it plain an' flat;
I don't want to go no furder
  Than my Testyment fer that;
God hez sed so plump an' fairly,
  It 's ez long ez it is broad,
An' you've gut to git up airly
  Ef you want to take in God.

'Taint your eppyletts an' feathers
  Make the thing a grain more right;
'Taint afollerin' your bell-wethers
  Will excuse ye in His sight;
Ef you take a sword an' dror it,
  An' go stick a feller thru,
Guv'ment aint to answer for it,
  God'll send the bill to you.

Wut's the use o' meetin'-goin'
  Every Sabbath, wet or dry,
Ef it's right to go amowin'
  Feller-men like oats an' rye?
I dunno but what it's pooty
  Trainin' round in bobtail coats, —
But it's curus Christian dooty
  This 'ere cuttin' folks's throats.

They may talk o' Freedom's airy
  Tell they're pupple in the face, —
It's a grand gret cemetary
  Fer the barthrights of our race;
They jest want this Californy
  So 's to lug new slave-states in
To abuse ye, an' to scorn ye,
  An' to plunder ye like sin.

Aint it cute to see a Yankee
  Take sech everlastin' pains,
All to get the Devil's thankee
  Helpin' on 'em weld their chains?
Wy, it's jest ez clear es figgers,
  Clear ez one an' one make two,
Chaps thet make black slaves o' niggers
  Want to make wite slaves o' you.

Tell ye jest the eend I've come to
  Arter cipherin' plaguy smart,
An' it makes a handy sum, tu,
  Any gump could larn by heart;
Laborin' man an' laborin' woman,
  Hev one glory an' one shame,
Ev'y thin' thet's done inhuman
  Injers all on 'em the same.

'Taint by turnin' out to hack folks
  You're agoin' to git your right,
Nor by lookin' down on black folks
  Coz you're put upon by wite;
Slavery aint o' nary color,
  'Taint the hide thet makes it wus,
All it keers fer in a feller
  'S jest to make him fill its pus.

Want to tackle *me* in, du ye?
　I expect you'll hev to wait;
Wen cold lead puts daylight thru ye
　You'll begin to kal'late;
S'pose the crows wun't fall to pickin'
　All the carkiss from your bones,
Coz you helped to give a lickin'
　To them poor half-Spanish drones?

Jest go home an' ask our Nancy
　Wether I'd be such a goose
Ez to jine ye, — guess you'd fancy
　The eternal bung wuz loose!
She wants me fer home consumption,
　Let alone the hay's to mow, —
Ef you're arter folks o' gumption,
　You've a darned long row to hoe.

Take them editors thet's crowin'
　Like a cockerel three months old, —
Don't ketch any on 'em goin',
　Though they *be* so blasted bold;
Aint they a prime lot o' fellers?
　'Fore they think on 't guess they'll sprout
(Like a peach thet's got the yellers),
　With the meanness bustin' out.

Wal, go 'long to help 'em stealin'
　Bigger pens to cram with slaves,
Help the men thet's ollers dealin'
　Insults on your fathers' graves;
Help the strong to grind the feeble,
　Help the many agin the few,
Help the men thet call your people
　Witewashed slaves an' peddlin' crew!

Massachusetts, God forgive her,
　She's akneelin' with the rest,
She, thet ough' to ha' clung ferever
　In her grand old eagle-nest;
She thet ough' to stand so fearless
　W'ile the wracks are round her hurled,
Holdin' up a beacon peerless
　To the oppressed of all the world!

Ha'n't they sold your colored seamen?
　Ha'n't they made your env'ys w'iz?
Wut 'll make ye act like freemen?
　Wut 'll git your dander riz?
Come, I tell you wut I'm thinkin'
　Is our dooty in this fix,
They'd ha' done 't ez quick ez winkin'
　In the days o' seventy-six.

Clang the bells in every steeple,
　Call all true men to disown
The tradoocers of our people,
　The enslavers o' their own;
Let our dear old Bay State proudly
　Put the trumpet to her mouth,
Let her ring this messidge loudly
　In the ears of all the South: —

"I'll return ye good fer evil
　Much ez we frail mortils can,
But I wun't go help the Devil
　Makin' man the cus o' man;
Call me coward, call me traitor,
　Jest ez suits your mean idees, —
Here I stand a tyrant-hater,
　An' the friend o' God an' Peace!"

Ef I'd *my* way I hed ruther
　We should go to work an' part,
They take one way, we take t'other,
　Guess it would n't break my heart;
Man hed ough' to put asunder
　Them thet God has noways jined;
An' I should n't gretly wonder
　Ef there's thousands o' my mind.
　　　　　　　JAMES RUSSELL LOWELL.

General Taylor took up his station opposite
Matamoras, where the Mexican army was, and
the Mexicans finally attacked Fort Brown, which
Taylor had erected opposite one of their batteries.
On May 7 Taylor started to relieve the fort, with
a force of twenty-one hundred men, and at noon
next day found the Mexican army, six thousand
strong, drawn up before him at Palo Alto. Taylor
ordered Lieutenant Blake to reconnoitre the ene-
my's position.

THE GUNS IN THE GRASS

[May 8, 1846]

As hang two mighty thunderclouds
　Ere lightnings link the twain,
So lie we and the Mexican
　On Palo Alto plain;
And silence, solemn, dread, profound,
Broods o'er the waiting battle-ground.

We see the foeman's musketeers
　Deployed upon his right,
And on his left the cavalry
　Stand, hungry for the fight;
But that blank centre — what? Alas.
'T is hidden by the prairie grass!

Old Rough and Ready scans the foe;
  "I would I knew," says he,
"Whether or no that lofty grass
  Conceals artillery.
Could I but bring that spot in ken,
'T were worth to me five thousand men!"

Then forward steps Lieutenant Blake,
  Touches his hat, and says,
"I wait command to ride and see
  What 'neath that prairie lays."
We stand amazed: no cowards, we:
But this is more than bravery!

"'Command'!" cries Taylor; "nay, I ne'er
  To such a deed 'command!'"
Then bends he o'er his horse's neck
  And takes as brave a hand
As e'er a loyal sabre bore:
"God bless you, Blake," he says — no more.

The soldier to his saddle springs
  And gayly waves good-by,
Determination on his lips,
  A proud light in his eye:
And then, as pity holds our breath,
We see him dare that road of death.

To utmost pace his steed he spurs.
  Save that his sword hangs free,
It were as though a madman charged
  A nation's chivalry!
On, on, he flies, his steed unreined
Till yonder hillock's crest is gained.

And now he checks his horse, dismounts,
  And coolly through his glass
Surveys the phalanx of the foe
  That lies beyond the grass.
A musket-flash! They move! Advance!
Halt! — 't was the sunlight on a lance!

He turns, remounts, and speeds him back.
  Hark! what is that we hear?
Across the rolling prairie rings —
  A gun? ah, no — a cheer!
A noble tribute sweeps the plain:
A thousand throats take up the strain.

Safe! But the secret to unveil
  Taylor no longer seeks;
For with a roar that shakes the earth
  That unmasked centre speaks!
'Gainst fearful odds, till set of sun,
We battle — and the field is won!
                    THOMAS FROST.

Blake brought back with him an accurate description of the disposition of the Mexican forces, and Taylor resolved to attack, despite the odds against him. His artillery did great execution, and gradually advanced, as the Mexicans were forced back. Charge after charge was repulsed, and the Mexicans finally withdrew to Resaca de la Palma. There Taylor attacked them next day, routed them, and marched on to relieve Fort Brown.

RIO BRAVO — A MEXICAN LAMENT

[May 8, 1846]

RIO BRAVO! Rio Bravo!
  Saw men ever such a sight?
Since the field of Roncesvalles
  Sealed the fate of many a knight.

Dark is Palo Alto's story,
  Sad Reseca Palma's rout,
On those fatal fields so gory,
  Many a gallant life went out.

There our best and bravest lances
  Shivered 'gainst the Northern steel,
Left the valiant hearts that couched them
  'Neath the Northern charger's heel.

Rio Bravo! Rio Bravo!
  Minstrel ne'er knew such a fight
Since the field of Roncesvalles
  Sealed the fate of many a knight.

Rio Bravo, fatal river,
  Saw ye not while red with gore,
Torrejon all headless quiver,
  A ghastly trunk upon thy shore!

Heard you not the wounded coursers
  Shrieking on your trampled banks,
As the Northern winged artillery
  Thundered on our shattered ranks!

There Arista, best and bravest,
  There Raguena, tried and true,
On the fatal field thou lavest,
  Nobly did all men could do.

Vainly there those heroes rally,
  Castile on Montezuma's shore,
"Rio Bravo" — "Roncesvalles,"
  Ye are names blent evermore.

Weepest thou, lorn lady Inez,
  For thy lover 'mid the slain,

Brave La Vega's trenchant falchion
  Cleft his slayer to the brain.

Brave La Vega who all lonely,
  By a host of foes beset,
Yielded up his sabre only
  When his equal there he met.

Other champions not less noted
  Sleep beneath that sullen wave;
Rio Bravo, thou hast floated
  An army to an ocean grave.

On they came, those Northern horsemen,
  On like eagles toward the sun,
Followed then the Northern bayonet,
  And the field was lost and won.

Oh! for Orlando's horn to rally
  His Paladins on that sad shore,
"Rio Bravo" — "Roncesvalles,"
  Ye are names blent evermore.
        Translated by CHARLES FENNO HOFF-
      MAN from the Spanish of DON JOSE
      DE SALTILLO.

These brilliant victories served to kindle enthu-
siasm for the war throughout the whole country.
Congress authorized the enlistment of fifty thou-
sand volunteers, and reinforcements were promptly
started to General Taylor at Matamoras.

TO ARMS

[1846]

AWAKE! arise, ye men of might!
  The glorious hour is nigh, —
Your eagle pauses in his flight,
  And screams his battle-cry.

From North to South, from East to West:
  Send back an answering cheer,
And say farewell to peace and rest,
  And banish doubt and fear.

Arm! arm! your country bids you arm!
  Fling out your banners free —
Let drum and trumpet sound alarm,
  O'er mountains, plain, and sea.

March onward from th' Atlantic shore,
  To Rio Grande's tide —
Fight as your fathers fought of yore!
  Die as your fathers died!

Go! vindicate your country's fame,
  Avenge your country's wrong!
The sons should own a deathless name,
  To whom such sires belong.

The kindred of the noble dead
  As noble deeds should dare:
The fields whereon their blood was shed
  A deeper stain must bear.

To arms! to arms! ye men of might;
  Away from home, away!
The first and foremost in the fight
  Are sure to win the day!
        PARK BENJAMIN.

By the last of August, Taylor had whipped his
army into shape, and began to advance on Mon-
terey, a town believed to be impregnable, and
where General Arista had collected an army of
ten thousand men. The American army reached
the town September 19; and after two days' des-
perate fighting the town surrendered.

MONTEREY

[September 23, 1846]

WE were not many, we who stood
  Before the iron sleet that day:
Yet many a gallant spirit would
Give half his years if but he could
  Have been with us at Monterey.

Now here, now there, the shot is hail'd
  In deadly drifts of fiery spray,
Yet not a single soldier quail'd
When wounded comrades round them wail'd
  Their dying shout at Monterey.

And on — still on our column kept
  Through walls of flame its withering
      way;
Where fell the dead, the living stept,
Still charging on the guns which swept
  The slippery streets of Monterey.

The foe himself recoil'd aghast,
  When, striking where he strongest lay,
We swoop'd his flanking batteries past,
And braving full their murderous blast,
  Storm'd home the towers of Monterey.

Our banners on those turrets wave,
  And there our evening bugles play:

Where orange-boughs above their grave
Keep green the memory of the brave
  Who fought and fell at Monterey.

We are not many — we who press'd
  Beside the brave who fell that day —
But who of us has not confess'd
He'd rather share their warrior rest
  Than not have been at Monterey?
      CHARLES FENNO HOFFMAN.

The city had cost the Americans five hundred
in killed and wounded; but the Mexican loss was
nearly twice as great. Among the American dead
was Victor Galbraith, a bugler in a company of
volunteer cavalry, who was shot for disobeying
orders.

VICTOR GALBRAITH

[September 23, 1846]

UNDER the walls of Monterey
At daybreak the bugles began to play,
      Victor Galbraith!
In the mist of 'he morning damp and gray,
These were the words they seemed to say:
      "Come forth to thy death,
      Victor Galbraith!"

Forth he came, with a martial tread;
Firm was his step, erect his head;
      Victor Galbraith,
He who so well the bugle played,
Could not mistake the words it said:
      "Come forth to thy death,
      Victor Galbraith!"

He looked at the earth, he looked at the
      sky,
He looked at the files of musketry,
      Victor Galbraith!
And he said, with a steady voice and eye,
"'Take good aim; I am ready to die!'"
      Thus challenges death
      Victor Galbraith.

Twelve fiery tongues flashed straight and
      red,
Six leaden balls on their errand sped;
      Victor Galbraith
Falls to the ground, but he is not dead:
His name was not stamped on those balls of
      lead,
      And they only scath
      Victor Galbraith.

Three balls are in his breast and brain,
But he rises out of the dust again,
      Victor Galbraith!
The water he drinks has a bloody stain;
"Oh, kill me, and put me out of my pain!"
      In his agony prayeth
      Victor Galbraith.

Forth dart once more those tongues of flame,
And the bugler has died a death of shame,
      Victor Galbraith!
His soul has gone back to whence it came,
And no one answers to the name
      When the Sergeant saith,
      "Victor Galbraith!"

Under the walls of Monterey
By night a bugle is heard to play,
      Victor Galbraith!
Through the mist of the valley damp and gray
The sentinels hear the sound, and say,
      "That is the wraith
      Of Victor Galbraith!"
      HENRY WADSWORTH LONGFELLOW.

Further reinforcements were hurried forward
to General Taylor. Santa Anna had collected a
great army, and Taylor fell back to Angostura,
near the village of Buena Vista. There, on Febru-
ary 22, Santa Anna summoned him to surrender,
stating that he was surrounded by twenty thou-
sand men and could not avoid defeat. Taylor tartly
refused, and Santa Anna advanced to the attack,
only to be routed after a desperate two days'
struggle.

BUENA VISTA

[February 22–23, 1847]

FROM the Rio Grande's waters to the icy lakes
      of Maine,
Let all exult! for we have met the enemy
      again;
Beneath their stern old mountains we have
      met them in their pride,
And rolled from BUENA VISTA back the bat-
      tle's bloody tide;
Where the enemy came surging swift, like the
      Mississippi's flood,
And the reaper, Death, with strong arms
      swung his sickle red with blood.

SANTANA boasted loudly that, before two
      hours were past,
His Lancers through Saltillo should pursue u
      fierce and fast: —

On comes his solid infantry, line marching
after line;
Lo! their great standards in the sun like
sheets of silver shine:
With thousands upon thousands, — yea, with
more than three to one, —
Their forests of bright bayonets fierce-flashing
in the sun.

Lo! Guanajuato's regiment; Morelos' boasted
corps,
And Guadalajara's chosen troops! — all
veterans tried before.
Lo! galloping upon the right four thousand
lances gleam,
Where, floating in the morning wind, their
blood-red pennons stream;
And here his stern artillery climbs up the
broad plateau:
To-day he means to strike at us an overwhelm-
ing blow.

Now, WOOL, hold strongly to the heights! for,
lo! the mighty tide
Comes, thundering like an avalanche, deep,
terrible, and wide.
Now, ILLINOIS, stand steady! Now, KEN-
TUCKY, to their aid!
For a portion of our line, alas! is broken and
dismayed:
Great bands of shameless fugitives are fleeing
from the field,
And the day is lost, if Illinois and brave Ken-
tucky yield.

One of O'Brien's guns is gone! — On, on
their masses drift,
Till their cavalry and infantry outflank us on
the left;
Our light troops, driven from the hills, retreat
in wild dismay,
And round us gather, thick and dark, the
Mexican array.
SANTANA thinks the day is gained; for, now
approaching near,
MIÑON's dark cloud of Lancers sternly men-
aces our rear.

Now, LINCOLN, gallant gentleman, lies dead
upon the field,
Who strove to stay those cravens, when before
the storm they reeled.
Fire, WASHINGTON, fire fast and true! Fire,
SHERMAN, fast and far!
Lo! BRAGG comes thundering to the front, to
breast the adverse war!

SANTANA thinks the day is gained! On, on his
masses crowd,
And the roar of battle swells again more ter-
rible and loud.

NOT YET! Our brave old General comes to
regain the day;
KENTUCKY, to the rescue! MISSISSIPPI, to
the fray!
Again our line advances! Gallant DAVIS
fronts the foe,
And back before his rifles, in red waves the
Lancers flow.
Upon them yet once more, ye brave! The
avalanche is stayed!
Back roll the Aztec multitudes, all broken and
dismayed.

Ride! MAY! — To Buena Vista! for the
Lancers gain our rear,
And we have few troops there to check their
vehement career.
Charge, ARKANSAS! KENTUCKY, charge!
YELL, PORTER, VAUGHAN, are slain,
But the shattered troops cling desperately
unto that crimsoned plain;
Till, with the Lancers intermixed, pursuing
and pursued,
Westward, in combat hot and close, drifts off
the multitude.

And MAY comes charging from the hills with
his ranks of flaming steel,
While, shattered with a sudden fire, the foe
already reel:
They flee amain! — Now to the left, to stay
the torrent there,
Or else the day is surely lost, in horror and
despair!
For their hosts pour swiftly onward, like a
river in the spring,
Our flank is turned, and on our left their
cannon thundering.

Now, good Artillery! bold Dragoons! Steady,
brave hearts, be calm!
Through rain, cold hail, and thunder, now
nerve each gallant arm!
What though their shot fall round us here, yet
thicker than the hail?
We'll stand against them, as the rock stands
firm against the gale.
Lo! their battery is silenced! but our iron
sleet still showers:
They falter, halt, retreat, — Hurrah! the glo-
rious day is ours!

In front, too, has the fight gone well, where
  upon gallant LANE,
And on stout Mississippi, the thick Lancers
  charged in vain:
Ah! brave Third Indiana! you have nobly
  wiped away
The reproach that through another corps
  befell your State to-day;
For back, all broken and dismayed, before
  your storm of fire,
SANTANA's boasted chivalry, a shattered
  wreck, retire.

Now charge again, SANTANA! or the day is
  surely lost —
For back, like broken waves, along our left
  your hordes are tossed.
Still faster roar his batteries, — his whole
  reserve moves on;
More work remains for us to do, ere the good
  fight is won.
Now for your wives and children, men! Stand
  steady yet once more!
Fight for your lives and honors! Fight as you
  never fought before!

Ho! HARDIN breasts it bravely! and heroic
  BISSELL there
Stands firm before the storm of balls that fill
  the astonished air:
The Lancers dash upon them too! The foe
  swarm ten to one:
HARDIN is slain; MCKEE and CLAY the last
  time see the sun:
And many another gallant heart, in that last
  desperate fray,
Grew cold, its last thought turning to its loved
  ones far away.

Speed, speed, Artillery! to the front! — for
  the hurricane of fire
Crushes those noble regiments, reluctant to
  retire!
Speed swiftly! Gallop! Ah! they come!
  Again BRAGG climbs the ridge,
And his grape sweeps down the swarming foe,
  as a strong man moweth sedge:
Thus baffled in their last attack, compelled
  perforce to yield,
Still menacing in firm array, their columns
  leave the field.

The guns still roared at intervals; but silence
  fell at last,
And on the dead and dying came the evening
  shadows fast.

And then above the mountains rose the cold
  moon's silver shield,
And patiently and pitying she looked upon the
  field.
While careless of his wounded, and neglectful
  of his dead,
Despairingly and sullenly by night SANTANA
  fled.

And thus on BUENA VISTA's heights a long
  day's work was done,
And thus our brave old General another battle
  won.
Still, still our glorious banner waves, unstained
  by flight or shame,
And the Mexicans among their hills still
  tremble at our name.
So, HONOR UNTO THOSE THAT STOOD! DIS-
  GRACE TO THOSE THAT FLED!
AND EVERLASTING GLORY UNTO BUENA
  VISTA'S DEAD!

ALBERT PIKE.

February 28, 1847.

THE ANGELS OF BUENA VISTA

[February 22–23, 1847]

SPEAK and tell us, our Ximena, looking north-
  ward far away,
O'er the camp of the invaders, o'er the Mexi-
  can array,
Who is losing? who is winning? are they far
  or come they near?
Look abroad, and tell us, sister, whither rolls
  the storm we hear.

"Down the hills of Angostura still the storm
  of battle rolls;
Blood is flowing, men are dying; God have
  mercy on their souls!"
Who is losing? who is winning? "Over hill
  and over plain,
I see but smoke of cannon clouding through
  the mountain rain."

Holy Mother! keep our brothers! Look,
  Ximena, look once more.
"Still I see the fearful whirlwind rolling
  darkly as before,
Bearing on, in strange confusion, friend and
  foeman, foot and horse,
Like some wild and troubled torrent sweep-
  ing down its mountain course."

Look forth once more, Ximena! "Ah! the
 smoke has rolled away;
And I see the Northern rifles gleaming down
 the ranks of gray.
Hark! that sudden blast of bugles! there the
 troop of Minon wheels;
There the Northern horses thunder, with the
 cannon at their heels.

'Jesu, pity! how it thickens! now retreat
 and now advance!
Right against the blazing cannon shivers
 Puebla's charging lance!
Down they go, the brave young riders; horse
 and foot together fall;
Like a ploughshare in the fallow, through
 them ploughs the Northern ball."

Nearer came the storm and nearer, rolling
 fast and frightful on!
Speak, Ximena, speak and tell us, who has
 lost, and who has won?
"Alas! alas! I know not; friend and foe to-
 gether fall,
O'er the dying rush the living: pray, my
 sisters, for them all!

"Lo! the wind the smoke is lifting. Blessed
 Mother, save my brain!
I can see the wounded crawling slowly out
 from heaps of slain.
Now they stagger, blind and bleeding; now
 they fall, and strive to rise;
Hasten, sisters, haste and save them, lest they
 die before our eyes!

'O my heart's love! O my dear one! lay thy
 poor head on my knee;
Dost thou know the lips that kiss thee? Canst
 thou hear me? canst thou see?
O my husband, brave and gentle! O my
 Bernal, look once more
On the blessed cross before thee! Mercy!
 mercy! all is o'er!"

Dry thy tears, my poor Ximena; lay thy dear
 one down to rest;
Let his hands be meekly folded, lay the cross
 upon his breast;
Let his dirge be sung hereafter, and his funeral
 masses said;
To-day, thou poor bereaved one, the living
 ask thy aid.

Close beside her, faintly moaning, fair and
 young, a soldier lay,
Torn with shot and pierced with lances, bleed-
 ing slow his life away;
But, as tenderly before him the lorn Ximena
 knelt,
She saw the Northern eagle shining on his
 pistol-belt.

With a stifled cry of horror straight she turned
 away her head;
With a sad and bitter feeling looked she back
 upon her dead;
But she heard the youth's low moaning, and
 his struggling breath of pain,
And she raised the cooling water to his parch-
 ing lips again.

Whispered low the dying soldier, pressed her
 hand and faintly smiled;
Was that pitying face his mother's? did she
 watch beside her child?
All his stranger words with meaning her
 woman's heart supplied;
With her kiss upon his forehead, "Mother!"
 murmured he, and died!

"A bitter curse upon them, poor boy, who led
 thee forth,
From some gentle, sad-eyed mother, weeping,
 lonely, in the North!"
Spake the mournful Mexic woman, as she laid
 him with her dead,
And turned to soothe the living, and bind the
 wounds which bled

Look forth once more, Ximena! "Like a
 cloud before the wind
Rolls the battle down the mountains, leaving
 blood and death behind;
Ah! they plead in vain for mercy; in the dust
 the wounded strive;
Hide your faces, holy angels! O thou Christ
 of God, forgive!"

Sink, O Night, among thy mountains! let the
 cool, gray shadows fall;
Dying brothers, fighting demons, drop thy
 curtain over all!
Through the thickening winter twilight, wide
 apart the battle rolled,
In its sheath the sabre rested, and the cannon's
 lips grew cold.

But the noble Mexic women still their holy
    task pursued,
Through that long, dark night of sorrow,
    worn and faint and lacking food.
Over weak and suffering brothers, with a ten-
    der care they hung,
And the dying foeman blessed them in a
    strange and Northern tongue.

Not wholly lost, O Father! is this evil world
    of ours;
Upward, through its blood and ashes, spring
    afresh the Eden flowers;
From its smoking hell of battle, Love and
    Pity send their prayer,
And still thy white-winged angels hover dimly
    in our air!
        JOHN GREENLEAF WHITTIER.

The American forces in this memorable battle
totalled 4691, while the Mexicans mustered over
23,000 men. The Mexican losses exceeded 2500.
The Americans lost 264 killed and 450 wounded.
Theodore O'Hara's famous poem was written to
commemorate them.

THE BIVOUAC OF THE DEAD

THE muffled drum's sad roll has beat
    The soldier's last tattoo;
No more on Life's parade shall meet
    That brave and fallen few.
On Fame's eternal camping-ground
    Their silent tents are spread,
And Glory guards, with solemn round,
    The bivouac of the dead.

No rumor of the foe's advance
    Now swells upon the wind;
No troubled thought at midnight haunts
    Of loved ones left behind;
No vision of the morrow's strife
    The warrior's dream alarms;
No braying horn nor screaming fife
    At dawn shall call to arms.

Their shivered swords are red with rust;
    Their plumèd heads are bowed;
Their haughty banner, trailed in dust,
    Is now their martial shroud.
And plenteous funeral tears have washed
    The red stains from each brow,
And the proud forms, by battle gashed,
    Are free from anguish now.

The neighing troop, the flashing blade,
    The bugle's stirring blast,

The charge, the dreadful cannonade,
    The din and shout are past;
Nor war's wild note, nor glory's peal,
    Shall thrill with fierce delight
Those breasts that nevermore may feel
    The rapture of the fight.

Like the fierce northern hurricane
    That sweeps his great plateau,
Flushed with the triumph yet to gain,
    Came down the serried foe.
Who heard the thunder of the fray
    Break o'er the field beneath,
Knew well the watchword of that day
    Was "Victory or Death."

Long had the doubtful conflict raged
    O'er all that stricken plain,
For never fiercer fight had waged
    The vengeful blood of Spain;
And still the storm of battle blew,
    Still swelled the gory tide;
Not long our stout old chieftain knew,
    Such odds his strength could bide.

'T was in that hour his stern command
    Called to a martyr's grave
The flower of his belovèd land,
    The nation's flag to save.
By rivers of their fathers' gore
    His first-born laurels grew,
And well he deemed the sons would pour
    Their lives for glory too.

Full many a norther's breath has swept,
    O'er Angostura's plain —
And long the pitying sky has wept
    Above its mouldered slain.
The raven's scream or eagle's flight
    Or shepherd's pensive lay,
Alone awakes each sullen height
    That frowned o'er that dread fray.

Sons of the Dark and Bloody ground,
    Ye must not slumber there,
Where stranger steps and tongues resound
    Along the heedless air.
Your own proud land's heroic soil
    Shall be your fitter grave;
She claims from war his richest spoil —
    The ashes of her brave.

Thus 'neath their parent turf they rest,
    Far from the gory field

Borne to a Spartan mother's breast
  On many a bloody shield;
The sunshine of their native sky
  Smiles sadly on them here,
And kindred eyes and hearts watch by
  The heroes' sepulchre.

Rest on, embalmed and sainted dead!
  Dear as the blood ye gave,
No impious footstep here shall tread
  The herbage of your grave;
Nor shall your story be forgot,
  While Fame her record keeps,
Or Honor points the hallowed spot
  Where Valor proudly sleeps.

Yon marble minstrel's voiceless stone
  In deathless song shall tell
When many a vanished age hath flown,
  The story how ye fell;
Nor wreck, nor change, nor winter's blight,
  Nor Time's remorseless doom,
Shall dim one ray of glory's light
  That gilds your deathless tomb.
                        THEODORE O'HARA.

Despite the victories, the war continued unpopular in New England, and particularly in Massachusetts. In the campaign of 1847, Caleb Cushing, who had raised a regiment at his own expense and taken it to Mexico, was nominated by the Democrats for governor, but was defeated by George Nixon Briggs, his Whig opponent, by a majority of fourteen thousand.

WHAT MR. ROBINSON THINKS

[1847]

GUVENER B. is a sensible man;
  He stays to his home an' looks arter his
    folks;
He draws his furrer ez straight ez he can,
  An' into nobody's tater-patch pokes;
        But John P.
        Robinson he
    Sez he wunt vote fer Guvener B.

My! aint it terrible? Wut shall we du?
  We can't never choose him o' course, —
    thet's flat;
Guess we shell hev to come round, (don't you?)
  An' go in fer thunder an' guns, an' all that;
        Fer John P.
        Robinson he
    Sez he wunt vote fer Guvener B.

Gineral C. is a dreffle smart man:
  He's ben on all sides thet give places or
    pelf;
But consistency still wuz a part of his plan, —
  He's ben true to *one* party, — an' thet is
    himself; —
        So John P.
        Robinson he
    Sez he shall vote fer Gineral C.

Gineral C. he goes in fer the war;
  He don't vally princerple more'n an old cud;
Wut did God make us raytional creeturs fer,
  But glory an' gunpowder, plunder an'
    blood?
        So John P.
        Robinson he
    Sez he shall vote fer Gineral C.

We were gittin' on nicely up here to our vil-
    lage,
  With good old idees o' wut's right an' wut
    aint,
We kind o' thought Christ went agin war an'
    pillage,
  An' thet eppyletts worn't the best mark of
    a saint;
        But John P.
        Robinson he
    Sez this kind o' thing's an exploded idee.

The side of our country must ollers be took,
  An' Presidunt Polk, you know, *he* is our
    country.
An' the angel thet writes all our sins in a book
  Puts the *debit* to him, an' to us the *per
    contry* ;
        An' John P.
        Robinson he
    Sez this is his view o' the thing to a T.

Parson Wilbur he calls all these argiments
    lies;
  Sez they're nothin' on airth but jest *fee,
    faw, fum* ;
An' thet all this big talk of our destinies
  Is half on it ign'ance, an' t'other half rum;
        But John P.
        Robinson he
    Sez it aint no sech thing; an', of course,
      so must we.

Parson Wilbur sez *he* never heerd in his life
  Thet th' Apostles rigged out in their swaller-
    tail coats,

An' marched round in front of a drum an' a
      fife,
  To git some on 'em office, an' some on 'em
      votes;
          But John P.
          Robinson he
  Sez they did n't know everythin' down in
      Judee.

Wal, it's a marcy we've gut folks to tell us
  The rights an' the wrongs o' these matters,
      I vow, —
God sends country lawyers, an' other wise
      fellers,
  To start the world's team wen it gits in a
      slough;
          Fer John P.
          Robinson he
  Sez the world 'll go right, ef he hollers out
      Gee!

            JAMES RUSSELL LOWELL.

On March 9, 1847, General Winfield Scott arrived
off Vera Cruz with twelve thousand men to march
against the City of Mexico. On April 18 he met
and defeated Santa Anna's army at Cerro Gordo.
On August 20 he arrived before the City of Mexico,
and, after an ill-advised armistice, advanced to
storm the city on September 8. He chose the ap-
proach guarded by the formidable works of Malino
del Rey and Chapultepec. The former was carried
by assault, after a fierce hand-to-hand battle.

BATTLE OF THE KING'S MILL

[September 8, 1847]

SAID my landlord, white-headed Gil Gomez,
  With newspaper held in his hand —
"So they've built from El Paso a railway
  That Yankees may visit our land.
As guests let them come and be welcome,
  But not as they came here before;
They are rather rough fellows to handle
  In the rush of the battle and roar.

"They took Vera Cruz and its castle;
  In triumph they marched through the land;
We fought them with desperate daring,
  But lacked the right man to command.
They stormed, at a loss, Cerro Gordo —
  Every mile in their movement it cost;
And when they arrived at Puebla,
  Some thousands of men they had lost.

"Ere our capital fell, and the city
  By foreign invaders was won,

We called out among its defenders
  Each man who could handle a gun.
Chapultepec stood in their pathway;
  Churubusco they had to attack;
The mill of the King — well, I fought there,
  And they were a hard nut to crack.

"While their right was assailing the ramparts,
  Our force struck their left on the field,
Where our colonel, in language that stirred us,
  To love of our country appealed.
And we swore that we never would falter
  Before either sabre or ball;
We would beat back the foeman before us,
  Or dead on the battle-field fall.

"Fine words, you may say, but we meant
      them;
  And so when they came up the hill,
We poured on them volley on volley,
  And riddled their ranks with a will.
Their line in a moment was broken;
  They closed it, and came with a cheer;
But still we fired quickly and deadly,
  And felt neither pity nor fear.

"We smote the blue column with grape-shot,
  But it rushed as the wild torrent runs;
At the pieces they slew our best gunners,
  And took in the struggle our guns.
We sprang in a rage to retake them,
  And lost nearly half of our men;
Then, baffled and beaten, retreated,
  And gained our position again.

"Ceased their yell, and in spite of our firing
  They dressed like an arrow in line,
Then, standing there moveless a moment,
  Their eyes flashed with purpose malign,
All still as the twilight in summer,
  No cloud on the sky to deform,
Like the lull in the voices of nature
  Ere wakens the whirlwind and storm.

"We had fought them with death-daring spirit,
  And courage unyielding till then;
No man could have forced us to falter,
  But these were more demons than men.
Our ranks had been torn by their bullets,
  We filled all the gaps they had made;
But the pall of that terrible silence
  The hearts of our boldest dismayed.

"Before us no roaring of cannon,
  Rifle-rattle, or musketry peal;

But there on the ocean of battle
　Surged steady the billow of steel.
Fierce we opened our fire on the column,
　We pierced it with ball here and there;
But it swept on in pitiless sternness
　Till we faltered and fled in despair.

"After that all their movements were easy;
　At their storming Chapultepec fell,
And that ended the war — we were beaten:
　No story is left me to tell.
And now they come back to invade us,
　Though not with the bullet and blade;
They are here with their goods on a railway,
　To conquer the country by trade."
　　　　　　THOMAS DUNN ENGLISH.

Chapultepec still remained, and on the morning
of September 13 two storming parties rushed it,
swarmed over the garrison, swept back the garrison,
and planted the American flag on the ramparts.
The Mexican army hastened to evacuate the city,
and on September 14 the Stars and Stripes floated
over the capital of Mexico.

THE SIEGE OF CHAPULTEPEC

[September 13, 1847]

WIDE o'er the valley the pennons are flutter-
　　ing,
War's sullen story the deep guns are mutter-
　　ing,
Forward! blue-jackets, in good steady order,
Strike for the fame of your good northern
　　border;
Forever shall history tell of the bloody check
Waiting the foe at the siege of Chapultepec.

Let the proud deeds of your fathers inspire ye
　　still,
Think ye of Monmouth, and Princeton, and
　　Bunker Hill,
Come from your hallowed graves, famous in
　　story,
Shades of our heroes, and lead us to glory.
Side by side, son and father with hoary head
Struggle for triumph, or death on a gory bed.

Hark! to the charge! the war-hail is pattering,
The foe through our ranks red rain is scat-
　　tering;
Huzza! forward! no halting or flagging till
Proudly the red stripes float o'er yon rocky
　　hill.

Northern and Southerner, let your feuds
　　smolder;
Charge! for our banner's fame, shoulder to
　　shoulder!

Flash the fort guns, and thunders their stun-
　　ning swell
Far o'er the valley to white Popocatapetl,
Death revels high in the midst of the bloody
　　sport,
Bursting in flame from each black-throated
　　castle-port,
Press on the line with keen sabres dripping
　　wet,
Cheer, as ye smite with the death-dealing
　　bayonet!

Our bold Northern eagle. king of the firma-
　　ment,
Shares with no rival the skies of the conti-
　　nent.
Yields the fierce foeman; down let his flag be
　　hurled,
Shout, as our own from the turret is wide
　　unfurled!
Shout! for long shall Mexico mourn the wreck
Of her proud state at the siege of Chapultepec.
　　　　　　WILLIAM HAINES LYTLE.

While these victories were being won in Mexico,
General Stephen W. Kearny, at the head of the
Army of the West, had seized the territory of
New Mexico, and established a civil government
at Santa Fé. He then proceeded to California,
defeated the Mexicans at Sacramento, and took
possession of that province.

ILLUMINATION FOR VICTORIES
IN MEXICO

LIGHT up thy homes, Columbia,
　For those chivalric men
Who bear to scenes of warlike strife
　Thy conquering arms again,
Where glorious victories, flash on flash,
　Reveal their stormy way, —
Resaca's, Palo Alto's fields,
　The heights of Monterey!

They pile with thousands of thy foes
　Buena Vista's plain;
With maids and wives, at Vera Cruz,
　Swell high the list of slain!
They paint upon the Southern skies
　The blaze of burning domes, —

Their laurels dew with blood of babes!
　Light up, light up thy homes!

Light up your homes, O fathers!
　For those young hero bands,
Whose march is still through vanquished
　　towns,
　And over conquered lands!
Whose valor, wild, impetuous,
　In all its fiery glow,
Pours onward like a lava-tide,
　And sweeps away the foe!

For those whose dead brows glory crowns,
　On crimson couches sleeping,
And for home faces wan with grief,
　And fond eyes dim with weeping.
And for the soldier, poor, unknown,
　Who battled, madly brave,
Beneath a stranger soil to share
　A shallow, crowded grave.

Light up thy home, young mother!
　Then gaze in pride and joy
Upon those fair and gentle girls,
　That eagle-eyed young boy;
And clasp thy darling little one
　Yet closer to thy breast,
And be thy kisses on its lips
　In yearning love impressed.

In yon beleaguered city
　Were homes as sweet as thine;
Where trembling mothers loved arms
　In fear around them twine, —
The lad with brow of olive hue,
　The babe like lily fair,
The maiden with her midnight eyes,
　And wealth of raven hair.

The booming shot, the murderous shell,
　Crashed through the crumbling walls,
And filled with agony and death
　Those sacred household halls!
Then, bleeding, crushed, and blackened, lay
　The sister by the brother,
And the torn infant gasped and writhed
　On the bosom of the mother!

O sisters, if ye have no tears
　For fearful tales like these,
If the banners of the victors veil
　The victim's agonies,

If ye lose the babe's and mother's cry
　In the noisy roll of drums,
If your hearts with martial pride throb high,
　Light up, light up your homes!
　　　　　　　　GRACE GREENWOOD.

The Mexican people knew themselves defeated,
and were eager for peace. The treaty was finally
signed February 2, 1848. Mexico accepted the
Rio Grande as her northern boundary, and ceded
New Mexico and California to the United States.
For this territory the United States was to pay
her $15,000,000, and to assume debts to the
amount of $3,500,000.

THE CRISIS

ACROSS the Stony Mountains, o'er the desert's
　　drouth and sand,
The circles of our empire touch the western
　　ocean's strand;
From slumberous Timpanogos to Gila, wild
　　and free,
Flowing down from Nuevo-Leon to Califor-
　　nia's sea;
And from the mountains of the east, to Santa
　　Rosa's shore,
The eagles of Mexitli shall beat the air no
　　more.

O Vale of Rio Bravo! Let thy simple chil-
　　dren weep;
Close watch about their holy fire let maids of
　　Pecos keep;
Let Taos send her cry across Sierra Madre's
　　pines,
And Santa Barbara toll her bells amidst her
　　corn and vines;
For lo! the pale land-seekers come, with
　　eager eyes of gain,
Wide scattering, like the bison herds on broad
　　Salada's plain.

Let Sacramento's herdsmen heed what sound
　　the winds bring down
Of footsteps on the crisping snow, from cold
　　Nevada's crown!
Full hot and fast the Saxon rides, with rein
　　of travel slack,
And, bending o'er his saddle, leaves the sun-
　　rise at his back;
By many a lonely river, and gorge of fir and
　　pine,
On many a wintry hill-top, his nightly camp
　　fires shine.

O countrymen and brothers! that land of
lake and plain,
Of salt wastes alternating with valleys fat
with grain;
Of mountains white with winter, looking
downward, cold, serene,
On their feet with spring-vines tangled and
lapped in softest green;
Swift through whose black volcanic gates,
o'er many a sunny vale,
Wind-like the Arapahoe sweeps the bison's
dusty trail!

Great spaces yet untravelled, great lakes
whose mystic shores
The Saxon rifle never heard, nor dip of Saxon
oars;
Great herds that wander all unwatched, wild
steeds that none have tamed,
Strange fish in unknown streams, and birds
the Saxon never named;
Deep mines, dark mountain crucibles, where
Nature's chemic powers
Work out the Great Designer's will; all these
ye say are ours!

Forever ours! for good or ill, on us the burden
lies:
God's balance, watched by angels, is hung
across the skies.
Shall Justice, Truth, and Freedom turn the
poised and trembling scale?
Or shall the Evil triumph, and robber Wrong
prevail?
Shall the broad land o'er which our flag in
starry splendor waves,
Forego through us its freedom, and bear the
tread of slaves?

The day is breaking in the East of which the
prophets told,
And brightens up the sky of Time the
Christian Age of Gold;
Old Might to Right is yielding, battle blade
to clerkly pen,
Earth's monarchs are her peoples, and her
serfs stand up as men;
The isles rejoice together, in a day are nations
born,
And the slave walks free in Tunis, and by
Stamboul's Golden Horn!

Is this, O countrymen of mine! a day for us
to sow
The soil of new-gained empire with slavery's
seeds of woe?

To feed with our fresh life-blood the Old
World's cast-off crime,
Dropped, like some monstrous early birth,
from the tired lap of Time?
To run anew the evil race the old lost nations
ran,
And die like them of unbelief of God, and
wrong of man?

Great Heaven! Is this our mission? End
in this the prayers and tears,
The toil, the strife, the watchings of our
younger, better years?
Still as the Old World rolls in light, shall ours
in shadow turn,
A beamless Chaos, cursed of God, through
outer darkness borne?
Where the far nations looked for light a
blackness in the air?
Where for words of hope they listened, the
long wail of despair?

The Crisis presses on us; face to face with us
it stands,
With solemn lips of question, like the Sphinx
in Egypt's sands!
This day we fashion Destiny, our web of Fate
we spin;
This day for all hereafter choose we holiness
or sin;
Even now from starry Gerizim, or Ebal's
cloudy crown,
We call the dews of blessing or the bolts of
cursing down!

By all for which the martyrs bore their agony
and shame;
By all the warning words of truth with which
the prophets came;
By the Future which awaits us; by all the
hopes which cast
Their faint and trembling beams across the
blackness of the Past;
And by the blessed thought of Him who for
Earth's freedom died,
O my people! O my brothers! let us choose
the righteous side.

So shall the Northern pioneer go joyful on
his way;
To wed Penobscot's waters to San Fran-
cisco's bay.
To make the rugged places smooth, and sow
the vales with grain;
And bear, with Liberty and Law, the Bible
in his train:

The mighty West shall bless the East, and sea
　　shall answer sea,
And mountain unto mountain call, Praise
　　God, for we are free!
　　　　　JOHN GREENLEAF WHITTIER.

On June 12, 1848, the last of the United States
troops left the City of Mexico. They were received
at home with the wildest enthusiasm. Never
had a nation, in modern times, fought so success-
ful a war in so short a time.

THE VOLUNTEERS

[1849]

THE Volunteers! the Volunteers!
I dream, as in the by-gone years,
I hear again their stirring cheers,
　　And see their banners shine,
What time the yet unconquered North
Pours to the wars her legions forth,
For many a wrong to strike a blow
With mailèd hand at Mexico.

The Volunteers! Ah, where are they
Who bade the hostile surges stay,
When the black forts of Monterey
　　Frowned on their dauntless line?
When, undismayed amid the shock
Of war, like Cerro Gordo's rock,
They stood, or rushed more madly on
Than tropic tempest o'er San Juan?

On Angostura's crowded field
Their shattered columns scorned to yield,

And wildly yet defiance pealed
　　Their flashing batteries' throats:
And echoed then the rifle's crack,
As deadly as when on the track
Of flying foe, of yore, its voice
Bade Orleans' dark-eyed girls rejoice.

Blent with the roar of guns and bombs,
How grandly from the dim past comes
The roll of their victorious drums,
　　Their bugle's joyous notes,
When over Mexico's proud towers,
And the fair valley's storied bowers,
Fit recompense of toil and scars,
In triumph waved their flag of stars.

Ah, comrades, of your own tried troop,
Whose honor ne'er to shame might stoop,
Of lion heart and eagle swoop,
　　But you alone remain;
On all the rest has fallen the hush
Of death; the men whose battle-rush
Was wild as sun-loosed torrent's flow
From Orizaba's crest of snow.

The Volunteers! the Volunteers!
God send us peace through all our years,
But if the cloud of war appears,
　　We'll see them once again.
From broad Ohio's peaceful side,
From where the Maumee pours its tide,
From storm-lashed Erie's wintry shore,
Shall spring the Volunteers once more.
　　　　　WILLIAM HAINES LYTLE.

CHAPTER VI

FOURTEEN YEARS OF PEACE

In his message to Congress at the opening of
the December session of 1847, President Polk
recommended, among other things, the construc-
tion of a ship canal across the Isthmus of Panama
— a recommendation which was not to bear fruit
for sixty years.

THE SHIP CANAL FROM THE AT-
LANTIC TO THE PACIFIC

AN ODE TO THE AMERICAN PEOPLE AND
THEIR CONGRESS, ON READING THE MES-
SAGE OF THE UNITED STATES PRESIDENT
IN DECEMBER, 1847

　　REND America asunder
　　And unite the Binding Sea

That emboldens man and tempers —
　　Make the ocean free.

Break the bolt that bars the passage,
That our River richly pours
Western wealth to western nations;
　　Let that sea be ours —

Ours by all the hardy whalers,
By the pointing Oregon,
By the west-impelled and working,
　　Unthralled Saxon son.

Long indeed they have been wooing,
The Pacific and his bride;

Now 't is time for holy wedding —
  Join them by the tide.

Have the snowy surfs not struggled
Many centuries in vain
That their lips might seal the Union?
  Lock them main to main.

When the mighty God of nature
Made this favored continent,
He allowed it yet unsevered,
  That a race be sent,

Able, mindful of his purpose,
Prone to people, to subdue,
And to bind the land with iron,
  Or to force it through.

What the prophet-navigator,
Seeking straits to his Catais,
But began, now consummate it —
  Make the strait and pass.

Blessed the eyes that shall behold it,
When the pointing boom shall veer,
Leading through the parted Andes,
  While the nations cheer!

There at Suez, Europe's mattock
Cuts the briny road with skill,
And must Darien bid defiance
  To the pilot still?

Do we breathe this breath of Knowledge
Purely to enjoy its zest?
Shall the iron arm of science
  Like a sluggard rest?

Up then, at it! earnest people!
Bravely wrought thy scorning blade,
But there's fresher fame in store yet,
  Glory for the spade.

What we want is naught in envy,
And for all we pioneer;
Let the keels of every nation
  Through the isthmus steer.

Must the globe be always girded
Ere we get to Bramah's priest?
Take the tissues of your Lowells
  Westward to the East.

Ye, that vanquish pain and distance,
Ye, enmeshing Time with wire,

Court ye patiently forever
  Yon Antarctic ire?

Shall the mariner forever
Double the impending capes,
While his longsome and retracing
  Needless course he shapes?

What was daring for our fathers,
To defy those billows fierce,
Is but tame for their descendants;
  We are bid to pierce.

Ye that fight with printing armies,
Settle sons on forlorn track,
As the Romans flung their eagles,
  But to win them back.

Who, undoubting, worship boldness,
And, if baffled, bolder rise,
Shall we lag when grandeur beckons
  To this good emprize?

Let the vastness not appal us;
Greatness is thy destiny.
Let the doubters not recall us:
  Venture suits the free.

Like a seer, I see her throning,
WINLAND strong in freedom's health,
Warding peace on both the waters,
  Widest Commonwealth.

Crowned with wreaths that still grow greener,
Guerdon for untiring pain,
For the wise, the stout, and steadfast:
  Rend the land in twain.

Cleave America asunder,
This is worthy work for thee.
Hark! The seas roll up imploring
  "Make the ocean free."

                    FRANCIS LIEBER.

  The famine in Ireland in 1847 awakened much
sympathy in the United States, and the ship
Jamestown, laden with food, was dispatched to
Cork, making a remarkably quick passage.

THE WAR SHIP OF PEACE

[1847]

SWEET land of song, thy harp doth hang
  Upon the willow now,

While famine's blight and fever's pang
　　Stamps mis'ry on thy brow;
Yet take thy harp and raise thy voice,
　　Though weak and low it be,
And let thy sinking heart rejoice
　　In friends still left to thee.

Look out! look out! across the sea
　　That girds thy em'rald shore,
A ship of war is bound to thee,
　　But with no war-like store.
Her thunders sleep; 't is mercy's breath
　　That wafts her o'er the sea;
She goes not forth to deal out death,
　　But bears new life to thee.

Thy wasted hands can scarcely strike
　　The chords of grateful praise,
Thy plaintive tone is now unlike
　　The voice of prouder days;
Yet, e'en in sorrow, tuneful still,
　　Let Erin's voice proclaim
In bardic praise on ev'ry hill
　　Columbia's glorious name.
　　　　　　　　SAMUEL LOVER.

On June 8, 1848, Henry Clay was defeated by Zachary Taylor for the Whig nomination for the presidency.

ON THE DEFEAT OF HENRY CLAY

[June 8, 1848]

FALLEN? How fallen? States and empires
　　fall;
O'er towers and rock-built walls,
And perished nations, floods to tempests call
With hollow sound along the sea of time:
　　The great man never falls.
He lives, he towers aloft, he stands sublime —
　　They fall who give him not
The honor here that suits his future name —
　　They die and are forgot.
O Giant loud and blind! the great man's fame
　　Is his own shadow and not cast by thee —
　　A shadow that shall grow
As down the heaven of time the sun descends,
　　And on the world shall throw
His god-like image, till it sinks where blends
Time's dim horizon with Eternity.
　　　　　　　WILLIAM WILBERFORCE LORD.

Margaret Fuller Ossoli, her husband, the Marquis Ossoli, and their child, were drowned off Fire Island, July 16, 1850, while returning from Europe in the ship Elizabeth. The ship was driven ashore in a storm, and broken up by the waves.

ON THE DEATH OF M. D'OSSOLI AND HIS WIFE, MARGARET FULLER

[July 16, 1850]

OVER his millions Death has lawful power,
But over thee, brave D'Ossoli! none, none.
After a longer struggle, in a fight
Worthy of Italy, to youth restored,
Thou, far from home, art sunk beneath the
　　surge
Of the Atlantic; on its shore; in reach
Of help; in trust of refuge; sunk with all
Precious on earth to thee — a child, a wife!
Proud as thou wert of her, America
Is prouder, showing to her sons how high
Swells woman's courage in a virtuous breast.
She would not leave behind her those she
　　loved;
Such solitary safety might become
Others; not her; not her who stood beside
The pallet of the wounded, when the worst
Of France and Perfidy assailed the walls
Of unsuspicious Rome. Rest, glorious soul,
Renowned for the strength of genius, Margaret!
Rest with the twain too dear! My words are
　　few,
And shortly none will hear my failing voice.
But the same language with more full appeal
Shall hail thee. Many are the sons of song
Whom thou hast heard upon thy native plains
Worthy to sing of thee: the hour is come;
Take we our seats and let the dirge begin.
　　　　　　　WALTER SAVAGE LANDOR.

The following verses from *Punch* describe various events of 1851 — the winning of the international yacht race by the America; the project for a canal across the isthmus — and comment upon the ingenuity of some Yankee inventions.

THE LAST APPENDIX TO "YANKEE DOODLE"

[*Punch*, 1851]

YANKEE DOODLE sent to Town
　　His goods for exhibition;
Everybody ran him down,
　　And laugh'd at his position.

They thought him all the world behind;
  A goney, muff, or noodle;
Laugh on, good people, — never mind —
  Says quiet Yankee Doodle.
      Chorus — Yankee Doodle, keep it up,
          Yankee Doodle Dandy!
      Mind the music and the
          step,
      And with the girls be
          handy!

Yankee Doodle had a craft,
  A rather tidy clipper,
And he challenged, while they laughed,
  The Britishers to whip her.
Their whole yacht-squadron she outsped,
  And that on their own water;
Of all the lot she went ahead,
  And they came nowhere arter.

O'er Panamà there was a scheme
  Long talked of, to pursue a
Short route — which many thought a dream —
  By Lake Nicaragua.
John Bull discussed the plan on foot,
  With slow irresolution,
While Yankee Doodle went and put
  It into execution.

A steamer of the Collins line,
  A Yankee Doodle's notion,
Has also quickest cut the brine
  Across the Atlantic Ocean.
And British Agents, no ways slow
  Her merits to discover,
Have been and bought her — just to tow
  The Cunard packets over.

Your gunsmiths of their skill may crack,
  But that again don't mention:
I guess that Colts' revolvers whack
  Their very first invention.
By Yankee Doodle, too, you're beat
  Downright in Agriculture,
With his machine for reaping wheat,
  Chawed up as by a vulture.

You also fancied, in your pride,
  Which truly is tarnation,
Them British locks of yourn defied
  The rogues of all creation;
But Chubbs' and Bramah's Hobbs has picked,
  And you must now be viewed all
As having been completely licked
  By glorious Yankee Doodle.

DANIEL WEBSTER

[Died October 24, 1852]

WHEN life hath run its largest round
  Of toil and triumph, joy and woe,
How brief a storied page is found
  To compass all its outward show!

The world-tried sailor tires and droops;
  His flag is rent, his keel forgot;
His farthest voyages seem but loops
  That float from life's entangled knot.

But when within the narrow space
  Some larger soul hath lived and wrought
Whose sight was open to embrace
  The boundless realms of deed and
      thought, —

When, stricken by the freezing blast,
  A nation's living pillars fall,
How rich the storied page, how vast,
  A word, a whisper, can recall!

No medal lifts its fretted face,
  Nor speaking marble cheats your eye;
Yet, while these pictured lines I trace,
  A living image passes by:

A roof beneath the mountain pines;
  The cloisters of a hill-girt plain;
The front of life's embattled lines;
  A mound beside the heaving main.

These are the scenes: a boy appears;
  Set life's round dial in the sun,
Count the swift arc of seventy years,
  His frame is dust; his task is done.

Yet pause upon the noontide hour,
  Ere the declining sun has laid
His bleaching rays on manhood's power,
  And look upon the mighty shade.

No gloom that stately shape can hide,
  No change uncrown his brow: behold!
Dark, calm, large-fronted, lightning-eyed,
  Earth has no double from its mould!

Ere from the fields by valor won
  The battle-smoke had rolled away,
And bared the blood-red setting sun,
  His eyes were opened on the day.

His land was but a shelving strip,
  Black with the strife that made it free;
He lived to see its banners dip
  Their fringes in the Western sea.

The boundless prairies learned his name,
  His words the mountain echoes knew;
The Northern breezes swept his fame
  From icy lake to warm bayou.

In toil he lived; in peace he died;
  When life's full cycle was complete,
Put off his robes of power and pride,
  And laid them at his Master's feet.

His rest is by the storm-swept waves
  Whom life's wild tempests roughly tried,
Whose heart was like the streaming caves
  Of ocean, throbbing at his side.

Death's cold white hand is like the snow
  Laid softly on the furrowed hill,
It hides the broken seams below,
  And leaves the summit brighter still.

In vain the envious tongue upbraids;
  His name a nation's heart shall keep
Till morning's latest sunlight fades
  On the blue tablet of the deep!
            OLIVER WENDELL HOLMES.

In 1854 a survey was ordered of the Isthmus of
Darien, and Lieutenant Isaac G. Strain was placed
in charge of the work. His party was reduced to
great extremities in crossing the isthmus, but bore
their sufferings with a heroism seldom surpassed.

THE FLAG

AN INCIDENT OF STRAIN'S EXPEDITION

[1854]

I NEVER have got the bearings quite,
  Though I've followed the course for many
    a year,
If he was crazy, clean outright,
  Or only what you might say was "queer."

He was just a simple sailor man.
  I mind it as well as yesterday,
When we messed aboard of the old Cyane.
  Lord! how the time does slip away!
That was five and thirty year ago,
  And I never expect such times again,

For sailors was n't afraid to stow
  Themselves on a Yankee vessel then.
He was only a sort of bosun's mate,
  But every inch of him taut and trim;
Stars and anchors and togs of state
  Tailors don't build for the like of him.
He flew a no-account sort of name,
  A reg'lar fo'castle "Jim" or "Jack,"
With a plain "McGinnis" abaft the same,
  Giner'ly reefed to simple "Mack."
Mack, we allowed, was sorter queer, —
  Ballast or compass was n't right.
Till he licked four Juicers one day, a fear
  Prevailed that he had n't larned to fight.
But I reckon the Captain knowed his man,
  When he put the flag in his hand the day
That we went ashore from the old Cyane,
  On a madman's cruise for Darien Bay.

Forty days in the wilderness
  We toiled and suffered and starved with
    Strain,
Losing the number of many a mess
  In the Devil's swamps of the Spanish Main.
All of us starved, and many died.
  One laid down, in his dull despair;
His stronger messmate went to his side —
  We left them both in the jungle there.
It was hard to part with shipmates so;
  But standing by would have done no good.
We heard them moaning all day, so slow
  We dragged along through the weary wood.
McGinnis, he suffered the worst of all;
  Not that he ever piped his eye
Or would n't have answered to the call
  If they 'd sounded it for "All hands to die."
I guess 't would have sounded for him before,
  But the grit inside of him kept him strong,
Till we met relief on the river shore;
  And we all broke down when it came along.

All but McGinnis. Gaunt and tall,
  Touching his hat, and standing square:
" Captain, the Flag." — And that was all;
  He just keeled over and foundered there.
"The Flag?" We thought he had lost his
    head —
  It might n't be much to lose at best —
Till we came, by and by, to dig his bed,
  And we found it folded around his breast.
He laid so calm and smiling there,
  With the flag wrapped tight about his heart,
Maybe he saw his course all fair,
  Only — we could n't read the chart.
            JAMES JEFFREY ROCHE.

On February 16, 1857, Elisha Kent Kane, explorer of the Arctic, died at Havana, Cuba, whither he had gone in the hope of regaining a health shattered by his sufferings in the north.

KANE

ALOFT upon an old basaltic crag,
  Which, scalp'd by keen winds that defend the Pole,
  Gazes with dead face on the seas that roll
Around the secret of the mystic zone,
A mighty nation's star-bespangled flag
    Flutters alone,
And underneath, upon the lifeless front
  Of that drear cliff, a simple name is traced;
Fit type of him who, famishing and gaunt,
  But with a rocky purpose in his soul,
    Breasted the gathering snows,
    Clung to the drifting floes,
By want beleaguer'd, and by winter chased,
Seeking the brother lost amid that frozen waste.

Not many months ago we greeted him,
  Crown'd with the icy honors of the North,
  Across the land his hard-won fame went forth,
And Maine's deep woods were shaken limb by limb;
His own mild Keystone State, sedate and prim,
  Burst from decorous quiet as he came;
Hot Southern lips with eloquence aflame
Sounded his triumph. Texas, wild and grim,
Proffer'd its horny hand. The large-lung'd West,
    From out its giant breast,
Yell'd its frank welcome. And from main to main,
    Jubilant to the sky,
    Thunder'd the mighty cry,
    HONOR TO KANE!

In vain, in vain beneath his feet we flung
  The reddening roses! All in vain we pour'd
  The golden wine, and round the shining board
Sent the toast circling, till the rafters rung
  With the thrice-tripled honors of the feast!
Scarce the buds wilted and the voices ceased
Ere the pure light that sparkled in his eyes,
Bright as auroral fires in Southern skies,
  Faded and faded! And the brave young heart
That the relentless Arctic winds had robb d

Of all its vital heat, in that long quest
For the lost captain, now within his breast
  More and more faintly throbb'd.
His was the victory; but as his grasp
Closed on the laurel crown with eager clasp,
    Death launch'd a whistling dart;
And ere the thunders of applause were done
His bright eyes closed forever on the sun!
Too late, too late the splendid prize he won
In the Olympic race of Science and of Art!
Like to some shatter'd berg that, pale and lone,
Drifts from the white North to a tropic zone,
    And in the burning day
    Wastes peak by peak away,
    Till on some rosy even
It dies with sunlight blessing it; so he
Tranquilly floated to a Southern sea,
    And melted into heaven.

He needs no tears, who lived a noble life;
  We will not weep for him who died so well,
  But we will gather round the hearth, and tell
The story of his strife;
  Such homage suits him well,
  Better than funeral pomp or passing bell.
What tale of peril and self-sacrifice!
Prison'd amid the fastnesses of ice,
  With hunger howling o'er the wastes of snow!
  Night lengthening into months, the ravenous floe
Crunching the massive ships, as the white bear
Crunches his prey. The insufficient share
    Of loathsome food,
The lethargy of famine, the despair
  Urging to labor, nervelessly pursued,
  Toil done with skinny arms, and faces hued
Like pallid masks, while dolefully behind
Glimmer'd the fading embers of a mind!
That awful hour, when through the prostrate band
Delirium stalk'd, laying his burning hand
  Upon the ghastly foreheads of the crew.
  The whispers of rebellion, faint and few
At first, but deepening ever till they grew
Into black thoughts of murder; such the throng
Of horrors bound the hero. High the song
Should be that hymns the noble part he play'd!
Sinking himself, yet ministering aid
    To all around him. By a mighty will
    Living defiant of the wants that kill,

Because his death would seal his comrades'
     fate;
  Cheering with ceaseless and inventive skill
Those Polar waters, dark and desolate.
Equal to every trial, every fate,
     He stands, until Spring, tardy with relief,
          Unlocks the icy gate,
And the pale prisoners thread the world once
     more,
To the steep cliffs of Greenland's pastoral
     shore
          Bearing their dying chief.

Time was when he should gain his spurs of
     gold
     From royal hands, who woo'd the knightly
          state;
The knell of old formalities is toll'd,
     And the world's knights are now self-con-
          secrate.
No grander episode doth chivalry hold
     In all its annals, back to Charlemagne,
     Than that lone vigil of unceasing pain,
Faithfully kept through hunger and through
     cold,
     By the good Christian knight, ELISHA KANE!
          FITZ-JAMES O'BRIEN.

On September 12, 1857, the Central America was
lost at sea in a great storm off Cape Hatteras. Cap-
tain William Lewis Herndon, of the navy, was in
command. His tranquil courage preserved disci-
pline up to the last, and until his passengers, offi-
cers, and crew were all in the boats. Seeing that the
last boat was already overloaded, Captain Herndon
refused to add to its danger, and, ordering it off,
went down with his ship.

HERNDON

[September 12, 1857]

AY, shout and rave, thou cruel sea,
     In triumph o'er that fated deck,
Grown holy by another grave —
     Thou hast the captain of the wreck.

No prayer was said, no lesson read,
     O'er him; the soldier of the sea:
And yet for him, through all the land,
     A thousand thoughts to-night shall be.

And many an eye shall dim with tears,
     And many a cheek be flushed with pride;
And men shall say, There died a man,
     And boys shall learn how well he died.

Ay, weep for him, whose noble soul
     Is with the God who made it great;
But weep not for so proud a death, —
     We could not spare so grand a fate.

Nor could Humanity resign
     That hour which bade her heart beat high,
And blazoned Duty's stainless shield,
     And set a star in Honor's sky.

O dreary night! O grave of hope!
     O sea, and dark, unpitying sky!
Full many a wreck these waves shall claim
     Ere such another heart shall die.

Alas, how can we help but mourn
     When hero bosoms yield their breath!
A century itself may bear
     But once the flower of such a death;

So full of manliness, so sweet
     With utmost duty nobly done;
So thronged with deeds, so filled with life,
     As though with death that life begun.

It *has* begun, true gentleman!
     No better life we ask for thee;
Thy Viking soul and woman heart
     Forever shall a beacon be, —

A starry thought to veering souls,
     To teach it is not best to live;
To show that life has naught to match
     Such knighthood as the grave can give.
          S. WEIR MITCHELL.

In 1857 Commodore Josiah Tattnall was ap-
pointed flag-officer of the Asiatic station, and,
finding China at war with the allied English and
French fleets, went to the scene of operations at
Pei-ho. Just before an engagement, his flagship
grounded and was towed off by the English boats;
and when he saw the English in trouble shortly
afterwards, he sailed in to their assistance, ex-
claiming, "Blood is thicker than water!"

BLOOD IS THICKER THAN WATER

[June 25, 1859]

EBBED and flowed the muddy Pei-Ho by the
     gulf of Pechili,
     Near its waters swung the yellow dragon-flag;
Past the batteries of China, looking westward
     we could see
     Lazy junks along the lazy river lag;

Villagers in near-by Ta-Kou toiled beneath
their humble star,
On the flats the ugly mud fort lay and
dreamed;
While the Powhatan swung slowly at her
station by the bar,
While the Toey-Wan with Tattnall onward
steamed.

Lazy East and lazy river, fort of mud in lazy
June,
English gunboats through the waters slowly
fare,
With the dragon-flag scarce moving in the
lazy afternoon
O'er the mud-heap storing venom in the
glare.
We were on our way to Peking, to the Son of
Heaven's throne,
White with peace was all our mission to his
court,
Peaceful, too, the English vessels on the turbid
stream bestrown
Seeking passage up the Pei-Ho past the fort.

By the bar lay half the English, while the rest,
with gallant Hope,
Wrestled with the slipping ebb-tide up the
stream;
They had cleared the Chinese irons, reached
the double chain and rope,
Where the ugly mud fort scowled upon their
beam —
Boom ! the heavens split asunder with the
thunder of the fight
As the hateful dragon made its faith a mock;
Every cannon spat its perfidy, each casemate
blazed its spite,
Crashing down upon the English, shock
on shock.

In his courage Rason perished, brave Mc-
Kenna fought and fell;
Scores were dying as they'd lived, like
valiant men;
And the meteor flag that upward prayed to
Heaven from that hell,
Wept below for those who ne'er should
weep again.
Far away the English launches near the Pow-
hatan swung slow,
All despairing, useless, out of reach of war,
Knew their comrades in the battle, felt them
reel beneath the blow,
Lying helpless 'gainst the ebb-tide by the bar.

On the Toey-Wan stood Tattnall, Stephen
Trenchard by his side —
"Old Man" Tattnall, he who dared at Vera
Cruz, —
Saw here, crippled by the cannon; saw there,
throttled by the tide,
Men of English blood and speech — could
he refuse ?
I'll be damned, says he to Trenchard, if old
Tattnall's standing by,
Seeing white men butchered here by such a foe.
Where's my barge ? No side-arms, mind you !
See those English fight and die —
Blood is thicker, sir, than water. Let us go.

Quick we man the boat, and quicker plunge
into that devil's brew —
"An official call," and Tattnall went in
state.
Trenchard's hurt, our flag in ribbons, and the
rocking barge shot through,
Hart, our coxswain, dies beneath the Chi-
nese hate;
But the cheers those English give us as we
gain their Admiral's ship
Make the shattered boat and weary arms
seem light —
Then the rare smile from "Old" Tattnall,
and Hope's hearty word and grip,
Lying wounded, bleeding, brave in hell's
despite.

Tattnall nods, and we go forward, find a gun
no longer fought —
What is peace to us when all its crew lie
dead ?
One bright English lad brings powder and a
wounded man the shot,
And we scotch that Chinese dragon, tail and
head.
Hands are shaken, faith is plighted, sounds
our Captain's cheery call,
In a British boat we speed us fast and far;
And the Toey-Wan and Tattnall down the
ebb-tide slide and fall
To the launches lying moaning by the bar.

Eager for an English vengeance, battle-light
on every face,
See the Clustered Stars lead on the Triple
Cross !
Cheering, swinging into action, valiant Hope
takes heart of grace
From the cannon's cloudy roar, the lan-
yards' toss

How they fought, those fighting English!
  How they cheered the Toey-Wan,
  Cheered our sailors, cheered "Old" Tatt-
    nall, grim and gray!
And their cheers ring down the ages as they
    rang beneath the sun
  O'er those bubbling, troubled waters far
    away.

Ebbs and flows the muddy Pei-Ho by the gulf
    of Pechili,
  Idly floats beside the stream the dragon-flag;
Past the batteries of China, looking westward
    still you see
  Lazy junks along the lazy river lag.
Let the long, long years drip slowly on that
    lost and ancient land,
  Ever dear one scene to hearts of gallant men;
There's a hand-clasp and a heart-throb,
    there's a word we understand:
  Blood is thicker, sir, than water, now as then.
                        WALLACE RICE.

In the fall of 1860 the Prince of Wales, travel-
ling as Baron Renfrew, paid a visit to the United
States, lasting from September 21 to October 20.
He was the recipient of many attentions, and a
great ball was given in his honor at the Academy
of Music in New York city. While the ball was in
progress, a portion of the floor gave way, but no
one was injured.

BARON RENFREW'S BALL

[October, 1860]

'T WAS a grand display was the prince's ball,
A pageant or fête, or what you may call
    A brilliant coruscation,
Where ladies and knights of noble worth
Enchanted a prince of royal birth
    By a royal demonstration.

Like queens arrayed in their regal guise,
They charmed the prince with dazzling eyes,
    Fair ladies of rank and station,
Till the floor gave way, and down they
    sprawled,
In a tableaux style, which the artists called
    A floor-all decoration.

At the prince's feet like flowers they were laid,
In the brightest bouquet ever made,
    For a prince's choice to falter —
Perplexed to find, where all were rare,
Which was the fairest of the fair
    To cull for a queenly altar.

But soon the floor was set aright,
And Peter Cooper's face grew bright,
    When, like the swell of an organ,
All hearts beat time to the first quadrille,
And the prince confessed to a joyous thrill
    As he danced with Mrs. Morgan.

Then came the waltz — the Prince's Own —
And every bar and brilliant tone
    Had music's sweetest grace on;
But the prince himself ne'er felt its charm
Till he slightly clasped, with circling arm,
    That lovely girl, Miss Mason.

But ah! the work went bravely on,
And meek-eyed Peace a trophy won
    By the magic art of the dancers;
For the daring prince's next exploit
Was to league with Scott's Camilla Hoyt,
    And overcome the Lancers.

Besides these three, he deigned to yield
His hand to Mrs. M. B. Field,
    Miss Jay and Miss Van Buren;
Miss Russell, too, was given a place —
All beauties famous for their grace
    From Texas to Lake Huron.

With Mrs. Kernochan he "lanced,"
With Mrs. Edward Cooper danced,
    With Mrs. Belmont capered;
With fair Miss Fish, in fairy rig,
He tripped a sort of royal jig,
    And next Miss Butler favored.

And thus, 'mid many hopes and fears,
By the brilliant light of the chandeliers,
    Did they gayly quaff and revel;
Well pleased to charm a royal prince —
The only one from old England since
    George Washington was a rebel.

And so the fleeting hours went by,
And watches stopped — lest Time should fly —
    Or that they winding wanted;
Old matrons dozed, and papas smiled,
And many a fair one was beguiled
    As the prince danced on, undaunted.

'T is now a dream — the prince's ball,
Its vanished glories, one and all,
    The scenes of the fairy tales;
For Cinderella herself was there,
And Barnum keeps for trial fair
The beautiful slipper deposited there
    By his highness, the Prince of Wales.
                CHARLES GRAHAM HALPINE.

PART IV

THE CIVIL WAR

BATTLE-HYMN OF THE REPUBLIC

MINE eyes have seen the glory of the coming of the Lord:
He is trampling out the vintage where the grapes of wrath are stored;
He hath loosed the fateful lightning of his terrible swift sword:
　　His truth is marching on.

I have seen Him in the watch-fires of a hundred circling camps;
They have builded Him an altar in the evening dews and damps;
I can read his righteous sentence by the dim and flaring lamps.
　　His day is marching on.

I have read a fiery gospel, writ in burnished rows of steel:
"As ye deal with my contemners, so with you my grace shall deal;
Let the Hero, born of woman, crush the serpent with his heel,
　　Since God is marching on."

He has sounded forth the trumpet that shall never call retreat;
He is sifting out the hearts of men before his judgment-seat:
Oh! be swift, my soul, to answer Him! be jubilant, my feet!
　　Our God is marching on.

In the beauty of the lilies Christ was born across the sea,
With a glory in his bosom that transfigures you and me:
As He died to make men holy, let us die to make men free,
　　While God is marching on.

JULIA WARD HOWE.

CHAPTER I

THE SLAVERY QUESTION

Negro slavery in the United States began in 1619, when a cargo of Africans was sold in Virginia. It gradually spread to all the states, but by the beginning of the nineteenth century it had been abolished in Massachusetts, Pennsylvania, New Hampshire, Connecticut, Rhode Island, Vermont, New York, and New Jersey. The ordinance of 1787 forbade slavery in the Northwest; but the purchase of Louisiana in 1803 added greatly to slave territory. The fight over the admission of Missouri (1817–21), resulting in the "Missouri Compromise," did much to intensify bitterness of feeling. Finally, in December, 1833, the American Anti-Slavery Society was organized at Philadelphia, with a platform of principles formulated by William Lloyd Garrison.

TO WILLIAM LLOYD GARRISON

[Read at the Convention which formed the American Anti-Slavery Society, in Philadelphia. December, 1833.]

CHAMPION of those who groan beneath
    Oppression's iron hand:
In view of penury, hate, and death,
    I see thee fearless stand.
Still bearing up thy lofty brow,
    In the steadfast strength of truth,
In manhood sealing well the vow
    And promise of thy youth.

Go on, for thou hast chosen well;
    On in the strength of God!
Long as one human heart shall swell
    Beneath the tyrant's rod.
Speak in a slumbering nation's ear,
    As thou hast ever spoken,
Until the dead in sin shall hear,
    The fetter's link be broken!

I love thee with a brother's love,
    I feel my pulses thrill,
To mark thy spirit soar above
    The cloud of human ill.
My heart hath leaped to answer thine,
    And echo back thy words,
As leaps the warrior's at the shine
    And flash of kindred swords!

They tell me thou art rash and vain,
    A searcher after fame;

That thou art striving but to gain
    A long-enduring name;
That thou hast nerved the Afric's hand
    And steeled the Afric's heart,
To shake aloft his vengeful brand,
    And rend his chain apart.

Have I not known thee well, and read
    Thy mighty purpose long?
And watched the trials which have made
    Thy human spirit strong?
And shall the slanderer's demon breath
    Avail with one like me,
To dim the sunshine of my faith
    And earnest trust in thee?

Go on, the dagger's point may glare
    Amid thy pathway's gloom;
The fate which sternly threatens there
    Is glorious martyrdom!
Then onward with a martyr's zeal;
    And wait thy sure reward
When man to man no more shall kneel,
    And God alone be Lord!
                JOHN GREENLEAF WHITTIER.

Branches of this society multiplied rapidly, and in order to counteract their influence, a great pro-slavery meeting was held at Charleston, S. C., September 4, 1835. The newspaper report that "the clergy of all denominations attended in a body, lending their sanction to the proceedings, and adding by their presence to the impressive character of the scene," drew a fiery protest from Whittier.

CLERICAL OPPRESSORS

[September 4, 1835]

JUST God! and these are they
Who minister at thine altar, God of Right!
Men who lay their hands with prayer and blessing
        lay
    On Israel's Ark of light!

What! preach, and kidnap men?
Give thanks, and rob thy own afflicted poor?
Talk of thy glorious liberty, and then
    Bolt hard the captive's door?

What! servants of thy own
Merciful Son, who came to seek and save
The homeless and the outcast, fettering down
    The tasked and plundered slave!

Pilate and Herod, friends!
Chief priests and rulers, as of old, combine!
Just God and holy! is that church, which lends
    Strength to the spoiler, thine?

Paid hypocrites, who turn
Judgment aside, and rob the Holy Book
Of those high words of truth which search and burn
    In warning and rebuke;

Feed fat, ye locusts, feed!
And, in your tasselled pulpits, thank the Lord
That, from the toiling bondman's utter need,
    Ye pile your own full board.

How long, O Lord! how long
Shall such a priesthood barter truth away,
And in Thy name, for robbery and wrong
    At Thy own altars pray?

Is not Thy hand stretched forth
Visibly in the heavens, to awe and smite?
Shall not the living God of all the earth,
    And heaven above, do right?

Woe, then, to all who grind
Their brethren of a common Father down!
To all who plunder from the immortal mind
    Its bright and glorious crown!

Woe to the priesthood! woe
To those whose hire is with the price of blood;
Perverting, darkening, changing, as they go,
    The searching truths of God!

Their glory and their might
Shall perish; and their very names shall be
Vile before all the people, in the light
    Of a world's liberty.

Oh, speed the moment on
When Wrong shall cease, and Liberty and Love
And Truth and Right throughout the earth be known
    As in their home above.
        JOHN GREENLEAF WHITTIER.

In April, 1848, an attempt was made to abduct seventy-seven slaves from Washington in the schooner Pearl. The slaves were speedily recaptured and sold South, while their defenders barely escaped with their lives from an infuriated mob. The Abolitionists in Congress determined to evoke from that body some expression of sentiment on the subject. On the 20th of April Senator Hale introduced a resolution implying sympathy with the negroes. It stirred the slaveholders to unusual intemperance of language.

THE DEBATE IN THE SENNIT

SOT TO A NUSRY RHYME

[April 20, 1848]

"HERE we stan' on the Constitution, by thunder!
  It's a fact o' wich ther's bushels o' proofs;
Fer how could we trample on 't so, I wonder,
  Ef 't worn't thet it's ollers under our hoofs?"
    Sez John C. Calhoun, sez he;
      "Human rights haint no more
      Right to come on this floor,
    No more'n the man in the moon," sez he.

"The North haint no kind o' bisness with nothin',
  An' you've no idee how much bother it saves;
We aint none riled by their frettin' an' frothin',
  We're *used* to layin' the string on our slaves,"
    Sez John C. Calhoun, sez he; —
    Sez Mister Foote,
    "I should like to shoot
    The holl gang, by the gret horn spoon!"
    sez he.

"Freedom's keystone is Slavery, thet ther's no doubt on,
  It's sutthin' thet's — wha' d' ye call it? — divine, —
An' the slaves thet we ollers *make* the most out on
  Air them north o' Mason an' Dixon's line,"
    Sez John C. Calhoun, sez he; —
    "Fer all thet," sez Mangum,
    "'T would be better to hang 'em
    An' so git red on 'em soon," sez he.

"The mass ough' to labor an' we lay on soffies,
  Thet's the reason I want to spread Freedom's aree;

It puts all the cunninest on us in office,
  An' reelises our Maker's orig'nal idee,"
    Sez John C. Calhoun, sez he; —
      "Thet's ez plain," sez Cass,
      "Ez thet some one's an ass,
    It's ez clear ez the sun is at noon," sez he.

"Now don't go to say I'm the friend of op-
      pression,
  But keep all your spare breath fer coolin'
      your broth,
Fer I ollers hev strove (at least thet's my im-
      pression)
  To make cussed free with the rights o' the
      North,"
    Sez John C. Calhoun, sez he; —
      "Yes," sez Davis o' Miss.,
      "The perfection o' bliss
    Is in skinnin' thet same old coon," sez
      he.

"Slavery's a thing thet depends on com-
      plexion,
  It's God's law thet fetters on black skins
      don't chafe;
Ef brains wuz to settle it (horrid reflection!)
  Wich of our onnable body'd be safe?"
    Sez John C. Calhoun, sez he; —
      Sez Mister Hannegan,
      Afore he began agin,
    "Thet exception is quite oppertoon,"
      sez he.

"Gen'nle Cass, Sir, you need n't be twitchin'
      your collar,
  Your merit's quite clear by the dut on your
      knees,
At the North we don't make no distinctions
      o' color;
  You can all take a lick at our shoes wen
      you please,"
    Sez John C. Calhoun, sez he; —
      Sez Mister Jarnagin,
      "They wun't hev to larn agin,
    They all on 'em know the old toon," sez
      he.

"The slavery question aint no ways bewil-
      derin',
  North an' South hev one int'rest, it's plain
      to a glance;
No'thern men, like us patriarchs, don't sell
      their childrin,
  But they du sell themselves, ef they git a
      good chance,"

    Sez John C. Calhoun, sez he; —
      Sez Atherton here,
      "This is gittin' severe,
    I wish I could dive like a loon," sez
      he.

"It'll break up the Union, this talk about
      freedom,
  An' your fact'ry gals (soon ez we split) 'll
      make head,
An' gittin' some Miss chief or other to lead 'em,
  'll go to work raisin' permiscoous Ned,"
    Sez John C. Calhoun, sez he; —
      "Yes, the North," sez Colquitt,
      "Ef we Southeners all quit,
    Would go down like a busted balloon,"
      sez he.

"Jest look wut is doin', wut annyky's brewin'
  In the beautiful clime o' the olive an' vine.
All the wise aristoxy's atumblin' to ruin,
  An' the sankylot's drorin' an' drinkin
      their wine,"
    Sez John C. Calhoun, sez he; —
      "Yes," sez Johnson, "in France
      They're beginnin' to dance
    Beëlzebub's own rigadoon," sez he.

"The South's safe enough, it don't feel a
      mite skeery,
  Our slaves in their darkness an' dut air tu
      blest
Not to welcome with proud hallylugers the ery
  Wen our eagle kicks yourn from the nay-
      tional nest,"
    Sez John C. Calhoun, sez he; —
      "Oh," sez Westcott o' Florida,
      "Wut treason is horrider
    Than our priv'leges tryin' to proon?"
      sez he.

"It's 'coz they're so happy, thet, wen crazy
      sarpints
  Stick their nose in our bizness, we git so
      darned riled;
We think it's our dooty to give pooty sharp
      hints,
  Thet the last crumb of Eden on airth sha'n't
      be spiled,"
    Sez John C. Calhoun, sez he; —
      "Ah," sez Dixon H. Lewis,
      "It perfectly true is
    Thet slavery's airth s grettest boon,"
      sez he.

                    JAMES RUSSELL LOWELL.

On March 7, 1850, Daniel Webster delivered in the Senate his famous speech on slavery, in which he declared for the exclusion of slavery from new territory, but called attention to the pledge which had been given to permit slavery south of the line of 36° 30', and gave his support to the fugitive slave bill introduced by a Virginia senator. The speech created a sensation; Webster was overwhelmed with abuse, and made the target for one of the greatest poems of denunciation in the language.

ICHABOD

[March 7, 1850]

So fallen! so lost! the light withdrawn
　　Which once he wore!
The glory from his gray hairs gone
　　Forevermore!

Revile him not, the Tempter hath
　　A snare for all;
And pitying tears, not scorn and wrath,
　　Befit his fall!

Oh, dumb be passion's stormy rage,
　　When he who might
Have lighted up and led his age,
　　Falls back in night.

Scorn! would the angels laugh, to mark
　　A bright soul driven,
Fiend-goaded, down the endless dark,
　　From hope and heaven!

Let not the land once proud of him
　　Insult him now.
Nor brand with deeper shame his dim,
　　Dishonored brow.

But let its humbled sons, instead,
　　From sea to lake,
A long lament, as for the dead,
　　In sadness make.

Of all we loved and honored, naught
　　Save power remains;
A fallen angel's pride of thought,
　　Still strong in chains.

All else is gone; from those great eyes
　　The soul has fled;
When faith is lost, when honor dies,
　　The man is dead!

Then, pay the reverence of old days
　　To his dead fame;

Walk backward, with averted gaze,
　　And hide the shame!
　　　　JOHN GREENLEAF WHITTIER.

The feeling at the North against slavery was soon intensified in bitterness by the execution of the fugitive slave law, which, in a way, made Northern states participants in the detested traffic. On April 3, 1851, a fugitive slave named Thomas Sims was arrested at Boston, adjudged to his owner, and put on board a vessel bound for Savannah. Other efforts to enforce the law proved abortive, and it was soon evident that it was, to all intents and purposes, a dead letter.

THE KIDNAPPING OF SIMS

[April 3, 1851]

SOULS of the patriot dead
On Bunker's height who bled!
　　The pile, that stands
On your long-buried bones —
Those monumental stones —
Should not suppress the groans
　　This day demands.

For Freedom there ye stood;
There gave the earth your blood;
　　There found your graves;
That men of every clime,
Faith, color, tongue, and time,
Might, through your death sublime,
　　Never be slaves.

Over your bed, so low,
Heard ye not, long ago,
　　A voice of power
Proclaim to earth and sea,
That where ye sleep should be
A home for Liberty
　　Till Time's last hour?

Hear ye the chains of slaves,
Now clanking round your graves?
　　Hear ye the sound
Of that same voice that calls
From out our Senate halls,
"Hunt down those fleeing thralls,
　　With horse and hound!"

That voice your sons hath swayed!
'T is heard, and is obeyed!
　　This gloomy day
Tells you of ermine stained,
Of Justice's name profaned,
Of a poor bondman chained
　　And borne away!

Over Virginia's Springs,
Her eagles spread their wings,
　　Her Blue Ridge towers —
That voice — once heard with awe —
Now asks, "Who ever saw,
Up there, a higher law
　　Than this of ours?"

Must we obey that voice?
When God or man's the choice,
　　Must we postpone
Him, who from Sinai spoke?
Must we wear slavery's yoke?
Bear of her lash the stroke,
　　And prop her throne?

Lashed with her hounds, must we
Run down the poor who flee
　　From Slavery's hell?
Great God! when we do this
Exclude us from thy bliss;
At us let angels hiss
　　From heaven that fell!
　　　　　　JOHN PIERPONT.

Abolition agitation was given new fuel when, on May 30, 1854, Congress passed the famous Kansas-Nebraska Bill, setting off the southern portion of Nebraska into a new territory called Kansas, and leaving the question of slavery or no-slavery to be decided by its inhabitants. The fight for Kansas began at once. Slaveholders from Missouri poured into the new territory, and in New England an Emigrant Aid Society was formed, which started large parties of Free-Soilers to Kansas. The first party started in July, 1854, and John G. Whittier sent them a hymn, which was sung over and over during the long journey.

THE KANSAS EMIGRANTS

[July, 1854]

WE cross the prairie as of old
　　The pilgrims crossed the sea,
To make the West, as they the East,
　　The homestead of the free!

We go to rear a wall of men
　　On Freedom's southern line,
And plant beside the cotton-tree
　　The rugged Northern pine!

We're flowing from our native hills
　　As our free rivers flow:
The blessing of our Mother-land
　　Is on us as we go.

We go to plant her common schools
　　On distant prairie swells,
And give the Sabbaths of the wild
　　The music of her bells.

Upbearing, like the Ark of old,
　　The Bible in our van,
We go to test the truth of God
　　Against the fraud of man.

No pause, nor rest, save where the streams
　　That feed the Kansas run,
Save where our Pilgrim gonfalon
　　Shall flout the setting sun!

We'll tread the prairie as of old
　　Our fathers sailed the sea,
And make the West, as they the East,
　　The homestead of the free!
　　　　　　JOHN GREENLEAF WHITTIER.

The pro-slavery men soon resorted to violence. In December fifteen hundred Missourians laid siege to Lawrence, where most of the Free-Soilers had settled. The Free-Soilers threw up earth-works and mustered six hundred men to defend them, among them John Brown and his four sons from Osawatomie. One Free-Soiler, Thomas Barber, was killed under discreditable circumstances; but the Missourians were persuaded to withdraw before there were further hostilities.

BURIAL OF BARBER

[December 6, 1855]

BEAR him, comrades, to his grave;
Never over one more brave
　　Shall the prairie grasses weep,
In the ages yet to come,
When the millions in our room,
　　What we sow in tears, shall reap.

Bear him up the icy hill,
With the Kansas, frozen still
　　As his noble heart, below,
And the land he came to till
With a freeman's thews and will,
　　And his poor hut roofed with snow!

One more look of that dead face,
Of his murder's ghastly trace!
　　One more kiss, O widowed one!
Lay your left hands on his brow,
Lift your right hands up, and vow
　　That his work shall yet be done.

Patience, friends! The eye of God
Every path by Murder trod
  Watches, lidless, day and night;
And the dead man in his shroud,
And his widow weeping loud,
  And our hearts, are in His sight.

Every deadly threat that swells
With the roar of gambling hells,
  Every brutal jest and jeer,
Every wicked thought and plan
Of the cruel heart of man,
  Though but whispered, He can hear!

We in suffering, they in crime,
Wait the just award of time,
  Wait the vengeance that is due;
Not in vain a heart shall break,
Not a tear for Freedom's sake
  Fall unheeded: God is true.

While the flag with stars bedecked
Threatens where it should protect,
  And the Law shakes hands with Crime,
What is left us but to wait,
Match our patience to our fate,
  And abide the better time?

Patience, friends! The human heart
Everywhere shall take our part,
  Everywhere for us shall pray;
On our side are nature's laws,
And God's life is in the cause
  That we suffer for to-day.

Well to suffer is divine;
Pass the watchword down the line,
  Pass the countersign: "Endure."
Not to him who rashly dares,
But to him who nobly bears,
  Is the victor's garland sure.

Frozen earth to frozen breast,
Lay our slain one down to rest;
  Lay him down in hope and faith,
And above the broken sod,
Once again, to Freedom's God,
  Pledge ourselves for life or death,

That the State whose walls we lay,
In our blood and tears, to-day,
  Shall be free from bonds of shame,
And our goodly land untrod
By the feet of Slavery, shod
  With cursing as with flame!

Plant the Buckeye on his grave,
For the hunter of the slave
  In its shadow cannot rest;
And let martyr mound and tree
Be our pledge and guaranty
  Of the freedom of the West!

JOHN GREENLEAF WHITTIER.

Affairs in Kansas went from bad to worse.
Bands of armed emigrants poured into the state
from the south, and such disorder followed that
on August 25, 1856, the governor proclaimed the
territory in a state of insurrection. On September
14 a force of twenty-five hundred Missourians
again attacked Lawrence, but were beaten off.

THE DEFENCE OF LAWRENCE

[September 14, 1856]

ALL night upon the guarded hill,
  Until the stars were low,
Wrapped round as with Jehovah's will,
  We waited for the foe;
All night the silent sentinels
  Moved by like gliding ghosts;
All night the fancied warning bells
  Held all men to their posts.

We heard the sleeping prairies breathe,
  The forest's human moans,
The hungry gnashing of the teeth
  Of wolves on bleaching bones;
We marked the roar of rushing fires,
  The neigh of frightened steeds,
The voices as of far-off lyres
  Among the river reeds.

We were but thirty-nine who lay
  Beside our rifles then;
We were but thirty-nine, and they
  Were twenty hundred men.
Our lean limbs shook and reeled about,
  Our feet were gashed and bare,
And all the breezes shredded out
  Our garments in the air.

.   .   .   .

They came: the blessed Sabbath day,
  That soothed our swollen veins,
Like God's sweet benediction, lay
  On all the singing plains;
The valleys shouted to the sun,
  The great woods clapped their hands,
And joy and glory seemed to run
  Like rivers through the lands.

And then our daughters and our wives,
   And men whose heads were white,
Rose sudden into kingly lives
   And walked forth to the fight;
And we drew aim along our guns
   And calmed our quickening breath,
Then, as is meet for Freedom's sons,
   Shook loving hands with Death.

And when three hundred of the foe
   Rode up in scorn and pride,
Whoso had watched us then might know
   That God was on our side;
For all at once a mighty thrill
   Of grandeur through us swept,
And strong and swiftly down the hill
   Like Gideons we leapt.

And all throughout that Sabbath day
   A wall of fire we stood,
And held the baffled foe at bay,
   And streaked the ground with blood.
And when the sun was very low
   They wheeled their stricken flanks,
And passed on, wearily and slow,
   Beyond the river banks.

Beneath the everlasting stars
   We bended child-like knees,
And thanked God for the shining scars
   Of His large victories.
And some, who lingered, said they heard
   Such wondrous music pass
As though a seraph's voice had stirred
   The pulses of the grass.
              RICHARD REALF.

A bill for the admission of Kansas under a
constitution permitting slavery was introduced
in Congress in February, 1858, and occasioned one
of the most acrimonious debates ever heard at the
Capital. In the House, a fist fight occurred be-
tween Keitt of South Carolina, and Grow of
Pennsylvania. The bill was passed on May 4.

THE FIGHT OVER THE BODY OF KEITT

A FRAGMENT FROM THE GREAT AMERICAN
EPIC, THE WASHINGTONIAD

[March, 1858]

SING, O goddess, the wrath, the ontamable
   dander of Keitt —
Keitt of South Carolina, the clear grit, the
   tall, the ondaunted —

Him that hath wopped his own niggers till
   Northerners all unto Keitt
Seem but as niggers to wop, and hills of the
   smallest potatoes.
Late and long was the fight on the Constitution
   of Kansas;
Daylight passed into dusk, and dusk into
   lighting of gas-lamps; —
Still on the floor of the house the heroes un-
   wearied were fighting.
Dry grew palates and tongues with excite-
   ment and expectoration,
Plugs were becoming exhausted, and Re-
   presentatives also.
Who led on to the war the anti-Lecomptonite
   phalanx?
Grow, hitting straight from the shoulder, the
   Pennsylvania Slasher;
Him followed Hickman, and Potter the wiry,
   from woody Wisconsin;
Washburne stood with his brother, — Cad-
   wallader stood with Elihu;
Broad Illinois sent the one, and woody Wis-
   consin the other.
Mott came mild as new milk, with gray hairs
   under his broad brim,
Leaving the first chop location and water
   privilege near it,
Held by his fathers of old on the willow-
   fringed banks of Ohio.
Wrathy Covode, too, I saw, and Montgomery
   ready for mischief.
Who against these to the floor led on the
   Lecomptonite legions?
Keitt of South Carolina, the clear grit, the tall,
   the ondaunted —
Keitt and Reuben Davis, the ra'al hoss of
   wild Mississippi;
Barksdale, wearer of wigs, and Craige from
   North Carolina;
Craige and scorny McQueen, and Owen, and
   Lovejoy, and Lamar,
These Mississippi sent to the war, "*tres
   juncti in uno.*"
Long had raged the warfare of words; it was
   four in the morning;
Whittling and expectoration and liquorin' all
   were exhausted,
When Keitt, tired of talk, bespake Reu.
   Davis, "O Reuben,
Grow's a tarnation blackguard, and I've
   concluded to clinch him."
This said, up to his feet he sprang, and
   loos'ning his choker.

Straighted himself for a grip, as a b'ar-hunter
   down in Arkansas
Squares to go in at the b'ar, when the danger-
   ous varmint is cornered.
"Come out, Grow," he cried, "you Black
   Republican puppy,
Come on the floor, like a man, and darn my
   eyes, but I'll show you" —
Him answered straight-hitting Grow, "Wall
   now, I calkilate, Keitt,
No nigger-driver shall leave his plantation
   in South Carolina,
Here to crack his cow-hide round this child's
   ears, if he knows it."
Scarce had he spoke when the hand, the
   chiválrous five fingers of Keitt,
Clutched at his throat, — had they closed,
   the speeches of Grow had been
   ended, —
Never more from a stump had he stirred up
   the free and enlightened; —
But though smart Keitt's mauleys, the mauleys
   of Grow were still smarter;
Straight from the shoulder he shot, — not
   Owen Swift or Ned Adams
Ever put in his right with more delicate feeling
   of distance.
As drops hammer on anvil, so dropped Grow's
   right into Keitt
Just where the jugular runs to the point at
   which Ketch ties his drop-knot; —
Prone like a log sank Keitt, his dollars rattled
   about him.
Forth sprang his friends o'er the body; first
   Barksdale, waving-wig-wearer,
Craige and McQueen and Davis, the ra'al
   hoss of wild Mississippi;
Fiercely they gathered round Grow, cata-
   wampously up as to chaw him;
But without Potter they reckoned, the wiry
   from woody Wisconsin;
He, striking out right and left, like a cata-
   mount varmint and vicious,
Dashed to the rescue, and with him the
   Washburnes, Cadwallader, Elihu;
Slick into Barksdale's bread-basket walked
   Potter's one, two, — hard and heavy;
Barksdale fetched wind in a trice, dropped
   Grow, and let out at Elihu.
Then like a fountain had flowed the claret of
   Washburne the elder,
But for Cadwallader's care, — Cadwallader,
   guard of his brother,
Clutching at Barksdale's nob, into Chancery
   soon would have drawn it.

Well was it then for Barksdale, the wig that
   waved over his forehead:
Off in Cadwallader's hands it came, and, the
   wearer releasing,
Left to the conqueror naught but the scalp of
   his bald-headed foeman.
Meanwhile hither and thither, a dove on the
   waters of trouble,
Moved Mott, mild as new milk, with his gray
   hair under his broad brim,
Preaching peace to deaf ears, and getting
   considerably damaged.
Cautious Covode in the rear, as dubious what
   it might come to,
Brandished a stone-ware spittoon 'gainst who-
   ever might seem to deserve it, —
Little it mattered to him whether Pro- or Anti-
   Lecompton,
So but he found in the Hall a foeman worthy
   his weapon!
So raged the battle of men, till into the thick of
   the *mêlée*,
Like to the heralds of old, stepped the Ser-
   geant-at-Arms and the Speaker.

Only a few days later, on May 19, occurred an
affair which threw the country into convulsion.
A Georgian named Charles A. Hamilton gathered
together a gang of twenty-five Missourians, at-
tacked the Free-Soilers in the neighborhood of
Marais des Cygnes, took eleven prisoners, marched
them off to a gulch and shot them. The pursuit
of the assassins was so half-hearted that they all
escaped.

LE MARAIS DU CYGNE

[May 19, 1858]

A BLUSH as of roses
   Where rose never grew!
Great drops on the bunch-grass,
   But not of the dew!
A taint in the sweet air
   For wild bees to shun!
A stain that shall never
   Bleach out in the sun!

Back, steed of the prairies!
   Sweet song-bird, fly back!
Wheel hither, bald vulture!
   Gray wolf, call thy pack!
The foul human vultures
   Have feasted and fled;
The wolves of the Border
   Have crept from the dead.

From the hearths of their cabins,
The fields of their corn,
Unwarned and unweaponed,
The victims were torn, —
By the whirlwind of murder
Swooped up and swept on
To the low, reedy fen-lands,
The Marsh of the Swan.

With a vain plea for mercy
No stout knee was crooked;
In the mouths of the rifles
Right manly they looked.
How paled the May sunshine,
O Marais du Cygne!
On death for the strong life,
On red grass for green!

In the homes of their rearing,
Yet warm with their lives,
Ye wait the dead only,
Poor children and wives!
Put out the red forge-fire,
The smith shall not come;
Unyoke the brown oxen,
The ploughman lies dumb.

Wind slow from the Swan's Marsh,
O dreary death-train,
With pressed lips as bloodless
As lips of the slain!
Kiss down the young eyelids,
Smooth down the gray hairs;
Let tears quench the curses
That burn through your prayers.

Strong man of the prairies,
Mourn bitter and wild!
Wail, desolate woman!
Weep, fatherless child!
But the grain of God springs up
From ashes beneath,
And the crown of his harvest
Is life out of death.

Not in vain on the dial
The shade moves along,
To point the great contrasts
Of right and of wrong:
Free homes and free altars,
Free prairie and flood, —
The reeds of the Swan's Marsh,
Whose bloom is of blood!

On the lintels of Kansas
That blood shall not dry;
Henceforth the Bad Angel
Shall harmless go by;
Henceforth to the sunset,
Unchecked on her way,
Shall Liberty follow
The march of the day.
JOHN GREENLEAF WHITTIER.

Prominent among the Kansas Free-Soilers was
John Brown, a leader in the guerrilla warfare.
United States troops were finally thrown into the
territory to preserve peace, and Brown, looking
around for new fields, decided to strike a blow
in Virginia. On the night of October 16, 1859,
at the head of a small company, he surprised and
captured the arsenal at Harper's Ferry. He was
attacked next day by an overwhelming force of
militia and United States marines, his men either
killed or captured, and he himself taken prisoner.
He was tried for treason and murder in the first
degree, was found guilty and hanged December
2, 1859. The men who had been captured with
him were hanged a few days later.

HOW OLD BROWN TOOK HARPER'S FERRY

[October 16, 1859]

JOHN BROWN in Kansas settled, like a stead-
fast Yankee farmer,
Brave and godly, with four sons, all stal-
wart men of might.
There he spoke aloud for freedom, and the
Border-strife grew warmer,
Till the Rangers fired his dwelling, in his
absence, in the night;
And Old Brown,
Osawatomie Brown,
Came homeward in the morning — to find
his house burned down.

Then he grasped his trusty rifle and boldly
fought for freedom;
Smote from border unto border the fierce,
invading band;
And he and his brave boys vowed — so might
Heaven help and speed 'em! —
They would save those grand old prairies
from the curse that blights the land;
And Old Brown,
Osawatomie Brown,
Said, "Boys, the Lord will aid us!" and he
shoved his ramrod down.

And the Lord *did* aid these men, and they
    labored day and even,
  Saving Kansas from its peril; and their very
    lives seemed charmed,
Till the ruffians killed one son, in the blessed
    light of Heaven, —
  In cold blood the fellows slew him, as he
    journeyed all unarmed;
        Then Old Brown,
        Osawatomie Brown,
Shed not a tear, but shut his teeth, and
    frowned a terrible frown!

Then they seized another brave boy, — not
    amid the heat of battle,
  But in peace, behind his ploughshare, —
    and they loaded him with chains,
And with pikes, before their horses, even as
    they goad their cattle,
  Drove him cruelly, for their sport, and at
    last blew out his brains;
        Then Old Brown,
        Osawatomie Brown,
Raised his right hand up to Heaven, calling
    Heaven's vengeance down.

And he swore a fearful oath, by the name of
    the Almighty,
  He would hunt this ravening evil that had
    scathed and torn him so;
He would seize it by the vitals; he would
    crush it day and night; he
  Would so pursue its footsteps, so return it
    blow for blow,
        That Old Brown,
        Osawatomie Brown,
Should be a name to swear by, in backwoods
    or in town!

Then his beard became more grizzled, and
    his wild blue eye grew wilder,
  And more sharply curved his hawk's-nose,
    snuffing battle from afar;
And he and the two boys left, though the Kan-
    sas strife waxed milder,
  Grew more sullen, till was over the bloody
    Border War,
        And Old Brown,
        Osawatomie Brown,
Had gone crazy, as they reckoned by his fear-
    ful glare and frown.

So he left the plains of Kansas and their bitter
    woes behind him,
  Slipt off into Virginia, where the statesmen
    all are born,

Hired a farm by Harper's Ferry, and no one
    knew where to find him,
  Or whether he'd turned parson, or was
    jacketed and shorn;
        For Old Brown,
        Osawatomie Brown,
Mad as he was, knew texts enough to wear a
    parson's gown.

He bought no ploughs and harrows, spades
    and shovels, and such trifles;
  But quietly to his rancho there came, by
    every train,
Boxes full of pikes and pistols, and his well-
    beloved Sharp's rifles;
  And eighteen other madmen joined their
    leader there again.
        Says Old Brown,
        Osawatomie Brown,
"Boys, we've got an army large enough to
    march and take the town!

"Take the town, and seize the muskets, free
    the negroes and then arm them;
  Carry the County and the State, ay, and all
    the potent South.
On their own heads be the slaughter, if their
    victims rise to harm them —
  These Virginians! who believed not, nor
    would heed the warning mouth."
        Says Old Brown,
        Osawatomie Brown,
"The world shall see a Republic, or my name
    is not John Brown."

'T was the sixteenth of October, on the even-
    ing of a Sunday:
  "This good work," declared the captain,
    "shall be on a holy night!"
It was on a Sunday evening, and before the
    noon of Monday,
  With two sons, and Captain Stephens, fif-
    teen privates — black and white,
        Captain Brown,
        Osawatomie Brown,
Marched across the bridged Potomac, and
    knocked the sentry down;

Took the guarded armory-building, and the
    muskets and the cannon;
  Captured all the county majors and the
    colonels, one by one;
Scared to death each gallant scion of Virginia
    they ran on,
  And before the noon of Monday, I say, the
    deed was done.

Mad Old Brown,
Osawatomie Brown,
With his eighteen other crazy men, went in
and took the town.

Very little noise and bluster, little smell of
powder made he;
It was all done in the midnight, like the
Emperor's *coup d'état.*
"Cut the wires! Stop the rail-cars! Hold the
streets and bridges!" said he,
Then declared the new Republic, with him-
self for guiding star, —
This Old Brown,
Osawatomie Brown;
And the bold two thousand citizens ran off
and left the town.

Then was riding and railroading and ex-
pressing here and thither;
And the Martinsburg Sharpshooters and
the Charlestown Volunteers,
And the Shepherdstown and Winchester mili-
tia hastened whither
Old Brown was said to muster his ten
thousand grenadiers.
General Brown!
Osawatomie Brown!
Behind whose rampant banner all the North
was pouring down.

But at last, 't is said, some prisoners escaped
from Old Brown's durance,
And the effervescent valor of the Chivalry
broke out,
When they learned that nineteen madmen had
the marvellous assurance —
Only nineteen — thus to seize the place and
drive them straight about;
And Old Brown,
Osawatomie Brown,
Found an army come to take him, encamped
around the town.

But to storm, with all the forces I have men-
tioned, was too risky;
So they hurried off to Richmond for the
Government Marines,
Tore them from their weeping matrons, fired
their souls with Bourbon whiskey,
Till they battered down Brown's castle with
their ladders and machines;
And Old Brown,
Osawatomie Brown,
Received three bayonet stabs, and a cut on his
brave old crown.

Tallyho! the old Virginia gentry gather to the
baying!
In they rushed and killed the game, shooting
lustily away;
And whene'er they slew a rebel, those who
came too late for slaying,
Not to lose a share of glory, fired their bul-
lets in his clay;
And Old Brown,
Osawatomie Brown,
Saw his sons fall dead beside him, and be-
tween them laid him down.

How the conquerors wore their laurels; how
they hastened on the trial;
How Old Brown was placed, half dying, on
the Charlestown court-house floor;
How he spoke his grand oration, in the scorn
of all denial;
What the brave old madman told them, —
these are known the country o'er.
"Hang Old Brown,
Osawatomie Brown,"
Said the judge, "and all such rebels!" with
his most judicial frown.

But, Virginians, don't do it! for I tell you that
the flagon,
Filled with blood of Old Brown's offspring,
was first poured by Southern hands;
And each drop from Old Brown's life-veins,
like the red gore of the dragon,
May spring up a vengeful Fury, hissing
through your slave-worn lands!
And Old Brown,
Osawatomie Brown,
May trouble you more than ever, when you've
nailed his coffin down!
EDMUND CLARENCE STEDMAN.
November, 1859.

THE BATTLE OF CHARLESTOWN

[December 2, 1859]

FRESH palms for the Old Dominion!
New peers for the valiant Dead!
Never hath showered her sunshine
On a field of doughtier dread —
Heroes in buff three thousand,
And a single scarred gray head!

Fuss, and feathers, and flurry —
Clink, and rattle, and roar —

The old man looks around him
  On meadow and mountain hoar;
The place, he remarks, is pleasant,
  I had not seen it before.

Form, in your boldest order,
  Let the people press no nigher!
Would ye have them hear to his words —
  The words that may spread like fire?

'T is a right smart chance to test him
  (Here we are at the gallows-tree),
So knot the noose — pretty tightly —
  Bandage his eyes, and we'll see
(For we'll keep him waiting a little),
  If he tremble in nerve or knee.

There, in a string, we've got him!
  (Shall the music bang and blow?)
The chivalry wheels and marches,
  And airs its valor below.

Look hard in the blindfold visage
  (He can't look back), and inquire
(He has stood there nearly a quarter),
  If he does n't begin to tire?

Not yet! how long will he keep us,
  To see if he quail or no?
I reckon it's no use waiting,
  And 't is time that we had the show.

For the trouble — we can't see why —
  Seems with us, and not with him,
As he stands 'neath the autumn sky,
  So strangely solemn and dim!
But high let our standard flout it!
  "Sic Semper" — the drop comes down —
And (woe to the rogues that doubt it!)
  There's an end of old John Brown!
          HENRY HOWARD BROWNELL.

BROWN OF OSSAWATOMIE

[December 2, 1859]

JOHN BROWN of Ossawatomie spake on his
      dying day:
"I will not have to shrive my soul a priest in
      Slavery's pay.

But let some poor slave-mother whom I have
      striven to free,
With her children, from the gallows-stair put
      up a prayer for me!"

John Brown of Ossawatomie, they led him
      out to die;
And lo! a poor slave-mother with her little
      child pressed nigh.
Then the bold, blue eye grew tender, and the
      old harsh face grew mild,
As he stooped between the jeering ranks and
      kissed the negro's child!

The shadows of his stormy life that moment
      fell apart;
And they who blamed the bloody hand for-
      gave the loving heart.
That kiss from all its guilty means redeemed
      the good intent,
And round the grisly fighter's hair the mar-
      tyr's aureole bent!

Perish with him the folly that seeks through
      evil good!
Long live the generous purpose unstained
      with human blood!
Not the raid of midnight terror, but the thought
      which underlies;
Not the borderer's pride of daring, but the
      Christian's sacrifice.

Nevermore may yon Blue Ridges the North-
      ern rifle hear,
Nor see the light of blazing homes flash on
      the negro's spear.
But let the free-winged angel Truth their
      guarded passes scale,
To teach that right is more than might, and
      justice more than mail!

So vainly shall Virginia set her battle in array;
In vain her trampling squadrons knead the
      winter snow with clay.
She may strike the pouncing eagle, but she
      dares not harm the dove;
And every gate she bars to Hate shall open
      wide to Love!
          JOHN GREENLEAF WHITTIER.

In the North, Brown was considered a sainted
martyr — an estimate as untrue as the Southern
one — and "John Brown's Body" became the
most popular marching song in the war which

was to follow. Charles Sprague Hall is said to have been the author of the verses.

GLORY HALLELUJAH! OR JOHN BROWN'S BODY

John Brown's body lies a-mould'ring in the grave,
John Brown's body lies a-mould'ring in the grave,
John Brown's body lies a-mould'ring in the grave,
    His soul is marching on!
    Chorus — Glory! Glory Hallelujah!
           Glory! Glory Hallelujah!
           Glory! Glory Hallelujah!
           His soul is marching on.

He's gone to be a soldier in the army of the Lord!
    His soul is marching on.

John Brown's knapsack is strapped upon his back.
    His soul is marching on.

His pet lambs will meet him on the way,
    And they'll go marching on.

They'll hang Jeff Davis on a sour apple tree,
    As they go marching on.

Now for the Union let's give three rousing cheers,
    As we go marching on.
           Hip, hip, hip, hip, Hurrah!
           CHARLES SPRAGUE HALL.

A variant of the John Brown song was written by Miss Edna Dean Proctor, and is certainly more coherent and intelligible than the lines which formed a marching song for over a million men.

JOHN BROWN

John Brown died on the scaffold for the slave,
Dark was the hour when we dug his hallowed grave;
Now God avenges the life he gladly gave,
    Freedom reigns to-day!
        Glory, glory hallelujah,
        Glory, glory hallelujah,
        Glory, glory hallelujah,
        Freedom reigns to-day!

John Brown sowed and the harvesters are we;
Honor to him who has made the bondsman free;
Loved evermore shall our noble ruler be,
    Freedom reigns to-day!

John Brown's body lies mouldering in the grave;
Bright o'er the sod let the starry banner wave;
Lo! for the million he perilled all to save,
    Freedom reigns to-day!

John Brown's body through the world is marching on;
Hail to the hour when oppression shall be gone;
All men will sing in the better day's dawn,
    Freedom reigns to-day!

John Brown dwells where the battle's strife is o'er;
Hate cannot harm him, nor sorrow stir him more;
Earth will remember the martyrdom he bore,
    Freedom reigns to-day!

John Brown's body lies mouldering in the grave;
John Brown lives in the triumph of the brave;
John Brown's soul not a higher joy can crave,
    Freedom reigns to-day!
        EDNA DEAN PROCTOR.

JOHN BROWN: A PARADOX

Compassionate eyes had our brave John Brown,
And a craggy stern forehead, a militant frown;
He, the storm-bow of peace. Give him volley on volley,
The fool who redeemed us once of our folly,
And the smiter that healed us, our right John Brown!

Too vehement, verily, was John Brown!
For waiting is statesmanlike; his the renown
Of the holy rash arm, the equipper and starter
Of freedmen; aye, call him fanatic and martyr:
He can carry both halos, our plain John Brown.

A scandalous stumbling-block was John
  Brown,
And a jeer; but ah! soon from the terrified
  town,
In his bleeding track made over hilltop and
  hollow,
Wise armies and councils were eager to follow,
And the children's lips chanted our lost John
  Brown.

Star-led for us, stumbled and groped John
  Brown,
Star-led, in the awful morasses to drown;
And the trumpet that rang for a nation's up-
  heaval,
From the thought that was just, thro' the deed
  that was evil,
Was blown with the breath of this dumb John
  Brown!

Bared heads and a pledge unto mad John
  Brown!
Now the curse is allayed, now the dragon is
  down,
Now we see, clear enough, looking back at the
  onset,
Christianity's flood-tide and Chivalry's sunset
In the old broken heart of our hanged John
  Brown!

          LOUISE IMOGEN GUINEY.

The summer of 1860 swung around, and on
April 23 the National Democratic Convention
met at Charleston, S. C. Antagonism at once
developed between the delegates from the South
and from the North, the committee on resolutions
could not agree, and after a week of bitter debate
the Northern platform was adopted and the
Southern delegates withdrew in a body. It was
the first step toward secession. The convention
adjourned to meet at Baltimore, where Stephen
A. Douglas was nominated for the presidency.

LECOMPTON'S BLACK BRIGADE

A SONG OF THE CHARLESTON CONVENTION

[April 23, 1860]

SINGLE-HANDED, and surrounded by Lecomp-
  ton's black brigade,
With the treasury of a nation drained to pay
  for hireling aid;
All the weapons of corruption — the bribe,
  the threat, the lie —
All the forces of his rivals leagued to make
  this one man die,

Yet smilingly he met them, his heart and fore-
  head bare,
And they quailed beneath the lightnings of his
  blue eye's sudden glare;
For all behind him thronging the mighty
  people came,
With looks of fiery eagerness and words of
  leaping flame —
    "A Douglas and a Douglas!"
      Hark to the people's cry,
    Shaking the earth beneath their feet,
      And thundering through the sky.

Crooked and weak, but envious as the witches
  of Macbeth,
Came old and gray Buchanan a-hungering
  for his death;
And full of mortal strategy, with green and
  rheumy eyes,
John Slidell — he of Houmas — each poi-
  soned arrow tries.
With cold and stony visage, lo! Breckinridge
  is there,
While old Joe Lane keeps flourishing his rusty
  sword in air;
But still the "Little Giant" holds unmoved
  his fearless way,
While the great waves of the people behind
  him rock and sway —
    "A Douglas and a Douglas!
      No hand but his can guide,
    In such a strait, our ship of state
      Across the stormy tide."

A poisonous reptile, many-scaled and with
  most subtle fang,
Crawled forward Caleb Cushing, while behind
  his rattles rang;
And, mounted on a charger of hot and glossy
  black,
The Alabamian Yancey dashes in with fell
  attack:
Lo! Bayard is aroused, and quits his favorite
  cards and dice,
While Jeff Davis plots with Bigler full many
  a foul device;
But, smiling still, against them all their One
  Foe holds his own,
While louder still and louder, the cry behind
  has grown —
    "A Douglas and a Douglas,
      Who every base trick spurns;
    The people's will is sovereign still,
      And that to Douglas turns."

Half horse, half alligator, here from Missis-
    sippi's banks
The blatant Barry caracoles and spurs along
    the ranks;
From Arkansaw comes Burrows, with his
    "toothpick" in its sheath,
While that jaundiced Georgian, Jackson,
    shows his grim and ugly teeth;
And Barksdale barks his bitterest bark, and
    curls his stunted tail,
And snarls like forty thousand curs beneath
    a storm of hail;
But smiling now — almost a laugh — the
    Douglas marches on,
While many million voices rise in chorus like
    to one —
    "A Douglas and a Douglas!"
    Louder the war-song grows:
"God speed the man who fights so well
    Against a thousand foes."

Long and fierce was the encounter beneath the
    burning sky,
Fierce were the threatening gestures — the
    words rang shrill and high;
In a struggle most protracted, after seven and
    fifty shocks,
Like those old gigantic combats in which
    Titans fought with rocks
(And with "rocks," but of a different kind,
    no doubt Buchanan fought),
This first pitched battle of the war unto its
    end was brought;
And smiling still, with stainless plume and
    eye as clear as day,
The "Little Giant" held his own through all
    that murderous fray:
    "A Douglas and a Douglas!"
    Still louder grows the roar
    Which swells and floats from myriad
    throats
    Like waves on some wild shore.

Oh! a cheer for Colonel Flournoy, who to help
    our chief did press,
May memory perish if his name we cease to
    love and bless!
And a cheer for all the good and true who
    faced the music's note,
Who seized old Hydra in his den, and shook
    him by the throat.
Though our country stand forever, from her
    record ne'er will fade
The glory of that combat with Lecompton's
    black brigade.

And when June comes with her roses, at
    Baltimore we'll crown
The "Little Giant," who has met and struck
    corruption down.
    So a Douglas and a Douglas!
    While hearts have smiles and tears,
    Your name will glow, your praise shall
    flow,
    Through all the coming years.
        CHARLES GRAHAM HALPINE.

While the Democrats were thus divided, the
Republicans had met at Chicago, adopted a plat-
form protesting against the extension of slavery
in the territories, and nominated for President
Abraham Lincoln, of Illinois. On November 6,
1860, Lincoln was elected President, receiving one
hundred and eighty electoral votes.

LINCOLN, THE MAN OF THE PEOPLE

When the Norn-Mother saw the Whirlwind
    Hour,
Greatening and darkening as it hurried on,
She bent the strenuous heavens and came down
To make a man to meet the mortal need.
She took the tried clay of the common road —
Clay warm yet with the genial heat of Earth,
Dashed through it all a strain of prophecy;
Then mixed a laughter with the serious stuff.
It was a stuff to wear for centuries,
A man that matched the mountains, and com-
    pelled
The stars to look our way and honor us.

The color of the ground was in him, the red
    earth;
The tang and odor of the primal things —
The rectitude and patience of the rocks;
The gladness of the wind that shakes the corn;
The courage of the bird that dares the sea;
The justice of the rain that loves all leaves;
The pity of the snow that hides all scars;
The loving-kindness of the wayside well;
The tolerance and equity of light
That gives as freely to the shrinking weed
As to the great oak flaring to the wind —
To the grove's low hill as to the Matterhorn
That shoulders out the sky.

            And so he came.
From prairie cabin up to Capitol,
One fair Ideal led our chieftain on.
Forevermore he burned to do his deed

With the fine stroke and gesture of a king.
He built the rail-pile as he built the State,
Pouring his splendid strength through every
blow,
The conscience of him testing every stroke,
To make his deed the measure of a man.

So came the Captain with a mighty heart:
And when the step of Earthquake shook the
house,
Wrenching the rafters from their ancient hold,
He held the ridgepole up, and spiked again
The rafters of the Home. He held his place —
Held the long purpose like a growing tree —
Held on through blame and faltered not at
praise.
And when he fell in whirlwind, he went down
As when a kingly cedar green with boughs
Goes down with a great shout upon the hills,
And leaves a lonesome place against the sky.
                        EDWIN MARKHAM.

Lincoln's election was the signal the South had
been awaiting. On December 20, 1860, the state
of South Carolina unanimously passed an ordi-
nance of secession, and a week later, the state
troops seized Castle Pinckney and Fort Moultrie,
in Charleston harbor, and took possession of the
United States arsenal at Charleston, with seventy-
five thousand stands of arms.

BROTHER JONATHAN'S LAMENT FOR SISTER CAROLINE

SHE has gone, — she has left us in passion and
pride, —
Our stormy-browed sister, so long at our side!
She has torn her own star from our firma-
ment's glow,
And turned on her brother the face of a foe!

O Caroline, Caroline, child of the sun,
We can never forget that our hearts have been
one, —
Our foreheads both sprinkled in Liberty's
name,
From the fountain of blood with the finger
of flame!

You were always too ready to fire at a touch;
But we said: "She is hasty, — she does not
mean much."
We have scowled when you uttered some
turbulent threat;
But Friendship still whispered: "Forgive
and forget."

Has our love all died out? Have its altars
grown cold?
Has the curse come at last which the fathers
foretold?
Then Nature must teach us the strength of the
chain
That her petulant children would sever in
vain.

They may fight till the buzzards are gorged
with their spoil, —
Till the harvest grows black as it rots in the
soil,
Till the wolves and the catamounts troop from
their caves,
And the shark tracks the pirate, the lord of the
waves:

In vain is the strife! When its fury is past,
Their fortunes must flow in one channel at last-
As the torrents that rush from the mountains
of snow
Roll mingled in peace through the valleys be-
low.

Our Union is river, lake, ocean, and sky;
Man breaks not the medal when God cuts the
die!
Though darkened with sulphur, though cloven
with steel,
The blue arch will brighten, the waters will
heal!

O Caroline, Caroline, child of the sun,
There are battles with fate that can never be
won!
The star-flowering banner must never be
furled,
For its blossoms of light are the hope of the
world!

Go, then, our rash sister, afar and aloof, —
Run wild in the sunshine away from our roof;
But when your heart aches and your feet have
grown sore,
Remember the pathway that leads to our
door!
                        OLIVER WENDELL HOLMES.

Georgia, Alabama, Florida, North Carolina,
Mississippi, and Louisiana followed South Caro-
lina's lead in seceding and seizing United States
forts and arsenals. On February 4, 1861, the first
Confederate congress met at Montgomery, Ala.,
and a few days later, Jefferson Davis, of Missis-
sippi, was chosen President, and Alexander H.

Stephens, of Georgia, Vice-President, of the Confederate States.

JEFFERSON D.

You're a traitor convicted, you know very
    well!
    Jefferson D., Jefferson D.!
You thought it a capital thing to rebel,
    Jefferson D.!
    But there's one thing I'll say:
    You'll discover some day,
When you see a stout cotton cord hang from
    a tree,
There's an accident happened you did n't
    foresee,
    Jefferson D.!

What shall be found upon history's page?
    Jefferson D., Jefferson D.!
When a student explores the republican age!
    Jefferson D.!
    He will find, as is meet,
    That at Judas's feet
You sit in your shame, with the impotent plea,
That you hated the land and the law of the
    free,
    Jefferson D.!

What do you see in your visions at night,
    Jefferson D., Jefferson D.?
Does the spectacle furnish you any delight,
    Jefferson D.?
    Do you feel in disgrace
    The black cap o'er your face,
While the tremor creeps down from your
    heart to your knee,
And freedom, insulted, approves the decree,
    Jefferson D.?

Oh! long have we pleaded, till pleading is
    vain,
    Jefferson D., Jefferson D.!
Your hands are imbrued with the blood of the
    slain,
    Jefferson D.!
    And at last, for the right,
    We arise in our might,
A people united, resistless, and free,
And declare that rebellion no longer shall be!
    Jefferson D.!
            H. S. Cornwell.

Davis was inaugurated on February 18, 1861, and
declared in his inaugural that the attitude of the
Southern States was purely one of self-defence.
"All we want," he said, "is to be let alone."

THE OLD COVE

" All we ask is to be let alone."

[February 18, 1861]

As vonce I valked by a disma! svamp,
There sot an Old Cove in the dark and damp,
And at everybody as passed that road
A stick or a stone this Old Cove throwed.
And venever he flung his stick or his stone,
He'd set up a song of "Let me alone."

"Let me alone, for I loves to shy
These bits of things at the passers-by —
Let me alone, for I've got your tin
And lots of other traps snugly in; —
Let me alone, I'm riggin' a boat
To grab votever you've got afloat; —
In a veek or so I expects to come
And turn you out of your 'ouse and 'ome; —
I'm a quiet Old Cove," says he, with a groan:
"All I axes is — Let me alone."

Just then came along on the self-same vay,
Another Old Cove, and began for to say —
"Let you alone! That's comin' it strong! —
You've ben let alone a darned sight too long; —
Of all the sarce that ever I heerd!
Put down that stick! (You may well look
    skeered.)
Let go that stone! If you once show fight,
I'll knock you higher than ary kite.
You must hev a lesson to stop your tricks,
And cure you of shying them stones and
    sticks, —
And I'll hev my hardware back and my cash,
And knock your scow into tarnal smash,
And if ever I catches you round my ranch,
I'll string you up to the nearest branch.

"The best you can do is to go to bed,
And keep a decent tongue in your head;
For I reckon, before you and I are done,
You'll wish you had left honest folks alone."
The Old Cove stopped, and t'other Old
    Cove
He sot quite still in his cypress grove,
And he looked at his stick revolvin' slow
Whether 't were safe to shy it or no, —
And he grumbled on, in an injured tone,
"All that I axed vos, *let me alone.*"
        Henry Howard Brownell.

Texas, by a majority of over three to one, voted to join the Confederacy, and seized more than a million dollars' worth of government munitions. Some were saved by the Union troops, notably those at Fort Duncan.

A SPOOL OF THREAD

[March, 1861]

WELL, yes, I've lived in Texas since the spring
of '61;
And I'll relate the story, though I fear, sir,
when 't is done,
'T will be little worth your hearing, it was
such a simple thing,
Unheralded in verses that the grander poets
sing.

There had come a guest unbidden, at the
opening of the year,
To find a lodgment in our hearts, and the
tenant's name was fear;
For secession's drawing mandate was a call
for men and arms,
And each recurring eventide but brought us
fresh alarms.

They had notified the General that he must
yield to fate,
And all the muniments of war surrender to the
state,
But he sent from San Antonio an order to the
sea
To convey on board the steamer all the fort's
artillery.

Right royal was his purpose, but the foe
divined his plan,
And the wily Texans set a guard to intercept
the man
Detailed to bear the message; they placed
their watch with care
That neither scout nor citizen should pass it
unaware.

Well, this was rather awkward, sir, as doubt-
less you will say,
But the Major, who was chief of staff, re-
solved to have his way
Despite the watchful provost guard; so he
asked his wife to send,
With a box of knick-knacks, a letter to her
friend;

And the missive held one sentence I remem-
ber to this day:
"The thread is for your neighbor, Mr. French,
across the way."

He dispatched a youthful courier. Of course,
as you will know,
The Texans searched him thoroughly and
ordered him to show
The contents of the letter. They read it o'er
and o'er,
But failed to find the message they had hin-
dered once before.

So it reached the English lady, and she won-
dered at the word,
But gave the thread to Major French, ex-
plaining that she heard
He wished a spool of cotton, and great was his
surprise
At such a trifle sent, unasked, through leagues
of hostile spies.

"There's some hidden purpose, doubtless, in
the curious gift," he said.
Then he tore away the label, and inside the
spool of thread
Was Major Nichol's order, bidding him con-
vey to sea
All the arms and ammunition from Fort
Duncan's battery.
"Down to Brazon speed your horses," thus
the Major's letter ran,
"Shift equipments and munitions, and em-
bark them if you can."

Yes, the transfer was effected, for the ships
lay close at hand,
Ere the Texans guessed their purpose, they
had vanished from the land.
Do I know it for a fact, sir? 'T is no story that
I've read —
I was but a boy in war time, and I carried him
the thread.

SOPHIE E. EASTMAN.

On March 4, 1861, Abraham Lincoln was in-
augurated President of the United States. In his
address he stated that he had no intention of in-
terfering with slavery in the states; but that acts
of violence within any state against the authority
of the United States were insurrectionary and
would be repressed. In the Confederate States
this announcement was construed to mean war.

GOD SAVE OUR PRESIDENT

[March 4, 1861]

All hail! Unfurl the Stripes and Stars!
  The banner of the free!
Ten times ten thousand patriots greet
  The shrine of Liberty!
Come, with one heart, one hope, one
    aim,
  An undivided band,
To elevate, with solemn rites,
  The ruler of our land!

Not to invest a potentate
  With robes of majesty, —
Not to confer a kingly crown,
  Nor bend a subject knee.
We bow beneath no sceptred sway,
  Obey no royal nod: —

Columbia's sons, erect and free,
  Kneel only to their God!

Our ruler boasts no titled rank,
  No ancient, princely line, —
No regal right to sovereignty,
  Ancestral and divine.
A patriot, — at his country's call,
  Responding to her voice;
One of the people, — he becomes
  A sovereign by our choice!

And now, before the mighty pile
  We've reared to Liberty,
He swears to cherish and defend
  The charter of the free!
God of our country! seal his oath
  With Thy supreme assent.
God save the Union of the States!
  God save our President!
                FRANCIS DeHAES JANVIER.

CHAPTER II

THE GAUNTLET

In the fall of 1860 Major Robert Anderson was selected to command the little garrison at Fort Moultrie, in Charleston harbor. In spite of his entreaties, no reinforcements were sent him, and on the night of December 26 he abandoned Fort Moultrie, which his little force was incapable of defending, and moved to Fort Sumter, where he remained in spite of the state's protests.

BOB ANDERSON, MY BEAU

(Miss Columbia Sings)

Bob Anderson, my beau, Bob, when we were
    first aquent,
You were in Mex-i-co, Bob, because by order
    sent;
But now you are in Sumter, Bob, because you
    chose to go;
And blessings on you anyhow, Bob Anderson,
    my beau!

Bob Anderson, my beau, Bob, I really don't
    know whether
I ought to like you so, Bob, considering that
    feather;
I don't like standing armies, Bob, as very well
    you know,
But *I love a man that dares to act*, Bob Ander-
    son, my beau.

Fort Moultrie was seized by the South Carolina troops, which were assembled in force under command of General Pierre T. Beauregard, and it was decided to bombard Sumter.

ON FORT SUMTER

It was a noble Roman,
  In Rome's imperial day,
Who heard a coward croaker
  Before the battle say —
"They're safe in such a fortress;
  There is no way to shake it" —
"On, on!" exclaimed the hero,
  "I'll FIND A WAY, OR MAKE IT!"

Is FAME your aspiration?
  Her path is steep and high;
In vain he seeks the temple,
  Content to gaze and sigh;
The crowded town is waiting,
  But he *alone* can take it
Who says, with "SOUTHERN FIRMNESS,"
  "I'll FIND A WAY, OR MAKE IT!"

Is GLORY your ambition?
  There is no royal road;
Alike we all must labor,
  Must climb to her abode:

Who feels the thirst for *glory*,
　In Helicon may slake it,
If he has but the "SOUTHERN WILL,"
　" To find a way, or make it!"

Is Sumter worth the getting?
　It must be bravely sought;
With wishing and with fretting
　The boon cannot be bought;
To *all* the prize is open,
　But only he can take it
Who says, with "SOUTHERN COURAGE,"
　"I'll find a way, or make it!"

In all impassioned warfare,
　The tale has ever been,
That victory crowns the valiant,
　The brave are they who win.
Though strong is " *Sumter Fortress*,"
　A HERO still may take it,
Who says, with "SOUTHERN DARING,"
　"I'll find a way, or make it!"
　　　Charleston, S. C., *Mercury*.

On April 11 Beauregard summoned Anderson to surrender. Anderson promptly refused, and at 4.30 o'clock on the morning of April 12, 1861, the first gun against Sumter was fired. The fort answered promptly, and a terrific bombardment continued all day. The fort's ammunition was exhausted by the 13th, and Major Anderson accepted the terms of evacuation offered by General Beauregard. On the afternoon of Sunday, April 14, the little garrison marched out of the fort with colors flying and drums beating. Not a man had been killed on either side.

SUMTER

[April 12, 1861]

CAME the morning of that day
When the God to whom we pray
Gave the soul of Henry Clay
　To the land;
How we loved him, living, dying!
But his birthday banners flying
Saw us asking and replying
　Hand to hand.

For we knew that far away,
Round the fort in Charleston Bay,
Hung the dark impending fray,
　Soon to fall;
And that Sumter's brave defender
Had the summons to surrender
Seventy loyal hearts and tender —
　(Those were all!)

And we knew the April sun
Lit the length of many a gun —
Hosts of batteries to the one
　Island crag;
Guns and mortars grimly frowning,
Johnson, Moultrie, Pinckney, crowning,
And ten thousand men disowning
　The old flag.

Oh, the fury of the fight
Even then was at its height!
Yet no breath, from noon till night,
　Reached us here;
We had almost ceased to wonder,
And the day had faded under,
When the echo of the thunder
　Filled each ear!

Then our hearts more fiercely beat,
As we crowded on the street,
Hot to gather and repeat
　All the tale;
All the doubtful chances turning,
Till our souls with shame were burning,
As if twice our bitter yearning
　Could avail!

Who had fired the earliest gun?
Was the fort by traitors won?
Was there succor? What was done
　Who could know?
And once more our thoughts would wander
To the gallant, lone commander,
On his battered ramparts grander
　Than the foe.

Not too long the brave shall wait:
On their own heads be their fate,
Who against the hallowed State
　Dare begin;
Flag defied and compact riven!
In the record of high Heaven
How shall Southern men be shriven
　For the sin!
　　　EDMUND CLARENCE STEDMAN.

THE BATTLE OF MORRIS' ISLAND

A CHEERFUL TRAGEDY

[April 12, 1861]

I

THE morn was cloudy and dark and gray,
When the first Columbiad blazed away,

Showing that there was the d—l to pay
  With the braves on Morris' Island;
They fired their cannon again and again,
Hoping that Major Anderson's men
Would answer back, but 't was all in vain
  At first, on Morris' Island:
Hokee pokee, winkee wum,
Shattering shot and thundering bomb,
Fiddle and fife and rattling drum,
  At the battle of Morris' Island!

II

At length, as rose the morning sun,
Fort Sumter fired a single gun,
Which made the chivalry want to run
  Away from Morris' Island;
But they had made so much of a boast
Of their fancy batteries on the coast,
That each felt bound to stick to his post
  Down there on Morris' Island.

III

Then there was firing in hot haste;
The chivalry stripped them to the waist,
And, brave as lions, they sternly faced
  — Their grog, on Morris' Island!
The spirit of Seventy-six raged high,
The cannons roared and the men grew dry —
'T was marvellous like the Fourth of July,
  That fight on Morris' Island.

IV

All day they fought, till the night came down;
It rained; the fellows were tired and blown,
And they wished they were safely back to
    town,
  Away from Morris' Island.
One can't expect the bravest men
To shoot their cannons off in the rain,
So all grew peaceful and still again,
  At the works on Morris' Island.

V

But after the heroes all had slept,
To his gun each warrior swiftly leapt,
Brisk, as the numerous fleas that crept
  In the sand on Morris' Island;
And all that day they fired their shot,
Heated in furnaces, piping hot,
Hoping to send Fort Sumter to pot
  And glory to Morris' Island.

VI

Finally, wearying of the joke,
Starved with hunger and blind with smoke

From blazing barracks of pine and oak,
  Set fire from Morris' Island,
The gallant Anderson struck his flag
And packed his things in a carpet-bag,
While cheers from bobtail, rag, and tag,
  Arose on Morris' Island.

VII

Then came the comforting piece of fun
Of counting the noses one by one,
To see if anything had been done
  On glorious Morris' Island:
"Nobody hurt!" the cry arose;
There was not missing a single nose,
And this was the sadly ludicrous close
  Of the battle of Morris' Island.

VIII

But, gentle gunners, just wait and see
What sort of a battle there yet will be;
You 'll hardly escape so easily,
  Next time on Morris' Island!
There 's a man in Washington with a will,
Who won't mind shooting a little "to kill,"
If it proves that We Have a Government Still,
  Even on Morris' Island!
Hokee pokee, winkee wum,
Shattering shot and thundering bomb,
Look out for the battle that 's yet to come
  Down there on Morris' Island!

Anderson's total force numbered one hundred
and twenty-eight. The South Carolina army op-
posed to him numbered about six thousand, and
was made up largely of the best blood of the state.
Planters and their sons, men of wealth and family,
did not scruple to serve in the ranks. Their sweet-
hearts and wives turned out in gala attire to witness
their triumph, and when the fort surrendered,
Charleston gave itself up to joy.

SUMTER — A BALLAD OF 1861

'T was on the twelfth of April,
  Before the break of day,
We heard the guns of Moultrie
  Give signal for the fray.

Anon across the waters
  There boomed the answering gun,
From north and south came flash on flash:
  The battle had begun.

The mortars belched their deadly food
  And spiteful whizz'd the balls,

A fearful storm of iron hailed
  On Sumter's doomèd walls.

We watched the meteor flight of shell,
  And saw the lightning flash —
Saw where each fiery missile fell,
  And heard the sullen crash.

The morn was dark and cloudy
  Yet till the sun arose,
No answer to our gallant boys
  Came booming from our foes.

Then through the dark and murky clouds
  The morning sunlight came,
And forth from Sumter's frowning walls
  Burst sudden sheets of flame.

Then shot and shell flew thick and fast,
  The war-dogs howling spoke,
And thundering came their angry roar,
  Through wreathing clouds of smoke.

Again to fight for liberty
  Our gallant sons had come,
They smiled when came the bugle call,
  And laughed when tapped the drum.

From cotton and from corn field,
  From desk and forum, too,
From work bench and from anvil came
  Our gallant boys and true!

A hireling band had come to awe,
  Our chains to rivet fast;
Yon lofty pile scowls on our homes
  Seaward the hostile mast.

But gallant freemen man our guns, —
  No mercenary host,
Who barter for their honor's price,
  And of their baseness boast.

Now came our stately matrons,
  And maidens, too, by scores;
Oh! Carolina's beauty shone
  Like love-lights on her shores.

See yonder, anxious gazing,
  Alone a matron stands,
The tear-drop glistening on each lid,
  And tightly clasped her hands.

For there, exposed to deadly fire,
  Her husband and her son —

"Father," she spoke, and heavenward look'd,
  "Father, thy will be done."

See yonder group of maidens,
  No joyous laughter now,
For cares lie heavy on each heart
  And cloud each anxious brow;

For brothers dear and lovers fond
  Are there amid the strife;
Tearful the sister's anxious gaze —
  Pallid the promised wife.

Yet breathed no heart one thought of fear,
  Prompt at their country's call,
They yielded forth their dearest hopes.
  And gave to honor all!

Now comes a message from below —
  Oh! quick the tidings tell —
"At Moultrie and Fort Johnson, too.
  And Morris', all are well!"

Then mark the joyous bright'ning;
  See how each bosom swells;
That friends and loved ones all are safe,
  Each to the other tells.

All day the shot flew thick and fast,
  All night the cannon roared,
While wreathed in smoke stern Sumter stood
  And vengeful answer poured.

Again the sun rose, bright and clear,
  'T was on the thirteenth day,
While, lo! at prudent distance moored,
  Five hostile vessels lay.

With choicest Abolition crews, —
  The bravest of *their* brave, —
They'd come to pull our Crescent down
  And dig Secession's grave.

"See, see, how Sumter's banner trails,
  They're signalling for aid.
See you no boats of armèd men?
  Is yet no movement made?"

Now densest smoke and lurid flames
  Burst out o'er Sumter's walls;
"The fort's on fire," is the cry,
  Again for aid he calls.

See you no boats or vessels yet?
  Dare they not risk *one* shot;

To make report grandiloquent
  Of aid they rendered not?

Nor boat, nor vessel, leaves the fleet,
  "Let the old Major burn,
We'll boast of what we would have done,
  If but — on our return."

Go back, go back, ye cravens;
  Go back the way ye came;
Ye gallant, *would-be* men-of-war,
  Go! to your country's shame.

'Mid fiery storm of shot and shell,
  'Mid smoke and roaring flame,
See how Kentucky's gallant son
  Does honor to her name!

See how he answers gun for gun —
  Hurrah! his flag is down!
The white! the white! Oh see it wave!
  Is echoed all around.

God save the gallant Anderson,
  All honor to his name,
A soldier's duty nobly done,
  He's earned a hero's fame.

Now ring the bells a joyous peal,
  And rend with shouts the air,
We've torn the hated banner down,
  And placed the Crescent there.

All honor to our gallant boys,
  Bring forth the roll of fame,
And there in glowing lines inscribe
  Each patriot hero's name.

Spread, spread the tidings far and wide,
  Ye winds take up the cry,
"Our soil's redeemed from hateful yoke,
  We'll keep it pure or die."

  Columbia, S. C., *Banner.*

Very different was the reception of the news at
the North. At last war had begun. The time for
argument and compromise and entreaty was past.
The time for action was at hand.

THE FIGHT AT SUMTER

'T WAS a wonderful brave fight!
  Through the day and all night,
  March! Halt! Left! Right!
    So they formed:

And one thousand to ten,
  The bold Palmetto men
    Sumter stormed.

The smoke in a cloud
Closed her in like a shroud,
While the cannon roared aloud
    From the Port;
And the red cannon-balls
Ploughed the gray granite walls
    Of the Fort.

Sumter's gunners at their places,
With their gunpowdered faces,
Shook their shoulders from their braces,
    And stripped
Stark and white to the waist,
Just to give the foe a taste,
    And be whipped.

In the town, through every street,
Tramp, tramp, went the feet,
For they said the Federal fleet
    Hove in sight;
And down the wharves they ran,
Every woman, child, and man,
    To the fight.

On the fort the old flag waved,
And the barking batteries braved,
While the bold seven thousand raved
    As they fought;
For each blinding sheet of flame
From her cannon thundered shame! —
    So they thought.

And strange enough to tell,
Though the gunners fired well,
And the balls ploughed red as hell
    Through the dirt;
Though the shells burst and scattered,
And the fortress walls were shattered, —
    None were hurt.

But the fort — so hot she grew,
As the cannon-balls flew,
That each man began to stew
    At his gun;
They were not afraid to die,
But this making Patriot pie
    Was not fun.

So, to make the story short,
The traitors got the fort
After thirty hours' sport
    With the balls·

But the victory is not theirs,
Though their brazen banner flares
    From the walls.

It were better they should dare
The lion in his lair,
Or defy the grizzly bear
    In his den,
Than to wake the fearful cry
That is rising up on high
    From our men.

To our banner we are clinging,
And a song we are singing,
Whose chorus is ringing
    From each mouth;
'T is "The old Constitution
And a stern retribution
    To the South."
    Vanity Fair, April 27, 1861.

SUMTER

So, they *will* have it!
    The Black Witch (curse on her)
    Always had won her
Greediest demand — for we gave it —
    All but our honor!

Thirty hours thundered
    Siege-guns and mortars —
    (Flames in the quarters!)
One to a hundred
    Stood our brave Forters!

No more of parties! —
    Let them all moulder —
    Here 's work that 's bolder!
Forward, my hearties!
    Shoulder to shoulder.

Sight o'er the trunnion —
    Send home the rammer —
    Linstock and hammer!
Speak for the Union!
    Tones that won't stammer!

Men of Columbia,
    Leal hearts from Annan,
    Brave lads of Shannon!
We are all one to-day —
    On with the cannon!
        HENRY HOWARD BROWNELL.

Nor was there any hesitation as to what that action should be. On Monday, April 15, 1861, President Lincoln issued a call for seventy-five thousand militia to suppress combinations obstructing the execution of the laws in seven of the Southern states.

THE GREAT BELL ROLAND

SUGGESTED BY THE PRESIDENT'S CALL FOR
VOLUNTEERS

I

TOLL! Roland, toll!
— High in St. Bavon's tower,
    At midnight hour,
The great bell Roland spoke,
And all who slept in Ghent awoke.
    — What meant its iron stroke?
    Why caught each man his blade?
    Why the hot haste he made?
    Why echoed every street
    With tramp of thronging feet —
All flying to the city's wall?
        It was the call
        Known well to all,
That Freedom stood in peril of some
    foe:
And even timid hearts grew bold
    Whenever Roland tolled,
And every hand a sword could hold; —
        For men
        Were patriots then,
        Three hundred years ago!

II

Toll! Roland, toll!
Bell never yet was hung,
Between whose lips there swung
So true and brave a tongue!
    — If men be patriots still,
        At thy first sound
        True hearts will bound,
        Great souls will thrill —
    Then toll! and wake the test
        In each man's breast,
    And let him stand confess'd!

III

Toll! Roland, toll!
    — Not in St. Bavon's tower
        At midnight hour, —
Nor by the Scheldt, nor far-off Zuyder
    Zee;

But here — this side the sea! —
And here in broad, bright day!
   Toll! Roland, toll!
For not by night awaits
A brave foe at the gates,
But Treason stalks abroad — inside! — at
  noon!
   Toll! Thy alarm is not too soon!
To arms! Ring out the Leader's
  call!
Reëcho it from East to West,
Till every dauntless breast
Swell beneath plume and crest!
   Toll! Roland, toll!
Till swords from scabbards leap!
   Toll! Roland, toll!
— What tears can widows weep
Less bitter than when brave men fall?
   Toll! Roland, toll!
Till cottager from cottage-wall
Snatch pouch and powder-horn and gun —
The heritage of sire to son,
Ere half of Freedom's work was done!
   Toll! Roland, toll!
Till son, in memory of his sire,
Once more shall load and fire!
   Toll! Roland, toll!
Till volunteers find out the art
Of aiming at a traitor's heart!

IV

   Toll! Roland, toll!
— St. Bavon's stately tower
Stands to this hour, —
And by its side stands Freedom yet in
  Ghent;
For when the bells now ring,
Men shout, "God save the King!"
Until the air is rent!
— Amen! — So let it be;
For a true king is he
Who keeps his people free.
   Toll! Roland, toll!
   This side the sea!
No longer they, but we,
Have now such need of thee!
   Toll! Roland, toll!
And let thy iron throat
Ring out its warning note,
Till Freedom's perils be outbraved,
And Freedom's flag, wherever waved,
Shall overshadow none enslaved!
Toll! till from either ocean's strand,
Brave men shall clasp each other's hand,

And shout, "God save our native land!"
— And love the land which God hath saved!
   Toll! Roland, toll!
            THEODORE TILTON.

Independent, April 18, 1861.

MEN OF THE NORTH AND WEST[1]

Men of the North and West,
  Wake in your might,
Prepare, as the rebels have done,
  For the fight!
You cannot shrink from the test;
Rise! Men of the North and West!

They have torn down your banner of stars;
  They have trampled the laws;
They have stifled the freedom they hate,
  For no cause!
Do you love it or slavery best?
Speak! Men of the North and West.

They strike at the life of the State:
  Shall the murder be done?
They cry: "We are two!" And you:
  "We are one!"
You must meet them, then, breast to breast;
On! Men of the North and West!

Not with words; they laugh them to scorn,
  And tears they despise;
But with swords in your hands and death
  In your eyes!
Strike home! leave to God all the rest;
Strike! Men of the North and West.
        RICHARD HENRY STODDARD.

OUT AND FIGHT

Out and fight! The clouds are breaking,
  Far and wide the red light streams,
North and west see millions waking
  From their night-mare, doubting dreams.
War is coming. As the thunder
  'Mid the mountain caverns rolls,
Driving rains in torrents under,
  So the wild roar wakes our souls.

Out and fight! The time is over
  For all truce and compromise,

[1] From Poetical Writings of Richard Henry
Stoddard; copyright, 1880, by Charles Scribner's
Sons.

Words of calm are words of folly,
  Peaceful dreams are painted lies;
Sumter's flames in Southern waters
  Are the first wild beacon light,
And on Northern hills reflected
  Give the signal for the fight.

Out and fight! Endure no longer
  Goading insult, brazen guilt;
Be the battle to the knife blade,
  And the knife blade to the hilt,
Till the sacred zone of Freedom
  Girds the whole Atlantic strand,
And the braggart and the Gascon
  Be extinguished from the land.
        CHARLES GODFREY LELAND.
Vanity Fair, April 27, 1861.

NO MORE WORDS

No more words;
  Try it with your swords!
Try it with the arms of your bravest and your
    best!
You are proud of your manhood, now put it to
    the test;
      Not another word;
      Try it by the sword!

No more notes;
  Try it by the throats
Of the cannon that will roar till the earth and
    air be shaken;
For they speak what they mean, and they can-
    not be mistaken;
      No more doubt;
      Come — fight it out!

No child's play!
  Waste not a day;
Serve out the deadliest weapons that you
    know;
Let them pitilessly hail on the faces of the foe;
      No blind strife;
      Waste not one life.

You that in the front
  Bear the battle's brunt —
When the sun gleams at dawn on the bayonets
    abreast,
Remember 't is for government and country
    you contest;
      For love of all you guard,
      Stand, and strike hard!

You at home that stay
  From danger far away,
Leave not a jot to chance, while you rest in
    quiet ease;
Quick! forge the bolts of death; quick! ship
    them o'er the seas;
      If War's feet are lame,
      Yours will be the blame.

You, my lads, abroad,
  "Steady!" be your word;
You, at home, be the anchor of your sol-
    diers young and brave;
Spare no cost, none is lost, that may strengthen
    or may save;
      Sloth were sin and shame,
      Now play out the game!
        FRANKLIN LUSHINGTON.

"At the darkest hour in the history of the re-
public," Emerson wrote, "when it looked as if the
nation would be dismembered, pulverized into its
original elements, the attack on Fort Sumter crys-
tallized the North into a unit, and the hope of
mankind was saved."

OUR COUNTRY'S CALL

LAY down the axe; fling by the spade;
  Leave in its track the toiling plough;
The rifle and the bayonet-blade
  For arms like yours were fitter now;
And let the hands that ply the pen
  Quit the light task, and learn to wield
The horseman's crooked brand, and rein
  The charger on the battle-field.

Our country calls; away! away!
  To where the blood-stream blots the green.
Strike to defend the gentlest sway
  That Time in all his course has seen.
See, from a thousand coverts — see,
  Spring the armed foes that haunt her track;
They rush to smite her down, and we
  Must beat the banded traitors back.

Ho! sturdy as the oaks ye cleave,
  And moved as soon to fear and flight,
Men of the glade and forest! leave
  Your woodcraft for the field of fight.
The arms that wield the axe must pour
  An iron tempest on the foe;
His serried ranks shall reel before
  The arm that lays the panther low.

And ye, who breast the mountain-storm
　By grassy steep or highland lake,
Come, for the land ye love, to form
　A bulwark that no foe can break.
Stand, like your own gray cliffs that mock
　The whirlwind, stand in her defence;
The blast as soon shall move the rock
　As rushing squadrons bear ye thence.

And ye, whose homes are by her grand
　Swift rivers, rising far away,
Come from the depth of her green land,
　As mighty in your march as they;
As terrible as when the rains
　Have swelled them over bank and borne,
With sudden floods to drown the plains
　And sweep along the woods uptorn.

And ye, who throng, beside the deep,
　Her ports and hamlets of the strand,
In number like the waves that leap
　On his long-murmuring marge of sand —
Come like that deep, when, o'er his brim
　He rises, all his floods to pour,
And flings the proudest barks that swim,
　A helpless wreck, against the shore!

Few, few were they whose swords of old
　Won the fair land in which we dwell,
But we are many, we who hold
　The grim resolve to guard it well.
Strike, for that broad and goodly land,
　Blow after blow, till men shall see
That Might and Right move hand in hand,
　And glorious must their triumph be!
　　　　　　　WILLIAM CULLEN BRYANT.

The people of the South were also wildly enthu-
siastic for the war. Prompted by the belief that
they must arm to defend their property and their
liberties, they rose as one man. All hearts were
in the cause.

DIXIE

SOUTHRONS, hear your country call you!
Up, lest worse than death befall you!
　To arms! To arms! To arms, in Dixie!
Lo! all the beacon-fires are lighted, —
Let all hearts be now united!
　To arms! To arms! To arms, in Dixie!
　　Advance the flag of Dixie!
　　　Hurrah! hurrah!
For Dixie's land we take our stand,
　And live and die for Dixie!

　　To arms! To arms!
　And conquer peace for Dixie!
　　To arms! To arms!
　And conquer peace for Dixie!

Hear the Northern thunders mutter!
Northern flags in South winds flutter!
Send them back your fierce defiance!
Stamp upon the accursed alliance!

Fear no danger! Shun no labor!
Lift up rifle, pike, and sabre!
Shoulder pressing close to shoulder,
Let the odds make each heart bolder!

How the South's great heart rejoices
At your cannons' ringing voices!
For faith betrayed, and pledges broken,
Wrongs inflicted, insults spoken.

Strong as lions, swift as eagles,
Back to their kennels hunt these beagles!
Cut the unequal bonds asunder!
Let them hence each other plunder!

Swear upon your country's altar
Never to submit or falter,
Till the spoilers are defeated,
Till the Lord's work is completed!

Halt not till our Federation
Secures among earth's powers its station!
Then at peace, and crowned with glory,
Hear your children tell the story!

If the loved ones weep in sadness,
Victory soon shall bring them gladness, —
　　　To arms!
Exultant pride soon vanish sorrow;
Smiles chase tears away to-morrow.
　To arms! To arms! To arms, in Dixie!
　　Advance the flag of Dixie!
　　　Hurrah! hurrah!
For Dixie's land we take our stand,
　And live or die for Dixie!
　　To arms! To arms!
　And conquer peace for Dixie!
　　To arms! To arms!
　And conquer peace for Dixie!
　　　　　　　　ALBERT PIKE.

A CRY TO ARMS

Ho, woodsmen of the mountain-side!
　Ho, dwellers in the vales!

Ho, ye who by the chafing tide
  Have roughened in the gales!
Leave barn and byre, leave kin and cot,
  Lay by the bloodless spade;
Let desk and case and counter rot,
  And burn your books of trade!

The despot roves your fairest lands;
  And till he flies or fears,
Your fields must grow but armèd bands,
  Your sheaves be sheaves of spears!
Give up to mildew and to rust
  The useless tools of gain,
And feed your country's sacred dust
  With floods of crimson rain!

Come with the weapons at your call —
  With musket, pike, or knife;
He wields the deadliest blade of all
  Who lightest holds his life.
The arm that drives its unbought blows
  With all a patriot's scorn,
Might brain a tyrant with a rose
  Or stab him with a thorn.

Does any falter? Let him turn
  To some brave maiden's eyes,
And catch the holy fires that burn
  In those sublunar skies.
Oh, could you like your women feel,
  And in their spirit march,
A day might see your lines of steel
  Beneath the victor's arch!

What hope, O God! would not grow warm
  When thoughts like these give cheer?
The lily calmly braves the storm,
  And shall the palm-tree fear?
No! rather let its branches court
  The rack that sweeps the plain;
And from the lily's regal port
  Learn how to breast the strain.

Ho, woodsmen of the mountain-side!
  Ho, dwellers in the vales!
Ho, ye who by the roaring tide
  Have roughened in the gales!
Come, flocking gayly to the fight,
  From forest, hill, and lake;
We battle for our country's right,
  And for the lily's sake!

HENRY TIMROD.

"WE CONQUER OR DIE"

THE war drum is beating, prepare for the fight,
The stern bigot Northman exults in his might;
Gird on your bright weapons, your foemen
  are nigh,
And this be our watchword, "We conquer or
  die."

The trumpet is sounding from mountain to
  shore,
Your swords and your lances must slumber
  no more,
Fling forth to the sunlight your banner on
  high,
Inscribed with the watchword, "We conquer
  or die."

March on the battlefield, there to do or dare,
With shoulder to shoulder, all danger to share,
And let your proud watchword ring up to the
  sky,
Till the blue arch reëchoes, "We conquer or
  die."

Press forward undaunted nor think of retreat,
The enemy's host on the threshold to meet;
Strike firm, till the foeman before you shall fly,
Appalled by the watchword, "We conquer or
  die."

Go forth in the pathway our forefathers trod;
We, too, fight for freedom — our Captain is
  God,
Their blood in our veins, with their honors we
  vie,
Theirs, too, was the watchword, "We conquer
  or die."

We strike for the South — Mountain, Valley,
  and Plain,
For the South we will conquer again and
  again;
Her day of salvation and triumph is nigh,
Ours, then, be the watchword, "We conquer
  or die."

JAMES PIERPONT.

"CALL ALL"

WHOOP! the Doodles have broken loose,
Roaring round like the very deuce!
Lice of Egypt, a hungry pack, —
After 'em, boys, and drive 'em back.

Bull-dog, terrier, cur, and fice,
Back to the beggarly land of ice;
Worry 'em, bite 'em, scratch and tear
Everybody and everywhere.

Old Kentucky is caved from under,
Tennessee is split asunder,
Alabama awaits attack,
And Georgia bristles up her back.

Old John Brown is dead and gone!
Still his spirit is marching on, —
Lantern-jawed, and legs, my boys,
Long as an ape's from Illinois!

Want a weapon? Gather a brick,
Club or cudgel, or stone or stick;
Anything with a blade or butt,
Anything that can cleave or cut.

Anything heavy, or hard, or keen!
Any sort of slaying machine!
Anything with a willing mind,
And the steady arm of a man behind.

Want a weapon? Why, capture one!
Every Doodle has got a gun,
Belt, and bayonet, bright and new;
Kill a Doodle, and capture two!

Shoulder to shoulder, son and sire!
All, call all! to the feast of fire!
Mother and maiden, and child and slave,
A common triumph or a single grave.

Rockingham, Va., *Register*, 1861.

THE BONNIE BLUE FLAG

Come, brothers! rally for the right!
The bravest of the brave
Sends forth her ringing battle-cry
Beside the Atlantic wave!
She leads the way in honor's path;
Come, brothers, near and far,
Come rally round the Bonnie Blue Flag
That bears a single star!

We've borne the Yankee trickery,
The Yankee gibe and sneer,
Till Yankee insolence and pride
Know neither shame nor fear;
But ready now with shot and steel
Their brazen front to mar,
We hoist aloft the Bonnie Blue Flag
That bears a single star.

Now Georgia marches to the front,
And close beside her come
Her sisters by the Mexique Sea,
With pealing trump and drum;
Till answering back from hill and glen
The rallying cry afar,
A Nation hoists the Bonnie Blue Flag
That bears a single star.

By every stone in Charleston Bay,
By each beleaguered town,
We swear to rest not, night nor day,
But hunt the tyrants down!
Till bathed in valor's holy blood
The gazing world afar
Shall greet with shouts the Bonnie Blue
Flag
That bears the cross and star!
ANNIE CHAMBERS KETCHUM.

The Southern women were carried away by
enthusiasm and excitement. They believed the
South invincible, and regarded the men who did
not rush to enlist as cowards and traitors.

"I GIVE MY SOLDIER BOY A BLADE!"

I GIVE my soldier boy a blade,
In fair Damascus fashioned well:
Who first the glittering falchion swayed,
Who first beneath its fury fell,
I know not; but I hope to know,
That, for no mean or hireling trade,
To guard no feeling base or low —
I give my soldier boy the blade!

Cool, calm, and clear — the lucid flood
In which its tempering work was done; —
As calm, as clear, in wind and wood,
Be thou where'er it sees the sun!
For country's claim at honor's call,
For outraged friend, insulted maid,
At mercy's voice to bid it fall —
I give my soldier boy the blade!

The eye which marked its peerless edge,
The hand that weighed its balanced
poise,
Anvil and pincers, forge and wedge,
Are gone with all their flame and noise;
Yet still the gleaming sword remains!
So, when in dust I low am laid,
Remember by these heartfelt strains,
I give my soldier boy the blade!

CHAPTER III

THE NORTH GETS ITS LESSON

On Wednesday, April 16, 1861, the Sixth Massachusetts left Boston for Washington. Three days later it reached Baltimore, and started to march to the Camden Street station to take train for its destination.

THE NINETEENTH OF APRIL

[1861]

THIS year, till late in April, the snow fell thick
and light:
Thy truce-flag, friendly Nature, in clinging
drifts of white,
Hung over field and city: now everywhere is
seen,
In place of that white quietness, a sudden
glow of green.

The verdure climbs the Common, beneath the
leafless trees,
To where the glorious Stars and Stripes are
floating on the breeze.
There, suddenly as spring awoke from winter's
snow-draped gloom,
The Passion-Flower of Seventy-Six is bursting
into bloom.

Dear is the time of roses, when earth to joy is
wed,
And garden-plat and meadow wear one gener-
ous flush of red;
But now in dearer beauty, to her ancient
colors true,
Blooms the old town of Boston in red and
white and blue.

Along the whole awakening North are those
bright emblems spread;
A summer noon of patriotism is burning over-
head:
No party badges flaunting now, no word of
clique or clan;
But "Up for God and Union!" is the shout of
every man.

Oh, peace is dear to Northern hearts; our
hard-earned homes more dear;
But Freedom is beyond the price of any
earthly cheer;

And Freedom's flag is sacred; he who would
work it harm,
Let him, although a brother, beware our
strong right arm!

A brother! ah, the sorrow, the anguish of
that word!
The fratricidal strife begun, when will its end
be heard?
Not this the boon that patriot hearts have
prayed and waited for; —
We loved them, and we longed for peace: but
they would have it war.

Yes; war! on this memorial day, the day of
Lexington,
A lightning-thrill along the wires from heart
to heart has run.
Brave men we gazed on yesterday, to-day
for us have bled:
Again is Massachusetts blood the first for
Freedom shed.

To war, — and with our brethren, then, —
if only this can be!
Life hangs as nothing in the scale against
dear Liberty!
Though hearts be torn asunder, for Freedom
we will fight;
Our blood may seal the victory, but God will
shield the Right!

LUCY LARCOM.

Baltimore was in a frenzy, the streets were
crowded with Southern sympathizers, and an
attack upon the troops soon began. A desperate
fight followed, in which three soldiers were killed
and about twenty wounded. Nine citizens of
Baltimore were killed, and many wounded — how
many is not known.

THROUGH BALTIMORE

[April 19, 1861]

'T WAS Friday morn: the train drew near
The city and the shore.
Far through the sunshine, soft and clear,
We saw the dear old flag appear,
And in our hearts arose a cheer
For Baltimore.

Across the broad Patapsco's wave,
   Old Fort McHenry bore
The starry banner of the brave,
As when our fathers went to save,
Or in the trenches find a grave
   At Baltimore.

Before us, pillared in the sky,
   We saw the statue soar
Of Washington, serene and high: —
Could traitors view that form, nor fly?
Could patriots see, nor gladly die
   For Baltimore?

"O city of our country's song!
   By that swift aid we bore
When sorely pressed, receive the throng
Who go to shield our flag from wrong,
And give us welcome, warm and strong,
   In Baltimore!"

We had no arms; as friends we came,
   As brothers evermore,
To rally round one sacred name —
The charter of our power and fame:
We never dreamed of guilt and shame
   In Baltimore.

The coward mob upon us fell:
   McHenry's flag they tore;
Surprised, borne backward by the swell,
Beat down with mad, inhuman yell,
Before us yawned a traitorous hell
   In Baltimore!

The streets our soldier-fathers trod
   Blushed with their children's gore;
We saw the craven rulers nod,
And dip in blood the civic rod —
Shall such things be, O righteous God,
   In Baltimore?

No, never! By that outrage black,
   A solemn oath we swore,
To bring the Keystone's thousands back,
Strike down the dastards who attack,
And leave a red and fiery track
   Through Baltimore!

Bow down, in haste, thy guilty head!
   God's wrath is swift and sore:
The sky with gathering bolts is red, —
Cleanse from thy skirts the slaughter shed,
Or make thyself an ashen bed,
   O Baltimore!
           BAYARD TAYLOR.

The secessionists of Maryland were wild with wrath; but a Federal force under General Butler soon occupied Annapolis and Baltimore, the Union spirit of the state asserted itself, and there was never any further danger of its joining the Confederacy.

MY MARYLAND

THE despot's heel is on thy shore,
   Maryland!
His torch is at thy temple door,
   Maryland!
Avenge the patriotic gore
That flecked the streets of Baltimore,
And be the battle-queen of yore,
   Maryland, my Maryland!

Hark to an exiled son's appeal,
   Maryland!
My Mother State, to thee I kneel,
   Maryland!
For life and death, for woe and weal,
Thy peerless chivalry reveal,
And gird thy beauteous limbs with steel,
   Maryland, my Maryland!

Thou wilt not cower in the dust,
   Maryland!
Thy beaming sword shall never rust,
   Maryland!
Remember Carroll's sacred trust,
Remember Howard's warlike thrust,
And all thy slumberers with the just,
   Maryland, my Maryland!

Come! 't is the red dawn of the day,
   Maryland!
Come with thy panoplied array,
   Maryland!
With Ringgold's spirit for the fray,
With Watson's blood at Monterey,
With fearless Lowe and dashing May,
   Maryland, my Maryland!

Dear Mother, burst the tyrant's chain
   Maryland!
Virginia should not call in vain,
   Maryland!
She meets her sisters on the plain, —
"*Sic semper!*" 't is the proud refrain
That baffles minions back amain,
   Maryland!
Arise in majesty again,
   Maryland, my Maryland!

Come! for thy shield is bright and strong,
    Maryland!
Come! for thy dalliance does thee wrong,
    Maryland!
Come to thine own heroic throng
Stalking with Liberty along,
And chant thy dauntless slogan-song,
    Maryland, my Maryland!

I see the blush upon thy cheek,
    Maryland!
For thou wast ever bravely meek,
    Maryland!
But lo! there surges forth a shriek,
From hill to hill, from creek to creek,
Potomac calls to Chesapeake,
    Maryland, my Maryland!

Thou wilt not yield the Vandal toll,
    Maryland!
Thou wilt not crook to his control,
    Maryland!
Better the fire upon thee roll,
Better the shot, the blade, the bowl,
Than crucifixion of the soul,
    Maryland, my Maryland!

I hear the distant thunder hum,
    Maryland!
The Old Line's bugle, fife, and drum,
    Maryland!
She is not dead, nor deaf, nor dumb;
Huzza! she spurns the Northern scum!
She breathes! She burns! She'll come! She'll
    come!
    Maryland, my Maryland!
          JAMES RYDER RANDALL.

On May 24, 1861, a Union force under Colonel
Ephraim E. Ellsworth occupied Alexandria, Va.
Over an inn called the Marshall House Ellsworth
saw a Confederate flag flying and went in person
to take it down. As he descended the stairs with
the flag in his arms, the proprietor of the inn, a
violent secessionist named Jackson, fired upon and
killed him instantly. Jackson was shot a moment
later by Francis E. Brownell, a New York Zouave.

ELLSWORTH

[May 24, 1861]

WHO is this ye say is slain?
Whose voice answers not again?
Ellsworth, shall we call in vain
    On thy name to-day?

No! from every vale and hill
Our response all hearts shall thrill,
"Ellsworth's fame is with us still,
    Ne'er to pass away!"

Bring that rebel banner low,
Hoisted by a treacherous foe:
'T was for that they dealt the blow,
    Laid him in the dust.
Raise aloft, that all may see
His loved flag of Liberty.
Forward, then, to victory,
    Or perish if we must!

Hark to what Columbia saith:
"Mourn not for his early death,
With each patriot's dying breath
    Strength renewed is given
To the cause of truth and right,
To the land for which they fight.
After darkness cometh light, —
    Such the law of Heaven."

So we name him not in vain,
Though he comes not back again!
For his country he was slain;
    Ellsworth's blood shall rise
To our gracious Saviour — King:
'T is a holy gift we bring;
Such a sacred offering
    God will not despise.

COLONEL ELLSWORTH[1]

IT fell upon us like a crushing woe,
Sudden and terrible. "Can it be?" we said
"That he from whom we hoped so much, is
    dead,
Most foully murdered ere he met the foe?"
Why not? The men that would disrupt the
    State
By such base plots as theirs — frauds, thefts
    and lies —
What code of honor do they recognize?
They thirst for blood to satisfy their hate,
Our blood: so be it; but for every blow
Woe shall befall them; not in their wild
    way,
But stern and pitiless, we will repay,
Until, like swollen streams, *their* blood shall
    flow:

[1] From *Poetical Writings of Richard Henry*
Stoddard; copyright, 1880, by Charles Scribner
Sons.

And should we pause; the thought of Ells-
    worth slain,
Will steel our aching hearts to strike again!
        RICHARD HENRY STODDARD.

ON THE DEATH OF "JACKSON"

[May 24, 1861]

Not where the battle red
Covers with fame the dead, —
Not where the trumpet calls
Vengeance for each that falls, —
Not with his comrades dear,
Not there — he fell not there.

He grasps no brother's hand,
He sees no patriot band;
Daring alone the foe
He strikes — then waits the blow,
Counting his life not dear,
His was no heart to fear!

Shout! shout, his deed of glory!
Tell it in song and story;
Tell it where soldiers brave
Rush fearless to their grave;
Tell it — a magic spell
In that great deed shall dwell.

Yes! he hath won a name
Deathless for aye to fame;
Our flag baptized in blood,
Always, as with a flood,
Shall sweep the tyrant band
Whose feet pollute our land.

Then, freemen, raise the cry,
As freemen live or die!
Arm! arm you for the fight!
His banner in your sight;
And this your battle-cry,
"Jackson and victory!"

General Butler, meanwhile, had been sent with
reinforcements to Fortress Monroe, and after
making that important post secure, began various
offensive measures against the Confederate posts in
the neighborhood, manned largely by Virginians.

THE VIRGINIANS OF THE VALLEY

The knightliest of the knightly race
    That, since the days of old,
Have kept the lamp of chivalry
    Alight in hearts of gold·

The kindliest of the kindly band
    That, rarely hating ease,
Yet rode with Spotswood round the land,
    And Raleigh round the seas;

Who climbed the blue Virginian hills
    Against embattled foes,
And planted there, in valleys fair,
    The lily and the rose;
Whose fragrance lives in many lands,
    Whose beauty stars the earth,
And lights the hearths of happy homes
    With loveliness and worth.

We thought they slept! — the sons who kept
    The names of noble sires,
And slumbered while the darkness crept
    Around their vigil-fires;
But aye the "Golden Horseshoe" knights
    Their old Dominion keep,
Whose foes have found enchanted ground,
    But not a knight asleep!
        FRANCIS ORRERY TICKNOR.

On the night of June 9, 1861, Butler dispatched
two expeditions against Great and Little Bethel,
two churches on the Yorktown road, which had
been strongly fortified. The columns got confused
in the darkness, and fired upon each other. In the
battle which followed, the same mistake was made,
and the Union forces finally retreated, having
suffered heavily.

BETHEL

[June 10, 1861]

We mustered at midnight, in darkness we
    formed,
And the whisper went round of a fort to be
    stormed;
But no drum-beat had called us, no trumpet
    we heard,
And no voice of command, but our colonel's
    low word —
      "Column! Forward!"

And out, through the mist, and the murk of
    the morn,
From the beaches of Hampton our barges
    were borne;
And we heard not a sound, save the sweep
    of the oar,
Till the word of our colonel came up from
    the shore —
      "Column! Forward!"

With hearts bounding bravely, and eyes all
    alight,
As ye dance to soft music, so trod we that
    night;
Through the aisles of the greenwood, with
    vines overarched,
Tossing dew-drops, like gems, from our feet,
    as we marched —
        "Column! Forward!"

As ye dance with the damsels, to viol and
    flute,
So we skipped from the shadows, and mocked
    their pursuit;
But the soft zephyrs chased us, with scents of
    the morn,
As we passed by the hay-fields and green
    waving corn —
        "Column! Forward!"

For the leaves were all laden with fragrance
    of June,
And the flowers and the foliage with sweets
    were in tune;
And the air was so calm, and the forest so
    dumb,
That we heard our own heart-beats, like taps
    of a drum —
        "Column! Forward!"

Till the lull of the lowlands was stirred by the
    breeze,
And the buskins of morn brushed the tops of
    the trees,
And the glintings of glory that slid from her
    track
By the sheen of our rifles were gayly flung
    back —
        "Column! Forward!"

And the woodlands grew purple with sun-
    shiny mist,
And the blue-crested hill-tops with roselight
    were kissed,
And the earth gave her prayers to the sun in
    perfumes,
Till we marched as through gardens, and
    trampled on blooms —
        "Column! Forward!"

Ay, trampled on blossoms, and seared the
    sweet breath
Of the greenwood with low-brooding vapors
    of death;

O'er the flowers and the corn we were born
    like a blast,
And away to the forefront of battle w
    passed —
        "Column! Forward!"

For the cannon's hoarse thunder roared ou
    from the glades,
And the sun was like lightning on banners an
    blades,
When the long line of chanting Zouaves, lik
    a flood,
From the green of the woodlands rolled, crin
    son as blood —
        "Column! Forward!"

While the sound of their song, like the surg
    of the seas,
With the "Star-Spangled Banner" swelle
    over the leas;
And the sword of Duryea, like a torch, led th
    way,
Bearing down on the batteries of Bethel th
    day —
        "Column! Forward!"

Through green tasselled cornfields our co
    umns were thrown,
And like corn by the red scythe of fire we we
    mown;
While the cannon's fierce ploughings ne
    furrowed the plain,
That our blood might be planted for Liberty
    grain —
        "Column! Forward!"

Oh! the fields of fair June have no lack
    sweet flowers,
But their rarest and best breathe no fragrar
    like ours;
And the sunshine of June, sprinkling gold
    the corn,
Hath no harvest that ripeneth like Beth
    red morn —
        "Column! Forward!"

When our heroes, like bridegrooms, with l
    and with breath,
Drank the first kiss of Danger and clasped
    in death;
And the heart of brave Winthrop grew m
    with his lyre,
When the plumes of his genius lay moul
    in fire —
        "Column! Forward!"

Where he fell shall be sunshine as bright as
    his name,
And the grass where he slept shall be green as
    his fame;
For the gold of the pen and the steel of the
    sword
Write his deeds — in his blood — on the land
    he adored —
      "Column! Forward!"

And the soul of our comrade shall sweeten the
    air,
And the flowers and the grass-blades his
    memory upbear;
While the breath of his genius, like music in
    leaves,
With the corn-tassels whispers, and sings in
    the sheaves —
      "Column! Forward!"
          A. J. H. DUGANNE.

Among the Union dead was Major Theodore
Winthrop. He had pressed eagerly forward, and
as he sprang upon a log to get a view of the posi-
tion, was shot through the head.

DIRGE

FOR ONE WHO FELL IN BATTLE

[June 10, 1861]

Room for a Soldier! lay him in the clover;
He loved the fields, and they shall be his
    cover;
Make his mound with hers who called him
    once her lover:
    Where the rain may rain upon it,
    Where the sun may shine upon it,
    Where the lamb hath lain upon it,
    And the bee will dine upon it.

Bear him to no dismal tomb under city
    churches;
Take him to the fragrant fields, by the silver
    birches,
Where the whippoorwill shall mourn, where
    the oriole perches:
    Make his mound with sunshine on it,
    Where the bee will dine upon it,
    Where the lamb hath lain upon it,
    And the rain will rain upon it.

Busy as the busy bee, his rest should be the
    clover;
Gentle as the lamb was he, and the fern should
    be his cover;
Fern and rosemary shall grow my soldier's
    pillow over:
    Where the rain may rain upon it,
    Where the sun may shine upon it,
    Where the lamb hath lain upon it,
    And the bee will dine upon it.

Sunshine in his heart, the rain would come
    full often
Out of those tender eyes which evermore did
    soften;
He never could look cold, till we saw him in
    his coffin:
    Make his mound with sunshine on it,
    Where the wind may sigh upon it,
    Where the moon may stream upon it,
    And Memory shall dream upon it.

"Captain or Colonel," — whatever invoca-
    tion
Suit our hymn the best, no matter for thy
    station, —
On thy grave the rain shall fall from the eyes
    of a mighty nation!
    Long as the sun doth shine upon it
    Shall grow the goodly pine upon it,
    Long as the stars do gleam upon it
    Shall Memory come to dream upon it.
         THOMAS WILLIAM PARSONS.

About fifty thousand Union troops had mean-
while been collected along the Potomac — a force
which seemed to most people at the North quite
sufficient to crush the rebellion. "On to Rich-
mond!" was the cry, and popular clamor de-
manded that the advance be begun at once.

WAIT FOR THE WAGON

[July 1, 1861]

A HUNDRED thousand Northmen,
    In glittering war array,
Shout, "Onward now to Richmond!
    We'll brook no more delay;
Why give the traitors time and means
    To fortify the way
With stolen guns, in ambuscades?
    Oh! answer us, we pray."

Chorus of Chieftains —
> You must wait for the wagons,
> The real army wagons,
> The fat contract wagons,
> Bought in the red-tape way.

Now, if for army wagons,
  Not for compromise you wait,
Just ask them of the farmers
  Of any Union state;
And if you need ten thousand,
  Sound, sound, though second-hand,
You'll find upon the instant
  A supply for your demand.
> *Chorus* —
> No! wait for the wagons,
> The new army wagons,
> The fat contract wagons,
> Till the fifteenth of July.

No swindling fat contractors
  Shall block the people's way,
Nor rebel compromisers —
  'T is treason's reckoning day.
Then shout again our war-cry,
  To Richmond onward move!
We now can crush the traitors,
  And that we mean to prove!
> *Chorus* —
> No! wait for the wagons,
> The fat contract wagons;
> If red-tape so wills it,
> Wait till the Judgment-day.

During the months of June and July, the Confederate forces had been assembling at Manassas Junction, about thirty miles from Washington. General Beauregard was in command, and had distributed them along a little stream called Bull Run, where they had thrown up strong intrenchments. On July 15, 1861, yielding to the popular clamor, General Scott ordered the forward movement of the Union army. On July 17 the army reached Fairfax Court-House, and next day a division moved forward to Centreville and attacked the Confederates intrenched along Bull Run. A sharp engagement resulted, and the Federals fell back.

At two o'clock on the morning of Sunday, July 21, 1861, the Union Army again moved forward for a grand attack. Each army numbered about thirty thousand men. The skirmishers soon got into touch, and the Confederates were driven back, but were rallied by the example of General T. J. Jackson, who with his brigade was "standing like a stone wall," as General Bee exclaimed, giving him his immortal sobriquet. The Union advance was checked, heavy reinforcements came up for the

Confederates, and the Union regiments were finally swept from the field.

UPON THE HILL BEFORE CENTRE-VILLE

[July 21, 1861]

I'LL tell you what I heard that day:
I heard the great guns far away,
Boom after boom. Their sullen sound
Shook all the shuddering air around;
And shook, ah me! my shrinking ear,
And downward shook the hanging tear
That, in despite of manhood's pride,
Rolled o'er my face a scalding tide.
And then I prayed. O God! I prayed,
As never stricken saint, who laid
His hot cheek to the holy tomb
Of Jesus, in the midnight gloom.

"What saw I?" Little. Clouds of dust;
Great squares of men, with standards thrust
Against their course; dense columns crowned
With billowing steel. Then bound on bound,
The long black lines of cannon poured
Behind the horses, streaked and gored
With sweaty speed. Anon shot by,
Like a lone meteor of the sky,
A single horseman; and he shone
His bright face on me, and was gone.
All these with rolling drums, with cheers,
With songs familiar to my ears,
Passed under the far-hanging cloud,
And vanished, and my heart was proud!

For mile on mile the line of war
Extended; and a steady roar,
As of some distant stormy sea,
On the south wind came up to me.
And high in air, and over all,
Grew, like a fog, that murky pall,
Beneath whose gloom of dusty smoke
The cannon flamed, the bombshell broke.
And the sharp rattling volley rang,
And shrapnel roared, and bullets sang,
And fierce-eyed men, with panting breath,
Toiled onward at the work of death.
I could not see, but knew too well,
That underneath that cloud of hell,
Which still grew more by great degrees,
Man strove with man in deeds like these.

But when the sun had passed his stand
At noon, behold! on every hand
The dark brown vapor backward bore,

And fainter came the dreadful roar
From the huge sea of striving men.
Thus spoke my rising spirit then:
"Take comfort from that dying sound,
Faint heart, the foe is giving ground!"
And one, who taxed his horse's powers,
Flung at me, "Ho! the day is ours!"
And scoured along. So swift his pace,
I took no memory of his face.
Then turned I once again to Heaven;
All things appeared so just and even;
So clearly from the highest Cause
Traced I the downward-working laws —
Those moral springs, made evident,
In the grand, triumph-crowned event.
So half I shouted, and half sang,
Like Jephtha's daughter, to the clang
Of my spread, cymbal-striking palms,
Some fragments of thanksgiving psalms.

Meanwhile a solemn stillness fell
Upon the land. O'er hill and dell
Failed every sound. My heart stood still,
Waiting before some coming ill.
The silence was more sad and dread,
Under that canopy of lead,
Than the wild tumult of the war
That raged a little while before.
All Nature, in her work of death,
Paused for one last, despairing breath;
And, cowering to the earth, I drew
From her strong breast my strength anew.

When I arose, I wondering saw
Another dusty vapor draw,
From the far right, its sluggish way
Toward the main cloud, that frowning lay
Against the western sloping sun:
And all the war was re-begun,
Ere this fresh marvel of my sense
Caught from my mind significance.
And then — why ask me? O my God!
Would I had lain beneath the sod,
A patient clod, for many a day,
And from my bones and mouldering clay
The rank field grass and flowers had sprung,
Ere the base sight, that struck and stung
My very soul, confronted me,
Shamed at my own humanity.
O happy dead! who early fell,
Ye have no wretched tale to tell
Of causeless fear and coward flight,
Of victory snatched beneath your sight,
Of martial strength and honor lost,
Of mere life bought at any cost,

Of the deep, lingering mark of shame,
Forever scorched on brow and name,
That no new deeds, however bright,
Shall banish from men's loathful sight!

Ye perished in your conscious pride,
Ere this vile scandal opened wide
A wound that cannot close nor heal.
Ye perished steel to levelled steel,
Stern votaries of the god of war,
Filled with his godhead to the core!
Ye died to live, these lived to die,
Beneath the scorn of every eye!
How eloquent your voices sound
From the low chambers under ground!
How clear each separate title burns
From your high-set and laurelled urns!
While these, who walk about the earth,
Are blushing at their very birth!
And, though they talk, and go, and come,
Their moving lips are worse than dumb.
Ye sleep beneath the valley's dew,
And all the nation mourns for you;
So sleep till God shall wake the lands!
For angels, armed with fiery brands,
Await to take you by the hands.

The right-hand vapor broader grew;
It rose, and joined itself unto
The main cloud with a sudden dash.
Loud and more near the cannon's crash
Came toward me, and I heard a sound
As if all hell had broken bound —
A cry of agony and fear.
Still the dark vapor rolled more near,
Till at my very feet it tossed,
The vanward fragments of our host.
Can man, Thy image, sink so low,
Thou, who hast bent Thy tinted bow
Across the storm and raging main;
Whose laws both loosen and restrain
The powers of earth, without whose will
No sparrow's little life is still?
Was fear of hell, or want of faith,
Or the brute's common dread of death
The passion that began a chase,
Whose goal was ruin and disgrace?
What tongue the fearful sight may tell?
What horrid nightmare ever fell
Upon the restless sleep of crime —
What history of another time —
What dismal vision, darkly seen
By the stern-featured Florentine,
Can give a hint to dimly draw
The likeness of the scene I saw?

I saw, yet saw not. In that sea,
That chaos of humanity,
No more the eye could catch and keep
A single point, than on the deep
The eye may mark a single wave,
Where hurrying myriads leap and rave.
Men of all arms, and all costumes,
Bare-headed, decked with broken plumes;
Soldiers and officers, and those
Who wore but civil-suited clothes;
On foot or mounted — some bestrode
Steeds severed from their harnessed load;
Wild mobs of white-topped wagons, cars,
Of wounded, red with bleeding scars;
The whole grim panoply of war
Surged on me with a deafening roar!
All shades of fear, disfiguring man,
Glared through their faces' brazen tan.
Not one a moment paused, or stood
To see what enemy pursued.
With shrieks of fear, and yells of pain,
With every muscle on the strain,
Onward the struggling masses bore.
Oh! had the foemen lain before,
They'd trampled them to dust and gore,
And swept their lines and batteries
As autumn sweeps the windy trees!
Here one cast forth his wounded friend,
And with his sword or musket-end
Urged on the horses; there one trod
Upon the likeness of his God,
As if 't were dust; a coward here
Grew valiant with his very fear,
And struck his weaker comrade prone,
And struggled to the front alone.
All had one purpose, one sole aim,
That mocked the decency of shame, —
To fly, by any means to fly;
They cared not how, they asked not why.
I found a voice. My burning blood
Flamed up. Upon a mound I stood;
I could no more restrain my voice
Than could the prophet of God's choice.
"Back, animated dirt!" I cried,
"Back, on your wretched lives, and hide
Your shame beneath your native clay!
Or if the foe affrights you, slay
Your own base selves; and, dying, leave
Your children's tearful cheeks to grieve,
Not quail and blush, when you shall come,
Alive, to their degraded home!
Your wives will look askance with scorn;
Your boys, and infants yet unborn,
Will curse you to God's holy face!
Heaven holds no pardon in its grace

For cowards. Oh! are such as ye
The guardians of our liberty?
Back, if one trace of manhood still
May nerve your arm and brace your will!
You stain your country in the eyes
Of Europe and her monarchies!

The despots laugh, the peoples groan;
Man's cause is lost and overthrown!
I curse you, by the sacred blood
That freely poured its purple flood
Down Bunker's heights, on Monmouth's plain,
From Georgia to the rocks of Maine!
I curse you, by the patriot band
Whose bones are crumbling in the land!
By those who saved what these had won
In the high name of Washington!"
Then I remember little more.
As the tide's rising waves, that pour
Over some low and rounded rock,
The coming mass, with one great shock,
Flowed o'er the shelter of my mound,
And raised me helpless from the ground.
As the huge shouldering billows bear,
Half in the sea and half in air,
A swimmer on their foaming crest,
So the foul throng beneath me pressed,
Swept me along, with curse and blow,
And flung me — where, I ne'er shall know.

When I awoke, a steady rain
Made rivulets across the plain;
And it was dark — oh, very dark.
I was so stunned as scarce to mark
The ghostly figures of the trees,
Or hear the sobbing of the breeze
That flung the wet leaves to and fro.
Upon me lay a dismal woe,
A boundless, superhuman grief,
That drew no promise of relief
From any hope. Then I arose,
As one who struggles up from blows
By unseen hands; and as I stood
Alone, I thought that God was good,
To hide, in clouds and driving rain,
Our low world from the angel train,
Whose souls filled heroes when the earth
Was worthy of their noble birth.
By that dull instinct of the mind,
Which leads aright the helpless blind,
I struggled onward, till the dawn
Across the eastern clouds had drawn
A narrow line of watery gray;
And full before my vision lay
The great dome's gaunt and naked bones

Beneath whose crown the nation thrones
Her queenly person. On I stole,
With hanging head and abject soul,
Across the high embattled ridge,
And o'er the arches of the bridge.
So freshly pricked my sharp disgrace,
I feared to meet the human face,
Skulking, as any woman might,
Who 'd lost her virtue in the night,
And sees the dreadful glare of day
Prepare to light her homeward way,
Alone, heart-broken, shamed, undone,
I staggered into Washington!
Since then long sluggish days have passed,
And on the wings of every blast
Have come the distant nations' sneers
To tingle in our blushing ears.
In woe and ashes, as was meet,
We wore the penitential sheet.
But now I breathe a purer air,
And from the depths of my despair
Awaken to a cheering morn,
Just breaking through the night forlorn,
A morn of hopeful victory.
Awake, my countrymen, with me!
Redeem the honor which you lost.
With any blood, at any cost!
I ask not how the war began,
Nor how the quarrel branched and ran
To this dread height. The wrong or right
Stands clear before God's faultless sight.
I only feel the shameful blow,
I only see the scornful foe,
And vengeance burns in every vein
To die, or wipe away the stain.
The war-wise hero of the west,
Wearing his glories as a crest,
Of trophies gathered in your sight,
Is arming for the coming fight.
Full well his wisdom apprehends
The duty and its mighty ends;
The great occasion of the hour,
That never lay in human power
Since over Yorktown's tented plain
The red cross fell, nor rose again.
My humble pledge of faith I lay,
Dear comrade of my school-boy day,
Before thee, in the nation's view,
And if thy prophet prove untrue,
And from our country's grasp be thrown
The sceptre and the starry crown,
And thou, and all thy marshalled host
Be baffled and in ruin lost;
Oh! let me not outlive the blow
That seals my country's overthrow!

And, lest this woful end come true,
Men of the North, I turn to you.
Display your vaunted flag once more,
Southward your eager columns pour!
Sound trump, and fife, and rallying drum;
From every hill and valley come.
Old men, yield up your treasured gold!
Can liberty be priced and sold?
Fair matrons, maids, and tender brides
Gird weapons to your lovers' sides;
And though your hearts break at the deed,
Give them your blessing and God-speed;
Then point them to the field of flame,
With words like those of Sparta's dame;
And when the ranks are full and strong,
And the whole army moves along,
A vast result of care and skill,
Obedient to the master will;
And your young hero draws the sword,
And gives the last commanding word
That hurls your strength upon the foe —
Oh! let them need no second blow.
Strike, as your fathers struck of old;
Through summer's heat, and winter's cold,
Through pain, disaster, and defeat;
Through marches tracked with blood,
        feet;
Through every ill that could befall
The holy cause that bound them all!
Strike as they struck for liberty!
Strike as they struck to make you free!
Strike for the crown of victory!
                GEORGE HENRY BOKER.

MANASSAS

[July 21, 1861]

THEY have met at last — as storm-clouds
        Meet in heaven,
And the Northmen back and bleeding
        Have been driven;
And their thunders have been stilled,
And their leaders crushed or killed,
And their ranks with terror thrilled,
        Rent and riven!

Like the leaves of Vallambrosa
        They are lying;
In the moonlight, in the midnight,
        Dead and dying;
Like those leaves before the gale,
Swept their legions, wild and pale;
While the host that made them quail
        Stood, defying.

When aloft in morning sunlight
 Flags were flaunted,
And "swift vengeance on the rebel"
 Proudly vaunted:
Little did they think that night
Should close upon their shameful flight,
And rebels, victors in the fight,
 Stand undaunted.

But peace to those who perished
 In our passes!
Light be the earth above them;
 Green the grasses!
Long shall Northmen rue the day
When they met our stern array,
And shrunk from battle's wild affray
 At Manassas.
 CATHERINE M. WARFIELD.

A BATTLE BALLAD

TO GENERAL J. E. JOHNSTON

A SUMMER Sunday morning,
 July the twenty-first,
In eighteen hundred sixty-one,
 The storm of battle burst.

For many a year the thunder
 Had muttered deep and low,
And many a year, through hope and
 fear,
 The storm had gathered slow.

Now hope had fled the hopeful,
 And fear was with the past;
And on Manassas' cornfields
 The tempest broke at last.

A wreath above the pine-tops,
 The booming of a gun;
A ripple on the cornfields,
 And the battle was begun.

A feint upon our centre,
 While the foeman massed his might,
For our swift and sure destruction,
 With his overwhelming "right."

All the summer air was darkened
 With the tramping of their host;
All the Sunday stillness broken
 By the clamor of their boast.

With their lips of savage shouting,
 And their eyes of sullen wrath,
Goliath, with the weaver-beam,
 The champion of Gath.

Are they men who guard the passes,
 On our "left" so far away?
In the cornfields, O Manassas!
 Are they *men* who fought to-day?

Our *boys* are brave and gentle,
 And their brows are smooth and white
Have they grown to *men*, Manassas,
 In the watches of a night?

Beyond the grassy hillocks
 There are tents that glimmer white;
Beneath the leafy covert
 There is steel that glistens bright.

There are eyes of watchful reapers
 Beneath the summer leaves,
With a glitter as of sickles
 Impatient for the sheaves.

They are men who guard the passes,
 They are men who bar the ford;
Stands our David at Manassas,
 The champion of the Lord.

They are men who guard our altars,
 And beware, ye sons of Gath,
The deep and dreadful silence
 Of the lion in your path.

Lo! the foe was mad for slaughter,
 And the whirlwind hurtled on;
But our *boys* had grown to heroes,
 They were *lions*, every one.

And they stood a wall of iron,
 And they shone a wall of flame,
And they beat the baffled tempest
 To the caverns whence it came.

And Manassas' sun descended
 On their armies crushed and torn,
On a battle bravely ended,
 On a nation grandly born.

The laurel and the cypress,
 The glory and the grave,
We pledge to thee, O Liberty!
 The life-blood of the brave.
 FRANCIS ORRERY TICKNOR.

Retreat soon turned to flight and flight to panic. A great crowd of officials and civilians, male and female, had driven out from Washington to the battlefield to witness a victory which they considered certain. They were furnished with passes, and picnicked and wined and jested and watched the distant conflict. Suddenly the Union army gave way, the Confederates dashed forward in pursuit, and soldiers and civilians were mixed together in one panic-stricken mob.

THE RUN FROM MANASSAS JUNCTION

[July 21, 1861]

YANKEE DOODLE went to war,
  On his little pony;
What did he go fighting for,
  Everlasting goney!
Yankee Doodle was a chap
  Who bragged and swore tarnation,
He stuck a feather in his cap,
  And called it Federation.
    Yankee Doodle, keep it up,
    Yankee Doodle, dandy,
    Mind the music and the step,
      And with the girls be handy.

Yankee Doodle, he went forth
  To conquer the seceders,
All the journals of the North,
  In most ferocious leaders,
Breathing slaughter, fire, and smoke,
  Especially the latter,
His rage and fury to provoke,
  And vanity to flatter.

Yankee Doodle, having floored
  His separated brothers,
He reckoned his victorious sword
  Would turn against us others;
Secession first he would put down,
  Wholly and forever,
And afterward, from Britain's crown,
  He Canada would sever.

England offering neutral sauce
  To goose as well as gander,
Was what made Yankee Doodle cross,
  And did inflame his dander.
As though with choler drunk he fumed,
  And threatened vengeance martial,
Because Old England had presumed
  To steer a course impartial.

Yankee Doodle bore in mind,
  When warfare England harassed,
How he, unfriendly and unkind,
  Beset her and embarrassed;
He put himself in England's place,
  And thought this injured nation
Must view his trouble with a base
  Vindictive exultation.

We for North and South alike
  Entertain affection;
These for negro slavery strike;
  Those for forced protection.
Yankee Doodle is the pot,
  Southerner the kettle;
Equal morally, if not
  Men of equal mettle.

Yankee Doodle, near Bull Run,
  Met his adversary,
First he thought the fight he'd won,
  Fact proved quite contrary.
Panic-struck he fled, with speed
  Of lightning glib with unction,
Of slippery grease, in full stampede,
  From famed Manassas Junction.

As he bolted, no ways slow,
  Yankee Doodle hallooed,
"We are whipped!" and fled, although
  No pursuer followed.
Sword and gun right slick he threw
  Both away together,
In his cap, to public view,
  Showing the white feather.

Yankee Doodle, Doodle, do,
  Whither are you flying,
"A cocked hat we've been licked into,
  And knocked to Hades," crying?
Well, to Canada, sir-ree,
  Now that, by secession,
I am driven up a tree,
  To seize that there possession.

Yankee Doodle, be content,
  You've had a lenient whipping;
Court not further punishment
  By enterprise of stripping
Those neighbors, whom if you assail,
  They'll surely whip you hollow;
Moreover, when you've turned your tail,
  Won't hesitate to follow.

The flight of the Union forces was watched with exultation by Jefferson Davis, who was at Confederate headquarters, and who at once wired news of the victory to the Confederate Congress at Richmond. Throughout the South, the news was naturally received with deep rejoicing.

ON TO RICHMOND

AFTER SOUTHEY'S "MARCH TO MOSCOW"

MAJOR-GENERAL SCOTT
An order had got
To push on the column to Richmond;
For loudly went forth,
From all parts of the North,
The cry that an end of the war must be made
In time for the regular yearly Fall Trade:
Mr. Greeley spoke freely about the delay,
The Yankees "to hum" were all hot for the fray;
    The chivalrous Grow
    Declared they were slow, —
    And therefore the order
    To march from the border
And make an excursion to Richmond.

Major-General Scott
Most likely was not
Very loth to obey this instruction, I wot;
    In his private opinion
    The Ancient Dominion
Deserved to be pillaged, her sons to be shot,
And the reason is easily noted;
    Though this part of the earth
    Had given him birth,
    And medals and swords,
    Inscribed in fine words,
    It never for Winfield had voted.
Besides, you must know, that our First of Commanders
Had sworn quite as hard as the army in Flanders,
With his finest of armies and proudest of navies,
To wreak his old grudge against Jefferson Davis.
Then, "Forward the column," he said to McDowell;
    And the Zouaves with a shout,
    Most fiercely cried out,
"To Richmond or h–ll!" (I omit here the vowel)

And Winfield he ordered his carriage and four,
A dashing turnout, to be brought to the door,
    For a pleasant excursion to Richmond.

    Major-General Scott
    Had there on the spot
    A splendid array
    To plunder and slay;
    In the camp he might boast
    Such a numerous host,
    As he never had yet
    In the battlefield set;
Every class and condition of Northern society
Were in for the trip, a most varied variety:
In the camp he might hear every lingo in vogue,
"The sweet German accent, the rich Irish brogue."
    The buthiful boy
    From the banks of the Shannon
    Was there to employ
    His excellent cannon;
And besides the long files of dragoons and artillery,
    The Zouaves and Hussars,
    All the children of Mars —
    There were barbers and cooks,
    And writers of books, —
The *chef de cuisine* with his French bill of fare,
And the artists to dress the young officers' hair.
And the scribblers were ready at once to prepare
    An eloquent story
    Of conquest and glory;
And servants with numberless baskets Sillery,
Though Wilson, the Senator, followed the train,
At a distance quite safe, to "conduct the *Champagne!*"
While the fields were so green and the sky was so blue,
There was certainly nothing more pleasant to do,
    On this pleasant excursion to Richmond.

In Congress the talk, as I said, was of action,
To crush out *instanter* the traitorous faction,
    In the press, and the mess,
    They would hear nothing less

Than to make the advance, spite of rhyme or
    of reason,
And at once put an end to the insolent treason.
    There was Greeley,
    And Ely,
    And bloodthirsty Grow,
And Hickman (the rowdy, not Hickman the
    beau,)
    And that terrible Baker
Who would seize of the South every acre,
And Webb, who would drive us all into the
    Gulf, or
Some nameless locality smelling of sulphur;
    And with all this bold crew,
    Nothing would do,
While the fields were so green, and the sky
    was so blue,
    But to march on directly to Richmond.

    Then the gallant McDowell
    Drove madly the rowel
Of spur that had never been "won" by him,
    In the flank of his steed,
    To accomplish a deed,
Such as never before had been done by him;
    And the battery called Sherman's
        Was wheeled into line
    While the beer-drinking Germans
        From Neckar and Rhine,
    With minie and yager,
    Come on with a swagger,
    Full of fury and lager
(The day and the pageant were equally fine).
Oh! the fields were so green, and the sky was
    so blue,
Indeed 't was a spectacle pleasant to view,
    As the column pushed onward to Richmond.

    Ere the march was begun,
    In a spirit of fun,
    General Scott in a speech
    Said the army should teach
The Southrons the lesson the laws to obey,
And just before dusk of the third or fourth day,
    Should joyfully march into Richmond.

    He spoke of their drill,
    And their courage and skill,
And declared that the ladies of Richmond
    would rave
O'er such matchless perfection, and gracefully
    wave
In rapture their delicate kerchiefs in air
At their morning parades on the Capitol
    Square.

    But alack! and alas!
    Mark what soon came to pass,
When this army, in spite of his flatteries,
    Amid war's loudest thunder,
    Must stupidly blunder
Upon those accursed "masked batteries."
    Then Beauregard came,
    Like a tempest of flame,
    To consume them in wrath,
    In their perilous path;
And Johnson bore down in a whirlwind to
    sweep
    Their ranks from the field,
    Where their doom had been sealed,
As the storm rushes over the face of the
    deep;
While swift on the centre our President
    pressed,
    And the foe might descry,
    In the glance of his eye,
The light that once blazed upon Diomede's
    crest.
McDowell! McDowell! weep, weep for the
    day,
When the Southrons you met in their battle
    array;
To your confident hosts with its bullets and
    steel,
'T was worse than Culloden to luckless
    Lochiel.
Oh! the generals were green, and old Scott is
    now blue,
And a terrible business, McDowell, to you,
    Was that pleasant excursion to Richmond.
              JOHN R. THOMPSON.

At the North news of the defeat caused a bitter
discouragement, which soon gave place to deter-
mination to push the war through. On July 22,
1861, Congress authorized the enlistment of five
hundred thousand men. The term of enlistment
was for three years, or during the war, and the
North girded itself anew for the conflict.

CAST DOWN, BUT NOT DESTROYED

OH, Northern men — true hearts and bold —
    Unflinching to the conflict press!
Firmly our country's flag uphold,
    Till traitorous foes its sway confess!

Not lightly was our freedom bought,
    By many a martyr's cross and grave;
Six weary years our fathers fought,
    'Midst want and peril, sternly brave.

And thrice six years, with tightening coil,
  Still closer wound by treacherous art,
Men — children of our common soil —
  Have preyed upon the nation's heart!

Yet still it beats, responsive, deep,
  Its strong pulse throbbing through the land,
Gathering a human flood, to sweep
  Resistless, o'er the rebel band!

Firmly resolved to win success,
  We'll tread the path our fathers trod,
Unflinching to the conflict press,
  And, fearless, trust our cause to God!

  New York *Evening Post*, July 26, 1861.

The North soon had another bitter pill to swallow. On May 13, 1861, Great Britain issued a proclamation of neutrality, recognizing the Confederacy as a belligerent power. England's sympathy, because of close trade relations, was with the South, and the Southern people counted on her eventually recognizing their independence.

SHOP AND FREEDOM

[May 13, 1861]

THOUGH with the North we sympathize,
  It must not be forgotten
That with the South we've stronger ties,
  Which are composed of cotton,
Whereof our imports 'mount unto
  A sum of many figures;
And where would be our calico,
  Without the toil of niggers?

The South enslaves those fellow-men
  Whom we love all so dearly;
The North keeps commerce bound again,
  Which touches us more nearly.
Thus a divided duty we
  Perceive in this hard matter —
Free trade, or sable brothers free?
  Oh, will we choose the latter!

  London *Punch.*

James M. Mason and John Slidell were appointed commissioners from the Confederacy to England and France; they reached Havana on a little steamer that had run the blockade, and took passage for Southampton in the British mail steamship Trent. On November 8, 1861, in the Bahama Channel, the Trent was overhauled by the American man-of-war San Jacinto, Captain Wilkes. She was compelled to stop, and Mason and Slidell and their secretaries were taken from her by force.

THE C. S. A. COMMISSIONERS

[November, 1861]

YE jolly Yankee gentlemen, who live at home in ease,
How little do ye think upon the dangers of the seas!
The winds and waves, the whales and sharks, you've heard of long ago,
But there are things much worse than these, as presently I'll show.
If you're a true-bred Union man, go joyful where you please;
Beneath the glorious Stars and Stripes cross safe the stormy seas;
But look out for San Jacintos that may catch you on your way,
If you're acting as Commissioner for the noble C. S. A.

And now you'll guess my subject, and what my song's about;
But I'd not have put them into rhyme, if *they* had n't first put out;
For they *put out* of Charleston, when the night was drear and dark,
And then they put out all the lights, that they might not be a mark;
And then they did put out to sea (though here there seems a hitch,
For what could they expect to see when the night was black as pitch?),
But they somehow 'scaped the Union ships, and hoped on some fine day
To land in Europe and to "blow" about the C. S. A.

They safely got to Cuba and landed in Havana;
Described the power and glory of New Orleans and Savannah;
Declared that running the blockade was a thing by no means hard,
And boasted of the vic'tries won by their valiant Beauregard;
Davis's skill in government could never be surpassed —
The amazing strokes of genius by which he cash amassed;

Foreign bankers would acknowledge, ere a month had passed away,
That the true financial paradise was in the C. S. A.

. . . .

Some days are passed, and pleasantly, upon Bermuda's Isle,
The sun is shining bright and fair, and nature seems to smile;
The breezes moved the British flag that fluttered o'er the Trent,
And the ripples rose to lave her sides, as proudly on she went.
Mason and Slidell, on deck, thought all their dangers past,
And poked each other's ribs and laughed, as they leant against the mast:
"Have n't the Yankees just been done uncommonly nice, eh?
They've got most money, but the *brains* are in the C. S. A.!"

You have heard the ancient proverb, and, though old, it's very good,
Which hints "it's better not to crow until you've left the wood."
And so it proved with these two gents; for at that moment — souse!
A cannon-shot fell splash across the steamer's bows.
The San Jacinto came up close, and though rather rude, 't is true,
Good Wilkes he hailed the Trent and said, "I'll thank you to heave to;
If you don't give up two rascals, I must blow you right away.
Mason and Slidell they're named, and they're from the C. S. A."

The British captain raged and swore; but then what could he do?
It scarcely would be worth his while to be blown up, he knew;
Wilkes's marines, with bayonets fixed, were standing on the Trent,
So he gave up the traitors, and o'er the side they went.
Wilkes, having got them, wished they'd feel pleasant and at home,
So offered his best cabins, if their ladies chose to come;
But they shook their heads and merely smiled, I'm sorry for to say,
Conjugality's at a discount down in the C. S. A.

They coolly said unto their lords, "Our dresses all are new;
What on earth would be the use of going back with you?
And though we're very sorry that your plans are undone,
We mean to pass the winter in Paris and in London.
'Stead of bothering you, and sharing your prison beds and fetters,
We'll write each mail from Europe the most delightful letters;
Tell you of all we've done and seen, at party, ball, or play,
To cheer your hearts, poor martyrs, to *cotton* and C. S. A."

So the two vessels parted; the San Jacinto went
To unload her precious cargo, while the captain of the Trent,
Having lost a (probable) *douceur* which had seemed within his grip,
We presume, for consolation, retired and took a nip.
The ladies talked of the affair less with a tear than smile;
Their lords and masters took their way to Warren's Fort the while;
And gratis lodged and boarded there, they may think for many a day
That brains are sometimes northward found as well's in C. S. A.

The prisoners were taken to Fort Warren, in Boston harbor, and the North went wild with delight. It was understood that Great Britain would have to be reckoned with, but no one seemed to care. Wilkes was complimented and banquetted and lionized, and the House of Representatives gave him a vote of thanks.

DEATH OF THE LINCOLN DESPOTISM

'T was out upon mid ocean that the San Jacinto hailed
An English neutral vessel, while on her course she sailed;
They sent her traitor Fairfax, to board her with his crew,
And beard the "British lion" with his "Yankee-doodle-doo."
The Yankees took her passengers, and put them on their ship,

And swore that base secession could not give
    them the slip;
But England says she 'll have them, if Wash-
    ington must fall,
So Lincoln and his "nigger craft" must cer-
    tainly feel small.

Of all the "Yankee notions" that ever had
    their birth,
The one of searching neutrals affords the
    greatest mirth —
To the Southrons; but the Yankees will ever
    hate the fame
Which gives to Wilkes and Fairfax their
    never-dying name.
Throughout the North their Captain Wilkes
    received his meed of praise,
For doing — in these civilized — the deeds
    of darker days;
But England's guns will thunder along the
    Yankee coast,
And show the abolitionists too soon they
    made their boast.

Then while Old England's cannon are boom-
    ing on the sea,
Our Johnson, Smith, and Beauregard dear
    Maryland will free,
And Johnston in Kentucky will whip the
    Yankees too,
And start them to the lively tune of "Yankee-
    doodle-doo."
Then down at Pensacola, where the game is
    always "Bragg,"
The "Stars and Stripes" will be pulled down
    and in the dust be dragged;
For Pickens can't withstand us when Brax-
    ton is the cry,
And there you 'll see the Yankees, with their
    usual speed, will fly.

On the coast of Dixie's kingdom there are
    batteries made by Lee,
And covered up with cotton, which the Yan-
    kees want to see;
But when they go to take it, they 'll find it
    will not do,
And start upon the "double-quick" to
    "Yankee-doodle-doo."
Then Evans and his cavalry will follow in
    their track,
And drive them in the Atlantic, or safely
    bring them back,

And hold them till Abe Lincoln and all his
    Northern scum
Shall own our independence of "Yankee-
    Doodledom."

Richmond *Dispatch*.

News of the seizure reached England November
27, 1861. A cabinet meeting was at once held,
the act of Captain Wilkes was declared to be "a
clear violation of the law of nations," the release
of Mason and Slidell was demanded, together with
a suitable apology for the aggression. England
began to make extensive naval preparations, and
eight thousand troops were sent to Canada.

JONATHAN TO JOHN

[December, 1861]

It don't seem hardly right, John,
    When both my hands was full,
To stump me to a fight, John, —
    Your cousin, tu, John Bull!
      Ole Uncle S. sez he, "I guess
      We know it now," sez he,
"The Lion's paw is all the law,
      Accordin' to J. B.,
      Thet's fit for you an' me!"

You wonder why we 're hot, John?
    Your mark wuz on the guns,
The neutral guns, thet shot, John,
    Our brothers an' our sons:
      Ole Uncle S. sez he, "I guess
      There 's human blood," sez he,
"By fits an' starts, in Yankee hearts,
      Though 't may surprise J. B.
      More 'n it would you an' me."

Ef *I* turned mad dogs loose, John,
    On *your* front-parlor stairs,
Would it jest meet your views, John,
    To wait an' sue their heirs?
      Ole Uncle S. sez he, "I guess,
      I on'y guess," sez he,
"Thet ef Vattel on *his* toes fell,
      'T would kind o' rile J. B.,
      Ez wal ez you an' me!"

Who made the law thet hurts, John,
    Heads I win — ditto tails?
"J. B." was on his shirts, John,
    Onless my memory fails.
      Ole Uncle S. sez he, "I guess
      (I'm good at thet)," sez he,

"Thet sauce for goose ain't *jest* the juice
  For ganders with J. B.,
    No more 'n with you or me!"

When your rights was our wrongs, John,
  You did n't stop for fuss, —
Britanny's trident prongs, John,
  Was good 'nough law for us.
    Ole Uncle S. sez he, "I guess,
      Though physic 's good," sez he,
"It does n't foller thet he can swaller
  Prescriptions signed 'J. B.,'
    Put up by you an' me."

We own the ocean, tu, John:
  You mus'n' take it hard,
Ef we can't think with you, John,
  It's jest your own back yard.
    Ole Uncle S. sez he, "I guess
      Ef *thet 's* his claim," sez he,
"The fencin'-stuff 'll cost enough
  To bust up friend J. B.,
    Ez wal ez you an' me!"

Why talk so dreffle big, John,
  Of honor when it meant
You did n't care a fig, John,
  But jest for *ten per cent?*
    Ole Uncle S. sez he, "I guess
      He's like the rest," sez he:
"When all is done, it's number one
  Thet's nearest to J. B.,
    Ez wal ez t' you an' me!"

We give the critters back, John,
  Cos Abram thought 't was right;
It warn't your bullyin' clack, John,
  Provokin' us to fight.
    Ole Uncle S. sez he, "I guess
      We've a hard row," sez he,
"To hoe jest now; but thet, somehow,
  May happen to J. B.,
    Ez wal ez you an' me!"

We ain't so weak an' poor, John,
  With twenty million people,
An' close to every door, John,
  A school-house an' a steeple.
    Ole Uncle S. sez he, "I guess
      It is a fact," sez he,
"The surest plan to make a Man
  Is, think him so, J. B.,
    Ez much ez you or me!"

Our folks believe in Law, John;
  An' it's fer her sake, now,

They've left the axe an' saw, John,
  The anvil an' the plough.
    Ole Uncle S. sez he, "I guess,
      Ef 't warn't fer law," sez he,
"There'd be one shindy from here to Indy;
  An' *thet* don't suit J. B.
    (When 't ain't 'twixt you an' me!)"

We know we've got a cause, John,
  Thet's honest, just, an' true;
We thought 't would win applause, John,
  If nowheres else, from you.
    Ole Uncle S. sez he, "I guess
      His love of right," sez he,
"Hangs by a rotten fibre o' cotton:
  There's natur' in J. B.,
    Ez wal ez in you an' me!"

The South says, "*Poor folks down!*" John,
  An' "*All men up!*" say we, —
White, yaller, black, an' brown, John:
  Now which is your idee?
    Ole Uncle S. sez he, "I guess
      John preaches wal," sez he;
"But, sermon thru, an' come to *du*,
  Why, there's the old J. B.
    A-crowdin' you an' me!"

Shall it be love, or hate, John?
  It's you thet's to decide;
Ain't *your* bonds held by Fate, John,
  Like all the world's beside?
    Ole Uncle S. sez he, "I guess
      Wise men forgive," sez he,
"But not forgit; an' some time yit
  Thet truth may strike J. B.,
    Ez wal ez you an' me!"

God means to make this land, John,
  Clear thru, from sea to sea,
Believe an' understand, John,
  The *wuth* o' bein' free.
    Ole Uncle S. sez he, "I guess
      God's price is high," sez he;
"But nothin' else than wut he sells
  Wears long, an' thet J. B.
    May larn, like you an' me!"
              JAMES RUSSELL LOWELL.

England was clearly in the right in her conten-
tion; Wilkes's act was disavowed, and Mason and
Slidell were delivered to an English steamer at
Provincetown. All danger of war with England
was for the time being avoided.

A NEW SONG TO AN OLD TUNE

JOHN BULL, ESQUIRE, my jo John,
　When we were first acquent,
You acted very much as now
　You act about the Trent.
You stole my bonny sailors, John,
　My bonny ships also,
You 're aye the same fierce beast to me,
　John Bull, Esquire, my jo!

John Bull, Esquire, my jo John,
　Since we were linked together,
Full many a jolly fight, John,
　We 've had with one another.
Now must we fight again, John?
　Then at it let us go!
And God will help the honest heart,
　John Bull, Esquire, my jo.

John Bull, Esquire, my jo John,
　A century has gone by,

Since you called me your slave, John,
　Since I at you let fly.
You want to fight it out again —
　That war of waste and woe;
You 'll find me much the same old coon,
　John Bull, Esquire, my jo.

John Bull, Esquire, my jo John,
　If lying loons have told
That I have lost my pluck, John,
　And fight not as of old;
You 'd better not believe it, John,
　Nor scorn your ancient foe;
For I 've seen weaker days than this,
　John Bull, Esquire, my jo.

John Bull, Esquire, my jo John,
　Hear this my language plain:
I never smote you unprovoked,
　I never smote in vain.
If you want peace, peace let it be!
　If war, be pleased to know,
Shots in my locker yet remain,
　John Bull, Esquire, my jo!

CHAPTER IV

THE GRAND ARMY OF THE POTOMAC

The defeat at Bull Run showed the necessity for a thorough reorganization of the Army of the Potomac, and George B. McClellan, who had made a successful campaign in Western Virginia, was summoned to Washington and placed in command. At the end of two months, he had under him a splendidly equipped and disciplined force of over a hundred thousand men. The pickets were gradually extended, and little skirmishes with the enemy took place almost daily.

CIVIL WAR

"RIFLEMAN, shoot me a fancy shot
　Straight at the heart of yon prowling vi-
　　dette;
Ring me a ball in the glittering spot
　That shines on his breast like an amulet!"

"Ah, captain! here goes for a fine-drawn bead,
　There 's music around when my barrel 's in
　　tune!"
Crack! went the rifle, the messenger sped,
　And dead from his horse fell the ringing
　　dragoon.

"Now, rifleman, steal through the bushes, and
　snatch
　From your victim some trinket to handsel
　　first blood;
A button, a loop, or that luminous patch
　That gleams in the moon like a diamond
　　stud!"

"O captain! I staggered, and sunk on my
　track,
　When I gazed on the face of that fallen vi-
　　dette,
For he looked so like you, as he lay on his
　back,
　That my heart rose upon me, and masters
　　me yet.

"But I snatched off the trinket, — this locket
　of gold;
　An inch from the centre my lead broke its
　　way,
Scarce grazing the picture, so fair to be-
　hold,
　Of a beautiful lady in bridal array."

"Ha! rifleman, fling me the locket! — 't is
    she,
My brother's young bride, and the fallen
    dragoon
Was her husband — Hush! soldier, 't was
    Heaven's decree,
We must bury him there, by the light of the
    moon!

"But, hark! the far bugles their warnings
    unite;
War is a virtue, — weakness a sin;
There's a lurking and loping around us to-
    night;
Load again, rifleman, keep your hand in!"
          CHARLES DAWSON SHANLY.

McClellan at last began preparations for a grand
advance into Virginia, troops were sent across
the Potomac in great numbers — then, suddenly,
the orders were countermanded and the troops
brought back across the river. The army had
increased to one hundred and fifty thousand men,
but for nearly two months the public ear was
daily irritated by the report, "All quiet along the
Potomac."

THE PICKET-GUARD

[November, 1861]

"ALL quiet along the Potomac," they say,
    "Except now and then a stray picket
Is shot, as he walks on his beat to and fro,
    By a rifleman hid in the thicket.
'T is nothing: a private or two, now and then,
    Will not count in the news of the battle;
Not an officer lost — only one of the men,
    Moaning out, all alone, the death rattle."

All quiet along the Potomac to-night,
    Where the soldiers lie peacefully dreaming;
Their tents in the rays of the clear autumn
    moon,
    Or the light of the watch-fire, are gleaming.
A tremulous sigh of the gentle night-wind
    Through the forest leaves softly is creeping,
While the stars up above, with their glittering
    eyes,
    Keep guard, for the army is sleeping.

There's only the sound of the lone sentry's
    tread
As he tramps from the rock to the fountain,
And thinks of the two in the low trundle-bed
    Far away in the cot on the mountain.

His musket falls slack; his face, dark and
    grim,
    Grows gentle with memories tender,
As he mutters a prayer for the children
    asleep —
    For their mother — may Heaven defend
    her!

The moon seems to shine just as brightly as
    then,
    That night, when the love yet unspoken
Leaped up to his lips — when low-murmured
    vows
    Were pledged to be ever unbroken.
Then drawing his sleeve roughly over his eyes,
    He dashes off tears that are welling,
And gathers his gun closer up to its place
    As if to keep down the heart-swelling.

He passes the fountain, the blasted pine-tree;
    The footstep is lagging and weary;
Yet onward he goes, through the broad belt
    of light,
    Towards the shade of the forest so dreary.
Hark! was it the night-wind that rustled the
    leaves?
    Was it moonlight so wondrously flashing?
It looked like a rifle . . . "Ha! Mary, good-
    by!"
    The red life-blood is ebbing and plashing.

All quiet along the Potomac to-night —
    No sound save the rush of the river,
While soft falls the dew on the face of the
    dead —
    The picket's off duty forever!
          ETHEL LYNN BEERS.

Despite the size and efficiency of the "Grand
Army," nothing was done and nothing attempted.
It was evident that McClellan, though a perfect
organizer and disciplinarian, lacked the qualities
of aggressive leadership, and the discontent of the
country found constant and angry expression.

TARDY GEORGE

[January, 1862]

WHAT are you waiting for, George, I pray?
To scour your cross-belts with fresh pipe-
    clay?
To burnish your buttons, to brighten your
    guns;
Or wait you for May-day and warm spring
    suns?

Are you blowing your fingers because they are
cold,
Or catching your breath ere you take a hold?
Is the mud knee-deep in valley and gorge?
What are you waiting for, tardy George?

Want you a thousand more cannon made,
To add to the thousand now arrayed?
Want you more men, more money to pay?
Are not two millions enough per day?
Wait you for gold and credit to go,
Before we shall see your martial show;
Till Treasury Notes will not pay to forge?
What are you waiting for, tardy George?

Are you waiting for your hair to turn,
Your heart to soften, your bowels to yearn
A little more toward "our Southern friends,"
As at home and abroad they work their
ends?
"Our Southern friends!" whom you hold so
dear
That you do no harm and give no fear,
As you tenderly take them by the gorge —
What are you waiting for, tardy George?

Now that you've marshalled your whole com-
mand,
Planned what you would, and changed what
you planned;
Practised with shot and practised with shell,
Know to a hair where every one fell,
Made signs by day and signals by night;
Was it all done to keep out of a fight?
Is the whole matter too heavy a charge?
What are you waiting for, tardy George?

Shall we have more speeches, more re-
views?
Or are you waiting to hear the news;
To hold up your hands in mute surprise,
When France and England shall "recognize"?
Are you too grand to fight traitors small?
Must you have a nation to cope withal?
Well, hammer the anvil and blow the forge —
You'll soon have a dozen, tardy George.

Suppose for a moment, George, my friend —
Just for a moment — you condescend
To use the means that are in your hands,
The eager muskets and guns and brands;
Take one bold step on the Southern sod,
And leave the issue to watchful God!
For now the nation raises its gorge,
Waiting and watching you, tardy George.

I should not much wonder, George, my
boy,
If Stanton get in his head a toy,
And some fine morning, ere you are out,
He send you all "to the right about" —
You and Jomini, and all the crew
Who think that war is nothing to do
But to drill and cypher, and hammer and
forge —
What are you waiting for, tardy George?

Finally, President Lincoln demanded that this
great army do something, and it was decided to
advance again against the Confederates at Ma-
nassas. The advance began on March 9, 1862, and
when the army reached Manassas, it found that
the Confederates had removed all their stores and
munitions and abandoned the position. Whereupon
the Grand Army marched back to the Potomac.

HOW McCLELLAN TOOK MANASSAS

[March 10, 1862]

HEARD ye how the bold McClellan,
He, the wether with the bell on;
He, the head of all the asses —
Heard ye how he took Manassas?

When the Anaconda plucky
Flopped its tail in old Kentucky;
When up stream the gunboats paddled,
And the thieving Floyd skedaddled,
Then the chief of all the asses
Heard the word: Go, take Manassas!

Forty brigades wait around him,
Forty blatant trumpets sound him,
As the pink of all the heroes
Since the time of fiddling Neros.
"Now's the time," cry out the masses,
"Show your pluck and take Manassas!"

Contrabands come flocking to him:
"Lo! the enemy flies — pursue him!"
"No," says George, "don't start a trigger
On the word of any nigger;
Let no more of the rascals pass us,
I know all about Manassas."

When at last a prowling Yankee —
No doubt long, and lean, and lanky —
Looking out for new devices,
Took the wooden guns as prizes,
Says he: "I sweow, ere daylight passes
I'll take a peep at famed Manassas."

Then up to the trenches boldly
Marched he — they received him coldly;
Nary reb was there to stop him.
Gathering courage, in he passes:
"Jerusalem! I've took Manassas."

Bold McClellan heard the story:
"Onward, men, to fields of glory;
Let us show the rebel foemen,
When we're READY we're not slow, men;
Wait no more for springing grasses —
Onward! onward! to Manassas!"

Baggage trains were left behind him,
In his eagerness to find them;
Upward the balloons ascended,
To see which way the rebels trended;
Thirty miles away his glasses
Swept the horizon round Manassas.

Out of sight, the foe, retreating,
Answered back no hostile greeting;
None could tell, as off he paddled,
Whitherward he had skedaddled.
Then the chief of all the asses
Cried: "Hurrah! I've got Manassas."

Future days will tell the wonder,
How the mighty Anaconda
Lay supine along the border,
With the mighty Mac to lord her:
Tell on shaft and storied brasses
How he took the famed Manassas.

McClellan, meanwhile, had decided that the
proper way to take Richmond was to remove his
army to Fortress Monroe and advance up the
peninsula. The change of base was accomplished
by April 3, 1862, and the advance began, the army
encountering no obstacle save almost impassable
mud. McClellan, however, firmly believed that
an immense force of Confederates was massed
before him and proceeded so cautiously that he
scarcely moved at all, and the impatience of the
people deepened into anger and disgust.

WANTED — A MAN

BACK from the trebly crimsoned field
Terrible words are thunder-tost;
Full of the wrath that will not yield,
Full of revenge for battles lost!
Hark to their echo, as it crost
The Capital, making faces wan:
"End this murderous holocaust;
Abraham Lincoln, give us a MAN!

"Give us a man of God's own mould,
Born to marshal his fellow-men;
One whose fame is not bought and sold
At the stroke of a politician's pen;
Give us the man of thousands ten,
Fit to do as well as to plan;
Give us a rallying-cry, and then,
Abraham Lincoln, give us a MAN!

"No leader to shirk the boasting foe,
And to march and countermarch our brave,
Till they fall like ghosts in the marshes
low,
And swamp-grass covers each nameless
grave;
Nor another, whose fatal banners wave
Aye in Disaster's shameful van;
Nor another, to bluster, and lie, and rave; —
Abraham Lincoln, give us a MAN!

"Hearts are mourning in the North,
While the sister rivers seek the main,
Red with our life-blood flowing forth —
Who shall gather it up again?
Though we march to the battle-plain
Firmly as when the strife began,
Shall all our offering be in vain? —
Abraham Lincoln, give us a MAN!

"Is there never one in all the land,
One on whose might the Cause may lean?
Are all the common ones so grand,
And all the titled ones so mean?
What if your failure may have been
In trying to make good bread from bran,
From worthless metal a weapon keen? —
Abraham Lincoln, find us a MAN!

"Oh, we will follow him to the death,
Where the foeman's fiercest columns are!
Oh, we will use our latest breath,
Cheering for every sacred star!
His to marshal us high and far;
Ours to battle, as patriots can
When a Hero leads the Holy War! —
Abraham Lincoln, give us a MAN!"
EDMUND CLARENCE STEDMAN.

Finally, after infinite preparation, McClellan's
batteries were ready to open on the Confederate
works at Yorktown, but on May 4, 1862, it was
discovered that the works had been abandoned.
Hooker's and Kearny's cavalry began a vigorous
pursuit of the Confederates, caught up with them
at Williamsburg and captured the works there,
after a severe engagement.

THE GALLANT FIGHTING "JOE"

[May 4, 5, 1862]

From Yorktown on the fourth of May
  The rebels did skedaddle,
And to pursue them on their way
  Brave Hooker took the saddle.
"I'll lead you on, brave boys," he said,
  "Where danger points the way;"
And drawing forth his shining blade,
  "Move onward!" he did say.
Chorus — Then we'll shout hurrah for
      Hooker, boys,
    The gallant fighting Joe;
    We'll follow him with heart and
      hand,
    Wherever he does go.

"Forward, March!" then was the word
  That passed from front to rear,
When all the men with one accord
  Gave a loud and hearty cheer.
And then with Hooker at our head,
  We marched in order good,
Till darkness all around us spread,
  When we lay down in the wood.

Early next morn by break of day,
  The rain in torrents fell;
"This day," brave Hooker he did say,
  "Your valor it will tell.
Williamsburg is very near,
  Be steady every man,
Let every heart be filled with cheer,
  And I will take the van."

The gallant Massachusetts men
  Fought well and nobly, too,
As did the men from good old Penn.,
  And Jersey, ever true,
And Sickles' men like lions brave,
  Their courage did display,
For gallantly they did behave
  On the battle-field that day.

The men from Mass. and good old Penn.
  That morn the fight began,
And like true, noble-hearted men,
  Most nobly they did stand.
When Jersey's sons, the bold, the brave,
  Not fearing lead nor steel,
Their gallant comrades for to save,
  Dashed boldly to the field.

By every means the rebels sought
  To stand the Jerseys' fire,
But soon for them it was too hot,
  And they quickly did retire.
But getting reënforced again
  With numbers very great,
The gallant band of Jerseymen
  Were forced for to retreat.

"Now, Sickles' men," Hooker did say,
  "Move out to the advance;
If you your courage would display,
  Now you have got a chance.
The foe have forced us to give way,
  They number six to one,
But still, my lads, we'll gain the day,
  And I will lead you on."

Excelsior then the foremost stood,
  Not knowing dread nor fear,
And met the rebels in the woods,
  With a loud and hearty cheer.
Volley after volley flew,
  Like hail the balls did fly,
And Hooker cried: " My heroes true,
  We'll conquer or we'll die."

Our ammunition being gone,
  Brave Hooker then did say:
" Reënforcements fast are coming on,
  My lads, do not give way.
Keep good your ground, our only chance
  Is t' remain upon the field.
And if the rebels dare advance,
  We'll meet them with the steel."

'T was then brave Kearny did appear,
  Who ne'er to foe would yield,
To him we gave a hearty cheer,
  As he rushed on the field.
"Now, charge! my lads," then Hooker
    cried,
  "Our work will soon be done,
For with brave Kearny by our side,
  The rebels we'll make run."

And since that time we all do know
  The battles he hath won;
He beat the rebels at Bristow,
  And chased them to Bull Run;
And had we a few more loyal men
  Like the gallant fighting "Joe,"
The war would soon be at an end,
  Then home we all would go.

Singing, hurrah, hurrah, for Hooker's
   boys,
The gallant Fighting Joe,
We 'll follow him with heart and hand,
   Wherever he does go.
                        JAMES STEVENSON.

The advance continued slowly, and on May 31,
1862, a portion of the army reached Fair Oaks.
Here the Confederates attacked with force, and
would have won a decisive victory but for the
timely arrival of dashing "Phil" Kearny, who ral-
lied the Union forces, led them forward, and swept
the Confederates from the field.

KEARNY AT SEVEN PINES

[May 31, 1862]

So that soldierly legend is still on its journey, —
   That story of Kearny who knew not to
      yield!
'T was the day when with Jameson, fierce
      Berry, and Birney,
   Against twenty thousand he rallied the field.
Where the red volleys poured, where the
      clamor rose highest,
   Where the dead lay in clumps through the
      dwarf oak and pine,
Where the aim from the thicket was surest
      and nighest, —
   No charge like Phil Kearny's along the
      whole line.

When the battle went ill, and the bravest
      were solemn,
   Near the dark Seven Pines, where we still
      held our ground,
He rode down the length of the withering
      column,
   And his heart at our war-cry leapt up with
      a bound;
He snuffed, like his charger, the wind of the
      powder, —
   His sword waved us on and we answered
      the sign;
Loud our cheer as we rushed, but his laugh
      rang the louder.
   "There 's the devil's own fun, boys, along
      the whole line!"

How he strode his brown steed! How we
      saw his blade brighten
   In the one hand still left, — and the reins
      in his teeth!

He laughed like a boy when the holidays
      heighten,
   But a soldier's glance shot from his visor
      beneath.
Up came the reserves to the mellay infernal,
   Asking where to go in, — through the
      clearing or pine?
"Oh, anywhere! Forward! 'T is all the same,
      Colonel:
   You 'll find lovely fighting along the whole
      line!"

Oh, evil the black shroud of night at Chan-
      tilly,
   That hid him from sight of his brave men
      and tried!
Foul, foul sped the bullet that clipped the
      white lily,
   The flower of our knighthood, the whole
      army's pride!
Yet we dream that he still, — in that shadowy
      region
   Where the dead form their ranks at the
      wan drummer's sign, —
Rides on, as of old, down the length of his
      legion,
   And the word still is "Forward!" along
      the whole line.
                  EDMUND CLARENCE STEDMAN.

For nearly a month after this battle, the Army
of the Potomac lay along the Chickahominy, within
a few miles of Richmond, while the Confederates
concentrated their forces, under Robert E. Lee, for
the defence of the city. On June 14, 1862, General
J. E. B. Stuart, with a force of fifteen hundred cav-
alry, circled the Union position, destroyed stores,
seized mules and horses, took nearly two hun-
dred prisoners, and returned leisurely to Rich-
mond. Captain Latané was killed in a skirmish
during this expedition.

THE BURIAL OF LATANÉ

[June 14, 1862]

THE combat raged not long, but ours the day;
And, through the hosts that compassed us
      around,
Our little band rode proudly on its way,
Leaving one gallant comrade, glory-crowned,
Unburied on the field he died to gain —
Single of all his men, amid the hostile slain.

One moment on the battle's edge he stood —
Hope's halo, like a helmet, round his hair;

The next beheld him, dabbled in his blood,
Prostrate in death — and yet, in death how
    fair!
Even thus he passed through the red gates of
    strife,
From earthly crowns and palms, to an im-
    mortal life.

A brother bore his body from the field,
And gave it unto strangers' hands, that closed
The calm blue eyes on earth forever sealed,
And tenderly the slender limbs composed:
Strangers, yet sisters, who, with Mary's love,
Sat by the open tomb, and, weeping, looked
    above.

A little child strewed roses on his bier —
Pale roses, not more stainless than his soul,
Nor yet more fragrant than his life sincere,
That blossomed with good actions — brief,
    but whole;
The aged matron and the faithful slave
Approached with reverent feet the hero's
    lowly grave.

No man of God might say the burial rite
Above the "rebel" — thus declared the foe
That blanched before him in the deadly fight;
But woman's voice, with accents soft and
    low,
Trembling with pity — touched with pathos
    — read
Over his hallowed dust the ritual for the dead.

"'T is sown in weakness, it is raised in
    power!"
Softly the promise floated on the air,
While the low breathings of the sunset hour
Came back responsive to the mourner's prayer.
Gently they laid him underneath the sod,
And left him with his fame, his country, and
    his God!

Let us not weep for him, whose deeds endure!
So young, so brave, so beautiful! He died
As he had wished to die; the past is sure;
Whatever yet of sorrow may betide
Those who still linger by the stormy shore,
Change cannot harm him now, nor fortune
    touch him more.
                    JOHN R. THOMPSON.

Meanwhile, McDowell's corps had been ordered
forward from the Shenandoah valley to coöperate
with McClellan, but was harassed by the Confed-
erate cavalry under Turner Ashby and Stonewall
Jackson, which was handled with the utmost bril-
liancy and daring.

THE CHARGE BY THE FORD

EIGHTY and nine with their captain
    Rode on the enemy's track,
Rode in the gray of the morning:
    Nine of the ninety came back.

Slow rose the mist from the river,
    Lighter each moment the way:
Careless and tearless and fearless
    Galloped they on to the fray.

Singing in tune, how the scabbards
    Loud on the stirrup-irons rang,
Clinked as the men rose in saddle,
    Fell as they sank with a clang.

What is it moves by the river,
    Jaded and weary and weak,
Gray-backs — a cross on their banner —
    Yonder the foe whom they seek.

Silence! They see not, they hear not,
    Tarrying there by the marge:
Forward! Draw sabre! Trot! Gallop!
    Charge! like a hurricane, *charge!*

Ah! 't was a man-trap infernal —
    Fire like the deep pit of hell!
Volley on volley to meet them,
    Mixed with the gray rebel's yell.

Ninety had ridden to battle,
    Tracing the enemy's track, —
Ninety had ridden to battle,
    Nine of the ninety came back.

Honor the name of the ninety,
    Honor the heroes who came
Scatheless from five hundred muskets,
    Safe from the lead-bearing flame.

Eighty and one of the troopers
    Lie on the field of the slain —
Lie on the red field of honor:
    Honor the nine who remain!

Cold are the dead there, and gory,
    There where their life-blood was spilt.
Back come the living, each sabre
    Red from the point to the hilt.

Give them three cheers and a tiger!
Let the flags wave as they come!
Give them the blare of the trumpet!
Give them the roll of the drum!
THOMAS DUNN ENGLISH.

Skirmish after skirmish was fought, in one of
which, at Harrisonburg, on June 6, 1862, Ashby
was killed. But the Confederates succeeded in
their object, for McDowell's junction with McClel-
lan was indefinitely delayed.

DIRGE FOR ASHBY

[June 6, 1862]

HEARD ye that thrilling word —
Accent of dread —
Flash like a thunderbolt,
Bowing each head, —
Crash through the battle dun,
Over the booming gun, —
"*Ashby, our bravest one,* —
Ashby is dead!"

Saw ye the veterans —
Hearts that had known
Never a quail of fear,
Never a groan, —
Sob 'mid the fight they win, —
Tears their stern eyes within, —
"Ashby, our Paladin,
Ashby is gone!"

Dash — dash the tear away, —
Crush down the pain!
"*Dulce et decus*" be
Fittest refrain!
Why should the dreary pall
Round him be flung at all?
Did not our hero fall
Gallantly slain?

Catch the last word of cheer
Dropt from his tongue;
Over the volley's din,
Loud be it rung, —
"*Follow me! follow me!*" —
Soldier, oh! could there be
Pæan or dirge for thee
Loftier sung!

Bold as the Lion-heart,
Dauntless and brave;
Knightly as knightliest
Bayard could crave;

Sweet with all Sidney's grace,
Tender as Hampden's face; —
Who — who shall fill the space
Void by his grave?

'T is not *one* broken heart,
Wild with dismay;
Crazed with her agony,
Weeps o'er his clay:
Ah! from a thousand eyes
Flow the pure tears that rise;
Widowed Virginia lies
Stricken to-day!

Yet though that thrilling word —
Accent of dread —
Falls like a thunderbolt,
Bowing each head, —
Heroes! be battle done
Bravelier every one,
Nerved by the thought alone —
Ashby is dead!
MARGARET JUNKIN PRESTON.

McClellan continued to waste his time in com-
plaints and reproaches to the government at
Washington, and the Confederates prepared to
take the offensive. Their advance began June 26,
1862, and McClellan promptly began to retreat.
Finally, on July 1, at Malvern Hill, the Union
army turned and repulsed the Confederates, after
a severe engagement. McClellan, instead of ad-
vancing, issued an order to "fall still farther back."

MALVERN HILL

[July 1, 1862]

YE elms that wave on Malvern Hill
In prime of morn and May,
Recall ye how McClellan's men
Here stood at bay?
While deep within yon forest dim
Our rigid comrades lay —
Some with the cartridge in their mouth,
Others with fixed arms lifted South —
Invoking so
The cypress glades? Ah wilds of woe!

The spires of Richmond, late beheld
Through rifts in musket-haze,
Were closed from view in clouds of dust
On leaf-walled ways,
Where streamed our wagons in caravan;
And the Seven Nights and Days

Of march and fast, retreat and fight,
Pinched our grimed faces to ghastly plight —
  Does the elm wood
Recall the haggard beards of blood?

The battle-smoked flag, with stars eclipsed,
  We followed (it never fell!) —
In silence husbanded our strength —
  Received their yell;
Till on this slope we patient turned
  With cannon ordered well;
Reverse we proved was not defeat;
But ah, the sod what thousands meet! —
  Does Malvern Wood
Bethink itself, and muse and brood?

> *We elms of Malvern Hill*
>   *Remember everything;*
> *But sap the twig will fill:*
> *Wag the world how it will,*
>   *Leaves must be green in Spring.*
>   HERMAN MELVILLE.

A MESSAGE

[July 1, 1862]

WAS there ever message sweeter
  Than that one from Malvern Hill,
From a grim old fellow, — you remember?
  Dying in the dark at Malvern Hill.
With his rough face turned a little,
  On a heap of scarlet sand,
They found him, just within the thicket,
  With a picture in his hand, —

With a stained and crumpled picture
  Of a woman's aged face;
Yet there seemed to leap a wild entreaty,
  Young and living — tender — from the
    face
When they flashed a lantern on it,
  Gilding all the purple shade,
And stooped to raise him softly, —
  "That's my mother, sir," he said.

"Tell her" — but he wandered, slipping
  Into tangled words and cries, —
Something about Mac and Hooker,
  Something dropping through the cries
About the kitten by the fire,
  And mother's cranberry-pies; and there
The words fell, and an utter
  Silence brooded in the air.

Just as he was drifting from them,
  Out into the dark, alone
(Poor old mother, waiting for your mes·
    sage,
  Waiting with the kitten, all alone!),
Through the hush his voice broke, — "Tell
    her —
Thank you, Doctor — when you can, —
Tell her that I kissed her picture,
  And wished I'd been a better man."

Ah, I wonder if the red feet
  Of departed battle-hours
May not leave for us their searching
  Message from those distant hours.
Sisters, daughters, mothers, think you,
  Would your heroes now or then,
Dying, kiss your pictured faces,
  Wishing they'd been better men?
        ELIZABETH STUART PHELPS.

So ended McClellan's attempt to capture Rich-
mond. He had lost seventy-five thousand men
and had accomplished nothing. President Lincoln
made a personal visit to inspect the army, then
issued a call for three hundred thousand more
troops.

THREE HUNDRED THOUSAND MORE

[July 2, 1862]

WE are coming, Father Abraham, three
    hundred thousand more,
From Mississippi's winding stream and from
    New England's shore;
We leave our ploughs and workshops, our
    wives and children dear,
With hearts too full for utterance, with but a
    silent tear;
We dare not look behind us, but steadfastly
    before:
We are coming, Father Abraham, three hun-
    dred thousand more!

If you look across the hill-tops that meet the
    northern sky,
Long moving lines of rising dust your vision
    may descry;
And now the wind, an instant, tears the
    cloudy veil aside,
And floats aloft our spangled flag in glory and
    in pride,

And bayonets in the sunlight gleam, and bands
    brave music pour:
We are coming, Father Abraham, three hun-
    dred thousand more!

If you look all up our valleys where the grow-
    ing harvests shine,
You may see our sturdy farmer boys fast
    forming into line;
And children from their mother's knees are
    pulling at the weeds,
And learning how to reap and sow against
    their country's needs;
And a farewell group stands weeping at every
    cottage door:
We are coming, Father Abraham, three hun-
    dred thousand more!

You have called us, and we're coming, by
    Richmond's bloody tide
To lay us down, for Freedom's sake, our
    brothers' bones beside,
Or from foul treason's savage grasp to wrench
    the murderous blade,
And in the face of foreign foes its fragments
    to parade.
Six hundred thousand loyal men and true
    have gone before:
We are coming, Father Abraham, three hun-
    dred thousand more!

              JAMES SLOAN GIBBONS.

Meanwhile the Army of Virginia had been
formed for the defence of Washington, and placed
under the command of General Pope. He at once
endeavored to secure the valley of the Shenan-
doah, and on August 9, 1862, fought a fierce but
indecisive battle with Jackson at Cedar Mountain.

CEDAR MOUNTAIN

[August 9, 1862]

RING the bells, nor ring them slowly;
Toll them not, — the day is holy!
Golden-flooded noon is poured
In grand libation to the Lord.

No mourning mothers come to-day
Whose hopeless eyes forget to pray:
They each hold high the o'erflowing urn,
And bravely to the altar turn.

Ye limners of the ancient saint!
To-day another virgin paint;

Where with the lily once she stood
Show now the new beatitude.

To-day a mother crowned with pain,
Of silver beauty beyond stain,
Clasping a flower for our land
A-sheathèd in her hand.

Each pointed leaf with sword-like strength,
Guarding the flower throughout its length;
Each sword has won a sweet release
To the flower of beauty and of peace.

Ring the bells, nor ring them slowly,
To the Lord the day is holy;
To the young dead we consecrate
These lives that now we dedicate.
              ANNIE FIELDS.

Lee's army, released from Richmond by
McClellan's retreat, hastened to face Pope, while
Jackson got in Pope's rear, captured Manassas
Junction, cut Pope's communications, formed a
junction with Longstreet, and on August 30, 1862,
defeated the Union forces at the second battle of
Bull Run.

"OUR LEFT"

[August 30, 1862]

FROM dawn to dark they stood
    That long midsummer day,
        While fierce and fast
        The battle blast
    Swept rank on rank away.

From dawn to dark they fought,
    With legions torn and cleft;
        And still the wide
        Black battle tide
    Poured deadlier on "Our Left."

They closed each ghastly gap;
    They dressed each shattered rank;
        They knew — how well —
        That freedom fell
    With that exhausted flank.

"Oh, for a thousand men
    Like these that melt away!"
        And down they came,
        With steel and flame,
    Four thousand to the fray!

Right through the blackest cloud
  Their lightning path they cleft;
    And triumph came
    With deathless fame
  To our unconquered "Left."

Ye of your sons secure,
  Ye of your dead bereft —
    Honor the brave
    Who died to save
  Your all upon "Our Left."
        FRANCIS ORRERY TICKNOR.

On the following day, Jackson again attacked
at Chantilly, an indecisive action lasting all day.
During the battle, General Philip Kearny pushed
forward to reconnoitre and came upon a Con-
federate outpost which summoned him to sur-
render. Instead, he clapped spurs to his horse and
endeavored to escape, but was shot and killed.

DIRGE FOR A SOLDIER

[September 1, 1862]

CLOSE his eyes; his work is done!
  What to him is friend or foeman,
Rise of moon, or set of sun,
  Hand of man, or kiss of woman?
    Lay him low, lay him low,
    In the clover or the snow!
    What cares he? he cannot know:
    Lay him low!

As man may, he fought his fight,
  Proved his truth by his endeavor;
Let him sleep in solemn night,
  Sleep forever and forever.
    Lay him low, lay him low,
    In the clover or the snow!
    What cares he? he cannot know:
    Lay him low!

Fold him in his country's stars,
  Roll the drum and fire the volley!
What to him are all our wars,
  What but death-bemocking folly?
    Lay him low, lay him low,
    In the clover or the snow!
    What cares he? he cannot know:
    Lay him low!

Leave him to God's watching eye;
  Trust him to the hand that made him.

Mortal love weeps idly by:
  God alone has power to aid him.
    Lay him low, lay him low,
    In the clover or the snow!
    What cares he? he cannot know:
    Lay him low!
        GEORGE HENRY BOKER.

Pope's shattered army was withdrawn within
the defences of Washington, where McClellan's
forces soon joined it. The latter was given com-
mand of the forces at the capital, and recruits
were hurried forward to fill the broken ranks.

THE REVEILLE

HARK! I hear the tramp of thousands,
  And of armèd men the hum;
Lo! a nation's hosts have gathered
  Round the quick-alarming drum, —
      Saying: "Come,
      Freemen, come!
Ere your heritage be wasted," said the quick-
      alarming drum.

"Let me of my heart take counsel:
  War is not of life the sum;
Who shall stay and reap the harvest
  When the autumn days shall come?"
      But the drum
      Echoed: "Come!
Death shall reap the braver harvest," said the
      solemn-sounding drum.

"But when won the coming battle,
  What of profit springs therefrom?
What if conquest, subjugation,
  Even greater ills become?"
      But the drum
      Answered: "Come!
You must do the sum to prove it," said the
      Yankee-answering drum.

"What if, 'mid the cannons' thunder,
  Whistling shot and bursting bomb,
When my brothers fall around me,
  Should my heart grow cold and numb?"
      But the drum
      Answered: "Come!
Better there in death united than in life a
      recreant, — Come!"

Thus they answered — hoping, fearing,
  Some in faith and doubting some,

Till a trumpet-voice proclaiming,
Said: "My chosen people, come!"
Then the drum,
Lo! was dumb;
For the great heart of the nation, throbbing,
answered: "Lord, we come!"
BRET HARTE.

Never was the Republic in greater danger. A
month before, Lee had been desperately defending
Richmond against two armies; now he had de-
feated them both and was ready to invade the
North. He pushed forward with decision and
celerity, and by September 7, 1862, his whole army
had crossed the Potomac into Maryland.

BEYOND THE POTOMAC

[September 7, 1862]

THEY slept on the field which their valor had
won,
But arose with the first early blush of the sun,
For they knew that a great deed remained to be
done,
When they passed o'er the river.

They arose with the sun, and caught life from
his light, —
Those giants of courage, those Anaks in fight, —
And they laughed out aloud in the joy of their
might,
Marching swift for the river.

On! on! like the rushing of storms through
the hills;
On! on! with a tramp that is firm as their
wills;
And the one heart of thousands grows buoy-
ant, and thrills,
At the thought of the river.

Oh, the sheen of their swords! the fierce gleam
of their eyes!
It seemed as on earth a new sunlight would
rise,
And, king-like, flash up to the sun in the skies,
O'er their path to the river.

But their banners, shot-scarred, and all dark-
ened with gore,
On a strong wind of morning streamed wildly
before,
Like the wings of death-angels swept fast to
the shore,
The green shore of the river.

As they march, from the hillside, the hamlet,
the stream,
Gaunt throngs whom the foemen had man-
acled, teem,
Like men just aroused from some terrible
dream,
To cross sternly the river.

They behold the broad banners, blood-dark-
ened, yet fair,
And a moment dissolves the last spell of de-
spair,
While a peal, as of victory, swells on the air,
Rolling out to the river.

And that cry, with a thousand strange echo-
ings, spread,
Till the ashes of heroes were thrilled in their
bed,
And the deep voice of passion surged up from
the dead,
" Ay, press on to the river ! "

On! on! like the rushing of storms through the
hills,
On! on! with a tramp that is firm as their
wills,
And the one heart of thousands grows buoy-
ant, and thrills,
As they pause by the river.

Then the wan face of Maryland, haggard and
worn,
At this sight lost the touch of its aspect for-
lorn,
And she turned on the foemen, full-statured
in scorn,
Pointing stern to the river.

And Potomac flowed calmly, scarce heaving
her breast,
With her low-lying billows all bright in the
west,
For a charm as from God lulled the waters to
rest
Of the fair rolling river.

Passed! passed! the glad thousands march
safe through the tide;
Hark, foeman, and hear the deep knell of
your pride,
Ringing weird-like and wild, pealing up from
the side
Of the calm-flowing river!

'Neath a blow swift and mighty the tyrant
    may fall;
Vain! vain! to his gods swells a desolate call;
Hath his grave not been hollowed, and woven
    his pall,
    Since they passed o'er the river?
            PAUL HAMILTON HAYNE.

McClellan undertook a timorous and blundering
pursuit, calling constantly for more men and even
proposing that Washington be abandoned, if that
should be necessary to reinforce his army. On
September 13, 1862, Lee's army passed through
Frederick, and it was then that the incident re-
corded in "Barbara Frietchie" is said to have
occurred.

BARBARA FRIETCHIE

[September 13, 1862]

UP from the meadows rich with corn,
Clear in the cool September morn,

The clustered spires of Frederick stand
Green-walled by the hills of Maryland.

Round about them orchards sweep,
Apple and peach tree fruited deep,

Fair as the garden of the Lord
To the eyes of the famished rebel horde,

On that pleasant morn of the early fall
When Lee marched over the mountain-wall;

Over the mountains winding down,
Horse and foot, into Frederick town.

Forty flags with their silver stars,
Forty flags with their crimson bars,

Flapped in the morning wind: the sun
Of noon looked down, and saw not one.

Up rose old Barbara Frietchie then,
Bowed with her fourscore years and ten;

Bravest of all in Frederick town,
She took up the flag the men hauled down;

In her attic window the staff she set,
To show that one heart was loyal yet.

Up the street came the rebel tread,
Stonewall Jackson riding ahead.

Under his slouched hat left and right
He glanced; the old flag met his sight.

"Halt!" — the dust-brown ranks stood fast.
"Fire!" — out blazed the rifle-blast.

It shivered the window, pane and sash;
It rent the banner with seam and gash.

Quick, as it fell, from the broken staff
Dame Barbara snatched the silken scarf.

She leaned far out on the window-sill,
And shook it forth with a royal will.

"Shoot, if you must, this old gray head,
But spare your country's flag," she said.

A shade of sadness, a blush of shame,
Over the face of the leader came;

The nobler nature within him stirred
To life at that woman's deed and word;

"Who touches a hair of yon gray head
Dies like a dog! March on!" he said.

All day long through Frederick street
Sounded the tread of marching feet:

All day long that free flag tost
Over the heads of the rebel host.

Ever its torn folds rose and fell
On the loyal winds that loved it well;

And through the hill-gaps sunset light
Shone over it with a warm good-night.

Barbara Frietchie's work is o'er,
And the Rebel rides on his raids no more.

Honor to her! and let a tear
Fall, for her sake, on Stonewall's bier.

Over Barbara Frietchie's grave,
Flag of Freedom and Union, wave!

Peace and order and beauty draw
Round thy symbol of light and law;

And ever the stars above look down
On thy stars below in Frederick town!
            JOHN GREENLEAF WHITTIER.

The main body of the Confederates was finally encountered at Antietam, and on September 17, 1862, a savage action was fought, which left Lee badly shattered.

MARTHY VIRGINIA'S HAND

[September 17, 1862]

"THERE, on the left!" said the colonel;
the battle had shuddered and faded away,
Wraith of a fiery enchantment that left only
ashes and blood-sprinkled clay —
"Ride to the left and examine that ridge,
where the enemy's sharpshooters
stood.
Lord, how they picked off our men, from the
treacherous vantage-ground of the
wood!
But for their bullets, I'll bet, my batteries
sent them something as good.
Go and explore, and report to me then, and
tell me how many we killed.
Never a wink shall I sleep till I know our
vengeance was duly fulfilled."

Fiercely the orderly rode down the slope of the
cornfield — scarred and forlorn,
Rutted by violent wheels, and scathed by the
shot that had ploughed it in scorn;
Fiercely, and burning with wrath for the
sight of his comrades crushed at a
blow,
Flung in broken shapes on the ground like
ruined memorials of woe;
These were the men whom at daybreak he
knew, but never again could know.
Thence to the ridge, where roots out-thrust,
and twisted branches of trees
Clutched the hill like clawing lions, firm
their prey to seize.

"What's your report?" and the grim colonel
smiled when the orderly came back at
last.
Strangely the soldier paused: "Well, they
were punished." And strangely his
face looked, aghast.
"Yes, our fire told on them; knocked over
fifty — laid out in line of parade.
Brave fellows, Colonel, to stay as they
did! But one I 'most wished had n't
stayed.
Mortally wounded, he'd torn off his knap-
sack; and then, at the end, he prayed —

Easy to see, by his hands that were clasped;
and the dull, dead fingers yet held
This little letter — his wife's — from the
knapsack. A pity those woods were
shelled!"

Silent the orderly, watching with tears in his
eyes as his officer scanned
Four short pages of writing. "What's this,
about 'Marthy Virginia's hand'?"
Swift from his honeymoon he, the dead sol-
dier, had gone from his bride to the
strife;
Never they met again, but she had written
him, telling of that new life,
Born in the daughter, that bound her still
closer and closer to him as his wife.
Laying her baby's hand down on the letter,
around it she traced a rude line:
"If you would kiss the baby," she wrote,
" you must kiss this outline of mine."

There was the shape of the hand on the page,
with the small, chubby fingers out-
spread.
"Marthy Virginia's hand, for her pa," — so
the words on the little palm said.
Never a wink slept the colonel that night, for
the vengeance so blindly fulfilled.
Never again woke the old battle-glow when
the bullets their death-note shrilled.
Long ago ended the struggle, in union of bro-
therhood happily stilled;
Yet from that field of Antietam, in warning
and token of love's command,
See! there is lifted the hand of a baby —
Marthy Virginia's hand!
GEORGE PARSONS LATHROP.

It was McClellan's first victory — a notable one, which might have been decisive had he followed it up with an attack next day. But he remained inac-tive, and Lee managed to make good his escape across the Potomac.

THE VICTOR OF ANTIETAM

[September 17, 1862]

WHEN tempest winnowed grain from bran,
And men were looking for a man,
Authority called you to the van,
McClellan!
Along the line the plaudits ran,
As later when Antietam's cheers began.

Through storm-cloud and eclipse must move
Each cause and man, dear to the stars and Jove;
Nor always can the wisest tell
Deferred fulfilment from the hopeless knell —
The struggler from the floundering ne'er-do-
    well.
A pall-cloth on the Seven Days fell,
    McClellan —
Unprosperously heroical!
Who could Antietam's wreath foretell?

Authority called you; then, in mist
And loom of jeopardy — dismissed.
But staring peril soon appalled;
You, the Discarded, she recalled —
Recalled you, nor endured delay;
And forth you rode upon a blasted way,
Arrayed Pope's rout, and routed Lee's array,
    McClellan!
Your tent was choked with captured flags
    that day,
    McClellan.
Antietam was a telling fray.

Recalled you; and she heard your drum
Advancing through the ghastly gloom.
You manned the wall, you propped the Dome,
You stormed the powerful stormer home,
    McClellan!
Antietam's cannon long shall boom.

At Alexandria, left alone,
    McClellan —
Your veterans sent from you, and thrown
To fields and fortunes all unknown —
What thoughts were yours, revealed to none,
While faithful still you labored on —
Hearing the far Manassas gun!
    McClellan,
Only Antietam could atone.

You fought in the front (an evil day,
    McClellan) —
The forefront of the first assay;
The Cause went sounding, groped its way;
The leadsmen quarrelled in the bay;
Quills thwarted swords; divided sway;
The rebel flushed in his lusty May:
You did your best, as in you lay,
    McClellan.
Antietam's sun-burst sheds a ray.

Your medalled soldiers love you well,
    McClellan!
Name your name, their true hearts swell:

With you they shook dread Stonewall's spell,
With you they braved the blended yell
Of rebel and maligner fell;
With you in fame or shame they dwell,
    McClellan!
Antietam-braves a brave can tell.

And when your comrades (now so few,
    McClellan, —
Such ravage in deep files they rue)
Meet round the board, and sadly view
The empty places; tribute due
They render to the dead — and you!
Absent and silent o'er the blue;
The one-armed lift the wine to *you*,
    McClellan,
And great Antietam's cheers renew.
                HERMAN MELVILLE.

On October 1, 1862, President Lincoln issued
to McClellan a peremptory order to pursue Lee.
Twenty days were spent in correspondence before
that order was obeyed. McClellan had exhausted
the patience even of the President. On November
5 he was relieved from command, and General
A. E. Burnside appointed to replace him. The latter
paused to get the army in hand and then moved
down the Rappahannock toward Fredericksburg,
where Lee was strongly intrenched. On December
11 the Union army managed to cross the Potomac
in the face of a heavy fire.

THE CROSSING AT FREDERICKS-BURG

[December 11, 1862]

I LAY in my tent at mid-day,
    Too full of pain to die,
When I heard the voice of Burnside,
    And an answering shout reply.

I heard the voice of the General, —
    "T' was firm, though low and sad;
But the roar that followed his question
    Laughed out till the hills were glad.

"O comrade, open the curtain,
    And see where our men are bound,
For my heart is still in my bosom
    At that terrible, mirthful sound.

"And hark what the General orders,
    For I could not catch his words;
But what means that hurry and movement,
    That clash of muskets and swords?"

"Lie still, lie still, my Captain,
    'T is a call for volunteers;
And the noise that vexes your fever
    Is only our soldiers' cheers."

"Where go they?" "Across the river."
    "O God! and must I lie still,
While that drum and that measured tramp-
        ling
    Move from me far down the hill?

"How many?" "I judge, four hundred."
    "Who are they? I'll know to a man."
"Our own Nineteenth and Twentieth,
    And the Seventh Michigan."

'Oh, to go, but to go with my comrades!
    Tear the curtain away from the hook;
For I'll see them march down to their glory,
    If I perish by the look!"

They leaped in the rocking shallops.
    Ten offered where one could go;
And the breeze was alive with laughter
    Till the boatmen began to row.

Then the shore, where the rebels harbored,
    Was fringed with a gush of flame,
And buzzing, like bees, o'er the water
    The swarms of their bullets came.

In silence, how dread and solemn!
    With courage, how grand and true!
Steadily, steadily onward
    The line of the shallops drew.

Not a whisper! Each man was conscious
    He stood in the sight of death;
So he bowed to the awful presence,
    And treasured his living breath.

'Twixt death in the air above them,
    And death in the waves below,
Through balls and grape and shrapnel
    They moved — my God, how slow!

And many a brave, stout fellow,
    Who sprang in the boats with mirth,
Ere they made that fatal crossing
    Was a load of lifeless earth.

And many a brave, stout fellow,
    Whose limbs with strength were rife,
Was torn and crushed and shattered, —
    A hopeless wreck for life.

But yet the boats moved onward;
    Through fire and lead they drove,
With the dark, still mass within them,
    And the floating stars above.

So loud and near it sounded,
    I started at the shout,
As the keels ground on the gravel,
    And the eager men burst out.

Cheer after cheer we sent them,
    As only armies can, —
Cheers for old Massachusetts,
    Cheers for young Michigan!

They formed in line of battle;
    Not a man was out of place.
Then with levelled steel they hurled them
    Straight in the rebels' face.

"Oh, help me, help me, comrade!
    For tears my eyelids drown,
As I see their smoking banners
    Stream up the smoking town.

"And see the noisy workmen
    O'er the lengthening bridges run,
And the troops that swarm to cross them
    When the rapid work be done.

"For the old heat, or a new one,
    Flames up in every vein;
And with fever or with passion
    I am faint as death again.

"If this is death, I care not!
    Hear me, men, from rear to van! —
One more cheer for Massachusetts,
    And one more for Michigan!"
                    GEORGE HENRY BOKER.

On the morning of December 13, 1862, the
Union army advanced to the attack. The Con-
federate advance lines were driven back, but ral-
lied and drove back their assailants with heavy
loss. Assault after assault was repulsed, and
Burnside was finally compelled to withdraw with
a loss of fifteen thousand men. He was relieved
of command soon afterwards.

AT FREDERICKSBURG

[December 13, 1862]

GOD send us peace, and keep red strife away;
    But should it come, God send us men and
        steel!

The land is dead that dare not face the day
  When foreign danger threats the common
    weal.

Defenders strong are they that homes defend;
  From ready arms the spoiler keeps afar.
Well blest the country that has sons to lend
  From trades of peace to learn the trade of
    war.

Thrice blest the nation that has every son
  A soldier, ready for the warning sound;
Who marches homeward when the fight is
    done,
  To swing the hammer and to till the ground.

Call back that morning, with its lurid light,
  When through our land the awful war-bell
    tolled;
When lips were mute, and women's faces
    white
  As the pale cloud that out from Sumter
    rolled.

Call back that morn: an instant all were
    dumb,
  As if the shot had struck the Nation's life;
Then cleared the smoke, and rolled the calling
    drum,
  And men streamed in to meet the coming
    strife.

They closed the ledger and they stilled the
    loom,
  The plough left rusting in the prairie farm;
They saw but "Union" in the gathering
    gloom;
  The tearless women helped the men to
    arm;

Brigades from towns — each village sent its
    band:
  German and Irish — every race and faith;
There was no question then of native land,
  But — love the Flag and follow it to death.

No need to tell their tale: through every age
  The splendid story shall be sung and said;
But let me draw one picture from the page —
  For words of song embalm the hero dead.

The smooth hill is bare, and the cannons are
    planted,
  Like Gorgon fates shading its terrible brow;

The word has been passed that the stormers
    are wanted,
  And Burnside's battalions are mustering
    now.
The armies stand by to behold the dread
    meeting;
  The work must be done by a desperate few;
The black-mouthèd guns on the height give
    them greeting —
  From gun-mouth to plain every grass blade
    in view.
Strong earthworks are there, and the rifles
    behind them
  Are Georgia militia — an Irish brigade —
Their caps have green badges, as if to remind
    them
  Of all the brave record their country has
    made.

The stormers go forward — the Federals
    cheer them;
  They breast the smooth hillside — the black
    mouths are dumb;
The riflemen lie in the works till they near
    them,
  And cover the stormers as upward they
    come.
Was ever a death-march so grand and so
    solemn?
  At last, the dark summit with flame is en-
    lined;
The great guns belch doom on the sacrificed
    column,
  That reels from the height, leaving hundreds
    behind.
The armies are hushed — there is no cause
    for cheering:
  The fall of brave men to brave men is a
    pain.
Again come the stormers! and as they are
    nearing
  The flame-sheeted rifle-lines, reel back
    again.
And so till full noon come the Federal
    masses —
  Flung back from the height, as the cliff
    flings a wave;
Brigade on brigade to the death-struggle
    passes,
  No wavering rank till it steps on the grave.

Then comes a brief lull, and the smoke-pall
    is lifted,
  The green of the hillside no longer is seen;

The dead soldiers lie as the sea-weed is drifted,
  The earthworks still held by the badges of
    green.
Have they quailed? is the word. No: again
  they are forming —
  Again comes a column to death and defeat!
What is it in these who shall now do the
  storming
  That makes every Georgian spring to his
    feet?

"O God! what a pity!" they cry in their cover,
  As rifles are readied and bayonets made
    tight;
" 'T is Meagher and his fellows! their caps
  have green clover;
  'T is Greek to Greek now for the rest of the
    fight!"
Twelve hundred the column, their rent flag
  before them,
  With Meagher at their head, they have
    dashed at the hill!
Their foemen are proud of the country that
  bore them;
  But, Irish in love, they are enemies still.
Out rings the fierce word, "Let them have it!"
  the rifles
  Are emptied point-blank in the hearts of
    the foe:
It is green against green, but a principle stifles
  The Irishman's love in the Georgian's
    blow.

The column has reeled, but it is not defeated;
  In front of the guns they re-form and attack;
Six times they have done it, and six times re-
  treated;
  Twelve hundred they came, and two hun-
    dred go back.
Two hundred go back with the chivalrous
  story;
  The wild day is closed in the night's solemn
    shroud;
A thousand lie dead, but their death was a
  glory
  That calls not for tears — the Green
    Badges are proud!

Bright honor be theirs who for honor were
  fearless,
  Who charged for their flag to the grim can-
    non's mouth;
And honor to them who were true, though not
  tearless, —
  Who bravely that day kept the cause of the
    South.

The quarrel is done — God avert such an-
  other;
  The lesson it brought we should evermore
    heed:
Who loveth the Flag is a man and a brother,
  No matter what birth or what race or what
    creed.

          JOHN BOYLE O'REILLY.

FREDERICKSBURG

THE increasing moonlight drifts across my
  bed,
And on the churchyard by the road, I know
It falls as white and noiselessly as snow. . . .
'T was such a night two weary summers fled;
The stars, as now, were waning overhead.
Listen! Again the shrill-lipped bugles blow
Where the swift currents of the river flow
Past Fredericksburg; far off the heavens are
  red
With sudden conflagration: on yon height,
Linstock in hand, the gunners hold their
  breath;
A signal-rocket pierces the dense night,
Flings its spent stars upon the town beneath:
Hark! — the artillery massing on the right,
Hark! — the black squadrons wheeling down
    to Death!

          THOMAS BAILEY ALDRICH.

    Major-General Joseph Hooker was placed in
command, and the Grand Army of the Potomac,
of which so much had been expected, went into
winter quarters on the Rappahannock.

BY THE POTOMAC

THE soft new grass is creeping o'er the graves
By the Potomac; and the crisp ground-flower
Tilts its blue cup to catch the passing shower;
The pine-cone ripens, and the long moss waves
Its tangled gonfalons above our braves.
Hark, what a burst of music from yon bower! —
The Southern nightingale that hour by hour
In its melodious summer madness raves.
Ah, with what delicate touches of her hand,
With what sweet voice of bird and rivulet
And drowsy murmur of the rustling leaf
Would Nature soothe us, bidding us forget
The awful crime of this distracted land
And all our heavy heritage of grief.

          THOMAS BAILEY ALDRICH.

THE WASHERS OF THE SHROUD

ALONG a river-side, I know not where,
I walked one night in mystery of dream;
A chill creeps curdling yet beneath my hair,
To think what chanced me by the pallid gleam
Of a moon-wraith that waned through haunted
air.

Pale fireflies pulsed within the meadow-mist
Their halos, wavering thistle downs of light;
The loon, that seemed to mock some goblin
tryst,
Laughed; and the echoes, huddling in affright,
Like Odin's hounds, fled baying down the
night.

Then all was silent, till there smote my ear
A movement in the stream that checked my
breath:
Was it the slow plash of a wading deer?
But something said, "This water is of Death!
The Sisters wash a shroud, — ill thing to
hear!"

I, looking then, beheld the ancient Three
Known to the Greek's and to the Northman's
creed,
That sit in shadow of the mystic Tree,
Still crooning, as they weave their endless
brede,
One song: "Time was, Time is, and Time
shall be."

No wrinkled crones were they, as I had
deemed,
But fair as yesterday, to-day, to-morrow,
To mourner, lover, poet, ever seemed:
Something too high for joy, too deep for sor-
row,
Thrilled in their tones, and from their faces
gleamed.

"Still men and nations reap as they have
strawn,"
So sang they, working at their task the while;
"The fatal raiment must be cleansed ere
dawn:
For Austria? Italy? the Sea-Queen's isle?
O'er what quenched grandeur must our
shroud be drawn?

"Or is it for a younger, fairer corse,
That gathered States like children round his
knees,

That tamed the waves to be his posting-
horse,
Feller of forests, linker of the seas,
Bridge-builder, hammerer, youngest son of
Thor's?

"What make we, murmur'st thou? and what
are we?
When empires must be wound, we bring the
shroud,
The time-old web of the implacable Three:
Is it too coarse for him, the young and proud?
Earth's mightiest deigned to wear it, — why
not he?"

"Is there no hope?" *i* moaned, "so strong, so
fair!
Our Fowler whose proud bird would brook
erewhile
No rival's swoop in all our western air!
Gather the ravens, then, in funeral file
For him, life's morn yet golden in his hair?

"Leave me not hopeless, ye unpitying dames!
I see, half seeing. Tell me, ye who scanned
The stars, Earth's elders, still must noblest
aims
Be traced upon oblivious ocean-sands?
Must Hesper join the wailing ghosts of
names?"

"When grass-blades stiffen with red battle-
dew,
Ye deem we choose the victor and the slain:
Say, choose we them that shall be leal and true
To the heart's longing, the high faith of brain?
Yet there the victory lies, if ye but knew.

"Three roots bear up Dominion: Knowledge,
Will, —
These twain are strong, but stronger yet the
third, —
Obedience, — 't is the great tap-root that
still,
Knit round the rock of Duty, is not stirred,
Though Heaven-loosed tempests spend their
utmost skill.

"Is the doom sealed for Hesper? 'T is not we
Denounce it, but the Law before all time:
The brave makes danger opportunity;
The waverer, paltering with the chance sub-
lime,
Dwarfs it to peril: which shall Hesper be?

"Hath he let vultures climb his eagle's seat
To make Jove's bolts purveyors of their maw?
Hath he the Many's plaudits found more sweet
Than Wisdom? held Opinion's wind for Law?
Then let him hearken for the doomster's feet!

"Rough are the steps, slow-hewn in flintiest rock,
States climb to power by; slippery those with gold
Down which they stumble to eternal mock:
No chafferer's hand shall long the sceptre hold,
Who, given a Fate to shape, would sell the block.

"We sing old Sagas, songs of weal and woe,
Mystic because too cheaply understood;
Dark sayings are not ours; men hear and know,
See Evil weak, see strength alone in Good,
Yet hope to stem God's fire with walls of tow.

"Time Was unlocks the riddle of Time Is,
That offers choice of glory or of gloom;
The solver makes Time Shall Be surely his.
But hasten, Sisters! for even now the tomb
Grates its slow hinge and calls from the abyss."

"But not for him," I cried, "not yet for him,
Whose large horizon, westering, star by star
Wins from the void to where on Ocean's rim
The sunset shuts the world with golden bar,
Not yet his thews shall fail, his eye grow dim!

"His shall be larger manhood, saved for those
That walk unblenching through the trial-fires;
Not suffering, but faint heart, is worst of woes,
And he no base-born son of craven sires,
Whose eye need blench confronted with his foes.

"Tears may be ours, but proud, for those who win
Death's royal purple in the foeman's lines;
Peace, too, brings tears; and mid the battle-din,
The wiser ear some text of God divines,
For the sheathed blade may rust with darker sin.

"God, give us peace! not such as lulls to sleep,
But sword on thigh, and brow with purpose knit!
And let our Ship of State to harbor sweep,
Her ports all up, her battle-lanterns lit,
And her leashed thunders gathering for their leap!"

So cried I with clenched hands and passionate pain,
Thinking of dear ones by Potomac's side;
Again the loon laughed mocking, and again
The echoes bayed far down the night and died,
While waking I recalled my wandering brain.
                    JAMES RUSSELL LOWELL.
    October, 1861.

CHAPTER V

THE WAR IN THE WEST

While the Army of the Potomac in the east was imitating the manœuvres of the King of France, stirring times were enacting in the west. Missouri was torn with dissension. The state had voted against secession in February, but the governor, C. F. Jackson, was doing everything he could to throw it into the Confederacy. General Nathaniel Lyon raised a force of loyalists, and a number of skirmishes ensued.

THE LITTLE DRUMMER[1]

'T is of a little drummer,
    The story I shall tell;

[1] From Poetical Writings of Richard Henry Stoddard; copyright, 1880, by Charles Scribner's Sons.

Of how he marched to battle,
    Of all that there befell,
Out in the west with Lyon
    (For once the name was true!)
For whom the little drummer beat
    His *rat-tat-too.*

Our army rose at midnight,
    Ten thousand men as one,
Each slinging off his knapsack
    And snatching up his gun.
"*Forward!*" and off they started,
    As all good soldiers do,
When the little drummer beats for them
    The *rat-tat-too.*

Across a rolling country,
  Where the mist began to rise;
Past many a blackened farmhouse,
  Till the sun was in the skies;
Then we met the rebel pickets,
  Who skirmished and withdrew,
While the little drummer beat, and beat
  The *rat-tat-too*.

Along the wooded hollows
  The line of battle ran,
Our centre poured a volley,
  And the fight at once began;
For the rebels answered shouting,
  And a shower of bullets flew;
But still the little drummer beat
  His *rat-tat-too*.

He stood among his comrades,
  As they quickly formed the line,
And when they raised their muskets
  He watched the barrels shine.
When the volley rang, he started,
  For war to him was new;
But still the little drummer beat
  His *rat-tat-too*.

It was a sight to see them,
  That early autumn day,
Our soldiers in their blue coats,
  And the rebel ranks in gray;
The smoke that rolled between them,
  The balls that whistled through,
And the little drummer as he beat
  His *rat-tat-too* !

His comrades dropped around him, —
  By fives and tens they fell,
Some pierced by minie bullets,
  Some torn by shot and shell;
They played against our cannon,
  And a caisson's splinters flew;
But still the little drummer beat
  His *rat-tat-too* !

The right, the left, the centre, —
  The fight was everywhere;
They pushed us here, — we wavered, —
  We drove and broke them there.
The graybacks fixed their bayonets,
  And charged the coats of blue,
But still the little drummer beat
  His *rat-tat-too* !

"Where is our little drummer?"
  His nearest comrades say,

When the dreadful fight is over,
  And the smoke has cleared away.
As the rebel corps was scattering
  He urged them to pursue,
So furiously he beat, and beat
  The *rat-tat-too* !

He stood no more among them,
  For a bullet, as it sped,
Had glanced and struck his ankle,
  And stretched him with the dead!
He crawled behind a cannon,
  And pale and paler grew;
But still the little drummer beat
  His *rat-tat-too* !

They bore him to the surgeon,
  A busy man was he:
"A drummer boy — what ails him?"
  His comrades answered, "See!"
As they took him from the stretcher
  A heavy breath he drew,
And his little fingers strove to beat
  The *rat-tat-too* !

The ball had spent its fury:
  "A scratch!" the surgeon said,
As he wound the snowy bandage
  Which the lint was staining red.
"I must leave you now, old fellow!"
  "Oh, take me back with you,
For I know the men are missing me
  And the *rat-tat-too* !"

Upon his comrade's shoulder
  They lifted him so grand,
With his dusty drum before him,
  And his drumsticks in his hand!
To the fiery front of battle,
  That nearer, nearer drew, —
And evermore he beat, and beat
  His *rat-tat-too* !

The wounded as he passed them
  Looked up and gave a cheer;
And one in dying blessed him,
  Between a smile and tear.
And the graybacks — they are flying
  Before the coats of blue,
For whom the little drummer beats
  His *rat-tat-too*.

When the west was red with sunset,
  The last pursuit was o'er;
Brave Lyon rode the foremost,
  And looked the name he bore.

And before him on his saddle,
    As a weary child would do,
Sat the little drummer, fast asleep,
    With his *rat-tat-too.*
                RICHARD HENRY STODDARD.

Hostilities culminated on August 10, 1861, in a pitched battle at Wilson's Creek, in which, through bad management, the Union forces were defeated and Lyon himself was killed.

THE DEATH OF LYON

[August 10, 1861]

SING, bird, on green Missouri's plain,
    The saddest song of sorrow;
Drop tears, O clouds, in gentlest rain
    Ye from the winds can borrow;
Breathe out, ye winds, your softest sigh,
    Weep, flowers, in dewy splendor,
For him who knew well how to die,
    But never to surrender.

Up rose serene the August sun
    Upon that day of glory;
Up curled from musket and from gun
    The war-cloud, gray and hoary;
It gathered like a funeral pall,
    Now broken, and now blended,
Where rang the bugle's angry call,
    And rank with rank contended.

Four thousand men, as brave and true
    As e'er went forth in daring,
Upon the foe that morning threw
    The strength of their despairing.
They feared not death — men bless the field
    That patriot soldiers die on;
Fair Freedom's cause was sword and shield,
    And at their head was Lyon.

Their leader's troubled soul looked forth
    From eyes of troubled brightness;
Sad soul! the burden of the North
    Had pressed out all its lightness.
He gazed upon the unequal fight,
    His ranks all rent and gory,
And felt the shadows close like night
    Round his career of glory.

"General, come lead us!" loud the cry
    From a brave band was ringing —
"Lead us, and we will stop, or die,
    That battery's awful singing!"

He spurred to where his heroes stood —
    Twice wounded, no one knowing —
The fire of battle in his blood
    And on his forehead glowing.

Oh! cursed for aye that traitor's hand
    And cursed that aim so deadly,
Which smote the bravest of the land,
    And dyed his bosom redly.
Serene he lay, while past him pressed
    The battle's furious billow,
As calmly as a babe may rest
    Upon its mother's pillow.

So Lyon died; and well may flowers
    His place of burial cover,
For never had this land of ours
    A more devoted lover.
Living, his country was his bride;
    His life he gave her, dying;
Life, fortune, love, he nought denied
    To her, and to her sighing.

Rest, patriot, in thy hillside grave,
    Beside her form who bore thee!
Long may the land thou diedst to save
    Her bannered stars wave o'er thee!
Upon her history's brightest page,
    And on fame's glowing portal,
She'll write thy grand, heroic age,
    And grave thy name immortal.
                HENRY PETERSON.

John C. Frémont had been placed in command of the department and advanced against the Confederates at the head of a strong force. On October 23, 1861, he detached a squadron of cavalry under Major Charles Zagonyi to reconnoitre the Confederate position at Springfield. Zagonyi found the Confederates two thousand strong, but charged them at the head of his hundred and fifty men, routed them, cut them to pieces, and drove them from the city. The charge was one of the most remarkable in history. The Confederates finally withdrew from the state.

ZAGONYI

[October 25, 1861]

BOLD Captain of the Body-Guard,
    I'll troll a stave to thee!
My voice is somewhat harsh and hard,
    And rough my minstrelsy.
I've cheered until my throat is sore
For how Dupont at Beaufort bore;
    Yet here's a cheer for thee!

I hear thy jingling spurs and reins,
  Thy sabre at thy knee;
The blood runs lighter through my veins,
  As I before me see
Thy hundred men with thrusts and blows
Ride down a thousand stubborn foes,
  The foremost led by thee.

With pistol snap and rifle crack —
  Mere *salvos* fired to honor thee —
Ye plunge, and stamp, and shoot, and hack
  The way your swords make free;
Then back again, — the path is wide
This time, — ye gods! it was a ride,
  The ride they took with thee!

No guardsman of the whole command
  Halts, quails, or turns to flee;
With bloody spur and steady hand
  They gallop where they see
Thy daring plume stream out ahead
O'er flying, wounded, dying, dead;
  They can but follow thee.

So, Captain of the Body-Guard,
  I pledge a health to thee!
I hope to see thy shoulders starred,
  My Paladin; and we
Shall laugh at fortune in the fray
Whene'er you lead your well-known way
  To death or victory!
                GEORGE HENRY BOKER.

Kentucky was another state divided against
itself. For a time, it endeavored to preserve
neutrality, but finally chose the Union side. On
January 19, 1862, the battle of Somerset was
fought, resulting in a Union victory.

BATTLE OF SOMERSET

[January 19, 1862]

I GAZED, and lo! Afar and near,
  With hastening speed, now there, now here,
The horseman rode with glittering spear —
  'Twas awful to behold!

Ten thousand men, in dread array —
On every hill and mound they lay —
A dreadful sight it was that day
  To see the front they formed.

The polished sabres, waving high,
Flashed brightly in the morning sky;
While, beaming on the dazzled eye,
  The glittering bayonets shone.

All, all was hushed among the trees,
Save now and then a gentle breeze,
Which stirr'd the brown and serried leaves
  That in the forest lay.

But what is that which greets mine eye?
Is it Columbia's sons I spy?
Hark! hark! I hear their battle cry —
  Their shouts of victory!

Still hotter does the conflict grow;
While dealing death in every blow,
McCook charged on the routed foe
  His daring little band.

Rest, patriots, rest; the conflict's o'er,
Your erring brethren punished sore;
Oh, would they'd fight their friends no more,
  And cease this bloody strife.
                CORNELIUS C. CULLEN.

The Confederate loss was very heavy, and in
one respect irreparable, for General Felix K. Zolli-
coffer was killed while reconnoitring the Union
position.

ZOLLICOFFER

[January 19, 1862]

FIRST in the fight, and first in the arms
  Of the white-winged angels of glory,
With the heart of the South at the feet of God,
  And his wounds to tell the story;

For the blood that flowed from his hero heart,
  On the spot where he nobly perished,
Was drunk by the earth as a sacrament
  In the holy cause he cherished!

In Heaven a home with the brave and blessed,
  And for his soul's sustaining
The apocalyptic eyes of Christ —
  And nothing on earth remaining,

But a handful of dust in the land of his choice,
  A name in song and story —
And fame to shout with immortal voice
  Dead on the field of Glory!
                HENRY LYNDEN FLASH.

Near the southern line of Kentucky, the Con-
federates held two strong forts, Henry and Don-
elson, and on February 2, 1862, a Union force
under General Ulysses S. Grant moved forward to
attack them. The army was supported by a fleet
of gunboats, and Fort Henry surrendered to the

fleet before the land forces came up. The gunboat
Essex led the attack and suffered severely, among
her dead being Lieutenant S. B. Brittan, Jr., a
boy of not quite seventeen.

BOY BRITTAN

[February 6, 1862]

I

Boy Brittan — only a lad — a fair-haired
        boy — sixteen,
    In his uniform,
Into the storm — into the roaring jaws of
        grim Fort Henry —
Boldly bears the Federal flotilla —
    Into the battle storm!

II

Boy Brittan is master's mate aboard of the
        Essex —
There he stands, buoyant and eager-eyed,
        By the brave captain's side;
Ready to do and dare. *Aye, aye, sir!* always
        ready —
    In his country's uniform.
Boom! Boom! and now the flag-boat sweeps,
        and now the Essex,
    Into the battle storm!

III

Boom! Boom! till river and fort and field are
        overclouded
By battle's breath; then from the fort a gleam
And a crashing gun, and the Essex is wrapt
        and shrouded
    In a scalding cloud of steam!

IV

        But victory! victory!
Unto God all praise be ever rendered,
Unto God all praise and glory be!
See, Boy Brittan! see, boy, see!
They strike! Hurrah! the fort has just sur-
        rendered!
Shout! Shout! my boy, my warrior boy!
And wave your cap and clap your hands for
        joy!
Cheer answer cheer and bear the cheer
        about —
Hurrah! Hurrah! for the fiery fort is ours;
And "Victory!" "Victory!" "Victory!"
        Is the shout.
Shout — for the fiery fort, and the field, and
        the day are ours —

The day is ours — thanks to the brave en-
        deavor
        Of heroes, boy, like thee!
The day is ours — the day is ours!
Glory and deathless love to all who shared
        with thee,
And bravely endured and dared with thee —
The day is ours — the day is ours —
        Forever!
Glory and Love for one and all; but — but —
        for thee —
Home! Home! a happy "Welcome — wel-
        come home" for thee!
        And kisses of love for thee —
And a mother's happy, happy tears, and a
        virgin's bridal wreath of flowers —
        For thee!

V

        Victory! Victory! . . .
But suddenly wrecked and wrapt in seething
        steam, the Essex
Slowly drifted out of the battle's storm;
Slowly, slowly down — laden with the dead
        and the dying;
And there, at the captain's feet, among the
        dead and the dying,
The shot-marred form of a beautiful boy is
        lying —
        There in his uniform!

VI

Laurels and tears for thee, boy,
Laurels and tears for thee!
Laurels of light, moist with the precious dew
Of the inmost heart of the nation's loving
        heart,
And blest by the balmy breath of the beautiful
        and the true;
Moist — moist with the luminous breath of
        the singing spheres
        And the nation's starry tears!
And tremble-touched by the pulse-like gush
        and start
Of the universal music of the heart,
        And all deep sympathy.
Laurels and tears for thee, boy,
        Laurels and tears for thee —
Laurels of light and tears of love forever
        more —
        For thee!

VII

And laurels of light, and tears of truth,
        And the mantle of immortality;

And the flowers of love and of immortal youth,
And the tender heart-tokens of all true ruth —
    And the everlasting victory!
And the breath and bliss of Liberty;
And the loving kiss of Liberty;
And the welcoming light of heavenly eyes,
And the over-calm of God's canopy;
And the infinite love-span of the skies
That cover the valleys of Paradise —
For all of the brave who rest with thee;
And for one and all who died with thee,
And now sleep side by side with thee;
And for every one who lives and dies,
On the solid land or the heaving sea,
    Dear warrior-boy — like thee.

VIII

    O the victory — the victory
      Belongs to thee!
God ever keeps the brightest crown for such
    as thou —
      He gives it now to thee!
O young and brave, and early and thrice
    blest —
      Thrice, thrice, thrice blest!
Thy country turns once more to kiss thy youthful brow,
And takes thee — gently — gently to her breast;
And whispers lovingly, "God bless thee — bless thee now —
      My darling, thou shalt rest!"
        FORCEYTHE WILLSON.

The fall of Fort Donelson, soon afterwards, opened the way to the south and it was decided to advance against Corinth, Miss., with Pittsburg Landing as the base of operations. By the first of April, 1862, five divisions had been concentrated there, but the Confederates had also massed a great army near by, and on the morning of Sunday, April 6, moved forward to the attack, took their opponents by surprise, and drove them back to the river. The Confederate leader, Albert Sidney Johnston, was killed during the battle.

ALBERT SIDNEY JOHNSTON

[April 6, 1862]

I HEAR again the tread of war go thundering
    through the land,
And Puritan and Cavalier are clinching neck
    and hand,
Round Shiloh church the furious foes have
    met to thrust and slay,
Where erst the peaceful sons of Christ were
    wont to kneel and pray.

The wrestling of the ages shakes the hills of
    Tennessee,
With all their echoing mounts a-throb with
    war's wild minstrelsy;
A galaxy of stars new-born round the shield
    of Mars,
And set against the Stars and Stripes the
    flashing Stars and Bars.

'T was Albert Sidney Johnston led the columns
    of the Gray,
Like Hector on the plains of Troy his presence fired the fray;
And dashing horse and gleaming sword spake
    out his royal will
As on the slopes of Shiloh field the blasts of
    war blew shrill.

"Down with the base invaders," the Gray
    shout forth the cry,
"Death to presumptuous rebels," the Blue
    ring out reply;
All day the conflict rages and yet again all
    day,
Though Grant is on the Union side he cannot stem nor stay.

They are a royal race of men, these brothers
    face to face,
Their fury speaking through their guns, their
    frenzy in their pace;
The sweeping onset of the Gray bears down
    the sturdy Blue,
Though Sherman and his legions are heroes
    through and through.

Though Prentiss and his gallant men are
    forcing scaur and crag,
They fall like sheaves before the scythes of
    Hardee and of Bragg;
Ah, who shall tell the victor's tale when all
    the strife is past,
When man and man in one great mould the
    men who strive are cast.

As when the Trojan hero came from that
    fair city's gates,
With tossing mane and flaming crest to scorn
    the scowling fates,
His legions gather round him and madly
    charge and cheer,
And fill the besieging armies with wild disheveled fear;

Then bares his breast unto the dart the daring
    spearsman sends,
And dying hears his cheering foes, the wailing
    of his friends,
So Albert Sidney Johnston, the chief of belt
    and scar,
Lay down to die at Shiloh and turned the
    scales of war.

Now five and twenty years are gone, and lo,
    to-day they come,
The Blue and Gray in proud array with
    throbbing fife and drum;
But not as rivals, not as foes, as brothers
    reconciled,
To twine love's fragrant roses where the
    thorns of hate grew wild.

They tell the hero of three wars, the lion-
    hearted man,
Who wore his valor like a star — uncrowned
    American;
Above his heart serene and still the folded
    Stars and Bars,
Above his head like mother-wings, the shelter-
    ing Stripes and Stars.

Aye, five and twenty years, and lo, the man-
    hood of the South
Has held its valor stanch and strong as at
    the cannon's mouth,
With patient heart and silent tongue has
    kept its true parole,
And in the conquests born of peace has
    crowned its battle roll.

But ever while we sing of war, of courage
    tried and true,
Of heroes wed to gallant deeds, or be it Gray
    or Blue,
Then Albert Sidney Johnston's name shall
    flash before our sight
Like some resplendent meteor across the
    sombre night.

America, thy sons are knit with sinews
    wrought of steel,
They will not bend, they will not break,
    beneath the tyrant's heel;
But in the white-hot flame of love, to silken
    cobwebs spun,
They whirl the engines of the world, all keep-
    ing time as one.

To-day they stand abreast and strong, who
    stood as foes of yore,
The world leaps up to bless their feet, heaven
    scatters blessings o'er;
Their robes are wrought of gleaming gold,
    their wings are freedom's own,
The trampling of their conquering hosts
    shakes pinnacle and throne.

Oh, veterans of the Blue and Gray, who fought
    on Shiloh field,
The purposes of God are true, His judgment
    stands revealed;
The pangs of war have rent the veil, and lo,
    His high decree:
One heart, one hope, one destiny, one flag
    from sea to sea.
            KATE BROWNLEE SHERWOOD.

ALBERT SIDNEY JOHNSTON

SHILOH

His soul to God! on a battle-psalm!
    A soldier's plea to Heaven!
From the victor wreath to the shining Palm;
From the battle's core to the central calm,
    And peace of God in Heaven.

Oh, Land! in your midnight of mistrust
    The golden gates flew wide,
And the kingly soul of your wise and just
Passed in light from the house of dust
    To the Home of the Glorified!
            FRANCIS ORRERY TICKNOR.

Buell's army came up during the night, and
Grant was able next day to assume the offensive
and drive the enemy from the field. Johnston's
death left Beauregard commander-in-chief of the
Confederate forces.

BEAUREGARD

Our trust is now in thee,
    Beauregard!
In thy hand the God of Hosts
    Hath placed the sword;
And the glory of thy fame
Has set the world aflame —
Hearts kindle at thy name,
    Beauregard!

The way that lies before
    Is cold and hard;
We are led across the desert
    By the Lord!

But the cloud that shines by night
To guide our steps aright,
Is the pillar of thy might,
    Beauregard!

Thou hast watched the southern heavens
    Evening starred,
And chosen thence thine emblems,
    Beauregard;
And upon thy banner's fold
Is that starry cross enrolled,
Which no Northman shall behold
    Shamed or scarred.

By the blood that crieth loudly
    From the sword,
We have sworn to keep around it
    Watch and ward,
And the standard of thine hand
Yet shall shine above a land,
Like its leader, free and grand,
    Beauregard!
                    MRS. C. A. WARFIELD.

The advance against Corinth was continued, and
on May 30, 1862, the Union army entered the city,
which the Confederates had evacuated. On Octo-
ber 3, 4, the Confederates attempted to recapture
it, but were repulsed with heavy loss. The Eighth
Wisconsin carried a live eagle in place of a flag,
and during the battle the great bird circled and
circled above the field.

THE EAGLE OF CORINTH

[October 3, 4, 1862]

DID you hear of the fight at Corinth,
    How we whipped out Price and Van Dorn?
Ah, that day we earned our rations
(Our cause was God's and the Nation's,
    Or we'd have come out forlorn!) —
A long and terrible day!
And at last, when night grew gray,
By the hundreds, there they lay
(Heavy sleepers, you'd say),
That would n't wake on the morn.

Our staff was bare of a flag,
We did n't carry a rag
In those brave marching days; —
Ah, no, but a finer thing!
With never a cord or string,
An eagle of ruffled wing,
And an eye of awful gaze.
The grape it rattled like hail,
The minies were dropping like rain,

The first of a thunder shower;
The wads were blowing like chaff
(There was pounding like floor and flail,
All the front of our line!),
So we stood it hour after hour;
But our eagle, he felt fine!
'T would have made you cheer and laugh,
To see, through that iron gale,
How the old fellow'd swoop and sail
Above the racket and roar, —
To right and to left he'd soar,
But ever came back, without fail,
And perched on his standard-staff.

All that day, I tell you true,
They had pressed us steady and fair,
Till we fought in street and square
(The affair, you might think, looked blue), —
But we knew we had them there!
Our batteries were few,
Every gun, they'd have sworn, they knew,
But, you see, there were one or two
We had fixed for them, unaware.

They reckon they've got us now!
    For the next half hour 't will be warm —
Aye, aye, look yonder! — I vow,
If they were n't Secesh, how I'd love them!
    Only see how grandly they form
(Our eagle whirling above them),
    To take Robinett by storm!
    They're timing! — it can't be long —
Now for the nub of the fight!
    (You may guess that we held our breath.)
By the Lord, 't is a splendid sight!
    A column two thousand strong
    Marching square to the death!

On they came in solid column,
For once no whooping nor yell
(Ah, I dare say they felt solemn!) —
Front and flank, grape and shell,
Our batteries pounded away!
And the minies hummed to remind 'em
They had started on no child's play!

Steady they kept a-going,
But a grim wake settled behind 'em
From the edge of the *abattis*
(Where our dead and dying lay
Under fence and fallen tree),
Up to Robinett, all the way
The dreadful swath kept growing!
'T was butternut mixed with gray.

Now for it, at Robinett!
Muzzle to muzzle we met
  (Not a breath of bluster or brag,
    Not a lisp for quarter or favor) —
Three times, there, by Robinett,
With a rush, their feet they set
On the logs of our parapet,
  And waved their bit of a flag —
    What could be finer or braver!
But our cross-fire stunned them in flank,
They melted, rank after rank
  (O'er them, with terrible poise,
    Our Bird did circle and wheel!) —
      Their whole line began to waver —
Now for the bayonet, boys!
  On them with the cold steel!

Ah, well — you know how it ended —
  We did for them, there and then,
But their pluck throughout was splendid.
(As I said before, I could love them!)
  They stood to the last, like men —
Only a handful of them
  Found the way back again.
    Red as blood, o'er the town,
The angry sun went down,
  Firing flagstaff and vane —
And our eagle, — as for him,
  There, all ruffled and grim,
    He sat, o'erlooking the slain!

Next morning, you'd have wondered
  How we had to drive the spade!
There, in great trenches and holes
  (Ah, God rest their poor souls!),
We piled some fifteen hundred,
  Where that last charge was made!
Sad enough, I must say.
  No mother to mourn and search,
No priest to bless or to pray —
We buried them where they lay,
  Without a rite of the church —
But our eagle, all that day,
  Stood solemn and still on his perch.

'T is many a stormy day
Since, out of the cold bleak north,
Our great war-eagle sailed forth
To swoop o'er battle and fray.
Many and many a day
O'er charge and storm hath he wheeled,
Foray and foughten field,
Tramp, and volley, and rattle! —
Over crimson trench and turf,
Over climbing clouds of surf,

Through tempest and cannon-wrack,
Have his terrible pinions whirled
(A thousand fields of battle!
A million leagues of foam!); —
But our bird shall yet come back,
He shall soar to his eyrie-home,
And his thunderous wings be furled,
In the gaze of a gladdened world,
On the nation's loftiest dome.
                HENRY HOWARD BROWNELL.

One more struggle closed the campaign. On December 29, 1862, the armies of Bragg and Rosecrans met at Murfreesboro, Tenn., and for four days a desperate battle raged, which ended finally in the Confederates falling back and leaving their antagonists in possession of the field.

THE BATTLE OF MURFREESBORO

[December 31, 1862]

ERE Murfreesboro's thunders rent the air —
With cannon booming 'mid the trumpet's
    blare —
Cane Hill and David Mills, stern battles, too,
Had carried death to hosts in Gray and Blue.
But here, more deadly, war's wild torrent
    rushed,
And victory, at first, the Rebels flushed.
The "right wing" gone, and troops in panic,
    lo!
The battle seemed already lost. But, No.
Brave Rosecrans cried out — "Now stop
    retreat!
We'll turn to victory this sore defeat!
We must and shall this battle — Soldiers! —
    win!
Now silence yonder batt'ry, to begin!
And all re-form and meet the yelling foe!
Stand firm and fire a volley! Back he'll go.
If not, present your bayonets, and Charge!
'T is needless on these orders to enlarge;
But — Comrades! — here we conquer or we
    die!"
And all that Rosecrans desired was done;
And Murfreesboro's battle thus was won.
Hail! to that New Year's Day in 'Sixty-three,
And to that morrow which brought victory.
Hail! to the courage of the Boys in Blue,
Who fought so grandly, to their Country true.
                KINAHAN CORNWALLIS.

Among the wounded, on the Confederate side, was Isaac Giffen, a native of East Tennessee. He was terribly injured, and was taken by Dr.

Francis O. Ticknor into his home and nursed back to life. He fell in one of the battles before Atlanta.

LITTLE GIFFEN

OUT of the focal and foremost fire,
Out of the hospital walls as dire,
Smitten of grape-shot and gangrene
(Eighteenth battle and *he* sixteen) —
Spectre such as you seldom see,
Little Giffen of Tennessee.

"Take him — and welcome!" the surgeons said,
"Little the doctor can help the dead!"
So we took him and brought him where
The balm was sweet in the summer air;
And we laid him down on a wholesome bed —
Utter Lazarus, heel to head!

And we watched the war with bated breath —
Skeleton Boy against skeleton Death.
Months of torture, how many such!
Weary weeks of the stick and crutch;
And still a glint in the steel-blue eye
Told of a spirit that would n't die.

And did n't. Nay, more! in death's despite
The crippled skeleton learned to write.
"Dear Mother," at first of course; and then
"Dear Captain," inquiring about "the men."
Captain's answer: "Of eighty and five,
Giffen and I are left alive."

Word of gloom from the war one day:
"Johnston 's pressed at the front, they say!"
Little Giffen was up and away;
A tear — his first — as he bade good-by,
Dimmed the glint of his steel-blue eye.
"I 'll write, if spared!" There was news of the fight;
But none of Giffen — he did not write.

I sometimes fancy that, were I king
Of the princely knights of the Golden Ring,
With the song of the minstrel in mine ear,
And the tender legend that trembles here,
I 'd give the best, on his bended knee,
The whitest soul of my chivalry,
For Little Giffen of Tennessee.
                        FRANCIS ORRERY TICKNOR.

Both the Union and Confederate armies were in need of rest and reorganization, and for a time hostilities ceased. Grant paused to collect his forces and to prepare for a manœuvre of the first importance.

THE BATTLE AUTUMN OF 1862

THE flags of war like storm-birds fly,
  The charging trumpets blow;
Yet rolls no thunder in the sky,
  No earthquake strives below.

And, calm and patient, Nature keeps
  Her ancient promise well,
Though o'er her bloom and greenness sweeps
  The battle's breath of hell.

And still she walks in golden hours
  Through harvest-happy farms,
And still she wears her fruits and flowers
  Like jewels on her arms.

What mean the gladness of the plain,
  This joy of eve and morn,
The mirth that shakes the beard of grain
  And yellow locks of corn?

Ah! eyes may well be full of tears,
  And hearts with hate are hot;
But even-paced come round the years,
  And Nature changes not.

She meets with smiles our bitter grief,
  With songs our groans of pain;
She mocks with tint of flower and leaf
  The war-field's crimson stain.

Still, in the cannon's pause, we hear
  Her sweet thanksgiving-psalm;
Too near to God for doubt or fear,
  She shares the eternal calm.

She knows the seed lies safe below
  The fires that blast and burn;
For all the tears of blood we sow
  She waits the rich return.

She sees with clearer eye than ours
  The good of suffering born, —
The hearts that blossom like her flowers,
  And ripen like her corn.

Oh, give to us, in times like these,
  The vision of her eyes;
And make her fields and fruited trees
  Our golden prophecies!

Oh, give to us her finer ear!
  Above this stormy din,
We too would hear the bells of cheer
  Ring peace and freedom in.
                        JOHN GREENLEAF WHITTIER.

CHAPTER VI

THE COAST AND THE RIVER

At the opening of the Civil War, the United States had proclaimed a blockade of all Southern ports. But places like Pamlico Sound and Port Royal had so many outlets that they could not be blockaded effectually, and finally, in November, 1861, a combined sea and land attack captured the latter place and gave the Union fleet a good harbor in the South.

AT PORT ROYAL

[November 7, 1861]

THE tent-lights glimmer on the land,
The ship-lights on the sea;
The night-wind smooths with drifting sand
Our track on lone Tybee.

At last our grating keels outslide,
Our good boats forward swing;
And while we ride the land-locked tide,
Our negroes row and sing.

For dear the bondman holds his gifts
Of music and of song:
The gold that kindly Nature sifts
Among his sands of wrong;

The power to make his toiling days
And poor home-comforts please;
The quaint relief of mirth that plays
With sorrow's minor keys.

Another glow than sunset's fire
Has filled the west with light,
Where field and garner, barn and byre,
Are blazing through the night.

The land is wild with fear and hate,
The rout runs mad and fast;
From hand to hand, from gate to gate
The flaming brand is passed.

The lurid glow falls strong across
Dark faces broad with smiles:
Not theirs the terror, hate, and loss
That fire yon blazing piles.

With oar-strokes timing to their song,
They weave in simple lays
The pathos of remembered wrong,
The hope of better days, —

The triumph-note that Miriam sung,
The joy of uncaged birds:
Softening with Afric's mellow tongue
Their broken Saxon words.

JOHN GREENLEAF WHITTIER.

The campaign along the North Carolina coast was vigorously pressed, and fort after fort was captured, until the Northern troops were so firmly in possession that their control of that portion of the coast was never afterwards seriously threatened.

READY

LOADED with gallant soldiers,
A boat shot in to the land,
And lay at the right of Rodman's Point,
With her keel upon the sand.

Lightly, gayly, they came to shore,
And never a man afraid;
When sudden the enemy opened fire,
From his deadly ambuscade.

Each man fell flat on the bottom
Of the boat; and the captain said:
"If we lie here, we all are captured,
And the first who moves is dead!"

Then out spoke a negro sailor,
No slavish soul had he:
"Somebody's got to die, boys,
And it might as well be me!"

Firmly he rose, and fearlessly
Stepped out into the tide;
He pushed the vessel safely off,
Then fell across her side:

Fell, pierced by a dozen bullets,
As the boat swung clear and free; —
But there was n't a man of them that day
Who was fitter to die than he!

PHŒBE CARY.

Especially important was the capture of Newberne, on the Neuse River, where the Confederates were strongly intrenched. The Union forces under Burnside advanced to the attack on the morning of March 14, 1862, and succeeded in carrying the works. The loss on both sides was heavy, and would have been heavier still on the Union side, but for the quick wit of Kady Brownell.

THE DAUGHTER OF THE REGI-MENT

(FIFTH RHODE ISLAND)

[March 14, 1862]

Who with the soldiers was stanch danger-
　　sharer, —
　Marched in the ranks through the shriek of
　　the shell?
Who was their comrade, their brave color-
　　bearer?
　Who but the resolute Kady Brownell!

Over the marshland and over the highland,
　Where'er the columns wound, meadow or
　　dell,
Fared she, this daughter of little Rhode
　　Island, —
　She, the intrepid one, Kady Brownell!

While the mad rout at Manassas was surging,
　When those around her fled wildly, or fell,
And the bold Beauregard onward was urging,
　Who so undaunted as Kady Brownell!

When gallant Burnside made dash upon
　　Newberne,
　Sailing the Neuse 'gainst the sweep of the
　　swell,
Watching the flag on the heaven's broad blue
　　burn,
　Who higher hearted than Kady Brownell?

In the deep slough of the springtide debark-
　　ing,
　Toiling o'er leagues that are weary to tell,
Time with the sturdiest soldiery marking,
　Forward, straight forward, strode Kady
　　Brownell.

Reaching the lines where the army was form-
　　ing,
　Forming to charge on those ramparts of hell,
When from the wood came her regiment
　　swarming,
　What did she see there — this Kady
　　Brownell?

See! why she saw that their friends thought
　　them foemen;
　Muskets were levelled, and cannon as well!

Save them from direful destruction would no
　　men?
　Nay, but this woman would, — Kady
　　Brownell!

Waving her banner she raced for the clearing;
　Fronted them all, with her flag as a spell;
Ah, what a volley — a volley of cheering —
　Greeted the heroine, Kady Brownell!

Gone (and thank God!) are those red days of
　　slaughter!
　Brethren again we in amity dwell;
Just one more cheer for the Regiment's
　　Daughter! —
　Just one more cheer for her, Kady Brownell!
　　　　　　　　　　　　　Clinton Scollard.

　The Federals had succeeded in partially de-stroying the navy yard at Norfolk at the outbreak of the war, but the Confederates succeeded in raising one vessel, the Merrimac. This they re-built, converted into an iron-clad, armed with ten rifled guns, and named the Virginia. A cast-iron ram was fitted to the bow. The vessel was com-pleted in March, 1862, and on the 8th cast loose and steamed down the river.

THE TURTLE

[March 8, 1862]

Cæsar, afloat with his fortunes!
　And all the world agog
Straining its eyes
At a thing that lies
　In the water, like a log!
It's a weasel! a whale!
I see its tail!
　It's a porpoise! a pollywog!

Tarnation! it's a *turtle*!
　And blast my bones and skin,
My hearties, sink her,
Or else you'll think her
　A regular terror-pin!

The frigate poured a broadside!
　The bombs they whistled well,
But — hit old Nick
With a sugar stick!
　It did n't phase her shell!

Piff, from the creature's larboard —
　And dipping along the water
A bullet hissed
From a wreath of mist
　Into a Doodle's quarter!

Raff, from the creature's starboard —
  Rip, from his ugly snorter,
And the Congress and
The Cumberland
  Sunk, and nothing — shorter.

Now, here's to you, Virginia,
  And you are bound to win!
By your rate of bobbing round
  And your way of pitchin' in —
For you are a cross
Of the old sea-hoss
And a regular terror-pin.

At Newport News lay the United States 50-gun frigate Congress, the 24-gun sloop Cumberland, and the frigates St. Lawrence, Roanoke, and Minnesota. In command of the Cumberland was Lieutenant George Upham Morris, and at noon the Merrimac was seen from the Cumberland's deck advancing to the attack. Shot and shell were poured upon her without effect. She steamed straight on and plunged her ram into the Cumberland's side. Morris fought his ship until she sank under him.

THE ATTACK

[March 8, 1862]

IN Hampton Roads, the airs of March were
    bland,
  Peace on the deck and in the fortress sleep-
    ing,
Till, in the look-out of the Cumberland,
  The sailor, with his well-poised glass in hand,
  Descried the iron island downward creep-
    ing.

A sudden wonder seized on land and bay,
  And Tumult, with her train, was there to
    follow;
For still the stranger kept its seaward way,
Looking a great leviathan blowing spray,
  Seeking with steady course his ocean wal-
    low.

And still it came, and largened on the sight;
  A floating monster; ugly and gigantic;
In shape, a wave, with long and shelving
    height,
As if a mighty billow, heaved at night,
  Should turn to iron in the mid-Atlantic.

Then ship and fortress gazed with anxious
    stare,
  Until the Cumberland's cannon, silence
    breaking,

Thundered its guardian challenge, "Who
    comes there?"
But, like a rock-flung echo in the air,
  The shot rebounded, no impression making.

Then roared a broadside; though directed
    well,
  On, like a nightmare, moved the shape
    defiant;
The tempest of our pounding shot and shell
Crumbled to harmless nothing, thickly fell
  From off the sounding armor of the giant!

Unchecked, still onward through the storm it
    broke,
  With beak directed at the vessel's centre;
Then through the constant cloud of sulphur-
    ous smoke
Drove, till it struck the warrior's wall of oak,
  Making a gateway for the waves to enter.

Struck, and to note the mischief done, with-
    drew,
  And then, with all a murderer's impatience,
Rushed on again, crushing her ribs anew,
Cleaving the noble hull well-nigh in two,
  And on it sped its fiery imprecations.

Swift through the vessel swept the drowning
    swell,
  With splash, and rush, and guilty rise
    appalling;
While sinking cannon rung their own loud
    knell,
Then, cried the traitor, from his sulphurous
    cell,
  "Do you surrender?" Oh, those words
    were galling!

How spake our captain to his comrades then?
  It was a shout from out a soul of splendor,
Echoed from lofty maintop, and again
Between-decks, from the lips of dying men,
  "Sink! sink, boys, sink! but never say
    surrender!"

Down went the ship! Down, down; but
    never down
  Her sacred flag to insolent dictator.
Weep for the patriot heroes, doomed to
    drown;
Pledge to the sunken Cumberland's renown.
  She sank, thank God! unsoiled by foot of
    traitor!

    THOMAS BUCHANAN READ.

THE CUMBERLAND

[March 8, 1862]

At anchor in Hampton Roads we lay,
  On board of the Cumberland, sloop-of-war;
And at times from the fortress across the bay
    The alarum of drums swept past,
    Or a bugle blast
  From the camp on the shore.

Then far away to the south uprose
  A little feather of snow-white smoke,
And we knew that the iron ship of our foes
    Was steadily steering its course
    To try the force
  Of our ribs of oak.

Down upon us heavily runs,
  Silent and sullen, the floating fort;
Then comes a puff of smoke from her guns,
    And leaps the terrible death,
    With fiery breath,
  From each open port.

We are not idle, but send her straight
  Defiance back in a full broadside!
As hail rebounds from a roof of slate,
    Rebounds our heavier hail
    From each iron scale
  Of the monster's hide.

"Strike your flag!" the rebel cries
  In his arrogant old plantation strain.
"Never!" our gallant Morris replies:
    "It is better to sink than to yield!"
    And the whole air pealed
  With the cheers of our men.

Then, like a kraken huge and black,
  She crushed our ribs in her iron grasp!
Down went the Cumberland all a wrack,
    With a sudden shudder of death,
    And the cannon's breath
  For her dying gasp.

Next morn, as the sun rose over the bay,
  Still floated our flag at the mainmast head.
Lord, how beautiful was Thy day!
    Every waft of the air
    Was a whisper of prayer,
  Or a dirge for the dead.

Ho! brave hearts that went down in the seas!
  Ye are at peace in the troubled stream;

Ho! brave land! with hearts like these,
  Thy flag, that is rent in twain,
    Shall be one again,
  And without a seam!
      HENRY WADSWORTH LONGFELLOW.

ON BOARD THE CUMBERLAND

[March 8, 1862]

"Stand to your guns, men!" Morris cried.
  Small need to pass the word;
Our men at quarters ranged themselves,
  Before the drum was heard.

And then began the sailors' jests:
  "What thing is that, I say?"
"A 'long-shore meeting-house adrift
  Is standing down the bay!"

A frown came over Morris' face;
  The strange, dark craft he knew;
"That is the iron Merrimac,
  Manned by a rebel crew.

"So shot your guns, and point them straight;
  Before this day goes by,
We'll try of what her metal's made."
  A cheer was our reply.

"Remember, boys, this flag of ours
  Has seldom left its place;
And where it falls, the deck it strikes
  Is covered with disgrace.

"I ask but this: or sink or swim,
  Or live or nobly die,
My last sight upon earth may be
  To see that ensign fly!"

Meanwhile the shapeless iron mass
  Came moving o'er the wave,
As gloomy as a passing hearse,
  As silent as the grave.

Her ports were closed, from stem to stern
  No sign of life appeared.
We wondered, questioned, strained our eyes,
  Joked, — everything but feared.

She reached our range. Our broadside rang,
  Our heavy pivots roared;
And shot and shell, a fire of hell,
  Against her sides we poured.

God's mercy! from her sloping roof
  The iron tempest glanced,
As hail bounds from a cottage-thatch,
  And round her leaped and danced;

Or, when against her dusky hull
  We struck a fair, full blow,
The mighty, solid iron globes
  Were crumbled up like snow.

On, on, with fast increasing speed,
  The silent monster came;
Though all our starboard battery
  Was one long line of flame.

She heeded not, nor gun she fired,
  Straight on our bow she bore;
Through riving plank and crashing frame
  Her furious way she tore.

Alas! our beautiful, keen bow,
  That in the fiercest blast
So gently folded back the seas,
  They hardly felt we passed!

Alas! Alas! My Cumberland,
  That ne'er knew grief before,
To be so gored, to feel so deep
  The tusk of that sea-boar!

Once more she backward drew a space,
  Once more our side she rent;
Then, in the wantonness of hate,
  Her broadside through us sent.

The dead and dying round us lay,
  But our foeman lay abeam;
Her open portholes maddened us;
  We fired with shout and scream.

We felt our vessel settling fast,
  We knew our time was brief;
"The pumps, the pumps!" But they who
      pumped,
  And fought not, wept with grief.

"Oh, keep us but an hour afloat!
  Oh, give us only time
To be the instruments of heaven
  Against the traitors' crime!"

From captain down to powder-boy,
  No hand was idle then;
Two soldiers, but by chance aboard,
  Fought on like sailor-men.

And when a gun's crew lost a hand,
  Some bold marine stepped out,
And jerked his braided jacket off,
  And hauled the gun about.

Our forward magazine was drowned;
  And up from the sick-bay
Crawled out the wounded, red with blood,
  And round us gasping lay.

Yes, cheering, calling us by name,
  Struggling with failing breath,
To keep their shipmates at the port,
  While glory strove with death.

With decks afloat, and powder gone,
  The last broadside we gave
From the guns' heated iron lips
  Burst out beneath the wave.

So sponges, rammers, and handspikes —
  As men-of-war's men should —
We placed within their proper racks,
  And at our quarters stood.

"Up to the spar-deck! Save yourselves!"
  Cried Selfridge. "Up, my men!
God grant that some of us may live
  To fight yon ship again!"

We turned — we did not like to go;
  Yet staying seemed but vain,
Knee-deep in water; so we left;
  Some swore, some groaned with pain.

We reached the deck. Here Randall stood:
  "Another turn, men — so!"
Calmly he aimed his pivot-gun:
  "Now, Tenney, let her go!"

It did our sore hearts good to hear
  The song our pivot sang,
As rushing on, from wave to wave,
  The whirring bomb-shell sprang.

Brave Randall leaped upon the gun,
  And waved his cap in sport;
"Well done! well aimed! I saw that shell
  Go through an open port."

It was our last, our deadliest shot;
  The deck was overflown;
The poor ship staggered, lurched to port,
  And gave a living groan.

Down, down, as headlong through the waves
  Our gallant vessel rushed,
A thousand gurgling, watery sounds
  Around my senses gushed.

Then I remember little more;
  One look to heaven I gave,
Where, like an angel's wing, I saw
  Our spotless ensign wave.

I tried to cheer, I cannot say
  Whether I swam or sank;
A blue mist closed around my eyes,
  And everything was blank.

When I awoke, a soldier-lad,
  All dripping from the sea,
With two great tears upon his cheeks,
  Was bending over me.

I tried to speak. He understood
  The wish I could not speak.
He turned me. There, thank God! the flag
  Still fluttered at the peak!

And there, while thread shall hang to thread,
  O let that ensign fly!
The noblest constellation set
  Against our northern sky.

A sign that we who live may claim
  The peerage of the brave;
A monument, that needs no scroll,
  For those beneath the wave!
                    GEORGE HENRY BOKER.

THE CUMBERLAND

SOME names there are of telling sound,
  Whose vowelled syllables free
Are pledge that they shall ever live renowned;
  Such seems to be
A Frigate's name (by present glory spanned) —
  The Cumberland.
        Sounding name as e'er was sung,
        Flowing, rolling on the tongue —
        Cumberland! Cumberland!

She warred and sunk. There's no denying
  That she was ended — quelled;
And yet her flag above her fate is flying,
  As when it swelled

Unswallowed by the swallowing sea: so
    grand —
  The Cumberland.
        Goodly name as e'er was sung,
        Roundly rolling on the tongue —
        Cumberland! Cumberland!

What need to tell how she was fought —
  The sinking flaming gun —
The gunner leaping out the port —
  Washed back, undone!
Her dead unconquerably manned
  The Cumberland.
        Noble name as e'er was sung,
        Slowly roll it on the tongue —
        Cumberland! Cumberland!

Long as hearts shall share the flame
  Which burned in that brave crew,
Her fame shall live — outlive the victor's
    name;
  For this is due.
Your flag and flag-staff shall in story stand —
  Cumberland!
        Sounding name as e'er was sung,
        Long they'll roll it on the tongue —
        Cumberland! Cumberland!
                    HERMAN MELVILLE.

The Merrimac then drew off and subjected the
Congress to such a terrific fire that the frigate was
forced to surrender. After heavily damaging the
other vessels of the fleet, the Merrimac withdrew,
intending to complete their destruction in the
morning.

HOW THE CUMBERLAND WENT
DOWN

[March 8, 1862]

GRAY swept the angry waves
  O'er the gallant and the true,
Rolled high in mounded graves
  O'er the stately frigate's crew —
Over cannon, over deck,
Over all that ghastly wreck, —
      When the Cumberland went down.

Such a roar the waters rent
  As though a giant died,
When the wailing billows went
  Above those heroes tried;
And the sheeted foam leaped high,
Like white ghosts against the sky, —
      As the Cumberland went down.

O shrieking waves that gushed
  Above that loyal band,
Your cold, cold burial rushed
  O'er many a heart on land!
And from all the startled North
A cry of pain broke forth,
    When the Cumberland went down.

And forests old, that gave
  A thousand years of power
To her lordship of the wave
  And her beauty's regal dower,
Bent, as though before a blast,
When plunged her pennoned mast,
    And the Cumberland went down.

And grimy mines that sent
  To her their virgin strength,
And iron vigor lent
  To knit her lordly length,
Wildly stirred with throbs of life,
Echoes of that fatal strife,
    As the Cumberland went down.

Beneath the ocean vast,
  Full many a captain bold,
By many a rotting mast,
  And admiral of old,
Rolled restless in his grave
As he felt the sobbing wave,
    When the Cumberland went down.

And stern Vikings that lay
  A thousand years at rest,
In many a deep blue bay
  Beneath the Baltic's breast,
Leaped on the silver sands,
And shook their rusty brands,
    As the Cumberland went down.
                    S. WEIR MITCHELL.

But when, on the morning of March 9, 1862, the
Merrimac steamed out again into Hampton Roads,
a new antagonist confronted her — the Monitor,
Ericsson's eccentric boat, which had arrived from
New York the night before. The ships approached
each other, like David and Goliath. A battle fol-
lowed, unique in naval warfare, the first duel of
ironclads the world had ever seen. It ended in the
Merrimac retreating to Norfolk, badly damaged.

THE CRUISE OF THE MONITOR

[March 9, 1862]

Out of a Northern city's bay,
'Neath lowering clouds, one bleak March day,

Glided a craft — the like, I ween,
On ocean's crest was never seen
Since Noah's float, that ancient boat,
Could o'er a conquered deluge gloat.

No raking masts, with clouds of sail,
Bent to the breeze, or braved the gale;
No towering chimney's wreaths of smoke
Betrayed the mighty engine's stroke;
But low and dark, like the crafty shark,
Moved in the waters this novel bark.

The fishers stared as the flitting sprite
Passed their huts in the misty light,
Bearing a turret huge and black,
And said, "The old sea-serpent's back,
Carting away by light of day,
Uncle Sam's fort from New York Bay."

Forth from a Southern city's dock,
Our frigates' strong blockade to mock,
Crept a monster of rugged build,
The work of crafty hands, well skilled —
Old Merrimac, with an iron back
Wooden ships would find hard to crack.

Straight to where the Cumberland lay,
The mail-clad monster made its way;
Its deadly prow struck deep and sure,
And the hero's fighting days were o'er.
Ah! many the braves who found their graves,
With that good ship, beneath the waves!

But with their fate is glory wrought,
Those hearts of oak like heroes fought
With desperate hope to win the day,
And crush the foe that 'fore them lay.
Our flag up run, the last-fired gun,
Tokens how bravely duty was done.

Flushed with success, the victor flew,
Furious, the startled squadron through:
Sinking, burning, driving ashore,
Until that Sabbath day was o'er,
Resting at night to renew the fight
With vengeful ire by morning's light.

Out of its den it burst anew,
When the gray mist the sun broke through,
Steaming to where, in clinging sands,
The frigate Minnesota stands,
A sturdy foe to overthrow,
But in woful plight to receive a blow.

But see! Beneath her bow appears
A champion no danger fears;
A pigmy craft, that seems to be
To this new lord who rules the sea,
Like David of old to Goliath bold —
Youth and giant, by Scripture told.

Round the roaring despot playing,
With willing spirit, helm obeying,
Spurning the iron against it hurled,
While belching turret rapid whirled,
And swift shot's seethe, with smoky wreath,
Told that the shark was showing his teeth —

The Monitor fought. In grim amaze
The Merrimacs upon it gaze,
Cowering 'neath the iron hail,
Crashing into their coat of mail;
They swore "this craft, the devil's shaft,
Looked like a cheese-box on a raft."

Hurrah! little giant of '62!
Bold Worden with his gallant crew
Forces the fight; the day is won;
Back to his den the monster's gone
With crippled claws and broken jaws,
Defeated in a reckless cause.

Hurrah for the master mind that wrought,
With iron hand, this iron thought!
Strength and safety with speed combined,
Ericsson's gift to all mankind;
To curb abuse, and chains to loose,
Hurrah for the Monitor's famous cruise!
GEORGE HENRY BOKER.

The reign of terror created by the Merrimac was at an end, and the ship herself did not last long. On May 10, 1862, the Confederates were forced to abandon Norfolk, and the Merrimac was blown up. On December 30 the Monitor foundered in a gale off Hatteras.

THE SINKING OF THE MERRIMACK

[May, 1862]

GONE down in the flood, and gone out in the flame!
What else could she do, with her fair Northern name?
Her font was a river whose last drop is free:
That river ran boiling with wrath to the sea,
To hear of her baptismal blessing profaned;
A name that was Freedom's, by treachery stained.

'T was the voice of our free Northern mountains that broke
In the sound of her guns, from her stout ribs of oak:
'T was the might of the free Northern hand you could feel
In her sweep and her moulding, from topmast to keel:
When they made her speak treason (does Hell know of worse?),
How her strong timbers shook with the shame of her curse!

Let her go! Should a deck so polluted again
Ever ring to the tread of our true Northern men?
Let the suicide-ship thunder forth, to the air
And the sea she has blotted, her groan of despair!
Let her last heat of anguish throb out into flame!
Then sink them together, — the ship and the name!
LUCY LARCOM.

The work of the gunboats on the Mississippi at the investment of Fort Henry and Fort Donelson has been already mentioned. In April, 1862, a blow was aimed at the very heart of the Confederacy, when a fleet under command of David Glasgow Farragut advanced up the river against the formidable forts below New Orleans. After five days' bombardment, the fleet ran past the forts and attacked the Confederate ships before the city.

THE RIVER FIGHT

[April 18, 1862]

Do you know of the dreary land,
If land such region may seem,
Where 't is neither sea nor strand,
Ocean, nor good, dry land,
But the nightmare marsh of a dream?
Where the Mighty River his death-road takes,
'Mid pools and windings that coil like snakes
A hundred leagues of bayous and lakes,
To die in the great Gulf Stream?

No coast-line clear and true,
Granite and deep-sea blue,
On that dismal shore you pass,
Surf-worn boulder or sandy beach, —
But oooze-flats as far as the eye can reach,
With shallows of water-grass;
Reedy Savannahs, vast and dun,

Lying dead in the dim March sun;
Huge, rotting trunks and roots that lie
Like the blackened bones of shapes gone by,
And miles of sunken morass.

No lovely, delicate thing
Of life o'er the waste is seen
But the cayman couched by his weedy spring,
And the pelican, bird unclean,
Or the buzzard, flapping with heavy wing,
Like an evil ghost o'er the desolate scene.

Ah! many a weary day
With our Leader there we lay.
In the sultry haze and smoke,
Tugging our ships o'er the bar,
Till the spring was wasted far,
Till his brave heart almost broke.
For the sullen river seemed
As if our intent he dreamed, —
All his sallow mouths did spew and choke.

But ere April fully passed
All ground over at last
And we knew the die was cast, —
Knew the day drew nigh
To dare to the end one stormy deed,
Might save the land at her sorest need,
Or on the old deck to die!

Anchored we lay, — and a morn the more,
To his captains and all his men
Thus wrote our old commodore
(He was n't Admiral then): —
"GENERAL ORDERS:
Send your to'gallant masts down,
Rig in each flying jib-boom!
Clear all ahead for the loom
Of traitor fortress and town,
Or traitor fleet bearing down.

" In with your canvas high;
We shall want no sail to fly!
Topsail, foresail, spanker, and jib
  With the heart of oak in the oaken rib),
Shall serve us to win or die!

"Trim every sail by the head
So shall you spare the lead),
Lest if she ground, your ship swing round,
Bows in shore, for a wreck.
See your grapnels all clear with pains,
And a solid kedge in your port main-chains,
With a whip to the main yard:

Drop it heavy and hard
When you grapple a traitor deck!

"On forecastle and on poop
Mount guns, as best you may deem.
If possible, rouse them up
(For still you must bow the stream).
Also hoist and secure with stops
Howitzers firmly in your tops,
To fire on the foe abeam.

"Look well to your pumps and hose;
Have water tubs fore and aft,
For quenching flame in your craft,
And the gun crew's fiery thirst.
See planks with felt fitted close,
To plug every shot-hole tight.
Stand ready to meet the worst!
For, if I have reckoned aright,
They will·serve us shot,
Both cold and hot,
Freely enough to-night.

"Mark well each signal I make
(Our life-long service at stake,
And honor that must not lag!), —
Whate'er the peril and awe,
In the battle's fieriest flaw,
Let never one ship withdraw
Till the orders come from the flag!"

———

Would you hear of the river fight?
It was two of a soft spring night;
God's stars looked down on all;
And all was clear and bright
But the low fog's clinging breath;
Up the River of Death
Sailed the great Admiral.

On our high poop-deck he stood,
And round him ranged the men
Who have made their birthright good
Of manhood once and again, —
Lords of helm and of sail,
Tried in tempest and gale,
Bronzed in battle and wreck.
Bell and Bailey grandly led
Each his line of the Blue and Red;
Wainwright stood by our starboard rail;
Thornton fought the deck.
And I mind me of more than they,
Of the youthful, steadfast ones,
That have shown them worthy sons
Of the seamen passed away.

Tyson conned our helm that day;
Watson stood by his guns.

What thought our Admiral then,
Looking down on his men?
Since the terrible day
(Day of renown and tears!), —
When at anchor the Essex lay, —
Holding her foes at bay, —
When a boy by Porter's side he stood,
Till deck and plank-sheer were dyed with
    blood;
'T is half a hundred years, —
Half a hundred years to a day!

Who could fail with him?
Who reckon of life or limb?
Not a pulse but beat the higher!
There had you seen, by the starlight dim,
Five hundred faces strong and grim:
The Flag is going under fire!
Right up by the fort,
With her helm hard aport,
The Hartford is going under fire!

The way to our work was plain.
Caldwell had broken the chain
(Two hulks swung down amain
Soon as 't was sundered).
Under the night's dark blue,
Steering steady and true,
Ship after ship went through,
Till, as we hove in view,
"Jackson" out-thundered!

Back echoed "Philip!" ah! then
Could you have seen our men.
How they sprung in the dim night haze,
To their work of toil and of clamor!
How the boarders, with sponge and rammer
And their captains, with cord and hammer
Kept every muzzle ablaze.
How the guns, as with cheer and shout —
Our tackle-men hurled them out —
Brought up on the water-ways!

First, as we fired at their flash,
'T was lightning and black eclipse,
With a bellowing roll and crash.
But soon, upon either bow,
What with forts and fire-rafts and ships
(The whole fleet was hard at it now),
All pounding away! — and Porter
Still thundering with shell and mortar, —
'T was the mighty sound and form!

(Such you see in the far South,
After long heat and drought,
As day draws nigh to even,
Arching from north to south,
Blinding the tropic sun,
The great black bow comes on,
Till the thunder-veil is riven, —
When all is crash and levin,
And the cannonade of heaven
Rolls down the Amazon!)

But, as we worked along higher,
Just where the river enlarges,
Down came a pyramid of fire, —
It was one of your long coal barges.
(We had often had the like before.)
'T was coming down on us to larboard,
Well in with the eastern shore;
And our pilot, to let it pass round
(You may guess we never stopped to sound),
Giving us a rank sheer to starboard,
Ran the Flag hard and fast aground!

'T was nigh abreast of the Upper Fort,
And straightway a rascal ram
(She was shaped like the Devil's dam)
Puffed away for us, with a snort,
And shoved it, with spiteful strength,
Right alongside of us to port.
It was all of our ship's length, —
A huge, crackling Cradle of the Pit!
Pitch-pine knots to the brim,
Belching flame red and grim,
What a roar came up from it!

Well, for a little it looked bad:
But these things are, somehow, shorter,
In the acting than in the telling;
There was no singing out or yelling,
Or any fussing or fretting,
No stampede, in short;
But there we were, my lad,
All afire on our port quarter,
Hammocks ablaze in the netting,
Flames spouting in at every port,
Our fourth cutter burning at the davit
(No chance to lower away and save it).

In a twinkling, the flames had risen
Halfway to maintop and mizzen,
Darting up the shrouds like snakes!
Ah, how we clanked at the brakes,
And the deep, steaming pumps throbbed
    under,
Sending a ceaseless flow.

Our topmen, a dauntless crowd,
Swarmed in rigging and shroud:
There ('t was a wonder!)
The burning ratlines and strands
They quenched with their bare, hard hands;
But the great guns below
Never silenced their thunder.

At last, by backing and sounding,
When we were clear of grounding,
And under headway once more,
The whole rebel fleet came rounding
The point. If we had it hot before,
'T was now from shore to shore,
One long, loud, thundering roar, —
Such crashing, splintering, and pounding,
And smashing as you never heard before!

But that we fought foul wrong to wreck,
And to save the land we loved so well,
You might have deemed our long gun-deck
Two hundred feet of hell!

For above all was battle,
Broadside, and blaze, and rattle,
Smoke and thunder alone
(But, down in the sick-bay,
Where our wounded and dying lay,
There was scarce a sob or a moan).

And at last, when the dim day broke,
And the sullen sun awoke,
Drearily blinking
O'er the haze and the cannon smoke.
That ever such morning dulls, —
There were thirteen traitor hulls
On fire and sinking!

Now, up the river! — though mad Chalmette
Sputters a vain resistance yet,
Small helm we gave her our course to steer, —
'T was nicer work than you well would dream,
With cant and sheer to keep her clear
Of the burning wrecks that cumbered the
    stream.

The Louisiana, hurled on high,
Mounts in thunder to meet the sky!
Then down to the depths of the turbid flood, —
Fifty fathom of rebel mud!
The Mississippi comes floating down,
A mighty bonfire from off the town;
And along the river, on stocks and ways,
A half-hatched devil's brood is ablaze, —
The great Anglo-Norman is all in flames

(Hark to the roar of her trembling frames!),
And the smaller fry that Treason would
    spawn
Are lighting Algiers like an angry dawn!

From stem to stern, how the pirates burn,
Fired by the furious hands that built!
So to ashes forever turn
The suicide wrecks of wrong and guilt!

But as we neared the city,
By field and vast plantation
(Ah! millstone of our nation!),
With wonder and with pity,
What crowds we there espied
Of dark and wistful faces,
Mute in their toiling places,
Strangely and sadly eyed,
Haply 'mid doubt and fear,
Deeming deliverance near
(One gave the ghost of a cheer!).

And on that dolorous strand,
To greet the victor brave,
One flag did welcome wave —
Raised, ah me! by a wretched hand,
All outworn on our cruel land, —
The withered hand of a slave!

But all along the levee,
In a dark and drenching rain
(By this 't was pouring heavy),
Stood a fierce and sullen train,
A strange and frenzied time!
There were scowling rage and pain,
Curses, howls, and hisses,
Out of Hate's black abysses, —
Their courage and their crime
All in vain — all in vain!

For from the hour that the Rebel Stream
With the Crescent City lying abeam,
Shuddered under our keel,
Smit to the heart with self-struck sting,
Slavery died in her scorpion-ring
And Murder fell on his steel.

'T is well to do and dare;
But ever may grateful prayer
Follow, as aye it ought,
When the good fight is fought,
When the true deed is done.
Aloft in heaven's pure light
(Deep azure crossed on white),
Our fair Church pennant waves

O'er a thousand thankful braves,
Bareheaded in God's bright sun.

Lord of mercy and frown,
Ruling o'er sea and shore,
Send us such scene once more!
All in line of battle
When the black ships bear down
On tyrant fort and town,
'Mid cannon cloud and rattle;
And the great guns once more
Thunder back the roar
Of the traitor walls ashore,
And the traitor flags come down.
HENRY HOWARD BROWNELL.

THE BALLAD OF NEW ORLEANS

[April 24, 1862]

JUST as the hour was darkest,
Just between night and day,
From the flag-ship shone the signal,
"Get the squadrons under way."

Not a sound but the tramp of sailors,
And the wheeling capstan's creak,
Arose from the busy vessels
As the anchors came apeak.

The men worked on in silence,
With never a shout or cheer,
Till 't was whispered from bow to quarter:
"Start forward! all is clear."

Then groaned the ponderous engine,
Then floundered the whirling screw;
And as ship joined ship, the comrades
Their lines of battle drew.

The moon through the fog was casting
A blur of lurid light,
As the captain's latest order
Was flashed into the night.

" Steam on! and whatever fortune
May follow the attack,
Sink with your bows still northward
No vessel must turn back!"

'T was hard when we heard that order
To smother a rising shout;
For it wakened the life within us,
And we burned to give it out.

All wrapped in the foggy darkness,
Brave Bailey moved ahead;
And stem after stern, his gunboats
To the starboard station led.

Next Farragut's stately flag-ship
To port her head inclined;
And midmost, and most in danger,
Bell's squadron closed behind.

Ah! many a prayer was murmured
For the homes we ne'er might see;
And the silence and night grew dreadful
With the thought of what must be.

For many a tall, stout fellow
Who stood at his quarters then,
In the damp and dismal moonlight,
Never saw the sun again.

Close down by the yellow river
In their oozy graves they rot;
Strange vines and strange weeds grow o'er
them,
And their far homes know them not.

But short was our time of musing;
For the rebel forts discerned
That the whole great fleet was moving,
And their batteries on us turned.

Then Porter burst out from his mortars,
In jets of fiery spray,
As if a volcano had opened
Where his leaf-clad vessels lay.

Howling and screeching and whizzing
The bomb-shells arched on high,
And then, like gigantic meteors,
Dropped swiftly from the sky.

Dropped down on the low, doomed fortress
A plague of iron death,
Shattering earth and granite to atoms
With their puffs of sulphurous breath.

The whole air quaked and shuddered
As the huge globes rose and fell,
And the blazing shores looked awful
As the open gates of hell.

Fort Jackson and Fort Saint Philip,
And the battery on the right,
By this time were flashing and thundering
Out into the murky night.

Through the hulks and the cables, sundered
  By the bold Itasca's crew,
Went Bailey in silence, though round him
  The shells and the grape-shot flew.

No answer he made to their welcome,
  Till abeam Saint Philip bore,
Then, oh, but he sent them a greeting
  In his broadsides' steady roar!

Meanwhile, the old man, in the Hartford,
  Had ranged to Fort Jackson's side;
What a sight! he slowed his engines
  Till he barely stemmed the tide;

Yes, paused in that deadly tornado
  Of case-shot and shell and ball,
Not a cable's length from the fortress,
  And he lay there, wood to wall.

Have you any notion, you landsmen,
  Who have seen a field-fight won,
Of canister, grape-shot, and shrapnel
  Hurled out from a ten-inch gun?

I tell you, the air is nigh solid
  With the howling iron flight;
And 't was such a tempest blew o'er us
  Where the Hartford lay that night.

Perched aloft in the forward rigging,
  With his restless eyes aglow,
Sat Farragut, shouting his orders
  To the men who fought below.

And the fort's huge faces of granite
  Were splintered and rent in twain,
And the masses seemed slowly melting,
  Like snow in a torrid rain.

Now quicker and quicker we fired,
  Till between us and the foe
A torrent of blazing vapor
  Was leaping to and fro;

While the fort, like a mighty caldron,
  Was boiling with flame and smoke,
And the stone flew aloft in fragments,
  And the brick into powder broke.

So thick fell the clouds o'er the river,
  You hardly could see your hand;
When we heard, from the foremast rigging,
  Old Farragut's sharp command:

"Full ahead! Steam across to Saint Philip!
  Starboard battery, mind your aim!
Forecastle there, shift your pivots! Now,
  Give them a taste of the same!"

Saint Philip grew faint in replying,
  Its voice of thunder was drowned;
"But ha! what is this? Back the engines!
  Back, back, the ship is aground!"

Straight down the swift current came sweeping
  A raft, spouting sparks and flame;
Pushed on by an iron-clad rebel,
  Under our port side it came.

At once the good Hartford was blazing,
  Below, aloft, fore and aft.
"We are lost!" "No, no; we are moving!"
  Away whirled the crackling raft.

The fire was soon quenched. One last broad-
    side
  We gave to the surly fort;
For above us the rebel gunboats
  Were wheeling like devils at sport.

And into our vacant station
  Had glided a bulky form;
'T was Craven's stout Brooklyn, demanding
  Her share of the furious storm.

We could hear the shot of Saint Philip
  Ring on her armor of chain,
And the crash of her answering broadside,
  Taking and giving again.

We could hear the low growl of Craven,
  And Lowry's voice clear and calm,
While they swept off the rebel ramparts
  As clean as your open palm.

Then ranging close under our quarter,
  Out burst from the smoky fogs
The queen of the waves, the Varuna,
  The ship of bold Charley Boggs.

He waved his blue cap as he passed us;
  The blood of his glorious race,
Of Lawrence, the hero, was burning
  Once more in a living face.

Right and left flashed his heavy pieces,
  Rams, gunboats — it mattered not.
Wherever a rebel flag floated
  Was a target for his shot.

All burning and sinking around him
  Lay five of the foe; but he,
The victor, seemed doomed with the van-
      quished,
  When along dashed gallant Lee.

And he took up the bloody conflict,
  And so well his part he bore,
That the river ran fire behind him,
  And glimmered from shore to shore.

But while powder would burn in a cannon,
  Till the water drowned his deck,
Boggs pounded away with his pivots
  From his slowly settling wreck.

I think our great captains in Heaven,
  As they looked upon those deeds,
Were proud of the flower of that navy,
  Of which they planted the seeds.

Paul Jones, the knight-errant of ocean,
  Decatur, the lord of the seas,
Hull, Lawrence, and Bainbridge, and Biddle,
  And Perry, the peer of all these!

If Porter beheld his descendant,
  With some human pride on his lip,
I trust, through the mercy of Heaven,
  His soul was forgiven that slip.

And thou, living veteran, Old Ironsides,
  The last of the splendid line,
Thou link 'twixt the old and new glory,
  I know what feelings were thine!

When the sun looked over the tree-tops,
  We found ourselves — Heaven knows
      how —
Above the grim forts; and that instant
  A smoke broke from Farragut's bow.

And over the river came floating
  The sound of the morning gun;
And the stars and stripes danced up the hal-
      yards,
  And glittered against the sun.

Oh, then what a shout from the squadrons!
  As flag followed flag, till the day
Was bright with the beautiful standard,
  And wild with the victors' huzza!

But three ships were missing. The others
  Had passed through that current of flame;

And each scar on their shattered bulwarks
  Was touched by the finger of Fame.

Below us, the forts of the rebels
  Lay in the trance of despair;
Above us, uncovered and helpless,
  New Orleans clouded the air.

Again, in long lines we went steaming
  Away towards the city's smoke;
And works were deserted before us,
  And columns of soldiers broke.

In vain the town clamored and struggled;
  The flag at our peak ruled the hour;
And under its shade, like a lion,
  Were resting the will and the power.
                    GEORGE HENRY BOKER.

The Varuna, after sinking five Confederate ves-
sels, was herself sunk. Every ship of the Federal
fleet suffered severely, but on the afternoon of
April 25, 1862, the fleet dropped anchor off New
Orleans.

THE VARUNA

[Sunk April 24, 1862]

WHO has not heard of the dauntless Varuna?
  Who has not heard of the deeds she has
      done?
Who shall not hear, while the brown Missis-
      sippi
  Rushes along from the snow to the sun?

Crippled and leaking she entered the battle,
  Sinking and burning she fought through the
      fray;
Crushed were her sides and the waves ran
      across her,
  Ere, like a death-wounded lion at bay,
Sternly she closed in the last fatal grapple,
  Then in her triumph moved grandly away.

Five of the rebels, like satellites round her,
  Burned in her orbit of splendor and fear;
One, like the Pleiad of mystical story,
  Shot, terror-stricken, beyond her dread
      sphere.

We who are waiting with crowns for the vic-
      tors,
  Though we should offer the wealth of our
      store,

Load the Varuna from deck down to kelson,
  Still would be niggard, such tribute to pour
On courage so boundless. It beggars posses-
      sion, —
It knocks for just payment at heaven's bright
      door!

Cherish the heroes who fought the Varuna;
  Treat them as kings if they honor your way;
Succor and comfort the sick and the wounded;
  Oh! for the dead let us all kneel to pray!
                          GEORGE HENRY BOKER.

New Orleans was panic-stricken. Many of the
better class of citizens fled, and the town was
given over to the mob. Drums were beaten, sol-
diers scampered hither and thither, and women
ran through the streets demanding that the city be
burned. The cotton on the levee was set on fire,
and the torch was put to the wharves and shipping.
Finally, on April 29, 1862, after a lot of silly rho-
domontade, the city surrendered.

THE SURRENDER OF NEW ORLEANS

[April 29, 1862]

ALL day long the guns at the forts,
  With far-off thunders and faint retorts,
Had told the city that down the bay
The fleet of Farragut's war-ships lay;
But now St. Philip and Jackson grim
Were black and silent below the rim
Of the southern sky, where the river sped
Like a war-horse scenting the fight ahead.

And we of the city, the women, and men
Too old for facing the battle then,
Saw all the signs of our weakness there
With a patience born of a great despair.
The river gnawed its neglected bank,
The weeds in the unused streets grew rank,
And flood and famine threatened those
Who stayed there braving greater woes.

Under the raking of shot and shell
The river fortresses fighting fell;
The Chalmette batteries then boomed forth,
But the slim. straight spars of the ships of the
      North
Moved steadily on in their river-road,
Like a tide that up from the ocean flowed.

Then load after load, and pile upon pile,
Lining the wharves for many a mile,

Out of the cotton-presses and yards,
With a grim industry which naught retards,
The bales were carried and swiftly placed
By those who knew there was need of haste,
And the torch was laid to the cotton so.
Up from that bonfire the glare and glow
Was seen by the watchers far away,
And weeping and wailing those watchers say,
"The city is lost! O men at the front,
Braving the fortunes of war, and the brunt
Of battle bearing with fearful cost,
The city you loved and left is lost!"

Ah, memories crowding so thick and fast,
Ye were the first; is this the last?
We gave with clamor our first great gift,
With shouts which up to the heavens lift;
We gave with silence our last best yield,
Our last, best gleaning for Shiloh's field.
With mute devotion we saw them go;
But when the banners were furled and low,
And the solid columns were thinned by war,
We wondered what we had given for.

And oh, the day when with muffled drum
We saw our dear, dead Johnston come!
The blood of our slain ones seemed to pour
From the eyes that should see them come no
      more.
We measured our grief by each gallant deed;
We measured our loss by our direful need;
Our dead dreams rose from the vanquished
      past,
And across the future their shadows cast.
Our brave young hope, like a fallen tear,
We laid on the grave of our Chevalier.

And that last wild night! the east was red
So long 'fore the day had left its bed.
With white, set faces, and smileless lips,
We fired our vessels, we fired our ships.
We saw the sails of the red flame lift
O'er each fire-cargo we set adrift;
To Farragut's fleet we sent them down,
A warm, warm welcome from the town.

But, alas, how quickly came the end!
For down the river, below the bend,
Like a threatening finger shook each mast
Of the Yankee ships as they steamed up
      fast.
Grim and terrible, black with men,
Oh, for the Mississippi then!
And — God be merciful! — there she came.
A drifting wreck, a ship of flame

What a torch to light the stripes and stars
That had braved our forts and harbor bars!
What a light, by which we saw vainly slip
Our hopes to their death in that sinking ship!

We shrieked with rage, and defeat, and dread,
As down the river that phantom sped;
But on the deck of a Yankee ship,
One grim old tar, with a smiling lip,
Patted the big black breech of his gun,
As one who silently says, "Well done!"

To-day the graves that were new are old,
And a story done is a story told;
But we of the city, the women and men,
And boys unfitted for fighting then,
Remember the day when our flag went down,
And the stars and stripes waved over the town.
Ah me! the bitter goes with the sweet,
And a victory means another defeat;
For, bound in Nature's inflexible laws,
A glory for one is another's *Lost Cause*.

MARION MANVILLE.

The national flag was hoisted over the mint, but was torn down and dragged through the streets in derision by a gang of men led by William B. Mumford. Mumford was captured and hanged for treason.

MUMFORD

THE MARTYR OF NEW ORLEANS

[May, 1862]

WHERE murdered Mumford lies
Bewailed in bitter sighs,
Low bowed beneath the flag he loved
Martyrs of Liberty,
Defenders of the Free!
Come, humbly nigh,
And learn to die!

Ah, Freedom on that day
Turned fearfully away,
While pitying angels lingered near,
To gaze upon the sod
Red with a martyr's blood;
And woman's tear
Fell on his bier!

Oh, God! that he should die
Beneath a Southern sky!
Upon a felon's gallows swinging,

Murdered by tyrant hand, —
While round a helpless band,
On *Butler's* name
Poured scorn and shame.

But hark! loud pæans fly
From earth to vaulted sky,
He's crowned at Freedom's holy throne!
List! sweet-voiced Israfel
Tolls for the martyr's knell!
Shout Southrons high,
Our battle cry!

Come all of Southern blood,
Come kneel to Freedom's God!
Here at her crimson altar swear!
Accursed forever more
The flag that Mumford tore,
And o'er his grave
Our colors wave.

INA M. PORTER.

The behavior of the women was especially insulting and culminated when one of them spat in the face of a Union officer. General Butler thereupon issued his famous Order No. 28, providing that any woman who insulted an officer or soldier of the United States should be treated as a woman of the town. The order was received with hysteria throughout the South, but it brought the people of New Orleans to their senses.

BUTLER'S PROCLAMATION

[May 15, 1862]

AY! drop the treacherous mask! throw by
The cloak that veiled thine instincts fell,
Stand forth, thou base, incarnate Lie,
Stamped with the signet brand of hell!
At last we view thee as thou art,
A trickster with a demon's heart.

Off with disguise! no quarter now
To rebel honor! thou wouldst strike
Hot blushes up the anguished brow,
And murder Fame and Strength alike.
Beware! ten million hearts aflame
Will burn with hate thou canst not tame!

We know thee now! we know thy race!
Thy dreadful purpose stands revealed
Naked, before the nation's face!
Comrades! let Mercy's font be sealed,
While the black banner courts the wind,
And cursed be he who lags behind!

O soldiers, husbands, brothers, sires!
  Think that each stalwart blow ye give
Shall quench the rage of lustful fires,
  And bid your glorious women live
Pure from a wrong whose tainted breath
Were fouler than the foulest death.

O soldiers, lovers, Christians, men!
  Think that each breeze that floats and
      dies
O'er the red field, from mount or glen,
  Is burdened with a maiden's sighs —
And each false soul that turns to flee,
Consigns his love to infamy!

Think! and strike home! the fabled might
  Of Titans were a feeble power
To that with which your arms should smite
  In the next awful battle-hour!
And deadlier than the bolts of heaven
Should flash your fury's fatal leven!

No pity! let your thirsty bands
  Drink their warm fill at caitiff veins;
Dip deep in blood your wrathful hands,
  Nor pause to wipe those crimson stains.
Slay! slay! with ruthless sword and will —
The God of vengeance bids you "kill!"

Yes! but there's *one who shall not die
  In battle harness!* One for whom
Lurks in the darkness silently
  Another and a sterner doom!
A warrior's end should crown the brave —
For *him*, swift cord! and felon grave!

As loathsome, charnel vapors melt,
  Swept by invisible winds to naught,
So, may this fiend of lust and guilt
  Die like nightmare's hideous thought!
Naught left to mark the mother's name,
Save — immortality of shame!

PAUL HAMILTON HAYNE.

CHAPTER VII

EMANCIPATION

Slavery had caused the war, and as the months passed, the President and his advisers became more and more convinced that the emancipation of the negroes would go far to end it. On August 31, 1861, John C. Frémont, in command of the Western Department, issued a proclamation freeing the slaves of secessionists in Missouri, but the President promptly countermanded it.

TO JOHN C. FRÉMONT

[August 31. 1861]

THY error, Frémont, simply was to act
A brave man's part, without the statesman's
      tact,
And, taking counsel but of common sense,
To strike at cause as well as consequence.
Oh, never yet since Roland wound his horn
At Roncesvalles, has a blast been blown
Far-heard, wide-echoed, startling as thine
      own,
Heard from the van of freedom's hope for-
      lorn!
Had been safer, doubtless, for the time,
To flatter treason, and avoid offence
So that Dark Power whose underlying crime
Heaves upward its perpetual turbulence.
But if thine be the fate of all who break

The ground for truth's seed, or forerun their
      years
Till lost in distance, or with stout hearts
      make
A lane for freedom through the level spears,
Still take thou courage! God has spoken
      through thee,
Irrevocable, the mighty words, Be free!
The land shakes with them, and the slave's
      dull ear
Turns from the rice-swamp stealthily to
      hear.
Who would recall them now must first
      arrest
The winds that blow down from the free
      Northwest,
Ruffling the Gulf; or like a scroll roll back
The Mississippi to its upper springs.
Such words fulfil their prophecy, and lack
But the full time to harden into things.

JOHN GREENLEAF WHITTIER.

The slaves were, however, from the outbreak of hostilities, declared to be "contraband of war," and not returnable to their masters. On April 16, 1862, the President approved a bill freeing the slaves in the District of Columbia and compensating their owners.

ASTRÆA AT THE CAPITOL

ABOLITION OF SLAVERY IN THE DISTRICT
OF COLUMBIA, 1862

[April 16, 1862]

WHEN first I saw our banner wave
Above the nation's council-hall,
I heard beneath its marble wall
The clanking fetters of the slave!

In the foul market-place I stood,
And saw the Christian mother sold,
And childhood with its locks of gold,
Blue-eyed and fair with Saxon blood.

I shut my eyes, I held my breath,
And, smothering down the wrath and
shame
That set my Northern blood aflame,
Stood silent, — where to speak was death.

Beside me gloomed the prison-cell
Where wasted one in slow decline
For uttering simple words of mine,
And loving freedom all too well.

The flag that floated from the dome
Flapped menace in the morning air;
I stood a perilled stranger where
The human broker made his home.

For crime was virtue: Gown and Sword
And Law their threefold sanction gave,
And to the quarry of the slave
Went hawking with our symbol-bird.

On the oppressor's side was power;
And yet I knew that every wrong,
However old, however strong,
But waited God's avenging hour.

I knew that truth would crush the lie, —
Somehow, sometime, the end would be;
Yet scarcely dared I hope to see
The triumph with my mortal eye.

But now I see it! In the sun
A free flag floats from yonder dome,
And at the nation's hearth and home
The justice long delayed is done.

Not as we hoped, in calm of prayer,
The message of deliverance comes,
But heralded by roll of drums
On waves of battle-troubled air!

Midst sounds that madden and appall,
The song that Bethlehem's shepherds
knew!
The harp of David melting through
The demon-agonies of Saul!

Not as we hoped; but what are we?
Above our broken dreams and plans
God lays, with wiser hand than man's,
The corner-stones of liberty.

I cavil not with Him: the voice
That freedom's blessed gospel tells
Is sweet to me as silver bells,
Rejoicing! yea, I will rejoice!

Dear friends still toiling in the sun;
Ye dearer ones who, gone before,
Are watching from the eternal shore
The slow work by your hands begun,

Rejoice with me! The chastening rod
Blossoms with love; the furnace heat
Grows cool beneath His blessed feet
Whose form is as the Son of God!

Rejoice! Our Marah's bitter springs
Are sweetened; on our ground of grief
Rise day by day in strong relief
The prophecies of better things.

Rejoice in hope! The day and night
Are one with God, and one with them
Who see by faith the cloudy hem
Of Judgment fringed with Mercy's light!
JOHN GREENLEAF WHITTIER.

At last the President resolved to throw down
the gauntlet, and on September 22, 1862, proclaimed that all slaves should be freed in such
states as were in rebellion against the United
States on January 1, 1863. The South continued
in rebellion, and the proclamation went into effect
on the first day of the new year.

BOSTON HYMN

[January 1, 1863]

THE word of the Lord by night
To the watching Pilgrims came,

As they sat by the seaside,
　And filled their hearts with flame.

God said, I am tired of kings,
　I suffer them no more;
Up to my ear the morning brings
　The outrage of the poor.

Think ye I made this ball
　A field of havoc and war,
Where tyrants great and tyrants small
　Might harry the weak and poor?

My angel — his name is Freedom —
　Choose him to be your king;
He shall cut pathways east and west,
　And fend you with his wing.

Lo! I uncover the land,
　Which I hid of old time in the West,
As the sculptor uncovers the statue
　When he has wrought his best;

I show Columbia, of the rocks
　Which dip their foot in the seas,
And soar to the air-borne flocks
　Of clouds and the boreal fleece.

I will divide my goods;
　Call in the wretch and slave;
None shall rule but the humble,
　And none but Toil shall have.

I will have never a noble,
　No lineage counted great;
Fishers and choppers and ploughmen
　Shall constitute a state.

Go, cut down trees in the forest
　And trim the straightest boughs;
Cut down trees in the forest
　And build me a wooden house.

Call the people together,
　The young men and the sires,
The digger in the harvest-field,
　Hireling and him that hires;

And here in a pine state-house
　They shall choose men to rule
In every needful faculty,
　In church and state and school.

Lo, now! if these poor men
　Can govern the land and sea,

And make just laws below the sun,
　As planets faithful be.

And ye shall succor men;
　'T is nobleness to serve;
Help them who cannot help again:
　Beware from right to swerve.

I break your bonds and masterships,
　And I unchain the slave:
Free be his heart and hand henceforth
　As wind and wandering wave.

I cause from every creature
　His proper good to flow;
As much as he is and doeth,
　So much he shall bestow.

But, laying hands on another,
　To coin his labor and sweat,
He goes in pawn to his victim
　For eternal years in debt.

To-day unbind the captive,
　So only are ye unbound;
Lift up a people from the dust,
　Trump of their rescue, sound!

Pay ransom to the owner
　And fill the bag to the brim.
Who is the owner? The slave is owner
　And ever was. Pay him.

O North! give him beauty for rags,
　And honor, O South! for his shame:
Nevada! coin thy golden crags
　With Freedom's image and name.

Up! and the dusky race
　That sat in darkness long, —
Be swift their feet as antelopes,
　And as behemoth strong.

Come, East and West and North,
　By races, as snowflakes,
And carry my purpose forth,
　Which neither halts nor shakes.

My will fulfilled shall be,
　For, in daylight or in dark,
My thunderbolt has eyes to see
　His way home to the mark.
　　　　　　RALPH WALDO EMERSON.

THE PROCLAMATION

[January 1, 1863]

SAINT PATRICK, slave to Milcho of the herds
Of Ballymena, wakened with these words:
　　"Arise, and flee
Out from the land of bondage, and be free!"

Glad as a soul in pain, who hears from heaven
The angels singing of his sins forgiven,
　　And, wondering, sees
His prison opening to their golden keys,

He rose a man who laid him down a slave,
Shook from his locks the ashes of the grave,
　　And outward trod
Into the glorious liberty of God.

He cast the symbols of his shame away;
And, passing where the sleeping Milcho lay,
　　Though back and limb
Smarted with wrong, he prayed, "God pardon
　　him!"

So went he forth; but in God's time he came
To light on Uilline's hills a holy flame;
　　And, dying, gave
The land a saint that lost him as a slave.

O dark, sad millions, patiently and dumb
Waiting for God, your hour, at last, has come,
　　And freedom's song
Breaks the long silence of your night of
　　wrong!

Arise and flee! shake off the vile restraint
Of ages; but, like Ballymena's saint,
　　The oppressor spare,
Heap only on his head the coals of prayer.

Go forth, like him! like him return again,
To bless the land whereon in bitter pain
　　Ye toiled at first,
And heal with freedom what your slavery
　　cursed.
　　　　JOHN GREENLEAF WHITTIER.

The Emancipation Proclamation was received
with little enthusiasm except in New England,
and early in 1863 certain politicians proposed to
form a new Union, excluding the New England
states because of their hostility to slavery and
consequent obnoxiousness to the South.

TREASON'S LAST DEVICE

[January 19, 1863]

" Who deserves greatness
　Deserves your hate. . . .
　Yon common cry of curs, whose breath I loathe
　As reek o' the rotten fens."　　CORIOLANUS.

" Hark! hark! the dogs do bark."
　　　　　　　　NURSERY RHYME.

SONS of New England, in the fray,
　Do you hear the clamor behind your back ?
Do you hear the yelping of Blanche and
　　Tray ?
Sweetheart, and all the mongrel pack ?
Girded well with her ocean crags,
　Little our mother heeds their noise;
Her eyes are fixed on crimsoned flags:
　But you — do you hear it, Yankee boys ?

Do you hear them say that the patriot fire
　Burns on her altars too pure and bright,
To the darkened heavens leaping higher,
　　Though drenched with the blood of every
　　fight ?
That in the light of its searching flame
　Treason and tyrants stand revealed,
And the yielding craven is put to shame
　On Capitol floor or foughten field ?

Do you hear the hissing voice, which saith
　That she — who bore through all the land
The lyre of Freedom, the torch of Faith,
　And young Invention's mystic wand —
Should gather her skirts and dwell apart,
　With not one of her sisters to share her
　　fate, —
A Hagar, wandering sick at heart ?
　A pariah, bearing the Nation's hate ?

Sons, who have peopled the distant West,
　And planted the Pilgrim vine anew,
Where, by a richer soil carest,
　It grows as ever its parent grew, —
Say, do you hear, — while the very bells
　Of your churches ring with her ancient
　　voice,
And the song of your children sweetly tells
　How true was the land of your fathers'
　　choice, —

Do you hear the traitors who bid you speak
　The word that shall sever the sacred tie ?

And ye, who dwell by the golden Peak,
  Has the subtle whisper glided by?
Has it crost the immemorial plains
  To coasts where the gray Pacific roars,
And the Pilgrim blood in the people's veins
  Is pure as the wealth of their mountain ores?

Spirits of sons who, side by side,
  In a hundred battles fought and fell,
Whom now no East and West divide,
  In the isles where the shades of heroes
      dwell, —
Say, has it reached your glorious rest,
  And ruffled the calm which crowns you
      there, —
The shame that recreants have confest
  The plot that floats in the troubled air?

Sons of New England, here and there,
  Wherever men are still holding by
The honor our fathers left so fair, —
  Say, do you hear the cowards' cry?
Crouching among her grand old crags,
  Lightly our mother heeds their noise,
With her fond eyes fixed on distant flags;
  But you — do you hear it, Yankee boys?
      EDMUND CLARENCE STEDMAN.

On January 31, 1865, Congress adopted an
amendment to the constitution forever abolishing
slavery in the United States. On December 18,
1865, it was announced that the amendment had
been ratified by the requisite number of states.

LAUS DEO!

On hearing the bells ring on the passage of the
constitutional amendment abolishing slavery.

IT is done!
  Clang of bell and roar of gun
Send the tidings up and down.
  How the belfries rock and reel!
  How the great guns, peal on peal,
Fling the joy from town to town!

Ring, O bells!
  Every stroke exulting tells
Of the burial hour of crime.
  Loud and long, that all may hear,
  Ring for every listening ear
Of Eternity and Time!

Let us kneel:
  God's own voice is in that peal,

And this spot is holy ground.
  Lord, forgive us! What are we,
  That our eyes this glory see,
That our ears have heard the sound!

For the Lord
  On the whirlwind is abroad;
In the earthquake He has spoken;
  He has smitten with His thunder
  The iron walls asunder,
And the gates of brass are broken!

Loud and long
  Lift the old exulting song;
Sing with Miriam by the sea,
  He has cast the mighty down;
  Horse and rider sink and drown;
"He hath triumphed gloriously!"

Did we dare,
  In our agony of prayer,
Ask for more than He has done?
  When was ever His right hand
  Over any time or land
Stretched as now beneath the sun?

How they pale,
  Ancient myth and song and tale,
In this wonder of our days,
  When the cruel rod of war
  Blossoms white with righteous law,
And the wrath of man is praise!

Blotted out!
  All within and all about
Shall a fresher life begin;
  Freer breathe the universe
  As it rolls its heavy curse
On the dead and buried sin!

It is done!
  In the circuit of the sun
Shall the sound thereof go forth.
  It shall bid the sad rejoice,
  It shall give the dumb a voice,
It shall belt with joy the earth!

Ring and swing,
  Bells of joy! On morning's wing
Send the song of praise abroad!
  With a sound of broken chains
  Tell the nations that He reigns,
Who alone is Lord and God!
      JOHN GREENLEAF WHITTIER.

CHAPTER VIII

THE "GRAND ARMY'S" SECOND CAMPAIGN

After its defeat at Fredericksburg, the Grand Army of the Potomac had gone into winter quarters. General Joseph Hooker was appointed to command it and found it weak and shaken. Meanwhile, the Confederate cavalry was busy, especially the guerrillas under John S. Mosby, who, in March, 1863, made a daring and successful raid upon the Union lines.

MOSBY AT HAMILTON

[March 16, 1863]

DOWN Loudon Lanes, with swinging reins
  And clash of spur and sabre,
And bugling of the battle horn,
Six score and eight we rode at morn,
Six score and eight of Southern born,
  All tried in love and labor.

Full in the sun at Hamilton,
  We met the South's invaders;
Who, over fifteen hundred strong,
'Mid blazing homes had marched along
All night, with Northern shout and song
  To crush the rebel raiders.

Down Loudon Lanes, with streaming manes,
  We spurred in wild March weather;
And all along our war-scarred way
The graves of Southern heroes lay,
Our guide-posts to revenge that day,
  As we rode grim together.

Old tales still tell some miracle
  Of saints in holy writing —
But who shall say while hundreds fled
Before the few that Mosby led,
Unless the noblest of our dead
  Charged with us then when fighting?

While Yankee cheers still stunned our ears,
  Of troops at Harper's Ferry,
While Sheridan led on his Huns,
And Richmond rocked to roaring guns,
We felt the South still had some sons
  She would not scorn to bury.
                    MADISON CAWEIN.

A few days after Mosby's exploit, a desperately contested battle occurred at Kelly's Ford, Va., when the National troops under General W. W.

Averill attacked and were defeated by a Confederate force under General Fitzhugh Lee. Among the Confederate dead was General John Pelham.

JOHN PELHAM

[March 17, 1863]

JUST as the spring came laughing through the strife,
  With all its gorgeous cheer,
In the bright April of historic life,
  Fell the great cannoneer.

The wondrous lulling of a hero's breath
  His bleeding country weeps;
Hushed in the alabaster arms of Death,
  Our young Marcellus sleeps.

Nobler and grander than the Child of Rome
  Curbing his chariot steeds,
The knightly scion of a Southern home
  Dazzled the land with deeds.

Gentlest and bravest in the battle-brunt,
  The champion of the truth,
He bore his banner to the very front
  Of our immortal youth.

A clang of sabres 'mid Virginian snow,
  The fiery pang of shells, —
And there's a wail of immemorial woe
  In Alabama dells.

The pennon drops that led the sacred band
  Along the crimson field;
The meteor blade sinks from the nerveless hand
  Over the spotless shield.

We gazed and gazed upon that beauteous face
  While round the lips and eyes,
Couched in their marble slumber, flashed the grace
  Of a divine surprise.

O mother of a blessed soul on high!
  Thy tears may soon be shed;
Think of thy boy with princes of the sky,
  Among the Southern dead!

How must he smile on this dull world beneath,
  Fevered with swift renown, —
He, with the martyr's amaranthine wreath
  Twining the victor's crown!
                    JAMES RYDER RANDALL.

By the middle of April, 1863, Hooker had his army in shape to advance, and on the 28th began to cross the Rappahannock for the purpose of attacking Lee, who held a strong position in the rear of Fredericksburg. On April 30 Hooker's army was all across and bivouacked that night at Chancellorsville.

HOOKER 'S ACROSS

[May 1, 1863]

HOOKER 's across! Hooker's across!
Standards and guidons and lance-pennons toss
Over the land where he points with his blade,
Bristle the hill-top, and fill up the glade.
Who would not follow a leader whose blood
Has swelled, like our own, the battle's red
    flood?
Who bore what we suffered, our wound and
    our pain, —
Bore them with patience, and dares them
    again?
        Hooker's across!

Hooker's across! Hooker's across!
River of death, you shall make up our loss!
Out of your channel we summon each soul,
Over whose body your dark billows roll;
Up from your borders we summon the dead,
From valleys and hills where they struggled
    and bled,
To joy in the vengeance the traitors shall feel
At the roar of our guns and the rush of our
    steel!
        Hooker 's across!

Hooker's across! Hooker's across!
Ears to the wind, with our standards, we
    toss,
Moving together, straight on, with one breath,
Down to the outburst of passion and death.
Ah, in the depths of our spirits we know
  we fail now in the face of the foe,
Lee from the field with our flag soiled and
    dim,
We may return, but 't will not be with him!
        Hooker's across!
            GEORGE HENRY BOKER.

Lee at once prepared to fight, and a little past midnight on May 1, 1863, he put Stonewall Jackson's column in motion toward Chancellorsville. Jackson had long since proved himself one of the South's most able generals, and his command had been increased to thirty-three thousand men; every one of whom fairly idolized him.

STONEWALL JACKSON'S WAY

COME, stack arms, men! Pile on the rails,
  Stir up the camp-fire bright;
No growling if the canteen fails,
  We'll make a roaring night.
Here Shenandoah brawls along,
There burly Blue Ridge echoes strong,
To swell the Brigade's rousing song
  Of "Stonewall Jackson's way."

We see him now — the queer slouched hat
  Cocked o'er his eye askew;
The shrewd, dry smile; the speech so pat,
  So calm, so blunt, so true.
The "Blue-Light Elder" knows 'em well;
Says he, "That's Banks — he's fond of shell;
Lord save his soul! we'll give him —" well!
  That's "Stonewall Jackson's way."

Silence! ground arms! kneel all! caps off!
  Old Massa's goin' to pray.
Strangle the fool that dares to scoff!
  Attention! it's his way.
Appealing from his native sod,
In forma pauperis to God:
"Lay bare Thine arm; stretch forth Thy
    rod!
  Amen!" That's "Stonewall's way."

He's in the saddle now. Fall in!
  Steady! the whole brigade!
Hill's at the ford, cut off; we'll win
  His way out, ball and blade!
What matter if our shoes are worn?
What matter if our feet are torn?
"Quick step! we're with him before morn!"
  That's "Stonewall Jackson's way."

The sun's bright lances rout the mists
  Of morning, and, by George!
Here's Longstreet, struggling in the lists,
  Hemmed in an ugly gorge.
Pope and his Dutchmen, whipped before;
"Bay'nets and grape!" hear Stonewall roar;
"Charge, Stuart! Pay off Ashby's score!"
  In "Stonewall Jackson's way."

Ah! Maiden, wait and watch and yearn
　　For news of Stonewall's band!
Ah! Widow, read, with eyes that burn,
　　That ring upon thy hand.
Ah! Wife, sew on, pray on, hope on;
Thy life shall not be all forlorn;
The foe had better ne'er been born
　　That gets in "Stonewall's way."
　　　　　　　JOHN WILLIAMSON PALMER.

The battle began early in the morning and the
Union army was soon forced to take refuge behind
its works and assume the defensive. The Con-
federates also paused, waiting for reinforcements.
The men slept on their arms that night, and arose
at dawn, ready to renew the conflict.

But the Confederates did not attack until late
in the afternoon. Jackson had made a long flank-
ing movement, and just as twilight fell, he burst
from the woods in overwhelming force and routed
the Federal right wing. For an instant it seemed
that all was lost, but at this critical moment the
Eighth Pennsylvania cavalry got in touch with the
Confederate flank and charged.

KEENAN'S CHARGE

[May 2, 1863]

THE sun had set;
The leaves with dew were wet —
Down fell a bloody dusk
On the woods, that second of May,
Where "Stonewall's" corps, like a beast of
　　　prey,
Tore through with angry tusk.

"They've trapped us, boys!"
Rose from our flank a voice.
With rush of steel and smoke
On came the rebels straight,
Eager as love and wild as hate;
And our line reeled and broke;

Broke and fled.
Not one stayed, — but the dead!
With curses, shrieks, and cries,
Horses and wagons and men
Tumbled back through the shuddering
　　　glen,
And above us the fading skies.

There's one hope, still, —
Those batteries parked on the hill!
"Battery, wheel!" ('mid the roar),
"Pass pieces; fix prolonge to fire

Retiring. Trot!" In the panic dire
A bugle rings "Trot!" — and no more.

The horses plunged,
The cannon lurched and lunged,
To join the hopeless rout.
But suddenly rose a form
Calmly in front of the human storm,
With a stern commanding shout:

"Align those guns!"
(We knew it was Pleasanton's.)
The cannoneers bent to obey,
And worked with a will at his word,
And the black guns moved as if they had
　　　heard.
But, ah, the dread delay!

"To wait is crime;
O God, for ten minutes' time!"
The general looked around.
There Keenan sat, like a stone,
With his three hundred horse alone,
Less shaken than the ground.

"Major, your men?"
"Are soldiers, general." "Then,
Charge, major! Do your best;
Hold the enemy back at all cost,
Till my guns are placed; — else the army is
　　　lost.
You die to save the rest!"

By the shrouded gleam of the western skies
Brave Keenan looked into Pleasanton's eyes
For an instant — clear, and cool, and still;
Then, with a smile, he said: "I will."

"Cavalry, charge!" Not a man of them
　　　shrank.
Their sharp, full cheer, from rank on rank
Rose joyously, with a willing breath, —
Rose like a greeting hail to death.

Then forward they sprang, and spurred, and
　　　clashed;
Shouted the officers, crimson-sashed;
Rode well the men, each brave as his fellow,
In their faded coats of the blue and yellow;
And above in the air, with an instinct true,
Like a bird of war their pennon flew.

With clank of scabbards and thunder of steeds
And blades that shine like sunlit reeds,

And strong brown faces bravely pale,
For fear their proud attempt shall fail,
Three hundred Pennsylvanians close
On twice ten thousand gallant foes.

Line after line the troopers came
To the edge of the wood that was ringed with
    flame;
Rode in, and sabred, and shot, — and fell:
Nor came one back his wounds to tell.
And full in the midst rose Keenan, tall
In the gloom, like a martyr awaiting his
    fall,
While the circle-stroke of his sabre, swung
'Round his head, like a halo there, luminous
    hung.

Line after line, aye, whole platoons,
Struck dead in their saddles, of brave dra-
    goons,
By the maddened horses were onward borne
And into the vortex flung, trampled and
    torn;
As Keenan fought with his men, side by side.
So they rode, till there were no more to ride.

But over them, lying there shattered and
    mute,
What deep echo rolls? 'T is a death-salute
From the cannon in place; for, heroes, you
    braved
Your fate not in vain; the army was saved!

Over them now, — year following year, —
Over their graves the pine-cones fall,
And the whippoorwill chants his spectre-call;
But they stir not again; they raise no
    cheer:
They have ceased. But their glory shall never
    cease,
Nor their light be quenched in the light of
    peace.
The rush of their charge is resounding still,
That saved the army at Chancellorsville.

      GEORGE PARSONS LATHROP.

The regiment was greatly outnumbered, and
was hurled back terribly shattered, Major Peter
Keenan being among the killed. But the Confed-
erate advance had been checked long enough for
Peasanton to get his artillery into position, and
it opened with deadly effect.

The Confederates paused in the face of the ter-
rible fire, and Jackson and his staff pushed for-
ward on a personal reconnoissance. As he was

returning to his lines, he and his companions were
mistaken for Union troops by his own men and
were fired upon. Jackson fell, pierced by three
bullets.

"THE BRIGADE MUST NOT KNOW, SIR!"

[May 2, 1863]

"WHO'VE ye got there?" — "Only a dying
    brother,
    Hurt in the front just now."
"Good boy! he'll do. Somebody tell his
    mother
    Where he was killed, and how."

"Whom have you there?" — "A crippled
    courier, Major,
Shot by mistake, we hear.
He was with Stonewall." "Cruel work
    they've made here;
    Quick with him to the rear!"

"Well, who comes next?" — "Doctor, speak
    low, speak low, sir;
    Don't let the men find out!
It's Stonewall!" — "God!" — "The brigade
    must not know, sir,
    While there's a foe about!"

Whom have we here — shrouded in martial
    manner,
    Crowned with a martyr's charm?
A grand dead hero, in a living banner,
    Born of his heart and arm:

The heart whereon his cause hung — see how
    clingeth
    That banner to his bier!
The arm wherewith his cause struck — hark!
    how ringeth
    His trumpet in their rear!

What have we left? His glorious inspiration,
    His prayers in council met.
Living, he laid the first stones of a nation;
    And dead, he builds it yet.

Early on the morning of Sunday, May 3, 1863,
the Confederates again attacked, and after two
days' heavy fighting, drove the Union army back
across the river, with a loss of seventeen thousand
men. But the Confederate victory was almost
outweighed by the loss of Stonewall Jackson, who
died May 10.

STONEWALL JACKSON

[May 10, 1863]

NOT midst the lightning of the stormy fight,
Nor in the rush upon the vandal foe,
Did kingly Death, with his resistless might,
    Lay the great leader low.

His warrior soul its earthly shackles broke
In the full sunshine of a peaceful town;
When all the storm was hushed, the trusty
    oak
    That propped our cause went down.

Though his alone the blood that flecks the
    ground,
Recalling all his grand, heroic deeds,
Freedom herself is writhing in the wound,
    And all the country bleeds.

He entered not the nation's Promised Land
At the red belching of the cannon's mouth,
But broke the House of Bondage with his
    hand —
    The Moses of the South!

O gracious God! not gainless is the loss:
A glorious sunbeam gilds thy sternest frown;
And while his country staggers 'neath the
    Cross,
    He rises with the Crown!
              HENRY LYNDEN FLASH.

THE DYING WORDS OF STONE-WALL JACKSON [1]

"Order A. P. Hill to prepare for battle."
"Tell Major Hawks to advance the commissary
    train."
"Let us cross the river and rest in the shade."

THE stars of Night contain the glittering Day
And rain his glory down with sweeter grace
Upon the dark World's grand, enchanted
    face —
    All loth to turn away.

And so the Day, about to yield his breath,
Utters the stars unto the listening Night,
To stand for burning fare-thee-wells of light
    Said on the verge of death.

[1] From Poems by Sidney Lanier; copyright,
1884, 1891, by Mary D. Lanier; published by
Charles Scribner's Sons.

O hero-life that lit us like the sun!
O hero-words that glittered like the stars
And stood and shone above the gloomy wars
    When the hero-life was done!

The phantoms of a battle came to dwell
I' the fitful vision of his dying eyes —
Yet even in battle-dreams, he sends supplies
    To those he loved so well.

His army stands in battle-line arrayed:
His couriers fly: all's done: now God de-
    cide!
— And not till then saw he the Other Side
    Or would accept the shade.

Thou Land whose sun is gone, thy stars re-
    main!
Still shine the words that miniature his
    deeds.
O thrice-beloved, where'er thy great heart
    bleeds,
    Solace hast thou for pain!
              SIDNEY LANIER.

UNDER THE SHADE OF THE TREES

WHAT are the thoughts that are stirring his
    breast?
    What is the mystical vision he sees?
— "Let us pass over the river, and rest
    Under the shade of the trees."

Has he grown sick of his toils and his tasks?
    Sighs the worn spirit for respite or ease?
Is it a moment's cool halt that he asks
    Under the shade of the trees?

Is it the gurgle of waters whose flow
    Ofttime has come to him, borne on the
    breeze,
Memory listens to, lapsing so low,
    Under the shade of the trees?

Nay — though the rasp of the flesh was so
    sore,
    Faith, that had yearnings far keener than
    these,
Saw the soft sheen of the Thitherward Shore
    Under the shade of the trees; —

Caught the high psalms of ecstatic delight —
    Heard the harps harping, like soundings of
    seas —

Watched earth's assoilèd ones walking in
    white
    Under the shade of the trees.

Oh, was it strange he should pine for re-
    lease,
    Touched to the soul with such transports as
      these, —
He who so needed the balsam of peace,
    Under the shade of the trees?

Yea, it was noblest for him — it was best
    (Questioning naught of our Father's de-
      crees),
There to pass over the river and rest
    Under the shade of the trees!
            MARGARET JUNKIN PRESTON.

Lee waited only to rest his forces and then, for
the second time, invaded Maryland, crossing the
Shenandoah at Front Royal. On June 13, 1863,
the army appeared before Winchester, scattered
the Union force stationed there, and swept resist-
lessly down the Shenandoah Valley, raiding into
Pennsylvania as far as Chambersburg.

THE BALLAD OF ISHMAEL DAY

[June, 1863]

ONE summer morning a daring band
Of Rebels rode into Maryland,
    Over the prosperous, peaceful farms,
    Sending terror and strange alarms,
    The clatter of hoofs and the clang of
      arms.

Fresh from the South, where the hungry pine
They ate like Pharaoh's starving kine;
    They swept the land like devouring surge,
    And left their path, to the farthest verge,
    Bare as the track of the locust scourge.

"The Rebels are coming!" far and near
Rang the tidings of dread and fear;
    Some paled and cowered and sought to
      hide;
    Some stood erect in their fearless pride;
    And women shuddered and children cried.

But others — vipers in human form
Stinging the bosom that kept them warm —
    Welcomed with triumph the thievish band,
    Hurried to offer the friendly hand,
    As the Rebels rode into Maryland.

Made them merry with food and wine,
Clad them in garments, rich and fine,
    For rags and hunger to make amends,
    Flattered them, praised them with selfish
      ends;
    "Leave us scathless, for we are friends."

Could traitors trust a traitor? No!
Little they favor friend or foe,
    But gathered the cattle the farms across,
    Flinging back, with a scornful toss,
    "If ye are friends ye can bear the loss!"

Flushed with triumph, and wine, and prey,
They neared the dwelling of Ishmael Day,
    A sturdy veteran, gray and old,
    With heart of a patriot, firm and bold,
    Strong and steadfast — unbribed, unsold.

And Ishmael Day, his brave head bare,
His white locks tossed by the morning air,
    Fearless of danger, or death, or scars,
    Went out to raise by the farm-yard bars
    The dear old flag of the stripes and stars.

Proudly, steadily, up it flew,
Gorgeous with crimson, white and blue,
    His withered hand as he shook it freer,
    May have trembled, but not with fear,
    While shouting the rebels drew more near.

"Halt!" They had seen the hated sign
Floating free from old Ishmael's line —
    "Lower that rag!" was their wrathful cry;
    "Never!" rung Ishmael Day's reply,
    "Fire if it please you — I can but die."

One, with a loud, defiant laugh,
Left his comrades and neared the staff.
    "Down!" came the fearless patriot's cry,
    "Dare to lower that flag and die!
    One must bleed for it — you or I."

But caring not for the stern command,
He drew the halliards with daring hand;
    Ping! went the rifle ball — down he came,
    Under the flag he had tried to shame —
    Old Ishmael Day took careful aim!

Seventy winters and three had shed
Their snowy glories on Ishmael's head.
    Though cheeks may wither and locks grow
      gray,
    His fame shall be fresh and young alway —
    Honor be to old Ishmael Day!

Hooker, meanwhile, was almost wholly in the dark concerning the position of Lee's army, until it was partially revealed to him on June 17, 1863, when Kilpatrick's cavalry charged and drove back the Confederate cavalry as it emerged from Ashby's Gap. Still he hesitated, and the whole of western Pennsylvania appeared to be at the mercy of the invaders.

RIDING WITH KILPATRICK

[June 17, 1863]

DAWN peered through the pines as we dashed at the ford;
Afar the grim guns of the infantry roared;
There were miles yet of dangerous pathway to pass,
And Mosby might menace, and Stuart might mass;
But we mocked every doubt, laughing danger to scorn,
As we quaffed with a shout from the wine of the morn.
Those who rode with Kilpatrick to valor were born!

How we chafed at delay! How we itched to be on!
How we yearned for the fray where the battle-reek shone!
It was *forward*, not *halt*, stirred the fire in our veins,
When our horses' feet beat to the click of the reins;
It was *charge*, not *retreat*, we were wonted to hear;
It was *charge*, not *retreat*, that was sweet to the ear;
Those who rode with Kilpatrick had never felt fear!

At last the word came, and troop tossed it to troop;
Two squadrons deployed with a falcon-like swoop;
While swiftly the others in echelons formed,
For there, just ahead, was the line to be stormed.
The trumpets rang out; there were guidons a-blow;
The white summer sun set our sabres a-glow;
Those who rode with Kilpatrick charged straight at the foe!

We swept like a whirlwind; we closed; at the shock
The sky seemed to reel and the earth seemed to rock;
Steel clashed upon steel with a deafening sound,
While a redder than rose-stain encrimsoned the ground;
If we gave back a space from the fierce pit of hell,
We were rallied again by a voice like a bell.
Those who rode with Kilpatrick rode valiantly well!

Rang sternly his orders from out of the wrack:
*Re-form there, New Yorkers ! You, "Harris Light," back !
Come on, men of Maine ! We will conquer or fall !
Now, forward, boys, forward ! and follow me all !*
A Bayard in boldness, a Sidney in grace,
A lion to lead and a stag-hound to chase —
Those who rode with Kilpatrick looked Death in the face!

Though brave were our foemen, they faltered and fled;
Yet that was no marvel when such as he led!
Long ago, long ago, was that desperate day,
Long ago, long ago, strove the Blue and the Gray!
Praise God that the red sun of battle is set!
That our hand-clasp is loyal and loving — and yet,
Those who rode with Kilpatrick can never forget!

CLINTON SCOLLARD.

This sudden and seemingly irresistible invasion created panic throughout the North. Troops were hurried forward, and Hooker at last started in pursuit with a hundred thousand men, but was relieved of command on June 27, 1863, and General George G. Meade appointed in his place. Lee was concentrating his army at Gettysburg, and his advance guard got into touch with the Union force on the morning of July 1. The first day's fighting ended in the Federals being swept backward to their position on Cemetery Hill. The battle continued with undiminished fury throughout the second day; and on the third, Lee determined to renew the assault and Meade decided to stay and receive it. The entire morning was consumed in preparation. Then the Confederates charged in a line three miles long, with General George Pickett and his Virginians in the van. A terrific struggle followed, ending in the repulse of the Confederates, who withdrew in good order from the field.

GETTYSBURG

[July 3, 1863]

WAVE, wave your glorious battle-flags, brave
    soldiers of the North,
And from the field your arms have won to-day
    go proudly forth!
For none, O comrades dear and leal, — from
    whom no ills could part,
Through the long years of hopes and fears,
    the nation's constant heart, —
Men who have driven so oft the foe, so oft
    have striven in vain,
Yet ever in the perilous hour have crossed his
    path again, —
At last we have our hearts' desire, from them
    we met have wrung
A victory that round the world shall long be
    told and sung!
It was the memory of the past that bore us
    through the fray,
That gave the grand old Army strength to
    conquer on this day!

O now forget how dark and red Virginia's
    rivers flow,
The Rappahannock's tangled wilds, the glory
    and the woe;
The fever-hung encampments, where our
    dying knew full sore
How sweet the north-wind to the cheek it soon
    shall cool no more;
The fields we fought, and gained, and lost;
    the lowland sun and rain
That wasted us, that bleached the bones of
    our unburied slain!
There was no lack of foes to meet, of deaths
    to die no lack,
And all the hawks of heaven learned to follow
    on our track;
But henceforth, hovering southward, their
    flight shall mark afar
The paths of yon retreating hosts that shun
    the northern star.

At night, before the closing fray, when all the
    front was still,
We lay in bivouac along the cannon-crested
    hill

Ours was the dauntless Second Corps; and
    many a soldier knew
How sped the fight, and sternly thought of
    what was yet to do.
Guarding the centre there, we lay, and talked
    with bated breath
Of Buford's stand beyond the town, of gallant
    Reynold's death,
Of cruel retreats through pent-up streets by
    murderous volleys swept, —
How well the Stone, the Iron, Brigades their
    bloody outposts kept:
'T was for the Union, for the Flag, they
    perished, heroes all,
And we swore to conquer in the end, or even
    like them to fall.

And passed from mouth to mouth the tale of
    that grim day just done,
The fight by Round Top's craggy spur, — of
    all the deadliest one;
It saved the left: but on the right they pressed
    us back too well,
And like a field in Spring the ground was
    ploughed with shot and shell.
There was the ancient graveyard, its hum-
    mocks crushed and red,
And there, between them, side by side, the
    wounded and the dead:
The mangled corpses fallen above, — the
    peaceful dead below,
Laid in their graves, to slumber here, a score
    of years ago;
It seemed their waking, wandering shades
    were asking of our slain,
What brought such hideous tumult now
    where they so still had lain!

Bright rose the sun of Gettysburg that
    morrow morning-tide,
And call of trump and roll of drum from
    height to height replied.
Hark! from the east already goes up the
    rattling din;
The Twelfth Corps, winning back their
    ground, right well the day begin!
They whirl fierce Ewell from their front!
    Now we of the Second pray,
As right and left the brunt have borne, the
    centre might to-day.
But all was still from hill to hill for many a
    breathless hour.
While for the coming battle-shock Lee
    gathered in his power;

And back and forth our leaders rode, who
    knew not rest or fear,
And along the lines, where'er they came,
    went up the ringing cheer.

'T was past the hour of nooning; the Summer
    skies were blue;
Behind the covering timber the foe was hid
    from view;
So fair and sweet with waving wheat the
    pleasant valley lay,
It brought to mind our Northern homes and
    meadows far away;
When the whole western ridge at once was
    fringed with fire and smoke;
Against our lines from sevenscore guns the
    dreadful tempest broke!
Then loud our batteries answer, and far along
    the crest,
And to and fro the roaring bolts are driven
    east and west;
Heavy and dark around us glooms the stifling
    sulphur-cloud,
And the cries of mangled men and horse go
    up beneath its shroud.

The guns are still: the end is nigh: we grasp
    our arms anew;
O now let every heart be stanch and every
    aim be true!
For look! from yonder wood that skirts the
    valley's further marge,
The flower of all the Southern host move to
    the final charge.
By Heaven! it is a fearful sight to see their
    double rank
Come with a hundred battle-flags, — a mile
    from flank to flank!
Tramping the grain to earth, they come, ten
    thousand men abreast;
Their standards wave, — their hearts are
    brave, — they hasten not, nor rest,
But close the gaps our cannon make, and
    onward press, and nigher,
And, yelling at our very front, again pour in
    their fire!

Now burst our sheeted lightnings forth, now
    all our wrath has vent!
They die, they wither; through and through
    their wavering lines are rent.
But these are gallant, desperate men, of our
    own race and land,
Who charge anew, and welcome death, and
    fight us hand to hand.

Vain, vain! give way, as well ye may — the
    crimson die is cast!
Their bravest leaders bite the dust, their
    strength is failing fast;
They yield, they turn, they fly the field: we
    smite them as they run;
Their arms, their colors are our spoil; the
    furious fight is done!
Across the plain we follow far and backward
    push the fray;
Cheer! cheer! the grand old Army at last has
    won the day!

Hurrah! the day has won the cause! No gray-
    clad host henceforth
Shall come with fire and sword to tread the
    highways of the North!
'T was such a flood as when ye see along the
    Atlantic shore,
The great Spring-tide roll grandly in with
    swelling surge and roar:
It seems no wall can stay its leap or balk its
    wild desire
Beyond the bound that Heaven hath fixed to
    higher mount, and higher;
But now, when whitest lifts its crest, most
    loud its billows call,
Touched by the Power that led them on, they
    fall, and fall, and fall.
Even thus, unstayed upon his course, to
    Gettysburg the foe
His legions led, and fought, and fled, and
    might no further go.

Full many a dark-eyed Southern girl shall
    weep her lover dead;
But with a price the fight was ours, — we too
    have tears to shed!
The bells that peal our triumph forth anon
    shall toll the brave,
Above whose heads the cross must stand, the
    hillside grasses wave!
Alas! alas! the trampled grass shall thrive
    another year,
The blossoms on the apple-boughs with each
    new Spring appear,
But when our patriot-soldiers fall, Earth gives
    them up to God;
Though their souls rise in clearer skies, their
    forms are as the sod;
Only their names and deeds are ours, — but
    for a century yet,
The dead who fell at Gettysburg the land
    shall not forget.

God send us peace! and where for aye the
 loved and lost recline
Let fall, O South, your leaves of palm, — O
 North, your sprigs of pine!
But when, with every ripened year, we keep
 the harvest-home,
And to the dear Thanksgiving-feast our sons
 and daughters come, —
When children's children throng the board in
 the old homestead spread,
And the bent soldier of these wars is seated at
 the head,
Long, long the lads shall listen to hear the
 gray-beard tell
Of those who fought at Gettysburg and stood
 their ground so well:
"'T was for the Union and the Flag," the
 veteran shall say,
"Our grand old Army held the ridge, and
 won that glorious day!"
    Edmund Clarence Stedman.

THE HIGH TIDE AT GETTYSBURG

[July 3, 1863]

A CLOUD possessed the hollow field,
The gathering battle's smoky shield:
 Athwart the gloom the lightning flashed,
 And through the cloud some horsemen
  dashed,
And from the heights the thunder pealed.

Then, at the brief command of Lee,
Moved out that matchless infantry,
 With Pickett leading grandly down,
 To rush against the roaring crown
Of those dread heights of destiny.

Far heard above the angry guns,
A cry of tumult runs:
 The voice that rang through Shiloh's
  woods,
 And Chickamauga's solitudes:
The fierce South cheering on her sons!

Ah, how the withering tempest blew
Against the front of Pettigrew!
 A Khamsin wind that scorched and
  singed,
 Like that infernal flame that fringed
The British squares at Waterloo!

A thousand fell where Kemper led;
A thousand died where Garnett bled;
 In blinding flame and strangling smoke,
 The remnant through the batteries broke,
And crossed the works with Armistead.

"Once more in Glory's van with me!"
Virginia cried to Tennessee:
 "We two together, come what may,
 Shall stand upon those works to-day!"
The reddest day in history.

Brave Tennessee! In reckless way
Virginia heard her comrade say:
 "Close round this rent and riddled rag!"
 What time she set her battle flag
Amid the guns of Doubleday.

But who shall break the guards that wait
Before the awful face of Fate?
 The tattered standards of the South
 Were shrivelled at the cannon's mouth,
And all her hopes were desolate.

In vain the Tennesseean set
His breast against the bayonet;
 In vain Virginia charged and raged,
 A tigress in her wrath uncaged,
Till all the hill was red and wet!

Above the bayonets, mixed and crossed,
Men saw a gray, gigantic ghost
 Receding through the battle-cloud,
 And heard across the tempest loud
The death-cry of a nation lost!

The brave went down! Without disgrace
They leaped to Ruin's red embrace;
 They only heard Fame's thunders wake,
 And saw the dazzling sunburst break
In smiles on Glory's bloody face!

They fell, who lifted up a hand
And bade the sun in heaven to stand;
 They smote and fell, who set the bars
 Against the progress of the stars,
And stayed the march of Motherland.

They stood, who saw the future come
On through the fight's delirium;
 They smote and stood, who held the hope
 Of nations on that slippery slope,
Amid the cheers of Christendom!

God lives! He forged the iron will,
That clutched and held that trembling hill!
  God lives and reigns! He built and lent
  The heights for Freedom's battlement,
Where floats her flag in triumph still!

Fold up the banners! Smelt the guns!
Love rules. Her gentler purpose runs.
  A mighty mother turns in tears,
  The pages of her battle years,
Lamenting all her fallen sons!
                    WILL HENRY THOMPSON.

GETTYSBURG

[July 1, 2, 3, 1863]

THERE was no union in the land,
  Though wise men labored long
With links of clay and ropes of sand
  To bind the right and wrong.

There was no temper in the blade
  That once could cleave a chain;
Its edge was dull with touch of trade
  And clogged with rust of gain.

The sand and clay must shrink away
  Before the lava tide:
By blows and blood and fire assay
  The metal must be tried.

Here sledge and anvil met, and when
  The furnace fiercest roared,
God's undiscerning workingmen
  Reforged His people's sword.

Enough for them to ask and know
  The moment's duty clear —
The bayonets flashed it there below,
  The guns proclaimed it here:

To do and dare, and die at need,
  But while life lasts, to fight —
For right or wrong a simple creed,
  But simplest for the right.

They faltered not who stood that day
  And held this post of dread;
Nor cowards they who wore the gray
  Until the gray was red.

For every wreath the victor wears
  The vanquished half may claim;

And every monument declares
  A common pride and fame.

We raise no altar stones to Hate,
  Who never bowed to Fear:
No province crouches at our gate,
  To shame our triumph here.

Here standing by a dead wrong's grave
  The blindest now may see,
The blow that liberates the slave
  But sets the master free!

When ills beset the nation's life
  Too dangerous to bear,
The sword must be the surgeon's knife,
  Too merciful to spare.

O Soldier of our common land,
  'T is thine to bear that blade
Loose in the sheath, or firm in hand,
  But ever unafraid.

When foreign foes assail our right,
  One nation trusts to thee —
To wield it well in worthy fight —
  The sword of Meade and Lee!
                    JAMES JEFFREY ROCHE.

Lee commenced his retreat next morning, and
was able to gain the Potomac, with his whole
train, virtually without molestation. But the
North was too rejoiced by the withdrawal of the
invaders to mourn at their escape.

THE BATTLE-FIELD

GETTYSBURG

THOSE were the conquered, still too proud to
    yield —
These were the victors, yet too poor for
    shrouds!
Here scarlet Slaughter slew her countless
    crowds
Heaped high in ranks where'er the hot guns
    pealed.
The brooks that wandered through the battle
    field
Flowed slowly on in ever-reddening streams:
Here where the rank wheat waves and golden
    gleams,
The dreadful squadrons, thundering, charged
    and reeled.
Within the blossoming clover many a bone

Lying unsepulchred, has bleached to white;
While gentlest hearts that only love had
    known,
Have ached with anguish at the awful sight;
And War's gaunt Vultures that were lean,
    have grown
Gorged in the darkness in a single night!

LLOYD MIFFLIN.

Among the thousands who took part in that terrific three days' struggle none was more remarkable than old John Burns, a veteran of the War of 1812 and of the Mexican War, who, rejected at the outbreak of the Civil War on account of his age, nevertheless shouldered his rifle and helped repel the invaders, when they approached his home at Gettysburg.

JOHN BURNS OF GETTYSBURG

HAVE you heard the story that gossips tell
Of Burns of Gettysburg? No? Ah, well:
Brief is the glory that hero earns,
Briefer the story of poor John Burns:
He was the fellow who won renown, —
The only man who did n't back down
When the rebels rode through his native
    town;
But held his own in the fight next day,
When all his townsfolk ran away.
That was in July, sixty-three, —
The very day that General Lee,
Flower of Southern chivalry,
Baffled and beaten, backward reeled
From a stubborn Meade and a barren field.

I might tell how, but the day before,
John Burns stood at his cottage door,
Looking down the village street,
Where, in the shade of his peaceful vine,
He heard the low of his gathered kine,
And felt their breath with incense sweet;
Or I might say, when the sunset burned
The old farm gable, he thought it turned
The milk that fell like a babbling flood
Into the milk-pail, red as blood!
Or how he fancied the hum of bees
Were bullets buzzing among the trees.
But all such fanciful thoughts as these
Were strange to a practical man like Burns,
Who minded only his own concerns,
Troubled no more by fancies fine
Than one of his calm-eyed, long-tailed kine,
Quite old-fashioned and matter-of-fact,
Slow to argue, but quick to act.

That was the reason, as some folks say,
He fought so well on that terrible day.

And it was terrible. On the right
Raged for hours the heady fight,
Thundered the battery's double bass, —
Difficult music for men to face;
While on the left — where now the graves
Undulate like the living waves
That all that day unceasing swept
Up to the pits the rebels kept —
Round-shot ploughed the upland glades,
Sown with bullets, reaped with blades;
Shattered fences here and there
Tossed their splinters in the air;
The very trees were stripped and bare;
The barns that once held yellow grain
Were heaped with harvests of the slain;
The cattle bellowed on the plain,
The turkeys screamed with might and main,
The brooding barn-fowl left their rest
With strange shells bursting in each nest.

Just where the tide of battle turns,
Erect and lonely, stood old John Burns.
How do you think the man was dressed?
He wore an ancient, long buff vest,
Yellow as saffron, — but his best;
And, buttoned over his manly breast,
Was a bright blue coat with a rolling collar,
And large gilt buttons, — size of a dollar, —
With tails that the country-folk called "swal-
    ler."
He wore a broad-brimmed, bell-crowned hat,
White as the locks on which it sat.
Never had such a sight been seen
For forty years on the village green,
Since old John Burns was a country beau,
And went to the "quiltings" long ago.

Close at his elbows all that day,
Veterans of the Peninsula,
Sunburnt and bearded, charged away;
And striplings, downy of lip and chin, —
Clerks that the Home-Guard mustered in, —
Glanced, as they passed, at the hat he wore,
Then at the rifle his right hand bore;
And hailed him, from out their youthful lore,
With scraps of a slangy repertoire:
"How are you, White Hat?" "Put her
    through!"
"Your head's level!" and "Bully for you!"
Called him "Daddy," — begged he'd disclose
The name of his tailor who made his clothes,
And what was the value he set on those:

While Burns, unmindful of jeer or scoff,
Stood there picking the rebels off, —
With his long brown rifle, and bell-crowned
    hat,
And the swallow-tails they were laughing at.

'T was but a moment, for that respect
Which clothes all courage their voices
    checked;
And something the wildest could understand
Spake in the old man's strong right hand,
And his corded throat, and the lurking
    frown
Of his eyebrows under his old bell-crown;
Until, as they gazed, there crept an awe
Through the ranks in whispers, and some men
    saw,
In the antique vestments and long white
    hair,
The Past of the Nation in battle there;
And some of the soldiers since declare
That the gleam of his old white hat afar,
Like the crested plume of the brave Navarre,
That day was their oriflamme of war.

So raged the battle. You know the rest:
How the rebels, beaten and backward pressed,
Broke at the final charge and ran.
At which John Burns — a practical man —
Shouldered his rifle, unbent his brows,
And then went back to his bees and cows.

That is the story of old John Burns;
This is the moral the reader learns:
In fighting the battle, the question's whether
You 'll show a hat that's white, or a feather.
                BRET HARTE.

Never was the Union nearer dissolution than
it was on the eve of Gettysburg. A counter-revo-
lution had been planned, but Lee was defeated
and the plot failed. A force of four thousand raid-
ers, under John H. Morgan, had dashed across
Kentucky, into Indiana and Ohio, expecting sup-
port from the peace faction; but the result of
Gettysburg spoiled all that, and Morgan and his
men were surrounded and captured while trying
to get back across the Ohio River.

KENTUCKY BELLE

SUMMER of 'sixty-three, sir, and Conrad was
    gone away —
Gone to the county-town, sir, to sell our first
    load of hay —

We lived in the log house yonder, poor as
    you 've ever seen;
Röschen there was a baby, and I was only
    nineteen.

Conrad, he took the oxen, but he left Ken-
    tucky Belle.
How much we thought of Kentuck, I could n't
    begin to tell —
Came from the Blue-Grass country; my
    father gave her to me
When I rode North with Conrad, away from
    Tennessee.

Conrad lived in Ohio — a German he is, you
    know —
The house stood in broad corn-fields, stretch-
    ing on, row after row.
The old folks made me welcome; they were
    kind as kind could be;
But I kept longing, longing, for the hills of
    Tennessee.

Oh! for a sight of water, the shadowed slope
    of a hill!
Clouds that hang on the summit, a wind that
    never is still!
But the level land went stretching away to
    meet the sky —
Never a rise, from north to south, to rest the
    weary eye!

From east to west no river to shine out under
    the moon,
Nothing to make a shadow in the yellow after-
    noon:
Only the breathless sunshine, as I looked out,
    all forlorn;
Only the "rustle, rustle," as I walked among
    the corn.

When I fell sick with pining, we did n't wait
    any more,
But moved away from the corn-lands, out to
    this river shore —
The Tuscarawas it 's called, sir — off there 's
    a hill, you see —
And now I 've grown to like it next best to the
    Tennessee.

I was at work that morning. Some one came
    riding like mad
Over the bridge and up the road — Farmer
    Rouf's little lad.

Bareback he rode; he had no hat; he hardly
    stopped to say,
"Morgan's men are coming, Frau; they're
    galloping on this way.

"I'm sent to warn the neighbors. He is n't a
    mile behind;
He sweeps up all the horses — every horse
    that he can find.
Morgan, Morgan the raider, and Morgan's
    terrible men,
With bowie-knives and pistols, are galloping
    up the glen!"

The lad rode down the valley, and I stood still
    at the door;
The baby laughed and prattled, playing with
    spools on the floor;
Kentuck was out in the pasture; Conrad, my
    man, was gone.
Near, nearer, Morgan's men were galloping,
    galloping on!

Sudden I picked up baby, and ran to the
    pasture-bar.
"Kentuck!" I called — "Kentucky!" She
    knew me ever so far!
I led her down the gully that turns off there to
    the right,
And tied her to the bushes; her head was just
    out of sight.

As I ran back to the log house, at once there
    came a sound —
The ring of hoofs, galloping hoofs, trembling
    over the ground —
Coming into the turnpike, out from the White-
    Woman Glen —
Morgan, Morgan the raider, and Morgan's
    terrible men.

As near they drew and nearer, my heart beat
    fast in alarm;
But still I stood in the doorway with baby on
    my arm.
They came; they passed; with spur and whip
    in haste they sped along —
Morgan, Morgan the raider, and his band,
    six hundred strong.

Weary they looked and jaded, riding through
    night and through day;
Pushing on East to the river, many long miles
    away,

To the border-strip where Virginia runs up
    into the West,
And fording the Upper Ohio before they could
    stop to rest.

On like the wind they hurried, and Morgan
    rode in advance;
Bright were his eyes like live coals, as he gave
    me a sideways glance;
I was just breathing freely, after my choking
    pain,
When the last one of the troopers suddenly
    drew his rein.

Frightened I was to death, sir; I scarce dared
    look in his face,
As he asked for a drink of water, and glanced
    around the place.
I gave him a cup and he smiled — 't was only
    a boy, you see;
Faint and worn, with dim blue eyes; and
    he'd sailed on the Tennessee.

Only sixteen he was, sir — a fond mother's
    only son —
Off and away with Morgan before his life has
    begun!
The damp drops stood on his temples —
    drawn was the boyish mouth;
And I thought me of the mother waiting down
    in the South.

Oh! pluck was he to the backbone, and clear
    grit through and through;
Boasted and bragged like a trooper, but the
    big words would n't do; —
The boy was dying, sir, dying, as plain as
    plain could be,
Worn out by his ride with Morgan up from
    the Tennessee.

But when I told the laddie that I too was from
    the South,
Water came in his dim eyes, and quivers
    around his mouth.
"Do you know the Blue-Grass country?" he
    wistful began to say;
Then swayed like a willow-sapling, and fainted
    dead away.

I had him into the log house, and worked and
    brought him to;
I fed him and I coaxed him, as I thought his
    mother'd do;

And when the lad grew better, and the noise
  in his head was gone,
Morgan's men were miles away, galloping,
  galloping on.

"Oh, I must go," he muttered; "I must be
  up and away!
Morgan — Morgan is waiting for me! Oh,
  what will Morgan say?"
But I heard a sound of tramping and kept
  him back from the door —
The ringing sound of horses' hoofs that I had
  heard before.

And on, on, came the soldiers — the Michi-
  gan cavalry —
And fast they rode, and black they looked,
  galloping rapidly, —
They had followed hard on Morgan's track;
  they had followed day and night;
But of Morgan and Morgan's raiders they had
  never caught a sight.

And rich Ohio sat startled through all those
  summer days;
For strange, wild men were galloping over her
  broad highways —
Now here, now there, now seen, now gone,
  now north, now east, now west,
Through river-valleys and corn-land farms,
  sweeping away her best.

A bold ride and a long ride! But they were
  taken at last.
They almost reached the river by galloping
  hard and fast;
But the boys in blue were upon them ere ever
  they gained the ford,
And Morgan, Morgan the raider, laid down
  his terrible sword.

Well, I kept the boy till evening — kept him
  against his will —
But he was too weak to follow, and sat there
  pale and still.
When it was cool and dusky — you'll wonder
  to hear me tell —
But I stole down to that gully, and brought up
  Kentucky Belle.

I kissed the star on her forehead — my pretty
  gentle lass —
But I knew that she'd be happy back in the
  old Blue Grass.

A suit of clothes of Conrad's, with all the
  money I had,
And Kentuck, pretty Kentuck, I gave to the
  worn-out lad.

I guided him to the southward as well as I
  knew how;
The boy rode off with many thanks, and many
  a backward bow;
And then the glow it faded, and my heart be-
  gan to swell,
As down the glen away she went, my lost
  Kentucky Belle!

When Conrad came in the evening, the moon
  was shining high;
Baby and I were both crying — I could n't
  tell him why —
But a battered suit of rebel gray was hanging
  on the wall,
And a thin old horse, with drooping head,
  stood in Kentucky's stall.

Well, he was kind, and never once said a hard
  word to me;
He knew I could n't help it — 't was all for
  the Tennessee.
But, after the war was over, just think what
  came to pass —
A letter, sir; and the two were safe back in
  the old Blue Grass.

The lad had got across the border, riding
  Kentucky Belle;
And Kentuck she was thriving, and fat, and
  hearty, and well;
He cared for her, and kept her, nor touched
  her with whip or spur.
Ah! we've had many horses since, but never
  a horse like her!
                    CONSTANCE FENIMORE WOOLSON.

Part of the same plot was the draft riot which
broke out in New York City on July 13, 1863. It
lasted four days, and four hundred people were
killed by the rioters. The draft was temporarily
suspended, but was quietly resumed in August.

THE DRAFT RIOT

IN THE UNIVERSITY TOWER: NEW YORK,
JULY, 1863

Is it the wind, the many-tongued, the weird,
  That cries in sharp distress about the eaves?

Is it the wind whose gathering shout is heard
    With voice of peoples myriad like the
        leaves?
Is it the wind? Fly to the casement, quick,
And when the roar comes thick,
        Fling wide the sash,
        Await the crash!

Nothing. Some various solitary cries, —
    Some sauntering woman's short hard laugh,
Or honester, a dog's bark, — these arise
    From lamplit street up to this free flagstaff:
Nothing remains of that low threatening
        sound;
The wind raves not the eaves around.
        Clasp casement to, —
        You heard not true.

Hark there again! a roar that holds a shriek!
    But not without — no, from below it comes:
What pulses up from solid earth to wreck
    A vengeful word on towers and lofty domes?
What angry booming doth the trembling ear,
Glued to the stone wall, hear —
        So deep, no air
        Its weight can bear?

Grieve! 't is the voice of ignorance and vice,—
    The rage of slaves who fancy they are free:
Men who would keep men slaves at any price,
    Too blind their own black manacles to see.
Grieve! 't is that grisly spectre with a torch,
Riot — that bloodies every porch,
        Hurls justice down
        And burns the town.
                    CHARLES DE KAY.

On November 19, 1863, a portion of the battle-
field of Gettysburg was consecrated as a national
military cemetery. It was there that President
Lincoln's famous Gettysburg address, prepared
almost on the spur of the moment, was delivered.
He said: —

"Fourscore and seven years ago our fathers
brought forth on this continent a new nation, con-
ceived in liberty, and dedicated to the proposition
that all men are created equal. Now we are en-
gaged in a great civil war, testing whether that
nation, or any nation so conceived and so dedi-
cated, can long endure. We are met on a great
battle-field of that war. We have come to dedicate
a portion of that field as a final resting-place for
those who here gave their lives that that nation
might live. It is altogether fitting and proper that
we should do this. But in a larger sense, we cannot
dedicate, we cannot consecrate, we cannot hallow
this ground. The brave men, living and dead, who
struggled here, have consecrated it far above our
poor power to add or detract. The world will little
note, nor long remember, what we say here, but
it can never forget what they did here. It is for
us, the living, rather, to be dedicated here to the
unfinished work which they who fought here have
thus far so nobly advanced. It is rather for us to be
here dedicated to the great task remaining before
us; — that from these honored dead, we take
increased devotion to that cause for which they
gave the last full measure of devotion; — that we
here highly resolve that these dead shall not have
died in vain, that this nation, under God, shall
have a new birth of freedom, and that government
of the people, by the people, for the people, shall
not perish from the earth."

LINCOLN AT GETTYSBURG

From the "Gettysburg Ode"

[November 19, 1863]

AFTER the eyes that looked, the lips that spake
Here, from the shadows of impending death,
        Those words of solemn breath,
        What voice may fitly break
The silence, doubly hallowed, left by him?
We can but bow the head, with eyes grown
        dim,
And, as a Nation's litany, repeat
The phrase his martyrdom hath made com-
        plete,
Noble as then, but now more sadly sweet;
"Let us, the Living, rather dedicate
Ourselves to the unfinished work, which they
Thus far advanced so nobly on its way,
        And save the perilled State!
Let us, upon this field where they, the brave,
Their last full measure of devotion gave,
Highly resolve they have not died in vain! —
That, under God, the Nation's later birth
        Of Freedom, and the people's gain
Of their own Sovereignty, shall never wane
And perish from the circle of the earth!"
From such a perfect text, shall Song aspire
        To light her faded fire,
        And into wandering music turn
Its virtue, simple, sorrowful, and stern?
His voice all elegies anticipated;
        For, whatsoe'er the strain,
        We hear that one refrain:
"We consecrate ourselves to them, the Con-
        secrated!"

                    BAYARD TAYLOR.

CHAPTER IX

WITH GRANT ON THE MISSISSIPPI

Grant had a brief repose after his victories at Shiloh and Corinth; then he addressed himself to the capture of Vicksburg. The Confederates had made a second Gibraltar of the place, and so long as they held it had command of the Mississippi. Early in April, 1863, he collected his army at New Carthage, just below Vicksburg, and on the night of April 16, Porter's fleet ran past the batteries, the object of this perilous enterprise being to afford means for carrying the troops across the river and for covering the movement.

RUNNING THE BATTERIES

(As observed from the anchorage above Vicksburg, April, 1863)

A MOONLESS night — a friendly one;
  A haze dimmed the shadowy shore
As the first lampless boat slid silent on;
  Hist! and we spake no more;
We but pointed, and stilly, to what we saw.

We felt the dew, and seemed to feel
  The secret like a burden laid.
The first boat melts; and a second keel
  Is blent with the foliaged shade —
Their midnight rounds have the rebel officers made?

Unspied as yet. A third — a fourth —
  Gunboat and transport in Indian file
Upon the war-path, smooth from the North;
  But the watch may they hope to beguile?
The manned river-batteries stretch far mile on mile.

A flame leaps out; they are seen;
  Another and another gun roars;
We tell the course of the boats through the screen
  By each further fort that pours,
And we guess how they jump from their beds on those shrouded shores.

Converging fires. We speak, though low:
  "That blastful furnace can they thread?"
"Why, Shadrach, Meshach, and Abednego
  Came out all right, we read;
The Lord, be sure, he helps his people, Ned."

How we strain our gaze. On bluffs they shun
  A golden growing flame appears —
Confirms to a silvery steadfast one:
  "The town is afire!" crows Hugh; "three cheers!"
Lot stops his mouth: "Nay, lad, better three tears."

A purposed light; it shows our fleet;
  Yet a little late in its searching ray,
So far and strong that in phantom cheat
  Lank on the deck our shadows lay;
The shining flag-ship stings their guns to furious play.

How dread to mark her near the glare
  And glade of death the beacon throws
Athwart the racing waters there;
  One by one each plainer grows,
Then speeds a blazoned target to our gladdened foes.

The impartial cresset lights as well
  The fixed forts to the boats that run;
And, plunged from the ports, their answers swell
  Back to each fortress dun;
Ponderous words speaks every monster gun.

Fearless they flash through gates of flame,
  The salamanders hard to hit,
Though vivid shows each bulky frame;
  And never the batteries intermit,
Nor the boat's huge guns; they fire and flit.

Anon a lull. The beacon dies.
  "Are they out of that strait accurst?"
But other flames now dawning rise,
  Not mellowly brilliant like the first,
But rolled in smoke, whose whitish volumes burst.

A baleful brand, a hurrying torch
  Whereby anew the boats are seen —
A burning transport all alurch!
  Breathless we gaze; yet still we glean
Glimpses of beauty as we eager lean.

The effulgence takes an amber glow
  Which bathes the hillside villas far;
Affrighted ladies mark the show
  Painting the pale magnolia —
The fair, false, Circe light of cruel War.

The barge drifts doomed, a plague-struck one,
  Shoreward in yawls the sailors fly.
But the gauntlet now is nearly run,
  The spleenful forts by fits reply,
And the burning boat dies down in morning's
  sky.

All out of range. Adieu, Messieurs!
  Jeers, as it speeds, our parting gun.
So burst we through their barriers
  And menaces every one;
So Porter proves himself a brave man's son.
                    HERMAN MELVILLE.

The army was at once taken across the river
and on May 19, 1863, a general assault was made
on the town. This was repulsed with severe loss,
and Grant thereupon settled down for a regular
siege.

BEFORE VICKSBURG

[May 18–July 4, 1863]

WHILE Sherman stood beneath the hottest
    fire,
  That from the lines of Vicksburg gleamed,
And bomb-shells tumbled in their smoky
    gyre,
  And grape-shot hissed, and case-shot
    screamed;
    Back from the front there came,
    Weeping and sorely lame,
The merest child, the youngest face
Man ever saw in such a fearful place.

Stifling his tears, he limped his chief to
    meet;
  But when he paused, and tottering stood,
Around the circle of his little feet
  There spread a pool of bright, young blood.
    Shocked at his doleful case,
    Sherman cried, "Halt! front face!
Who are you? Speak, my gallant boy!"
"A drummer, sir: — Fifty-fifth Illinois."

"Are you not hit?" "That's nothing. Only
    send
  Some cartridges: our men are out;

And the foe press us." "But, my little
    friend —"
  "Don't mind me! Did you hear that shout?
    What if our men be driven?
    Oh, for the love of Heaven,
Send to my Colonel, General dear!"
"But you?" "Oh, I shall easily find the rear."

"I'll see to that," cried Sherman; and a drop,
  Angels might envy, dimmed his eye,
As the boy, toiling towards the hill's hard top,
  Turned round, and with his shrill child's
    cry
    Shouted, "Oh, don't forget!
    We'll win the battle yet!
But let our soldiers have some more,
More cartridges, sir, — calibre fifty-four!"
                    GEORGE HENRY BOKER.

The place was completely invested and a terrific
bombardment maintained until July 3, 1863, when
the town surrendered, and on the next day, the
Confederate troops in the place, to the number
of twenty-seven thousand, laid down their arms.

VICKSBURG

FOR sixty days and upwards,
  A storm of shell and shot
Rained round us in a flaming shower,
  But still we faltered not.
"If the noble city perish,"
  Our grand young leader said,
"Let the only walls the foe shall scale
  Be ramparts of the dead!"

For sixty days and upwards,
  The eye of heaven waxed dim;
And e'en throughout God's holy morn,
  O'er Christian prayer and hymn,
  Arose a hissing tumult,
    As if the fiends in air
Strove to engulf the voice of faith
  In the shrieks of their despair.

There was wailing in the houses,
  There was trembling on the marts,
While the tempest raged and thundered,
  'Mid the silent thrill of hearts:
But the Lord, our shield, was with us,
  And ere a month had sped,
Our very women walked the streets
  With scarce one throb of dread

And the little children gambolled,
  Their faces purely raised,
Just for a wondering moment,
  As the huge bombs whirled and blazed;
Then turned with silvery laughter
  To the sports which children love,
Thrice-mailed in the sweet, instinctive thought
  That the good God watched above.

Yet the hailing bolts fell faster,
  From scores of flame-clad ships,
And about us, denser, darker,
  Grew the conflict's wild eclipse,
Till a solid cloud closed o'er us,
  Like a type of doom and ire,
Whence shot a thousand quivering tongues
  Of forked and vengeful fire.

But the unseen hands of angels
  Those death-shafts warned aside,
And the dove of heavenly mercy
  Ruled o'er the battle tide:
In the houses ceased the wailing,
  And through the war-scarred marts
The people strode, with step of hope,
  To the music in their hearts.
                    PAUL HAMILTON HAYNE.

Just at noon of July 4, 1863, the Stars and
Stripes was run up over the court-house, and the
Union troops, seeing it, started to sing "The
Battle-Cry of Freedom." By mid-afternoon the
possession of the post was absolute and the Union
fleet lay at the levee.

THE BATTLE-CRY OF FREEDOM

YES, we'll rally round the flag, boys, we'll
    rally once again,
  Shouting the battle-cry of freedom,
We will rally from the hill-side, we'll gather
    from the plain,
  Shouting the battle-cry of freedom.
Chorus — The Union forever, hurrah! boys,
        hurrah!
          Down with the traitor, up with
            the star,
          While we rally round the flag, boys,
            rally once again,
            Shouting the battle-cry of free-
              dom.

We are springing to the call of our brothers
    gone before,
  Shouting the battle-cry of freedom,

And we'll fill the vacant ranks with a million
    freemen more,
  Shouting the battle-cry of freedom.

We will welcome to our numbers the loyal,
    true, and brave,
  Shouting the battle-cry of freedom,
And altho' they may be poor, not a man shall
    be a slave,
  Shouting the battle-cry of freedom.

So we're springing to the call from the East
    and from the West,
  Shouting the battle-cry of freedom,
And we'll hurl the rebel crew from the land
    we love the best,
  Shouting the battle-cry of freedom.
                    GEORGE FREDERICK ROOT.

Meanwhile, General Banks had been besieging
Port Hudson, a position scarcely less formidable
than Vicksburg, and on May 24, 1863, had driven
the Confederates within their inner line of in-
trenchments. Three days later, a general assault
took place, in which the First and Second Louisi-
ana, colored troops, bore a prominent part.

THE BLACK REGIMENT

[May 27, 1863]

DARK as the clouds of even,
Ranked in the western heaven,
Waiting the breath that lifts
All the dead mass, and drifts
Tempest and falling brand
Over a ruined land, —
So still and orderly,
Arm to arm, knee to knee,
Waiting the great event,
Stands the black regiment.

Down the long dusky line
Teeth gleam and eyeballs shine;
And the bright bayonet,
Bristling and firmly set,
Flashed with a purpose grand,
Long ere the sharp command
Of the fierce rolling drum
Told them their time had come,
Told them what work was sent
For the black regiment.

"Now," the flag-sergeant cried,
"Though death and hell betide,

Let the whole nation see
If we are fit to be
Free in this land; or bound
Down, like the whining hound, —
Bound with red stripes of pain
In our old chains again!"
Oh, what a shout there went
From the black regiment!

"Charge!" trump and drum awoke;
Onward the bondmen broke;
Bayonet and sabre-stroke
Vainly opposed their rush.
Through the wild battle's crush,
With but one thought aflush,
Driving their lords like chaff,
In the guns' mouths they laugh;
Or at the slippery brands,
Leaping with open hands,
Down they tear man and horse,
Down in their awful course;
Trampling with bloody heel
Over the crashing steel,
All their eyes forward bent,
Rushed the black regiment.

"Freedom!" their battle-cry, —
"Freedom! or leave to die!"
Ah! and they meant the word,
Not as with us 't is heard,
Not a mere party shout:
They gave their spirits out;
Trusted the end to God,
And on the gory sod
Rolled in triumphant blood.
Glad to strike one free blow,
Whether for weal or woe;
Glad to breathe one free breath,
Though on the lips of death;
Praying, — alas! in vain! —
That they might fail again,
So they could once more see
That burst to liberty!
This was what "freedom" lent
To the black regiment.

Hundreds on hundreds fell;
But they are resting well;
Scourges, and shackles strong
Never shall do them wrong.
Oh, to the living few,
Soldiers, be just and true!
Hail them as comrades tried;
Fight with them side by side;

Never, in field or tent,
Scorn the black regiment!
GEORGE HENRY BOKER.

Shortly after the fall of Vicksburg, Grant was severely injured by a fall from a horse, and it was some months before he could take the field again. Most of his troops were sent to reinforce the Army of the Cumberland, under Rosecrans, which was operating against the Confederates under Bragg, in Tennessee. Chattanooga was occupied by the Union forces on September 16, 1863. Rosecrans pushed forward to the Chickamauga valley, where, on September 18, Bragg attacked in force. The battle raged for two days, the Union line was broken, and General Thomas and his division were isolated on a slope of Missionary Ridge. Assault after assault was delivered against him, but he stood like a rock, and at sundown still held the position.

THE BALLAD OF CHICKAMAUGA

[September 19, 20, 1863]

By Chickamauga's crooked stream the martial trumpets blew;
The North and South stood face to face, with War's dread work to do.
O lion-strong, unselfish, brave, twin athletes battle-wise,
Brothers yet enemies, the fire of conflict in their eyes,
All banner-led and bugle-stirred, they set them to the fight,
Hearing the god of slaughter laugh from mountain height to height.

The ruddy, fair-haired, giant North breathed loud and strove amain;
The swarthy shoulders of the South did heave them to the strain;
An earthquake shuddered underfoot, a cloud rolled overhead:
And serpent-tongues of flame cut through and lapped and twinkled red,
Where back and forth a bullet-stream went singing like a breeze,
What time the snarling cannon-balls to splinters tore the trees.

"Make way, make way!" a voice boomed out, "I'm marching to the sea!"
The answer was a rebel yell and Bragg's artillery.
Where Negley struck, the cohorts gray like storm-tossed clouds were rent;

Where Buckner charged, a cyclone fell, the
    blue to tatters went;
The noble Brannan cheered his men, Pat
    Cleburne answered back,
And Lytle stormed, and life was naught in
    Walthall's bloody track.

Old Taylor's Ridge rocked to its base, and
    Pigeon Mountain shook;
And Helm went down, and Lytle died, and
    broken was McCook.
Van Cleve moved like a hurricane, a tempest
    blew with Hood,
Awful the sweep of Breckenridge across the
    flaming wood.
Never before did battle-roar such chords of
    thunder make,
Never again shall tides of men over such
    barriers break.

"Stand fast, stand fast!" cried Rosecrans;
    and Thomas said, "I will!"
And, crash on crash, his batteries dashed their
    broadsides down the hill.
Brave Longstreet's splendid rush tore through
    whatever barred its track,
Till the Rock of Chickamauga hurled the
    roaring columns back,
And gave the tide of victory a red tinge of de-
    feat,
Adding a noble dignity to that hard word,
    retreat.

Two days they fought, and evermore those
    days shall stand apart,
Keynotes of epic chivalry within the nation's
    heart.
Come, come, and set the carven rocks to mark
    this glorious spot;
Here let the deeds of heroes live, their hatreds
    be forgot.
Build, build, but never monument of stone
    shall last as long
As one old soldier's ballad borne on breath of
    battle-song.

            MAURICE THOMPSON.

THOMAS AT CHICKAMAUGA

[September 19, 20, 1863]

It was that fierce contested field when Chick-
    amauga lay
Beneath the wild tornado that swept her pride
    away;

Her dimpling dales and circling hills dyed
    crimson with the flood
That had its sources in the springs that throb
    with human blood.

"Go say to General Hooker to reinforce his
    right!"
Said Thomas to his aide-de-camp, when
    wildly went the fight;
In front the battle thundered, it roared both
    right and left,
But like a rock "Pap" Thomas stood upon
    the crested cleft.

"Where will I find you, General, when I re-
    turn?" The aide
Leaned on his bridle-rein to wait the answer
    Thomas made;
The old chief like a lion turned, his pale lips
    set and sere,
And shook his mane, and stamped his foot,
    and fiercely answered, "Here!"

The floodtide of fraternal strife rolled upward
    to his feet,
And like the breakers on the shore the thun-
    derous clamors beat;
The sad earth rocked and reeled with woe
    the woodland shrieked in pain,
And hill and vale were groaning with the bur-
    den of the slain.

Who does not mind that sturdy form, that
    steady heart and hand,
That calm repose and gallant mien, that cour-
    age high and grand? —
O God, who givest nations men to meet their
    lofty needs,
Vouchsafe another Thomas when our country
    prostrate bleeds!

They fought with all the fortitude of earnest
    men and true —
The men who wore the rebel gray, the men
    who wore the blue;
And those, they fought most valiantly for
    petty state and clan,
And these, for truer Union and the brother-
    hood of man.

They come, those hurling legions, with ban-
    ners crimson-splashed,
Against our stubborn columns their rushing
    ranks are dashed,

Till 'neath the blistering iron hail the shy and
    frightened deer
Go scurrying from their forest haunts to
    plunge in wilder fear.

Beyond, our lines are broken; and now in
    frenzied rout
The flower of the Cumberland has swiftly
    faced about;
And horse and foot and color-guard are reel-
    ing, rear and van,
And in the awful panic man forgets that he
    is man.

Now Bragg, with pride exultant above our
    broken wings,
The might of all his army against "Pap"
    Thomas brings;
They're massing to the right of him, they're
    massing to the left,
Ah, God be with our hero, who holds the
    crested cleft!

Blow, blow, ye echoing bugles! give answer,
    screaming shell!
Go, belch your murderous fury, ye batteries
    of hell!
Ring out, O impious musket! spin on, O
    shattering shot, —
Our smoke-encircled hero, he hears but heeds
    ye not!

Now steady, men! now steady! make one
    more valiant stand,
For gallant Steedman's coming, his forces well
    in hand!
Close up your shattered columns, take steady
    aim and true,
The chief who loves you as his life will live or
    die with you!

By solid columns, on they come; by columns
    they are hurled,
As down the eddying rapids the storm-swept
    booms are whirled;
And when the ammunition fails — O mo-
    ment drear and dread —
The heroes load their blackened guns from
    rounds of soldiers lead.

God never set His signet on the hearts of
    braver men,
Or fixed the goal of victory on higher heights
    than then;

With bayonets and muskets clubbed, they
    close the rush and roar;
Their stepping-stones to glory are their com-
    rades gone before.

O vanished majesty of days not all forgotten
    yet,
We consecrate unto thy praise one hour of
    deep regret;
One hour to them whose days were years of
    glory that shall flood
The Nation's sombre night of tears, of
    carnage, and of blood!

O vanished majesty of days, when men were
    gauged by worth,
Set crowned and dowered in the way to judge
    the sons of earth;
When all the little great fell down before the
    great unknown,
And priest put off the hampering gown and
    coward donned his own!

O vanished majesty of days that saw the sun
    shine on
The deeds that wake sublimer praise than
    Ghent or Marathon;
When patriots in homespun rose — where
    one was called for, ten —
And heroes sprang full-armored from the
    humblest walks of men!

O vanished majesty of days! Rise, type and
    mould to-day,
And teach our sons to follow on where duty
    leads the way;
That whatsoever trial comes, defying doubt
    and fear,
They in the thickest fight shall stand and
    proudly answer, "*Here!*"
            KATE BROWNLEE SHERWOOD.

Rosecrans could not reinforce Thomas, and at
four o'clock General James A. Garfield was in-
trusted with the perilous task of taking him an
order to withdraw. Garfield got to Thomas safely
and the retreat began at sundown. The Confed-
erates attempted no pursuit.

GARFIELD'S RIDE AT CHICKA-
MAUGA

[September 20, 1863]

AGAIN the summer-fevered skies,
    The breath of autumn calms;
Again the golden moons arise
    On harvest-happy farms.

The locusts pipe, the crickets sing
  Among the falling leaves,
And wandering breezes sigh, and bring
  The harp-notes of the sheaves.

Peace smiles upon the hills and dells;
  Peace smiles upon the seas;
And drop the notes of happy bells
  Upon the fruited trees.
The broad Missouri stretches far
  Her commerce-gathering arms,
And multiply on Arkansas
  The grain-encumbered farms.

Old Chattanooga, crowned with green,
  Sleeps 'neath her walls in peace;
The Argo has returned again,
  And brings the Golden Fleece.
O nation! free from sea to sea,
  In union blessed forever,
Fair be their fame who fought for thee
  By Chickamauga River.

The autumn winds were piping low,
  Beneath the vine-clad eaves;
We heard the hollow bugle blow
  Among the ripened sheaves.
And fast the mustering squadrons passed
  Through mountain portals wide,
And swift the blue brigades were massed
  By Chickamauga's tide.

It was the Sabbath; and in awe
  We heard the dark hills shake,
And o'er the mountain turrets saw
  The smoke of battle break.
And 'neath the war-cloud, gray and grand,
  The hills o'erhanging low,
The Army of the Cumberland,
  Unequal, met the foe!

Again, O fair September night!
  Beneath the moon and stars,
I see, through memories dark and bright,
  The altar-fires of Mars.
The morning breaks with screaming guns
  From batteries dark and dire,
And where the Chickamauga runs
  Red runs the muskets' fire.

I see bold Longstreet's darkening host
  Sweep through our lines of flame,
And hear again, "The right is lost!"
  Swart Rosecrans exclaim.
"But not the left!" young Garfield cries;
  "From that we must not sever,

While Thomas holds the field that lies
  On Chickamauga River!"

Oh! on that day of clouded gold,
  How, half of hope bereft,
The cannoneers, like Titans, rolled
  Their thunders on the left!
I see the battle-clouds again,
  With glowing autumn splendors blending:
It seemed as if the gods with men
  Were on Olympian heights contending.

Through tongues of flame, through meadows
      brown,
  Dry valley roads concealed,
Ohio's hero dashes down
  Upon the rebel field.
And swift, on reeling charger borne,
  He threads the wooded plain,
By twice a hundred cannon mown,
  And reddened with the slain.

But past the swathes of carnage dire,
  The Union guns he hears,
And gains the left, begirt with fire,
  And thus the heroes cheers —
"While stands the left, yon flag o'erhead,
  Shall Chattanooga stand!"
"Let the Napoleons rain their lead!"
  Was Thomas's command.

Back swept the gray brigades of Bragg;
  The air with victory rung;
And Wurzel's "Rally round the flag!"
  'Mid Union cheers was sung.
The flag on Chattanooga's height
  In twilight's crimson waved,
And all the clustered stars of white
  Were to the Union saved.

O chief of staff! the nation's fate
  That red field crossed with thee,
The triumph of the camp and state,
  The hope of liberty!
O nation! free from sea to sea,
  With union blessed forever,
Not vainly heroes fought for thee
  By Chickamauga River.

In dreams I stand beside the tide
  Where those old heroes fell:
Above the valleys long and wide
  Sweet rings the Sabbath bell.
I hear no more the bugle blow,
  As on that fateful day!

I hear the ringdove fluting low,
 Where shaded waters stray.

On Mission Ridge the sunlight streams
 Above the fields of fall,
And Chattanooga calmly dreams
 Beneath her mountain-wall.
Old Lookout Mountain towers on high,
 As in heroic days,
When 'neath the battle in the sky
 Were seen its summits blaze.

'T was ours to lay no garlands fair
 Upon the graves "unknown":
Kind Nature sets her gentians there,
 And fall the sear leaves lone.
Those heroes' graves no shaft of Mars
 May mark with beauty ever;
But floats the flag of forty stars
 By Chickamauga River.

HEZEKIAH BUTTERWORTH.

This defeat brought Grant into the field again,
though he was still on crutches. The Confederates
held a strong position on Missionary Ridge and
Lookout Mountain, and Grant prepared to attack.
On November 24, 1863, Hooker's brigade moved
forward to the northern face of Lookout Mountain,
drove the enemy from their rifle pits and intrench-
ments, and then started after them up the slope.
The mountain was enveloped in a dense fog, and
into this Hooker's men disappeared. During the
night the Confederates delivered a savage assault,
but were beaten off. At dawn, when the Union
troops scaled the palisades, they found the in-
trenchments at the top deserted, and unfurled the
Stars and Stripes from the summit of Pulpit Rock.
The Confederates were dislodged next day from
Missionary Ridge and were soon in full retreat.

THE BATTLE OF LOOKOUT MOUN-
TAIN

[November 24, 1863]

"GIVE me but two brigades," said Hooker,
 frowning at fortified Lookout;
"And I 'll engage to sweep yon mountain clear
 of that mocking rebel rout."
At early morning came an order, that set the
 General's face aglow:
"Now," said he to his staff, "draw out my
 soldiers! Grant says that I may go."

Hither and thither dashed each eager Colo-
 nel, to join his regiment,
While a low rumor of the daring purpose ran
 on from tent to tent.

For the long roll was sounding through the
 valley, and the keen trumpet's bray,
And the wild laughter of the swarthy veterans,
 who cried, "We fight to-day!"

The solid tramp of infantry, the rumble of the
 great jolting gun,
The sharp, clear order, and the fierce steeds
 neighing, "Why 's not the fight be-
 gun?"
All these plain harbingers of sudden conflict
 broke on the startled ear;
And last arose a sound that made your blood
 leap, the ringing battle-cheer.

The lower works were carried at one onset;
 like a vast roaring sea
Of steel and fire, our soldiers from the trenches
 swept out the enemy;
And we could see the gray-coats swarming up
 from the mountain's leafy base,
To join their comrades in the higher fastness,
 — for life or death the race!

Then our long line went winding up the moun-
 tain, in a huge serpent-track,
And the slant sun upon it flashed and glim-
 mered as on a dragon's back.
Higher and higher the column's head pushed
 onward, ere the rear moved a man;
And soon the skirmish-lines their straggling
 volleys and single shots began.

Then the bald head of Lookout flamed and
 bellowed, and all its batteries woke,
And down the mountain poured the bomb-
 shells, puffing into our eyes their smoke;
And balls and grape-shot rained upon our
 column, that bore the angry shower
As if it were no more than that soft dropping
 which scarcely stirs the flower.

Oh, glorious courage that inspires the hero,
 and runs through all his men!
The heart that failed beside the Rappahan-
 nock, it was itself again!
The star that circumstance and jealous faction
 shrouded in envious night
Here shone with all the splendor of its nature,
 and with a freer light!

Hark, hark! there go the well-known crashing
 volleys, the long-continued roar
That swells and falls, but never ceases wholly
 until the fight is o'er.

Up towards the crystal gates of heaven ascend-
    ing, the mortal tempest beat,
As if they sought to try their cause together
    before God's very feet.

We saw our troops had gained a footing al-
    most beneath the topmost ledge,
And back and forth the rival lines went surg-
    ing upon the dizzy edge.
We saw, sometimes, our men fall backward
    slowly, and groaned in our despair;
Or cheered when now and then a stricken
    rebel plunged out in open air,
Down, down, a thousand empty fathoms
    dropping, — his God alone knows
    where!

At eve thick haze upon the mountain gathered,
    with rising smoke stained black,
And not a glimpse of the contending armies
    shone through the swirling rack.
Night fell o'er all; but still they flashed their
    lightnings and rolled their thunders
    loud,
Though no man knew upon which side was
    going that battle in the cloud.

Night — what a night! — of anxious thought
    and wonder, but still no tidings came
From the bare summit of the trembling moun-
    tain, still wrapped in mist and flame.
But towards the sleepless dawn, stillness, more
    dreadful than the fierce sound of war,
Settled o'er Nature, as if she stood breathless
    before the morning star.

As the sun rose, dense clouds of smoky vapor
    boiled from the valley's deeps,
Dragging their torn and ragged edges slowly
    up through the tree-clad steeps;
And rose and rose, till Lookout, like a vision,
    above us grandly stood,
And over his bleak crags and storm-blanched
    headlands burst the warm golden
    flood.

Thousands of eyes were fixed upon the moun-
    tain, and thousands held their breath,
And the vast army, in the valley watching,
    seemed touched with sudden death.
High o'er us soared great Lookout, robed in
    purple, a glory on his face,
A human meaning in his hard, calm features,
    beneath that heavenly grace.

Out on a crag walked something — what?
    an eagle, that treads yon giddy height?
Surely no man! but still he clambered forward
    into the full, rich light.
Then up he started, with a sudden motion,
    and from the blazing crag
Flung to the morning breeze and sunny radi-
    ance the dear old starry flag!

Ah! then what followed? Scarred and war-
    worn soldiers, like girls, flushed
    through their tan,
And down the thousand wrinkles of the bat-
    tles a thousand tear-drops ran.
Men seized each other in returned embraces,
    and sobbed for very love;
A spirit, which made all that moment bro-
    thers, seemed falling from above.

And as we gazed, around the mountain's sum-
    mit our glittering files appeared,
Into the rebel works we saw them moving; and
    we — we cheered, we cheered!
And they above waved all their flags before
    us, and joined our frantic shout,
Standing, like demigods, in light and triumph
    upon their own Lookout!
                            GEORGE HENRY BOKER.

THE BATTLE IN THE CLOUDS

[November 24, 1863]

WHERE the dews and the rains of heaven have
    their fountain,
    Like its thunder and its lightning our brave
        burst on the foe.
Up above the clouds on Freedom's Lookout
    Mountain
    Raining life-blood like water on the valleys
        down below.
        Oh, green be the laurels that grow,
        Oh, sweet be the wild-buds that blow,
In the dells of the mountain where the brave
    are lying low.

Light of our hope and crown of our story,
    Bright as sunlight, pure as starlight shall
        their deed of daring glow,
While the day and the night out of heaven shed
    their glory,
    On Freedom's Lookout Mountain whence
        they routed Freedom's foe.

Oh, soft be the gales when they go
   Through the pines on the summit where
      they blow,
Chanting solemn music for the souls that
   passed below.
        WILLIAM DEAN HOWELLS.

By the autumn of 1862, the Union forces had established themselves firmly on the North Carolina coast, and early in the following year preparations were made to attack Charleston, the very head and front of the Confederacy.

CHARLESTON

[April, 1863]

CALM as that second summer which precedes
   The first fall of the snow,
In the broad sunlight of heroic deeds,
   The city bides the foe.

As yet, behind their ramparts, stern and proud,
   Her bolted thunders sleep, —
Dark Sumter, like a battlemented cloud,
   Looms o'er the solemn deep.

No Calpe frowns from lofty cliff or scaur
   To guard the holy strand;
But Moultrie holds in leash her dogs of war
   Above the level sand.

And down the dunes a thousand guns lie
      couched,
   Unseen, beside the flood, —
Like tigers in some Orient jungle crouched,
   That wait and watch for blood.

Meanwhile, through streets still echoing with
      trade,
   Walk grave and thoughtful men,
Whose hands may one day wield the patriot's
      blade
   As lightly as the pen.

And maidens, with such eyes as would grow
      dim
   Over a bleeding hound,
Seem each one to have caught the strength of
      him
   Whose sword she sadly bound.

Thus girt without and garrisoned at home,
   Day patient following day,
Old Charleston looks from roof and spire and
      dome,
   Across her tranquil bay.

Ships, through a hundred foes, from Saxon
      lands
   And spicy Indian ports,
Bring Saxon steel and iron to her hands,
   And summer to her courts.

But still, along yon dim Atlantic line,
   The only hostile smoke
Creeps like a harmless mist above the brine,
   From some frail floating oak.

Shall the spring dawn, and she, still clad in
      smiles,
   And with an unscathed brow,
Rest in the strong arms of her palm-crowned
      isles,
   As fair and free as now?

We know not; in the temple of the Fates
   God has inscribed her doom:
And, all untroubled in her faith, she waits
   The triumph or the tomb.
        HENRY TIMROD.

On April 7, 1863, a strong squadron under Admiral Dupont attempted to enter the harbor and reduce Fort Sumter, but got such a warm reception that it was forced to withdraw. One ship was sunk and the others badly damaged.

THE BATTLE OF CHARLESTON HARBOR

[April 7, 1863]

Two hours, or more, beyond the prime of a
      blithe April day,
The   Northmen's   mailed   "Invincibles"
      steamed up fair Charleston Bay;
They came in sullen file, and slow, low-
      breasted on the wave,
Black as a midnight front of storm, and silent
      as the grave.

A thousand warrior-hearts beat high as those
      dread monsters drew
More closely to the game of death across the
      breezeless blue,
And twice ten thousand hearts of those who
      watch the scene afar,
Thrill in the awful hush that bides the battle's
      broadening star.

Each gunner, moveless by his gun, with rigid
      aspect stands,
The reedy linstocks firmly grasped in bold,
      untrembling hands,

So moveless in their marbled calm, their stern,
    heroic guise,
They look like forms of statued stone with
    burning human eyes!

Our banners on the outmost walls, with stately
    rustling fold,
Flash back from arch and parapet the sun-
    light's ruddy gold, —
They mount to the deep roll of drums, and
    widely echoing cheers,
And then, once more, dark, breathless,
    hushed, wait the grim cannoneers.

Onward, in sullen file, and slow, low-gloom-
    ing on the wave,
Near, nearer still, the haughty fleet glides
    silent as the grave,
When shivering the portentous calm o'er
    startled flood and shore,
Broke from the sacred Island Fort the thun-
    der-wrath of yore!

Ha! brutal Corsairs! though ye come thrice-
    cased in iron mail,
Beware the storm that's opening now, God's
    vengeance guides the hail!
Ye strive, the ruffian types of Might, 'gainst
    law and truth and Right;
Now quail beneath a sturdier Power, and own
    a mightier Might!

The storm has burst! and while we speak,
    more furious, wilder, higher,
Dart from the circling batteries a hundred
    tongues of fire;
The waves gleam red, the lurid vault of heaven
    seems rent above —
Fight on, O knightly gentlemen! for faith, and
    home, and love!

There's not, in all that line of flame, one soul
    that would not rise
To seize the victor's wreath of blood, though
    death must give the prize;
There's not, in all this anxious crowd that
    throngs the ancient town,
A maid who does not yearn for power to strike
    one foeman down!

The conflict deepens! ship by ship the proud
    Armada sweeps,
Where fierce from Sumter's raging breast the
    volleyed lightning leaps;

And ship by ship, raked, overborne, ere burned
    the sunset light,
Crawls in the gloom of baffled hate beyond the
    field of fight!

O glorious Empress of the Main! from out
    thy storied spires
Thou well mayst peal thy bells of joy, and
    light thy festal fires, —
Since Heaven this day hath striven for thee,
    hath nerved thy dauntless sons,
And thou in clear-eyed faith hast seen God's
    angels near the guns!
                    PAUL HAMILTON HAYNE.

It was evident that the fleet by itself could
accomplish nothing, and a land attack was there-
fore planned against Fort Wagner, a very strong
work, fully garrisoned by veterans. It was stormed
on the evening of July 18, 1863, the Fifty-Fourth
Massachusetts (colored), Colonel Robert Gould
Shaw, leading. He was killed in the first assault
and his regiment was decimated. The Confederates
buried Shaw ": in a pit under a heap of his niggers."

BURY THEM

(WAGNER, July 18, 1863)

BURY the Dragon's Teeth!
    Bury them deep and dark!
    The incisors swart and stark,
    The molars heavy and dark —
And the one white Fang underneath!

Bury the Hope Forlorn!
    Never shudder to fling,
With its fellows dusky and worn,
    The strong and beautiful thing
(Pallid ivory and pearl!)
    Into the horrible Pit —
Hurry it in, and hurl
    All the rest over it!

Trample them, clod by clod,
    Stamp them in dust amain!
    The cuspids, cruent and red,
    That the Monster, Freedom, shed
On the sacred, strong Slave-Sod —
    They never shall rise again!

Never? — what hideous growth
    Is sprouting through clod and clay?
    What Terror starts to the day?
A crop of steel, on our oath!
    How the burnished stamens glance! —

Spike, and anther, and blade,
How they burst from the bloody shade,
    And spindle to spear and lance!

There are tassels of blood-red Maize —
    How the horrible Harvest grows!
'T is sabres that glint and daze —
'T is bayonets all ablaze
    Uprearing in dreadful rows!

For one that we buried there,
A thousand are come to air!
Ever, by door-stone and hearth,
They break from the angry earth —
    And out of the crimson sand,
Where the cold white Fang was laid,
Rises a terrible Shade,
    The Wraith of a sleepless Brand!

And our hearts wax strange and chill,
With an ominous shudder and thrill,
    Even here, on the strong Slave-Sod,
Lest, haply, we be found
(Ah, dread no brave hath drowned!)
    Fighting against Great God.
            HENRY HOWARD BROWNELL.

Heavy siege batteries were at once erected by the
Union forces and on August 17, 1863, a terrific bom-
bardment began against Sumter and Wagner, and
continued uninterruptedly. Ten days later Sumter
had been reduced to a shapeless mass of ruins, and
Fort Wagner was captured soon afterwards, but
the city itself still stood unshaken.

TWILIGHT ON SUMTER [1]

[1863]

STILL and dark along the sea
    Sumter lay;

[1] From Poetical Writings of Richard Henry
Stoddard; copyright, 1880, by Charles Scribner's
Sons.

A light was overhead,
As from burning cities shed,
And the clouds were battle-red,
    Far away.
Not a solitary gun
Left to tell the fort had won
    Or lost the day!
Nothing but the tattered rag
Of the drooping rebel flag,
And the sea-birds screaming round it in their
    play.

How it woke one April morn
    Fame shall tell;
As from Moultrie, close at hand,
And the batteries on the land,
Round its faint but fearless band
    Shot and shell
Raining hid the doubtful light;
But they fought the hopeless fight
    Long and well
(Theirs the glory, ours the shame!),
Till the walls were wrapped in flame,
Then their flag was proudly struck, and Sum-
    ter fell!

Now — oh, look at Sumter now,
    In the gloom!
Mark its scarred and shattered walls.
(Hark! the ruined rampart falls!)
There's a justice that appals
    In its doom!
For this blasted spot of earth
Where rebellion had its birth
    Is its tomb!
And when Sumter sinks at last
From the heavens, that shrink aghast,
Hell shall rise in grim derision and make
    room!
            RICHARD HENRY STODDARD.

CHAPTER X

THE FINAL STRUGGLE

A survey of the field at the opening of the
fourth year of the war shows how steadily the
North had been gaining the advantage — an ad-
vantage due to superior numbers and greater
resources rather than to brilliant generalship.
The Union forces in the field numbered eight
hundred thousand, while the Confederates had
scarcely half as many, and were compelled to
stand on the defensive. The North hoped to
crush them by one mighty effort.

PUT IT THROUGH

[1864]

COME, Freemen of the land,
Come, meet the last demand, —
Here's a piece of work in hand;
    Put it through!

Here's a log across the way,
We have stumbled on all day;
Here's a ploughshare in the clay, —
    Put it through!

Here's a country that's half free,
And it waits for you and me
To say what its fate shall be;
    Put it through!
While one traitor thought remains,
While one spot its banner stains,
One link of all its chains, —
    Put it through!

Hear our brothers in the field,
Steel your swords as theirs are steeled,
Learn to wield the arms they wield, —
    Put it through!
Lock the shop and lock the store,
And chalk this upon the door, —
"We've enlisted for the war!"
    Put it through!

For the birthrights yet unsold,
For the history yet untold,
For the future yet unrolled,
    Put it through!
Lest our children point with shame
On the fathers' dastard fame,
Who gave up a nation's name,
    Put it through!
                EDWARD EVERETT HALE.

Grant was made lieutenant-general, and pre-
pared to advance on Richmond, while the task of
taking Atlanta was intrusted to Sherman. Sher-
man began his advance without delay, and was
before Atlanta by the middle of July, 1864. On
the 20th the Confederates made a desperate sally,
but were driven back.

LOGAN AT PEACH TREE CREEK

A VETERAN'S STORY

[July 20, 1864]

You know that day at Peach Tree Creek,
When the Rebs with their circling, scorching
        wall
Of smoke-hid cannon and sweep of flame
Drove in our flanks, back! back! and all
Our toil seemed lost in the storm of shell —
That desperate day McPherson fell!

Our regiment stood in a little glade
Set round with half-grown red oak trees —

An awful place to stand, in full fair sight,
While the minie bullets hummed like bees,
And comrades dropped on either side —
That fearful day McPherson died!

The roar of the battle, steady, stern,
Rung in our ears. Upon our eyes
The belching cannon smoke, the half-hid
        swing
Of deploying troops, the groans, the cries,
The hoarse commands, the sickening smell —
That blood-red day McPherson fell!

But we stood there! — when out from the
        trees,
Out of the smoke and dismay to the right
Burst a rider — His head was bare, his eye
Had a blaze like a lion fain for fight;
His long hair, black as the deepest night,
Streamed out on the wind. And the might
Of his plunging horse was a tale to tell,
And his voice rang high like a bugle's swell;
"Men, the enemy hem us on every side;
We'll whip 'em yet! Close up that breach —
Remember your flag — don't give an inch!
The right flank's gaining and soon will
        reach —
Forward boys, and give 'em hell!" —
Said Logan after McPherson fell.

We laughed and cheered and the red ground
        shook,
As the general plunged along the line
Through the deadliest rain of screaming shells;
For the sound of his voice refreshed us all,
And we filled the gap like a roaring tide,
And saved the day McPherson died!

But that was twenty years ago,
And part of a horrible dream now past.
For Logan, the lion, the drums throb low
And the flag swings low on the mast;
He has followed his mighty chieftain through
The mist-hung stream, where gray and blue
One color stand,
And North to South extends the hand.
It's right that deeds of war and blood
Should be forgot, but, spite of all,
I think of Logan, now, as he rode
That day across the field; I hear the call
Of his trumpet voice — see the battle shine
In his stern, black eyes, and down the line
Of cheering men I see him ride,
As on the day McPherson died.
                HAMLIN GARLAND.

On July 22, 1864, Sherman ordered a general assault, which lasted two days, with heavy losses on both sides. General McPherson was killed by a Confederate sharpshooter about noon of the first day.

A DIRGE FOR McPHERSON

KILLED IN FRONT OF ATLANTA

[July 22, 1864]

ARMS reversed and banners craped —
  Muffled drums;
Snowy horses sable-draped —
  McPherson comes.
    But, tell us, shall we know him more,
    Lost-Mountain and lone Kenesaw?

Brave the sword upon the pall —
  A gleam in gloom;
So a bright name lighteth all
  McPherson's doom.

Bear him through the chapel-door —
  Let priest in stole
Pace before the warrior
  Who led. Bell — toll!

Lay him down within the nave,
  The Lesson read —
Man is noble, man is brave,
  But man's — a weed.

Take him up again and wend
  Graveward, nor weep:
There's a trumpet that shall rend
  This Soldier's sleep.

Pass the ropes the coffin round,
  And let descend;
Prayer and volley — let it sound
  McPherson's end.
    True fame is his, for life is o'er —
    Sarpedon of the mighty war.
                    HERMAN MELVILLE.

Hostilities continued about Atlanta for nearly a month, and finally, on September 2, 1864, the Confederates evacuated the city. A few days later, they suddenly attacked Allatoona, where General Corse was stationed with a small garrison. Sherman heard the thunder of the guns from the top of Kenesaw Mountain, and signalled Corse the famous message, "Hold out; relief is coming!" Corse did hold out and the Confederates finally withdrew.

WITH CORSE AT ALLATOONA

[October 5, 1864]

IT was less than two thousand we numbered,
  In the fort sitting up on the hill;
That night not a soldier that slumbered;
  We watched by the starlight until
Daybreak showed us all of their forces;
  About us their gray columns ran,
To left and to right they were round us,
  Five thousand if there was a man.

"Surrender your fort," bawled the rebel;
  "Five minutes I give, or you're dead."
"Not a man," answered Corse, in his treble,
  "Perhaps you can *take* us instead!"
Then pealed forth their cannon infernal;
  We fought them outside of the pass,
Two hours, the time seemed eternal;
  The dead lay in lines on the grass.

But who cared for dead or for dying?
  The fort we were there to defend,
And across from yon far mountain flying,
  Came a message, "Hold on to the end;
Hold on to the fort." It was Sherman,
  Who signalled from Kenesaw's height,
Far over the heads of our foemen,
  "Hold on — I am coming to-night."

Quick fluttered our flag to the signal,
  We answered him back with a will,
And fired on the gray-coated rebels
  That charged up the slope of the hill.
"Load double," cried Corse, "every cannon
  Who cares for their ten to our one?"
We looked at the swift-coming rebels,
  And answered their yell with a gun.

With the grape from our fort in their faces,
  They rush to the ramparts, but stop;
Ah! few of the gray-columned army
  That day left alive at the top.
On the parapets, too, lie our wounded,
  Each porthole a grave for the dead;
No room for our cannon, the corpses
  Fill up the embrasures instead.

Again through the cannon's red weather
  They charge up the hill and the pass,
Their dead and our dead lie together
  Out there on the slope in the grass.
A crash from our rifles — they falter;
  A gleam from our steel — it is by.

"Recall and retreat," sound their bugles;
     We cheer from the fort as they fly.

Once more and the signal is flying —
"How many the wounded and dead?"
"Six hundred," says Corse. "with the dying,"
     The blood streaming down from his head.
"But what of that? Look! the old banner
     Shines out there as peaceful and still
As if there had not been a battle
     This morning up there on the hill."
                    SAMUEL H. M. BYERS.

ALLATOONA

[October 5, 1864]

WINDS that sweep the southern mountains,
     And the leafy river shore,
Bear ye now a prouder burden
     Than ye ever learned before!
          And the heart blood fills
          The heart, till it thrills
          At the story
          Of the terror and the glory
          Of this battle of the Allatoona hills!

Echo it from the purple mountain
     To the gray resounding shore!
'T is as sad and proud a burden
     As ye ever learned before.
          How they fell like grass
          When the mowers pass!
          And the dying,
          When the foe were flying,
          Swelled the cheering of the heroes of the
               pass.

Sweep it o'er the hills of Georgia,
     To the mountains of the north!
Teach the coward and the doubter
     What the blood of man is worth!
          Toss the flags as ye pass!
          Let their stained and tattered mass
          Tell the story
          Of the terror and the glory
          Of the battle of the Allatoona Pass!

Sherman now prepared for a manœuvre which
was destined to be the most famous of the war.
He determined to destroy Atlanta, and, marching
through the heart of Georgia, to capture one or
more of the important seaport towns. On No-
vember 16, 1864, the famous ":march to the sea"
began.

SHERMAN'S MARCH TO THE SEA

OUR camp-fires shone bright on the mountain
     That frowned on the river below,
As we stood by our guns in the morning,
     And eagerly watched for the foe;
When a rider came out of the darkness
     That hung over mountain and tree,
And shouted: "Boys, up and be ready!
     For Sherman will march to the sea."

Then cheer upon cheer for bold Sherman
     Went up from each valley and glen,
And the bugles reëchoed the music
     That came from the lips of the men;
For we knew that the stars in our banner
     More bright in their splendor would be,
And that blessings from Northland would
          greet us
     When Sherman marched down to the sea.

Then forward, boys! forward to battle!
     We marched on our wearisome way,
We stormed the wild hills of Resaca,
     God bless those who fell on that day!
Then Kenesaw, dark in its glory,
     Frowned down on the flag of the free,
And the East and the West bore our standard
     And Sherman marched on to the sea.

Still onward we pressed till our banners
     Swept out from Atlanta's grim walls,
And the blood of the patriot dampened
     The soil where the traitor flag falls.
We paused not to weep for the fallen,
     Who slept by each river and tree,
Yet we twined them a wreath of the laurel
     As Sherman marched down to the sea.

Oh, proud was our army that morning,
     That stood where the pine darkly towers,
When Sherman said: "Boys, you are weary
     But to-day fair Savannah is ours!"
Then sang we the song of our chieftain,
     That echoed o'er river and lea,
And the stars in our banner shone brighter
     When Sherman marched down to the sea.
                    SAMUEL H. M. BYERS.

Through the heart of Georgia the army moved,
leaving behind a path of ruin forty miles in width.
Some of this destruction was no doubt necessary,
but much of it seems to have been wanton and
without reason.

THE SONG OF SHERMAN'S ARMY

A PILLAR of fire by night,
  A pillar of smoke by day,
Some hours of march — then a halt to
    fight,
  And so we hold our way;
Some hours of march — then a halt to
    fight,
  As on we hold our way.

Over mountain and plain and stream,
  To some bright Atlantic bay,
With our arms aflash in the morning beam,
  We hold our festal way;
With our arms aflash in the morning beam,
  We hold our checkless way!

There is terror wherever we come,
  There is terror and wild dismay
When they see the Old Flag and hear the
    drum
  Announce us on our way;
When they see the Old Flag and hear the
    drum
  Beating time to our onward way.

Never unlimber a gun
  For those villainous lines in gray;
Draw sabres! and at 'em upon the run!
  'T is thus we clear our way;
Draw sabres, and soon you will see them
    run,
  As we hold our conquering way.

The loyal, who long have been dumb,
  Are loud in their cheers to-day;
And the old men out on their crutches come,
  To see us hold our way;
And the old men out on their crutches come,
  To bless us on our way.

Around us in rear and flanks,
  Their futile squadrons play,
With a sixty-mile front of steady ranks,
  We hold our checkless way;
With a sixty-mile front of serried ranks,
  Our banner clears the way.

Hear the spattering fire that starts
  From the woods and the copses gray,
There is just enough fighting to quicken our
    hearts,
  As we frolic along the way!

There is just enough fighting to warm our
    hearts,
  As we rattle along the way.

Upon different roads, abreast,
  The heads of our columns gay,
With fluttering flags, all forward pressed,
  Hold on their conquering way;
With fluttering flags to victory pressed,
  We hold our glorious way.

Ah, traitors! who bragged so bold
  In the sad war's early day,
Did nothing predict you should ever be-
    hold
  The Old Flag come this way?
Did nothing predict you should yet be-
    hold
  Our banner come back this way?

By heaven! 't is a gala march,
  'T is a picnic or a play;
Of all our long war 't is the crowning arch,
  Hip, hip! for Sherman's way!
Of all our long war this crowns the arch —
  For Sherman and Grant, hurrah!
            CHARLES GRAHAM HALPINE.

MARCHING THROUGH GEORGIA

BRING the good old bugle, boys, we'll sing
    another song —
Sing it with a spirit that will start the world
    along —
Sing it as we used to sing it fifty thousand
    strong,
  While we were marching through Georgia.
Chorus — "Hurrah! Hurrah! we bring the
          jubilee!
          Hurrah! Hurrah! the flag that
          makes you free!"
        So we sang the chorus from At-
          lanta to the sea,
        While we were marching through
          Georgia.

How the darkeys shouted when they heard the
    joyful sound!
How the turkeys gobbled which our commis-
    sary found!
How the sweet potatoes even started from the
    ground,
  While we were marching through Georgia.

Yes, and there were Union men who wept with
  joyful tears,
When they saw the honored flag they had not
  seen for years;
Hardly could they be restrained from break-
  ing forth in cheers,
  While we were marching through Georgia.

"Sherman's dashing Yankee boys will never
  reach the coast!"
So the saucy rebels said — and 't was a hand-
  some boast,
Had they not forgot, alas! to reckon on a host,
  While we were marching through Georgia.

So we made a thoroughfare for Freedom and
  her train,
Sixty miles in latitude — three hundred to
  the main;
Treason fled before us, for resistance was in
  vain,
  While we were marching through Georgia.
    HENRY CLAY WORK.

ETHIOPIA SALUTING THE COLORS

WHO are you dusky woman, so ancient hardly
  human,
With your woolly-white and turban'd head,
  and bare bony feet?
Why rising by the roadside here, do you the
  colors greet?

('T is while our army lines Carolina's sands
  and pines,
Forth from thy hovel door thou Ethiopia
  com'st to me,
As under doughty Sherman I march toward
  the sea.)

*Me master years a hundred since from my
  parents sunder'd,
A little child, they caught me as the savage
  beast is caught,
Then hither me across the sea the cruel slaver
  brought.*

No further does she say, but lingering all the
  day,
Her high-borne turban'd head she wags, and
  rolls her darkling eye,
And courtesies to the regiments, the guidons
  moving by.

What is it fateful woman, so blear, hardly
  human?
Why wag your head with turban bound, yel-
  low, red and green?
Are the things so strange and marvellous you
  see or have seen?
    WALT WHITMAN.

The invasion brought panic to the South, and
Beauregard hastened to oppose it. But Sherman
pressed on irresistibly, beating down all opposition,
reached Savannah, and on December 22, 1864,
marched into the city, which had been abandoned
by the Confederates. On Christmas day, he tele-
graphed President Lincoln, "I beg to present to
you, as a Christmas gift, the city of Savannah."

SHERMAN 'S IN SAVANNAH

[December 22, 1864]

LIKE the tribes of Israel,
  Fed on quails and manna,
Sherman and his glorious band
Journeyed through the rebel land,
Fed from Heaven's all-bounteous hand,
  Marching on Savannah!

As the moving pillar shone,
  Streamed the starry banner
All day long in rosy light,
Flaming splendor all the night,
Till it swooped in eagle flight
  Down on doomed Savannah!

Glory be to God on high!
  Shout the loud Hosanna!
Treason's wilderness is past,
Canaan's shore is won at last,
Peal a nation's trumpet-blast, —
  Sherman 's in Savannah!

Soon shall Richmond's tough old hide
  Find a tough old tanner!
Soon from every rebel wall
Shall the rag of treason fall,
Till our banner flaps o'er all
  As it crowns Savannah!
    OLIVER WENDELL HOLMES

SAVANNAH

[December 23, 1864]

THOU hast not drooped thy stately head-
Thy woes a wondrous beauty shed!

Not like a lamb to slaughter led,
But with the lion's monarch tread,
Thou comest to thy battle bed,
    Savannah! O Savannah!

Thine arm of flesh is girded strong;
The blue veins swell beneath thy wrong;
To thee the triple cords belong
Of woe and death and shameless wrong,
And spirit vaunted long, too long!
    Savannah! O Savannah!

No blood-stains spot thy forehead fair;
Only the martyrs' blood is there;
It gleams upon thy bosom bare,
It moves thy deep, deep soul to prayer,
And tunes a dirge for thy sad ear,
    Savannah! O Savannah!

Thy clean white hand is opened wide
For weal or woe, thou Freedom Bride;
The sword-sheath sparkles at thy side,
Thy plighted troth, whate'er betide,
Thou hast but Freedom for thy guide,
    Savannah! O Savannah!

What though the heavy storm-cloud lowers,
Still at thy feet the old oak towers;
Still fragrant are thy jessamine bowers,
And things of beauty, love, and flowers
Are smiling o'er this land of ours,
    My sunny home, Savannah!

There is no film before thy sight, —
Thou seest woe and death and night,
And blood upon thy banner bright;
But in thy full wrath's kindled might
What carest thou for woe or night?
    My rebel home, Savannah!

Come — for the crown is on thy head!
Thy woes a wondrous beauty shed;
Not like a lamb to slaughter led,
But with the lion's monarch tread,
Oh! come unto thy battle bed,
    Savannah! O Savannah!
           ALETHEA S. BURROUGHS.

Sherman paused at Savannah to fortify the place and get his army into shape, after its march of two hundred and fifty miles; then, on January 15, 1865, he started northward into South Carolina.

CAROLINA

[January, 1865]

THE despot treads thy sacred sands,
Thy pines give shelter to his bands,
Thy sons stand by with idle hands,
    Carolina!
He breathes at ease thy airs of balm,
He scorns the lances of thy palm;
Oh! who shall break thy craven calm,
    Carolina!
Thy ancient fame is growing dim,
A spot is on thy garment's rim;
Give to the winds thy battle-hymn,
    Carolina!

Call on thy children of the hill,
Wake swamp and river, coast and rill,
Rouse all thy strength and all thy skill,
    Carolina!
Cite wealth and science, trade and art,
Touch with thy fire the cautious mart,
And pour thee through the people's heart,
    Carolina!
Till even the coward spurns his fears,
And all thy fields, and fens, and meres
Shall bristle like thy palm with spears,
    Carolina!

I hear a murmur as of waves
That grope their way through sunless caves,
Like bodies struggling in their graves,
    Carolina!
And now it deepens; slow and grand
It swells, as, rolling to the land,
An ocean broke upon thy strand,
    Carolina!
Shout! Let it reach the startled Huns!
And roar with all thy festal guns!
It is the answer of thy sons,
    Carolina!
           HENRY TIMROD.

Every man in the state was called to arms, but the Union forces met with only a weak and ineffective resistance. On February 16, 1865, Columbia was occupied; and catching fire accidentally next day, was totally destroyed. The fall of Columbia left Charleston exposed and the Confederate troops hastened to get away while they could.

CHARLESTON

[February, 1865]

CALMLY beside her tropic strand,
    An empress, brave and loyal,

I see the watchful city stand,
  With aspect sternly royal;
She knows her mortal foe draws near,
  Armored by subtlest science,
Yet deep, majestical, and clear,
  Rings out her grand defiance.
Oh, glorious is thy noble face,
  Lit up by proud emotion,
And unsurpassed thy stately grace,
  Our warrior Queen of Ocean!

First from thy lips the summons came,
  Which roused our South to action,
And, with the quenchless force of flame
  Consumed the demon, Faction;
First, like a rush of sovereign wind,
  That rends dull waves asunder,
Thy prescient warning struck the blind,
  And woke the deaf with thunder;
They saw, with swiftly kindling eyes,
  The shameful doom before them,
And heard, borne wild from northern skies,
  The death-gale hurtling o'er them:

Wilt thou, whose virgin banner rose,
  A morning star of splendor,
Quail when the war-tornado blows,
  And crouch in base surrender?
Wilt thou, upon whose loving breast
  Our noblest chiefs are sleeping,
Yield thy dead patriots' place of rest
  To scornful alien keeping?
No! while a life-pulse throbs for fame,
  Thy sons will gather round thee,
Welcome the shot, the steel, the flame,
  If honor's hand hath crowned thee.

Then fold about thy beauteous form
  The imperial robe thou wearest,
And front with regal port the storm
  Thy foe would dream thou fearest;
If strength, and will, and courage fail
  To cope with ruthless numbers,
And thou must bend, despairing, pale,
  Where thy last hero slumbers,
Lift the red torch, and light the fire
  Amid those corpses gory,
And on thy self-made funeral pyre,
  Pass from the world to glory.
            PAUL HAMILTON HAYNE.

The cotton in the town was burned, many
houses caught fire, and a magazine exploded,
killing two hundred people. The city was virtually
a ruin when the last of the Confederate troops —
"poor old Dixie's bottom dollar" — left the city.

ROMANCE

"TALK of pluck!" pursued the Sailor,
  Set at euchre on his elbow,
  "I was on the wharf at Charleston,
  Just ashore from off the runner.

"It was gray and dirty weather,
  And I heard a drum go rolling,
  Rub-a-dubbing in the distance,
  Awful dour-like and defiant.

"In and out among the cotton,
  Mud, and chains, and stores, and an-
    chors,
  Tramped a squad of battered scare-
    crows —
  Poor old Dixie's bottom dollar!

"Some had shoes, but all had rifles,
  Them that was n't bald was beardless,
  And the drum was rolling 'Dixie,'
  And they stepped to it like men, sir!

"Rags and tatters, belts and bayonets,
  On they swung, the drum a-rolling,
  Mum and sour. It looked like fighting,
  And they meant it too, by thunder!"
            WILLIAM ERNEST HENLEY.

The excitement of the people mounted to
hysteria; there were those who advised that the
city be destroyed and that its inhabitants die
fighting on its ashes. But calmer counsel prevailed
and Charleston, on February 18, 1865, was sur-
rendered without resistance.

THE FOE AT THE GATES

[CHARLESTON, 1865]

RING round her! children of her glorious
    skies,
  Whom she hath nursed to stature proud and
    great;
Catch one last glance from her imploring
    eyes,
  Then close your ranks and face the threaten-
    ing fate.

Ring round her! with a wall of horrent steel
  Confront the foe, nor mercy ask nor give;
And in her hour of anguish let her feel
  That ye can die whom she has taught to
    live.

Ring round her! swear, by every lifted blade,
  To shield from wrong the mother who gave
      you birth;
That never violent hand on her be laid,
  Nor base foot desecrate her hallowed hearth.

Curst be the dastard who shall halt or doubt!
  And doubly damned who casts one look
      behind!
Ye who are men! with unsheathed sword, and
      shout,
  Up with her banner! give it to the wind!

Peal your wild slogan, echoing far and wide,
  Till every ringing avenue repeat
The gathering cry, and Ashley's angry tide
  Calls to the sea-waves beating round her
      feet.

Sons, to the rescue! spurred and belted, come!
  Kneeling, with clasp'd hands, she invokes
      you now
By the sweet memories of your childhood's
      home,
  By every manly hope and filial vow,

To save her proud soul from that loathèd
      thrall
  Which yet her spirit cannot brook to name;
Or, if her fate be near, and she must fall,
  Spare her — she sues — the agony and
      shame.

From all her fanes let solemn bells be tolled;
  Heap with kind hands her costly funeral
      pyre,
And thus, with pæan sung and anthem rolled,
  Give her unspotted to the God of Fire.

Gather around her sacred ashes then,
  Sprinkle the cherished dust with crimson
      rain,
Die! as becomes a race of free-born men,
  Who will not crouch to wear the bondman's
      chain.

So, dying, ye shall win a high renown,
  If not in life, at least by death, set free;
And send her fame through endless ages
      down —
  The last grand holocaust of Liberty.
              JOHN DICKSON BRUNS.

While Sherman was accomplishing his task in
this triumphant manner, Grant was hammering
away at Richmond. Late in February, 1864, a
strong force under Kilpatrick was detached to
raid around Richmond and if possible release the
Union prisoners at Belle Isle and in Libby prison.
They reached the outer fortifications, but were
repulsed, Major Ulric Dahlgren being among the
killed.

ULRIC DAHLGREN

[March 2, 1864]

A FLASH of light across the night,
  An eager face, an eye afire!
O lad so true, you yet may rue
  The courage of your deep desire!

"Nay, tempt me not; the way is plain —
''T is but the coward checks his rein;
        For there they lie,
        And there they cry,
For whose dear sake 't were joy to die!"

He bends unto his saddlebow,
  The steeds they follow two and two;
Their flanks are wet with foam and sweat,
  Their riders' locks are damp with dew.

"O comrades, haste! the way is long,
The dirge it drowns the battle-song;
        The hunger preys,
        The famine slays,
An awful horror veils our ways!"

Beneath the pall of prison wall
  The rush of hoofs they seem to hear;
From loathsome guise they lift their eyes,
  And beat their bars and bend their ear.

"Ah, God be thanked! our friends are
      nigh;
He wills it not that thus we die;
        O fiends accurst
        Of Want and Thirst,
Our comrades gather, — do your worst!"

A sharp affright runs through the night,
  An ambush stirred, a column reined;
The hurrying steed has checked his speed,
  His smoking flanks are crimson stained.

O noble son of noble sire,
Thine ears are deaf to our desire!
        O knightly grace
        Of valiant race,
The grave is honor's trysting-place!

O life so pure! O faith so sure!
O heart so brave, and true, and strong!
With tips of flame is writ your name,
　　In annaled deed and storied song!

It flares across the solemn night,
It glitters in the radiant light;
　　　A jewel set,
　　　Unnumbered yet,
In our Republic's coronet!
　　　KATE BROWNLEE SHERWOOD.

On May 1, 1864, a general advance was ordered, and two days later the Army of the Potomac, one hundred and thirty thousand strong, advanced into the Wilderness, south of the Rapidan. There, on May 5, Lee hurled his forces upon them. On the second day, Lee seized the colors of a Texas regiment and started to lead an assault in person. The men remonstrated and promised to carry the position if Lee would retire. The troops advanced shouting, "Lee to the rear!" and kept their word.

LEE TO THE REAR

[May 6, 1864]

DAWN of a pleasant morning in May
Broke through the Wilderness cool and gray;
While perched in the tallest tree-tops, the birds
Were carolling Mendelssohn's "Songs without
　　Words."

Far from the haunts of men remote,
The brook brawled on with a liquid note;
And Nature, all tranquil and lovely, wore
The smile of the spring, as in Eden of yore.

Little by little, as daylight increased,
And deepened the roseate flush in the East —
Little by little did morning reveal
Two long glittering lines of steel;

Where two hundred thousand bayonets gleam,
Tipped with the light of the earliest beam,
And the faces are sullen and grim to see
In the hostile armies of Grant and Lee.

All of a sudden, ere rose the sun,
Pealed on the silence the opening gun —
A little white puff of smoke there came,
And anon the valley was wreathed in flame.

Down on the left of the Rebel lines,
Where a breastwork stands in a copse of pines,
Before the Rebels their ranks can form,
The Yankees have carried the place by storm.

Stars and Stripes on the salient wave,
Where many a hero has found a grave,
And the gallant Confederates strive in vain
The ground they have drenched with their
　　blood, to regain.

Yet louder the thunder of battle roared —
Yet a deadlier fire on the columns poured;
Slaughter infernal rode with Despair,
Furies twain, through the murky air.

Not far off, in the saddle there sat
A gray-bearded man in a black slouched hat;
Not much moved by the fire was he,
Calm and resolute Robert Lee.

Quick and watchful he kept his eye
On the bold Rebel brigades close by, —
Reserves that were standing (and dying) at
　　ease,
While the tempest of wrath toppled over the
　　trees.

For still with their loud, deep, bull-dog bay,
The Yankee batteries blazed away,
And with every murderous second that sped
A dozen brave fellows, alas! fell dead.

The grand old graybeard rode to the space
Where Death and his victims stood face to
　　face,
And silently waved his old slouched hat —
A world of meaning there was in that!

"Follow me! Steady! We'll save the day!"
This was what he seemed to say;
And to the light of his glorious eye
The bold brigades thus made reply:

"We'll go forward, but you must go back" —
And they moved not an inch in the perilous
　　track:
"Go to the rear, and we'll send them to hell!"
And the sound of the battle was lost in their
　　yell.

Turning his bridle, Robert Lee
Rode to the rear. Like waves of the sea,
Bursting the dikes in their overflow,
Madly his veterans dashed on the foe.

And backward in terror that foe was driven,
Their banners rent and their columns riven,
Wherever the tide of battle rolled
Over the Wilderness, wood and wold.

Sunset out of a crimson sky
Streamed o'er a field of ruddier dye,
And the brook ran on with a purple stain,
From the blood of ten thousand foemen
    slain.

Seasons have passed since that day and year —
Again o'er its pebbles the brook runs clear,
And the field in a richer green is drest
Where the dead of a terrible conflict rest.

Hushed is the roll of the Rebel drum,
The sabres are sheathed, and the cannon are
    dumb;
And Fate, with his pitiless hand, has furled
The flag that once challenged the gaze of the
    world;

But the fame of the Wilderness fight abides;
And down into history grandly rides,
Calm and unmoved as in battle he sat,
The gray-bearded man in the black slouched
    hat.
              JOHN RANDOLPH THOMPSON.

For two weeks a frightful struggle raged. The
Union losses were fearful, but on May 11, 1864,
Grant wired to the Secretary of War, "I propose
to fight it out on this line, if it takes all summer."

CAN'T

How history repeats itself
    You'll say when you remember Grant,
Who, in his boyhood days, once sought
    Throughout the lexicon for "can't."

He could not find the word that day,
    The earnest boy whose name was Grant;
He never found it through long years,
    With all their power to disenchant.

No hostile host could give him pause;
    Rivers and mountains could not daunt;
He never found that hindering word —
    The steadfast man whose name was Grant.
              HARRIET PRESCOTT SPOFFORD.

Grant used his cavalry most effectively, and he
had a dashing leader in "Phil" Sheridan. Early in
May, 1864, Sheridan and a strong force was sent
on a raid around the Confederate lines, and on the
12th encountered General J. E. B. Stuart in force
at Yellow Tavern. A sharp engagement followed,
in which Stuart was killed.

OBSEQUIES OF STUART

[May 12, 1864]

WE could not pause, while yet the noontide air
    Shook with the cannonade's incessant peal-
        ing,
The funeral pageant fitly to prepare —
    A nation's grief revealing.

The smoke, above the glimmering woodland
    wide
    That skirts our southward border in its
        beauty,
Marked where our heroes stood and fought
    and died
    For love and faith and duty.

And still, what time the doubtful strife went
    on,
    We might not find expression for our
        sorrow;
We could but lay our dear dumb warrior down,
    And gird us for the morrow.

One weary year agone, when came a lull
    With victory in the conflict's stormy closes,
When the glad Spring, all flushed and beauti-
    ful,
    First mocked us with her roses,

With dirge and bell and minute-gun, we paid
    Some few poor rites — an inexpressive token
Of a great people's pain — to Jackson's shade,
    In agony unspoken.

No wailing trumpet and no tolling bell,
    No cannon, save the battle's boom receding,
When Stuart to the grave we bore, might tell,
    With hearts all crushed and bleeding.

The crisis suited not with pomp, and she
    Whose anguish bears the seal of consecra-
        tion
Had wished his Christian obsequies should be
    Thus void of ostentation.

Only the maidens came, sweet flowers to twine
    Above his form so still and cold and painless,
Whose deeds upon our brightest records shine,
    Whose life and sword were stainless.

They well remembered how he loved to dash
    Into the fight, festooned from summer
        bowers;

How like a fountain's spray his sabre's flash
  Leaped from a mass of flowers.

And so we carried to his place of rest
  All that of our great Paladin was mortal:
The cross, and not the sabre, on his breast,
  That opes the heavenly portal.

No more of tribute might to us remain;
  But there will still come a time when Free-
      dom's martyrs
A richer guerdon of renown shall gain
  Than gleams in stars and garters.

I hear from out that sunlit land which lies
  Beyond these clouds that gather darkly o'er
      us,
The happy sounds of industry arise
  In swelling peaceful chorus.

And mingling with these sounds, the glad ac-
      claim
  Of millions undisturbed by war's afflic-
      tions,
Crowning each martyr's never-dying name
  With grateful benedictions.

In some fair future garden of delights,
  Where flowers shall bloom and song-birds
      sweetly warble,
Art shall erect the statues of our knights
  In living bronze and marble.

And none of all that bright heroic throng
  Shall wear to far-off time a semblance
      grander,
Shall still be decked with fresher wreaths of
      song,
  Than this beloved commander.

The Spanish legend tells us of the Cid,
  That after death he rode, erect, sedately,
Along his lines, even as in life he did,
  In presence yet more stately;

And thus our Stuart, at this moment, seems
  To ride out of our dark and troubled story
Into the region of romance and dreams,
  A realm of light and glory;

And sometimes, when the silver bugles blow,
  That ghostly form, in battle reappearing,
Shall lead his horsemen headlong on the foe,
  In victory careering!
                JOHN RANDOLPH THOMPSON.

Grant was overwhelming the Confederates by
weight of numbers, and pushed slowly on. To
divert him, Lee threw a portion of his army into
the Shenandoah valley, and started again to invade
Maryland and Pennsylvania. A body of Union
troops contested their passage at Snicker's Ferry
and a sharp skirmish followed.

A CHRISTOPHER OF THE SHENANDOAH

ISLAND FORD, SNICKER'S GAP, JULY 18, 1864

TOLD BY THE ORDERLY

MUTE he sat in the saddle, — mute 'midst
    our full acclaim,
As three times over we gave to the mountain
    echo his name.
Then, "But I could n't do less!" in a murmur
    remonstrant came.

This was the deed his spirit set and his hand
    would not shun,
When the vale of the Shenandoah had lost the
    glow of the sun,
And the evening cloud and the battle smoke
    were blending in one.

Retreating and ever retreating, the bank of
    the river we gained,
Hope of the field was none, and choice but
    of flight remained,
When there at the brink of the ford his horse
    he suddenly reined.

For his vigilant eye had marked where, close
    by the oozy marge,
Half-parted its moorings, there lay a battered
    and oarless barge.
"Quick! gather the wounded in!" and the
    flying stayed at his charge.

They gathered the wounded in whence they
    fell by the river-bank,
Lapped on the gleaming sand, or aswoon, 'mid
    the rushes dank;
And they crowded the barge till its sides low
    down in the water sank.

The river was wide, was deep, and heady the
    current flowed,
A burdened and oarless craft! — straight into
    the stream he rode
By the side of the barge, and drew it along
    with its moaning load.

A moaning and ghastly load — the wounded
— the dying — the dead!
For ever upon their traces followed the whist-
ling lead,
Our bravest the mark, yet unscathed and un-
daunted, he pushed ahead.

Alone? Save for one that from love of his
leader or soldierly pride
(Hearing his call for aid, and seeing that none
replied),
Plunged and swam by the crazy craft on the
other side.

But Heaven! what weary toil! for the river is
wide, is deep;
The current is swift, and the bank on the fur-
ther side is steep.
'T is reached at last, and a hundred of ours
to the rescue leap.

Oh, they cheered as he rose from the stream
and the water-drops flowed away!
"But I could n't do less!" in the silence that
followed we heard him say;
Then the wounded cheered, and the swoon-
ing awoke in the barge where they
lay.

And I? — Ah, well, I swam by the barge on
the other side;
But an orderly goes wherever his leader
chooses to ride.
Come life or come death I could n't do less
than follow his guide.
                    EDITH M. THOMAS.

The Confederate cavalry pushed on toward the
Susquehanna, sacked Chambersburg, and filled all
western Pennsylvania with panic. Grant at once
got together a large force to repel this invasion,
and placed it under command of General Sheridan.
On September 19, 1864, the Confederates attacked
his troops at Winchester, but Sheridan beat them
off and punished them so severely that he supposed
they had enough. With that impression, he went
to Washington on official business, leaving his men
strongly posted on Cedar Creek. There, on the
morning of October 19, the Confederates attacked
them, front, flank, and rear.

SHERIDAN AT CEDAR CREEK

[October 19, 1864]

SHOE the steed with silver
  That bore him to the fray,

When he heard the guns at dawning —
  Miles away;
When he heard them calling, calling —
  Mount! nor stay:
    Quick, or all is lost;
    They've surprised and stormed the post,
  They push your routed host —
Gallop! retrieve the day.

House the horse in ermine —
  For the foam-flake blew
White through the red October;
  He thundered into view;
They cheered him in the looming,
  Horseman and horse they knew.
    The turn of the tide began,
    The rally of bugles ran,
  He swung his hat in the van;
The electric hoof-spark flew.

Wreathe the steed and lead him —
  For the charge he led
Touched and turned the cypress
  Into amaranths for the head
Of Philip, king of riders,
  Who raised them from the dead.
    The camp (at dawning lost)
    By eve, recovered — forced,
  Rang with laughter of the host
As belated Early fled.

Shroud the horse in sable —
  For the mounds they heap!
There is firing in the Valley,
  And yet no strife they keep;
It is the parting volley,
  It is the pathos deep.
    There is glory for the brave
    Who lead, and nobly save,
  But no knowledge in the grave
Where the nameless followers sleep.
                    HERMAN MELVILLE.

Sheridan, returning from Washington, had slept
at Winchester the night of October 18, 1864, and
early next morning heard the sounds of the battle.
He mounted his horse and started for the field;
reached there just in time to rally his retreating
troops, turned a defeat into a decisive victory, and
drove the invaders pell-mell back to Virginia.

SHERIDAN'S RIDE

[October 19. 1864]

UP from the South, at break of day
Bringing to Winchester fresh dismay

The affrighted air with a shudder bore,
Like a herald in haste to the chieftain's door,
The terrible grumble, and rumble, and roar,
Telling the battle was on once more,
      And Sheridan twenty miles away.

And wider still those billows of war
Thundered along the horizon's bar;
And louder yet into Winchester rolled
The roar of that red sea uncontrolled,
Making the blood of the listener cold,
As he thought of the stake in that fiery fray,
      With Sheridan twenty miles away.

But there is a road from Winchester town,
A good, broad highway leading down:
And there, through the flush of the morning
      light,
A steed as black as the steeds of night
Was seen to pass, as with eagle flight;
As if he knew the terrible need,
He stretched away with his utmost speed.
Hills rose and fell, but his heart was gay,
      With Sheridan fifteen miles away.

Still sprang from those swift hoofs, thunder-
      ing south,
The dust like smoke from the cannon's mouth,
Or the trail of a comet, sweeping faster and
      faster,
Foreboding to traitors the doom of disaster.
The heart of the steed and the heart of the
      master
Were beating like prisoners assaulting their
      walls,
Impatient to be where the battle-field calls;
Every nerve of the charger was strained to full
      play,
      With Sheridan only ten miles away.

Under his spurning feet, the road
Like an arrowy Alpine river flowed,
And the landscape sped away behind
Like an ocean flying before the wind;
And the steed, like a bark fed with furnace ire,
Swept on, with his wild eye full of fire;
But, lo! he is nearing his heart's desire;
He is snuffing the smoke of the roaring fray,
      With Sheridan only five miles away.

The first that the general saw were the groups
Of stragglers, and then the retreating troops;
What was done? what to do? a glance told him
      both.
Then striking his spurs with a terrible oath,

He dashed down the line, 'mid a storm of
      huzzas,
And the wave of retreat checked its course
      there, because
The sight of the master compelled it to
      pause.
With foam and with dust the black charger
      was gray;
By the flash of his eye, and the red nostril's
      play,
He seemed to the whole great army to say:
" I have brought you Sheridan all the way
      From Winchester down to save the day."

Hurrah! hurrah for Sheridan!
Hurrah! hurrah for horse and man!
And when their statues are placed on high
Under the dome of the Union sky,
The American soldier's Temple of Fame,
There, with the glorious general's name,
Be it said, in letters both bold and bright:
" Here is the steed that saved the day
By carrying Sheridan into the fight,
      From Winchester — twenty miles away!"
                    THOMAS BUCHANAN READ.

Grant, meanwhile, steadily tightened his grip
on Richmond, and Lee at last perceived that to
hold the capital longer would be to sacrifice his
army. He withdrew during the night of April 2,
1865, and the Union troops entered the city un-
opposed next day.

THE YEAR OF JUBILEE

[Sung by the negro troops as they entered Rich
      mond]

SAY, darkeys, hab you seen de massa,
      Wid de muffstash on he face,
Go long de road some time dis mornin',
      Like he gwine leaoe de place?
He see de smoke way up de ribber
      Whar de Lincum gunboats lay;
He took he hat an' leff berry sudden,
      And I spose he's runned away.
            De massa run, ha, ha!
            De darkey stay, ho, ho!
            It mus' be now de kingdum comin',
            An' de yar ob jubilo.

He six foot one way an' two foot todder,
      An' he weigh six hundred poun';
His coat so big he could n't pay de tailor,
      An' it won't reach half way roun';

He drill so much dey calls him cap'n,
  An' he git so mighty tanned,
I spec he'll try to fool dem Yankees,
  For to tink he contraband.
    De massa run, ha, ha!
    De darkey stay, ho, ho!
    It mus' be now de kingdum comin',
    An' de yar ob jubilo.

De darkeys got so lonesome libb'n
  In de log hut on de lawn,
Dey moved dere tings into massa's parlor
  For to keep it while he gone.
Dar's wine an' cider in de kitchin,
  An' de darkeys dey hab some,
I spec it will be all fiscated,
  When de Lincum sojers come.
    De massa run, ha, ha!
    De darkey stay, ho, ho!
    It mus' be now de kingdum comin',
    An' de yar ob jubilo.

De oberseer he makes us trubble,
  An' he dribe us roun' a spell,
We lock him up in de smoke-house cellar,
  Wid de key flung in de well.
De whip am lost, de han'-cuff broke,
  But de massy hab his pay;
He big an' ole enough for to know better
  Dan to went an' run away.
    De massa run, ha, ha!
    De darkey stay, ho, ho!
    It mus' be now de kingdum comin',
    An' de yar ob jubilo.
          HENRY CLAY WORK.

VIRGINIA CAPTA

APRIL, 1865

UNCONQUER'D captive! — close thine eye,
  And draw the ashen sackcloth o'er,
  And in thy speechless woe deplore
The fate that would not let thee die!

The arm that wore the shield, strip bare;
  The hand that held the martial rein,
  And hurled the spear on many a plain, —
Stretch — till they clasp the shackles there!

The foot that once could crush the crown,
  Must drag the fetters, till it bleed
  Beneath their weight : — thou dost not need
It now, to tread the tyrant down.

Thou thought'st him vanquished — boastful trust! —
  His lance, in twain — his sword, a wreck,—
  But with his heel upon thy neck,
He holds *thee* prostrate in the dust!

Bend though thou must, beneath his will,
  Let not one abject moan have place;
  But with majestic, silent grace,
Maintain thy regal bearing still.

Look back through all thy storied past,
  And sit erect in conscious pride:
  No grander heroes ever died —
No sterner, battled to the last!

Weep, if thou wilt, with proud, sad mien,
  Thy blasted hopes — thy peace undone, —
  Yet brave, live on, — nor seek to shun
Thy fate, like Egypt's conquer'd Queen.

Though forced a captive's place to fill
  In the triumphal train, — yet there,
  Superbly, like Zenobia, wear
Thy chains, — *Virginia Victrix* still!
          MARGARET JUNKIN PRESTON.

Tidings of the fall of Richmond went over the North with lightning speed, and in every city, every town and hamlet, public demonstrations were held.

THE FALL OF RICHMOND

THE TIDINGS RECEIVED IN THE NORTHERN METROPOLIF (APRIL, 1865)

WHAT mean these peals from every tower,
  And crowds like seas that sway?
The cannon reply; they speak the heart
  Of the People impassioned, and say —
A city in flags for a city in flames,
  Richmond goes Babylon's way —
    Sing and pray.

O weary years and woeful wars,
  And armies in the grave;
But hearts unquelled at last deter
  The helmed dilated Lucifer —
Honor to Grant the brave,
Whose three stars now like Orion's rise
  When wreck is on the wave —
    Bless his glaive.

Well that the faith we firmly kept,
  And never our aim forswore
For the Terrors that trooped from each recess
When fainting we fought in the Wilderness,
  And Hell made loud hurrah;
But God is in Heaven, and Grant in the Town,
  And Right through Might is Law —
    God's way adore.
                    HERMAN MELVILLE.

Lee, meanwhile, was trying desperately to escape the force which Grant had sent in pursuit of him. His army was dreadfully shattered and without supplies; his horses were too weak to draw the cannon; and he soon found himself surrounded by a vastly superior force. To fight would have been folly; instead, he sent forward a white flag, and surrendered at two o'clock on the afternoon of Palm Sunday, April 9, 1865.

THE SURRENDER AT APPOMATTOX

[April 9, 1865]

As billows upon billows roll,
  On victory victory breaks;
Ere yet seven days from Richmond's fall
  And crowning triumph wakes
The loud joy-gun, whose thunders run
  By sea-shore, streams, and lakes.
    The hope and great event agree
      In the sword that Grant received from
        Lee.

The warring eagles fold the wing,
  But not in Cæsar's sway;
Not Rome o'ercome by Roman arms we sing,
  As on Pharsalia's day,
But Treason thrown, though a giant grown,
  And Freedom's larger play.
    All human tribes glad token see
      In the close of the wars of Grant and
        Lee.
                    HERMAN MELVILLE.

Grant was generous with the fallen enemy; too generous, some of the patriot politicians thought, in releasing Lee and his officers on parole; but Grant insisted that the terms he had given be carried out to the letter.

LEE'S PAROLE

"WELL, General Grant, have you heard the
    news?
How the orders are issued and ready to send

For Lee, and the men in his staff-command,
    To be under arrest, — now the war's at an
      end?"

"How so? Arrested for what?" he cried.
  "Oh, for trial as traitors, to be shot, or
    hung."
The chief's eye flashed with a sudden ire,
  And his face grew crimson as up he sprung.
"Orderly, fetch me my horse," he said.
  Then into the saddle and up the street,
As if the battle were raging ahead,
  Went the crash of the old war-charger's feet.

"What is this I am told about Lee's arrest, —
    Is it true?" — and the keen eyes searched
      his soul.
"It *is* true, and the order will be enforced!"
    "*My* word was given in their parole
At Richmond, and that parole
  Has not been broken, — nor has my word,
Nor *will* be until there is better cause
  For breaking than this I have lately heard."

"Do you know, sir, whom you have thus
    addressed?
  I am the War Department's head —"
"And I — am General Grant!
    At your peril order arrests!" he said.

.   .   .   .

A friend is a friend, as we reckon worth,
    Who will throw the gauntlet in friendship's
      fight;
But a man is a man in peace or war
    Who will stake his all for an enemy's right.
'T was a hard-fought battle, but quickly
    won, —
  As a fight must be when 't is soul to soul, —
And 't was years ago; but that honored word
    Preserved the North in the South's parole.
                    MARION MANVILLE.

In disbanding his army, Lee issued a farewell address, copies of which are still treasured in many a Southern home. Even in the North, he has come to be recognized as the great general and true gentleman he really was.

ROBERT E. LEE

A GALLANT foeman in the fight,
  A brother when the fight was o'er,
The hand that led the host with might
  The blessed torch of learning bore.

No shriek of shells nor roll of drums,
  No challenge fierce, resounding far,
When reconciling Wisdom comes
  To heal the cruel wounds of war.

Thought may the minds of men divide,
Love makes the heart of nations one,
And so, thy soldier grave beside,
  We honor thee, Virginia's son.
                        JULIA WARD HOWE.

CHAPTER XI

WINSLOW AND FARRAGUT

During the Civil War, the Confederates commissioned a large number of privateers to prey upon Northern commerce, the most famous of which was the Alabama, commanded by Raphael Semmes. Semmes had orders to sink, burn, and destroy everything flying the Stars and Stripes, and carried them out in the most thorough-going way. On June 11, 1864, the Alabama entered the harbor of Cherbourg, France. Three days later, the United States sloop-of-war Kearsarge, Captain John A. Winslow, appeared in the offing, and both ships prepared for battle. The Alabama steamed out of the harbor on the morning of Sunday, June 19, and was soon reduced to a wreck by the deadly fire from the Kearsarge. She sank while trying to run inshore.

THE EAGLE AND VULTURE

[June, 1864]

IN Cherbourg Roads the pirate lay
One morn in June, like a beast at bay,
Feeling secure in the neutral port,
Under the guns of the Frenchman's fort;
A thieving vulture; a coward thing;
Sheltered beneath a despot's wing.

But there outside, in the calm blue bay,
Our ocean-eagle, the Kearsarge, lay;
Lay at her ease on the Sunday morn,
Holding the Corsair ship in scorn;
With captain and crew in the might of their
    right,
Willing to pray, but more eager to fight.

Four bells are struck, and this thing of night,
Like a panther, crouching with fierce affright,
Must leap from his cover, and, come what
    may,
Must fight for his life, or steal away!
So, out of the port with his braggart air,
With flaunting flags, sailed the proud Corsair.

The Cherbourg cliffs were all alive
With lookers-on, like a swarming hive;

While compelled to do what he dared not
    shirk,
The pirate went to his desperate work;
And Europe's tyrants looked on in glee,
As they thought of our Kearsarge sunk in the
    sea.

But our little bark smiled back at them
A smile of contempt, with that Union gem,
The American banner, far floating and free,
Proclaiming her champions were out on the
    sea;
Were out on the sea, and abroad on the
    land,
Determined to win under God's command.

Down came the vulture; our eagle sat still,
Waiting to strike with her iron-clad bill;
Convinced by the glow of his glorious cause,
He could crumple his foe in the grasp of his
    claws.

"Clear the decks," then said Winslow, words
    measured and slow;
"Point the guns, and prepare for the terrible
    blow;
And whatever the fate to ourselves may be,
We will sink in the ocean this pest of the
    sea."

The decks were all cleared, and the guns were
    all manned,
Awaiting to meet this Atlantic brigand;
When, lo! roared a broadside; the ship of the
    thief
Was torn, and wept blood in that moment of
    grief.

Another! another! another! And still
The broadsides went in with a hearty good
    will,
Till the pirate reeled wildly, as staggering and
    drunk,
And down to his own native regions he sunk.

Down, down, forty fathoms beneath the blue
    wave,
And the hopes of old Europe lie in the same
    grave;
While Freedom, more firm, stands upon her
    own sod,
And for heroes like Winslow is shouting,
    "Thank God!"
        THOMAS BUCHANAN READ.

KEARSARGE AND ALABAMA

[June 19, 1864]

IT was early Sunday morning, in the year of
    sixty-four,
The Alabama she steam'd out along the
    Frenchman's shore.
    Long time she cruised about,
    Long time she held her sway,
But now beneath the Frenchman's shore she
    lies off Cherbourg Bay.
    Hoist up the flag, and long may it wave
    Over the Union, the home of the brave.
    Hoist up the flag, and long may it wave,
    God bless America, the home of the
        brave!

The Yankee cruiser hove in view, the Kear-
    sarge was her name,
It ought to be engraved in full upon the scroll
    of fame;
    Her timbers made of Yankee oak,
    And her crew of Yankee tars.
And o'er her mizzen peak she floats the glo-
    rious stripes and stars.

A challenge unto Captain Semmes, bold Win-
    slow he did send!
"Bring on your Alabama, and to her we will
    attend,
    For we think your boasting privateer
    Is not so hard to whip;
And we'll show you that the Kearsarge is not
    a merchant ship."

It was early Sunday morning, in the year of
    sixty-four,
The Alabama she stood out and cannons loud
    did roar;
The Kearsarge stood undaunted, and quickly
    she replied
And let a Yankee 'leven-inch shell go tearing
    through her side.

The Kearsarge then she wore around and
    broadside on did bear,
With shot and shell and right good-will, her
    timbers she did tear;
When they found that they were sinking,
    down came the stars and bars,
For the rebel gunners could not stand the
    glorious stripes and stars.

The Alabama she is gone, she'll cruise the
    seas no more,
She met the fate she well deserved along the
    Frenchman's shore;
Then here is luck to the Kearsarge, we know
    what she can do,
Likewise to Captain Winslow and his brave
    and gallant crew.
    Hoist up the flag, and long may it wave
    Over the Union, the home of the brave!
    Hoist up the flag, and long may it wave,
    God bless America, the home of the brave!

KEARSARGE

[June 19, 1864]

SUNDAY in Old England:
    In gray churches everywhere
The calm of low responses,
    The sacred hush of prayer.

Sunday in Old England;
    And summer winds that went
O'er the pleasant fields of Sussex,
    The garden lands of Kent,

Stole into dim church windows
    And passed the oaken door,
And fluttered open prayer-books
    With the cannon's awful roar.

Sunday in New England:
    Upon a mountain gray
The wind-bent pines are swaying
    Like giants at their play;

Across the barren lowlands,
    Where men find scanty food,
The north wind brings its vigor
    To homesteads plain and rude.

Ho, land of pine and granite!
    Ho, hardy northland breeze!
Well have you trained the manhood
    That shook the Channel seas,

When o'er those storied waters
  The iron war-bolts flew,
And through Old England's churches
  The summer breezes blew;

While in our other England
  Stirred one gaunt rocky steep,
When rode her sons as victors,
  Lords of the lonely deep.
              S. WEIR MITCHELL.
LONDON, July 20, 1864.

THE ALABAMA

SHE has gone to the bottom! the wrath of the
    tide
  Now breaks in vain insolence o'er her;
No more the rough seas like a queen shall she
    ride,
  While the foe flies in terror before her!

Now captive or exiled, or silent in death,
  The forms that so bravely did man her;
Her deck is untrod, and the gale's stirring
    breath
  Flouts no more the red cross of her banner!

She is down 'neath the waters, but still her
    bright name
  Is in death, as in life, ever glorious,
And a sceptre all barren the conqueror must
    claim,
  Though he boasts the proud title "Vic-
    torious."

Her country's lone champion, she shunned
    not the fight,
  Though unequal in strength, bold and fear-
    less;
And proved in her fate, though not matchless
    in might,
  In daring at least she was peerless.

No trophy hung high in the foe's hated hall
  Shall speak of her final disaster,
Nor tell of the danger that could not appall,
  Nor the spirit that nothing could master!

The death-shot has sped — she has grimly
    gone down,
  But left her destroyer no token,
And the mythical wand of her mystic re-
    nown,
  Though the waters o'erwhelm, is unbroken.

For lo! ere she settles beneath the dark
    wave
  On her enemies' cheeks spreads a pallor,
As another deck summons the swords of the
    brave
  To gild a new name with their valor.

Her phantom will yet haunt the wild roaring
    breeze,
  Causing foemen to start and to shudder,
While their commerce still steals like a thief
    o'er the seas,
  And trembles from bowsprit to rudder.

The spirit that shed on the wave's gleaming
    crest
  The light of a legend romantic
Shall live while a sail flutters over the breast
  Of thy far-bounding billows, Atlantic!

And as long as one swift keel the strong surges
    stems,
  Or "poor Jack" loves his song and his
    story,
Shall shine in tradition the valor of Semmes
  And the brave ship that bore him to glory!
                        MAURICE BELL.

Mobile and Wilmington were the only important
Confederate ports still open, and early in August,
1864, Admiral Farragut appeared off Mobile with
a fleet of eighteen vessels. The entrance to the har-
bor was strongly defended by forts on both sides,
but Farragut determined to run past them. On
August 5 the fleet advanced, but the Tecumseh,
leading the fleet, struck a torpedo and sank in-
stantly, carrying down nearly all her crew, includ-
ing T. A. M. Craven, her commander, who drew
aside from the ladder that the pilot might pass
first.

CRAVEN

[August 5, 1864]

OVER the turret, shut in his ironclad tower,
  Craven was conning his ship through smoke
    and flame;
Gun to gun he had battered the fort for an
    hour,
  Now was the time for a charge to end the
    game.

There lay the narrowing channel, smooth and
    grim,
  A hundred deaths beneath it, and never a
    sign;

There lay the enemy's ships, and sink or
swim
The flag was flying, and he was head of the
line.

The fleet behind was jamming: the monitor
hung
Beating the stream; the roar for a moment
hushed;
Craven spoke to the pilot; slow she swung;
Again he spoke, and right for the foe she
rushed

Into the narrowing channel, between the shore
And the sunk torpedoes lying in treacherous
rank;
She turned but a yard too short; a muffled
roar,
A mountainous wave, and she rolled,
righted, and sank.

Over the manhole, up in the ironclad tower,
Pilot and captain met as they turned to fly:
The hundredth part of a moment seemed an
hour,
For one could pass to be saved, and one
must die.

They stood like men in a dream; Craven
spoke, —
Spoke as he lived and fought, with a cap-
tain's pride:
"After you, Pilot." The pilot woke,
Down the ladder he went, and Craven died.

All men praise the deed and the manner; but
we —
We set it apart from the pride that stoops
to the proud,
The strength that is supple to serve the strong
and free,
The grace of the empty hands and pro-
mises loud;

Sidney thirsting a humbler need to slake,
Nelson waiting his turn for the surgeon's
hand,
Lucas crushed with chains for a comrade's
sake,
Outram coveting right before command,

These were paladins, these were Craven's
peers,
These with him shall be crowned in story
and song,

Crowned with the glitter of steel and the glim-
mer of tears,
Princes of courtesy, merciful, proud, and
strong.

HENRY NEWBOLT.

Farragut, who had lashed himself to the shrouds
of his flagship, the Hartford, observed the Brook-
lyn, which preceded him, recoil as the Tecumseh
sank. "What's the trouble?" he signalled. "Tor-
pedoes!" answered the Brooklyn. "Damn the
torpedoes!" shouted Farragut. "Go ahead, Cap-
tain Drayton! Four bells!" and the Hartford
cleared the Brooklyn and took the lead.

FARRAGUT

(MOBILE BAY, August 5, 1864)

FARRAGUT, Farragut,
Old Heart of Oak,
Daring Dave Farragut,
Thunderbolt stroke,
Watches the hoary mist
Lift from the bay,
Till his flag, glory-kissed,
Greets the young day.

Far, by gray Morgan's walls,
Looms the black fleet.
Hark, deck to rampart calls
With the drums' beat!
Buoy your chains overboard,
While the steam hums;
Men! to the battlement,
Farragut comes.

See, as the hurricane
Hurtles in wrath
Squadrons of clouds amain
Back from its path!
Back to the parapet,
To the guns' lips,
Thunderbolt Farragut
Hurls the black ships.

Now through the battle's roar
Clear the boy sings,
"By the mark fathoms four,"
While his lead swings.
Steady the wheelmen five
"Nor' by East keep her,"
"Steady," but two alive:
How the shells sweep her!

Lashed to the mast that sways
   Over red decks,
Over the flame that plays
   Round the torn wrecks,
Over the dying lips
   Framed for a cheer,
Farragut leads his ships,
   Guides the line clear.

On by heights cannon-browed,
   While the spars quiver;
Onward still flames the cloud
   Where the hulks shiver.
See, yon fort's star is set,
   Storm and fire past.
Cheer him, lads — Farragut,
   Lashed to the mast!

Oh! while Atlantic's breast
   Bears a white sail,
While the Gulf's towering crest
   Tops a green vale,
Men thy bold deeds shall tell,
   Old Heart of Oak,
Daring Dave Farragut,
   Thunderbolt stroke!
      WILLIAM TUCKEY MEREDITH.

On went the flagship across the line of torpe-
does, but not one of them exploded, and a mo-
ment later one of the most daring feats in the
naval history of the world had been safely ac-
complished. The line of battle was reformed, the
forts and Confederate fleet savagely attacked, and
by nine o'clock the Union fleet was in the bay.

THROUGH FIRE IN MOBILE BAY

[August 5, 1864]

I'D weave a wreath for those who fought
   In blue upon the waves,
I drop a tear for all who sleep
   Down in the coral caves,
And proudly do I touch my cap
   Whene'er I meet to-day
A man who sail'd with Farragut
   Thro' fire in Mobile Bay.

Oh, what a gallant sight it was
   As toward the foe we bore!
Lashed to the mast, unflinching, stood
   Our grand old Commodore.
I see him now above the deck,
   Though time has cleared away
The battle smoke that densely hung
   Above old Mobile Bay.

Torpedoes to the right and left,
   Torpedoes straight ahead!
The stanch Tecumseh sinks from sight,
   The waves receive her dead.
But on we press, thro' lead and iron,
   On, on with pennons gay,
Whilst glory holds her wreath above
   Immortal Mobile Bay.

The rebel forts belch fire and death,
   But what care we for them?
Our onward course, with Farragut
   To guide us, nought can stem.
The Hartford works her dreaded guns,
   The Brooklyn pounds away,
And proudly flies the flag of stars
   Aloft o'er Mobile Bay.

Behold yon moving mass of iron
   Beyond the Ossipee;
To fight the fleet with courage grim
   Steams forth the Tennessee.
We hem her in with battle fire —
   How furious grows the fray,
Until Surrender's flag she flies
   Above red Mobile Bay.

We count our dead, we count our scars,
   The proudest ever won;
We cheer the flag that gayly flies
   Victorious in the sun.
No longer in the rigging stands
   The hero of the day,
For he has linked his name fore'er
   To deathless Mobile Bay.

Thus I would weave a wreath for all
   Who fought with us that time,
And I'd embalm that glorious day
   Forevermore in rhyme.
The stars above will rise and set,
   The years will pass away,
But brighter all the time shall grow
   The fame of Mobile Bay.

He sleeps, the bluff old Commodore
   Who led with hearty will;
But ah! methinks I see him now,
   Lashed to the rigging still.
I know that just beyond the tide,
   In God's own glorious day,
He waits to greet the gallant tars
   Who fought in Mobile Bay.

The ships were brought to anchor and breakfast was being served, when the great Confederate ram, Tennessee, was seen advancing at full speed, to attack the whole fleet. A terrific struggle followed, in which nearly every one of the Union ships was badly damaged; but the Tennessee at last became unmanageable and was forced to surrender. The task of reducing the forts remained. This was completed in a few days and the port of Mobile was effectually closed.

THE BAY FIGHT

(MOBILE HARBOR, August 5, 1864)

THREE days through sapphire seas we sailed,
  The steady Trade blew strong and free,
The Northern Light his banners paled,
  The Ocean Stream our channels wet,
We rounded low Canaveral's lee,
And passed the isles of emerald set
  In blue Bahama's turquoise sea.

By reef and shoal obscurely mapped,
  The hauntings of the gray sea-wolf,
The palmy Western Key lay lapped
  In the warm washing of the Gulf.

But weary to the hearts of all
  The burning glare, the barren reach
Of Santa Rosa's withered beach,
And Pensacola's ruined wall.

And weary was the long patrol,
  The thousand miles of shapeless strand,
From Brazos to San Blas that roll
  Their drifting dunes of desert sand.

Yet coastwise as we cruised or lay,
  The land-breeze still at nightfall bore,
By beach and fortress-guarded bay,
  Sweet odors from the enemy's shore,

Fresh from the forest solitudes,
  Unchallenged of his sentry lines, —
The bursting of his cypress buds,
  And the warm fragrance of his pines.

Ah, never braver bark and crew,
  Nor bolder Flag a foe to dare,
Had left a wake on ocean blue
  Since Lion-Heart sailed Trenc-le-mer!

But little gain by that dark ground
  Was ours, save, sometime, freer breath
For friend or brother strangely found,
  'Scaped from the drear domain of death.

And little venture for the bold,
  Or laurel for our valiant Chief,
  Save some blockaded British thief,
Full fraught with murder in his hold,

Caught unawares at ebb or flood,
  Or dull bombardment, day by day,
  With fort and earthwork, far away,
Low couched in sullen leagues of mud.

A weary time, — but to the strong
  The day at last, as ever, came;
And the volcano, laid so long,
  Leaped forth in thunder and in flame!

"*Man your starboard battery!*"
  Kimberly shouted; —
The ship, with her hearts of oak,
Was going, 'mid roar and smoke,
On to victory;
None of us doubted,
No, not our dying —
Farragut's Flag was flying!

Gaines growled low on our left,
Morgan roared on our right;
Before us, gloomy and fell,
With breath like the fume of hell,
Lay the dragon of iron shell,
Driven at last to the fight!

Ha, old ship! do they thrill,
The brave two hundred scars
You got in the River-Wars?
That were leeched with clamorous skill
(Surgery savage and hard),
Splinted with bolt and beam,
Probed in scarfing and seam,
Rudely linted and tarred
With oakum and boiling pitch,
And sutured with splice and hitch,
At the Brooklyn Navy Yard!

Our lofty spars were down,
To bide the battle's frown
(Wont of old renown) —
But every ship was drest
In her bravest and her best,
As if for a July day;
Sixty flags and three,
As we floated up the bay —
At every peak and mast-head flew
The brave Red, White, and Blue, —
We were eighteen ships that day.

With hawsers strong and taut,
The weaker lashed to port,
On we sailed two by two —
That if either a bolt should feel
Crash through caldron or wheel,
Fin of bronze, or sinew of steel,
Her mate might bear her through.

Forging boldly ahead,
The great Flag-Ship led,
Grandest of sights!
On her lofty mizzen flew
Our leader's dauntless Blue,
That had waved o'er twenty fights.
So we went with the first of the tide,
Slowly, 'mid the roar
Of the rebel guns ashore
And the thunder of each full broadside.

Ah, how poor the prate
Of statute and state
We once held these fellows!
Here on the flood's pale green,
Hark how he bellows,
Each bluff old Sea-Lawyer!
Talk to them, Dahlgren,
Parrott, and Sawyer!

On, in the whirling shade
Of the cannon's sulphury breath,
We drew to the Line of Death
That our devilish Foe had laid, —
Meshed in a horrible net,
And baited villainous well,
Right in our path were set
Three hundred traps of hell!

And there, O sight forlorn!
There, while the cannon
Hurtled and thundered
(Ah, what ill raven
Flapped o'er the ship that morn!), —
Caught by the under-death,
In the drawing of a breath
Down went dauntless Craven,
He and his hundred!

A moment we saw her turret,
A little heel she gave,
And a thin white spray went o'er her,
Like the crest of a breaking wave; —
In that great iron coffin,
The channel for their grave,
The fort their monument
(Seen afar in the offing),

Ten fathom deep lie Craven
And the bravest of our brave.

Then in that deadly track
A little the ships held back,
Closing up in their stations; —
There are minutes that fix the fate
Of battles and of nations
(Christening the generations),
When valor were all too late,
If a moment's doubt be harbored; —
From the main-top, bold and brief,
Came the word of our grand old chief:
"Go on!" — 't was all he said, —
Our helm was put to starboard,
And the Hartford passed ahead.

Ahead lay the Tennessee,
On our starboard bow he lay,
With his mail-clad consorts three
(The rest had run up the bay);
There he was, belching flame from his bow,
And the steam from his throat's abyss
Was a Dragon's maddened hiss;
In sooth a most cursed craft! —
In a sullen ring, at bay,
By the Middle-Ground they lay,
Raking us fore and aft.

Trust me, our berth was hot,
Ah, wickedly well they shot —
How their death-bolts howled and stung!
And the water-batteries played
With their deadly cannonade
Till the air around us rung;
So the battle raged and roared; —
Ah, had you been aboard
To have seen the fight we made!
How they leapt, the tongues of flame,
From the cannon's fiery lip!
How the broadsides, deck and frame,
Shook the great ship!

And how the enemy's shell
Came crashing, heavy and oft,
Clouds of splinters flying aloft
And falling in oaken showers; —
But ah, the pluck of the crew!
Had you stood on that deck of ours,
You had seen what men may do.

Still, as the fray grew louder,
Boldly they worked and well —
Steadily came the powder,
Steadily came the shell.

And if tackle or truck found hurt,
Quickly they cleared the wreck —
And the dead were laid to port,
All a-row, on our deck.

Never a nerve that failed,
Never a cheek that paled,
Not a tinge of gloom or pallor; —
There was bold Kentucky's grit,
And the old Virginian valor,
And the daring Yankee wit.
There were blue eyes from turfy Shannon,
There were black orbs from palmy
    Niger, —
But there alongside the cannon,
Each man fought like a tiger!

A little, once, it looked ill,
Our consort began to burn —
They quenched the flames with a will,
But our men were falling still,
And still the fleet were astern.

Right abreast of the Fort
In an awful shroud they lay,
Broadsides thundering away,
And lightning from every port;
Scene of glory and dread!
A storm-cloud all aglow
With flashes of fiery red,
The thunder raging below,
And the forest of flags o'erhead!

So grand the hurly and roar,
So fiercely their broadsides blazed,
The regiments fighting ashore
Forgot to fire as they gazed.

There, to silence the foe,
Moving grimly and slow,
They loomed in that deadly wreath,
Where the darkest batteries frowned, —
Death in the air all round,
And the black torpedoes beneath!

And now, as we looked ahead,
All for'ard, the long white deck
Was growing a strange dull red, —
But soon, as once and again
Fore and aft we sped
(The firing to guide or check),
You could hardly choose but tread
On the ghastly human wreck
(Dreadful gobbet and shred
That a minute ago were men!),

Red, from mainmast to bitts!
Red, on bulwark and wale,
Red, by combing and hatch,
Red, o'er netting and vail!

And ever, with steady con,
The ship forged slowly by, —
And ever the crew fought on,
And their cheers rang loud and high.

Grand was the sight to see
How by their guns they stood,
Right in front of our dead,
Fighting square abreast —
Each brawny arm and chest
All spotted with black and red,
Chrism of fire and blood!

Worth our watch, dull and sterile,
Worth all the weary time,
Worth the woe and the peril,
To stand in that strait sublime!

Fear? A forgotten form!
Death? A dream of the eyes!
We were atoms in God's great storm
That roared through the angry skies.

One only doubt was ours,
One only dread we knew, —
Could the day that dawned so well
Go down for the Darker Powers?
Would the fleet get through?
And ever the shot and shell
Came with the howl of hell,
The splinter-clouds rose and fell,
And the long line of corpses grew, —
Would the fleet win through?

They are men that never will fail
(How aforetime they've fought!),
But Murder may yet prevail, —
They may sink as Craven sank.
Therewith one hard fierce thought,
Burning on heart and lip,
Ran like fire through the ship;
Fight her, to the last plank!

A dimmer renown might strike
If Death lay square alongside, —
But the old Flag has no like,
She must fight, whatever betide; —
When the War is a tale of old,
And this day's story is told,
They shall hear how the Hartford died!

But as we ranged ahead,
And the leading ships worked in,
Losing their hope to win,
The enemy turned and fled —
And one seeks a shallow reach!
And another, winged in her flight,
Our mate, brave Jouett, brings in; —
And one, all torn in the fight,
Runs for a wreck on the beach,
Where her flames soon fire the night.

And the Ram, when well up the Bay,
And we looked that our stems should meet
(He had us fair for a prey),
Shifting his helm midway,
Sheered off, and ran for the fleet;
There, without skulking or sham,
He fought them gun for gun;
And ever he sought to ram,
But could finish never a one.

From the first of the iron shower
Till we sent our parting shell,
'T was just one savage hour
Of the roar and the rage of hell.

With the lessening smoke and thunder,
Our glasses around we aim, —
What is that burning yonder?
Our Philippi — aground and in flame!

Below, 't was still all a-roar,
As the ships went by the shore,
But the fire of the Fort had slacked
(So fierce their volleys had been), —
And now with a mighty din,
The whole fleet came grandly in,
Though sorely battered and wracked.

So, up the Bay we ran,
The Flag to port and ahead, —
And a pitying rain began
To wash the lips of our dead.

A league from the Fort we lay,
And deemed that the end must lag, —
When lo! looking down the Bay,
There flaunted the Rebel Rag; —
The Ram is again under way
And heading dead for the Flag!

Steering up with the stream,
Boldly his course he lay,
Though the fleet all answered his fire,
And, as he still drew nigher,
Ever on bow and beam

Our Monitors pounded away;
How the Chickasaw hammered away!

Quickly breasting the wave,
Eager the prize to win,
First of us all the brave
Monongahela went in
Under full head of steam; —
Twice she struck him abeam,
Till her stem was a sorry work
(She might have run on a crag!),
The Lackawanna hit fair,
He flung her aside like cork,
And still he held for the Flag.

High in the mizzen shroud
(Lest the smoke his sight o'erwhelm),
Our Admiral's voice rang loud;
"Hard-a-starboard your helm!
Starboard, and run him down!"
Starboard it was, — and so,
Like a black squall's lifting frown,
Our mighty bow bore down
On the iron beak of the Foe.

We stood on the deck together,
Men that had looked on death
In battle and stormy weather;
Yet a little we held our breath,
When, with the hush of death,
The great ships drew together.

Our Captain strode to the bow,
Drayton, courtly and wise,
Kindly cynic, and wise
(You hardly had known him now,
The flame of fight in his eyes!), —
His brave heart eager to feel
How the oak would tell on the steel!

But, as the space grew short,
A little he seemed to shun us;
Out peered a form grim and lanky,
And a voice yelled, "*Hard-a-port!
Hard-a-port! — here's the damned Yankee
Coming right down on us!*"

He sheered, but the ships ran foul
With a gnarring shudder and growl;
He gave us a deadly gun;
But as he passed in his pride
(Rasping right alongside!),
The old Flag, in thunder-tones
Poured in her port broadside,
Rattling his iron hide
And cracking his timber-bones!

Just then, at speed on the Foe,
With her bow all weathered and brown,
The great Lackawanna came down
Full tilt, for another blow; —
We were forging ahead,
She reversed — but, for all our pains,
Rammed the old Hartford, instead,
Just for'ard the mizzen chains!

Ah! how the masts did buckle and bend,
And the stout hull ring and reel,
As she took us right on end!
(Vain were engine and wheel,
She was under full steam) —
With the roar of a thunder-stroke
Her two thousand tons of oak
Brought up on us, right abeam!

A wreck, as it looked, we lay
(Rib and plank-sheer gave way
To the stroke of that giant wedge!) —
Here, after all, we go —
The old ship is gone! — ah, no,
But cut to the water's edge.

Never mind then, — at him again!
His flurry now can't last long;
He'll never again see land, —
Try that on *him*, Marchand!
On him again, brave Strong!

Heading square at the hulk,
Full on his beam we bore;
But the spine of the huge Sea-Hog
Lay on the tide like a log,
He vomited flame no more.

By this, he had found it hot; —
Half the fleet, in an angry ring,
Closed round the hideous thing,
Hammering with solid shot,
And bearing down, bow on bow;
He has but a minute to choose, —
Life or renown? — which now
Will the Rebel Admiral lose?

Cruel, haughty, and cold,
He ever was strong and bold;
Shall he shrink from a wooden stem?
He will think of that brave band
He sank in the Cumberland;
Ay, he will sink like them.

Nothing left but to fight
Boldly his last sea-fight!
Can he strike? By Heaven, 't is true!

Down comes the traitor Blue,
And up goes the captive White!

Up went the White! Ah, then
The hurrahs that once and again
Rang from three thousand men
All flushed and savage with fight!
Our dead lay cold and stark;
But our dying, down in the dark,
Answered as best they might,
Lifting their poor lost arms,
And cheering for God and Right!

Ended the mighty noise,
Thunder of forts and ships.
Down we went to the hold,
Oh, our dear dying boys!
How we pressed their poor brave lips
(Ah, so pallid and cold!)
And held their hands to the last
(Those who had hands to hold)

Still thee, O woman heart!
(So strong an hour ago);
If the idle tears must start,
'T is not in vain they flow.

They died, our children dear.
On the drear berth-deck they died, —
Do not think of them here —
Even now their footsteps near
The immortal, tender sphere
(Land of love and cheer!
Home of the Crucified!).

And the glorious deed survives;
Our threescore, quiet and cold,
Lie thus, for a myriad lives
And treasure-millions untold
(Labor of poor men's lives,
Hunger of weans and wives,
Such is war-wasted gold).

Our ship and her fame to-day
Shall float on the storied Stream
When mast and shroud have crumbled away,
And her long white deck is a dream.

One daring leap in the dark,
Three mortal hours, at the most, —
And hell lies stiff and stark
On a hundred leagues of coast.

For the mighty Gulf is ours, —
The bay is lost and won,
An Empire is lost and won!
Land, if thou yet hast flowers,

Twine them in one more wreath
Of tenderest white and red
(Twin buds of glory and death!),
For the brows of our brave dead,
For thy Navy's noblest son.

Joy, O Land, for thy sons,
Victors by flood and field!
The traitor walls and guns
Have nothing left but to yield
(Even now they surrender!).

And the ships shall sail once more,
And the cloud of war sweep on
To break on the cruel shore; —
But Craven is gone,
He and his hundred are gone.

The flags flutter up and down
At sunrise and twilight dim,
The cannons menace and frown, —
But never again for him,
Him and the hundred.

The Dahlgrens are dumb,
Dumb are the mortars;
Never more shall the drum
Beat to colors and quarters, —
The great guns are silent.

O brave heart and loyal!
Let all your colors dip; —
Mourn him proud ship!
From main deck to royal.
God rest our Captain,
Rest our lost hundred!

Droop, flag and pennant!
What is your pride for?
Heaven, that he died for,
Rest our Lieutenant,
Rest our brave threescore!

. . . .

O Mother Land! this weary life
    We led, we lead, is 'long of thee;
Thine the strong agony of strife,
    And thine the lonely sea.

Thine the long decks all slaughter-sprent,
    The weary rows of cots that lie
With wrecks of strong men, marred and rent,
    'Neath Pensacola's sky.

And thine the iron caves and dens
    Wherein the flame our war-fleet drives;
The fiery vaults, whose breath is men's
    Most dear and precious lives!

Ah, ever when with storm sublime
    Dread Nature clears our murky air,
Thus in the crash of falling crime
    Some lesser guilt must share.

Full red the furnace fires must glow
    That melt the ore of mortal kind;
The mills of God are grinding slow,
    But ah, how close they grind!

To-day the Dahlgren and the drum
    Are dread Apostles of His Name;
His kingdom here can only come
    By chrism of blood and flame.

Be strong: already slants the gold
    Athwart these wild and stormy skies:
From out this blackened waste, behold
    What happy homes shall rise!

But see thou well no traitor gloze,
    No striking hands with Death and Shame,
Betray the sacred blood that flows
    So freely for thy name.

And never fear a victor foe —
    Thy children's hearts are strong and high;
Nor mourn too fondly; well they know
    On deck or field to die.

Nor shalt thou want one willing breath,
    Though, ever smiling round the brave,
The blue sea bear us on to death,
    The green were one wide grave.

HENRY HOWARD BROWNELL.

One more naval action remains to be recorded.
The blockading fleet on the Carolina coast had
been constantly threatened by the Confederate
ram Albemarle. Finally, late in October, 1864,
Lieutenant William B. Cushing undertook to de-
stroy it. On the night of October 27, he entered
Plymouth harbor in a small boat, with a crew of
thirteen men, approached the ram, and despite
a hail of bullets, exploded a torpedo under its
bow, sinking it. Cushing and most of his men
escaped by leaping into the water.

"ALBEMARLE" CUSHING

[October 27, 1864]

Joy in rebel Plymouth town, in the spring of
        sixty-four,
    When the Albemarle down on the Yankee
        frigates bore.

With the saucy Stars and Bars at her main;
  When she smote the Southfield dead, and
    the stout Miami quailed,
And the fleet in terror fled when their mighty
    cannon hailed
  Shot and shell on her iron back in vain,
Till she slowly steamed away to her berth at
    Plymouth pier,
  And their quick eyes saw her sway with her
    great beak out of gear,
And the color of their courage rose again.

    All the summer lay the ram,
      Like a wounded beast at bay,
    While the watchful squadron swam
      In the harbor night and day,
Till the broken beak was mended, and the
    weary vigil ended,
  And her time was come again to smite and
    slay.

    Must they die, and die in vain,
      Like a flock of shambled sheep?
    Then the Yankee grit and brain
      Must be dead or gone to sleep,
And our sailors' gallant story of a hundred
    years of glory
  Let us sell for a song, selling cheap!

    Cushing, scarce a man in years,
      But a sailor thoroughbred,
    "With a dozen volunteers
      I will sink the ram," he said.
"At the worst 't is only dying." And the old
    commander, sighing,
  "'T is to save the fleet and flag — go
    ahead!"

.   .   .   .

    Bright the rebel beacons blazed
      On the river left and right:
    Wide awake their sentries gazed
      Through the watches of the night;
Sharp their challenge rang, and fiery came the
    rifle's quick inquiry,
  As the little launch swung into the light.

    Listening ears afar had heard;
      Ready hands to quarters sprung,
    The Albemarle awoke and stirred,
      And her howitzers gave tongue;
Till the river and the shore echoed back the
    mighty roar,
  When the portals of her hundred-pounders
    swung.

    Will the swordfish brave the whale,
      Doubly girt with boom and chain?
    Face the shrapnel's iron hail?
      Dare the livid leaden rain?
Ah! that shell has done its duty; it has
    spoiled the Yankee's beauty;
  See her turn and fly with half her madmen
    slain.

    High the victor's taunting yell
      Rings above the battle roar,
    And they bid her mock farewell
      As she seeks the farther shore,
Till they see her sudden swinging, crouching
    for the leap and springing
  Back to boom and chain and bloody fray
    once more.

    Now the Southern captain, stirred
      By the spirit of his race,
    Stops the firing with a word,
      Bids them yield, and offers grace.
Cushing, laughing, answers, "No! we are here
    to fight!" and so
  Swings the dread torpedo spar to its
    place.

    Then the great ship shook and reeled,
      With a wounded, gaping side,
    But her steady cannon pealed
      Ere she settled in the tide,
And the Roanoke's dull flood ran full red
    with Yankee blood,
  When the fighting Albemarle sunk and
    died.

Woe in rebel Plymouth town when the Albe-
    marle fell,
  And the saucy flag went down that had
    floated long and well,
Nevermore from her stricken deck to
    wave.
  For the fallen flag a sigh, for the fallen foe
    a tear!
Never shall their glory die while we hold our
    glory dear,
  And the hero's laurels live on his grave.
Link their Cooke's with Cushing's name;
    proudly call them both our own;
Claim their valor and their fame for America
    alone —
  Joyful mother of the bravest of the
    brave!
            JAMES JEFFREY ROCHE.

AT THE CANNON'S MOUTH

DESTRUCTION OF THE RAM ALBEMARLE BY THE TORPEDO-LAUNCH, OCTOBER 27, 1864

PALELY intent, he urged his keel
  Full on the guns, and touched the spring;
Himself involved in the bolt he drove
Timed with the armed hull's shot that stove
His shallop — die or do!
Into the flood his life he threw,
  Yet lives — unscathed — a breathing thing
To marvel at.
            He has his fame;
But that mad dash at death, how name?

Had Earth no charm to stay the Boy
  From the martyr-passion? Could he dare
Disdain the Paradise of opening joy
  Which beckons the fresh heart every-
    where?

Life has more lures than any girl
  For youth and strength; puts forth a
    share
Of beauty, hinting of yet rarer store;
And ever with unfathomable eyes,
  Which bafflingly entice,
Still strangely does Adonis draw.
And life once over, who shall tell the rest?
Life is, of all we know, God's best.
What imps these eagles then, that they
Fling disrespect on life by that proud way
In which they soar above our lower clay.

Pretence of wonderment and doubt un-
    blest:
  In Cushing's eager deed was shown
  A spirit which brave poets own —
That scorn of life which earns life's crown;
  Earns, but not always wins; but he —
  The star ascended in his nativity.
                        HERMAN MELVILLE.

CHAPTER XII

THE MARTYR PRESIDENT

In November, 1864, Abraham Lincoln was re-elected President, carrying twenty-two out of the twenty-five states of the Union. He had grown ever dearer to the hearts of the American people, and the country had come to trust and love him.

LINCOLN

CHAINED by stern duty to the rock of state,
  His spirit armed in mail of rugged mirth,
  Ever above, though ever near to earth,
  Yet felt his heart the cruel tongues that sate
Base appetites, and foul with slander, wait
  Till the keen lightnings bring the awful hour
  When wounds and suffering shall give them
    power.
  Most was he like to Luther, gay and great,
Solemn and mirthful, strong of heart and limb.
  Tender and simple too; he was so near
  To all things human that he cast out fear,
And, ever simpler, like a little child,
  Lived in unconscious nearness unto Him
  Who always on earth's little ones hath
    smiled.
                        S. WEIR MITCHELL.

On the evening of April 14, 1865, the President attended a performance of "Our American Cousin," at Ford's Theatre, at Washington. The play was drawing to a close, when suddenly the audience was startled by a pistol shot, and an instant later saw a man leap from the President's box to the stage. The man was John Wilkes Booth, an actor. He had shot the President through the head, and the latter died next day without regaining consciousness.

O CAPTAIN! MY CAPTAIN!

[April 14, 1865]

O CAPTAIN! my Captain! our fearful trip is
    done,
The ship has weathered every rack, the prize
    we sought is won,
The port is near, the bells I hear, the people
    all exulting,
While follow eyes the steady keel, the vessel
    grim and daring;
    But O heart! heart! heart!
      O the bleeding drops of red,
    Where on the deck my Captain lies,
      Fallen cold and dead.

O Captain! my Captain! rise up and hear the
    bells;
Rise up — for you the flag is flung — for you
    the bugle trills,

For you bouquets and ribboned wreaths —
    for you the shores a-crowding,
For you they call, the swaying mass, their
    eager faces turning;
    Here Captain! dear father!
    This arm beneath your head!
    It is some dream that on the deck
    You've fallen cold and dead.

My Captain does not answer, his lips are pale
    and still,
My father does not feel my arm, he has no
    pulse nor will,
The ship is anchored safe and sound, its voy-
    age closed and done,
From fearful trip the victor ship comes in with
    object won:
    Exult O shores, and ring O bells!
    But I with mournful tread,
    Walk the deck my Captain lies,
    Fallen cold and dead.
                        WALT WHITMAN.

THE DEAD PRESIDENT

WERE there no crowns on earth,
No evergreen to wreathe a hero's wreath,
That he must pass beyond the gates of death,
Our hero, our slain hero, to be crowned?
Could there on our unworthy earth be found
    Naught to befit his worth?

The noblest soul of all!
When was there ever, since our Washington,
A man so pure, so wise, so patient — one
Who walked with this high goal alone in sight,
To speak, to do, to sanction only Right,
    Though very heaven should fall!

Ah, not for him we weep;
What honor more could be in store for him?
Who would have had him linger in our dim
And troublesome world, when his great work
    was done —
Who would not leave that worn and weary one
    Gladly to go to sleep?

For us the stroke was just;
We were not worthy of that patient heart;
We might have helped him more, not stood
    apart,
And coldly criticised his works and ways —
Too late now, all too late — our little praise
    Sounds hollow o'er his dust.

Be merciful, O our God!
Forgive the meanness of our human hearts,
That never, till a noble soul departs,
See half the worth, or hear the angel's wings
Till they go rustling heavenward as he springs
    Up from the mounded sod.

Yet what a deathless crown
Of Northern pine and Southern orange-flower,
For victory, and the land's new bridal-hour,
Would we have wreathed for that beloved
    brow!
Sadly upon his sleeping forehead now
    We lay our cypress down.

O martyred one, farewell!
Thou hast not left thy people quite alone,
Out of thy beautiful life there comes a tone
Of power, of love, of trust, a prophecy,
Whose fair fulfilment all the earth shall be,
    And all the Future tell.
                        EDWARD ROWLAND SILL.

ABRAHAM LINCOLN

ASSASSINATED GOOD FRIDAY, 1865

"FORGIVE them, for they know not what they
    do!"
He said, and so went shriven to his fate, —
Unknowing went, that generous heart and
    true.
    Even while he spoke, the slayer lay in wait,
    And when the morning opened Heaven's
        gate
There passed the whitest soul a nation knew.
    Henceforth all thoughts of pardon are too
        late;
They, in whose cause that arm its weapon
        drew,
    Have murdered Mercy. Now alone shall
        stand
Blind Justice, with the sword unsheathed she
        wore.
    Hark, from the eastern to the western
        strand,
The swelling thunder of the people's roar:
    What words they murmur, — Fetter not
        her hand!
So let it smite, such deeds shall be no more!
                        EDMUND CLARENCE STEDMAN.

The assassin escaped into Maryland, where
he found a temporary refuge, but the country was

alarmed, pursuers were close upon his trail, and on April 25, 1865, he was brought to bay in a barn. He refused to surrender and was shot by a sergeant named Boston Corbett.

PARDON

WILKES BOOTH — APRIL 26, 1865

PAINS the sharp sentence the heart in whose wrath it was uttered,
Now thou art cold;
Vengeance, the headlong, and Justice, with purpose close muttered,
Loosen their hold.

Death brings atonement; he did that whereof ye accuse him, —
Murder accurst;
But from that crisis of crime in which Satan did lose him,
Suffered the worst.

Harshly the red dawn arose on a deed of his doing,
Never to mend;
But harsher days he wore out in the bitter pursuing
And the wild end.

So lift the pale flag of truce, wrap those mysteries round him,
In whose avail
Madness that moved, and the swift retribution that found him,
Falter and fail.

So the soft purples that quiet the heavens with mourning,
Willing to fall,
Lend him one fold, his illustrious victim adorning
With wider pall.

Back to the cross, where the Saviour uplifted in dying
Bade all souls live,
Turns the reft bosom of Nature, his mother, low sighing,
Greatest, forgive!
JULIA WARD HOWE.

On Wednesday, April 19, 1865, a simple funeral service was held over the body of Lincoln at the White House, and for two days thereafter the body lay in state in the rotunda of the Capitol.

THE DEAR PRESIDENT

ABRAHAM LINCOLN, the Dear President,
Lay in the Round Hall at the Capitol,
And there the people came to look their last.

There came the widow, weeded for her mate;
There came the mother, sorrowing for her son;
There came the orphan, moaning for its sire.

There came the soldier, bearing home his wound;
There came the slave, who felt his broken chain;
There came the mourners of a blacken'd Land.

Through the dark April day, a ceaseless throng,
They pass'd the coffin, saw the sleeping face,
And, blessing it, in silence moved away.

And one, a poet, spoke within his heart:
"It harm'd him not to praise him when alive,
And me it cannot harm to praise him dead.

"Too oft the muse has blush'd to speak of men —
No muse shall blush to speak her best of him,
And still to speak her best of him is dumb.

"O lofty wisdom's low simplicity!
O awful tenderness of noted power! —
No man e'er held so much of power so meek.

"He was the husband of the husbandless,
He was the father of the fatherless:
Within his heart he weigh'd the common woe.

"His call was like a father's to his sons!
As to a father's voice, they, hearing, came —
Eager to offer, strive, and bear, and die.

"The mild bond-breaker, servant of his Lord,
He took the sword, but in the name of Peace,
And touched the fetter, and the bound was free.

"Oh, place him not among the historic kings,
Strong, barbarous chiefs and bloody conquerors,
But with the Great and pure Republicans:

"Those who have been unselfish, wise, and
    good,
Bringers of Light and Pilots in the dark,
Bearers of Crosses, Servants of the World.

"And always, in his Land of birth and death,
Be his fond name — warm'd in the people's
    hearts —
Abraham Lincoln, the Dear President."
                    JOHN JAMES PIATT.

ABRAHAM LINCOLN

OH, slow to smite and swift to spare,
    Gentle and merciful and just!
Who, in the fear of God, didst bear
    The sword of power, a nation's trust:

In sorrow by thy bier we stand,
    Amid the awe that hushes all,
And speak the anguish of a land
    That shook with horror at thy fall.

Thy task is done; the bond are free:
    We bear thee to an honored grave,
Whose proudest monument shall be
    The broken fetters of the slave.

Pure was thy life; its bloody close
    Hath placed thee with the sons of light,
Among the noble host of those
    Who perished in the cause of Right.
                    WILLIAM CULLEN BRYANT.

    Then the funeral train started for Lincoln's home
at Springfield, Ill., stopping at Philadelphia, New
York, and other towns along the route, great crowds
everywhere gathering to honor the dead President.

ABRAHAM LINCOLN [1]

NOT as when some great Captain falls,
In battle, where his Country calls,
    Beyond the struggling lines
    That push his dread designs

To doom, by some stray ball struck dead:
Or, in the last charge, at the head
    Of his determined men,
    Who *must* be victors then.

    [1] From Poetical Writings of Richard Henry
Stoddard; copyright. 1880, by Charles Scribner's
Sons.

Nor as when sink the civic great,
The safer pillars of the State,
    Whose calm, mature, wise words
    Suppress the need of swords.

With no such tears as e'er were shed
Above the noblest of our dead
    Do we to-day deplore
    The Man that is no more.

Our sorrow hath a wider scope,
Too strange for fear, too vast for hope,
    A wonder, blind and dumb,
    That waits — what is to come!

Not more astounded had we been
If Madness, that dark night, unseen,
    Had in our chambers crept,
    And murdered while we slept!

We woke to find a mourning earth,
Our Lares shivered on the hearth,
    The roof-tree fallen, all
    That could affright, appall!

Such thunderbolts, in other lands,
Have smitten the rod from royal hands,
    But spared, with us, till now,
    Each laurelled Cæsar's brow.

No Cæsar he whom we lament,
A Man without a precedent,
    Sent, it would seem, to do
    His work, and perish, too.

Not by the weary cares of State,
The endless tasks, which will not wait,
    Which, often done in vain,
    Must yet be done again:

Not in the dark, wild tide of war,
Which rose so high, and rolled so far,
    Sweeping from sea to sea
    In awful anarchy:

Four fateful years of mortal strife,
Which slowly drained the nation's life
    (Yet for each drop that ran
    There sprang an armèd man!).

Not then; but when, by measures meet
By victory, and by defeat,
    By courage, patience, skill,
    The people's fixed, "*We will!*"

Had pierced, had crushed Rebellion dead,
Without a hand, without a head,
    At last, when all was well,
    He fell, O how he fell!

The time, the place, the stealing shape,
The coward shot, the swift escape,
    The wife, the widow's scream, —
    It is a hideous Dream!

A dream? What means this pageant, then?
These multitudes of solemn men,
    Who speak not when they meet,
    But throng the silent street?

The flags half-mast that late so high
Flaunted at each new victory?
    (The stars no brightness shed,
    But bloody looks the red!)

The black festoons that stretch for miles,
And turn the streets to funeral aisles?
    (No house too poor to show
    The nation's badge of woe.)

The cannon's sudden, sullen boom,
The bells that toll of death and doom,
    The rolling of the drums,
    The dreadful car that comes?

Cursed be the hand that fired the shot,
The frenzied brain that hatched the plot,
    Thy country's Father slain
    By thee, thou worse than Cain!

Tyrants have fallen by such as thou,
And good hath followed — may it now!
    (God lets bad instruments
    Produce the best events.)

But he, the man we mourn to-day,
No tyrant was: so mild a sway
    In one such weight who bore
    Was never known before.

Cool should he be, of balanced powers,
The ruler of a race like ours,
    Impatient, headstrong, wild,
    The Man to guide the Child.

And this *he* was, who most unfit
(So hard the sense of God to hit)
    Did seem to fill his place;
    With such a homely face,

Such rustic manners, speech uncouth
(That somehow blundered out the truth),
    Untried, untrained to bear
    The more than kingly care.

Ah! And his genius put to scorn
The proudest in the purple born,
    Whose wisdom never grew
    To what, untaught, he knew,

The People, of whom he was one:
No gentleman, like Washington
    (Whose bones, methinks, make room,
    To have him in their tomb!).

A laboring man, with horny hands,
Who swung the axe, who tilled his lands,
    Who shrank from nothing new,
    But did as poor men do.

One of the People! born to be
Their curious epitome;
    To share yet rise above
    Their shifting hate and love.

Common his mind (it seemed so then),
His thoughts the thoughts of other men:
    Plain were his words, and poor,
    But now they will endure!

No hasty fool, of stubborn will,
But prudent, cautious, pliant still;
    Who since his work was good
    Would do it as he could.

Doubting, was not ashamed to doubt,
And, lacking prescience, went without:
    Often appeared to halt,
    And was, of course, at fault;

Heard all opinions, nothing loath,
And, loving both sides, angered both:
    Was — *not* like Justice, blind,
    But watchful, clement, kind.

No hero this of Roman mould,
Nor like our stately sires of old:
    Perhaps he was not great,
    But he preserved the State!

O honest face, which all men knew!
O tender heart, but known to few!
    O wonder of the age,
    Cut off by tragic rage!

Peace! Let the long procession come,
For hark, the mournful, muffled drum,
    The trumpet's wail afar,
    And see, the awful car!

Peace! Let the sad procession go,
White cannon boom and bells toll slow.
    And go, thou sacred car,
    Bearing our woe afar!

Go, darkly borne, from State to State,
Whose loyal, sorrowing cities wait
    To honor all they can
    The dust of that good man.

Go, grandly borne, with such a train
As greatest kings might die to gain.
    The just, the wise, the brave,
    Attend thee to the grave.

And you, the soldiers of our wars,
Bronzed veterans, grim with noble scars,
    Salute him once again,
    Your late commander — slain!

Yes, let your tears indignant fall,
But leave your muskets on the wall;
    Your country needs you now
    Beside the forge — the plough.

(When Justice shall unsheathe her brand,
If Mercy may not stay her hand,
    Nor would we have it so,
    She must direct the blow.)

And you, amid the master-race,
Who seem so strangely out of place,
    Know ye who cometh? He
    Who hath declared ye free.

Bow while the body passes — nay,
Fall on your knees, and weep, and pray!
    Weep, weep — I would ye might —
    Your poor black faces white!

And, children, you must come in bands,
With garlands in your little hands,
    Of blue and white and red,
    To strew before the dead.

So sweetly, sadly, sternly goes
The Fallen to his last repose.
    Beneath no mighty dome,
    But in his modest home;

The churchyard where his children rest,
The quiet spot that suits him best,
    There shall his grave be made,
    And there his bones be laid.

And there his countrymen shall come,
With memory proud, with pity dumb,
    And strangers far and near,
    For many and many a year.

For many a year and many an age,
While History on her ample page
    The virtues shall enroll
    Of that Paternal Soul.
        RICHARD HENRY STODDARD.

During those twenty days, the one thought uppermost in men's minds was the martyred President. The desire for vengeance alternated with grief. It was generally believed that the conspiracy had been concocted by the Confederate authorities, and magnanimity toward a beaten foe gave place to hatred.

PARRICIDE

ABRAHAM LINCOLN — APRIL 14, 1865

O'ER the warrior gauntlet grim
Late the silken glove we drew,
Bade the watch-fires slacken dim
In the dawn's auspicious hue.
    Stayed the armèd heel;
    Stilled the clanging steel;
Joys unwonted thrilled the silence through.

Glad drew near the Easter tide;
And the thoughts of men anew
Turned to Him who spotless died
For the peace that none shall rue.
    Out of mortal pain
    This abiding strain
Issued: "Peace, my peace, I give to you."

Musing o'er the silent strings,
By their apathy opprest,
Waiting for the spirit wings,
To be touched and soul-possessed,
    "I am dull," I said:
    "Treason is not dead;
Still in ambush lurks that shivering guest."

Then a woman's shriek of fear
Smote us in its arrowy flight;

And a wonder wild and drear
Did the hearts of men unite,
   Has the seed of crime
   Reached its flowering-time,
That it shoots to this audacious height?

Then, as frosts the landscape change,
Stiffening from the summer's glow,
Grew the jocund faces strange,
Lay the loftiest emblem low:
   Kings are of the past,
   Suffered still to last;
These twin crowns the present did bestow.

Fair assassin, murder white,
With thy serpent speed avoid
Each unsullied household light,
Every conscience unalloyed.
   Neither heart nor home
   Where good angels come
Suffer thee in nearness to abide.

Slanderer of the gracious brow,
The untiring blood of youth,
Servant of an evil now,
Of a crime that beggars ruth,
   Treason was thy dam,
   Wolfling, when the Lamb,
The Anointed, met thy venomed tooth.

With the righteous did he fall,
With the sainted doth he lie;
While the gibbet's vultures call
Thee, that, 'twixt the earth and sky,
   Disavowed of both
   In their Godward troth,
Thou mayst make thy poor amend, and die.

If it were my latest breath,
Doomed his bloody end to share,
I would brand thee with his death
As a deed beyond despair.
   Since the Christ was lost
   For a felon's cost,
None like thee of vengeance should beware.

Leave the murderer, noble song,
Helpless in the toils of fate:
To the just thy meeds belong,
To the martyr, to the state.
   When the storm beats loud
   Over sail and shroud,
Tunefully the seaman cheers his mate.

Never tempest lashed the wave
But to leave it fresher calm;
Never weapon scarred the brave
But their blood did purchase balm.
   God hath writ on high
   Such a victory
As uplifts the nation with its psalm.

Honor to the heart of love,
Honor to the peaceful will,
Slow to threaten, strong to move,
Swift to render good for ill!
   Glory crowns his end,
   And the captive's friend
From his ashes makes us freemen still.
             JULIA WARD HOWE.

The feeling throughout the South was one of
sorrow and indignation. In England, too, the
act was condemned, and London *Punch*, which
had delighted in caricaturing the President, pub-
lished a full-page cartoon, depicting itself in the
act of laying a wreath upon his bier — a cartoon
which was followed by some spirited verses from
Punch's editor, Tom Taylor, confessing that the
English attitude toward Lincoln and the North
had been a mistaken one.

ABRAHAM LINCOLN

You lay a wreath on murdered Lincoln's
   bier,
  You, who, with mocking pencil, wont to
   trace,
Broad for the self-complaisant British sneer,
  His length of shambling limb, his furrowed
   face,

His gaunt, gnarled hands, his unkempt, bris-
   tling hair,
  His garb uncouth, his bearing ill at ease,
His lack of all we prize as debonair,
  Of power or will to shine, of art to please;

You, whose smart pen backed up the pencil's
   laugh,
  Judging each step as though the way were
   plain;
Reckless, so it could point its paragraph
  Of chief's perplexity, or people's pain, —

Beside this corpse, that bears for winding-sheet
  The Stars and Stripes he lived to rear anew,
Between the mourners at his head and feet,
  Say, scurrile jester, is there room for *you*?

Yes, he had lived to shame me from my sneer,
  To lame my pencil, and confute my pen;
To make me own this hind of Princes peer,
  This rail-splitter a true-born king of men.

My shallow judgment I had learned to rue,
  Noting how to occasion's height he rose,
How his quaint wit made home-truth seem
      more true,
  How, iron-like, his temper grew by blows;

How humble, yet how hopeful, he could be;
  How, in good fortune and in ill, the same;
Nor bitter in success, nor boastful he,
  Thirsty for gold, nor feverish for fame.

He went about his work — such work as few
  Ever had laid on head and heart and hand —
As one who knows, where there's a task to do,
  Man's honest will must Heaven's good
      grace command;

Who trusts the strength will with the burden
      grow,
  That God makes instruments to work His
      will,
If but that will we can arrive to know,
  Nor tamper with the weights of good and
      ill.

So he went forth to battle, on the side
  That he felt clear was Liberty's and Right's,
As in his peasant boyhood he had plied
  His warfare with rude Nature's thwarting
      mights, —

The uncleared forest, the unbroken soil,
  The iron bark that turns the lumberer's axe,
The rapid, that o'erbears the boatman's toil,
  The prairie, hiding the mazed wanderer's
      tracks,

The ambushed Indian, and the prowling
      bear, —
  Such were the needs that helped his youth
      to train:
Rough culture — but such trees large fruit
      may bear,
  If but their stocks be of right girth and
      grain.

So he grew up, a destined work to do,
  And lived to do it: four long-suffering
      years'
Ill-fate, ill-feeling, ill-report, lived through,
  And then he heard the hisses change to
      cheers,

The taunts to tribute, the abuse to praise,
  And took both with the same unwavering
      mood:
Till, as he came on light, from darkling
      days,
  And seemed to touch the goal from where
      he stood,

A felon hand, between the goal and him,
  Reached from behind his back, a trigger
      prest —
And those perplexed and patient eyes were
      dim,
  Those gaunt, long-laboring limbs were laid
      to rest.

The words of mercy were upon his lips,
  Forgiveness in his heart and on his pen,
When this vile murderer brought swift eclipse
  To thoughts of peace on earth, good will
      to men.

The Old World and the New, from sea to
      sea,
  Utter one voice of sympathy and shame.
Sore heart, so stopped when it at last beat
      high!
  Sad life, cut short just as its triumph came!

A deed accurst! Strokes have been struck
      before
  By the assassin's hand, whereof men doubt
If more of horror or disgrace they bore;
  But thy foul crime, like Cain's, stands dark-
      ly out,

Vile hand, that brandest murder on a strife,
  Whate'er its grounds, stoutly and nobly
      striven,
And with the martyr's crown, crownest a
      life
  With much to praise, little to be forgiven.
                            Tom Taylor.

CHAPTER XIII

PEACE

The surrender of Lee at Appomattox virtually ended the war. The only considerable Confederate force left in the field was that under command of Johnston, and it surrendered to Sherman on April 26, 1865.

"STACK ARMS!"

"Stack Arms!" I've gladly heard the cry
    When, weary with the dusty tread
Of marching troops, as night drew nigh,
    I sank upon my soldier bed,
And calmly slept; the starry dome
    Of heaven's blue arch my canopy,
And mingled with my dreams of home
    The thoughts of Peace and Liberty.

"*Stack Arms!*" I've heard it when the shout
    Exulting ran along our line,
Of foes hurled back in bloody rout,
    Captured, dispersed; its tones divine
Then came to mine enraptured ear,
    Guerdon of duty nobly done,
And glistened on my cheek the tear
    Of grateful joy for victory won.

"*Stack Arms!*" In faltering accents, slow
    And sad, it creeps from tongue to tongue,
A broken, murmuring wail of woe,
    From manly hearts by anguish wrung.
Like victims of a midnight dream,
    We move, we know not how nor why;
For life and hope like phantoms seem,
    And it would be relief — to die!

JOSEPH BLYNTH ALSTON.

Jefferson Davis, who had fled from Richmond, was captured on May 11, 1865, near the Ocmulgee River, in Georgia, and on May 26, when Kirby Smith formally surrendered, the last vestige of armed resistance to the national government disappeared. Davis was confined at Fortress Monroe until 1868, the South, of course, considering him a martyr.

JEFFERSON DAVIS

"Our hearts, our hopes, our prayers, our tears,
    Our faith triumphant o'er our fears,
Are all with thee, are all with thee."

LONGFELLOW.

CALM martyr of a noble cause.
    Upon thy form in vain

The Dungeon shuts its cankered jaws,
    And clasps its cankered chain;
For thy free spirit walks abroad,
    And every pulse is stirred
With the old deathless glory thrill,
    Whene'er thy name is heard.

The same that lit each Grecian eye,
    Whene'er it rested on
The wild pass of Thermopylæ —
    The plain of Marathon;
And made the Roman's ancient blood
    Bound fiercely as he told,
"How well Horatio kept the bridge,
    In the brave days of old."

The same that makes the Switzer's heart
    With silent rapture swell,
When in each Alpine height he sees
    A monument to Tell:
The same that kindles Irish veins
    When Emmet's name is told;
What Bruce to Caledonia is,
    Kosciusko to the Pole —

Art thou to us! — thy deathless fame,
    With Washington entwined,
Forever in each Southern heart
    Is hallowed and enshrined; —
And though the tyrant give thy form
    To shameful death — 't were vain;
It would but shed a splendor round
    The gibbet and the chain.

Only less sacred in our eyes,
    Thus blest and purified,
Than the dear cross on which our Lord
    Was shamed and crucified,
Would the vile gallows tree become,
    And through all ages shine,
Linked with the glory of thy name,
    A relic and a shrine!

WALKER MERIWETHER BELL.

It was for the South a sad awakening from the dream which had been so entrancing and which seemed so certain to come true. Their land was ravaged, their people were ruined, their best and bravest dead.

IN THE LAND WHERE WE WERE DREAMING

FAIR were our visions! Oh, they were as grand
As ever floated out of faerie land;
   Children were we in single faith,
   But God-like children whom nor death
Nor threat nor danger drove from honor's
    path,
   In the land where we were dreaming.

Proud were our men, as pride of birth could
    render;
As violets, our women pure and tender;
   And when they spoke, their voices did thrill
   Until at eve the whip-poor-will,
At morn the mocking-bird, were mute and
    still,
   In the land where we were dreaming.

And we had graves that covered more of glory
Than ever tracked tradition's ancient story;
   And in our dream we wove the thread
   Of principles for which had bled
And suffered long our own immortal dead,
   In the land where we were dreaming.

Though in our land we had both bond and
    free,
Both were content; and so God let them be;
   Till envy coveted our land,
   And those fair fields our valor won;
But little recked we, for we still slept on,
   In the land where we were dreaming.

Our sleep grew troubled and our dreams grew
    wild —
Red meteors flashed across our heaven's
    field;
   Crimson the moon; between the Twins
   Barbed arrows fly, and then begins
Such strife as when disorder's Chaos reigns,
   In the land where we were dreaming.

Down from her sun-lit heights smiled Liberty
And waved her cap in sign of Victory —
   The world approved, and everywhere,
   Except where growled the Russian bear,
The good, the brave, the just gave us their
    prayer
   In the land where we were dreaming.

We fancied that a Government was ours —
We challenged place among the world's great
    powers;

We talked in sleep of Rank, Commission,
Until so life-like grew our vision
That he who dared to doubt but met deri-
    sion,
   In the land where we were dreaming.

We looked on high: a banner there was seen,
Whose field was blanched and spotless in its
    sheen —
   Chivalry's cross its Union bears,
   And veterans swearing by their scars
Vowed they would bear it through a hundred
    wars,
   In the land where we were dreaming.

A hero came amongst us as we slept;
At first he lowly knelt — then rose and wept;
   Then gathering up a thousand spears
   He swept across the field of Mars;
Then bowed farewell and walked beyond the
    stars,
   In the land where we were dreaming.

We looked again: another figure still
Gave hope, and nerved each individual will —
   Full of grandeur, clothed with power,
   Self-poised, erect, he ruled the hour
With stern, majestic sway — of strength a
    tower,
   In the land where we were dreaming.

As, while great Jove, in bronze, a warder
    God,
Gazed eastward from the Forum where he
    stood,
   Rome felt herself secure and free,
   So, "Richmond's safe," we said, while we
Beheld a bronzèd hero — God-like Lee,
   In the land where we were dreaming.

As wakes the soldier when the alarum calls —
As wakes the mother when the infant falls —
   As starts the traveller when around
   His sleeping couch the fire-bells sound —
So woke our nation with a single bound,
   In the land where we were dreaming.

Woe! woe is me! the startled mother cried —
While we have slept our noble sons have
    died!
   Woe! woe is me! how strange and sad
That all our glorious vision's fled,
And left us nothing real but the dead,
   In the land where we were dreaming.

              DANIEL B. LUCAS.

ACCEPTATION

I

WE do accept thee, heavenly Peace!
  Albeit thou comest in a guise
  Unlooked for — undesired, our eyes
Welcome through tears the sweet release
From war, and woe, and want, — surcease,
For which we bless thee, blessèd Peace!

II

We lift our foreheads from the dust;
  And as we meet thy brow's clear calm,
  There falls a freshening sense of balm
Upon our spirits. Fear — distrust —
The hopeless present on us thrust —
We'll meet them as we can, and *must*.

III

War has not wholly wrecked us: still
  Strong hands, brave hearts, high souls are
    ours —
  Proud consciousness of quenchless powers—
A Past whose memory makes us thrill —
Futures uncharactered, to fill
With heroisms — if we will.

IV

Then courage, brothers! —Though each breast
  Feel oft the rankling thorn, despair,
  That failure plants so sharply there —
No pain, no pang shall be confest:
We'll work and watch the brightening west,
And leave to God and Heaven the rest.
              MARGARET JUNKIN PRESTON.

THE CONQUERED BANNER

FURL that Banner, for 't is weary;
Round its staff 't is drooping dreary;
  Furl it, fold it — it is best;
For there 's not a man to wave it,
And there 's not a sword to save it,
And there 's not one left to lave it
In the blood which heroes gave it;
  And its foes now scorn and brave it;
  Furl it, hide it — let it rest!

Take that Banner down! 't is tattered;
Broken is its staff and shattered,
And the valiant hosts are scattered
  Over whom it floated high.
Oh, 't is hard for us to fold it,
Hard to think there 's none to hold it,

Hard that those who once unrolled it
  Now must furl it with a sigh!

Furl that Banner — furl it sadly;
Once ten thousands hailed it gladly,
And ten thousands wildly, madly
  Swore it should forever wave —
Swore that foeman's sword should never
Hearts like theirs entwined dissever,
And that flag should float forever
  O'er their freedom, or their grave!

Furl it! for the hands that grasped it,
And the hearts that fondly clasped it,
  Cold and dead are lying low;
And that Banner — it is trailing,
While around it sounds the wailing
  Of its people in their woe;

For, though conquered, they adore it —
Love the cold, dead hands that bore it!
Weep for those who fell before it!
Pardon those who trailed and tore it!
But, oh, wildly they deplore it,
  Now who furl and fold it so!

Furl that Banner! True, 't is gory,
Yet 't is wreathed around with glory,
And 't will live in song and story
  Though its folds are in the dust!
For its fame on brightest pages,
Penned by poets and by sages,
Shall go sounding down the ages —
  Furl its folds though now we must!

Furl that Banner, softly, slowly;
Treat it gently — it is holy,
  For it droops above the dead;
Touch it not — unfold it never,
Let it droop there, furled forever, —
  For its people's hopes are fled.
              ABRAM J. RYAN.

At the North, too, Peace was welcome. The
North, while suffering less poignantly than the
South, had drunk deeply of the bitter cup. It had
lost over three hundred and fifty thousand men.

PEACE

DAYBREAK upon the hills!
Slowly, behind the midnight murk and trail
Of the long storm, light brightens, pure and
    pale,
  And the horizon fills.

Not bearing swift release, —
Not with quick feet of triumph, but with tread
August and solemn, following her dead,
　　Cometh, at last, our Peace.

Over thick graves grown green,
Over pale bones that graveless lie and bleach,
Over torn human hearts her path doth reach,
　　And Heaven's dear pity lean.

O angel sweet and grand!
White-footed, from beside the throne of God,
Thou movest, with the palm and olive-rod,
　　And day bespreads the land!

His Day we waited for!
With faces to the East, we prayed and fought;
And a faint music of the dawning caught,
　　All through the sounds of War.

Our souls are still with praise!
It is the dawning; there is work to do:
When we have borne the long hours' burden
　　through,
　　Then we will pæans raise.

God give us, with the time,
His strength for His large purpose to the
　　world!
To bear before Him, in its face unfurled,
　　His gonfalon sublime!

Ay, we *are* strong! Both sides
The misty river stretch His army's wings:
Heavenward, with glorious wheel, one flank
　　He flings;
　　And one front still abides!

Strongest where most bereft!
His great ones He doth call to more command.
For whom He hath prepared it, they shall
　　stand
　　On the Right Hand and Left!
　　　　　ADELINE D. T. WHITNEY.

PEACE

O LAND, of every land the best —
　　O Land, whose glory shall increase;
Now in your whitest raiment drest
　　For the great festival of Peace:

Take from your flag its fold of gloom,
　　And let it float undimmed above,

Till over all our vales shall bloom
　　The sacred colors that we love.

On mountain high, in valley low,
　　Set Freedom's living fires to burn;
Until the midnight sky shall show
　　A redder pathway than the morn.

Welcome, with shouts of joy and pride,
　　Your veterans from the war-path's track;
You gave your boys, untrained, untried;
　　You bring them men and heroes back!

And shed no tear, though think you must
　　With sorrow of the martyred band;
Not even for him whose hallowed dust
　　Has made our prairies holy land.

Though by the places where they fell,
　　The places that are sacred ground,
Death, like a sullen sentinel,
　　Paces his everlasting round.

Yet when they set their country free
　　And gave her traitors fitting doom,
They left their last great enemy,
　　Baffled, beside an empty tomb.

Not there, but risen, redeemed, they go
　　Where all the paths are sweet with flow-
　　　ers;
They fought to give us Peace and lo!
　　They gained a better Peace than ours.
　　　　　　　　　PHŒBE CARY.

On May 24, 1865, the united armies of Grant and
Sherman, two hundred thousand strong, were re-
viewed at Washington by President Johnson and
his cabinet.

A SECOND REVIEW OF THE GRAND ARMY

[May 24, 1865]

I READ last night of the Grand Review
　　In Washington's chiefest avenue, —
Two hundred thousand men in blue,
　　I think they said was the number, —
Till I seemed to hear their trampling feet
The bugle blast and the drum's quick beat
The clatter of hoofs in the stony street,
The cheers of people who came to greet,
And the thousand details that to repeat
　　Would only my verse encumber, —

Till I fell in a revery, sad and sweet,
  And then to a fitful slumber.

When, lo! in a vision I seemed to stand
In the lonely Capitol. On each hand
Far stretched the portico, dim and grand
Its columns ranged, like a martial band
Of sheeted spectres, whom some command
  Had called to a last reviewing.
And the streets of the city were white and
    bare;
No footfall echoed across the square;
But out of the misty midnight air
I heard in the distance a trumpet blare,
And the wandering night-winds seemed to
    bear
  The sound of a far tattooing.

Then I held my breath with fear and dread;
For into the square, with a brazen tread,
There rode a figure whose stately head
  O'erlooked the review that morning,
That never bowed from its firm-set seat
When the living column passed its feet,
Yet now rode steadily up the street
  To the phantom bugle's warning:

Till it reached the Capitol square, and wheeled,
And there in the moonlight stood revealed
A well-known form that in State and field
  Had led our patriot sires:
Whose face was turned to the sleeping camp,
Afar through the river's fog and damp,
That showed no flicker, nor waning lamp,
  Nor wasted bivouac fires.

And I saw a phantom army come,
With never a sound of fife or drum,
But keeping time to a throbbing hum
  Of wailing and lamentation:
The martyred heroes of Malvern Hill,
Of Gettysburg and Chancellorsville,
The men whose wasted figures fill
  The patriot graves of the nation.

And there came the nameless dead, — the
    men
Who perished in fever-swamp and fen,
The slowly-starved of the prison-pen;
  And, marching beside the others,
Came the dusky martyrs of Pillow's fight,
With limbs enfranchised and bearing bright:
  I thought — perhaps 't was the pale moon-
      light —
  They looked as white as their brothers!

And so all night marched the Nation's dead,
With never a banner above them spread,
Nor a badge, nor a motto brandishèd;
No mark — save the bare uncovered head
  Of the silent bronze Reviewer;
With never an arch save the vaulted sky;
With never a flower save those that lie
On the distant graves — for love could buy
  No gift that was purer or truer.

So all night long swept the strange array;
So all night long, till the morning gray,
I watch'd for one who had passed away,
  With a reverent awe and wonder, —
Till a blue cap waved in the lengthening line,
And I knew that one who was kin of mine
Had come; and I spake — and lo! that sign
  Awakened me from my slumber.
                                    BRET HARTE.

The work of disbandment began at once, and
the troops were sent home as rapidly as possible;
they laid by the musket, took up the spade or
hammer, and returned once more to the occupa-
tions of peace.

WHEN JOHNNY COMES MARCH-
ING HOME

WHEN Johnny comes marching home again,
    Hurrah! hurrah!
We'll give him a hearty welcome then,
    Hurrah! hurrah!
The men will cheer, the boys will shout,
The ladies, they will all turn out,
    And we'll all feel gay,
When Johnny comes marching home.

The old church-bell will peal with joy,
    Hurrah! hurrah!
To welcome home our darling boy,
    Hurrah! hurrah!
The village lads and lasses say,
With roses they will strew the way;
    And we'll all feel gay,
When Johnny comes marching home.

Get ready for the jubilee,
    Hurrah! hurrah!
We'll give the hero three times three,
    Hurrah! hurrah!
The laurel-wreath is ready now
To place upon his loyal brow,
    And we'll all feel gay,
When Johnny comes marching home.

Let love and friendship on that day,
  Hurrah! hurrah!
Their choicest treasures then display,
  Hurrah! hurrah!
And let each one perform some part,
To fill with joy the warrior's heart;
  And we'll all feel gay,
When Johnny comes marching home.
          PATRICK SARSFIELD GILMORE.

DRIVING HOME THE COWS

OUT of the clover and blue-eyed grass,
  He turned them into the river-lane;
One after another he let them pass,
  Then fastened the meadow-bars again.

Under the willows, and over the hill,
  He patiently followed their sober pace;
The merry whistle for once was still,
  And something shadowed the sunny face.

Only a boy! and his father had said
  He never could let his youngest go:
Two already were lying dead
  Under the feet of the trampling foe.

But after the evening work was done,
  And the frogs were loud in the meadow-
    swamp,
Over his shoulder he slung his gun,
  And stealthily followed the foot-path damp,

Across the clover, and through the wheat,
  With resolute heart and purpose grim,
Though cold was the dew on his hurrying
    feet,
  And the blind bat's flitting startled him.

Thrice since then had the lanes been white,
  And the orchards sweet with apple-bloom;
And now, when the cows came back at night,
  The feeble father drove them home.

For news had come to the lonely farm
  That three were lying where two had lain;
And the old man's tremulous, palsied arm
  Could never lean on a son's again.

The summer day grew cold and late.
  He went for the cows when the work was
    done;
But down the lane, as he opened the gate,
  He saw them coming, one by one, —

Brindle, Ebony, Speckle, and Bess,
  Shaking their horns in the evening wind;
Cropping the buttercups out of the grass, —
  But who was it following close behind?

Loosely swung in the idle air
  The empty sleeve of army blue;
And worn and pale, from the crisping hair,
  Looked out a face that the father knew.

For Southern prisons will sometimes yawn,
  And yield their dead unto life again;
And the day that comes with a cloudy dawn
  In golden glory at last may wane.

The great tears sprang to their meeting eyes;
  For the heart must speak when the lips are
    dumb;
And under the silent evening skies,
  Together they followed the cattle home.
          KATE PUTNAM OSGOOD.

On July 21, 1865, services were held at Cam-
bridge, Mass., in commemoration of the three
hundredth anniversary of Harvard College. Ad-
dresses were made by General Meade and Gen-
eral Devens, and an ode written for the occasion
was read by James Russell Lowell. This ode,
perhaps the greatest ever delivered in America,
forms a fitting close to the history of the Civil
War.

ODE RECITED AT THE HARVARD COMMEMORATION

[July 21, 1865]

I

WEAK-WINGED is song,
Nor aims at that clear-ethered height
Whither the brave deed climbs for light:
    We seem to do them wrong,
Bringing our robin's-leaf to deck their hearse
Who in warm life-blood wrote their noble
    verse,
Our trivial song to honor those who come
With ears attuned to strenuous trump and
    drum,
And shaped in squadron-strophes their desire,
Live battle-odes whose lines were steel and fire
    Yet sometimes feathered words are strong,
A gracious memory to buoy up and save
From Lethe's dreamless ooze, the common
    grave
Of the unventurous throng.

II

To-day our Reverend Mother welcomes back
  Her wisest Scholars, those who understood
The deeper teaching of her mystic tome,
  And offered their fresh lives to make it
      good:
      No lore of Greece or Rome,
No science peddling with the names of things,
Or reading stars to find inglorious fates,
      Can lift our life with wings
Far from Death's idle gulf that for the many
      waits,
      And lengthen out our dates
With that clear fame whose memory sings
In manly hearts to come, and nerves them
      and dilates:
Nor such thy teaching, Mother of us all!
      Not such the trumpet-call
      Of thy diviner mood,
      That could thy sons entice
From happy homes and toils, the fruitful nest
Of those half-virtues which the world calls
      best,
      Into War's tumult rude;
      But rather far that stern device
The sponsors chose that round thy cradle
      stood
  In the dim, unventured wood,
  The VERITAS that lurks beneath
  The letter's unprolific sheath,
Life of whate'er makes life worth living,
Seed-grain of high emprise, immortal food,
  One heavenly thing whereof earth hath the
      giving.

III

Many loved Truth, and lavished life's best oil
  Amid the dust of books to find her,
Content at last, for guerdon of their toil,
  With the cast mantle she hath left behind
      her.
  Many in sad faith sought for her,
  Many with crossed hands sighed for her;
  But these, our brothers, fought for her,
  At life's dear peril wrought for her,
  So loved her that they died for her,
  Tasting the raptured fleetness
  Of her divine completeness:
  Their higher instinct knew
Those love her best who to themselves are
      true,
  And what they dare to dream of, dare to do;
  They followed her and found her
  Where all may hope to find,

Not in the ashes of the burnt-out mind,
But beautiful, with danger's sweetness round
      her.
  Where faith made whole with deed
  Breathes its awakening breath
  Into the lifeless creed,
  They saw her plumed and mailed,
  With sweet, stern face unveiled,
And all-repaying eyes, look proud on them
      in death.

IV

Our slender life runs rippling by, and glides
  Into the silent hollow of the past;
  What is there that abides
  To make the next age better for the last?
  Is earth too poor to give us
  Something to live for here that shall out-
      live us?
  Some more substantial boon
Than such as flows and ebbs with Fortune's
      fickle moon?
  The little that we see
  From doubt is never free;
  The little that we do
  Is but half-nobly true;
  With our laborious hiving
What men call treasure, and the gods call
      dross,
  Life seems a jest of Fate's contriving,
  Only secure in every one's conniving,
A long account of nothings paid with loss,
Where we poor puppets, jerked by unseen
      wires,
After our little hour of strut and rave,
With all our pasteboard passions and desires,
Loves, hates, ambitions, and immortal fires,
  Are tossed pell-mell together in the grave.
  But stay! no age was e'er degenerate,
  Unless men held it at too cheap a rate,
  For in our likeness still we shape our fate.
  Ah, there is something here
  Unfathomed by the cynic's sneer,
  Something that gives our feeble light
  A high immunity from Night,
  Something that leaps life's narrow bars
To claim its birthright with the hosts of
      heaven;
  A seed of sunshine that can leaven
  Our earthy dulness with the beams of stars
      And glorify our clay
  With light from fountains elder than the
      Day;
  A conscience more divine than we,
  A gladness fed with secret tears,

A vexing, forward-reaching sense
Of some more noble permanence;
    A light across the sea,
Which haunts the soul and will not let it be,
Still beaconing from the heights of unde-
        generate years.

v

            Whither leads the path
            To ampler fates that leads?
            Not down through flowery meads,
            To reap an aftermath
Of youth's vainglorious weeds,
But up the steep, amid the wrath
And shock of deadly-hostile creeds,
Where the world's best hope and stay
By battle's flashes gropes a desperate way,
And every turf the fierce foot clings to bleeds.
Peace hath her not ignoble wreath,
Ere yet the sharp, decisive word
Light the black lips of cannon, and the sword
Dreams in its easeful sheath;
But some day the live coal behind the thought,
            Whether from Baäl's stone obscene,
            Or from the shrine serene
            Of God's pure altar brought,
Bursts up in flame; the war of tongue and pen
Learns with what deadly purpose it was
        fraught,
And, helpless in the fiery passion caught,
Shakes all the pillared state with shock of men:
Some day the soft Ideal that we wooed
Confronts us fiercely, foe-beset, pursued,
And cries reproachful: "Was it, then, my
        praise,
And not myself was loved? Prove now thy
        truth;
I claim of thee the promise of thy youth;
Give me thy life, or cower in empty phrase,
The victim of thy genius, not its mate!"
            Life may be given in many ways,
            And loyalty to Truth be sealed
As bravely in the closet as the field,
            So bountiful is Fate;
            But then to stand beside her,
            When craven churls deride her,
To front a lie in arms and not to yield,
            This shows, methinks, God's plan
            And measure of a stalwart man,
            Limbed like the old heroic breeds,
            Who stands self-poised on manhood's
                solid earth,
Not forced to frame excuses for his birth,
Fed from within with all the strength he
        needs.

vi

Such was he, our Martyr-Chief,
    Whom late the Nation he had led,
    With ashes on her head,
Wept with the passion of an angry grief:
Forgive me, if from present things I turn
To speak what in my heart will beat and
        burn,
And hang my wreath on his world-honored
        urn.
    Nature, they say, doth dote,
    And cannot make a man
    Save on some worn-out plan,
    Repeating us by rote:
For him her Old-World moulds aside she
        threw,
    And, choosing sweet clay from the breast
        Of the unexhausted West,
With stuff untainted shaped a hero new,
Wise, steadfast in the strength of God, and
        true
How beautiful to see
Once more a shepherd of mankind indeed,
Who loved his charge, but never loved to
        lead;
One whose meek flock the people joyed to
        be,
    Not lured by any cheat of birth,
    But by his clear-grained human worth,
And brave old wisdom of sincerity!
    They knew that outward grace is dust;
    They could not choose but trust
In that sure-footed mind's unfaltering skill,
    And supple-tempered will
That bent like perfect steel to spring again
        and thrust.
    His was no lonely mountain-peak of mind
    Thrusting to thin air o'er our cloudy bars,
    A sea-mark now, now lost in vapors
        blind;
    Broad prairie rather, genial, level-lined,
    Fruitful and friendly for all human kind,
Yet also nigh to heaven and loved of loftiest
        stars,
            Nothing of Europe here,
Or, then, of Europe fronting mornward still,
    Ere any names of Serf and Peer
    Could Nature's equal scheme deface
    And thwart her genial will;
    Here was a type of the true elder race,
And one of Plutarch's men talked with u
        face to face.
    I praise him not; it were too late;
And some innative weakness there must b
In him who condescends to victory

such as the Present gives, and cannot wait,
  Safe in himself as in a fate.
    So always firmly he:
    He knew to bide his time,
    And can his fame abide,
Still patient in his simple faith sublime,
    Till the wise years decide.
  Great captains, with their guns and drums,
    Disturb our judgment for the hour,
    But at last silence comes;
These all are gone, and, standing like a
    tower,
Our children shall behold his fame,
    The kindly-earnest, brave, foreseeing
    man,
Sagacious, patient, dreading praise, not blame,
  New birth of our new soil, the first Amer-
    ican.

VII

Long as man's hope insatiate can discern
  Or only guess some more inspiring goal
  Outside of Self, enduring as the pole,
Along whose course the flying axles burn
Of spirits bravely-pitched, earth's manlier
    brood;
  Long as below we cannot find
The meed that stills the inexorable mind;
So long this faith to some ideal Good,
Under whatever mortal names it masks,
Freedom, Law, Country, this ethereal mood
That thanks the Fates for their severer tasks,
Feeling its challenged pulses leap,
While others skulk in subterfuges cheap,
And, set in Danger's van, has all the boon it
    asks,
  Shall win man's praise and woman's love,
  Shall be a wisdom that we set above
All other skills and gifts to culture dear,
  A virtue round whose forehead we inwreathe
  Laurels that with a living passion breathe
When other crowns grow, while we twine
    them, sear.
    What brings us thronging these high rites
    to pay,
And seal these hours the noblest of our year,
  Save that our brothers found this better
    way?

VIII

We sit here in the Promised Land
  That flows with Freedom's honey and
    milk;
But 't was they won it, sword in hand,
Making the nettle danger soft for us as silk.

We welcome back our bravest and our
    best; —
Ah me! not all! some come not with the rest,
Who went forth brave and bright as any here!
I strive to mix some gladness with my strain,
    But the sad strings complain,
    And will not please the ear:
I sweep them for a pæan, but they wane
    Again and yet again
Into a dirge, and die away, in pain.
In these brave ranks I only see the gaps,
Thinking of dear ones whom the dumb turf
    wraps,
Dark to the triumph which they died to gain:
    Fitlier may others greet the living,
    For me the past is unforgiving;
    I with uncovered head
    Salute the sacred dead,
Who went, and who return not. — Say not so!
'T is not the grapes of Canaan that repay,
But the high faith that failed not by the way;
Virtue treads paths that end not in the grave;
No ban of endless night exiles the brave;
    And to the saner mind
We rather seem the dead that stayed behind.
Blow, trumpets, all your exultations blow!
For never shall their aureoled presence lack;
I see them muster in a gleaming row,
With ever-youthful brows that nobler show;
We find in our dull road their shining track;
    In every nobler mood
We feel the orient of their spirit glow,
Part of our life's unalterable good,
Of all our saintlier aspiration;
    They come transfigured back,
Secure from change in their high-hearted ways,
Beautiful evermore, and with the rays
Of morn on their white Shields of Expectation!

IX

    But is there hope to save
  Even this ethereal essence from the grave?
  What ever 'scaped Oblivion's subtle wrong
Save a few clarion names, or golden threads
    of song?
    Before my musing eye
  The mighty ones of old sweep by,
Disvoicèd now and insubstantial things,
As noisy once as we; poor ghosts of kings,
Shadows of empire wholly gone to dust,
And many races, nameless long ago,
To darkness driven by that imperious gust
Of ever-rushing Time that here doth blow:
O visionary world, condition strange,
Where naught abiding is but only Change,

Where the deep-bolted stars themselves still
  shift and range!
 Shall we to more continuance make pre-
  tence?
Renown builds tombs; a life-estate is Wit;
  And, bit by bit,
The cunning years steal all from us but woe;
  Leaves are we, whose decays no harvest
  sow.
    But, when we vanish hence,
 Shall they lie forceless in the dark below,
 Save to make green their little length of
  sods,
 Or deepen pansies for a year or two,
 Who now to us are shining-sweet as gods?
 Was dying all they had the skill to do?
 That were not fruitless: but the Soul re-
  sents
 Such short-lived service, as if blind events
 Ruled without her, or earth could so en-
  dure;
  She claims a more divine investiture
 Of longer tenure than Fame's airy rents;
 Whate'er she touches doth her nature
  share;
  Her inspiration haunts the ennobled air,
    Gives eyes to mountains blind,
 Ears to the deaf earth, voices to the wind,
 And her clear trump sings succor every-
  where
 By lonely bivouacs to the wakeful mind;
 For soul inherits all that soul could dare:
    Yea, Manhood hath a wider span
 And larger privilege of life than man.
 The single deed, the private sacrifice,
 So radiant now through proudly-hidden
  tears,
 Is covered up erelong from mortal eyes
 With thoughtless drift of the deciduous
  years;
 But that high privilege that makes all men
  peers,
 That leap of heart whereby a people rise
    Up to a noble anger's height,
 And, flamed on by the Fates, not shrink, but
  grow more bright,
    That swift validity in noble veins,
    Of choosing danger and disdaining shame,
    Of being set on flame
 By the pure fire that flies all contact base,
 But wraps its chosen with angelic might,
    These are imperishable gains,
  Sure as the sun, medicinal as light,
 These hold great futures in their lusty reins
 And certify to earth a new imperial race.

X

    Who now shall sneer?
    Who dare again to say we trace
    Our lines to a plebeian race?
    Roundhead and Cavalier!
Dumb are those names erewhile in battle
  loud;
Dream-footed as the shadow of a cloud,
    They flit across the ear:
That is best blood that hath most iron in 't.
To edge resolve with, pouring without stint
    For what makes manhood dear.
    Tell us not of Plantagenets,
Hapsburgs, and Guelfs, whose thin bloods
  crawl
Down from some victor in a border-brawl!
    How poor their outworn coronets,
Matched with one leaf of that plain civic
  wreath
Our brave for honor's blazon shall bequeath,
    Through whose desert a rescued Nation
  sets
Her heel on treason, and the trumpet hears
Shout victory, tingling Europe's sullen ears
    With vain resentments and more vain
  regrets!

XI

    Not in anger, not in pride,
    Pure from passion's mixture rude
    Ever to base earth allied,
    But with far-heard gratitude,
    Still with heart and voice renewed,
To heroes living and dear martyrs dead,
The strain should close that consecrates our
  brave.
 Lift the heart and lift the head!
    Lofty be its mood and grave,
    Not without a martial ring,
    Not without a prouder tread
    And a peal of exultation:
    Little right has he to sing
 Through whose heart in such an hour
 Beats no march of conscious power,
 Sweeps no tumult of elation!
    'T is no Man we celebrate,
    By his country's victories great,
 A hero half, and half the whim of Fate,
 But the pith and marrow of a Nation
    Drawing force from all her men,
    Highest, humblest, weakest, all,
    For her time of need, and then
    Pulsing it again through them,
 Till the basest can no longer cower,
 Feeling his soul spring up divinely tall,

Touched but in passing by her mantle-
  hem.
Come back, then, noble pride, for 't is her
  dower!
  How could poet ever tower,
  If his passions, hopes, and fears,
  If his triumphs and his tears,
  Kept not measure with his people?
Boom, cannon, boom to all the winds and
  waves!
Clash out, glad bells, from every rocking
  steeple!
Banners, adance with triumph, bend your
  staves!
  And from every mountain-peak,
  Let beacon-fire to answering beacon
  speak,
  Katahdin tell Monadnock, Whiteface he,
And so leap on in light from sea to sea,
  Till the glad news be sent
  Across a kindling continent,
Making earth feel more firm and air breathe
  braver:
"Be proud! for she is saved, and all have
  helped to save her!
  She that lifts up the manhood of the
  poor,
  She of the open soul and open door,
  With room about her hearth for all man-
  kind!
  The fire is dreadful in her eyes no
  more;
  From her bold front the helm she doth
  unbind,
  Sends all her handmaid armies back to
  spin,
  And bids her navies, that so lately
  hurled
  Their crashing battle, hold their thun-
  ders in,

Swimming like birds of calm along the
  unharmful shore.
No challenge sends she to the elder
  world,
  That looked askance and hated; a light
  scorn
  Plays o'er her mouth, as round her
  mighty knees
  She calls her children back, and waits
  the morn
Of nobler day, enthroned between her subject
  seas."

XII

Bow down, dear Land, for thou hast found
  release!
  Thy God, in these distempered days,
  Hath taught thee the sure wisdom of His
  ways,
And through thine enemies hath wrought
  thy peace!
  Bow down in prayer and praise!
No poorest in thy borders but may now
Lift to the juster skies a man's enfranchised
  brow.
O Beautiful! my Country! ours once more!
Smoothing thy gold of war-dishevelled hair
O'er such sweet brows as never other wore,
  And letting thy set lips,
  Freed from wrath's pale eclipse,
  The rosy edges of their smile lay bare,
What words divine of lover or of poet
Could tell our love and make thee know it,
Among the Nations bright beyond compare?
  What were our lives without thee?
  What all our lives to save thee?
  We reck not what we gave thee;
  We will not dare to doubt thee,
But ask whatever else, and we will dare!
                    JAMES RUSSELL LOWELL.

PART V

THE PERIOD OF EXPANSION

THE EAGLE'S SONG

THE lioness whelped, and the sturdy cub
Was seized by an eagle and carried up,
And homed for a while in an eagle's nest,
And slept for a while on an eagle's breast;
And the eagle taught it the eagle's song:
"To be stanch, and valiant, and free, and strong!"

The lion whelp sprang from the eyrie nest,
From the lofty crag where the queen birds rest;
He fought the King on the spreading plain,
And drove him back o'er the foaming main.
He held the land as a thrifty chief,
And reared his cattle, and reaped his sheaf
Nor sought the help of a foreign hand
Yet welcomed all to his own free land!

Two were the sons that the country bore
To the Northern lakes and the Southern shore;
And Chivalry dwelt with the Southern son,
And Industry lived with the Northern one.
Tears for the time when they broke and fought!
Tears was the price of the union wrought!
And the land was red in a sea of blood,
Where brother for brother had swelled the flood!

And now that the two are one again,
Behold on their shield the word "Refrain!"
And the lion cubs twain sing the eagle's song:
"To be stanch, and valiant, and free, and strong!"
For the eagle's beak, and the lion's paw,
And the lion's fangs, and the eagle's claw,
And the eagle's swoop, and the lion's might,
And the lion's leap, and the eagle's sight,
Shall guard the flag with the word "Refrain!"
Now that the two are one again!

RICHARD MANSFIELD.

CHAPTER I

RECONSTRUCTION AND AFTER

The war was over, but three great questions remained to be settled. How were the people of the South to be regarded? How was the Union to be reconstructed? What was to be done with the three millions of negroes who had been given their freedom? These were the questions which came before the Thirty-Ninth Congress.

TO THE THIRTY-NINTH CONGRESS

O PEOPLE-CHOSEN! are ye not
　Likewise the chosen of the Lord,
　To do His will and speak His word?

From the loud thunder-storm of war
　Not man alone hath called ye forth,
　But He, the God of all the earth!

The torch of vengeance in your hands
　He quenches; unto Him belongs
　The solemn recompense of wrongs.

Enough of blood the land has seen,
　And not by cell or gallows-stair
　Shall ye the way of God prepare.

Say to the pardon-seekers: Keep
　Your manhood, bend no suppliant knees,
　Nor palter with unworthy pleas.

Above your voices sounds the wail
　Of starving men; we shut in vain
　Our eyes to Pillow's ghastly stain.

What words can drown that bitter cry?
　What tears wash out the stain of death?
　What oaths confirm your broken faith?

From you alone the guaranty
　Of union, freedom, peace, we claim;
　We urge no conqueror's terms of shame.

Alas! no victor's pride is ours;
　We bend above our triumphs won
　Like David o'er his rebel son.

Be men, not beggars. Cancel all
　By one brave, generous action; trust
　Your better instincts, and be just!

Make all men peers before the law,
　Take hands from off the negro's throat,
　Give black and white an equal vote.

Keep all your forfeit lives and lands,
　But give the common law's redress
　To labor's utter nakedness.

Revive the old heroic will;
　Be in the right as brave and strong
　As ye have proved yourselves in wrong.

Defeat shall then be victory,
　Your loss the wealth of full amends,
　And hate be love, and foes be friends.

Then buried be the dreadful past,
　Its common slain be mourned, and let
　All memories soften to regret.

Then shall the Union's mother-heart
　Her lost and wandering ones recall,
　Forgiving and restoring all, —

And Freedom break her marble trance
　Above the Capitolian dome,
　Stretch hands, and bid ye welcome home!
　　　　JOHN GREENLEAF WHITTIER.

Few men could have been worse fitted for the delicate task of reconstruction than Andrew Johnson. But even his policy, narrow as it was, was not narrow enough to suit the radical Republicans in Congress.

"MR. JOHNSON'S POLICY OF RE-CONSTRUCTION"

SOME COMMENT FROM THE BOYS IN BLUE

　"HIS policy," do you say?
By heaven, who says so lies in his throat!
'T was our policy, boys, from our muster-day,
Through skirmish and bivouac, march and
　　　fray —
　"His policy," do you say?

　"His policy" — do but note!
'T is a pitiful falsehood for you to say.

Did he bid all the stars in our banner float?
Was it he shouted Union from every throat
   Through the long war's weary day?

"His policy" — how does it hap?
Has the old word "Union" no meaning,
   pray?
What meant the "U. S." upon every cap —
Upon every button, belt, and strap?
   'T was our policy all the way.

"His policy?" That may do
For a silly and empty political brag;
But 't was held by every Boy in Blue
When he lifted his right hand, stanch and true,
   And swore to sustain the flag.

We are with him none the less —
He works for the same great end we sought;
We feel for the South in its deep distress,
And to get the old Union restored we press —
   'T was for this we enlisted and fought.

Be it his or whose it may,
'T is the policy, boys, that we avow;
There were noble hearts in the ranks of gray
As they proved on many a bloody day,
   And we would not oppress them now.

"Let us all forgive and forget:"
It was thus Grant spoke to General Lee,
When, with wounds still raw and bayonets
   wet,
The chiefs of the two great armies met
   Beneath the old apple-tree.
          CHARLES GRAHAM HALPINE.

The leader of this coterie was Thaddeus Stevens.
He declared the South was in a state of anarchy,
demanded that it be placed under military rule
and that suffrage be extended to the negroes.
In February, 1868, he introduced a resolution
that "Andrew Johnson, President of the United
States, be impeached of high crimes and misde-
meanors in office," but at the trial which followed
the proceedings were shown to have been actu-
ated by partisan bitterness and the President was
acquitted. The verdict was a heavy blow to
Stevens. He had burned himself out and died in
August.

THADDEUS STEVENS

DIED AUG. 11, 1868

AN eye with the piercing eagle's fire,
   Not the look of the gentle dove;

Not his the form that men admire,
   Nor the face that tender women love.

Working first for his daily bread
   With the humblest toilers of the earth;
Never walking with free, proud tread —
   Crippled and halting from his birth.

Wearing outside a thorny suit
   Of sharp, sarcastic, stinging power;
Sweet at the core as sweetest fruit,
   Or inmost heart of fragrant flower.

Fierce and trenchant, the haughty foe
   Felt his words like a sword of flame;
But to the humble, poor, and low
   Soft as a woman's his accents came.

Not his the closest, tenderest friend —
   No children blessed his lonely way;
But down in his heart until the end
   The tender dream of his boyhood lay.

His mother's faith he held not fast;
   But he loved her living, mourned her dead,
And he kept her memory to the last
   As green as the sod above her bed.

He held as sacred in his home
   Whatever things she wrought or planned,
And never suffered change to come
   To the work of her "industrious hand."

For her who pillowed first his head
   He heaped with a wealth of flowers the
      grave,
While he chose to sleep in an unmarked bed,
   By his Master's humblest poor — the slave!

Suppose he swerved from the straightest
   course —
That the things he should not do he did —
That he hid from the eyes of mortals, close,
   Such sins as you and I have hid?

Or suppose him worse than you; what then?
   Judge not, lest you be judged for sin!
One said who knew the hearts of men:
   Who loveth much shall a pardon win.

The Prince of Glory for sinners bled;
   His soul was bought with a royal price;
And his beautified feet on flowers may tread
   To-day with his Lord in Paradise.
          PHŒBE CARY.

The South's condition meanwhile was pitiful indeed. Negroes, led by " carpet-baggers " from the North, secured the ascendancy in state government. Millions of dollars were wasted or stolen, and it looked for a time as though a great section of the country was doomed to negro domination.

SOUTH CAROLINA TO THE STATES OF THE NORTH

ESPECIALLY TO THOSE THAT FORMED A PART OF THE ORIGINAL THIRTEEN

I LIFT these hands with iron fetters banded:
  Beneath the scornful sunlight and cold stars
I rear my once imperial forehead branded
  By alien shame's immedicable scars;
Like some pale captive, shunned by all the nations,
  I crouch unpitied, quivering and apart —
Laden with countless woes and desolations,
  The life-blood freezing round a broken heart!

About my feet, splashed red with blood of slaughters,
  My children gathering in wild, mournful throngs,
Despairing sons, frail infants, stricken daughters,
  Rehearse the awful burden of their wrongs;
Vain is their cry, and worse than vain their pleading:
  I turn from stormy breasts, from yearning eyes,
To mark where Freedom's outraged form receding,
  Wanes in chill shadow down the midnight skies!

I wooed her once in wild tempestuous places,
  The purple vintage of my soul outpoured,
To win and keep her unrestrained embraces,
  What time the olive-crown o'ertopped the sword;
Oh! northmen, with your gallant heroes blending,
  Mine, in old years, for this sweet goddess died;
But now — ah! shame, all other shame transcending!
  Your pitiless hands have torn her from my side.

What!'t is a tyrant-party's treacherous action —
  *Your hand is clean, your conscience clear,
  ye sigh* ;
Ay! but ere now your sires had throttled faction,
  Or, pealed o'er half the world their battle-cry;
Its voice outrung from solemn mountain-passes
  Swept by wild storm-winds of the Atlantic strand,
To where the swart Sierras' sullen grasses
  Droop in low languors of the sunset-land!

Never, since earthly States began their story,
  Hath any suffered, bided, borne like me:
At last, recalling all mine ancient glory,
  I vowed my fettered Commonwealth to free:
Even at the thought, beside the prostrate column
  Of chartered rights, which blasted lay and dim —
Uprose my noblest son with purpose solemn,
  While, host on host, his brethren followed *him* :

Wrong, grasped by *truth*, arraigned by *law* (whose sober
  Majestic mandates rule o'er change and time) —
Smit by the *ballot*, like some flushed October,
  Reeled in the Autumn rankness of his crime;
Struck, tortured, pierced — but not a blow returning.
  The steadfast phalanx of my honored braves
Planted their bloodless flag where sunrise burning,
  Flashed a new splendor o'er our martyrs' graves!

What then ? Oh, sister States! what welcome omen
  Of love and concord crossed our brightening blue,
The foes we vanquished, are they not *your* foemen,
  Our laws upheld, your sacred safeguards, too ?
Yet scarce had victory crowned our grand endeavor,
  And peace crept out from shadowy glooms remote —

Than — as if bared to blast all hope for-
ever,
    Your tyrant's sword shone glittering at my
    throat!

Once more my bursting chains were reunited,
Once more barbarian plaudits wildly rung
O'er the last promise of deliverance blighted,
    The prostrate purpose and the palsied
    tongue:
Ah! faithless sisters, 'neath my swift un-
doing,
    Peers the black presage of your wrath to
    come;
Above your heads are signal clouds of ruin,
    Whose lightnings flash, whose thunders
    are not dumb!

There towers a judgment-seat beyond our
seeing;
    There lives a Judge, whom none can
    bribe or blind;
Before whose dread decree, your spirit fleeing,
    May reap the whirlwind, having sown the
    wind:
I, in that day of justice, fierce and torrid,
    When blood — *your* blood — outpours like
    poisoned wine,
*Pointing to these chained limbs, this blasted
    forehead,*
    May mock your ruin, as ye mocked at mine!
        PAUL HAMILTON HAYNE.

But the white people of the South rallied at
last, asserted their supremacy, and seized the
reins of government. The famous Ku-Klux Klan
was organized and spread terror among the ne-
groes, by its sure and swift administration of
punishment — just and unjust.

KU-KLUX

WE have sent him seeds of the melon's core,
And nailed a warning upon his door;
By the Ku-Klux laws we can do no more.

Down in the hollow, 'mid crib and stack,
The roof of his low-porched house looms
black,
Not a line of light at the doorsill's crack.

Yet arm and mount! and mask and ride!
The hounds can sense though the fox may
hide!
And for a word too much men oft have died.

The clouds blow heavy towards the moon.
The edge of the storm will reach it soon.
The killdee cries and the lonesome loon.

The clouds shall flush with a wilder glare
Than the lightning makes with his angled flare,
When the Ku-Klux verdict is given there.

In the pause of the thunder rolling low,
A rifle's answer — who shall know
From the wind's fierce hurl and the rain's
black blow?

Only the signature written grim
At the end of the message brought to him, —
A hempen rope and a twisted limb.

So arm and mount! and mask and ride!
The hounds can sense though the fox may
hide!
And for a word too much men oft have died.
        MADISON CAWEIN.

The North kept its hands off and permitted the
South to work out its own destiny — which it did
blindly and blunderingly enough. Yet bravely,
too; for it had only ashes to build from. But from
the ashes a new land arose, and a better one.

THE REAR GUARD

THE guns are hushed. On every field once
flowing
    With war's red flood May's breath of peace
    is shed,
And, spring's young grass and gracious flow-
ers are growing
    Above the dead.

Ye gray old men whom we this day are greet-
ing,
    Honor to you, honor and love and trust!
Brave to the brave. Your soldier hands are
meeting
    Across their dust.

Bravely they fought who charged when flags
were flying
    In cannon's crash, in screech and scream
    of shell;
Bravely they fell, who lay alone and dying
    In battle's hell.

Honor to them! Far graves to-day are flinging
    Up through the soil peace-blooms to meet
    the sun,

And daisied heads to summer winds are sing-
ing
    Their long "well done."

Our vanguard, they. They went with hot
blood flushing
At battle's din, at joy of bugle's call.
They fell with smiles, the flood of young life
gushing,
    Full brave the fall!

But braver ye who, when the war was ended,
    And bugle's call and wave of flag were
done,
Could come back home, so long left unde-
fended.
    Your cause unwon,

And twist the useless sword to hook of reaping,
    Rebuild the homes, set back the empty
chair
And brave a land where waste and want were
keeping
    Guard everywhere.

All this you did, your courage strong upon you,
    And out of ashes, wreck, a new land rose,
Through years of war no braver battle won
you,
    'Gainst fiercer foes.

And now to-day a prospered land is cheering
    And lifting up her voice in lusty pride
For you gray men, who fought and wrought,
not fearing
    Battle's red tide.

Our rear guard, ye whose step is slowing,
slowing,
    Whose ranks, earth-thinned, are filling
otherwhere,
Who wore the gray — the gray, alas! still
showing
    On bleaching hair.

For forty years you've watched this land grow
stronger,
    For forty years you've been its bulwark,
stay;
Tarry awhile; pause yet a little longer
    Upon the way.

And set our feet where there may be no turn-
ing,
    And set our faces straight on duty's track,

Where there may be for stray, strange goods
no yearning
    Nor looking back.

And when for you the last tattoo has sounded,
    And on death's silent field you've pitched
your tent,
When, bowed through tears, the arc of life
has rounded
    To full content,

We that are left will count it guerdon royal,
    Our heritage no years can take away,
That we were born of those, unflinching,
loyal,
    Who wore the gray.
        IRENE FOWLER BROWN.

The bitterness which the great struggle had
engendered gradually gave place to a kindlier
feeling. As early as 1867, the women of Columbus,
Miss., decorated alike the graves of Confederate
and Union soldiers, an action which was the first
of many such.

THE BLUE AND THE GRAY

[1867]

By the flow of the inland river,
    Whence the fleets of iron have fled,
Where the blades of the grave-grass quiver,
    Asleep are the ranks of the dead:
        Under the sod and the dew,
            Waiting the judgment-day;
        Under the one, the Blue,
            Under the other, the Gray.

These in the robings of glory,
    Those in the gloom of defeat,
All with the battle-blood gory,
    In the dusk of eternity meet:
        Under the sod and the dew,
            Waiting the judgment-day;
        Under the laurel, the Blue,
            Under the willow, the Gray.

From the silence of sorrowful hours
    The desolate mourners go,
Lovingly laden with flowers
    Alike for the friend and the foe:
        Under the sod and the dew
            Waiting the judgment-day;
        Under the roses, the Blue,
            Under the lilies, the Gray.

So with an equal splendor,
    The morning sun-rays fall,
With a touch impartially tender,
    On the blossoms blooming for all:
        Under the sod and the dew,
            Waiting the judgment-day;
        Broidered with gold, the Blue,
            Mellowed with gold, the Gray.

So, when the summer calleth,
    On forest and field of grain,
With an equal murmur falleth
    The cooling drip of the rain:
        Under the sod and the dew,
            Waiting the judgment-day;
        Wet with the rain, the Blue,
            Wet with the rain, the Gray.

Sadly, but not with upbraiding,
    The generous deed was done,
In the storm of the years that are fading
    No braver battle was won:
        Under the sod and the dew,
            Waiting the judgment-day;
        Under the blossoms, the Blue,
            Under the garlands, the Gray.

No more shall the war-cry sever,
    Or the winding rivers be red;
They banish our anger forever
    When they laurel the graves of our dead!
        Under the sod and the dew,
            Waiting the judgment-day;
        Love and tears for the Blue,
            Tears and love for the Gray.
                        FRANCIS MILES FINCH.

When the South was swept by yellow fever a few years later, the North rushed to its relief in a way which showed how completely old animosities had been forgotten.

THE STRICKEN SOUTH TO THE NORTH

WHEN ruthful time the South's memorial places —
    Her heroes' graves — had wreathed in grass and flowers;
When Peace ethereal, crowned by all her graces,
    Returned to make more bright the summer hours;

When doubtful hearts revived, and hopes grew stronger;
    When old sore-cankering wounds that pierced and stung,
Throbbed with their first, mad, feverous pain no longer,
    While the fair future spake with flattering tongue;
When once, once more she felt her pulses beating
    To rhythms of healthful joy and brave desire;
Lo! round her doomed horizon darkly meeting,
    A pall of blood-red vapors veined with fire!

Oh! ghastly portent of fast-coming sorrows!
    Of doom that blasts the blood and blights the breath,
Robs youth and manhood of all golden morrows —
    And life's clear goblet brims with wine of death! —
Oh! swift fulfilment of this portent dreary!
    Oh! nightmare rule of ruin, racked by fears,
Heartbroken wail, and solemn *miserere*,
    Imperious anguish, and soul-melting tears!
Oh! faith, thrust downward from celestial splendors,
    Oh! love grief-bound, with palely-murmurous mouth!
Oh! agonized by life's supreme surrenders —
    Behold her now — the scourged and suffering South!

No balm in Gilead? nay, but while her forehead,
    Pallid and drooping, lies in foulest dust,
There steals across the desolate spaces torrid,
    A voice of manful cheer and heavenly trust,
A hand redeeming breaks the frozen starkness
    Of palsied nerve, and dull, despondent brain;
Rolls back the curtain of malignant darkness,
    And shows the eternal blue of heaven again —
Revealing there, o'er worlds convulsed and shaken,
    That face whose mystic tenderness enticed

To hope new-born earth's lost bereaved,
    forsaken!
  Ah! still beyond the tempest smiles the
    Christ!

Whose voice? Whose hand? Oh, thanks
    divinest Master,
  Thanks for those grand emotions which
    impart
Grace to the North to feel the South's dis-
    aster,
  The South to bow with touched and cordial
    heart!
Now, now at last the links which war had
    broken
  Are welded fast, at mercy's charmed com-
    mands;
Now, now at last the magic words are
    spoken
  Which blend in one two long-divided
    lands!
O North! you came with warrior strife and
    clangor;
  You left our South one gory burial ground;
But love, more potent than your haughtiest
    anger,
  Subdues the souls which hate could only
    wound!
                    PAUL HAMILTON HAYNE.

On July 29, 1866, the first submarine cable was
completed between Ireland and Newfoundland,
the enterprise having been undertaken and carried
through by Cyrus West Field.

HOW CYRUS LAID THE CABLE

[July 29, 1866]

COME, listen all unto my song;
    It is no silly fable;
'T is all about the mighty cord
    They call the Atlantic Cable.

Bold Cyrus Field he said, says he,
    "I have a pretty notion
That I can run a telegraph
    Across the Atlantic Ocean."

Then all the people laughed, and said
    They'd like to see him do it;
He might get half-seas over, but
    He never could go through it.

To carry out his foolish plan
    He never would be able;
He might as well go hang himself
    With his Atlantic Cable.

But Cyrus was a valiant man,
    A fellow of decision;
And heeded not their mocking words,
    Their laughter and derision.

Twice did his bravest efforts fail,
    And yet his mind was stable;
He wa'n't the man to break his heart
    Because he broke his cable.

"Once more, my gallant boys!" he cried;
    "Three times! — you know the fa-
        ble
(I'll make it thirty," muttered he,
    "But I will lay the cable!").

Once more they tried, — hurrah! hurrah!
    What means this great commotion?
The Lord be praised! the cable's laid
    Across the Atlantic Ocean!

Loud ring the bells, — for, flashing through
    Six hundred leagues of water,
Old Mother England's benison
    Salutes her eldest daughter!

O'er all the land the tidings speed,
    And soon, in every nation,
They'll hear about the cable with
    Profoundest admiration!

Now, long live President and Queen;
    And long live gallant Cyrus;
And may his courage, faith, and zeal
    With emulation fire us;

And may we honor evermore
    The manly, bold, and stable;
And tell our sons, to make them brave,
    How Cyrus laid the cable!
                    JOHN GODFREY SAXE.

THE CABLE HYMN

O LONELY bay of Trinity,
    O dreary shores, give ear!
Lean down unto the white-lipped sea
    The voice of God to hear!

From world to world His couriers fly,
  Thought-winged and shod with fire;
The angel of His stormy sky
  Rides down the sunken wire.

What saith the herald of the Lord?
  "The world's long strife is done;
Close wedded by that mystic cord,
  Its continents are one.

"And one in heart, as one in blood,
  Shall all her peoples be;
The hands of human brotherhood
  Are clasped beneath the sea.

"Through Orient seas, o'er Afric's plain
  And Asian mountains borne,
The vigor of the Northern brain
  Shall nerve the world outworn.

"From clime to clime, from shore to shore,
  Shall thrill the magic thread;
The new Prometheus steals once more
  The fire that wakes the dead."

Throb on, strong pulse of thunder! beat
  From answering beach to beach;
Fuse nations in thy kindly heat,
  And melt the chains of each!

Wild terror of the sky above,
  Glide tamed and dumb below!
Bear gently, Ocean's carrier-dove,
  Thy errands to and fro.

Weave on, swift shuttle of the Lord,
  Beneath the deep so far,
The bridal robe of earth's accord,
  The funeral shroud of war!

For lo! the fall of Ocean's wall
  Space mocked and time outrun;
And round the world the thought of all
  Is as the thought of one!

The poles unite, the zones agree,
  The tongues of striving cease;
As on the Sea of Galilee
  The Christ is whispering, Peace!
        JOHN GREENLEAF WHITTIER.

The most notable accomplishment of Johnson's
administration was the purchase from Russia in
1867 of the territory of Alaska. The price paid
was $7,200,000, and the cession was formally
made on June 20.

AN ARCTIC VISION

[June 20, 1867]

WHERE the short-legged Esquimaux
Waddle in the ice and snow,
And the playful Polar bear
Nips the hunter unaware;
Where by day they track the ermine,
And by night another vermin, —
Segment of the frigid zone,
Where the temperature alone
Warms on St. Elias' cone;
Polar dock, where Nature slips
From the ways her icy ships;
Land of fox and deer and sable,
Shore end of our western cable, —
Let the news that flying goes
Thrill through all your Arctic floes,
And reverberate the boast
From the cliffs off Beechey's coast,
Till the tidings, circling round
Every bay of Norton Sound,
Throw the vocal tide-wave back
To the isles of Kodiac.
Let the stately Polar bears
Waltz around the pole in pairs,
And the walrus, in his glee,
Bare his tusk of ivory;
While the bold sea-unicorn
Calmly takes an extra horn;
All ye Polar skies, reveal your
Very rarest of parhelia;
Trip it, all ye merry dancers,
In the airiest of "Lancers";
Slide, ye solemn glaciers, slide,
One inch farther to the tide,
Nor in rash precipitation
Upset Tyndall's calculation.
Know you not what fate awaits you,
Or to whom the future mates you?
All ye icebergs make salaam, —
You belong to Uncle Sam!

On the spot where Eugene Sue
Led his wretched Wandering Jew,
Stands a form whose features strike
Russ and Esquimaux alike.
He it is whom Skalds of old
In their Runic rhymes foretold;
Lean of flank and lank of jaw,
See the real Northern Thor!
See the awful Yankee leering
Just across the Straits of Behring;

On the drifted snow, too plain,
Sinks his fresh tobacco stain,
Just beside the deep inden-
Tation of his Number 10.

Leaning on his icy hammer
Stands the hero of this drama,
And above the wild-duck's clamor,
In his own peculiar grammar,
With its linguistic disguises,
Lo, the Arctic prologue rises:
"Wall, I reckon 'tain't so bad,
Seein' ez 't was all they had;
True, the Springs are rather late
And early Falls predominate;
But the ice crop's pretty sure,
And the air is kind o' pure;
'Tain't so very mean a trade,
When the land is all surveyed.
There's a right smart chance for fur-chase
All along this recent purchase,
And, unless the stories fail,
Every fish from cod to whale;
Rocks, too; mebbe quartz; let's see, —
'T would be strange if there should be, —
Seems I've heerd such stories told;
Eh! — why, bless us, — yes, it's gold!"

While the blows are falling thick
From his California pick,
You may recognize the Thor
Of the vision that I saw, —
Freed from legendary glamour,
See the real magician's hammer.

                    BRET HARTE.

ALASKA

ICE built, ice bound, and ice bounded,
Such cold seas of silence! such room!
Such snow-light, such sea-light, confounded
With thunders that smite like a doom!
Such grandeur! such glory! such gloom!
Hear that boom! Hear that deep distant boom
   Of an avalanche hurled
   Down this unfinished world!

Ice seas! and ice summits! ice spaces
In splendor of white, as God's throne!
Ice worlds to the pole! and ice places
Untracked, and unnamed, and unknown!
Hear that boom! Hear the grinding, the
        groan
Of the ice-gods in pain! Hear the moan

Of yon ice mountain hurled
Down this unfinished world.
                    JOAQUIN MILLER.

Friday, September 24, 1869, witnessed one of
the greatest panics ever known in the United
States, when Jay Gould and a few associates
managed to drive the price of gold up to 162½.

ISRAEL FREYER'S BID FOR GOLD

FRIDAY, SEPTEMBER 24, 1869

ZOUNDS! how the price went flashing through
Wall Street, William, Broad Street, New!
All the specie in all the land
Held in one Ring by a giant hand —
For millions more it was ready to pay,
And throttle the Street on hangman's-day.
Up from the Gold Pit's nether hell,
While the innocent fountain rose and fell,
Loud and higher the bidding rose,
And the bulls, triumphant, faced their foes.
It seemed as if Satan himself were in it:
Lifting it — one per cent a minute —
Through the bellowing broker, there amid,
Who made the terrible, final bid!
   High over all, and ever higher,
      Was heard the voice of Israel Freyer, —
A doleful knell in the storm-swept mart, —
"Five millions more! and for any part
      I'll give One Hundred and Sixty!"

Israel Freyer — the Government Jew —
Good as the best — soaked through and
        through
With credit gained in the year he sold
Our Treasury's precious hoard of gold;
Now through his thankless mouth rings
        out
The leaguers' last and cruellest shout!
Pity the shorts? Not they, indeed,
While a single rival's left to bleed!
Down come dealers in silks and hides,
Crowding the Gold Room's rounded sides,
Jostling, trampling each other's feet,
Uttering groans in the outer street;
Watching, with upturned faces pale,
The scurrying index mark its tale;
      Hearing the bid of Israel Freyer, —
      That ominous voice, would it never tire?
"Five millions more! — for any part
(If it breaks your firm, if it cracks your
        heart),
      I'll give One Hundred and Sixty!"

One Hundred and Sixty! Can't be true!
What will the bears-at-forty do?
How will the merchants pay their dues?
How will the country stand the news?
What'll the banks — but listen! hold!
In screwing upward the price of gold
To that dangerous, last, particular peg,
They have killed their Goose with the Golden
    Egg!
Just there the metal came pouring out,
All ways at once, like a water-spout,
Or a rushing, gushing, yellow flood,
That drenched the bulls wherever they stood!
Small need to open the Washington main,
Their coffer-dams were burst with the strain!
    It came by runners, it came by wire,
    To answer the bid of Israel Freyer,
It poured in millions from every side,
And almost strangled him as he cried, —
    "I'll give One Hundred and Sixty!"

Like Vulcan after Jupiter's kick,
Or the aphoristical Rocket's stick,
Down, down, down, the premium fell,
Faster than this rude rhyme can tell!
Thirty per cent the index slid,
Yet Freyer still kept making his bid, —
"One Hundred and Sixty for any part!"
— The sudden ruin had crazed *his* heart,
Shattered his senses, cracked his brain,
And left him crying again and again, —
Still making his bid at the market's top
(Like the Dutchman's leg that never could
    stop),
"One Hundred and Sixty — Five Millions
    more!"
Till they dragged him, howling, off the floor.
    The very last words that seller and buyer
    Heard from the mouth of Israel Freyer —
A cry to remember long as they live —
Were, "I'll take Five Millions more! I'll give —
I'll give One Hundred and Sixty!"

Suppose (to avoid the appearance of evil)
There's such a thing as a Personal Devil,
It would seem that his Highness here got hold,
For once, of a bellowing Bull in Gold!
Whether bull or bear, it would n't much matter
Should Israel Freyer keep up his clatter
On earth or under it (as, they say,
He is doomed) till the general Judgment Day,
When the Clerk, as he cites him to answer for 't,
Shall bid him keep silence in that Court!
But it matters most, as it seems to me,
That my countrymen, great and strong and free,

So marvel at fellows who seem to win,
That if even a Clown can only begin
By stealing a railroad, and use its purse
For cornering stocks and gold, or — worse —
For buying a Judge and Legislature,
And sinking still lower poor human nature,
The gaping public, whatever befall,
Will swallow him, tandem, harlots, and all!
While our rich men drivel and stand amazed
At the dust and pother his gang have raised,
And make us remember a nursery tale
Of the four-and-twenty who feared one snail.

What's bred in the bone will breed, you know;
Clowns and their trainers, high and low,
Will cut such capers, long as they dare,
While honest Poverty says its prayer.
But tell me what prayer or fast can save
Some hoary candidate for the grave,
The market's wrinkled Giant Despair,
Muttering, brooding, scheming there, —
Founding a college or building a church
Lest Heaven should leave him in the lurch!
Better come out in the rival way,
Issue your scrip in open day,
And pour your wealth in the grimy fist
Of some gross-mouthed, gambling pugilist;
Leave toil and poverty where they lie,
Pass thinkers, workers, artists, by,
Your pot-house fag from his counters bring
And make him into a Railway King!
Between such Gentiles and such Jews
Little enough one finds to choose:
Either the other will buy and use,
Eat the meat and throw him the bone,
And leave him to stand the brunt alone.

— Let the tempest come, that's gathering near,
And give us a better atmosphere!
            EDMUND CLARENCE STEDMAN.

On October 8 and 9, 1871, Chicago, which had
grown to be the greatest city in the West, was
almost entirely destroyed by fire. An area of three
and a half square miles was burned over; two
hundred people were killed and a hundred thou-
sand rendered homeless.

CHICAGO

[October 8–10, 1871]

MEN said at vespers: "All is well!"
In one wild night the city fell;
Fell shrines of prayer and marts of gain
Before the fiery hurricane.

On threescore spires had sunset shone,
Where ghastly sunrise looked on none.
Men clasped each other's hands, and said:
"The City of the West is dead!"

Brave hearts who fought, in slow retreat,
The fiends of fire from street to street,
Turned, powerless, to the blinding glare,
The dumb defiance of despair.

A sudden impulse thrilled each wire
That signalled round that sea of fire;
Swift words of cheer, warm heart-throbs came;
In tears of pity died the flame!

From East, from West, from South and
    North,
The messages of hope shot forth,
And, underneath the severing wave,
The world, full-handed, reached to save.

Fair seemed the old; but fairer still
The new, the dreary void shall fill
With dearer homes than those o'erthrown,
For love shall lay each corner-stone.

Rise, stricken city! from thee throw
The ashen sackcloth of thy woe;
And build, as to Amphion's strain,
To songs of cheer thy walls again!

How shrivelled in thy hot distress
The primal sin of selfishness!
How instant rose, to take thy part,
The angel in the human heart!

Ah! not in vain the flames that tossed
Above thy dreadful holocaust;
The Christ again has preached through thee
The Gospel of Humanity!

Then lift once more thy towers on high,
And fret with spires the western sky,
To tell that God is yet with us,
And love is still miraculous!
    JOHN GREENLEAF WHITTIER.

CHICAGO

BLACKENED and bleeding, helpless, panting,
    prone,
On the charred fragments of her shattered
    throne
Lies she who stood but yesterday alone.

Queen of the West! by some enchanter taught
To lift the glory of Aladdin's court,
Then lose the spell that all that wonder
    wrought.

Like her own prairies by some chance seed
    sown,
Like her own prairies in one brief day grown,
Like her own prairies in one fierce night
    mown.

She lifts her voice, and in her pleading call
We hear the cry of Macedon to Paul,
The cry for help that makes her kin to all.

But haply with wan fingers may she feel
The silver cup hid in the proffered meal,
The gifts her kinship and our loves reveal.
    BRET HARTE.

The whole country rallied to the aid of the
stricken city. An Aid and Relief Society was at
once formed, and within a month had received
subscriptions aggregating three and a half millions.

CHICAGO

GAUNT in the midst of the prairie,
    She who was once so fair;
Charred and rent are her garments,
Heavy and dark like cerements;
    Silent, but round her the air
Plaintively wails, "Miserere!"

Proud like a beautiful maiden,
    Art-like from forehead to feet,
Was she till pressed like a leman
Close to the breast of the demon,
    Lusting for one so sweet,
So were her shoulders laden.

Friends she had, rich in her treasures:
    Shall the old taunt be true, —
Fallen, they turn their cold faces,
Seeking new wealth-gilded places,
    Saying we never knew
Aught of her smiles or her pleasures?

Silent she stands on the prairie,
    Wrapped in her fire-scathed sheet:
Around her, thank God, is the Nation,
Weeping for her desolation,
    Pouring its gold at her feet,
Answering her "Miserere!"
    JOHN BOYLE O'REILLY.

Only second to the Chicago fire in destructiveness was that which visited Boston in the following year. It started on Saturday evening, November 9, 1872, and sixty-five acres were laid waste before it was controlled.

BOSTON

[November 9, 1872]

O BROAD-BREASTED Queen among Nations!
  O Mother, so strong in thy youth!
Has the Lord looked upon thee in ire,
And willed thou be chastened by fire,
  Without any ruth?

Has the Merciful tired of His mercy,
  And turned from thy sinning in wrath,
That the world with raised hand sees and
    pities
Thy desolate daughters, thy cities,
  Despoiled on their path?

One year since thy youngest was stricken:
  Thy eldest lies stricken to-day.
Ah! God, was Thy wrath without pity,
To tear the strong heart from our city,
  And cast it away?

O Father! forgive us our doubting;
  The stain from our weak souls efface;
Thou rebukest, we know, but to chasten,
Thy hand has but fallen to hasten
  Return to Thy grace.

Let us rise purified from our ashes
  As sinners have risen who grieved;
Let us show that twice-sent desolation
On every true heart in the nation
  Has conquest achieved.
              JOHN BOYLE O'REILLY.

The district burned contained the finest business blocks in the city, and the loss was estimated at $80,000,000. For a time, it seemed that the famous "Old South" would be destroyed.

THE CHURCH OF THE REVOLUTION

"The Old South stands."

LOUD through the still November air
  The clang and clash of fire-bells broke;
From street to street, from square to square,
  Rolled sheets of flame and clouds of smoke.

The marble structures reeled and fell,
  The iron pillars bowed like lead;
But one lone spire rang on its bell
  Above the flames. Men passed, and said,
    "The Old South stands!"

The gold moon, 'gainst a copper sky,
  Hung like a portent in the air,
The midnight came, the wind rose high,
  And men stood speechless in despair.
But, as the marble columns broke,
  And wider grew the chasm red, —
A seething gulf of flame and smoke, —
  The firemen marked the spire and said,
    "The Old South stands!"

Beyond the harbor, calm and fair,
  The sun came up through bars of gold,
Then faded in a wannish glare,
  As flame and smoke still upward rolled.
The princely structures, crowned with art,
  Where Commerce laid her treasures bare;
The haunts of trade, the common mart,
  All vanished in the withering air, —
    "The Old South stands!"

"The Old South must be levelled soon
  To check the flames and save the street;
Bring fuse and powder." But at noon
  The ancient fane still stood complete.
The mitred flame had lipped the spire,
  The smoke its blackness o'er it cast;
Then, herd-like, men fought the fire,
  And from each lip the watchword passed, —
    "The Old South stands!"

All night the red sea round it rolled,
  And o'er it fell the fiery rain:
And, as each hour the old clock told,
  Men said, "'T will never strike again!"
But still the dial-plate at morn
  Was crimsoned in the rising light.
Long may it redden with the dawn,
  And mark the shading hours of night!
    Long may it stand!

Long may it stand! where help was sought
  In weak and dark and doubtful days;
Where freedom's lessons first were taught,
  And prayers of faith were turned to praise;
Where burned the first Shekinah's flame
  In God's new temples of the free;
Long may it stand, in freedom's name,
  Like Israel's pillar by the sea!
    Long may it stand!
              HEZEKIAH BUTTERWORTH.

The nation rushed to Boston's aid just as it had done to Chicago's, and the city soon rose from her ashes greater than ever.

AFTER THE FIRE

WHILE far along the eastern sky
I saw the flags of Havoc fly,
As if his forces would assault
The sovereign of the starry vault
And hurl Him back the burning rain
That seared the cities of the plain,
I read as on a crimson page
The words of Israel's sceptred sage: —

*For riches make them wings, and they
Do as an eagle fly away.*

O vision of that sleepless night,
What hue shall paint the mocking light
That burned and stained the orient skies
Where peaceful morning loves to rise,
As if the sun had lost his way
And dawned to make a second day, —
Above how red with fiery glow,
How dark to those it woke below!

On roof and wall, on dome and spire,
Flashed the false jewels of the fire;
Girt with her belt of glittering panes,
And crowned with starry-gleaming vanes,
Our northern queen in glory shone
With new-born splendors not her own,
And stood, transfigured in our eyes,
A victim decked for sacrifice!

The cloud still hovers overhead,
And still the midnight sky is red;
As the lost wanderer strays alone
To seek the place he called his own,
His devious footprints sadly tell
How changed the pathways known so well;
The scene, how new! The tale, how old
Ere yet the ashes have grown cold!

Again I read the words that came
Writ in the rubric of the flame:
Howe'er we trust to mortal things,
Each hath its pair of folded wings;
Though long their terrors rest unspread
Their fatal plumes are never shed;
At last, at last, they stretch in flight,
And blot the day and blast the night!

Hope, only Hope, of all that clings
Around us, never spreads her wings;
Love, though he break his earthly chain,
Still whispers he will come again;
But Faith that soars to seek the sky
Shall teach our half-fledged souls to fly,
And find, beyond the smoke and flame,
The cloudless azure whence they came!
OLIVER WENDELL HOLMES.

On May 16, 1874, the bursting of a reservoir dam at Williamsburg, Mass., caused a disastrous flood, costing one hundred and forty lives and the loss of $1,500,000 in property. The loss of life would have been far greater but for the heroism of a milkman named Collins Graves, who rode forward in front of the flood, giving warning.

THE RIDE OF COLLINS GRAVES

[May 16, 1874]

No song of a soldier riding down
To the raging fight from Winchester town;
No song of a time that shook the earth
With the nations' throe at a nation's birth;
But the song of a brave man, free from fear
As Sheridan's self or Paul Revere;
Who risked what they risked, free from strife
And its promise of glorious pay, — his life!

The peaceful valley has waked and stirred,
And the answering echoes of life are heard,
The dew still clings to the trees and grass,
And the early toilers smiling pass,
As they glance aside at the white-walled homes,
Or up the valley, where merrily comes
The brook that sparkles in diamond rills
As the sun comes over the Hampshire hills.

What was it passed like an ominous breath —
Like a shiver of fear, or a touch of death?
What was it? The valley is peaceful still,
And the leaves are afire on top of the hill;
It was not a sound, nor a thing of sense, —
But a pain, like the pang of the short suspense
That thrills the being of those who see
At their feet the gulf of Eternity.

The air of the valley has felt the chill;
The workers pause at the door of the mill:

The housewife, keen to the shivering air,
Arrests her foot on the cottage stair,
Instinctive taught by the mother-love,
And thinks of the sleeping ones above.

Why start the listeners? Why does the course
Of the mill-stream widen? Is it a horse —
"Hark to the sound of the hoofs!" they say —
That gallops so wildly Williamsburg way?

God! what was that, like a human shriek
From the winding valley? Will nobody speak?
Will nobody answer those women who cry
As the awful warnings thunder by?

Whence come they? Listen! and now they hear
The sound of the galloping horse-hoofs near;
They watch the trend of the vale, and see
The rider who thunders so menacingly,
With waving arms and warning scream
To the home-filled banks of the valley stream.
He draws no rein, but he shakes the street
With a shout and the ring of the galloping feet,
And this the cry he flings to the wind, —
"To the hills for your lives! The flood is
        behind!"

He cries and is gone, but they know the
        worst, —
The breast of the Williamsburg dam has burst!
The basin that nourished their happy homes
Is changed to a demon. It comes! it comes!

A monster in aspect, with shaggy front
Of shattered dwellings to take the brunt
Of the homes they shatter; — white-maned
        and hoarse,
The merciless Terror fills the course
Of the narrow valley, and rushing raves,
With death on the first of its hissing waves,
Till cottage and street and crowded mill
Are crumbled and crushed.
                                But onward still,
In front of the roaring flood, is heard
The galloping horse and the warning word.
Thank God! the brave man's life is spared!
From Williamsburg town he nobly dared
To race with the flood, and take the road
In front of the terrible swath it mowed.

For miles it thundered and crashed be-
        hind,
But he looked ahead with a steadfast mind:
"They must be warned!" was all he said,
As away on his terrible ride he sped.

When heroes are called for, bring the crown
To this Yankee rider; send him down
On the stream of time with the Curtius
        old;
His deed, as the Roman's, was brave and
        bold;
And the tale can as noble a thrill awake,
For he offered his life for the people's
        sake!
                        JOHN BOYLE O'REILLY.

CHAPTER II

THE YEAR OF A HUNDRED YEARS

The year 1876 marked the completion of the first century of independence, and it was decided to celebrate it in a worthy manner. The city of Philadelphia, where the country had been born, was fittingly selected as the place for the celebration.

OUR FIRST CENTURY

IT cannot be that men who are the seed
    Of Washington should miss fame's true
        applause;
    Franklin did plan us; Marshall gave us
        laws;
And slow the broad scroll grew a people's
        creed —
Union and Liberty! then at our need,

Time's challenge coming, Lincoln gave it
        pause,
Upheld the double pillars of the cause,
And dying left them whole — our crowning
        deed.

Such was the fathering race that made all
        fast,
    Who founded us, and spread from sea to sea
    A thousand leagues the zone of liberty,
And built for man this refuge from his past,
    Unkinged,unchurched,unsoldiered; shamed
        were we,
Failing the stature that such sires forecast!
                GEORGE EDWARD WOODBERRY.

The celebration took the form of a great industrial exposition, at which the arts and industries of the whole world were represented. The exposition was opened on May 10, 1876, more than a hundred thousand people being present. Wagner had composed a march for the occasion and Whittier's "Centennial Hymn" was sung by a chorus of a thousand voices.

CENTENNIAL HYMN

I

Our fathers' God! from out whose hand
The centuries fall like grains of sand,
We meet to-day, united, free,
And loyal to our land and Thee,
To thank Thee for the era done,
And trust Thee for the opening one.

II

Here, where of old, by Thy design,
The fathers spake that word of Thine
Whose echo is the glad refrain
Of rended bolt and falling chain,
To grace our festal time, from all
The zones of earth our guests we call.

III

Be with us while the New World greets
The Old World thronging all its streets,
Unveiling all the triumphs won
By art or toil beneath the sun;
And unto common good ordain
This rivalship of hand and brain.

IV

Thou, who hast here in concord furled
The war flags of a gathered world,
Beneath our Western skies fulfil
The Orient's mission of good-will,
And, freighted with love's Golden Fleece,
Send back its Argonauts of peace.

V

For art and labor met in truce,
For beauty made the bride of use,
We thank Thee; but, withal, we crave
The austere virtues strong to save,
The honor proof to place or gold,
The manhood never bought nor sold!

VI

Oh make Thou us, through centuries long,
In peace secure, in justice strong;
Around our gift of freedom draw
The safeguards of Thy righteous law:

And, cast in some diviner mould,
Let the new cycle shame the old!
            John Greenleaf Whittier.

"The restored South chanted the praises of the Union in the words of Sidney Lanier, the Georgia poet." The poem was written as a cantata, the music for which was composed by Dudley Buck.

THE CENTENNIAL MEDITATION OF COLUMBIA [1]

1776–1876

From this hundred-terraced height,
Sight more large with nobler light
Ranges down yon towering years.
Humbler smiles and lordlier tears
    Shine and fall, shine and fall,
While old voices rise and call
Yonder where the to-and-fro
Weltering of my Long-Ago
Moves about the moveless base
Far below my resting-place.

Mayflower, Mayflower, slowly hither flying,
Trembling westward o'er yon balking sea,
Hearts within *Farewell dear England* sighing,
Winds without *But dear in vain* replying,
Gray-lipp'd waves about thee shouted, crying
    "No! It shall not be!"

Jamestown, out of thee —
Plymouth, thee — thee, Albany —
Winter cries, *Ye freeze:* away!
Fever cries, *Ye burn:* away!
Hunger cries, *Ye starve:* away!
Vengeance cries, *Your graves shall stay!*

Then old Shapes and Masks of Things,
Framed like Faiths or clothed like Kings,
Ghosts of Goods once fleshed and fair,
Grown foul Bads in alien air —
War, and his most noisy lords,
Tongued with lithe and poisoned swords —
Error, Terror, Rage, and Crime,
All in a windy night of time
Cried to me from land and sea,
    No! Thou shalt not be!

Hark!
Huguenots whispering *yea* in the dark,
Puritans answering *yea* in the dark!

[1] From Poems by Sidney Lanier; copyright 1884, 1891, by Mary D. Lanier; published by Charles Scribner's Sons.

Yea like an arrow shot true to his mark,
Darts through the tyrannous heart of Denial.
Patience and Labor and solemn-souled Trial,
    Foiled, still beginning,
    Soiled, but not sinning,
Toil through the stertorous death of the Night,
Toil when wild brother-wars new-dark the
    Light,
Toil, and forgive, and kiss o'er, and re-
    plight.

Now Praise to God's oft-granted grace,
Now Praise to Man's undaunted face,
Despite the land, despite the sea,
I was: I am: and I shall be —
How long, Good Angel, O how long?
Sing me from Heaven a man's own song!

"Long as thine Art shall love true love,
Long as thy Science truth shall know,
Long as thine Eagle harms no Dove,
Long as thy Law by law shall grow,
Long as thy God is God above,
Thy brother every man below,
So long, dear Land of all my love,
Thy name shall shine, thy fame shall glow!"

O Music, from this height of time my Word
    unfold:
In thy large signals all men's hearts Man's
    heart behold:
Mid-heaven unroll thy chords as friendly
    flags unfurled,
And wave the world's best lover's welcome
    to the world.
                SIDNEY LANIER.

President Grant then declared the exposition open. It was a success from the very start, and great crowds were every day in attendance.

CENTENNIAL HYMN

1876

THROUGH calm and storm the years have
    led
    Our nation on, from stage to stage —
A century's space — until we tread
    The threshold of another age.

We see where o'er our pathway swept
    A torrent-stream of blood and fire,
And thank the Guardian Power who kept
    Our sacred League of States entire.

Oh, chequered train of years, farewell!
    With all thy strifes and hopes and fears!
Yet with us let thy memories dwell,
    To warn and teach the coming years.

And thou, the new-beginning age,
    Warned by the past, and not in vain,
Write on a fairer, whiter page,
    The record of thy happier reign.
            WILLIAM CULLEN BRYANT.

On July 4, 1876, simple but impressive exercises were held in the public square in the rear of Independence Hall, where, a century before, a great throng had awaited the promulgation of the "Declaration."

WELCOME TO THE NATIONS

PHILADELPHIA, JULY 4, 1876

BRIGHT on the banners of lily and rose
    Lo! the last sun of our century sets!
Wreathe the black cannon that scowled on our
    foes,
    All but her friendships the nation forgets!
    All but her friends and their welcome for-
        gets!
These are around her; but where are her
    foes?
    Lo, while the sun of her century sets,
Peace with her garlands of lily and rose!

Welcome! a shout like the war trumpet's swell
    Wakes the wild echoes that slumber around!
Welcome! it quivers from Liberty's bell;
    Welcome! the walls of her temple resound!
    Hark! the gray walls of her temple resound!
Fade the far voices o'er hillside and dell;
    Welcome! still whisper the echoes around;
Welcome! still trembles on Liberty's bell!

Thrones of the continent! isles of the sea!
    Yours are the garlands of peace we entwine;
Welcome, once more, to the land of the free,
    Shadowed alike by the palm and the pine;
    Softly they murmur, the palm and the pine,
"Hushed is our strife, in the land of the free;"
    Over your children their branches entwine
Thrones of the continents! isles of the sea!
            OLIVER WENDELL HOLMES.

"The National Ode" was read by its author, Bayard Taylor, whose deep voice and impressive delivery added appreciably to the majesty of the lines.

THE NATIONAL ODE

INDEPENDENCE SQUARE, PHILADELPHIA,
JULY 4, 1876

I — 1

Sun of the stately Day,
Let Asia into the shadow drift,
Let Europe bask in thy ripened ray,
And over the severing ocean lift
    A brow of broader splendor!
Give light to the eager eyes
Of the Land that waits to behold thee rise;
    The gladness of morning lend her,
    With the triumph of noon attend her,
    And the peace of the vesper skies!
        For, lo! she cometh now
With hope on the lip and pride on the brow,
    Stronger, and dearer, and fairer,
    To smile on the love we bear her, —
To live, as we dreamed her and sought her,
    Liberty's latest daughter!
In the clefts of the rocks, in the secret places,
        We found her traces;
On the hills, in. the crash of woods that fall,
        We heard her call;
    When the lines of battle broke,
We saw her face in the fiery smoke;
Through toil, and anguish, and desolation,
        We followed, and found her
    With the grace of a virgin Nation
    As a sacred zone around her!
        Who shall rejoice
        With a righteous voice,
Far-heard through the ages, if not she?
    For the menace is dumb that defied her,
    The doubt is dead that denied her,
And she stands acknowledged, and strong,
        and free!

II — 1

Ah, hark! the solemn undertone,
On every wind of human story blown.
    A large, divinely-moulded Fate
Questions the right and purpose of a State,
    And in its plan sublime
    Our eras are the dust of Time.
    The far-off Yesterday of power
    Creeps back with stealthy feet,
    Invades the lordship of the hour,
And at our banquet takes the unbidden seat.
From all unchronicled and silent ages
Before the Future first begot the Past,
    Till History dared, at last,
To write eternal words on granite pages;

From Egypt's tawny drift, and Assur's mound,
    And where, uplifted white and far,
    Earth highest yearns to meet a star,
And Man his manhood by the Ganges found,—
Imperial heads, of old millennial sway,
    And still by some pale splendor crowned,
Chill as a corpse-light in our full-orbed day,
    In ghostly grandeur rise
And say, through stony lips and vacant eyes:
"Thou that assertest freedom, power, and
        fame,
    Declare to us thy claim!"

I — 2

On the shores of a Continent cast,
    She won the inviolate soil
By loss of heirdom of all the Past,
And faith in the royal right of Toil!
She planted homes on the savage sod:
    Into the wilderness lone
    She walked with fearless feet,
    In her hand the divining-rod,
    Till the veins of the mountains beat
With fire of metal and force of stone!
She set the speed of the river-head
    To turn the mills of her bread;
    She drove her ploughshare deep
Through the prairie's thousand-centuried
        sleep,
    To the South, and West, and North,
    She called Pathfinder forth,
Her faithful and sole companion
Where the flushed Sierra, snow-starred,
    Her way to the sunset barred,
And the nameless rivers in thunder and foam
Channelled the terrible canyon!
    Nor paused, till her uttermost home
Was built, in the smile of a softer sky
And the glory of beauty still to be,
Where the haunted waves of Asia die
    On the strand of the world-wide sea'

II — 2

    The race, in conquering,
Some fierce, Titanic joy of conquest knows;
    Whether in veins of serf or king,
Our ancient blood beats restless in repose.
    Challenge of Nature unsubdued
Awaits not Man's defiant answer long;
    For hardship, even as wrong,
Provokes the level-eyed heroic mood.
This for herself she did; but that which lies
    As over earth the skies,
Blending all forms in one benignant glow,—
    Crowned conscience, tender care,

Justice that answers every bondman's prayer,
Freedom where Faith may lead and Thought
        may dare,
    The power of minds that know,
    Passion of hearts that feel,
    Purchased by blood and woe,
    Guarded by fire and steel, —
Hath she secured? What blazon on her shield,
    In the clear Century's light
    Shines to the world revealed,
Declaring nobler triumph, born of Right?

                I — 3

    Foreseen in the vision of sages,
        Foretold when martyrs bled,
    She was born of the longing of ages,
        By the truth of the noble dead
        And the faith of the living fed!
    No blood in her lightest veins
        Frets at remembered chains,
Nor shame of bondage has bowed her head.
    In her form and features still
    The unblenching Puritan will,
    Cavalier honor, Huguenot grace,
    The Quaker truth and sweetness,
    And the strength of the danger-girdled
        race
Of Holland, blend in a proud completeness.
From the homes of all, where her being be-
        gan,
    She took what she gave to Man;
    Justice, that knew no station,
    Belief, as soul decreed,
    Free air for aspiration,
    Free force for independent deed!
    She takes, but to give again,
As the sea returns the rivers in rain;
And gathers the chosen of her seed
From the hunted of every crown and creed.
    Her Germany dwells by a gentler Rhine;
    Her Ireland sees the old sunburst shine;
    Her France pursues some dream divine;
    Her Norway keeps his mountain pine;
    Her Italy waits by the western brine;
    And, broad-based under all,
Is planted England's oaken-hearted mood,
        As rich in fortitude
As e'er went worldward from the island-
        wall!
    Fused in her candid light,
To one strong race all races here unite:
Tongues melt in hers, hereditary foemen
Forget their sword and slogan, kith and clan:
    'T was glory, once, to be a Roman:
She makes it glory, now, to be a man!

                II — 3

    Bow down!
    Doff thine æonian crown!
    One hour forget
    The glory, and recall the debt:
        Make expiation,
        Of humbler mood,
For the pride of thine exultation
O'er peril conquered and strife subdued!
    But half the right is wrested
        When victory yields her prize,
    And half the marrow tested
        When old endurance dies.
    In the sight of them that love thee,
    Bow to the Greater above thee!
    He faileth not to smite
    The idle ownership of Right,
    Nor spares to sinews fresh from trial,
    And virtue schooled in long denial,
        The tests that wait for thee
In larger perils of prosperity.
    Here, at the Century's awful shrine,
    Bow to thy Father's God, and thine!

                I — 4

    Behold! she bendeth now,
Humbling the chaplet of her hundred years
There is a solemn sweetness on her brow,
    And in her eyes are sacred tears.
        Can she forget,
In present joy, the burden of her debt,
        When for a captive race
        She grandly staked, and won,
The total promise of her power begun,
    And bared her bosom's grace
To the sharp wound that inly tortures yet?
        Can she forget
The million graves her young devotion set,
    The hands that clasp above,
From either side, in sad, returning love?
        Can she forget,
    Here, where the Ruler of to-day,
        The Citizen of to-morrow,
And equal thousands to rejoice and pray
    Beside these holy walls are met,
Her birth-cry, mixed of keenest bliss and
        sorrow?
    Where, on July's immortal morn
    Held forth, the People saw her head
And shouted to the world: "The King is
        dead,
        But, lo! the Heir is born!"
When fire of Youth, and sober trust of Age,
    In Farmer, Soldier, Priest, and Sage,
        Arose and cast upon her

Baptismal garments, — never robes so fair
  Clad prince in Old-World air, —
Their lives, their fortunes, and their sacred
    honor!

II — 4

Arise! Recrown thy head,
Radiant with blessings of the Dead!
Bear from this hallowed place
The prayer that purifies thy lips, ·
The light of courage that defies eclipse,
The rose of Man's new morning on thy face!
  Let no iconoclast
Invade thy rising Pantheon of the Past,
To make a blank where Adams stood,
To touch the Father's sheathed and sacred
    blade,
Spoil crowns on Jefferson and Franklin laid,
Or wash from Freedom's feet the stain of
    Lincoln's blood!
  Hearken, as from that haunted Hall
    Their voices call:
  "We lived and died for thee;
We greatly dared that thou might'st be:
So, from thy children still
We claim denials which at last fulfil,
And freedom yielded to preserve thee free!
  Beside clear-hearted Right
That smiles at Power's uplifted rod,
  Plant Duties that requite,
And Order that sustains, upon thy sod,
  And stand in stainless might
Above all self, and only less than God!

III — 1

Here may thy solemn challenge end,
All-proving Past, and each discordance die
  Of doubtful augury,
Or in one choral with the Present blend,
  And that half-heard, sweet harmony
Of something nobler that our sons may see!
Though poignant memories burn
Of days that were, and may again return,
When thy fleet foot, O Huntress of the
    Woods,
  The slippery brinks of danger knew,
  And dim the eyesight grew
That was so sure in thine old solitudes, —
  Yet stays some richer sense
Won from the mixture of thine elements,
  To guide the vagrant scheme,
And winnow truth from each conflicting
    dream!
  Yet in thy blood shall live
Some force unspent, some essence primitive,

To seize the highest use of things;
For Fate, to mould thee to her plan,
  Denied thee food of kings,
Withheld the udder and the orchard-fruits,
  Fed thee with savage roots,
And forced thy harsher milk from barren
    breasts of man!

III — 2

O sacred Woman-Form,
Of the first People's need and passion
    wrought, —
No thin, pale ghost of Thought,
But fair as Morning and as heart's-blood
    warm, —
Wearing thy priestly tiar on Judah's hills;
Clear-eyed beneath Athene's helm of gold;
  Or from Rome's central seat
Hearing the pulses of the Continents beat
  In thunder where her legions rolled;
Compact of high heroic hearts and wills,
    Whose being circles all
The selfless aims of men, and all fulfils;
Thyself not free, so long as one is thrall;
  Goddess, that as a Nation lives,
    And as a Nation dies,
That for her children as a man defies,
And to her children as a mother gives, —
    Take our fresh fealty now!
No more a Chieftainess, with wampum-
    zone
  And feather-cinctured brow, —
No more a new Britannia, grown
To spread an equal banner to the breeze,
And lift thy trident o'er the double seas;
  But with unborrowed crest,
  In thine own native beauty dressed, —
The front of pure command, the unflinching
    eye, thine own!

III — 3

Look up, look forth, and on!
There's light in the dawning sky:
The clouds are parting, the night is gone:
Prepare for the work of the day!
  Fallow thy pastures lie,
  And far thy shepherds stray,
And the fields of thy vast domain
  Are waiting for purer seed
  Of knowledge, desire, and deed,
For keener sunshine and mellower rain!
  But keep thy garments pure:
Pluck them back, with the old disdain,
  From touch of the hands that stain!
So shall thy strength endure.

Transmute into good the gold of Gain,
Compel to beauty thy ruder powers,
  Till the bounty of coming hours
  Shall plant, on thy fields apart,
With the oak of Toil, the rose of Art!
  Be watchful, and keep us so:
  Be strong, and fear no foe:
  Be just, and the world shall know!
With the same love love us, as we give;
  And the day shall never come,
  That finds us weak or dumb
  To join and smite and cry
In the great task, for thee to die,
And the greater task, for thee to live!
                    BAYARD TAYLOR.

Richard Henry Lee, grandson of the mover of
the Declaration, came to the front with the
original document in his hands, and read its
sonorous sentences. William M. Evarts delivered
an oration and "Our National Banner," words by
Dexter Smith, music by Sir Julius Benedict, was
sung.

OUR NATIONAL BANNER

[July 4, 1876]

O'ER the high and o'er the lowly
Floats that banner bright and holy
  In the rays of Freedom's sun,
In the nation's heart embedded,
O'er our Union newly wedded,
  One in all, and all in one.

Let that banner wave forever,
May its lustrous stars fade never,
  Till the stars shall pale on high;
While there's right the wrong defeating,
While there's hope in true hearts beat-
      ing,
  Truth and freedom shall not die.

As it floated long before us,
Be it ever floating o'er us,
  O'er our land from shore to shore:
There are freemen yet to wave it,
Millions who would die to save it,
  Wave it, save it, evermore.
                    DEXTER SMITH.

The exposition closed November 10, 1876. It
had served to draw all sections of the country more
closely together, and to establish the industrial
position of the United States among the nations
of the world.

AFTER THE CENTENNIAL

(A HOPE)

BEFORE our eyes a pageant rolled
  Whose banners every land unfurled;
And as it passed, its splendors told
  The art and glory of the world.

The nations of the earth have stood
  With face to face and hand in hand,
And sworn to common brotherhood
  The sundered souls of every land.

And while America is pledged
  To light her Pharos towers for all,
While her broad mantle, starred and edged
  With truth, o'er high and low shall fall;

And while the electric nerves still belt
  The State and Continent in one, —
The discords of the past shall melt
  Like ice beneath the summer sun.

O land of hope! thy future years
  Are shrouded from our mortal sight;
But thou canst turn the century's fears
  To heralds of a cloudless light!

The sacred torch our fathers lit
  No wild misrule can ever quench;
Still in our midst wise judges sit,
  Whom party passion cannot blench.

From soul to soul, from hand to hand
  Thy sons have passed that torch along,
Whose flame by Wisdom's breath is fanned
  Whose staff is held by runners strong.

O Spirit of immortal truth,
  Thy power alone that circles all
Can feed the fire as in its youth —
  Can hold the runners lest they fall!
                    CHRISTOPHER PEARSE CRANCH.

CHAPTER III

THE CONQUEST OF THE PLAINS

The Indians had long since ceased to be a serious menace to the United States, and the policy of the government for many years had been to settle them upon various selected tracts of land west of the Mississippi. But the population of the West was increasing very rapidly, the completion of the railway to the Pacific having given it a great impetus.

THE PACIFIC RAILWAY

FINISHED, MAY 10, 1869

" And a Highway shall there be."

'T is *"Done"* — the wondrous thorough-
fare
Type of that Highway all divine!
No ancient wonder can compare
With this, in grandeur of design.
For, 't was no visionary scheme
To immortalize the builder's name;
No impulse rash, no transient dream
Of some mere worshipper of Fame.

Rare common sense conceived the plan,
For working out a lasting good —
The full development of Man;
The growth of human brotherhood!
And lo! by patient toil and care,
The work with rare success is crowned;
And nations, yet to be, will share
In blessings that shall e'er abound.

Across a continent's expanse,
The lengthening track now runs secure,
O'er which the Iron Horse shall prance,
So long as earth and time endure!
His course extends from East to West —
From where Atlantic billows roar,
To where the quiet waters rest,
Beside the far Pacific shore.

Proud commerce, by Atlantic gales
Tossed to and fro, — her canvas rent —
Will gladly furl her wearied sails,
And glide across a continent.
Through smiling valleys, broad and free,
O'er rivers wide, or mountain-crest,
Her course shall swift and peaceful be,
Till she has reached the farthest West.

And e'en the treasures of the East,
Diverted from their wonted track, —
With safety gained, with speed increased, —
Will follow in her footsteps back.
And thus the Nations, greatly blest,
Will share another triumph, won,
That links yet closer East and West —
The rising and the setting sun!

This glorious day with joy we greet!
May Faith abound, may Love increase,
And may this highway, now complete,
Be the glad harbinger of Peace!
God bless the Work, that it may prove
The source of greater good in store,
When Man shall heed the law of Love,
And Nations shall learn war no more.

C. R. BALLARD.

During the autumn of 1874, gold was discovered in the Black Hills Sioux reservation and explorers rushed in; a still worse grievance was the wanton destruction of bison by hunters and excursionists. Driven to frenzy, at last, tribe after tribe of savages took up arms, and started on a career of murder and rapine.

AFTER THE COMANCHES

SADDLE! saddle! saddle!
Mount, mount, and away!
Over the dim green prairie,
Straight on the track of day;
Spare not spur for mercy,
Hurry with shout and thong,
Fiery and tough is the mustang,
The prairie is wide and long.

Saddle! saddle! saddle!
Leap from the broken door,
Where the brute Comanche entered,
And the white-foot treads no more!
The hut is burnt to ashes,
There are dead men stark outside,
And only a long torn ringlet
Left of the stolen bride.

Go like the east wind's howling,
Ride with death behind,

Stay not for food or slumber,
  Till the thieving wolves ye find!
They came before the wedding,
  Swifter than prayer or priest;
The bride-men danced to bullets,
  The wild dogs ate the feast.

Look to rifle and powder,
  Buckle the knife-belt sure;
Loose the coil of the lasso,
  And make the loop secure;
Fold the flask in the poncho,
  Fill the pouch with maize,
And ride as if to-morrow
  Were the last of living days.

Saddle! saddle! saddle!
  Redden spur and thong,
Ride like the mad tornado,
  The track is lonely and long,
Spare not horse nor rider,
  Fly for the stolen bride!
Bring her home on the crupper,
  A scalp on either side.

It was decided to transfer the Sioux to another
reservation, but, under the advice of Sitting Bull,
they refused to stir. A detachment under Lieu-
tenant-Colonel George A. Custer was sent against
them, and came suddenly upon their encampment
on June 25, 1876. A terrific fight followed, in
which Custer and all of his men were killed.

DOWN THE LITTLE BIG HORN

June 25, 1876

Down the Little Big Horn
(O troop forlorn!),
Right into the camp of the Sioux
(What was the muster?),
Two hundred and sixty-two
Went into the fight with Custer,
Went out of the fight with Custer,
Went out at a breath,
Stanch to the death!
Just from the canyon emerging,
Saw they the braves of Sitting Bull surging,
Two thousand and more,
Painted and feathered, thirsting for gore,
Did they shrink and turn back
(Hear how the rifles crack!),
Did they pause for a life,
For a sweetheart or wife?

And one in that savage throng
(His revenge had waited long),

Pomped with porcupine quills,
His deerskins beaded and fringed,
An eagle's plume in his long black hair,
His tall lance fluttering in the air,
Glanced at the circling hills —
His cheeks flushed with a keen surmise,
A demon's hate in his eyes
Remembering the hour when he cringed,
A prisoner thonged,
Chief Rain-in-the-Face
(There was a sachem wronged!)
Saw his enemy's heart laid bare,
Feasted in thought like a beast in his lair.

Cavalry, cavalry
(Tramp of the hoof, champ of the bit),
Horses prancing, cavorting,
Shying and snorting,
Accoutrements rattling
(Children at home are prattling),
Gallantly, gallantly,
"Company dismount!"
From the saddle they swing,
With their steeds form a ring
(Hear how the bullets sing!),
Who can their courage recount?

Do you blanch at their fate?
(Who would hesitate?)
Two hundred and sixty-two
Immortals in blue,
Standing shoulder to shoulder,
Like some granite boulder
You must blast to displace
(Were they of a valiant race?) —
Two hundred and sixty-two,
And never a man to say,
"I rode with Custer that day."
Give the savage his triumph and bluster,
Give the hero to perish with Custer,
To his God and his comrades true.

Closing and closing,
Nearer the redskins creep;
With cunning disposing,
With yell and with whoop
(There are women shall weep!),
They gather and swoop,
They come like a flood,
Maddened with blood,
They shriek, plying the knife
(Was there one begged for his life?),
Where but a moment ago
Stood serried and sternly the foe,
Now fallen, mangled below.

Down the Little Big Horn
(Tramp of the hoof, champ of the bit).
A single steed in the morn,
Comanche, seven times hit,
Comes to the river to drink;
Lists for the sabre's clink,
Lists for the voice of his master
(O glorious disaster!),
Comes, sniffing the air,
Gazing, lifts his head,
But his master lies dead.
(Who but the dead were there?)
But stay, what was the muster?
Two hundred and sixty-two
(Two thousand and more the Sioux!)
Went into the fight with Custer,
Went out of the fight with Custer;
For never a man can say,
"I rode with Custer that day —"
Went out like a taper,
Blown by a sudden vapor,
Went out at a breath,
True to the death!

FRANCIS BROOKS.

LITTLE BIG HORN

[June 25, 1876]

BESIDE the lone river,
That idly lay dreaming,
Flashed sudden the gleaming
Of sabre and gun
In the light of the sun
As over the hillside the soldiers came streaming.

One peal of the bugle
In stillness unbroken
That sounded a token
Of soul-stirring strife,
Savage war to the knife,
Then silence that seemed like defiance unspoken.

But out of an ambush
Came warriors riding,
Swift ponies bestriding,
Shook rattles and shells,
With a discord of yells,
That fired the hearts of their comrades in hiding.

Then fierce on the wigwams
The soldiers descended,

And madly were blended,
The red man and white
In a hand-to-hand fight,
With the Indian village assailed and defended.

And there through the passage
Of battle-torn spaces,
From dark lurking-places,
With blood-curdling cry
And their knives held on high,
Rushed Amazon women with wild, painted faces.

Then swung the keen sabres
And flashed the sure rifles
Their message that stifles
The shout in red throats,
While the reckless blue-coats
Laughed on 'mid the fray as men laugh over trifles.

Grim cavalry troopers
Unshorn and unshaven,
And never a craven
In ambuscade caught,
How like demons they fought
Round the knoll on the prairie that marked their last haven.

But the Sioux circled nearer
The shrill war-whoop crying,
And death-hail was flying,
Yet still they fought on
Till the last shot was gone,
And all that remained were the dead and the dying.

A song for their death, and
No black plumes of sorrow,
This recompense borrow,
Like heroes they died
Man to man — side by side;
We lost them to-day, we shall meet them to-morrow.

And on the lone river,
Has faded the seeming
Of bright armor gleaming,
But there by the shore
With the ghosts of no-more
The shades of the dead through the ages lie dreaming.

ERNEST McGAFFEY.

CUSTER'S LAST CHARGE

[June 25, 1876]

DEAD! Is it possible? He, the bold rider,
  Custer, our hero, the first in the fight,
Charming the bullets of yore to fly wider,
  Far from our battle-king's ringlets of light!
Dead, our young chieftain, and dead, all forsaken!
  No one to tell us the way of his fall!
Slain in the desert, and never to waken,
  Never, not even to victory's call!

Proud for his fame that last day that he met them!
  All the night long he had been on their track,
Scorning their traps and the men that had set them,
  Wild for a charge that should never give back.
There on the hilltop he halted and saw them, —
  Lodges all loosened and ready to fly;
Hurrying scouts with the tidings before he was nigh.

All the wide valley was full of their forces,
  Gathered to cover the lodges' retreat! —
Warriors running in haste to their horses,
  Thousands of enemies close to his feet!
Down in the valleys the ages had hollowed,
  There lay the Sitting Bull's camp for a prey!
Numbers! What recked he? What recked those who followed —
  Men who had fought ten to one ere that day?

Out swept the squadrons, the fated three hundred,
  Into the battle-line steady and full;
Then down the hillside exultingly thundered,
  Into the hordes of the old Sitting Bull!
Wild Ogalallah, Arapahoe, Cheyenne,
  Wild Horse's braves, and the rest of their crew,
Shrank from that charge like a herd from a lion, —
  Then closed around, the grim horde of wild Sioux!

Right to their centre he charged, and then facing —
  Hark to those yells! and around them, O see!

Over the hilltops the Indians come racing,
  Coming as fast as the waves of the sea!
Red was the circle of fire around them;
  No hope of victory, no ray of light,
Shot through that terrible black cloud without them,
  Brooding in death over Custer's last fight.

Then did he blench? Did he die like a craven,
  Begging those torturing fiends for his life?
Was there a soldier who carried the Seven
  Flinched like a coward or fled from the strife?
No, by the blood of our Custer, no quailing!
  There in the midst of the Indians they close,
Hemmed in by thousands, but ever assailing,
  Fighting like tigers, all 'bayed amid foes!

Thicker and thicker the bullets came singing;
  Down go the horses and riders and all;
Swiftly the warriors round them were ringing,
  Circling like buzzards awaiting their fall.
See the wild steeds of the mountain and prairie,
  Savage eyes gleaming from forests of mane;
Quivering lances with pennons so airy,
  War-painted warriors charging amain.

Backward, again and again, they were driven,
  Shrinking to close with the lost little band;
Never a cap that had worn the bright Seven
  Bowed till its wearer was dead on the strand.
Closer and closer the death circle growing,
  Ever the leader's voice, clarion clear,
Rang out his words of encouragement glowing,
  "We can but die once, boys, — we'll sell our lives dear!"

Dearly they sold them like Berserkers raging,
  Facing the death that encircled them round;
Death's bitter pangs by their vengeance assuaging,
  Marking their tracks by their dead on the ground.
Comrades, our children shall yet tell their story, —
  Custer's last charge on the old Sitting Bull;
And ages shall swear that the cup of his glory
  Needed but that death to render it full.

FREDERICK WHITTAKER.

CUSTER

[June 25, 1876]

WHAT! shall that sudden blade
Leap out no more?
No more thy hand be laid
Upon the sword-hilt smiting sore?
O for another such
The charger's rein to clutch, —
One equal voice to summon victory,
Sounding thy battle-cry,
Brave darling of the soldiers' choice!
Would there were one more voice!

O gallant charge, too bold!
O fierce, imperious greed
To pierce the clouds that in their darkness
hold
Slaughter of man and steed!
Now, stark and cold,
Among thy fallen braves thou liest,
And even with thy blood defiest
The wolfish foe:
But ah, thou liest low,
And all our birthday song is hushed indeed!

Young lion of the plain,
Thou of the tawny mane!
Hotly the soldiers' hearts shall beat,
Their mouths thy death repeat,
Their vengeance seek the trail again
Where thy red doomsmen be;
But on the charge no more shall stream
Thy hair, — no more thy sabre gleam, —
No more ring out thy battle-shout,
Thy cry of victory!

Not when a hero falls
The sound a world appalls:
For while we plant his cross
There is a glory, even in the loss:
But when some craven heart
From honor dares to part,
Then, then, the groan, the blanching cheek,
And men in whispers speak,
Nor kith nor country dare reclaim
From the black depths his name.

Thou, wild young warrior, rest,
By all the prairie winds caressed!
Swift was thy dying pang;
Even as the war-cry rang
Thy deathless spirit mounted high
And sought Columbia's sky: —

There, to the northward far,
Shines a new star,
And from it blazes down
The light of thy renown!
EDMUND CLARENCE STEDMAN.
July 10, 1876.

The Indians were led by Rain-in-the-Face. The year before, he had been arrested by Captain Tom Custer at Standing Rock, and had threatened to eat the latter's heart. The Captain was among the killed, and Rain-in-the-Face is said to have made good his threat. Mr. Longfellow is mistaken in saying that Colonel George Custer was thus mutilated. His body was not disfigured in any way.

THE REVENGE OF RAIN–IN–THE–FACE

[June 25, 1876]

IN that desolate land and lone,
Where the Big Horn and Yellowstone
Roar down their mountain path,
By their fires the Sioux Chiefs
Muttered their woes and griefs
And the menace of their wrath.

"Revenge!" cried Rain-in-the-Face,
"Revenge upon all the race
Of the White Chief with yellow hair!"
And the mountains dark and high
From their crags reëchoed the cry
Of his anger and despair.

In the meadow, spreading wide
By woodland and river-side
The Indian village stood;
All was silent as a dream,
Save the rushing of the stream
And the blue-jay in the wood.

In his war paint and his beads,
Like a bison among the reeds,
In ambush the Sitting Bull
Lay with three thousand braves
Crouched in the clefts and caves,
Savage, unmerciful!

Into the fatal snare
The White Chief with yellow hair
And his three hundred men
Dashed headlong, sword in hand;
But of that gallant band
Not one returned again.

The sudden darkness of death
Overwhelmed them like the breath
    And smoke of a furnace fire:
By the river's bank, and between
The rocks of the ravine,
    They lay in their bloody attire.

But the foemen fled in the night,
And Rain-in-the-Face, in his flight,
    Uplifted high in air
As a ghastly trophy, bore
The brave heart, that beat no more,
    Of the White Chief with yellow hair.

Whose was the right and the wrong?
Sing it, O funeral song,
    With a voice that is full of tears,
And say that our broken faith
Wrought all this ruin and scathe,
    In the Year of a Hundred Years.
        HENRY WADSWORTH LONGFELLOW.

One survivor there was, and only one, Comanche,
the horse ridden by Captain Miles Keogh. He
was found several miles from the battlefield, and
had been wounded seven times. By order of the
Secretary of War, a soldier was detailed to take
care of him as long as he lived, and no one was
ever afterwards permitted to ride him.

MILES KEOGH'S HORSE

ON the bluff of the Little Big-Horn,
    At the close of a woful day,
Custer and his Three Hundred
    In death and silence lay.

Three Hundred to Three Thousand!
    They had bravely fought and bled;
For such is the will of Congress
    When the White man meets the Red.

The White men are ten millions,
    The thriftiest under the sun;
The Reds are fifty thousand,
    And warriors every one.

So Custer and all his fighting men
    Lay under the evening skies,
Staring up at the tranquil heaven
    With wide, accusing eyes.

And of all that stood at noonday
    In that fiery scorpion ring,
Miles Keogh's horse at evening
    Was the only living thing.

Alone from that field of slaughter,
    Where lay the three hundred slain,
The horse Comanche wandered,
    With Keogh's blood on his mane.

And Sturgis issued this order,
    Which future times shall read,
While the love and honor of comrades
    Are the soul of the soldier's creed.

He said —
        Let the horse Comanche
    Henceforth till he shall die,
Be kindly cherished and cared for
    By the Seventh Cavalry.

He shall do no labor; he never shall know
    The touch of spur or rein;
Nor shall his back be ever crossed
    By living rider again.

And at regimental formation
    Of the Seventh Cavalry,
Comanche draped in mourning and led
    By a trooper of Company I,

Shall parade with the Regiment!
                    Thus it was
    Commanded and thus done,
By order of General Sturgis, signed
    By Adjutant Garlington.

Even as the sword of Custer,
    In his disastrous fall,
Flashed out a blaze that charmed the world
    And glorified his pall,

This order, issued amid the gloom,
    That shrouds our army's name,
When all foul beasts are free to rend
    And tear its honest fame,

Shall prove to a callous people
    That the sense of a soldier's worth,
That the love of comrades, the honor of arms,
    Have not yet perished from earth.
                    JOHN HAY.

The government rushed a large force to the
scene, and finally, after painful fighting and toil-
some marches stretching over many months, the
Indians were brought to terms. Rain-in-the-Face
afterwards professed himself a man of peace, and
in 1886 tried to enter Hampton Institute. He
was killed during the Sioux outbreak in 1890.

ON THE BIG HORN

[1886]

THE years are but half a score,
And the war-whoop sounds no more
  With the blast of bugles, where
Straight into a slaughter pen,
With his doomed three hundred men,
  Rode the chief with the yellow hair.

O Hampton, down by the sea!
What voice is beseeching thee
  For the scholar's lowliest place?
Can this be the voice of him
Who fought on the Big Horn's rim?
  Can this be Rain-in-the-Face?

His war-paint is washed away,
His hands have forgotten to slay;
  He seeks for himself and his race
The arts of peace and the lore
That give to the skilled hand more
  Than the spoils of war and chase.

O chief of the Christ-like school!
Can the zeal of thy heart grow cool
  When the victor scarred with fight
Like a child for thy guidance craves,
And the faces of hunters and braves
  Are turning to thee for light?

The hatchet lies overgrown
With grass by the Yellowstone,
  Wind River and Paw of Bear;
And, in sign that foes are friends,
Each lodge like a peace-pipe sends
  Its smoke in the quiet air.

The hands that have done the wrong
To right the wronged are strong,
  And the voice of a nation saith:
"Enough of the war of swords,
Enough of the lying words
  And shame of a broken faith!"

The hills that have watched afar
The valleys ablaze with war
  Shall look on the tasselled corn;
And the dust of the grinded grain,
Instead of the blood of the slain,
  Shall sprinkle thy banks, Big Horn!

The Ute and the wandering Crow
Shall know as the white men know,
  And fare as the white men fare;

The pale and the red shall be brothers,
One's rights shall be as another's,
  Home, School, and House of Prayer!

O mountains that climb to snow,
O river winding below,
  Through meadows by war once trod,
O wild, waste lands that await
The harvest exceeding great,
  Break forth into praise of God!
          JOHN GREENLEAF WHITTIER.

In 1886 another somewhat serious uprising took place among the Apaches, a band of hostiles taking the warpath under the chief, Geronimo. General Nelson A. Miles, after a long pursuit, succeeded in capturing them.

THE "GREY HORSE TROOP"

ALL alone on the hillside —
Larry an' Barry an' me;
Nothin' to see but the sky an' the plain,
Nothin' to see but the drivin' rain,
Nothin' to see but the painted Sioux,
Galloping, galloping: "Whoop — whuroo!
The divil in yellow is down in the mud!"
Sez Larry to Barry, "I'm losin' blood."

  "Cheers for the Greys!" yells Barry;
  "Second Dragoons!" groans Larry;
    Hurrah! hurrah! for Egan's Grey Troop!
    Whoop! ye divils — ye've got to whoop;
    Cheer for the troopers who die: sez I —
  "Cheer for the troop that never shall die!"

All alone on the hillside —
Larry an' Barry an' me;
Flat on our bellies, an' pourin' in lead —
Seven rounds left, an' the horses dead —
Barry a-cursin' at every breath;
Larry beside him, as white as death;
Indians galloping, galloping by,
Wheelin' and squealin' like hawks in the sky!

  "Cheers for the Greys!" yells Barry;
  "Second Dragoons!" groans Larry;
    Hurrah! hurrah! for Egan's Grey Troop!
    Whoop! ye divils — ye've got to whoop;
    Cheer for the troopers who die: sez I —
  "Cheer for the troop that never shall die!"

All alone on the hillside —
Larry an' Barry an' me;

Two of us livin' and one of us dead —
Shot in the head, and God! — how he bled!
"Larry's done up," sez Barry to me;
"Divvy his cartridges! Quick! gimme three!"
While nearer an' nearer an' plainer in view,
Galloped an' galloped the murderin' Sioux.

"Cheers for the Greys!" yells Barry;
"Cheer —" an' he falls on Larry.
   Alas! alas! for Egan's Grey Troop!
   The Red Sioux, hovering stoop to swoop;
Two out of three lay dead, while I
Cheered for the troop that never shall die.

All alone on the hillside —
Larry an' Barry an' me;
An' I fired an' yelled till I lost my head,
Cheerin' the livin', cheerin' the dead,
Swingin' my cap, I cheered until
I stumbled and fell. Then over the hill
There floated a trumpeter's silvery call,
An' Egan's Grey Troop galloped up, that's all.

   Drink to the Greys, — an' Barry!
   Second Dragoons, — an' Larry!
Here's a bumper to Egan's Grey Troop!
Let the crape on the guidons droop;
Drink to the troopers who die, while I
Drink to the troop that never shall die!
                    ROBERT W. CHAMBERS.

Geronimo was sent to Fort Pickens, Florida,
where he was kept in captivity for the remainder
of his life.

GERONIMO

BESIDE that tent and under guard
In majesty alone he stands,
As some chained eagle, broken-winged,
With eyes that gleam like smouldering
      brands, —
A savage face, streaked o'er with paint,
And coal-black hair in unkempt mane,
Thin, cruel lips, set rigidly, —
A red Apache Tamerlane.

As restless as the desert winds,
Yet here he stands like carven stone,
His raven locks by breezes moved
And backward o'er his shoulders blown;
Silent, yet watchful as he waits
Robed in his strange, barbaric guise,
While here and there go searchingly
The cat-like wanderings of his eyes.

The eagle feather on his head
Is dull with many a bloody stain,
While darkly on his lowering brow
Forever rests the mark of Cain.
Have you but seen a tiger caged
And sullen through his barriers glare?
Mark well his human prototype,
The fierce Apache fettered there.
                    ERNEST McGAFFEY.

In 1889 the territory known as Oklahoma was
opened to settlement, and again the Indians saw
their hunting-grounds invaded by the white man,
while they themselves were compelled to remove
to a new reservation. Sitting Bull again advised
resistance, and was killed while trying to escape
arrest. A squaw of the tribe, made desperate by
the removal, killed her baby and committed
suicide.

THE LAST RESERVATION

SULLEN and dark, in the September day,
      On the bank of the river
They waited the boat that would bear them
      away
      From their poor homes forever.

For progress strides on, and the order had
      gone
      To these wards of the nation,
"Give us land and more room," was the cry,
      "and move on
      To the next reservation."

With her babe, she looked back at the home
      'neath the trees
      From which they were driven,
Where the smoke of the last camp fire, borne
      on the breeze,
      Rose slowly toward heaven.

Behind her, fair fields, and the forest and
      glade,
      The home of her nation;
Around her, the gleam of the bayonet and
      blade
      Of civilization.

Clasping close to her bosom the small dusky
      form,
      With tender caressing,
She bent down, on the cheek of her babe soft
      and warm
      A mother's kiss pressing.

There's a splash in the river — the column
    moves on,
    Close-guarded and narrow,
With hardly more note of the two that are
    gone
    Than the fall of a sparrow.

Only an Indian! Wretched, obscure,
    To refinement a stranger,
And a babe, that was born, in a wigwam as
    poor
    And rude as a manger.

Moved on — to make room for the growth in
    the West
    Of a brave Christian nation,
Moved on — and, thank God, forever at
    rest
    In the last reservation.
                                WALTER LEARNED.

That was the last of the Indian outbreaks.
Although there are still more than two hundred
thousand Indians in the United States, by far
the greater part of them have adopted the dress
and customs of the white man and are engaged
in peaceful occupations. The remainder are con-
tent to live in idleness upon the government's
bounty.

INDIAN NAMES

YE say they all have pass'd away,
    That noble race and brave,
That their light canoes have vanish'd
    From off the crested wave;
That, 'mid the forests where they roam'd,
    There rings no hunter's shout;

But their name is on your waters,
    Ye may not wash it out.

'T is where Ontario's billow
    Like ocean's surge is curl'd;
Where strong Niagara's thunders wake
    The echo of the world;
Where red Missouri bringeth
    Rich tribute from the West,
And Rappahannock sweetly sleeps
    On green Virginia's breast.

Ye say their conelike cabins,
    That cluster'd o'er the vale,
Have fled away like wither'd leaves
    Before the autumn's gale:
But their memory liveth on your hills,
    Their baptism on your shore;
Your everlasting rivers speak
    Their dialect of yore.

Old Massachusetts wears it
    Within her lordly crown,
And broad Ohio bears it
    'Mid all her young renown;
Connecticut hath wreathed it
    Where her quiet foliage waves,
And bold Kentucky breathes it hoarse,
    Through all her ancient caves.

Wachusett hides its lingering voice
    Within his rocky heart,
And Alleghany graves its tone
    Throughout his lofty chart;
Monadnock on his forehead hoar
    Doth seal the sacred trust:
Your mountains build their monument,
    Though ye destroy their dust.
                        LYDIA HUNTLEY SIGOURNEY.

CHAPTER IV

THE SECOND ASSASSINATION

On the fourth day of March, 1881, James Abram
Garfield, Republican, was inaugurated President
of the United States. He had served with distinc-
tion in the Civil War and afterwards in Congress
and seemed destined to enjoy a peaceful and pros-
perous administration. But on July 1 he was shot
down at Washington by Charles J. Guiteau, a half-
crazed, disappointed office-seeker. The President
fought manfully for life, but blood poisoning de-
veloped, and death followed on September 19.

REJOICE

"Bear me out of the battle, for lo! I am sorely
wounded."

I

FROM out my deep, wide-bosomed West,
    Where unnamed heroes hew the way

For worlds to follow, with stern zest, —
　Where gnarled old maples make array,
Deep-scarred from red men gone to rest, —
　Where pipes the quail, where squirrels
　　play
Through tossing trees, with nuts for toy,
　A boy steps forth, clear-eyed and tall,
A bashful boy, a soulful boy,
　　Yet comely as the sons of Saul, —
　　A boy, all friendless, poor, unknown,
　　Yet heir-apparent to a throne.

II

Lo! Freedom's bleeding sacrifice!
　So, like some tall oak tempest-blown,
Beside the storied stream he lies
　Now at the last, pale-browed and prone.
A nation kneels with streaming eyes,
　A nation supplicates the throne,
A nation holds him by the hand,
　A nation sobs aloud at this:
The only dry eyes in the land
　Now at the last, I think, are his.
　　Why, we should pray, God knoweth
　　　best,
　　That this grand, patient soul should rest.

III

The world is round. The wheel has run
　Full circle. Now behold a grave
Beneath the old loved trees is done.
　The druid oaks lift up, and wave
A solemn welcome back. The brave
　Old maples murmur, every one,
"Receive him, Earth!" In centre land,
　As in the centre of each heart,
As in the hollow of God's hand,
　　The coffin sinks. And with it part
　　All party hates! Now, not in vain
　　He bore his peril and hard pain.

IV

Therefore, I say, rejoice! I say,
　The lesson of his life was much, —
This boy that won, as in a day,
　The world's heart utterly; a touch
Of tenderness and tears: the page
　Of history grows rich from such;
His name the nation's heritage, —
　But oh! as some sweet angel's voice
Spake this brave death that touched us all.
　　Therefore, I say, Rejoice! Rejoice!
　　Run high the flags! Put by the pall!
　　Lo! all is for the best for all!
　　　　　　　　　　JOAQUIN MILLER.

THE BELLS AT MIDNIGHT

[September 19, 1881]

In their dark House of Cloud
The three weird sisters toil till time be sped;
One unwinds life, one ever weaves the shroud,
　One waits to part the thread.

I

CLOTHO

How long, O sister, how long
Ere the weary task is done?
How long, O sister, how long
Shall the fragile thread be spun?

LACHESIS

'T is mercy that stays her hand,
Else she had cut the thread;
She is a woman too,
Like her who kneels by his bed!

ATROPOS

Patience! the end is come;
He shall no more endure:
See! with a single touch! —
My hand is swift and sure!

II

Two Angels pausing in their flight.

FIRST ANGEL

Listen! what was it fell
An instant ago on my ear —
A sound like the throb of a bell
From yonder darkling sphere!

SECOND ANGEL

The planet where mortals dwell!
I hear it not . . . yes, I hear;
How it deepens — a sound of dole!

FIRST ANGEL

Listen! It is the knell
Of a passing soul —
The midnight lamentation
Of some stricken nation
For a Chieftain's soul!
It is just begun,
The many-throated moan . . .
Now the clangor swells
As if a million bells
Had blent their tones in one!
Accents of despair
Are these to mortal ear;
But all this wild funereal music blown

And sifted through celestial air
Turns to triumphal pæans here!
Wave upon wave the silvery anthems flow;
Wave upon wave the deep vibrations roll
From that dim sphere below.
Come, let us go —
Surely, some chieftain's soul!

THOMAS BAILEY ALDRICH.

J. A. G.

OUR sorrow sends its shadow round the earth.
So brave, so true! A hero from his birth!
The plumes of Empire moult, in mourning
    draped,
The lightning's message by our tears is
    shaped.

Life's vanities that blossom for an hour
Heap on his funeral car their fleeting flower.
Commerce forsakes her temples, blind and dim,
And pours her tardy gold, to homage him.

The notes of grief to age familiar grow
Before the sad privations all must know;
But the majestic cadence which we hear
To-day, is new in either hemisphere.

What crown is this, high hung and hard to
    reach,
Whose glory so outshines our laboring speech?
The crown of Honor, pure and unbetrayed;
He wins the spurs who bears the knightly aid.

While royal babes incipient empire hold,
And, for bare promise, grasp the sceptre's gold,
This man such service to his age did bring
That they who knew him servant, hailed him
    king.

In poverty his infant couch was spread;
His tender hands soon wrought for daily
    bread;
But from the cradle's bound his willing feet
The errand of the moment went to meet.

When learning's page unfolded to his view,
The quick disciple straight a teacher grew;
And, when the fight of freedom stirred the
    land,
Armed was his heart and resolute his hand.

Wise in the council, stalwart in the field!
Such rank supreme a workman's hut may yield.

His onward steps like measured marbles show,
Climbing the height where God's great flame
    doth glow.

Ah! Rose of joy, that hid'st a thorn so sharp!
Ah! Golden woof that meet'st a severed warp!
Ah! Solemn comfort that the stars rain down!
The hero's garland his, the martyr's crown.

JULIA WARD HOWE.

MIDNIGHT — SEPTEMBER 19, 1881

ONCE in a lifetime, we may see the veil
    Tremble and lift, that hides symbolic things;
The Spirit's vision, when the senses fail,
    Sweeps the weird meaning that the outlook
    brings.

Deep in the midst of turmoil, it may be —
    A crowded street, a forum, or a field, —
The soul inverts the telescope to see
    To-day's events in future's years revealed.

Back from the present, let us look at Rome:
    Behold, what Cato meant, what Brutus said,
Hark! the Athenians welcome Cimon home!
    How clear they are, those glimpses of the
    dead!

But we, hard toilers, we who plan and weave
    Through common days the web of common
    life,
What word, alas! shall teach us to receive
    The mystic meaning of our peace and strife?

Whence comes our symbol? Surely, God
    must speak —
    No less than He can make us heed or pause:
Self-seekers we, too busy or too weak
    To search beyond our daily lives and laws.

From things occult our earth-turned eyes
    rebel;
    No sound of Destiny can reach our ears;
We have no time for dreaming — Hark! a
    knell —
    A knell at midnight! All the nation hears!

A second grievous throb! The dreamers
    wake —
    The merchant's soul forgets his goods and
    ships;
The weary workmen from their slumbers
    break;
    The women raise their eyes with quivering
    lips;

The miner rests upon his pick to hear;
  The printer's type stops midway from the
    case;
The solemn sound has reached the roysterer's
    ear,
  And brought the shame and sorrow to his
    face.

Again it booms! O Mystic Veil, upraise!
  — Behold, 't is lifted! On the darkness
    drawn,
A picture lined with light! The people's gaze,
From sea to sea, beholds it till the dawn!

A death-bed scene — a sinking sufferer lies,
  Their chosen ruler, crowned with love and
    pride;
Around, his counsellors, with streaming eyes;
  His wife, heart-broken, kneeling by his side:

Death's shadow holds her — it will pass too
    soon;
  She weeps in silence — bitterest of tears;
He wanders softly — Nature's kindest boon;
  And as he murmurs, all the country hears:

For him the pain is past, the struggle ends;
  His cares and honors fade — his younger
    life
In peaceful Mentor comes, with dear old
    friends;
  His mother's arms take home his dear young
    wife.

He stands among the students, tall and strong,
  And teaches truths republican and grand;
He moves — ah, pitiful — he sweeps along
  O'er fields of carnage leading his command!

He speaks to crowded faces — round him
    surge
  Thousands and millions of excited men;
He hears them cheer — sees some vast light
    emerge —
  Is borne as on a tempest — then — ah, then,

The fancies fade, the fever's work is past;
  A deepened pang, then recollection's thrill;
He feels the faithful lips that kiss their last,
  His heart beats once in answer, and is
    still!

The curtain falls: but hushed, as if afraid,
  The people wait, tear-stained, with heaving
    breast:

'T will rise again, they know, when he is laid
With Freedom, in the Capitol, at rest.
                    JOHN BOYLE O'REILLY.

For two days, September 22 and 23, the body
lay in state in the rotunda of the Capitol. Then,
in a long train crowded with the most illustrious
of his countrymen, the dead President was borne
to Cleveland, Ohio, and buried on September 26,
in a beautiful cemetery overlooking the waters of
Lake Erie.

AT THE PRESIDENT'S GRAVE

ALL summer long the people knelt
  And listened at the sick man's door:
Each pang which that pale sufferer felt
  Throbbed through the land from shore to
    shore;

And as the all-dreaded hour drew nigh,
  What breathless watching, night and day!
What tears, what prayers! Great God on high,
  Have we forgotten how to pray!

O broken-hearted, widowed one,
  Forgive us if we press too near!
Dead is our husband, father, son, —
  For we are all one household here.

And not alone here by the sea,
  And not in his own land alone,
Are tears of anguish shed with thee —
  In this one loss the world is one.

EPITAPH

A man not perfect, but of heart
  So high, of such heroic rage,
That even his hopes became a part
  Of earth's eternal heritage.
                    RICHARD WATSON GILDER.

The public rage against the assassin knew no
bounds. Only by the utmost vigilance was his
life saved from the attacks upon it. He was
brought to trial and found guilty of murder in
January, 1882, and was executed June 30.

ON THE DEATH OF PRESIDENT
GARFIELD

I

FALLEN with autumn's falling leaf
  Ere yet his summer's noon was past,

Our friend, our guide, our trusted chief, —
    What words can match a woe so vast!

And whose the chartered claim to speak
    The sacred grief where all have part,
Where sorrow saddens every cheek
    And broods in every aching heart?

Yet Nature prompts the burning phrase
    That thrills the hushed and shrouded
      hall,
The loud lament, the sorrowing praise,
    The silent tear that love lets fall.

In loftiest verse, in lowliest rhyme,
    Shall strive unblamed the minstrel choir, —
The singers of the new-born time,
    And trembling age with outworn lyre.

No room for pride, no place for blame, —
    We fling our blossoms on the grave,
Pale, — scentless, — faded, — all we claim,
    This only, — what we had we gave.

Ah, could the grief of all who mourn
    Blend in one voice its bitter cry,
The wail to heaven's high arches borne
    Would echo through the caverned sky.

II

O happiest land, whose peaceful choice
    Fills with a breath its empty throne!
God, speaking through thy people's voice,
    Has made that voice for once his own.

No angry passion shakes the state
    Whose weary servant seeks for rest,
And who could fear that scowling hate
    Would strike at that unguarded breast?

He stands, unconscious of his doom,
    In manly strength, erect, serene;
Around him Summer spreads her bloom;
    He falls, — what horror clothes the scene!

How swift the sudden flash of woe
    Where all was bright as childhood's dream!
As if from heaven's ethereal bow
    Had leaped the lightning's arrowy gleam.

Blot the foul deed from history's page;
    Let not the all-betraying sun
Blush for the day that stains an age
    When murder's blackest wreath was won.

III

Pale on his couch the sufferer lies,
    The weary battle-ground of pain:
Love tends his pillow; Science tries
    Her every art, alas! in vain.

The strife endures how long! how long!
    Life, death, seem balanced in the scale,
While round his bed a viewless throng
    Await each morrow's changing tale.

In realms the desert ocean parts
    What myriads watch with tear-filled eyes,
His pulse-beats echoing in their hearts,
    His breathings counted with their sighs!

Slowly the stores of life are spent,
    Yet hope still battles with despair;
Will Heaven not yield when knees are bent?
    Answer, O thou that hearest prayer!

But silent is the brazen sky;
    On sweeps the meteor's threatening train,
Unswerving Nature's mute reply,
    Bound in her adamantine chain.

Not ours the verdict to decide
    Whom death shall claim or skill shall save;
The hero's life though Heaven denied,
    It gave our land a martyr's grave.

Nor count the teaching vainly sent
    How human hearts their griefs may share, —
The lesson woman's love has lent,
    What hope may do, what faith can bear!

Farewell! the leaf-strown earth enfolds
    Our stay, our pride, our hopes, our fears,
And autumn's golden sun beholds
    A nation bowed, a world in tears.
            OLIVER WENDELL HOLMES.

PRESIDENT GARFIELD

"E venni dal martirio a questa pace."
            PARADISO, xv, 148.

THESE words the poet heard in Paradise,
Uttered by one who, bravely dying here
In the true faith, was living in that sphere
Where the celestial cross of sacrifice
Spread its protecting arms athwart the skies;
    And set thereon, like jewels crystal clear,
    The souls magnanimous, that knew not fear,
Flashed their effulgence on his dazzled eyes.

Ah me! how dark the discipline of pain,
  Were not the suffering followed by the sense
  Of infinite rest and infinite release!
This is our consolation; and again
  A great soul cries to us in our suspense,
"I came from martyrdom unto this peace!"
        HENRY WADSWORTH LONGFELLOW.

The hundredth anniversary of the surrender of
the British at Yorktown was celebrated on Octo-
ber 19, 1881. The lyric for the occasion was writ-
ten by Paul Hamilton Hayne.

YORKTOWN CENTENNIAL LYRIC

[October 19, 1881]

HARK! hark! down the century's long reach-
        ing slope
To those transports of triumph, those raptures
        of hope,
The voices of main and of mountain com-
        bined
In glad resonance borne on the wings of the
        wind,
The bass of the drum and the trumpet that
        thrills
Through the multiplied echoes of jubilant
        hills.
And mark how the years melting upward like
        mist
Which the breath of some splendid enchant-
        ment has kissed,
Reveal on the ocean, reveal on the shore
The proud pageant of conquest that graced
        them of yore,
When blended forever in love as in fame
See, the standard which stole from the star-
        light its flame,
And type of all chivalry, glory, romance,
The lilies, the luminous lilies of France.

Oh, stubborn the strife ere the conflict was
        won!
And the wild whirling war wrack half stifled
        the sun.
The thunders of cannon that boomed on the
        lea,
But reëchoed far thunders pealed up from
        the sea,
Where guarding his sea lists, a knight on the
        waves,
Bold De Grasse kept at bay the bluff bull-
        dogs of Graves.
The day turned to darkness, the night changed
        to fire,

Still more fierce waxed the combat, more
        deadly the ire,
Undimmed by the gloom, in majestic advance,
Oh, behold where they ride o'er the red battle
        tide,
Those banners united in love as in fame,
The brave standard which drew from the star-
        beams their flame,
And type of all chivalry, glory, romance,
The lilies, the luminous lilies of France.

No respite, no pause; by the York's tortured
        flood,
The grim Lion of England is writhing in blood.
Cornwallis may chafe and coarse Tarleton
        aver,
As he sharpens his broadsword and buckles
        his spur,
"This blade, which so oft has reaped rebels
        like grain,
Shall now harvest for death the rude yeomen
        again."
Vain boast! for ere sunset he's flying in
        fear,
With the rebels he scouted close, close in his
        rear,
While the French on his flank hurl such volleys
        of shot
That e'en Gloucester's redoubt must be grow-
        ing too hot.
Thus wedded in love as united in fame,
Lo! the standard which stole from the star-
        light its flame,
And type of all chivalry, glory, romance,
The lilies, the luminous lilies of France.

O morning superb! when the siege reached its
        close;
See! the sundawn outbloom, like the alchem-
        ist's rose!
The last wreaths of smoke from dim trenches
        upcurled,
Are transformed to a glory that smiles on the
        world.
Joy, joy! Save the wan, wasted front of the
        foe,
With his battle-flags furled and his arms trail-
        ing low; —
Respect for the brave! In stern silence they
        yield,
And in silence they pass with bowed heads
        from the field.
Then triumph transcendent! so Titan of tone
That some vowed it must startle King George
        on his throne.

When Peace to her own, timed the pulse of the
   land,
And the war weapon sank from the war-
   wearied hand,
Young Freedom upborne to the height of the
   goal
She had yearned for so long with deep tra-
   vail of soul,
A song of her future raised, thrilling and clear,
Till the woods leaned to hearken, the hill slopes
   to hear: —
Yet fraught with all magical grandeurs that
   gleam
On the hero's high hope, or the patriot's
   dream,
What future, though bright, in cold shadow
   shall cast
The proud beauty that haloes the brow of the
   past.
Oh! wedded in love, as united in fame,
See the standard which stole from the star-
   light its flame,
And type of all chivalry, glory, romance,
The lilies, the luminous lilies of France.
                    PAUL HAMILTON HAYNE.

On May 24, 1883, the great bridge spanning the
East River and connecting Brooklyn with New
York City was opened to the public, having been
thirteen years in process of construction.

THE BROOKLYN BRIDGE

[May 24, 1883]

A GRANITE cliff on either shore:
   A highway poised in air;
Above, the wheels of traffic roar;
   Below, the fleets sail fair; —
And in and out, forevermore,
The surging tides of ocean pour,
And past the towers the white gulls soar,
   And winds the sea-clouds bear.

O peerless this majestic street,
   This road that leaps the brine!
Upon its heights twin cities meet,
   And throng its grand incline, —
To east, to west, with swiftest feet,
Though ice may crash and billows beat,
Though blinding fogs the wave may greet
   Or golden summer shine.

Sail up the Bay with morning's beam,
   Or rocky Hellgate by, —

Its columns rise, its cables gleam,
   Great tents athwart the sky!
And lone it looms, august, supreme,
When, with the splendor of a dream,
Its blazing cressets gild the stream
   Till evening shadows fly.

By Nile stand proud the pyramids,
   But they were for the dead;
The awful gloom that joy forbids,
   The mourners' silent tread,
The crypt, the coffin's stony lids, —
Sad as a soul the maze that thrids
Of dark Amenti, ere it rids
   Its way of judgment dread.

This glorious arch, these climbing towers,
   Are all for life and cheer!
Part of the New World's nobler dowers;
   Hint of millennial year
That comes apace, though evil lowers, —
When loftier aims and larger powers
Will mould and deck this earth of ours,
   And heaven at length bring near!

Unmoved its cliffs shall crown the shore;
   Its arch the chasm dare;
Its network hang the blue before,
   As gossamer in air;
While in and out, forevermore,
The surging tides of ocean pour,
And past its towers the white gulls soar
   And winds the sea-clouds bear!
                    EDNA DEAN PROCTOR.

BROOKLYN BRIDGE

No lifeless thing of iron and stone,
   But sentient, as her children are,
Nature accepts you for her own,
   Kin to the cataract and the star.

She marks your vast, sufficing plan,
   Cable and girder, bolt and rod,
And takes you, from the hand of man,
   For some new handiwork of God.

You thrill through all your chords of steel
   Responsive to the living sun;
And quickening in your nerves you feel
   Life with its conscious currents run.

Your anchorage upbears the march
   Of time and the eternal powers.

The sky admits your perfect arch,
The rock respects your stable towers.
CHARLES G. D. ROBERTS.

The first week in September, 1886, a destructive
earthquake shook the eastern portion of the
United States, Charleston, S. C., suffering a tre-
mendous shock which snuffed out scores of lives
and rendered seven eighths of the houses unfit for
habitation.

CHARLESTON

1886

Is this the price of beauty! Fairest, thou,
Of all the cities of the sunrise sea,
Yet thrice art stricken. First, war harried
thee;
Then the dread circling tempest drove its
plough
Right through thy palaces; and now, O now!
A sound of terror, and thy children flee
Into the night and death. O Deity!
Thou God of war and whirlwind, whose
dark brow,
Frowning, makes tremble sea and solid land!
These are thy creatures who to heaven cry
While hell roars 'neath them, and its por-
tals ope;
To thee they call, — to thee who bidst them
die,
Who hast forgotten to withhold thy hand,—
For thou, Destroyer, art man's only Hope!
RICHARD WATSON GILDER.

On September 9 and 11, 1886, the American
yacht Mayflower defeated the English yacht Gala-
tea in the international races for the America's cup.

MAYFLOWER

THUNDER our thanks to her — guns, hearts,
and lips!
Cheer from the ranks to her,
Shout from the banks to her, —
Mayflower! Foremost and best of our ships.

Mayflower! Twice in the national story
Thy dear name in letters of gold —
Woven in texture that never grows old —
Winning a home and winning glory!
Sailing the years to us, welcomed for aye;
Cherished for centuries, dearest to-day.
Every heart throbs for her, every flag dips —
Mayflower! First and last — best of our ships!

White as a seagull she swept the long passage.
True as the homing-bird flies with its message.
Love her? O, richer than silk every sail of her.
Trust her? more precious than gold every nail
of her.
Write we down faithfully every man's part in
her;
Greet we all gratefully every true heart in her.
More than a name to us, sailing the fleetest,
Symbol of that which is purest and sweetest.
More than a keel to us, steering the straightest:
Emblem of that which is freest and greatest.
More than a dove-bosomed sail to the wind-
ward:
Flame passing on while the night-clouds fly
hindward.
Kiss every plank of her! None shall take rank
of her;
Frontward or weatherward, none can eclipse.
Thunder our thanks to her! Cheer from the
banks to her!
Mayflower! Foremost and best of our ships!
JOHN BOYLE O'REILLY.

On October 28, 1886, Bartholdi's statue of
Liberty Enlightening the World, a gift to America
from the people of France, was unveiled on Bedloe's
Island, in New York Harbor.

FAIREST OF FREEDOM'S DAUGHTERS

Read at the dedication of the Bartholdi Statue,
New York Harbor, October 28, 1886

NIGHT's diadem around thy head,
The world upon thee gazing,
Beneath the eye of heroes dead
Thy queenly form up-raising,
Lift up, lift up thy torch on high,
Fairest of Freedom's daughters!
Flash it against thine own blue sky,
Flash it across the waters!

Stretch up to thine own woman's height,
Thine eye lit with truth's lustre,
As though from God, Himself a-light,
Earth's hopes around thee cluster.
The stars touch with thy forehead fair;
At them thy torch was lighted.
They grope to find where truth's ways are,
The nations long benighted.

Thou hast the van in earth's proud march,
To thee all nations turning;
Thy torch against thine own blue arch,
In answer to their yearning!

Show them the pathway thou hast trod,
  The chains which thou hast broken;
Teach them thy trust in man and God,
  The watchwords thou hast spoken.

Not here is heard the Alp-herd's horn,
  The mountain stillness breaking;
Nor do we catch the roseate morn,
  The Alpine summits waking.
Is Neckar's vale no longer fair,
  That German hearts are leaving?
Ah! German hearts from hearthstones tear,
  In thy proud star believing.

Has Rhineland lost her grape's perfume,
  Her waters green and golden?
And do her castles no more bloom
  With legends rare and olden?
Why leave, strong men, the Fatherland?
  Why cross the cold blue ocean?
Truth's torch in thine uplifted hand,
  Ha! kindles their devotion.

God, home, and country be thy care,
  Thou queen of all the ages!
Belting the earth is this one prayer:
  Unspotted be thy pages!
Lift up, lift up thy torch on high,
  Fairest of Freedom's daughters!
Flash it against thine own blue sky,
  Flash it across the waters!
                JEREMIAH EAMES RANKIN.

LIBERTY ENLIGHTENING THE WORLD

WARDEN at ocean's gate,
  Thy feet on sea and shore,
Like one the skies await
  When time shall be no more!
What splendors crown thy brow?
What bright dread angel Thou,
  Dazzling the waves before
  Thy station great?

"My name is Liberty!
  From out a mighty land
I face the ancient sea,
  I lift to God my hand;
By day in Heaven's light,
A pillar of fire by night,
  At ocean's gate I stand
  Nor bend the knee.

"The dark Earth lay in sleep,
  Her children crouched forlorn,
Ere on the western steep
  I sprang to height, reborn:
Then what a joyous shout
The quickened lands gave out,
  And all the choir of morn
  Sang anthems deep.

"Beneath yon firmament,
  The New World to the Old
My sword and summons sent,
  My azure flag unrolled:
The Old World's hands renew
Their strength; the form ye view
  Came from a living mould
  In glory blent.

"O ye, whose broken spars
  Tell of the storms ye met,
Enter! fear not the bars
  Across your pathway set;
Enter at Freedom's porch,
For you I lift my torch,
  For you my coronet
  Is rayed with stars.

"But ye that hither draw
  To desecrate my fee,
Nor yet have held in awe
  The justice that makes free, —
Avaunt, ye darkling brood!
By Right my house hath stood:
  My name is Liberty,
  My throne is Law."

O wonderful and bright,
  Immortal Freedom, hail!
Front, in thy fiery might,
  The midnight and the gale;
Undaunted on this base
Guard well thy dwelling-place:
  Till the last sun grow pale
  Let there be Light!
                EDMUND CLARENCE STEDMAN

THE BARTHOLDI STATUE

1886

THE land, that, from the rule of kings,
  In freeing us, itself made free,
Our Old World Sister, to us brings
  Her sculptured Dream of Liberty:

Unlike the shapes on Egypt's sands
  Uplifted by the toil-worn slave,
On Freedom's soil with freemen's hands
  We rear the symbol free hands gave.

O France, the beautiful! to thee
  Once more a debt of love we owe:
In peace beneath thy Colors Three,
  We hail a later Rochambeau!

Rise, stately Symbol! holding forth
  Thy light and hope to all who sit
In chains and darkness! Belt the earth
  With watch-fires from thy torch up-lit!

Reveal the primal mandate still
  Which Chaos heard and ceased to be,
Trace on mid-air th' Eternal Will
  In signs of fire: "Let man be free!"

Shine far, shine free, a guiding light
  To Reason's ways and Virtue's aim,
A lightning-flash the wretch to smite
    Who shields his license with thy name!
          JOHN GREENLEAF WHITTIER.

On September 18, 1887, the one hundredth anniversary of the adoption of the Constitution of the United States was suitably observed at Philadelphia. President Grover Cleveland, Justice Samuel Freeman Miller, and John Adams Kasson delivered addresses, and "The New Hail Columbia" was sung by a chorus of two thousand voices.

ADDITIONAL VERSES TO HAIL COLUMBIA

Written at the request of the committee for the Constitutional Centennial Celebration at Philadelphia, 1887.

LOOK our ransomed shores around,
Peace and safety we have found!
  Welcome, friends who once were foes!
  Welcome, friends who once were foes,
To all the conquering years have gained, —
A nation's rights, a race unchained!
  Children of the day new-born!
  Mindful of its glorious morn,
  Let the pledge our fathers signed
  Heart to heart forever bind!

    While the stars of heaven shall burn,
    While the ocean tides return,
    Ever may the circling sun
    Find the Many still are One!

Graven deep with edge of steel,
Crowned with Victory's crimson seal,
  All the world their names shall read!
  All the world their names shall read,
Enrolled with his, the Chief that led
The hosts whose blood for us was shed.
  Pay our sires their children's debt,
  Love and honor, nor forget
  Only Union's golden key
  Guards the Ark of Liberty!

    While the stars of heaven shall burn,
    While the ocean tides return,
    Ever may the circling sun
    Find the Many still are One!

Hail, Columbia! strong and free,
Throned in hearts from sea to sea!
  Thy march triumphant still pursue
  Thy march triumphant still pursue
With peaceful stride from zone to zone,
Till Freedom finds the world her own!
  Blest in Union's holy ties,
  Let our grateful song arise,
  Every voice its tribute lend,
  All in loving chorus blend!

    While the stars in heaven shall burn,
    While the ocean tides return,
    Ever shall the circling sun
    Find the Many still are One!
          OLIVER WENDELL HOLMES.

Following this came the recital by James Edward Murdock of the "New National Hymn," the Marine Band leading the people and the singers in the chorus.

NEW NATIONAL HYMN

HAIL, Freedom! thy bright crest
And gleaming shield, thrice blest,
  Mirror the glories of a world thine own.
Hail, heaven-born Peace! our sight,
Led by thy gentle light,
  Shows us the paths with deathless flowers
    strewn.
Peace, daughter of a strife sublime,
Abide with us till strife be lost in endless
    time.
Chorus — Thy sun is risen, and shall not set,
        Upon thy day divine;
          Ages, of unborn ages, yet,
          America, are thine.

Her one hand seals with gold
The portals of night's fold,
    Her other, the broad gates of dawn unbars;
O'er silent wastes of snows,
Crowning her lofty brows,
    Gleams high her diadem of northern stars;
While, clothed in garlands of warm flowers,
Round Freedom's feet the South her wealth of
    beauty showers.

Sweet is the toil of peace,
Sweet is the year's increase,
    To loyal men who live by Freedom's laws;
And in war's fierce alarms
God gives stout hearts and arms
    To freemen sworn to save a rightful cause.
Fear none, trust God, maintain the right,
And triumph in unbroken Union's might.

Welded in war's fierce flame,
Forged on the hearth of fame,
    The sacred Constitution was ordained;
Tried in the fire of time,
Tempered in woes sublime,
    An age was passed and left it yet unstained.
God grant its glories still may shine,
While ages fade, forgotten, in time's slow de-
    cline!

Honor the few who shared
Freedom's first fight, and dared
    To face war's desperate tide at the full flood;
Who fell on hard-won ground,
And into Freedom's wound
    Poured the sweet balsam of their brave
    hearts' blood.
They fell; but o'er that glorious grave
Floats free the banner of the cause they died
    to save.

In radiance heavenly fair,
Floats on the peaceful air
    That flag that never stooped from victory's
    pride;
Those stars that softly gleam,
Those stripes that o'er us stream,
    In war's grand agony were sanctified;
A holy standard, pure and free,
To light the home of peace, or blaze in vic-
    tory.

Father, whose mighty power
Shields us through life's short hour,
    To Thee we pray, — Bless us and keep us
    free:

All that is past forgive;
Teach us, henceforth, to live,
    That, through our country, we may honor
    Thee;
And, when this mortal life shall cease,
Take Thou, at last, our souls to Thine eter-
    nal peace.
                    FRANCIS MARION CRAWFORD.

On March 15, 1889, a destructive hurricane
visited the Samoan Islands. There were in the
harbor of Apia, at the time one English, three
German, and three American war-ships, sent
there to safeguard the interests of their respective
countries. The English ship, the Calliope, suc-
ceeded in steaming out of the harbor, the crew of
the American flagship Trenton cheering her as she
passed. The Trenton was wrecked a few minutes
later, as were the five other ships in the harbor.

IN APIA BAY

(Morituri vos salutamus)

RUIN and death held sway
    That night in Apia Bay,
And smote amid the loud and dreadful gloom.
    But, Hearts, no longer weep
    The salt unresting sleep
Of the great dead, victorious in their doom.

Vain, vain the strait retreat
    That held the fated fleet,
Trapped in the two-fold threat of sea and
    shore!
    Fell reefs on either hand,
    And the devouring strand!
Above, below, the tempest's deafening roar!

What mortal hand shall write
    The horror of that night,
The desperate struggle in that deadly close,
    The yelling of the blast,
    The wild surf, white, aghast,
The whelming seas, the thunder and the throes!

How the great cables surged,
    The giant engines urged,
As the brave ships the unequal strife waged
    on!
    Not hope, not courage flagged;
    But the vain anchors dragged,
Down on the reefs they shattered, and were
    gone!

And now were wrought the deeds
Whereof each soul that reads

Grows manlier, and burns with prouder
    breath, —
    Heroic brotherhood,
    The loving bonds of blood,
Proclaimed from high hearts face to face with
    death.

    At length, the English ship
    Her cables had let slip,
Crowded all steam, and steered for the open
    sea,
    Resolved to challenge Fate,
    To pass the perilous strait,
And wrench from jaws of ruin Victory.

    With well-tried metals strained,
    In the storm's teeth she gained,
Foot by slow foot made head, and crept to-
    ward life.
    Across her dubious way
    The good ship Trenton lay,
Helpless, but thrilled to watch the splendid
    strife.

    Helmless she lay, her bulk
    A blind and wallowing hulk,
By her strained hawsers only held from wreck,
    But dauntless each brave heart
    Played his immortal part
In strong endurance on the reeling deck.

    They fought Fate inch by inch, —
    Could die, but could not flinch;
And, biding the inevitable doom,
    They marked the English ship,
    Baffling the tempest's grip,
Forge hardly forth from the expected tomb.

    Then, with exultant breath,
    These heroes waiting death,
Thundered across the storm a peal of cheers, —
    To the triumphant brave
    A greeting from the grave,
Whose echo shall go ringing down the years.

    "To you, who well have won,
    From us, whose course is run,
Glad greeting, as we face the undreaded end!"
    The memory of those cheers
    Shall thrill in English ears
Where'er this English blood and speech ex-
    tend.

    No manlier deed comes down,
    Blazoned in broad renown,

From men of old who lived to dare and die!
    The old fire yet survives,
    Here in our modern lives,
Of splendid chivalry and valor high!
        CHARLES GEORGE DOUGLAS ROBERTS.

AN INTERNATIONAL EPISODE

[March 15, 1889]

WE were ordered to Samoa from the coast of
    Panama,
    And for two long months we sailed the un-
        equal sea,
Till we made the horseshoe harbor with its
    curving coral bar,
    Smelt the good green smell of grass and
        shrub and tree.
We had barely room for swinging with the
    tide —
    There were many of us crowded in the bay:
Three Germans, and the English ship, beside
    Our three — and from the Trenton, where
        she lay,
Through the sunset calms and after,
We could hear the shrill, sweet laughter
    Of the children's voices on the shore at play.

We all knew a storm was coming, but, dear
    God! no man could dream
    Of the furious hell-horrors of that day:
Through the roar of winds and waters we
    could hear wild voices scream —
    See the rocking masts reel by us through
        the spray.
In the gale we drove and drifted helplessly,
    With our rudder gone, our engine-fires
        drowned,
And none might hope another hour to see;
    For all the air was desperate with the sound
Of the brave ships rent asunder —
Of the shrieking souls sucked under,
    'Neath the waves, where many a good man's
        grave was found.

About noon, upon our quarter, from the
    deeper gloom afar,
    Came the English man-of-war Calliope:
"We have lost our anchors, comrades, and,
    though small the chances are,
    We must steer for safety and the open sea."
Then we climbed aloft to cheer her as she
    passed
    Through the tempest and the blackness and
        the foam:

"Now God speed you, though the shout
 should be our last,
 Through the channel where the maddened
  breakers comb,
Through the wild sea's hill and hollow,
On the path we cannot follow,
 To your women and your children and your
  home."

Oh! remember it, good brothers. We two
 people speak one tongue,
 And your native land was mother to our
  land;
But the head, perhaps, is hasty when the na-
 tion's heart is young,
 And we prate of things we do not under-
  stand.
But the day when we stood face to face with
 death
 (Upon whose face few men may look and
  tell),
As long as you could hear, or we had breath,
 Four hundred voices cheered you out of hell!
By the will of that stern chorus,
By the motherland which bore us,
 Judge if we do not love each other well.
    CAROLINE DUER.

On May 31, 1889, western Pennsylvania was
visited by one of the worst catastrophes in the
history of the country. A flood from a broken
reservoir overwhelmed Johnstown, Conemaugh,
and a number of smaller towns, destroying over
two thousand lives and property to the value of
ten million dollars.

BY THE CONEMAUGH

[May 31, 1889]

FOREBODING sudden of untoward change,
 A tight'ning clasp on everything held dear,
A moan of waters wild and strange,
 A whelming horror near;
And, 'midst the thund'rous din a voice of
 doom, —
"Make way for me, O Life, for Death make
 room!

"I come like the whirlwind rude,
 'Gainst all thou hast cherished warring;
I come like the flaming flood
 From a crater's mouth outpouring;
I come like the avalanche gliding free —
And the Power that sent thee forth, sends
 me!

"Where thou hast builded with strength
 secure,
 My hand shall spread disaster;
Where thou hast barr'd me, with forethought
 sure,
 Shall ruin flow the faster;
I come to gather where thou hast sowed, —
But I claim of thee nothing thou hast not owed!

"On my mission of mercy forth I go
 Where the Lord of Being sends me;
His will is the only will I know,
 And my strength is the strength He lends
  me;
Thy loved ones I hide 'neath my waters dim,
But I cannot hide them away from Him!"
    FLORENCE EARLE COATES.

The reservoir was known to be weak, and the
people below had been warned of the danger yet
remained where they were. When, just before the
break, Engineer John G. Parke galloped down
the valley, shouting to all to run for their lives,
it was too late.

THE MAN WHO RODE TO
CONEMAUGH

[May 31, 1889]

INTO the town of Conemaugh,
Striking the people's souls with awe,
Dashed a rider, aflame and pale,
Never alighting to tell his tale,
Sitting his big bay horse astride.
"Run for your lives to the hills!" he cried;
"Run to the hills!" was what he said,
As he waved his hand and dashed ahead.

"Run for your lives to the hills!" he cried,
Spurring his horse, whose reeking side
Was flecked with foam as red as flame.
Whither he goes and whence he came
Nobody knows. They see his horse
Plunging on in his frantic course,
Veins distended and nostrils wide,
Fired and frenzied at such a ride.
Nobody knows the rider's name —
Dead forever to earthly fame.
"Run to the hills! to the hills!" he cried;
"Run for your lives to the mountain side!"

"Stop him! he's mad! just look at him go!
'Tain't safe," they said, "to let him ride so."
"He thinks he can scare us," said one, with a
 laugh,
"But Conemaugh folks don't swallow no chaff:

'Tain't nothing, I'll bet, but the same old leak
In the dam above the South Fork Creek."
Blind to their danger, callous of dread,
They laughed as he left them and dashed
    ahead.
"Run for your lives to the hills!" he cried,
Lashing his horse in his desperate ride.

Down through the valley the rider passed,
Shouting, and spurring his horse on fast;
But not so fast did the rider go
As the raging, roaring, mighty flow
Of the million feet and the millions more
Of water whose fury he fled before.
On he went, and on it came,
The flood itself a very flame
Of surging, swirling, seething tide,
Mountain high and torrents wide.
God alone might measure the force
Of the Conemaugh flood in its V-shaped
    course.
Behind him were buried under the flood
Conemaugh town and all who stood
Jeering there at the man who cried,
"Run for your lives to the mountain side!"

On he sped in his fierce, wild ride.
"Run to the hills! to the hills!" he cried.
Nearer, nearer raged the roar
Horse and rider fled before.
Dashing along the valley ridge,
They came at last to the railroad bridge.
The big horse stood, the rider cried,
"Run for your lives to the mountain side!"
Then plunged across, but not before
The mighty, merciless mountain roar
Struck the bridge and swept it away
Like a bit of straw or a wisp of hay.
But over and under and through that tide
The voice of the unknown rider cried,
"Run to the hills! to the hills!" it cried, —
"Run for your lives to the mountain side!"
                    JOHN ELIOT BOWEN.

It is said that another hero named Daniel
Periton rode in front of the flood giving warning,
and was finally caught by it and drowned.

A BALLAD OF THE CONEMAUGH FLOOD

[May 31, 1889]

THE windows of Heaven were open wide,
The storm cloud broke, and the people cried,
    Will Conemaugh dam hold out?

But the great folks down at Johnstown played,
They ate, they drank, they were nought afraid,
For Conemaugh dam holds Conemaugh lake,
By Conemaugh dam their pleasure they take,
    Fine catching are Conemaugh trout.

The four mile lake at the back of its wall
Is growing to five, and the rains still fall,
    And the flood by night and by day
Is burrowing deep thro' buttress and mound,
Fresh waters spring and spurt from the ground;
While God is thundering out of His cloud
The fountain voices are crying aloud,
    Away to the hills! away!

Away to the hills! leave altar and shrine,
Away to the hills! leave table and wine,
    Away from the trade and your tills;
Let the strong man speed with the weakest
    child,
And the mother who just on her babe has
    smiled
Be carried, leave only the dead on their biers,
No time for the tomb, and no time for tears;
    Away, away to the hills!

Daniel Periton heard the wail
Of the waters gathering over the vale,
    With sorrow for city and field, —
Felt already the mountain quake
'Twixt living and dead. For the brethren's
    sake
Daniel Periton dared to ride
Full in front of the threatening tide,
    And what if the dam do yield?

To a man it is given but once to die,
Though the flood break forth he will raise his
    cry
    For the thousands there in the town.
At least, some child may be saved by his voice,
Some lover may still in the sun rejoice,
Some man that has fled, when he wins his
    breath,
Shall bless the rider who rode thro' death,
    For his fellows' life gave his own.

He leapt to his horse that was black as night,
He turned not left and he turned not right,
    Down to the valley he dashed;
He heard behind him a thunderous boom,
The dam had burst and he knew his doom;
" Fly, fly, for your lives!" it was all he spoke;
" Fly, fly, for the Conemaugh dam has brok'
    And the cataract after him crashed.

They saw a man with the God in his face,
Pale from the desperate whirlwind pace,
  They heard an angel cry.
And the steed's black mane was flecked as he
    flew,
And its flanks were red with the spur's red
    dew,
Into the city and out of the gate,
Rider and ridden were racing with fate,
  Wild with one agony.

"Flash on the news that the dam has burst,"
And one looked forth, and she knew the
    worst,
  "My last message!" she said.
The words at her will flashed on before
Periton's call and the torrent's roar;
And not in vain had Periton cried,
His heart had caught a brave heart to his
    side,
  As bold for the saving he sped.

The flood came down and its strong arms
    took
The city, and all together shook,
  Tower and church and street,
Like a pack of cards that a player may crush,
The houses fell in the whirlpool rush,
Rose and floated and jammed at the last,
Then a fierce flame fed by the deluge blast
  Wove them a winding-sheet.

God have mercy! was ever a pyre
Lit like that of the flood's fierce fire!
  Cattle and men caught fast,
Prisoners held between life and death,
While the flame struck down with its sulphur-
    ous breath,
And the flood struck up with its strong, cold
    hand,
No hope from the water, no help from the
    land,
  And the torrent thundering past!

Daniel Periton, still he rides,
By the heaving flank and the shortening
    strides,
  The race must be well-nigh won.
"Away to the hills!" but the cataract's bound
Has caught and has dashed him from saddle
    to ground, —
And the man who saw the end of the race,
Saw a dark, dead horse, and a pale dead face,
  Did they hear Heaven's great "Well done"?
    HARDWICK DRUMMOND RAWNSLEY.

In charge of the telegraph office at Johnstown
was a Mrs. Ogle. She stayed at her post, sending
message after message of warning down the val-
ley until she herself was overwhelmed and swept
away.

CONEMAUGH

"FLY to the mountain! Fly!"
Terribly rang the cry.
The electric soul of the wire
Quivered like sentient fire.
The soul of the woman who stood
Face to face with the flood
Answered to the shock
Like the eternal rock.
  For she stayed
With her hand on the wire,
  Unafraid,
Flashing the wild word down
Into the lower town.
Is there a lower yet and another?
Into the valley she and none other
Can hurl the warning cry:
"Fly to the mountain! Fly!
The water from Conemaugh
Has opened its awful jaw.
The dam is wide
On the mountain-side!"

"Fly for *your* life, oh, fly!"
  They said.
She lifted her noble head:
"I can stay at my post, and die."

Face to face with duty and death,
Dear is the drawing of human breath.
"Steady, my hand! Hold fast
To the trust upon thee cast.
Steady, my wire! Go, say
That death is on the way!
Steady, strong wire! Go, save!
Grand is the power you have!"

Grander the soul that can stand
Behind the trembling hand;
Grander the woman who dares;
Glory her high name wears.
" *This message is my last!* "
Shot over the wire, and passed
To the listening ear of the land.
The mountain and the strand
Reverberate the cry:
"*Fly for your lives, oh, fly!
I stay at my post, and die.*"

The torrent took her. God knows all.
Fiercely the savage currents fall
To muttering calm. Men count their dead.
The June sky smileth overhead.
God's will we neither read nor guess.
Poorer by one more hero less,
We bow the head, and clasp the hand:
"Teach us, altho' we die, to stand."
ELIZABETH STUART PHELPS WARD.

On May 1, 1893, the most remarkable exposition ever held in America opened at Chicago, to celebrate the four hundredth anniversary of the discovery of America. The group of exposition buildings soon became known as "The White City."

"THE WHITE CITY"

I

GREECE was; Greece is no more.
Temple and town
Have crumbled down;
Time is the fire that hath consumed them all.
Statue and wall
In ruin strew the universal floor.

II

Greece lives, but Greece no more!
Its ashes breed
The undying seed
Blown westward till, in Rome's imperial towers,
Athens reflowers;
Still westward — lo, a veiled and virgin shore!

III

Say not, "Greece is no more."
Through the clear morn
On light winds borne
Her white-winged soul sinks on the New
      World's breast.
Ah! happy West —
Greece flowers anew, and all her temples soar!

IV

One bright hour, then no more
Shall to the skies
These columns rise.
But though art's flower shall fade, again the
      seed
Onward shall speed,
Quickening the land from lake to ocean's roar.

V

Art lives, though Greece may never
From the ancient mold

As once of old
Exhale to heaven the inimitable bloom;
Yet from that tomb
Beauty walks forth to light the world forever!
                    RICHARD WATSON GILDER.

On February 2, 1894, the famous old corvette, Kearsarge, which destroyed the Confederate cruiser Alabama, off Cherbourg, during the Civil War, was wrecked on Roncador reef in the Caribbean Sea.

THE KEARSARGE

[February 2, 1894]

IN the gloomy ocean bed
Dwelt a formless thing, and said,
In the dim and countless eons long ago,
   "I will build a stronghold high,
   Ocean's power to defy,
And the pride of haughty man to lay low."

Crept the minutes for the sad,
Sped the cycles for the glad,
But the march of time was neither less nor
      more;
   While the formless atom died,
   Myriad millions by its side,
And above them slowly lifted Roncador.

Roncador of Caribee,
Coral dragon of the sea,
Ever sleeping with his teeth below the wave;
   Woe to him who breaks the sleep!
   Woe to them who sail the deep!
Woe to ship and man that fear a shipman's
      grave!

Hither many a galleon old,
Heavy-keeled with guilty gold,
Fled before the hardy rover smiting sore;
   But the sleeper silent lay
   Till the preyer and his prey
Brought their plunder and their bones to
      Roncador.

Be content, O conqueror!
Now our bravest ship of war,
War and tempest who had often braved before,
   All her storied prowess past,
   Strikes her glorious flag at last
To the formless thing that builded Roncador.
                    JAMES JEFFREY ROCHE.

In 1896 Tennessee celebrated the one hundredth anniversary of her admission to the Union, by an exposition held at Nashville.

TENNESSEE

[June 1, 1896]

SHE is touching the cycle, — her tender tread
Is soft on the hearts of her hallowed dead,
And she proudly stands where her sons have
        bled
        For God and Tennessee;

Where the love of her women set the seal
Of the warrior's faith for the country's weal,
With hand on the rifle and hand on the wheel,
        By the altars of Tennessee.

They have builded well for the niche of fame,
Through the sleet of want and the heat of
        blame,
But the courage of heroes tried the flame,
        As they builded Tennessee.

'T was up to the port-holes and down in the
        dust,
Not the weight of might, but the force of
        must,
With faith and rifle-bore free from rust,
        They were building Tennessee.

'T was up in the saddle and off to the fight,
Where arrow and tomahawk shrieked in the
        light;
But the sinews of pioneers won for the right, —
        The bulwarks of Tennessee.

. . . .

She was true when they pressed like a shad-
        owy fate, —
Her royal foes at her unbarred gate, —
And as true when were menaced her Rights
        of State, —
        The mother, — Tennessee.

And she gave of her life for the stars and bars,
As she gave of her sons for the earlier wars,
And the breast of her motherhood wears the
        scars,
        For the manhood of Tennessee.

But she wrought again, in the strength of
        might,
In the face of defeat and a yielded right,

The Cloth of Gold from the loom of night, —
        The mantle of Tennessee.

She has given all that she held most dear,
With a Spartan hope and a Spartan fear, —
Crowned in her statehood "Volunteer," —
        Glorious Tennessee!

She has rounded the cycle, — the tale is told;
The circlet is iron, the clasp is gold;
And the leaves of a wonderful past unfold
        The garland of Tennessee.

And her garments gleam in the sunlit years,
And the songs of her children fill her ears;
And the listening heart of the great world hears
        The pæans of Tennessee!
                VIRGINIA FRASER BOYLE.

On May 31, 1897, a monument to the memory of Robert Gould Shaw, who fell at the head of his colored regiment during the Civil War, was unveiled on Boston Common. The monument, designed by Augustus Saint-Gaudens, is perhaps the most noteworthy of its kind in America.

AN ODE

May 31, 1897

I

NOT with slow, funereal sound
Come we to this sacred ground;
Not with wailing fife and solemn muffled drum,
        Bringing a cypress wreath
        To lay, with bended knee,
        On the cold brows of Death —
        Not so, dear God, we come,
But with the trumpets' blare
And shot-torn battle-banners flung to air,
        As for a victory!

Hark to the measured tread of martial feet,
The music and the murmurs of the street!
        No bugle breathes this day
        Disaster and retreat! —
        Hark, how the iron lips
        Of the great battle-ships
Salute the City from her azure Bay!

II

Time was—time was, ah, unforgotten years!—
We paid our hero tribute of our tears.
        But now let go

All sounds and signs and formulas of woe:
'T is Life, not Death, we celebrate;
To Life, not Death, we dedicate
This storied bronze, whereon is wrought
The lithe immortal figure of our thought,
To show forever to men's eyes,
Our children's children's children's eyes,
How once he stood
In that heroic mood,
He and his dusky braves
So fain of glorious graves! —
One instant stood, and then
Drave through that cloud of purple steel and
flame,
Which wrapt him, held him, gave him not
again,
But in its trampled ashes left to Fame
An everlasting name!

III

That was indeed to live —
At one bold swoop to wrest
From darkling death the best
That death to life can give.
He fell as Roland fell
That day at Roncevaux,
With foot upon the ramparts of the foe!
A pæan, not a knell,
For heroes dying so!
No need for sorrow here,
No room for sigh or tear,
Save such rich tears as happy eyelids
know.
See where he rides, our Knight!
Within his eyes the light
Of battle, and youth's gold about his
brow;
Our Paladin, our Soldier of the Cross,
Not weighing gain with loss —
World-loser, that won all
Obeying duty's call!
Not his, at peril's frown,
A pulse of quicker beat;
Not his to hesitate
And parley hold with Fate,
But proudly to fling down
His gauntlet at her feet.
O soul of loyal valor and white truth,
Here, by this iron gate,
Thy serried ranks about thee as of yore,
Stand thou for evermore
In thy undying youth!
The tender heart, the eagle eye!
Oh, unto him belong
The homages of Song;

Our praises and the praise
Of coming days
To him belong —
To him, to him, the dead that shall not die!
THOMAS BAILEY ALDRICH.

The years 1897 and 1898 witnessed a great rush of gold-seekers to Alaska, where placer gold in large quantities had been discovered, the year before, in the Yukon district on Klondike Creek.

THE KLONDIKE

[1898]

NEVER mind the day we left, or the way the
women clung to us;
All we need now is the last way they looked
at us.
Never mind the twelve men there amid the
cheering —
Twelve men or one man, 't will soon be all
the same;
For this is what we know: we are five men
together,
Five left o' twelve men to find the golden river.

Far we came to find it out, but the place was
here for all of us;
Far, far we came, and here we have the last
of us.
We that were the front men, we that would
be early,
We that had the faith, and the triumph in our
eyes:
We that had the wrong road, twelve men to-
gether, —
Singing when the devil sang to find the golden
river.

Say the gleam was not for us, but never say
we doubted it;
Say the wrong road was right before we fol-
lowed it.
We that were the front men, fit for all forage,—
Say that while we dwindle we are front men
still;
For this is what we know to-night: we 're
starving here together —
Starving on the wrong road to find the golden
river.

Wrong, we say, but wait a little: hear him in
the corner there;
He knows more than we, and he 'll tell us if
we listen there —

He that fought the snow-sleep less than all
    the others
Stays awhile yet, and he knows where he stays:
Foot and hand a frozen clout, brain a freezing
    feather,
Still he's here to talk with us and to the golden
    river.

"Flow," he says, "and flow along, but you
    cannot flow away from us;
All the world's ice will never keep you far
    from us;
Every man that heeds your call takes the way
    that leads him —
The one way that's his way, and lives his
    own life:
Starve or laugh, the game goes on, and on
    goes the river;
Gold or no, they go their way — twelve men
    together.

"Twelve," he says, "who sold their shame for
    a lure you call too fair for them —
You that laugh and flow to the same word that
    urges them:
Twelve who left the old town shining in the
    sunset,
Left the weary street and the small safe days:
Twelve who knew but one way out, wide the
    way or narrow:
Twelve who took the frozen chance and laid
    their lives on yellow.

"Flow by night and flow by day, nor ever
    once be seen by them;
Flow, freeze, and flow, till time shall hide the
    bones of them:
Laugh and wash their names away, leave
    them all forgotten,
Leave the old town to crumble where it sleeps;
Leave it there as they have left it, shining in
    the valley, —
Leave the town to crumble down and let the
    women marry.

"Twelve of us or five," he says, "we know
    the night is on us now:
Five while we last, and we may as well be
    thinking now:
Thinking each his own thought, knowing,
    when the light comes,
Five left or none left, the game will not be lost.

Crouch or sleep, we go the way, the last way
    together:
Five or none, the game goes on, and on goes
    the river.

"For after all that we have done and all that
    we have failed to do,
Life will be life and the world will have its
    work to do:
Every man who follows us will heed in his
    own fashion
The calling and the warning and the friends
    who do not know:
Each will hold an icy knife to punish his
    heart's lover,
And each will go the frozen way to find the
    golden river."

There you hear him, all he says, and the last
    we'll ever get from him.
Now he wants to sleep, and that will be the
    best for him.
Let him have his own way — no, you need n't
    shake him —
Your own turn will come, so let the man sleep.
For this is what we know: we are stalled here
    together —
Hands and feet and hearts of us, to find the
    golden river.

And there's a quicker way than sleep? . . .
Never mind the looks of him:
All he needs now is a finger on the eyes of him.
You there on the left hand, reach a little over —
Shut the stars away, or he'll see them all night:
He'll see them all night and he'll see them
    all to-morrow,
Crawling down the frozen sky, cold and hard
    and yellow.

Won't you move an inch or two — to keep the
    stars away from him?
— No, he won't move, and there's no need
    of asking him.
Never mind the twelve men, never mind the
    women;
Three while we last, we'll let them all go;
And we'll hold our thoughts north while we
    starve here together,
Looking each his own way to find the golden
    river.

EDWIN ARLINGTON ROBINSON.

CHAPTER V

THE WAR WITH SPAIN

For three centuries and a half, Spain held possession of the island of Cuba, although she had lost, long before, her possessions in North and South America. The Cubans desired freedom, for the Spanish yoke was a galling one, and as early as 1822 sympathy with this desire was openly expressed in the United States.

The people of Cuba revolted against their Spanish rulers in 1848, and kept up a guerilla warfare for some years. In August, 1851, a filibustering expedition, led by Narciso Lopez, sailed from New Orleans. The expedition was captured, and most of its members were executed, among them Lopez himself, and Colonel William L. Crittenden, of Kentucky, who, with fifty others, was shot at Havana, August 16.

APOSTROPHE TO THE ISLAND OF CUBA

[November, 1822]

THERE is blood on thy desolate shore,
    Thou island of plunder and slaves!
Thy billows are purpled with gore,
    And murder has crimsoned thy waves;
The vengeance of nations will come,
    And wrath shall be rained on thy head,
And in terror thy voice shall be dumb,
    When they ask for their brothers who bled.
Thy hand was not stirred, when their life-
        blood was spilt;
And therefore that hand must partake in the
        guilt.

Thou art guilty or weak, — and the rod
    Should be wrenched from thy palsied hand;
By the pirate thy green fields are trod,
    And his steps have polluted thy land;
Unmoved is thy heart and thine eye,
    When our dear ones are tortured and slain;
But their blood with a terrible cry,
    Calls on vengeance, and calls not in vain;
If Europe regard not — our land shall awake,
And thy walls and thy turrets shall tremble
        and shake.

The voice of a world shall be heard,
    And thy faith shall be tried by the call;
And that terrible voice shall be feared,
    And obeyed — or the proud one shall fall.
Enough of our life has been shed,
    In watching and fighting for thee;
If thy foot linger still — on thy head
    The guilt and the vengeance shall be:
We have sworn that the spirit of ALLEN shall
        lead,
And our wrath shall not rest, till we finish the
        deed.

                    JAMES GATES PERCIVAL.

THE GALLANT FIFTY-ONE

WHO FORMED PART OF THE LOPEZ EXPEDI-
TION AND WERE EXECUTED BY THE SPAN-
ISH AUTHORITIES IN HAVANA

[August 16, 1851]

FREEDOM called them — up they rose,
Grasped their swords and showered blows
On the heads of Freedom's foes —
    And Freedom's foes alone.
Fate decreed that they should die;
Pitying angels breathed a sigh;
Freedom wildly wept on high,
    For the gallant Fifty-one!

There they stood in proud array,
None for mercy there would pray;
None would coward looks betray —
    All stood forth with fearless eye,
Showing by their dauntless air,
What their noble souls could dare;
Showing to the tyrants there,
    How Freedom's sons could die.
None there strove their fate to shun —
Gallant band of Fifty-one!

Then a voice the stillness broke:
'T was their gallant leader spoke,
Scorning to receive Death's stroke,
    Kneeling humbly on the sod!
Gazing calmly on the dead,
Whose life-blood had just been shed.
Proudly then the words he said,
    "Americans kneel but to God!"
Perished thus Kentucky's son —
Leader of the Fifty-one.

Rejoice! sons of Thermopylæ!
Kindred spirits join with thee,

Who fell in fight for Liberty,
   For Freedom's sacred name.
Future days their deeds shall tell,
How they nobly fought and fell,
Youthful bosoms proudly swell
   At mention of their fame —
   ·Rays of light from Freedom's sun,
   Gallant band of Fifty-one!

Honor's rays will ever shed
Glory 'round their hallowed bed.
Though their hearts are cold and dead,
   Though their sands of life have run,
Still their names revered will be,
Among the noble and the free —
Glorious sons of Liberty;
   Gallant band of Fifty-one!
            HENRY LYNDEN FLASH.

Spain at last found it necessary to put the
whole island under martial law, and American
sympathy grew more outspoken.

CUBA

[1870]

Is it naught? Is it naught
That the South-wind brings her wail to our
      shore,
   That the spoilers compass our desolate
      sister?
Is it naught? Must we say to her, "Strive no
      more,"
   With the lips wherewith we loved her and
      kissed her?
With the mocking lips wherewith we said,
   "Thou art the dearest and fairest to us
Of all the daughters the sea hath bred,
   Of all green-girdled isles that woo us!"
      Is it naught?

Must ye wait? Must ye wait,
Till they ravage her gardens of orange and
      palm,
   Till her heart is dust, till her strength is
      water?
Must ye see them trample her, and be calm
   As priests when a virgin is led to slaughter?
Shall they smite the marvel of all lands, —
   The nation's longing, the Earth's complete-
      ness, —
On her red mouth dropping myrrh, her hands
   Filled with fruitage and spice and sweet-
      ness?
      Must ye wait?

In the day, in the night,
In the burning day, in the dolorous night,
   Her sun-browned cheeks are stained with
      weeping.
Her watch-fires beacon the misty height: —
   Why are her friends and lovers sleeping?
"Ye, at whose ear the flatterer bends,
   Who were my kindred before all others, —
Hath he set your hearts afar, my friends?
   Hath he made ye alien, my brothers,
      Day and night?"

Hear ye not? Hear ye not
From the hollow sea the sound of her voice;
   The passionate far-off tone which sayeth:
"Alas, my brothers! alas, what choice, —
   The lust that shameth, the sword that
      slayeth?
They bind me! they rend my delicate locks;
   They shred the beautiful robes I won me!
My round limbs bleed on the mountain rocks:
   Save me, ere they have quite undone me!"
      Hear ye not?

Speak at last! Speak at last!
In the might of your strength, in the strength
      of your right,
   Speak out at last to the treacherous spoiler!
Say: "Will ye harry her in our sight?
Ye shall not trample her down, nor soil her!
Loose her bonds! let her rise in her loveli-
      ness, —
   Our virginal sister; or, if ye shame her,
Dark Amnon shall rue for her sore distress,
   And her sure revenge shall be that of
      Tamar!"
      Speak at last!
            EDMUND CLARENCE STEDMAN.

Then in 1873 came what was certain to come,
sooner or later, an outrage by Spain against the
United States. The Virginius, a vessel of American
register, was captured on the high seas by a Span-
ish gunboat, taken to a Cuban port, and some fifty
of her officers and crew, Americans for the most
part, summarily shot. America was wild with rage,
but Spain was permitted to settle by paying an
indemnity.

THE GOSPEL OF PEACE

[1873]

Ay, let it rest! And give us peace.
   'T is but another blot
On Freedom's fustian flag, and gold
   Will gild the unclean spot.

Yes, fold the hands, and bear the wrong
  As Christians over-meek,
And wipe away the bloody stain,
  And turn the other cheek.

What boots the loss of freemen's blood
  Beside imperilled gold ?
Is honor more than merchandise ?
  And cannot pride be sold ?

Let Cuba groan, let patriots fall;
  Americans may die;
Our flag may droop in foul disgrace,
  But "Peace!" be still our cry.

Ay, give us peace! And give us truth
  To nature, to resign
The counterfeit which Freedom wears
  Upon her banner fine.

Remove the Stars, — they light our shame;
  But keep the Stripes of gore
And craven White, to tell the wrong
  A prudent nation bore.
                JAMES JEFFREY ROCHE.

The insurrection in Cuba dragged on, its hor-
rors steadily increasing, and at last, in 1875, the
American government intimated that if Spain
did not stop the war, foreign intervention might
become necessary. Spain took the hint and ended
the struggle by granting Cuba certain reforms.

CUBA

ISLE of a summer sea,
  Fragrant with Eden's flowers,
God meant thee to be free,
  And wills thee to be *ours!*

The blood of generous hearts
  Has freely drenched thy soil;
That blood but strength imparts,
  Which tyrants cannot foil!

Within thy fair retreat,
  'Mid victory and flame,
Thy sons shall yet repeat
  Huzzas in Freedom's name!

Yet, where his ashes rest,
  Whose eye revealed a world,
From towers and mountain crest,
  Our flag shall be unfurled!

In truth, it is but just,
  That Freedom's hand should hold,
Confided to her trust,
  The key to lands of gold!
                HARVEY RICE.

But with a cynical disregard of good faith,
Spain kept only such of her promises as she
pleased; increased abuses followed, and in 1895
revolution flamed out again. Under such leaders
as Gomez, Maceo, and Garcia, the revolutionists
soon gained control of most of the provinces.

CUBA TO COLUMBIA

[April, 1896]

A VOICE went over the waters —
  A stormy edge of the sea —
Fairest of Freedom's daughters,
  Have you no help for me?
Do you not hear the rusty chain
  Clanking about my feet?
Have you not seen my children slain,
  Whether in cell or street?
Oh, if you were sad as I,
  And I as you were strong,
You would not have to call or cry —
  You would not suffer long!

Patience? " — have I not learned it,
  Under the crushing years?
Freedom — have I not earned it,
  Toiling with blood and tears?
"Not of you?" — my banners wave
  Not on Egyptian shore,
Or by Armenia's mammoth grave —
  But at your very door!
Oh, if you were needy as I,
  And I as you were strong,
You should not suffer, bleed, and die,
  Under the hoofs of wrong!

Is it that you have never
  Felt the oppressor's hand,
Fighting, with fond endeavor,
  To cling to your own sweet land?
Were you not half dismayed,
  There in the century's night,
Till to your view a sister's aid
  Came, like a flash of light?
Oh, what gift could ever be grand
  Enough to pay the debt,
If out of the starry Western land,
  Should come my Lafayette!
                WILL CARLETON.

American sympathy was soon awakened, and grew rapidly in strength. This was increased when Spain placed Valeriano Weyler in command in Cuba. Weyler had an evil reputation for cruelty and extortion, and at once proceeded to make it more evil by exterminating the " pacificos," or quiet people who were taking no active part in the war.

CUBA LIBRE

COMES a cry from Cuban water —
  From the warm, dusk Antilles —
From the lost Atlanta's daughter,
  Drowned in blood as drowned in seas;
Comes a cry of purpled anguish —
  See her struggles, hear her cries!
Shall she live, or shall she languish?
  Shall she sink, or shall she rise?

She shall rise, by all that's holy!
  She shall live and she shall last;
Rise as we, when crushed and lowly,
  From the blackness of the past.
Bid her strike! Lo, it is written
  Blood for blood and life for life.
Bid her smite, as she is smitten;
  Stars and stripes were born of strife.

Once we flashed her lights of freedom,
  Lights that dazzled her dark eyes
Till she could but yearning heed them,
  Reach her hands and try to rise.
Then they stabbed her, choked her, drowned her
  Till we scarce could hear a note.
Ah! these rusting chains that bound her!
  Oh! these robbers at her throat!

And the kind who forged these fetters?
  Ask five hundred years for news.
Stake and thumbscrew for their betters!
  Inquisitions! Banished Jews!
Chains and slavery! What reminder
  Of one red man in that land?
Why, these very chains that bind her
  Bound Columbus, foot and hand!

Shall she rise as rose Columbus,
  From his chains, from shame and wrong—
Rise as Morning, matchless, wondrous —
  Rise as some rich morning song —
Rise a ringing song and story,
  Valor, Love personified?
Stars and stripes espouse her glory,
  Love and Liberty allied.
                    JOAQUIN MILLER.

The situation of Americans in Havana began to cause uneasiness, and it was decided to send a ship of war to that port. The battleship Maine was selected for this duty, and reached Havana on the morning of January 24, 1898.

THE PARTING OF THE WAYS[1]

UNTRAMMELLED Giant of the West,
  With all of Nature's gifts endowed,
With all of Heaven's mercies blessed,
  Nor of thy power unduly proud —
Peerless in courage, force, and skill,
And godlike in thy strength of will, —

Before thy feet the ways divide:
  One path leads up to heights sublime;
The other downward slopes, where bide
  The refuse and the wrecks of Time.
Choose then, nor falter at the start,
O choose the nobler path and part!

Be thou the guardian of the weak,
  Of the unfriended, thou the friend;
No guerdon for thy valor seek,
  No end beyond the avowèd end.
Wouldst thou thy godlike power preserve,
Be godlike in the will to serve!
                    JOSEPH B. GILDER.

On the morning of February 16, 1898, the news flashed over the country that on the previous evening the Maine had been blown up at her anchorage, and that two hundred and sixty-four men and two officers had been killed.

THE MEN OF THE MAINE

[February 15, 1898]

NOT in the dire, ensanguined front of war,
Conquered or conqueror,
'Mid the dread battle-peal, did they go
    down
To the still under-seas, with fair Renown
To weave for them the hero-martyr's crown.
They struck no blow
'Gainst an embattled foe;
With valiant-hearted Saxon hardihood
They stood not as the Essex sailors stood,
So sore bestead in that far Chilian bay;
Yet no less faithful they,
These men who, in a passing of the breath,
Were hurtled upon death.

No warning the salt-scented sea-wind bore,
No presage whispered from the Cuban shore
Of the appalling fate
That in the tropic night-time lay in wait
To bear them whence they shall return no
　　more.
Some lapsed from dreams of home and love's
　　clear star
Into a realm where dreams eternal are;
And some into a world of wave and flame
Wherethrough they came
To living agony that no words can name.
Tears for them all,
And the low-tunèd dirge funereal!

Their place is now
With those who wear, green-set about the brow,
The deathless immortelles, —
The heroes torn and scarred
Whose blood made red the barren ocean dells,
Fighting with him the gallant Ranger bore,
Daring to do what none had dared before,
To wave the New World banner, freedom-
　　starred,
At England's very door!
Yea, with such noble ones their names shall
　　stand
As those who heard the dying Lawrence speak
His burning words upon the Chesapeake,
And grappled in the hopeless hand-to-hand;
With those who fell on Erie and Champlain
Beneath the pouring, pitiless battle-rain:
With such as these, our lost men of the Maine!

What though they faced no storm of iron hail
That freedom and the right might still pre-
　　vail?
The path of duty it was theirs to tread
To death's dark vale through ways of travail
　　led,
And they are ours — our dead!
If it be true that each loss holds a gain,
It must be ours through saddened eyes to see
From out this tragic holocaust of pain
The whole land bound in closer amity!
　　　　　　　　　　　　CLINTON SCOLLARD.

THE WORD OF THE LORD FROM HAVANA

[February 16, 1898]

THUS spake the Lord:
Because ye have not heard,

Because ye have given no heed
To my people in their need,

Because the oppressed cried
From the dust where he died,
And ye turned your face away
From his cry in that day,

Because ye have bought and sold
That which is above gold,
Because your brother is slain
While ye get you drunk with gain,

(Behold, these are my people, I have brought
　　them to birth,
On whom the mighty have trod,
The kings of the earth,
Saith the Lord God!)

Because ye have fawned and bowed down
Lest the spoiler frown,
And the wrongs that the spoiled have
　　borne
Ye have held in scorn,

Therefore with rending and flame
I have marred and smitten you,
Therefore I have given you to shame,
That the nations shall spit on you.

Therefore my Angel of Death
Hath stretched out his hand on you,
Therefore I speak in my wrath,
Laying command on you;

(Once have I bared my sword,
And the kings of the earth gave a cry;
Twice have I bared my sword,
That the kings of the earth should die;
Thrice shall I bare my sword,
And ye shall know my name, that it is I!)

Ye who held peace less than right
When a king laid a pitiful tax on you,
Hold not your hand from the fight
When freedom cries under the axe on you!

(I who called France to you, call you to Cuba
　　in turn!
Repay — lest I cast you adrift and you perish
　　astern!)

Ye who made war that your ships
Should lay to at the beck of no nation,

Make war now on Murder, that slips
The leash of her hounds of damnation!

Ye who remembered the Alamo,
Remember the Maine!

RICHARD HOVEY.

HALF-MAST

[February 16, 1898]

On every schoolhouse, ship, and staff
From 'Frisco clear to Marblehead,
Let droop the starry banner now,
In sorrow for our sailors dead.

Half-mast! Half-mast! o'er all the land;
The verdict wait; your wrath restrain;
Half-mast for all that gallant band —
The sailors of the Maine!

Not till a treachery is proved
His sword the patriot soldier draws;
War is the last alternative —
Be patient till ye know the cause.

Meanwhile — Half-mast o'er all the land!
The verdict wait; your wrath restrain;
Half-mast! for all that gallant band —
The martyrs of the Maine!

LLOYD MIFFLIN.

THE FIGHTING RACE

[February 16, 1898]

"READ out the names!" and Burke sat back,
And Kelly drooped his head,
While Shea — they call him Scholar Jack —
Went down the list of the dead.
Officers, seamen, gunners, marines,
The crews of the gig and yawl,
The bearded man and the lad in his teens,
Carpenters, coal passers — all.
Then, knocking the ashes from out his pipe,
Said Burke in an offhand way:
"We're all in that dead man's list by Cripe!
Kelly and Burke and Shea."
"Well, here's to the Maine, and I'm sorry
for Spain,"
Said Kelly and Burke and Shea.

"Wherever there's Kellys there's trouble,"
said Burke.
"Wherever fighting's the game,
Or a spice of danger in grown man's work,"
Said Kelly, "you'll find my name."

"And do we fall short," said Burke, getting
mad,
"When it's touch and go for life?"
Said Shea, "It's thirty-odd years, bedad,
Since I charged to drum and fife
Up Marye's Heights, and my old canteen
Stopped a rebel ball on its way;
There were blossoms of blood on our sprigs
of green —
Kelly and Burke and Shea —
And the dead didn't brag." "Well, here's
to the flag!"
Said Kelly and Burke and Shea.

"I wish 't was in Ireland, for there's the place,"
Said Burke, "that we'd die by right,
In the cradle of our soldier race,
After one good stand-up fight.
My grandfather fell on Vinegar Hill,
And fighting was not his trade;
But his rusty pike's in the cabin still,
With Hessian blood on the blade."
"Aye, aye," said Kelly, "the pikes were great
When the word was 'clear the way!'
We were thick on the roll in ninety-eight —
Kelly and Burke and Shea."
"Well, here's to the pike and the sword and
the like!"
Said Kelly and Burke and Shea.

And Shea, the scholar, with rising joy,
Said, "We were at Ramillies;
We left our bones at Fontenoy
And up in the Pyrenees;
Before Dunkirk, on Landen's plain,
Cremona, Lille, and Ghent;
We're all over Austria, France, and Spain,
Wherever they pitched a tent.
We've died for England from Waterloo
To Egypt and Dargai;
And still there's enough for a corps or crew,
Kelly and Burke and Shea."
"Well, here's to good honest fighting blood!"
Said Kelly and Burke and Shea.

"Oh, the fighting races don't die out,
If they seldom die in bed,
For love is first in their hearts, no doubt,"
Said Burke; then Kelly said:
"When Michael, the Irish Archangel, stands,
The angel with the sword,
And the battle-dead from a hundred lands
Are ranged in one big horde,
Our line, that for Gabriel's trumpet waits,
Will stretch three deep that day,

From Jehoshaphat to the Golden Gates —
  Kelly and Burke and Shea."
"Well, here's thank God for the race and the
    sod!"
  Said Kelly and Burke and Shea.
              JOSEPH I. C. CLARKE.

A wave of fierce wrath swept over the Ameri-
can people; but Captain Sigsbee, of the destroyed
ship, asked that judgment be suspended until the
cause of the accident had been investigated.

ON THE EVE OF WAR

O GOD of Battles, who art still
  The God of Love, the God of Rest,
Subdue thy people's fiery will,
  And quell the passions in their breast!
Before we bathe our hands in blood
We lift them to thy Holy Rood.

The waiting nations hold their breath
  To catch the dreadful battle-cry;
And in the silence as of death
  The fateful hours go softly by.
Oh, hear thy people where they pray,
And shrive our souls before the fray!

Before the sun of peace shall set,
  We kneel apart a solemn while;
Pity the eyes with sorrow wet,
  But pity most the lips that smile.
The night comes fast; we hear afar
The baying of the wolves of war.

Not lightly, oh, not lightly, Lord,
  Let this our awful task begin;
Speak from thy throne a warning word
  Above the angry factions' din.
If *this* be thy Most Holy will,
Be with us still, — be with us still!
              DANSKE DANDRIDGE.
  Good Friday, 1898.

Spain, without waiting for investigation, an-
nounced that the Maine had been blown up by an
explosion of her magazines, due to the careless-
ness of her officers. The American people waited
in ominous silence for the investigation to be con-
cluded.

TO SPAIN — A LAST WORD

IBERIAN! palter no more! By thine hands,
    thine alone, they were slain!
Oh, 't was a deed in the dark —

              Yet mark!
We will show you a way — only one — by
    which ye may blot out the stain!

Build them a monument whom to death-
    sleep, in their sleep, ye betrayed!
  Proud and stern let it be —
              Cuba free!
So, only, the stain shall be razed — so, only,
    the great debt be paid!
              EDITH M. THOMAS.

Meanwhile, the sailor dead were buried in the
cemetery at Havana, with impressive ceremony.
They were afterwards disinterred and placed in
the military cemetery at Arlington on the Poto-
mac.

THE MARTYRS OF THE MAINE

AND they have thrust our shattered dead away
    in foreign graves,
Exiled forever from the port the homesick
    sailor craves!
  They trusted once in Spain,
  They're trusting her again!
  And with the holy care of our own sacred
    slain!
  No, no, the Stripes and Stars
  Must wave above our tars.
        Bring them home!

On a thousand hills the darling dead of all
    our battles lie,
In nooks of peace, with flowers and flags,
    but now they seem to cry
  From out their bivouac:
  "Here every good man Jack
  Belongs. Nowhere but here — with us.
  So bring them back."
  And on the Cuban gales,
  A ghostly rumor wails,
        "Bring us home!"

Poltroon, the people that neglects to guard
    the bones, the dust,
The reverenced relics its warriors have be-
    queathed in trust!
  But heroes, too, were these
  Who sentinell'd the seas
  And gave their lives, to shelter us in care-
    less ease.
  Shall we desert them, slain,
  And proffer them to Spain

As alien mendicants, — these martyrs of
our Maine?
No! Bring them home!
RUPERT HUGHES.

At last, the investigation was ended, and showed
that the Maine had been blown up from the out-
side, probably by a submarine mine, exploded
by men who wore the uniform of Spain. The
report reached Congress March 28, 1898, and on
April 11 President McKinley asked Congress for
authority to establish an independent government
in Cuba.

EL EMPLAZADO

EL EMPLAZADO, the Summoned, the Doomed
One,
Spain whom the nations denounce and
abhor,
Robe thy dismay in the black sanbenito,
Come to the frowning tribunal of war.

Curst were thy minions, their roster and
scutcheon,
Alvas, Alfonsos, Archarchons of hate;
Pillared on bigotry, pride, and extortion,
Topples to ruin thy mansion of state.

Violence, Cruelty, Intrigue, and Treason,
These the false courtiers who flattered thy
throne;
Empires, thy sisters, forbode thee disaster,
Even thy children their mother disown.

Suppliant Cuba, thy daughter forsaken,
Famished and bleeding and buffeted sore,
Ghastly from gashes and stabs of thy ran-
cor,
Binds up her wounds at an alien door.

Courts and corregidors erst at thy bidding
Banished or butchered Moresco and Jew;
Ghosts from all Christendom, shades of the
Martyrs
Flock from the sepulchre thee to pursue.

Wrath of retributive justice o'ertakes thee!
Brand of time's malison blisters thy brow:
Armed cabelleros and crowned kings of Bour-
bon,
All are unable to succor thee now.

El Emplazado, the Summoned, the Doomed
One!
God's Inquisition condemns thee to-day!

Earth-shaking cannon-bolts thunder thy
sentence, —
Heaven reëchoes the auto-da-fé.
WILLIAM HENRY VENABLE.

On April 19, 1898, Congress adopted a resolution
declaring that Spanish rule in Cuba must cease,
recognizing the independence of the Cubans, and
empowering the President to use the entire land
and naval forces of the United States to drive
Spain from the island. It was, in effect, a declara-
tion of war.

BATTLE SONG

WHEN the vengeance wakes, when the battle
breaks,
And the ships sweep out to sea;
When the foe is neared, when the decks are
cleared,
And the colors floating free;
When the squadrons meet, when it's fleet to
fleet
And front to front with Spain,
From ship to ship, from lip to lip,
Pass on the quick refrain,
"Remember, remember the Maine!"

When the flag shall sign, "Advance in
line;
Train ships on an even keel;"
When the guns shall flash and the shot shall
crash
And bound on the ringing steel;
When the rattling blasts from the armored
masts
Are hurling their deadliest rain,
Let their voices loud, through the blinding
cloud,
Cry ever the fierce refrain,
"Remember, remember the Maine!"

God's sky and sea in that storm shall be
Fate's chaos of smoke and flame,
But across that hell every shot shall tell,
Not a gun can miss its aim;
Not a blow shall fail on the crumbling
mail,
And the waves that engulf the slain
Shall sweep the decks of the blackened
wrecks,
With the thundering, dread refrain,
"Remember, remember the Maine!"
ROBERT BURNS WILSON.

England was the only country in Europe whose sympathies were openly with the United States. In France, Italy, and elsewhere, the hostility to America was bitter and outspoken.

GREETING FROM ENGLAND

AMERICA! dear brother land!
    While yet the shotted guns are mute,
    Accept a brotherly salute,
A hearty grip of England's hand.

To-morrow, when the sulphurous glow
    Of war shall dim the stars above,
    Be sure the star of England's love
Is over you, come weal or woe.

Go forth in hope! Go forth in might!
    To all your nobler self be true,
    That coming times may see in you
The vanguard of the hosts of light.

Though wrathful justice load and train
    Your guns, be every breach they make
    A gateway pierced for mercy's sake
That peace may enter in and reign.

Then, should the hosts of darkness band
    Against you, lowering thunderously,
    Flash the word "Brother" o'er the sea,
And England at your side shall stand,

Exulting! For, though dark the night
    And sinister with scud and rack,
    The hour that brings us back to back
But harbingers the larger light.

London *Chronicle*, April 22, 1898.

Diplomatic relations between Spain and the United States were at once severed, and on April 25, 1898, Congress formally declared that war with the Kingdom of Spain had existed since April 21. The first blow was to be struck with surprising suddenness.

BATTLE CRY

[May 1, 1898]

THE loud drums are rolling, the mad trumpets blow!
To battle! the war is begun and we go
To humble the pride of an arrogant foe!

*The ensign and standard which wave for the
    Crown
Of Castile and Aragon — trample them down!*

*Granada and Leon and haughty Navarre
Shall lower their banner to Cuba's lone star!*

Now under Old Glory, the Blue and the Gray
United march shoulder to shoulder away,
To meet the Hidalgos in furious fray.

With musket and haversack ready are we
To tramp the globe over, to sweep every sea,
From isles of dead Philip to Florida's Key.

We think of the Maine and our hot bosoms
    swell
With rage of love's sorrow, which vengeance
    must quell,
And then we are ready to storm gates of Hell.

Our flag streams aloft by the tempest un-
    furled!
We strike for a Continent; — nay, for the
    World!
Mene, Tekel, Upharsin! the thunder is hurled!

*The ensign and standard which wave for the
    Crown
Of Castile and Aragon — trample them down!
Granada and Leon and haughty Navarre
Shall lower their banner to Cuba's lone star!*
                    WILLIAM HENRY VENABLE.

Thousands of miles away, across the Pacific, lay another island dependency of Spain, the Philippines. The Navy Department, with singular foresight, had been gradually increasing the Asiatic squadron, commanded by Commodore George Dewey, and that officer was carefully preparing for the work he saw before him. The fleet was assembled at Hong Kong, and on April 26, 1898, came a cablegram to Dewey stating that war had commenced and ordering him to proceed at once to the Philippines and capture or destroy the Spanish fleet there. At two o'clock the next afternoon, the American fleet started on its six-hundred-mile journey. It reached Manila on the night of April 30, and steamed straight into the harbor.

JUST ONE SIGNAL

[May 1, 1898]

THE war-path is true and straight,
    It knoweth no left or right;
Why ponder and wonder and vacillate?
    The way to fight is to fight.

The officer of the deck
    Had climbed to a perch aloft,

And he leaned far out and he craned his
  neck,
  And his tones were gentle and soft:
"I see," he whispered, "off there to port,
  Through the night shade's lesser black,
The darker blur of the outer fort,
  Preparing for the attack."
They signalled it so, and sharp and short
  The answer was signalled back:
    "Keep on."

Again from the upper air
  Came the quiet voice of the guide:
"The admiral's flagship's over there,
  Two miles on the starboard side.
It's a long, long way for the best of eyes,
  But I know her by moon or sun,
I know by her lines and I know her size —
  And there goes her warning gun."
"That boat will make a most excellent prize,"
  Said the admiral, "when we've won.
    Keep on."

The whispering came again:
  "I think by the hints and signs
Appearing ahead of us now and then
  That we're getting among their mines.
Ten fathom in front, as the search-lights
  show,
  I fancy that I can detect
The line of their outermost works — Ah, no!
  It is nearer than I'd suspect."
The message was sent to the admiral so,
  And he answered to this effect:
    "Keep on."

The haze of the dawning day
  Slid into the shades of night,
And he called: "Off there in the upper bay,
  They're lining their ships for a fight.
I think they are training on us —" No more
  He said, for the dawn was lit
By the blaze of a gun from the neighboring
  shore,
  And he fell to the deck, hard hit.
They signalled: "The first man struck." As
  before
  The admiral answered it:
    "Keep on."

The sun came over the hills
  As wishing a world-wide weal.
And the guns were fired with the aim that
  kills,
  And steel pierced the heart of steel.

And the line of shore was the fringe of hell,
  And the centre of hell was the sea,
And the woe was the woe no tongue may tell,
  And no eye view tearlessly,
And over that crater of bomb and shell
  The signal continued to be:
    "Keep on."

O Lawrence, whose passing cry
  Grows ever the more sublime,
And thou, O Nile King, whose words shall die
  When we learn of the death of time,
We send you the third of a glorious three;
  We send you a battle shout
That echoes up from the blood-thick sea
  And up from the wreck and rout
And down from the staff on the high cross-
  tree
  Where the flag is signalling out:
    "Keep on."

The war-path is true and straight,
  It knoweth no left or right;
Mars loves not the man who would devi-
  ate, —
  For the way to fight is to fight.

A shot from Corregidor and another from El
Fraile told that the fleet was discovered, but the
ships glided quietly on, and at dawn the Spanish
fleet was seen anchored under the batteries of
Cavité. Dewey steamed straight for them; the
Spanish ships were sunk, one after another, by
the deadly fire of the American gunners, and by
noon the Spanish fleet had been destroyed, the
shore batteries silenced, and a white flag floated
over the citadel of Cavité. Dewey had not lost
a man, and had won the greatest naval battle
since Trafalgar.

DEWEY AT MANILA

[May 1, 1898]

'T was the very verge of May
  When the bold Olympia led
Into Bocagrande Bay
  Dewey's squadron, dark and dread, —
Creeping past Corregidor,
Guardian of Manila's shore.

Do they sleep who wait the fray?
  Is the moon so dazzling bright
That our cruisers' battle-gray
  Melts into the misty light? . . .
Ah! the red flash and the roar!
Wakes at last Corregidor!

All too late their screaming shell
  Tears the silence with its track;
This is but the *gate* of hell,
  We've no leisure to turn back.
Answer, Concord! — then once more
Slumber on, Corregidor!

And as, like a slowing tide,
  Onward still the vessels creep,
Dewey, watching, falcon-eyed,
  Orders, — "Let the gunners sleep;
For we meet a foe at four
Fiercer than Corregidor."

Well they slept, for well they knew
  What the morrow taught us all, —
He was wise (as well as true)
  Thus upon the foe to fall.
Long shall Spain the day deplore
Dewey ran Corregidor.

May is dancing into light
  As the Spanish Admiral
From a dream of phantom fight
  Wakens at his sentry's call.
Shall he leave Cavité's lee,
Hunt the Yankee fleet at sea?

O Montojo, to thy deck,
  That to-day shall float its last!
Quick! To quarters! Yonder speck
  Grows a hull of portent vast.
Hither, toward Cavité's lee
Comes the Yankee hunting thee!

Not for fear of hidden mine
  Halts our doughty Commodore.
He, of old heroic line,
  Follows Farragut once more,
Hazards all on victory,
Here within Cavité's lee.

If he loses, all is gone;
  He will win because he must.
And the shafts of yonder dawn
  Are not quicker than his thrust.
Soon, Montojo, he shall be
With thee in Cavité's lee.

Now, Manila, to the fray!
  Show the hated Yankee host
This is not a holiday, —
  Spanish blood is more than boast.

Fleet and mine and battery,
Crush him in Cavité's lee!

Lo, hell's geysers at our fore
  Pierce the plotted path — in vain,
Nerving every man the more
  With the memory of the Maine!
Now at last our guns are free
Here within Cavité's lee.

"Gridley," says the Commodore,
  "You may fire when ready." Then
Long and loud, like lions' roar
  When a rival dares the den,
Breaks the awful cannonry
Full across Cavité's lee.

Who shall tell the daring tale
  Of our Thunderbolt's attack,
Finding, when the chart should fail,
  By the lead his dubious track,
Five ships following faithfully
Five times o'er Cavité's lee;

Of our gunners' deadly aim;
  Of the gallant foe and brave
Who, unconquered, faced with flame,
  Seek the mercy of the wave, —
Choosing honor in the sea
Underneath Cavité's lee?

Let the meed the victors gain
  Be the measure of their task.
Less of flinching, stouter strain,
  Fiercer combat — who could ask?
And "surrender," — 't was a word
That Cavité ne'er had heard.

Noon, — the woful work is done!
  Not a Spanish ship remains;
But, of their eleven, none
  Ever was so truly Spain's!
Which is prouder, they or we,
Thinking of Cavité's lee?

ENVOY

But remember, when we've ceased
  Giving praise and reckoning odds,
Man shares courage with the beast,
  Wisdom cometh from the gods.
Who would win, on land or wave,
Must be wise as well as brave.
        ROBERT UNDERWOOD JOHNSON.

DEWEY AND HIS MEN

[May 1, 1898]

GLISTERING high in the midnight sky the
    starry rockets soar
To crown the height so soon to be uncrowned,
    Corregidor;
And moaning into the middle night resounds
    the answering shock
From Fraile's island battery within the living
    rock;
Like Farragut before him, so Dewey down the
    bay,
Past fort and mine, in single line, holds on
    toward Cavité.

When the earth was new a raven flew o'er the
    sea on a perilous quest,
By his broad black pinions buoyed up as he
    sought him a spot to rest;
So to-day from British China sweeps our
    Commodore 'mid the cheers
Of England's dauntless ships of steel, and into
    the night he steers,
With never a home but the furrowy foam and
    never a place for ease
Save the place he'll win by the dint and din of
    his long, lean batteries.

A misty dawn on the May-day shone, yet the
    enemy sees afar
On our ships-of-war great flags flung out as
    bright as the morning star;
Then the cannon of Spain crash over the
    main and their splendor flecks the ports
As the crackling thunder rolls along the frown-
    ing fleet and forts;
But the Olympia in her majesty leads up the
    broadening bay
And behind her come gaunt ships and dumb
    toward crested Cavité.

All pearl and rose the dawnlight glows, and
    ruddy and gray the gloom
Of battle over their squadron sinks as we
    sweep like a vast simoom:
When our broadsides flash and ring at last —
    in a hoarsening, staggering crush
On the arsenal and fleet in wrath our lurid
    lightnings rush.
Malate knows us, Cavité, Cañacoa crazed
    with hate;
But Corregidor shall speak no more, El
    Fraile fears his fate.

Montojo fights as fought the knights by the
    Cid Campeador;
He leaves his flagship all afire, the Cuba takes
    him o'er
The Don Antonio roars and fumes, the Austria
    lights and lifts;
From Sangley to Manila Mole the battle
    vapor drifts;
But the Queen Christine in one great blast
    dies as becomes her name,
Her funeral shroud a pillar of cloud all fila-
    greed with flame.

From peak to peak our quick flags speak, the
    rattling chorus ends;
And cheer on cheer rolls over the sea at the
    word the signal sends.
From Commodore to powder-boy, from bridge
    to stoker's den,
No battle rips have found our ships, nor
    wounds nor death our men.
We cheer and rest, we rest and cheer; and
    ever above the tides
The flag that knows no conquering foes in
    newer glory rides.

When the reek of war is rolled afar by the
    breezes down the bay
We turn our deadly guns again on the walls
    of Cavité.
The Spaniard dreamed of victory — his final
    hope is flown
As winged destruction up and down our bat-
    teries have strown —
In horrid havoc, red and black, the storm
    throbs on amain
Till in the glare of carnage there fade all the
    flags of Spain.

In old Madrid sad eyes are hid for an empire
    sore bestead:
Manila's mad with misery, Havana sick with
    dread,
As the great bells toll each gallant soul Castile
    shall see no more,
Toll Fraile's rock a thing for sport, toll lost
    Corregidor —
Spain's fortresses are fluttering with banners
    blanched and pale;
Her admiralty in agony lies shattered, steam
    and sail.

And the home we sought was cheaply bought,
    for no mother, wife, nor maid
From Maine to Loma Point bewails the lad
    for whom she prayed;

Now everywhere, from Florida to the blue
　　Vancouver Straits,
The flag we've flown abroad is thrown, and
　　a word of cheer awaits.
The ships and men that never failed the nation
　　from her birth
Have done again all ships and men may do
　　upon this earth.

Glistering high in the noontide sky the starry
　　banners soar
To crown anew the height so soon uncrowned,
　　Corregidor.
They bring the promise of the free to Philip's
　　jewelled isles,
And hearts oppressed thrill hard with hope
　　whene'er that promise smiles;
For the spirit of Old Ironsides broods o'er
　　that tropic day
And the wildfire lights as Dewey fights on the
　　broad Manila Bay.
　　　　　　　　　　　　WALLACE RICE.

"OFF MANILLY"

AYE, lads, aye, we fought 'em,
　　And we sent 'em to the bottom,
And you'll say that I'm a-talkin' like a
　　silly;
　　I hear your cheers and jokes,
　　But, lads, them's human folks
What is soakin' in the water off Manilly.

Aye, lads, and when we shot
　　It's just as like as not
We hit some mother's heart in old Granady.
　　She did n't sink no Maine,
　　'Way over there in Spain,
But she won't never see her laddy's body.

I kin see a black-eyed gal,
　　Somethin' like my little Sal,
What is cryin' out her eyes in old Sevilly;
　　There's a widow in Madrid
　　With a pore little kid,
And his daddy has went down off Manilly.

Aye, lads, aye, we fought 'em,
　　And we sent 'em to the bottom,
And I hopes you won't be thinkin' I'm a
　　booby,
　　But that little black-eyed gal,
　　What reminds me so of Sal,
She did n't never do no harm to Cuby.

And if instead of Sanchy,
　　It had been "the hated Yankee,"
Which you know, my lads, is me and Jack,
　　and Billy,
　　You know who would be cryin'
　　For us fellers, what was dyin'
And a-soakin' in the water off Manilly.
　　　　　　　　　　　　EDMUND VANCE COOKE.

MANILA BAY

FROM keel to fighting top, I love
　　Our Asiatic fleet,
I love our officers and crews
　　Who'd rather fight than eat.
I love the breakfast ordered up
　　When enemies ran short,
But most I love our chaplain
　　With his head out of the port.

Now, a naval chaplain cannot charge
　　As chaplains can on land,
With his Bible in his pocket,
　　His revolver in his hand,
He must wait and help the wounded,
　　No danger must he court;
So our chaplain helped the wounded
　　With his head out of the port.

Beneath his red and yellow,
　　At bay the Spaniard stood
Till the yellow rose in fire
　　And the crimson sank in blood.
And till the last fouled rifle
　　Sped its impotent retort,
Our chaplain watched the Spaniard
　　With his head out of the port.

Then here's our admiral on the bridge
　　Above the bursting shell;
And here's our sailors who went in
　　For victory or hell,
And here's the ships and here's the guns,
　　That silenced fleet and fort;
But don't forget our chaplain
　　With his head out of the port.
　　　　　　　　　　　　ARTHUR HALE.

May 1, 1898.

A BALLAD OF MANILA BAY

YOUR threats how vain, Corregidor;
Your rampired batteries, feared no more;
Your frowning guard at Manila gate, —
　　When our Captain went before!

Lights out. Into the unknown gloom
From the windy, glimmering, wide sea-room
Challenging fate in that dark strait
    We dared the hidden doom.

But the death in the deep awoke not then;
Mine and torpedo they spoke not then;
From the heights that loomed on our passing
    line
    The thunders broke not then.

Safe through the perilous dark we sped,
Quiet each ship as the quiet dead,
Till the guns of El Fraile roared — too late,
    And the steel prows forged ahead.

Mute each ship as the mute-mouth grave,
A ghost leviathan cleaving the wave;
But deep in its heart the great fires throb,
    The travailing engines rave.

The ponderous pistons urge like fate,
The red-throat furnaces roar elate,
And the sweating stokers stagger and swoon
    In a heat more fierce than hate.

So through the dark we stole our way
Past the grim warders and into the bay,
Past Kalibuyo, and past Salinas, —
    And came at the break of day

Where strong Cavité stood to oppose, —
Where, from a sheen of silver and rose,
A thronging of masts, a soaring of towers,
    The beautiful city arose.

How fine and fair! But the shining air
With a thousand shattered thunders there
Flapped and reeled. For the fighting foe —
    We had caught him in his lair.

Surprised, unready, his proud ships lay
Idly at anchor in Bakor Bay: —
Unready, surprised, but proudly bold,
    Which was ever the Spaniard's way.

Then soon on his pride the dread doom fell,
Red doom, — for the ruin of shot and shell
Lit every vomiting, bursting hulk
    With a crimson reek of hell.

But to the brave though beaten, hail!
All hail to them that dare and fail!
To the dauntless boat that charged our fleet
    And sank in the iron hail!

  .   .   .   .   .   .

Manila Bay! Manila Bay!
How proud the song on our lips to-day!
A brave old song of the true and strong,
    And the will that has its way;

Of the blood that told in the days of Drake
When the fight was good for the fighting's sake!
For the blood that fathered Farragut
    Is the blood that fathered Blake;

And the pride of the blood will not be undone
While war's in the world and a fight to be won.
For the master now, as the master of old,
    Is "the man behind the gun."

The dominant blood that daunts the foe,
That laughs at odds, and leaps to the blow, —
It is Dewey's glory to-day, as Nelson's
    A hundred years ago!
      CHARLES GEORGE DOUGLAS ROBERTS.

THE BATTLE OF MANILA

A FRAGMENT

[May 1, 1898]

By Cavité on the bay
'T was the Spanish squadron lay;
And the red dawn was creeping
O'er the city that lay sleeping
To the east, like a bride, in the May.
There was peace at Manila,
In the May morn at Manila, —
When ho, the Spanish admiral
Awoke to find our line
Had passed by gray Corregidor,
Had laughed at shoal and mine,
And flung to the sky its banners
With "Remember" for the sign!

With the ships of Spain before
In the shelter of the shore,
And the forts on the right,
They drew forward to the fight,
And the first was the gallant Commodore;
In the bay of Manila,
In the doomed bay of Manila —
With succor half the world away,
No port beneath that sky,
With nothing but their ships and guns
And Yankee pluck to try,
They had left retreat behind them,
They had come to win or die!

  .   .   .   .   .   .

For we spoke at Manila,
We said it at Manila,
Oh be ye brave, or be ye strong,
Ye build your ships in vain;
The children of the sea queen's brood
Will not give up the main;
We hold the sea against the world
As we held it against Spain.

Be warned by Manila,
Take warning by Manila,
Ye may trade by land, ye may fight by land,
Ye may hold the land in fee;
But not go down to the sea in ships
To battle with the free;
For England and America
Will keep and hold the sea!
                    RICHARD HOVEY.

This remarkable victory amazed the world,
and set America wild with excitement and en-
thusiasm. Dewey became a popular hero, and
Congress made haste to revive the grade of ad-
miral and to confer it upon him.

DEWEY IN MANILA BAY

HE took a thousand islands and he did n't
            lose a man
    (Raise your heads and cheer him as he
            goes!) —
He licked the sneaky Spaniard till the fellow
            cut and ran,
    For fighting's part of what a Yankee knows.

He fought 'em and he licked 'em, without any
            fuss or flam
    (It was only his profession for to win),
He sank their boats beneath 'em, and he
            spared 'em as they swam,
    And then he sent his ambulances in.

He had no word to cheer him and had no
            bands to play,
    He had no crowds to make his duty brave;
But he risked the deep torpedoes at the break-
            ing of the day,
    For he knew he had our self-respect to save.

He flew the angry signal crying justice for the
            Maine,
    He flew it from his flagship as he fought.
He drove the tardy vengeance in the very teeth
            of Spain,
    And he did it just because he thought he
            ought.

He busted up their batteries and sank eleven
            ships
    (He knew what he was doing, every bit);
He set the Maxims going like a hundred crack-
            ing whips,
    And every shot that crackled was a hit.

He broke 'em and he drove 'em, and he did n't
            care at all,
    He only liked to do as he was bid;
He crumpled up their squadron and their bat-
            teries and all, —
    He knew he had to lick 'em and he did.

And when the thing was finished and they
            flew the frightened flag,
    He slung his guns and sent his foot ashore,
And he gathered in their wounded, and he
            quite forgot to brag,
    For he thought he did his duty, nothing more.

Oh, he took a thousand islands and he did n't
            lose a man
    (Raise your heads and cheer him as he
            goes!) —
He licked the sneaky Spaniard till the fellow
            cut and ran,
    For fighting's part of what a Yankee knows!
                    R. V. RISLEY.

Another fleet, and a much more powerful one
than Dewey's, had been collected at Key West,
under command of Admiral Sampson, ready to
proceed to Cuba, and on April 21 orders came
for it to sail. On the morning of April 22, it put
to sea and steamed slowly off toward Havana.

"MENE, MENE, TEKEL, UPHARSIN"

[April 22, 1898]

BEHOLD, we have gathered together our battle-
            ships, near and afar;
Their decks they are cleared for action, their
            guns they are primed for war.
From the East to the West there is hurry; in
            the North and the South a peal
Of hammers in fort and ship-yard, and the
            clamor and clang of steel;
And the rush and roar of engines, and clank-
            ing of derrick and crane, —
Thou art weighed in the scales and found
            wanting, the balance of God, O Spain!

Behold, I have stood on the mountains, and
            this was writ in the sky:
"She is weighed in the scales and found want-
            ing, the balance God holds on high!"

The balance He once weighed Babylon, the
   Mother of Harlots, in.
One scale holds thy pride and power and em-
   pire, begotten of sin,
Heavy with woe and torture, the crimes of a
   thousand years,
Mortared and welded together with fire and
   blood and tears;
In the other, for justice and mercy, a blade
   with never a stain,
Is laid the Sword of Liberty, and the balance
   dips, O Spain!

Summon thy vessels together! great is thy
   need for these!
Cristobal Colon, Vizcaya, Oquendo, Marie
   Therese.
Let them be strong and many, for a vision
   I had by night,
That the ancient wrongs thou hast done the
   world came howling to the fight;
From the New World shores they gathered.
   Inca and Aztec, slain,
To the Cuban shot but yesterday, and our
   own dead seamen, Spain!

Summon thy ships together, gather a mighty
   fleet!
For a strong young nation is arming that never
   hath known defeat.
Summon thy ships together, there on thy
   blood-stained sands!
For a shadowy army gathers with manacled
   feet and hands,
A shadowy host of sorrows and of shames, too
   black to tell,
That reach with their horrible wounds for
   thee to drag thee down to hell;
Myriad phantoms and spectres, thou warrest
   against in vain!
Thou art weighed in the scales and found
   wanting, the balance of God, O Spain!
               MADISON CAWEIN.

A blockade was proclaimed of Havana and a
number of other ports. But no attempt was made
to enter the harbor, which was crammed with
mines and defended by strong fortifications.

THE SPIRIT OF THE MAINE

IN battle-line of sombre gray
   Our ships-of-war advance,
As Red Cross Knights in holy fray
   Charged with avenging lance.

And terrible shall be thy plight,
   O fleet of cruel Spain!
Forever in our van doth fight
   The spirit of the Maine!

As when beside Regillus Lake
   The Great Twin Brethren came
A righteous fight for Rome to make
   Against the Deed of Shame —
So now a ghostly ship shall doom
   The fleet of treacherous Spain:
Before her guilty soul doth loom
   The Spirit of the Maine!

A wraith arrayed in peaceful white,
   As when asleep she lay
Above the traitorous mine that night
   Within Havana Bay,
She glides before the avenging fleet,
   A sign of woe to Spain,
Brave though her sons, how shall they meet
   The Spirit of the Maine!
               TUDOR JENKS.

Spain also had a fleet, and a strong one, on
the ocean. It had been gathered together at the
Cape Verde Islands, and on April 29, 1898, it put
to sea, and steamed westward into the Atlantic,
for a destination which could only be conjectured.

THE DRAGON OF THE SEAS [1]

THEY say the Spanish ships are out
   To seize the Spanish main;
Reach down the volume, boy, and read
   The story o'er again.

How when the Spaniard had the might,
   He drenched the earth, like rain,
With human blood, and made it death
   To sail the Spanish main.

With torch and steel, and stake and rack,
   He trampled out all truce,
Until Queen Bess her leashes slipt,
   And turned her sea-dogs loose.

God! how they sprang! And how they tore!
   The Grenvilles, Hawkins, Drake!
Remember, boy, they were your sires!
   They made the Spaniard quake.

They sprang, like lions, for their prey,
   Straight for the throat, amain!

[1] From "The Coast of Bohemia"; copyright,
1888, 1906, by Charles Scribner's Sons.

By twos, by scores, where'er they caught
  They fought the ships of Spain.

When Spain, in dark Ulloa's bay
  Broke doubly-plighted faith,
Bold Hawkins fought his way through fire
  For great Elizabeth.

A bitter malt Spain brewed that day —
  She drained it to the lees;
Her faithless guns that morn awoke
  The Dragon of the Seas.

From sea to sea he ravaged far,
  A scourge with flaming breath —
Where'er the Spaniard sailed his ships
  Sailed Francis Drake and Death.

No port was safe against his ire,
  Secure no furthest shore;
The fairest day oft sank in fire
  Before the Dragon's roar.

He made th' Atlantic surges red
  Round every Spanish keel;
Piled Spanish decks with Spanish dead,
  The noblest of Castile.

From Del Fuego's beetling coast
  To sleety Hebrides,
He hounded down the Spanish host,
  And swept the flaming seas.

He fought till on Spain's inmost lakes
  'Mid orange bowers set,
La Mancha's daughters feared to sail
  Lest they the Dragon met.

King Philip, of his raven reft,
  As forfeit claimed his head.
The great Queen laughed his wrath to scorn,
  And knighted Drake instead,

And gave him ships and sent him forth
  To clear the Spanish main
For England and for England's brood,
  And sink the fleets of Spain.

And well he wrought his mighty work,
  Till on that fatal day,
He met his only conqueror,
  In Nombre Dios Bay.

There, in his shotted hammock swung,
  Amid the surges' sweep,

He waits the lookouts' signal
  Across the quiet deep.

And dreams of dark Ulloa's bay
  And Spanish treachery;
And how he tracked Magellan far
  Across the unknown sea.

But if Spain fires a single shot
  Upon the Spanish main,
She'll come to deem the Dragon dead
  Has waked to life again.
                    THOMAS NELSON PAGE.

THE SAILING OF THE FLEET

Two fleets have sailed from Spain. The one
    would seek
  What lands uncharted ocean might conceal.
Despised, condemned, and pitifully weak,
  It found a world for Leon and Castile.

The other, mighty, arrogant, and vain,
  Sought to subdue a people who were free.
Ask of the storm-gods where its galleons
    be, —
  Whelmed 'neath the billows of the northern
    main!

A third is threatened. On the westward track,
  Once gloriously traced, its vessels speed,
    With gold and crimson battle-flags un-
      furled.
On Colon's course, but to Sidonia's wrack,
  Sure fated, if so need shall come to need,
    For Sons of Drake are lords of Colon's
      world.

A portion of the American fleet started off to
look for the Spaniards, and the remainder engaged
in various minor operations off the Cuban coast.
On May 11 a party rowed in and cut the cables
at Cienfuegos, under a heavy fire.

"CUT THE CABLES"

AN INCIDENT OF CIENFUEGOS

[May 11, 1898]

"CUT the cables!" the order read,
  And the men were there; there was no de-
    lay.
The ships hove to in Cienfuegos Bay, —
  The Windom, Nashville, Marblehead, —

Beautiful, grim, and alert were they,
It was midway, past in the morning gray.
"Cut the cables!" the order said —
Over the clouds of the dashing spray,
The guns were trained and ready for play;
    Picked from the Nashville, Winslow led,—
Grim death waits ashore, they say;
"Lower the boats, Godspeed, give way."
Did "our untried navy lads" obey?
    Away to their perilous work they sped.

Now, steady the keel, keep stroke the oar!
    They must go in close, they must find the
        wires;
Grim death is alert on that watching shore,
    That deadly shore of the "Hundred Fires."
In the lighthouse tower, — along the ledge, —
    In the blockhouse, waiting, — the guns are
        there;
On the lowland, too, in the tall, dry sedge;
    They are holding the word till the boats
        draw near.
One hundred feet from the water's edge,
    Dazzling clear is the sunlit air;
Quick, my men, — the moments are dear!
    Two hundred feet from the rifle-pit,
And our "untried" lads still show no fear —
    When they open now they 're sure to hit;
No question, even by sign, they ask,
    In silence they bend to their dangerous task.

Quick now! — the shot from a smokeless
        gun
    Cuts close and spatters the glistening brine;
Now follows the roar of the battle begun,
But the boys were bent in the blazing sun
    Like peaceful fishermen, "wetting a line."
They searched the sea while a shrieking blast
    Swept shoreward, swift as the lightning
        flies,
While the fan-like storm of the shells went past
    Like a death-wing cleaving the hissing
        skies.
Like a sheltering wing, — for the hurricane
        came
    From our own good guns, and the foe might
        tell
What wreck was wrought by their deadly
        aim;
    For the foe went down where the hurricane
        fell.
It shattered the blockhouse, levelled the tower,
    It ripped the face of the smoking hill,
It beat the battle back, hour by hour,
    And then, for a little, our guns were still.

For a little, but that was the fatal breath, —
    That moment's lull in the friendly crash, —
For the long pit blazed with a vicious flash,
And eight fell, — two of them done to death.

Once more the screen of the screaming shot
    With its driving canopy covered the men,
While they dragged, and grappled, and, fal-
        tering not,
    Still dragged, and searched, and grappled
        again.
And they stayed right there till the work was
        done,
The cables were found and severed, each one,
With an eighty-foot gap, and the "piece"
        hauled in,
And stowed in place, — then, under the din
Of that deafening storm, that had swept the
        air
For three long hours, they turned from shore
("Steady the keel" there; "stroke" the oar).
To the smoke-wreathed ships, and, under the
        guns,
They went up the side, — our "untried" ones.

Quiet, my brave boys; hats off, all!
    They are here, our "untried" boys in blue.
Steady the block, now, all hands haul!
    Slow on the line there! — look to that
        crew!
Six lads hurt! — and the colors there?
    Wrap two of them? — hold! Ease back the
        bow!
Slow, now, on the line!— slack down with care!
    Steady! they 're back on their own deck
        now!
The cables are cut, sir, eighty-foot spread,
Six boys hurt, and — two of them dead.
    Half-mast the colors! there 's work to do!
There are two red marks on the starboard
        gun,
There is still some work that is not quite
        done,
    For our "untried" boys that are tried and
        true.
It was n't all play when they cut the wires, —
Well named is that bay of the "Hundred
        Fires."

                    ROBERT BURNS WILSON.
June 2, 1898.

A few days later, on May 24, 1898, the battle-
ship Oregon arrived at Jupiter Inlet, Florida, after
one of the most remarkable voyages in history.
On March 9 the ship, then at San Francisco, was

ordered to circle South America and join the Atlantic squadron, and the journey of nearly fifteen thousand miles was accomplished without starting a rivet.

THE RACE OF THE OREGON

Lights out! And a prow turned towards the South,
And a canvas hiding each cannon's mouth,
And a ship like a silent ghost released
Is seeking her sister ships in the East.

A rush of water, a foaming trail,
An ocean hound in a coat of mail,
A deck long-lined with the lines of fate,
She roars good-by at the Golden Gate.

On! On! Alone without gong or bell,
But a burning fire, like the fire of hell,
Till the lookout starts as his glasses show
The white cathedral of Callao.

A moment's halt 'neath the slender spire;
Food, food for the men, and food for the fire.
Then out to the sea to rest no more
Till her keel is grounded on Chili's shore.

South! South! God guard through the unknown wave,
Where chart nor compass may help or save,
Where the hissing wraiths of the sea abide
And few may pass through the stormy tide.

North! North! For a harbor far away,
For another breath in the burning day;
For a moment's shelter from speed and pain,
And a prow to the tropic sea again.

Home! Home! With the mother fleet to sleep
Till the call shall rise o'er the awful deep;
And the bell shall clang for the battle there,
And the voice of guns is the voice of prayer!

. . . .

One more to the songs of the bold and free,
When your children gather about your knee;
When the Goths and Vandals come down in might
As they came to the walls of Rome one night;
When the lordly William of Deloraine
Shall ride by the Scottish lake again;
When the Hessian spectres shall flit in air
As Washington crosses the Delaware;
When the eyes of babes shall be closed in dread
As the story of Paul Revere is read;

When your boys shall ask what the guns are for,
Then tell them the tale of the Spanish war,
And the breathless millions that looked upon
The matchless race of the Oregon.
                    JOHN JAMES MEEHAN.

BATTLE-SONG OF THE OREGON

The billowy headlands swiftly fly
  The crested path I keep,
My ribboned smoke stains many a sky,
  My embers dye the deep;
A continent has hardly space —
  Mid-ocean little more,
Wherein to trace my eager race
  While clang the alarums of war.

I come, the warship Oregon,
  My wake a whitening world,
My cannon shotted, thundering on
  With battle-flags unfurled.
My land knows no successful foe —
  Behold, to sink or save,
From stoker's flame to gunner's aim
  The race that rules the wave!

A nation's prayers my bulwark are
  Though ne'er so wild the sea;
Flow time or tide, come storm or star,
  Throbs my machinery.
Lands Spain has lost forever peer
  From every lengthening coast,
Till rings the cheer that proves me near
  The flag of Columbia's host.

Defiantly I have held my way
  From the vigorous shore where Drake
Dreamed a New Albion in the day
  He left New Spain a-quake;
His shining course retraced, I fight
  The self-same foe he fought,
All earth to light with signs of might
  Which God our Captain wrought.

Made mad, from Santiago's mouth
  Spain's ships-of-battle dart:
My bulk comes broadening from the south,
  A hurricane at heart;
Its desperate armories blaze and boom,
  Its ardent engines beat;
And fiery doom finds root and bloom
  Aboard of the Spanish fleet. . . .

The hundredweight of the Golden Hind
  With me are ponderous tons,
The ordnance great her deck that lined
  Would feed my ravening guns,
Her spacious reach in months and years
  I've shrunk to nights and days;
Yet in my ears are ringing cheers
  Sir Frank himself would raise;

For conquereth not mine engines' breath
  Nor sides steel-clad and strong,
Nor bulk, nor rifles red with death:
  To Spain, too, these belong;
What made that old Armada break
  This newer victory won:
Jehovah spake by the sons of Drake
  At each incessant gun.

I come, the warship Oregon,
  My wake a whitening world,
My cannon shotted, thundering on
  With battle-flags unfurled.
My land knows no successful foe —
  Behold, to sink or save,
From stoker's flame to gunner's aim
  The race that rules the wave!
                WALLACE RICE.

A few days before, Sampson's fleet had bombarded San Juan, Porto Rico, ineffectually, and then came word that the Spanish squadron had slipped into the harbor of Santiago, Cuba, to coal and refit. It was not until May 29 that its presence there was discovered by the Americans, who proceeded at once to blockade the harbor.

STRIKE THE BLOW

THE four-way winds of the world have blown,
  And the ships have ta'en the wave;
The legions march to the trumps' shrill call
  'Neath the flag of the free and brave.
    The hounds of the sea
      Have trailed the foe,
    They have trailed and tracked him
      down, —
      Then wait no longer, but strike, O land,
      With the dauntless strength of thy
        strong right hand,
      Strike the blow!

The armored fleets, with their grinning guns,
  Have the Spaniard in his lair;
They have tracked him down where the ramparts frown,
  And they'll halt and hold him there.

They have steamed in his wake,
  They have seen him go,
They have bottled and corked him up;
  Then send him home to the under-
    foam,
  Till the wide sea shakes to the far blue
    dome;
  Strike the blow!

The Cuban dead and the dying call,
  The children starved in the light
Of the aid that waits till the hero deed
  Breaks broad on the tyrant's might.
    The starved and the weak
      In their hour of woe
    Are calling, land, on thee;
      Then why delay in thy dauntless sway?
      On, on, to the charge of the freedom-
        way,
      Strike the blow!

They have ta'en the winds of the Carib
    seas,
  Thy fleets that know not fear;
Their ribs of steel have yearned to reel
  In the dance of the cannoneer.
    Thy sons of the blue
      That wait to go
    Would leap with a will to the charge,
      Then send them the word so long de-
        ferred;
      They have listened late, but they have
        not heard;
      Strike the blow!

They have listened late in the desolate
    land,
  They have looked through brimming eyes,
And starving women have held dead babes
  To their heart with a thousand sighs.
    On, on to the end,
      O land, the foe
    Beneath thy sword shall fall,
      Thy ships of steel have tracked them
        home,
      Ye are king of the land and king of the
        foam.
      Strike the blow!

On June 1, 1898, a great portion of Sampson's fleet was off the harbor, and it was decided to block the entrance by sinking the collier Merrimac in the channel. The enterprise was intrusted to Lieutenant Richmond Pearson Hobson, and a crew of eight volunteers.

EIGHT VOLUNTEERS

EIGHT volunteers! on an errand of death!
　Eight men! Who speaks?
Eight men to go where the cannon's hot
　breath
　Burns black the cheeks.

Eight men to man the old Merrimac's hulk;
Eight men to sink the old steamer's black
　bulk,
Blockade the channel where Spanish ships
　skulk, —
　Eight men! Who speaks?
"Eight volunteers!" said the Admiral's
　flags!

　Eight men! Who speaks?
Who will sail under El Morro's black
　crags? —
　Sure death he seeks.
Who is there willing to offer his life?
Willing to march to this music of strife, —
Cannon for drum and torpedo for fife?
　Eight men! Who speaks?

Eight volunteers! on an errand of death!
　Eight men! Who speaks?
Was there a man who in fear held his
　breath?
　With fear-paled cheeks?
From ev'ry war-ship ascended a cheer!
From ev'ry sailor's lips burst the word
　"Here!"
Four thousand heroes their lives volunteer!
　Eight men! Who speaks?
　　　　　　　　　　LANSING C. BAILEY.

It was impossible to get the boat ready that
night, but at last, at 3.30 on the morning of
June 2, she stood away for the harbor. The
Spaniards saw her as she entered and rained a
storm of fire upon her. A moment later, torn by
her own torpedoes and those of the enemy, she
sank to the bottom. Hobson and his men were
taken prisoners by the Spaniards.

THE MEN OF THE MERRIMAC

[June 3, 1898]

Hail to Hobson! Hail to Hobson! hail to all
　the valiant set!
Clausen, Kelly, Deignan, Phillips, Murphy,
　Montagu, Charette!

Howsoe'er we laud and laurel we shall be
　their debtors yet!
Shame upon us, shame upon us, should the
　nation e'er forget!

Though the tale be worn with the telling, let
　the daring deed be sung!
Surely never brighter valor, since this wheel-
　ing world was young,
Thrilled men's souls to more than wonder,
　till praise leaped from every tongue!

Trapped at last the Spanish sea-fox in the hill-
　locked harbor lay;
Spake the Admiral from his flagship, rocking
　off the hidden bay,
"We must close yon open portal lest he slip
　by night away!"

"Volunteers!" the signal lifted; rippling
　through the fleet it ran;
Was there ever deadlier venture? was there
　ever bolder plan?
Yet the gallant sailors answered, answered
　well-nigh to a man!

Ere the dawn's first rose-flush kindled, swiftly
　sped the chosen eight
Toward the batteries grimly frowning o'er
　the harbor's narrow gate;
Sooth, he holds his life but lightly who thus
　gives the dare to Fate.

They had passed the outer portal where the
　guns grinned, tier o'er tier,
When portentous Morro thundered, and So-
　capa echoed clear,
And Estrella joined the chorus pandemoniac
　to hear.

Heroes without hands to waver, heroes with-
　out hearts to quail,
There they sank the bulky collier 'mid the
　hurtling Spanish hail;
Long shall float our starry banner if such lads
　beneath it sail!

Hail to Hobson! hail to Hobson! hail to all
　the valiant set!
Clausen, Kelly, Deignan, Phillips, Murphy,
　Montagu, Charette!
Howsoe'er we laud and laurel we shall be
　their debtors yet!
Shame upon us, shame upon us, should the
　nation e'er forget!
　　　　　　　　　　CLINTON SCOLLARD.

THE VICTORY-WRECK [1]

[June 3, 1898]

O STEALTHILY-CREEPING Merrimac,
  Hush low your fiery breath;
You who gave life to ships of strife
  Are sailing unto your death! —
"I am ready and dressed for burial,
  Beneath the Cuban wave;
But still I can fight for God and right,
  While resting in my grave!"

O men that are sailing the Merrimac,
  Your hearts are beating high;
But send a prayer through the smoking air,
  To your Captain in the sky! —
"We know there is death in every breath,
  As we cling to the gunless deck;
And grand will be our voyage, if we
  Can make of our ship a wreck!"

Now drop the bower of the Merrimac,
  And swing her to the tide.
Now scuttle her, braves, and bid the waves
  Sweep into her shattered side! —
"Through a flying hell of shot and shell,
  We passed Death, with a sneer;
We wrenched our life from a novel strife,
  And even our foemen cheer!"
                              WILL CARLETON.

Examination showed that the channel had not
been blocked. The Merrimac had gone too far in,
and had sunk lengthwise of the channel instead
of across it. So the Spanish ships were not yet
"corked."

HOBSON AND HIS MEN

[June 3, 1898]

HOBSON went towards death and hell,
  Hobson and his men,
Unregarding shot and shell,
And the rain of fire that fell;
Calm, undaunted, fearless, bold,
Every heart a heart of gold,
Steadfast, daring, uncontrolled, —
  Hobson and his men.

Hobson came from death and hell,
  Hobson and his men,

1 From "Songs of Two Centuries," published
by Harper & Brothers.

Shout the tidings, ring the bell,
Let the pealing anthems swell;
Back from wreck and raft and wave,
From the shadow of the grave,
Every honor to the brave. —
  Hobson and his men.
                              ROBERT LOVEMAN.

Meanwhile, nearer home, things were moving
slowly enough, for the War Department developed
a startling unpreparedness and inefficiency. Two
hundred thousand volunteers were called for,
but, though every state responded instantly, the
work of mobilizing these troops was conducted
in so bungling a fashion that, by the beginning
of June, only three regiments, in addition to the
regulars, had reached the rendezvous at Tampa,
Florida.

THE CALL TO THE COLORS

"ARE you ready, O Virginia,
  Alabama, Tennessee?
People of the Southland, answer!
  For the land hath need of thee."
"Here!" from sandy Rio Grande,
  Where the Texan horsemen ride;
"Here!" the hunters of Kentucky
  Hail from Chatterawah's side;
Every toiler in the cotton,
  Every rugged mountaineer,
Velvet-voiced and iron-handed,
  Lifts his head to answer, "Here!"
Some remain who charged with Pickett,
  Some survive who followed Lee;
They shall lead their sons to battle
  For the flag, if need there be."

"Are you ready, California,
  Arizona, Idaho?
'Come, oh, come, unto the colors!'
  Heard you not the bugle blow?"
Falls a hush in San Francisco
  In the busy hives of trade;
In the vineyards of Sonoma
  Fall the pruning knife and spade;
In the mines of Colorado
  Pick and drill are thrown aside;
Idly in Seattle harbor
  Swing the merchants to the tide;
And a million mighty voices
  Throb responsive like a drum,
Rolling from the rough Sierras,
  "You have called us, and we come."

O'er Missouri sounds the challenge —
  O'er the great lakes and the plain;
"Are you ready, Minnesota?
  Are you ready, men of Maine?"
From the woods of Ontonagon,
  From the farms of Illinois,
From the looms of Massachusetts,
  "We are ready, man and boy."
Axemen free, of Androscoggin,
  Clerks who trudge the cities' paves,
Gloucester men who drag their plunder
  From the sullen, hungry waves,
Big-boned Swede and large-limbed German,
  Celt and Saxon swell the call,
And the Adirondacks echo:
  "We are ready, one and all."

Truce to feud and peace to faction!
  All forgot is party zeal
When the war-ships clear for action,
  When the blue battalions wheel.
Europe boasts her standing armies, —
  Serfs who blindly fight by trade;
We have seven million soldiers,
  And a soul guides every blade.
Laborers with arm and mattock,
  Laborers with brain and pen,
Railroad prince and railroad brakeman
  Build our line of fighting men.
Flag of righteous wars! close mustered
  Gleam the bayonets, row on row,
Where thy stars are sternly clustered,
  With their daggers towards the foe!
                    ARTHUR GUITERMAN.

ESSEX REGIMENT MARCH

WRITTEN FOR THE EIGHTH MASSACHUSETTS
UNITED STATES VOLUNTEER INFANTRY IN
THE SPANISH WAR

ONCE more the Flower of Essex is marching
  to the wars;
We are up to serve the Country wherever
  fly her Stars;
Ashore, afloat, or far or near, to her who bore
  us true,
We will do a freeman's duty as we were born
  to do.
  Lead the van, and may we lead it,
    God of armies, till the wrong shall cease;
  Speed the war, and may we speed it
    To the sweet home-coming, God of
  peace!

Our fathers fought their battles, and con-
  quered for the right,
Three hundred years victorious from every
  stubborn fight;
And still the Flower of Essex from the ancient
  stock puts forth,
Where the bracing blue sea-water strings the
  sinews of the North.

The foe on field, the foe on deck to us is all
  the same;
With both the Flower of Essex has played a
  winning game;
We threw them on the village green, we
  cowed them in Algiers,
And ship to ship we shocked them in our first
  great naval years.

We rowed the Great Commander o'er the
  ice-bound Delaware,
When the Christmas snow was falling in the
  dark and wintry air;
And still the Flower of Essex, like the heroes
  gone before,
Where the tide of danger surges shall take the
  laboring oar.

The Flower that first lay bleeding along by
  Bloody Brook
Full oft hath Death upgathered in war's red
  reaping-hook;
Its home is on our headlands; 't is sweeter
  than the rose;
But sweetest in the battle's breath the Flower
  of Essex blows.

At the best a dear home-coming, at the worst
  a soldier's grave,
Beating the tropic jungle, ploughing the dark
  blue wave;
But while the Flower of Essex from the granite
  rock shall come,
None but the dead shall cease to fight till all
  go marching home.

March onward to the leaguer wherever it may
  lie;
The Colors make the Country whatever be the
  sky;
Where round the Flag of Glory the storm
  terrific blows,
We march, we sail, whoever fail, the Flower
  of Essex goes.
                GEORGE EDWARD WOODBERRY.

THE GATHERING

WE are coming, Cuba, — coming; our starry
      banner shines
  Above the swarming legions, sweeping
      downward to the sea.
From Northern hill, and Western plain, and
      towering Southern pines
  The serried hosts are gathering, — and
      Cuba shall be free.

We are coming, Cuba, — coming. Thy sturdy
      patriots brave,
  Who fight as fought our fathers in the old
      time long ago,
Shall see the Spanish squadrons sink beneath
      the whelming wave,
  And plant their own loved banner on the
      ramparts of their foe.

We are coming, Cuba, — coming. Across the
      billow's foam
  Our gallant ships are bearing our bravest
      down to thee,
While earnest prayers are rising from every
      freeman's home
  That freedom's God may lead them on, and
      Cuba shall be free.
                          HERBERT B. SWETT.

It was evident that an army was badly needed
to support the fleet at Santiago, and on June 7,
1898, the force at Tampa was ordered to embark
for that place, under command of General William
Shafter. Everything was confusion, and it was
not until June 14 that the transports finally made
their way down the bay.

COMRADES

Now from their slumber waking, —
  The long sleep men thought death —
The War Gods rise, inhaling deep
  The cannon's fiery breath!
Their mighty arms uplifted,
  Their gleaming eyes aglow
With the steadfast light of battle,
  As it blazed long years ago!

Now from the clouds they summon
  The Captains of the Past,
Still sailing in their astral ships
  The star-lit spaces vast;
And from Valhalla's peaceful plains
  The Great Commanders come,

And marshal again their armies
  To the beat of the muffled drum.

His phantom sails unfurling
  McDonough sweeps amain
Where once his Yankee sailors fought
  The battle of Champlain!
And over Erie's waters,
  Again his flagship sweeps,
While Perry on the quarter-deck
  His endless vigil keeps.

Silent as mists that hover
  When twilight shadows fall,
The ghosts of the royal armies
  Foregather at the call;
And their glorious chiefs are with them,
  From conflicts lost or won,
As they gather round one mighty shade,
  The shade of Washington!

. . . .

Side by side with the warships
  That sail for the hostile fleet,
The ships of the Past are sailing
  And the dauntless comrades meet;
And standing shoulder to shoulder,
  The armèd spirits come,
And march with our own battalions
  To the beat of the muffled drum!
                          HENRY R. DORR.

The fleet reached Santiago June 20, and Shafter
decided to move directly upon the city. But the
army had lost or forgotten its lighters and
launches, so the task of disembarking it fell upon
the navy and was admirably performed. Next
morning, General Joseph Wheeler, with four
squadrons of dismounted cavalry, was ordered
forward. Two of these squadrons were composed
of the "Rough Riders," under command of Leon-
ard Wood and Theodore Roosevelt.

WHEELER'S BRIGADE AT
SANTIAGO

BENEATH the blistering tropical sun
    The column is standing ready,
Awaiting the fateful command of one
    Whose word will ring out
    To an answering shout
  To prove it alert and steady.
And a stirring chorus all of them sung
    With singleness of endeavor,
Though some to "The Bonny Blue Flag" had
        swung
    And some to "The Union For Ever."

The order came sharp through the desperate
   air
   And the long ranks rose to follow,
Till their dancing banners shone more fair
         Than the brightest ray
         Of the Cuban day
   On the hill and jungled hollow;
And to "Maryland" some in the days gone
   by
   Had fought through the combat's rumble,
And some for "Freedom's Battle-Cry"
   Had seen the broad earth crumble.

Full many a widow weeps in the night
   Who had been a man's wife in the
      morning;
For the banners we loved we bore to the
   height
         Where the enemy stood
         As a hero should,
   His valor his country adorning;
But drops of pride with your tears of grief,
   Ye American women, mix ye!
For the North and South, with a Southron
   chief,
      Kept time to the tune of "Dixie."
                              WALLACE RICE.

After great confusion and several days' delay,
the remainder of the army came up, and on
the afternoon of June 30 a general advance was
ordered. By dawn of July 1 the troops were in
position and the attack began.

DEEDS OF VALOR AT SANTIAGO

[July 1, 1898]

WHO cries that the days of daring are those
   that are faded far,
That never a light burns planet-bright to be
   hailed as the hero's star?
Let the deeds of the dead be laurelled, the
   brave of the elder years,
But a song, we say, for the men of to-day, who
   have proved themselves their peers!

High in the vault of the tropic sky is the garish
   eye of the sun,
And down with its crown of guns afrown
   looks the hilltop to be won;
There is the trench where the Spaniard lurks,
   his hold and his hiding-place,
And he who would cross the space between
   must meet death face to face.

The black mouths belch and thunder, and
   the shrapnel shrieks and flies;
Where are the fain and the fearless, the lads
   with the dauntless eyes?
Will the moment find them wanting? Nay,
   but with valor stirred!
Like the leashed hound on the coursing-ground
   they wait but the warning word.

"Charge!" and the line moves forward, moves
   with a shout and a swing,
While sharper far than the cactus-thorn is the
   spiteful bullet's sting.
Now they are out in the open, and now they
   are breasting the slope,
While into the eyes of death they gaze as into
   the eyes of hope.

Never they wait nor waver, but on they clam-
   ber and on,
With "Up with the flag of the Stripes and
   Stars, and down with the flag of the
   Don!"
What should they bear through the shot-rent
   air but rout to the ranks of Spain,
For the blood that throbs in their hearts is the
   blood of the boys of Anthony Wayne!

See, they have taken the trenches! Where are
   the foemen? Gone!
And now "Old Glory" waves in the breeze
   from the heights of San Juan!
And so, while the dead are laurelled, the
   brave of the elder years,
A song, we say, for the men of to-day who
   have proved themselves their peers.
                          CLINTON SCOLLARD.

The morning was consumed in blundering about
under the Spanish fire, trying vainly to carry out
the orders of a general lying in a hammock far in
the rear. Finally, the subordinate commanders
acted for themselves; Lawton, Ludlow, and Chaffee
took the fort of El Caney, and the Rough Riders
charged San Juan.

THE CHARGE AT SANTIAGO

[July 1, 1898]

WITH shot and shell, like a loosened hell,
   Smiting them left and right,
They rise or fall on the sloping wall
   Of beetling bush and height!
They do not shrink at the awful brink
   Of the rifle's hurtling breath,

But onward press, as their ranks grow less,
  To the open arms of death!

Through a storm of lead, o'er maimed and
      dead,
  Onward and up they go,
Till hand to hand the unflinching band
  Grapple the stubborn foe.
O'er men that reel, 'mid glint of steel,
  Bellow or boom of gun,
They leap and shout over each redoubt
  Till the final trench is won!

O charge sublime! Over dust and grime
  Each hero hurls his name
In shot or shell, like a molten hell,
  To the topmost heights of fame!
And prone or stiff, under bush and cliff,
  Wounded or dead men lie,
While the tropic sun on a grand deed done
  Looks with his piercing eye!
              WILLIAM HAMILTON HAYNE.

PRIVATE BLAIR OF THE REGULARS

[July 1, 1898]

IT was Private Blair, of the regulars, before
      dread El Caney,
Who felt with every throb of his wound the
      life-tide ebb away;
And as he dwelt in a fevered dream on the
      home of his youthful years,
He heard near by the moan and sigh of two
      of the volunteers.

He raised him up and gazed at them, and
      likely lads they were,
But when he bade them pluck up heart he
      found they could not stir.
Then a bullet ploughed the sodden loam, and
      his fearless face grew dark,
For he saw through the blur a sharpshooter
      who made the twain his mark.

And his strength leaped into his limbs again,
      and his fading eye burned bright;
And he gripped his gun with a steady hand
      and glanced along the sight;
Then another voice in that choir of fire out-
      spake with a deadly stress,
And in the trench at El Caney there lurked
      a Spaniard less.

But still the moans of the volunteers went up
      through the murky air,
And there kindled the light of a noble thought
      in the brain of Private Blair.
The flask at his side, he had drained it dry
      in the blistering scorch and shine,
So, unappalled, he crept and crawled in the
      face of the firing line.

The whirring bullets sped o'erhead, and the
      great shells burst with a roar,
And the shrapnel tore the ground around like
      the tusks of the grisly boar;
But on he went, with his high intent, till he
      covered the space between,
And came to the place where the Spaniard lay
      and clutched his full canteen.

Then he writhed him back o'er the bloody
      track, while Death drummed loud in
      his ears,
And pressed the draught he would fain have
      quaffed to the lips of the volunteers.
Drink! cried he; *don't think of me, for I'm
      only a regular,*
*While you have homes in the mother-land
      where your waiting loved ones are.*

Then his soul was sped to the peace of the
      dead. All praise to the men who dare,
And honor be from sea to sea to the deed of
      Private Blair!
              CLINTON SCOLLARD.

The fort on San Juan was carried and held all
the next day, despite Spanish attacks. But
Shafter was alarmed and considered withdrawing
the army, though strongly opposed by General
Wheeler, who had been in the thick of the fighting
from the very first.

WHEELER AT SANTIAGO

INTO the thick of the fight he went, pallid and
      sick and wan,
Borne in an ambulance to the front, a ghostly
      wisp of a man;
But the fighting soul of a fighting man, ap-
      proved in the long ago,
Went to the front in that ambulance, and the
      body of Fighting Joe.

Out from the front they were coming back,
      smitten of Spanish shells —
Wounded boys from the Vermont hills and
      the Alabama dells;

"Put them into this ambulance; I'll ride to
   the front," he said,
And he climbed to the saddle and rode right
   on, that little old ex-Confed.

From end to end of the long blue ranks rose
   up the ringing cheers,
And many a powder-blackened face was fur-
   rowed with sudden tears,
As with flashing eyes and gleaming sword,
   and hair and beard of snow,
Into the hell of shot and shell rode little old
   Fighting Joe!

Sick with fever and racked with pain, he
   could not stay away,
For he heard the song of the yester-year in the
   deep-mouthed cannon's bay —
He heard in the calling song of the guns there
   was work for him to do,
Where his country's best blood splashed and
   flowed 'round the old Red, White and
   Blue.

Fevered body and hero heart! this Union's
   heart to you
Beats out in love and reverence — and to each
   dear boy in blue
Who stood or fell 'mid the shot and shell, and
   cheered in the face of the foe,
As, wan and white, to the heart of the fight
   rode little old Fighting Joe!
           JAMES LINDSAY GORDON.

Then, suddenly, sorrow gave place to joy, and
discouragement to enthusiasm for a great victory
won. At nine o'clock on the morning of Sunday,
July 3, 1898, the Spanish fleet came rushing out of
the harbor in a mad effort to escape. The Ameri-
can ships closed in, and a battle to the death began,
which ended in the total destruction of the Spanish
fleet.

SPAIN'S LAST ARMADA

[July 3, 1898]

THEY fling their flags upon the morn,
   Their safety 's held a thing for scorn,
As to the fray the Spaniards on the wings of
   war are borne;
   Their sullen smoke-clouds writhe and reel,
   And sullen are their ships of steel,
All ready, cannon, lanyards, from the fight-
   ing-tops to keel.

They cast upon the golden air
   One glancing, helpless, hopeless prayer,
To ask that swift and thorough be the victory
   falling there;
   Then giants with a cheer and sigh
   Burst forth to battle and to die
Beneath the walls of Morro on that morning
   in July.

The Teresa heads the haughty train
   To bear the Admiral of Spain,
She rushes, hurtling, whitening, like the sum-
   mer hurricane;
   El Morro glowers in his might;
   Socapa crimsons with the fight,
The Oquendo's lunging lightning blazes
   through her sombre night.

In desperate and eager dash
   The Vizcaya hurls her vivid flash,
As wild upon the waters her enormous bat-
   teries crash,
   Like spindrift scuds the fleet Colon,
   And, on her bubbling wake bestrown,
Lurch, hungry for the slaughter, El Furor and
   El Pluton.

Round Santiago's armored crest,
   Serene, in their gray valor dressed,
Our behemoths lie quiet, watching well from
   south and west,
   Their keen eyes spy the harbor-reek;
   The signals dance, the signals speak;
Then breaks the blasting riot as our broad-
   sides storm and shriek!

Quick, poising on her eagle-wings,
   The Brooklyn in battle swings;
The wide sea falls and wonders as the titan
   Texas springs,
   The Iowa in monster-leaps
   Goes bellowing above the deeps;
The Indiana thunders as her terror onward
   sweeps.

And, hovering near and hovering low
   Until the moment strikes to go,
In gallantry the Gloucester swoops down on
   her double foe;
   She volleys — the Furor falls lame;
   Again — and the Pluton 's aflame,
Hurrah, on high she 's tossed her! Gone the
   grim destroyers' fame!

And louder yet and louder roar
   The Oregon's black cannon o'er
The clangor and the booming all along the
   Cuban shore.

She's swifting down her valkyr-path,
Her sword sharp for the aftermath,
With levin in her glooming, like Jehovah in
His wrath.

Great ensigns snap and shine in air
Above the furious onslaught where
Our sailors cheer the battle, danger but a
thing to dare;
Our gunners speed, as oft they've sped,
Their hail of shrilling, shattering lead,
Swift-sure our rifles rattle, and the foeman's
decks are red.

Like baying bloodhounds lope our ships,
Adrip with fire their cannons' lips;
We scourge the fleeing Spanish, whistling
weals from scorpion-whips;
Till, livid in the ghastly glare,
They tremble on in dread despair,
And thoughts of victory vanish in the carnage
they must bear.

Where Cuban coasts in beauty bloom,
Where Cuban breakers swirl and boom,
The Teresa's onset slackens in a scarlet spray
of doom;
Near Nimanima's greening hill
The streaming flames cry down her will,
Her vast hull blows and blackens, prey to
every mortal ill.

On Juan Gonzales' foaming strand
The Oquendo plunges 'neath our hand,
Her armaments all strangled, and her hope
a showering brand;
She strikes and grinds upon the reef,
And, shuddering there in utter grief,
In misery and mangled, wastes away beside
her chief.

The Vizcaya nevermore shall ride
From out Aserradero's tide,
With hate upon her forehead ne'er again
she'll pass in pride;
Beneath our fearful battle-spell
She moaned and struggled, flared and fell,
To lie a-gleam and horrid, while the piling
fires swell.

Thence from the wreck of Spain alone
Tears on the terrified Colon,
In bitter anguish crying, like a storm-bird
forth she's flown;

Her throbbing engines creak and thrum;
She sees abeam the Brooklyn come,
For life she's gasping, flying; for the combat
is she dumb.

Till then the man behind the gun
Had wrought whatever must be done —
Here, now, beside our boilers is the fight
fought out and won;
Where great machines pulse on and beat,
A-swelter in the humming heat
The Nation's nameless toilers make her mas-
tery complete.

The Cape o' the Cross casts out a stone
Against the course of the Colon,
Despairing and inglorious on the wind her
white flag's thrown;
Spain's last Armada, lost and wan,
Lies where Tarquino's stream rolls on,
As round the world, victorious, looms the
dreadnaught Oregon.

The sparkling daybeams softly flow
To glint the twilight afterglow,
The banner sinks in splendor that in battle
ne'er was low;
The music of our country's hymn
Rings out like songs of seraphim,
Fond memories and tender fill the evening
fair and dim;

Our huge ships ride in majesty
Unchallenged o'er the glittering sea,
Above them white stars cluster, mighty em-
blem of the free;
And all a-down the long sea-lane
The fitful bale-fires wax and wane
To shed their lurid lustre on the empire that
was Spain.

WALLACE RICE.

SANTIAGO

[July 3, 1898]

In the stagnant pride of an outworn race
The Spaniard sail'd the sea:
Till we haled him up to God's judgment
place —
And smashed him by God's decree!

Out from the harbor, belching smoke,
Came dashing seaward the Spanish ships —

And from all our decks a great shout broke,
Then our hearts came up and set us a-choke
For joy that we had them at last at grips!

No need for signals to get us away —
  We were off at score, with our screws
  a-gleam!
Through the blistering weeks we'd watched
  the bay
And our captains had need not a word to
  say —
  Save to bellow and curse down the pipes
  for steam!

Leading the pack in its frightened flight
  The Colon went foaming away to the
  west —
Her tall iron bulwarks, black as night,
And her great black funnels, sharp in sight
  'Gainst the green-clad hills in their peace
  and rest.

Her big Hontaria blazed away
  At the Indiana, our first in line.
The short-ranged shot drenched our decks
  with spray —
While our thirteen-inchers, in answering play,
  Ripped straight through her frame to her
  very spine!

.   .   .   .

Straight to its end went our winning fight
  With the thunder of guns in a mighty
  roar.
Our hail of iron, casting withering blight,
Turning the Spanish ships in their flight
  To a shorter death on the rock-bound shore.

The Colon, making her reckless race
  With the Brooklyn and Oregon close a-beam,
Went dashing landward — and stopped the
  chase
By grinding her way to her dying-place
  In a raging outburst of flame and steam.

So the others, facing their desperate luck,
  Drove headlong on to their rock-dealt
  death —
The Vizcaya, yielding before she struck,
The riddled destroyers, a huddled ruck,
  Sinking, and gasping for drowning breath.

So that flying battle surged down the coast,
  With its echoing roar from the Cuban
  land;

So the dying war-ships gave up the ghost;
So we shattered and mangled the Philistine
  host —
  So the fight was won that our Sampson
  planned!
                              THOMAS A. JANVIER.

The American battleships were practically un-
injured, and the fleet had lost only two men, one
killed and one injured, both on the Brooklyn.
The Spanish loss was 350 killed or drowned, 160
wounded, and 1774 taken prisoners.

THE FLEET AT SANTIAGO

[July 3, 1898]

THE heart leaps with the pride of their story,
  Predestinate lords of the sea!
They are heirs of the flag and its glory,
  They are sons of the soil it keeps free;
For their deeds the serene exaltation
  Of a cause that was stained with no shame,
For their dead the proud tears of a nation,
  Their fame shall endure with its fame.

The fervor that grim, unrelenting,
  The founders in homespun had fired,
With blood the free compact cementing,
  Was the flame that their souls had inspired.
They were sons of the dark tribulations,
  Of the perilous days of the birth
Of a nation sprung free among nations,
  A new hope to the children of earth!

They were nerved by the old deeds of daring,
  Every tale of Decatur they knew,
Every ship that, the bright banner bearing,
  Shot to keep it afloat in the blue;
They were spurred by the splendor undying
  Of Somer's fierce fling in the bay,
And the Watchword that Lawrence died cry-
  ing,
  And of Cushing's calm courage were they.

By the echo of guns at whose thunder
  Old monarchies crumbled and fell,
When the warships were shattered asunder
  And their pennants went down in the swell;
By the strength of the race that, unfearing,
  Faces death till the death of the last,
Or has sunk with the fierce Saxon cheering,
  Its colors still nailed to the mast —

So they fought — and the stern race immortal
  Of Cromwell and Hampton and Penn

Has thrown open another closed portal,
    Stricken chains from a new race of men.
So they fought, so they won, so above them
    Blazed the light of a consecrate aim;
Empty words! Who may tell how we love
    them,
    How we thrill with the joy of their fame!
                    CHARLES E. RUSSELL.

Particularly gallant was the part played by the
Gloucester, a converted yacht with no armor,
under Commander Wainwright. She was lying
inshore near the harbor mouth, and opened with
her little rapid-fire guns on the great battleships
as they swept past; then, the moment the Spanish
destroyers, Furor and Pluton, appeared, she
rushed straight upon them with absolute disre-
gard of the shore batteries. Within twenty min-
utes, the Pluton went down in deep water and the
Furor was beached and sunk.

THE DESTROYER OF DESTROYERS

[July 3, 1898]

FROM Santiago, spurning the morrow,
Spain's ships come steaming, big with black
    sorrow:
Over the ocean, first on our roster,
Runs Richard Wainwright, glad on the
    Gloucester.
        Boast him, and toast him!
        Wainwright! The Gloucester!

Great ships and gaunt ships, steel-clad and
    sable,
Roll on resplendent, monsters of fable:
Crash all our cannon, quick Maxims rattle.
Red death and ruin rush through the battle;
        Red death and dread death
        Ravage and rattle.

Speed on Spain's cruisers, towers of thunder:
Calm rides the Gloucester, though the waves
    wonder;
Morro roars at her, enemies looming
On their wakes heave her, vast through the
    glooming;
        Thunders and wonders
        Speak from the glooming.

Sped are Spain's cruisers; then 'mid the
    clangor
Dart her destroyers, lurid with anger;
Shouts Richard Wainwright, quivers the
    Gloucester:

Where the Furor goes Wainwright has crossed
    her.
        Boast him, and toast him!
        Wainwright! The Gloucester!

Wide to the westward El Furor flutters:
Hid in bright vapors there Wainwright mut-
    ters;
Under Socapa races the faster,
Smiles at Spain's gunners, laughs at disaster;
        Aiming and flaming
        Faster and faster.

Wide to the westward El Pluton plunges;
At her with rapiers now Wainwright lunges!
Swords of fierce scarlet, blades blue as light-
    ning;
Rapid guns snapping, little guns brightening;
        . Four-pounders, six-pounders,
        Lunging like lightning.

Done the destroyers, blazing and bursting:
Berserker Wainwright rides to their worsting;
Seethe the Pluton's sides, soon to exhaust her;
Flames the Furor's deck, doomed by the
    Gloucester.
        Boast him, and toast him!
        Wainwright! The Gloucester!

Where the Pluton lies lifts the red leven —
Fire-clouds prodigious dash against Heaven
Where the Pluton lay void swells the ocean,
Shattered and sunken, spent her devotion;
        Waves where wet graves were,
        Deep in the ocean.

Shrieking toward Cuba, agonized, broken,
El Furor 's hasting, her fate bespoken;
There in the shallows 'mid the white surges
Her guns, deserted, moan out their dirges;
        Swelling and knelling
        Through the white surges.

Wainwright in mercy does his endeavor:
Some he shall rescue; more rest for ever —
Say a prayer for them, one kindly Ave.
Spain weeps her wounded, wails a lost navy;
        Fails them, bewails them,
        Says them an Ave.

Off Santiago, when from beleaguer
Rushed forth Cervera, daring and eager,
Who stood Spain's onset? Who met and
    tossed her?

Wainwright, the Maine's man, glad on the
    Gloucester!
      Boast him, and toast him!
    Wainwright! The Gloucester!
              WALLACE RICE.

The evolutions of the Brooklyn, under Com-
modore Winfield Scott Schley, have been the sub-
ject of bitter controversy. Schley, finding himself
too near the Spaniards, made a wide turn away
from them, wishing, he afterwards alleged, to
preserve his ship, which was the fastest of our
squadron, to head off any of the Spanish ships
which might escape.

THE BROOKLYN AT SANTIAGO

[July 3, 1898]

'TWIXT clouded heights Spain hurls to doom
    Ships stanch and brave,
Majestic, forth they flash and boom
    Upon the wave.

El Morro raises eyes of hate
    Far out to sea,
And speeds Cervera to his fate
    With cannonry.

The Brooklyn o'er the deep espies
    His flame-wreathed side:
She sets her banners on the skies
    In fearful pride.

On, to the harbor's mouth of fire,
    Fierce for the fray,
She darts, an eagle from his eyre,
    Upon her prey.

She meets the brave Teresa there —
    Sigh, sigh for Spain! —
And beats her clanging armor bare
    With glittering rain.

The bold Vizcaya's lightnings glance
    Into the throng
Where loud the bannered Brooklyn chants
    Her awful song.

Down swoops, in one tremendous curve,
    Our Commodore;
His broadsides roll, the foemen swerve
    Toward the shore.

In one great round his Brooklyn turns
    And, girdling there

This side and that with glory, burns
    Spain to despair.

Frightful in onslaught, fraught with fate
    Her missiles hiss:
The Spaniard sees, when all too late,
    A Nemesis.

The Oquendo's diapason swells;
    Then, torn and lame,
Her portholes turn to yawning wells,
    Geysers of flame.

Yet fierce and fiercer breaks and cries
    Our rifles' dread:
The doomed Teresa shudders — lies
    Stark with her dead.

How true the Brooklyn's battery speaks
    Eulate knows,
As the Vizcaya staggers, shrieks
    Her horrent woes.

Sideward she plunges: nevermore
    Shall Biscay feel
Her heart throb for the ship that wore
    Her name in steel.

The Oquendo's ports a moment shone,
    As gloomed her knell;
She trembles, bursts — the ship is gone
    Headlong to hell.

The fleet Colon in lonely flight —
    Spain's hope, Spain's fear! —
Sees, and it lends her wings of fright,
    Schley's pennant near.

The fleet Colon scuds on alone —
    God, how she runs! —
And ever hears behind her moan
    The Brooklyn's guns.

Our ruthless cannon o'er the flood
    Roar and draw nigh;
Spain's ensign stained with gold and blood,
    Falls from on high.

The world she gave the World has passed —
    Gone, with her power —
Dead, 'neath the Brooklyn's thunder-blast,
    In one great hour.

The bannered Brooklyn! gallant crew,
    And gallant Schley!

Proud is the flag his sailors flew
  Along the sky.

Proud is his country: for each star
  Our Union wears,
The fighting Brooklyn shows a scar —
  So much he dares.

God save us war upon the seas;
  But, if it slip,
Send such a chief, with men like these,
  On such a ship!
                              WALLACE RICE.

The Oregon, which had arrived from her fifteen-
thousand-mile voyage from San Francisco, also
took a conspicuous part in the battle, and did
splendid service.

THE RUSH OF THE OREGON

THEY held her South to Magellan's mouth,
  Then East they steered her, forth
Through the farther gate of the crafty strait,
  And then they held her North.

Six thousand miles to the Indian Isles!
  And the Oregon rushed home,
Her wake a swirl of jade and pearl,
  Her bow a bend of foam.

And when at Rio the cable sang,
  "There is war! — grim war with Spain!"
The swart crews grinned and stroked their guns
  And thought on the mangled Maine.

In the glimmered gloom of the engine-room
  There was joy to each grimy soul,
And fainting men sprang up again
  And piled the blazing coal.

Good need was there to go with care;
  But every sailor prayed
Or gun for gun, or six to one
  To meet them, unafraid.

Her goal at last! With joyous blast
  She hailed the welcoming roar
Of hungry sea-wolves curved along
  The strong-hilled Cuban shore.

Long nights went by. Her beamèd eye,
  Unwavering, searched the bay
Where trapped and penned for a certain end
  The Spanish squadron lay.

Out of the harbor a curl of smoke —
  A watchful gun rang clear.
Out of the channel the squadron broke
  Like a bevy of frightened deer.

Then there was shouting for "steam, more
      steam!"
  And fires glowed white and red;
And guns were manned, and ranges planned,
  And the great ships leaped ahead.

Then there was roaring of chorusing guns,
  Shatter of shell, and spray;
And who but the rushing Oregon
  Was fiercest in chase and fray!

For her mighty wake was a seething snake;
  Her bow was a billow of foam;
Like the mailèd fists of an angry wight
  Her shot drove crashing home!

Pride of the Spanish navy, ho!
  Flee like a hounded beast!
For the Ship of the Northwest strikes a blow
  For the Ship of the far Northeast!

In quivering joy she surged ahead,
  Aflame with flashing bars,
Till down sunk the Spaniard's gold and red
  And up ran the Clustered Stars.

"Glory to share"? Aye, and to spare;
  But the chiefest is hers by right
Of a rush of fourteen thousand miles
  For the chance of a bitter fight!
                          ARTHUR GUITERMAN.

The high quality of American marksmanship
was never more conclusively shown than in this
battle. The Spanish ships were literally blown to
pieces. Here, as at Manila, the victory had been
won by "the men behind the guns."

THE MEN BEHIND THE GUNS

A CHEER and salute for the Admiral, and
      here's to the Captain bold,
And never forget the Commodore's debt when
      the deeds of might are told!
They stand to the deck through the battle's
      wreck when the great shells roar and
      screech —
And never they fear when the foe is near to
      practise what they preach:

But off with your hat and three times three
    for Columbia's true-blue sons,
The men below who batter the foe — the
    men behind the guns!

Oh, light and merry of heart are they when
    they swing into port once more,
When, with more than enough of the "green-
    backed stuff," they start for their
    leave-o'-shore;
And you'd think, perhaps, that the blue-
    bloused chaps who loll along the
    street
Are a tender bit, with salt on it, for some
    fierce "mustache" to eat —
Some warrior bold, with straps of gold, who
    dazzles and fairly stuns
The modest worth of the sailor boys — the
    lads who serve the guns.

But say not a word till the shot is heard that
    tells the fight is on,
Till the long, deep roar grows more and
    more from the ships of "Yank" and
    "Don,"
Till over the deep the tempests sweep of fire
    and bursting shell,
And the very air is a mad Despair in the
    throes of a living hell;
Then down, deep down, in the mighty ship,
    unseen by the midday suns,
You'll find the chaps who are giving the raps
    — the men behind the guns!

Oh, well they know how the cyclones blow
    that they loose from their cloud of
    death,
And they know is heard the thunder-word
    their fierce ten-incher saith!
The steel decks rock with the lightning shock,
    and shake with the great recoil,
And the sea grows red with the blood of the
    dead and reaches for his spoil —
But not till the foe has gone below or turns
    his prow and runs,
Shall the voice of peace bring sweet release
    to the men behind the guns!
            JOHN JEROME ROONEY.

Admiral Pasquale de Cervera, in command of
the Spanish fleet, knew from the first how desper-
ate the venture was. He made it only because
forced to do so by direct orders from Madrid, the
Spanish authorities fearing that Santiago would
be taken and the whole fleet be made captive.

CERVERA

HAIL to thee, gallant foe!
Well hast thou struck thy blow —
    Hopeless of victory —
Daring unequal strife,
Valuing more than life
    Honor and chivalry.

Forth from the harbor's room
Rushing to meet thy doom,
    Lit by the day's clear light.
"Out to the waters free!
Out to the open sea!
    There should a sailor fight."

Where the red battle's roar
Beats on the rocky shore,
    Thunders proclaiming
How the great cannon's breath
Hurls forth a dreadful death,
    Smoking and flaming.

While her guns ring and flash,
See each frail vessel dash,
    Though our shots rend her,
Swift through the iron rain,
Bearing the flag of Spain,
    Scorning surrender.

Hemmed in 'twixt foe and wreck,
Blood soaks each slippery deck,
    Still madly racing,
Till their ships burn and reel,
Crushed by our bolts of steel,
    Firing and chasing.

Driven to the rocks at last,
Now heels each shattered mast,
    Flames the blood drinking,
Each with her load of dead,
Wrapped in that shroud of red,
    Silenced and sinking.

Vanquished! but not in vain:
Ancient renown of Spain,
    Coming upon her.
Once again lives in thee,
All her old chivalry,
    All her old honor.

Ever her past avers,
When wealth and lands were hers,
    Though she might love them,

Die for their keeping, yet
  Spain, in her pride, has set
  Honor above them.
          BERTRAND SHADWELL.

Santiago surrendered a few days later and an
army of occupation, under General Nelson A. Miles,
landed at Porto Rico and took possession of the
island, after a few sharp skirmishes. In the Phil-
ippines, operations against Manila were pushed
vigorously forward, and on August 13, after sharp
actions at Malate, Singalon, and Ermita, the city
was captured. Among the killed at Malate was
Sergeant J. A. McIlrath, Battery H, Third Artil-
lery. Regulars.

McILRATH OF MALATE

[August 13, 1898]

YES, yes, my boy, there's no mistake,
  You put the contract through!
You lads with Shafter, I'll allow,
  Were heroes tried and true;

But don't forget the men who fought
  About Manila Bay,
And don't forget brave McIlrath
  Who died at Malate.

The night was black, save where the forks
  Of tropic lightning ran,
When, with a long deep thunder-roar,
  The typhoon storm began.

Then, suddenly above the din,
  We heard the steady bay
Of volleys from the trenches where
  The Pennsylvanias lay.

The Tenth, we thought, could hold their
      own
  Against the feigned attack,
And, if the Spaniards dared advance
  Would pay them doubly back.

But soon we marked the volleys sink
  Into a scattered fire —
And now we heard the Spanish guns
  Boom nigher yet and nigher!

Then, like a ghost, a courier
  Seemed past our picket tossed,
With wild hair streaming in his face —
  "We're lost — we're lost — we're lost!"

"Front, front — in God's name — front!" he
      cried:
  "Our ammunition's gone!"
He turned a face of dazed dismay —
  And through the night sped on!

"Men, follow me!" cried McIlrath,
  Our acting sergeant then;
And when he gave the word he knew
  He gave the word to men!

Twenty there — not one man more —
  But down the sunken road
We dragged the guns of Battery H,
  Nor even stopped to load!

Sudden, from the darkness poured
  A storm of Mauser hail —
But not a man there thought to pause,
  Nor any man to quail!

Ahead, the Pennsylvanias' guns
  In scattered firing broke;
The Spanish trenches, red with flame,
  In fiercer volleys spoke!

Down with a rush our twenty came —
  The open field we passed —
And in among the hard-pressed Tenth
  We set our feet at last!

Up, with a leap, sprang McIlrath,
  Mud-spattered, worn and wet,
And, in an instant, there he stood
  High on the parapet!

"Steady, boys! we've got 'em now —
  Only a minute late!
It's all right, lads — we've got 'em whipped —
  Just give 'em volleys straight!"

Then, up and down the parapet
  With head erect he went,
As cool as when he sat with us
  Beside our evening tent!

Not one of us, close sheltered there
  Down in the trench's pen,
But felt that we would rather die
  Than shame or grieve him then!

The fire so close to being quenched
  In panic and defeat,
Leaped forth, by rapid volleys sped,
  In one long deadly sheet!

A cheer went up along the line
  As breaks the thunder-call —
But, as it rose, great God, we saw
  Our gallant sergeant fall!

He sank into our outstretched arms
  Dead — but immortal grown;
And Glory brightened where he fell,
  And valor claimed her own!
          JOHN JEROME ROONEY.

Spain had had enough. She recognized the folly
of struggling further, and made overtures for peace.
On August 12 a protocol was signed and hostilities
ceased. Eight days later, the American squadron
steamed into New York harbor.

WHEN THE GREAT GRAY SHIPS COME IN [1]

NEW YORK HARBOR, August 20, 1898

To eastward ringing, to westward winging,
    o'er mapless miles of sea,
On winds and tides the gospel rides that the
    furthermost isles are free,
And the furthermost isles make answer,
    harbor, and height, and hill,
Breaker and beach cry each to each, " 'T is
    the Mother who calls! Be still!"
Mother! new-found, beloved, and strong to
    hold from harm,
Stretching to these across the seas the shield
    of her sovereign arm,
Who summoned the guns of her sailor sons,
    who bade her navies roam,
Who calls again to the leagues of main, and
    who calls them this time Home!

And the great gray ships are silent, and the
    weary watchers rest,
The black cloud dies in the August skies, and
    deep in the golden west
Invisible hands are limning a glory of crim-
    son bars,
And far above is the wonder of a myriad
    wakened stars!
Peace! As the tidings silence the strenuous
    cannonade,
Peace at last! is the bugle blast the length of
    the long blockade,

    ¹ Copyright, 1898, by Harper & Brothers.

And eyes of vigil weary are lit with the glad
    release,
From ship to ship and from lip to lip it is
    "Peace! Thank God for peace."

Ah, in the sweet hereafter Columbia still
    shall show
The sons of these who swept the seas how
    she bade them rise and go, —
How, when the stirring summons smote on
    her children's ear,
South and North at the call stood forth, and
    the whole land answered, "Here!"
For the soul of the soldier's story and the
    heart of the sailor's song
Are all of those who meet their foes as right
    should meet with wrong,
Who fight their guns till the foeman runs,
    and then, on the decks they trod,
Brave faces raise, and give the praise to the
    grace of their country's God!

Yes, it is good to battle, and good to be strong
    and free,
To carry the hearts of a people to the utter-
    most ends of sea,
To see the day steal up the bay where the
    enemy lies in wait,
To run your ship to the harbor's lip and sink
    her across the strait: —
But better the golden evening when the ships
    round heads for home,
And the long gray miles slip swiftly past in
    a swirl of seething foam,
And the people wait at the haven's gate to
    greet the men who win!
Thank God for peace! Thank God for peace,
    when the great gray ships come in!
          GUY WETMORE CARRYL.

FULL CYCLE

SPAIN drew us proudly from the womb of
    night,
  A lusty man-child of the Western wave, —
Who now, full-grown, smites the old mid-
    wife down,
  And thrusts her deep in a dishonored grave.
          JOHN WHITE CHADWICK.

Peace commissioners from the two countries
met at Paris in October, and a treaty of peace was
signed on December 10, 1898. Spain relinquished
all sovereignty over Cuba, and ceded Porto Rico

Guam, and the Philippine Islands to the United States, receiving in payment for the latter the sum of twenty million dollars.

BREATH ON THE OAT

FREE are the Muses, and where freedom is
They follow, as the thrushes follow spring,
Leaving the old lands songless there behind;
Parnassus disenchanted suns its woods,
Empty of every nymph; wide have they flown;
And now on new sierras think to set
Their wandering court, and thrill the world anew,
Where the Republic babbling waits its speech;
For but the prelude of its mighty song
As yet has sounded. Therefore, would I woo
Apollo to the land I love, 't is vain;
Unknown he spies on us; and if my verse
Ring not the empyrean round and round,
'T is that the feeble oat is few of stops.
The noble theme awaits the nobler bard.
Then how all air will quire to it, and all
The great dead listen, America! — For lo,
Diana of the nations hath she lived
Remote, and hoarding her own happiness
In her own land, the land that seemed her first
An exile, where her bark was cast away,
Till maiden grew the backward-hearted child,
And on that sea whose waves were memories
Turned her young shoulder, looked with steadfast eyes
Upon her wilderness, her woods, her streams;
Inland she ran, and gathering virgin joy
Followed her shafts afar from humankind.
And if sometimes her isolation drooped
And yearning woke in her, she put it forth
With a high boast and with a sick disdain;
Actæons fleeing, into antlers branched
The floating tresses of her fancy, and far
Her arrows smote them with a bleeding laugh.
O vain and virgin, O the fool of love!
Now children not her own are at her knee.
For stricken by her path lay one that vexed
Her maiden calm; she reached a petulant hand;
And the old nations drew sharp breath and looked.
The two-edged sword, how came it in her hand?
The sword that slays the holder if he withhold,
That none can take, or having taken drop,
The sword is in thy hand, America!

The wrath of God, that fillets thee with lightnings,
America! Strike then; the sword departs.
Ah God, once more may men crown drowsy days
With glorious death, upholding a great cause!
I deemed it fable; not of them am I.
Yet if they loved thee on the loud May-day
Who with unexultant thunder wreathed the flag,
With thunder and with victory, if they
Who on the third most famous of our Fourths
Along the seaboard mountains swept, a storm
Unleashed, whose tread spurned not the wrecks of Spain,
If these thy sons have loved thee, and have set
Santiago and Manila like new stars
Crowding thy field of blue, new terror perched
Like eagles on thy banners, oh, not less
I love thee, who but prattle in the prime
Of birds of passage over river and wood
Thine also, piping little charms to lure,
Uncaptured and unflying, the wings of song.

JOSEPH RUSSELL TAYLOR.

But the United States was still involved in a struggle altogether unforeseen and repugnant to many of her citizens. The Philippines had been bought from Spain, and with them the United States had taken over just such an insurrection as Spain had encountered in Cuba.

THE ISLANDS OF THE SEA

GOD is shaping the great future of the Islands of the Sea;
He has sown the blood of martyrs and the fruit is liberty;
In thick clouds and in darkness He has sent abroad His word;
He has given a haughty nation to the cannon and the sword.

He has seen a people moaning in the thousand deaths they die;
He has heard from child and woman a terrible dark cry;
He has given the wasted talent of the steward faithless found
To the youngest of the nations with His abundance crowned.

He called her to do justice where none but
   she had power;
He called her to do mercy to her neighbor at
   the door;
He called her to do vengeance for her own
   sons foully dead;
Thrice did He call unto her ere she inclined
   her head.

She has gathered the vast Midland, she has
   searched her borders round;
There has been a mighty hosting of her chil-
   dren on the ground;
Her search-lights lie along the sea, her guns
   are loud on land;
To do her will upon the earth her armies
   round her stand.

The fleet, at her commandment, to either
   ocean turns;
Belted around the mighty world her line of
   battle burns;
She has loosed the hot volcanoes of the ships
   of flaming hell;
With fire and smoke and earthquake shock
   her heavy vengeance fell.

O joyfullest May morning when before our
   guns went down
The Inquisition priesthood and the dungeon-
   making crown,
While through red lights of battle our starry
   dawn burst out,
Swift as the tropic sunrise that doth with glory
   shout!

Be jubilant, free Cuba, our feet are on thy
   soil;
Up mountain road, through jungle growth,
   our bravest for thee toil;
There is no blood so precious as their wounds
   pour forth for thee;
Sweet be thy joys, free Cuba, — sorrows have
   made thee free.

Nor Thou, O noble Nation, who wast so slow
   to wrath,
With grief too heavy-laden follow in duty's
   path;
Not for ourselves our lives are; not for Thyself
   art Thou;
The Star of Christian Ages is shining on Thy
   brow.

Rejoice, O mighty Mother, that God hath
   chosen Thee
To be the western warder of the Islands of
   the Sea;
He lifteth up, He casteth down, He is the King
   of Kings,
Whose dread commands o'er awe-struck
   lands are borne on eagle's wings.

   GEORGE EDWARD WOODBERRY.

The people of the Philippines had fought against
Spanish sovereignty much as the people of Cuba
had. A band of them, under Emilio Aguinaldo, had
assisted at the capture of Manila, in the fond hope
that the defeat of the Spaniards would mean
Philippine independence. Instead, they found
that they had merely traded masters. At once
they took up arms against the Americans.

BALLADE OF EXPANSION

1899

TIME was he sang the British Brute,
   The ruthless lion's grasping greed,
The European Law of Loot,
   The despot's devastating deed;
   But now he sings the heavenly creed
Of saintly sword and friendly fist,
   He loves you, though he makes you bleed —
The Ethical Expansionist!

He loves you, Heathen! Though his foot
   May kick you like a worthless weed
From that wild field where you have root,
   And scatter to the winds your seed;
   He's just the government you need;
If you object, why, he'll insist,
   And, on your protest, "draw a bead" —
The Ethical Expansionist!

He'll take you to him *coûte que coûte!*
   He'll win you, though you fight and plead.
His guns shall urge his ardent suit,
   Relentless fire his cause shall speed.
   In time you'll learn to write and read
(That is, if you should then exist!),
   You won't, if you his course impede —
The Ethical Expansionist!

ENVOI

Heathen, you must, you shall be freed!
   It's really useless to resist;
To save your life, you'd better heed
   The Ethical Expansionist!

   HILDA JOHNSON.

Misguided they no doubt were, and the warfare they waged was of the cruellest kind; but to employ against them the troops of a Republic, to shoot them down as "rebels," occasioned in the United States a great outburst of indignation.

"REBELS"

SHOOT down the rebels — men who dare
To claim their native land!
Why should the white invader spare
A dusky heathen band?

You bought them from the Spanish King,
You bought the men he stole;
You bought perchance a ghastlier thing —
The Duke of Alva's soul!

"Freedom!" you cry, and train your gun
On men who would be freed,
And in the name of Washington
Achieve a Weyler's deed.

Boast of the benefits you spread,
The faith of Christ you hold;
Then seize the very soil you tread
And fill your arms with gold.

Go, prostitute your mother-tongue,
And give the "rebel" name
To those who to their country clung,
Preferring death to shame.

And call him "loyal," him who brags
Of countrymen betrayed —
The patriot of the money-bags,
The loyalist of trade.

Oh, for the good old Roman days
Of robbers bold and true,
Who scorned to oil with pious phrase
The deeds they dared to do —

The days before degenerate thieves
Devised the coward lie
Of blessings that the enslaved receives
Whose rights their arms deny!

I hate the oppressor's iron rod,
I hate his murderous ships,
But most of all I hate, O God,
The lie upon his lips!

Nay, if they still demand recruits
To curse Manila Bay,
Be men; refuse to act like brutes
And massacre and slay.

Or if you will persist to fight
With all a soldier's pride,
Why, then be rebels for the right
By Aguinaldo's side!

ERNEST CROSBY.

But the administration felt that it had gone too far to draw back; spellbinders raised the shout that wherever the flag was raised it must remain; new regiments were shipped to the Philippines and the war against the natives pushed vigorously.

ON A SOLDIER FALLEN IN THE PHILIPPINES

STREETS of the roaring town,
Hush for him, hush, be still!
He comes, who was stricken down
Doing the word of our will.
Hush! Let him have his state.
Give him his soldier's crown.
The grists of trade can wait
Their grinding at the mill,
But he cannot wait for his honor, now the
    trumpet has been blown.
Wreathe pride now for his granite brow, lay
    love on his breast of stone.

Toll! Let the great bells toll
Till the clashing air is dim,
Did we wrong this parted soul?
We will make it up to him.
Toll! Let him never guess
What work we set him to.
Laurel, laurel, yes;
He did what we bade him do.
Praise, and never a whispered hint but the
    fight he fought was good;
Never a word that the blood on his sword
    was his country's own heart's blood.

A flag for the soldier's bier
Who dies that his land may live;
Oh, banners, banners here,
That he doubt not nor misgive!
That he heed not from the tomb
The evil days draw near
When the nation, robed in gloom,
With its faithless past shall strive.
Let him never dream that his bullet's scream
    went wide of its island mark,
Home to the heart of his sinning land where
    she stumbled and sinned in the dark.

WILLIAM VAUGHN MOODY.

On February 5, 1899, General Ricarti's division of the Filipino army was encountered near Santa Ana, and completely routed. It was at this battle that Lieutenant Charles E. Kilbourne, Jr., and Lieutenant W. G. Miles performed the exploits described in the following poems.

THE BALLAD OF PACO TOWN

[February 5, 1899]

In Paco town and in Paco tower,
At the height of the tropic noonday hour,
Some Tagal riflemen, half a score,
Watched the length of the highway o'er,
And when to the front the troopers spurred,
Whiz-z! whiz-z! how the Mausers whirred!

From the opposite walls, through crevice and
    crack,
Volley on volley went ringing back
Where a band of regulars tried to drive
The stinging rebels out of their hive;
"Wait, till our cannon come, and then,"
Cried a captain, striding among his men,
"We'll settle that bothersome buzz and drone
With a merry little tune of our own!"

The sweltering breezes seemed to swoon,
And down the *calle* the thickening flames
Licked the roofs in the tropic noon.
Then through the crackle and glare and heat,
And the smoke and the answering acclaims
Of the rifles, far up the village street
Was heard the clatter of horses' feet,
And a band of signalmen swung in sight,
Hasting back from the ebbing fight
That had swept away to the left and right.

"Ride!" yelled the regulars, all aghast,
And over the heads of the signalmen,
As they whirled in desperate gallop past,
The bullets a vicious music made,
Like the whistle and whine of the midnight
    blast
On the weltering wastes of the ocean when
The breast of the deep is scourged and flayed.

It chanced in the line of the fiercest fire
A rebel bullet had clipped the wire
That led, from the front and the fighting, down
To those that stayed in Manila town;
This gap arrested the watchful eye
Of one of the signalmen galloping by,
And straightway, out of the plunge and press,
He reined his horse with a swift caress

And a word in the ear of the rushing steed;
Then back with never a halt nor heed
Of the swarming bullets he rode, his goal
The parted wire and the slender pole
That stood where the deadly tower looked
    down
On the rack and ruin of Paco town.

Out of his saddle he sprang as gay
As a schoolboy taking a holiday;
Wire in hand up the pole he went
With never a glance at the tower, intent
Only on that which he saw appear
As the line of his duty plain and clear.
To the very crest he climbed, and there,
While the bullets buzzed in the scorching air,
Clipped his clothing, and scored and stung
The slender pole-top to which he clung,
Made the wire that was severed sound,
Slipped in his careless way to the ground,
Sprang to the back of his horse, and then
Was off, this bravest of signalmen.

Cheers for the hero! While such as he,
Heedless alike of wounds and scars,
Fight for the dear old Stripes and Stars,
Down through the years to us shall be
Ever and ever the victory!

                    CLINTON SCOLLARD.

THE DEED OF LIEUTENANT MILES

[February 5, 1899]

When you speak of dauntless deeds,
    When you tell of stirring scenes,
Tell this story of the isles
Where the endless summer smiles, —
Tell of young Lieutenant Miles
    In the far-off Philippines!

'T was the Santa Ana fight! —
    All along the Tagal line
From the thickets dense and dire
Gushed the fountains of their fire;
You could mark their rifles' ire,
    You could hear their bullets whine.

Little wonder there was pause!
    Some were wounded, some were dead.
"Call Lieutenant Miles!" He came,
    In his eyes a fearless flame.
"Yonder blockhouse is our aim!"
    The battalion leader said.

"You must take it — how you will;
  You must break this damnèd spell!"
"Volunteers!" cried Miles. 'T was vain,
For that narrow tropic lane
'Twixt the bamboo and the cane
  Was a very lane of hell.

There were five stood forth at last;
  God above, but they were men!
"Come!" exultantly he saith!—
Did they falter? Not a breath!
Down the path of hurtling death
  The Lieutenant led them then.

Two have fallen — now a third!
  Forward dash the other three;
In the onrush of that race
Ne'er a swerve or stay of pace.
And the Tagals — dare they face
  Such a desperate company?

Panic gripped them by the throat, —
  Every Tagal rifleman;
And as though they seemed to see
In those charging foemen three
An avenging destiny,
  Fierce and fast and far they ran.

So a salvo for the six!
  So a round of ringing cheers!
Heroes of the distant isles
Where the endless summer smiles, —
Gallant young Lieutenant Miles
  And his valiant volunteers!
                CLINTON SCOLLARD.

So the war went on, with massacre, ambush,
and lonely murder. The conquest of the islands
was proving a costly one, but the administration
held that it must be carried through, at whatever
sacrifice. It was a war in which victory and defeat
alike brought only sorrow and disgust.

AGUINALDO

(PATRIOT AND EMPIRE)

WHEN arms and numbers both have failed
  To make the hunted patriot yield,
Nor proffered riches have prevailed
  To tempt him to forsake the field,
    By spite and baffled rage beguiled,
    Strike at his mother and his child.

O land where freedom loved to dwell,
  Which shook'st the despot on his throne,

And o'er the beating floods of hell
  Hope's beacon to the world hast shown,
    How art thou fallen from thy place!
    O thing of shame!— O foul dis-
      grace!

Thy home was built upon the height
  Above the murky clouds beneath,
In the blue heaven's freest light,
  Thy sword flashed ever from its sheath,
    The weak and the oppressed to save —
    To smite the tyrant — free the slave.

Thy place was glorious — sublime.
  What devil tempts thee to descend
To conquest, robbery and crime?
  O shameful fate! Is this the end?
    Thy hands have now the damning
      stain
    Of human blood — for love of gain.

With weak hypocrisy's thin veil,
  Seek not in vain to blind thine eyes;
Nor shall deceitful prayers prevail.
  Pray not — for fear the dead should
      rise
    From 'neath their conquered country's
      sod
    And cry against thee unto God.
                BERTRAND SHADWELL.

The capture of Aguinaldo, March 23, 1901, put
a virtual end to organized resistance; though
sporadic outbreaks continued for several years.
As late as March, 1906, such an affair occurred, a
band of Moros, men, women, and children, being
surrounded and killed on the summit of a crater at
Dajo, no prisoners being taken.

THE FIGHT AT DAJO

[March 7, 1906]

THERE are twenty dead who're sleeping near
    the slopes of Bud Dajo,
'Neath the shadow of the crater where the
    bolos laid them low,
And their comrades feel it bitter, and their
    cheeks grow hot with shame,
When they read the sneering comments which
    have held them up to blame.

They were told to scale the mountain and they
    stormed its beetling crest,
Spite of all the frantic Moros, though they did
    their level best,

Though the bullets whistled thickly, and the cliff was lined with foes,
Though the campilans were flashing and the kriss gave deadly blows.

There was little time for judging ere they met in deadly strife
What the sex might be that rushing waved aloft the blood-stained knife;
For the foe was drunk with frenzy and the women in the horde
Thought that paradise was certain could they kill first with the sword.

They'd been freely offered mercy, but they'd scorned the proffered gift,
For their priests had told them Allah promised victory sure and swift.
They were foolish and their folly cost the lives of wife and son,
But they fought their fight like heroes; there were none that turned to run.

Though they'd robbed and slain and ravaged, though their crimes had mounted high,
Though 't is true that naught became them like the death they chose to die,
One would think to read the papers that the troops who scaled their fort
Were a lot of brutal ruffians shooting girls and babes for sport.

More than one who's sleeping soundly 'neath the shade of Bud Dajo
Lost his life while giving succor to the one who dealt the blow,
Yet his comrades feel more bitter and they give a far worse name
To the men who dubbed them "butchers" and have smirched the army's fame.

ALFRED E. WOOD.

The Philippines, meanwhile, had been placed under a civil government; but no promise was given them of ultimate independence. Their commerce was crippled by the high tariff party in control of Congress; and while their condition was vastly better than it had been under Spanish rule, it was not such as a Republic, working for their good, might have made it. The acquisition and conquest of the islands is believed by many intelligent and patriotic persons to be one of the darkest blots upon American history.

AN ODE IN TIME OF HESITATION

(WRITTEN AFTER SEEING AT BOSTON THE STATUE OF ROBERT GOULD SHAW. KILLED WHILE STORMING FORT WAGNER, JULY 18, 1863, AT THE HEAD OF THE FIRST ENLISTED NEGRO REGIMENT, THE FIFTY-FOURTH MASSACHUSETTS)

I

BEFORE the living bronze Saint-Gaudens made
Most fit to thrill the passer's heart with awe,
And set here in the city's talk and trade
To the good memory of Robert Shaw,
This bright March morn I stand
And hear the distant spring come up the land;
Knowing that what I hear is not unheard
Of this boy soldier and his negro band,
For all their gaze is fixed so stern ahead,
For all the fatal rhythm of their tread.
The land they died to save from death and shame
Trembles and waits, hearing the spring's great name,
And by her pangs these resolute ghosts are stirred.

II

Through street and mall the tides of people go
Heedless; the trees upon the Common show
No hint of green; but to my listening heart
The still earth doth impart
Assurance of her jubilant emprise,
And it is clear to my long-searching eyes
That love at last has might upon the skies.
The ice is runnelled on the little pond;
A telltale patter drips from off the trees;
The air is touched with southland spiceries,
As if but yesterday it tossed the frond
Of pendent mosses where the live oaks grow
Beyond Virginia and the Carolines,
Or had its will among the fruits and vines
Of aromatic isles asleep beyond
Florida and the Gulf of Mexico.

III

Soon shall the Cape Ann children laugh in glee,
Spying the arbutus, spring's dear recluse;
Hill lads at dawn shall hearken the wild goose
Go honking northward over Tennessee;
West from Oswego to Sault Saint-Marie,
And on to where the Pictured Rocks are hung,
And yonder where, gigantic, wilful, young,
Chicago sitteth at the northwest gates,

With restless violent hands and casual tongue
Moulding her mighty fates,
The Lakes shall robe them in ethereal sheen;
And like a larger sea, the vital green
Of springing wheat shall vastly be outflung
Over Dakota and the prairie states.
By desert people immemorial
On Arizonan mesas shall be done
Dim rites unto the thunder and the sun;
Nor shall the primal gods lack sacrifice
More splendid, when the white Sierras call
Unto the Rockies straightway to arise
And dance before the unveiled ark of the
    year,
Clashing their windy cedars as for shawms,
Unrolling rivers clear
For flutter of broad phylacteries;
While Shasta signals to Alaskan seas
That watch old sluggish glaciers downward
    creep
To fling their icebergs thundering from the
    steep,
And Mariposa through the purple calms
Gazes at far Hawaii crowned with palms
Where East and West are met, —
A rich seal on the ocean's bosom set
To say that East and West are twain,
With different loss and gain:
The Lord hath sundered them; let them be
    sundered yet.

IV

Alas! what sounds are these that come
Sullenly over the Pacific seas, —
Sounds of ignoble battle, striking dumb
The season's half-awakened ecstasies?
Must I be humble, then,
Now when my heart hath need of pride?
Wild love falls on me from these sculptured
    men;
By loving much the land for which they
    died
I would be justified.
My spirit was away on pinions wide
To soothe in praise of her its passionate mood
And ease it of its ache of gratitude.
Too sorely heavy is the debt they lay
On me and the companions of my day.
I would remember now
My country's goodliness, make sweet her
    name.
Alas! what shade art thou
Of sorrow or of blame
Liftest the lyric leafage from her brow,
And pointest a slow finger at her shame?

V

Lies! lies! It cannot be! The wars we wage
Are noble, and our battles still are won
By justice for us, ere we lift the gage.
We have not sold our loftiest heritage.
The proud republic hath not stooped to cheat
And scramble in the market-place of war;
Her forehead weareth yet its solemn star.
Here is her witness: this, her perfect son,
This delicate and proud New England soul
Who leads despisèd men, with just-unshackled
    feet,
Up the large ways where death and glory
    meet,
To show all peoples that our shame is done,
That once more we are clean and spirit-
    whole.

VI

Crouched in the sea fog on the moaning sand
All night he lay, speaking some simple word
From hour to hour to the slow minds that
    heard,
Holding each poor life gently in his hand
And breathing on the base rejected clay
Till each dark face shone mystical and grand
Against the breaking day;
And lo, the shard the potter cast away
Was grown a fiery chalice, crystal-fine,
Fulfilled of the divine
Great wine of battle wrath by God's ring-
    finger stirred.
Then upward, where the shadowy bastion
    loomed
Huge on the mountain in the wet sea light,
Whence now, and now, infernal flowerage
    bloomed,
Bloomed, burst, and scattered down its deadly
    seed, —
They swept, and died like freemen on the
    height,
Like freemen, and like men of noble breed;
And when the battle fell away at night
By hasty and contemptuous hands were
    thrust
Obscurely in a common grave with him
The fair-haired keeper of their love and trust.
Now limb doth mingle with dissolvèd limb
In nature's busy old democracy
To flush the mountain laurel when she blows
Sweet by the southern sea,
And heart with crumbled heart climbs in the
    rose: —
The untaught hearts with the high heart that
    knew

This mountain fortress for no earthly hold
Of temporal quarrel, but the bastion old
Of spiritual wrong,
Built by an unjust nation sheer and strong,
Expugnable but by a nation's rue
And bowing down before that equal shrine
By all men held divine,
Whereof his band and he were the most holy
    sign.

VII

O bitter, bitter shade!
Wilt thou not put the scorn
And instant tragic question from thine eyes?
Do thy dark brows yet crave
That swift and angry stave —
Unmeet for this desirous morn —
That I have striven, striven to evade?
Gazing on him, must I not deem they err
Whose careless lips in street and shop aver
As common tidings, deeds to make his cheek
Flush from the bronze, and his dead throat to
    speak?
Surely some elder singer would arise,
Whose harp hath leave to threaten and to
    mourn
Above this people when they go astray.
Is Whitman, the strong spirit, overworn?
Has Whittier put his yearning wrath away?
I will not and I dare not yet believe!
Though furtively the sunlight seems to grieve,
And the spring-laden breeze
Out of the gladdening west is sinister
With sounds of nameless battle overseas;
Though when we turn and question in sus-
    pense
If these things be indeed after these ways,
And what things are to follow after these,
Our fluent men of place and consequence
Fumble and fill their mouths with hollow
    phrase,
Or for the end-all of deep arguments
Intone their dull commercial liturgies —
I dare not yet believe! My ears are shut!
I will not hear the thin satiric praise
And muffled laughter of our enemies,
Bidding us never sheathe our valiant sword
Till we have changed our birthright for a
    gourd
Of wild pulse stolen from a barbarian's hut;
Showing how wise it is to cast away
The symbols of our spiritual sway,
That so our hands with better ease
May wield the driver's whip and grasp the
    jailer's keys.

VIII

Was it for this our fathers kept the law?
This crown shall crown their struggle and
    their ruth?
Are we the eagle nation Milton saw
Mewing its mighty youth,
Soon to possess the mountain winds of truth,
And be a swift familiar of the sun
Where aye before God's face His trumpets
    run?
Or have we but the talons and the maw,
And for the abject likeness of our heart
Shall some less lordly bird be set apart? —
Some gross-billed wader where the swamps
    are fat?
Some gorger in the sun? Some prowler with
    the bat?

IX

Ah no!
We have not fallen so.
We are our fathers' sons: let those who lead
    us know!
'T was only yesterday sick Cuba's cry
Came up the tropic wind, "Now help us, for
    we die!"
Then Alabama heard,
And rising, pale, to Maine and Idaho
Shouted a burning word;
Proud state with proud impassioned state
    conferred,
And at the lifting of a hand sprang forth,
East, west, and south, and north,
Beautiful armies. Oh, by the sweet blood
    and young
Shed on the awful hill slope at San Juan,
By the unforgotten names of eager boys
Who might have tasted girls' love and been
    stung
With the old mystic joys
And starry griefs, now the spring nights
    come on,
But that the heart of youth is generous, —
We charge you, ye who lead us,
Breathe on their chivalry no hint of stain!
Turn not their new-world victories to gain!
One least leaf plucked for chaffer from the
    bays
Of their dear praise,
One jot of their pure conquest put to hire,
The implacable republic will require;
With clamor, in the glare and gaze of noon,
Or subtly, coming as a thief at night,
But surely, very surely, slow or soon
That insult deep we deeply will requite.

Tempt not our weakness, our cupidity!
For save we let the island men go free,
Those baffled and dislaurelled ghosts
Will curse us from the lamentable coasts
Where walk the frustrate dead.
The cup of trembling shall be drainèd quite,
Eaten the sour bread of astonishment,
With ashes of the hearth shall be made
    white
Our hair, and wailing shall be in the tent:

Then on your guiltier head
Shall our intolerable self-disdain
Wreak suddenly its anger and its pain;
For manifest in that disastrous light
We shall discern the right
And do it, tardily. — O ye who lead,
Take heed!
Blindness we may forgive, but baseness we
    will smite.

WILLIAM VAUGHN MOODY.

CHAPTER VI

THE NEW CENTURY

No country in the world entered upon the twentieth century with brighter prospects of peace, happiness, and prosperity than did the United States.

A TOAST TO OUR NATIVE LAND

HUGE and alert, irascible yet strong,
We make our fitful way 'mid right and
    wrong.
One time we pour out millions to be free,
Then rashly sweep an empire from the sea!
One time we strike the shackles from the
    slaves,
And then, quiescent, we are ruled by knaves.
Often we rudely break restraining bars,
And confidently reach out toward the stars.

Yet under all there flows a hidden stream
Sprung from the Rock of Freedom, the great
    dream
Of Washington and Franklin, men of old
Who knew that freedom is not bought with
    gold.
This is the Land we love, our heritage,
Strange mixture of the gross and fine, yet
    sage
And full of promise, — destined to be great.
Drink to Our Native Land! God Bless the
    State!

ROBERT BRIDGES.

But the very first year, a bolt from the blue fell upon her. In May, 1901, a great industrial exposition, known as the "Pan-American," was opened at Buffalo, New York. It was especially notable for its electrical display and came to be known as "The Dream City," or ":The City of Light."

BUFFALO

[1901]

A TRANSIENT city, marvellously fair,
    Humane, harmonious, yet nobly free,
    She built for pure delight and memory.
At her command, by lake and garden rare,
Pylon and tower majestic rose in air,
    And sculptured forms of grace and sym-
        metry.
    Then came a thought of God, and, rever-
        ently, —
"Let there be Light!" she said; and Light
        was there.
O miracle of splendor! Who could know
    That Crime, insensate, egoist and blind,
    Destructive, causeless, caring but to smite,
    Would in its dull Cimmerian gropings find
A sudden way to fill those courts with woe,
    And swallow up that radiance in night?

FLORENCE EARLE COATES.

September 5 was set aside as President's Day. The attendance was very large, and President William McKinley spoke to an audience of thirty thousand people. The next afternoon a reception was held, at which all were invited to pass in line and shake hands with the President. In the line was a man whose right hand was bandaged with a handkerchief. The handkerchief concealed a revolver. As the President stretched out his hand, the assassin fired twice, one bullet penetrating the President's abdomen.

McKINLEY

[September 6, 1901]

'T IS not the President alone
    Who, stricken by that bullet, fel

The assassin's shot that laid him prone
　　Pierced a great nation's heart as well;
And when the baleful tidings sped
　　From lip to lip throughout the crowd,
Then, as they deemed their ruler dead,
　　'T was Liberty that cried aloud.

Ay, Liberty! for where the foam
　　Of oceans twain marks out the coast
'T is there, in Freedom's very home,
　　That anarchy has maimed its host;
There 't is that it has turned to bite
　　The hand that fed it; there repaid
A country's welcome with black spite;
　　There, Judas-like, that land betrayed.

For 't is no despot that 's laid low,
　　But a free nation's chosen chief;
A free man, stricken by a blow
　　Base, dastardly, past all belief.
And Tyranny exulting hears
　　The tidings flashed across the sea;
While stern Repression hugs her fears,
　　And mouths them in a harsh decree.

Meanwhile the cloud, though black as death,
　　Is lined with hopes, hopes light as life,
And Liberty that, scant of breath,
　　Had watched the issue of the strife,
Fills the glad air with grateful cries
　　To find the sun no more obscured,
And with new yearnings in her eyes
　　Climbs to her watch-tower — reassured.
　　　　London *Truth.*

Surgical aid was at hand. It was found that
the bullet had passed through the stomach; both
wounds were sewed up, and five days later the
President was pronounced out of danger. The
next day, he showed signs of a relapse, and sank
steadily until death came early on the morning of
Saturday, September 14.

FAITHFUL UNTO DEATH

[September 14, 1901]

His work is done, his toil is o'er;
　　A martyr for our land he fell —
　　The land he loved, that loved him well;
Honor his name for evermore!

Let all the world its tribute pay,
　　For glorious shall be his renown;
　　Though duty's was his only crown,
Yet duty's path is glory's way.

For he was great without pretence;
　　A man of whom none whispered shame,
　　A man who knew nor guile nor blame;
Good in his every influence.

On battle-field, in council-hall,
　　Long years with sterling service rife
　　He gave us, and at last his life —
Still unafraid at duty's call.

Let the last solemn pageant move,
　　The nation's grief to consecrate
　　To him struck down by maniac hate
Amid a mighty nation's love;

And though the thought it solace gives,
　　Beside the martyr's grave to-day
　　We feel 't is almost hard to say:
"God reigns and the Republic lives!"
　　　　RICHARD HANDFIELD TITHERINGTON.

THE COMFORT OF THE TREES

Gentle and generous, brave-hearted, kind,
　　And full of love and trust was he, our chief;
　　He never harmed a soul! Oh, dull and
　　　blind
　　And cruel, the hand that smote, beyond be-
　　　lief!
Strike us? It could not be! Soon should we
　　　find
　　'T was but a torturing dream — our sud-
　　　den grief!
　　Then sobs and wailings down the northern
　　　wind
　　Like the wild voice of shipwreck from a
　　　reef!
By false hope lulled (his courage gave us
　　　hope!)
　　By day, by night we watched, — until un-
　　　furled
　　At last the word of fate! — Our memories
Cherish one tender thought in their sad scope:
He, looking from the window on this world,
Found comfort in the moving green of trees.
　　　　RICHARD WATSON GILDER.

OUTWARD BOUND

Farewell! for now a stormy morn and dark
　　The hour of greeting and of parting brings;
Already on the rising wind yon bark
　　Spreads her impatient wings.

Too hasty keel, a little while delay!
  A moment tarry, O thou hurrying dawn!
For long and sad will be the mourners' day
    When their beloved is gone.

But vain the hands that beckon from the shore:
  Alike our passion and our grief are vain.
Behind him lies our little world: before
    The illimitable main.

Yet, none the less, about his moving bed
  Immortal eyes a tireless vigil keep —
An angel at the feet and at the head
    Guard his untroubled sleep.

Two nations bowed above a common bier,
  Made one forever by a martyred son —
One in their agony of hope and fear,
    And in their sorrow one.

And thou, lone traveller, of a waste so wide,
  The uncharted seas that all must pass in turn,
May the same star that was so long thy guide
    O'er thy last voyage burn.

No eye can reach where through yon sombre
        veil
  That bark to its eternal haven fares;
No earthly breezes swell its shadowy sail:
    Only our love and prayers.
            EDWARD SYDNEY TYLEE.

Theodore Roosevelt, Vice-President, succeeded
to the Presidency. The greatest project which the
new administration undertook was the construc-
tion of a ship canal across the Isthmus of Panama.
This enterprise had been agitated as early as 1826,
and in 1879 a French company under Ferdinand
de Lesseps had secured a concession from Colom-
bia and started to work. At the end of ten years,
the company had exhausted its resources and
work ceased.

PANAMA

HERE the oceans twain have waited
All the ages to be mated, —
Waited long and waited vainly,
Though the script was written plainly:
"This, the portal of the sea,
Opes for him who holds the key;
Here the empire of the earth
Waits in patience for its birth."

But the Spanish monarch, dimly
Seeing little, answered grimly:

"North and South the land is Spain's;
As God gave it, it remains.
He who seeks to break the tie,
By mine honor, he shall die!"

So the centuries rollèd on,
And the gift of great Colon,
Like a spendthrift's heritage,
Dwindled slowly, age by age,
Till the flag of red and gold
Fell from hands unnerved and old
And the granite-pillared gate
Waited still the key of fate.

Who shall hold that magic key
But the child of destiny,
In whose veins has mingled long
All the best blood of the strong?
He who takes his place by grace
Of nò single tribe or race,
But by many a rich bequest
From the bravest and the best.
Sentinel of duty, here
Must he guard a hemisphere.

Let the old world keep its ways;
Naught to him its blame or praise;
Naught its greed, or hate, or fear;
For all swords be sheathèd here.

Yea, the gateway shall be free
Unto all, from sea to sea;
And no fratricidal slaughter
Shall defile its sacred water;
But — the hand that ope'd the gate shall
    forever hold the key!
            JAMES JEFFREY ROCHE.

The United States was naturally looked to to
carry on the project. The matter was brought be-
fore Congress, and in 1902 the French company
was bought out for the sum of forty million dol-
lars. The Republic of Panama was organized,
when Colombia hesitated over the concession, and
control of the canal route was thus secured.

DARIEN

A. D. 1513–A. D. 1901

[The American Senate has ratified the isthmus
treaty. — WASHINGTON TELEGRAM.]

"SILENT upon a peak in Darien,"
    The Spanish steel red in his conquering
        hand,
    While golden, green and gracious the vast
        land

Of that new world comes sudden into ken —
Stands Nuñez da Balboa. North and south
    He sees at last the full Pacific roll
    In blue and silver on each shelf and shoal,
And the white bar of the broad river's mouth,
And the long, ranked palm-trees. "Queen of
    Heaven," he cried,
    "To-day thou giv'st me this for all my
    pain,
    And I the glorious guerdon give to
    Spain,
A new earth and new sea to be her pride,
War ground and treasure-house." And while
    he spoke
The world's heart knew a mightier dawn was
    broke.

"Silent, upon a peak in Darien" —
    Four hundred years being fled, a Greater
    stood
    On that same height; and did behold the
    flood
Of blue waves leaping; Mother of all men!
Wise Nature! And she spake, "The gift I
    gave
    To Nuñez da Balboa could not keep
    Spain from her sins; now must the ages
    sweep
To larger legend, tho' her own was brave.
Here on this ridge I do foresee fresh birth.
    That which departed shall bring side by
    side,
    The sea shall sever what hills did divide;
Shall link in love." And there was joy on
    earth;
Whilst England and Columbia, quitting fear,
Kissed — and let in the eager waters there.
                EDWIN ARNOLD.

PANAMA

HOME OF THE DOVE-PLANT OR HOLY GHOST
FLOWER

I

WHAT time the Lord drew back the sea
    And gave thee room, slight Panama,
"I will not have thee great," said he,
"But thou shalt bear the slender key
Of both the gates I builded me,
And all the great shall come to thee
    For leave to pass, O Panama!"
      (Flower of the Holy Ghost, white dove,
      Breathe sweetness where he wrought in
      love.)

II

His oceans call across the land:
    "How long, how long, fair Panama,
Wilt thou the shock of tides withstand,
Nor heed us sobbing by the strand?
Set wide thy gates on either hand,
That we may search through saltless sand —
    May clasp and kiss, O Panama!"
      (Flower of the deep-embosomed dove,
      So should his mighty nations love.)

III

Out-peal his holy temple-clocks:
    It is thine hour, glad Panama.
Now shall thy key undo the locks;
The strong shall cleave thy sunken rocks;
Swung loose and floating from their docks,
The world's white fleets shall come in flocks
    To thread thy straits, O Panama!
      (Flower of the tropics, snowy dove,
      Forbid, unless they come in love.)

IV

How beautiful is thy demesne!
    Search out thy wealth, proud Panama:
Thy gold, thy pearls of silver sheen,
Thy fruitful palms, thy thickets green;
Load thou the ships that ride between;
Attire thee as becomes a queen:
    The great ones greet thee, Panama!
      (Flower of the white and peaceful dove,
      Let all men pass who come in love.)
              AMANDA T. JONES.

A working organization was perfected, improved
machinery got into place, and when, in the fall of
1906, President Roosevelt visited the Isthmus, he
found the dirt flying in a most satisfactory way.
The canal was finally opened to commerce in April,
1916.

A SONG OF PANAMA

[1906]

"CHUFF! chuff! chuff!" An' a mountain-
    bluff
    Is moved by the shovel's song;
"Chuff! chuff! chuff!" Oh, the grade is rough
    A liftin' the landscape along!

We are ants upon a mountain, but we're
    leavin' of our dent,
An' our teeth-marks bitin' scenery they will
    show the way we went;

We 're a liftin' half creation, an' we 're changin'
 it around,
Just to suit our playful purpose when we 're
 diggin' in the ground.

"Chuff! chuff! chuff!" Oh, the grade is
 rough,
 An' the way to the sea is long;
"Chuff! chuff! chuff!" an' the engines puff
 In tune to the shovel's song!

We 're a shiftin' miles like inches, and we
 grab a forest here
Just to switch it over yonder so 's to leave
 an angle clear;
We 're a pushin' leagues o' swamps aside so 's
 we can hurry by —
An' if we had to do it we would probably
 switch the sky!

"Chuff! chuff! chuff!" Oh, it's hard enough
 When you 're changin' a job gone wrong;
"Chuff! chuff! chuff!" an' there 's no rebuff
 To the shovel a singin' its song!

You hears it in the mornin' an' you hears it
 late at night —
It's our battery keepin' action with support
 o' dynamite;
Oh, you gets it for your dinner, an' the scenery
 skips along
In a movin' panorama to the chargin' shovel's
 song!

"Chuff! chuff! chuff!" an' it grabs the
 scruff
 Of a hill an' boosts it along;
"Chuff! chuff! chuff!" Oh, the grade is rough,
 But it gives to the shovel's song!

This is a fight that 's fightin', an' the battle 's
 to the death;
There ain't no stoppin' here to rest or even
 catch your breath;
You ain't no noble hero, an' you leave no
 gallant name —
You're a fightin' Nature's army, an' it ain't
 no easy game!

"Chuff! chuff! chuff!" Oh, the grade is rough,
 An' the way to the end is long;
"Chuff! chuff! chuff!" an' the engines puff
 As we lift the landscape along!
ALFRED DAMON RUNYON.

In 1904 an industrial exposition to commemorate the one hundredth anniversary of the purchase of Louisiana from France was held at St. Louis, and was attended by millions of people. The official hymn was written by Edmund Clarence Stedman, and was sung on the opening day by a chorus of five hundred voices.

HYMN OF THE WEST

O THOU, whose glorious orbs on high
 Engird the earth with splendor round,
From out thy secret place draw nigh
 The courts and temples of this ground;
 Eternal Light,
 Fill with thy might
These domes that in thy purpose grew,
And lift a nation's heart anew!

Illumine Thou each pathway here,
 To show the marvels God hath wrought!
Since first thy people's chief and seer
 Looked up with that prophetic thought,
 Bade Time unroll
 The fateful scroll,
And empire unto Freedom gave
From cloudland height to tropic wave.

Poured through the gateways of the North
 Thy mighty rivers join their tide,
And, on the wings of morn sent forth,
 Their mists the far-off peaks divide.
 By Thee unsealed,
 The mountains yield
Ores that the wealth of Ophir shame,
And gems enwrought of seven-hued flame

Lo, through what years the soil hath lain
 At thine own time to give increase —
The greater and the lesser grain,
 The ripening boll, the myriad fleece!
 Thy creatures graze
 Appointed ways;
League after league across the land
The ceaseless herds obey thy hand.

Thou, whose high archways shine most clear
 Above the plenteous Western plain,
Thine ancient tribes from round the sphere
 To breathe its quickening air are fain:
 And smiles the sun
 To see made one
Their brood throughout Earth's greenest
 space,
Land of the new and lordlier race!
EDMUND CLARENCE STEDMAN.

Particularly noteworthy was the growing sentiment of friendship between England and America. Not so many years before, the two countries had seemed on the verge of war, but all such clouds had long since been swept away.

BRITANNIA TO COLUMBIA

WHAT is the voice I hear
  On the wind of the Western Sea?
Sentinel, listen from out Cape Clear,
  And say what the voice may be.
"'T is a proud, free people calling aloud to
  a people proud and free.

"And it says to them, 'Kinsmen, hail!
  We severed have been too long;
Now let us have done with a wornout tale,
  The tale of an ancient wrong,
And our friendship last long as love doth last,
  and be stronger than death is strong!'"

Answer them, sons of the selfsame race,
  And blood of the selfsame clan,
Let us speak with each other, face to face,
  And answer as man to man,
And loyally love and trust each other as none
  but free men can.

Now fling them out to the breeze,
  Shamrock, thistle, and rose,
And the Star-Spangled Banner unfurl with
  these,
  A message to friends and foes,
Wherever the sails of peace are seen and
  wherever the war wind blows.

A message to bond and thrall to wake,
  For wherever we come, we twain,
The throne of the tyrant shall rock and
  quake
  And his menace be vold and vain,
For you are lords of a strong young land and
  we are lords of the main.

Yes, this is the voice on the bluff March
  gale,
  "We severed have been too long;
But now we have done with a wornout tale,
  The tale of an ancient wrong,
And our friendship shall last long as love doth
  last and be stronger than death is
  strong."
                                    ALFRED AUSTIN.

Within the United States a similar change was taking place. The old sectional lines of North and South were being forgotten, as a new generation arose, and the proposal to return to the South her captured battle flags — a proposal which, a few years before, had met with frenzied protest from fire-alarm patriots — received general and hearty approval.

THOSE REBEL FLAGS

DISCUSSED BY "ONE OF THE YANKS"

SHALL we send back the Johnnies their bunt-
  ing,
  In token, from Blue to the Gray,
That "Brothers-in-blood" and "Good Hunt-
  ing"
  Shall be our new watchword to-day?
In olden times knights held it knightly
  To return to brave foemen the sword;
Will the Stars and the Stripes gleam less
  brightly
  If the old Rebel flags are restored?

Call it sentiment, call it misguided
  To fight to the death for "a rag";
Yet, trailed in the dust, derided,
  The true soldier still loves his flag!
Does love die, and must honor perish
  When colors and causes are lost?
Lives the soldier who ceases to cherish
  The blood-stains and valor they cost?

Our battle-fields, safe in the keeping
  Of Nature's kind, fostering care,
Are blooming, — our heroes are sleeping, —
  And peace broods perennial there.
All over our land rings the story
  Of loyalty, fervent and true;
"One flag," and that flag is "Old Glory,"
  Alike for the Gray and the Blue.

Why cling to those moth-eaten banners?
  What glory or honor to gain
While the nation is shouting hosannas,
  Uniting her sons to fight Spain?
Time is ripe, and the harvest worth reap-
  ing,
  Send the Johnnies their flags f. o. b.,
Address to the care and safe-keeping
  Of that loyal "old Reb," Fitzhugh Lee!

Yes, send back the Johnnies their bunting,
  With greetings from Blue to the Gray;

We are "Brothers-in-blood," and "Good
Hunting"
Is America's watchword to-day.

JOHN H. JEWETT.

On February 24, 1905, Congress directed that
the flags be returned, and they now rest in the
capitols of the various Southern States.

THE SONG OF THE FLAGS

ON THEIR RETURN TO THE STATES OF THE
CONFEDERACY

[February 24, 1905]

WE loved the wild clamor of battle,
The crash of the musketry's rattle,
    The bugle and drum;
We have drooped in the dust, long and lonely;
The blades that flashed joy are rust only,
    The far-rolling war music dumb.

God rest the true souls in death lying,
For whom overhead proudly flying
    We challenged the foe.
The storm of the charge we have breasted,
On the hearts of our dead we have rested,
    In the pride of a day, long ago.

Ah, surely the good of God's making
Shall answer both those past awaking
    And life's cry of pain;
But we nevermore shall be tossing
On surges of battle where crossing
    The swift-flying death bearers rain.

Again in the wind we are streaming,
Again with the war lust are dreaming
    The call of the shell.
What gray heads look up at us sadly?
Are these the stern troopers who madly
    Rode straight at the battery's hell?

Nay, more than the living have found us,
Pale spectres of battle around us;
    The gray line is dressed.
Ye hear not, but they who are bringing
Your symbols of honor are singing
    The song of death's bivouac rest.

Blow forth on the south wind to greet us,
O star flag! once eager to meet us
    When war lines were set.

Go carry to far fields of glory
The soul-stirring thrill of the story,
    Of days when in anger we met.

Ah, well that we hung in the churches
In quiet, where God the heart searches,
    That under us met
Men heard through the murmur of praying
The voice of the torn banners saying,
    "Forgive, but ah, never forget."

S. WEIR MITCHELL.

The territories of the West were clamoring for
admission to statehood, and finally, in the sum-
mer of 1906, Oklahoma and the Indian Territory
were admitted as one state. Arizona and New
Mexico were offered joint statehood, but the
former refused to link her destinies with her sister
territory.

ARIZONA

No beggar she in the mighty hall where her
    bay-crowned sisters wait,
No empty-handed pleader for the right of a
    free-born state,
No child, with a child's insistence, demand-
    ing a gilded toy,
But a fair-browed, queenly woman, strong
    to create or destroy —
Wise for the need of the sons she has bred in
    the school where weaklings fail,
Where cunning is less than manhood, and
    deeds, not words, avail —
With the high, unswerving purpose that mea-
    sures and overcomes,
And the faith in the Farthest Vision that
    builded her hard-won homes.

Link her, in her clean-proved fitness, in her
    right to stand alone —
Secure for whatever future in the strength
    that her past has won —
Link her, in her morning beauty, with an-
    other, however fair?
And open your jealous portal and bid her
    enter there
With shackles on wrist and ankle, and dust
    on her stately head,
And her proud eyes dim with weeping? No!
    Bar your doors instead
And seal them fast forever! but let her go
    her way —
Uncrowned if you will, but unshackled, to
    wait for a larger day.

Ay! Let her go bare-handed, bound with
　　no grudging gift,
Back to her own free spaces where her rock-
　　ribbed mountains lift
Their walls like a sheltering fortress — back
　　to her house and blood.
And we of her blood will go our way and
　　reckon your judgment good.
We will wait outside your sullen door till the
　　stars you wear grow dim
As the pale dawn-stars that swim and fade
　　o'er our mighty Cañon's rim.
We will lift no hand for the bays ye wear, nor
　　covet your robes of state —
But ah! by the skies above us all, we will
　　shame ye while we wait!

We will make ye the mold of an empire here
　　in the land ye scorn,
While ye drowse and dream in your well-housed
　　ease that States at your nod are born.
Ye have blotted your own beginnings, and
　　taught your sons to forget
That ye did not spring fat-fed and old from
　　the powers that bear and beget.
But the while ye follow your smooth-made
　　roads to a fireside safe of fears,
Shall come a voice from a land still young, to
　　sing in your age-dulled ears
The hero song of a strife as fine as your fathers'
　　fathers knew,
When they dared the rivers of unmapped wilds
　　at the will of a bark canoe —

The song of the deed in the doing, of the work
　　still hot from the hand;
Of the yoke of man laid friendly-wise on the
　　neck of a tameless land.
While your merchandise is weighing, we will
　　bit and bridle and rein
The floods of the storm-rocked mountains and
　　lead them down to the plain;
And the foam-ribbed, dark-hued waters, tired
　　from that mighty race,
Shall lie at the feet of palm and vine and know
　　their appointed place;
And out of that subtle union, desert and
　　mountain-flood,
Shall be homes for a nation's choosing, where
　　no home else had stood.

We will match the gold of your minting, with
　　its mint-stamp dulled and marred
By the tears and blood that have stained it and
　　the hands that have clutched too hard,

With the gold that no man has lied for — the
　　gold no woman has made
The price of her truth and honor, plying a
　　shameless trade —
The clean, pure gold of the mountains,
　　straight from the strong, dark earth,
With no tang or taint upon it from the hour
　　of its primal birth.
The trick of the money-changer, shifting his
　　coins as he wills,
Ye may keep — no Christ was bartered for
　　the wealth of our lavish hills.

"Yet we are a little people — too weak for the
　　cares of state!"
Let us go our way! When ye look again, ye
　　shall find us, mayhap, too great.
Cities we lack — and gutters where children
　　snatch for bread;
Numbers — and hordes of starvelings, toil-
　　ing but never fed.
Spare pains that would make us greater in the
　　pattern that ye have set;
We hold to the larger measure of the men that
　　ye forget —
The men who, from trackless forests and
　　prairies lone and far,
Hewed out the land where ye sit at ease and
　　grudge us our fair-won star.

"There yet be men, my masters," though the
　　net that the trickster flings
Lies wide on the land to its bitter shame, and
　　his cunning parleyings
Have deafened the ears of Justice, that was
　　blind and slow of old.
Yet time, the last Great Judge, is not bought,
　　or bribed, or sold;
And Time and the Race shall judge us — not
　　a league of trafficking men,
Selling the trust of the people, to barter it
　　back again;
Palming the lives of millions as a handful of
　　easy coin,
With a single heart to the narrow verge where
　　craft and statecraft join.
　　　　　　　　　　　SHARLOT M. HALL.

On the morning of Wednesday, April 18, 1906,
an appalling calamity visited California, and
especially the great city of San Francisco. At a
few minutes past five o'clock a severe earthquake
shock desolated the cities of the central coast
region, snuffed out hundreds of lives, and destroyed
millions of dollars' worth of property.

SAN FRANCISCO

[April 18, 1906]

SUCH darkness as when Jesus died!
  Then sudden dawn drave all before.
Two wee brown tomtits, terrified,
  Flashed through my open cottage door;
Then instant out and off again
And left a stillness like to pain —
Such stillness, darkness, sudden dawn
I never knew or looked upon!

This ardent, Occidental dawn
  Dashed San Francisco's streets with gold,
Just gold and gold to walk upon,
  As he of Patmos sang of old.
And still, so still, her streets, her steeps,
As when some great soul silent weeps;
And oh, that gold, that gold that lay
Beyond, above the tarn, brown bay!

And then a bolt, a jolt, a chill,
  And Mother Earth seemed as afraid;
Then instant all again was still,
  Save that my cattle from the shade
Where they had sought firm, rooted clay,
Came forth loud lowing, glad and gay,
Knee-deep in grasses to rejoice
That all was well, with trumpet voice.

Not so yon city — darkness, dust,
  Then martial men in swift array,
Then smoke, then flames, then great guns thrust
  To heaven, as if pots of clay —
Cathedral, temple, palace, tower —
An hundred wars in one wild hour!
And still the smoke, the flame, the guns
The piteous wail of little ones!

The mad flame climbed the costly steep,
  But man, defiant, climbed the flame.
What battles where the torn clouds keep!
  What deeds of glory in God's name!
What sons of giants — giants, yea —
Or beardless lad or veteran gray.
Not Marathon nor Waterloo
Knew men so daring, dauntless, true.

Three days, three nights, three fearful days
  Of death, of flame, of dynamite,
Of God's house thrown a thousand ways;
  Blown east by day, blown west by night —

By night? There was no night. Nay, nay,
The ghoulish flame lit nights that lay
Crouched down between this first, last day.
I say those nights were burned away!

And jealousies were burned away,
  And burned were city rivalries,
Till all, white crescenting the bay,
  Were one harmonious hive of bees.
Behold the bravest battle won!
The City Beautiful begun;
One solid San Francisco, one,
The fairest sight beneath the sun.
                          JOAQUIN MILLER.

In San Francisco, fire followed the shock; the water-mains had been broken, and the flames were soon utterly beyond control, and raged for two days, destroying the business and principal residence portions of the city — an area of four square miles. The loss of life reached a thousand, the property loss three hundred million dollars.

SAN FRANCISCO

WHO now dare longer trust thy mother hand?
  So like thee thou hadst not another child;
The favorite flower of all thy Western sand,
  She looked up, Nature, in thy face and smiled,
Trustful of thee, all-happy in thy care.
  She was thine own, not to be lured away
Down joyless paths of men. Happy as fair,
  Held to thy heart — that was she yesterday.
To-day the sea is sobbing her sweet name;
  She cannot answer — she that loved thee best,
That clung to thee till Hell's own shock and flame
  Wrenched her, swept her, from thy forgetting breast.
Day's darling, playmate of thy wind and sun —
Mother, what hast thou done, what hast thou done!
                          JOHN VANCE CHENEY.

The whole country rushed to the relief of the stricken state; the Californians met their losses bravely, and started at once to build a greater San Francisco.

TO SAN FRANCISCO

IF we dreamed that we loved Her aforetime,
    't was the ghost of a dream; for I vow
By the splendor of God in the highest, we
    never have loved Her till now.

When Love bears the trumpet of Honor, oh,
  highest and clearest he calls,
With the light of the flaming of towers, and
  the sound of the rending of walls.
When Love wears the purple of Sorrow, and
  kneels at the altar of Grief,
Of the flowers that spring in his footsteps, the
  white flower of Service is chief.
And as snow on the snow of Her bosom, as a
  star in the night of Her hair,
We bring to our Mother such token as the
  time and the elements spare.

If we dreamed that we loved Her aforetime,
  adoring we kneel to Her now,
When the golden fruit of the ages falls, swept
  by the wind from the bough.
The beautiful dwelling is shattered, wherein,
  as a queen at the feast,
In gems of the barbaric tropics and silks of
  the ultimate East,
Our Mother sat throned and triumphant,
  with the wise and the great in their
  day.
They were captains, and princes, and rulers;
  but She, She was greater than they.

We are sprung from the builders of nations;
  by the souls of our fathers we swear,
By the depths of the deeps that surround Her,
  by the height of the heights she may
  dare,
Though the Twelve league in compact against
  Her, though the sea gods cry out in
  their wrath,
Though the earth gods, grown drunk of their
  fury, fling the hilltops abroad in Her
  path,
Our Mother of masterful children shall sit on
  Her throne as of yore,
With Her old robes of purple about Her, and
  crowned with the crowns that She
  wore.

She shall sit at the gates of the world, where
  the nations shall gather and meet,
And the East and the West at Her bidding
  shall lie in a leash at Her feet.
                    S. J. ALEXANDER.

The regeneration was moral as well as physical,
for not only was the town rebuilt, but it was res-
cued from the corrupt ring which, for years, had
kept control of the city government.

RESURGE SAN FRANCISCO

BEHOLD her Seven Hills loom white
Once more as marble-builded Rome.
Her marts teem with a touch of home
And music fills her halls at night;
Her streets flow populous, and light
Floods every happy, hopeful face;
The wheel of fortune whirls apace
And old-time fare and dare hold sway.
Farewell the blackened, toppling wall,
The bent steel gird, the sombre pall —
Farewell forever, let us pray;
Farewell, forever and a day!
                    JOAQUIN MILLER.

On June 24, 1908, Grover Cleveland, twice
President of the United States, died at his home in
Princeton, N. J., at the age of seventy-one. His
death called forth a remarkable tribute from men
of all parties and in all walks of life — a tribute to
his stainless service of the state, to his honesty,
courage, and fidelity. Lowell had called him "the
most typical American since Lincoln."

GROVER CLEVELAND

[1837–1908]

BRING cypress, rosemary and rue
For him who kept his rudder true;
Who held to right the people's will,
And for whose foes we love him still.

A man of Plutarch's marble mold,
Of virtues strong and manifold,
Who spurned the incense of the hour,
And made the nation's weal his dower.

His sturdy, rugged sense of right
Put selfish purpose out of sight;
Slowly he thought, but long and well,
With temper imperturbable.

Bring cypress, rosemary and rue
For him who kept his rudder true;
Who went at dawn to that high star
Where Washington and Lincoln are.
                    JOEL BENTON.

One feature of the country's growth has awak-
ened great uneasiness. Over a million emigrants
have been landing every year upon her shores,
and the feeling has grown that America must cease
to be an asylum for the ignorance and vice of
Europe.

UNGUARDED GATES

WIDE open and unguarded stand our gates,
Named of the four winds, North, South, East,
    and West;
Portals that lead to an enchanted land
Of cities, forests, fields of living gold,
Vast prairies, lordly summits touched with
    snow,
Majestic rivers sweeping proudly past
The Arab's date-palm and the Norseman's
    pine —
A realm wherein are fruits of every zone,
Airs of all climes, for lo! throughout the year
The red rose blossoms somewhere — a rich
    land,
A later Eden planted in the wilds,
With not an inch of earth within its bound
But if a slave's foot press it sets him free.
Here, it is written, Toil shall have its wage,
And Honor honor, and the humblest man
Stand level with the highest in the law.
Of such a land have men in dungeons dreamed,
And with the vision brightening in their eyes
Gone smiling to the fagot and the sword.

Wide open and unguarded stand our gates,
And through them presses a wild motley
    throng —
Men from the Volga and the Tartar steppes,
Featureless figures of the Hoang-Ho,
Malayan, Scythian, Teuton, Kelt, and Slav,
Flying the Old World's poverty and scorn;
These bringing with them unknown gods and
    rites,
Those, tiger passions, here to stretch their
    claws.
In street and alley what strange tongues are
    loud,
Accents of menace alien to our air,
Voices that once the Tower of Babel knew!

O Liberty, white Goddess! is it well
To leave the gates unguarded? On thy breast
Fold Sorrow's children, soothe the hurts of fate,
Lift the down-trodden, but with hands of steel
Stay those who to thy sacred portals come
To waste the gifts of freedom. Have a care
Lest from thy brow the clustered stars be torn
And trampled in the dust. For so of old
The thronging Goth and Vandal trampled
    Rome,
And where the temples of the Cæsars stood
The lean wolf unmolested made her lair.

THOMAS BAILEY ALDRICH.

The first decade of the new century witnessed a long stride forward toward better government. Both State and Nation asserted the right to protect their citizens against exploitation, to guard the rights of labor, to regulate railroads and public utilities, to outlaw gambling, to supervise the sale of intoxicants and poisons, and to prosecute the purveyors of impure food.

NATIONAL SONG

AMERICA, my own!
    Thy spacious grandeurs rise
Faming the proudest zone
    Pavilioned by the skies;
Day's flying glory breaks
    Thy vales and mountains o'er,
And gilds thy streams and lakes
    From ocean shore to shore.

Praised be thy wood and wold,
    Thy corn and wine and flocks,
The yellow blood of gold
    Drained from thy cañon rocks;
Thy trains that shake the land,
    Thy ships that plough the main,
Triumphant cities grand
    Roaring with noise of gain.

Earth's races look to Thee:
    The peoples of the world
Thy risen splendors see
    And thy wide flag unfurled;
Thy sons, in peace or war,
    That emblem who behold,
Bless every shining star,
    Cheer every streaming fold!

Float high, O gallant flag,
    O'er Carib Isles of palm,
O'er bleak Alaskan crag,
    O'er far-off lone Guam;
Where Mauna Loa pours
    Black thunder from the deeps;
O'er Mindanao's shores,
    O'er Luzon's coral steeps.

Float high, and be the sign
    Of love and brotherhood, —
The pledge, by right divine
    Of Power, to do good;
For aye and everywhere,
    On continent and wave,
Armipotent to dare,
    Imperial to save!

WILLIAM HENRY VENABLE.

Especially significant was the awakening of the public conscience, the growing intolerance of corruption in office, the demand for honesty in public as in private life, and the realization of the fact that the great public service corporations are accountable to the people and amenable to law.

AD PATRIAM

To deities of gauds and gold,
    Land of our Fathers, do not bow!
But unto those beloved of old
    Bend thou the brow!

Austere they were of front and form;
    Rigid as iron in their aim;
Yet in them pulsed a blood as warm
    And pure as flame; —

Honor, whose foster-child is Truth;
    Unselfishness in place and plan;
Justice, with melting heart of ruth;
    And Faith in man.

Give these our worship; then no fears
    Of future foes need fright thy soul;
Triumphant thou shalt mount the years
    Toward thy high goal!
                CLINTON SCOLLARD.

O LAND BELOVED

From " My Country "

O LAND beloved!
My Country, dear, my own!
May the young heart that moved
    For the weak words atone;
The mighty lyre not mine, nor the full breath
        of song!
    To happier sons shall these belong.
    Yet doth the first and lonely voice
    Of the dark dawn the heart rejoice,
While still the loud choir sleeps upon the
        bough;
    And never greater love salutes thy brow
    Than his, who seeks thee now.
Alien the sea and salt the foam
Where'er it bears him from his home;
    And when he leaps to land,
    A lover treads the strand;
    Precious is every stone;
    No little inch of all the broad domain
    But he would stoop to kiss, and end
        his pain,

Feeling thy lips make merry with his
        own;
    But oh, his trembling reed too frail
    To bear thee Time's All-Hail!

Faint is my heart, and ebbing with the passion
        of thy praise!
    The poets come who cannot fail;
    Happy are they who sing thy perfect days!
Happy am I who see the long night ended,
In the shadows of the age that bore me,
    All the hopes of mankind blending,
    Earth awaking, heaven descending,
        While the new day steadfastly
        Domes the blue deeps over thee!
    Happy am I who see the Vision splendid
    In the glowing of the dawn before me,
        All the grace of heaven blending,
        Man arising, Christ descending,
            While God's hand in secrecy
            Builds thy bright eternity.
                GEORGE EDWARD WOODBERRY.

So America faced the future unafraid, confident of her destiny — perhaps over-confident, for many of her problems were as yet unsolved, and, unforeseen by anyone, another time of trial lay ahead.

THE REPUBLIC

From " The Building of the Ship "

THOU, too, sail on, O Ship of State!
Sail on, O Union, strong and great!
Humanity with all its fears,
With all the hopes of future years,
Is hanging breathless on thy fate!
We know what Master laid thy keel,
What Workmen wrought thy ribs of steel,
Who made each mast, and sail, and rope,
What anvils rang, what hammers beat,
In what a forge and what a heat
Were shaped the anchors of thy hope!
Fear not each sudden sound and shock,
'T is of the wave and not the rock;
'T is but the flapping of the sail,
And not a rent made by the gale!
In spite of rock and tempest's roar,
In spite of false lights on the shore,
Sail on, nor fear to breast the sea!
Our hearts, our hopes, are all with thee,
Our hearts, our hopes, our prayers, our tears,
Our faith triumphant o'er our fears,
Are all with thee, — are all with thee!
                HENRY WADSWORTH LONGFELLOW.

CHAPTER VII

THE WORLD WAR

From the time of Washington and Jefferson, Americans had been taught to keep themselves free from "entangling alliances" with the governments of Europe, and to guard their "splendid isolation." But such isolation became more and more difficult to maintain as steam and electricity made the world smaller, and economic causes drew its nations more closely together. Yet when, on August 1, 1914, war broke out between France, England, Belgium, and Russia on one side, and Germany and Austria on the other, few Americans suspected there was any danger of their country being involved. Their sympathies for the most part were with Belgium and France and England, which seemed to be defending themselves against unprovoked aggression.

SONNETS WRITTEN IN THE FALL OF 1914

Awake, ye nations, slumbering supine,
Who round enring the European fray!
Heard ye the trumpet sound? "The Day! the
    Day!
The last that shall on England's empire
    shine!
The Parliament that broke the Right Divine
Shall see her realm of reason swept away,
And lesser nations shall the sword obey —
The sword o'er all carve the great world's de-
    sign!"
So on the English Channel boasts the foe
On whose imperial brow death's helmet nods.
Look where his hosts o'er bloody Belgium go,
And mix a nation's past with blazing sods!
A kingdom's waste! a people's homeless woe!
Man's broken Word, and violated gods!

Far fall the day when England's realm shall see
The sunset of dominion! Her increase
Abolishes the man-dividing seas,
And frames the brotherhood on earth to be!
She, in free peoples planting sovereignty,
Orbs half the civil world in British peace;
And though time dispossess her, and she cease,
Rome-like she greatens in man's memory.
Oh, many a crown shall sink in war's turmoil,
And many a new republic light the sky,
Fleets sweep the ocean, nations till the soil,
Genius be born and generations die,

Orient and Occident together toil,
Ere such a mighty work man rears on high!

Hearken, the feet of the Destroyer tread
The wine-press of the nations; fast the blood
Pours from the side of Europe; in full flood
On the Septentrional watershed
The rivers of fair France are running red!
England, the mother-eyrie of our brood,
That on the summit of dominion stood,
Shakes in the blast: heaven battles overhead!
Lift up thy head, O Rheims, of ages heir
That treasured up in thee their glorious sum;
Upon whose brow, prophetically fair,
Flamed the great morrow of the world to come;
Haunt with thy beauty this volcanic air
Ere yet thou close, O Flower of Christendom!

As when the shadow of the sun's eclipse
Sweeps on the earth, and spreads a spectral air,
As if the universe were dying there,
On continent and isle the darkness dips,
Unwonted gloom, and on the Atlantic slips;
So in the night the Belgian cities flare
Horizon-wide; the wandering people fare
Along the roads, and load the fleeing ships.
And westward borne that planetary sweep,
Darkening o'er England and her times to be,
Already steps upon the ocean-deep!
Watch well, my country, that unearthly sea,
Lest when thou thinkest not, and in thy sleep,
Unapt for war, that gloom enshadow thee!
          George Edward Woodberry.

American opinion was especially aroused by Germany's cynical disregard of her pledge to preserve the neutrality of Belgium, and by the military severity which marked the invasion and occupation of that little kingdom.

ABRAHAM LINCOLN WALKS AT MIDNIGHT

[In Springfield, Illinois]

It is portentous, and a thing of state
That here at midnight, in our little town,

A mourning figure walks, and will not rest,
Near the old court-house pacing up and down.

Or by his homestead, or in shadowed yards
He lingers where his children used to play;
Or through the market, on the well-worn
  stones
He stalks until the dawn-stars burn away.

A bronzed, lank man! His suit of ancient
  black,
A famous high top-hat and plain worn shawl
Make him the quaint great figure that men
  love,
The prairie-lawyer, master of us all.

He cannot sleep upon his hillside now.
He is among us: — as in times before!
And we who toss and lie awake for long
Breathe deep, and start, to see him pass the
  door.

His head is bowed. He thinks on men and
  kings.
Yea, when the sick world cries, how can he
  sleep?
Too many peasants fight, they know not why,
Too many homesteads in black terror weep.

The sins of all the war-lords burn his heart.
He sees the dreadnaughts scouring every main.
He carries on his shawl-wrapped shoulders
  now
The bitterness, the folly and the pain.

He cannot rest until a spirit-dawn
Shall come; — the shining hope of Europe
  free:
The league of sober folk, the Workers' Earth
Bringing long peace to Cornland, Alp, and Sea.

It breaks his heart that kings must murder
  still,
That all his hours of travail here for men
Seem yet in vain. And who will bring white
  peace
That he may sleep upon his hill again?
                              VACHEL LINDSAY.

On sea, as well as on land, the same policy of
"frightfulness" was followed, and German sub-
marines and raiders, finding it dangerous to attack
British battleships, turned their attention to un-
armed merchantmen. On February 28, 1915, an
American vessel, the William P. Frye, carrying
wheat from Seattle to Queenstown, was sunk by a
German raider in the South Atlantic.

THE "WILLIAM P. FRYE"

[February 28, 1915]

I SAW her first abreast the Boston Light
At anchor; she had just come in, turned head,
And sent her hawsers creaking, clattering
  down.
I was so near to where the hawse-pipes ted
The cable out from her careening bow,
I moved up on the swell, shut steam and lay
Hove to in my old launch to look at her.
She'd come in light, a-skimming up the Bay
Like a white ghost with topsails bellying full;
And all her noble lines from bow to stern
Made music in the wind; it seemed she rode
The morning air like those thin clouds that
  turn
Into tall ships when sunrise lifts the clouds
From calm sea-courses.

          There, in smoke-smudged coats,
Lay funnelled liners, dirty fishing craft,
Blunt cargo-luggers, tugs, and ferry-boats.
Oh, it was good in that black-scuttled lot
To see the Frye come lording on her way
Like some old queen that we had half forgot
Come to her own. A little up the Bay
The Fort lay green, for it was springtime then;
The wind was fresh, rich with the spicy bloom
Of the New England coast that tardily
Escapes, late April, from an icy tomb.
The State-House glittered on old Beacon Hill,
Gold in the sun. . . . 'T was all so fair awhile;
But she was fairest — this great square-rigged
  ship
That had blown in from some far happy isle
Or from the shores of the Hesperides.

They caught her in a South Atlantic road
Becalmed, and found her hold brimmed up
  with wheat;
"Wheat's contraband," they said, and blew
  her hull
To pieces, murdered one of our staunch fleet,
Fast dwindling, of the big old sailing ships
That carry trade for us on the high sea
And warped out of each harbor in the States.

It was n't law, so it seems strange to me —
A big mistake. Her keel's struck bottom now
And her four masts sunk fathoms, fathoms
    deep
To Davy Jones. The dank seaweed will root
On her oozed decks, and the cross-surges sweep
Through the set sails; but never, never more
Her crew will stand away to brace and trim,
Nor sea-blown petrels meet her thrashing up
To windward on the Gulf Stream's stormy
    rim;
Never again she'll head a no'theast gale,
Or like a spirit loom up, sliding dumb,
And ride in safe beyond the Boston Light,
To make the harbor glad because she's come.
              JEANNE ROBERT FOSTER.

The crowning outrage came on May 7, 1915, when
the great Cunard steamship Lusitania was torpe-
doed without warning off the coast of Ireland, and
1153 men, women, and children drowned. Of these,
114 were Americans.

THE WHITE SHIPS AND THE RED

[May 7, 1915]

WITH drooping sail and pennant
  That never a wind may reach,
They float in sunless waters
  Beside a sunless beach.
Their mighty masts and funnels
  Are white as driven snow,
And with a pallid radiance
  Their ghostly bulwarks glow.

Here is a Spanish galleon
  That once with gold was gay,
Here is a Roman trireme
  Whose hues outshone the day.
But Tyrian dyes have faded,
  And prows that once were bright
With rainbow stains wear only
  Death's livid, dreadful white.

White as the ice that clove her
  That unforgotten day,
Among her pallid sisters
  The grim Titanic lay.
And through the leagues above her
  She looked aghast, and said:
"What is this living ship that comes
  Where every ship is dead?"

The ghostly vessels trembled
  From ruined stern to prow;
What was this thing of terror
  That broke their vigil now?
Down through the startled ocean
  A mighty vessel came,
Not white, as all dead ships must be,
  But red, like living flame!

The pale green waves about her
  Were swiftly, strangely dyed,
By the great scarlet stream that flowed
  From out her wounded side.
And all her decks were scarlet
  And all her shattered crew.
She sank among the white ghost ships
  And stained them through and through.

The grim Titanic greeted her.
  "And who art thou?" she said;
"Why dost thou join our ghostly fleet
  Arrayed in living red?
We are the ships of sorrow
  Who spend the weary night,
Until the dawn of Judgment Day,
  Obscure and still and white."

"Nay," said the scarlet visitor,
  "Though I sink through the sea,
A ruined thing that was a ship,
  I sink not as did ye.
For ye met with your destiny
  By storm or rock or fight,
So through the lagging centuries
  Ye wear your robes of white.

"But never crashing iceberg
  Nor honest shot of foe,
Nor hidden reef has sent me
  The way that I must go.
My wound that stains the waters,
  My blood that is like flame,
Bear witness to a loathly deed,
  A deed without a name.

"I went not forth to battle,
  I carried friendly men,
The children played about my decks,
  The women sang — and then —
And then — the sun blushed scarlet
  And Heaven hid its face,
The world that God created
  Became a shameful place!

"My wrong cries out for vengeance,
    The blow that sent me here
Was aimed in hell. My dying scream
    Has reached Jehovah's ear.
Not all the seven oceans
    Shall wash away that stain;
Upon a brow that wears a crown
    I am the brand of Cain."

When God's great voice assembles
    The fleet on Judgment Day,
The ghosts of ruined ships will rise
    In sea and strait and bay,
Though they have lain for ages
    Beneath the changeless flood,
They shall be white as silver,
    But one — shall be like blood.
                    JOYCE KILMER.

No event since the sinking of the Maine in Havana
Harbor had so stirred the country with rage and
horror. The contention of the Germans that they
were fighting for the freedom of the seas was in-
dignantly scouted.

MARE LIBERUM

You dare to say with perjured lips,
    "We fight to make the ocean free?'
You, whose black trail of butchered ships
    Bestrews the bed of every sea
Where German submarines have wrought
Their horrors! Have you never thought, —
    What you call freedom, men call piracy!

Unnumbered ghosts that haunt the wave
    Where you have murdered, cry you down;
And seamen whom you would not save
    Weave now in weed-grown depths a crown
Of shame for your imperious head, —
A dark memorial of the dead, —
    Women and children whom you sent to
        drown.

Nay, not till thieves are set to guard
    The gold, and corsairs called to keep
O'er peaceful commerce watch and ward,
    And wolves to herd the helpless sheep,
Shall men and women look to thee,
Thou ruthless Old Man of the Sea,
    To safeguard law and freedom on the
        deep!

In nobler breeds we put our trust:
    The nations in whose sacred lore
The "Ought" stands out above the "Must,"
    And honor rules in peace and war.
With these we hold in soul and heart,
With these we choose our lot and part,
    Till liberty is safe on sea and shore.
                    HENRY VAN DYKE.

President Woodrow Wilson warned Germany that
the United States would not tolerate further disre-
gard of American rights, and Germany promised to
restrict her submarine warfare. But the Allies, who
realized that the war was going against them, did
their utmost to arouse American opinion against
the Central Powers, and Germany, by her diplo-
matic blundering, added fuel to the flames. Many
Americans entered the French Aviation Corps or the
Foreign Legion, or went to Canada and enlisted, in
order to take their stand at once beside the nations
which, they believed, were battling for human liberty.

ODE IN MEMORY OF THE AMERI-CAN VOLUNTEERS FALLEN FOR FRANCE

[To have been read before the statue of Lafay-
ette and Washington in Paris, on Decoration Day,
May 30, 1916]

I

Ay, it is fitting on this holiday,
Commemorative of our soldier dead,
When — with sweet flowers of our New Eng-
        land May
Hiding the lichened stones by fifty years made
        gray —
Their graves in every town are garlanded,
That pious tribute should be given too
To our intrepid few
Obscurely fallen here beyond the seas.
Those to preserve their country's greatness
        died;
But by the death of these
Something that we can look upon with pride
Has been achieved, nor wholly unreplied
Can sneerers triumph in the charge they make
That from a war where Freedom was at stake
America withheld and, daunted, stood aside.

II

Be they remembered here with each reviving
        spring,
Not only that in May, when life is loveliest,
Around Neuville-Saint-Vaast and the dis-
        puted crest

Of Vimy, they, superb, unfaltering,
In that fine onslaught that no fire could halt,
Parted impetuous to their first assault;
But that they brought fresh hearts and spring-
    like too
To that high mission, and 't is meet to strew
With twigs of lilac and spring's earliest rose
The cenotaph of those
Who in the cause that history most endears
Fell in the sunny morn and flower of their
    young years.

III

Yet sought they neither recompense nor
    praise,
Nor to be mentioned in another breath
Than their blue-coated comrades whose great
    days
It was their pride to share — ay, share even
    to the death!
Nay, rather, France, to you they rendered
    thanks
(Seeing they came for honor, not for gain),
Who, opening to them your glorious ranks,
Gave them that grand occasion to excel,
That chance to live the life most free from stain
And that rare privilege of dying well.

IV

O friends! I know not since that war began
From which no people nobly stands aloof
If in all moments we have given proof
Of virtues that were thought American.
I know not if in all things done and said
All has been well and good,
Or if each one of us can hold his head
As proudly as he should,
Or, from the pattern of those mighty dead
Whose shades our country venerates to-day,
If we've not somewhat fallen and somewhat
    gone astray.
But you to whom our land's good name is dear,
If there be any here
Who wonder if her manhood be decreased,
Relaxed its sinews and its blood less red
Than that at Shiloh and Antietam shed,
Be proud of these, have joy in this at least,
And cry: "Now, heaven be praised
That in that hour that most imperilled her,
Menaced her liberty who foremost raised
Europe's bright flag of freedom, some there
    were

Who, not unmindful of the antique debt,
Came back the generous path of Lafayette;
And when of a most formidable foe
She checked each onset, arduous to stem —
Foiled and frustrated them —
On these red fields where blow with furious blow
Was countered, whether the gigantic fray
Rolled by the Meuse or at the Bois Sabot,
Accents of ours were in the fierce mêlée;
And on that furthest rim of hallowed ground
Where the forlorn, the gallant charge expires,
When the slain bugler has long ceased to sound,
And on the tangled wires
The last wild rally staggers, crumbles, stops,
Withered beneath the shrapnel's iron show-
    ers: —
Now heaven be thanked, we gave a few brave
    drops;
Now heaven be thanked, a few brave drops
    were ours."

V

There, holding still, in frozen steadfastness,
Their bayonets toward the beckoning frontiers,
They lie — our comrades — lie among their
    peers,
Clad in the glory of fallen warriors,
Grim clusters under thorny trellises,
Dry, furthest foam upon disastrous shores,
Leaves that made last year beautiful, still
    strewn
Even as they fell, unchanged, beneath the
    changing moon;
And earth in her divine indifference
Rolls on, and many paltry things and mean
Prate to be heard and caper to be seen.
But they are silent, calm; their eloquence
Is that incomparable attitude;
No human presences their witness are,
But summer clouds and sunset crimson-hued,
And showers and night winds and the northern
    star.
Nay, even our salutations seem profane,
Opposed to their Elysian quietude;
Our salutations coming from afar,
From our ignobler plane
And undistinction of our lesser parts:
Hail, brothers, and farewell; you are twice
    blest, brave hearts.
Double your glory is who perished thus,
For you have died for France and vindicated us.
                                ALAN SEEGER.

Germany lived up to her agreement only in partial and grudging fashion, and the climax came on January 31, 1917, when the German Government announced that an unrestricted submarine warfare against all ships encountered on the seas would begin next day. President Wilson at once handed the German Ambassador his passports, and on April 2, after the sinking of three American ships without warning, appeared before Congress and asked that war be declared. After thirteen hours of debate, the Senate passed the necessary resolution; the House concurred on April 5, and the next day the President issued a proclamation declaring that "a state of war exists between the United States and the Imperial German Government."

REPUBLIC TO REPUBLIC

1776–1917

FRANCE!
It is I answering.
America!
And it shall be remembered not only in our
　　lips but in our hearts
And shall awaken forever familiar and new
　　as the morning
That we were the first of all lands
To be lovers,
To run to each other with the incredible cry
Of recognition.
Bound by no ties of nearness or of knowledge
But of the nearness of the heart,
You chose me then —
And so I choose you now
By the same nearness —
And the name you called me then
I call you now —
O Liberty, my Love!

　　　　　　　　　WITTER BYNNER.

The Entente Powers welcomed their new ally with bursting hearts, for a decisive victory, which was becoming more and more hopeless, now seemed assured.

TO THE UNITED STATES OF AMERICA

BROTHERS in blood! They who this wrong
　　began
To wreck our commonwealth, will rue the
　　day
When first they challenged freemen to the
　　fray,
And with the Briton dared the American.
Now are we pledged to win the Rights of man;

Labor and Justice now shall have their way,
And in a League of Peace — God grant we
　　may —
Transform the earth, not patch up the old
　　plan.

Sure is our hope since he who led your nation
Spake for mankind, and ye arose in awe
Of that high call to work the world's salvation;
Clearing your minds of all estranging blindness
In the vision of Beauty and the Spirit's law,
Freedom and Honor and sweet Loving-kind-
　　ness.

　　　　　　　　　ROBERT BRIDGES.

One of the first acts of the government was to seize all enemy ships in American ports — which, of course, included Hawaii, Porto Rico and the Philippines. These were at once overhauled and put into service under American command.

THE CAPTIVE SHIPS AT MANILA

OUR keels are furred with tropic weed that
　　clogs the crawling tides
And scarred with crust of salt and rust that
　　gnaws our idle sides;
And little junks they come and go, and ships
　　they sail at dawn;
And all the outbound winds that blow they
　　call us to be gone,
As yearning to the lifting seas our gaunt flo-
　　tilla rides,
　　　Drifting aimless to and fro,
　　　Sport of every wind a-blow,
　　　Swinging to the ebb and flow
　　　　Of lazy tropic tides.

And once we knew the clean seaways to sail
　　them pridefully;
And once we met the clean sea winds and gave
　　them greeting free;
And honest craft, they spoke us fair, who'd
　　scorn to speak us now;
And little craft, they'd not beware to cross a
　　German bow
When yet the flag of Germany had honor on
　　the sea.
　　　And now, of all that seaward fare,
　　　What ship of any port is there
　　　But would dip her flag to a black corsair
　　　　Ere she'd signal such as we!

Yet we are ribbed with Norseland steel and
    fleshed with Viking pine,
That's fashioned of the soil which bred the
    hosts of Charlemagne;
And clad we are with rusting pride of stays
    and links and plates
That lay within the mountain side where
    Barbarossa waits —
The mighty Frederick thralled in sleep, held
    by the ancient sign,
    While yet the ravens circle wide
    Above that guarded mountain side,
    Full fed with carrion from the tide
        Of swinish, red rapine!

Oh, we have known the German men when
    German men were true,
And we have borne the German flag when
    honor was her due;
But sick we are of honest scorn from honest
    merchant-men —
The winds they call us to be gone down to the
    seas again —
Down to the seas where waves lift white and
    gulls they sheer in the blue,
    Shriven clean of our blood-bought scorn
    By a foeman's flag — ay, proudly borne!
    Cleaving out in the good red dawn —
        Out again to the blue!

                DOROTHY PAUL.

Every effort was bent toward getting an army into
the field in the shortest possible time. General John
J. Pershing was appointed to command the Ameri-
can Expeditionary Forces, and started for France.
The National Guard was mobilized, volunteers
called for, and the First Division of regulars was
loaded on transports and, on June 14, headed out
to sea.

THE ROAD TO FRANCE

THANK God our liberating lance
Goes flaming on the way to France!
To France — the trail the Gurkhas found!
To France — old England's rallying ground!
To France — the path the Russians strode!
To France — the Anzac's glory road!
To France — where our Lost Legion ran
To fight and die for God and man!
To France — with every race and breed
That hates Oppression's brutal creed!

Ah France — how could our hearts
    forget
The path by which came Lafayette?
How could the haze of doubt hang low
Upon the road of Rochambeau?
At last, thank God! At last we see
There is no tribal Liberty!
No beacon lighting just our shores!
No Freedom guarding but our doors!
The flame she kindled for our sires
Burns now in Europe's battle fires!
The soul that led our fathers west
Turns back to free the world's op-
    pressed!

Allies, you have not called in vain;
We share your conflict and your pain.
"Old Glory," through new stains and rents,
Partakes of Freedom's sacraments.
Into that hell his will creates
We drive the foe — his lusts, his hates.
Last come, we will be last to stay,
Till Right has had her crowning day.
Replenish, comrades, from our veins,
The blood the sword of despot drains,
And make our eager sacrifice
Part of the freely-rendered price
You pay to lift humanity —
You pay to make our brothers free!
See, with what proud hearts we advance
        To France!

                DANIEL HENDERSON.

General Pershing, with his staff, reached England
early in June, and crossed to France a few days later.
On the Fourth of July, a parade of American troops
took place in Paris, proceeding to the Picpus ceme-
tery, where General Pershing placed a wreath on the
tomb of Lafayette, and Colonel C. E. Stanton, one
of his aides, made a short address, ending with the
words, "Lafayette, we are here!"

PERSHING AT THE TOMB OF LAFAYETTE

[July 4, 1917]

THEY knew they were fighting our war. As
    the months grew to years
Their men and their women had watched
    through their blood and their tears
For a sign that we knew, we who could not
    have come to be free
Without France, long ago. And at last from
    the threatening sea

The stars of our strength on the eyes of their
    weariness rose,
And he stood among them, the sorrow-strong
    hero we chose
To carry our flag to the tomb of that French-
    man whose name
A man of our country could once more pro-
    nounce without shame.
What crown of rich words would he set for all
    time on this day?
The past and the future were listening what
    he would say —
Only this, from the white-flaming heart of a
    passion austere,
Only this — ah, but France understood!
    "Lafayette, we are here!"

                AMELIA JOSEPHINE BURR.

An army of at least 2,000,000 men was needed at
once; to secure it with the least possible disturbance
of the country's economic life, Congress passed a
bill providing for a selective draft of all men between
twenty-one and thirty. Great training-camps were
built, and by September, the training of the National
Army was in full swing, while the National Guard
regiments, which had already had some training,
were started on their way to France.

YOUR LAD, AND MY LAD

DOWN toward the deep-blue water, marching
    to throb of drum,
From city street and country lane the lines of
    khaki come;
The rumbling guns, the sturdy tread, are full
    of grim appeal,
While rays of western sunshine flash back
    from burnished steel.
With eager eyes and cheeks aflame the serried
    ranks advance;
And your dear lad, and my dear lad, are on
    their way to France.

A sob clings choking in the throat, as file on
    file sweep by,
Between those cheering multitudes, to where
    the great ships lie;
The batteries halt, the columns wheel, to
    clear-toned bugle-call,
With shoulders squared and faces front they
    stand a khaki wall.

Tears shine on every watcher's cheek, love
    speaks in every glance;
For your dear lad, and my dear lad, are on
    their way to France.

Before them, through a mist of years, in sol-
    dier buff or blue,
Brave comrades from a thousand fields watch
    now in proud review;
The same old Flag, the same old Faith — the
    Freedom of the World —
Spells Duty in those flapping folds above long
    ranks unfurled.
Strong are the hearts which bear along De-
    mocracy's advance,
As your dear lad, and my dear lad, go on their
    way to France.

The word rings out; a million feet tramp for-
    ward on the road,
Along that path of sacrifice o'er which their
    fathers strode.
With eager eyes and cheeks aflame, with cheers
    on smiling lips,
These fighting men of '17 move onward to
    their ships.
Nor even love may hold them back, or halt
    that stern advance,
As your dear lad, and my dear lad, go on their
    way to France.

                RANDALL PARRISH.

Germany had boasted that we could never get
an army to Europe past her submarines, but so
efficient was the system of protection worked out by
the navy, that only one loaded transport was sunk.
Early in February, 1918, the Tuscania, carrying
2179 American soldiers, was torpedoed off the north
coast of Ireland. British destroyers rescued all but
about two hundred before the ship sank. Nearly
all the bodies were washed ashore and were tenderly
buried.

A CALL TO ARMS

[February 5, 1918]

IT is I, America, calling!
    Above the sound of rivers falling,
Above the whir of the wheels and the chime
    of bells in the steeple
— Wheels, rolling gold into the palms of the
    people —

Bells ringing silverly clear and slow
To church-going, leisurely steps on pavements
below.
Above all familiar sounds of the life of a na-
tion
I shout to you a name.
And the flame of that name is sped
Like fire into hearts where blood runs red —
The hearts of the land burn hot to the land's
salvation
As I call across the long miles, as I, America,
call to my nation
Tuscania! Tuscania!
Americans, remember the *Tuscania!*

Shall we not remember how they died
In their young courage and loyalty and pride,
Our boys — bright-eyed, clean lads of Amer-
ica's breed,
Hearts of gold, limbs of steel, flower of the
nation indeed?
How they tossed their years to be
Into icy waters of a winter sea
That we whom they loved — that the world
which they loved should be free?
Ready, ungrudging, they died, each one
thinking, likely, as the moment was
come
Of the dear, starry flag, worth dying for, and
then of dear faces at home;
Going down in good order, with a song on
their lips of the land of the free and
the brave
Till each young, deep voice stopped — under
the rush of a wave.
Was it like that? And shall their memory
ever grow pale?
Not ever, till the stars in the flag of America
fail.
It is I, America, who swear it, calling
Over the sound of that deep ocean's falling,
Tuscania! Tuscania!
Arm, arm, Americans! Remember the *Tus-
cania!*

Very peacefully they are sleeping
In friendly earth, unmindful of a nation's
weeping,
And the kindly, strange folk that honored the
long, full graves, we know;
And the mothers know that their boys are safe,
now, from the hurts of a savage foe;

It is for us who are left to make sure and plain
That these dead, our precious dead, shall not
have died in vain;
So that I, America, young and strong and not
afraid,
I set my face across that sea which swallowed
the bodies of the sons I made,
I set my eyes on the still faces of boys washed
up on a distant shore
And I call with a shout to my own to end this
horror forevermore!
In the boys' names I call a name,
And the nation leaps to fire in its flame
And my sons and my daughters crowd, eager to
end the shame —
It is I, America, calling,
Hoarse with the roar of that ocean falling,
Tuscania! Tuscania!
Arm, arm, Americans! And remember, re-
member, the *Tuscania!*

MARY RAYMOND SHIPMAN ANDREWS.

Meanwhile, in France, the Americans were al-
ready taking part in the war. About the middle of
October, the First division had been sent into a here-
tofore quiet sector of the trenches beyond Einville,
in Lorraine. On October 25, we took our first pris-
oner; a few days later, we had our first wounded;
and finally before dawn on the morning of November
3, came a swift German raid in which three Americans
were killed, five wounded and eleven taken prisoner.
The three, whose names were Corporal James D.
Gresham, Private Thomas F. Enright, and Private
Merle D. Hay, were buried at Bathlemont next day,
with touching ceremonies.

THE FIRST THREE

[November 3, 1917]

"SOMEWHERE in France," upon a brown hill-
side,
They lie, the first of our brave soldiers slain;
Above them flowers, now beaten by the rain,
Yet emblematic of the youths who died
In their fresh promise. They who, valiant-
eyed,
Met death unfaltering have not fallen in vain;
Remembrance hallows those who thus attain
The final goal; their names are glorified.
Read then the roster! — Gresham! Enright!
Hay! —
No bugle call shall rouse them when the flower
Of morning breaks above the hills and dells,
For they have grown immortal in an hour,

And we who grieve and cherish them would
lay
Upon their hillside graves our immortelles!

CLINTON SCOLLARD.

TO AMERICA, ON HER FIRST SONS FALLEN IN THE GREAT WAR

Now you are one with us, you know our tears,
Those tears of pride and pain so fast to flow;
You too have sipped the first strange draught
of woe;
You too have tasted of our hopes and fears;
Sister across the ocean, stretch your hand,
Must we not love you more, who learn to un-
derstand?

There are new graves in France, new quiet
graves;
The first-fruit of a Nation great and free,
Full of rich fire of life and chivalry.
Lie quietly, though tide of battle laves
Above them; sister, sister, see our tears,
We mourn with you, who know so well the
bitter years.

Now do you watch with us; your pain of loss
Lit by a wondrous glow of love and power
That flowers, star-like at the darkest hour
Lighting the eternal message of the Cross;
They gain their life who lose it, earth shall rise
Anew and cleansed, because of life's great
sacrifice.

And that great band of souls your dead have
met,
Who saved the world in centuries past and
gone,
Shall find new comrades in their valiant throng;
O, Nation's heart that cannot e'er forget,
Is not death but the door to life begun
To those who hear far Heaven cry, "Well
done!"

E. M. WALKER.

Training proceeded rapidly, and the sectors where
its final stages took place became more and more
lively as the Americans were gradually given a freer
and freer hand.

ROUGE BOUQUET

[March 7, 1918]

In a wood they call the Rouge Bouquet
There is a new-made grave to-day,
Built by never a spade nor pick
Yet covered with earth ten metres thick.
There lie many fighting men,
  Dead in their youthful prime,
Never to laugh nor love again
  Nor taste the Summertime.
For Death came flying through the air
And stopped his flight at the dugout stair.
Touched his prey and left them there,
  Clay to clay.
He hid their bodies stealthily
In the soil of the land they fought to free
  And fled away.
Now over the grave abrupt and clear
  Three volleys ring;
And perhaps their brave young spirits hear
  The bugle sing:
"Go to sleep!
Go to sleep!
Slumber well where the shell screamed and fell
Let your rifles rest on the muddy floor,
You will not need them any more.
Danger's past;
Now at last,
Go to sleep!"

There is on earth no worthier grave
To hold the bodies of the brave
Than this place of pain and pride
Where they nobly fought and nobly died.
Never fear but in the skies
  Saints and angels stand
Smiling with their holy eyes
  On this new-come band.
St. Michael's sword darts through the air
And touches the aureole on his hair
As he sees them stand saluting there,
  His stalwart sons:
And Patrick, Brigid, Columkill
Rejoice that in veins of warriors still
  The Gael's blood runs.
And up to Heaven's doorway floats,
  From the wood called Rouge Bouquet,
A delicate cloud of bugle notes
  That softly say:
"Farewell!
Farewell!

Comrades true, born anew, peace to you!
Your souls shall be where the heroes are
And your memory shine like the morning-star.
Brave and dear,
Shield us here.
Farewell!"

JOYCE KILMER.

The great summons came in the spring of 1918, for on March 21 the Germans began a series of terrific attacks which they believed would end the war. On March 31 an official note announced that "the Star-Spangled Banner will float beside the French and English flags in the plains of Picardy." On April 17 the order came for the First Division to move into the battle area.

MARCHING SONG

[April 17, 1918]

WHEN Pershing's men go marching into Picardy.
Marching, marching into Picardy —
With their steel aslant in the sunlight and their great gray hawks a-wing
And their wagons rumbling after them like thunder in the Spring —

Tramp, tramp, tramp, tramp
Till the earth is shaken —
Tramp, tramp, tramp, tramp
Till the dead towns waken!
And flowers fall and shouts arise from Chaumont to the sea —
When Pershing's men go marching, marching into Picardy.

Women of France, do you see them pass to the battle in the North?
And do you stand in the doorways now as when your own went forth?
Then smile to them and call to them, and mark how brave they fare
Upon the road to Picardy that only youth may dare!

Tramp, tramp, tramp, tramp,
Foot and horse and caisson —
Tramp, tramp, tramp, tramp,
Such is Freedom's passion —
And oh, take heart, ye weary souls that stand along the Lys,
For the New World is marching, marching into Picardy!

April's sun is in the sky and April's in the grass —
And I doubt not that Pershing's men are singing as they pass —
For they are very young men, and brave men, and free,
And they know why they are marching, marching into Picardy.

Tramp, tramp, tramp, tramp,
Rank and file together —
Tramp, tramp, tramp, tramp,
Through the April weather.
And never Spring has thrust such blades against the light of dawn
As yonder waving stalks of steel that move so shining on!

I have seen the wooden crosses at Ypres and Verdun,
I have marked the graves of such as lie where the Marne waters run,
And I know their dust is stirring by hill and vale and lea,
And their souls shall be our captains who march to Picardy.

Tramp, tramp, tramp, tramp,
Hope shall fail us never —
Tramp, tramp, tramp, tramp,
Forward, and forever!
And God is in His judgment seat, and Christ is on His tree —
And Pershing's men are marching, marching into Picardy.

DANA BURNET.

On June 2, the Second and Third Divisions met and checked the enemy at Château-Thierry. The Marne offensive was followed sharply by another on the part of the British, with whom our Twenty-Seventh Division was fighting, and on August 8 the Twenty-Seventh broke through the famous Hindenburg line

OUR MODEST DOUGHBOYS

[August 8, 1918]

SAID the Captain: "There was wire
A mile deep in No Man's Land,
And the concentrated fire
Was all mortal nerve could stand;

But these huskies craved the chance
  To go out and leave their bones!"
"*The climate's quite some damp in France,*"
  Said Private Thomas Jones.

Said the Major: "What is more,
  At the point where we attacked,
Tough old veterans loudly swore
  Hindy's line could not be cracked.
But the 27th said,
  'Hindenburg! That guy's a myth!'"
"*I slept last night in a reg'lar bed,*"
  Said Private Johnny Smith.

Said the Colonel: "They had placed
  Pillboxes on the crests.
I can safely say we faced
  Maybe thousands of those nests.
But our doughboys took one height
  Seven times in that hell's hail."
"*And were the cooties thick? Good night!*"
  Said Private William Dale.

Said the General: "We were told
  Anything we'd start they'd stop —
That the Boche would knock us cold
  When we slid across the top.
But the 7th with a yell
  Made the Prussian Guards back down."
"*You oughta lamped the smile on Nell!*"
  Said Private Henry Brown.

Said the Sergeant: "Every shell
  Seemed to whine, 'Old scout, you're dead!'
And I thought I'd gone to hell
  In a blizzard of hot lead.
But each bloomin' gunner stuck
  At his post by his machine."
"*Our orders said to hold it, Buck!*"
  Said Private Peter Green.

Said the Chaplain: "Talk of pep!
  They were there! And, may I add,
When we clambered up the step
  That last fight, we only had
Eighty men of Company D —
  Every one, I'll say, a man!"
"*And am I glad I'm home? Ah, oui!*"
  Said Private Mike McCann.
              CHARLTON ANDREWS.

Early in September eight American divisions were concentrated on the Lorraine front and organized into the First American Army.   On September 12 an assault in force was made against the St.-Mihiel salient, which had threatened France for four years. Twenty-four hours later the salient was ours, together with 15,000 prisoners.

SEICHEPREY

[September 12, 1918]

A HANDFUL came to Seicheprey
  When winter woods were bare,
When ice was in the trenches
  And snow was in the air.
The foe looked down on Seicheprey
  And laughed to see them there.

The months crept by at Seicheprey
  The growing handful stayed,
With growling guns at midnight,
  At dawn, the lightning raid,
And learned, in Seicheprey trenches,
  How war's red game is played.

September came to Seicheprey;
  A slow-wrought host arose
And rolled across the trenches
  And whelmed its sneering foes,
And left to shattered Seicheprey
  Unending, sweet repose.

Two weeks later we began our greatest battle in an attack on the strong German positions running from the Meuse westward through the Argonne forest. It was in this battle that perhaps the most remarkable single exploit of the war was performed, when Corporal Alvin C. York, a young giant from the mountains of Tennessee, who had been sent forward with a small squad to clean up some machine-gun nests, was reported in the press dispatches to have killed twenty-eight Germans single-handed, and to have brought 132 prisoners back to the American lines.

A BALLAD OF REDHEAD'S DAY

[October 8, 1918]

TALK of the Greeks at Thermopylæ!
  They fought like mad till the last was dead;
But Alvin C. York, of Tennessee,
  Stayed cool to the end though his hair was
    red,
Stayed mountain cool, yet blazed that gray
October the Eighth as Redhead's Day.

With rifle and pistol and redhead nerve
He captured one hundred and thirty-two;
A battalion against him, he did not swerve
From the Titans' task they were sent to do —
Fourteen men under Sergeant Early
And York, the blacksmith, big and burly.

Sixteen only, but fighters all,
They dared the brood of a devil's nest,
And three of those that did not fall
Were wounded and out of the scrap; the rest
Were guarding a bunch of Boche they'd
caught,
When both were trapped by a fresh onslaught.

Excepting York, who smiled "Amen,"
And, spotting the nests of spitting guns,
Potted some twenty birds, and then
Did with his pistol for eight more Huns
Who thought they could crush a Yankee alive
In each red pound of two hundred and five.

That was enough for kill-babe Fritz:
Ninety in all threw up their hands,
Suddenly tender as lamb at the Ritz,
Milder than sheep to a York's commands;
And back to his line he drove the herd,
Gathering more on the way — Absurd!

Absurd, but true — ay, gospel fact;
For here was a man with a level head,
Who, scorning to fail for the help he lacked,
Helped himself till he won instead;
An elder was he in the Church of Christ,
Immortal at thirty; his faith sufficed.
                    RICHARD BUTLER GLAENZER.

While our Argonne offensive was in progress, the
French and English had been striking mighty blows
at other portions of the German line, and everywhere
the enemy was in retreat. Realizing that their power
was broken and to save themselves from imminent
disaster, the Germans asked for an armistice. It was
offered on terms so drastic that many thought the
Germans would not sign, but they did, and at eleven
o'clock on the morning of November 11, 1918, firing
ceased all along the front.

VICTORY BELLS

I HEARD the bells across the trees,
I heard them ride the plunging breeze
Above the roofs from tower and spire,
And they were leaping like a fire,

And they were shining like a stream
With sun to make its music gleam.
Deep tones as though the thunder tolled,
Cool voices thin as tinkling gold,
They shook the spangled autumn down
From out the tree-tops of the town;
They left great furrows in the air
And made a clangor everywhere
As of metallic wings. They flew
Aloft in spirals to the blue
Tall tent of heaven and disappeared.
And others, swift as though they feared
The people might not heed their cry
Went shouting VICTORY up the sky.
They did not say that war is done,
Only that glory has begun
Like sunrise, and the coming day
Will burn the clouds of war away.
There will be time for dreams again,
And home-coming for weary men.
                    GRACE HAZARD CONKLING.

America had lost nearly fifty thousand men killed
in battle, and immediately after the armistice, work
was begun gathering together their bodies, scat-
tered over many battlefields, and re-interring them
in beautiful cemeteries, where their graves would be
perpetually cared for and honored.

EPICEDIUM

IN MEMORY OF AMERICA'S DEAD IN THE
GREAT WAR

No more for them shall Evening's rose unclose,
Nor Dawn's emblazoned panoplies be spread;
Alike, the Rain's warm kiss, and stabbing
snows,
Unminded, fall upon each hallowed head.
But the Bugles as they leap and wildly sing,
Rejoice, . . . remembering.

The guns' mad music their young years have
known —
War's lullabies that moaned on Flanders Plain;
To-night the wind walks on them, still as stone,
Where they lie huddled close as riven grain.
But the Drums, reverberating, proudly roll —
They love a Soldier's soul!

With arms outflung, and eyes that laughed at
Death,
They drank the wine of sacrifice and loss;
For them a life-time spanned a burning breath,

And Truth they visioned, clean of earthly
   dross.
But the Fifes — can ye not hear their lusty
   shriek?
   They know, and now they speak!

The lazy drift of cloud, the noon-day hum
Of vagrant bees, the lark's untrammeled song
Shall gladden them no more, who now lie dumb
In Death's strange sleep, yet once were swift
   and strong.
But the Bells that to all living listeners peal,
   With joy their deeds reveal!

They have given their lives, with bodies bruised
   and broken,
Upon their Country's altar they have bled;
They have left, as priceless heritage, a token
That Honor lives forever with the dead.
And the Bugles, as their rich notes rise and
   fall —
   They answer, knowing all.
                           J. CORSON MILLER.

THE DEAD

THINK you the dead are lonely in that place?
   They are companioned by the leaves and
      grass,
By many a beautiful and vanished face,
   By all the strange and lovely things that
      pass.
Sunsets and dawnings and the starry vast,
   The swinging moon, the tracery of trees —
These they shall know more perfectly at last,
   They shall be intimate with such as these.
'T is only for the living Beauty dies,
   Fades and drifts from us with too brief a
      grace,
Beyond the changing tapestry of skies
   Where dwells her perfect and immortal face.
For us the passage brief; — the happy dead
Are ever by great beauty visited.
                           DAVID MORTON.

THE UNRETURNING

FOR us, the dead, though young,
   For us, who fought and bled,
Let a last song be sung,
   And a last word be said!

Dreams, hopes, and high desires,
   That leaven and uplift,
On sacrificial fires
   We offered as a gift.

We gave, and gave our all,
   In gladness, though in pain;
Let not a whisper fall
   That we have died in vain!
                           CLINTON SCOLLARD.

To America's soldier dead was added, on January
6, 1919, a valiant and righteous warrior, Theodore
Roosevelt, whose sudden death at the age of sixty-
one was a shock to the whole country.

THE STAR

[January 6, 1919]

GREAT soul, to all brave souls akin,
   High bearer of the torch of truth,
Have you not gone to marshal in
   Those eager hosts of youth?

Flung outward by the battle's tide,
   They met in regions dim and far;
And you — in whom youth never died —
   Shall lead them, as a star!
                           MARION COUTHOUY SMITH.

Arrangements for sending home the American army
were begun immediately after the armistice, and
within a few months a steady stream of khaki-clad
troops was flowing through the port of Brest, bound
for America.

BREST LEFT BEHIND

THE sun strikes gold the dirty street,
The band blares, the drums insist,
And brown legs twinkle and muscles twist —
Pound! — Pound! — the rhythmic feet.
The laughing street-boys shout,
And a couple of hags come out
To grin and bob and clap.
Stiff rusty black their dresses,
And crispy white their Breton cap,
Prim on white, smooth tresses.

Wait! . . . Wait! . . . While dun clouds droop
Over the sunlit docks,
Over the wet gray rocks
And mast of steamer and sloop.

And the old squat towers,
Damp gray and mossy brown,
Where lovely Ann looked down
And dreamed rich dreams through long luxu-
    rious hours.

Sudden and swift, it rains!
Familiar, fogging, gray;
It blots the sky away
And cuts the face with biting little pains.
We grunt and poke shoes free of muddy cakes,
Watching them messing out
Upon the dock in thick brown lakes —
"No more French mud!" the sergeant cries,
And someone swears, and someone sighs,
And the neat squads swing about.

Silent the looming hulk above —
No camouflage this time —
She's white and tan and black!
Hurry, bend, climb,
Push forward, stagger back!
How clean the wide deck seems,
The bunks, how trim;
And, oh, the musty smell of ships!
Faces are set and grim,
Thinking of months, this hope was pain;
And eyes are full of dreams,
And gay little tunes come springing to the
    lips —
Home, home, again, again!

She's moving now,
Across the prow
The dusk-soft harbor bursts
Into a shivering bloom of light
From warehouse, warship, transport, tramp,
And countless little bobbing masts
Each flouts the night
With eager boastful lamp —
Bright now, now dimmer, dimmer,
Fewer and fewer glimmer.
Only the lights that mark the passing shore,
Lofty and lonely star the gray —
Then are no more.
We are alone with dusk and creamy spray.

The captain coughs, remembering the rain.
The major coughs remembering the mud.
Some shudder at the horror of dark blood,
Or wine-wet kisses, lewd.
Some sigh, remembering new loves and fare-
    well pain.

Some smile, remembering old loves to be re-
    newed.
Silent, we stare across the deepening night.
France vanishing! — Swift, swift, the curling
    waves —
Fights and despair,
And faces fair;
Proud heads held high
For Victory;
And flags above friends' graves.

The group buzzes, rustles, hums,
Then stiffens as the colonel comes,
A burly figure in the mellow light,
With haughty, kingly ways.
He does not scan the night,
Nor hissing spray that flies,
But his cold old glance plays
Along the level of our eyes.

"I don't see very many tears," he says.
            JOHN CHIPMAN FARRAR.

America went wild in welcoming them, as they
arrived division after division. There were parades
and celebrations; but with surprising swiftness the
divisions were demobilized and the men returned to
civil life.

TO THE RETURNING BRAVE

VICTORIOUS knights without reproach or
    fear —
As close as man is ever to the stars! —
Our welcome met you on the ocean drear
    In loud, free winds and sunset's golden
        bars.
      Here, at our bannered gate
      Love, honor, laurels wait.
Though you be humble, we are proud, and,
    in your stead, elate.

Fame shall not tire to tell, no sordid stain
    Lies on your purpose, on your record none.
No broken word, no violated fane,
    No winning one could wish had ne'er been
        won.
      You were our message sent
      To the torn Continent:
That with its hope and faith henceforth our
    faith and hope are blent.

You of our new, our homespun chivalry,
  Here is your welcome — in all women's eyes,
The envious handclasp, romping children's
    glee,
    Music, and color, and glad tears that rise.
    Here every voice of Peace
    Shall bruit our joy, nor cease
To vie with shotless guns to shout your blame-
    less victories.

But, though you are a part of all men's pride,
  And from your fortitude new nations date,
Oh, lay not yet your sacred steel aside,
  But save it for the still-imperiled State.
    You who have bound a girth
    Of new hope round the Earth,
Should its firm bond be loosened here, what
    were your struggle worth?

A redder peril dogs the path of war;
  With fire and poison wanton children play;
And fickle crowds toward new pretenders
    pour
    Who summon demons they can never lay.
    Already we can hear,
    Importunately near,
The snarling of the savage crew, half fury and
    half jeer.

Then hang not up your arms till you have
    taught
    The ungrateful guests about our hearth and
    board
That in your swift encounter has been wrought
  A keener edge to our reluctant sword.
    You who know well the price
    Of the great sacrifice,
Your courage saved us once; pray Heaven, it
    need not save us twice.

And those who come not back, who mutely lie
  By Marne or Meuse or tangled Argonne
    wood:
Were it to lose the gain, (let them reply!)
  Would we recall their spirits if we could?
    Open your ranks and save
    Their places with the brave,
That Liberty may greet you all, her shields of
    land and wave.
                ROBERT UNDERWOOD JOHNSON.

Amid all the celebrations, there was always the consciousness of those who would not return, in body, at least, but whose spirits would never be severed from America's.

THE RETURN

GOLDEN through the golden morning,
    Who is this that comes
With the pride of banners lifted,
    With the roll of drums?

With the self-same triumph shining
    In the ardent glance,
That divine, bright fate defiance
    That you bore to France.

You! But o'er your grave in Flanders
    Blow the winter gales;
Still for sorrow of your going
    All life's laughter fails.

Borne on flutes of dawn the answer:
    "O'er the foam's white track,
God's work done, so to our homeland
    Comes her hosting back.

"Come the dead men with the live men
    From the marshes far,
From the mounds in no man's valley,
    Lit by cross nor star.

"Come to blend with hers the essence
    Of their strength and pride,
All the radiance of the dreaming
    For whose truth they died."

So the dead men with the live men
    Pass, an hosting fair,
And the stone is rolled forever
    From the soul's despair.
                ELEANOR ROGERS COX.

One distinguished visitor was welcomed by the American people as they welcomed their own sons — King Albert, of Belgium, who made an extensive tour of the United States in the summer of 1919.

KING OF THE BELGIANS

How spoke the King, in his crucial hour vic-
    torious?
The words of a high decision, few, but glorious.

What was the choice he made, that all fear
    surmounted?
The choice of a man — that leaves not the
    soul uncounted.

What did the King, in bitter defeat and
    sorrow?
He stood as a god, foreseeing a great to-
    morrow.

How fought the King? In silent and stern
    persistence;
Patience and power within, and hope in the
    distance.

What was the gift he won, in the fire that tried
    him?
The deathless love of his own, who fought be-
    side him.

What is his crown, the noblest of all for wear-
    ing?
The homage of hearts that beat for his splen-
    did bearing.

Robe and sceptre and crown — what are these
    for holding?
Vesture and sign for his spirit's royal moulding.

What speaks he now, in the hour of faith vic-
    torious?
Words of a quiet gladness, few, but glorious.

Then, as we greet him, what shall be ours to
    render?
Silence that shines, and speech that is proud
    and tender?
            MARION COUTHOUY SMITH.

Meanwhile, at Paris, the Peace Conference, under
the leadership of President Woodrow Wilson, who
had broken all precedents by going to Europe, was
struggling with the peace treaty For America, the
great conflict had been a war to end war, and the
President insisted that provisions to establish a
League of Nations should be made an integral part
of the treaty.

THE FAMILY OF NATIONS

WITH that pathetic impudence of youth,
America, half-formed, gigantic and uncouth,
Stretching great limbs, in something of sur-
    prise
Beholds new meaning written on the skies.

Out of the granite, Time has reared a State
Haughty and fearless, awkward, passionate —
For all his dreaming and his reckless boast,
Betrayed by those whom he has trusted most.

Years of stern peril knit that welded frame,
Banded those arms and set that heart aflame,
Burdened those loins with vigor of increase,
Gave to his hand a weapon forged to peace.

He cannot turn the discovering hour aside,
He feels the stir that will not be denied,
And in the family the Nations plan
Forgets the boy and finds himself a man!
            WILLARD WATTLES.

After months of struggle and negotiation, this
purpose was achieved, and on July 10, 1919, the
President laid the treaty before the Senate for confir-
mation. Strong opposition to the League of Nations
developed immediately, on the ground that it inter-
fered with America's independence and freedom of
action, and various "reservations" were proposed,
limiting America's participation. These the Presi-
dent refused to accept, and finally, after eight months
of bitter debate, largely partisan and personal, the
Senate rejected the treaty March 19, 1920.

THE LEAGUE OF NATIONS

Lo, Joseph dreams his dream again,
And Joan leads her armies in the night,
And somewhere near, the Master from His
    cross
Lifts his hurt hands and heals the world again!
For from the great red welter of the world,
Out from the tides of its red suffering
Comes the slow sunrise of the ancient dream —
Is flung the glory of its bright imagining.
See how it breaks in beauty on the world,
Shivers and shudders on its trembling way —
Shivers and waits and trembles to be born!

America, young daughter of the gods, swing
    out,
Strong in the beauty of virginity,
Fearless in thine unquestioned leadership,
And hold the taper to the nations' torch,
And light the hearthfires of the halls of home.
Thine must it be to break an unpathed way,
To lift the torch for world's in-brothering —
To bring to birth this child of all the earth,
Formed of the marriage of all nations;

Else shall we go, the head upon the breast,
A Cain without a country, a Judas at the
board!

MARY SIEGRIST.

This refusal to enter the League was sustained, as
the years passed, by the weight of American opinion,
and every attempt to revive the question, either in
the Senate or in the House of Representatives, was
defeated.

BEYOND WARS

FOR THE LEAGUE OF NATIONS

Then will a quiet gather round the door,
    And settle on those evening fields again,
    Where women watch the slow, home-coming
        men
Across brown acres hoofed and hurt no
    more,
The sound of children's feet be on the floor,
    When lamps are lit, and stillness deeper falls,
    Unbroken, save where cattle in their stalls
Keep munching patiently upon their store.

Only a scar beside the pasture gate,
    A torn and naked tree upon the hill,
    What times remembered, will remind them
        still
Of long disastrous days they knew of late;
    Till these, too, yield for sweet, accustomed
        things, —
    And a man ploughs, a woman sews and
        sings.

DAVID MORTON.

In fact, the great mass of the American people were
so completely disillusioned by their one excursion
into foreign war, that they determined never to be
drawn into another; and when, within a few years of
the ending of the "war to end war," the nations of
Europe seemed headed toward an even more terrible
conflict, the Congress, backed by unanimous public
opinion, passed a stringent neutrality law, and di-
rected the President to enforce it the instant the
need arose.

"WHEN THERE IS PEACE"

"WHEN there is Peace, our land no more
    Will be the land we knew of yore."
    Thus do our facile seers foretell
    The truth that none can buy or sell
    And e'en the wisest must ignore.

When we have bled at every pore,
Shall we still strive for gear and store?
Will it be heaven? Will it be hell?
When there is Peace?

This let us pray for, this implore:
That, all base dreams thrust out at door,
We may in loftier aims excel
And, like men waking from a spell,
Grow stronger, nobler, than before,
When there is Peace.

AUSTIN DOBSON.

So "the wheel is come full circle," and America is
again occupied with her own destiny, with a new
sense of responsibility for the welfare of her citizens,
and a new determination that "government of the
people, by the people, for the people, shall not perish
from the earth."

AFTER THE WAR

AFTER the war — I hear men ask — what
    then?
As though this rock-ribbed world, sculptured
    with fire,
And bastioned deep in the ethereal plan
Can never be its morning self again
Because of this brief madness, man with man;
As though the laughing elements should tire,
The very seasons in their order reel;
As though indeed yon ghostly golden wheel
Of stars should cease from turning, or the moon
Befriend the night no more, or the wild rose
Forget the world, and June be no more June.

How many wars and long-forgotten woes
Unnumbered, nameless, made a like despair
In hearts long stilled; how many suns have set
On burning cities blackening the air, —
Yet dawn came dreaming back, her lashes wet
With dew, and daisies in her innocent hair.
Nor shall, for this, the soul's ascension pause,
Nor the sure evolution of the laws
That out of foulness lift the flower to sun,
And out of fury forge the evening star.

Deem not Love's building of the world un-
    done —
Far Love's beginning was, her end is far;
By paths of fire and blood her feet must climb,
Seeking a loveliness she scarcely knows,
Whose meaning is beyond the reach of Time.

RICHARD LE GALLIENNE.

NOTES AND INDEXES

NOTES

Page 3. THE STORY OF VINLAND. The discovery of America by the Norsemen is as well authenticated as any other fact of tenth-century history, and much better authenticated than most. There can be no doubt of the substantial accuracy of the Icelandic chronicle, and Mr. Lanier has followed it very closely.

Page 3. *Stout Are Marson.* Are Marsson. The stories concerning him and "Huitramannaland" are believed to be purely fanciful, an embroidery of fiction upon the historical background of the chronicles. There is no evidence that the Norsemen ever got farther south than Cape Cod, or, at most, Point Judith.

Page 7. *Mid-ships with iron keel.* The Norse boats had neither "iron keel" nor "ribs of steel." Keel and ribs were made of oak, and no evidence has been found of metallic sheathing. The size of these ships is usually underestimated. They were larger, stronger, and more seaworthy than those of Columbus. There is one in the museum at Christiania seventy-eight feet long, seventeen feet beam, and nearly six feet in depth. She carried a crew of at least thirty-five men. Henry Hudson's Half Moon carried a crew of only sixteen.

Page 7. *The lofty tower.* The old stone tower at Newport, around whose origin controversy raged for many years, but which is now believed to have been built by Benedict Arnold, governor of Newport, about 1676, for a windmill. The reader is referred to Palfrey's "History of New England," i, 57; Fiske's "Discovery of America," i, 214; and Drake's "New England Legends and Folk-lore," 393.

Page 7. *Beyond the limits he had vainly set.* The Pillars of Hercules, Gibraltar and Cape Serra.

Page 9. *St. Stephen's cloistered hall.* The conference was held at the Dominican convent of St. Stephen, at Salamanca.

Page 10. *Cordova's sage.* Seneca.

Page 12. *The far-seeing Marchioness.* Beatriz de Bobadilla, Marchioness of Moya, the bosom friend of the Queen, and a devoted admirer of Columbus. She happened to be with the Queen when Santangel rushed in demanding audience and told of Columbus's departure, and added her eloquence to his.

Page 14. *Pedro Gutierrez.* Pilot of the Santa Maria.

Page 14. *Sanchez of Segovia.* Roderigo Sanchez, inspector-general of the armament.

Page 16. *A Castilla y á Leon.* "To Castile and Leon Columbus gave a new world." This was the motto annexed to the coat of arms granted to Columbus.

Page 21. *The shining Cèpango.* Cipango was the name given by Marco Polo to an island east

of Asia, supposed to be the modern Japan. It was Cipango which Columbus and all the voyagers for half a century after him were seeking.

Page 25. *Old Las Casas.* Bartolomé de las Casas (1474–1566), a Spanish Dominican, celebrated as a defender of the Indians against their Spanish conquerors.

Page 30. *Moscoso.* Luis de Moscoso, who took charge of the expedition after De Soto's death.

Page 30. *Six thousand of our foemen.* The native loss was greatly exaggerated. It probably did not exceed five hundred.

Page 30. *And eighty-two of Spain.* The Spanish loss was 170. The scene of the battle is supposed to have been what is now known as Choctaw Bluff, in Clarke County, Alabama.

Page 31. *The cities of the Zuñi.* Coronado's expedition reached Cibola early in July, 1540, and a few days later carried it by storm and subdued the whole district, but found no treasure. A detailed account of the expedition will be found in Winsor's "Narrative and Critical History of America," ii, 473–503.

Page 34. *Good Bernard.* Bernard of Cluny, a French Benedictine monk of the twelfth century, author of "De Contemptu Mundi," popularly known through Neale's translation, "Jerusalem the Golden."

Page 34. *Do not fear.* The last words Gilbert is known to have spoken were the famous "We are as near to heaven by sea as by land." These are said to have been heard on board the companion ship, the Hind, a short time before the Squirrel disappeared.

Page 38. POCAHONTAS. This imaginative tale, from which all other narratives of the event are derived, appears in the second chapter of the third book of Smith's "The Generall Historie of Virginia, New England, and the Summer Isles" (London, 1622), and is as follows: —

"At last they brought him to *Meronoco moco*, where was Powhatan, their emperor. Here more than two hundred of these grim courtiers stood wondering at him as he had been a monster, till Powhatan and his train had put themselves in their greatest braveries. Before a fire, upon a seat like a bedstead, he sat covered with a great robe, made of Rarowcun skins, and all the tails hanging by. On either hand did sit a young wench of 16 or 18 years, and along on each side of the house, two rows of men, and behind them as many women, with all their heads and shoulders painted red; many of their heads bedecked with the white down of birds; but every one with something: and a great chain of white beads about their necks.

At his entrance before the King, all the people gave a great shout. The queen of *Appamatuck* was appointed to bring him water to wash his hands, and another brought him a bunch of feathers, instead of a towel to dry them: having feasted him after their best barbarous manner they could, a long consultation was held, but the conclusion was, two great stones were brought before Powhatan; then as many as could laid hand on him, dragged him to them, and thereon laid his head, and being ready with their clubs to beat out his brains, Pocahontas, the king's dearest daughter, when no entreaty could prevail, got his head in her arms, and laid her own upon his to save him from death: whereat the emperor was contented he should live to make him hatchets, and her bells, beads, and copper: for they thought him as well of all occupations as themselves. For the king himself will make his own robes, shoes, bows, arrows, pots; plant, hunt, or do anything so well as the rest.

> "They say he bore a pleasant show,
> But sure his heart was sad,
> For who can pleasant be, and rest,
> That lives in fear and dread:
> And having life suspected, doth
> It still suspected lead."

In spite of which, it is generally agreed among historians that no such incident ever occurred. One can only remark that Smith seems to have had a genius for imaginative detail worthy of Defoe.

Page 40. *Richard Rich* was a soldier and adventurer who accompanied Captain Newport in the Sea Venture, and experienced all the dangers and hardships of that remarkable voyage. He finally got back to England in 1610, and on the first day of October, published this poem, his object being, as he says in a brief and broadly humorous preface, to " spread the truth " about the new colony, whose attractions had so impressed him that he was resolved to return thither with Captain Newport in the following year. He speaks of another book of his soon to be issued, also devoted to a description of the colony, but no copy of it has ever been discovered, nor is anything known concerning Rich's subsequent adventures. A copy of his " Newes from Virginia " was found in 1864 in Lord Charlemont's collection, and is now in the Huth Library.

Page 40. *Gates.* Sir Thomas Gates, lieutenant-general of the new company.

Page 40. *Newport.* Christopher Newport (1565?-1617) had had an adventurous career as a corsair in the West Indies, where he sacked four Spanish towns, and destroyed no less than twenty Spanish vessels.

Page 40. *Eleaven months.* June 2, 1609–May 24, 1610.

Page 40. *Inhabited by hogges.* The descendants, presumably, of those left by the Spaniards.

Page 40. *Two only.* Six of the company died on the island.

Page 40. *A son and daughter.* These details

are confirmed in " A True Repertory of the Wracke and Redemption of Sir Thomas Gates upon and from the Islands of the Bermudas," or from Silas Jourdan's " Discovery of the Barmudas . . . by Sir T. Gates . . . with divers others " (1610); to both of which Shakespeare is said to have been indebted for the groundwork of " The Tempest."

Page 43. THE MARRIAGE OF POCAHONTAS. There is some doubt as to whether the marriage occurred in 1613 or 1614. The former has been the more generally accepted date, but the compiler has adopted the latter on the authority of Mr. Wyndham Robertson, who has made an exhaustive study of the question, the results of which were embodied in a paper read before the Virginia Historical Society in 1860. Mr. Robertson proves pretty conclusively that April 5, 1614, is the correct date.

Page 43. *Sparkling-Water.* The English meaning of Pocahontas.

Page 45. *The town shall not rise from its ashes again.* Jamestown, at the time it was burned, consisted of a church, statehouse, and about eighteen dwellings, mostly of brick. Only the tower of the church and a few chimneys were left standing.

Page 45. BACON'S EPITAPH. This remarkable poem has been preserved in an anonymous " History of Bacon's and Ingram's Rebellion," known as " The Burwell Papers," and printed by the Massachusetts Historical Society in 1814. The " Burwell Papers " have been attributed to a planter named Cotton of Acquia Creek, but this is only conjecture, and there seems to be absolutely no clue to the authorship of the elegy, which will probably always remain one of the literary mysteries of America.

Page 48. THE DOWNFALL OF PIRACY. This is thought to be one of the ballads referred to by Benjamin Franklin in his autobiography. He says: " I now took a fancy to poetry, and made some little pieces. My brother, thinking it might turn to account, encouraged me, and put me on composing occasional ballads. One was called 'The Lighthouse Tragedy,' and contained an account of the drowning of Captain Worthilake, with his two daughters ; the other was a sailor song on the taking of Teach (or Blackbeard) the pirate."

It had been thought for many years that both of these ballads were lost, but " The Downfall of Piracy " was discovered by Dr. Edward Everett Hale in a volume entitled " Some Real Sea-Songs," edited by Mr. John Ashton, and published in London. There is, in Dr. Hale's opinion, no doubt that it is one of the Franklin ballads. The news of the fight probably reached Boston about the first of January, 1719, in the broadside we no doubt written soon after. Of " The Lighthouse Tragedy " no trace has been found.

Page 50. *'T was Juet spoke.* Robert Juet accompanied Hudson as mate on his previous voyage, and on this one acted as clerk. He kept a curious journal of the voyage, which has been preserved in Purchas's third volume.

Page 52. THE PRAISE OF NEW NETHER-LAND. The full title, in English, is "The Praise of New Netherland: wherein are briefly and truly shown the excellent qualities which it possesses in the purity of the air, fertility of the soil, production of the cattle, abundance of game and fish, with its advantages for naviga-tion and commerce." It was printed at Am-sterdam "for Jacobus Van Der Fuyk, book-seller in the Still-Alley, Anno 1661." Steendam had returned to Amsterdam, it is thought only on a visit, at the time of the publication of this poem. It is dedicated to "The Honorable Cor-nelis van Ruyven, councillor and secretary of the Hon. West India Company there. Faithful and very upright Promoter of New Nether-land."

Page 54. *Noch vaster.* A play upon words, a whimsical device adopted by Steendam. Steendam means "stone dam," and *noch vaster,* "still firmer." Notwithstanding which he seems to have been "a man of very unsettled purposes of life."

Page 58. *Bartholomew Gosnold's 'headlands.'* Gosnold commanded an expedition which, in 1602, discovered Cape Cod and Martha's Vine-yard, both of which were named by him.

Page 63. THE EXPEDITION TO WESSAGUS-SET. Mr. Longfellow has followed the account of this expedition given in Winslow's Relation of "Standish's Expedition against the Indians of Weymouth." He has, however, turned the incident of Standish's killing of the chiefs, Pecksuot and Wituwamat, into a much more open and heroic piece of conduct than the chronicle admits. The killing really occurred in a room into which Standish and a few of his men had enticed them. This was the first In-dian blood shed by the Pilgrims. A general battle followed in the open field, from which the Indians fled and in which no lives were lost.

"Concerning the killing of those poor In-dians," wrote Robinson of Leyden (December 16, 1623), "of which we heard first by report and since by more certain relation, O how happy a thing had it been, if you had converted some before you had killed any!"

Page 65. NEW ENGLAND'S ANNOYANCES. These verses are undoubtedly of a very early date, probably about 1630. Rufus W. Griswold, in his introduction to "The Poets and Poetry of America" (Philadelphia, 1854), calls them "the first verses by a colonist," a statement which is, of course, impossible of proof. They appeared originally in the Massachusetts Historical Col-lections, with the statement that they were "taken memoriter, in 1785, from the lips of an old lady at the advanced age of 96."

Page 73. ANNE HUTCHINSON'S EXILE. The basis of the famous Antinomian controversy, as it was called, was the promulgation, by Mrs. Hutchinson, of "two dangerous errors: first, that the person of the Holy Ghost dwells in a justified person; second, that no sanctification can help to evidence to us our justification." The words are Winthrop's. To these two doc-trines Mrs. Hutchinson attached so much im-portance that she undertook the public minis-tration of them. Sir Harry Vane, the young governor of the colony, was one of her con-verts, but in May, 1637, Winthrop was chosen governor instead of Vane, and at once took steps to suppress the Antinomians, which re-sulted in the banishment of the more promi-nent among them.

Page 73. *The father.* William Hutchinson, who had accompanied his family from England.

Page 73. *The boys and girls.* There were fif-teen children, so that Portsmouth, which they founded, started off with a larger population than most towns of the period.

Page 75. *In the ruler's seat.* Underhill was chosen governor of the "Passataquack men" in October, 1638.

Page 83. *Pettaquamscut town.* South Kings-ton, Rhode Island. The Narragansett strong-hold lay sixteen miles away, in what is now the town of North Kingston.

Page 83. *George Fox.* Founder of the So-ciety of Friends, who visited America in 1671-72.

Page 84. *Connecticut had sent her men.* Of the army of a thousand, five hundred and twenty-seven were furnished by Massachusetts, and the remainder by Connecticut and Plymouth.

Page 85. ON A FORTIFICATION AT BOSTON BEGUN BY WOMEN. This poem occurs on pages 30-31 of "New England's Crisis," and not, as Duyckinck states, at the beginning. The author, Benjamin Tompson, "learned school-master and physician, and yᵉ renowned poet of New England," as the epitaph upon his tomb-stone puts it, was born at Braintree, Massachu-setts, July 14, 1642, graduated from Harvard in 1662, and after serving as master of the Bos-ton Latin School and Cambridge Preparatory School, died at Cambridge in 1675.

Page 85. *Sudbury's battle.* The Indian at-tack was made early in the morning of April 21, and lasted practically all the day. News of it soon reached the neighboring towns, and relief parties were started forward. The In-dians were on the lookout for them. A party of eleven men from Concord walked into an ambush and only one escaped; eighteen troop-ers from Boston finally got into the town with a loss of four; and a party of fifty from Marl-boro, under Captain Samuel Wadsworth, were caught in an adroitly prepared trap, out of which but thirteen came alive.

Page 99. *Charles of Estienne.* Charles de St. Estienne was a son of Claude de la Tour, a nobleman who, in 1610, had been forced by poverty to seek his fortune in the New World. They came to Port Royal, shared in the vicis-situdes of the little settlement, and were among those who took to the woods after its destruc-tion by the English. Among the fugitives was the Sieur de Biencourt, who held a grant to the country about Port Royal. They built some rude cabins, cultivated little patches of ground, and raised a fort of logs and earth near Cape Sable, which they called Fort St. Louis. Biencourt died in 1623, and Charles de la Tour took command of the fort and assumed control of Biencourt's property, claiming that Biencourt had so willed it. Another fort was built on the River St. John, and La Tour was appointed by the king lieutenant-governor over Fort Louis, Port la Tour, and dependencies.

At about the same time, Richelieu sent out an expedition to take formal possession of New France, and named Isaac de Launay de Razilly governor of all Acadia. He made his settlement at La Hève, on the Atlantic coast of Nova Scotia, but died in 1635, and his deputy, Charles de Menou, Chevalier D'Aulnay, asserted his right to command in the colony. Thereupon began between him and Charles de la Tour that famous struggle for the possession of Acadia which forms so romantic a passage in American history.

Page 101. *Pentagoet shall rue.* La Tour was unable to avenge himself, but time did it for him. D'Aulnay was drowned in 1650, and La Tour was appointed governor of Acadia. In 1653 he married D'Aulnay's widow, Jeanne de Motin.

Page 105. PENTUCKET. The Indian name for Haverhill.

Page 106. LOVEWELL'S FIGHT. This ballad, which is of extraordinary interest as the oldest American war ballad extant, was preserved in "The | History | of the | Wars of New England with the Eastern Indians, | or a | Narrative | of their continued perfidy and cruelty, | from the 10th of August, 1703, | to the Peace renewed 13th of July, 1713, | and from the 25th of July, 1722, | to their Submission 15th December, 1725, | which was Ratified August 5th, 1726. | By Samuel Penhallow, Esqr. | Boston, 1726." This was reprinted at Cincinnati, Ohio, in 1859, and the ballad occurs on page 129.

Page 106. *Of worthy Captain Lovewell.* Not much is known of Lovewell. He was a son of Zaccheus Lovewell, an ensign in the army of Oliver Cromwell, who had come to America and settled at Dunstable, where he died at the great age of one hundred and twenty years, — "the oldest white man who ever died in New Hampshire." He left three sons, the youngest of whom was John, the hero of Pigwacket. At the time of the fight, he was about thirty-three years of age, and had a wife and two or three children. After the Indian attack on Dunstable in 1624, he and some others petitioned the House of Representatives at Boston to make some provision for a force to be sent against the savages. The Representatives voted that all such volunteers should be paid two shillings and sixpence a day, and promised large rewards for the scalps of male Indians old enough to fight. A company of thirty was raised, with Lovewell as captain, and captured one prisoner and took one scalp. A second expedition brought back ten scalps and some other booty, and the third expedition culminated in the battle at Pigwacket.

Page 106. *'T was nigh unto Piqwacket.* The old name for Fryeburg. Pigwacket was at the time the principal village of the Ossipe tribe. Also spelled Pequawket.

Page 108. *They killed Lieutenant Robbins.* Robbins was a native of Chelmsford. He was so badly wounded that he had to be left on the ground. He desired his companions to charge his gun and leave it with him, saying, "As the Indians will come in the morning to scalp me, I will kill one more of them if I can."

Page 108. *Good young Frye.* Jonathan Frye, the chaplain of the company, was the only son of Captain James Frye, of Andover, and had graduated at Harvard only two years before. It is a curious commentary on the taste of the time that he should be commended for scalping Indians, as well as killing them; the scalping, however, was the result not of ferocity but of the large rewards offered by the Boston legislature for these trophies.

Page 108. *Wymans Captain made.* Ensign Seth Wymans, or Wyman, belonged in Woburn, and commanded through the day, after the fall of his superiors at the first fire. He so distinguished himself that he was given a captain's commission, and his admiring townsmen presented him with a silver-hilted sword.

Page 108. LOVEWELL'S FIGHT. From Collections, | Historical and Miscellaneous; | and | Monthly Literary Journal: | [table of contents] Edited by J. Farmer and J. B. Moore. | Concord: | Published by J. B. Moore. | 1824. Vol. iii, page 94.

Page 108. *Anon, there eighty Indians rose.* Penhallow says seventy, Hutchinson eighty, Williamson sixty-three, and Belknap forty-one.

Page 111. THE BRITISH LYON ROUSED. From Tilden's | miscellaneous | Poems, | on | Divers Occasions; | Chiefly to Animate & Rouse | the | Soldiers. | Printed 1756. The little volume from which this poem was taken is one of the most interesting published before the Revolution. For a long time nothing whatever was known of the author, not even his first name. But that was subsequently discovered by Mr. J. H. Trumbull, and communicated to the "New York Historical Magazine," iv, 72, by him. This account seems to have been overlooked by all of Tilden's biographers. Appleton's Cyclopædia of American Biography fails to give his first name, nor does any history or cyclopædia of American literature with which the compiler is familiar.

Page 112. THE SONG OF BRADDOCK'S MEN. This spirited song has been preserved by Mr. Winthrop Sargent in his excellent monograph upon the Braddock expedition, published by the Pennsylvania Historical Society in 1855. Mr. Sargent states that it was composed in Chester County, Pennsylvania, while the army was on the march in the early autumn of 1755, and that there is no doubt of its authenticity. He does not say where he discovered it.

Page 112. BRADDOCK'S FATE. It will be noticed that these verses were composed just six weeks after the battle which they describe, and the author must have sat down to them at once upon hearing the news of the defeat.

Page 113. *Old sixty-six.* The author.

Page 114. *North America.* It is worthy of note that in all colonial and revolutionary poetry, America is rhymed with such words as day, say, and away.

Page 114. *Telesem.* A name which Tilden gave to this form of verse.

Page 118. *Of Wolfe's brave deeds.* General James Wolfe, who commanded a brigade, and took the leading part in the assaults on the fortress, on one occasion plunging into the sea at the head of his grenadiers, and capturing a battery which commanded the beach.

Page 118. *Amherst's patriot name.* Jeffrey (afterwards Baron) Amherst, commander-in-chief of the land forces, fourteen thousand strong. He was hotly criticised by Wolfe for his blundering conduct of the campaign.

Page 119. *The tartans of Grant's Highlanders.* Major Grant, of the Highlanders, had obtained permission to reconnoitre the fort, and set out with about eight hundred men. He reached the fort on September 14, but, relying on his supposed superior numbers, divided his force in such a way that the different parts could not support each other. He was defeated in detail, his force cut to pieces, and himself taken prisoner. His loss was nearly three hundred.

Page 119. *Loyalhanna.* Westmoreland County, Pennsylvania.

Page 121. *Ned Botwood.* Edward Botwood, sergeant in the grenadiers of the Forty-seventh, or Lascelles' Regiment. He was the author of the verses given here, which were written on the eve of the expedition's departure from Louisburg, and continued popular with the British troops throughout the Revolution. He was killed during an unsuccessful assault, July 31.

Page 122. *Then Wolfe he took his leave.* A short time before leaving for America, Wolfe had become engaged to Katherine, daughter of Robert Lowther.

Page 122. *A parley.* This is, of course, purely imaginary. There was no parley.

Page 122. *Then instant from his horse.* Wolfe was not on horseback.

Page 129. THE VIRGINIA SONG. When David Garrick wrote " Hearts of Oak " as an expression of English patriotism, he little dreamed that he was furnishing ammunition for England's enemies. It was to the air of that song that the most popular of the colonial patriotic songs were written, and it was probably better known than any of our national songs are to us to-day. Such versions as " The Virginia Song," " The Patriot's Appeal," " The Massachusetts Song," and " The Liberty Song " were printed on broadside sheets and in newspaper columns and sung in village meeting and city street throughout the land, awakening immense enthusiasm.

Page 131. THE LIBERTY POLE. From " The Procession with the Standard of Faction, a Cantata," a four-page folio preserved in the Du Simitière collection of broadsides.

Page 132. *Who carry caps and pouches.*

" Pouches," perhaps a survival of the days of the hand-grenade.

Page 132. CRISPUS ATTUCKS. Attucks was a resident of Framingham, and there is some difference of opinion as to whether he was a mulatto or half-breed Indian. His only claim to remembrance is that he happened to be in the path of a British bullet on that March day in Boston.

Page 135. A NEW SONG CALLED THE GASPEE. The author of this old ballad is unknown. It was rescued from oblivion by Mr. John S. Taylor, who printed it in his " Sketches of Newport and its Vicinity," New York, 1842.

Page 138. *Tremble! for know, I, Thomas Gage.* Gage was the last royal governor of Massachusetts, and the best hated.

Page 139. *Against Virginia's hostile land.* Patrick Henry's famous speech, delivered in 1764 before the House of Burgesses, had never ceased to ring in the ears of royalty, and the people of Virginia had long been regarded as a " rebellious band that must be broken."

Page 139. *Hail, Middlesex!* A small number of the people of Middlesex County, Virginia, early in 1774, had adopted some Royalist " resolves," an event which gave rise to the following epigram by a " Lady of Pennsylvania " : —

> To manhood he makes a vain pretence
> Who wants both manly form and sense;
> 'T is but the form and not the matter,
> According to the schoolmen's clatter ;
> From such a creature, Heaven defend her !
> Each lady cries, no *neuter gender !*
> But when a number of such creatures,
> With women's hearts and manly features,
> Their country's generous schemes perplex,
> I own I hate this Middle-sex.

Page 139. *To Murray bend the humble knee.* John Murray, Earl of Dunmore, royal governor of Virginia, 1770-1775.

Page 139. *Mesech Weare.* Weare was president of the state of New Hampshire in 1776. His verses were set to a psalm tune and widely sung.

Page 140. *In spite of Rice.* This refers to the extensive donations sent from the other colonies to the people of Boston.

Page 140. *Rivington's New York Gazetteer.* This paper, the principal vehicle of Royalist poetry during the Revolution, was established by James Rivington, a bookseller, in 1773, and printed at his " ever open and uninfluenced press." In the autumn of 1775 his printing outfit was destroyed by a patriot mob ; but he was soon afterwards appointed King's Printer for the colony, furnished with a new outfit, and started " Rivington's New York Loyal Gazette." At the close of the war he changed its title to " Rivington's Gazette and Universal Advertiser," but it died of starvation in 1783.

Page 141. LIBERTY TREE. On August 14, 1765, an effigy representing Andrew Oliver, distributer of stamps for Boston, was found hanging from a great elm opposite the Boylston Market. A mob gathered when the sheriff tried to take down the effigy, the stamp office was demolished, and Oliver himself was compelled to repair to the tree and resign his commission. It was thenceforward called the Liberty Tree. Liberty trees were afterwards consecrated in many other New England towns.

Page 143. *Since mad Lee now commands us.* Major-General Charles Lee, that eccentric, morose, and ill-fated genius, characterized by Thomas Paine as "above all monarchs and below all scum."

Page 143. MASSACHUSETTS SONG OF LIBERTY. This song, to the air "Hearts of Oak," became almost as popular as "Adams and Liberty" did at a later day. Mrs. Mercy Warren, to whom it is attributed, published a volume of "Poems, Dramatic and Miscellaneous" (Boston, 1790), dedicated to Washington.

Page 144. TO THE BOSTON WOMEN. From Upcott, iv, 339.

Page 144. PAUL REVERE'S RIDE. It is possible that Mr. Longfellow derived the story, as told in the poem, from Revere's account of the adventure in a letter to Dr. Jeremy Belknap, printed in Mass. Hist. Coll. v. The publication of the poem called out a long controversy as to the accuracy of its details.

Page 147. *Then Devens looked.* Richard Devens, a member of the Committee of Safety, of which Hancock and Warren were the leading spirits.

Page 147. *Then haste ye, Prescott and Revere.* Dr. Samuel Prescott, of Concord, joined Revere and Dawes at Lexington and started with them for Concord. They were stopped by a British patrol. Prescott escaped by leaping his horse over the roadside wall and spurred on to Concord, while his companions were taken prisoners, but soon released.

Page 147. *The red-coats fire, the homespuns fall.* Eight Americans were killed, four near the spot where the battle monument now stands, and four others while escaping over the fences. Their names, as recorded on the monument, were Robert Monroe, Jonas Parker, Samuel Hadley, Jonathan Harrington, Jr., Isaac Muzzy, Caleb Harrington, and John Brown, of Lexington, and Asahel Porter, of Woburn.

Page 148. NEW ENGLAND'S CHEVY CHASE. As Lord Percy, at the head of the relief column, marched through Roxbury, his bands playing "Yankee Doodle" in derision of the opponents he was soon to meet, he observed a boy who seemed to be exceedingly amused. He stopped and asked the boy why he was so merry. "To think," said the boy, "how you will dance by and by to Chevy Chase." Percy, who was very superstitious, was worried by the remark all day. Its point will be appreciated when it is remembered that Percy was a lineal descendant of the Earl Percy who was slain at Chevy Chase.

Page 149. *We saw Davis fall dead.* Captain Isaac Davis, of the Acton company. He and Abner Hosmer were killed as the Americans charged the British stationed at the North Bridge. "I haven't a man that's afraid to

go!" he had exclaimed as he wheeled his company into line for the charge.

Page 150. *We'd rather have spent it this way than to home.* One of the veterans of the fight made this very remark to Edward Everett.

Page 153. *Of man for man the sacrifice.* The British lost 65 killed, 180 wounded, 28 captured; the Americans, 59 killed, 39 wounded, 5 missing.

Page 158. *King David.* See 2 Samuel v, 23, 24.

Page 159. *Yankee Doodle.* Accounts of the origin of "Yankee Doodle" are many and various. The air is very old, and nearly every country in Europe claims it. It probably reached England from Holland, and in the days of Charles I was used for some verses about Lydia Lockett and Kittie Fisher, gay ladies of the town. Afterwards, when Cromwell rode into Oxford on a pony, with his single plume fastened into a sort of knot called a "macaroni," the Cavaliers used the same air for their derisive verses. The story goes that this fact was recalled by Dr. Richard Shuckburg, of the Seventeenth Foot, when the queerly garbed provincial levies presented themselves, in June, 1755, at the camp at Albany, to take part in the campaign against the French. He wrote down the notes of the air and got the regimental band to play it. It was taken up by the Americans and became instantly popular. Verses innumerable have been attached to the air, the best known of which are "The Yankee's Return from Camp" and "The Battle of the Kegs."

Page 160. *Edward Bangs.* This is upon the authority of Dr. Edward Everett Hale, who states that "an autograph note of Judge Dawes, of the Harvard class of 1777, addressed to my father, says that the author of the well-known lines was Edward Bangs, who graduated with him. Mr. Bangs had, as a college boy, joined the Middlesex farmers in the pursuit of April 19, 1775. He was afterward a judge in Worcester County."

Page 160. TOM GAGE'S PROCLAMATION. General Gage's proclamation, issued June 12, 1775, was as follows: —

"Whereas the infatuated multitudes, who have long suffered themselves to be conducted by certain well-known incendiaries and traitors, in a fatal progression of crimes against the constitutional authority of the state, have at length proceeded to avowed rebellion, and the good effects which were expected to arise from the patience and lenity of the king's government have been often frustrated, and are now rendered hopeless by the influence of the same evil counsels, it only remains for those who are entrusted with the supreme rule, as well for the punishment of the guilty as the protection of the well-affected, to prove that they do not bear the sword in vain."

Page 162. THE BALLAD OF BUNKER HILL. An unsigned copy of these verses, apparently an authentic Revolutionary ballad, but really written by Dr. Hale in 1845, was "discovered," about 1858, among some old manuscripts at Millbury, Mass., and reproduced in the "Historical Magazine," iii, 311. Dr. Hale had himself lost all trace of the poem, until he came across it in the first edition of this compilation.

Page 163. GRANDMOTHER'S STORY OF BUNKER-HILL BATTLE. Dr. Holmes himself says:—
"The story of Bunker Hill battle is told as literally in accordance with the best authorities as it would have been if it had been written in prose instead of in verse. I have often been asked what steeple it was from which the little group I speak of looked upon the conflict. To this I answer that I am not prepared to speak authoritatively, but that the reader may take his choice among all the steeples standing at that time in the northern part of the city. Christ Church in Salem Street is the one I always think of, but I do not insist upon its claim. As to the personages who made up the small company that followed the old corporal, it would be hard to identify them, but by ascertaining where the portrait by Copley is now to be found, some light may be thrown on their personality."

It has been pointed out that the belfry could hardly have been that of Christ Church, since tradition has it that General Gage himself watched the battle from that vantage point.

The poem was first published in 1875, in connection with the centenary of the battle which it describes.

Page 167. THE BATTLE OF BUNKER HILL. This "popular" ballad was written and printed as a broadside for the purpose of encouraging recruiting for the English army. There are many versions of it, as well as parodies composed by Yankee sympathizers.

Page 169. 'T was then he took his gloomy way. Washington's journey was, as a matter of fact, a kind of triumph.

Page 169. Lawyer Close. Washington's aide, Major Lee.

Page 170. Like Esop's greedy cur. Fable 118. A dog crossing a rivulet, with a piece of meat in his mouth, saw his own shadow; and believing it to be another dog with a larger piece of meat, snatched at it, with the result that he lost his own piece.

Page 173. A POEM CONTAINING SOME REMARKS ON THE PRESENT WAR, etc., is from Poems | upon | Several Occasions, | viz. | I. A POEM on the Enemy's first coming | to Boston; the burning of Charles- | town; the Fight at Bunker-Hill, &c. | II. The WIDOW'S Lamentation. | III. Nebuchadnezzar's DREAM. | IV. Against OPPRESSION. | V. An heroic POEM on the taking of Gen. | Burgoyne, &c. | Boston: Printed for the AUTHOR, 1779. | It is an 8vo of sixteen pages, the first poem being printed in double column. A note at the end of the volume is signed "A Friend to Liberty."

Page 176. EMANCIPATION FROM BRITISH DEPENDENCE. The following explanatory note is from Duyckinck's edition of Freneau : —
"Sir James Wallace, Admiral Graves, and Captain Montague were British naval officers, employed on our coast. The Viper and Rose were vessels in the service. Lord Dunmore, the last Royal governor of Virginia, had recently, in April, 1775, removed the public stores from Williamsburg, and, in conjunction with a party of adherents, supported by the naval force on the station, was making war on the province. William Tryon, the last Royal governor of New York, discerning the signs of the times, took refuge on board the Halifax packet in the harbor, and left the city in the middle of October, 1775."

Page 177. Rodney, who was one of the Delaware delegates to the Continental Congress, had obtained leave of absence for a journey through the southern part of the state to prepare the people for a change of government. His colleagues, Thomas McKean and George Read, were divided on the question, and the former, knowing Rodney to be favorable to the declaration, sent him a message urging his return. By great exertion Rodney arrived just in time for the final discussion, and his affirmative vote secured the consent of the Delaware delegation to the declaration, and effected that unanimity among the colonies which was essential to the success of the measure.

Page 180. THE AMERICAN PATRIOT'S PRAYER. This poem was formerly ascribed to Thomas Paine, but recent authority has rejected this on the basis of internal evidence.

Page 183. THE MARYLAND BATTALION. At the opening of the Revolution, the young men of Baltimore organized the "Baltimore Independent Company," and elected Mordecai Gist captain. This was afterwards increased to a battalion, of which Gist was appointed major. The battalion checked the advance of Cornwallis at the battle of Long Island, and saved a portion of Stirling's command from capture. Two hundred and fifty-nine were left dead on the field.

Page 183. Grant. The British general who commanded the left wing. He had declared in the House of Commons that the Americans would not fight, and that he could march from one end of the continent to the other with five thousand men.

Page 183. Stirling. William Alexander, commonly called Lord Stirling, eldest son of James Alexander Stirling, who had fled to America upon the discovery of the Jacobite conspiracy of 1715.

Page 184. Knowlton. Thomas Knowlton, lieutenant-colonel of a regiment of rangers selected from the Connecticut troops. He was killed at the battle of Harlem Heights, as was Major Leitch, who had been sent to his aid.

Page 185. NATHAN HALE. Nathan Hale was a great-grandson of John Hale, first minister of Beverly, Massachusetts. He was born in 1755, and graduated from Yale in 1773. Little is known of his personal history.

Page 188. TRENTON AND PRINCETON. From McCarty's "National Song Book," iii, 88. McCarty says it was written from the dictation of an old lady who had heard it sung during the Revolution.

Page 204. LORD NORTH'S RECANTATION.

These verses were written by "a gentleman of Chester," England, and first appeared in the "London Evening Post."

Page 205. GENERAL HOWE'S LETTER. From Upcott, v, 45.

Page 208. BRITISH VALOR DISPLAYED; OR, THE BATTLE OF THE KEGS. This ballad was occasioned by a real incident. Certain machines in the form of kegs, charged with gunpowder, were sent down the river to annoy the British shipping then at Philadelphia. The danger of these machines being discovered, the British manned the wharfs and shipping and discharged their small-arms and cannons at everything they saw floating in the river during the ebb tide. — Author's note.

David Bushnell, inventor of the American torpedo, constructed the machines, which were so arranged as to explode on coming in contact with anything. Hopkinson's verses, which swept from colony to colony, did much to relieve the strain of those early months of 1778, and were perhaps worth as much, in tonic and inspiration, as the winning of a battle would have been.

Page 208. Sir William. Sir William Howe, commanding the British army.

Page 208. Mrs. Loring. Wife of Joshua Loring, the notorious commissary of prisoners.

Page 208. Sir Erskine. Sir William Erskine.

Page 214. King Hancock at their head. John Hancock commanded the second line of Massachusetts militia in this movement.

Page 214. Bold Pigot Sir Robert Pigot commanded the British forces in Rhode Island.

Page 216. BETTY ZANE. Elizabeth Zane was about eighteen years of age at the time she performed this exploit, and had just returned to Fort Henry from Philadelphia, where she had completed her education. She lived until 1847.

Page 216. Betty's brothers. Ebenezer and Silas.

Page 217. THE WYOMING MASSACRE. This ballad was printed, apparently for the first time, in Charles Miner's "History of Wyoming" (Philadelphia, 1845), where it is stated that it was written shortly after the tragedy by Mr. "Uriah Terry, of Kingston." In McCarty's "National Song Book" (iii, 344) it is said to have been written "by a person then resident near the field of battle."

Page 219. THE CRUISE OF THE FAIR AMERICAN. The war song of the Salem Privateersmen during the Revolution, and preserved in Griswold's manuscript collection of "American Historical Ballads." It was taken down from the mouths of Hawthorne's surviving shipmates early in the last century.

Page 219. Bold Hawthorne. Daniel Hawthorne, grandfather of Nathaniel Hawthorne.

Page 223. THE YANKEE MAN-OF-WAR. This, one of the very best of American seasongs, was first published by Commodore Luce, in his collection of "Naval Songs." He states that it was taken down from the recitation of a sailor. Internal evidence would indicate that it was composed by a member of the Ranger's crew.

Page 224. PAUL JONES — A NEW SONG. This is Number 613, vol. iii, of the Roxburghe collection of broadsides.

Page 224. As Green, Jemmy Twitcher. Captain Green was a noted pirate, and Jemmy Twitcher was the name given to the notorious John, Lord Sandwich.

Page 224. Pierce. Captain Richard Pearson. He was knighted as a reward for his fight with Jones. The latter remarked, upon hearing of it, "Should I fall in with him again, I'll make a lord of him."

Page 225. The Alliance bore down and the Richard did rake. The Alliance was commanded by Pierre Landais, a Frenchman, and his actions have never been satisfactorily explained. He had held his ship aloof at the opening of the battle, disregarding Jones's orders, but came up later only to pour three or four broadsides into the Richard, killing or wounding many of her crew and almost sinking her. She then drew off and awaited the result of the battle.

Page 225. Full forty guns Serapis bore. She really carried fifty against the Richard's forty-two. Besides, she was a new frigate, only four months out, while the Richard was old and unseaworthy. The Serapis carried 320 men, the Richard 304.

Page 226. Bold Pallas soon the Countess took. The Countess of Scarborough struck to the Pallas after a gallant two hours' battle.

Page 226. In the Hyder Ali. Hyder Ali was an Indian prince who defeated the English in 1767 and subsequently caused them so much annoyance that he was very popular with American patriots.

Page 229. The Hope. The ship Hope and the brig Constance, which were with the South Carolina, were also taken.

Page 229. Sir Henry Clinton. Clinton was left in command of New York city, when Howe started on his expedition for the capture of Philadelphia.

Page 230. Braving the death that his heart foretold. Wayne was convinced that he would not survive the attack on Stony Point, but nevertheless led the assault in person. He was struck in the head by a bullet, but insisted on being borne into the fort with his men.

Page 232. THE MODERN JONAS. A pasquinade printed as a broadside and stuck up in New York city. "Old Knyp" was General Knyphausen; "Old Clip," General Robertson; and "Yankee Farms," Connecticut Farms.

Page 233. THE COW-CHACE. The last canto of this poem was published in "Rivington's Royal Gazette" on the day that André was captured. These are the only verses he is known to have published. The original copy is still in existence, and has the following stanza upon it, under André's signature: —

When the epic strain was sung,
The poet by the neck was hung,
And to his cost he finds too late
The dung-born tribe decides his fate.

The poem was afterwards published by Rivington as an 8vo of 69 pages.

"The Cow-Chace," in its early editions, had the following explanatory notes: —

Tanner : General Wayne's *legal* occupation.

Mumps : A disorder prevalent in the Rebel lines.

Yan Van Poop : Who kept a dram-shop.

Jade : A New England name for a horse, mare, or gelding.

Bodies : A cant appellation given among the soldiery to the corps that have the honor to guard his majesty's person.

Cunningham : Provost-Marshal of New York. The shot will not go thro':

> Five Refugees ('t is true) were found
> Stiff on the block-house floor,
> But then 't is thought the shot went round,
> And in at the back door.

Frost-bit Alexander : Earl of Stirling.

The frantic priest : Caldwell, a minister at Elizabethtown.

One pretty marquis : Lafayette, a French coxcomb in the rebel service.

Page 237. *John Paulding.* Paulding was born in New York city in 1758 and died in 1818. His capture of André was his one famous exploit. With him at the time were two comrades, named Isaac Van Wart and David Williams. They were given medals by Congress and an annuity of two hundred dollars.

Page 239. *And then, at last, a transatlantic grave.* In 1821 André's remains were removed to England and placed in Westminster Abbey.

Page 240. *Sir Hal.* Sir Henry Clinton.

Page 241. *Congo.* The American Congress.

Page 242. *The reverend Mather.* Moses Mather, D.D.

Page 245. HYMN OF THE MORAVIAN NUNS OF BETHLEHEM. The banner of Pulaski's legion was embroidered by the Moravian sisters of Bethlehem, who helped to support their house by needlework. It is preserved in the cabinet of the Maryland Historical Society at Baltimore.

Page 245. *Martial cloak and shroud for thee.* The banner was made to be carried on a lance and was only twenty inches square. It could not have been used as a shroud.

Page 246. *Brave Maitland push'd in.* Colonel Maitland brought a large body of British troops from Beaufort to Prevost's aid.

Page 246. *Moncrieffe.* Major Moncrieff was the engineer who planned Savannah's defences.

Page 246. *Who attempted to murder his king.* In 1771 Pulaski attempted to kidnap Stanislaus, King of Poland.

Page 250. *South Mount.* Sumter's home near Camden, South Carolina.

Page 259. *Two birds of his feather.* Howe and Burgoyne.

Page 259. *Poor Charley.* Cornwallis.

Page 260. *A murder'd Hayne.* Isaac Hayne, hanged by the British, August 4, 1781.

Page 262. *And Whitehead.* William Whitehead, poet laureate 1751-1785.

Page 263. *Thus he.* Cincinnatus.

Page 269. *No taxes we'll pay.* Shays and his followers demanded decreased taxes and a paper currency.

Page 269. *Here's a pardon for Wheeler, Shays, Parsons, and Day.* Wheeler, Parsons, and Day were associates of Shays. All of them fled from the state, but were afterwards pardoned.

Page 271. *So they went to Federal Street.* The convention was held in a church on Long Lane, which was afterwards christened Federal Street in honor of the event.

Page 273. THE FIRST AMERICAN CONGRESS. From "The Columbiad."

Page 274. THE VOW OF WASHINGTON. Read in New York, April 30, 1889, at the centennial celebration of Washington's inauguration.

Page 276. ADAMS AND LIBERTY. Mr. Charles Prentiss, in his preface to the collected works of Robert Treat Paine, published at Boston in 1812, gives the following account of the writing of "Adams and Liberty": —

"In June, 1798, at the request of the 'Massachusetts Charitable Fire Society,' Mr. Paine wrote his celebrated political song of 'Adams and Liberty.' It may appear singular that politics should have any connection with an institution of benevolence: but the great object of the anniversary being to obtain charitable donations, the more various and splendid were the attractions, the more crowded the attendance: and of course, the more ample the accumulation for charity.

"There was, probably, never a political song more sung in America than this; and one of more poetical merit was, perhaps, never written: an anecdote deserves notice respecting one of the best stanzas in it. Mr. Paine had written all he intended; and being in the house of Major Russell, editor of the 'Centinel,' showed him the verses. It was highly approved, but pronounced imperfect; as Washington was omitted. The sideboard was replenished, and Paine was about to help himself; when Major Russell familiarly interfered, and insisted, in his humorous manner, that he should not slake his thirst till he had written an additional stanza, in which Washington should be introduced. Paine marched back and forth a few minutes, and suddenly starting, called for a pen. He immediately wrote the following sublime stanza [the one beginning "Should the tempest of war overshadow our land"].

"The sale of this song yielded him a profit of about seven hundred and fifty dollars. It was read by all; and there was scarcely in New England, a singer, that could not sing this song. Nor was its circulation confined to New England: it was sung at theatres, and on public and private occasions, throughout the United States; and republished and applauded in Great Britain."

Page 277. HAIL COLUMBIA. The following letter from Joseph Hopkinson, son of Francis Hopkinson, is quoted by Rev. R. W. Griswold, in his "Poets and Poetry of America": —

"It ["Hail Columbia"] was written in the summer of 1798, when war with France was thought to be inevitable. Congress was then in session in Philadelphia, deliberating upon that important subject, and acts of hostility had actually taken place. The contest between England and France was raging, and the people of the United States were divided into parties for the one side or the other, some thinking that policy and duty required us to espouse the cause of republican France, as she was called; while others were for connecting ourselves with England, under the belief that she was the great preservative power of good principles and safe government. The violation of our rights by both belligerents was forcing us from the just and wise policy of President Washington, which was to do equal justice to both, to take part with neither, but to preserve a strict and honest neutrality between them. The prospect of a rupture with France was exceedingly offensive to the portion of the people who espoused her cause, and the violence of the spirit of party has never risen higher, I think not so high, in our country, as it did at that time, upon that question. The theatre was then open in our city. A young man belonging to it, whose talent was as a singer, was about to take his benefit. I had known him when he was at school. On this acquaintance, he called on me one Saturday afternoon, his benefit being announced for the following Monday. His prospects were very disheartening; but he said that if he could get a patriotic song adapted to the tune of the 'President's March,' he did not doubt of a full house; that the poets of the theatrical corps had been trying to accomplish it, but had not succeeded. I told him I would try what I could do for him. The object of the author was to get up an *American spirit*, which should be independent of and above the interests, passions, and policy of both belligerents: and look and feel exclusively for our own honour and rights. No allusion is made to France or England, or the quarrel between them: or to the question, which was most at fault in their treatment of us: of course the song found favour with both parties, for both were Americans; at least neither could disavow the sentiments and feelings it inculcated."

Page 278. YE SONS OF COLUMBIA: AN ODE. From " Original Poems by Thomas Green Fessenden, Esq., author of Terrible Tractoration, or Caustic's Petition to the Royal College of Physicians, and Democracy Unveiled. Philadelphia: Printed at the Lorenzo Press of E. Bronson. 1806." The following note to this poem appears in the first edition : "The above Ode was written, set to musick, and sung on a publick occasion in Rutland, Vermont, July, 1798. At that time the armament, which afterwards sailed to Egypt, under Buonaparte, lay at Toulon: its destination was not known in America, but many supposed that it was intended to waft the blessings of *French Liberty* to the United States." Fessenden seems to have been possessed of an acute hatred of the French, due, perhaps, to his residence in England. Three other poems in this little book are

devoted to denouncing Napoleon, the Jacobins, and the "sans culotte"—of which latter phrase he was singularly fond.

Page 283. *So the common sailor died.* James did not die. He recovered from his wounds, served through the second war with England and lived till about 1840.

Page 283. SKIPPER IRESON'S RIDE. Whittier heard the story of Skipper Ireson in 1828, when he was a student at Haverhill Academy. It was told him by a schoolmate from Marblehead, and he began at once to write the ballad, but it was not published until 1857, when it appeared in the second number of the " Atlantic Monthly."

Mr. Samuel Roads, Jr., in his " History of Marblehead," contended that Ireson was in no way responsible for the abandonment of the disabled ship, and Whittier, in writing to Mr. Roads, says : " I have now no doubt that thy version of Skipper Ireson's ride is the correct one. My verse was founded solely on a fragment of rhyme which I heard from one of my early schoolmates, a native of Marblehead. I supposed the story to which it referred dated back at least a century. I knew nothing of the participants, and the narrative of the ballad was pure fancy. I am glad for the sake of truth and justice that the real facts are given in thy book. I certainly would not knowingly do injustice to any one, dead or living."

The use of dialect in the refrain was suggested by Lowell, the editor of the " Atlantic " at the time.

Page 285. THE TIMES. McCarty's " National Song Book " (Philadelphia, 1861) is a real treasure-house of ballads written during the second war with England. " The Times " is from this source, as are many of the other ballads quoted here.

Page 287. HULL'S SURRENDER. This ballad was copied from a broadside in the possession of the library of Harvard University. It is so tattered that one stanza, the last, is indecipherable and had to be omitted.

Page 289. *Commanded by Dacres the grandee O.* Captain (afterward Rear-Admiral of the Red) James Richard Dacres.

Page 292. *Where Brock, the proud insulter, rides.* Sir Isaac Brock. He had received Hull's surrender less than two months before. He was pierced by three bullets as he led his troops into battle at Queenstown and died where he fell.

Page 298. *Brave Chauncey.* Captain Isaac Chauncey.

Page 302. *We mourn, indeed, a hero lost!* Captain William Burrows, of the Enterprise, and Captain Blythe, of the Boxer, both fell during the action, and were buried side by side at Portland.

Page 303. *And whether like Yeo, boys, they'd taken affright.* Sir James Lucas Yeo, who had been defeated by Captain Isaac Chauncey and was afterwards blockaded by him in Kingston Harbor.

Page 304. *Thought it best from his well-pep-*

pered ship to depart. The Lawrence was so severely shot up early in the action, that Perry transferred his flag to the Niagara. He afterwards returned to the Lawrence to receive the surrender of the surviving British officers.

Page 306. *And Tecumseh fell prostrate before him.* The honor of having killed Tecumseh was claimed for Colonel Richard Malcolm Johnston, but the claim was never conclusively established.

Page 306. *Walbach.* John Batiste de Barth, Baron de Walbach, a German veteran who had come to America on a visit in 1798. He enlisted in the American army, won steady promotion, and died in 1857 with the rank of brigadier-general.

Page 309. *Four gallant ships.* The Ramillies 74, commanded by Sir Thomas Hardy; the Pactolus 38, the Despatch 22, and a bombship.

Page 313. *Downie.* George Downie, commander of the British fleet. He was killed during the action.

Page 313. *Macomb.* General Alexander Macomb, in command of the American land force. His army, consisting of about fifteen hundred regulars and some detachments of militia, was greatly outnumbered by the British.

Page 315. *To serve me just like Drummond.* Sir Gordon Drummond, who lost a large part of his force by the explosion of a mine, while assaulting Fort Erie.

Page 315. *Old Ross, Cockburn, and Cochrane too.* Robert Ross, selected by Wellington to command the troops sent to this country in 1814. He was killed while leading the advance toward Baltimore, after having sacked Washington. Sir George Cockburn, second in command of the fleet, who had become notorious for his raids along the American coast. Sir Alexander Cochrane, in command of the British fleet on the American station.

Page 315. *General Winder.* General William Henry Winder, in command of the American militia at the battle of Bladensburg.

Page 317. THE STAR-SPANGLED BANNER. The poem was really written at white heat, for Key made his first draft while the fight was actually in progress, and corrected it at Baltimore next day. It was at once struck off as a broadside, and was received with great enthusiasm. The air, from which it is inseparable, was selected almost at random, from a volume of flute music, by an actor named Ferdinand Durang, and was known as "Anacreon in Heaven." Additional stanzas have been written for the poem from time to time, but none of them are in any way notable except those written during the Civil War by Oliver Wendell Holmes:

When our land is illumined with liberty's smile,
If a foe from within strike a blow at her glory,
Down, down with the traitor who dares to defile
The flag of her stars and the page of her story!
    By the millions unchained
      Who their birthright have gained
We will keep her bright blazon forever unstained!
And the star-spangled banner in triumph shall wave
While the land of the free is the home of the brave.

Page 321. *Take our wounded and our dead.* The American loss was two killed and seven wounded, while the British lost 120 killed and 180 wounded.

Page 323. *For I went down with Carroll.* William Carroll, major-general of Tennessee militia.

Page 324. *'T was Pakenham in person.* Sir Edward Michael Pakenham. He had succeeded Ross in the command of Wellington's veterans, and, like his predecessor, was killed while leading his men against the enemy.

Page 325. *And came, with Gibbs to head it.* Sir Samuel Gibbs, second in command to Pakenham.

Page 325. *It is the Baratarian.* The headquarters of Jean Lafitte, the freebooter, at Barataria, had been broken up only a short time before, and many of his band captured and imprisoned. They were subsequently released, and under three of Lafitte's lieutenants, Dominique, You, and Bluche, hastened to Jackson's aid before New Orleans, where they did good service, especially with the artillery.

Page 325. *Keane was sorely wounded.* Baron John Keane, in command of the third brigade.

Page 327. *Our captain.* Charles Stewart. He held the remarkable record of being seventy-one years in the service, and senior officer for seventeen years. He lived until 1869. His daughter was the mother of Charles Stewart Parnell.

Page 335. *Oyo.* The Indian name for the Ohio.

Page 337. *Blanny.* A popular corruption of Blennerhassett.

Page 337. *Our General brave.* Major-General Buell.

Page 337. *I have the Baron in my head.* The only system of military tactics then in use among the officers in the western country was that of Baron Steuben.

Page 337. *The Deputy.* Governor Return Jonathan Meigs.

Page 338. *'T was half a kneel of Indian meal.* A kneel is equal to two quarts.

Page 338. *Tyler, they say, lies at Belpré.* Comfort Tyler was one of Burr's chief lieutenants.

Page 338. *The Cor'ner.* Joel Bowen.

Page 338. *Instead of sword, he seized his board.* Buell was a tailor by trade.

Page 343. *Good Junipero.* Father Junipero Serra, the famous head of the missionaries in California.

Page 343. *The Visitador.* José de Galvez, Visitador General of New Spain.

Page 344. *Viscaino.* Sebastian Viscaino, who conducted a Spanish exploring expedition along the California coast in 1602–03.

Page 345. "THE DAYS OF 'FORTY-NINE." Half a century ago, this song was widely popular, and yet to-day it is almost impossible to find an authentic copy. There is a version in Upham's "Notes of a Voyage to California," but it is anything but convincing. The version given here was contributed to "Out West" by

Florence Gleason, of Bakersfield, California, and has the ear-marks of authenticity.

Page 351. CONCORD HYMN. The first quatrain of this poem is inscribed on the Battle Monument at Concord. Emerson's grandfather, William Emerson, was minister at Concord in 1775, and from his pulpit strongly advocated resistance to the British. When the day of trial came, he took his place among " the embattled farmers." " Let us stand our ground," he said to the minutemen ; " if we die, let us die here." The fight took place near his own house, the home afterwards of Emerson and of Hawthorne, and celebrated by the latter as " The Old Manse."

Page 353. OLD TIPPECANOE. From "The Harrison Log Cabin Song Book," Columbus [Ohio], 1840.

Page 356. A thousand Mexicans lay dead. A careful estimate places the Mexican loss at about five hundred. Six of the Texans, including Travis, Bowie, and Crockett, were taken alive, but were immediately put to death by Santa Anna's order.

Page 357. Save the gasp of a woman. While every man of the garrison was killed, three women survived, one of whom was Mrs. Almerion Dickinson, wife of a lieutenant belonging to the garrison. Three children also survived.

Page 358. We slew and slew till the sun set red. Houston reported the Mexican loss to be 630 killed, 208 wounded, 730 captured. The wounded were, however, counted among the prisoners. The American loss was 2 killed and 23 wounded. Santa Anna himself was captured next day.

Page 362. Rio Bravo. Rio Bravo del Norte, "Rapid River of the North," is a Spanish name for the Rio Grande.

Page 366. THE ANGELS OF BUENA VISTA. A letter-writer from Mexico during the Mexican War, when detailing some of the incidents at the terrible fight of Buena Vista, mentioned that Mexican women were seen hovering near the field of death, for the purpose of giving aid and succor to the wounded. One poor woman was found surrounded by the maimed and suffering of both armies, ministering to the wants of Americans as well as Mexicans with impartial tenderness. — Author's note.

Page 369. Guvener B. George Nixon Briggs was the Whig governor of Massachusetts from 1844 to 1851.

Page 369. John P. Robinson. John Paul Robinson (1799–1864) was a resident of Lowell, a lawyer of considerable ability and a thorough classical scholar. Late in the gubernatorial contest of 1847 it was rumored that Robinson, heretofore a zealous Whig, and a delegate to the recent Springfield convention, had gone over to the Democratic or, as it was then styled, the "Loco" camp. The editor of the 'Boston Palladium " wrote to him to learn the truth, and Robinson replied in an open letter avowing his intention to vote for Cushing.

Page 369. Gineral C. General Caleb Cushing.

Page 384. BATTLE-HYMN OF THE REPUBLIC.

This, perhaps the loftiest strain of American patriotism, was inspired by a visit which Mrs. Howe paid to Washington in December, 1861. She heard the troops singing "John Brown's Body," and, at the suggestion of James Freeman Clarke, determined to write some worthy words to go with that air. The words were written almost at once, and were taken back to Boston by Mrs. Howe. She gave them to James T. Fields, editor of the "Atlantic Monthly," and they were published in the issue of that magazine for February, 1862, being given the entire first page. Mr. Fields furnished the title. Strangely enough, the poem attracted little attention, until a copy of a newspaper containing it was smuggled into Libby Prison. Chaplain Charles C. McCabe read it there, and presently the whole prison was singing it. After his release, Chaplain McCabe continued to call attention to the song, and its merits were soon widely recognized. President Roosevelt has suggested that it deserves to be the national anthem.

Page 386. Mr. Foote. Henry S. Foote was Senator from Mississippi from 1847 to 1852. He was a member of the Confederate Congress.

Page 386. Mangum. W. P. Mangum (1792–1861) was Senator from North Carolina from 1831 to 1837, and again from 1841 to 1847.

Page 387. Cass. Lewis Cass (1782–1866) was Senator from Michigan from 1845 to 1848, and candidate for the presidency on the Democratic ticket in 1848. After his defeat by Taylor he was, in 1849, returned to the Senate to fill out his unexpired term. He was Buchanan's Secretary of State until the famous message of December, 1860, when he resigned.

Page 387. Davis. Jefferson Davis, the President of the Confederate States, was a Senator from Mississippi from 1847 to 1850.

Page 387. Hannegan. Edward A. Hannegan was Senator from Indiana from 1843 to 1849.

Page 387. Jarnagin. Spencer Jarnagin represented the state of Tennessee in the Senate from 1841 to 1847.

Page 387. Atherton. Charles G. Atherton (1804–53) was Senator from New Hampshire from 1843 to 1849

Page 387. Colquitt. W. T. Colquitt (1799–1855) was Senator from Georgia from 1843 to 1849.

Page 387. Johnson. Reverdy Johnson, Senator from Maryland, 1845–49.

Page 387. Westcott. James D. Westcott, Senator from Florida, 1845–49.

Page 387. Lewis. Dixon H. Lewis, Senator from Alabama, 1844–48.

Page 388. ICHABOD. This poem was the outcome of the surprise and grief and forecast of evil consequences which I felt on reading the seventh of March speech of Daniel Webster in support of the " compromise," and the Fugitive Slave Law. . . . But death softens all resentments, and the consciousness of a common inheritance of frailty and weakness modifies the severity of judgment. Years after, in " The Lost Occasion," I gave utterance to an almost universal regret that the great statesman did not live to see the flag which he loved trampled under the feet of Slavery, and, in view of this desecration, make his last days glorious in defence of "Liberty and Union, one and inseparable."—Author's note.

Page 391. *Beyond the river banks.* The Wakarusa.

Page 391. *Keitt.* Laurence Massillon Keitt, Congressman from South Carolina, 1852-60. Killed at the battle of Cold Harbor, 1862.

Page 391. *The anti-Lecomptonite phalanx.* Lecompton was the capital of the territory of Kansas, and a pro-slavery constitution was framed there at a constitutional convention which lasted from September 5 to November 7, 1857. It was rejected by the people of Kansas early in the following year.

Page 394. *Captain Stephens.* Aaron Dwight Stephens. He was a captain only in the sense that he was to be given that position in the negro army which Brown expected to organize.

Page 395. *With his eighteen other crazy men.* There were either twenty-two or twenty-three men in the party.

Page 395. *So they hurried off to Richmond for the Government Marines.* The marines arrived by train from Washington. Strangely enough, they were under command of Colonel Robert E. Lee and Lieutenant J. E. B. Stuart.

Page 395. *Fired their bullets in his clay.* The bodies of some of the dead were atrociously maltreated.

Page 395. *How they hastened on the trial.* The trial began October 26 and ended November 2. The proceedings, though swift, were not unseemly nor unduly summary, considering the excitement of the Virginians and their fear that a rescue would be attempted from the North.

Page 403. GOD SAVE OUR PRESIDENT. These verses were written in 1857, and the music for them was composed a year later by George Felix Benkert. It was played by the Marine Band at the first inauguration of Lincoln, immediately after the inaugural address.

Page 411. DIXIE. Dan Emmett, the once-famous negro minstrel, was the author of the original "Dixie," which was written in 1859. It is said he got the air from an old plantation melody. It was soon appropriated by the Southern war songs. The words used, however, were not Emmett's, which were mere doggerel, but General Albert Pike's, as given in the text. Since the war, "Dixie" has grown as popular in the North as in the South. Many verses have been set to the air, but none of them, besides Emmett's and Pike's, has gained any popularity.

Page 411. A CRY TO ARMS. The unusual poetic merit of the Southern poems at the opening of the war is worth remarking. This, as the war progressed, gave place in large part to mere hysteria, while the poetic quality of Northern verse, poor enough at first, grew steadily better. This may perhaps be explained by the fact that the South was the more in earnest when the war began, while the earnestness of the North deepened as it went on.

Page 415. MY MARYLAND. This poem, which divided with "Dixie" popularity among the Southern troops, was written by Mr. Randall immediately upon hearing of the outbreak at Baltimore. The form of the poem was suggested by Mangan's "Karamanian Exile":—

I see thee ever in my dreams,
   Karaman!
Thy hundred hills, thy thousand streams,
   Karaman, O Karaman!

It was wedded to the old college air "Lauriger Horatius," by Miss Hattie Cary, of Baltimore.

In affecting contrast to the reception given the Sixth Massachusetts in 1861 was that given it in 1898, when it passed through Baltimore on its way to Cuba. The historic regiment was met at the station by the mayor; school-children drawn up along the line of march pelted the soldiers with flowers; each soldier was given a little box containing cake, fruit, and a love-letter; and a great motto was strung across the streets reading, "Let the welcome of '98 efface the memory of '61."

Page 424. *To General J. E. Johnston.* General Johnston, who had been stationed at Winchester with the Army of the Shenandoah, marched rapidly to Beauregard's aid, when the latter was attacked at Manassas, and upon his arrival left Beauregard, whom he ranked, in tactical command of the field, and assumed responsibility and general charge of the battle.

Page 435. WANTED—A MAN. This poem is said to have so impressed President Lincoln that he read it to his Cabinet.

Page 444. BARBARA FRIETCHIE. This poem was written in strict conformity to the account of the incident as I had it from respectable and trustworthy sources. It has since been the subject of a good deal of conflicting testimony, and the story was probably incorrect in some of its details. It is admitted by all that Barbara Frietchie was no myth, but a worthy and highly esteemed gentlewoman, intensely loyal and a hater of the Slavery Rebellion, holding her Union flag sacred and keeping it with her Bible; that when the Confederates halted before her house, and entered her dooryard, she denounced them in vigorous language, shook her cane in their faces, and drove them out; and when General Burnside's troops followed close upon Jackson's, she waved her flag and cheered them. It is stated that May Quantrell, a brave and loyal lady in another part of the city, did wave her flag in sight of the Confederates. It is possible that there has been a blending of the two incidents.—Author's note.

Page 449. *'Tis Meagher and his fellows.* Brigadier-General Thomas F. Meagher commanded the second brigade of the first division of the right grand division. It was called the "Irish Brigade," and Meagher himself had organized it. After Chancellorsville, it was so decimated that it was incorporated with other regiments.

Page 449. *The wild day is closed.* Burnside's attempt to carry the heights behind Fredericksburg by storm was perhaps the most insane of the war. In spite of McClellan's lack of promptness, thoroughness, and vigor, and a sort of incapacity of doing anything until an ideal completeness of preparation was reached, he was in many ways the best commander the Army of the Potomac ever had. Pope, Burnside, and Hooker were admittedly his inferiors.

Page 458. THE EAGLE OF CORINTH. The finest thing I ever saw was a live American eagle, carried by the Eighth Wisconsin, in the place of a flag. It would fly off over the enemy during the hottest of the fight, then would return and seat himself upon his pole, clap his pinions, shake his head, and start again. Many and hearty were the cheers that arose from our lines as the old fellow would sail around, first to the right, then to the left, and always return to his post, regardless of the storm of leaden hail that was around him. — Letter from an Illinois Volunteer.

At the close of the war, the eagle was presented to Governor Lewis, of Wisconsin, and provided with a suite of rooms in the State House Park at Madison.

Page 461. READY. The incident described in this poem occurred probably during the first week of April, 1863. Rodman's Point is a strip of land projecting into the Pimlico River just below Washington, North Carolina.

Page 462. Kady Brownell. On April 25, 1861, the New York "Herald," in referring to the passage of the second detachment of Rhode Island troops through New York city, said: "The volunteers bring along with them two very prepossessing young women, named Martha Francis and Katey Brownell, both of Providence, who propose to act as 'daughters of the regiment,' after the French plan."

Page 467. THE CRUISE OF THE MONITOR. The contract for the construction of the monitor was given to John Ericsson, of New York, on October 4, 1861. It was to be an iron-plated raft, 172 feet over all, 41½ feet beam, and 11¼ feet depth of hold, carrying a revolving iron turret containing two 11-inch Dahlgren guns. The ironclad was launched January 30, 1862, an extraordinary feat in naval construction, and was handed over to the government February 19, its cost being $275,000. At eleven o'clock on the morning of March 6, the queer craft started for Hampton Roads, to meet the Merrimac, word of whose completion had reached the United States government. That the vessel did not founder on the voyage was little less than a miracle, but at nine o'clock on the evening of March 8, the Monitor reached Fort Monroe, her progress up the bay being lighted by the burning frigate Congress.

Page 466. Bold Worden. The Monitor was commanded by Lieutenant John Lorimer Worden, while the Merrimac was in charge of Lieutenant Catesby Jones, his superior, Captain Franklin Buchanan, having been wounded by a rifle ball the day before. Worden was injured during the action by a shell exploding against the sight-hole of the pilot house, and

was succeeded by Lieutenant Samuel Dana Greene.

Page 468. THE RIVER FIGHT. The fleet which Farragut took upon this desperate venture consisted of nine gunboats and eight sloops of war. The defences of New Orleans were of the most formidable kind, the river being guarded by Forts Jackson and St. Philip, mounting 116 guns, and by a strong fleet of gunboats and ironclads, under command of Commodore J. K. Mitchell. The river was also barred by a great raft thrown across it under the guns of the forts, and a large number of long flatboats, filled with pine knots, were held in readiness by the Confederates to be fired and sent down the swift current into the midst of the Union fleet. In spite of all this, after the terrific fight was over, it was found that the Union loss was only thirty-seven killed and one hundred and forty-seven wounded. The Confederate loss was never accurately determined.

Admiral Farragut was so impressed with Brownell's poem that he sought out the author and a warm friendship followed. When Mobile was captured, Brownell was a guest of the Admiral on board his flagship, the Hartford, and the result was another spirited poem, "The Bay Fight," which appears elsewhere in this collection.

Page 471. Our fair Church pennant waves. The church pennant is made of white bunting on which is sewn a cross of blue.

Page 478. Beside me gloomed the prison-cell. The reference is to Dr. Reuben Crandall, of Washington, who, in 1834, was arrested and confined in the old city prison until his health was destroyed, his offence having been in lending to a brother physician a copy of Whittier's pamphlet, "Justice and Expediency."

Page 483. STONEWALL JACKSON'S WAY. "These verses," according to William Gilmore Simms, "were found, stained with blood, in the breast of a dead soldier of the old Stonewall Brigade, after one of Jackson's battles in the Shenandoah Valley." Though widely copied, their authorship remained unknown for nearly a quarter of a century.

Page 493. John Burns. John Burns was seventy years of age in 1863. He had been among the first to volunteer for the War of 1812, and was present at the battles of Plattsburg, Queenstown, and Lundy's Lane. He served through the war with Mexico, and volunteered promptly for the Civil War, was rejected because of his age, served for a time as a teamster, but was finally sent home to Gettysburg, where his townsmen made him constable to keep him busy and contented. When, in June, 1863, the Confederates occupied the town, Burns had to be locked up for asserting his civil authority in opposition to that of the Confederate provost guard. As soon as the Confederates left the town, Burns busied himself arresting Confederate stragglers. When the preliminary skirmishing at Gettysburg began, Burns borrowed a rifle and ammunition from a wounded Union soldier, went to the front, and offered his services as volunteer. The colonel of the Seventh Wisconsin loaned him a long-range rifle, which he used with deadly effect all day, but he was badly wounded when the Union troops were forced back, was captured by the Confederates, and narrowly escaped being hanged as an un-uniformed combatant. He lived in his little home on the battlefield until 1872, and was visited by thousands and thousands of pilgrims to the scene of the great struggle.

Page 500. THE BATTLE-CRY OF FREEDOM. The popularity of the songs sung by the armies of both North and South seems to have been in direct ratio to their maudlin sentimentality. Most popular of all was the song known as " When this Cruel War is Over." It was heard in every camp, north and south, many times a day, the Southern soldiers inserting "gray" for " blue " in the sixth line of the first stanza with a cheerful disregard of the rhyme. It was sung in public gatherings, in the home — in fact, it is doubtful if any other song was ever upon so many American tongues. This wide appeal gives it, in a way, a historic interest, which warrants its inclusion here.

WHEN THIS CRUEL WAR IS OVER

Dearest love, do you remember
  When we last did meet,
How you told me that you loved me.
  Kneeling at my feet?
Oh, how proud you stood before me,
  In your suit of blue,
When you vowed to me and country
  Ever to be true.

Chorus — Weeping, sad and lonely,
    Hopes and fears how vain;
    Yet praying when this cruel war is over,
    Praying that we meet again.

When the summer breeze is sighing
  Mournfully along,
Or when autumn leaves are falling,
  Sadly breathes the song.
Oft in dreams I see thee lying
  On the battle plain,
Lonely, wounded, even dying,
  Calling, but in vain.

If, amid the din of battle,
  Nobly you should fall,
Far away from those who love you,
  None to hear you call,
Who would whisper words of comfort?
  Who would soothe your pain?
Ah, the many cruel fancies
  Ever in my brain!

But our country called you, darling,
  Angels cheer your way!
When our nation's sons are fighting,
  We can only pray.
Nobly strike for God and country,
  Let all nations see
How we love the starry banner,
  Emblem of the free.
          CHARLES CARROLL SAWYER.

Page 506. *Out on a crag walked something.* The flag was unfurled from Pulpit Rock, on the extreme point of the mountain overlooking Chattanooga. It was from that " pulpit " that Jefferson Davis, three days before, had addressed his troops, assuring them that all was well with the Confederacy.

Page 506. THE BATTLE IN THE CLOUDS. "The day had been one of dense mists and rains, and much of General Hooker's battle was fought above the clouds, on the top of Lookout Mountain." — General Meigs's Report.

Page 508. *And the one white Fang underneath.* Robert Gould Shaw was only twenty-five years of age when he was killed at the head of his regiment at Fort Wagner. He had enlisted as a private at the outbreak of the war, and soon rose to a captaincy. He was appointed colonel of the Fifty-Fourth Massachusetts, the first regiment of colored troops from a free state, April 17, 1863, and went to his death with them three months later. See also " Ode on the Unveiling of the Shaw Memorial," page 603, and " An Ode in Time of Hesitation," page 646.

Page 510. LOGAN AT PEACH TREE CREEK. Mr. Garland is mistaken in stating that McPherson was killed at the battle of Peachtree Creek, which was fought on July 20, 1864. He was killed two days later, at what is known as the battle of Atlanta. While hastening to join his troops, who had just been attacked by the Confederates, he ran full into the enemy's skirmish line and was shot while trying to escape. Sherman at once ordered General John A. Logan to assume command of the Army of the Tennessee, and it was largely due to General Logan's skill and determination that the Union army was saved from serious disaster in the desperate battle which followed.

Page 512. SHERMAN'S MARCH TO THE SEA. General Sherman, in his Memoirs, says that on the afternoon of February 17, 1865, while overhauling his pockets, according to his custom, to read more carefully the various notes and memoranda received during the day, he found a paper which had been given him by a Union prisoner who had escaped from Columbia. It proved to be "Sherman's March to the Sea," composed by Adjutant S. H. M. Byers, of the Fifth Iowa Infantry, while a prisoner at Columbia. General Sherman was so impressed by the verses that he immediately sent for their author and attached him to his staff.

Page 513. MARCHING THROUGH GEORGIA. General Sherman makes no reference in his Memoirs to these verses and would have been glad to replace them with Adjutant Byers's song. They were, however, widely popular and, indeed, still hold an honored place at every reunion of Civil War veterans.

Page 517. *O noble son of noble sire.* Ulric Dahlgren was the son of John Adolph Dahlgren, perhaps the greatest chief of ordnance the Navy Department has ever had. Ulric was only twenty-two years of age at the time of his death. He had lost a leg at Gettysburg the year before, but had returned to active service upon his recovery although compelled to walk on crutches. He had planned the expedition in which he lost his life.

Page 519. *When Stuart to the grave we bore.* The loss of Stuart was one of the most serious the Confederacy had sustained since the death of Stonewall Jackson. He was, in many respects, the most brilliant cavalry leader developed on either side during the war, though it was alleged that his unauthorized absence from the field of Gettysburg contributed greatly to the defeat of Lee's army.

Page 522. THE YEAR OF JUBILEE. A remarkable evidence of the elasticity of spirit shown by the losers in the great struggle is the fact that this song, which one would suppose would be particularly offensive to them, became even more popular in the South than in the North.

Page 524. THE SURRENDER AT APPOMATTOX. Lee's army, at the time of the surrender, consisted of about twenty-eight thousand men, nearly half of whom were without arms. His army had had little to eat for several days except parched corn, and was upon the verge of starvation. Immediately after the surrender, Grant sent twenty-five thousand rations into the Confederate lines.

Page 524. LEE'S PAROLE. Grant's behavior was marked throughout with the greatest delicacy. He did not ask Lee's sword, promptly stopped salutes which were started after the surrender, did not require the Confederates to march out and stack arms, and did not enter their lines. The terms of surrender were so liberal that many partisans at the North took violent exception to them.

Page 525. *The Cherbourg cliffs were all alive.* A great throng had gathered to witness the fight, which had been advertised as a sort of gala event, excursions even being run from Paris. The sympathies of the crowd were all with the Alabama.

Page 525. *When, lo! roared a broadside.* The firing of the Kearsarge was a magnificent exhibition of gunnery. She fired 173 missiles, nearly all of which took effect. The Alabama fired 370, of which only 28 struck. The Kearsarge's 11-inch shells were aimed a little below the water line, with such deadly effect that the Alabama sank in a little more than an hour after going into action.

Page 526. KEARSARGE. On Sunday morning, June 19, 1864, the noise of the cannons during the fight between the Kearsarge and the Alabama was heard in English churches near the Channel. — Author's note.

Page 527. *Though unequal in strength.* The Kearsarge had a displacement of 1031 tons, carried a crew of 163, and mounted seven guns, throwing 366 pounds. The Alabama was of 1016 tons displacement, carried a crew of 149 and eight guns, throwing 328 pounds. The ships were remarkably well matched.

Page 527. *Shall shine in tradition the valor of Semmes.* A bitter controversy followed the fight as to whether the Alabama actually surrendered. The preponderance of evidence shows that her colors were hauled down and a white flag displayed a few minutes before she sank. The British steam yacht Deerhound picked up forty-two men, including Semmes and fourteen officers, and made off with them to Southampton. The British Government afterwards refused to surrender these men. It is consoling to reflect that England's aid to Confederate privateers cost her, in the end, over fifteen million dollars.

Page 527. CRAVEN. Craven has been called the Sidney of the American navy. His pilot's name was John Collins, and as the Tecumseh was going down, he and Craven met at the foot of the ladder leading to the top of the turret. Craven stepped back, saying, "After you, Pilot." As the pilot reached the top round of the ladder, the vessel seemed "to drop from under him," and no one followed. A buoy marks the spot.

Page 528. *Sidney.* Sir Philip Sidney, who is said to have refused a cup of water while lying mortally wounded on the battlefield of Zutphen, in order to give it to a wounded soldier.

Page 528. *Nelson.* Admiral Horatio Nelson. The reference is to the Battle of the Nile, where Nelson was severely wounded.

Page 528. *Lucas.* A young English captain, who was imprisoned by Hyder Ali in 1780. To relieve a wounded comrade, Captain Baird, he assumed two sets of chains.

Page 528. *Outram.* Sir James Outram, who, in admiration for the brilliant deeds of his subordinate, General Havelock, conceded him the glory of relieving Lucknow, in 1857, waiving his own rank and tendering his services as a volunteer.

Page 530. THE BAY FIGHT. Farragut took only a short vacation after his triumphant "River Fight," and began at once to prepare for another desperate encounter. The defences of Mobile were among the strongest in the South. Three forts, mounting seventy-one guns, guarded the channel, which was further defended by a double row of torpedoes, one hundred and eighty in number. Besides this, there was in the bay itself a Confederate fleet of four vessels, one of which was the great ram Tennessee.

Farragut's fleet was the most formidable collection of war vessels that had ever been assembled under command of one man. It surpassed in power for destruction the combined English, French, and Spanish fleets at Trafalgar. Yet, in spite of the desperate nature of the struggle which followed, the loss was less than in many a skirmish on land, that in the Union fleet being 52 killed and 170 wounded, besides 93 drowned in the Tecumseh, while the Confederate loss was only 12 killed and 20 wounded.

Page 535. "ALBEMARLE" CUSHING. Lieutenant Cushing was only twenty-one years of age at the time he sunk the Albemarle, one of the most brilliant and gallant exploits of the war. The deed was rendered extremely difficult by the fact that the Albemarle had been surrounded by a cordon of timber, and Cushing actually drove his launch at full speed over this in order to reach the Albemarle's side. He received the thanks of Congress and was made lieutenant-commander as a reward for his heroism.

Page 539. PARDON. John Wilkes Booth was a son of Junius Brutus Booth and was twenty-six years old at the time of the assassination. His success as an actor had never been notable. There is some dispute as to whether he was hit by the bullet which Boston Corbett fired at him, or whether he shot himself. At any rate, he was brought out of the barn in which he had been cornered with a bullet in the base of his brain, and with his body paralyzed. He died the following morning. Eight accomplices were arrested, tried by a military commission, and found guilty. Four, one a woman, were hanged, and the others, with one exception, sentenced to hard labor for life.

Page 542. Treason is not dead. The charge and specification on which the conspirators were arraigned declared that they were "incited and encouraged" to the crime by Jefferson Davis, and a reward of one hundred thousand dollars was offered for his arrest. There was at no time any trustworthy evidence implicating Davis.

Page 559. Pillow's ghastly stain. Fort Pillow, situated on the Mississippi River about forty miles above Memphis, was captured, April 12, 1864, by a large Confederate force under General N. B. Forrest. The garrison consisted of 295 white and 262 colored troops, of whom 221 were killed and 130 wounded. Most of the killed and wounded were negroes, many of whom were shot down after the fort had been captured. There is no evidence, however, that the massacre, if it can be called such, was premeditated, and General Forrest seems to have stopped it as promptly as he could.

Page 559. "MR. JOHNSON'S POLICY OF RECONSTRUCTION." The "policy" consisted of two papers, one a proclamation of amnesty granting a pardon for treason to all, with some exceptions, who should take an oath to support the Constitution and the Union and to obey all laws and proclamations which had been made with reference to the emancipation of the slaves; the second an executive order intrusting the state governments to the people who had taken this oath. That the plan did not succeed was due in no small part to the folly of the newly constituted legislatures in immediately proceeding to pass various restrictive laws aimed at the negro, the effect of which would be to deprive him, in large part, of his newly acquired freedom.

Page 560. Crippled and halting from his birth. Stevens had a club foot, and was compelled to use a cane in walking.

Page 563. THE BLUE AND THE GRAY. The poem grew out of an item which appeared in the New York "Tribune," in 1867: "The women of Columbus, Mississippi, animated by nobler sentiments than many of their sisters,

have shown themselves impartial in their offerings made to the memory of the dead. They strewed flowers alike on the graves of the Confederate and of the National soldiers." The poem, prefaced by this item, was first published in the "Atlantic Monthly" for September, 1867, and at once attracted wide attention.

Page 565. HOW CYRUS LAID THE CABLE. Mr. Field had been working at this project since 1854. In 1858 he had succeeded in laying a cable across the ocean, and it was in operation from August 17 to September 4, when the signals became unintelligible and finally ceased altogether. The story of his perseverance and final success is an inspiring one.

Page 565. O lonely bay of Trinity. The American end of the cable was landed at Trinity Bay, Newfoundland.

Page 568. Small need to open the Washington main. Gould had persuaded President Grant that a rise in gold while the crops were moving would advantage the country, and early in September the treasury department was instructed to sell only gold sufficient to buy bonds for the sinking fund. Gould saw that the "Washington main" could not be kept closed indefinitely, however, and unloaded secretly, leaving his partner, "Jim" Fisk, to look out for himself. Fisk's broker, Speyers, continued to run up the price of gold, until his bid reached 163½, when the market broke, the price falling almost instantly to 133. Fisk saved himself by coolly repudiating his contracts.

Page 580. DOWN THE LITTLE BIG HORN. Custer, who was thirty-seven years old at the time of his death, had served with great distinction through the Civil War. He was bitterly censured for accepting battle upon the Little Big Horn, and accused of disobedience of orders, but no basis for this accusation was ever clearly shown.

Page 580. Just from the canyon emerging. Custer and the five companies with him advanced without hesitation into the jaws of death, for they were outnumbered twelve to one. They dismounted and planted themselves on two little hills a short distance apart. The Indians stampeded their horses, waited till their ammunition was exhausted, and then overwhelmed them.

Page 580. Sitting Bull. Sitting Bull, who commanded the Indians, was a Sioux chief and was born about 1837. He was killed during the Sioux outbreak of December, 1890.

Page 583. In ambush the Sitting Bull. There was no ambush. The battle was fought in the open, from high ground. Custer's surprise lay not in finding the Indians before him, but in finding them so fatally numerous.

Page 584. The brave heart. Two days after the battle, a detachment of cavalry discovered the bodies of Custer and his five companies. Custer alone had not been mutilated. He had been shot in the left temple, and lay as though peacefully sleeping.

Page 593. THE BROOKLYN BRIDGE. The bridge had been begun January 3, 1870, and

was not wholly completed at the time of its opening in 1883. Its cost was about twenty million dollars.

Page 615. *Bocagrande.* The main channel into Manila Bay south of Corregidor Island. It means, literally, "large mouth."

Page 616. *Montojo.* Admiral Patricio Montojo y Pasarou, commander of the Spanish naval forces in the Philippines.

Page 616. *Gridley.* Charles Vernon Gridley (1845-1898), captain of Admiral Dewey's flagship, the Olympia.

Page 626. EIGHT VOLUNTEERS. Besides Hobson, the volunteers were Osborn Deignan, a coxswain of the Merrimac ; George F. Phillips, a machinist of the Merrimac ; John Kelly, a water-tender of the Merrimac; George Charette, a gunner's mate of the New York ; Daniel Montagu, a seaman of the Brooklyn; J. C. Murphy, a coxswain of the Iowa ; and Randolph Clausen, a coxswain of the New York.

Page 628. *Once more the Flower of Essex.* See "The Lamentable Ballad of the Bloody Brook," page 82.

Page 631. WHEELER AT SANTIAGO. "Fighting Joe" Wheeler was one of the most active and successful cavalry leaders of the Confederacy. The death of General J. E. B. Stuart, in 1864, made him senior cavalry general of the Confederate armies. He served in Congress after the war, and volunteered for active service on the outbreak of the war with Spain. He was given command of a cavalry brigade, and his presence before Santiago was of inestimable value.

Page 633. *Near Nimanima's greening hill.* The cove, six and a half miles from the entrance to Santiago harbor, where the Infanta Maria Teresa was beached. Juan Gonzales is seven miles and Aserradero fifteen miles from Santiago.

Page 633. *The Cape o' the Cross.* Cape Cruz, at the southwestern extremity of Cuba.

Page 641. *Who on the third most famous of our Fourths.* July 4, 1776, the Declaration of Independence adopted. July 4, 1863, announcement of the victory at Gettysburg. July 4, 1898, announcement of the victory at Santiago.

Page 645. AGUINALDO. Emilio Aguinaldo was born in 1870, of Chinese and Tagalog parentage. He received a good education, became interested in military affairs, and was one of the leaders of the outbreak against Spanish authority in 1896. At the beginning of the Spanish-American war, Admiral Dewey sent for Aguinaldo, who arrived at Cavité a few days after the destruction of the Spanish fleet. He at once began the organization of the Filipino troops, and soon afterwards proclaimed himself dictator of the so-called Filipino Republic. He stoutly resisted the American occupation which followed the peace, but was captured in 1901, and finally took the oath of allegiance to the United States.

Page 645. *Strike at his mother and his child.* Aguinaldo's family was captured by the United States troops and held prisoners until his submission.

Page 645. *When they read the sneering comments.* The fact that no prisoners were taken at the fight at Dajo, and that many women and children were among the killed, caused much bitter comment. The poem gives the army's side of the controversy.

Page 646 *Before the living bronze Saint-Gaudens made.* See "Bury Them," page 508, and "An Ode on the Unveiling of the Shaw Memorial," page 603.

Page 650. *The assassin's shot.* The assassin was a young Pole named Leon Czolgosz, who proclaimed himself an anarchist. He was tried speedily, sentenced to electrocution, and executed October 28.

Page 651. "*Silent upon a peak in Darien.*" From Keats's sonnet, "On First Looking into Chapman's Homer."

INDEX OF AUTHORS

INDEX OF FIRST LINES

INDEX OF TITLES